D0474938

THE

FOOTBALL CLUB
DIRECTORY 1993

Editor: Tony Williams

House Editor: Adrian Barber

A

Burlington Publishing

Publication

Sponsored by BARCLAYS BANK PLC

First edition published 1985

ISBN 1 873057-12-1

Typeset by Kentones Inc., Taunton, Somerset.
Created and Typeset using Spellbinder Desktop Publisher
and a Hewlett Packard Laserjet series II. Additional data
imported directly from Dbase IV and Supacalc 5.
All photos, reproduced by kind permission at Character
Graphics, Taunton, Somerset and ISCA Repro, Exeter, Devon.
Printed by Richard Clay Ltd, Bungay, Suffolk

Front cover photo:
Action from the Division One clash between Leeds United
and Sheffield Wednesday.

CONTENTS

ACKNOWLEDGEMENTS

EDITOR: Tony Williams

HOUSE EDITOR: Adrian Barber

Editorial Committee: Tony Williams, Adrian Barber, George Brown, Michael Williams

Editorial Assistants: Steve Whitney, Greg Tesser, Ken Bithell, James Wright & Keith Rye

Editorial Address:

Football Directories,
24A Queen Square,
North Curry, Taunton,
Somerset. TA3 6LE
Tel: (0823) 490469
Fax: (0823) 490281

The editorial views expressed in this Directory are not necessarily those of either, Barclays Bank, The Publishers or indeed any individual on the Good News Awards panel.

WITH senior football in this country now split into an F.A. Premier League with The Barclays Football League feeding it, a major change in structures has been introduced for the first time since the regional Third Divisions became the third and fourth divisions in 1958.

The change in status certainly hasn't helped us with our compilation as both club and league administration is still settling down after the changes. However, we do thank all the kind club officials who have sent the required information to us.

Once again the rush to ensure summer transfers and new signings are recorded has been hectic, but House Editor Adrian Barber, who has looked after the book all year has been helped by the rest of the team in his hours of particular need. There have been one or two all night typesetting sessions over the last weekend and hopefully it will all be proved worthwhile.

The co-operation we received from The Barclays Public Relations Department was, as usual, splendid and of course the encouragement and support from the administrators at The Football League and The F.A. Premier League was greatly appreciated.

When the pressure is on a good printer can make or break the launch by ensuring the book arrives on time and in good condition. Clays of Bungay have been great over the years and their experience has been invaluable again this season.

For many years now our statisticians have loyally produced facts, figures and reviews for The Directory and we would especially like to thank them all again this season. The extra work of Duncan Hoskins, Frank Grande, Ronald Baker and Graham Lucas has also been very special.

Every year more readers and football professionals (writers, scouts, managers, secretaries and players) let us know how much they appreciate the special players pages and once again to all those who make them possible – a very big thank you.

We hope to be presenting our 10th Football Club Directory next season and certainly a lot has changed in the game since the idea was born way back in 1984.

Tony Williams

We can recommend two other books that feature for the football enthusiast: *League Players 1945-92*, by Barry Hugman (£19.95) – featuring every appearance by every player in a League match since the War to the end of the 1991-92 season.
The Supporters Guide to Football League Clubs, by John Robinson (£4.99) – A complete guide to all Premier, League and National Stadiums.

EDITORIAL

THIS season sees the beginning of a new era for full time professional football in England. The much publicised F.A. Premier League has been launched and although it is extremely difficult to appreciate the benefits of the new scheme, we accept that Premier club chairmen are happy with their extra income.

The Barclays Football Club Directory will continue to present all clubs in the comprehensive manner which our regular readers expect and do seem to appreciate.

As usual, we sent the copy to the printers after the season had started so we have a better chance of including the hectic pre-season transfers. And sadly we have to record the demise of Maidstone United who like Aldershot, a few months before them, resigned from the Barclays Football League.

More and more clubs are under very real pressure just to keep going and surely the time must have come for club directors in the new Second and Third Divsions to re-appraise the wisdom of full time national football at their level.

It can only be misguided or pig-headed pride that prevents chairmen of struggling little clubs attracting under 3,000 to home matches, accepting the common-sense facts of life that part-time regional football would be far more cost effective. Supporters would also be happier with more local derbies rather than all day outings of hundreds of miles to stand on windswept terraces and soak up an atmosphere of a three quarter empty ground.

Surely we should be thinking along the lines of the very successful Italian League, who have two full time highly paid top class leagues fed by three regional leagues where most clubs are part time but can go full time if they are determined to challenge for a place amongst the elite.

Every club would find its comfortable level and the level of facilities with which it could afford to surround itself.

The pressure would be off and just as the non-league pyramid of football leagues has proved, the strong and ambitious can continue to grow, those happy with their level within the game can relax and enjoy themselves and of course those who really are not capable of competing at certain levels will drop down to a level in which they can cope and be happy.

So lets hope that the Premier League can lead the way to more common sense being shown within senior clubs, less silly pride and greed and more sensible, realistic planning by those in charge of town clubs throughout the country.

Everybody seems to agree on these principles except many of the club chairmen - how do they get into power?

TONY WILLIAMS

GOOD NEWS STORIES

FOLLOWING a season in which a thrilling Barclays League championship created more impact on the football world than England's challenge at the European Nations Championship or the constant media promotion of political interests concerning the Premier League; 'good news' was not given much space in the press.

However, we once again thank the team of **Graham Taylor, Gordon Taylor (PFA), Bob Wilson (BBC), Brian Moore (ITV), Peter Stewart (Shoot Magazine)** and **Jeff Powell (Daily Mail)** who have considered the 'good news of the season.

Perhaps the wonderful season enjoyed by **Gary Lineker** within his role as the busiest footballer ever in the promotional scene did the game more good than any other one factor. Gary won one of our awards last season but his appearance on all sorts of television programmes and his quotes or articles in the press brought nothing but respect and admiration to the game of Association Football.

For him and his wife to suffer such terrible distress through son George's illness, seemed so very sad for the whole family.

Another illness that football attempted to do something about was Multiple Sclerosis as the **Wallace brothers** (Danny, Rod and Ray) introduced 'The Football against M.S.' scheme which made valiant efforts to raise money to fight the disease.

Manchester United suffered the disappointment of throwing away a lead at the top of the First Division, but in young striker **Ryan Giggs** they introduced another exciting talent, while popular goalkeeper **Peter Schmeichel** followed a great season with a hero's contribution in Sweden. **Neil Webb** having shown immense character to win back his England place after a really unpleasant injury, also showed rare qualities in these days of selling stories to tabloid newspapers, when he refused to make a story out of his mystifying treatment by United's management in the latter part of the season.

Managers always feature strongly in our seasonal round ups but how **Barry Fry** must wish he didn't hit the headlines so often! However, full marks to Barry for always showing a sense of humour however frustrating the situation. Also a thank you for Barnet's insistence on attacking football.

Chris Turner also proved a few points at Peterborough United who enjoyed a memorable season, while **Jim Smith**, one of football's favourite personalities, gave the game some wonderful moments through the performances of his young and talented Portsmouth side in the F.A. Cup.

John Lyall has also won a previous 'Good News Award' but it was good to see his principles and ideas once again producing a successful side at Ipswich.

Exciting footballers of real quality do not appear too often in these days of all action, super fit, battling all rounders, but last season we were able to enjoy the pure skills of the aforementioned **Ryan Giggs** plus **Steve McManaman** (Liverpool), **Tony Daley** (Aston Villa) and **Darren Anderton** (Spurs signing from Portsmouth).

It was also good to see the skills and attitude of **Alan Shearer** blossoming to create a striker that has every chance of being as well respected as Gary Lineker.

Sadly a lot of disappointment after the England matches in Sweden inspired some fairly bitter comments within the media. Yes we were all disappointed, surely no more so than the England players and management, but those of us who heard **Lawrie McMenemy** stand up to an hour long grilling on many sensitive matters, will have certainly had their football education improved and the way he handled the situation was definitely 'Good News'.

We can only hope that the new look to English domestic football is an unqualified success for the game in this country. We can only wait and see!

Tony Williams

GOOD NEWS AWARDS 1992

DANNY BERGARA: (Manager of Stockport County)

THERE are certain clubs who have always traditionally appeared amongst the real strugglers at the foot of the Football League. Not even their most ardent fans would argue that Stockport County didn't feature amongst this group – that is until the last three seasons under the inspirational managership of **Danny Bergara**. Real management skills plus hard work earned promotion from Division Four, took County to Wembley twice and although they failed to achieve a trophy or promotion last season, the sportsmanship of the manager, the effort of his team, plus the rapturous enjoyment of the appreciative fans brought Stockport County the respect of the football world.

LEE CHAPMAN: (Leeds United)

EVERY Championship winning side produces its heroes and Leeds United were indeed a side bursting with talent. However, a tall, fair striker has more chance than most to collect a fan club and **Lee Chapman** also showed great physical bravery in leading United's attack and becoming one of the most popular footballers in or out of the City of Leeds. He epitomised most of the good traditional features of English football and also impressed with his articulate work on television.

LENNIE LAWRENCE: (Manager of Middlesbrough)

WHEN a Southerner takes up a managerial job in the North East he is often described as brave or desperate! 'Lennie', however, is another manager without experience at senior levels who has shown that shrewd commonsense and man-management, plus a true love and understanding of the game, can command respect from professionals and indeed bring results. Last season he not only guided Middlesbrough to the semi-final of the Rumbelows Cup and the fifth round of the F.A. Cup, but then when all at the club could have been forgiven for feeling deflated and tired he took Middlesbrough into the Premier Division without even battling with the play-offs.

CARLTON PALMER: (Sheffield Wednesday & England)

MOST managers have an idea of their perfect player. He would be skilfull, very fit, willing to run all day, prepared to play wherever he is told and has the ability to follow orders within a game plan. Well I should imagine that both his club and international managers would confirm that **Carlton Palmer** filled most of those criteria. He certainly worked extremely hard for England's cause in Sweden and impressed the watching English television millions who had little else to cheer them.

TERRY VENABLES: (Chief Executive, Tottenham Hotspur)

A very famous club, respected for its insistence to stand by quality football played on the ground with a special style, nearly died a year ago. Amid all sorts of bad publicity for his club **Terry Venables** fought for Tottenham Hotspur football club and their survival. He has achieved more than that, as the club is now in the Premier Division, still keeping its playing standards and has eliminated most of the daunting debts that had so depressed all involved at White Hart Lane. Terry's all round contribution to football since first playing for England as a schoolboy international has been immense.

THE OFFICIAL

F.A. NON-LEAGUE

CLUB DIRECTORY

1993

(FIFTHTEENTH EDITION)

A RECORD 1072 PAGES

OVER 600 PHOTOS

**Large sections on – F.A. Trophy – F.A.
Vase & F.A. Cup**

**Full squad lists for all Conference &
Premier Feeder Leagues**

**Comprehensive coverage of all leagues
in the national Semi-Professional
Pyramid & many below**

**Large sections on Sunday, Welsh,
Scottish, A.F.A & Women's Football**

All County Senior Cup scores

Available at **£12.95** (postage & packing free) from:
**FOOTBALL DIRECTORIES, FREEPOST, TAUNTON,
SOMERSET TA3 6BR**

(Cheques or postal orders to made payable to **FOOTBALL DIRECTORIES**)

Foreword by:

Alastair Robinson
Group Vice Chairman, Barclays Bank

Alastair Robinson, group vice chairman of Barclays Bank, presents the Barclays League Championship trophy to Leeds United skipper Gordon Strachan: as Lee Chapman is congratulated and Howard Wilkinson applauds.

TRAUMATIC is the only word one can think of which would adequately describe the happenings last season in the Barclays League – both **on field** and **off**.

The traumas on field centred mainly on the North – a 'War of the Roses' tussle between Lancs (Manchester United) and Yorks (Leeds United) – and it was a long-running epic.

The title victory meant a great deal to the Elland Road club – as indeed it would have done to the Reds of Old Trafford – and to all neutrals it was desperately hard to separate the two.

The duel also became a personal one between the two managers, who almost monopolised the Barclays Bank Managers Awards throughout the season: both Alex Ferguson and Howard Wilkinson claiming three awards each, with the latter taking the big one at the end of the season.

It was some achievement for the canny and studied Leeds boss to chart this championship course over three and a half years from the nether regions of the Second Division. And it was a success, publicly and sportingly acknowledged by the volatile and likeable Scot after the heart-breaking finale of the final fortnight.

Barclays feels honoured to salute the achievements of these managerial giants – and all their colleagues – and we announced at the 1992 Managers Awards luncheon our intention to continue with these prestigous prizes (along with the other awards in the Barclays portfolio) as official sponsors of the League Managers Association. These awards will go across the board – through the new F.A. Premier League and the new-style Barclays League.

The 'new era for football' promised by The F.A. Premier League and the new Barclays League set up has occupied acres of media space and agonising comment for over the best part of a year in establishing a new administrative framework for the game.

But underneath all of that we can be sure that the battles for all four championships will be as fiercely contested as ever and provide a season of excitement and excellence for all of us to enjoy.

We wish them all well.

HOWARD WILKINSON: LEEDS UNITED
Barclays Bank Manager of the Year 1992

Howard Wilkinson, who led Leeds United to become Barclays League Champions, displays the personal accolade he received: the Barclays Bank Manager of the Year award for 1992. It is exactly 20 years since the title last came to Elland Road when Don Revie completed a hat-trick of Manager of the Year selections ('69, '70 & '72).

It was appropriate that Wilkinson was the winner in the first full year of the inception of the League Managers Association. As chairman of this influential (and high-profile) body, which includes top club managers Alex Ferguson and George Graham on its committee, Howard announced the signing of a three year sponsorship of the association by Barclays Bank at the annual Barclays Managers Awards luncheon.

He said: "I'd like to thank Barclays for their tremendous support in the past and the introduction of the Achievement Award (voted for by the LMA members and won for the first time by Dave Bassett). This new Barclays sponsorship of the LMA is vital if managers are to make a positive contribution to the future of the game."

Howard stressed that the Association had made great strides in its short life and negotiations for it to play a formal part in the game's decision-making progress were well advanced.

BARCLAYS BANK MANAGERS AWARDS 1991-92

	Division 1	Division 2	Division 3	Division 4
August	**ALEX FERGUSON** (Manchester United)	JOHN BECK (Cambridge United)	TERRY COOPER (Birmingham City)	BILLY AYRE (Blackpool)
September	**ALEX FERGUSON** (Manchester United	LENNIE LAWRENCE (Middlesbrough)	BOBBY GOULD (West Bromwich Alb.)	BARRY FRY (Barnet)
October	**HOWARD WILKINSON** (Leeds United)	ALAN CURBISHLEY/ STEVE GRITT (Charlton Athletic)	TERRY COOPER (Birmingham City)	GEORGE FOSTER (Mansfield Town)
November	**HOWARD WILKINSON** (Leeds United)	DAVID WEBB (Southend United)	PHIL HOLDER (Brentford)	JIMMY MULLEN (Burnley)
December	**ALEX FERGUSON** (Manchester United)	GRAHAM TURNER (Wolverhampton W.)	ALAN MURRAY (Hartlepool United)	BILL GREEN (Scunthorpe United)
January	**GRAEME SOUNESS** (Liverpool)	MALCOLM CROSBY (Sunderland)	DANNY BERGARA (Stockport County)	BRIAN FLYNN (Wrexham)
February	**BRIAN CLOUGH** (Nottingham Forest)	JOHN LYALL (Ipswich Town)	CHRIS TURNER (Peterborough United)	DARIO GRADI (Crewe Alexandra)
March	**GERRY FRANCIS** (Queens Park Rngrs)	ALAN CURBISHLEY/ STEVE GRITT (Charlton Athletic)	DAVID PHILPOTTS (Wigan Athletic)	PHIL HENSON (Rotherham United)
April	**TREVOR FRANCIS** (Sheffield Wednesday)	ARTHUR COX (Derby County)	PHIL HOLDER (Brentford)	STEVE THOMPSON (Lincoln City)

Bold Type: Barclays Bank Manager of the Month

BARCLAYS BANK MANAGER OF THE YEAR 1991-1992: **HOWARD WILKINSON** (Leeds United)

BARCLAYS BANK DIVISION TWO MANAGER OF THE SEASON: **JOHN LYALL** (Ipswich Town)

BARCLAYS BANK DIVISION THREE MANAGER OF THE SEASON: **PHIL HOLDER** (Brentford)

BARCLAYS BANK DIVISION FOUR MANAGER OF THE SEASON: **JIMMY MULLEN** (Burnley)

BARCLAYS BANK ACHIEVEMENT AWARD: **DAVE BASSETT** (Sheffield United)

HAPPY MANAGERS DISPLAY BARCLAYS BANK AWARDS

ALL SMILES: Barclays Bank Manager of the Year 1992, **Howard Wilkinson** (Leeds United) displays the giant trophy; flanked by a happy band of prize-winning colleagues – l to r. Divisional Managers of the Season: **John Lyall** (Ipswich Town), Division Two; **Phil Holder** (Brentford), Division Three; **Brian Flynn**, accepting on behalf of **Jimmy Mullen** (Burnley), Division Four, and **Dave Bassett** (Sheffield United) inaugural selection of his fellow LMA members for the new Barclays Bank Special Achievement Award.

ALEX FERGUSON of MAN. UTD:
His third 'Barclays Bubbly' prize of '91-'92

Alex Ferguson received three of the first five Barclays Bank Manager of the Month awards for season 1991-92 as the Old Trafford Reds set sail at the top of the Barclays League.

His side suffered the severe disappointment of a final day of the season debacle. But his recognition for achievements at Manchester United with a major trophy in each of the past three seasons – FA Cup 1990, European Cup Winners Cup 1991 and League Cup 1992 – taking his career total to 12 national and international trophies, remains undiminished.

A Daily Mirror Photograph

BARCLAYS YOUNG EAGLE AWARDS 1991-92

	Overall Winner	North East	North West	Yorks
August	TOMMY JOHNSON (Notts County)	LEE CLARK (Newcastle United)	STEVE McMANAMAN (Liverpool)	SIMON CHARLTON (Huddersfield Town)
September	RYAN GIGGS (Manchester United)	LEE CLARK (Newcastle United)	RYAN GIGGS (Manchester United)	WES REID (Bradford City)
October	GARY SPEED (Leeds United)	LEE ELLISON (Darlington)	MICHAEL SHERON (Manchester City)	GARY SPEED (Leeds United)
November	RYAN GIGGS (Manchester United)	MATTIE APPLEBY (Newcastle United)	MICHAEL HUGHES (Manchester City)	ALAN FETTIS (Hull City)
December	DWIGHT YORKE (Aston Villa)	MATTIE APPLEBY (Newcastle United)	ALAN WRIGHT (Blackburn Rovers)	CHRIS BART-WILLIAMS (Sheffield Wednesday)
January	ROB JONES (Liverpool)	BRIAN ATKINSON (Sunderland)	ROB JONES (Liverpool)	DANE WHITEHOUSE (Sheffield United)
February	ROY KEANE (Nottingham Forest)	ALAN NEILSON (Newcastle United)	ROB JONES (Liverpool)	GERRY TAGGART (Barnsley)
March	SCOT GEMMILL (Nottingham Forest)	JAMIE POLLOCK (Middlesbrough)	ROB JONES (Liverpool)	DEAN KIELY (York City)

TWO YOUNG VILLA TOP MEN . . .

(left) 19 year old **Steve Froggatt**, named Barclays Man of the Match on his first team home debut at Villa Park; and shooting star, **Dwight Yorke**, were two of the brightest Barclays Young Eagles of last season.

	Midlands	London & E. Anglia	London & South	Wales & West
August	SIMON STURRIDGE (Birmingham City)	DARREN PITCHER (Charlton Athletic)	ALAN SHEARER (Southampton)	–
September	DWIGHT YORKE (Aston Villa)	CHRIS BART-WILLIAMS (Leyton Orient)	SANDY AWFORD (Portsmouth)	ROB EDWARDS (Bristol City)
October	DARYL BURGESS (West Bromwich Alb.)	KEVIN CAMPBELL (Arsenal)	JOHN ROBINSON (Brighton & H. A.)	LEE BADDELEY (Cardiff City)
November	SCOT GEMMILL (Nottingham Forest)	DAVID HILLIER (Arsenal)	FITZROY SIMPSON (Swindon Town)	SHAUN CHAPPLE (Swansea City)
December	DAVID EDWARDS (Walsall)	MARK PEMBRIDGE (Luton Town)	KEITH ROWLAND (Bournemouth)	STEVE WATKIN (Wrexham)
January	STEVE FROGGATT (Aston Villa)	DARREN ANDERTON (Portsmouth)*	DARREN ANDERTON (Portsmouth)*	ANDY GORMAN (Cardiff City)
February	ROY KEANE (Nottingham Forest)	GRAHAM STUART (Chelsea)	ANTHONY BARNESS (Charlton Athletic)	PHIL HARDY (Wrexham)
March	M. BREITKREUTZ (Aston Villa)	BRADLEY ALLEN (Queens Park R.)	PAUL McCARTHY (Brighton & H. A.)	ANDREW COLE (Bristol City)

Bill Nicholson & Bill Dodgin selected Darren Anderton as their joint selection for London, East Anglia and the South

TWO BARCLAYS YOUNG EAGLES FOR THE PRICE OF ONE

Not just one but **two** Barclays Young Eagle of the Year winners – and **both** from Nottingham Forest: left, the 1992 winner 21 year-old **Roy Keane**, Forest & Republic of Ireland midfield dynamo and goal-scorer extraordinaire; and right, **Nigel Clough**, the very first winner of this prestigious award in 1988, who made the presentation to his team-mate.

The award was nominated by England team manager Graham Taylor who said: "I just wish he was an English laddie" and his panel including Jack Charlton, Jimmy Armfield, Stan Cullis, Trever Cherry, Bill Nicholson, Bill Dodgin & Terry Yorath.

Rupublic of Ireland manager Charlton concluded: "Roy is now one of the most wanted players in the world."

His award comprised the Barclays Silver Eagle trophy and a Barclays Higher Rate Deposit cheque for £5,000.

ROB JONES MADE GRANDAD PROUD AT ANFIELD

Top young discovery of the year, Liverpool's **Rob Jones** – whose Roy of the Rovers rise to fame included international acclaim (and three Barclays Young Eagle nominations on the trot) – pictured here with Grandad, a former Liverpool stalwart, and Barclays Liverpool regional director, Brian Thaxter.

BARCLAYS

BARCLAYS PERFORMANCE OF THE WEEK

Each week a panel of leading managers, chaired by the England team manager, select the outstanding performance by a League club in the Premier League, Barclays League or F.A. Cup competition. The selected club then nominates a local Boy's Club to receive the Barclays award from the local manager, on the pitch, at the next home match. The award consists of a complete strip in the bank's colours and a cheque for £300, half of which must be spent on a local community project. The club receives an inscribed silver trophy. Thirty-eight awards were presented last season to clubs from all four divisions.

1. DARLINGTON	14. PORTSMOUTH	27. ARSENAL
2. SOUTHEND UNITED	15. SWANSEA CITY	28. DERBY COUNTY
3. WALSALL	16. CHESTERFIELD	29. OXFORD UNITED
4. BARNET	17. PLYMOUTH ARGYLE	30. HULL CITY
5. ARSENAL	18. HARTLEPOOL UNITED	31. NEWCASTLE UNITED
6. GRIMSBY TOWN	19. NORTHAMPTON TOWN	32. CHARLTON ATHLETIC
7. MANCHESTER UNITED	20. LUTON TOWN	33. TORQUAY UNITED
8. BARNSLEY	21. QUEENS PARK RANGERS	34. WATFORD
9. DERBY COUNTY	22. ROTHERHAM UNITED	35. MIDDLESBROUGH
10. CHESTER CITY	23. CHARLTON ATHLETIC	36. LINCOLN CITY
11. MANSFIELD TOWN	24. SWINDON TOWN	37. CHESTER CITY
12. TRANMERE ROVERS	25. SHEFFIELD UNITED	38. OXFORD CITY
13. BRISTOL ROVERS	26. BURY	

Arsenal took the Barclays Performance of the Week twice during the 1991-92 season: and this was the second one, for their 7-1 triumph over Sheffield Wednesday on Saturday, February 15. The club nominated Colverstone Boys Club for the award (Barclays set of strip plus cheque for £300); and the Highbury first team coach Stewart Houston received the silver trophy memento from Barclays London Northern Regional Office corporate director, Barry James.

INTRODUCTION TO CLUB PAGES

MOST readers have found their way around The Directory without to much trouble for a few years and the lay out this year is much the same as in previous editions.

However, you will notice that club statistics still refer to the old Football League Four Divisions and these will be amended after the first season of Premier Division Football.

We have included season by season leading League goalscorers and telephone numbers are now within the grounds details.

As readers seem to enjoy the present layout we hope that this years presentations also meets with your approval. The following notes should act as a guide to the club pages.

First Page:
Review of the 1991-92 season; Senior club personnel; 1992-93 playing squad photograph (if available at time of going to press).

Second & Third Pages
Complete match by match details of the 1991-92 season
Notations used: Left Hand Page: †=After extra-time
Right Hand Page: †=Player Sent Off;   *=Player substituted by No.12;
*=Player substituted by No.14;   S=Non playing substitute;   (L)=Player on Loan;   (M)=Player on monthly contract;   (T)=Trainee;   (NC)=Player on non-contract registration

Records Page(s)
Second and Third Division clubs' records and statistics are covered on one page.

Premier and First Division clubs' records and statistics cover two complete pages.

Players Page
The ever expanding detailed section on players of all clubs as at the start of the 1992-93 season including: heights, weights, birthdates and birthplace (where available) League and Cup appearances and goals, honours, contract dates, previous clubs and transfer fees. Please note that any competitions (including Play-Offs) other than League, FA Cup and League (Rumbelows) Cup are shown as others.
(Notations and Abbreviations):

E: England	S: Scotland	W: Wales	Ei: Eire	NI: Northern Ireland
D: Denmark	Sw: Sweden	H: Holland	I: Iceland	Sp: Spain
R: U.S.S.R.	U: Uraguay	A: Argentina	Pi: Poland	F: France

u21/23 – Under 21/23 International Cap   Y/u19 – Youth International Cap
S – Schoolboy International Cap   S-P – Semi Professional Cap
B – 'B' International Cap   F.lg – Football League Representative 'cap'

Div 1/2/3/4 – Div League Championship   FAC – F.A. Cup
LC – League Cup (incl. Milk, Littlewoods & Rumbelows)   CS – Charity Shield
SC/FMC/ZDS – Simod Cup/Full Members Cup/Zenith Data Cup   SVT/FRT/AGT – Sherpa Van/Freight Rover/Autoglass Trophy

EC – European Cup   ECWC – European Cup Winners Cup
UEFA – UEFA Cup (inc. Fairs)   ESC – European Super Cup
SPD – Scottish Premier Div Championship   SDiv1/2 – Scottish League Championship
ScC – Scottish Cup   SLC – Scottish League Cup (incl Skol)
AS – Anglo-Scottish Cup   GMVC General Motors Vauxhall Conference
FAYC – FA Youth Cup   FoY – Sports writers 'Footballer of the Year'
PoY – Player of the Year
FAAC – F.A. Amateur Cup   FAT – F.A. Trophy

Seventh Page
(Prem. & 1st Div)
This page accommodates any overspill of the players details along with a detailed career of the club manager and details of the club programme. Where a players page has been kept to one page we have included the record win and loss against each club in their current division.

Grounds Page
Containing this seasons match day prices along with record attendances and receipts, directions to the ground and the telephone numbers of the ground, ticket office (if different from ground) and Clubcall number. This year we have introduced on to this page the leading League goalscores of past seasons.

ARSENAL

Formed: 1886   **Turned Professional:** 1891   **PLC:** 1990

Premier

SPONSORED BY: JVC (UK) Ltd.   **NICKNAME:** The Gunners

Chairman
P D Hill-Wood

Directors
D Dein(Vice-Chairman)
Sir Robert Bellinger CBE,DSO
R G Gibbs   C E B L Carr
R C L Carr   K J Friar
D Fiszman

Secretary/Managing Director
K J Friar(071-226 0304)

Assistant Secretary
D Miles

Marketing Manager
Phillip Carling (071-359 0808)

Commercial Manager
John Hazell (071-359 0808)

Team Manager
George Graham

First Team Coach
Stewart Houston

Reserve Team Coach
George Armstrong

Youth Team Coach
Pat Rice

Chief Scout
S Burtenshaw

Physiotherapist
Gary Lewin

Groundsman
Steve Braddock

Club Statistician for the Directory
Chris Thompson

O NCE again the burden of being defending champions proved too big a a cross to bear for the Gunners. After losing just one game in the previous League campaign Arsenal suffered two defeats in the first week of the season, confirming that a successful defence of the title would be difficult.

There were no summer signings to augment George Grahams' squad although the prolific Ian Wright was signed for a club record £2.5 million in September. Norwegian defender Pal Lydersen was signed later in the season, as was Jimmy Carter with Michael Thomas joining Liverpool.

Arsenal's pre-season games included the high profile Makita Tournament – lost on penalties to holders Sampdoria – and a share of the Charity Shield after drawing 0-0 with Spurs at Wembley.

Leicester City were defeated over two legs in the Rumbelows Cup before the team were eliminated by Coventry at Highfield Road. At the time the result was greeted almost as a blessing in disguise but a week later, after losing at home to West Ham and Benfica, the F.A. Cup was seen as the most realistic chance of honours.

Arsenal progressed to the second round of the European Cup after comprehensively despatching Austria Vienna 6-2 on aggregate. The first leg against Benfica was played in the Estadio De La Luz and the Gunners came away with a creditable draw thanks to Kevin Campbell's equaliser. The second-leg at Highbury was lost 1-3 after Colin Pates had given Arsenal an early lead. This result proved to be a real watershed. George Graham had stressed the importance of the European Cup and the early elimination seemed to sap morale. Indeed the 12 league games following the Benfica defeat brought only two victories – against Tottenham and Everton – and it was this barren spell that doomed any chance of retaining the title.

The real nadir came in early January at Wrexham, when the Gunners suffered their first ever F.A. Cup defeat by a fourth division side, albeit that two contentious refereeing decisions were significant factors.

Wrexham also marked the turning point of the club's season with defeat at Anfield, at the end of January, being the only other defeat in 1992. Arsenal's, now traditional long unbeaten spell, then began and remained unbroken on seventeen at the season's end. The team played some superb football during this period and their victories included Sheffield Wednesday 7-1, Liverpool 4-0 and Southampton 5-1.

The Arsenal players of the season were Paul Merson, Ian Wright and Anders Limpar, and with George Graham looking to strengthen his squad in the close season, Arsenal should again be the team they all have to beat. Come on you Gunners!   **Chris Thompson**

Back row L-R: Gary Lewin (Physio), Pat Rice (Youth Team Coach), Perry Groves, Steve Bould, Alan Miller, David O'Leary, Alan Smith, Andy Linigan, Colin Pates, David Seaman, Tony Adams, Lee Dixon, Stewart Houston (First Team Coach), George Armstrong (Reserve Team Coach). **Front:** Nigel Winterburn, Paul Davis, Kevin Campbell, Pal Lydersen, Ian Wright, Ray Parlour, George Graham (Manager), Anders Limpar, Jimmy Carter, Neil Heaney, Paul Merson, John Jensen, David Hillier.

ARSENAL

DIVISION ONE: 4th **FA CUP:** 3rd RND **RUMBELOWS CUP:** 3rd RND **EUROPEAN CUP:** 2nd RND

M	DATE		COMP.	VEN	OPPONENTS	RESULT	H/T	LGE POS	GOALSCORERS/GOAL TIMES	ATTEN-DANCE
1	A	10	C Sh'ld	N	Tottenham Hotspur	D 0-0	0-0			(65,483)
2		17	BL	H	Queens Park R.	D 1-1	0-0		Merson 89	38,099
3		20	BL	A	Everton	L 1-3	0-1		Winterburn 87	(31,200)
4		24	BL	A	Aston Villa	L 1-3	1-1	21	Smith 45	(29,684)
5		28	BL	H	Luton Town	W 2-0	1-0	16	Merson 18, Smith 50	25,898
6		31	BL	H	Manchester City	W 2-1	0-1	12	Smith 46, Limpar 77	35,009
7	S	3	BL	A	Leeds United	D 2-2	1-0	10	Smith 20, 48	(29,396)
8		7	BL	H	Coventry City	L 1-2	0-1	15	Adams 58	28,142
9		14	BL	A	Crystal Palace	W 4-1	1-0	10	Campbell 14, 80, Smith 54, Thomas 57	(24,228)
10		18	EC 1/1	H	Austria Vienna	W 6-1	1-0		Linighan 39, Smith 4 (51, 54, 65, 66), Limpar 79	24,124
11		21	BL	A	Sheffield United	W 5-2	4-0	7	Smith 12, Dixon (p) 16, Groves 25, Rocastle 34, Campbell 67	30,244
12		25	RC 2/1	A	Leicester City	D 1-1	1-0		Wright 45	(20,679)
13		28	BL	A	Southampton	W 4-0	1-0	3	Rocastle 39, Wright 3 (47, 52, 73)	(18,050)
14	O	2	EC 1/2	A	Austria Vienna	L 0-1	0-0			(11,000)
15		5	BL	H	Chelsea	W 3-2	1-2	3	Dixon (pen) 30, Wright 47, Campbell 70	42,074
16		8	RC 2/2	H	Leicester City	W 2-0	0-0		Wright 54, Merson 76	28,580
17		19	BL	A	Manchester United	D 1-1	1-1	4	Rocastle 39	(46,594)
18		23	EC 2/1	A	Benfica	D 1-1	0-1		Campbell 17	(80,000)
19		26	BL	H	Notts County	W 2-0	0-0	4	Smith 69, Wright 75	30,011
20		30	RC 3	A	Coventry City	L 0-1	0-1			(15,337)
21	N	2	BL	H	West Ham United	L 0-1	0-0	5		33,539
22		6	EC 2/2	H	Benfica	L 1-3	1-1		Pates 20	35,815
23		16	BL	A	Oldham Athletic	D 1-1	0-0	6	Wright 86	(15,681)
24		23	BL	A	Sheffield Wed.	D 1-1	0-1	6	Bould 64	(32,174)
25	D	1	BL	H	Tottenham Hotspur	W 2-0	0-0	4	Wright 68, Campbell 77	38,892
26		8	BL	A	Nottingham Forest	L 2-3	0-1	6	Merson 74, Smith 78	(22,095)
27		21	BL	H	Everton	W 4-2	3-2	6	Wright 4 (3, 13, 26, 70)	29,684
28		26	BL	A	Luton Town	L 0-1	0-0	7		(12,665)
29		28	BL	A	Manchester City	L 0-1	0-0	7		(32,325)
30	J	1	BL	H	Wimbledon	D 1-1	0-1	7	Merson 46	26,839
31		4	FAC 3	A	Wrexham	L 1-2	1-0		Smith 44	(13,343)
32		11	BL	H	Aston Villa	D 0-0	0-0	7		31,413
33		18	BL	A	Queens Park R.	D 0-0	0-0	7		(20,497)
34		28	BL	A	Liverpool	L 0-2	0-1	7		(33,753)
35	F	1	BL	H	Manchester United	D 1-1	1-1	8	Rocastle 44	41,703
36		8	BL	A	Notts County	W 1-0	1-0	6	Smith 19	(11,221)
37		11	BL	H	Norwich City	D 1-1	0-0	6	Merson 63	22,352
38		15	BL	H	Sheffield Wed.	W 7-1	1-1	6	Smith 13, Campbell 71, 81, Limpar 74, 89, Merson 84, Wright 86	26,805
39		22	BL	A	Tottenham Hotspur	D 1-1	0-0	6	Wright 89	(33,124)
40	M	10	BL	H	Oldham Athletic	W 2-1	1-0	6	Wright 36, Merson 59	22,096
41		14	BL	A	West Ham United	W 2-0	1-0	6	Wright 13, 51	(22,640)
42		22	BL	H	Leeds United	D 1-1	0-0	6	Merson 81	27,844
43		28	BL	A	Wimbledon	W 3-1	2-0	5	Parlour 1, Wright 7, Campbell 64	(11,299)
44		31	BL	H	Nottingham Forest	D 3-3	1-2	5	Dixon (pen) 5, Merson 85, Adams 89	27,036
45	A	4	BL	A	Coventry City	W 1-0	1-0	4	Campbell 28	(14,133)
46		8	BL	A	Norwich City	W 3-1	0-0	4	Wright (pen) 32, 84, Campbell 46	(12,971)
47		11	BL	H	Crystal Palace	W 4-1	3-1	4	Merson 3 (9, 12, 64), Campbell 16	36,016
48		18	BL	A	Sheffield United	D 1-1	0-1	4	Campbell 58	(25,034)
49		20	BL	H	Liverpool	W 4-0	3-0	4	Hillier 6, Wright 16, 47, Limpar 40	38,517
50		25	BL	A	Chelsea	D 1-1	0-0	4	Dixon 88	(26,003)
51	M	2	BL	H	Southampton	W 5-1	0-0	4	Campbell 66, Wright 3 (71, 89, 90 pen), Smith 85	37,702

Best Home League Attendance: 42,074 v Chelsea **Smallest:** 22,096 v Oldham Athletic **Av Home Att:** 31,901

Goal Scorers: **Compared with 90-91:** -4,964

League (81): Wright 24 (2 pen), Campbell 13, Smith 12, Merson 12, Dixon 4 (3 pens), Limpar 4, Rocastle 4, Adams 2, Groves, Parlour, Winterburn, Hillier, Bould, Thomas

R/lows C (3): Wright 2, Merson

FA Cup (1): Smith

Euro Cup (8): Smith 4, Pates, Limpar, Campbell, Linighan

Seaman D.	Dixon L.	Winterburn N.	Hillier D.	O'Leary D.	Adams T.	Rocastle D.	Davis P.	Smith A.	Merson P.	Campbell K.	Thomas M.	Cole A.	Miller A.	Linighan A.	Jonsson S.	Limpar A.	Groves P.	Pates C.	Wright I.	Parlour R.	Bould S.	Carter J.	Lydersen P.	Morrow S.	Heaney N.	Referee	
1	2	3	4	5	6	7*	8	9	10	11•	12	14	S	S	S											T Holbrook	1
1	2	3	4	5*	6	12	8	9	10	7•						11	14									R Groves	2
1	2	3	4•	5	6	7	8	9	10					14		11*	12									D Phillips	3
1	2	3		5*	6	7•	8	9	10			14		4		11	12									D Allison	4
1	2	3			6	7	8	9	10			4	S	5		11†	S									P Foakes	5
1	2	3			6	7*	8	9	10	12		4		5		11•	14									B Hill	6
1	2	3	7		6	12	8	9	10	11		4*		5			S									R Nixon	7
1	2	3	12		6	7	8•	9	10	4		14		5		11*										R Gifford	8
1	2	3	4•	14	6	7		9	10	11	12			5			8*									K Hackett	9
1	2	3	S		6	7	8	9	10	4	S	S		5	S	11*	12									R Larsson	10
1	2	3*	12		6	7	8	9	10	4		14		5		11•										J Worrall	11
1	2		12		6	7	8		10	4	3			5*		11		9	S							N Midgley	12
1	2	3	S		6	7		9*	10	12		4		5		11		8								P Durkin	13
1	2	3	11		6	7	S	9*	10	8		4	S	5	S		12	S								A Spirin	14
1	2	3	14			7		9	10	12		4		5		11*	6	8•								A Buksh	15
1	2	3			6	7		9	10	11		4				S	12	5	8*							J Borrett	16
1	2	3			6	7	4	9	10	11		S		S				5	8							T Holbrook	17
1	2	3	S		6	7	4	9	10	8*		14	S	S		11•	12	5								T Lanese	18
1	2	3			6	7	4	9	10	11*						S	12	5	8							A Gunn	19
1	2	3			6	7	4	9	10					14		11*	12	5•	8							M Bodenham	20
1	2	3				7		9	10			4*		6		11	12	5	8			S				J Martin	21
1	2	3	S	S	6	7	4	9	10	8					S	11*	12	5•				14				A Schmidhuber	22
1	2	3	4	12		7		9	10					6		14	11•	8	5*							J Watson	23
1	2	3	4*	12		7		9	10					6		S	11	8	5							V Callow	24
1	2	3	4	14		7•		9	10	11				6		12		8*	5							K Redfern	25
1	2	3	4	14		7		9	10	8				6		11*		5•					12			R Milford	26
1	2	3	4	12	6	7*		9	10•	14						11			8		5					P Vanes	27
1	2	3	4		6	7		9	10	12				S		11*			8		5*					R Wiseman	28
1	2	3	4•		6	7	11	9	10					12†		14			8		5*					J Rushton	29
1	2	3	4	S	6	7		9	10	12				5					8*			11				D Axcell	30
1	2	3	4	5	6	7		9	10	8*				S				12				11				K Breen	31
1	2	3	4	5	6	7		9	10*	8								12	S			11				K Hackett	32
1	2	3		5	6	7	4	9	10							S	S		8			11				A Buksh	33
1	2	3	4		6	7*		9	10							14			8	4•		12	11			M Reed	34
1	2	3	4		6	7*		9	10							14		12	8		5*	11				R Groves	35
1	2	3*	4		6			9	10	14						11•	7		8		12	5				W Burns	36
1	2	3*	4		6			9	10	12						11*	7		8		14	5				J Key	37
1	2	3	4		6	7		9	10	12						11		S	8		5					A Gunn	38
1	2	3	4	12	6	7*		9	10	11						14	6		8		5					K Barratt	39
1	2	3	4	12	6	7		9	10	S						11*			8		5					I Borrett	40
1	2	3	4	14	6	7		9*	10	12						11•			8		5					B Hill	41
1	2	3	4*	9	6	7•			10	11				12					8	14	5					M Bodenham	42
1	2	3	4		6			9	10•	12						11*	8	7			5	14				R Lewis	43
1	2	3	4		6	7*		9	10	14						11			8•		5	12				P Foakes	44
1	2	3*	4		6	12		9	10	14						11•			8		5	7				R Gifford	45
1		4	2*		6	7		9	10	14						11•			8		5	3	12			P Wright	46
1	3•	4			6	7		9	10	12						11•			8		5	2	14			R Bigger	47
1		3	4	S	6	7		9	10	8						11*					5	2		12		H King	48
1	2	3	4	12	6	7	S	9	10							11			8		5	2*				K Hackett	49
1	2	3	4	14	6	7		9	10•	12						11*			8		5					P Danson	50
1	2	3	4		6	7		9	10•	12						11*			8	14	5					D Phillips	51
42	38	41	27	11	35	36	12	33	41	22	6			15		23	5	9	30	2	24	5	5			**League Appearances**	
			14		3			6	1	9	4			2		6	8	2		4	1	1	2	2	1	**Substitute Appearances**	
3	3	2	0+1	3	3	2	2	3	2	2				1+1		1	1+2	2	3							**R/lows Appearances**	
1	1	1	1	1	1	1		1	1	1									0+1			1				**FA Cup Appearances**	
4	4	4	1	4	4	3	4	4	4	4				0+1	0+1	2		3	0+4	2			0+1			**European Cup Apps**	
1	1	1	1	1	1	1	1	1	1	1	1	0+1	0+1													**Charity Shield Apps**	

† = Sent Off

ARSENAL

Club Colours: Red with white sleeve shirts, white shorts, red and white stockings.
Change Colours: Yellow shirts, navy blue shorts, yellow stockings.
Reserves League: Football Combination. **Youth League:** South Eastern Counties.

COMPETITIONS				
Div. 1	Div. 2	Euro C	ECWC	UEFA
04-13	93-04	71-72	79-80	63-64
19-	13-19	91-92		69-70
				70-71
				78-79
				81-82
				82-83

HONOURS				
Div. 1	FA Cup	Lge C	UEFA	C/Shield
30-31	29-30	86-87	69-70	1930
32-33	35-36			1931
33-34	49-50			1933
34-35	70-71			1934
37-38	78-79			1938
47-48				1948
52-53				1953
70-71				1992
88-89				shared
90-91				

MOST APPEARANCES: DAVID O'LEARY 674+33 (1975-)				
Year	League	FAC	Lge C	Europe
1975-76	27	1	2	
1976-77	33	3	4	
1977-78	41	6	6	
1978-79	37	11	1	5
1979-80	34	9	6	9
1980-81	24	1	2	
1981-82	40	1	5	4
1982-83	36	5	7	2
1983-84	36	1	4	
1984-85	36	3	3	
1985-86	35	5	7	
1986-87	39	4	9	
1987-88	23	4	6	
1988-89	26	2		
1989-90	28+6	3	4	
1990-91	11+10	5+1	0+1	
1991-92	11+14	1	0+1	1
	517+30	65+1	66+2	21
Plus 3 Charity Shield & 2 Others				
Previous holder: George Armstrong 607+14 (1961-77)				

MOST GOALS IN A CAREER		
CLIFF BASTIN: 178 (1929-37) inc. 2 in Charity Shield		
Season	League	FA Cup
1929-30	7	4
1930-31	28	1
1931-32	15	6
1932-33	33	
1933-34	13	2
1934-35	20	1
1935-36	11	6
1936-37	5	3
1937-38	15	2
1938-39	3	1
Total	150	26
Previous holder: Jimmy Brain, 137 (1924-31)		

RECORD TRANSFER FEE RECEIVED			
Amount	Club	Player	Date
£1,500,000	Liverpool	Michael Thomas	12/91
£1,250,000	Crystal Palace	Clive Allen	8/80
£450,000	Liverpool	Ray Kennedy	7/74
£100,000	Leicester City	Jon Sammels	7/71

RECORD TRANSFER FEE PAID			
Amount	Club	Player	Date
£2,500,000	Crystal Palace	Ian Wright	9/91
£1,300,000	Queens Park R	David Seaman	5/90
£1,250,000	Queens Park R	Clive Allen	6/80
£450,000	Ipswich Town	Brian Talbot	1/79

MANAGERS			
Name	Seasons	Best	Worst
T E Mitchell	1897-98	5(2)	5(2)
George Excoat	1898-99	7(2)	7(2)
Harry Bradshaw	1899-04	2(2)	8(2)
Phil Kelso	1904-08	7(1)	15(1)
George Morrell	1908-15	6(1)	15(1)
Leslie Knighton	1919-25	9(1)	20(1)
Herbert Chapman	1925-34	1(1)	14(1)
George Allison	1934-47	1(1)	6(1)
Tom Whittaker	1947-56	1(1)	6(1)
Jack Crayston	1956-58	5(1)	12(1)
George Swindin	1958-62	3(1)	15(1)
Billy Wright	1962-66	8(1)	17(1)
Bertie Mee	1966-76	1(1)	17(1)
Terry Neill	1976-83	3(1)	17(1)
Don Howe	1983-86	6(1)	7(1)
George Graham	1986-		

LONGEST LEAGUE RUNS	
of undefeated matches:	26 (28.4.1990-19.1.1991)
of undefeated home matches:	33 (1.10.1902-22.10.1904)
without home win:	16 (23.4.1912-1.3.1913)
of league wins:	10 (12.9.1987-14.11.1987)
of league defeats:	7 (12.2.1977-12.3.1977)
of league matches without a win:	23 (28.9.1912-1.3.1913)
of undefeated away matches:	13 (5.5.1990-12.1.1991)
without an away win:	15 (7.1.1928-6.10.1928)
of home wins:	15 (5.9.1903-4.4.1904)
of away wins:	6 (22.10.1977-27.12.1977)

BIGGEST VICTORIES

League: 12-0 v Loughborough Town, Division 2, 12.3.1900
F.A. Cup: 11-1 v Darwen, Round 3, 9.1.1932
League Cup: 7-0 v Leeds Utd., Round 2, 4.9.1979
Europe (UEFA): 7-1 v Staevnet, Round 1, 25.9.1963
7-1 v Dinamo Bacau, Fairs Cup Q/Final, 18.3.1970

BIGGEST DEFEATS

League: 0-8 v Loughborough Town, Division 2, 12.12.1896
F.A. Cup: 0-6 v Sunderland, Round 1, 21.1.1893
0-6 v Derby County, Round 1, 28.1.1899
0-6 v West Ham, Round 3, 5.1.1946
League Cup: 2-6 v Manchester Utd, Round 4, 28.11.1990
0-3 v Liverpool, Round4, 8.12.1981
Europe (UEFA): 2-5 v Spartak Moscow, Round 1, 29.9.1982

MOST POINTS

3 points a win: 83, 1990-91.
2 points a win: 66, 1930-31.

MOST GOALS

127, Division 1, 1930-31.
Lambert 38, Jack 31, Bastin 28, Hulme 14, James 5, Brain 4, John 2, Williams 2, Johnson 1, Roberts 1, Jones 1.

MOST GOALS IN A MATCH

7. Ted Drake v Aston Villa, Division 1, 14.12.1935 (7-1).

MOST GOALS IN A SEASON

Ted Drake: 42 goals in 1934-35.
4 goals 4 times = 16; 3 goals 3 times = 9; 2 goals 2 times = 4;
1 goal 13 times = 13.
Previous holders: I Shanks 25; J Tanley 28; J Brain 34, J Lambert 39.

MOST FIRST CLASS MATCHES IN A SEASON

70 (42 League, 11 FA Cup, 7 League Cup, 1 Charity Shield, 9 European Cup Winners Cup) 1979-80

MOST LEAGUE GOALS CONCEDED

86, Division 1, 1926-27; Div 1, 1927-28

MOST LEAGUE WINS

29, Division 1, 1970-71

MOST LEAGUE DRAWS

18, Division 1, 1969-70

MOST LEAGUE DEFEATS

23, Division 1, 1912-13; Div 1, 1924-25

OLDEST PLAYER

Jock Rutherford, 42 years v Liverpool 23.1.1926

YOUNGEST PLAYER

Gerry Ward, 16 years 321 days v Huddersfield, 22.8.1953

MOST CAPPED PLAYER

Kenny Sansom (England) 77 1981-86

BEST PERFORMANCES BY ARSENAL

League: 1930-31: Matches played 42, Won 29, Drawn 10, Lost 4, Goals for 127, Goals against 59, Points 66. First in Division 1

Highest: Division 1 Champions.

F.A. Cup: 1929-30: 3rd rnd. Chelsea 2-1; 4th rnd. Birmingham City 2-2, 1-0; 5th rnd. Middlesbrough 2-0; 6th rnd. West Ham 3-0; Semi-Final Hull 2-2, 1-0; Final Huddersfield 2-0.

1935-36: 3rd rnd. Bristol Rovers 5-1; 4th rnd. Liverpool 2-0; 5th rnd. Newcastle Utd. 3-3, 3-0; 6th rnd Barnsley 4-1; Semi-Final Grimsby 1-0; Final Sheffield United 1-0.

1949-50: Sheffield Wednesday 1-0; 4th rnd. Swansea 2-1; 5th rnd. Burnley 2-0; 6th rnd. Leeds 1-0; Semi-Final Chelsea 2-2, 1-0; Final Liverpool 2-0

1970-71: 3rd rnd. Yeovil 3-0; 4th rnd. Portsmouth 1-1, 3-2; 5th rnd. Manchester City 2-1; 6th rnd. Leicester City 0-0, 1-0; Semi-Final Stoke City 0-0, 1-0; Final Liverpool 2-1.

1978-79: 3rd rnd. Sheffield Wednesday 1-1, 1-1, 2-2, 3-3, 2-0; 4th rnd. Notts County 2-0; 5th rnd. Nottingham Forest 1-0; 6th rnd. Southampton 1-1, 2-0; Semi-Final Wolves 2-0; Final Manchester Utd. 3-2.

League Cup: 1986-87: 2nd rnd. Huddersfield 1-1, 2-0; 3rd rnd. Manchester City 3-1; 4th rnd. Charlton 2-0; 5th rnd. Nottingham Forest 2-0; Semi-Final Tottenham 0-1, 2-1, 2-1; Final Liverpool 2-1.

Europe (UEFA): 1969-70: 1st rnd. Glentoran 5-0, 0-1; 2nd rnd. Sp. ch. de port 0-0, 3-0; 3rd rnd. Rouen 0-0, 1-0; Dinemo Bacau 2-0, 7-1; Semi-Final Ajax 3-0, 0-1; Final Anderlect 1-3, 3-0.

DIVISIONAL RECORDS

	Played	Won	Drawn	Lost	For	Against	Points
DIVISION 1	3096	1321	797	978	5020	4177	**3653**
DIVISION 2	428	216	73	139	825	550	**505**
TOTALS	**3524**	**1537**	**870**	**1117**	**5845**	**4727**	**4158**

ARSENAL

PLAYERS NAME / Honours	Ht	Wt	Birthdate	Birthplace / Transfers	Contract Date	Clubs	League	L/Cup	FA Cup	Other	Lg	L/C	FAC	Oth
GOALKEEPERS														
Alan Miller	6.2	13.8	29.03.70	Epping	05.05.88	Arsenal (A)								
E:u21.4,GMFAS,FAYC'88				Loan	24.11.88	Portsmouth								
				Loan	24.11.88	Plymouth A	13		2					
Loan WBA (15.08.91) 2 lge app. 1 L/Cup				Loan	19.12.91	Birmingham City	15			1				
David Seaman	6.2	13.0	19.09.63	Rotherham	22.09.81	Leeds Utd. (A)								
E:9,u21.10				£4,000	13.08.82	Peterborough U	91	10	5					
				£100,000	05.10.84	Birmingham City	75	4	5					
				£225,000	07.08.86	Q.P.R	141	13	17	4				
				£1,300,000	18.05.90	Arsenal	80	7	9	5				
James Will	6.1		07.10.72	Aberdeen	15.11.90	Arsenal								
				Loan	21.11.91	Sheffield Utd								
DEFENDERS														
Tony Adams	6.1	12.1	10.10.66	Romford	30.01.84	Arsenal (A)	248+1	33+1	18	9	20	2	1	1
E:19,B:4,u21.5,Y.5,ES; CT'89; Div.1'89; LC'87														
Steve Bould	6.2	11.13	16.11.62	Stoke	15.11.80	Stoke City (A)	179+4	13	10	5	6	1		
Div1'89. CT'89				Loan	19.10.82	Torquay Utd	9		2					
				£390,000	13.06.88	Arsenal	107+5	9	12	1+1	3			
Lee Dixon	5.9	10.12	17.03.64	Manchester	21.07.82	Burnley (A)	4	1						
E:4, Div.1'89. CT'89				Free	16.02.84	Chester City	56+1	2	1	3	1			
				Free	15.07.85	Bury	45	4	8	1	6		1	
				£40,000	18.07.86	Stoke City	71	6	7	4	5			
				£400,000	29.01.88	Arsenal	151+2	16	13	8	16		1	
Andy Linighan	6.3	12.6	18.06.62	Hartlepool	19.09.80	Hartlepool Utd	110	7+1	8	1	4	1		1
EB 4				£200,000	15.05.84	Leeds Utd	66	6	2	2	3	1		
				£65,000	17.01.86	Oldham Ath	87	8	3	4	6	2		
				£350,000	04.03.88	Norwich City	86	6	10	4	8			
				£1,250,000	04.07.90	Arsenal	22+5	1+1	3+1	2				1
Steve Morrow	6.0	11.3	02.07.70	Belfast	05.05.88	Arsenal (T)	0+2							
NI:7,U23:1;FAYC'88				Loan	16.01.91	Reading	10							
				Loan	14.08.91	Watford	7+1				1			
Loan Reading (30.10.91) 3lg app.				Loan	04.03.92	Barnet								
David O'Leary	5.11	11.3	02.05.58	London		Arsenal (A)								
Ei:67,FAC'79;LC'87;Div1'89					01.07.75	Arsenal	517+30	66+2	65	26	11	2	3	
Colin Pates	6.0	11.0	10.08.61	Carshalton	19.07.79	Chelsea (A)	280+1	32	20	13	10			
E:Y1,UEFAY'80,Div2'84,FMC'86				£430,000	26.10.88	Charlton Ath	37+1	3	3					
				£500,000	22.01.90	Arsenal	10+4	2		2				1
				Loan	28.02.91	Brighton & H.A	17			3				
Nigel Winterburn	5.10	10.7	11.12.63	Nuneaton	14.08.81	Birmingham City (A)								
E:1,u21.1,Y(1);Div1'89.CT'89				Free	04.08.83	Oxford Utd								
				Free	22.09.83	Wimbledon	164+1	13	12	2	8			
				£407,000	26.05.87	Arsenal	169+1	19	17	9	4	2		
MIDFIELD														
Paul Davis	5.8	9.7	09.12.61	London	11.07.79	Arsenal (A)	301+18	42+3	19+5	9+1	29	4	3	1
E: ,u21.11; LC'87. Div1'89; CT'89														
David Hillier	5.10	11.6	18.12.69	London	11.02.88	Arsenal (T)	36+7	2	4+1	1	1			
FAYC'88														
John Jenson			03.05.65			Brondby								
				£1,100,000	01.08.92	Arsenal								
Anders Limpar						Cremonese								
				£1,000,000	06.08.90	Arsenal	55+8	3	5	3	15		2	1
Raymond Parlour			07.03.73	Romford	06.03.91	Arsenal	2+4				1			
FORWARDS														
Kevin Campbell	6.0	13.1	04.02.70	London	11.02.88	Arsenal (T)	45+24	2+4	5+2	5	24		1	1
FAYC'88				Loan	16.01.89	Leyton Orient	16				9			
				Loan	08.11.89	Leicester City	11			1	5			1
Jimmy Carter	5.10	10.4	09.11.65	Hammersmith	15.11.83	Crystal Palace (A)								
Div2'88				Free	12.12.85	Q.P.R								
				£15,000	12.03.87	Millwall	99+11	6+1	6+1	5+1	11		2	
				£800,000	10.01.91	Liverpool	2+3		2+1					
				£500,000	08.10.91	Arsenal	5+1		1					
Paul Merson	5.10	11.9	20.03.68	Brent	22.01.87	Brentford	6+1			1+1				
E:7,u21.3,u19.3,Y; Div1'89; CT'89					01.12.85	Arsenal (A)	139+28	13+2	13+2	7+1	50	5	3	
Alan Smith	6.3	12.0	02.11.62	Bromsgrove		Alvechurch								
E:13,S-P.3; F.Lg.1; Div1'89; CT'89				£22,000	14.06.82	Leicester City	190+10	8+1	8		76	4	4	
				£800,000	26.03.87	Arsenal	177+12	22+1	16	9	78	12	4	4
Ian Wright	5.10	11.0	03.11.63	Woolwich		Greenwich								
E:5,B.1,FMC'91				Free	02.08.85	Crystal Palace	206+19	19	9+2	19+3	89	9	3	16
				£2,500,000	24.09.91	Arsenal	30	3			24	2		
ADDITIONAL CONTRACT PLAYERS														
(F) Neil Heaney	5.9		03.11.71	Middlesbrough	14.11.89	Arsenal (T)	0+1							
E: Y				Loan	03.01.91	Hartlepool Utd	2+1							
				Loan	09.01.92	Cambridge Utd	9+4		1		2			
Pal Lydersen						Start (Norway)								
				£500,000	22.11.91	Arsenal	5+2							

(F) John Bacon, (M) Steven Clements, (F) Paul Dickov, (M) Mark Flatts, (D) Craig Gaunt, Justin Lee, (D) Scott Marshall, Paul Reed, Ian Selley, Paul Shaw, (D) Kenneth Webster.

ARSENAL

RECORD WIN & LOSS AGAINST EACH CLUB IN CURRENT DIVISION
(Where a score has occured on several occasions the most recent is given)

Club	Rec. Win	Season	Rec. Loss	Season
ASTON VILLA	7-1	1935-36 (away)	5-0	1920-21
BLACKBURN ROVERS	8-0	1922-23	7-0	1909-10
CHELSEA	5-1	1930-31 (away)	4-1	1960-61 (home)
COVENTRY CITY	6-1	1990-91	3-0	1974-75
CRYSTAL PALACE	5-1	1969-70 (away)	1-0	1979-80
EVERTON	6-0	1963-64	6-1	1985-86
IPSWICH TOWN	6-0	1963-64	4-1	1976-77 (home)
LEEDS UNITED	6-1	1924-25	6-1	1972-73
LIVERPOOL	8-1	1934-35	5-0	1963-64
MANCHESTER CITY	7-3	1956-57	4-0	1912-13
MANCHESTER UNITED	6-2	1946-47	6-1	1951-52
MIDDLESBROUGH	8-0	1934-35	5-0	1979-80
NORWICH CITY	5-0	1988-89	3-1	1982-83
NOTTINGHAM FOREST	7-0	1914-15	4-0	1957-58
OLDHAM ATHLETIC	2-0	1922-23	3-0	1919-20
QUEENS PARK RANGERS	5-1	1978-79	2-0	1989-90
SHEFFIELD UNITED	9-2	1932-33	5-0	1973-74
SHEFFIELD WEDNESDAY	7-1	1991-92	6-0	1907-08
SOUTHAMPTON	5-1	1991-92	3-0	1985-86
TOTTENHAM HOTSPUR	6-0	1934-35 (away)	5-0	1982-83
WIMBLEDON	5-1	1988-89 (away)	3-1	1987-88

MANAGER: GEORGE GRAHAM

DATE OF BIRTH: 30.11.1944   **PLACE OF BIRTH:** Bargeddie

DATE OF APPOINTMENT: MAY 1986

PREVIOUS CLUBS
   as Manager: Millwall
   as Coach: Crystal Palace
   as Player: A Villa; Chelsea; Arsenal; Manchester Utd; Portsmouth; C Palace

HONOURS
   as Manager: Millwall: Football League Trophy Winners;   Arsenal: League Cup Winners 1987; League Championship 1989; 1991
   as Player: A Villa: Lge/Cup Finalists 1963; Chelsea: Lge Cup Winners 1965; Arsenal: Inter-Cities Fairs Cup Winners 1970; Lge Cup Winners 1965; Finalists 1968, 1969; League Championship 1971; FAC Winners 1971; Finalists 1972
   International: Scotland: 12 Full Caps, U23 (2) Schools

Value Rating: ★ ★ ★ ★ ★

Programme Editor: Kevin Connolly

Price of 1991-92 Programme: £1.50

Number of Pages: 48

Subscriptions: Subscription price on application to club shop.

Local Newspapers: Islington Gazette.

Local Radio Stations: Capital Radio, LBC, BBC Radio London.

Additional Club Publications: Arsenal 1886-1986. Official Centenary History of the Club (Phil Soar, Martin Tyler) hardback £12.95.
Arsenal – Complete Record (Fred Ollier), Breedon Books, Hardback, £14.95
Arsenal – History & Full Record (Scott Grant & Colin White), Lingfield Press, Hardback, £26.95

LEADING LEAGUE GOALSCORERS
SEASONS 1979-80 – 1991-92

1979-80	FRANK STAPLETON	14		1980-81	FRANK STAPLETON	14
	ALAN SUNDERLAND	14				
1981-82	ALAN SUNDERLAND	11		1982-83	TONY WOODCOCK	14
1983-84	TONY WOODCOCK	21		1984-85	IAN ALLINSON	10
1985-86	TONY WOODCOCK	11		1986-87	MARTIN HAYES	19
1987-88	ALAN SMITH	11		1988-89	ALAN SMITH	23
1989-90	ALAN SMITH	10		1990-91	ALAN SMITH	22
			1991-92	**IAN WRIGHT**	**24**	

ARSENAL STADIUM Highbury, London N5 1BU

Capacity: 30,000   **Covered Standing:** 10,000   **Seating:** 17,000

Tel: Ground: 071 226 0304   **Ticket Sales:** 071 354 5404   **Clubcall:** 0898 20 20 20

All premium rate calls (0898/0891) cost 36p per minute cheap rate and 48p per minute at all other times. Call costings correct at time of going to press.

GROUNDS
Plumstead Common 1886-1887; Sportsman's Ground 1887-1888, Manor Road 1888-1890/1893-1913; Invicta Ground 1890-1893; Highbury 1913-

ATTENDANCES
Highest: 73,295 v Sunderland, Division 1, 9.3.1935

Lowest: 600 v Loughborough Town, Division 2, 12.3.1900

RECORD RECEIPTS (with previous records):
£482,513 Liverpool v Portsmouth, FA Cup Semi-Final, 5.4.1992
£233,595 v Everton, Littlewoods Cup, 24.2.1988
£116,498 v Juventus, ECWC, 9.4.1980
£51,477 v Anderlecht, UEFA, 28.8.1970
£21,470 v Spartak, 9.11.1954

HIGHBURY
First game: Arsenal v Leicester Fosse, Division 2, 6.9.1913
First floodlit game: Arsenal v Glasgow Rangers, 1951

Season Tickets:
Stands: from £252 to £504 (no reductions)
Ground: from £95 jun/OAP, £190 adults

Cost of Stand Tickets: (seats): Centre £22, next to Centre £16, Wings £14.50, Lower Tier £10.50.
Terraces: £3 junior Gunners, £4 Cannon Club, £8 adults.
Family Enclosure: Adult £10.50, juveniles/OAP £5

Car Parking: Parking is permitted in adjacent street

Nearest Railway Station: Finsbury Park and Highbury and Islington

Nearest Underground Station: Arsenal, on the Piccadilly Line

How to get to the ground

From North: Leave Motorway M1 at Junction 2 and follow signs City. In 6.2m pass Holloway Road Station and then take 3rd turning on left into Drayton Park Road. In 0.7m turn right into Avenell Road for Arsenal FC

From South: From London Bridge follow signs, to Bank of England, then follow signs to Angell (Islington). At traffic signals turn right (S.P. The North) and in 1m at Highbury roundabout forward into Holloway Road. Then take 3rd turning on right into Drayton Park Road. In 0.7m turn right into Avenell Road for Arsenal FC

From West: Leave Motorway M4 at junction 1 Chiswick and follow A315 (S.P. Chiswick). In 0.9m turn left A40 then follow signs City to join Motorway M41, then A40(M) at end forward into Ring Road A501. At Angell (Islington) turn left to Highbury roundabout, keep forward into Holloway Road. Then take 3rd turning on right into Drayton Park Road. In 0.7m turn right into Avenell Road for Arsenal FC

ASTON VILLA
Premier

Formed: 1874   **Turned Professional:** 1885   **Ltd Co:** 1896

SPONSORED BY: Mita Copystar (UK) Ltd   **NICKNAME:** The Villa

President
Harold Musgrove

Chairman
Doug Ellis

Directors
J A Alderson, Dr D H Targett
P D Ellis

Secretary
Steven Stride (021-327 2299)

Assistant Secretary
Arthur Moseley

Team Manager
Ron Atkinson

Assistant Manager
Jim Barron

First Team Coach
Dave Sexton

Youth Coach
Richard Money

Director of Youth Development
Dave Richardson

Chief Scout
Brian Whitehouse

Commercial Manager
Abdul Rashid (021-327 5399)

Stadium Manager
Ted Small

Promotions Manager
John Greenfield

Physiotherapist
Jim Walker

Fitness Consultant
Roger Spry

Groundsman
Tony Eden

Club Statistician for the Directory
Dave Hodges

HAVING survived the trauma of returning to Sheffield Wednesday on the first day of the season, Ron Atkinson must surely have been justified in looking forward to a season full of excitement and certainly full of goals. The pace, skills and general presence of such entertainers as Tony Daley, Dalian Atkinson, Dwight Yorke and Cyrille Regis would surely be too much for most defences and how the fans would be entertained.

But football can play funny tricks and despite eight goals in the first five league games it was scoring that proved the problem of the season for Ron Atkinson's club. The popular veteran, Regis more than repaid the manager's faith in him by finishing top league scorer with 11 goals but only Yorke, with seventeen in all competitions, also reached double figures. Indeed, at the turn of the year, only eight goals were scored before April!

Ron Atkinson's sides have always been known for their style and entertainment value and to be fair the Villa were never unattractive and during their lean period the club never fell lower than twelfth position. Their persistance brought eleven goals in the last six league matches and a thrilling quarter-final at Anfield saw the end of a good F.A. Cup run which included victories over Spurs, Derby County and Swindon Town. Unfortunately the other cup competitions failed to bring any excitement but home attendances were around the 25,000 mark and there is plenty to look forward to in the coming season.

The attacking potential will always be present in the manager's teams and the solid reliability of Kevin Richardson, Shaun Teale and Paul McGrath will benefit from the flair to be added by Ray Houghton and the very promising Steve Froggatt.

Hopefully the playing surface at the superb Villa Park stadium will be a vast improvement from last season. The midlands needs a successful club and Aston Villa have always been considered the senior member of 'the family' in that area. When Villa are successful the midlands comes alive and I expect just that to happen in the coming season. **T.W.**

Back row L-R: Richard Money, Stefan Beinlich, Matthias Breitkreutz, Neil Cox, Mark Blake, Stephen Froggatt, Bryan Small, Roger Spry. **Middle row:** Dave Sexton (First team coach), Dwight Yorke, Garry Parker, Paul McGrath, Les Sealey, Nigel Spink, Martin Carruthers, Ugo Ehiogum, Cyrille Regis, Jim Walker (Physio). **Front row:** Shaun Teale, Earl Barratt, Dariusz Kubicki, Jim Barron (Asst. Manager), Ron Atkinson (Manager), Kevin Richardson, Dalian Atkinson, Steve Staunton.

ASTON VILLA

DIVISION ONE: 7th   **FA CUP:** 6th RND   **RUMBELOWS CUP:** 2nd RND   **ZDS CUP:** 3rd RND

M	DATE		COMP.	VEN	OPPONENTS	RESULT		H/T	LGE POS	GOALSCORERS/GOAL TIMES	ATTEN-DANCE
1	A	17	BL	A	Sheffield Wed.	W	3-2	1-2	2	Regis 42, Atkinson 52, Staunton 86	(36,749)
2		21	BL	H	Manchester United	L	0-1	0-1	9		39,995
3		24	BL	H	Arsenal	W	3-1	1-1	4	Staunton (pen) 40, Penrice 53, Daley 76	29,684
4		28	BL	A	West Ham United	L	1-3	0-0	9	Daley 50	(23,644)
5		31	BL	A	Southampton	D	1-1	1-1	11	Richardson 2	(16,161)
6	S	4	BL	H	Crystal Palace	L	0-1	0-1	16		20,740
7		7	BL	H	Tottenham Hotspur	D	0-0	0-0	14		33,096
8		14	BL	A	Liverpool	D	1-1	1-1	16	Richardson 25	(38,400)
9		18	BL	A	Chelsea	L	0-2	0-1	18		(17,182)
10		21	BL	H	Nottingham Forest	W	3-1	0-1	15	Blake 48, Richardson 62, Yorke 63	28,506
11		25	RC 2/1	A	Grimsby Town	D	0-0	0-0			(13,835)
12		28	BL	A	Coventry City	L	0-1	0-1	16		(17,851)
13	O	5	BL	H	Luton Town	W	4-0	1-0	14	Richardson 4, Regis 47, Yorke 59, Mortimer 80	18,722
14		9	RC 2/2	H	Grimsby Town	D	†1-1	0-0		Teale 69 (Lost on away goals)	15,338
15		19	BL	A	Everton	W	2-0	1-0	8	Regis 32, Daley 66	(27,048)
16		23	ZDS 2	A	Coventry City	W	2-0	1-0		Olney 16, Yorke 72	(6,447)
17		26	BL	H	Wimbledon	W	2-1	2-0	6	Olney 10, Yorke 29	16,928
18	N	2	BL	A	Queens Park R.	W	1-0	1-0	6	Yorke 45	(10,642)
19		16	BL	H	Notts County	W	1-0	1-0	4	Yorke 29	23,020
20		19	ZDS 3	H	Nottingham Forest	L	0-2	0-1			7,859
21		24	BL	H	Leeds United	L	1-4	0-1	4	Yorke 68	23,713
22		30	BL	A	Oldham Athletic	L	2-3	1-1	5	Blake 10, Regis 58	(15,370)
23	D	7	BL	H	Manchester City	W	3-1	2-0	5	Regis 26, Yorke 40, Daley 70	26,265
24		14	BL	A	Sheffield United	L	0-2	0-1	5		(18,401)
25		26	BL	H	West Ham United	W	3-1	2-0	6	Yorke 34, Daley 35, Richardson 89	31,959
26		28	BL	H	Southampton	W	2-1	1-0	5	Regis 15, Yorke 60	23,094
27	J	1	BL	A	Norwich City	L	1-2	0-0	6	Regis 74	(15,318)
28		4	FAC 3	H	Tottenham Hotspur	D	0-0	0-0			29,316
29		11	BL	A	Arsenal	D	0-0	0-0	6		(31,413)
30		14	FAC 3R	A	Tottenham Hotspur	W	1-0	1-0		Yorke 10	(25,462)
31		18	BL	H	Sheffield Wed.	L	0-1	0-0	6		28,036
32		22	BL	A	Manchester United	L	0-1	0-0	6		(45,022)
33	F	2	BL	H	Everton	D	0-0	0-0	6		17,451
34		5	FAC 4	A	Derby County	W	4-3	4-2		Yorke 3 (9, 19, 39), Parker 24	(22,452)
35		8	BL	A	Wimbledon	L	0-2	0-1	8		(5,534)
36		16	FAC 5	A	Swindon Town	W	2-1	1-0		Yorke 39, Froggatt 63	(16,402)
37		22	BL	H	Oldham Athletic	W	1-0	0-0	7	Regis 52	20,509
38		29	BL	A	Manchester City	L	0-2	0-1	8		(28,268)
39	M	3	BL	A	Leeds United	D	0-0	0-0	7		(28,896)
40		8	FAC 6	A	Liverpool	L	0-1	0-0			(29,109)
41		10	BL	A	Notts County	D	0-0	0-0	8		(8,389)
42		14	BL	H	Queens Park R.	L	0-1	0-0	11		19,630
43		21	BL	A	Crystal Palace	D	0-0	0-0	12		(15,368)
44		28	BL	H	Norwich City	W	1-0	0-0	10	Staunton 78	16,985
45		31	BL	H	Sheffield United	D	1-1	0-0	9	Regis 89	15,745
46	A	4	BL	A	Tottenham Hotspur	W	5-2	2-2	8	Richardson 20, Olney 31, Yorke 58, Daley 86, Regis 89	(26,370)
47		11	BL	H	Liverpool	W	1-0	0-0	7	Daley 64	35,755
48		18	BL	A	Nottingham Forest	L	0-2	0-1	9		(22,800)
49		20	BL	H	Chelsea	W	3-1	1-0	9	Staunton 32, McGrath 64, Parker 89	19,269
50		25	BL	A	Luton Town	L	0-2	0-1	9		(11,178)
51	M	2	BL	H	Coventry City	W	2-0	2-0	7	Regis 20 secs, Yorke 36	31,984

Best Home League Attendance: 39,995 v Manchester United   **Smallest:** 15,745 v Sheffield Utd   **Av Home Att:** 24,814

Goal Scorers: **Compared with 90-91: -849**

League (48): Regis 11, Yorke 11, Daley 7, Richardson 6, Staunton 4 (1 pen), Blake 2, Olney 2, Parker, Atkinson, Mortimer, McGrath, Penrice

R/lows C (1): Teale
FA Cup (7): Yorke 5, Parker, Froggatt
ZDS Cup (2): Yorke, Olney

† = After extra-time

26

Spink N.	Staunton S.	Teale S.	McGrath P.	Richardson K.	Yorke D.	Regis C.	Atkinson D.	Cowans G.	Mortimer P.	Ehiogu U.	Penrice G.	Olney I.	Daley A.	Price C.	Kubicki D.	Nielsen K.	Blake M.	Sealey L.	Small B.	Cox N.	Carruthers M.	Parker G.	Froggatt S.	Breitkreutz M.	Barrett E.	Referee	
1	3	4	5	6	7	8	9•	10	11	S	14															R Milford	1
1	3	4	5	6	7	9		10	11•	S	8	14														K Cooper	2
1	3*	4	5	6	14	9		10	11	2	8•		7	12												D Allison	3
1		4	5	6	12	9		10	11	2	8		7	3*												A Gunn	4
1	3	4	5	6		8	9	10	11	S	S		7		2											K Burge	5
1	3	4	5	6		9		10	11	S	8•		7		2											T Fitzharris	6
1	3	4	5	6		8	9	10	11	S			7		2	S										K Hackett	7
1	3	4	5	6	12	8*	9	10•	11				7		2	14										M Peck	8
1	3	4	5	6	7	8*		10•	11	12		9			2	14										B Hill	9
1	3	4	5	6	7	9			12	14	8*				2	10•	11									K Breen	10
1	3	4	5	6	7	9		10	11	S					2		8									D Phillips	11
1	3	4	5	6	7	9		14	11•	10	S				2	8										P Alcock	12
1	3	4	5	6	7	8	9	10	12	S					2	11*										P Don	13
1	3	4	5	6	7	8	9	10	11*	12					2											J Lloyd	14
		4	5	6	11	8	9	S	S				7		2		10	1	3							S Lodge	15
		4	6*	11	S	14	5	9					7	2			8	1	3							R Wiseman	16
	3	4	5	6	11	8		S				9	7		2		10	1								R Nixon	17
	3	4	5	6	11*	8	14		12			9•	7		2		10	1								L Shapter	18
	3	4	5	6	11•	8	14		12			9*	7		2		10	1								K Barrett	19
		4		6		8						9•	7		2*	5	10	1	3	11	12					G Ashby	20
	3	4	5	6	11	8	9	14				S	7		2		10•	1								A Buksh	21
	3	4	5	6	11	9	10					S	14		2	7		1				8•				R Hart	22
	3	4	5	6	11*	9			12			S	7		2		10	1				8				R Groves	23
	3	4	5	6	11	9			12			S	7		2		10*	1				8				R Milford	24
	3	4	5	6	11*	9							7		2	S	8	1				10	12			R Dilkes	25
	3*	4	5	6	11	9							7		2	14	8	1				S	10			C Bailey	26
		4	5	6	11	9						12	7	3	2	S	8*	1				10				J Martin	27
	3•	4	5	6	11	9						14		S	7	2	8	1				10				I Borrett	28
		4	5	6	11	9							7		2		1	3	S			10	8	S		K Hackett	29
	3	4	5	6	11	9							7		2		1		8	S		10		S		I Borrett	30
	3	4	5	6	11	9							7		2		1		8*	S		10	12			G Courtney	31
	3*	4	5	6	11	9						S	7		2		1		8			10	12			D Elleray	32
	3	4	5	6	11	9*						12	7		2		1		10			8		S		P Don	33
		4	5	6	8	9							7	2†			1	3	12	10	11*			S		K Morton	34
	11	4	5	6		9							2			7	1	3•	S	8		10	14			R Bigger	35
	3	4	5	6	8*	9							7		2		1		12			10	11	S		R Lewis	36
	3	4	5	6		9							7		2		1		S	7		10	11	8		J Carter	37
	3	4	5	6	8•	9							7				S	1	14			10	11		2	C Wilkes	38
1	3	4	5	6	S	9	10						7			11						8	S		2	P Wright	39
1	3	4	5	6	11•	9	10						7	12	2*							8	14			P Don	40
1	3	4	5	6		S	10					9	12				7					8	11		2	D Elleray	41
1	3	4	5	6	12	10						9*	14				7					8	11•		2	R Nixon	42
1	3	4	5	6	11•	9	10					9	14									8	7*		2	J Worrall	43
1	3	4	5	6	11•	9	10					12	14				7					8			2	A Buksh	44
1	3	4	5	6	12	9						10	7				S					8*	11		2	R Lewis	45
1	3	4	5	6	11•	9						10	12				14					8	7*		2	R Groves	46
1		4		6		9	S				5	10	7				3		14			8	11•		2	R Pawley	47
1	3	4	5	6		9•						10	7									8	11•		2	B Burns	48
1	3	4	5	6								9†	7				11•	10				8	S		2	D Gallagher	49
	3	4	5	6		9	12					10*	7					S	11			8			2	G Pooley	50
1	3	4	5	6	10*	9						12	7				11	S				8			2	A Ward	51
23	37	42	41	42	27	39	11	10	10	4	5	14	29	2	23	3	14	18	8	4	2	25	6	7	13	League Appearances	
					5		3	2	2	4	3	6	5	1		3						3		1		Substitute Appearances	
2	2	2	2	2	2	2	1	2	2			0+1			2		1									R/lows Appearances	
1	4	5	5	5	5	1					0+1			5	4+1	2	4	2+1			0+1	5	2+1			FA Cup Appearances	
	2		2	1		1		0+1	1			1		2	2	1	1	1	2	2	2	1	0+1			ZDS Cup Appearances	

Also Played: Mountfield 2(1,2)S(11,14), Gage S(4), Ormondroyd 14(6), McLoughlin 10(16)S(17), Bosnich 1(50), Beinlich 14(20,48,49)S(37)

Players on Loan: McLoughlin (Southampton)

ASTON VILLA

Club Colours: Claret shirts with blue sleeves white shorts with claret/blue trim, blue stockings with claret trim
Change Colours: White shirts with blue & black trim, black shorts with blue & white trim, black stockings with white trim
Reserves League: Pontins Central League Div 1   **Youth League:** Midland Purity Youth League

COMPETITIONS					
Div. 1	Div. 2	Div. 3	Eur Cup	UEFA	W.C.C.
88-36	36-38	70-72	81-82	75-76	82-83
38-59	59-60		82-83	77-78	
60-67	67-70			83-84	
75-87	72-75		E S Cup	90-91	
88-	87-88		82-83		

HONOURS					
Div. 1	Div. 2	Div. 3	FA Cup	Lge Cup	Euro C
93-94	37-38	71-72	1887	1961	81-82
95-96	59-60		1895	1975	
96-97			1897	1977	E.S.C.
98-99			1905		82-83
99-00			1913	C/Sh'ld	
09-10			1920	1981	
80-81			1957		

MOST APPEARANCES: CHARLIE AITKEN 656 + 3 (60-76)				
Year	League	FA Cup	Lge Cup	Europe
60-61	1			
61-62	35	4	3	
62-63	42	3	8	
63-64	34	2	1	
64-65	42	5	6	
65-66	42	1	5	
66-67	39	2	1	
67-68	30 + 2	2	1	
68-69	42	4	1	
69-70	31	1	2	
70-71	44	1	10	
71-72	43	1	6	
72-73	33	1	4	
73-74	38	4	1	
74-75	42	3	10	
75-76	21	0 + 1	2	2
	559 + 2	34 + 1	61	2
Previous holder: Billy Walker 532 (1919-33)				

MOST GOALS IN A CAREER		
BILLY WALKER: 244 (1919-1934)		
Season	League	FA Cup
1919-20	8	5
1920-21	27	4
1921-22	21	6
1922-23	23	0
1923-24	14	3
1924-25	19	6
1925-26	21	1
1926-27	15	0
1927-28	10	1
1928-29	19	0
1929-30	8	3
1930-31	15	1
1931-32	9	0
1932-33	5	0
1933-34	0	0
Total	214	30
Previous holder: Harry Hampton 242 (1904-1920)		

RECORD TRANSFER FEE RECEIVED			
Amount	Club	Player	Date
£5,500,000	Bari	David Platt	7/91
£1,750,000	Wolverhampton W	Andy Gray	9/79
£200,000	Derby County	Bruce Rioch	3/74
£100,000	Chelsea	Tony Hateley	10/66

RECORD TRANSFER FEE PAID			
Amount	Club	Player	Date
£1,700,000	Oldham Athletic	Earl Barrett	2/92
£1,600,000	Real Sociedad	Dalian Atkinson	7/91
£1,500,000	Millwall	Tony Cascarino	3/90
£650,000	Bradford City	Ian Ormondroyd	2/89

MANAGERS			
Name	Seasons	Best	Worst
Jim McMullen	1934-36	13(1)	21(1)
Jim Hogan	1936-39	12(1)	9(2)
Alex Massie	1945-50	6(1)	12(1)
George Martin	1950-53	6(1)	15(1)
Eric Houghton	1953-58	6(1)	20(1)
Joe Mercer	1958-64	7(1)	1(2)
Dick Taylor	1964-67	16(1)	21(1)
Tony Cummings	1967-68	16(2)	16(2)
Arthur Cox (caretaker)	1968		
Tommy Docherty	1968-70	18(2)	21(2)
Vic Crowe	1970-74	3(2)	4(3)
Ron Saunders	1974-82	1(1)	2(2)
Tony Barton	1982-84	6(1)	11(1)
Graham Turner	1984-86	10(1)	16(1)
Billy McNeil	1986-87		22(1)
Graham Taylor	1987-90	2(1)	2(2)
Jozef Venglos	1990-91	17(1)	17(1)
Ron Atkinson	1991-		

LONGEST LEAGUE RUNS	
of undefeated matches:	15 (16.1.1897-18.9.1897)
of undefeated home matches:	37 (24.4.1909-22.4.1911)
without home win:	8 (11.12.1920-28.3.1921)
of league wins:	9 (22.3.1897-18.9.1897)
of league defeats:	11 (22.3.1963-4.4.1963)
of league matches without a win:	12 (10.11.1973-2.2.1974)
of undefeated away matches:	13 (5.9.1987-23.1.1988)
without an away win:	27 (21.9.1963-26.12.1964)
of home wins:	14 (11.1.1903-25.11.1903)
of away wins:	6 (6.2.1897-11.9.1897)

BIGGEST VICTORIES
League: 12-2 v Accrington, Division 1, 12.3.1892
11-1 v Charlton Athletic, Division 2, 24.11.1959
10-0 v Sheffield Wednesday, Division 1, 5.10.1912
10-0 v Burnley, Division 1, 29.8.1925
F.A. Cup: 13-0 v Wednesbury Old Ath., 3.10.1886
League Cup: 8-1 v Exeter, Round 2 2nd leg, 7.10.1985
Europe: 5-0 v Valur, Round 1, 16.9.1981.

BIGGEST DEFEATS
League: 0-7 v Blackburn Rovers, Division 1, 19.10.1889
0-7 v Everton, Division 1, 4.1.1890
0-7 v West Bromwich Albion, Division 1, 19.10.1935
0-7 v Manchester Utd, Division 1, 8.3.1950
0-7 v Manchester United, Division 1, 24.10.1964
F.A. Cup: 1-8 v Blackburn Rovers, Round 3, 16.2.1889
League Cup: 1-6 v West Bromwich Alb, Round 2, 14.9.1966
Europe (UEFA): 1-4 v Antwerp, Round 2, 17.9.1975
0-3 v Inter Milan, Round 2, 17.11.1990

MOST GOALS
128, 1930/31 (Division 1 record)
Waring 49, Houghton 30, Walker 15, Beresford 14, Mandley 8, Brown 5, Chester 3, Gibson 2, Talbot 1, Tate 1.

MOST GOALS IN A MATCH
5, Harry Hampton v Sheffield Wednesday 10-0, 5.10.1912
5, Harold Halse v Derby County, 5-1, 19.10.1912
5, Len Capwell v Burnley, 10-0, 29.8.1925
5, George Brown v Leicester (a), 8-3, 2.1.1932
5, Gerry Hitchens v Charlton Ath., 11-1, 18.11.1959

MOST GOALS IN A SEASON
Tom 'Pongo' Waring, 50 (49 Lge, 1 FA Cup) 1930-31
4 goals 3 times = 12; 3 goals once = 3; 2 goals 9 times = 18; 1 goal 17 times = 17

MOST POINTS
3 points a win: 78, Division 2, 1987-88
2 points a win: 70, Division 3, 1971-72. (Division 3 record)

MOST FIRST CLASS MATCHES IN A SEASON
61 (42 League, 3 FA Cup, 6 League Cup, 1 Charity Shield, 9 European Cup) 1981-82

MOST LEAGUE GOALS CONCEDED
110, Division 1, 1935-36

MOST LEAGUE WINS
32, Division 3, 1971-72

MOST LEAGUE DRAWS
17, Division 1, 1975-76

MOST LEAGUE DEFEATS
24, Division 1, 1966-67

OLDEST PLAYER
Ernie Callaghan, 39 yrs 249 days v Sunderland, Div 1, 4.4.1947.

YOUNGEST PLAYER
Jimmy Brown, 15 years 349 days v Bolton (a), 17.9.1969.

MOST CAPPED PLAYER
Peter McParland (Northern Ireland) 33
(For England) David Platt 22

BEST PERFORMANCES BY ASTON VILLA

League: 1971-72: Matches played 46, Won 32, Drawn 6, Lost 8, Goals for 88, Goals against 32, Points 70. First in Division 3
Highest: Division 1 Champions

F.A. Cup: 1886-87: 1st rnd. Wedesbury Old Ath., 13-0; 2nd rnd. Derby Midland, 6-0; 3rd rnd. Wolverhampton W., 2-2, 1-1, 3-3, 2-0; 4th rnd. Bye; 5th rnd. Horncastle, 5-0; 6th rnd. Darwen, 3-2; Semi-Final Rangers, 3-1; Final West Bromwich Albion, 2-0.
1894-95: 4th rnd. Derby, 2-1; 5th rnd. Newcastle Utd., 7-1; 6th rnd. Nottingham Forest, 6-1; Semi-Final Sunderland, 2-1; Final West Bromwich Albion 1-0
1896-97: 4th rnd. Newcastle Utd, 5-0; 5th rnd. Notts County, 2-1; 6th rnd. Preston North End, 1-1, 0-0, 3-2; Semi-Final Liverpool, 3-0; Final Everton, 3-2.
1904-05: 4th rnd. Leicestr, 5-1; 5th rnd. Bury, 3-2; 6th rnd. Fulham, 5-0; Semi-Final Everton, 1-1, 2-1; Final Newcastle Utd, 2-0.
1912-13: 3rd rnd. Derby, 3-1; 4th rnd. West Ham, 5-0; 5th rnd. Crystal Palace, 5-0; 6th rnd. Bradford, 5-0; Semi-Final Oldham Athletic, 1-0; Final Sunderland, 0-1.
1919-20: 3rd rnd. Queens Park Rangers, 2-1; 4th rnd. Manchester Utd., 2-1; 5th rnd. Sunderland, 1-0; 6th rnd. Tottenham Hotspur, 1-0; Semi-Final Chelsea, 3-1; Final Huddersfield, 1-0.
1956-57: 3rd rnd. Luton Town, 2-2, 2-0; 4th rnd. Middlesbrough 3-2; 5th rnd. Bristol City 2-1; 6th rnd. Burnley, 1-1, 2-0; Semi-Final West Bromwich Albion 2-2, 1-0; Final Manchester Utd. 2-1.

League Cup: 1960-61: 2nd rnd. Huddersfield, 4-1; 3rd rnd. Preston North End, 3-3, 3-1; 4th rnd. Plymouth, 3-3, 0-0, 5-3; 5th rnd. Wrexham, 3-0; Semi-Final Burnley, 1-1, 2-2, 2-1; Final Rotherham 0-2, 3-0.
1974-75: 2nd rnd. Everton 1-1, 3-0; 3rd rnd. Crewe, 2-2, 1-0; 4th rnd. Hartlepool 1-1, 6-1; 5th rnd. Colchester 2-1; Semi-Final Chester 2-2, 3-2; Final Norwich 1-0.
1976-77: 2nd rnd. Manchester City, 3-0; 3rd rnd. Norwich, 2-1; 4th rnd. Wrexham, 5-1; 5th rnd. Millwall, 2-0; Semi-Final Queens Park Rangers, 0-0, 2-2, 3-0; Final Everton 0-0, 1-1, 3-2.

European Cup: 1981-82: 1st rnd. Valur, 5-0, 2-0; 2nd rnd. Dynamo Berlin, 2-1, 0-1; 3rd rnd. Dynamo Kiev, 0-0, 2-0; Semi-Final Anderlecht, 1-0, 0-0; Final Bayern Munich, 1-0.

DIVISIONAL RECORDS

	Played	Won	Drawn	Lost	For	Against	Points
DIVISION 1	3146	1327	693	1126	5491	4891	**3489**
DIVISION 2	422	179	111	132	617	487	**491**
DIVISION 3	92	51	21	20	139	78	**123**
TOTALS	**3660**	**1557**	**825**	**1278**	**6247**	**5456**	**4103**

ASTON VILLA | APPEARANCES | GOALS

PLAYERS NAME Honours	Ht	Wt	Birthdate	Birthplace Transfers	Contract Date	Clubs	League	L/Cup	FA Cup	Other	Lg	L/C	FAC	Oth
GOALKEEPERS														
Les Sealey	6.0	11.6	29.09.57	Bethnal Green	01.03.76	Coventry City (A)	158	11	9					
FAC'90;ECWC'91;CS'90				£100,000	03.08.83	Luton Town	207	21	28	3				
				Loan		Plymouth A	6							
				Loan	14.12.89	Manchester Utd								
				Loan	21.03.90	Manchester Utd	2		1					
				Free	06.06.90	Manchester Utd	31	8	3	9				
				Free	19.07.91	Aston Villa	18		4	2				
				Loan	25.03.92	Coventry City	2							
Nigel Spink	6.2	14.6	08.08.58	Chelmsford		Chelmsford								
E:1,B:2,EC'82,ESC'82				£4,000	01.01.77	Aston Villa	306	39	24	19+1				
DEFENDERS														
Earl Barrett	5.10	11.2	28.04.67	Rochdale		Manchester City	2+1	1						
E:1,u21.4				Loan		Chester City	12							
				£35,000	24.11.87	Oldham Ath	152+2	16	12	3	5	1	1	
				£1,700,000	25.02.92	Aston Villa	32	4	2	1	2			
Mark A Blake	5.11	12.7	16.12.70	Nottingham	01.07.89	Aston Villa (T)	26+4	1+1	2	2	2			
E: u21.2, Y.4, S				Loan	17.01.91	Wolverhampton W	2							
Neil Cox	6.0	12.10	08.10.71	Scunthorpe	20.03.90	Scunthorpe Utd. (T)	17		4	4+1	1			
				£400,000	12.02.91	Aston Villa	4+3			1				
Ugochuku Ehiogu	6.1	12.0	03.11.72	London		West Brom A. (T)	0+2							
				£40,000	12.07.91	Aston Villa	4+4		0+1	1				
Dariusz Kubicki	5.10	11.7	06.06.63	Warsaw		Legia Warsaw								
				£200,000	28.08.91	Aston Villa	23	2	4+1	1				
Paul McGrath	6.0	14.0	04.12.59	Ealing		St Patrick								
Ei:55,FAC'85,Flg				£30,000	30.04.82	Manchester Utd	159+4	13	15+2	9	12	2	2	
				£400,000	03.08.89	Aston Villa	111	9	12	7	2			
Bryan Small	5.9	11.9	15.11.71	Birmingham	09.07.90	Aston Villa (T)	8		2+1	2				
E: Y.8														
Steve Staunton	5.11	11.2	19.01.69	Drogheda	02.09.86	Liverpool (A)	55+10	6+2	14+2	1		4	1	1
Ei:34;u21.4, Div.1'90; FAC'89;CS'89				Loan	01.11.88	Bradford City	7+1	2						
				£1.100,000	07.08.91	Aston Villa	37	2	4		4			
Shaun Teale	6.0	13.7	10.03.64	Southport		Weymouth								
ESP 1				£50,000	22.01.89	Bournemouth	99+1	8	5	3	4		1	
				£300,000	25.07.91	Aston Villa	42	2	5	2		1		
MIDFIELD														
Matthias Breikreutz	5.9	11.3	12.05.71	Crivitz		Borussia Borsig								
				£100,000	27.11.91	Aston Villa	7+1							
Stephen Froggatt	5.10	11.0	09.03.73	Lincoln	26.01.91	Aston Villa	6+3		2+1				1	
Ray Houghton	5.7	10.10	09.01.62	GLASGOW	05.07.79	West Ham U	0+1							
Ei:46,LC'86,Div1'88'90; CS'88; FAC'89'92				07.07.82	Fulham	129	12	4		16	2	3		
				P.E	13.09.85	Oxford Utd	83	13	3	6	10	3		1
				£800,000	19.10.87	Liverpool	177+6	14	26+1	8	28	3	4	3
				£900,000	28.07.92	Aston Villa								
Gary Parker	5.8	11.0	07.09.65	Oxford	05.05.83	Luton Town (A)	31+11	1+3	6+2		3	1		
E:u21.6,u19.3,Y.1; LC'89'90; SC'89				£72,000	21.02.86	Hull City	82+2	5	4	2	8			1
				£250,000	24.03.88	Nottm. Forest	99+3	22+1	16	9	17	4	5	3
				£650,000	29.11.91	Aston Villa	25		5		1		1	
Kevin Richardson	5.9	10.12	04.12.62	Newcastle	08.12.80	Everton (A)	95+14	10+3	13	7+2	16	3	1	
Div1'85'89;FAC'84,CS'84'86,ECWC'85				£225,000	04.09.86	Watford	39	3	7	1	2			
				£200,000	26.08.87	Arsenal	88+8	13+3	9	3	5	2	1	
				£750,000	01.07.90	Real Sociedad								
				£450,000	06.08.91	Aston Villa	42	2	5	2	6			
FORWARDS														
Dalian Atkinson	5.11	11.7	21.03.68	Shrewsbury	04.06.85	Ipswich Town (A)	49+11	5+1		2+1	18	3		
E:B.1				£450,000	16.06.89	Sheffield Wed	38	3	2	2	10	3	1	1
				£1,750,000		Real Sociedad								
				£1,600,000	11.07.91	Aston Villa	11+3	1	1	1	1			
Martin Carruthers	5.11	11.9	07.08.72	Nottingham	04.07.90	Aston Villa (T)	2+1		0+1	0+1				
Tony Daley	5.8	10.8	18.10.67	Aston	31.05.85	Aston Villa (A)	162+31	17+1	13+1	13+2	28	4	2	1
E:7,B1,Y8														
Mark Parrott	5.10	11.5	14.03.71	Cheltenham	01.07.89	Aston Villa (T)								
E: Y.1, S														
Cyrille Regis	6.0	13.4	09.02.58	French Guyana		Molesey								
E:5,B3,U21.6,FAC'87						Hayes								
				£5,000	01.05.77	West Brom A	233+4	27+1	25	10	82	16	10	4
				£300,000	11.10.84	Coventry City	231+7	24	15+1	4	46	12	3	
				Free	02.07.91	Aston Villa	39	2	5		11			
Dwight Yorke	5.10	11.12	03.11.71	Canaan (Tobago)		Signal Hill (Tobago)								
T&T: 20				£120,000	19.12.89	Aston Villa	35+17	3	7	1	13		5	1

ADDITIONAL CONTRACT PLAYERS

Stefan Beinlich 0+2lg 0+1oth, Chris Boden, (G) Mark Bosnich 3lg, (M) Richard Crisp, Neil Davis, David Farrell, Graham Fenton, Glen Livingstone, Scott Macintyre, Michael Oakes, Lee Williams.

ASTON VILLA

RECORD WIN & LOSS AGAINST EACH CLUB IN CURRENT DIVISION
(Where a score has occured on several occasions the most recent is given)

Club	Rec. Win	Season	Rec. Loss	Season
ARSENAL	5-0	1920-21	7-1	1935-36 (home)
BLACKBURN ROVERS	5-0	1932-33 (away)	0-7	1889-90
CHELSEA	7-1	1951-52	6-2	1966-67 (home)
COVENTRY CITY	4-0	1982-83	2-0	1989-90
CRYSTAL PALACE	4-1	1987-88	4-2	1968-69
EVERTON	6-2	1989-90	7-0	1889-90
IPSWICH TOWN	6-1	1977-78	3-0	1984-85
LEEDS UNITED	9-1	1926-27	6-0	1924-25
LIVERPOOL	6-1	1931-32	6-1	1953-54
MANCHESTER CITY	7-1	1900-01	5-0	1935-36
MANCHESTER UNITED	7-0	1930-31	7-0	1964-65
MIDDLESBROUGH	8-1	1930-31	6-0	1948-49
NORWICH CITY	4-1	1974-75 (away)	5-1	1936-37
NOTTINGHAM FOREST	7-3	1903-04 (away)	6-0	1986-87
OLDHAM ATHLETIC	7-1	1912-13	3-1	1921-22
QUEENS PARK RANGERS	5-2	1984-85	3-0	1967-68
SHEFFIELD UNITED	6-1	1903-04	6-0	1901-02
SHEFFIELD WEDNESDAY	10-0	1912-13	4-0	1902-03
SOUTHAMPTON	4-0	1936-37	5-0	1986-87
TOTTENHAM HOTSPUR	4-0	1982-83	6-2	1960-61
WIMBLEDON	2-0	1989-90 (away)	3-0	1989-90 (home)

MANAGER: RON ATKINSON

DATE OF BIRTH: 18.03.1939   **PLACE OF BIRTH:** Liverpool

DATE OF APPOINTMENT: JULY 1991

PREVIOUS CLUBS
as Manager: Kettering Town, Cambridge Utd, West Bromwich Albion, Manchester Utd, Atletico Madrid, Sheffield Wed.
as Player: Aston Villa (A), Oxford United.

HONOURS
as Manager: Promotion to Div 3 1977, Promotion to Div 2 1978, (with Cambridge); F.A. Cup Winners 1983, 1985 (with Manchester Utd.); League Cup Winners & Promotion to Div 1, 1991 (with Sheff. Wed.)
as Player: Promotion to Div 3 1965, Division 3 Champions 1968

Value Rating: ★ ★ ★ ★ ★

Programme Editor: Bernard Gallagher

Price of 1992-93 Programme: £1.20
Number of Pages: 32
Subscriptions: £43.50 within the UK

Local Newspapers: Birmingham Post & Mail, Sports Argus (Sat Football Special), Express & Star, Daily News, Sunday Mercury

Local Radio Stations: BRMB, BBC Radio W.M.

Additional Publications on Club: Aston Villa a Complete Record, Tony Matthews/Dave Goodyear (Breedon Books)
The Aston Villa Quiz Book, Derrick Spinks (Mainstream)
Aston Villa Who's Who, Tony Matthews (Paper Plane)
Aston Villa Greats, Leon Hickman (Sportsprint)

LEADING LEAGUE GOALSCORERS
SEASONS 1979-80 – 1991-92

1979-80	GARY SHAW	9		1980-81	PETER WITHE	20
1981-82	PETER WITHE	10		1982-83	GARY SHAW	17
1983-84	PETER WITHE	15		1984-85	PAUL RIDEOUT	14
1985-86	SIMON STAINROD	10		1986-87	ALLEN EVANS	6
	MARK WALTERS	10			GARRY THOMPSON	6
1987-88	GARRY THOMPSON	11		1988-89	ALAN McINALLY	14
	WARREN ASPINALL	11				
1989-90	DAVID PLATT	19		1990-91	DAVID PLATT	19
	1991-92	**CYRILLE REGIS**	**11**			

VILLA PARK Trinity Road, Birmingham B6 6HE

Capacity: 40,312   **Covered Standing:**   **Seating:** 20,281

Tel: Ground: 021 327 2299   **Ticket Sales:** 021 327 5353   **Clubcall:** 0898 12 11 48

All premium rate calls (0898/0891) cost 36p per minute cheap rate and 48p per minute at all other times. Call costings correct at time of going to press.

GROUNDS
Aston Park 1874-96; Perry Bar 1876-1897; Villa Park 1897-

ATTENDANCES
Highest: 76,588 v Derby County, FAC 6th Rnd, 2.3.1946

Lowest: 2,600 v Accrington, Div 1, 27.10.1888
(at Villa Pk.): 2,900 v Bradford City, Div 1, 13.2.1915 (0-0)

RECORD RECEIPTS (with previous records):
£390,935 Nott'm Forest v West Ham, FAC S/Final, 14.4.1991
£335,372 Everton v Norwich, FAC S/Final, 15.4.1989
£294,447.29p Tottenham v Watford, FAC S/Final, 11.4.1987
£211,155 Arsenal v Manchester Utd, FAC S/Final, 16.4.1983
£167,753 Everton v West Ham Utd, FAC S/Final, 12.4.1980
£165,481 v Juventus, European Cup S/Final, 2.3.1983

GROUND NAME
First game: Aston v Blackburn, Div 1, 17.4.1897 (3-0)
First Floodlit game: v Portsmouth, Div 1, 25.8.1958 (3-2)
Internationals: England v Scotland: 8.4.1899, 3.5.1902, 8.4.1922
England v Wales: 10.11.1948, 26.11.1958
England v Ireland: 14.11.1951
Spain v Argentina: 13.7.1966
Argentina v West Germany: 16.7.1966
Spain v West Germany: 20.7.1966

Season Tickets:
Stands: from £180 to £210, juv/OAP £80
Ground: £160 (no reduction)

Executive Box Season Tickets: 79 boxes leased on three year basis. Information can be obtained from Commercial Manager

Cost of Stand Tickets: Stand: £12, £11, juveniles/OAP: £6, £5.50
Terraces: £10, juv/OAP £5

Match and Ticket Information: By post or in person, applications accepted anytime during season

Car Parking: Asda Park in Aston Hall Road, a Park & Ride. Street parking also available

Nearest Railway Station: Witton or Aston

Villa Soccer Special: Activity days for 8-14 year olds every Saturday. Includes football games, coaching and match ticket.
Panini sponsored Family Section is at the top of the Witton End, North Stand

---

How to get to the ground

From North, East, South and West: Use Motorway M6 Junction 6. Leave motorway and follow signs Birmingham (NE). Shortly at roundabout take 4th exit A38 (S.P. Aston). In 0.5m turn right into Aston Hall Road for Aston Villa FC

BARNET

Division 3

Formed: 1888 **Turned Professional:** 1965 **Ltd Co:**

SPONSORED BY: **NICKNAME:** The Bees

Chairman
Stan Flashman

Directors
J Quill
L Rose

Manager
Barry Fry

Assistant Manager
Edwin Stein

Secretary
Bryan Ayres

Commercial Manager
Mick Hooker

Physiotherapist
Andy McDade

Club Doctor
Dr V Khiroya

Club Statistician for the Directory
Bryan Ayres/Tony Holmes

IF you want to be entertained with fresh, flowing football probably laced with some smart finishing and a smile or two, then Barnet is your club!

The players mirror the character of their manager and a look at the club's league record last season shows that his attitudes pay off. Eighty-one League goals plus another 29 in the cups testified that and gave 'Spike' Carter, England's record semi-professional international goalscorer, an amazing 32 goals in his first Football League season and of course the much publicised Gary Bull also totalled an excellent 27 goals.

Most of the side were experienced semi-professionals and many continued with their other careers alongside their 'fun in the fourth'. Barnet averaged 3,720 for their home games and usually gave great value for money. Apart from the all round attacking ability the side benefitted from Dave Howell and Mick Bodley's steadiness in the middle of the back line and the exciting skills of Paul Showler and Kenny Lowe.

The Cups brought goals but no lasting success but the play offs were reached in the club's first season in the Football League. You would think everyone would be extremely happy and satisfied but according to the media all is not well at the Underhill Stadium.

No one outside the club can really comment on internal matters but it is a terrible shame that a club so admired for it's style and attitude on the field cannot enjoy similar success off the park.

Only one club can win the championship and three others can win promotion from the Fourth Division but there is more to football than instant success. The club has proved its worth in the Football League, it has also impressed with it's playing style and attitudes so that Barnet now have more friends than ever throughout football.

Barnet have laid the foundations for a very successful life in 'The League' and hopefully Barry Fry, their very popular manager, will be able to enjoy the club's development along with his chairman and a very talented squad of players.

T.W.

Back row L-R: Tim Alexander, Mark Carter, Mark Flashman, Andy Pape, Gary Phillips, Nicky Evans, Hakan Hayrettin. **Middle row:** Gordon Ogbourne (Kit Manager), Tony Lynch, Jonathan Hunt, Derek Payne, Dave Barnett, Mick Bodley, David Howell, Richard Huxford, Roger Willis, Carl Hoddle. **Front row:** Dominic Naylor, Gary Bull, Gavin MacPherson, Duncan Horton, Barry Fry (Manager), Edwin Stein (Asst. Manager), Geoff Cooper, Paul Showler, Kenny Lowe.

BARNET

DIVISION FOUR: 7th **FA CUP:** 3rd RND **RUMBELOWS CUP:** 1st RND **AUTOGLASS:** Q/FINALS

M	DATE	COMP.	VEN	OPPONENTS	RESULT	H/T	LGE POS	GOALSCORERS/GOAL TIMES	ATTEN-DANCE
1	A 17	BL	H	Crewe Alexandra	L 4-7	2-3		Bull 7, 75, Carter 40, 89	5,090
2	20	RC 1/1	H	Brentford	D 5-5	2-2		Evans 9, 48, Carter 43, Bull 51, 80	2,927
3	24	BL	A	Mansfield Town	W 2-1	2-1	12	Bull 14, Carter 38	(2,668)
4	27	RC 1/2	A	Brentford	L 1-3	0-3		Carter 88	(5,563)
5	31	BL	H	Hereford United	W 1-0	0-0	6	Willis 90	2,872
6	S 4	BL	A	Lincoln City	W 6-0	2-0	3	Bull 20, 69, Murphy 30, Willis 64, Finney (og) 70, Evans 90	3,067
7	7	BL	A	Northampton Town	D 1-1	0-1	3	Bull 90	(4,339)
8	14	BL	H	Doncaster Rovers	W 1-0	1-0	3	Bull 45	3,762
9	17	BL	H	Scunthorpe United	W 3-2	1-1	2	Carter 35, Willis 64, Bull (pen) 88	3,094
10	21	BL	A	Gillingham	D 3-3	2-2	2	Wilson 18, Lowe 28, Bull 80	(4,864)
11	28	BL	H	Cardiff City	W 3-1	2-1	2	Showler 30, Bull 35, 83 (pen)	4,000
12	O 5	BL	A	Walsall	L 0-2	0-2	4		(4,981)
13	12	BL	H	York City	W 2-0	0-0	2	Murphy 70, 72	4,474
14	19	BL	H	Blackpool	W 3-0	1-0	2	Willis 7, Poole 51, Showler 61	5,085
15	26	BL	A	Scarborough	W 4-0	2-0	2	Showler 15, Willis 23, 88, Bull 58	(1,942)
16	N 2	BL	A	Wrexham	L 0-1	0-1	2		(1,886)
17	5	BL	H	Carlisle United	W 4-2	0-1	2	Howell 56, Poole 60, Bull 66, Carter 87	2,983
18	9	BL	H	Halifax Town	W 3-0	1-0	1	Bull 9, Lowe 56, Willis 73	4,837
19	16	FAC 1	H	Tiverton Town	W 5-0	2-0		Bull 22, Naylor 36, Carter 63, Evans 68, Showler 81	3,964
20	19	AGT Pre	H	Aldershot	W 3-0	1-0		Carter 2, Willis 65, Evans 72	1,312
21	23	BL	A	Rochdale	L 0-1	0-1	2		(3,033)
22	30	BL	H	Chesterfield	L 1-2	0-1	4	Carter 55	3,725
23	D 7	FAC 2	A	Enfield	W 4-1	1-0		Bull 36, Carter 3 (60, 69, 75)	(5,120)
24	17	AGT Pre	A	Brentford	W 6-3	1-1		Carter 3 (51, 57, 67), Bull 65, 79, Poole 82	(1,871)
25	21	BL	A	Mansfield Town	W 2-0	1-0	3	Showler 32, Willis 85	4,209
26	26	BL	A	Crewe Alexandra	L 0-3	0-2	3		(4,736)
27	28	BL	A	Hereford United	D 2-2	1-2	3	Howell 18, Carter 54	(4,654)
28	J 1	BL	H	Lincoln City	W 1-0	1-0	2	Bull 36	3,739
29	5	FAC 3	A	Charlton Athletic	L 1-3	1-1		Carter 30	(9,618)
30	8	BL	A	Maidstone United	D 1-1	0-1	3	Carter 49	(1,988)
31	11	BL	H	Rotherham United	L 2-5	0-3	4	Carter 53, Bull (pen) 89	3,552
32	14	AGT 1	H	Northampton Town	W 3-2	2-1		Johnson (og) 4, Carter 36, Murphy 84	1,422
33	F 4	AGT QF	H	Leyton Orient	L 0-1	0-1			2,969
34	8	BL	H	Scarborough	W 5-1	2-0	3	Horton 24, Willis 45, Lowe 69, Carter 76, Bull 89	2,851
35	11	BL	A	Chesterfield	L 2-3	1-1	4	Bodley 43, Horton 61	(3,076)
36	15	BL	H	Maidstone United	W 3-2	2-0	3	Showler 32, Willis 34, Carter 90	2,871
37	18	BL	A	Blackpool	L 2-4	2-2	3	Bull 14, Showler 43	(5,149)
38	22	BL	A	Rotherham United	L 0-3	0-1	4		(3,841)
39	M 7	BL	A	Burnley	L 0-3	0-1	7		(12,018)
40	10	BL	A	Carlisle United	W 3-1	2-0	5	Carter 9, Horton 31, Willis 46	(1,888)
41	14	BL	H	Wrexham	W 2-0	0-0	5	Carter 77, Murphy 87	2,917
42	21	BL	A	Halifax Town	L 1-3	0-0	5	Murphy 83	(1,756)
43	24	BL	H	Burnley	D 0-0	0-0	6		4,881
44	28	BL	H	Rochdale	W 3-0	2-0	6	Bull 10, 78 (pen), Carter 21	3,099
45	31	BL	A	Doncaster Rovers	L 0-1	0-1	6		(1,247)
46	A 4	BL	H	Northampton Town	W 3-0	1-0	6	Carter 40, 79, Showler 72	2,816
47	11	BL	A	Scunthorpe United	D 1-1	1-0	6	Howell 28	(3,361)
48	18	BL	H	Gillingham	W 2-0	1-0	5	Payne 24, Carter 71	4,049
49	20	BL	A	Cardiff City	L 1-3	0-2	5	Cooper 83	(7,720)
50	25	BL	H	Walsall	L 0-1	0-1	7		3,207
51	M 2	BL	A	York City	W 4-1	0-0	7	Bull 60, Carter 75, 84, Willis 88	(2,643)
52	10	PO SF1	H	Blackpool	W 1-0	1-0		Carter 29	5,629
53	13	PO SF2	A	Blackpool	L 0-2	0-1			(7,588)

Best Home League Attendance: 5,090 v Crewe Alexandra   **Smallest:** 2,816 v Northampton Town   **Av Home Att:** 3,720

Goal Scorers: **Compared with 90-91:** +802

League (81): Bull 21 (4 pens), Carter 19, Willis 12, Showler 7, Murphy 5, Lowe 3, Horton 3, Howell 3, Poole 2, Payne, Opponents, Cooper, Wilson, Evans, Bodley
R/lows C (6): Carter 2, Bull 2, Evans 2
FA Cup (10): Carter 5, Bull 2, Evans, Showler, Naylor
Autoglass (12): Carter 5, Bull 2, Willis, Evans, Poole, Murphy, Opponents
Play-offs (1): Carter

Phillips G.	Blackford G.	Cooper G.	Horton D.	Bodley M.	Johnson R.	Showler P.	Carter M.	Bull G.	Lowe K.	Evans N.	Murphy F.	Naylor D.	Howell D.	Poole G.	Hoddle C.	Lynch A.	Willis R.	Pape A.	Wilson P.	Nugent R.	Payne D.	Cawley P.	Hunt J.	Nethercott S.	Barnett D.	Referee	
1	2	3•	4	5*	6	7	8	9	10	11	14															P Jones	1
	2		4•		6		8	9	10	S	3	5	7	11	14											D Elleray	2
1	2		4		S	11	8	9	10		S	3	7	5		5	6									W Flood	3
1	2		4	12	11		8	9	10•			3	7		5*	14	6									M James	4
			4		6	11	8*	9	10			3	7•	5	2			1				12				P Scoble	5
S			4			11	8	9	10	6		3		5	2			1	7							M Bailey	6
12			4			11	8*	9	10•	6		3		5	2			1	7							S Bell	7
			4			11*	8	9	10	6		3		5	2			1	7•				14			D Axcell	8
12			4			11	8	9	10	6•		3			2*			1	7		14		5			J Carter	9
12			4			11	8	9	10•			3			2			1	7		6		5*			M Pierce	10
			4			11	8*	9	10			3		5	2	14	6	1	7•				12			G Willard	11
			4•			11		9	10			3		5	2	14	6	1	7				12			I Hendrick	12
			4			11		9	10*	12		3		5•	2		6	1	7			8				D Gallagher	13
		14	4			11		9	10	12		3		5*	2		6	1	7			8•				J Moules	14
		14	4			11		9	10•			3		5	2		6	1	7*			8				P Wright	15
		14	4			11	12	9	10			3		5	2•		6*	1	7			8				P Harrison	16
		14	4			11	12	9	10*			3		5	2		6	1	7			8•				I Hemley	17
			4			11	8•	9	10*			3		5	2	12	6	1	7	14						P Alcock	18
1		12	4			11	8	9	10	14		3*			2*		6		7							M Pierce	19
1		12	4			11	8	9	10*	14		3		5•	2		6		7							K Morton	20
		12	4			11	8*	9	10•	14		3		5	2		6	1	7							R Poulain	21
12		10*	4			11	8	9		14		3		5	2		6	1	7•							P Foakes	22
12		6	4			11	8	9	10	14		3		5	2*			1	7							M Brandwood	23
		6*	4			11	8	9	10			3			2	14		1	7			5•	12			I Borrett	24
		6	4			11	8	9	10*			3		5	2•	12		1	7				14			D Axcell	25
		6	4*			11	8	9				3		5•	2	12		1	7				14			K Hackett	26
		10*	4			11	14	9	12	8		3•		5	2		6	1	7							R Gifford	27
		11•	4				8	9	10*	12		3		5	2		6	1	7				14			G Willard	28
	11	6	4				8	9	10•	12		3*		5	2	14		1	7							P Don	29
	12	3	4			11	8*	9	10				7	5	2	14	6•	1								J Deakin	30
		3†	4†			11	8	9	10•	12				5	2		6*	1	7				14			R Hamer	31
1	6	3*	4			11•	8	9	10	12				5	2	14			7							M Reed	32
		6	4*			11	8	9	10			3		5	2	14		1	7•				12			P Foakes	33
		6	4			11*	8*	9	10	14		3		5	2			1	7				12			P Scoble	34
		6	4			11	8	9	10*			3		5	2			1	7		S		12			T Holbrook	35
			4			11*	8	9	10			3			2		6	1	7•			12		5		J Martin	36
		6	4			11	8	9		14		3		5	2•			1	7			12	10*			J Key	37
		6	4*			11	8	9•	12	14		3		5	2			1	7				10			A Wilkie	38
1		6	4•			11	8	9	10					5	2	12			7*	14						P Vanes	39
1	3	6	4			11•	8	9	10					5	2				7*	14						R Shepherd	40
1	3	6	4			11•	8	9	12	14				5*	2				7	10						R Bigger	41
1	3	6•	4			11*	8	9	12	14				5	2				7	10						R Hart	42
	3		4			11*		9		14			10	5	2•		6	1	7			8	12			R Pawley	43
	3	6	4			11	8	9					10•	5	2			1	7*	14			12			A Gunn	44
	3	6	4			11	8*	9		12			14	5	2			1	7•	10						K A Cooper	45
	3	6	4			11	8	9	10•	14				5	2*			1	7					12		M Pierce	46
	3	6	4†			11	8	9						5	2		S	1	7	10				S		T Fitzharris	47
	3	6				11•	8*	9	12					5	2		14	1	7	10				4		A Bennett	48
	3	6					8	9	14	12				5	2		11	1	7*	10				4•		J Carter	49
	3					11•	8	9	6*	14				5	2			1	7				10		4	H King	50
	3	6				11•	8	9	12					5	2	4	14	1		10*	7					J Kirkby	51
	3	6	4			11*	8	9						5	2	10	12	1		S	7					G Courtney	52
	3	6	4			11	8	9						5	2	10•	12	1		14	7*					J Martin	53
6	2	13	24	36	2	39	32	42	26	7	3	26	34	39	10	1	33	36	23	2	13	3	2	3	3	League Appearances	
4	1	6			4				10	2	12				1	3	5	5		2		1	12		1	Substitute Appearances	
1	2		1	1		1+1	1	2	2	1	1		2	1	2	2	0+2	1								R/lows Appearances	
1	0+1	1		2+1	3		2	3	3	3		0+1	0+2	3	3		1+1	2	3							FA Cup Appearances	
2		1	3+1	4		4	4	4	3	0+1	0+1	3	1	4	1+1		1+2	3	2		1		1+2			Autoglass Appearances	
		2	2	2		2	2	2					2	2	0+2		2	2			0+1					Play-Offs Appearances	

Also Played: Stein 12(1), Berryman 1(2), Hayrettin 14(5,36)S(6)12(40,50), Tomlinson 14(7,10)12(8), Joseph 8*(12), Morrow 3(39)
Players on Loan: Nethercott (Tottenham), Morrow (Arsenal)
† = Sent Off

BARNET

Club Colours: Amber shirts, black shorts, black stockings
Change Colours: All white
Reserves League: Capital League

Previous Leagues: Olympian, London Athenian, Southern, Alliance, Gola, GM Vauxhall Conference
Previous Name: Barnet Alston F.C.
Previous Managers: (Since 1946): Lester Finch George Wheeler Dexter Adams Tommy Coleman Gerry Ward Gordon Ferry Brian Kelly Bill Meadows Barry Fry Roger Thompson Don McAllister Barry Fry
Honours: F.A. Amateur Cup 1945-46 Athenian League 1930-31, 1931-32, 1946-47, 1947-48, 1958-59, 1963-64, 1964-65 Southern League Div 1 1965-66 Southern League Div 1 (South) 1976-77 Southern League Cup 1971-72 Clubcall Cup (Bob Lord Trophy) 1988-89 GMVC Champions 1990-91 Herts Senior Cup Winners 13 times
League Career: Promoted to Division 4 1990-91

CLUB RECORDS (As a League Club)

Most Appearances for Club: Gary Bull: League 42 + FA Cup 9 + League Cup 2 + AMC 2 + 2 Play-offs. **Total 59** (1989-92)
Most Capped Player: No Barnet player has won a full cap
Record Goalscorer in a Match: Ron Phipps, Denis Kelleher, Peter Burridge, Steve Ragan, Tony Brimacombe, Roger Figg, Tony Harding (All 5, whilst a Non-League club). No player has scored more than 2 goals in a Football League match
Record League Goalscorer in a Season: Gary Bull 21, 1991-92 **In All Competitions:** Mark Carter, 32, (League 19 + League Cup 2 + FA Cup 5 + AMC 5 + Play-offs 1) 1991-92
Record League Goalscorer in a Career: Gary Bull 21, 1991-92 **In All Competitions:** Mark Carter, 32, (League 19 + League Cup 2 + FA Cup 5 + AMC 5 + Play-offs 1) 1991-92
Record Transfer Fee Received: £350,000 from Wimbledon for Andrew Clarke, 1991
Record Transfer Fee Paid: £40,000 to Barrow for Kenny Lowe, 1991 £40,000 to Runcorn for Mark Carter, 1991
Best Performances: League: 7th Division 4, 1991-92 **FA Cup:** 3rd Round 1964-65, 1970-71, 1972-73, 1981-82, 1990-91, 1991-92
League Cup: 1st Round 1991-92
Most League Points: (3pts for win) 69, Division 4, 1991-92
Most League Goals: 81, Division 4, 1991-92
Record League Victory and Most Goals Scored in a League Match: 6-0 v Lincoln City (away), Division 4, 4.9.1992
Most Goals Scored in a Cup Tie: 9-0 v Wealdstone, FA Cup, 1961-62 **First Class Cup Tie:** 6-3 v Brentford, Autoglass Trophy (AMC), 17.12.1991
Record Victory in a First Class Cup tie: 5-0 v Tiverton Town, FA Cup Round 1, 16.11.1992
Record League Defeat: 4-7 v Crewe Alex. (h), Div 4, 17.8.1991 2-5 v Rotherham Utd (h), Div 4, 11.1.1992 0-3 v Crewe Alex., Div 4, 26.12.1991 0-3 v Rotherham Utd, Div 4, 22.2.1992 0-3 v Burnley, Div 4, 7.3.1992
Oldest Player in a League Match: Edwin Stein, 35 years 323 days v Crewe Alex., Div 4, 17.8.1991
Youngest Player in a League Match: Mark Flashman 18 years 314 days

LONGEST RUNS	
of undefeated matches: 8 (1991)	**of league matches without a win:** 3 (1992)
of undefeated home matches: 8 (1991)	**of undefeated away matches:** 4 (1991)
without home win: (Not more than 1)	**without an away win:** 9 (1991-92)
of league wins: 3 (1991 twice)	**of home wins:** 8 (1991)
of league defeats: 3 (1992)	**of away wins:** 2 (1991)

BARNET

PLAYERS NAME Honours	Ht	Wt	Birthdate	Birthplace Transfers	Contract Date	Clubs	League	L/Cup	FA Cup	Other	Lg	L/C	FAC	Oth
GOALKEEPERS														
Mark Flashman			25.06.71	London		Barnet								
Andy Pape			22.03.62	Hammersmith		Feltham								
ESP:15, FAT, GL						QPR		1						
						Charlton								
						Ikast (Den)								
						C.Palace								
						Harrow								
						Enfield								
						Barnet	36							
Gary Phillips	5.11	14.5	20.09.61	St. Albans		Barnet								
E: S.1				£5,000		Brentford	143	8	5	15				
					25.08.88	Reading	24		7	3				
				Loan	01.09.89	Hereford	6							
				£12,500	01.12.89	Barnet	6	1	1	2				
DEFENDERS														
Dave Barnett			16.04.67	Brimingham		Kidderminster								
						Barnet	3							
Michael Bodley	5.11	12.0	14.09.67	Hayes	17.09.85	Chelsea (A)	6		1		1			
				£50,000	12.01.89	Northampton T	20			2				
				£15,000	01.10.89	Barnet	36	1	3	6	1			
Duncan Horton			18.02.67	Maidstone		Maidstone Utd								
						Charlton Ath								
via Welling United to						Barnet	24+6	1	2+1	5+1	3			
David Howell			10.10.58	London		Harrow Borough								
E: S-P.15						Hounslow								
						Hillingdon Bor.								
						Fulham								
via Enfield to						Barnet	34	1	3	3	3			
Dominic Naylor	5.9	11.7	12.08.70	Watford		Watford								
						Halifax	6+1							
						Barnet	26							
Paul Wilson			26.09.64	London		West Ham U								
						Billericay Town								
via Barking to						Barnet	23		3	3	1			
MIDFIELD														
Hakan Hayrettin			04.02.70	London	04.07.88	Leyton Orient (T)								
					01.06.89	Barnet	0+4							
Carl Hoddle			08.03.67	Harlow		Bishops Stortford								
				£10,000	24.07.89	Leyton Orient	19+9	1		2	2			
				Free		Barnet	10+3	2		3+1				
Kenny Lowe			06.11.64	Sedgefield		Hartlepool Utd								
E: S-P.2						Billingham Syn.								
via Gateshead, Morecambe & Barrow to						Barnet								
Derek Payne					22.07.91	Barnet								
Paul Showler			10.10.66	Doncaster		Sheffield Wed. (A)								
E: S-P.2						Sunderland								
via Bentley Vics & Goole Town to						Colne Dynamoes								
via Altrincham to						Barnet	39	1	2	6	7	1		
Edwin Stein			28.09.55	Cape Town		Luton Town								
						Edgware								
via Harrow Borough & Dagenham to						Barnet	0+1							
FORWARDS														
Gary Bull	5.9	11.7	12.06.66	Tipton		Paget Rangers								
					15.10.86	Southampton								
					29.03.88	Cambridge Utd	4+6	0+1		0+1	1			
						Barnet	42	2	3	6	21	2	2	2
Nicky Evans			06.07.58	Bedford		Kettering Town								
						Q.P.R								
						Peterborough U								
via Wycombe Wanderers to						Barnet	7+2	1	0+1	0+1	1	2	1	1
Tony Lynch			20.01.66	London		Maidstone Utd								
						Brentford								
via Wealdstone to						Barnet	1+5	0+2						
Brian Stein	5.10	11.8	09.10.57	S.Africa		Edgware T.								
E:11,u21,3, Div.2'82						Luton Town	378+10				127			
						Cannes								
						Luton Town	32+7	1+1	1		3			
						Barnet								
Frank Murphy			01.06.59	Glasgow		Corby Town								
via Nuneaton Town & Kettering Town to						Barnet	3+12		0+2	0+1	5			1
Roger Willis	6.1	11.6	17.06.67	Sheffield		Grimsby Town	9							
						Barnet	33+5	1	1+1	1+4	12			1

LEADING LEAGUE GOALSCORERS SEASONS 1985-86 – 1991-92

1985-86	Not in League		1986-87	Not in League
1987-88	Not in League		1988-89	Not in League
1989-90	Not in League		1990-91	Not in League

1991-92   **GARY BULL**   **21**

UNDERHILL STADIUM   Barnet Lane, Herts EN5 2BE

Capacity: 7,500   **Covered Standing:** 3,500   **Seating:** 1,000

Tel: Ground: 081 440 0277   **Ticket Sales:**   **Clubcall:** 0898 12 15 44

All premium rate calls (0898/0891) cost 36p per minute cheap rate and 48p per minute at all other times. Call costings correct at time of going to press.

ATTENDANCES
Highest: 11,026 v Wycombe Wanderers, FA Amateur Cup 4th Round, 1951-52

Lowest: 248 v Milton Keynes City, Southern League First Division North, 1975-76

Record Receipts: £31,202 v Portsmouth, FA Cup 3rd Round, 1990-91

UNDERHILL STADIUM
First game: v Crystal Palace, 7.9.1907 (London League)

Season Tickets: Seats £260
Terraces: £156, £78 jun/OAP's

Cost of Stand Tickets: Reserved seats (mains stand) £10; Unreserved £7.50
Terraces: £6 (adults); £3 (Juveniles & Senior Citizens)

Car Parking: Surrounding roads under police control

Nearest Railway Station: High Barnet (LT Northern Line) New Barnet (British Rail)

How to get to the ground

From North, South, East and West: Use M1 then M25, turn off at Junction 23. Follow signs for Barnet (A1000). Ground is located at the footb of Barnet Hill, behind the Old Red Lion Public House.

Value Rating: ★ ★ ★

Programme Editor: Tony Holmes

Price of 1992-93 Programme: £1
Number of Pages: 48
Subscriptions: Apply to club

Local Newspapers: Barnet & Finchley Press, Barnet Advertiser, Barnet Independent, Barnet Borough Times, Hendon & Finchley Times, Barnet Post

Local Radio Stations: L.B.C., Capital, BBC Radio Bedfordshire, Chiltern

BARNSLEY

Division 1

Formed: 1887   **Turned Professional:** 1888   **Ltd Co:** 1899

SPONSORED BY: T. Hayselden Ltd   **NICKNAME:** The Tykes

President
Arthur Raynor

Chairman
John Dennis

Vice-Chairman
Barry Taylor

Directors
Christopher Harrison
Michael Hayselden
Stuart Manley

Secretary
Michael Spinks

Team Manager
Mel Machin

Club Coach
Michael Wadsworth

Chief Scout
John Benson

Youth Team Coach
Eric Winstanley

Commercial Manager
Gerry Whewall (0226 286718)

Physiotherapist
Andrew Thomas

Groundsman
Roy Hatton

Club Statistician for the Directory
Ian Sawyer

THE first half of the season was nothing to write home about as far as performances on the field were concerned. Maybe two or three outstanding performances; firstly against Leicester City at home with a 3-1 victory in September, then came a 3-0 win against Newcastle United at the end of November. A fine 4-1 win against Grimsby Town in December even brought fame from the local television news programme 'Calendar'. A 2-1 away win against Wolverhampton in October earned the Reds the Barclays Bank 'Performance of the Week' award for the second season in succession for the same fixture.

A couple of good runs spanning mid-season saw Barnsley climb to their highest league position of the season – twelfth at the end of March. The first string of good performances, an unbeaten run of six matches, took place through December. The next started with a 2-0 away victory at Bristol City on 1st February ending with a 2-0 defeat at the hands of Ipswich Town at Portman Road at the end of March. The period December to March saw Barnsley lose only three League matches.

The 1-0 away victory against Grimsby Town saw Barnsley notch up their 5,000 league goal.

There were early exits from the major cup competitions; a third round departure against Middlesbrough in the Rumbelows Cup, while a last minute penalty from Scottish International Robert Fleck put Barnsley off course in the F.A. Cup, beaten by Norwich City who eventually lost to Sunderland in the semis. An exciting tie in the ZDS Cup against Leicester City saw Barnsley narrowly beaten by the odd goal in seven in extra-time after being 3-0 down to Leicester at one point.

Continued International recognition for Gerry Taggart saw him win his 11th cap for Northern Ireland against Lithuania, which beat the club record for International appearances previously held by Eddie McMorran. Gary Fleming also won international recognition with Northern Ireland, the first time Barnsley have had two current internationals on their books since 1950 when Pat Kelly and Eddie McMorran both appeared during the season for Northern Ireland.

Off the field profits rose to a healthy £756,391 for the year ending May 1991, a record profit beating the previous best of £535,271 – both were mainly due to dealings in the transfer market.

Ian Sawyer

Back row L-R: Alan Wilkinson, Colin Hoyle, Andy Rammell, Gerry Taggart, Phil Whitehead, Lee Butler, John Pearson, Mark Smith, Andy Saville, Phil Gridelet. **Middle row:** Mark Nile (Physio), Brendan O'Connell, Andrew Liddell, Nicky Eaden, Mark Burton, Ian Banks, Charlie Bishop, Daniel Graham, Wayne Bullimore, Gareth Williams, Steve Davis, Eric Winstanley (Youth Coach). **Front row:** John Deehan (First Team Coach), Michael Jackson, Gary Fleming, Brian McCord, Mark Robinson, Mel Machin (Team Manager), Colin Marshall, Owen Archdeacon, Dean Connelly, Paul Cross, John Benson (Chief Scout)

BARNSLEY

DIVISION TWO: 14TH **FA CUP:** 3rd RND **RUMBELOWS CUP:** 3rd RND **ZDS CUP:** 1st RND

M	DATE		COMP.	VEN	OPPONENTS	RESULT	H/T	LGE POS	GOALSCORERS/GOAL TIMES	ATTEN-DANCE
1	A	17	BL	A	Plymouth Argyle	L 1-2	0-1		Pearson 74	(6,352)
2		20	BL	H	Sunderland	L 0-3	0-2			12,454
3		24	BL	H	Brighton & H A	L 1-2	1-0	23	O'Connell 41	6,066
4		27	BL	A	Port Vale	D 0-0	0-0	23		(8,058)
5		31	BL	A	Swindon Town	L 1-3	1-0	23	Banks 1	(7,449)
6	S	3	BL	H	Watford	L 0-3	0-1	23		6,500
7		7	BL	A	Derby County	D 1-1	0-1	23	Saville 77	(10,559)
8		14	BL	H	Ipswich Town	W 1-0	0-0	21	Currie 80	6,449
9		17	BL	H	Leicester City	W 3-1	1-1	18	Rammell 2, Taggart 52, Redfearn (pen) 72	9,318
10		21	BL	A	Tranmere Rovers	L 1-2	0-1	20	Banks 50	(8,452)
11		24	RC 2/1	A	Blackpool	L 0-1	0-0			(4,123)
12		28	BL	H	Millwall	L 0-2	0-1	20		6,544
13	O	1	ZDC 1	A	Leicester City	L 3-4	0-3		Archdeacon 55, Currie 64, Saville 70	(3,995)
14		5	BL	A	Wolverhampton W	W 2-1	0-1	20	Saville 77, O'Connell 81	(14,082)
15		8	RC 2/2	H	Blackpool	W †2-0	1-0		O'Connell 37, Pearson 93	6,315
16		12	BL	H	Portsmouth	W 2-0	1-0	19	Taggart 16, Graham 88	6,579
17		19	BL	H	Bristol City	L 1-2	0-1	21	Currie 75	5,678
18		26	BL	A	Cambridge United	L 1-2	0-0	21	Rammell 64	(5,334)
19		29	RC 3	A	Middlesbrough	L 0-1	0-0			(9,381)
20	N	2	BL	A	Oxford United	W 1-0	1-0	18	Redfearn 3	(3,419)
21		5	BL	H	Middlesbrough	W 2-1	2-0	15	Rammell 34, Taggart 36	6,525
22		9	BL	H	Bristol Rovers	L 0-1	0-0	17		6,688
23		16	BL	A	Blackburn Rovers	L 0-3	0-0	19		(13,797)
24		23	BL	A	Southend United	L 1-2	0-0	20	Saville 78	(5,060)
25		30	BL	H	Newcastle United	W 3-0	3-0	19	Saville 26, Robinson 42, Rammell 45	9,648
26	D	7	BL	A	Charlton Athletic	D 1-1	0-0	18	Saville 66	(4,581)
27		14	BL	H	Grimsby Town	W 4-1	2-0	15	Currie 28, 48, Archdeacon 44, 73	6,056
28		22	BL	A	Watford	D 1-1	1-0	14	Robinson 42	(7,522)
29		26	BL	H	Port Vale	D 0-0	0-0	15		8,843
30		28	BL	H	Swindon Town	D 1-1	0-1	16	Saville 56	8,357
31	J	1	BL	A	Sunderland	L 0-2	0-1	18		(16,107)
32		4	FAC 3	A	Norwich City	L 0-1	0-0			(12,189)
33		11	BL	A	Brighton & H A	L 1-3	0-1	19	Currie 58	(6,107)
34		18	BL	H	Plymouth Argyle	L 1-3	0-3	21	Saville 60	5,374
35	F	1	BL	A	Bristol City	W 2-0	0-0	21	Archdeacon 69, O'Connell 90	(9,508)
36		8	BL	H	Cambridge United	D 0-0	0-0	17		6,196
37		15	BL	H	Southend United	W 1-0	0-0	16	O'Connell 75	5,328
38		22	BL	A	Newcastle United	D 1-1	0-0	17	Currie 84	(27,670)
39		29	BL	H	Charlton Athletic	W 1-0	0-0	14	Archdeacon 82	6,050
40	M	7	BL	A	Grimsby Town	W 1-0	0-0	13	Archdeacon 40	(6,513)
41		14	BL	H	Oxford United	W 1-0	0-0	13	Currie 60	5,436
42		21	BL	A	Bristol Rovers	D 0-0	0-0	14		(5,665)
43		28	BL	H	Blackburn Rovers	W 2-1	0-1	12	Smith 60, Rammell 79	13,346
44		31	BL	A	Ipswich Town	L 0-2	0-1	12		(14,148)
45	A	4	BL	H	Derby County	L 0-3	0-2	16		10,121
46		11	BL	A	Leicester City	L 1-3	1-0	17	Currie 35	(14,438)
47		13	BL	A	Middlesbrough	W 1-0	0-0	16	Redfearn 46	(12,743)
48		18	BL	H	Tranmere Rovers	D 1-1	1-1	16	Archdeacon 34	5,811
49		22	BL	A	Millwall	D 1-1	1-1	16	Rammell 44	(5,703)
50		25	BL	H	Wolverhampton W	W 2-0	1-0	14	Bullimore 29, Rammell 87	7,244
51	M	2	BL	A	Portsmouth	L 0-2	0-0	14		(11,169)

Best Home League Attendance: 13,346 v Blackburn Rovers   **Smallest:** 5,328 v Southend Utd   **Av Home Att:** 7,418

Goal Scorers: **Compared with 90-91:** -1,516

League (46): Currie 8, Rammell 7, Saville 7, Archdeacon 6, O'Connell 4, Redfearn 3 (1 pen), Taggart 3, Robinson 2, Banks 2, Bullimore, Pearson, Graham, Smith

R/lows C(2): Pearson, O'Connell

FA Cup (0):

ZDS Cup (3): Currie, Archdeacon, Saville

† = After extra-time

Whitehead P.	Bishop C.	Williams G.	Banks I.	Davis S.	Taggart G.	O'Connell B.	Rammell A.	Pearson J.	McCord B.	Graham D.	Fleming G.	Connelly D.	Smith M.	Butler L.	Robinson M.	Cross P.	Saville A.	Redfearn N.	Currie D.	Archdeacon O.	Bullimore W.	Whitworth N.	Referee	#
1	2	3	4	5	6	7	8	9	10*	11	12		S										G Ashby	1
1	2	3	4	5	6*	7	8	9		11●	10	12	14										J Brandwood	2
1	2		4	5	6	7	8	9*		12	10	11	3	S									P Taylor	3
	10		4		6	7	8	9		S	11	S	5	1	2	3							T Holbrook	4
	10		4	S	6	7	8	9*		12	11		5	1	2	3							M Bodenham	5
	10		4	5	6	7	8	S		9	2	11*		1				12	3				T West	6
2	4●				6	7	8*	14			3		5	1				12	9	10	11		I Borrett	7
	4				6	7	12	S			3		5	1	2			9*	8	10	11		P Wright	8
	4				6	7	9	S			3		5	1	2			12	8	10*	11		K Lupton	9
	4		S		6	7*	9			10	3		5	1	2			12	8		11		B Hill	10
	4				6	7	9			10*	3	S	5	1	2			12	8		11		A Flood	11
	4*				6	7	9				3		5	1	2			12	8	10	11	S	B Courtney	12
4*	14				6	7*	11	9			3			1	2			5	8	10	12		R Groves	13
		12			6	7	11	9		S	4			1	2			5	8	10*	3		T Lunt	14
		12			6	7	11*	9		14	4			1	2			5*	8	10	3		A Wilkie	15
		12			6	7	11	9		10	4			1	2			5	8	S	3*		N Midgeley	16
		14			6	7	11	9*		12	4			1	2			5*	8	10	3		R Hart	17
		9			6	7	11			12	4		5	1	2				8	10*	3	S	P Foakes	18
		9			6	7	11			12	4●		5	1	2				8	10*	3	14	M Peck	19
		9*			6	7	11				4		5	1	2		S	8	12	3	10		J Worrall	20
		9			6	7	11				4		5	1	2		S	8	10	3	S		M Reed	21
5	9				6	7	11			12	4*			1	2				8	10	3	S	R Nixon	22
14	9*				6	7	11	12			4		5	1	2				8	10*	3		T Ward	23
10					6	S	11†				4*		5	1	2			9	8	12	3	7	R Bigger	24
3					6	S	10*				2		5	1	7			9	8	12	11	4	V Callow	25
3		S			6			12			2		5	1	7			9	8	10*	11	4	M Pierce	26
3		12			6			14			2		5	1	7			9	8*	10*	11	4	I Cruikshanks	27
3		S			6			12			2		5	1	7			9	8	10*	11	4	R Pawley	28
3		S			6			12			2		5	1	7			9	8	10	11	4*	J Parker	29
		14	3		6			10			2*		5	1	7			9●	8	12	11	4	P Harrison	30
	3*	14			6			10			2		5	1	7			9	8	12	11	4●	P Jones	31
3	6				9		10				2	5*	1	7			14	8	12*	11	4		A Buksh	32
5				4	6*	10†					14	3		1	2●			12	7	11	9	8	A Smith	33
5			4	3	12	9					14	2●		1				10	6	11	8	7*	A Dawson	34
6		7	S		11			8	3		4		1	2			S		10	9			P Alcock	35
6		7			5	11*		8	3		4		1	2			12	S	10	9			T Holbrook	36
	3*	8		6	7			9●	4		5		1	2			12	14	10	11			T Fitzharris	37
		8	3*		7●			4			5		1	2			12	9	10	11		6	N Midgley	38
3		8			7	12		14	4*		5		1	2			9●		10	11		6	I Hendrick	39
3	S	8	4		7						5		1	2	S			10	11	9		6	I Hemley	40
4	3	8			7			S			5		1	2			9	10	11	S		6	C Trussell	41
4	3	8			7			S			5		1	2			9	10	11	S		6	G Ashby	42
4	3	8			7						5		1	2			9*	10	11	S		6	J Watson	43
	3	8	4*		7			10			5		1	2			9●	14	11			6	P Danson	44
	3	8*			7			10		14	4		5	1	2			9	12	11		6●	R Hart	45
		8●			7*	3		12	4				5	1	2			9	10	11	14	6	P Scoble	46
					3	7*	12	S	4				5	1	2			9	10	11	8	6	T Lunt	47
12					3	7*	10	14	4				5	1	2			9		11	8	6	A Flood	48
6					3	12	10*		4				5	1	2			9	7	11	8	S	R Hamer	49
6	12				3*		10	S	4				5	1	2			9	7	11	8		P Harrison	50
	6●				3		10	14	4				5	1	2			9	7*	11	8	12	R Foakes	51
3	25	15	23	8	38	34	31	8	1	8	40	2	37	43	40	3	14	35	30	40	17	11	**League Appearances**	
3	2	3	1		2	6	2	2		13	2	1	1		1		8	1	7		1	1	**Substitute Appearances**	
0+1	1	1		3	3	3	1		1+2	3		2	3	3		1+1	3	2	3	0+1			**R/lows Appearances**	
1	1			1	1			1		1		1	1	1		1	0+1	1	1				**FA Cup Appearances**	
1	0+1		1	1	1	1			1		1	1	1		1	1	1	0+1					**ZDS Cup Appearances**	

Players on Loan: Neil Whitworth (Manchester Utd)

†= Sent Off

BARNSLEY

Club Colours: Red shirts, white shorts, red stockings.
Change Colours: White shirts, red shorts, white stockings.
Reserves League: Pontins Central League Division 1.   **Youth League:** Northern League.

COMPETITIONS			
Div. 2	Div. 3	Div. 3N	Div. 4
98-32	59-65	32-34	65-68
34-38	68-72	38-39	72-79
39-53	79-81	53-55	
55-59			
81-			

HONOURS	
Div. 3N	FA Cup
33-34	11-12
38-39	
54-55	

MOST APPEARANCES: BARRY MURPHY 564 (1962-78)			
Year	League	FA Cup	League Cup
1962-63	21		2
1963-64	4		1
1964-65	22	1	1
1965-66	7+3		2
1966-67	14		
1967-68	46	1	1
1968-69	46	6	3
1969-70	46	4	1
1970-71	45	4	1
1971-72	46	3	3
1972-73	42	2	2
1973-74	10+1		2
1974-75	35	1	1
1975-76	36+1		2
1976-77	46	2	4
1977-78	43	2	3
	509+5	26	29
Previous holder: Eric Winstanley 460 (1961-73)			

MOST GOALS IN A CAREER		
ERNIE HINE 130 (1921-26 & 34-38)		
Season	League	FA Cup
1921-22	12	1
1922-23	23	1
1923-24	19	
1924-25	15	
1925-26	12	
1934-35	9	
1935-36	14	5
1936-37	13	
1937-38	6	
Total	123	7

RECORD TRANSFER FEE RECEIVED			
Amount	Club	Player	Date
£1,400,000	Nott'm Forest	Carl Tiler	5/91
£750,000	Nott'm Forest	David Currie	1/90
£300,000	Portsmouth	John Beresford	3/89
£200,000	Manchester City	Mick McCarthy	12/83

MANAGERS			
Name	Seasons	Best	Worst
John McCartney	1901-04	8(2)	11(2)
Arthur Fairclough	1904-12	6(2)	19(2)
John Hastie	1912-14	4(2)	5(2)
Harry Lewis	1914-19	3(2)	13(2)
Peter Sant	1919-26	3(2)	16(2)
John Commins	1926-29	11(2)	16(2)
Arthur Fairclough	1929-30	17(2)	17(2)
Brough Fletcher	1930-37	14(2)	8(3N)
Angus Seed	1937-53	9(2)	1(3N)
Tim Ward	1953-60	16(2)	17(3N)
John Steel	1960-71	7(3)	18(4)
John McSeventy	1971-72	22(3)	22(3)
John Steel	1972-73	14(4)	14(4)
Jim Iley	1973-78	6(4)	13(4)
Allan Clarke	1978-80	11(3)	4(4)
Norman Hunter	1980-84	6(2)	2(3)
Bobby Collins	1984-85	11(2)	11(2)
Allan Clarke	1985-89	7(2)	14(2)
Mel Machin	1989-	8(2)	19(2)

RECORD TRANSFER FEE PAID			
Amount	Club	Player	Date
£250,000	Oldham Athletic	David Currie	9/91
£200,000	Aston Villa	Gareth Williams	8/91
£180,000	Burnley	Steve Davis	7/91
£175,000	Barnet	Phil Gridelet	9/90

BARCLAYS

BARCLAYS BUSINESS CENTRE
Barnsley Church Street
PO Box No 20
27 Church Street
Barnsley
South Yorkshire S70 2AJ
Tel: 0226 73300

BARCLAYBANK MACHINE

LONGEST LEAGUE RUNS	
of undefeated matches:	21 (1.10.1933-5.5.1934)
of undefeated home matches:	36 (6.2.1933-24.11.1934)
without home win:	11 (6.12.1952-24.9.1953)
of league wins:	10 (5.2.1955-23.4.1955)
of league defeats:	9 (14.3.1953-25.4.1953)
of league matches w/out a win:	26 (13.12.1952-29.8.1953)
of undefeated away matches:	10 (27.12.1938-15.4.1939)
without an away win:	29 (14.3.1908-19.11.1910)
of home wins:	12 (3.10.1914-8.3.1915)
of away wins:	5 (27.12.1938-25.2.1939)

PREVIOUS NAMES
Barnsley St. Peters

PREVIOUS LEAGUE
Midland

BIGGEST VICTORIES
League: 9-0 v Loughborough Town, Division 2, 28.1.1899.
9-0 v Accrington Stanley, Division 3N, 3.2.1934 (a).
F.A. Cup: 8-0 v Leeds City, Qualifying, 3.11.1894.
League Cup: 6-0 v Peterborough, Round 1, 15.9.1981.

BIGGEST DEFEATS
League: 0-9 v Notts County, Division 2, 19.11.1927.
F.A. Cup: 1-8 v Derby County, Round 1, 30.1.1897.
League Cup: No defeat by more than 3 goals.

MOST POINTS
3 points a win: 74, Division 2, 1988-89.
2 points a win: 67, Division 3N, 1938-39.

MOST GOALS
118 Division 3(N), 1933-34

MOST GOALS IN A MATCH
5. F Eaton v South Sheilds, Division 3N, 9.4.1927 (6-1)
5. P Cunningham v Darlington, Division 3N, 4.2.1933. (6-2)
5. B Asquith v Darlington, Division 3N, 12.11.1938. (7-1)
5. C McCormack v Luton, Division 2, 9.9.1950. (6-1)

MOST GOALS IN A SEASON
Cecil McCormack: 34 (League 33, FAC 1) 1950-51, Div 2.
5 goals once = 5; 3 goals twice = 6; 2 goals five times = 10; 1
goal thirteen times = 13.
Previous holder: Abe Blight 31 (1933-34).

MOST FIRST CLASS MATCHES IN A SEASON
58 (46 League, 10 FA Cup, 2 League Cup) 1960-61
58 (46 League, 6 FA Cup, 6 League Cup) 1980-81

MOST LEAGUE GOALS CONCEDED
108, Division 2, 1952-53

MOST LEAGUE WINS
30, Division 3(N), 1938-39
30, Division 3(N), 1954-55

MOST LEAGUE DRAWS
18, Division 3, 1971-72

MOST LEAGUE DEFEATS
29, Division 2, 1952-53

OLDEST PLAYER
Beaumont Asquith, 37 years 3 months, v Coventry City,
19.11.1927

YOUNGEST PLAYER
Glyn Riley, 16 years 171 days, v Torquay Utd, 11.1.1975

MOST CAPPED PLAYER
Gerry Taggart (N. Ireland) 11 caps

BEST PERFORMANCES BY BARNSLEY

League: 1938-39: Matches played 42, Won 30, Drawn 7, Lost 5, Goals for 94, Goals against 34, Points 67. First in Division 3N.

Highest: 1914-15, 1921-22: Third Division 2.

F.A. Cup: 1911-12: 3rd rnd. Birmingham City 0-0, 3-1; 4th rnd. Leicester City 1-0; 5th rnd. Bolton Wanderers 2-1; 6th rnd. Bradford City 0-0, 0-0,
0-0, 3-0; Semi-Final Swindon Town 0-0, 1-0; Final West Bromwich Albion 0-0, 1-0.

League Cup: 1981-82: 1st rnd. Peterborough United 3-2, 6-0; 2nd rnd. Swansea City 2-0, 2-3; 3rd rnd. Brighton & Hove Albion 4-1; 4th rnd. Manchester City 1-0; 5th rnd. Liverpool 0-0, 1-3.

DIVISIONAL RECORDS

	Played	Won	Drawn	Lost	For	Against	Points
DIVISION 2	2274	782	562	930	3164	3605	2302
DIVISION 3	552	183	159	210	736	838	525
DIVISION 3N	218	130	38	50	467	278	298
DIVISION 4	460	177	127	156	628	555	481
TOTALS	3504	1272	886	1346	4995	5276	3606

BARNSLEY

PLAYERS NAME / Honours	Ht	Wt	Birthdate	Birthplace / Transfers	Contract Date	Clubs	League	L/Cup	FA Cup	Other	Lg	L/C	FAC	Oth
GOALKEEPERS														
Lee Butler	6.2	13.0	30.05.66	Sheffield		Haworth Co								
					16.06.86	Lincoln City	30	1	1					
				£100,000	21.08.87	Aston Villa	8			2				
Loan Hull City (18.0391) 4lg				£165,000	22.07.91	Barnsley	43	3	1	1				
Philip Whitehead	6.3	13.07	17.12.69	Halifax	01.07.88	Halifax Town (T)	42	2	4	4				
				£60,000	09.03.90	Barnsley	3							
Loan Halifax Town (07.03.91) 9lg				Loan	29.11.91	Scunthorpe Utd	8			2				
DEFENDERS														
Charlie Bishop	6.0	12.11	16.02.68	Nottingham		Stoke City (A)								
via Watford				Free	10.08.87	Bury	104+10	5	4	12+1	6		1	
				£50,000	24.07.91	Barnsley	25+3	0+1	1	1				
Steve Davis	6.0	12.7	26.07.65	Birmingham		Stoke City (A)								
E:Y1				f	17.08.83	Crewe Alexandra	140+5	10	3	7+1	1			
				£15,000	03.10.87	Burnley	147	7	9	19	11			1
				£180,000	26.07.91	Barnsley	8+1							
Gary Fleming	5.9	11.1	17.02.67	Londonderry	19.11.84	Nottm. Forest	71+3	5+1	2+1	0+1				
NI:12				£150,000	17.08.89	Manchester City	13+1	4		1				
Loan Notts County (08.0390) 3lg 1oth				£85,000	23.03.90	Barnsley	96+2	6	3	5				
Mark Smith	6.1	12.2	21.03.60	Sheffield	22.03.78	Sheffield Wed. (A)	281+1	30	39		16	1	3	
E:u21.5				£170,000	28.07.87	Plymouth A	82	9	5	1	6	1		
				£145,000	18.12.89	Barnsley	98+2	6	6	3+1	10		1	1
Gerald Taggart	6.1	13.4	18.10.70	Belfast	01.07.89	Manchester City (T)	10+2			1	1			
NI:7				£75,000	10.01.90	Barnsley	86+3	7	6	3	7		1	
MIDFIELD														
Wayne Bullimore	5.9	10.6	12.09.70	Sutton-in-Ashfield	16.09.88	Manchester Utd. (T)								
				Free	09.03.91	Barnsley	17+1	0+1	1		1			
Mark Burton	5.9		07.05.73	Barnsley	06.07.91	Barnsley (T)								
Dean Connelly	5.9	10.8	06.01.70	Jersey	11.02.88	Arsenal (T)								
				Free	01.07.90	Barnsley	7+5			0+1				1
				Loan	09.10.91	Wigan Athletic	12		3	2	2			
Deiniol Graham	5.9	10.7	04.10.69	Cannock	08.10.87	Manchester Utd. (T)	1+1	0+1	0+1				1	
W:u21.1				£50,000	08.08.91	Barnsley	8+13	1+2			1			
Phil Gridelet	5.11	12.0	30.04.67	Edgeware		Hendon			1					
E:SP.4				£25,000		Barnet			0+1					
				£175,000	21.09.90	Barnsley	1+3			1				
Neil Redfearn	5.10	12.4	20.06.65	Dewsbury		Nottm. Forest								
Div2'91				Free	23.06.82	Bolton W	35	2	4		1			
					23.08.84	Lincoln City	96+4	4	3	7	13		1	
					22.08.86	Doncaster Rovers	46	2	3	2	14		1	
				£100,000	31.07.87	Crystal Palace	57	6	1	1	10			
				£150,000	21.11.88	Watford	22+2	1	6	5	3		3	1
				£150,000	12.01.90	Oldham Ath	56+6	3	7+1	1	16	1	3	
				£150,000	05.09.91	Barnsley	35+1	3	1	1	3			
Mark Robinson	5.9	10.6	21.11.68	Manchester	10.01.87	West Brom A. (A)	2	0+1						
				Free	29.01.88	Barnsley	89+19	5+2	4+1	2+2	5			1
FORWARDS														
Owen Archdeacon	5.7	11.0	04.03.66	Greenock		Gourock Utd								
S: u21.1, Y; SPD'86						Celtic	38+38	1+4	3+1	1+3	8	1		
				£80,000	07.07.89	Barnsley	102+4	8+1	4+1	5+1	11	1		3
David Currie	6.0	11.13	27.11.62	Stockton	05.02.82	Middlesbrough	94+19	6	5+1	2	30	1		
FLgXI.1; Div2'91				Free	17.06.86	Darlington	76	6	3	5	33			3
				£150,000	26.02.88	Barnsley	80	3	5	1	30	1	4	
				£750,000	19.01.90	Nottm. Forest	4+4				1			
				£460,000	23.08.90	Oldham Ath	17+14	2+1	1	0+1	3	2		
				£250,000	05.09.91	Barnsley	30+7	2	0+1	1	8			1
Colin Hoyle	5.11	12.03	15.01.72	Derby	29.01.90	Arsenal (T)								
				Loan	08.02.90	Chesterfield	3							
				Free	01.07.90	Barnsley								
Andrew Liddell	5.8	10.5	28.06.73	Leeds	06.07.91	Barnsley (T)	0+1							
Brian McCord	5.10	11.6	24.06.68	Derby	05.06.87	Derby County (A)	3+2	1	3	0+1				1
				£100,000	09.03.90	Barnsley	40+3	4		2	2			
Brendan O'Connell	5.10	10.9	12.11.66	London	01.07.85	Portsmouth								
				Free	04.08.86	Exeter City	73+8	3+1	3	4	19	2		
				Free	01.07.88	Burnley	62+2	6	3	5	17	3	1	2
Loan Huddersfield T. (30.11.89) 11lg 1gl				£50,000	23.03.90	Barnsley	75+17	4+1	3	5	15	1		
John Pearson	6.2	13.2	01.09.63	Sheffield	18.05.81	Sheffield Wed	64+41	7+3	8+5		24	1	2	
E: Y.3				£100,000	20.05.85	Charlton Ath	52+9	3+1	4	1	15			1
				£70,000	15.01.87	Leeds Utd	51+48	5+4	5+5	6+3	12			
Loan Rotherham Utd (28.03.91) 11lg 5gl				£135,000	08.07.91	Barnsley	8+2	1		1	1	1		
				Loan	09.01.92	Hull City	15		2					1
Andrew Rammell	5.10	11.7	10.02.67	Nuneaton		Atherstone			0+1					
				£40,000	26.09.89	Manchester Utd								
				£100,000	14.09.90	Barnsley	63+14	4+1	3	4	19			1
Gareth Williams	5.10	11.8	12.03.67	Isle of Wight		Gosport Bo								
				£30,000	09.01.88	Aston Villa	6+6	0+1	2	0+1				
				£200,000	06.08.91	Barnsley	15+2	1	1	0+1				

BARNSLEY

RECORD WIN & LOSS AGAINST EACH CLUB IN CURRENT DIVISION

(Where score has occured on several occasions the most recent is given)

Club	Rec. Win	Season	Rec. Loss	Season
BIRMINGHAM CITY	5-1	1909-10	5-0	1919-20 (home)
BRENTFORD	3-0	1967-68	8-1	1934-35
BRISTOL CITY	7-1	1912-13	5-0	1957-58
BRISTOL ROVERS	4-0	1962-63	4-0	1970-71 (home)
CAMBRIDGE UNITED	4-0	1975-76	2-0	1974-75
CHARLTON ATHLETIC	7-1	1958-59	4-0	1958-59
DERBY COUNTY	5-0	1922-23	7-0	1914-15
GRIMSBY TOWN	7-2	1949-50	8-1	1899-00
LEICESTER CITY	3-0	1989-90	6-0	1946-47
LUTON TOWN	6-1	1950-51	6-0	1952-53
MILLWALL	4-1	1987-88	4-1	1990-91
NEWCASTLE UNITED	3-0	1937-38	5-0	1982-83 (home)
NOTTS COUNTY	5-2	1960-61	9-0	1926-27
OXFORD UNITED	3-0	1990-91	4-0	1984-85
PETERBOROUGH UTD	3-2	1964-65	6-3	1972-73
PORTSMOUTH	4-0	1990-91	4-1	1924-25 (home)
SOUTHEND UNITED	4-1	1959-60	4-1	1964-65 (home)
SUNDERLAND	3-0	1988-89	4-2	1989-90
SWINDON TOWN	6-2	1961-62	3-0	1987-88
TRANMERE ROVERS	5-1	1933-34	5-2	1933-34
WATFORD	4-0	1964-65	4-0	1988-89
WEST HAM UNITED	7-0	1919-20	4-0	1955-56 (home)
WOLVERHAMPTON WNDRS	7-1	1909-10	9-1	1926-27

MANAGER: MELVIN MACHIN

DATE OF BIRTH: 16.04.1945 **PLACE OF BIRTH:** Stoke on Trent

DATE OF APPOINTMENT: 29 December 1989

PREVIOUS CLUBS
as Manager: Manchester City
as Asst. Man./Coach: Norwich City
as Player: Port Vale; Gillingham; Bournemouth; Norwich City

HONOURS
as Manager: Promotion to Division One
as Asst. Man./Coach: Promotion to Division One
as Player:
International:

BARCLAYS LEAGUE DIVISION TWO
BARNSLEY v WATFORD
Saturday, 2nd March, 1991
Kick-off 3.00p.m.

Value Rating: ★ ★ ★ ★

Programme Editor: Keith Lodge

Price of 1992-93 Programme: £1
Number of Pages: 32
Subscriptions: £29.90 for 23 home fixtures (inc post & packing)

Local Newspapers: Barnsley Chronicle (weekly), Barnsley Star (daily), Morning Telegraph, Yorkshire Post.

Local Radio Stations: Radio Sheffield, Radio Hallam.

Books Available about Club: Oakwell Heroes – Who's Who of Barnsley Football Club. (Graham Noble), paperback £4.95.
Oakwell Centurions. (David Watson), paperback £7.95,

LEADING LEAGUE GOALSCORERS
SEASONS 1979-80 – 1991-92

1979-80	RONNIE GLAVIN	20	1980-81	RONNIE GLAVIN	18
1981-82	IAN BANKS	15	1982-83	RONNIE GLAVIN	17
1983-84	DAVID GEDDES	15	1984-85	GORDON OWEN	14
1985-86	IAN WALSH	15	1986-87	STUART GRAY	11
1987-88	STEVE LOWNDES	9	1988-89	DAVID CURRIE	16
1989-90	STEVE AGNEW	8	1990-91	ANDY SAVILLE	12
				ANDY RAMMELL	12

1991-92   **DAVID CURRIE**   **8**

OAKWELL GROUND Grove Street, Barnsley, Yorkshire S71 1ET

Capacity: 27,386   **Covered Standing:** 17,822   **Seating:** 9,564

Tel: Ground: 0226 295353   **Clubcall:** 0898 12 11 52

All premium rate calls (0898/0891) cost 36p per minute cheap rate and 48p per minute at all other times. Call costings correct at time of going to press.

ATTENDANCES
Highest: 40,255 v Stoke City, FA Cup 5th Round, 15.2.1936

Lowest: 1,972 v Wrexham, Division 3, 8.3.1972

Record Receipts:
Not Disclosed

OAKWELL
First game: Barnsley v Gawber (Friendly), 0-0, 15.10.1887
First floodlit game: v Bolton Wanderers (Friendly), 23.1.1962

Season Tickets:
Stands: from £155 (£108 jun/OAP)
Ground: from £99-£108 (£70-£72 jun/OAP)

Executive Box Season Tickets: None

Cost of Stand Tickets: Seats: £10.00 (no reductions)
Terraces: adult £5.50-£6.00 (£3.80-£4.00 jun/OAP)

Car Parking: Official car parks for 1,200 vehicles adjacent to ground. Cost £1. Visitors use Queens Ground car park

Nearest Railway Station: Exchange Station, Barnsley (Tel 0742 26411)

How to get to the ground

From North: M1 to J37. Take A628 towards Barnsley and follow signs for Football Ground

From South: M1 to J37. Proceed as above

From East: A635 towards Barnsley and follow signs for Football Ground

From West: A628 towards Barnsley and shortly after crossing M1 Jnt 37 follow signs for Football Ground

BIRMINGHAM CITY
Division 1

Formed: 1875   **Turned Professional:** 1885   **Ltd Co:** 1888

SPONSORED BY: Triton Showers   **NICKNAME:** The Blues

Chairman
S Kumar B.A.

Directors
R Kumar B.Sc (Vice-Chairman)
B Kumar B.Sc
J F Wiseman
T Cooper
B H Slater

Secretary
Alan G Jones, BA, MBA
(021-772 0101)

Manager
Terry Cooper

Coaches
Ian Atkins
Brian Caswell

Chief Scout
Bill Coldwell

Commercial Manager
Joan Hill

Physiotherapist
Paul Heath

Groundsman
Brian Harris

Club Statistician for the Directory
Dave Drage

BEFORE the season started the chances of Blues gaining promotion were extremely remote. The club was in turmoil following the departure of manager Lou Macari to Stoke with 21 players out of contract and seemingly reluctant to pledge their future to the club.

Caretaker boss Bill Coldwell must take a great deal of credit for persuading the players to re-sign and in the end only Vince Overson refused and followed former boss Macari to Stoke.

On the eve of the season Terry Cooper was appointed manager and the rest as they say is history. Just one defeat in 15 games got Blues off to a flying start. This was supplemented by a good run in the Rumbelows Cup when the Blues took First Division Crystal Palace to 3 matches before bowing out. However, the F.A. Cup ended at the first hurdle following an abysmal performance at Torquay.

Once again Blues seemed to lose their way around Christmas and a dismal run of only three wins in 12 games began to sow the seeds of doubt. Also hope of a return to Wembley in the Autoglass Trophy ended ignominiously at the qualifying stage.

Matters came to a head during the match against Stoke when a refereeing decision gifted Stoke an equaliser and sparked off a disgraceful riot.

Meanwhile victory over Brentford in March ended the dismal spell and Blues never looked back after that as promotion was gained with victory over Shrewsbury, and the three year exile in Division Three was finally over. However, two unnecessary defeats in the last 2 games cost Blues the championship they deserved.

Terry Cooper has done a magnificent job and the fact that Birmingham had to use 32 players during the season makes his achievement even greater. Blues' supporters can now look forward to the future with confidence. The phoenix has risen from the ashes and the rebirth of the Blues is under way.

Dave Drage

Back row L-R: Simon Sturridge, Louie Donowa, Paul Tait, Martin Thomas, Martin Hicks, John Gayle, Andy Gosney, Matthew Fox, Jason Beckford, Paul Holmes. **Middle row:** Brian Caswell (Reserve Coach), Graham Potter, Trevor Matthewson, Nigel Gleghorn, Dean Peer, Paul Mardon, Ian Atkins (Asst. Manager), Mark Sale, Alan O'Neil, David Foy, Darren Rogers, David Rennie, Tony Taylor (Youth Coach). **Front row:** Paul Heath (Physio), Ian Rodgerson, Carl Adams, Eric Hogan, Paul Jones, Darren Rowbotham, Mark Cooper, Ian Clarkson, John Frain, Terry Cooper (Manager)

BIRMINGHAM CITY

DIVISION THREE: RUNNERS-UP **FA CUP:** 1st RND **RUMBELOWS CUP:** 3rd RND **AUTOGLASS:** Prelim.

M	DATE		COMP.	VEN	OPPONENTS	RESULT	H/T	LGE POS	GOALSCORERS/GOAL TIMES	ATTEN-DANCE
1	A	17	BL	H	Bury	W 3-2	2-1		Gleghorn 6, Gayle 29, Okenla 46	9,033
2		20	RC 1/1	A	Exeter City	W 1-0	1-0		Rodgerson 30	(4,071)
3		24	BL	A	Fulham	W 1-0	1-0	6	Rodgerson 37	(4,762)
4		27	RC 1/2	H	Exeter City	W 4-0	2-0		Hicks 12, Yates 31, Peer 52, Gleghorn 67	6,177
5		31	BL	H	Darlington	W 1-0	1-0	1	Sturridge 39	8,768
6	S	3	BL	A	Hull City	W 2-1	0-0		Sturridge 56, Rodgerson 89	(4,801)
7		7	BL	A	Reading	D 1-1	1-1	2	Sturridge 30	(6,649)
8		14	BL	H	Peterborough Utd	D 1-1	0-0	1	Cooper 90	9,408
9		17	BL	H	Chester City	W 3-2	2-2	1	Sturridge 23, Frain (pen) 33, Gleghorn 77	8,154
10		21	BL	A	Hartlepool United	L 0-1	0-1	2		(4,643)
11		25	RC 2/1		Luton Town	D 2-2	1-1		Rodgerson 3, Gleghorn 59	(6,315)
12		28	BL	H	Preston North End	W 3-1	1-1	2	Matthewson 35, Gleghorn 72, Rodgerson 80	8,760
13	O	5	BL	A	Shrewsbury Town	D 1-1	1-0	2	Gleghorn 32	(7,035)
14		8	RC 2/1	H	Luton Town	W 3-2	1-0		Peer 29, Gleghorn 60, 90	13,252
15		12	BL	H	Stockport County	W 3-0	2-0	1	Cooper 32, Drinkell 41, Donowa 87	12,634
16		19	BL	H	Wigan Athletic	D 3-3	1-2	2	Sturridge 13, Gleghorn 52, Rodgerson 90	9,662
17		26	BL	A	West Bromwich A.	W 1-0	0-0	1	Drinkell 49	(26,169)
18		29	RC 3	H	Crystal Palace	D 1-1	0-0		Sturridge 83	17,270
19	N	2	BL	A	Torquay United	W 3-0	0-0	1	Gleghorn (pen) 33, Sturridge 51, Donowa 72	9,408
20		6	BL	A	Brentford	D 2-2	1-1	1	Sturridge 24, Cooper 55	(8,798)
21		9	BL	A	Huddersfield Town	L 2-3	0-1	2	Gleghorn 58, Matthewson 81	(11,688)
22		16	FAC 1	A	Torquay United	L 0-3	0-2			(4,123)
23		19	RC 3R	A	Crystal Palace	D †1-1	0-0		Gleghorn 93	(10,698)
24		23	BL	H	Exeter City	W 1-0	0-0	2	Gleghorn 78	11,319
25		30	BL	H	Bradford City	W 2-0	1-0	2	Peer 25, Gleghorn 65	10,468
26	D	3	RC 3R2	A	Crystal Palace	L 1-2	1-2		Peer 45	(11,384)
27		14	BL	A	Bournemouth	L 1-2	0-1	2	Paskin 52	(6,168)
28		18	AGT Pre	A	Stoke City	L 1-3	1-2		Tait 11	(5,942)
29		21	BL	H	Fulham	W 3-1	1-0	1	Gleghorn 38, Rodgerson 72, 78	8,877
30		26	BL	A	Darlington	D 1-1	0-1	2	Rodgerson 59	(4,422)
31		28	BL	A	Bury	L 0-1	0-1	3		(4,253)
32	J	1	BL	H	Hull City	D 2-2	1-1	2	Paskin 34, Gleghorn 71	12,983
33		4	BL	A	Stoke City	L 1-2	0-0	2	Beckford 51	(18,914)
34		7	AGT Pre	H	Walsall	L 0-1	0-0			5,239
35		11	BL	H	Leyton Orient	D 2-2	0-1	3	Cooper 52, Paskin 69	10,445
36		18	BL	A	Swansea City	W 2-0	1-0	2	Rodgerson 26, Rowbotham 87	(4,147)
37	F	8	BL	H	West Bromwich A.	L 0-3	0-2	4		27,508
38		11	BL	H	Bradford City	W 2-1	1-0	4	Gleghorn 9, Sturridge 53	(7,008)
39		15	BL	H	Bournemouth	L 0-1	0-0	5		10,898
40		22	BL	A	Leyton Orient	D 0-0	0-0	5		(5,995)
41		29	BL	H	Stoke City	D 1-1	1-0	6	Frain (pen) 22	22,162
42	M	3	BL	A	Swansea City	D 1-1	1-0	5	Rowbotham 26	9,475
43		10	BL	H	Brentford	W 1-0	1-0	5	Matthewson 33	13,290
44		17	BL	A	Bolton Wanderers	D 1-1	1-0	6	Rodgerson 42	(7,329)
45		21	BL	H	Huddersfield Town	W 2-0	1-0	6	Sturridge 29, Gleghorn 88	12,482
46		24	BL	A	Torquay United	W 2-1	0-1	2	Rowbotham 63, Matthewson 82	(2,446)
47		28	BL	A	Exeter City	L 1-2	1-1	3	Hicks 25	(5,479)
48		31	BL	A	Peterborough Utd	W 3-2	1-1	3	Frain (pen) 27, Sturridge 60, Matthewson 70	(12,081)
49	A	4	BL	H	Reading	W 2-0	2-0	2	Rowbotham 9, Frain (pen) 45	12,229
50		11	BL	A	Chester City	W 1-0	0-0	2	Gleghorn 89	(4,895)
51		14	BL	H	Bolton Wanderers	W 2-1	2-1	1	Frain (pen) 32, Rennie 38	14,440
52		18	BL	H	Hartlepool United	W 2-1	0-0	1	Matthewson 55, Gleghorn 75	13,698
53		21	BL	A	Preston North End	L 2-3	0-2	1	Gleghorn 47, Rennie 76	(7,738)
54		25	BL	H	Shrewsbury Town	W 1-0	1-0	1	Gleghorn 34	19,868
55		28	BL	A	Wigan Athletic	L 0-3	0-2	1		(5,950)
56	M	2	BL	A	Stockport County	L 0-2	0-2	2		(7,840)

Best Home League Attendance: 27,508 v West Bromwich A.	Smallest: 8,154 v Chester City	Av Home Att: 12,433
Goal Scorers:		
		Compared with 90-91: +5,403

League (69): Gleghorn 17 (1 pen), Sturridge 10, Rodgerson 9, Matthewson 6, Frain 5 (5 pens), Cooper 4, Rowbotham 4, Paskin 3, Rennie 2, Donowa 2, Drinkell 2, Hicks, Peer, Gayle, Beckford, Okenla

R/lows C(13): Gleghorn 5, Peer 3, Rodgerson 2, Yates, Sturridge, Hicks

FA Cup (0):

Autoglass (1): Tait

† = After extra-time

Thomas M.	Clarkson I.	Matthewson T.	Frain J.	Hicks M.	Mardon P.	Rogerson I.	Gayle J.	Peer D.	Gleghorn N.	Sturridge S.	Yates M.	Okenla F.	Dolan E.	Aylott T.	Donowa L.	Cooper M.	atkins I.	Tait P.	Drinkell K.	Paskin J.	Miller A.	Rowbotham D.	Beckford J.	Rennie D.	Dearden K.	Referee	
1	2	3*	4	5	6	7	8•	9	10	11	12	14														P Alcock	1
1	2		3	5	6	7		9	10	11	4	S	8†													P Scoble	2
1	2		3	5	6	7		9	10	11	4	14	8•													D Axcell	3
1	2		3	5	6	7		9	10	11	4	S	8	S												P Danson	4
1	2		3	5	6	7	8*	9	10	11		S	12		4											P Jones	5
1	2		3	5	6	7		9	10	11		S	8		4											J Watson	6
1	2		3	5	6	7*		9	10	11		S	8		4	12										R Bigger	7
1	2		3	5	6*			9	10	11	7•				4	8	12									J Rushton	8
1	2		3	5	6	7		9	10	11					4	8	S									A Bennett	9
1	2		3	5	6	7		9	10	11					4	8	S									T Fitzharris	10
1	2	3	8	5	6	7		9	10	11		S			4		S									R Pawley	11
1	2	3	8	5	6	7		S	10	11		S			4	9										B Coddington	12
1	2	3	8	5	6	7		12	10	11					4•	9*		14								D Gallagher	13
1	2	3	8	5	6	7		9	10	11		S			4		S									W Burge	14
1	2	3	8	5	6	7		S	10	11					14	4		9•								E Parker	15
1	2	3	8	5	6	7		12	10	11					14	4		9•								G Courtney	16
1	2	3	8	5	6			S	10	11	7				4		S	9								R Gifford	17
1	2	3	8	5	6			4	10	11	7•				9		S									S Lodge	18
1	2	3	8	5	6		S	4	10	11	7				S	9										T West	19
1	2	3	8	5	6	14		12	10	11	7				4*	9•										K Cooper	20
1	2	3	8	5	6	7		4*	10	11		S			9	12										J Worrall	21
1	2	3	8	5*	6	7		12	10	11		S			9	4†										M Bodenham	22
1	2	5	3	6	7			4	10	11		S			9	8*										R Hamer	23
	2	5	3	6	7			4*	10	11					9	8		12								A Wilkie	24
	2	5	3	S	6	7		4	10	11*					9	8		12								J Deakin	25
	2	5	3	12	6	7		4	10	11•					9	8*	14									B Hill	26
	2	5	3	12	6	7		4	10						9•	8*	11									I Hemley	27
	2	3	5	6	7			4	10	11					12	9*	8									K Cooper	28
	2	5	3	S	6	7		4	10	11					S	8	9	1								W Flood	29
	2	5	3	S	6	7		4	10	11					14	8•	9	1								T Phillips	30
	2	12	3	6	7			4*	10	11					8	9	1									M Peck	31
3	2	5	6	7				10	11•	14	8*	4	12	9	1											J Kirby	32
3	2	5	6*	7				10		12	4	S	9	1	8	11										R Milford	33
	2	6	3	5	7	8		10	11*	4					1		9									S Bell	34
	2	6	3	5	7	8		10	12	4		9	1	11*	S											D Allison	35
	2	6	3	5	7	8*		10	4	9		1	11	12												W Burge	36
	2	6	3	5	7	12		10	14	9	4•		1	8*	11											K Barratt	37
	2	6		5	7			10	11*	9	4	3	1	8	S											R Nixon	38
	2	6		5	7			10	11	9•	4	3*	12	1	8	14										R Poulain	39
	2	11		5	7			10	4	9	S	3	8	1	S	6										M James	40
	2	3	5	6	7			10	11*	12•	8			1	9	4										R Wiseman	41
	2	3	5	6	7			10		12	8•			1	9	4										P Taylor	42
	2	6	3	5	7			10	11*	12•	14	8		1	9	4										I Hendrick	43
S	6	3	5	2	7			10	12	11	8*			1	9	4										A Bennett	44
	2	3	8	5	6	7		10	11*	12	S			9	4	1										P Alcock	45
S	3	8	5	6	7			10	11	S	2			9	4	1										R Groves	46
	2	3	8	5	6*	7		10	11	12				9•	4	1										J Deakin	47
	2	6	3	5	7•			10	11	8	S			9	4	1										G Willard	48
	2	6	3	5				10	11•	8				9	4	1										R Dilkes	49
	2	6	3	5				10	11	8				9	4	1										J Key	50
2•	6	3	5	12	7*			10	11	8				9	4	1										A Dawson	51
	2	6	3	5	S			10	11	7				8	9	4	1									R Lewis	52
	2	6	3	5	14			10	11	12				8	9•	7*	4	1								K Redfearn	53
	2	6	3	5	14	7		10	11	S				8	9•	4	1									E Parker	54
	2	6	3	5	9*	7		10	11•	8				14	4	1										K Hackett	55
	2	6	3	5	12	7		10	14	8				9	4	1										G Courtney	56
16	42	35	44	41	31	38	2	18	46	38	1	2	1	2	20	27	5	10	5	8	15	21	2	17	12	League Appearances	
	1		1	4	1	1	3		2	1	5	1			6	6	3	2		2		1		2		Substitute Appearances	
6	7	5	7	5+1	7	6		7	7	7		2	1	2	5			2	0+1							R/lows Appearances	
1	1	1	1	1	1	1		0+1	1	1					1			1								FA Cup Appearances	
2	1	2	2	1	2	1		1+1	1	1					1						1			1		Autoglass Appearances	

Also Played: Posn.(Game): Fox S(2,3,6,24), Taylor S(9), Gray S(10), Foy 12(23)S(34), Carter 1(24,25,26), Cheesewright 1(27,28), Jones 14(8,18), Hogan S(28,31,36)12(34)14(27), Francis 12(38)14(42,49)S(50), Sale 14(47,48,51)S(49,52)7(50)12(55)11•(56), O'Neil 14(41)11*(42)7(49)12(50)

BIRMINGHAM CITY

Club Colours: Royal blue/white & red trim shirts, white with blue trim shorts, red stockings
Change Colours:
Reserves League: Midland Intermediate

COMPETITIONS		
Div. 1	Div. 2	Div. 3
94-96	92-94	89-92
01-02	96-01	
03-08	02-03	
21-39	08-21	
48-50	39-48	
55-65	50-55	
72-79	65-72	
80-84	79-80	
85-86	84-85	
	86-89	
	92-	

HONOURS		
Div. 2	Lge. Cup	Ley/Daf
92-93	62-63	1991
20-21		
47-48		
54-55		

MOST APPEARANCES: GIL MERRICK 551 (1945-60)			
Year	League	FA Cup	Europe
1945-46		8	
1946-47	41	4	
1947-48	36		
1948-49	41	2	
1949-50	42	1	
1950-51	42	6	
1951-52	41	2	
1952-53	35	7	
1953-54	38	2	
1954-55	27	4	
1955-56	38	6	2
1956-57	40	7	2
1957-58	28	1	3
1958-59	34	6	2
1959-60	2		1
	485	56	10

MOST GOALS IN A CAREER		
JOE BRADFORD 267 (1920-35)		
Season	League	FA Cup
1920-21	1	
1921-22	10	
1922-23	18	1
1923-24	24	
1924-25	11	
1925-26	26	1
1926-27	22	1
1927-28	29	3
1928-29	22	2
1929-30	23	
1930-31	14	8
1931-32	26	2
1932-33	14	
1933-34	5	
1934-35	4	
Total	249	18

RECORD TRANSFER FEE RECEIVED			
Amount	Club	Player	Date
£975,000	Nottingham Forest	Trevor Francis	2/79
£350,000	Everton	B Latchford + PE	2/74
£100,000	Stoke City	Jimmy Greenhoff	8/69

RECORD TRANSFER FEE PAID			
Amount	Club	Player	Date
£350,000	Derby County	David Langan	6/80
£300,000	Everton	Colin Todd	7/79
£180,000	Everton	H Kendall + PE	2/74
£140,000	Arsenal	John Roberts	10/72

MANAGERS			
Name	Seasons	Best	Worst
Bob McRoberts	1910-15	3(2)	20(2)
Bill Beer	1923-27	8(1)	17(1)
Les Knighton	1928-33	9(1)	15(1)
George Liddell	1933-39	12(1)	20(1)
Willie Camkin	1939-45		
Ted Goodier	1945		
Harry Storer	1945-48	1(2)	3(2)
Bob Brocklebank	1949-54	17(1)	6(2)
Arthur Turner	1954-58	6(1)	1(2)
Albert Beasley	1958-60	9(2)	19(2)
Gil Merrick	1960-64	17(2)	20(2)
Joe Mallett	1964-65	22(2)	22(2)
Stan Cullis	1965-70	4(2)	18(2)
Fred Goodwin	1970-75	10(1)	9(2)
Willie Bell	1975-77	13(2)	19(2)
Sir Alf Ramsey	1977-78	11(1)	11(1)
Jim Smith	1978-82	13(1)	3(2)
Ron Saunders	1982-86	17(1)	2(2)
John Bond	1986-87	19(2)	19(2)
Gary Pendry	1987-89	19(2)	12(3)
Dave Mackay	1989-90	7(3)	7(3)
Lou Macari	1991		
Terry Cooper	1991-	2(3)	2(3)

LONGEST LEAGUE RUNS	
of undefeated matches:	18 (8.1.1972-2.5.1972)
of undefeated home matches:	36 (20.10.1970-25.4.1972)
without home win:	11 (10.11.1962-20.4.1963)
of league wins:	13 (17.12.1992-16.9.1993)
of league defeats:	8 (2.12.1978-13.2.1979)
	(28.9.1985-27.11.85)
of league matches w/out a win:	17 (28.9.1985-18.1.1986)
of undefeated away matches:	15 (13.12.1947-4.9.1948)
without an away win:	32 (15.11.1980-28.4.1982)
of home wins:	17 (13.9.1902-20.4.1902)
of away wins:	9 (2.1.1897-18.9.1897)

PREVIOUS LEAGUE: Football Alliance

PREVIOUS NAMES: Small Heath Alliance (1875-88); Small Heath (1888-1905; Birmingham (1905-45)

BIGGEST VICTORIES
League: 12-0 v Walsall Town Swifts, Div 2, 17.12.1892
12-0 v Doncaster Rov, Div 2, 1.4.1903
F.A. Cup: 10-0 v Druids, 9.11.1889
League Cup: 6-0 v Manchester City, 11.12.1962
Europe: 5-0 v Boldklub Copenhag., 7.12.1960

BIGGEST DEFEATS
League: 1-9 v Sheff Wed, Div 1, 13.12.1930
1-9 v Blackburn Rov., Div 1, 5.1.1895
0-8 v Derby County, Div 1, 30.11.1895
0-8 v Newcastle Utd, Div 1, 23.11.1907
0-8 v Preston N. End, Div 1, 1.2.1958
F.A. Cup: 0-6 v Wendesbury O.B., Qual., 17.10.1981
0-6 v Tottenham H., 6th Rnd., 12.4.1967
League Cup: 0-5 v Tottenham H., 3rd Rnd., 29.10.1986
Europe: (Fairs) 1-4 v Barcelona, Final, 4.5.1960

MOST POINTS
3 points a win: 82, Division 2, 1984-85
2 points a win: 59, Division 2, 1947-48

MOST GOALS
103, Division 2, 1893-94.
Mobley 24, Wheldon 22, Walton 16, Hands 14, Hallam 9, Jenkyns 6, Izon 4, Lee 3, Jolley 2, Pumfrey, Devey, Jackson 1 each
Leadbetter 4, Acres 2, Brown 2, Myles 1, Snell 1, og 2

MOST GOALS IN A MATCH
5. Walter Abbott v Darwen (h), 8-0, Div 2, 26.11.1898
5. John McMillan & R McRoberts v Blackpool (h), 10-1, Div 2, 2.3.1901
5. Ben Green v Middlesbrough (h), 7-0, Div 1, 26.12.1905
5. Jimmy Windridge v Glossop (h), 11-1, Div 2, 23.1.1915

MOST GOALS IN A SEASON
Walter Abbott 42, (League 34, FAC 8) 1898-99.
5 goals once = 5, 3 goals 5 times = 15, 2 goals 7 times = 14, 1 goal 8 times = 8

MOST FIRST CLASS MATCHES IN A SEASON
56 (46 League, 1 FA Cup, 7 League Cup, 2 AMC) 1991-92

MOST LEAGUE GOALS CONCEDED
96, Division 1, 1964-65

MOST LEAGUE WINS
27, Division 2, 1979-80

MOST LEAGUE DRAWS
18, Div 1, 1937-38 & Div 2, 1971-72

MOST LEAGUE DEFEATS
29, Division 1, 1985-86

OLDEST PLAYER
Dennis Jennings, 40 years 190 days. 6.5.1950

YOUNGEST PLAYER
Trevor Francis, 16 years 7 months v Cardiff, 5.9.1970.

MOST CAPPED PLAYER
Malcolm Page (Wales) 28, 1971-79
(For England) Harry Hibbs, 25, 1951-54

BEST PERFORMANCES BY BIRMINGHAM CITY

League: 1947-48: Matches played 42, Won 22, Drawn 15, Lost 5, Goals for 55, Goals against 24, Points 59. First in Division 2.

Highest: 1955-56: 6th in Division 1.

F.A. Cup: 1930-31: 3rd rnd. Liverpool 2-0 (a); 4th rnd. Port Vale 2-0 (h); 5th rnd. Watford 3-0 (h); 6th rnd. Chelsea 2-2 (h), 3-0 (a); Semi-Final Sunderland 3-0 (n); Final. West Bromwich Albion 1-2
1955-56: 3rd rnd. Torquay 7-1 (a); 4th rnd. Leyland Orient 4-0 (a); 5th rnd. West Bromwich 1-0 (a); 6th rnd. Arsenal 3-1 (a); Semi-Final Sunderland 3-0 (n); Final. Manchester City 1-3

League Cup: 1962-63: 2nd rnd. Doncaster Rov 5-0; 3rd rnd. Barrow 1-1 (a), 5-1 (h); 4th rnd. Notts County 3-2 (h); 5th rnd. Manchester City 6-0 (h); Semi-Final Bury 1-1 (a), 3-2 (h); Final. Aston Villa 0-0 (a), 3-1 (h)

Fairs Cup: 1958-60: 1st rnd. F.C. Cologne 2-2 (a), 2-0 (h); 2nd rnd. Dinamo Zagreb 1-0 (h), 3-3 (a); Semi-Final Union Giulluise 4-2 (a), 4-2 (h); Final Barcelona 0-0 (h), 1-4 (a)
1960-61: 1st rnd. Ujpest Dozsa 3-2 (h), 2-1 (a); 2nd rnd. Boldklub Copenhagen 4-4 (a), 5-0 (h); Semi-Final Inter Milan 2-1 (a), 2-1 (h); Final A.S. Roma 2-2 (h), 0-2 (a)

DIVISIONAL RECORDS

	Played	Won	Drawn	Lost	For	Against	Points
DIVISION 1	2040	651	501	888	2776	3296	1845
DIVISION 2	1400	632	324	444	2346	1818	1643
DIVISION 3	138	57	41	40	174	160	221
TOTALS	3578	1340	866	1372	5296	5274	3709

BIRMINGHAM CITY

PLAYERS NAME Honours	Ht	Wt	Birthdate	Birthplace Transfers	Contract Date	Clubs	League	L/Cup	FA Cup	Other	Lg	L/C	FAC	Oth
GOALKEEPERS														
Martyn Thomas	6.1	13.0	28.11.59	Senghenydd	10.09.77	Bristol Rovers	162	12	9					
W:1,u21.2				Loan	13.07.82	Cardiff City	15	4						
Loan Southend Utd (03.02.83) 6lg				£35,000	28.07.83	Newcastle Utd	118	7	5	1				
Loan Middlesborough (25.10.84) 4lg				£75,000	03.10.88	Birmingham City	139	12	6	11				
DEFENDERS														
Ian Atkins	5.10	11.0	16.01.57	Birmingham	01.01.75	Shrewsbury Town (A)	273+5	13	23		58	3	3	
Div3'79,WC'79				PE	14.08.72	Sunderland	76+1	6	4		6			
				£70,000	07.11.84	Everton	6+1		0+1		1			
				£100,000	25.10.85	Ipswich Town	73+4	8	2	7	4			
					21.04.88	Birmingham City	93	8	4	3	5+1	2		
				Player-Man		Colchester Utd								
				Player-Coa	26.11.91	Birmingham City	5+3			1				
Ian Clarkson	5.11	11.8	04.12.70	Birmingham	15.12.88	Birmingham City (A)	100+8	10	5+1	11+1				
AMC'91														
Matthew Fox	6.0	12.3	13.07.71	Birmingham		Birmingham City (A)	12+2	1						
Martin Hicks	6.3	13.6	27.02.57	Stratford-on-Avon		Stratford								
Div.4'79,Div.3'86,SC'88				N.C		Reading								
via Charlton Athletic (Free)				£3,000	15.02.78	Reading	499+1	38	38	17+1	23	3	1	
				Free	15.08.91	Birmingham City	41+1	5	1	2	1	1		
Paul Holmes	5.10	11.0	18.02.68	Wortley	24.02.86	Doncaster Rovers (A)	42+5		3+1	1	1		1	
				£6,000	12.08.88	Torquay Utd	127+11	9	9+2	13+3	4			
					05.06.92	Birmingham City								
Paul Mardon	6.0	12.0	14.09.69	Bristol	29.01.88	Bristol City	29+13	3+3		1	1		1	
Loan Doncaster R. (13.09.90) 3lg				£65,000+	16.08.91	Birmingham City	31+4	7	1	1				
Trevor Matthewson	6.1	12.5	12.02.63	Sheffield	12.02.81	Sheffield Wed. (A)	3		2					
GMVC (APL)'88, AMC'91				15.10.83	Newport Co	73+2	2	7	6				
				27.09.85	Stockport Co	79+1	3	2	3				
				£13,000 (V		Lincoln City			3					
					03.08.88	Lincoln City	43	3	3	2	2			
				£45,000	03.08.89	Birmingham City	127+1	11	7	11	10			1
David Rennie	6.0	12.0	29.08.64	Edinburgh	18.05.82	Leicester City	21	2			1			
S:Y				£50,000	17.01.86	Leeds Utd	95+6	7	7	4	5		1	1
				£175,000	31.07.89	Bristol City	103+3	8	9	5	8			
				£120,000	20.02.92	Birmingham City	17				2			
Darren Rogers	5.9	11.2	09.04.70	Birmingham	05.07.88	West Brom A. (T)	7+7		0+1	1	1			1
				Free	01.07.92	Birmingham City								
MIDFIELD														
Mark N Cooper	5.8	10.10	18.12.68	Wakefield	10.09.87	Bristol City (A)								
					01.06.89	Exeter City	46+4	4+1	3+1	5	12		1	
				Loan	22.03.90	Southend Utd	4+1							
				Swap	05.09.91	Birmingham City	27+6		1	1	4			
John Frain	5.9	11.9	08.10.68	Birmingham	10.10.86	Birmingham City (A)	165+8	14	8	14	15			
AMC'91														
Nigel Gleghorn	6.0	12.13	12.08.62	Seaham		Seaham R S								
AMC'91, FLg.XI						Ipswich Town	54+12	3+2	3+1	7+2	11			2
				£47,500	04.08.88	Manchester City	27+7	2	0+1	1	7	2	1	1
				£175,000	09.09.89	Birmingham City	131	11	7	12	31	5	3	1
Dean Peer	6.2	11.5	08.08.69	Dudley	09.07.87	Birmingham City (A)	93+14	13+1	2+1	10	7	3		1
Ian Rodgerson	5.8	10.7	09.04.66	Hereford	03.07.85	Hereford Utd	95+5	7	4	7+1	6			
				£35,000	03.08.88	Cardiff City	98+1	8	10	6+1	4			
				£50,000	03.01.91	Birmingham City	63+1	6	1	6	11	2		1
Paul Tait	6.1	10.0	31.07.71	Birmingham	02.08.88	Birmingham City (A)	40+14	5	2+1	2+1	5			1
FORWARDS														
Jason Beckford	5.9	12.4	14.02.70	Manchester	18.08.87	Manchester City (T)	8+12	1+4			1	1		
E:Y2				Loan	14.03.91	Blackburn Rovers	3+1							
				Loan	26.09.91	Port Vale	4+1				1			
				£50,000	02.01.92	Birmingham City	2+2			1	1			
Louie Donowa	5.9	12.2	24.09.64	Ipswich		Norwich City (A)	56+6	13+2	1+2		11	3	1	
E: u21(3); FAYC'83; MC'85				Loan		Stoke City	4		0+1		1			
						Willem II (Hol)								
				Free		Ipswich Town	17+6	0+2	2	2+1	1			1
				£55,000	10.08.90	Bristol City	11+13	1	0+1		3			
				£60,000	30.08.91	Birmingham City	20+6	5	1		2			
John Gayle	6.4	13.01	30.07.64	Birmingham		Burton Albion								
AMC'91				£30,000*	01.03.89	Wimbledon	17+3	3			2			
				£175,000	21.11.90	Birmingham City	22+3		1	5+1	7			4
Ronnie Morris	6.0	11.8	25.09.70	Birmingham		Birmingham City (A)	3+8	2+1		0+1				
Darren Rowbotham	5.10	11.5	22.10.66	Cardiff	07.11.84	Plymouth A. (A)	22+24	1	0+3	1+1	2		1	
W: Y; Div.4'90				P.E	31.10.87	Exeter City	110+8	11	8	8	46	6	5	1
				£25,000	13.09.91	Torquay Utd	14		3	2	3		1	
				£20,000	02.01.92	Birmingham City	21+1				4			
Mark Sale	6.5		27.02.72	Rugeley	12.01.91	Stoke City	0+2							
Loan Yeovil Town					31.07.91	Cambridge Utd								
				Nominal	26.03.92	Birmingham City	2+4							
Simon Sturridge	5.5	10.7	09.12.69	Birmingham	08.07.88	Birmingham City (A)	114+16	9+4	7	11	29	1	2	3
AMC'91														

BIRMINGHAM CITY

Club	Rec. Win	Season	Rec. Loss	Season
BARNSLEY	5-0	1919-20	5-1	1909-10
BRENTFORD	5-1	1953-54	2-0	1990-91 (home)
BRISTOL CITY	4-0	1966-67	4-0	1989-90 (home)
BRISTOL ROVERS	2-1	1954-55	1-0	1979-80
CAMBRIDGE UNITED	1-0	1990-91 (away)	3-0	1990-91 (home)
CHARLTON ATHLETIC	4-0	1967-68	3-1	1968-69
DERBY COUNTY	5-1	1976-77	8-0	1895-96
GRIMSBY TOWN	6-0	1901-02	4-0	1937-38
LEICESTER CITY	5-0	1920-21	5-1	1961-62 (home)
LUTON TOWN	9-0	1899-00	4-1	1974-75 (home)
MILLWALL	4-0	1946-47	6-2	1969-70
NEWCASTLE UNITED	6-1	1956-57	8-0	1907-08
NOTTS COUNTY	4-1	1981-82 (away)	6-1	1901-02
OXFORD UNITED	3-1	1985-86	3-0	1988-89
PETERBOROUGH UTD	3-2	1991-92 (away)	1-1	1991-92 (home)
PORTSMOUTH	5-0	1955-56	3-0	1949-50 (home)
SOUTHEND UNITED	1-1	1990-91	2-1	1990-91
SUNDERLAND	6-1	1957-58 (away)	7-2	1935-36 (home)
SWINDON TOWN	4-1	1971-72	4-1	1969-70
TRANMERE ROVERS	2-1	1989-90	5-1	1989-90
WATFORD	4-1	1971-72	3-0	1985-86
WEST HAM UNITED	4-0	1961-62	5-0	1982-83
WOLVERHAMPTON WNDRS	4-1	1913-14	7-2	1895-96

MANAGER: TERRY COOPER

DATE OF BIRTH: 12.7.1944   **PLACE OF BIRTH:** Castleford

DATE OF APPOINTMENT: AUGUST 1991

PREVIOUS CLUBS
as Manager: Bristol City; Bristol Rovers (Player-Manager); Exeter City
as Asst. Man./Coach: Bristol Rovers
as Player: Leeds Utd; Middlesbrough; Bristol City; Bristol Rovers; Doncaster Rovers

HONOURS
as Manager: Division 4 champions 1990 (Exeter); Promotion to Div 3 (Bristol City); Freight Rover winners (Bristol City), Promotion to New Div 1 1992 (Birmingham)
as Player: Div 1 '69; LC '68; EUFA '68 ' 71
International: England 20 full caps

Value Rating: ★ ★ ★

Programme Editor: David Teague

Price of 1992-93 Programme: £1.20
Number of Pages: 40
Subscriptions: £40 for first 26 issues

Local Newspapers: Birmingham Post & Evening Mail, Sports Argus (Sat Football Special)

Local Radio Stations: B.B.C. Radio W.M. & BRMB

LEADING LEAGUE GOALSCORERS
SEASONS 1979-80 – 1991-92

1979-80	KEITH BERTSCHIN	12		1980-81	FRANK WORTHINGTON	16
1981-82	TONY EVANS	15		1982-83	MICK FERGUSON	8
1983-84	HOWARD GAYLE	8		1984-85	WAYNE CLARKE	17
1985-86	ANDY KENNEDY	7		1986-87	WAYNE CLARKE	16
1987-88	STEVE WHITTON	14		1988-89	COLIN ROBINSON	5
1989-90	DENNIS BAILEY	18		1990-91	JOHN GAYLE	6
					NIGEL GLEGHORN	6
					SIMON STURRIDGE	6

1991-92	**NIGEL GLEGHORN**	**17**

ST ANDREWS Birmingham B9 4NH

Capacity: 28,235   **Covered Standing:** 9,400   **Seating:** 5,500

Tel: Ground: 021 772 0101   **Ticket Sales:** 021 766 8274   **Clubcall:** 0891 88 86 82

All premium rate calls (0898/0891) cost 36p per minute cheap rate and 48p per minute at all other times. Call costings correct at time of going to press.

ATTENDANCES
Highest: 66,844 v Everton, FA Cup 5th Round, 11.2.1939

Lowest: 1,500 v Chesterfield, Division 2, 17.4.1909
(as Small Heath): 500 v Manchester City, Div 2, 19.4.1897

Record Receipts (with previous records):
£116,372.50 v Nottingham Forest, FA Cup 5th Rnd, 20.2.88
£110,000 v Watford, FA Cup 6th Round
£48,505 v Aston Villa, Division 1, 11.10.1980
£37,949 v Leeds United, FA Cup 4th Round, 29.1.1977
£29,379 v Middlesbrough, FA Cup 6th Round, 8.3.1975
£19,587 v Leeds United, Division 1, 29.12.1973

Season Tickets:
Stands: from £168-£221 (£84-£111 jun/OAP)
Ground: from £137 (£69 jun/OAP)

Cost of Stand Tickets: Seats: £8-£10, juveniles/OAP £4-£5
Terraces: £6.50, juveniles/OAP £4, Non-members £7

Car Parking: Car parks in Coventry Road and Cattell Road. £2 per car on match days

Nearest Railway Station: Buses from Birmingham New Street or Snow Hill, or walk from Bordesley Station from Birmingham Moor Street

How to get to the ground

From North and East: M6 to J6, A38(M). Branch left, first exit from roundabout. A45 along Dartmouth Middleway. Left into St. Andrews Road for ground

From South: M5 to J4, or A435 or A41 into Birmingham. A45 to Coventry road then left into St Andrews Road for ground

From West: A456, A41 then A45 into Coventry Road, left into St Andrews Road for ground

BLACKBURN ROVERS

Premier

Formed: 1875   **Turned Professional:** 1880   **Ltd Co:** 1897

SPONSORED BY: Matthew Brown   **NICKNAME:** The Rovers

President
W H Bancroft

Vice-Presidents
E Pickering
A L Fryars   J Walker

Hon Vice-President
Rt Hon Margaret Thatcher, MP

Chairman
R D Coar, BSc

Directors
T W Ibbotson, LLB (Vice-Chairman & Managing Director)
K C Lee   I R Stanners
G R Root, FCMA   R Matthewman

Secretary
John W Howarth FAAI(0254 55432)

Commercial Manager
Ken Beamish (0254 55432)

Manager
Kenny Dalglish

Assistant Manager
Ray Harford

Reserve Team Manager
Asa Hartford

Youth Team Manager
Jim Furnell

Physiotherapist
Mike Pettigrew

Head Groundsman
Steve Patrick

Club Statistician for the Directory
Harry Berry

CYNICS may suggest that promotion to the Premier League was the minimum return anticipated on an investment of £5.4 million pounds, and that delaying this achievement until the final minute of the Football League season was scant reason for self congratulation. The availability of apparently limitless funds from the club's major shareholder Jack Walker was the main feature of a season that made the club the cynosure of English football. Fortunes roller coasted throughout the season, starting with Don Mackay in charge. One point from the first three League games and an exit from the Rumbelows Cup at the hands of Third Division Hull, were not the chief reasons for the manager's dismissal. Rather it was the lack of credibility present that prompted several star players to turn down the chance of a move to Ewood.

The club again turned to coach Tony Parkes to act as temporary manager. As he had done before, Parkes changed the season round. Retaining only Mimms and Speedie of the expensive signings financed by Walker, he bought in youngsters Wilcox, Skinner and Johnrose, the dependable Sulley, switched Mark Atkins from full-back to the centre of midfield and filled the vacancy by giving a debut to an unknown central-defender Richard Brown. The combination was tight and spirited and by the time the shock news came that Kenny Dalglish had been tempted from the golf course to return to the game as the club's manager, the platform for a promotion chase had been created.

Dalglish spent Walker's money gradually, phasing his signings so that the players could be blended in. His first four acquisitions were to be crucial. Tiny Alan Wright arrived to bring attacking options to the left-back position, and the popular Colin Hendry returned to provide grit and club spirit. However, even these two signings paled compared with the next pair. For a club record of £1.1 million Mike Newell became leader of the line and a bargain fee of £250,000 bought Gordon Cowans to be the play-maker and organiser.

By mid-December the club had taken over the leadership of the division. By mid-February they were seven points clear of the third placed club and the bookmakers were refusing to take any more bets on their promotion. Then Newell fractured his tibia, and the season was transformed.

Seven points were gained from the next thirteen games, including six consecutive defeats. Dalglish's transfer touch appeared to elude him. Chris Price was brought back to the club, but never settled into a regular role on the right flank. Tim Sherwood from Norwich was unable to oust Atkins from midfield. £750,000 was spent on the prolific Duncan Shearer and £1.1 million on Roy Wegerle. Neither was able to gain a regular place.

Results continued to go against the club so that on the final day of the season they had not only missed one of the two automatic promotion places but were unsure of being involved in the play offs. Happily by then the lucky mascot Newell had returned, the club ended in sixth place and an epic three games in the play offs took them to the Premier League.

Harry Berry

Back Row L-R: Nicky Reid, Craig Skinner, Wayne Burnett, David May, Frank Talia, Bobby Mimms, Matt Dickens, Darren Collier, Keith Hill, Jason Wilcox, Mark Atkins, Peter Thorne. **Middle row:** Mike Pettigrew, Ray Harford, Tim Sherwood, Stuart Ripley, Mike Newell, Colin Hendry, Robert Dewhurst, Lee Richardson, Richard Brown, Steve Agnew, Darren Donnelly, Stuart Munro, Ian McGarry, Gordon Cowans, Tony Parkes, Asa Hartford. **Front row:** Gary Tallon, Roy Wegerle, Alan Shearer, Chris Price, Alan Wright, Brendan O'Shaughnessy, Kenny Dalglish, Kevin Moran, Tony Dobson, Steve Livingstone, John Pickup, Scott Lyndsay, Lee Makel.

BLACKBURN ROVERS

DIVISION TWO: 6th   **FA CUP:** 4th RND   **RUMBELOWS CUP:** 1st RND   **ZDS CUP:** 1st RND

M	DATE	COMP.	VEN	OPPONENTS	RESULT	H/T	LGE POS	GOALSCORERS/GOAL TIMES	ATTENDANCE
1	A 17	BL	H	Portsmouth	D 1-1	0-1		Moran 90	11,118
2	20	RC 1/1	H	Hull City	D 1-1	1-0		Buckley (og) 24	6,300
3	24	BL	A	Bristol City	L 0-1	0-1	21		(11,317)
4	27	RC 1/2	A	Hull City	L 0-1	0-1			(3,227)
5	31	BL	H	Ipswich Town	L 1-2	0-1	21	Speedie 90	8,898
6	S 4	BL	A	Derby County	W 2-0	1-0	18	Wilcox 1, Speedie 53	(12,078)
7	7	BL	A	Sunderland	D 1-1	1-1	18	Speedie 9	(17,043)
8	11	BL	H	Port Vale	W 1-0	1-0	14	Speedie 13	10,225
9	14	BL	H	Watford	W 1-0	1-0	10	Richardson 37	9,542
10	21	BL	A	Leicester City	L 0-3	0-2	15		(13,278)
11	28	BL	H	Tranmere Rovers	D 0-0	0-0	15		11,449
12	O 1	ZDS 1	A	Port Vale	L 0-1	0-1			(2,355)
13	5	BL	A	Millwall	W 3-1	1-0	11	Speedie 43, Johnrose 71, Garner 78	(8,026)
14	12	BL	H	Plymouth Argyle	W 5-2	2-0	8	Moran 10, Garner 43, 61, Speedie 48, 56 (pen)	10,830
15	19	BL	A	Swindon Town	L 1-2	0-0	9	Speedie 73	(10,717)
16	26	BL	H	Grimsby Town	W 2-1	1-1	7	Garner 2, Atkins 60	11,096
17	N 2	BL	H	Brighton & H A	W 1-0	0-0	8	Livingstone (pen) 77	9,877
18	5	BL	A	Southend United	L 0-3	0-1	8		(4,860)
19	9	BL	A	Charlton Athletic	W 2-0	1-0	8	Sellars 5, Speedie 74	(7,114)
20	16	BL	H	Barnsley	W 3-0	1-0	5	Speedie 24, Wilcox 71, Newell 75	13,797
21	23	BL	A	Newcastle United	D 0-0	0-0	5		(23,639)
22	30	BL	H	Middlesbrough	W 2-1	1-1	4	Newell (pen) 44, Atkins 77	15,541
23	D 7	BL	A	Oxford United	W 3-1	2-0	3	Sellars 12, Cowans 29, Garner 51	(5,924)
24	14	BL	H	Bristol Rovers	W 3-0	3-0	1	Atkins 22, 28, Sellars 23	12,295
25	26	BL	A	Wolverhampton W	D 0-0	0-0	1		(18,277)
26	28	BL	H	Ipswich Town	L 1-2	1-0	2	Wright 11	(17,675)
27	J 1	BL	A	Cambridge United	W 2-1	0-0	1	Speedie 56, Reid 87	15,001
28	4	FAC 3	H	Kettering Town	W 4-1	1-0		Speedie 32, Newell 59, 70, Cowans 64	13,821
29	11	BL	H	Bristol City	W 4-0	3-0	1	Newell 2, 41, Scott (og) 31, Speedie 73	12,994
30	18	BL	A	Portsmouth	D 2-2	0-0	1	Speedie 26, 54	(20,106)
31	F 1	BL	H	Swindon Town	W 2-1	0-1	1	Hendry 74, Speedie 82	14,887
32	4	FAC 4	A	Notts County	L 1-2	0-1		Newell 89	(12,173)
33	8	BL	A	Grimsby Town	W 3-2	3-1	1	Price 5, Sellars 9, Wilcox 29	(10,014)
34	11	BL	H	Derby County	W 2-0	0-0	1	Price 49, Atkins 70	15,350
35	15	BL	H	Newcastle United	W 3-1	1-1	1	Speedie 3 (42, 60, 75)	19,511
36	22	BL	A	Middlesbrough	D 0-0	0-0	1		(19,353)
37	25	BL	A	Cambridge United	L 1-2	0-2	1	Hendry 82	(7,857)
38	29	BL	H	Oxford United	D 1-1	1-1	1	Sellars (pen) 17	13,917
39	M 7	BL	A	Bristol Rovers	L 0-3	0-2	1		(6,313)
40	10	BL	H	Southend United	D 2-2	1-2	1	Price 44, Speedie 89	14,404
41	14	BL	A	Brighton & H A	W 3-0	2-0	1	Speedie 6, Hendry 16, Wegerle 82	(10,845)
42	21	BL	H	Charlton Athletic	L 0-2	0-0	1		14,844
43	28	BL	H	Barnsley	L 1-2	1-0	1	Shearer 25	(13,346)
44	31	BL	A	Port Vale	L 0-2	0-1	2		(10,384)
45	A 11	BL	A	Watford	L 1-2	1-1	4	Wegerle 43	(10,522)
46	14	BL	H	Wolverhampton W	L 1-2	1-0	4	Sellars 25	14,114
47	18	BL	H	Leicester City	L 0-1	0-0	7		18,078
48	20	BL	A	Tranmere Rovers	D 2-2	1-1	6	Wilcox 12, Newell (pen) 72	(13,705)
49	25	BL	H	Millwall	W 2-1	0-0	7	Newell 49, Atkins 56	12,820
50	29	BL	H	Sunderland	D 2-2	1-0	6	Hendry 19, Sellars 86	15,079
51	M 2	BL	A	Plymouth Argyle	W 3-1	2-1	6	Speedie 3 (44, 45, 67)	(17,459)
52	10	PO SF 1	H	Derby County	W 4-2	2-2		Sellars 35, Newell 44, Speedie 66, 70	19,677
53	13	PO SF 2	A	Derby County	L 1-2	0-1		Moran 49	(22,920)
54	25	PO Fin	N	Leicester City	W 1-0	1-0		Newell (pen) 45	(68,147)

Best Home League Attendance: 19,511 v Newcastle United   **Smallest:** 8,898 v Ipswich Town   **Av Home Att:** 13,290

Goal Scorers: **Compared with 90-91:** +5,190

League (70): Speedie 23 (1 pen), Sellars 7 (1 pen), Newell 6 (2 pens), Atkins 6, Garner 5, Hendry 4, Wilcox 4, Price 3, Moran 2, Wegerle 2, Livingstone (1 pen), Richardson, Wright, Cowans, Reid, Opponents, Shearer, Johnrose

R/lows C (1): Opponents
FA Cup (5): Newell 3, Cowans, Speedie
ZDS Cup (0):
Play-Offs (6): Newell 2 (1 pen), Speedie 2, Sellars, Moran

Mimms R.	Atkins M.	Sulley C.	Richardson L.	Moran K.	Dobson A.	Irvine J.	Livingstone S.	Speedie D.	Sellars S.	Garner S.	Reid N.	Wilcox J.	May D.	Skinner C.	Johnrose L.	Brown R.	Hill K.	Wright A.	Hendry E.	Newell M.	Cowans G.	Price C.	Sherwood T.	Wegerle R.	Shearer D.	Referee	
1	2	3	4	5	6	7	9*	10	11	14																M Reed	1
1	2	3		5	6	7		9		10	4	S														A Wilkie	2
1	2	3	14	5	6		9*	10	11•		4	7														R Bigger	3
1	2	3	S	5	6		11•	9	10		4	7														J Key	4
1	2		8	6				9		S	4	11	5	12												R Shepherd	5
1	8	3	4	5				9		14		11•	6	7*	10											V Callow	6
1	8	3	4	5				9		S	12	11	6*	7	10											D Phillips	7
1	8	3	4*	5				9		12	S	11	6	7	10•	2										S Lodge	8
1	8	3	4*	5				9		12	14	11	6	7	10•	2										J Watson	9
1	8*	3•	4	5				9		12	14	11	6	7	10	2										K Hackett	10
1		4	5	3			12	9		8	14	11*	6	7•	10	2										K Redfearn	11
1		4		3	12		8			14	11	6	7	10	2•	5										H King	12
1	14	4	3				12	9		10*		6	7*	8		5										M Bodenham	13
1	3	11	8*			7*	14	9	12	10	4		6			5										T Holbrook	14
1	3	8	6			12	10•	9	11	14	4	7*				5										R Groves	15
1	2•	4	6		7	9*	8	11	10	14	12					5	3									M Peck	16
1	2	4	6		7*	14	8	11	10	12	9•					5	3									G Courtney	17
1	2	10*	6	14		8	9	11•	12	4		7				5	3									J Carter	18
1	8	4	6			9	11	10*	12	7		S				2	3	5								D Axcell	19
1	8	4	6			9•	11	14		7						2	3	5		10						T Ward	20
1	8	4	6			9	11		12	7		S				2	3	5*		10						I Cruickshank	21
1	8		S	6			11	9*	12	7						2	5	3		10	4					K Barratt	22
1	8			14			11•	9*	12	7						2	6	3	5	10	4					G Poll	23
1	8	S	6				11*	10	12	7						2		3	5	9	4					R Hart	24
1	8		6				12	10*		7						2	14	3	5•	9	4					C Wilkes	25
1	8*	12	6				10	S		7						2	11•	3	5	9	4					R Hamer	26
1	8		6				10	S		12	7					2	11	3	5•	9	4					P Vanes	27
1	8		6				10*	11•	12	14		7				2	5	3		9	4					D Phillips	28
1	8*		6•				9	11		12	7					2	5	3	14	10	4					A Wilkie	29
1			6				9•	11		8	7		14			2	5	3	12	10	4					P Durkin	30
1	8		6				9	11	14	7*						2	5	3	12	10	4					G Ashby	31
1	8		6				9†	11•	14	7*						2	5	3	12	10	4					R Nixon	32
1	8		6				9*	11•	14	7						S	5	3	12	10	4	2				M Bailey	33
1	8*		6				9	11*	14	7						12	5	3	6	10	4	2				K Lupton	34
1	8		6				9*	12	S	7						11	5	3	6	10	4	2				P Jones	35
1	8	S		6			9*	10		7						11	5	3	6		4	2	12			D Phillips	36
1	8	3						14		10•		7	2*			11	5		12	6	4		9			P Don	37
1	12		14					9*	11	10		7•					5	3	6	4	2	8				K Breen	38
1	14		12					9	11*			7					5	3	6	4*	2	8	10			P Danson	39
1	8		7					9		12		11•					5	3	6	4	2	14	10*			S Lodge	40
1	8		7*					9•		12		11					5	3	6	4	2	14	10			R Milford	41
1	8		7*		4			9		14		11					5	3	6	4	2	12	10*			D Gallagher	42
1	8							9	11*	12							5	3	6	4	2	7•	14	10		J Watson	43
1	8		14					9•	11								5	3	6	4	2	7*	12	10		T Holbrook	44
1	14		2					11*		9	12						5	3	6		4	7•	10	8		M Brandwood	45
	9	S	2					11		7							5	3	6	12	4		10	8*		A Flood	46
1	9	12	2					11		7							5	3	6	14*	4		10	8•		P Wright	47
1	8	14	5					11		7					2		3	6	9*	4•			10	12		A Bennett	48
1	8	14	5					12	11	7					2		3	6	9		4•		10			B Coddington	49
1	8	4	5					9*	11	7					2*		3	6	10		12		14			R Nixon	50
1	8	14	5					9*	11	7*					2		3	6	10	4		12	14			W Burge	51
1	8	12	5*					9*	11					2			3	6	10	4	7			14		K Hackett	52
1	8	7	5					9	11					2			3	6	10	4	S			S		D Elleray	53
1	8	12	5					9	11*					2			3	6	10	4	7		S			G Courtney	54
45	40	7	18	37	4	4	6	34	28	14	8	33	12	7	7	24	31	32	26	18	26	11	7	9	5	**League Appearances**	
4		6	4	1	2	4	2	2	11	13	5		2			2	1	1	4	2		2	4	3	1	**Substitute Appearances**	
2	2		2		1	2		2	2	2		2			1											**R/lows Appearances**	
2	2		2			2	2	0+2	1+1		1		2	2	2	0+1	2	2								**FA Cup Appearances**	
1		1		1	0+1		1	0+1	1	1	1	1	1	1												**ZDS Cup Appearances**	
3	3		1+2	3		0+1		3	3			3				3	3	3	3	2					0+1	**Play-Offs Appearances**	

Also Played: Posn.(Game): Agnew 8(1,2,3,4*), Gayle 12(1,2,3,6)14(4)7(5)9*(12), Shepstone 11*(2)10*(5), Munro 3(5), Duxbury 2(6,7,13,14,15), Baah 11(13), Beardsmore 11(25)14(26), Dickins 1(46)

† = Sent Off

BLACKBURN ROVERS

Club Colours: Blue & white halves shirts, blue shorts, blue with red and white tops stockings.
Change Colours: Yellow/blue pin striped shirts, yellow shorts, yellow stockings.
Reserves League: Pontins Central League Division 1

COMPETITIONS			
Div. 1	Div. 2	Div. 3	A/Scot
88-36	36-39	71-75	75-76
39-47	47-57	79-80	76-77
57-66	66-71		77-78
92-	75-79		78-79
	80-92		79-80
			80-81

HONOURS					
Div. 1	Div. 2	Div. 3	FAC	FMC	C/Sh'ld
11-12	38-39	74-75	1884	86-87	1912
13-14			1885		
			1886		
			1890		
			1891		
			1928		

MOST APPEARANCES: D FAZACKERLEY 689 + 3 (70-87)			
(includes 18 Anglo-Scottish Cup)			
Year	League	FA Cup	League Cup
1970-71	14		
1971-72	39	2	2
1972-73	46	3	1
1973-74	46	5	3
1974-75	22 + 1	1	2
1975-76	42	1	2
1976-77	37 + 1	4	3
1977-78	28	2	2
1978-79	37	2	1
1979-80	46	7	4
1980-81	38	1	5
1981-82	39	1	3
1982-83	38	1	2
1983-84	39	3	2
1984-85	39	4	2
1985-86	36 + 1	3	2
1986-87	7		2
	593 + 3	40	38

MOST GOALS IN A CAREER				
SIMON GARNER 191 (1978-present)				
Season	League	FA Cup	Lge Cup	Others
1978-79	8			
1979-80	6			
1980-81	7		1	
1981-82	14	2	2	
1982-83	22	1		
1983-84	19	1	3	
1984-85	13		2	
1985-86	12			
1986-87	10		1	4
1987-88	14	1		
1988-89	20	1	2	
1989-90	18			2
1990-91	1	1		
1991-92	5			
Total	169	7	11	6

RECORD TRANSFER FEE RECEIVED			
Amount	Club	Player	Date
£700,000	Manchester City	Colin Hendry	11/89
£400,000	Queens Park R	Simon Barker	7/88
£357,000	Leeds United	Kevin Hird	2/79
£140,000	Wolverhampton W	Paul Bradshaw	9/77

RECORD TRANSFER FEE PAID			
Amount	Club	Player	Date
£1,200,000	Queens Park R	Roy Wegerle	3/92
£1,100,000	Everton	Mike Newell	11/91
£700,000	Manchester City	Colin Hendry	11/91
£700,000	Barnsley	Steve Agnew	7/91

MANAGERS			
Name	Seasons	Best	Worst
Eddie Hapgood	1946-48	17(1)	21(1)
Will Scott	1948-50	14(2)	16(2)
Jack Britton	1950-52	6(2)	14(2)
Jackie Bestall	1952-53	9(2)	9(2)
John Carey	1953-58	2(2)	9(2)
Dally Duncan	1958-61	8(1)	17(1)
Jack Marshall	1961-69	7(1)	19(2)
Eddie Quigley	1969-71	8(2)	21(2)
John Carey	1971-72	10(3)	10(3)
Ken Furphy	1972-74	3(3)	13(3)
Gordon Lee	1974-75	1(3)	1(3)
Jim Smith	1975-78	5(2)	11(2)
Jim Iley	1978-79	22(2)	22(2)
Howard Kendall	1979-81	4(2)	2(3)
Bobby Saxton	1981-86	6(2)	19(2)
Don Mackay	1986-91		
Kenny Dalglish	1991-		

LONGEST LEAGUE RUNS	
of undefeated matches:	23 (30.9.1987-27.2.1988)
of undefeated home matches:	30 (14.4.1911.-21.12.1912)
without home win:	11 (16.9.1978-24.3.1979)
of league wins:	8 (1.3.1980-7.4.1980)
of league defeats:	7 (12.3.1966-16.4.1966)
of league matches w/out a win:	16 (25.11.1978-28.3.1979)
of undefeated away matches:	11 (15.2.1912-1.11.1913)
	(30.9.1987-27.2.1988)
without an away win:	24 (12.2.1910-14.4.1911)
of home wins:	13 (2.1.1954-20.11.1954)
of away wins:	7 (12.1.1980-12.4.1980)

PREVIOUS NAME
Blackburn Grammar School Old Boys

BIGGEST VICTORIES
League: 9-0 v Middlesbrough, Division 2, 6.11.1954
F.A. Cup: 11-0 v Rossendale, Round 1, 13.10.1884
League Cup: 5-1 v Bolton Wanderers, 23.9.1964
4-0 v Leeds United, 17.10.1962
4-0 v Bristol Rovers, 16.10.1961

BIGGEST DEFEATS
League: 0-8 v Arsenal, Division 1, 25.2.1933
0-8 v Lincoln City, Division 2, 29.8.1953
F.A. Cup: 0-6 v Nott'm Forest, Rnd 3, 1879-80
1-6 v Manchester United, 1908-09
1-6 v Luton Town, Rnd 3, 1952-53
League Cup: 0-5 v Wimbledon, 24.9.1985
1-6 v Nott'm Forest, 15.9.1979

MOST POINTS
3 points a win: 77, Division 2, 1987-88, 1988-89
2 points a win: 60, Division 3, 1974-75

MOST GOALS
114, 1954-55, Division 2.
Briggs 33, Quigley 28, Crossan 18, Mooney 16, Langton 13, Clayton 2, Bell 1, og 3.

MOST GOALS IN A MATCH
7. Tommy Briggs v Bristol Rovers, Division 2, 5.2.1953.

MOST GOALS IN A SEASON
Ted Harper 45 (League 43, FAC 2) 1925-26.
5 goals once = 5; 4 goals once = 4; 3 goals twice = 6; 2 goals 7 times = 14; 1 goal 16 times = 16.
Previous holder: D Shea 28.

MOST FIRST CLASS MATCHES IN A SEASON
60 (46 League, 7 FA Cup, 4 League Cup, 3 Anglo-Scottish Cup) 1979-80
60 (46 League, 3 FA Cup, 4 League Cup, 3 Simod Cup, 4 League Play-offs) 1988-89

MOST LEAGUE GOALS CONCEDED
102, Division 1, 1932-33

MOST LEAGUE WINS
25, Division 2, 1938-39;   25, Division 3, 1979-80

MOST LEAGUE DRAWS
18, Division 2, 1980-81

MOST LEAGUE DEFEATS
30, Division 1, 1980-81

OLDEST PLAYER
Bob Crompton, 40 years 151 days, 23.2.1920.

YOUNGEST PLAYER
Harry Dennison, 16 years 155 days, 8.4.1911.

MOST CAPPED PLAYER
Robert Crompton (England) 41

BEST PERFORMANCES BY BLACKBURN ROVERS

League: 1974-75: Matches played 46, Won 22, Drawn 16, Lost 8, Goals for 68, Goals against 45, Points 60. First in Division 3.

Highest: 1911-12 & 1912-13, Division 1 Champions.

F.A. Cup: 1884: 3rd rnd. Padiham 3-0; 4th rnd. Staveley 5-0; 5th rnd. Upton 3-0; Semi-Final Notts County 1-0; Final Queens Park 2-1.
1885: 3rd rnd. Witton 6-1; 4th rnd. Romford 8-0; 5th rnd Bye; 6th rnd. West Bromwich 2-0; Semi-Final Carthusians 5-0; Final Queens Park 2-0.
1886: 3rd rnd. Darwen 6-1; 4th rnd. Bye; 5th rnd. Staveley 7-1; 6th rnd. Brentwood 3-1; Semi-Final Swifts 2-1; Final West Bromiwich 0-0, 2-0.
1890: 4th rnd. Sunderland 4-2; 5th rnd. Grimsby 3-0; 6th rnd. Bootle 7-0; Semi-Final Wolves 1-0; Final Sheffield Wed 6-1.
1891: 1st rnd. Middlesbrough 3-0; 2nd rnd. Chester 7-0; 3rd rnd. Wolves 2-0; Semi-Final West Bromwich 3-2; Final Notts County 3-1.
1928: 3rd rnd. Newcastle United 4-1; 4th rnd. Exeter 2-2, 3-1; 5th rnd. Port Vale 2-1; 6th rnd. Manchester United 2-0; Semi-Final Arsenal 1-0; Final Huddersfield Town 3-1.

League Cup: 1961-62: 1st rnd. Peterborough United 3-1; 2nd rnd. Bristol Rovers 1-1, 4-0; 3rd rnd. Nottingham Forest 2-1; 4th rnd. Ipswich Town 4-1; 5th rnd. Rotherham United 1-0; Semi-Final Rochdale 1-3.

DIVISIONAL RECORDS

	Played	Won	Drawn	Lost	For	Against	Points
DIVISION 1	2024	755	467	802	3379	3441	**1977**
DIVISION 2	1446	583	364	499	2134	1981	**1723**
DIVISION 3	230	104	59	67	299	249	**267**
TOTALS	3700	1442	890	1368	5812	5671	**3967**

BLACKBURN ROVERS

PLAYERS NAME Honours	Ht	Wt	Birthdate	Birthplace Transfers	Contract Date	Clubs	League	L/Cup	FA Cup	Other	Lg	L/C	FAC	Oth
APPEARANCES											**GOALS**			
GOALKEEPERS														
Darren Collier	5.11	11.09	01.12.67	Stockton		Middlesbrough								
					20.06.88	Blackburn Rovers	27	3		1				
Bobby Mimms	6.2	12.10	12.10.63	York	05.08.81	Halifax Town (A)								
E: u21.3; CS'86 '87				£15,000	06.11.81	Rotherham Utd	83	7	3	1				
					30.05.85	Everton	29	2	2	4				
Loans: Notts Co. 03.86 2lg, Sund. 12.86 4lg, BlRo. 01.87 6lg,					24.09.87	Manchester City	3							
				£325,000	25.02.88	Tottenham H	37	5	2					
Loan Aberdeen 16.0290 6lg 2SCup				£250,000	22.12.90	Blackburn Rovers	67	17	20	16				
DEFENDERS														
Mark Atkins	6.0	12.5	14.08.68	Doncaster	09.07.86	Scunthorpe Utd. (A)	45+5	3+1	5	6+1	2			
				£45,000	16.06.88	Blackburn Rovers	162+11	11	7	14	22	3		1
Robert Dewhurst	6.3		10.09.71	Keighley	15.10.90	Blackburn Rovers	13	2		1				
				Loan	20.12.91	Darlington	11			1	1			
Tony Dobson	6.1	12.10	05.02.69	Coventry	07.07.86	Coventry City	51+3	5+3		0+1	1			
E: u21.4				£300,000	17.01.91	Blackburn Rovers	21+1	2		1				
Colin Hendry	6.1	12.2	07.12.65	Keith		Dundee United	17+24		2+3		2		1	
S:B.1,FMC'87				£30,000	11.03.87	Blackburn Rovers	99+3	4	3	7	22			1
				£700,000	16.11.89	Manchester City	57+6	4+1	5	4	5	1	2	2
				£700,000	08.11.91	Blackburn Rovers	26+4		0+1	3	4			
Keith Hill	6.0	11.3	17.05.69	Bolton	09.05.87	Blackburn R. (A)	89+6	6	5+1	3+2	4	1		
David May	6.0	11.4	24.06.70	Oldham	16.06.88	Blackburn R. (T)	49	3	3	5	1			
Kevin Moran	5.11	12.8	29.04.56	Dublin		Manchester Utd	228+3	24+1	18	15+1	21	2	1	
Eire:60,EiXl.1,FAC'83'85 via Sporting Gijion				Free	26.01.90	Blackburn Rovers	88+4	5	4	6	5			1
Stuart Munro	5.8	10.5	15.09.62	Falkirk		Alloa Athletic	58+2	14	2		2	1	1	
SPD'87'89'90'91, SLC'87'88'91						Glasgow Rangers	173+6	19+1	12+2	15+1	3			
				£350,000	12.08.91	Blackburn Rovers	1							
Chris Price	5.9	11.11	30.03.60	Bridgnorth	12.01.78	Hereford Utd. (A)	327+3	17	19	7+1	27	1	1	
FMC'87				£25,000	31.07.86	Blackburn Rovers	83	6	2	7	11			
				£125,000	01.06.88	Aston Villa	109+2	14	7	11+1	2			
				£150,000	07.02.92	Blackburn Rovers	11+2			2	3			
Chris Sulley	5.9	11.00	03.12.59	Camberwell	07.08.78	Chelsea (A)								
AMC'84; FMC'87					12.03.81	Bournemouth	205+1	14	18	10	3			
via Dundee Utd (07.07.84) £15,000 7lg, 1SCup £15,000					10.04.87	Blackburn Rovers	134	5	6	10	3			
Alan Wright	5.4	9.0	28.10.71	Ashton-u-Lyne	13.04.89	Blackpool (T)	79+7	6+2	8	10+2				
E: Y.13, S		via Wrexham (N.C)				Blackpool	12	4		1				
				£400,000	25.10.91	Blackburn Rovers	32+1		2	3	1			
MIDFIELD														
Steve Agnew	5.9	10.6	09.11.65	Shipley	04.10.86	Barnsley (A)	185+9	13	20	6+1	29	3	4	
				£700,000	25.06.91	Blackburn Rovers	2	2						
Gordon Cowans	5.7	10.6	27.10.58	Durham	01.09.76	Aston Villa (A)	276+10	23+4	19+1	23+1	42	5	3	2
E:10,B1,u21.5,Y,Div1'81,EC'82,ESC'82,CS'81,LC'77						Bari								
				£250,000	13.07.88	Aston Villa	124+1	15	9	11+1	7			
				£200,000	28.11.91	Blackburn Rovers	26		2	3	1		1	
Nicky Reid	5.10	11.0	30.10.60	Ormston	04.11.78	Manchester City	211+6	20	17	6	2			
E:u21.6				Free	10.07.87	Blackburn Rovers	160+14	13	6+2	13+1	9			1
Lee Richardson	5.11	11.0	12.03.69	Halifax	06.07.87	Halifax Town	43+13	4	4+2	6	2			
				£175,000	09.02.89	Watford	40+1	1+1	1		1			
				£250,000	15.08.90	Blackburn Rovers	50+12	1		2+2	3			
Stewart Ripley	5.11	12.6	20.11.67	Middlesbrough	23.12.85	Middlesbrough (A)	210+39	21+2	17+1	20+1	26	3	1	1
E:Y4,u21.8				Loan	18.02.86	Bolton W	5		0+1		1			
				£1,300,000	20.07.92	Blackburn Rovers								
Paul Shepstone	5.6	10.6	08.11.70	Coventry	13.11.87	Coventry City								
E: S				Free		Birmingham City								
		via Birmingham (Free)	Free	03.05.90	Blackburn Rovers	16+10	1	0+1	1	1			
				Loan	05.03.92	York City	2							
Tim Sherwood	6.0	11.6	06.02.69	St.Albans	07.02.87	Watford (A)	23+9	4+1	9	4+1	2			
E:u21.4,u19.2				£175,000	18.07.89	Norwich City	66+5	7	4	5+1	10	1		2
				£500,000	12.02.92	Blackburn Rovers	7+4							
FORWARDS														
Steve Livingstone	6.1	12.7	08.09.69	Middlesbrough	16.07.86	Coventry City	17+14	8+2		0+1	5	10		
				£450,000	17.01.91	Blackburn Rovers	24+4	1			10			
Mike Newell	6.0	11.0	27.01.65	Liverpool	28.09.83	Crewe Alexandra	3							
E: B.2, u21.4; FRT'85				Free	31.10.83	Wigan Ath	64+8	6	8	5+1	25	1	6	3
					09.01.86	Luton Town	62+1		5		18		1	
				£350,000	16.09.87	Leicester City	81	9	2	4	21	5		
				£1,100,000	27.07.89	Everton	48+20	7+2	6+4	6	15	4		2
				£1,100,000	15.11.91	Blackburn Rovers	18+2		2	3	6		3	2
Alan Shearer	5.11	11.3	13.08.70	Newcastle	14.04.88	Southampton (T)	105+13	16+2	11+3	8	23	11	4	5
E:3,B,u21.7,Y				£3,600,000	24.07.92	Blackburn Rovers								
Craig Skinner	5.11		21.10.70	Bury	13.06.89	Blackburn Rovers (T)	11+5	0+1	1	3				1
Roy Wegerle	5.11	11.0	19.03.64	South Africa		Tampa Bay Rowdies								
				£100,000	21.07.86	Chelsea	15+8		1+1	2+1	3		1	
Loan Swindon (24.03.88) 7lg 1gl				£75,000	27.07.88	Luton Town	39+6	10	1	2+1	10	8		
				£1,000,000	14.12.89	Q.P.R	71+4	5	11	1	29	1	1	
				£1,200,000	06.03.92	Blackburn Rovers	9+3				2			
Jason Wilcox	5.10		15.07.71	Bolton	13.06.89	Blackburn Rovers (T)	49+8	2		2	4			

BLACKBURN ROVERS

RECORD WIN & LOSS AGAINST EACH CLUB IN CURRENT DIVISION
(Where a score has occured on several occasions the most recent is given)

Club	Rec. Win	Season	Rec. Loss	Season
ARSENAL	7-0	1909-10	8-0	1932-33
ASTON VILLA	7-0	1889-90	6-1	1988-89
CHELSEA	6-1	1912-13 (away)	5-1	1964-65
COVENTRY CITY	2-0	1948-49	6-1	1950-51
CRYSTAL PALACE	3-0	1982-83	5-0	1977-78
EVERTON	6-0	1913-14	7-1	1933-34
IPSWICH TOWN	4-1	1962-63	3-1	1989-90
LEEDS UNITED	4-1	1926-27	5-1	1934-35
LIVERPOOL	6-2	1913-14	4-0	1933-34
MANCHESTER CITY	4-0	1988-89	8-2	1919-20
MANCHESTER UNITED	7-0	1925-26	6-1	1961-62
MIDDLESBROUGH	9-0	1954-55	7-1	1947-48 (home)
NORWICH CITY	6-0	1938-39	4-0	1938-39
NOTTINGHAM FOREST	9-1	1936-37	5-2	1962-63 (home)
OLDHAM ATHLETIC	7-1	1912-13	5-0	1978-79
QUEENS PARK RANGERS	4-2	1951-52	4-2	1951-52
SHEFFIELD UNITED	6-1	1985-86	7-0	1896-97
SHEFFIELD WEDNESDAY	6-1	1910-11	6-0	1896-97
SOUTHAMPTON	4-0	1937-38	6-1	1952-53
TOTTENHAM HOTSPUR	7-2	1963-64	5-0	1924-25
WIMBLEDON	3-0	1979-80	1-0	1979-80

MANAGER: KENNY DALGLISH

DATE OF BIRTH: 04.03.1951   **PLACE OF BIRTH:** Glasgow
DATE OF APPOINTMENT: October 1991
PREVIOUS CLUBS
  as Manager: Liverpool   **as Player:** Celtic; Liverpool
HONOURS
  as Manager: (Liverpool): Division 1 Championship 1986, 1988, 1990; FA Cup Winners 1986, 1989
  as Player: Celtic: Scottish League Championship 1972, 1973, 1974, 1977; Scottish Cup Winners 1972, 1974, 1975, 1977; Finalists 1973; Scottish League Cup Winners 1975; Finalists 1973, 1974, 1977; Liverpool: League Championship 1979, 1980, 1982, 1983, 1984; FA Cup 1986; League Cup Winners 1981, 1982, 1983, 1984; Finalists 1978; European Cup Winners 1978, 1981; Finalists 1985
  International: Scotland: 102+ Full Caps, U23 (4)

Value Rating: ✱ ✱ ✱ ✱

Programme Editor: Peter White

Price of 1992-93 Programme: £1.20
Number of Pages: 32

Subscriptions: £70 home & away, £35 home

Local Newspapers: Lancashire Evening Telegraph.

Local Radio Stations: Red Rose Radio, BBC Radio Lancashire.

LEADING LEAGUE GOALSCORERS
SEASONS 1979-80 – 1991-92

1979-80	**ANDY CRAWFORD**	18	1980-81	**KEVIN STONEHOUSE**	9
1981-82	**SIMON GARNER**	14	1982-83	**SIMON GARNER**	22
1983-84	**SIMON GARNER**	19	1984-85	**CHRIS THOMPSON**	15
1985-86	**SIMON GARNER**	12	1986-87	**SIMON BARKER**	11
1987-88	**SIMON GARNER**	14	1988-89	**SIMON GARNER**	22
1989-90	**SIMON GARNER**	18	1990-91	**FRANK STAPLETON**	10

1991-92   **DAVID SPEEDIE**   **23**

EWOOD PARK Blackburn, Lancs BB2 4JF

Capacity: 20,292   **Covered Standing:** 10,080   **Seating:** 7,542

Tel: Ground: 0254 55432   **Ticket Sales:** 0254 696767   **Clubcall:** 0898 12 11 79

All premium rate calls (0898/0891) cost 36p per minute cheap rate and 48p per minute at all other times. Call costings correct at time of going to press.

GROUNDS
Brookhouse Ground 1875-76. Alexandra Meadow 1876-81. Leamington Road 1881-1890. Ewood Park 1890-

ATTENDANCES
Highest: 61,783 v Bolton Wanderers, FA Cup, 2.3.1929

Lowest: 1,200 v West Bromwich Albion, Division 1, 22.12.1894

RECORD RECEIPTS (with previous records):
£108,000 v Derby County, Play-off Semi-Final, 10.5.1992
£85,510 v Liverpool, FA Cup 3rd Round, 5.1.1991
£60,612 v Liverpool, FA Cup 3rd Round, 2.1.1983
£40,686 v Aston Villa, FA Cup 5th Round, 16.2.1980
£25,307 v Bolton Wanderers, Division 2, 26.4.1978
£16,723 v Burnley, Division 2, 27.12.1976
£13,280 v Manchester City, FA Cup 5th Round, 5.2.1969

EWOOD PARK
First game: v Accrington, (Friendly), 13.9.1890
First floodlit game: v Werder (Friendly), 1958-59
Second Set: v Aberdeen (Friendly), 7.12.1976
Internationals: England v Scotland: 6.4.1891
England v Wales: 3.3.1924

Season Tickets:
Stands: from £216-£252 adults, £114 jun/OAP
Ground: £147 (no reductions)

Executive Box Season Tickets: None

Cost of Stand Tickets: Walkersteel adults £12.00, jun/OAP £8.00; Nuttall Street adult £10.00, jun/OAP £6.00
Terraces: £7 (no reductions)

Car Parking: Ewood car park within walking distance

Nearest Railway Station: Blackburn Central (0254 662537/8)

How to get to the ground

From North and West: M6 to Junction 31 or A666 into Blackburn. A666 into Bolton Road, left into Kidder Street for Ewood Park

From South: M6 to Junction 31 as from North or A666 via Bolton. After Darwen turn right into Kidder Street for Ewood Park

From East: A679 or A677 to Blackburn then A666 toward Bolton into Bolton Road. Left into Kidder Street for Ewood Park.

BLACKPOOL

Division 2

Formed: 1887   **Turned Professional:** 1887   **Ltd Co:** 1896

SPONSORED BY: Inenco Group Plc   **NICKNAME:** The Seasiders

President
C A Sagar B.E.M

Hon Vice-Presidents
R P Gibrail
J Armfield
K Chadwick

Chairman
O J Oyston

Directors
W Ayre
D Hatton
J Wilde, MBE
G Warburton
J Allitt
J Crowther LLB
Mrs V Oyston

Club Secretary
J Miskelly (0253 404331)

Team Manager
Bill Ayre

Physiotherapist
Steve Redmond

Commercial Manager
Geoff Warburton (0253 404331)

Honorary Medical Officer
Dr G Celikkol.M.D

Honorary Dental Surgeon
W G Mair BDS

Club Statistician for the Directory
Roger Harrison

AFTER the disappointment of losing on penalties at Wembley last season in the play offs, we had to endure the same fate this season, but fortunately at the second time of asking we gained promotion 4-3 on penalties, not good for the heart! Manager Billy Ayre had done another magnificent job throughout the season.

We were always in contention for an automatic promotion spot but losing the last three away games cost us that chance. The magnificent home record, the best in the league, of 17 wins from 21 games with one defeat was not matched by the away form of only 5 wins.

Dave Bamber was again superb with 27 league goals and was well supported by nine each from Dave Eyres and Paul Groves and eight from Tony Rodwell (robbed of a hat-trick by Aldershot's demise).

The play off semi finals against Barnet were tense, losing 1-0 at Barnet but goals either side of the interval gave us a 2-0 home win and a meeting at Wembley with Scunthorpe United.

We did not progress far in the cups this season. In the Rumbelows we beat Mansfield Town 7-2 on aggregate but lost at Barnsley 2-1 (aet) on aggregate with Dave Bamber scoring six of our goals in the competition. In the F.A. Cup we beat Grimsby Town before losing to Hull City an in the Autoglass Trophy we progressed through the group games but lost on penalties at Huddersfield Town.

Blackpool will look forward to season 1992-93 with many local derbies and with Billy Ayre, in charge who knows what this time next year might bring.

Roger Harrison

Back row L-R: Grant Leitch, Ian Gore, Andy Garner, Paul Groves, David Eyres, Mark Taylor, Tony Rodwell. **Middle row:** Steve Redmond, Trevor Sinclair, Paul Stoneman, Phil Horner, Carl Richards, Steve McIlhargey, Dave Bamber, Dave Lancaster, Chris Hedworth, Mike Davies, Neil Bailey. **Front row:** Alan Wright, Mark Murray, Gary Brook, Billy Ayre, Dave Burgess, Andy Gouck, Nigel Hawkins.

BLACKPOOL

DIVISION FOUR: 4th **FA CUP:** 2nd RND **RUMBELOWS CUP:** 2nd RND **AUTOGLASS:** 1st RND

M	DATE		COMP.	VEN	OPPONENTS	RESULT	H/T	LGE POS	GOALSCORERS/GOAL TIMES	ATTEN-DANCE
1	A	17	BL	H	Walsall	W 3-0	1-0		Horner 9, Eyres 60, Garner 76	4,141
2		20	RC 1/1	A	Mansfield Town	W 3-0	2-0		Bamber 12, 52, Charles (og) 31	(2,134)
3		24	BL	A	Carlisle United	W 2-1	2-1	1	Bamber 19, Rodwell 40	(4,369)
4		27	RC 1/2	H	Mansfield Town	W 4-2	1-1		Bamber 3 (28, 48, 53), Groves 60	2,155
5		31	BL	H	Scunthorpe United	W 2-1	1-1	1	Hicks (og) 41, Groves 82	3,273
6	S	3	BL	A	York City	L 0-1	0-0	6		(2,686)
7		7	BL	A	Mansfield Town	D 1-1	0-1	5	Bamber 61	(2,629)
8		14	BL	H	Cardiff City	D 1-1	1-1	7	Horner 34	3,931
9		17	BL	H	Gillingham	W 2-0	1-0	4	Bamber 18, 65	3,035
10		20	BL	A	Doncaster Rovers	W 2-0	2-0	1	Bamber 20, Taylor 29	(2,428)
11		24	RC 2/1	H	Barnsley	W 1-0	0-0		Bamber 89	4,123
12		28	BL	H	Rotherham United	W 3-0	1-0	1	Eyres 45, Groves 61, Rodwell 80	5,356
13	O	5	BL	A	Northampton Town	D 1-1	1-0	1	Sinclair 5	(3,355)
14		8	RC 2/2	A	Barnsley	L †0-2	0-1			(6,315)
15		13	BL	H	Lincoln City	W 3-0	1-0	1	Horner 34, Groves (pen) 70, Bamber 83	5,086
16		19	BL	A	Barnet	L 0-3	0-1	3		(5,085)
17		22	AGT Pre	H	Burnley	L 1-3	1-3		Rodwell 16	2,805
18	N	2	BL	A	Scarborough	D 1-1	1-1	5	Groves 3	3,057
19		9	BL	A	Chesterfield	D 1-1	0-0	4	Taylor 66	(4,917)
20		16	FAC 1	H	Grimsby Town	W 2-1	1-0		Groves 8, Bamber 72	4,074
21		19	BL	H	Wrexham	W 4-0	2-0	3	Sinclair 7, 26, Bamber 47, 58	2,842
22		23	BL	H	Crewe Alexandra	L 0-2	0-0	4		4,534
23		30	BL	H	Halifax Town	W 3-0	3-0	3	Groves 4, Bamber 33, 45	3,118
24	D	7	FAC 2	H	Hull City	L 0-1	0-0			4,554
25		14	BL	A	Rochdale	L 2-4	1-2	4	Bamber 13, Rodwell 48	(2,892)
26		17	AGT Pre	A	Doncaster Rovers	D 2-2	0-0		Rodwell 67, Bamber 79	(613)
27		21	BL	H	Carlisle United	W 1-0	0-0	4	Bamber 60	3,440
28		26	BL	A	Walsall	L 2-4	0-2	4	Eyres 53, Bamber 58	(4,675)
29		28	BL	A	Scunthorpe United	L 1-2	1-1	4	Groves 44	(4,271)
30	J	1	BL	H	York City	W 3-1	2-0	4	Eyres 17, Bamber 31, Gouch 88	3,534
31		4	BL	A	Maidstone United	D 0-0	0-0	4		(1,774)
32		11	BL	H	Burnley	W 5-2	2-0	3	Rodwell 17, 89, Kerr 39, Garner 66, Bamber 73	8,007
33		18	BL	A	Hereford United	W 2-0	1-0	3	Bamber 18, 81	(3,008)
34		21	AGT 1	A	Huddersfield Town	D †1-1	1-1		Garner 40 (Lost 3-1 on pens)	(1,585)
35	F	8	BL	A	Wrexham	D 1-1	1-1	2	Garner (pen) 33	(4,053)
36		12	BL	A	Halifax Town	W 2-1	2-0	2	Bamber 21, Rodwell 34	(2,158)
37		15	BL	A	Rochdale	W 3-0	3-0	2	Gouch 28, Groves 34, Eyres 41	4,632
38		18	BL	H	Barnet	W 4-2	2-2	2	Bamber 20, Groves 45, Rodwell 50, Eyres 57	5,186
39		22	BL	A	Burnley	D 1-1	1-1	2	Bamber 31	(18,265)
40		29	BL	H	Maidstone United	D 1-1	1-1	2	Garner 25	4,136
41	M	3	BL	A	Hereford United	W 2-0	0-0	2	Bamber 49, Groves 74	3,560
42		14	BL	A	Scarborough	W 2-1	2-1	1	Eyres 38, Bamber 42	(1,965)
43		21	BL	H	Chesterfield	W 3-1	3-1	1	Davies 33, Rodwell 35, Bamber 37	4,447
44		28	BL	A	Crewe Alexandra	L 0-1	0-0	2		(4,913)
45		31	BL	A	Cardiff City	D 1-1	1-1	2	Bamber 42	(8,430)
46	A	4	BL	H	Mansfield Town	W 2-1	1-1	2	Bamber 14, 78	6,055
47		11	BL	A	Gillingham	L 2-3	1-1	2	Eyres 28, Horner 75	(3,684)
48		14	BL	H	Doncaster Rovers	W 1-0	0-0	1	Eyres (pen) 90	4,353
49		20	BL	A	Rotherham United	L 0-2	0-1	3		(8,992)
50		25	BL	H	Northampton Town	W 1-0	0-0	2	Bamber 52	5,915
51	M	2	BL	A	Lincoln City	L 0-2	0-1	4		(7,884)
52		10	PO SF 1	A	Barnet	L 0-1	0-1			(5,629)
53		13	PO SF 2	H	Barnet	W 2-0	1-0		Groves 42, Garner (pen) 57	7,588
54		23	PO Fin	A	Scunthorpe United	D †1-1	1-0		Bamber 40 (Won 4-3 on pens)	(22,741)

Best Home League Attendance: 8,007 v Burnley   **Smallest:** 2,842 v Wrexham   **Av Home Att:** 4,362

Goal Scorers: Compared with 90-91: +304

League (71): Bamber 27, Groves 9 (1 pen), Eyres 9 (1 pen), Rodwell 8, Horner 4, Garner 4 (1 pen), Sinclair 3, Taylor 2, Gouch 2, Kerr Davies, Opponents

R/lows C(8): Bamber 6, Groves, Opponents
FA Cup (2): Groves, Bamber
Autoglass (4): Rodwell 2, Bamber, Garner
Play-offs (3): Bamber, Garner (pen), Groves

1991-92

McIlhargey S.	Davies M.	Wright A.	Groves P.	Stoneman P.	Gore I.	Rodwell A.	Horner P.	Bamber J.	Garner A.	Eyres D.	Richards C.	Gouck A.	Bonner M.	Hedworth C.	Sinclair T.	Taylor P.	Briggs G.	Brook G.	Burgess D.	Murray M.	Murphy	Kerr D. (L)	Kearton J. (L)	Leitch G.	Cook M.	Referee	
1	2*	3	4	5	6	7	8•	9	10	11	14	12														R Hart	1
1	2	3	4	5	6	7		9	10	11	S	8	S													B Coddington	2
1	2	3	4	5	6	7		9	10	11	S	8		S												A Dawson	3
1	2	3	4*	5	6	7		9	10	11	12	8		S												D Phillips	4
1	2	3	4	S	6	7	5	9	10	11	12	8*														A Bennett	5
1	2	3	4	5•	6	7	8	9	10*	11	12	14														I Cruikshanks	6
1	2	3	4		6	7	8	9	10	11	S			5	S											J Deakin	7
1	2	3	4		6	7	8	9	10*	11				5	12	S										J Lloyd	8
1	2	3	4		6	7	8	9•	12	11					14	10*	5									J Kirkby	9
1	2	3*	4		6	7	8	9	S	11					10	12	5									I Borrett	10
1	2*	3	4		6	7	8	9	12	11					10	S	5									W Flood	11
1	2	3	4		6	7	8	9	S	11					10	S	5									M Peck	12
1	2	3	4	S	6	7	8	9		11					10	S	5									P Vanes	13
1	2	3	4	S	6	7*	8	9		11					10	12	5									A Wilkie	14
1	2	3	4		6	7	8	9		11					10	S	5	S								C Trussell	15
1	2•	3	4	14	6	7	8	9		11					10*	12	5									J Moules	16
1	2*	3	4		6	7	8•	9		11					10	14	5	12								R Nixon	17
1			4		6	7	8	9		11					12		5	10•	2	3*						K Barrett	18
1			4	3	6	7		9		11			8		10	12	5*		2							R Poulain	19
1	S		4	3	6	7	8	9		11					10	S	5		2							A Wilkie	20
1	12		4	3	6	7	8•	9		11					10	14	5		2*							S Bell	21
1	12		4	3	6*	7	8•	9		11†					10	14	5		2							G Singh	22
1	2		4	3		7		9	12	11			8•	6	10*	14	5									W Burns	23
1	2*		4	3		7		9	12				8	6	10•	11				5						C Trussell	24
1	2*		4	3	6	7		9	11				8•	12	5	10	14									J Watson	25
1	2•		4	3	6	7		9	11*				8	12	5	10	14									K Redfearn	26
1			4	3	6	7		9	S	11			8		10	S	5		2							P Jones	27
1			4	3	6	7		9	12	11			8*		10*	14	5		2							J Carter	28
1			4	3	6	7		9	5	11			8	S	S	10			2							S Lodge	29
1			4	3	6	7		9	10	11			8		S	S	5		2							P Danson	30
1			4	3	6	7		9	10	11			8		S	S			2	5						B Hill	31
			4	3	6	7		9	10	11			8		S	S			2	5			1			M Reed	32
	2		4		6	7	S	9	10	11			8		S		5					3	1			P Alcock	33
1	2*		4		6	7	14	9	10	11			8•		12		5					3				P Wright	34
	2*		4		6	7	S	9	10	11			8		12		5					3	1			P Vanes	35
	2		4		6	7	S	9	10	11			8		12		5					3	1			K Lupton	36
	2		4		6	7*	14	9	10	11			8•		12		5					3	1			J Brandwood	37
	2		4		6	7	S	9	10	11			8		S		5					3	1			J Key	38
	2		4		6	7*	S	9	10	11			8		12		5					3	1			J Worrall	39
	2		4		6		14	9	10	11			8•		7*		5					3	1	12		D Shadwell	40
	2		4		6		8	9•	10*	11			14		12		5					3	1	7		K Breen	41
	2		4		6		8	9	10	11			S		14		5*					3	1			D Phillips	42
	2		4		6		8	9	10	11					14		5*					3	1	12•		J Rushton	43
			4	S	6	7	8	9	10	11		5			S				2				1		3	G Poll	44
			4	S	6	7*	8	9	10	11		5			12				2				1		3	M Bodenham	45
	2		4	S	6	7*	8	9	10	11		5											1	12	3	G Courtney	46
1	2*		4	14	6	7	8	9	10†	11		5•											12		3	G Pooley	47
1			4	5	6	7	8	9	10*	11		14			12				2						3	K Barratt	48
1			4		6	7*	8	9	10	11		14			12		5†		2						3*	P Danson	49
1	14		4	5	6	7*	8	9		11					10•				2				12		3	V Callow	50
1	S		4	5	6	7	8	9		11					10				2						3	R Hamer	51
1	7•		4		6	12	8	9		11		5*			10				2	14					3	G Courtney	52
1	5*		4		6	7	8	9	10	11					S				2	12					3	J Martin	53
1	5*		4		6	7	8•	9	10	11					14				2	12					3	K Hackett	54
28	26	12	42	17	41	40	25	42	27	41		20	2	4	15	2	24	1	16	2		12	14	1	8	League Appearances	
	3			2			2		3	3		4	1		12	8							5			Substitute Appearances	
4	4	4	4	2	4	4	2	4	2+1	4		0+1	2			2	0+1	2								R/lows Appearances	
2	1		2	2	1	2	1	2		1			1	1	2	1	1		1		1					FA Cup Appearances	
3	3	1	3	1	3	3	1+1	3	2	2		2	0+1	1	2+1	0+2	2	0+1					1			Autoglass Appearances	
3	3		3		3	3	2+1	3	2	3		1			1+1			3		0+3					3	Play-offs Appearances	

Also played: Posn.(Game): Mitchell 14(18), Howard S(19) 14(24)

Players on Loan: Kerr (Leeds Utd), Kearton (Everton)

BLACKPOOL

Club Colours: Tangerine shirts with white collar, white shorts with navy & tangerine side panel, tangerine stockings with white turnovers
Change Colours: White shirts with navy/tangerine trim; tangerine shorts, tangerine stockings with navy & white tops
Reserves League: Pontins Central League Div 2   **Youth League:** Lancashire League

Previous League: Lancashire League
Previous Name: In 1899 South Shore amalgamated with Blackpool who had been formed when Blackpool St John disbanded in 1887
Previous Managers: (Since 1946): Joe Smith Ron Stuart Stan Mortensen Les Shannon Jimmy Meadows Bob Stokoe Harry Potts Allan Brown Jimmy Meadows Bob Stokoe Stan Ternent Alan Ball (jnr) Allan Brown Sam Ellis Jimmy Mullen Graham Carr
Honours: Div 2 Champions 1929-30 FA Cup Winners 1953 Anglo-Italian Cup Winners 1971
League Career: Elected to Div 2 1896 Failed to gain re-election 1899 Re-elected to Div 2 1900
Promoted to Div 1 1929-30 Relegated to Div 2 1932-33 Promoted to Div 1 1936-37 Relegated to Div 2 1966-67
Promoted to Div 1 1969-70 Relegated to Div 2 1970-71 Relegated to Div 3 1977-78 Relegated to Div 4 1980-81
Promoted to Div 3 1984-85 Relegated to Div 4 1989-90 Promoted to Div 3 1991-92

CLUB RECORDS

Most Appearances for Club: Jimmy Armfield: League 568 + Cup ties 101 **Total 669** (1952-71)
Most Capped Player: Jimmy Armfield, 43 England
Record League Goalscorer in a Season: Jimmy Hampson 45, Div 2 **In All Competitions:** Jimmy Hampson 50 (League 45 + FA Cup 5), 1929-30
Record League Goalscorer in a Career: Jimmy Hampson 247, 1927-38 **In All Competitions:** Jimmy Hampson 271 (League 247, FA Cup 24) 1927-38
Record Transfer Fee Received: £633,333 from Manchester City for Paul Stewart
Record Transfer Fee Paid: £116,666 to Sunderland for Jack Ashurst, October 1979
Best Performances: League: 2nd Div 1, 1955-56 **FA Cup:** Winners 1953 **League Cup:** Semi-final 1962
Most League Points: (3pts for win) 86 Div 4, 1984-85 (2pts for win) 58, Div 2, 1929-30, 1967-68
Most League Goals: 98, Div 2, 1929-30
Most Goals in a Match: 5, Jimmy Hampson v Reading, 7-0, Div 2, 10.11.1928 5, Jimmy McIntosh v Preston North End (a), 7-0, Div 1, 1.5.1948
Record League Victory and Most Goals Scored in a League Match: 8-4 v Charlton Athletic, Div 1, 27.9.1952 7-0 v Reading, Div 2, 10.11.1928 7-0 v Preston North End, Div 1, 1.5.1948 7-0 v Sunderland, Div 1, 13.10.1957
Most Goals Scored in a Cup Tie: 10-0 v Lanerossi Vicenza, Anglo-Italian Cup, 10.6.1972
Record League Defeat: 1-10 v Small Heath, Div 2, 2.3.1901 1-10 v Huddersfield Town, Div 1, 13.12.1930
Record Cup Defeat: 0-6 v Barnsley, FA Cup Round 1 Replay, 1909-10
Oldest Player in a League Match: Sir Stanley Matthews 46
Youngest Player in a League Match: Trevor Sinclair, 16 years 170 days, v Wigan Athletic, 19.8.1989
Youngest Player: Eammon Collins, 14 years 323 days v Kilmarnock, Anglo-Scottish Cup 1980

LONGEST RUNS	
of undefeated matches: 17 (1968)	of league matches without a win: 19 (1970-71)
of undefeated home matches: 24 (1990-91)	of undefeated away matches: 10 (1973-74)
without home win: 16 (1966-67)	without an away win: 41 (1907-09)
of league wins: 9 (1936-37)	of home wins: 15 (1990-91)
of league defeats: 8 (1898-99)	of away wins: 6 (1936-37)

BLACKPOOL

PLAYERS NAME Honours	Ht	Wt	Birthdate	Birthplace Transfers	Contract Date	Clubs	League	L/Cup	FA Cup	Other	Lg	L/C	FAC	Oth
GOALKEEPERS														
Steve McIlhargey	6.1	13.0	23.08.64	Glasgow		Blantyre Celtic								
					01.07.87	Walsall (A)								
				Loan	23.03.89	Rotherham Utd								
				Free	03.08.89	Blackpool	94	4	2	6				
DEFENDERS														
Gary Briggs	6.3	12.10	21.06.59	Leeds	01.05.77	Middlesbrough (A)								
Div.3.84,Div.2.85,LgC86				£12,500	07.01.78	Oxford Utd	418+2	49	24	8	18	3		1
				Free	27.06.89	Blackpool	71	9	4	8	2	2		
David Burgess	5.10	11.5	20.01.60	Liverpool	13.10.81	Tranmere Rovers	217+1	16	15	11	1			
				20.08.86	Grimsby Town	66+3	6	4	3				
				£30,000	07.07.88	Blackpool	81	10	5	11	1		1	
Ian Gore	5.11	12.04	10.01.68	Liverpool		Birmingham City								
					Southport								
					Blackpool	134+3	12+1	11	19+2				
Phillip Horner	6.1	12.1	10.11.66	Lincoln	15.11.84	Leicester City (A)	7+3	1	0+1					
				Loan	27.03.86	Rotherham Utd	3+1							
					03.08.88	Halifax Town	70+2	6	6	8	4		2	1
				£40,000	14.09.90	Blackpool	64+2	2	4	11+1	11			1
James A Murphy					23.08.90	Blackpool			1	0+3				
Paul Stoneman			26.02.73	Whitley Bay	26.07.91	Blackpool	17+2	2	2	1				
MIDFIELD														
Mark Bonner			07.06.74	Ormskirk	18.06.92	Blackpool (T)	2+1		1	0+1				
Mitch Cook	5.10	12.0	15.10.61	Scarborough		Scarborough			1					
APL Lg Cup'84;GMVC'87					13.08.84	Darlington	34	1	6	3	4			
					13.09.85	Middlesbrough	3+3			1+1				
					01.08.86	Scarborough	61+20	6+2	3	7+1	10	4	1	
				£25,000	02.08.89	Halifax Town	52+2	7		5	2	1		2
				Loan	01.10.90	Scarborough	9		1		1			
				Free	26.03.91	Darlington	35+1	2	2		4	1		
				nominal	26.03.92	Blackpool	8			3				
Mike Davies	5.7	10.7	19.01.66	Stretford	19.01.84	Blackpool (A)	221+34	16+1	14+6	20+5	15	1		2
Andrew Gouck	5.9	11.12	08.06.72	Blackpool	04.07.90	Blackpool (T)	26+11	2		3	3			
Paul Groves	5.11	11.5	28.02.66	Derby	01.10.86	Burton Alb			2				1	
				£12,000	18.04.88	Leicester City	7+9	1	0+1	0+1	1	1		
				Loan	20.08.89	Lincoln City	8	2			1			
				£60,000	25.01.90	Blackpool	106+1	6	9	13	21	1	4	3
Trevor Sinclair	5.10	11.2	02.03.73	Dulwich	21.08.90	Blackpool (T)	39+28	4	4+1	5+5	4			1
E:Y.1, S														
FORWARDS														
Dave Bamber	6.3	13.10	01.02.59	St.Helens	20.09.79	Blackpool	81+5	6	7+1		29	5	2	
				£50,000	09.06.83	Coventry City	18+1	2	0+1		3	1		
				£20,000	22.03.84	Walsall	17+3	3			7			
					19.12.84	Portsmouth	4				1			
				£12,500	10.03.86	Swindon Town	103+3	10	6	15	31	6	5	4
				£105,000	28.06.88	Watford	16+2	2		2	3	1		
				£190,000	21.12.88	Stoke City	43	2	3	1	9		2	1
				£130,000	01.02.90	Hull City	25+3	2			5			
				Loan	29.11.90	Blackpool								
				£25,000	16.01.91	Blackpool	65	4	3	10	44	6	1	2
David Eyres	5.10	11.0	26.02.64	Liverpool		Rhyl								
				£10,000	15.06.89	Blackpool	101+11	7+1	9	10+2	22		2	2
Andy Garner	5.11	11.9	08.03.66	Chesterfield	22.12.83	Derby County (A)	48+23	1+4	4+3	5	17		2	1
				£75,000	26.08.88	Blackpool	147+7	14+1	13	20+1	36	3	4	4
Grant Leitch			31.10.72	South Africa	23.08.90	Blackpool	1+5							
David Robinson	6.0	13.02	27.11.69	Newcastle	07.06.88	Newcastle Utd. (T)	0+8	0+1	0+1				1	
				Loan		Peterborough U	7				3			
				N.C	26.03.92	Reading	8							
				Free		Blackpool								
Anthony Rodwell	5.11	11.2	26.08.62	Southport		Runcorn			3				1	
NPL Prem'90						Colne Dynamoes								
					15.08.90	Blackpool	83+2	4+1	5	14+1	15			3
ADDITIONAL CONTRACT PLAYERS														
Richard Bond						Blyth Spartans								
				£10,000	20.12.91	Blackpool								
(D) Stephen Burns	6.0	12.7	28.10.68	Salford	01.06.89	Blackpool								
George Costa					22.03.90	Blackpool								
David Johnson					23.08.90	Blackpool								
Simon Marsh					23.08.90	Blackpool								
Neil N Mitchell			07.11.74	Lytham		Blackpool (T)	1							
Mark Murphy					23.08.90	Blackpool								
Steven Murphy					23.08.90	Blackpool								
Mark Murray			13.06.73		20.10.90	Blackpool	2							
Chris Speak					06.07.92	Blackpool								
Simon Westwell					09.08.90	Blackpool								

LEADING LEAGUE GOALSCORERS SEASONS 1985-86 – 1991-92

1985-86	EAMONN O'KEEFE	15		1986-87	PAUL STEWART	21
1987-88	MARK TAYLOR	21		1988-89	ANDY GARNER	11
1989-90	ANDY GARNER	8		1990-91	DAVE BAMBER	17

1991-92 **DAVE BAMBER** 27

BLOOMFIELD ROAD Blackpool, Lancs FY1 6JJ

Capacity: 10,337   **Covered Standing:** 2,800   **Seating:** 2,987

Tel: Ground: 0253 404331   **Clubcall:** 0898 12 16 48

All premium rate calls (0898/0891) cost 36p per minute cheap rate and 48p per minute at all other times. Call costings correct at time of going to press.

ATTENDANCES
Highest: 38,098 v Wolverhampton Wanderers, Div 1, 17.9.1955

Lowest: 1,228 v Rochdale, S.V. Trophy, 6.12.1988

Record Receipts: £72,949 v Tottenham H., FA Cup Round 3, 5.1.1991

BLOOMFIELD ROAD
First game: (League) v Gainsborough Town, 1-1, 8.9.1900
First floodlit game: v Hearts, 2-1, 13.10.1958

Season Tickets:
Stands: from £156-£166 (jun/OAP £114-£125)
Ground: from £109

Executive Box Season Tickets: £350

Admission Prices: Paddocks: adult £6, jun/OAP £4; Stands: adult £7.50, jun/OAP £5.50; West Stand Reserve Box: adults £8, jun/OAP £6
Family Block Tickets: 1+1 £10.50, 1+2 £13.50, 2+1 £18, 2+2 £21

Match and Ticket Information: Bookable four weeks prior to match

Car Parking: Parking for 1,000 cars. Street parking available

Nearest Railway Station: Blackpool North (0772 59439)

How to get to the ground

From North, East and South: Leave M6 Motorway at junction 32 and follow signs Blackpool M55. At end of motorway the ground is immediately on the right hand side of the Municipal Car Park

Value Rating: ★ ★ ★

Programme Editor: Geoff Warburton

Price of 1992-93 Programme: £1.20
Number of Pages: 32
Subscriptions: £47.50 for all home programmes

Local Newspapers: Blackpool Evening Gazette

Local Radio Stations: Red Rose Radio, Radio Lancashire

Additional Club Publications: Centenary Book £4.95+£1p+p

BOLTON WANDERERS — Division 2

Formed: 1874   **Turned Professional:** 1880   **Ltd Co:** 1895

SPONSORED BY: Reebok   **NICKNAME:** The Trotters

President
Nat Lofthouse

Chairman
G Hargreaves

Directors
G Ball
G Seymour
G Warburton
W B Warburton
P Gartside

Secretary/Chief Excutive
D McBain (0204 389200)

Team Manager
Bruce Rioch

Coach
Colin Todd

Reserve Team Manager
Steve Carroll

Physiotherapist
Ewan Simpson

Youth Development Officer
Dean Crombie

Commercial Manager
T. Holland

Club Historian/Club Statistician for the Directory
Simon Marland

AFTER two disappointments in the play-offs in previous seasons, much was expected of the Wanderers in 1991-92.

Tony Kelly and Michael Brown were added to the squad from Shrewsbury whilst the club's longest serving player, Steve Thompson, was an early season departure to Luton Town.

Early results were promising, just one defeat in the opening eight league games coming at Darlington where Bolton just failed to recover from a three goal half-time deficit.

Three defeats in the next four games, culminating in a 3-0 home reverse by Fulham, set the alarm bells ringing as the club slumped to 14th in the league. An undefeated run of seven games put the club back into contention with David Reeves enjoying his best goalscoring spell since joining the Wanderers. Unfortunately he was injured in a home win over Hull just before Christmas and failed to find the net again.

Steady progress had been made in the F.A. Cup and when a weakened Bolton side defeated Reading at Burnden to earn a Fourth Round home tie against second division Brighton, cup tie fever took over. Added to this was the signing of Andy Walker, initially on loan from Celtic, who scored within seconds of his introduction as substitute in a 2-2 draw at Exeter City. Walker was a revelation with his goals helping to keep the club in the Third Division.

Goals from Walker and Philliskirk defeated Brighton to put Bolton in the Fifth Round of the F.A. Cup for the first time since 1980 and a home tie against Southampton who had conquered Manchester United in the previous round. The Wanderers showed plenty of character by earning a replay after being two goals down with only eleven minutes left and kept up their record of never having lost on a Sunday.

At the Dell, Julian Darby appeared to have given Bolton a 2-1 win with an 89th minute strike, but then everything went wrong as the Saints equalised in the third minute of injury time and won it in extra time.

After the cup exit there were still hopes of a play-off place as the club had games in hand over their rivals. A 4-0 win at Hartlepool, the clubs best away win since February 1988, kept them in contention but then injuries and a number of players off form began to take their toll. The final eleven games produced just one win, a 3-1 defeat of Stoke on the last day.

Manager Phil Neal and coach Mick Brown parted company with the club and promotion hopes have now been placed in the hands of Bruce Rioch and Colin Todd.
Simon Marland

Back row L-R: Jason Lydiate, Mark Seagraves, Mark Winstanley, Mark Came, Alan Stubbs, Julian Darby, Nicky Spooner. **First row:** Andy Roscoe, Jason McAteer, David Reeves, Tony Philliskirk, Stuart Storer, Barry Smith, Craig Lewin. **Second row:** Ewan Simpson, Darren Oliver, David Burke, Keith Branagan, Chris Clarke, Dave Felgate, Scott Green, Michael Brown, Dean Crombie. **Front row:** Steve Carroll, Mark Patterson, Neil Fisher, Bruce Rioch (Manager), Phil Brown, Colin Todd (Asst. Manager), Andy Walker, Tony Kelly

BOLTON WANDERERS

DIVISION THREE: 13th   **FA CUP:** 5th RND   **RUMBELOWS CUP:** 2nd RND   **AUTOGLASS:** 1st RND

M	DATE		COMP.	VEN	OPPONENTS	RESULT	H/T	LGE POS	GOALSCORERS/GOAL TIMES	ATTEN-DANCE
1	A	17	BL	H	Huddersfield Town	D 1-1	0-1		Philliskirk 83	7,606
2		20	RC 1/1	H	York City	D 2-2	1-0		Philliskirk 44, Darby 79	3,017
3		24	BL	A	Swansea City	D 1-1	1-1		Reeves 2	(3,578)
4		27	RC 1/2	A	York City	W 2-1	1-1		Darby 12, Patterson 66	(2,757)
5		31	BL	H	Leyton Orient	W 1-0	0-0		Reeves 49	5,058
6	S	3	BL	A	Darlington	L 2-3	0-3		Philliskirk 61, Reeves 87	(3,385)
7		7	BL	H	West Bromwich A.	W 3-0	1-0	5	Philliskirk 28, 84, M Brown 64	7,980
8		14	BL	H	Bournemouth	W 2-1	1-0		Reeves 38, P Brown 58	(5,690)
9		17	BL	A	Bradford City	D 4-4	1-0		Darby 26, 74, Patterson (pen) 65, Reeves 88	(5,669)
10		21	BL	H	Wigan Athletic	D 1-1	0-1	7	Darby 80	6,923
11		25	RC 2/1	A	Nottingham Forest	L 0-4	0-2			(19,936)
12		28	BL	A	Brentford	L 2-3	0-2		Reeves 55, Darby 85	(5,658)
13	O	5	BL	H	Torquay United	W 1-0	1-0	6	Green 1	5,092
14		8	RC 2/2	H	Nottingham Forest	L 2-5	2-3		Darby 20, Kelly 21	5,469
15		12	BL	A	Stoke City	L 0-2	0-1			(12,420)
16		19	BL	H	Fulham	L 0-3	0-1	14		5,152
17		26	BL	A	Chester City	W 1-0	0-0	11	Darby 90	(1,867)
18	N	2	BL	H	Reading	D 1-1	0-0	11	Philliskirk (pen) 61	3,632
19		5	BL	A	Stockport County	D 2-2	2-1		Philliskirk (pen) 9, 31	(5,036)
20		9	BL	A	Bury	D 1-1	1-0	11	M Brown 14	(5,886)
21		17	FAC 1	A	Emley	W 3-0	1-0		Reeves 39, 57, Philliskirk 78	(9,035)
22		19	AGT Pre	A	Preston North End	L 1-2	0-1		Reeves 87	(2,709)
23		23	BL	H	Preston North End	W 1-0	0-0		Reeves 90	7,033
24		30	BL	A	Shrewsbury Town	W 3-1	1-1	7	Philliskirk (pen) 21, Kelly 72, Reeves 86	(3,937)
25	D	7	FAC 2	H	Bradford City	W 3-1	2-0		Burke 1, Reeves 4, Philliskirk (pen) 90	7,129
26		10	AGT Pre	H	Rochdale	W 4-1	0-0		Reeves 3 (62, 69, 73), Philliskirk 83	1,507
27		14	BL	A	Hull City	W 1-0	0-0	7	Philliskirk (pen) 70	5,273
28		26	BL	A	Leyton Orient	L 1-2	1-0		Green 25	(4,896)
29		28	BL	A	Huddersfield Town	L 0-1	0-1	9		(11,884)
30	J	1	BL	H	Darlington	W 2-0	0-0		Fisher 69, Philliskirk 75	5,841
31		4	FAC 3	H	Reading	W 2-0	0-0		Philliskirk 74, 85	7,301
32		11	BL	A	Exeter City	D 2-2	1-1		Philliskirk 25, Walker 69	(3,336)
33		14	AGT 1	A	Crewe Alexandra	L 0-2	0-1			(2,155)
34		18	BL	H	Hartlepool United	D 2-2	0-1	8	Walker 58, Darby 59	6,129
35		25	FAC 4	H	Brighton & H A	W 2-1	0-0		Walker 51, Philliskirk (pen) 71	12,635
36	F	1	BL	A	Fulham	D 1-1	0-1	9	Walker 64	(3,804)
37		8	BL	H	Chester City	D 0-0	0-0			6,609
38		11	BL	H	Shrewsbury Town	W 1-0	0-0		Walker 6	5,276
39		16	FAC 5	H	Southampton	D 2-2	0-2		Walker 79, Green 86	20,131
40		22	BL	H	Exeter City	L 1-2	1-1	11	Walker 27	5,631
41		26	FAC 5R	A	Southampton	L †2-3	1-1		Walker 34, Darby 89	(18,009)
42		29	BL	A	Peterborough Utd	L 0-1	0-0			(6,270)
43	M	3	BL	A	Hartlepool United	W 4-0	3-0		Kelly 8, Walker 18, 85, M Brown 30	(2,244)
44		10	BL	H	Stockport County	D 0-0	0-0			7,635
45		14	BL	A	Reading	L 0-1	0-1	15		(3,515)
46		17	BL	H	Birmingham City	D 1-1	0-0		P Brown 90	7,329
47		21	BL	H	Bury	W 2-1	1-0		Walker 40, 55	7,619
48		24	BL	H	Peterborough Utd	W 2-1	2-1		Walker 22, Charlery (og) 38	5,421
49		28	BL	A	Preston North End	L 1-2	0-1	12	Philliskirk 63	(7,327)
50		31	BL	H	Bournemouth	L 0-2	0-1			4,955
51	A	4	BL	A	West Bromwich A.	D 2-2	1-1	12	Walker 32, Stubbs 46	(10,287)
52		7	BL	H	Swansea City	D 0-0	0-0			3,535
53		11	BL	H	Bradford City	D 1-1	1-0	12	Walker 21	4,892
54		14	BL	A	Birmingham City	L 1-2	1-2	12	Walker 17	(14,440)
55		18	BL	A	Wigan Athletic	D 1-1	0-1	12	Spooner 86	(3,357)
56		20	BL	H	Brentford	L 1-2	0-2	12	Walker 68	4,382
57		25	BL	A	Torquay United	L 0-2	0-1	13		(2,178)
58		29	BL	A	Hull City	L 0-2	0-1			(3,997)
59	M	2	BL	H	Stoke City	W 3-1	0-1	13	Patterson 49, Seagraves 69, Walker 90	10,000

Best Home League Attendance: 10,000 v Stoke City   **Smallest:** 3,535 v Swansea City   **Av Home Att:** 6,044

Goal Scorers: **Compared with 90-91:** -1,233

League (57):   Walker 15, Philliskirk 12 (4 pens), Reeves 8, Darby 6, M Brown 3, P Brown 2, Green 2, Kelly 2, Patterson 2 (1 pen), Spooner Opponents, Seagraves, Fisher, Stubbs

R/lows C(6):   Darby 3, Philliskirk, Patterson, Kelly
FA Cup (14):   Philliskirk 5 (2 pens), Reeves 3, Walker 3, Green, Darby, Burke
Autoglass (5):   Reeves 4, Philliskirk

1991-92

Felgate D.	Brown P.	Cowdrill B.	Kelly T.	Seagraves M.	Stubbs A.	Thompson S.	Reeves D.	Philliskirk T.	Darby J.	Brown M.	Burke D.	Rose K.	Storer S.	Comstive P.	Jeffrey M.	Fisher N.	Patterson M.	Winstanley M.	Dibble A.	Came M.	Spooner N.	Kennedy A.	Walker A.	Charnley C.	Referee	
1	2	3	4	5	6	7*	8	9	10	11	12	S													P Wright	1
	2	3	4	5	6			9	10	11		12	1	7	8*	S									**C Wilkes**	2
	2		4	5	6	8†		9	10	11		3	1	7	S	S									K Cooper	3
	2		4	5	6			9	10	11		3	1	7•		8*	12	14							**A Dawson**	4
	2		4	5*	12			9	10	11	7	3	1		S		8	6							J Watson	5
	2		4	5	S			9	10	11	7	3	1				14	8	6						J Key	6
	2		4	5	S			9	10	11	7	3		S			8	6	1						J Lloyd	7
	2		4	5	S	14		9	10	11	7*	3					8	6	1						G Willard	8
	2		4	5•	14	S		9	10†	11	7	3					8	6	1						A Wilkie	9
	2	4•		6	14			9	10	11	7*	3		12			8		1		5				J Rushton	10
	2		4	6	7*			9	10•	11		3	1	12	14		8				5				**M Bailey**	11
	2	4*	S	6	7			9	10	11		3	1	12			8				5				J Carter	12
	2		4	6	10			9		11		3		7		S	8		1	5	S				B Coddington	13
	2		4	6	10			9		11		3	1	7		S	8			5	S				**W Burns**	14
	2		4	14	6	10*		9		11	7	3		12			8		1	5					R Gifford	15
	2		4	5	6	12		9	10	11	7	3					8	S	1						J Kirkby	16
	2		4	5		14		12	10	11	7*	3					8•	6	1			9			R Pawley	17
	2		4	5	S			9	10	11	7	3					8	6	1	S					A Bennett	18
	2		4	5	S	12		9	10	11	7	3					8*	6	1						M Peck	19
	2		4	5	S	S		9	10	11	7	3					8	6	1						K Hackett	20
1	2		4	5	12	8*		9	10	11	7•	3		14				6							**R Hart**	21
	2	14	4		S	8•		9		11	7	3		10				6	1		5				**P Harrison**	22
	2		4	5	S	8		9	10	11	7	3		S				6	1						D Allison	23
	2		4	5	12	8		9	10	11	7	3		S				6*	1						R Hamer	24
1	2		4	5	6•	8		9	10	11	7	3		S				6				14			**J Lloyd**	25
1	2		4	5		8		9	10	11	7	3		S				6				S			**P Danson**	26
1	2		4	5	S	8	9•		10	11	7	3		14				6				S			T Holbrook	27
1	2		4	5	S	S			10	11	7*	3		12				8				6			D Gallagher	28
1	2		4	6	12	9			10	11		3		7*				8				5			G Courtney	29
1	2*		4	5	12	9			10	11		3		7•				14	8			6			A Smith	30
1			4	5	2	7			10			3		S	9		11	8				6		S	**G Singh**	31
1			4	5	2	7			10	11		3			9*		S	8				6			J Martin	32
1			4	5	2	7*			10	11		3		12				8•				6	14	9	P Vanes	33
1			4	5	2	7*		S	10	11		3					S	8				6		9	D Shadwell	34
1			4	5	2	7*		12	10	11		3					S	8				6		9	**R Hamer**	35
1			4	5		7*		12	10	11	14	3						8•				6	2	9	A Gunn	36
1			4	5		7*		12	10	11		3					14	8•				6	2	9	K Redfern	37
1			4	5		7•		12	10*	11	7*	3						8				6	2	9	M Brandwood	38
1			4	5		14		12	10	11	7*	3						8*				6	2	9	**M Peck**	39
	12	4*		5		14		7	10	11		3						8				6	2*	9	V Callow	40
1			4	5	14	7*		12	10	11		3						8•				6	2	9	**K Barrett**	41
1	S		4	5	11	7		12	10								8*		3		6	2		9	D Axcell	42
1	2		4	5	11	S		S	10		7						8	3			6			9	M Peck	43
1	2	4*		5	8			12	10	14	7						11*	3			6			9	K Barrett	44
1	2			5	8	14		12	10	4	7•						11	3*			6			9	A Ward	45
1	2			8•	4*	7		10	5	12	3						11	6					14	9	A Bennett	46
1	2			5	8	4		7	10*	12	3						11	6			S			9	T Holbrook	47
1	2			5	8	7		10	S	4	3						11	6			S			9	R Poulain	48
1	2			5	7*			12	10	4		3					11	6				9		8	J Lloyd	49
1	2			5	14			10	12	4	7	3					11	6				9		8*	P Wright	50
1			5	12	14				10	4	7*	3					11†	6			2	9		8*	J Deakin	51
1	S		5	8	12				10	4	7*	3					11	6			2	9			S Lodge	52
			5	8	11			S	10	4	7	3					S	6			2	9			J Rushton	53
	14		5	8	7			12	10*	4		3					11	6			2	9			A Dawson	54
14	7		5	8	4				10	11		3						6			2	9			K Barratt	55
1	3		5	8	4*			12	10	11					7			6			2	9			R Shepherd	56
1	3		5	8	4*			12	10	11					7			6			2	9			R Lewis	57
1	3		5	6	12			8	10	4					7*		11				2	9			R Pawley	58
1	3		5	8	7			S	10	4		S					11				2	9			K Lupton	59
25	35	1	31	39	26	26	2	24	42	42	23	37	4	4		1	4	36	27	13	18	14	1	23	League Appearances	3
2					1		6	11		11	1	2	4								1		1		Substitute Appearances	
4	1		4	2	4	2		4	3	4		3+1	4		3+1	1		2+1	0+1		2				R/lows Appearances	
6	2		6	6	3+2	5+1		2+3	6	5	3	6			1		1	4	1		4+1	2		3	FA Cup Appearances	
2	2	0+1	3	2	1	3		2	2	3	2	3		1				1	1		3	0+1		1	Autoglass Appearances	

Also Played: Posn.(Game): G Peyton 1(40), Maxwell 1(53,54,55), J Lydiate S(55,56,58)6(59), D Oliver S(57)

BOLTON WANDERERS

Club Colours: White shirts with red and blue trim, navy blue shorts, red stockings
Change Colours: Blue check shirts, white shorts, blue stockings or yellow shirts
Reserves League: Pontins Central League Div 1   **'A' Team:** Lancashire League

Previous Name: Christ Church FC from 1874-1877
Previous Managers: 1908-10 John Somerville   1910-15 Will Settle   1915-19 Tom Mather   1919-45 Charles Foweraker   1945-50 Walter Rowley   1950-68 Bill Ridding   1968-70 Nat Lofthouse   1970-71 Jimmy McIlroy   1971 Jimmy Meadows   1971 Nat Lofthouse   1971-74 Jimmy Armfield   1974-80 Ian Greaves   1980-81 Stan Anderson   1981-82 George Mulhall   1982-85 John McGovern   1985 Charlie Wright   1985-92 Phil Neal
Honours: Champions Div 2, 1908-09, 1977-78   Champions Div 3, 1972-73   FA Cup Winners 1923, 1926, 1929, 1958   Sherpa Van Trophy Winners 1989
League Career: Founder members of the Football League 1888   Relegated to Div 2 1898-89
Promoted to Div 1 1899-1900   Relegated to Div 2 1902-03   Promoted to Div 1 1904-05   Relegated to Div 2 1907-08
Promoted to Div 1 1908-09   Relegated to Div 2 1909-10   Promoted to Div 1 1910-11   Relegated to Div 2 1932-33
Promoted to Div 1 1934-35   Relegated to Div 2 1963-64   Relegated to Div 3 1970-71   Promoted to Div 2 1972-73
Promoted to Div 1 1977-78   Relegated to Div 2 1979-80   Relegated to Div 3 1982-83   Relegated to Div 4 1986-87
Promoted to Div 3 1987-88

CLUB RECORDS

Most Appearances for Club: Eddie Hopkinson: League 519 + FA Cup 38 + League Cup 21 **Total 578** (1956-70)
Most Capped Player: Nat Lofthouse 33, England (1951-58)
Record Goalscorer in a Match: J Cassidy, 5 v Sheffield United, F.A. Cup, 13-0, 1890   T Caldwell, 5 v Walsall, Div 3, 8-1, 1983
Record League Goalscorer in a Season: Joe Smith 38, Div 1, 1920-21   **In All Competitions:** Joe Smith 38, 1920-21
Record League Goalscorer in a Career: Nat Lofthouse 255, 1946-61   **In All Competitions:** Nat Lofthouse 285 (League 255 + FA Cup 27 + League Cup 3)
Record Transfer Fee Received: £340,000 from Birmingham City for Neil Whatmore, Aug 1974
Record Transfer Fee Paid: £350,000 to West Bromwich Albion for Len Cantello, May 1979
Best Performances: League: 3rd in Div 1, 1891-92, 1920-21, 1924-25   **FA Cup:** Winners 1923, 1926, 1929, 1958   **League Cup:** Semi-final 1976-77
Most League Points: (2pts for Win) 61, Div 3, 1972-73   (3pts for win) 83, Div 3, 1990-91
Most League Goals: 96, Div 2, 1934-35
Record League Victory: 8-0 v Barnsley, Div 2, 6 Oct 1934
Most Goals Scored in a Cup Tie: 13-0 v Sheffield United, FA Cup 2nd Round, Feb 1890
Record League Defeat: 0-7 v Manchester City, Div 1, 21.3.1936   0-7 v Burnley, Div 1, 1.3.1890   0-7 Sheffield Wednesday, Div 1, 1.3.1915
Record Cup Defeat: 1-9 v Preston North End, FA Cup First Series Rnd 2, 1887-88
Oldest Player in a League Match: Ted Vizard 41 yrs 287 days
Youngest Player in a League Match: Ray Parry 15 years 267 days

LONGEST LEAGUE RUNS	
of undefeated matches: 23 (1990-91)	**of league matches without a win:** 26 (1902, 1903)
of undefeated home matches: 27 (1920-21)	**of undefeated away matches:** 11 (1904-05, 1990-91)
without home win: 11 (1902-03)	**without an away win:** 36 (1948-50)
of league wins: 11 (1904)	**of home wins:** 17 (1924-25)
of league defeats: 11 (1902-03)	**of away wins:** 5 (1904-05)

BARCLAYS

BARCLAYS BUSINESS CENTRE
Bolton Business Centre
The Wellsprings
Victoria Square
Bolton BL1 1BY
Tel: 0204 387452

BARCLAYBANK MACHINE

BOLTON WANDERERS

PLAYERS NAME / Honours	Ht	Wt	Birthdate	Birthplace / Transfers	Contract Date	Clubs	League	L/Cup	FA Cup	Other	Lg	L/C	FAC	Oth
							APPEARANCES				GOALS			
GOALKEEPERS														
Keith Branagan	6.0	11.0	10.07.66	Fulham	04.08.83	Cambridge Utd	110	12	6	6				
				£100,000	25.03.88	Millwall	46	1	5	1				
				Loan	24.11.89	Brentford	2			1				
Loan Gillingham				Loan	06.02.92	Fulham	1							
				Free	03.07.92	Bolton W								
David Felgate	6.1	13.3	04.03.60	Blaenau Festiniog	01.08.78	Bolton W								
W: 1,S; SVT'89				Loan	07.10.78	Rochdale	35							
				Loan	27.09.79	Crewe Alexandra	14							
				Loan	09.03.80	Rochdale	12							
				£25,000	05.09.80	Lincoln City	198	16	10	2				
Loan Cardiff (01.12.84) 4lg				£27,000	23.02.85	Grimsby Town	36	2	1					
				Loan	14.02.86	Bolton W	15			4				
				Loan	10.12.86	Rotherham Utd				1				
					17.02.87	Bolton W	223	14	17	27				
DEFENDERS														
Phil Brown	5.11	11.6	30.05.57	Hartlepool	07.07.78	Hartlepool Utd	210+7	12	11	3	8			1
SVT'89				Free	30.07.85	Halifax Town	135	6	8	9	19	1	1	
				£17,000	23.06.88	Bolton W	172+2	18	10	22	7	1		1
David Burke	5.10	10.7	06.08.60	Liverpool	25.08.77	Bolton W	65+4	5	1+1		1			
E:Y2				Free	16.06.81	Huddersfield Town	189	19	15		3			
				£78,000	09.10.87	Crystal Palace	80+1	4	3	9				
					27.07.90	Bolton W	50+1	6+1	6	3			1	
Mark Came	6.1	13.0	14.09.61	Exeter		Winsford Utd								
					28.04.84	Bolton W	185+6	14+4	16+2	27	7	2		2
Julian Darby	6.0	11.4	03.10.67	Bolton	22.07.86	Bolton W (T)	237+7	21	19	30	32	8	3	5
Mark Seagraves	6.0	12.10	22.10.66	Bootle	04.11.83	Liverpool		1	1					
E:Y4				Loan	21.11.86	Norwich City	3							
				£100,000	25.09.87	Manchester City	36+6	3	3	2				
				£100,000	24.09.90	Bolton W	71+1	3	8	6	1			
Nicholas Spooner	5.10	11.0	05.06.71	Manchester	12.07.89	Bolton W (T)	14+1		2	0+1	1			
Allan Stubbs	6.2	12.12	06.10.71	Kirkby	24.07.90	Bolton W (T)	42+13	6	3+3	4	1	1		
Mark Winstanley	6.1	12.4	22.01.68	St. Helens	22.07.86	Bolton W (T)	169+1	15+1	9	18	2			3
SVT'89														
MIDFIELD														
Neil Fisher	5.10	11.0	07.11.70	St.Helens	12.07.89	Bolton W (T)	4+3	1	1		1			
Scott Green	5.10	11.12	15.01.70	Walsall		Derby County								
				£50,000	17.03.90	Bolton W	63+20	6	7+2	7+2	10		1	
Tony G Kelly	5.10	13.2	01.10.64	Prescott	30.09.82	Liverpool (A)								
FRT85				f	04.01.84	Wigan Ath	98+3	4	10	12	15	2	1	4
				26.04.86	Stoke City	33+3	2	5	1	4			
				£60,000	13.07.87	West Brom A	26	2	1	1	1			
				Loan	22.09.88	Chester City	5	2						
				Loan	24.10.88	Colchester Utd	13		4	3	2			
					10.03.89	Shrewsbury Town	100+1	8	7	4	15	1	1	
				£100,000	15.08.91	Bolton W	31	4	6	3	2	1		
Mark Patterson	5.6	10.10	24.05.65	Darwen	01.05.83	Blackburn R (A)	89+12	4	3+1	2+4	20	1		1
FMC'87				£20,000	15.06.88	Preston N.E	54+1	4+1	4	7	19			2
				£80,000+P	01.02.90	Bury	42	2	1	4	10			
				£65,000	10.01.91	Bolton W	54+1	2+1	4	1	4	1		
FORWARDS														
Mickey Brown	5.9	10.12	08.02.68	Birmingham		Shrewsbury T (A)								
						Shrewsbury Town	174+16	17	10	11	9	2	1	
				£100,000	15.08.91	Bolton W	23+4		3	2	3			
Tony Philliskirk	6.1	11.2	10.02.65	Sunderland	16.08.83	Sheffield Utd	62+18	4+1	5	3+2	20	1	1	
E:S				Loan		Rotherham Utd	6							
					13.07.88	Oldham Ath	3+7	0+2		1	1	1		
					10.02.89	Preston N.E	13+1				6			
				£50,000	22.06.89	Bolton W	130+1	14	10	13	49	11	7	5
David Reeves	6.0	11.7	19.11.67	Birkenhead		Heswall								
				Free	06.08.86	Sheffield Wed	8+9	1+1	1+1	0+1	2	1		
				Loan	17.12.86	Scunthorpe Utd	3+1				2			
				Loan	01.10.87	Scunthorpe Utd	6				4			
				Loan	20.11.87	Burnley	16			2	8			1
				£80,000	17.08.89	Bolton W	101+19	14	7+3	9+1	28	1	4	7
Stuart Storer	5.11	11.8	16.01.67	Harborough	23.08.83	Mansfield Town (T)	0+1							
SVT'89				Free	10.01.85	Birmingham City	5+3	1						
				P.E	06.03.87	Everton								
				Loan	23.07.87	Wigan Ath	9+3	4						
				£25,000	24.12.87	Bolton W	94+26	9+2	6+2	15+3	12		2	1
Andrew Walker	5.8	10.7	06.04.65	Glasgow		Motherwell	65+4	2+4	9+2		17	1	2	
S:1, u21.1; SPD'88, SFAC'88				£350,000		Celtic	86+22	9+6	8+3	5+2	40	8	6	3
				Loan	01.09.91	Newcastle Utd	3	3		1				
				£160,000	01.02.92	Bolton W	23+1		3	1	15		3	

ADDITIONAL CONTRACT PLAYERS

Peter Barnes, Chris J Clarke, Craig Lewin, (D) Jason Lydiate, Jason McAteer, (D) Darren Oliver, David Price, Andrew Roscoe, Barry Smith.

LEADING LEAGUE GOALSCORERS SEASONS 1985-86 – 1991-92

1985-86	TONY CALDWELL	10	1986-87	TONY CALDWELL	11
1987-88	JOHN THOMAS	22	1988-89	TREVOR MORGAN	10
1989-90	TONY PHILLISKIRK	18	1990-91	TONY PHILLISKIRK	19
			1991-92	ANDY WALKER	15

BURNDEN PARK Manchester Road, Bolton, Lancs BL3 2QR

Capacity: 22,000   **Standing:** 14,000   **Seating:** 8,000

Tel: Ground: 0204 404331   **Ticket Sales:** 0204 21101   **Clubcall:** 0898 12 11 64

All premium rate calls (0898/0891) cost 36p per minute cheap rate and 48p per minute at all other times. Call costings correct at time of going to press.

ATTENDANCES
Highest: 69,912 v Manchester City, FA Cup Round 5, 18.2.1933

Lowest: Approx 700 v Aston Villa, Div 1, 18.11.1893 or 1,507 v Rochdale, Autoglass Trophy, 10.12.1991

Record Receipts: £113,395.75 v Southampton, FA Cup 5th Round, 16.2.1992

BURNDEN PARK
First game: v Preston North End, Dai Jones Benefit, 11.9.1895
First floodlit game: v Heart of Midlothian, 14.10.1957

Season Tickets:
Stands: from £133 to £171 (jun/OAP £85 to £104)
Ground: £133 (Jun/OAP £85)

Executive Box Season Tickets: None

Cost of Stand Tickets: Manchester Road Stand: adults £9, juv/OAP £5.50; Block 'A' (Wing): adults £9, juv/OAP £5; Burnden Stand: adults £9, juv/OAP £5.50; Great Lever

Stand: adults £7, juv/OAP £4.50, adult + jun £11
Terraces: Manchester Road Terrace: adults £5.50, juv/OAP £4; Burnden Terrace: adults £5.50, juv/OAP £4

Car Parking: Private car parking only in forecourt. Large car park 200 yards from ground. Limited street parking nearby. Multi-storey car parks are in town centre

Nearest Railway Station: Bolton (0204 28216)

How to get to the ground

From North: Leave M61 at junction 5 or enter Bolton via A666 or A676. Then follow signs Farnworth B653 into Manchester Road. In 0.6m turn left into Croft Lane to Bolton Wanderers FC

From South, East and West: Use M62 until junction 14 then join M61. In 2.1m leave Motorway and at roundabout take 1st exit B6536. In 2.1m turn right into Croft Lane for Bolton Wanderers FC

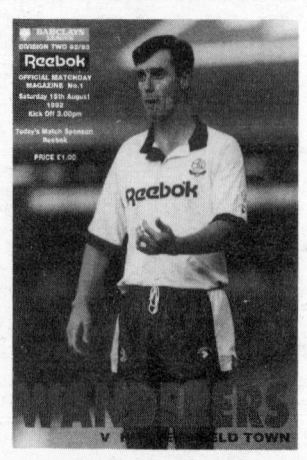

Value Rating: ★ ★ ★

Programme Editor: Gary Porter

Price of 1992-93 Programme: £1
Number of Pages: 32
Subscriptions: £29.90 (League games only), Cup matches £1+30p P+P

Local Newspapers: Bolton Evening News

Local Radio Stations: Piccadilly Radio, G.M.R.

Additional Publications on Club: A Complete Record 1877-1989 & A Complete Record Season 1990-91. Both by Simon Marland – available from the club

AFC BOURNEMOUTH

Division 2

Formed: 1899   **Turned Professional:** 1912   **Ltd Co:** 1914

SPONSORED BY: Exchange & Mart   **NICKNAME:** The Cherries

President
P W Hayward

Chairman
N Hayward

Vice-Chairman
B E Willis

Directors
E G Keep   G M C Hayward
G W Legg   K Gardiner

Chief Executive
Annie Bassett

Company Secretary
Colin McMillan

Club Secretary
Keith MacAlister

Team Manager
Tony Pulis

Assistant Manager
David Williams

Administration
Lisa Swift
Diane Plummer
Sue Heyward
Mandy Willis

Physiotherapist
Mick Newman

Groundsman
John Harriss

Club Statistician for the Directory
Roger Cooke

THE previous two seasons had shown the last game of the season to be a 'nail-biting' experience for the Club. The 1991-92 campaign proved to be different. Once again the Cherries fate was decided by other teams results.

'If' Stockport County lost at home to Birmingham or 'if' Peterborough United lost to Brentford by three clear goals, the club would be in the play-offs for a place in the new first division. Of course they also needed to win at Hartlepool – unfortunately none of these things happened, leaving AFC Bournemouth to contest another year in the lower division.

The season started in a disappointing fashion, a home defeat by Darlington 1-2, who ironically ended up at the foot of the table. So much was expected by the home supporters after the acquisition of new recruits such as Jimmy Case, Jimmy Quinn, Vince Bartram, Mark Morris and Steve Baker. Poor home form and a mixture of niggling injuries kept the Cherries in a mid-table position by the New Year.

Although they had lost narrowly to Middlesbrough by the odd goal in the Rumbelows Cup, the success in the F.A. Cup seemed to help the club's league position in 1992. Exciting wins against Bromsgrove Rovers, Brentford and Newcastle (a penalty shoot-out epic!) finally ended in the F.A. Cup 4th Round at Ipswich Town, losing 3-0. It has to be said that both Ipswich and Middlesbrough went on to gain promotion to the Premier League so the Cherries were not disgraced in anyway.

Jimmy Quinn must be congratulated on scoring 24 goals in his first season with the club, and 'veteran' Kevin Bond was named 'Player of the Year'.

Out of contract players, Jimmy Case, Kevin Bond and Sean O'Driscoll were reluctantly released by the club.

In June, long serving manager, Harry Redknapp, resigned his position and team coach Tony Pulis was immediately promoted to the manager's position.

Roger Cooke

Back row L-R: Sean O'Driscoll (Player/Community Officer), David Morris, Paul Wood, Scott Mean, Brian McGorry, Neil Masters, Denny Mundee, Peter Scott, Paul Mitchell, Mick Newman (Physio). **Middle:** Ken Sullivan (Youth trainer), Adrian Pennock, Efan Ekoku, Alex Watson, Steven Fletcher, Sammy Bibbo, Vince Bartram, Mark Morris, Paul Morrell, Peter Shearer, Brett Phillips, Mike Trusson (Youth Manager). **Front:** Richard Cooke, Shaun Brooks, Keith Rowland, David Williams (Asst. Manager/Coach), Tony Pullis (Manager), John Kirk (Trainer), Danny Holmes, Paul Smith, David Puckett (now at Woking), Matthew Lovell.

BOURNEMOUTH

DIVISION THREE: 8th   **FA CUP:** 4th RND   **RUMBELOWS CUP:** 2nd RND   **AUTOGLASS:** Prelim.

M	DATE		COMP.	VEN	OPPONENTS	RESULT		H/T	LGE POS	GOALSCORERS/GOAL TIMES	ATTEN-DANCE
1	A	17	BL	H	Darlington	L	1-2	0-0		Morris 84	6,210
2		21	RC 1/1	A	Cardiff City	L	2-3	1-1		Morrell 25, Cooke 74	(3,439)
3		24	BL	A	Stoke City	D	1-1	1-1		Quinn 42	(10,011)
4		27	RC 1/2	H	Cardiff City	W	4-1	1-1		Jones 17, 80, Quinn 60, Watson 75	4,292
5		31	BL	H	Hull City	D	0-0	0-0	19		5,015
6	S	3	BL	A	Preston North End	D	2-2	1-0	20	Holmes 18, Case 88	(3,170)
7		7	BL	A	Chester City	W	1-0	0-0	13	O'Driscoll 73	(1,117)
8		14	BL	H	Bolton Wanderers	L	1-2	0-1	19	Quinn 88	5,690
9		17	BL	H	Shrewsbury Town	W	1-0	0-0	12	Morris 56	4,454
10		21	BL	H	Huddersfield Town	D	0-0	0-0	13		6,802
11		24	RC 2/1	A	Middlesbrough	D	1-1	0-0		Lawrence 90	(10,577)
12		27	BL	H	Fulham	D	0-0	0-0	13		6,450
13	O	5	BL	A	Reading	D	0-0	0-0	14		(4,033)
14		8	RC 2/2	H	Middlesbrough	L	†1-2	0-0		Quinn 74	5,528
15		12	BL	H	Hartlepool United	W	2-0	1-0	11	Holmes 19, Quinn 89	4,817
16		19	BL	A	Leyton Orient	D	1-1	1-0	12	Quinn 33	(3,878)
17		22	AGT Pre	H	Swansea City	W	3-0	2-0		Wood 10, 15, McGorry 81	1,814
18		26	BL	H	Bradford City	L	1-3	0-1	15	Quinn 77	4,445
19	N	1	BL	H	Stockport County	W	1-0	0-0	13	Morris 53	4,649
20		6	BL	A	Torquay United	L	0-1	0-0	15		(1,884)
21		8	BL	A	Swansea City	L	1-3	0-1	16	Quinn 89	(2,698)
22		16	FAC 1	H	Bromsgrove Rovers	W	3-1	0-1		Bond 62, Mundee 65, 80	4,301
23		22	BL	H	Brentford	D	0-0	0-0	16		6,035
24		30	BL	A	Bury	W	1-0	1-0	13	Mundee 25	(1,886)
25	D	7	FAC 2	H	Brentford	W	2-1	0-0		Quinn 71, 89	6,538
26		10	AGT Pre	A	Cardiff City	D	3-3	2-3		Mundee 25, Ekoku 36, Quinn 51	(1,337)
27		14	BL	H	Birmingham City	W	2-1	1-0	10	Wood 54, Quinn 73	6,048
28		21	BL	H	Stoke City	L	1-2	1-1	12	Wood 5	5,436
29		26	BL	A	Hull City	W	1-0	0-0	10	Quinn 53	(4,741)
30		28	BL	A	Darlington	D	0-0	0-0	10		(3,172)
31	J	1	BL	H	Preston North End	W	1-0	0-0	10	Wood 5	5,508
32		4	FAC 3	H	Newcastle United	D	0-0	0-0			10,639
33		11	BL	A	West Bromwich A.	L	0-4	0-1	12		(10,932)
34		18	BL	H	Wigan Athletic	W	3-0	0-0	11	Bond 63, Wood 64, Quinn 84	4,338
35		22	FAC 3R	A	Newcastle United	D	†2-2	0-1		Wood 79, Bond 112 (Won 6-5 on pens)	(25,954)
36	F	1	BL	H	Leyton Orient	L	0-1	0-1	12		6,544
37		5	FAC 4	A	Ipswich Town	L	0-3	0-2			(17,163)
38		8	BL	A	Bradford City	L	1-3	0-1	12	Quinn 62	(5,820)
39		11	BL	H	Bury	W	4-0	1-0	11	Quinn 19, Mundee 58, Ekoku 73, 80	3,558
40		15	BL	A	Birmingham City	W	1-0	0-0	10	Quinn 69	(10,898)
41		22	BL	H	West Bromwich A.	W	2-1	1-0	9	Wood 33, Ekoku 89	7,721
42		29	BL	A	Exeter City	W	3-0	1-0	9	Quinn 30, 66, Morrell 77	(4,538)
43	M	3	BL	A	Wigan Athletic	L	0-2	0-1	9		(1,790)
44		7	BL	H	Peterborough Utd	L	1-2	1-1	9	Shearer 1	5,379
45		10	BL	H	Torquay United	W	2-1	2-0	9	Quinn 12, Ekoku 25	4,083
46		13	BL	A	Stockport County	L	0-5	0-3	10		(3,576)
47		20	BL	H	Swansea City	W	3-0	2-0	8	Ekoku 35, 43	4,358
48		24	BL	H	Exeter City	W	1-0	0-0	8	Quinn 32	4,959
49		29	BL	A	Brentford	D	2-2	0-1	9	Holmes 57, Ekoku 86	(7,605)
50		31	BL	H	Bolton Wanderers	W	2-0	1-0	9	Ekoku 17, Wood 51	(4,905)
51	A	3	BL	H	Chester City	W	2-0	1-0	7	Wood 29, Ekoku 89	5,974
52		8	BL	A	Peterborough Utd	L	0-2	0-2	8		(4,910)
53		11	BL	A	Shrewsbury Town	W	2-1	0-1	6	Quinn 46, Ekoku 75	(2,586)
54		14	BL	H	Huddersfield Town	D	1-1	1-0	6	Wood 42	7,655
55		20	BL	A	Fulham	L	0-2	0-0	6		(7,619)
56		25	BL	H	Reading	W	3-2	1-1	6	Quinn 26, 90, Ekoku 50	6,442
57	M	2	BL	A	Hartlepool United	L	0-1	0-0	8		(2,612)

Best Home League Attendance: 7,721 v West Bromwich A.   **Smallest: 3,558 v Bury**   Av Home Att: 5,468

Goal Scorers: Compared with 90-91: -548

League (51):	Quinn 19, Ekoku 11, Wood 8, Holmes 3, Morris 3, Mundee 2, Shearer, Case, O'Driscoll, Morrell, Bond
R/lows C (8):	Jones 2, Quinn 2, Cooke, Morrell, Lawrence, Watson
FA Cup (7):	Mundee 2, Bond 2, Quinn 2, Wood
Autoglass (6):	Wood 2, Quinn, McGorry, Ekoku, Mundee

† = After extra-time

Bartram V.	Baker S.	Morrell P.	Morris M.	Watson A.	O'Driscoll S.	Cooke R.	Jones A.	Quinn J.	Case J.	Holmes J.	Rowlands K.	Mundee D.	Bond K.	Lawrence G.	Fereday W.	Mitchell P.	Wood P.	McGorry B.	Masters	Pulis	Statham B.	Ekoku E.	Brooks S.	Shearer P.	Puckett D.	Referee	
1	2	3	4	5	6•	7	8	9*	10	11	12	14														R Pawley	1
1	2	3	5	4	6	14	8	9	10	11	7*	S														D Shadwell	2
1	2	3	4	5	6	12	8*	9	10	11*		14	7													S Bell	3
1	2	3	4	5	6			8	9	10	11	S	7	S												J Moules	4
1	7	3*	4	5	6	12	8	9	10	11•		14	2													G Ashby	5
1	2	3	4	5	6	12	8*	9	10	11		14			7*											K Redfearn	6
1	7	3	4	5	6		8	9	10	11•		14		12		2*										J Brandwood	7
1		3	4	5	6	14	8*	9	10	11•		12	2	7												G Willard	8
1			4	5	6	S	12	9	10†	11	3	8	2	7*												R Wiseman	9
1			4	5	6	7*	S	9	10	11	3	8	2	12												N Midgley	10
1			4	5	6	7*		9	10	11•	3	8	2	12	14											J Key	11
1			4	5	6*	7		9	10	11	3	8	2•	12	14											P Scoble	12
1	14		4	5	6	S		9		11•	3	8	2				7	10								I Borrett	13
1			4	5	6	7•		9		11	3	12	2		14		8	10*								R Hamer	14
1			4	5	6	10		9		11•	3	8	2		S		7	12								D Axcell	15
1			4		6	7•		9	10	11	3	5	2		S		8	14								R Bigger	16
1			4		2	7		9•	10	11*	3	5			14	12	8	6								M Pierce	17
1			4		5	7		9	10	11*	3	12	2		S		8	6								G Pooley	18
1			4		5	S		9	10	11	3	2			7		8	6	S							B Hill	19
1			4		6	S		9	10	11	3	5	2		7*		8	12								J Griffiths	20
1			4		5	12		9	10	11*	3	7•	2		14		8	6								P Vanes	21
1					5	6		9	10	11	3	7	2		4*		8	12	S							G Willard	22
1			4		6	S		9	10	11	3	7	2				8	S			5					M Bodenham	23
1			4		6	S		9	10	11	3	7*	2				8				5	12				G Courtney	24
1			4		6	12		9	10	11*	3	5	2				8•	14				7				A Gunn	25
1			4		6	10		9		11	3	5	2		12	S	8				5	7*				G Singh	26
1			4		6	12		9	10	11	3	5	2				8	S				7*				T Holbrook	27
1			4		6	7		9	10	11*	3	5	2	12		14	8•									W Flood	28
1			4		6	12		9	10	11	3	5	2				8•					14	7*			R Shepherd	29
1			4		6			9	10	11*	3	5	2				8	S				12	7			J Kirby	30
1			4		6	12		9*	10	14	3	5	2				8					7•	11			A Gunn	31
1			4		6	12•		9*	10	14	3	5	2				8					11	7			V Callow	32
1			4		6				10	11*	3	5	2	12			8†		S			9	7			D Elleray	33
1			4		12	S		9	10	6	3	5	2				8					11	7*			D Axcell	34
1			4		6	12		9	10•	7*	3	5	2				8					11	14			V Callow	35
1	14		4		6	12		9	10	8*	3	5	2				8					11•	7			P Scoble	36
1		14	4		6			9	10	12	3	5†	2				8					11*	7•			K Barratt	37
1		3	4		6	12		9	10*	14	7	5	2				8					11				R Lewis	38
1		5	4		6	7		9		10	3	11	2*				8					12	14			A Ward	39
1		5			6	7		9	12	10•	3	4	2*				8					11				R Poulain	40
1		5	4		6	7			10*	11	3		2	14•		12	8					9				P Don	41
1		5	4		10	7*		9		6	3	14	2				8					11•		12		K Cooper	42
1		5	4			7		9		6	3	2				14	8*	12				11		10•		K Redfearn	43
1		5*	4			7		9		6	3	8	2				S					11	10	12		R Groves	44
1		4			10	7*		9	12	6	3	2		5			8					11			S	P Alcock	45
1		4			6			9*	10•	7	3	2		5			8		14			11			12	K Lupton	46
1		5	4			12		S	9	10	6	3	2				8					11		7*		M Bailey	47
1		5	4			12		7*	9	10	6	3	2				8					11		S		A Buksh	48
1		5	4			7		12	9	10	6*	3	2	S			8					11				G Pooley	49
1		3	4		5	7*		9	10	6	14	12	2				8					11•				P Wright	50
1		3	4		5	7*		9	10	6	S	12	2				8					11				M James	51
1		3	4†		5			9	10	6	12	3	2*				8					11	7			P Taylor	52
1		3	4	5	2			9	10	6	S	14					8•					11		7		R Nixon	53
1		3	4	5	2	7*		9		10•	12	14					8					11		9•	14	R Pawley	54
1		3	4	5	2	7*		9		10•	12		14				8					11		6		P Foakes	55
1			5		12	7*		9		10*	6	3	2	4			8					11		S		M Pierce	56
1		5			2	7*		9		10*	6	3	14	4			8					11		12		C Trussell	57
46	5	23	43	15	40	20	6	43	38	43	34	28	38	2	3	1	35	4			2	24	6	6	1	League Appearances	
	1	1	4		4	11	1		2	3	3	13		6	2	4		4		1		4	1	2	3	Substitute Appearances	
4	2	2	4	4	4	2+1	2	4	3	4	3	1+1	3	0+1	0+2		1	1								R/lows Appearances	
5		0+1	4		5	1+3		5	5	3+2	5	5	5		1		5	0+2				4	2+1			FA Cup Appearances	
2		2		2	2	2		2	1	2	2	2				0+1	1	2			1	1				Autoglass Appearances	

†=Sent Off

AFC BOURNEMOUTH

Club Colours: Red shirts with white 'V' shaped & reverse 'V' shaped 3" pattern, black shorts and socks
Change Colours: Purple shirts with green & navy 'V' shaped & reverse 'V' shaped 3" pattern, white shorts and socks
Reserves League: Clifton Stockbrokers League

Previous League: Southern
Previous Name: Boscombe St. Johns 1899; Boscombe FC 1899-1923; Bournemouth & Boscombe AFC 1923-72
Previous Managers: Harry Kinghorn 1920-25 Leslie Knighton 1925-28 Frank Richards 1928-30 Billy Birrell 1930-35 Bob
Crompton 1935-36 Charles Bell 1936-39 Harry Kinghorn 1939-47 Harry Lowe 1947-50 Jack Bruton 1950-56 Freddie Cox
1956-58 Don Welsh 1958-61 Bill McGarry 1961-63 Reg Flewin 1963-65 Freddie Cox 1965-70 John Bond 1970-73 Trevor
Hartley 1973-75 John Benson 1975-79 Alec Stock 1979-1980 Dave Webb 1980-82 Don Megson 1982 Harry Redknapp 1983-
92 Tony Pulis 1992-
Honours: Division 3 Champions 1986-87   Associate Members Cup 1983-84
League Career: Elected to Div 3S 1923 Transferred to Div 3 1957-58 Relegated to Div 4 1969-70
Promoted to Div 3 1970-71 Relegated to Div 4 1974-75 Promoted to Div 3 1981-82 Promoted to Div 2 1986-87
Relegated to Div 3 1989-90

CLUB RECORDS

Most Appearances for Club: Ray Bumstead, 460+2 (League 412+2, FA Cup 26, League Cup 22) 1958-70
Most Capped Player: Colin Clarke (N. Ireland) 6 Gerry Peyton (Eire) 6
Record Goalscorer in a Match: Ted MacDougall, 9 v Margate, FA Cup Rnd 1, (11-0), 20.11.1971 (All time FA Cup record)
Record League Goalscorer in a Season: Ted MacDougall, 42, 1970-71 **In All Competitions:** Ted MacDougall, 49 (League 42, FA
Cup 7) 1970-71
Record League Goalscorer in a Career: Ron Eyre, 227 (League 202, FA Cup 25) 1924-33
Record Transfer Fee Received: £750,000 from Manchester City for Ian Bishop, July 1989
Record Transfer Fee Paid: £300,000 to Manchester City for Paul Moulden, July 1989
Best Performances: League: 1988-89: 12th Div 2 **FA Cup:** 6th rnd. 1956-57 **League Cup:** 4th rnd, 1961-62, 1963-64
Most League Points: (3pts a win) 97, Division 3, 1986-87 (2pts a win) 62, Division 3, 1971-72
Record League Victory and Most Goals Scored in a League Match: 7-0 v Swindon Town, Div 3(S), 22.9.1956
Most Goals Scored in a Cup Tie: 11-0 v Margate, FA Cup, 20.11.1971
Record League Defeat: 0-9 v Lincoln, Div 3, 1.12.1982
Record Cup Defeat: 0-7 v Burnley, Rnd 3 Replay, 1965-66 0-7 v Sheffield Wednesday, Round 4, 1931-32
Oldest Player in a League Match: Harry Kinghorn, 48 years v Brentford, 11.3.1929
Youngest Player in a League Match: Jimmy White, 15 years v Brentford, 30.4.1958

LONGEST RUNS	
of undefeated matches: 18 (1982)	of league matches without a win: 14 (1973-74)
of undefeated home matches: 33 (1962-63)	of undefeated away matches: 13 (1961)
without home win: 10 (1931-32)	without an away win: 26 (1976-77)
of league wins: 7 (1970)	of home wins: 12 (1968, 1971)
of league defeats: 7 (1955)	of away wins: 5 (1948)

AFC BOURNEMOUTH

PLAYERS NAME Honours	Ht	Wt	Birthdate	Birthplace Transfers	Contract Date	Clubs	League	L/Cup	FA Cup	Other	Lg	L/C	FAC	Oth
GOALKEEPERS														
Vince Bartram	6.2	13.4	07.08.68	Birmingham	17.08.85	Wolves (A)	5	2	3					
				Loan	27.10.89	Blackpool	9			2				
				Loan	20.02.91	West Brom A								
				£65,000	24.07.91	Bournemouth	46	4	5	2				
DEFENDERS														
Paul Mitchell	5.10	12.0	20.10.71	Bournemouth	07.08.89	Bournemouth (T)	3+4			0+1				
Mark J Morris	6.1	13.8	26.09.62	Morden	12.10.81	Wimbledon (A)	167+1	11	11	1+1	9			
Div4'83				Loan	05.09.85	Aldershot	14		1					
				£35,000	21.07.87	Watford	41	5	7		1	1		
				£175,000	11.07.89	Sheffield Utd	53+3	5	5	2	3			
				£100,000	31.07.91	Bournemouth	43	4	4	2	3			
Denny Mundee	5.10	11.0	10.10.68	Swindon	03.04.85	Q.P.R. (A)								
					21.08.86	Swindon Town								
					04.04.89	Bournemouth	53+21	3+1	5+1	2+1	4		2	1
				Loan		Yeovil Town			3					
				Loan		Weymouth								
				Loan	07.08.89	Torquay Utd	9							
Alec Watson	6.0	11.9	05.04.68	Liverpool	18.05.85	Liverpool (A)	3+1	1+1	1+1	1				
E:Y.4,CS'88				Loan	30.08.90	Derby County	5							
				£150,000	18.01.91	Bournemouth	38	4	1		3	1		
MIDFIELD														
Shaun Brooks	5.7	11.0	09.10.62	London	16.10.79	Crystal Palace	47+7	5+2	5		4	1		
E:Y,S,Y7					17.10.83	Leyton Orient	140+8	10	12	7+3	26	1	4	1
					22.06.87	Bournemouth	114+14	12	4+1	3	13		1	
Matthew J Holmes	5.7	10.7	01.08.69	Luton	23.09.88	Bournemouth								
					19.12.88	Bournemouth	105+9	7	8+2	4	8			
				Loan	23.03.89	Cardiff City	0+1							
Paul Morrell	5.11	13.5	23.03.61	Poole		Poole Town								
AMC'84; Div3'87				£3,000		Bath City								
						Weymouth			5					
					01.06.83	Bournemouth	317+5	24	25+1	19	8	1	1	1
Keith Rowland	5.10	10.0	01.09.71	Portadown	02.10.89	Bournemouth (T)	34+3	3	5	2				
				Loan	01.08.90	Farnborough T.			1					
Peter Shearer	6.0	11.6	04.02.67	Birmingham		Birmingham City	2+2	1				1		
ESP.1						Rochdale	1	1				2		
						Nuneaton Boro			1					
						Cheltenham Town								
				£18,000	09.03.89	Bournemouth	42+9	6	1	0+1	6	1		1
FORWARDS														
Richard Cooke	5.6	9.0	04.09.65	Islington	18.05.83	Tottenham H. (A)	9+2	1+1	1	1+4	2			
E:u21.1,u19.6,Y.8,Div3'87				Loan	18.09.86	Birmingham City	5			1				
					23.01.87	Bournemouth	63+9	6+2	4+1	2+1	16	3	1	1
				£140,000	23.03.89	Luton Town	3+14			1+1	1			
				Free	28.03.91	Bournemouth	30+11	2+1	1+3	2	2	1		
Efan Ekoku	6.1	12.0	08.06.67	Manchester		Sutton Utd			1					
				£100,000	11.05.90	Bournemouth	29+19	0+2	4+2	1+1	14		1	1
Steven M Fletcher			26.06.72	Hartlepool	23.06.90	Hartlepool Utd. (T)	19+13	0+2	0+2	3+2	4	1		1
				£30,000	28.07.92	Bournemouth								
David Puckett	5.7	10.5	29.10.60	Southampton	01.11.78	Southampton (A)	52+43	5+7	2+1	1+2	14	2		
Div3'87					17.07.86	Bournemouth	29+6	4	2+1	2	14		3	
				Loan	01.03.88	Stoke City	7							
				Loan	23.11.88	Swansea City	7+1		0+1	2	3			
				£25,000	26.01.89	Aldershot	113	6	5	6	50	6	2	1
				Free	05.03.92	Bournemouth	1+3							
Paul A Wood	5.9	10.1	01.11.64	Middlesbrough	03.11.82	Portsmouth (A)	25+22	5+3	2	2+2	6	1		3
				£40,000	28.08.87	Brighton & H.A	77+15	4	2+2	5	8			
				£90,000	09.02.90	Sheffield Utd	16+8	1		1	3			
				Loan	31.01.91	Bournemouth	20+1							
				£40,000	03.10.91	Bournemouth	35	1	5	1	8		1	2
ADDITIONAL CONTRACT PLAYERS														
Richard Hill					18.10.90	Bournemouth								
Brian McGorry	5.10	11.0	16.04.70	Liverpool		Weymouth								
				£30,000	13.08.91	Bournemouth	4+4	1	0+2	2				1

LEADING LEAGUE GOALSCORERS SEASONS 1985-86 – 1991-92

1985-86	**COLIN CLARKE**	**16**		1986-87	**CARL RICHARDS**	**12**
1987-88	**TREVOR AYLOTT**	**9**		1988-89	**LUTHER BLISSETT**	**18**
1989-90	**LUTHER BLISSETT**	**18**		1990-91	**LUTHER BLISSETT**	**19**

1991-92   **JIMMY QUINN**   **19**

DEAN COURT GROUND Bournemouth, Dorset BH7 7AF

Capacity: **Covered Standing:**   **Seating:**

Tel: Ground: 0202 395381   **Ticket Sales:** As ground number   **Clubcall:** 0898 12 11 63

All premium rate calls (0898/0891) cost 36p per minute cheap rate and 48p per minute at all other times. Call costings correct at time of going to press.

GROUNDS
Castleman Road, Pokedown 1899-1910; Dean Court 1910-

ATTENDANCES
Highest: 28,799 v Manchester United, FA Cup 6th Round, 2.3.1957

Lowest: 1,482 v Cardiff City, Freight Rover Trophy, 6.1.1987

RECORD RECEIPTS (with previous records):
£33,723 v Manchester United, FA Cup, 7.1.1984
£24,145 v Portsmouth, Division 3, 26.2.1983
£15,466 v Portsmouth, Division 4, 2.10.1979
£9,525 v Portsmouth, Division 4, 29.9.1978
£7,326 v Brighton & H.A., Division 3, 1.4.1972

Season Tickets:
Stands: from £160 to £180, juv/OAP £105
Ground: £100, juv/OAP £60

Executive Box Season Tickets: None

Cost of Stand Tickets: Seats: £7 to £9
Terraces: £5, juv/OAP £3

Match and Ticket Information: Phone number above

Car Parking: Parking for 1,500 cars

Nearest Railway Station: Bournemouth. Tel: 0202 558216

How to get to the ground

From North and East: A338 to roundabout junction with A3060. Take second exit then first from next roundabout into Littledown Avenue. Turn right into Thistlebarrow Road for Dean Court.

From West: A3049 to Bournemouth. In 2 miles after lights at Wallisdown turn left into Talbot Road. Take first exit from roundabout into Queens Park South Drive, then second exit from next roundabout into Littledown Avenue. Turn right into Thistlebarrow Road for Dean Court.

Value Rating: ★ ★ ★ ★

Programme Editor: Archway Panbourne

Price of 1992-93 Programme: £1
Number of Pages: 32
Subscriptions: £32

Local Newspapers: Evening Echo

Local Radio Stations: Two Counties Radio, BBC Radio Solent

BRADFORD CITY   Division 2

Formed: 1903   **Turned Professional:** 1903   **Ltd Co:** 1908

SPONSORED BY: Freemans Plc   **NICKNAME:** The Bantams

Chairman
Dave Simpson

Vice-Chairman
D Thompson, FCA

Directors
T Goddard, FCCA
D Taylor, FCA
M Woodhead

Associate Directors
P Brearley
M Scott
M Smith
H Williams

Secretary
Terry Newman (0274 306062)

Manager
Frank Stapleton

Assistant Manager
Stuart Pearson

Coach
Steve Smith

Physiotherapist
Bryan Edwards

Stadium Manager
Allan Gilliver

Commercial Manager
Russell Gaunt (0274 306062)

Lottery and Promotions Manager
Russell Gaunt (0274 306062)

Doctor
Andrew Henderson

Club Statistician for the Directory
T Frost

IF only Bradford City's season could have begun in January 1992 instead of August 1991!

Such had been the transformation in the Bantams playing fortunes since the turn of the year, their supporters had become optimistic about a genuine promotion challenge next term. For them the season had ended prematurely, for despite a final game defeat at Fulham, they had seen their team overturn the threat of relegation to finish in a respectable 16th place in Division Three, following an impressive late surge that featured a nine match unbeaten run.

Had their League programme not included 19 draws – just one less than the club record – then Bradford City could have been contesting the promotion play-offs with the likes of Peterborough United and Stockport County, both of whom were Valley Parade victims in the final two months of the season.

Bradford City were languishing in 20th position, and had already been dismissed from the Rumbelows and F.A. Cup competitions, when Frank Stapleton was recruited from Huddersfield Town, on 9th December, to become their player/manager.

However, the union with Colin Todd – who arrived as his assistant a month later, via Middlesbrough – proved to be the catalyst the Bradford City board had been hoping for since gambling on the appointment of the ex-Arsenal, Manchester United and Republic of Ireland striker to his first managerial post.

The former international duo not only won over the fans with a style of entertaining football that was in direct contrast to that of their predecessors, John Docherty and Leighton James – the latter of whom acted as caretaker for a brief spell – but also tightened up the team's defensive frailties.

In just five months, a sieve-like defence which, in November, had leaked six goals against Swansea City, had become so uncharitable that the Bantams were to suffer only six defeats in the 28 matches under Stapleton's control.

During that period, however, Bradford City enjoyed a 4-3 success at champions-elect, Brentford, which was to prove the turning point of their season. It coincided with a return to scoring form of Sean McCarthy who, despite being out of the team through injury for the first three months of the season, finished as the club's top scorer for the second successive occasion. His 17-goal haul – made all the more important in view of the mid-season loss of in-form Brian Tinnion with a knee problem – included a run of ten in seven matches.

The advent of youngsters like Michael McHugh, Jeremy Howe and goalscoring debutant, Dean Richards, coupled with the continued progress of Steve Torpey and Paul Jewell, and the cultured play of veteran Bradford City newcomer Gary Williams, auger well for the future, but with the added disappointment of a breakdown in talks concerning ground sharing with Bradford Northern Rugby Football Club, it remains to be seen whether Frank Stapleton and Co. can achieve the expected promotion under the kind of financial constraints that has become synonymous with today's game.

Terry Frost

Back row L-R: Lee Margerison, Dean Richards, Stephen Torpey, Noel Blake, Scott Bairstow, Brian Tinnion, Sean McCarthy. **Middle row:** Steve Smith (Youth Development Officer), Andy Hanson (Chief Scout), Stuart Pearson (Asst. Manager), Paul West, Michael McHugh, Paul Tomlinson, Chris Pearce, Gary Williams, Paul Coy, Craig Lawford, Frank Stapleton (Manager), Bryan Edwards (Physio). **Front row:** Paul Reid, Paul Jewell, Scott Partridge, Gavin Oliver, Jeremy Howe, Lee Duxbury, Mike Duxbury.

BRADFORD CITY

DIVISION THREE: 16th   **FA CUP:** 2nd RND   **RUMBELOWS CUP:** 2nd RND   **AUTOGLASS:** Prelim.

M	DATE	COMP.	VEN	OPPONENTS	RESULT	H/T	LGE POS	GOALSCORERS/GOAL TIMES	ATTEN-DANCE
1	A 17	BL	H	Stoke City	W 1-0	1-0		Tinnion 17	7,556
2	20	RC 1/1	A	Stockport County	D 1-1	1-0		Tinnion (pen) 45	(3,834)
3	25	BL	A	Huddersfield Town	L 0-1	0-1	14		(9,234)
4	28	RC 1/2	H	Stockport County	W †3-1	1-0		Duxbury 44, 92, Stuart 107	3,806
5	31	BL	H	Hartlepool United	D 1-1	0-0	12	Tinnion (pen) 89	5,872
6	S 3	BL	A	Leyton Orient	D 1-1	0-1	13	Tinnion 83	(3,435)
7	7	BL	A	Preston North End	D 1-1	0-0	15	Stuart 64	(4,160)
8	14	BL	H	Chester City	D 1-1	0-1	15	Stuart 80	4,843
9	17	BL	H	Bolton Wanderers	D 4-4	0-1	14	Stuart 46, Babb 58, Torpey 63, Tinnion 85	5,669
10	21	BL	A	Reading	W 2-1	1-1	10	Babb 27, W Reid 64	(3,765)
11	24	RC 2/1	H	West Ham United	D 1-1	1-1		Leonard 5	7,034
12	28	BL	H	Shrewsbury Town	W 3-0	0-0	6	Torpey 57, 58, W Reid 85	5,324
13	O 5	BL	A	Stockport County	L 1-4	1-2	13	Tinnion (pen) 41	(5,825)
14	9	RC 2/2	A	West Ham United	L 0-4	0-2			(17,232)
15	12	BL	H	Fulham	L 3-4	1-3	16	Tinnion 30, 52, Babb 85	5,143
16	19	BL	H	Torquay United	W 2-0	0-0	10	Duxbury 51, Babb 77	4,543
17	22	AGT Pre	A	Hull City	L 1-2	1-2		Tinnion 23	(1,218)
18	26	BL	A	Bournemouth	W 3-1	1-0	9	Torpey 31, Richards 54, Tinnion 89	(4,445)
19	N 2	BL	H	Brentford	L 0-1	0-0	12		5,359
20	6	BL	A	Exeter City	L 0-1	0-0	13		(2,625)
21	9	BL	A	Peterborough Utd	L 1-2	0-1	13	D Robinson (og) 80	(9,224)
22	16	FAC 1	A	Bury	W 1-0	0-0		Tinnion 85	(3,805)
23	19	AGT Pre	H	Hartlepool United	D 3-3	2-2		Torpey 19, 29, McCarthy 66	1,562
24	23	BL	H	Swansea City	L 4-6	1-4	15	McCarthy 40, Duxbury 50, Torpey 55, 79	5,728
25	30	BL	A	Birmingham City	L 0-2	0-1	17		(10,468)
26	D 7	FAC 2	A	Bolton Wanderers	L 1-3	0-2		Tinnion 48	(7,129)
27	14	BL	H	West Bromwich A.	D 1-1	1-0	17	McCarthy 15	7,195
28	22	BL	H	Huddersfield Town	D 1-1	1-0	16	Jewell 6	10,050
29	26	BL	A	Hartlepool United	L 0-1	0-1	16		(5,412)
30	28	BL	A	Stoke City	D 0-0	0-0	16		(12,208)
31	J 1	BL	A	Leyton Orient	D 1-1	1-1	19	Jewell 39	6,810
32	4	BL	H	Bury	D 1-1	1-0	20	Torpey 22	6,354
33	11	BL	A	Wigan Athletic	L 1-2	1-2	21	Torpey 17	(2,548)
34	18	BL	H	Hull City	W 2-1	0-0	17	James (pen) 70, McCarthy 89	6,369
35	F 1	BL	A	Torquay United	D 1-1	0-1	18	McCarthy 46	(2,243)
36	8	BL	H	Bournemouth	W 3-1	1-0	17	McCarthy 45, 70, Jewell 60	5,820
37	11	BL	H	Birmingham City	L 1-2	0-1	18	W Reid 90	7,008
38	15	BL	A	West Bromwich A.	D 1-1	1-1	19	James (pen) 34	(12,607)
39	22	BL	H	Wigan Athletic	D 1-1	0-0	19	Johnson (og) 85	5,621
40	29	BL	A	Bury	W 1-0	0-0	17	Jewell 89	(2,983)
41	M 3	BL	A	Hull City	D 0-0	0-0	17		(4,244)
42	7	BL	H	Darlington	L 0-1	0-1	18		5,579
43	10	BL	H	Exeter City	D 1-1	0-0	19	Jewell 58	4,170
44	14	BL	A	Brentford	W 4-3	2-1	16	McCarthy 25, 61, Torpey 29, L Duxbury 72	(6,791)
45	21	BL	H	Peterborough Utd	W 2-1	2-0	15	McCarthy 6, James (pen) 20	6,896
46	28	BL	A	Swansea City	D 2-2	1-2	16	L Duxbury 30, Willis 76	(3,748)
47	31	BL	A	Chester City	D 0-0	0-0	16		(1,149)
48	A 4	BL	H	Preston North End	D 1-1	1-0	16	Jewell 22	6,044
49	7	BL	A	Darlington	W 3-1	2-1	15	McCarthy 30, 32, L Duxbury 83	(1,946)
50	11	BL	A	Bolton Wanderers	D 1-1	0-1	14	McCarthy 54	(4,892)
51	18	BL	H	Reading	W 1-0	0-0	13	McCarthy 60	5,492
52	21	BL	A	Shrewsbury Town	L 2-3	0-2	13	McCarthy 51, 63	(2,707)
53	25	BL	H	Stockport County	W 1-0	0-0	12	McCarthy 54	7,099
54	M 2	BL	A	Fulham	L 1-2	1-2	16	Torpey 8	(8,671)

Best Home League Attendance: 10,050 v Huddersfield Town   **Smallest: 4,170 v Exeter City**   **Av Home Att: 6,111**

Goal Scorers: **Compared with 90-91: -533**

League (62): McCarthy 16, Torpey 10, Tinnion 8 (2 pens), Jewell 6, L Duxbury 5, Babb 4, Stuart 3, James 3 (3 pens), W Reid 3, Opponents 2, Richards, Willis

R/lows C(5): L Duxbury 2, Tinnion (1 pen), Stuart, Leonard

FA Cup (2): Tinnion 2

Autoglass (4): Torpey 2, Tinnion, McCarthy   †=After extra-time

Tomlinson P.	Mitchell C.	Dowson A.	James R.	Oliver G.	Gardner S.	Babb P.	Duxbury M. (L)	Torpey S.	Tinnion B.	Stuart M.	Leonard M.	Reid W.	McHugh M.	Morgan D.	Howe J.	McCarthy S.	Richards D.	Jewell P.	Evans M.	Stapleton F.	Williams G.	Duxbury M.	Blake N.	Reid P.	Willis J.	Referee	
1	2	3	4	5	6	7	8	9	10	11	S															C Trussell	1
1	2	3	4	5	6	7	8	9	10	11	S															**T West**	2
1	2	3	4	5	6	7	8	9	10	11*	12	S														I Cruikshanks	3
1	2	3	4	5	6	7	8	9	10	11	S	S														**J Lloyd**	4
1	2	3	4	5	6	7*	8	9	10	11*		14		12												P Vanes	5
1	2	3	4	5	6	7	8	9	10	S	S	11														R Pawley	6
1	2	3	4	5	6	7	8	9				11	S	10		S										A Dawson	7
1	2*	3	4	5	6	7*	8	9				11	14	12	10											R Hart	8
1	2	3	4	5*	6	7	8	9*	10		12	14	11													A Wilkie	9
1	2	3	4		6	7*	8	9		11	12		5	10		S										C Wilkes	10
1	2	3	4		6	7	8	9	10	S			5	11		S										**R Nixon**	11
1	2	3	4		6	7	8	9	10	S	S		5	11		S										D Shadwell	12
1	2	3	4	6		S	7	8	9	10			5			S	11									R Hamer	13
1	2	3	4	5	6	7	8	9*	10		12			11*		14										**M James**	14
1	2	3	4	6		7	8	9	10			5*		11	S	12										G Courtney	15
1	2	3	4	5	S	7	8	9	10	11		6				S										J Rushton	16
1	2*	3	4	5•	6	7	8	9	10	14		11				12										**P Harrison**	17
1		3	4		6	7	8	9	10			11		2	S		5	S								G Pooley	18
1		3	4		6	7*	8	9	10•			11		2		14	5	12								J Parker	19
1		3*	4		6	7	8	9	10	12		11		2		2	S	5								K Cooper	20
1			4			7	8	9	10			11	6	2			5	S	3							L Dilkes	21
1		3	4		5	6	8	9	10			11	S	2			7		S							**T Holbrook**	22
	2	3	4			6	8	9	10	S		11					7	5	S	1						**A Flood**	23
1		3	4		5*	6	8	9	10	12		11		2•		7		14								K Lupton	24
1	2		4		5*	6	8	9	10			12		S		7	3	11								J Deakin	25
1	2		4			6	8	9	10	12	5			S		7	3*	11								**J Lloyd**	26
1	2	S	4			6	8	9	10	11	5			S		7		3								K Redfearn	27
1	2		4			6	8	9	10	S	5		S			7		11	3							V Callow	28
1	2		4			6	8	9	10*	12	5		14			7•		11	3							A Wilkie	29
1	2					6	8	9		S	5	10	S			7		11		4	3					K Barratt	30
1	2					6	8	9		S	5	10	12			7		11		4	3*					J Worrall	31
1	2					6	8	9		S	5	10	S			7		11		4	3					J Watson	32
1	S		2			6	7*	9			5	12	10					11		4	3	8				G Ashby	33
	S		2			6	7	9*			5	4				10		11	1	12	3	8				G Singh	34
1			2			6	7	S			5	4	S			10		11		9	3	8				J Carter	35
1			2			6	7				5*	4	14		9•	10		11		12	3	8				R Lewis	36
1			2			6	7				4	14		9•	10	12	11		5	3*	8					R Nixon	37
1			2			6	7	12			9	4*				10	S	11		5	3	8				R Groves	38
1	8*	14	2			6	7	12				4*				10	5	11		9	3					R Bigger	39
1	S		2			6	7	8		S			4			10		11		9	3		5			D Gallagher	40
1	S		2			6	7	8*		12			4			10		11		9	3		5			M Bailey	41
1	S		2			6	7	8		4						10*	12	11		9	3		5			A Flood	42
1	S		2			6	7	8		4						10	S	11		9	3		5			T West	43
1	12		2			6	7	8		4*						10	S	11		9	3		5			P Foakes	44
1	S		2			6	7	8					S			10		9		3	4	5		11		T Fitzharris	45
1			2			6	7	8	S				S			10		9		3	4		11	5		K Cooper	46
1			2			6	7	8	12				S			10		9		3	4	11*	5*			J Parker	47
1	S		2			6	7	8	12							10		9		3	4	11*	5			T Holbrook	48
1			2			6	7	8	12							9		10*		S	3	4	11	5		W Burns	49
1			2			6	7	8	12							9		10		3	4		11	5*		J Rushton	50
1			2			6	7*	8	12							9		10		3	4		11	5		A Dawson	51
1			2			6	7	8	11							9		10		3	4			5		I Hendrick	52
1			2			6	7	8					S			9		10		11	3	4		5		I Cruikshanks	53
1	S		2			6	7	8					12			9		10		11*	3	4		5		M Bailey	54
45	20	16	43	10	14	46	46	41	21	9	15	17	5	9	3	27	5	28	1	25	22	16	6	7	9	League Appearances	
	2							2	5	7	4	2	4	2		1		2		2	2	2				Substitute Appearances	
4	4	4	4	3	4	4	4	4	4	2	1+1	1				1		0+1								R/lows Appearances	
2	1	1	2		1	2	2	2	2	0+1	1	1				1		2		1	1					FA Cup Appearances	
2	2	1	2		1	2	2	2	2	0+1	0	2				1		1		1	1					Autoglass Appearances	

Also Played: Posn.(Game): Treacy S(1), McGinley S(2), Lawford S(21), Margerison S(50,51,52,53)
Players on Loan: Noel Blake (Stoke City), Paul Reid (Leicester City), Jimmy Willis (Leicester City)

BRADFORD CITY (1983) LTD

Club Colours: Amber/claret stripes, claret shorts, amber stockings
Change Colours: White shirts, white shorts, white stockings
Reserves League: Pontins Central League Division 2

Previous League: None (One of only two clubs to gain admission to Football League without playing a senior fixture – Chelsea being the other)
Previous Name: None
Previous Managers: Robert Campbell 1903-05 Peter O'Rourke 1905-21 David Menzies 1921-26 Colin Veitch 1926-28 Peter O'Rourke 1928-30 Jack Peart 1930-35 Richard Ray 1935-38 Fred Westgarth 1938-43 Robert Sharp (Hon.) 1943-46 Jack Barker 1946-47 John Milburn 1947-48 David Steele 1948-52 Albert Harris (Hon.) 1952 Ivor Powell 1952-55 Peter Jackson Snr. 1955-61 Robert Brocklebank 1961-64 William Harris 1965-66 William Watson 1966-68 Grenville Hair 1968 Jimmy Wheeler 1968-71 Bryan Edwards 1971-75 Robert Kennedy 1975-78 John Napier 1978 George Mulhall 1978-81 Roy McFarland 1981-82 Trevor Cherry 1982-87 Terry Dolan 1987-89 Terry Yorath 1989-90 John Docherty 1990-91 Frank Stapleton 1991-
Honours: Champions Div 2 1907-08; Champions Div 3 1984-85; Champions Div 3N 1928-29; FA Cup Winners 1911; Div 3N Cup 1939
League Career: Elected to Div 2 1903   Promoted to Div 1 1908   Relegated to Div 2 1922   Relegated to Div 3N 1927   Promoted to Div 2 1929   Relegated to Div 3N 1937   Transferred to Div 3 1958   Relegated to Div 4 1961   Promoted to Div 3 1969   Relegated to Div 4 1972   Promoted to Div 3 1977   Relegated to Div 4 1978   Promoted to Div 3 1982   Promoted to Div 2 1985   Relegated to Div 3 1990

CLUB RECORDS

Most Appearances for Club: Cyril 'Cec' Podd, 1970-84: League 494 + 8, FA Cup 30, League Cup 33 + 1, Others 8. **Total 574**
Most Capped Player: Harry Hampton, 9, N. Ireland   England: Evelyn Lintott, 4
Record Goalscorer in a Match: Albert Whitehurst, 7 v Tranmere Rovers, 8-0, Div 3N, 6.3.1929
Record League Goalscorer in a Season: David Layne, 34   **In All Competitions:** David Layne, 36 (League 34, F.A. Cup 2), Div 4, 1961-62
Record League Goalscorer in a Career: Bobby Campbell, 121, 1979-87   **In All Competitions:** Bobby Campbell, 143 (League 121, FA Cup 5, League Cup 11, Others 6), 1979-87
Record Transfer Fee Received: £875,000 from Everton for Stuart McCall, June 1988
Record Transfer Fee Paid: £290,000 to Newcastle Utd for Peter Jackson, September 1988
Best Performances: League: 5th in Div 1, 1910-11   **FA Cup:** Winners 1911   **League Cup:** 5th Round, 1964-65, 1987-88, 1988-89
Most League Points: (3pts a win) 94, Division 3, 1984-85   (2pts a win) 63, Division 3(N), 1928-29
Record League Victory and Most Goals Scored in a League Match: 11-1 v Rotherham United, Division 3N, 25.8.1928
Most Goals Scored in a Cup Tie: 11-3 v Walker Celtic, FA Cup Rnd 1 Replay, 1.12.1937
Record League Defeat: 0-8 v Manchester City, Div 2, 7.5.1927, 1-9 v Colchester Utd, Div 4, 30.12.1961
Oldest Player in a League Match: Tommy Cairns, 41 years 7 days v Bradford, 7.11.1931
Youngest Player in a League Match: Robert Cullingford, 16 years 141 v Mansfield Town, 22.4.1970

<table>
<tr><td colspan="2" align="center">LONGEST LEAGUE RUNS</td></tr>
<tr><td>of undefeated matches: 21 (1968-69)</td><td>of league matches without a win: 16 (1948-49)</td></tr>
<tr><td>of undefeated home matches: 25 (1975-78)</td><td>of undefeated away matches: 10 (1968-69)</td></tr>
<tr><td>without home win: 10 (1962-64)</td><td>without an away win: 29 (1925-27)</td></tr>
<tr><td>of league wins: 10 (1983-84)</td><td>of home wins: 9 (1952-53, 1961-64)</td></tr>
<tr><td>of league defeats: 8 (1932-33)</td><td>of away wins: 5 (1928-29, 1981-82, 1984-85)</td></tr>
</table>

BRADFORD CITY

PLAYERS NAME Honours	Ht	Wt	Birthdate	Birthplace Transfers	Contract Date	Clubs	League	L/Cup	FA Cup	Other	Lg	L/C	FAC	Oth
GOALKEEPERS														
Chris Pearce	6.0	11.4	07.08.61	Newport	13.08.77	Wolves (A)								
W:Y,S				Free	01.10.79	Blackburn Rovers								
				Free	07.08.80	Rochdale	41	6	1					
				Free	01.06.83	Port Vale	48	3	2	3				
				Free	15.08.86	Wrexham	25	4	3	7				
				£4,000	14.07.87	Burnley	181	16	15	22				
				Free	03.07.92	Bradford City								
Paul Tomlinson	6.2	12.10	22.02.64	Brierley Hill		Middlewood								
					01.06.83	Sheffield Utd	37	1	5	3				
				Loan	20.03.87	Birmingham City	11							
				£47,500	23.06.87	Bradford City	209	21	10	11				
DEFENDERS														
Alan Dowson	5.10	11.2	17.06.70	Gateshead		Millwall	1							
				Loan	11.01.90	Fulham	4							
				Free	02.07.91	Bradford City	16+2	4	1	2				
Mike Duxbury	5.9	10.12	01.09.59	Blackburn	01.10.76	Manchester Utd. (A)	274+25	32+2	20+5	23+1	6		1	
E:10,u21.7,UEFA u21'82;FAC'83'85,CS'83				Free	10.08.90	Blackburn Rovers	25+2	1	2	0+1				
				Free	09.01.92	Bradford City	16							
Craig Lawford	5.10	11.0	25.11.72	Dewsbury	02.07.91	Bradford City (T)	0+1							
Gavin Oliver	5.11	13.2	06.09.62	Felling	07.08.80	Sheffield Wed. (A)	14+6	2+3	2+1					
Loan Tranmere Rovers (14.01.83) 17lg 1gl				Free	12.08.85	Brighton & H.A	15+1			1				
				£20,000	22.11.85	Bradford City	223+4	22+1	11	16	7	2		
Dean Richards			09.06.74	Bradford	10.07.92	Bradford City (T)	5+2		1	1				
Brian Tinnion	5.11	11.5	22.02.68	Stanley	26.02.86	Newcastle Utd. (A)	30+2	5		1+1	2			
				£150,000	09.03.89	Bradford City	113+5	10	6	6+1	19	1	3	1
Paul West					15.02.91	Port Vale								
				Free	03.07.92	Bradford City								
MIDFIELD														
Lee Duxbury	5.8	11.0	07.10.69	Keighley	04.07.88	Bradford City (T)	100+4	9	4	6	11	2		
				Loan	18.01.90	Rochdale	9+1		1					
Robbie James	5.11	13.1	23.03.57	Swansea	01.04.74	Swansea City (A)	386+8	21	19	7	99	6	5	
W: 47, u21.3; WC'81'82'83'89;				£160,000	25.07.83	Stoke City	48	7	1		6	1		
				£100,000	23.10.84	Q.P.R	78+9	9	5		5		1	
				£70,000	24.06.87	Leicester City	21+2	4		1				
				£35,000	16.01.88	Swansea City	82+8	4	3+1	9	16			1
				P.E	23.08.90	Bradford City	98	9	4	6	6	1		1
Paul Reid	5.9	10.8	19.01.68	Oldbury	09.01.86	Leicester City (A)	140+22	13	5+1	6+2	21	4		
				Loan	19.03.92	Bradford City	7							
				£25,000	27.07.92	Bradford City								
Gary Williams	5.9	11.1	17.06.60	Wolverhampton	01.06.78	Aston Villa (A)	235+5	29	14	18		2		
Div.1'81; EC'82; ESC'82				Loan	01.03.80	Walsall	9							
				£235,000	31.07.87	Leeds Utd	39	4	1+1		3			
				Free	18.01.90	Watford	39+3	2	3					
					19.12.91	Bradford City	22							
FORWARDS														
Paul Jewell	5.8	10.8	28.08.64	Liverpool	01.06.83	Liverpool (A)								
FRT'85				£15,000	05.02.85	Wigan Ath	117+20	5+2	9	14+4	35		5	7
				£80,000	21.07.88	Bradford City	105+32	6+1	6+1	4+1	19	2	1	1
Sean McCarthy	6.1	11.7	12.09.67	Bridgend		Bridgend T								
					22.09.85	Swansea City	76+15	4+1	5+2	9+1	25	3	4	6
				£50,000	18.08.88	Plymouth A	67+3	7	3	0+1	19	5	1	1
				£250,000	04.07.90	Bradford City	69+2	5+2	4	5	29	2		2
Michael McHugh	5.11	11.0	03.04.71	Donegal	15.09.89	Bradford City	5+5							
Frank Stapleton	5.11	13.0	10.07.56	Dublin	01.09.73	Arsenal (A)	223+2	26	32	15	75	14	15	4
Ei: 71, Xl.2,Y; FAC'79'83'85				£900,000	28.08.81	Manchester Utd	204+19	26+1	21	19+1	60	6	7	5
via Ajax (Amsterdam)				Loan	18.03.88	Derby County	10				1			
via Le Harve (France) Free				Free		Blackburn Rovers	90+1	5	4	3	13	1		
				Free N.C	15.09.91	Aldershot								
				N.C	28.10.91	Huddersfield Town	5	0+1	1	1			1	
				Free	11.12.91	Bradford City	25+2							
Stephen Torpey	6.3	13.3	08.12.70	Islington	14.02.89	Millwall (T)	3+4	0+1						
				£70,000	21.11.90	Bradford City	69+3	4	2	5	17			5
ADDITIONAL CONTRACT PLAYERS														
(M) Scott Bairstow	6.1	12.0	01.06.72	Bradford	03.07.90	Bradford City								
Paul Coy					14.07.92	Bradford City (T)								
Alan Dawson					02.07.91	Bradford City								
Jeremy Howe			05.09.73	Stancliffe	06.07.92	Bradford City (T)	3							
Lee Margerison					10.07.92	Bradford City (T)								
Ian McCall	5.10	11.07	13.09.64	Dumfries		Read	59+7	2	2		9			
SLC'90						Dunfermline	33+14	3	0+1		8	2		
						Glasgow Rangers	12+9	0+1	0+1	0+1	2			
				£200,000		Bradford City	11+1				1			
Scott Partridge					10.07.92	Bradford City (T)								
(M) Darren Treacey	5.11	12.4	06.09.70	Lambeth	21.02.89	Millwall (T)	7		1					
				£30,000	21.11.90	Bradford City	16			3	2			

LEADING LEAGUE GOALSCORERS SEASONS 1985-86 – 1991-92

1985-86	BOBBY CAMPBELL	10		1986-87	JOHN HENDRIE	14
	GREG ABBOTT	10				
1987-88	RON FUTCHER	14		1988-89	JIMMY QUINN	7
1989-90	JIMMY QUINN	6		1990-91	SEAN McCARTHY	13
	1991-92	SEAN McCARTHY	16			

VALLEY PARADE GROUND Bradford, West Yorkshire BD8 7DY

Capacity: 14,359   **Covered Standing:** 8,089   **Seating:** 6,270

Tel: Ground: 0274 306062   **Ticket Sales:** 0274 307050

ATTENDANCES
Highest: 39,146 v Burnley, FA Cup 4th Round, 11.3.1911

Lowest: 1,178 v Hartlepool, Associate Members Cup, 22.2.1984

RECORD RECEIPTS
£59,250 v Tottenham Hotspur, FA Cup 3rd Round, 7.1.1989

VALLEY PARADE
First game: v Gainsborough, Division 2, 5.9.1893
First floodlit game: v Mansfield, 12.9.1956

Season Tickets:
N & P Stands: £189, juv/OAP £94.50: Family Stand: £147, OAP £73.50, Jnr Bantam £64
Ground: £115.50, juv/OAP £63

Executive Box Season Tickets: 8-20 persons from £4,000 per person. Contact Chief Commercial Executive for more details

Cost of Stand Tickets: N & P Stand: £9 adults, £5 juniors/OAP; Family Stand: £7 adults, OAP £4, Junior Bantams £3.50; Midland Road: adults £5.50, jun/OAP £5.50. **Terraces:** Spion Kop: £5.50 adults, juniors/OAP £3

Match and Ticket Information: N & P Stand tickets available four weeks in advance of matches

Car Parking: Street parking in side streets and private car park at £2.25 per car

Nearest Railway Station: Bradford Exchange (0274 733994/8)

How to get to the ground

From North: A650 to Bradford. Join Ring Road A6036 and turn left into Valley Parade for ground

From South and West: M62 and A606(M) to Bradford. Fourth exit from roundabout to A6036 Ring Road. Left at crossroads A650, left into Valley parade.

From East: A647 to Bradford. Right at crossroads A6036, left at crossroads A650, left into Valley Parade

Value Rating: ★ ★ ★

Programme Editor: Keith Hanvey

Price of 1992-93 Programme: £1
Number of Pages: 16
Subscriptions: £25 per season

Local Newspapers: Telegraph and Argus, Bradford Star

Local Radio Stations: Pennine Radio (235 medium wave), BBC Radio Leeds (388 medium wave), Radio Aire (362 medium wave)

Additional Publications on Club: The Complete Record 1903-88 (Breedon Books)

BRENTFORD

Division 1

Formed: 1889   **Turned Professional:** 1899   **Ltd Co:** 1901

SPONSORED BY: KLM Royal Dutch Airlines   **NICKNAME:** The Bees

President
W Wheatley

Deputy President
E V J White

Chairman
G V Potter

Vice-Chairman
E J Radley-Smith MS,FRCS,LRCR

Directors
R J J Blindell,LL.B.
D Tana
M M Lange

Ceif Executive
Keith Loring

Secretary
Polly Kates

Manager
Phil Holder

Physiotherapist
Roy Clare

Community Liaison Officer
Martyn Spong

Press Officer/Programme Editor
Eric White (081-578 0101)

Club Statistician for the Directory
Frank Coumbe

CHAMPIONS! At last the Bees realised their potential and won the Third Division, albeit at the fourteenth attempt.

After an average start the side won six consecutive games, topping the table after the fifth of them, a victory over Fulham. They slipped back but regained the leadership following a 4-0 victory over Wigan on 9 November, a position they held, apart from a few days, for the next three months. This was maintained thanks to a fine home record, yet away from Griffin Park Brentford did little right. A home reverse against Bury saw the lead lost but it was re-claimed a week later. A defeat and two wins saw Brentford settle into second place but four consecutive defeats followed by two draws saw the Bees slip to fourth and a play-off spot didn't look likely, let alone automatic promotion. Amazingly the side found their form again to win their last six games, and with Birmingham losing on the last day, the Bees took the championship by one point!

In the cups the Bees beat Barnet and Brighton in the Rumbelows before defeat at Norwich while the F.A. Cup saw Gillingham defeated in a replay before elimination at Bournemouth. The Autoglass Trophy saw a win at Aldershot, a defeat to Barnet and then a defeat to Orient.

There were so many heroes of the season with goalkeeper Graham Benstead again performing well. In defence 'Player of the Year' Keith Millen, captain Terry Evans and Jamie Bates stood out as did midfielder Simon Ratcliffe. The front four of Neil Smillie, 38 goal Dean Holdsworth, Gary Blissett and Marcus Gayle had no equals in the division while Kevin Godfrey also impressed. Late season acquisitions Brian Statham and Chris Hughton also played their parts.

So what of next season in the new First Division? It seems that Holdsworth will depart but who Phil Holder recruits will give an indication of the Bees chances. At the moment though we're just happy to be there!

Frank Coumbe

Back row L-R: Marcus Gayle, Danny Tripp, Murray Jones, Keith Millen, Ashley Bayes, Terry Evans, Graham Benstead, Bob Booker, Chris Sparks, Jamie Bates. **Middle row:** Joe Gadston (Youth Team Manager), Micky Bennett, Detzi Kruszynski, Lee Luscombe, Gary Blissett, Simon Ratcliffe, Grant Chalmers, Kevin Godfrey, Robert Peters, Roy Clare (Physiotherapist). **Front row:** Wilf Rostron (Asst. Manager), Brian Statham, Billy Manuel, Chris Hughton, Phil Holder (Manager), Neil Smillie, Paul Buckle, Steven Bircham, Graham Pearce (First Team Coach).

BRENTFORD

DIVISION THREE: CHAMPIONS **FA CUP:** 2nd RND **RUMBELOWS CUP:** 3rd RND **AUTOGLASS:** 1st RND

M	DATE		COMP.	VEN	OPPONENTS	RESULT	H/T	LGE POS	GOALSCORERS/GOAL TIMES	ATTEN-DANCE
1	A	17	BL	H	Leyton Orient	W 4-3	1-1		Holdsworth 3 (30, 61, 69), Evans 77	6,156
2		20	RC 1/1	A	Barnet	D 5-5	2-2		Cadette 21, 38, Godfrey 60, Holdsworth 83, 89	(2,927)
3		24	BL	A	Exeter City	W 2-1	2-0	2	Gayle 3, Blissett 45	(3,518)
4		27	RC 1/2	H	Barnet	W 3-1	3-0		Holdsworth 9, Godfrey 22, Evans 38	5,563
5		31	BL	H	Huddersfield Town	L 2-3	1-1	8	Jones 45, Godfrey 58	5,459
6	S	3	BL	A	Hartlepool United	L 0-1	0-0			(3,660)
7		7	BL	A	Shrewsbury Town	L 0-1	0-0	16		(3,193)
8		14	BL	H	Reading	W 1-0	0-0	8	Cadette 87	5,775
9		17	BL	H	Hull City	W 4-1	4-0	7	Evans 9, Smillie 11, Buckley (og) 14, Holdsworth 43	4,586
10		21	BL	A	Darlington	W 2-1	2-1	5	Smillie 6, Holdsworth 8	(3,900)
11		24	RC 2/1	H	Brighton & H A	W 4-1	3-0		Godfrey 6, Cadette 15, Holdsworth 28, 57	4,927
12		28	BL	H	Bolton Wanderers	W 3-2	2-0	3	Holdsworth 3, 50, Gayle 25	5,865
13	O	5	BL	A	Fulham	W 1-0	1-0	1	Evans 31	(7,710)
14		9	RC 2/2	A	Brighton & H A	L †2-4	1-3		Cadette 37, Holdsworth 109	(4,502)
15		12	BL	A	Peterborough Utd	W 2-1	1-1	1	Evans 5, Smillie 85	7,705
16		19	BL	H	West Bromwich A.	L 1-2	0-1	3	Gayle 80	8,575
17		22	AGT Pre	A	Aldershot	W 2-0	1-0		Sealy 9, 50	(1,348)
18		26	BL	A	Bury	W 3-0	2-0	2	Holdsworth 40, 44, Gayle 58	(2,280)
19		30	RC 3	A	Norwich City	L 1-4	0-0		Manuel 90	(7,394)
20	N	2	BL	A	Bradford City	W 1-0	0-0	2	Smillie 84	(5,359)
21		6	BL	H	Birmingham City	D 2-2	1-1	2	Smillie 29, Blissett 72	8,798
22		9	BL	H	Wigan Athletic	W 4-0	1-0	1	Blissett 18, 51, Holdsworth 73, 77	6,675
23		18	FAC 1	H	Gillingham	D 3-3	2-1		Holdsworth 9, 25, Blissett 68	5,830
24		22	BL	A	Bournemouth	D 0-0	0-0	1		(6,035)
25		26	FAC 1R	A	Gillingham	W 3-1	1-0		Holdsworth 36, 63, Sealy 89	(7,328)
26		30	BL	H	Swansea City	W 3-2	0-2	1	Holdsworth 51, Ratcliffe 74, Blissett 84	6,669
27	D	7	FAC 2	A	Bournemouth	L 1-2	0-0		Bates 70	(6,538)
28		14	BL	A	Torquay United	D 1-1	1-0	1	Godfrey 14	(2,475)
29		17	AGT Pre	H	Barnet	L 3-6	1-1		Luscombe 4, Holdsworth 46, 89	1,871
30		22	BL	H	Exeter City	W 3-0	2-0	1	Blissett 27, 36, Gayle 85	7,226
31		26	BL	A	Huddersfield Town	L 1-2	0-1	1	Blissett (pen) 83	(10,605)
32		28	BL	A	Leyton Orient	L 2-4	2-2	2	Luscombe 12, 28	(7,333)
33	J	1	BL	H	Hartlepool United	W 1-0	0-0	1	Holdsworth 67	7,103
34		4	BL	A	Stockport County	L 1-2	1-0	1	Francis (og) 20	(4,421)
35		11	BL	A	Stoke City	W 2-0	1-0	1	Luscombe 4, Holdsworth 58	9,004
36		18	BL	A	Chester City	D 1-1	1-0	1	Booker 3	(1,447)
37		21	AGT 1	A	Leyton Orient	L 2-3	0-2		Holdsworth 52, 89	(1,856)
38		25	BL	H	Preston North End	W 1-0	1-0	1	Evans 14	7,559
39	F	1	BL	A	West Bromwich A.	L 0-2	0-2	1		(15,984)
40		8	BL	H	Bury	L 0-3	0-2	3		6,789
41		11	BL	A	Swansea City	D 1-1	1-0		Millen 41	(3,582)
42		15	BL	H	Torquay United	W 3-2	1-0	1	Booker 19, Blissett 49, Bates 72	6,079
43		22	BL	A	Stoke City	L 1-2	0-1	2	Blissett 47	(16,417)
44		29	BL	H	Stockport County	W 2-1	2-1	2	Smillie 38, Holdsworth 43	7,484
45	M	3	BL	H	Chester City	W 2-0	1-0	1	Blissett 39, Holdsworth (pen) 86	6,869
46		7	BL	A	Preston North End	L 2-3	2-2	2	Smillie 23, Buckle 44	(3,548)
47		10	BL	A	Birmingham City	L 0-1	0-1			(13,290)
48		14	BL	H	Bradford City	L 3-4	1-2	2	Evans 10, Blissett 50, Holdsworth 63	6,791
49		20	BL	A	Wigan Athletic	L 1-2	0-1		Holdsworth 90	(2,371)
50		29	BL	H	Bournemouth	D 2-2	1-0	4	Godfrey 38, Blissett 49	7,605
51	A	1	BL	A	Reading	D 0-0	0-0	4		(5,660)
52		4	BL	H	Shrewsbury Town	W 2-0	1-0	4	Holdsworth 31, Evans 67	5,561
53		11	BL	A	Hull City	W 3-0	1-0	4	Holdsworth 3, 77, Blissett 84	(3,770)
54		17	BL	H	Darlington	W 4-1	3-0	3	Holdsworth 18, 22, Blissett 45, Toman (og) 88	8,383
55		20	BL	A	Bolton Wanderers	W 2-1	2-0	3	Evans 9, Spooner (og) 28	(4,382)
56		26	BL	H	Fulham	W 4-0	4-0	2	Holdsworth 19, Gayle 20, Blissett 27, Ratcliffe 42	12,071
57	M	2	BL	A	Peterborough Utd	W 1-0	1-0	1	Blissett 26	(14,539)

Best Home League Attendance: 12,071 v Fulham **Smallest:** 4,586 v Hull City **Av Home Att:** 7,165

Goal Scorers: Compared with 90-91: +1,017

League (81): Holdsworth 24 (1 pen), Blissett 17 (1 pen), Evans 8, Smillie 7, Gayle 6, Opponents 4, Godfrey 3, Luscombe 3, Ratcliffe 2, Booker 2, Bates, Cadette, Millen, Jones, Buckle

R/lows C(15): Holdsworth 6, Cadette 4, Godfrey 3, Evans, Manuel

FA Cup (7): Holdsworth 4, Bates, Sealy, Blissett

Autoglass (7): Holdsworth 4, Sealy 2, Luscombe

† = After extra-time

Bayes A.	Ratcliffe S.	Rostron W.	Bates J.	Evans T.	Buckle P.	Jones K.	Godfrey K.	Holdsworth D.	Cadette R.	Smillie N.	Gayle M.	Blissett G.	Manuel W.	Benstead G.	Peters R.	Millen K.	Suckling P. (L)	Sealy A.	Booker R.	Luscombe L.	Statham B.	Finnigan A. (M)	Driscoll A.	Hughton C.	Kruszynski Z.	Referee	
	2*	3	4	5	6	7	8	9•	10	11	12	14														K Morton	1
1	2*		4	5	6	7	8	9	10•	11	12	14	3													D Elleray	2
		14	4	5	6	7	8	9		11	2*	10	3•	1		12										R Hamer	3
		S	4	5	6	7	8	9		11		10	3	1	2*											M James	4
		14	4	5	6•	7	8		9	11	12	10	3	1	2*											P Foakes	5
	2		4	5	6		8	9	10*	11	7•	12	3	1		14										R Dilkes	6
	6		4	5	12	7*	8	9	10	2	11•		3	1		14										H King	7
	2		4	5		7	9	12	11	8•	10*		3	1		14	6									J Moules	8
	2		4	5		7	9	10*	11	8	12		3	1	S	6										G Pooley	9
	2		4	5		7	9	10*	11	8	12		3*	1		14	6									T Lunt	10
	6		2	5		8	9	10*	11	7•	12		3	1		14	4									R Gifford	11
	6		2	5		8	9	10*	11	7	12		3	1	S	4										J Carter	12
	S	6	2	5		7	8		10*	11	9		3	1		14	4									B Hill	13
1	4	6	2	5		7	8	12	10•	11	9		3*			14										I Hemley	14
	14	6	2	5		3	8	9	10	11	7•		S			4	1									G Poll	15
	14	6	2	5		7		10•	11	8	12	3			4	1	9*									M Bailey	16
	5	6	2		7		12	11	8	10•	3			14	4	1	9*									D Axcell	17
	6	S	2	5		7	9*		11	8	10	3			4	1	12									T West	18
1	6*	12	2	5	14	7*	9		11	8	10	3			4											A Gunn	19
	6	8	2	5	S	7	9		11		10	3	S		4	1										J Parker	20
	6	14	2	5		7*	9	S	11	8	10	3			4	1										K Cooper	21
	6	S	2	5		7	9		11	8*	10	3			4	1	12									L Shapter	22
1	6		2	5	S	7	9		11	8	10•	3			4		14									J Carter	23
	6	S	2	5		12	9		11	8*		3			4	1	7	10								M Bodenham	24
1	6•		2	5	14	7	9	S	11		10	3			4		8									J Carter	25
	6	11*	2	5	14	8•	9		12	10	3			4	1	7										M James	26
	6		2	5	8	14	9		11	12	10*	3*	1		4		7									A Gunn	27
		2	5	8	3	9*		11	6†	10†		1	12	4		7		S								A Smith	28
	12	S	2	5	6	8	9		11*	4	10		1	3		7										I Borrett	29
	6	3	2	5	12	8		11*	14	10		1		4		7	9•									G Willard	30
	6	11	2	5	8	3		9	10	S	1		4	7*		12										D Shadwell	31
	6	3*	2	5	11	8•	14	10		12	1	4		7		9										D Elleray	32
	6		2	12	8	9	11		3	1	14	4		7			5*	10•								R Pawley	33
	6		2	5	S	8	9	11		3•	1	4		14		10	7									C Wilkes	34
	6		2	5	14	9		11	12	10*	3•	1	4		8	7										P Scoble	35
	6		5		S	9		11	10	3	1	4		S	8	7			2							V Callow	36
	6		5	14	2	9		11	12	10*	3•	1	4		7			8								M Bailey	37
	6	3	5	12		9		11	10	S	1	4		8	7*			2								D Gallagher	38
	6	3	5		9		11	10		14	1	4	12	8	7*			2								B Coddington	39
	6•	3*	5		9		11	7	10	14	1	4		8			2		12							D Frampton	40
		6	5	14		9*		11	12	10	3•	1	4		8		2	7								P Durkin	41
	14	3	5		9		11	12	10•	6	1	4		8•			2	7*								P Vanes	42
	6		2	5		9		11	12	10•	3	1	4	14	8			7*								G Ashby	43
	6		2	5		9		11	7*	10	3•	1	4	12	14		8									J Deakin	44
	6			5		9		11	7	10•	S	1	4	14	8		2				4					M Pierce	45
	6	4	5	8		S	9		11	7	10		1		S		2				3					R Hart	46
	6*	5		12		7	9		11	14			1		4	8	10•	2			3					I Hendrick	47
		4	5			12	9		11		10	6•	1		14	8	7*	2			3					P Foakes	48
	8	4	5			7	9		11		10*	6*	1		14	12		2†			3					J Key	49
	6	3	5	S		7	9		11	12	10	8*	1					2				4				G Pooley	50
	6	S	5			9		11	7	10	S	1		4				2			3	8				P Taylor	51
	6		2	5			9		11	7•	10	12	1		4			14			3	8*				I Hemley	52
	6		2	5			9		11	7•	10	12	1		4*			14			3	8				K Hackett	53
	6		4	5		14	9		11	7•	10	12	1					2			3	8*				M James	54
	6		4	5		14*	9		11	7	10•	12	1					2			3	8				R Shepherd	55
	6	S	5				9		11	7	10	S	1		4			2			3	8				I Borrett	56
	6	14	5				9		11	7	10•	12	1		4			2			3	8				G Ashby	57
1	31	15	41	44	8	6	26	40	10	44	28	31	27	37	1	34	8	9	14	10	18	3		12	8	League Appearances	
	3	3	1		7		5	1	1		10	6	8		8				9	2	3			1		Substitute Appearances	
3	3	2+1	5	5	2+1	3		5		4+1	3		5	3+1	2+2	5		2	1+2	2						R/lows Appearances	
2	3		3	3	1		2+1	3		3	1	3	3	1		3		2+1								FA Cup Appearances	
2+1	1		2	2		2	2		3	2	3	2		1+1	2	1	1		2		1					Autoglass Appearances	

Also Played: Posn.(Game): Line 12(4)

Players on Loan: Perry Suckling (Crystal Palace), Detsi Kruszynski (Wimbledon)

† = Sent Off

BRENTFORD

Club Colours: Red & white striped shirts, black shorts, red stockings with white turnover
Change Colours: Blue & black striped shirts, navy shorts, sky stockings with 3 stripes
Reserves League: Capital League   **Youth League:** S. E. Counties

COMPETITIONS				
Div. 1	Div. 2	Div. 3	Div. 3S	Div. 4
35-46	33-35	58-62	20-33	62-63
	46-54	63-64	54-58	64-72
	92-	72-73		73-78
		78-92		

HONOURS			
Div. 2	Div. 3	Div. 3S	Div. 4
34-35	91-92	32-33	62-63

MOST APPEARANCES: KEN COOTE 559 (1949-64)			
Year	League	FA Cup	Lge Cup
1949-50	20		
1950-51	5	1	
1951-52	24	4	
1952-53	17		
1953-54	40	3	
1954-55	37	6	
1955-56	45	2	
1956-57	44	3	
1957-58	45	1	
1958-59	44	4	
1959-60	42	2	
1960-61	41	2	3
1961-62	45	5	1
1962-63	46	1	2
1963-64	19	1	4
	514	**35**	**10**

MOST GOALS IN A CAREER		
JIM TOWERS 163 (1954-61)		
Season	League	FA Cup
1954-55	16	1
1955-56	21	1
1956-57	12	1
1957-58	29	
1958-59	32	5
1959-60	23	1
1960-61	21	
Total	**154**	**9**

MANAGERS			
Name	Seasons	Best	Worst
William Lewis	1900-03		
Richard Molyneaux	03-06		
W. G. Brown	06-08		
Fred Halliday	08-12		
Emphrair Rhodes	12-15		
Fred Halliday	15-21	9(3S)	17(3S)
Archie Mitchell	21-24	18(3S)	21(3S)
Fred Halliday	24-26	22(2)	18(3S)
Harry Curtis	26-49	5(1)	10(2)
A. H. Gibbons	49-52	9(2)	17(2)
Jim Bain	52-53	17(2)	
Tommy Lawton	1953		11(3S)
Bill Dodgin (Snr)	53-57	21(2)	1(4)
Malcolm McDonald	57-65	3(3)	23(3)
Tommy Cavanagh	65-66	23(3)	9(4)
Billy Gray	66-67	9(4)	14(4)
Jimmy Sirrell	67-69	11(4)	14(4)
Frank Bluntstone	69-73	22(3)	19(4)
Mike Everitt	73-75	8(4)	18(4)
John Docherty	75-76	14(4)	14(4)
Bill Dodgin (Jnr)	76-80	10(3)	4(4)
Fred Callaghan	80-84	8(3)	13(3)
Frank McClintock	84-87	10(3)	13(3)
Steve Perryman	87-90	7(3)	13(3)
Phil Holder	90-	1(3)	6(3)

RECORD TRANSFER FEE RECEIVED			
Amount	Club	Player	Date
£1,000,000	Wimbledon	Dean Holdsworth	7/92
£350,000	Queens Park R	Andy Sinton	5/89
£93,000	Reading	Terry Hurlock	2/86
£60,000	Sheffield Wed.	Andy McCulloch	7/79

RECORD TRANSFER FEE PAID			
Amount	Club	Player	Date
£167,000	Hibernians	Eddie May	7/89
£100,000	Norwich City	Simon Ratcliffe	1/89
£78,000	Bury	Alan Whitehead	7/81
£55,000	Gillingham	Tony Funnell	3/80

LONGEST LEAGUE RUNS	
of undefeated matches:	16 (30.4.1932-12.11.1932)
	(14.1.1967-15.4.1967)
of undefeated home matches:	24 (14.4.1934-5.9.1935)
without home win:	11 (1.2.1947-30.8.1947)
of league wins:	9 (30.4.1932-24.9.1932)
of league defeats:	9 (13.4.1925-12.9.1925)
	(20.10.1928-25.12.1928)
of league matches w/out a win:	14 (13.4.1925-10.10.1925)
	(15.9.1928-25.12.1928) (7.4.1947-6.9.1947)
of undefeated away matches:	8 (4.1.1936-18.4.1936)
without an away win:	21 (24.4.1965-16.4.1966)
of home wins:	21 (31.8.1929-26.4.1930)
of away wins:	5 (21.4.1956-29.8.1956)
	(24.10.1981-28.12.1981)

PREVIOUS LEAGUE
Southern League

BIGGEST VICTORIES
League: 9-0 v Wrexham, Division 3, 15.10.1963
F.A. Cup: (Proper) 9-0 v Windsor & Eton, Rnd 1, 20.11.1982
(Played at Griffin Park)
League Cup: No more than 3 goals

BIGGEST DEFEATS
League: 0-7 v Walsall, Division 3S, 19.1.1957
0-7 v Swansea, Division 3S, 8.11.1924
F.A. Cup: 1-7 v Manchester Utd, Rnd 3, 14.1.1928
League Cup: 0-5 v Charlton Ath, Rnd 1, 12.8.1980

MOST POINTS
3 points a win: 82, Division 3, 1991-92
2 points a win: 62, Div 3S, 1932-33; Div 4, 1962-63

MOST GOALS
98, 1962-63, Division 4
Dick 23, Brooks 22, McAdams 22, Block 8, Summers 6, McLeod
4, Fielding 3, Hales 2, Higginson, Edgley, Anthoney, Scott 1
each, 4 own goals

MOST GOALS IN A MATCH
5, Jack Holliday v Luton (a), 5-5, Div 3S, 28.1.1933
5, Billy Scott v Barnsley, 8-1, Div 2, 15.12.1934
5, Peter McKennan v Bury, 8-2, Div 2, 18.2.1949

MOST GOALS IN A SEASON
Jack Holliday 39 (League 38, FA Cup 1), 1932-33.
5 goals once = 5, 4 goals once = 4, 3 goals 3 times = 9, 2 goals 6
times = 12, 1 goal 9 times = 9

MOST FIRST CLASS MATCHES IN A SEASON
63 (46 League, 8 FA Cup, 4 League Cup, 5 AMC) 1988-89

MOST LEAGUE GOALS CONCEDED
93, Division 3, 1961-62

MOST LEAGUE WINS
27, Division 4, 1962-63

MOST LEAGUE DRAWS
19, Division 3, 1980-81

MOST LEAGUE DEFEATS
26, Division 2, 1946-47

OLDEST PLAYER
Idris Hopkins, 39 years 7 months 13 days, 26.5.1947

YOUNGEST PLAYER
Danis Salman, 15 years 8 months 3 days, 15.11.1975

MOST CAPPED PLAYER
I Hopkins (Wales) 12
(For England): B Scott & L Smith 1 each

BEST PERFORMANCES BY BRENTFORD

League: 1932-33: Matches played 42, Won 26, Drawn 10, Lost 6, Goals for 90, Goals against 41, Points 62. 1st Division 3S

Highest: 5th Division 1, 1935-36

F.A. Cup: 1937-38: 3rd rnd. Fulham 3-1 (h); 4th rnd. Portsmouth 2-1 (h); 5th rnd. Manchester Utd 2-0 (h); 6th rnd. Preston N. E. 0-3 (h).
1945-46: 3rd rnd. Tottenham 2-2 (a), 2-0 (h); 4th rnd. Bristol City 1-2 (a), 5-0 (h); 5th rnd. Queens Park R 0-0 (h), 3-1 (a); 6th rnd. Charlton Ath 3-6 (a), 1-3 (h).
1948-49: 3rd rnd. Middlesbrough 3-2 (h); 4th rnd. Torquay 1-0 (h); 5th rnd. Burnley 4-2 (h); 6th rnd. Leicester 0-2 (h).
1988-89: 1st rnd. Halesowen 2-0 (h); 2nd rnd. Peterborough 0-0 (a), 3-2 (h); 3rd rnd. Walsall 1-1 (a), 1-0 (h); 4th rnd. Manchester City 3-1 (h); 5th rnd. Blackburn Rov 2-0 (a); 6th rnd. Liverpool 0-4 (a).

League Cup: 1982-83: 1st rnd. Wimbledon 1-1 (a), 2-0 (h); 2nd rnd. Blackburn Rov 3-2 (h), 0-0 (a); 3rd rnd. Swansea 1-1 (h), 2-1 (a); 4th rnd. Nottingham Forest 0-2 (a).

DIVISIONAL RECORDS

	Played	Won	Drawn	Lost	For	Against	Points
DIVISION 1	210	76	46	88	330	359	**198**
DIVISION 2	378	143	99	136	536	554	**385**
DIVISION 3	1012	375	263	374	1418	1399	**1183**
DIVISION 3S	730	290	173	267	1151	1101	**753**
DIVISION 4	552	226	138	188	801	679	**590**
TOTALS	**2882**	**1110**	**719**	**1053**	**4236**	**4092**	**3109**

PLAYERS NAME Honours	Ht	Wt	Birthdate	Birthplace Transfers	Contract Date	Clubs	League	L/Cup	FA Cup	Other	Lg	L/C	FAC	Oth
GOALKEEPERS														
Ashley Bayes	6.1	12.9	19.04.72	Lincoln	05.07.90	Brentford (T)	2	3	2					
Graham Benstead	6.1	12.11	20.08.63	Aldershot	08.07.81	Q.P.R. (A)			1					
E:Y.1; Div.3'92					28.03.85	Norwich City	16	3						
				Loan	14.08.87	Colchester Utd	18			1				
				£35,000	19.07.88	Sheffield Utd	47	5	8	2				
				£60,000	30.07.90	Brentford	82	6	4	11				
DEFENDERS														
Jamie Bates	6.1	13.0	24.02.68	London	01.06.87	Brentford (A)	152+20	13+3	4+1	18	6		1	
Div'3														
Terry Evans	6.4	12.7	12.04.65	London			SAfr								
Div'3				£5,000	22.07.85	Brentford	217+1	15+1	17	23	23	4	2	1
Chris Hughton	5.7	11.5	11.12.58	Forest Gate	02.06.77	Tottenham H	293+4	33+2	34+2	36+2	12	2	1	4
Ei: 50, u21.1; FAC'81'82; UEFA'84, CS'81;				Free	04.01.91	West Ham U	32+1		7	1				
Div.3'92				Free	02.03.92	Brentford	12							
Billy Manuel	5.8	11.6	28.06.69	Hackney	28.07.87	Tottenham H. (T)								
Div.3'92					10.02.89	Gillingham	74+13	2	3	5	5			
					14.06.91	Brentford	27+8	5	3	2			1	
Keith Millen	6.1	12.0	26.09.66	Croydon	17.06.85	Brentford (A)	258+4	22	18	22+1	13	1	1	
Div.3'92														
Simon Ratcliffe	5.11	11.9	08.02.67	Davyhulme	13.02.85	Manchester Utd								
E: u19(3);Y.1;S; Div.3'92				£40,000	16.06.87	Norwich City	6+3	2+1						
				£100,000	13.01.89	Brentford	107+9	7	8+1	15+2	7			
Wilf Rostron	5.6	11.1	29.09.56	Sunderland	01.10.73	Arsenal (A)	12+5	1	1		2			
E:S; Div.3'92				£40,000	01.07.77	Sunderland	75+1	4	4		17	1		
				£150,000	01.10.79	Watford	306+11	30+1	43+1	7	22	3	2	3
				Free	13.01.89	Sheffield Wed	7		1	1				
				Free	13.08.90	Sheffield Utd	33+3	2+1	0+2		3			
				Free	10.01.91	Brentford	33+7	2+1	3	5+2	2			
Brian Statham	5.8	11.6	21.05.69	Zimbabwe	03.08.87	Tottenham H. (T)	20+4	2	0+1					
E: u21.3, u19.2.; Div.3'92				Loan	28.03.91	Reading	8							
				Loan	20.11.91	Bournemouth	2		1					
				£70,000	16.01.92	Brentford	18							
MIDFIELD														
Bob Booker	6.2	12.4	25.01.58	Watford		Bedmond								
Div.3'92				Free	24.10.78	Brentford	207+44	19+3	10+4	9+2	42	1	1	2
					24.11.88	Sheffield Utd	91+8	3+1	8+2	6+1	13			1
				Free	22.11.91	Brentford	14+2				2			
FORWARDS														
Gary Blissett	6.0	12.7	29.06.64	Manchester		Manchester City								
Div.3'92						Manchester Utd								
						Altrincham								
					23.08.83	Crewe Alexandra	112+10	9	4	6+1	39	3		4
				£60,000	26.03.87	Brentford	174+13	12+3	13	15+1	58	5	7	6
Neil Smillie	5.6	10.7	19.07.58	Barnsley	01.10.75	Crystal Palace (A)	71+12	7	7		7		1	
SC88; Div.3'92				Loan	01.01.77	Brentford	3							
				PE	09.08.82	Brighton & H.A	62+13	2	8+1		2		1	
				£100,000	24.06.85	Watford	10+6	1	2		3		1	
				Free	27.03.87	Reading	38+1	3		5+1				2
				Free	15.08.88	Brentford	145+6	13	5	14	17		1	3
ADDITIONAL CONTRACT PLAYERS														
Paul Buckle	5.8	10.8	16.12.70	Hertford	01.07.89	Brentford (T)	38+14	4+1	3	6+1	1			
E:Y.1; Div.3'92														
Marcus Gayle	6.1	12.9	27.09.70	Hammersmith		Brentford (T)	52+31	3+1	3+1	7+3	12			1
E:Y.1														
Murray L Jones					23.08.90	Bristol City								
				£30,000	25.01.91	Exeter City	16+4		1	3	3			
				Loan		Doncaster Rovers	5			1				
				£75,000	15.07.91	Grimsby Town	14+14	1+2	0+1	0+1	3	1		
				£75,000	27.07.92	Brentford								
Lee Luscombe	6.0	11.10	16.07.71	Guernsey	25.04.89	Southampton (T)								
Div.3'92				Free	18.10.91	Brentford	10+3		2		3			1
Robert Peters	5.6	11.6	18.05.71	London		Brentford (T)	8+9	1+2	1	1+2	1			
Chris Sparks					03.07.92	Brentford (T)								
Daniel Tripp					03.07.92	Brentford (T)								

BRENTFORD

RECORD WIN & LOSS AGAINST EACH CLUB IN CURRENT DIVISION

(Where a score has occured on several occasions the most recent is given)

Club	Rec. Win	Season	Rec. Loss	Season
BARNSLEY	8-1	1934-35	3-0	1967-68
BIRMINGHAM CITY	2-0	1990-91 (away)	5-1	1953-54
BRISTOL CITY	4-0	1922-23	3-0	1961-62
BRISTOL ROVERS	5-1	1982-83	5-0	1965-66 (home)
CAMBRIDGE UNITED	2-0	1984-85	3-0	1990-91 (home)
CHARLTON ATHLETIC	4-0	1925-26	3-0	1924-25
DERBY COUNTY	6-0	1935-36	4-1	1953-54
GRIMSBY TOWN	6-1	1937-38	7-2	1950-51
LEICESTER CITY	4-2	1952-53	6-0	1953-54
LUTON TOWN	3-0	1924-25	6-2	1963-64 (home)
MILLWALL	6-1	1927-28	4-0	1955-56
NEWCASTLE UNITED	5-2	1934-35 (away)	1-0	1947-48
NOTTS COUNTY	5-0	1952-53	4-0	1952-53
OXFORD UNITED	5-1	1965-66	2-0	1965-66
PETERBOROUGH UTD	5-1	1971-72	6-0	1961-62
PORTSMOUTH	4-0	1936-37	4-0	1961-62
SOUTHEND UNITED	6-1	1958-59	6-0	1983-84
SUNDERLAND	4-0	1937-38	5-1	1935-36 (home)
SWINDON TOWN	5-2	1930-31	4-0	1979-80
TRANMERE ROVERS	4-0	1962-63	6-2	1972-73
WATFORD	5-0	1929-30	6-1	1960-61
WEST HAM UNITED	4-1	1934-35	4-1	1952-53 (home)
WOLVERHAMPTON WNDRS	5-0	1935-36	4-0	1936-37

MANAGER: PHIL HOLDER

DATE OF BIRTH: 19.01.1952   **PLACE OF BIRTH:** Kilburn

DATE OF APPOINTMENT: September 1990

PREVIOUS CLUBS
- **as Manager:**
- **as Asst. Man./Coach:**
- **as Player:** Tottenham, Brentford, Crystal Palace, Bournemouth

HONOURS
- **as Manager:**
- **as Asst. Man./Coach:**
- **as Player:**
- **International:** England Youth

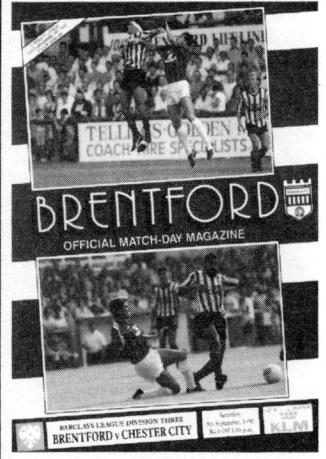

Value Rating: ★ ★ ★ ★ ★

Programme Editor: Eric White

Price of 1992-93 Programme: £1.50
Number of Pages: 40
Subscriptions: £50

Local Newspapers: Brentford & Chiswick Times, Ealing Gazette, Middlesex Chronicle, Hounslow Informer, Weekend Recorder

Local Radio Stations: Capital Gold, Talk Back Radio

LEADING LEAGUE GOALSCORERS
SEASONS 1979-80 – 1991-92

1979-80	STEVE PHILLIPS	12		1980-81	BOB BOOKER	7
1981-82	KEITH BOWEN	8		1982-83	FRANCIS JOSEPH	23
	GARY JOHNSON	8				
	GARY ROBERTS	8				
1983-84	FRANCIS JOSEPH	18		1984-85	KEITH CASSELLS	12
1985-86	ROBBIE COOKE	17		1986-87	ROBBIE COOKE	20
1987-88	ANDY SINTON	11		1988-89	RICHARD CADETTE	12
1989-90	DEAN HOLDSWORTH	24		1990-91	GARY BLISSETT	10

1991-92   **DEAN HOLDSWORTH   24**

GRIFFIN PARK Braemar Road, Brentford, Middx TW8 0NT

Capacity: 13,800   **Covered Standing:** 6,500   **Seating:** 3,500

Tel: Ground: 081 560 2021   **Clubcall:** 0898 12 11 08

All premium rate calls (0898/0891) cost 36p per minute cheap rate and 48p per minute at all other times. Call costings correct at time of going to press.

ATTENDANCES
Highest: 39,626 v Preston North End, FA Cup Round 6.
5.3.1938

Lowest: 1,110 v Swindon Town, Freight Rover Trophy,
6.1.1987

Record Receipts: £61,348 v Fulham, Division 3,
26.4.1992

GRIFFIN PARK
First game: v Plymouth Argyle, 1.9.1904
First floodlit game: v Chelsea, 5.10.1954

Season Tickets:
Stands: from £170 to £250 (juv/OAP £100 to £200)
Ground: £125 (juv/OAP £75, under-12 £23)

Cost of Stand Tickets: £9.00 **Terraces:** £5.00
(£3.00 juveniles/OAPs), (£1 extra for non-members)

Match and Ticket Information: Postal applications with
sae and remittance by post or by personal application.
Latest information on the Club ring Club Call on 0898 121
108

Car Parking: Street parking available

Nearest Railway Station: Brentford or South Ealing
(Tube), Piccadilly Line

How to get to the ground

From North: Use M1 or A1 then A406 North Circular
Road to Chiswick then follow signs South Circular Road.
In 0.3m turn right A315 (S.P. Brentford). In 0.5m turn right
into Ealing Road for Brentford FC

From East: Use either A406 North Circular Road then as
above or South Circular Road A205. Cross Kew Bridge
and turn left A315 (S.P. Brentford). In 0.5m turn right into
Ealing Road for Brentford FC

From South: Use A240/A3/M3/ or A316 to junction with
South Circular Road. A205. Cross Kew Bridge and turn
left A315 (S.P. Brentford). In 0.5m turn right into Ealing
Road for Brentford FC

From West: Use M4 until junction 1, leave Motorway and
follow signs South Circular Road. In 0.3m turn right A315
(S.P. Brentford). In 0.5m turn right into Ealing Road for
Brentford FC. Alternative use M25/M4

BRIGHTON & HOVE ALBION Division 2

Formed: 1900   **Turned Professional:** 1901   **Ltd Co:** 1904

SPONSORED BY: TSB Bank   **NICKNAME:** The Seagulls

President/Chairman
D C Sizen

Vice-Chairman
D Sullivan

Directors
B E Clarke
W A Archer
R A Bloom

Managing Director
B Lloyd

Chief Executive/Secretary
Ron Pavey

Team Manager
Barry Lloyd

Coach
Martin Hinshelwood

Youth Development Officer
Ted Streeter

Chief Scout
Bill Dodgin

Physiotherapist
Malcolm Stuart

Marketing Manager
Terry Gill (0273 26412)

Hon.Medical Officer
Dr H Sless
MB,BCh,BAO,LM,DObst,RCOG

Football in the Community Officer
Stephen Ford

Club Statistician for the Directory
Malcolm Boyes

A Wembley play-off place at the end of 1990-91 to a relegation place in 1991-92. That was a fate hardly imaginable to any follower of Brighton & Hove Albion following a day out at the national stadium.

Many supporters might have agreed that the team was not good enough for the First Division but felt it was more than good enough to hold its own in the Second Division.

Therein though lies the true tail of Brighton's demise. With the spectre of a £3 million debt hanging heavy like a thunder storm over the club, it had to sell its best players to survive on a week to week basis.

Mike Small left and chose to go to West Ham for £400,000. His striking partner John Byrne was also allowed to leave for a give-away £225,000 to Sunderland. It must have hurt many a Seagulls fan to hear football commentators at Sunderland's F.A. Cup matches saying what a steal he was at that price. If the debt was not there perhaps Small and Byrne could have stayed. As it was, losing these two players hurt the team most.

An early exit in Round 2 of the Rumbelows Cup at the hands of Brentford 5-6 on aggregate seemed to follow a pattern in this competition for Brighton in recent years.

The F.A. Cup draw paired local non-league club, Crawley Town, with Brighton at the Goldstone Ground. This fixture really caught the imagination of the Sussex people as 18,031 turned up to watch the game. A 5-0 win, Brighton being 3-0 up at half-time, soon put paid to the headline writers. A 2-1 defeat at Bolton Wanderers in Round 4, left the supporters with only Second Division survival to look forward to.

It would seem that what ended Brighton's spell in the Second Division was the lack of consistency throughout the season.

Changes at boardroom level as well did not help the cause. The sad loss of Mr Appleby whose association with the club was long standing was obviously not expected and caused much heartache with the club. Manager Barry Lloyd was made-up to Managing Director and this might also have added to the clubs poor form. If the manager is not spending time with the players during the week at training and only seeing them on match days due to other commitments surely this can't help morale.

The largest hangover still seems to be the £3 million debt, with eleven player being given free transfers at the end of the 1991-92 season. Mr Lloyd still having to search for bargain basement signings, as with Mark Gall last season, £45,000 from Maidstone United, who ended up being the supporters 'Player of the Year', but surely he cannot keep on doing this.

The 1992-93 season looks like being a struggle for Brighton. One I am sure most fans are not looking forward to very much.   **Malcolm Boyes**

Back row L-R: Larry May (Reserve Team Coach), Stuart Myall, John Crumplin, Simon Funnell, Nicky Bissett, Gary O'Reilly, Paul McCarthy, Robert Codner, Ted Streeter (Youth Development Officer). **Middle row:** Malcolm Stuart (Physio), Mark Farrington, Andy Polston, Perry Digweed, Gary Chivers, Mark Beeney, Mark Gall, Billy Logan, Martin Hinshelwood (Coach). **Front row:** Dean Wilkins, Bernard Gallacher, John Robinson, Barry Lloyd (Managing Director), Clive Walker, Matthew Edwards, Ian Chapman.

BRIGHTON & HOVE ALBION

DIVISION TWO: 24th   **FA CUP:** 4th RND   **RUMBELOWS CUP:** 2nd RND   **ZDS CUP:** Q/FINALS

M		DATE	COMP.	VEN	OPPONENTS	RESULT		H/T	LGE POS	GOALSCORERS/GOAL TIMES	ATTEN-DANCE
1	A	17	BL	H	Tranmere Rovers	L	0-2	0-2			9,679
2		20	BL	A	Bristol City	L	1-2	0-1		Bissett 88	(11,299)
3		24	BL	A	Barnsley	W	2-1	1-1	16	Wade 2, Barham 90	(6,066)
4		31	BL	H	Wolverhampton W	D	3-3	2-2	17	O'Reilly 28, Barham 30, Robinson 81	10,621
5	S	4	BL	A	Millwall	W	2-1	1-1	13	Byrne 23, Codner 58	(9,266)
6		7	BL	A	Portsmouth	D	0-0	0-0	14		(10,567)
7		14	BL	H	Watford	L	0-1	0-1	16		8,741
8		18	BL	H	Port Vale	W	3-1	3-0	13	Byrne 6, Meade 13, Robinson 43	5,790
9		21	BL	A	Derby County	L	1-3	0-1	16	Meade 85	(12,004)
10		24	RC 2/1	A	Brentford	L	1-4	0-3		Robinson 62	(4,927)
11		28	BL	H	Bristol Rovers	W	3-1	1-1	12	Codner 45, 48, Byrne 86	6,392
12	O	5	BL	A	Sunderland	L	2-4	2-1	14	Byrne 5, Robinson 43	(15,119)
13		9	RC 2/2	H	Brentford	W	†4-2	3-1		Byrne 4, 55, Codner 13, Meade 44	4,502
14		12	BL	H	Ipswich Town	D	2-2	0-1	15	Byrne 53, Chivers 69	9,010
15		19	BL	A	Charlton Athletic	L	0-2	0-2	18		(5,598)
16		23	ZDS 2	H	Wimbledon	W	3-2	2-1		Barham 10, Robinson 45, Chivers 90	2,796
17		26	BL	H	Swindon Town	L	0-2	0-1	19		7,370
18		30	BL	H	Leicester City	L	1-2	0-1	19	Codner 55	6,424
19	N	2	BL	A	Blackburn Rovers	L	0-1	0-0	20		(9,877)
20		6	BL	H	Grimsby Town	W	3-0	3-0	20	Meade 12, 20, Gall 15	4,420
21		9	BL	H	Middlesbrough	D	1-1	1-0	20	Gall 35	8,720
22		16	BL	A	Cambridge United	D	0-0	0-0	17		(7,625)
23		23	BL	A	Oxford United	L	1-3	0-1	19	Gall 58	(4,563)
24		26	ZDS QF	A	West Ham United	L	0-2	0-1			(8,146)
25		30	BL	H	Plymouth Argyle	W	1-0	0-0	18	O'Reilly 90	6,713
26	D	7	BL	A	Southend United	L	1-2	0-1	22	Wade 82	(6,303)
27		14	BL	A	Newcastle United	D	2-2	1-2	20	O'Reilly 25, Farrington 75	7,658
28		21	BL	H	Millwall	L	3-4	0-1	21	Gall 49, 84, Chapman 74	7,598
29		26	BL	A	Leicester City	L	1-2	0-1	23	Gallacher 77	(16,767)
30		28	BL	A	Wolverhampton W	L	0-2	0-2	23		(13,606)
31	J	1	BL	H	Bristol City	D	0-0	0-0	23		7,555
32		4	FAC 3	H	Crawley Town	W	5-0	3-0		Gall 24, Walker 31, Chapman 39, 59, Meade 84	18,031
33		11	BL	H	Barnsley	W	3-1	2-0	23	Robinson 16, Wade 27, Chapman 63	6,107
34		17	BL	A	Tranmere Rovers	D	1-1	0-0	22	Meade 80	(7,179)
35		25	FAC 4	A	Bolton Wanderers	L	1-2	0-0		Meade 55	(12,635)
36	F	1	BL	H	Charlton Athletic	L	1-2	1-1	22	Walker 17	8,870
37		8	BL	A	Swindon Town	L	1-2	1-0	23	Gall 6	(9,127)
38		15	BL	H	Oxford United	L	1-2	0-1	24	Robinson 15	6,096
39		22	BL	A	Plymouth Argyle	D	1-1	0-1	24	Gall 82	(5,259)
40		29	BL	H	Southend United	W	3-2	1-1	24	Meade 32, Codner 65, Munday 88	8,271
41	M	7	BL	A	Newcastle United	W	1-0	0-0	20	Gall 78	(24,597)
42		10	BL	A	Grimsby Town	W	1-0	0-0	18	Walker 58	(4,583)
43		14	BL	H	Blackburn Rovers	L	0-3	0-2	20		10,845
44		21	BL	A	Middlesbrough	L	0-4	0-2	22		(13,054)
45		28	BL	H	Cambridge United	D	1-1	0-0	23	Gall 52	7,702
46		31	BL	H	Watford	W	1-0	0-0	20	Meade 58	(7,783)
47	A	11	BL	A	Port Vale	L	1-2	0-0	23	Gall 59	(6,441)
48		15	BL	H	Derby County	L	1-2	0-1	23	Gall 80	8,159
49		20	BL	A	Bristol Rovers	L	1-4	0-2	24	Gall 55	(6,092)
50		24	BL	H	Sunderland	D	2-2	2-2	24	Gall 11, Codner 19	9,851
51		29	BL	H	Portsmouth	W	2-1	1-0	24	Robinson 43, Meade 46	11,647
52	M	2	BL	A	Ipswich Town	L	1-3	1-2	24	Meade 45	(26,803)

Best Home League Attendance: 11,647 v Portsmouth   **Smallest:** 4,420 v Grimsby Town   **Av Home Att:** 8,010

Goal Scorers: **Compared with 90-91:** -361

League (56): Gall 13, Meade 9, Robinson 6, Codner 6, Byrne 5, Wade 3, O'Reilly 3, Walker 2, Barham 2, Chapman 2, Farrington, Munday Bissett, Gallacher, Chivers

R/lows C (5): Byrne 2, Robinson, Meade, Codner

FA Cup (6): Meade 2, Chapman 2, Walker, Gall

ZDS Cup (3): Chivers, Barham, Robinson

†=After extra-time

96

1991-92

Digweed P.	Crumplin J.	Chapman I.	Wilkins D.	Chivers G.	O'Reilly G.	Iovan S.	Byrne J.	Wade B.	Codner R.	Walker C.	Robinson J.	Bissett N.	Barham M.	Meade R.	McGrath	Beeney M.	Farrington M.	Briley L.	Clarkson D.	Gall M.	Gallacher B.	Sommer J. (L)	McCarthy P.	Reed	Munday S.	Referee	
1	2	3	4	5	6	7*	8	9	10•	11	12	14														A Buksh	1
1	2	3	4	5	6	7•	8	9*	10	11			14	12												D Frampton	2
1	12	3	4	2	6		8	9*	10	11•	14	5	7													P Taylor	3
1	S	3	4	2	6		8		10	11		5	7	9	S											R Milford	4
	2*	3	4	1	6		8		10	11		5	7	9	S	12										K Barratt	5
	2	3	4	5	6		8		10	11			7	9		1	S	S								G Ashby	6
		3•	4	2	6		8		10	11	5	7	9*			1	12	14								M Bailey	7
		3	4	2•	6		8		10	11	5	7	9			1	S	14								M Pierce	8
		3	4	2	6		8*		10	11•	5	7	9			1	12	14								P Foakes	9
		3	4	2	6		8		10	11	5	7	9*			1	12	S								**R Gifford**	**10**
	2	3	4•	5	6		8		10	11		7	9			1	S	14								R Lewis	11
	2	3		5	6		8*		10	11		7	9•			1	12	4	14							J Worrall	12
	2	3	4	5	6		8		10	11		7	9*			1	12	S								**I Hemley**	**13**
	2	3	4	5	6		8		10	11		7	9			1	S	S								R Wiseman	14
	2	3		5			8		10	11		6	7	9		1	S	4	S							J Martin	15
	2	3		5				S	10	11		6	7	9		1	8	4	S							**J Moules**	**16**
	2	3		5					10	11		6•	7*	12		1	8	4	14	9						J Carter	17
	2	3	12	5	6				10	11•			7			1	8	4*		9						D Ellery	18
	2	4		5	6†	11			10			14	7•			1†	8	S		9	3					G Courtney	19
	2	4		5	6				10	11	7			8		1	S	4	14	9	3					B Hamer	20
	2			5	6				10	11	7•			8		1	S	4	14	9	3					P Durkin	21
	2			5		7			10	11				8			S	4	S	9	3	1	6			D Gallagher	22
	2	S		5	6				10	11	7			8		1	S	4		9	3					P Don	23
	2•	S		5	6	7			10	14				8•		1	11	4		9	3					**P Danson**	**24**
	2	12		5	6				10	11	7			8•		1	14	4*		9	3					D Axcell	25
	2	12		5	6		8		10	11	7					1		4		9*	3	S				P Jones	26
	2	4		5	6				10	11	7					1	8	S		9	3					C Wilkes	27
	2	4		5	6†				10	11	7					1	8	S		9	3					J Brandwood	28
	2	4		5†	6				10	11	7			12		1	8*	S		9	3					R Pawley	29
	2	4		5	6•				10	11	7			12		1	8*		14	9	3					A Ward	30
	2	4		5					10	11	7	6		12		1	8*	S		9	3					G Pooley	31
	2	4	14	5			12			11	7*	6		8		1			10	9*	3					**M Bailey**	**32**
	2	4		S				9	S	11	7	6		8		1			10		3		5			A Smith	33
	2	4		S				9	12	11	7	6		8		1			10*		3		5			J Kirkby	34
	2	4		S				9	12	11	7	6		8		1			10*		3		5			**R Hamer**	**35**
	2	4	14		6			9*	10	11•	7			8		1			12		3		5			P Foakes	36
1	2	4	11		6			S	10		7			8						9	3		5			D Chadwell	37
1	2	4			6				10		7		S	8•		11*			14	9	3		5			I Borrett	38
1		4			6	S			10		7			8		S	11			9	3		5		2	H King	39
1		4			6	S			10		7			8		S	11			9	3		5		2	M Reed	40
1	6	4							10	11	7			8*			12			9	3		5		2	D Allison	41
1	6	4	12						10	11	7			8*			S			9	3		5		2	A Dawson	42
1	6	4*		12					10	11	7•			8					14	9	3		5		2	R Milford	43
1		4		6				S	10	11				8•				7		9	3		5		2	P Wright	44
1	7	4		6					10	11				8*				S	12	9	3		5		2	G Ashby	45
1	7	4		6					10	11				8				S	S	9	2		5		2	R Bigger	46
1	11	4		6					10	S	7			8				S		9	3		5		2	V Callow	47
1		4		S	6				10	11	7			8						9	3		5		2	D Axcell	48
1	11	4		6					10	S	7			8•					14	9	3		5		2	P Scoble	49
1		4			6				10	11	7			8				S		9	3		5		2	G Poll	50
1		4			6				10	11	7			8†				S		9	3		5		2	P Alcock	51
1	12	4			6				10	11	7*			8•						9	3		5		2	P Vanes	52
20	27	35	24	36	28	4	13	7	44	23	34	11	22	35		24	8	11	4	30	31	1	20		14	League Appearances	
2	2	2	2						1			2	2	2	5	1	6	4	9	1						Substitute Appearances	
1	2	2	2	2			2			2	1	2	2		2	0+2			2	1	2		1			R/lows Appearances	
2	2	0+1	1				1+1	0+1	2		2		2	2		2			2	1	2		1			FA Cup Appearances	
2	1		2	1		1		2	0+1	1	1	1	2		2	2	2		1	1	2					ZDS Cup Appearances	

Also Played: Posn.(Game): O'Dowd 14(44), Funnell S(50,51)14(52)
Players on Loan: Juergen Sommer (Luton Town)   † = Sent Off

BRIGHTON & HOVE ALBION

Club Colours: Blue & white striped shirts, blue & white striped shorts, blue stockings
Change Colours: White shirts with red navy lines, red shorts, red stockings with blue & white trim
Reserves League: Neville Ovenden Football Combination

Previous Name: Brighton United 1898-1900, Brighton & Hove Rangers 1900-1901
Previous League: Southern League
Previous Managers: John Jackson 1900-05   Frank Scott Walford 1905-08   Jack Robson 1908-15   Charles Webb 1919-47   Tommy Cook 1947   Don Welsh 1947-51   Billy Lane 1951-61   George Curtis 1961-63   Archie Macauley 1963-68   Freddie Goodwin 1968-70   Pat Saward 1970-73   Brian Clough 1973-74   Peter Taylor 1974-76   Alan Mullery 1976-81   Mike Bailey 1981-82   Jimmy Melia 1982-83   Chris Cattlin 1983-86   Alan Mullery 1986-87   Barry Lloyd 1987-
Honours: Champions Division 3S 1957-58   Champions Division 4 1964-65   Charity Shield Winners 1910
League Career: Original Members of Division 3 1920   Transfered to Div 3S 1921   Promoted to Div 2 1957-58   Relegated to Div 3 1961-62   Relegated to Div 4 1962-63   Promoted to Div 3 1964-65   Promoted to Div 2 1971-72   Relegated to Div 3 1972-73   Promoted to Div 2 1976-77   Promoted to Div 1 1978-79   Relegated to Div 2 1982-83   Relegated to Div 3 1986-87   Promoted to Div 2 1987-88   Relegated to Div 3 1991-92

CLUB RECORDS

Most Appearances for Club: E 'Tug' Wilson (1922-36): League 509, FA Cup 49, Divisional Cup 8 **Total 566**
Most Capped Player: Steve Penney (N. Ireland) 17
Record Goalscorer in a Match: Arthur Attwood, 6 v Shoreham, 12-0, FA Cup, 1.10.1932
Record League Goalscorer in a Season: Peter Ward, 32, 1976-77 **In All Competitions:** Peter Ward, 36 (League 32, FA Cup 1, League Cup 3) 1976-77
Record League Goalscorer in a Career: Tommy Cook, 113, 1922-29 **In All Competitions:** Tommy Cook, 123 (League 113, FA Cup 9) 1922-29
Record Transfer Fee Received: £900,000 from Liverpool for Mark Lawrenson, August 1981
Record Transfer Fee Paid: £500,000 to Manchester United for Andy Ritchie, October 1980
Best Performances: League: 13th Division 1 1981-82   **FA Cup:** Finalists 1982-83   **League Cup:** 5th Round 1978-79
Most League Points: (3pts for win) 84, Division 3, 1987-88   (2pts for win) 65, Division 3S, 1955-56 & Division 3, 1971-72
Most Goals: 112, Division 3, 1955-56
Record League Victory and Most Goals Scored in a League Match: 9-1 v Newport, Division 3S, 18.4.1951   9-1 v Southend, Division 3, 27.11.1965
Record Victory and Most Goals Scored in a Cup Tie: 10-1 v Wisbech, FA Cup Round 1, 13.11.1965
Record League Defeat: 0-9 v Middlesbrough, Division 2, 23.8.1958
Record Cup Defeat: 0-8 v Northampton, League Cup Rnd 4 replay, 1.11.1966
Oldest Player in a League Match: Herbert Jones, 39 years 8 months, 13.4.1935
Youngest Player in League Match: Ian Chapman, 16 years 259 days v Birmingham City, Div 2, 14.2.1987 (First Lilleshall School of Excellence player to make League debut)

LONGEST LEAGUE RUNS	
of undefeated matches: 16 (1930-31)	**of league matches without a win:** 15 (1947-48, 1972-73)
of undefeated home matches: 27 (1975-76)	**of undefeated away matches:** 9 (1938)
without home win: 10 (1972-73)	**without an away win:** 21 (1982-83)
of league wins: 9 (1926)	**of home wins:** 14 (1955-56, 1975-76)
of league defeats: 12 (1972-73)	**of away wins:** 4 (1926, 1936 twice)

BRIGHTON & HOVE ALBION

PLAYERS NAME Honours	Ht	Wt	Birthdate	Birthplace Transfers	Contract Date	Clubs	League	L/Cup	FA Cup	Other	Lg	L/C	FAC	Oth
GOALKEEPERS														
Mark Beeney	6.4	14.7	30.12.67	Pembury		Gillingham	2	1						
E:Semi.Pro.1,GMVC'89				Free	28.07.89	Maidstone Utd	50	3	11	6				
				Loan	22.03.90	Aldershot	7							
				£30,000		Brighton & H.A	26+1	2	2	2				
Perry Digweed	6.0	11.4	26.10.59	London	01.09.76	Fulham (A)	15							
				£150,000	15.01.81	Brighton & H.A	175	5	9	8				
				Loan	01.10.83	West Brom A								
				Loan	01.01.85	Charlton Ath								
				Loan	01.12.87	Newcastle Utd								
				Loan	02.03.88	Chelsea	3							
DEFENDERS														
Nicholas Bissett	6.1	12.10	05.04.64	Fulham		Dagenham			1					
				£20,000		Barnet								
				£125,000	08.09.88	Brighton & H.A	58+3	3	2	6	6			
Ian Chapman	5.8	11.6	31.05.70	Brighton	05.06.87	Brighton & H.A	114+12	5+1	4+2	3+4	2		2	
E: S														
Gary Chivers	5.11	11.5	15.05.60	Stockwell	07.08.78	Chelsea (A)	128+5	8	8		4			
					01.08.83	Swansea City	10							
					15.02.84	Q.P.R	58+2	6	2	1				
					10.09.87	Watford	14	1	4					
					18.03.88	Brighton & H.A	162+2	8	7	9	13			1
Bernard Gallacher	5.8	11.4	22.03.67	Johnstone	04.04.85	Aston Villa (A)	55+2	8+1	3	3				1
				Loan		Blackburn Rovers	4							
				Free N.C	26.09.91	Doncaster Rovers								
				Free	31.10.91	Brighton & H.A	31		2	1	1			
Paul McCarthy	6.0	13.6	04.08.71	Cork	26.04.89	Brighton & H.A. (T)	43+1	2	4	3				
Eire:u21.1														
Gary O'Reilly	6.0	12.2	21.03.61	Isleworth	05.09.79	Tottenham H	39+6	4	2	3+2				
Ei: Y, S				£45,000	28.08.84	Brighton & H.A	78+1	4	7	2	3			
				£40,000	03.01.87	Crystal Palace	65+5	3	7	3+2	2		2	
				Loan	28.03.91	Birmingham City	1							
				Free	31.07.91	Brighton & H.A	28	2		1	3			
MIDFIELD														
Robert Codner	5.11	11.05	23.06.65	Walthamstow		Dagenham			2					
E: S-P.1						Barnet			1					
				£125,000	08.09.88	Brighton & H.A	153+7	6	4+1	10	24	1	1	3
John Crumplin	5.7	11.2	26.05.67	Bath		Bognor Reg			4				1	
				£3,500	25.03.87	Brighton & H.A	117+26	5+1	8	9	4			1
John Robinson	5.10	11.2	29.08.71	Bulawayo	21.04.89	Brighton & H.A. (T)	51+5	3	2+1	1+2	6	1		2
Dean Wilkins	5.8	11.8	12.07.62	Hillingdon	17.05.80	Q.P.R. (A)	1+5	1						
				Free	04.08.83	Brighton & H.A	2		1					
				Loan	22.04.84	Leyton Orient	10							
						Zwolle,Hol								
					28.07.87	Brighton & H.A	201+4	10	10+1	13	17	1		3
FORWARDS														
Mark Gall	5.10	12.0	14.05.63	Tulse Hill		Wandsworth								
GMVC'89						Grennwich Boro								
				£2,000	01.07.89	Maidstone Utd	69+16	3+2	7+1	9+1	31		4	8
				£45,000	24.10.91	Brighton & H.A	30+1		1	1	13		1	
Clive Walker	5.9	11.4	26.05.57	Oxford	01.04.75	Chelsea (A)	168+30	9+1	14+2		60	2	3	
E: S				£70,000	26.07.84	Sunderland	48+2	11	1	1+1	10	6		1
				£75,000	14.12.85	Q.P.R	16+5	2+1	4		1	1		
					13.10.87	Fulham	102+7	5+1	4	8	29	1	1	1
				£20,000	23.08.90	Brighton & H.A	68	2	5	5+1	5		1	1
ADDITIONAL CONTRACT PLAYERS														
Michael Barrett					04.09.91	Brighton & H.A. (T)								
Mark Benney						Maidstone Utd								
					28.03.91	Brighton & H.A								
David J Clarkson				16.09.91		Brighton & H.A	4+9		2					
Mark Farrington						Feyenoord								
				£100,000	24.08.91	Brighton & H.A	8+6	0+2			1			
Simon Funnell		08.07.74	Brighton		02.07.92	Brighton & H.A. (T)	0+1							
Igor Gurinovich					06.11.90	Brighton & H.A	3+1		1	1	1		1	
Ari Heikkinen					06.12.90	Brighton & H.A								
Ari Keikinnen						Tutka								
				£150,000		Brighton & H.A								
(D) Stuart Munday	5.11	10.0	28.09.72	London	06.07.90	Brighton & H.A. (T)	14				1			

LEADING LEAGUE GOALSCORERS SEASONS 1985-86 – 1991-92

1985-86	**DEAN SAUNDERS**	**15**		1986-87	**TERRY CONNOR**	**9**
1987-88	**GARRY NELSON**	**22**		1988-89	**GARRY NELSON**	**15**
					KEVIN BREMNER	**15**
1989-90	**KEVIN BREMNER**	**13**		1990-91	**MIKE SMALL**	**15**
	1991-92	**MARK GALL**	**13**			

THE GOLDSTONE GROUND Newtown Road, Hove, East Sussex BN3 7DE

Capacity: 17,607   **Covered Standing:** 12,497   **Seating:** 5,110

Tel: Ground: 0273 739535   **Ticket Sales:** 0273 778855   **Clubcall:** 0891 800 609

All premium rate calls (0898/0891) cost 36p per minute cheap rate and 48p per minute at all other times. Call costings correct at time of going to press.

ATTENDANCES
Highest: 36,747 v Fulham, Div 2, 27.12.1958

Lowest: 1,150 v Norwich City, Div 3(S), 2.2.1929

RECORD RECEIPTS:
£87,946 v Millwall, Div 2 P/Off S/F 1st leg, 19.5.1991

Season Tickets:
Stands: (West) from £174 to £309; (South) adult £153, OAP £82, Family £82
Ground: £92, jnr/OAP £62

Executive Box Season Tickets:

Cost of Stand Tickets: Seats: £5.50 to £15 (no reductions)
Terraces: Members £5, juniors under 16/OAP £2.50; Non-members and Visiting Supporters £6

Match and Ticket Information: Postal bookings depending on availability four weeks before each match. Visa and Access bookings up to day of match

Car Parking: Available at the Greyhound Stadium (Nevill Road). Limited parking adjacent to ground. Visitors beware – Police tow-away squad on duty on match days

Nearest Railway Station: Hove (0273 206755)

How to get to the ground

From North: Use A23 with Pyecombe, then in 2m turn right (S.P. Hove). In 1.1m bear left into Nevill Road A2023. In 0.9m at cross roads turn left A27 into Old Shoreham Road for Brighton and Hove Albion.

From East: From Lewes use A27 to Brighton then follow signs Worthing A27 along Old Shoreham Road for Brighton and Hove Albion

From West: Use A27 (S.P. Brighton) along Old Shoreham Road for Brighton and Hove Albion

Value Rating: ★ ★ ★ ★

Programme Editor: Tony Millard Associates

Price of 1992-93 Programme: £1.20
Number of Pages: 32
Subscriptions: 23 home programmes £27.60 (saved) + £8.74 if sent by post; 23 away programmes £24.70 (saved) + £8.74 if sent by post.

Local Newspapers: Evening Argus
Seagull News (Clubs own paper)

Local Radio Stations: BBC Radio Sussex, Southern Sound

BRISTOL CITY

Division 1

Formed: 1894   **Turned Professional:** 1897   **Ltd Co:** 1897

SPONSORED BY: Thorn Security   **NICKNAME:** The Robins

Chairman
L J Kew

Directors
W I Williams (Vice-Chairman)
K Sage (Vice-Chairman)
D Coller
O W Newland
P Manning
M Fricker

Secretary
Miss Jean Harrison (0272 632812)

Commercial Manager
John Cox

Team Manager
Denis Smith

Asst. Player/Manager
Russell Osman

Chief Scout
Tony Fawthrop

Physiotherapist
Buster Footman

Groundsman
Gary Vile

Club Statisticians for the Directory
David Woods & David Peacey

MOST City fans would have probably viewed the start of the '91-92 campaign with confidence. The previous season, the club's first back in Division Two, had seen them more than hold their own, finishing ninth, just three three points off a play-off place. By mid-September, sixth place seemed to confirm this confidence and by the end of the month further evidence was provided in the shape of an away win over rivals Bristol Rovers in the Rumbelows League Cup. Although Rovers were to win the return at Ashton and progress on the away goals rule league form continued to offer hope and victory over Plymouth on 5 November saw them established in ninth spot. Four months later, on 10 March, and defeat at Plymouth left City one place off the bottom of the table in 23rd place. The run of league games between those two fixtures against Argyle read like a nightmare: Played 17, Won 2, Drawn 6, Lost 9, and can by attributed to any amount of reasons; bad luck (particularly with injuries) partly, but bad form and inconsistency to a great degree.

By the second game against Plymouth, former Sunderland boss Denis Smith had replaced Jimmy Lumsden and, as is often the case, a new face with the injection of a few new players had the desired effect and an impressive run of eight games unbeaten ensured safety in the now re-christened 'Division One' for season '92-93, even allowing time for three straight defeats to end the season. It is, perhaps, that last game, away to Watford, that summed up one of the club's problems during the season. In the space of a few minutes three City players were sent off at Vicarage Road and if the club are to consolidate and progress they certainly aren't going to achieve it by shooting themselves in the foot in this way.

There were successes during the season; Martin Scott and Matt Bryant were virtual ever-presents in defence and are a good foundation for the club to build on. The goalkeeping spot has become a problem with neither Keith Welch nor Andy Leaning showing sufficient consistency to make the spot his own however. Former manager Jimmy Lumsden did sign something of a 'folk hero' in Jacki Dziekonowski but at times he does seem to play 'outside' the team – not always successfully. He did feature strongly in the team's F.A. Cup run, however, which accounted for First Division Wimbledon and Division Two pacesetters Leicester City before ending at the City ground, Nottingham in Round Five.   Denis Smith's appointment in early March left him with little time to assess the squad prior to the transfer deadline and the signings that were made, Leroy Rosenior and Ray Atteveld have both made their mark. But the burning question for City followers is whether he can make Andrew Cole's loan signing from Arsenal a permanent move. Cole's all round ability, pace and goalscoring – 8 goals in 12 games – was a major factor in City's survival.

Changes in playing staff are inevitable before the new season in August – a season, I feel, that will be as much a test of the patience of the supporters as anything else. No predictions this time around, but with his success in building the side that took Sunderland to Wembley in May who's to say that a cup run isn't on the cards for City under Denis Smith?   **Dave Peacey**

Back row L-R: Micky Mellon, Nicky Morgan, Gerry Harrison, James McIntyre, Ray Atteveld, Mark Gavin, Terry Connor. **Middle row:** Buster Footman, Denis Smith, Wayne Allison, Dariusz Dziekanowski, Robert Edwards, Gary Campbell, Andy Leaning, Keith Welch, David Thompson, Matt Bryant, Brian Mitchell, Leroy Rosenior, Steve Benton, Mark Harrison, Alan Crawford. **Front row:** Deion Vernon, Andy Paterson, Shaun Rouse, Andy Cole, Russell Osman, Gary Shelton, Mark Aizelwood, Andy Llewellyn, Martin Scott, Junior Bent, Andy Hogg

BRISTOL CITY

DIVISION TWO: 17th **FA CUP:** 5th RND **RUMBELOWS CUP:** 2nd RND **ZDS CUP:** 2nd RND

M	DATE		COMP.	VEN	OPPONENTS	RESULT		H/T	LGE POS	GOALSCORERS/GOAL TIMES	ATTEN-DANCE
1	A	17	BL	A	Southend United	D	1-1	0-1		Taylor 57	(6,720)
2		20	BL	H	Brighton & H A	W	2-1	1-0		Scott 22, Bryant 66	11,299
3		24	BL	H	Blackburn Rovers	W	1-0	1-0	2	Allison 43	11,317
4		31	BL	A	Port Vale	D	1-1	0-1	4	Morgan 67	(7,057)
5	S	4	BL	H	Bristol Rovers	W	1-0	0-0	2	Allison 64	20,183
6		7	BL	A	Leicester City	L	1-2	1-2	5	Morgan 36	(17,815)
7		14	BL	H	Tranmere Rovers	D	2-2	2-1	5	Allison 10, Shelton 25	11,235
8		17	BL	H	Millwall	D	2-2	1-2	6	Bryant 45, Scott (pen) 86	10,862
9		21	BL	A	Ipswich Town	L	2-4	1-1	10	Allison 4, Smith 56	(9,692)
10		**25**	**RC 2/1**	**A**	**Bristol Rovers**	**W**	**3-1**	**2-1**		**Morgan 6, Smith 38, Allison 75**	**(5,155)**
11		28	BL	H	Portsmouth	L	0-2	0-2	14		9,830
12	O	5	BL	A	Derby County	L	1-4	0-1	18	Edwards 74	(11,880)
13		**8**	**RC 2/2**	**H**	**Bristol Rovers**	**L**	**†2-4**	**1-1**		**Morgan 14, Smith 114**	**9,880**
14		12	BL	H	Watford	W	1-0	1-0	11	Connor 44	7,882
15		19	BL	A	Barnsley	W	2-1	1-0	8	May 24, Shelton 79	(6,566)
16		**22**	**ZDS 2**	**H**	**Southampton**	**L**	**1-2**	**1-0**		**Taylor 9**	**5,672**
17		26	BL	H	Newcastle United	D	1-1	0-1	9	Taylor 87	8,613
18	N	2	BL	A	Cambridge United	D	0-0	0-0	9		(4,810)
19		5	BL	H	Plymouth Argyle	W	2-0	2-0	9	Morgan 14, Allison 27	7,735
20		9	BL	H	Sunderland	W	1-0	1-0	9	Allison 25	10,570
21		16	BL	A	Oxford United	D	1-1	0-0	10	Allison 54	(5,779)
22		23	BL	A	Middlesbrough	L	1-3	1-2	11	Taylor 40	(12,928)
23		30	BL	H	Charlton Athletic	L	0-2	0-1	11		9,125
24	D	7	BL	A	Grimsby Town	L	1-3	1-1	12	Rennie 34	(4,866)
25		21	BL	A	Bristol Rovers	L	2-3	1-2	14	Rennie 11, Bent 89	(6,306)
26		26	BL	H	Swindon Town	D	1-1	0-1	16	Taylor 48	14,636
27		28	BL	H	Port Vale	W	3-0	2-0	12	Allison 1, Osman 14, Bent 49	9,235
28	J	1	BL	A	Brighton & H A	D	0-0	0-0	13		(7,555)
29		4	FAC 3	H	Wimbledon	D	1-1	0-1		Barton (og) 88	12,679
30		11	BL	A	Blackburn Rovers	L	0-4	0-3	14		(12,964)
31		14	FAC 3R	A	Wimbledon	W	1-0	1-0		May 10	(3,747)
32		18	BL	H	Southend United	D	2-2	0-1	14	Dziekanowski 67, Powell (og) 78	9,883
33		25	FAC 4	A	Leicester City	W	2-1	1-0		Bent 27, Dziekanowski 57	(19,313)
34	F	1	BL	H	Barnsley	L	0-2	0-0	16		9,508
35		4	BL	A	Swindon Town	L	0-2	0-0	16		(9,627)
36		8	BL	A	Newcastle United	L	0-3	0-0	18		(29,054)
37		15	FAC 5	A	Nottingham Forest	L	1-4	0-1		Dziekanowski 76	(24,054)
38		22	BL	A	Charlton Athletic	L	1-2	1-0	21	Shelton 43	(5,900)
39		29	BL	H	Grimsby Town	D	1-1	1-0	20	Aizelwood 43	8,992
40	M	7	BL	A	Wolverhampton W	D	1-1	1-1	22	Osman 41	(12,542)
41		10	BL	A	Plymouth Argyle	L	0-1	0-0	23		(9,734)
42		14	BL	H	Cambridge United	L	1-2	1-0	23	Scott 17	9,579
43		17	BL	H	Wolverhampton W	W	2-0	0-0	21	Dziekanowski 85, 87	11,623
44		21	BL	A	Sunderland	W	3-1	3-0	20	Cole 7, Allison 19, 39	(18,933)
45		28	BL	H	Oxford United	D	1-1	0-0	20	Dziekanowski 88	12,402
46		31	BL	A	Tranmere Rovers	D	2-2	0-0	19	Cole 71, Rosenior 75	(5,797)
47	A	4	BL	H	Leicester City	W	2-1	1-1	17	Rosenior 5, Cole 55	13,020
48		7	BL	H	Middlesbrough	D	1-1	0-1	17	Cole 66	12,814
49		11	BL	A	Millwall	W	3-2	0-1	16	Rosenior 53, 75, Cole 64	(6,989)
50		18	BL	H	Ipswich Town	W	2-1	1-0	17	Rosenior 37, Cole 53	16,941
51		20	BL	A	Portsmouth	L	0-1	0-1	17		(17,151)
52		25	BL	H	Derby County	L	1-2	1-1	17	Atteveld 44	16,648
53	M	2	BL	A	Watford	L	2-5	1-1	17	Cole 26, 48	(10,582)

Best Home League Attendance: 20,183 v Bristol Rovers **Smallest:** 7,735 v Plymouth Argyle **Av Home Att:** 11,475

Goal Scorers: **Compared with 90-91:** -2,018

League (55): Allison 10, Cole 8, Rosenior 5, Taylor 4, Dziekanowski 4, Morgan 3, Scott 3 (1 pen), Shelton 3, Rennie 2, Bent 2, Bryant 2, Osman 2, May, Opponents, Atteveld, Edwards, Aizelwood, Smith, Connor

R/lows C (5): Morgan 2, Smith 2, Allison

FA Cup (5): Dziekanowski 2, Opponents, May, Bent

ZDS Cup (1): Taylor

† = After extra-time

Welch K.	Llewellyn A.	Scott M.	May A.	Bryant M.	Aizlewood M.	Shelton G.	Rennie D.	Allison W.	Taylor R.	Smith D.	Morgan N.	Edwards R.	Bent J.	Harrison G.	Mellon M.	Caesar G.	Connor T.	Leaning A.	Osman R.	Gavin M.	Dziekanowski D.	McIntyre J.	Cole A.	Rosenior L.	Atteveld R.	Referee	
1	2	3	4	5	6	7	8	9	10	11	S	S														R Lewis	1
1	2	3	4	5	6	7	8	9	10	11	S	S														D Frampton	2
1	2	3	4	5	6	7	8	9	10*	11	12		S													R Bigger	3
1	2	3	4	5	6	7	8	9	10*	11	12		S													M Reed	4
1	2•	3	4	5	6	7	8	9	S	11	10				14											M Bodenham	5
1		3	2	5	6•	7	8	9		11	10	4	7*		12	S										P Don	6
1		3	2	5	6•	7	8	9		11	10	4			12	S										P Vanes	7
1		3	2	5		7	8	9	12	11	10*	4*	14			6										C Wilkes	8
1	2	3	4	5		7	8	9		11	S	S				6	10									A Buksh	9
1	2	3	4	5		7•	8	9	S	11	10	14				6										K Cooper	10
1	2	3	4	5		7*	8	9		11	10	14				6•	12									D Elleray	11
1	2	3	4•	5	6		8	9		11	S	7	14				10									W Flood	12
1	2	3		5*	6		8	9	14	11	10	7	12	4•												J Deakin	13
	2	3	4				8	9	12	11	10*		14		5	7•		1	6							H King	14
	2	3	4			7	8	9	12	S	10*				5	11		1	6							R Hart	15
	2	3	4	5	12	7*	8	9	10		S					6	11	1								T Ward	16
	2	3	4			7	8	12	9	14	10*				5	11	6•	1								D Gallagher	17
	2	3	S	5	6		8	10	9	S						4	11	1								R Shepherd	18
	2	3	4	5	6†	7	8	9		11	10	S						1	S							K Barratt	19
	2•	3	4	5	6	7	8	9		11	10•						14	1	12							B Hill	20
	2	3	4	5	6	7	8	9	14	11							10•	1	S							P Taylor	21
	2•	3	4	5		7	8	9	14	11						12	10*	1	6							P Jones	22
	2	3	12	5		7	8•	9	10	11			14				4*	1	6							G Ashby	23
	2	3	4	5			8	9	10		S	7			S	6		1		11						R Poulain	24
	2•	3	7	5	6		8	9	10			14			S			1	4	11						P Durkin	25
	2	3	4	5	6		8	9	10			S			S			1	7	11						R Gifford	26
	2	3*	4•	5	6		8	9	10			14			12			1	7	11						A Smith	27
	2	3	4	5	6		8*	9	10			S			12			1	7	11						G Pooley	28
	2*	3	4	5	6		8	9	10			S			12			1	7	11						K Cooper	29
		3	2	5	6		8*	9	10•			14	7	12				1	4	11						A Wilkie	30
		3	8	5	6				14		9	10	7•		S	2		1	4	11						K Cooper	31
		3	7	5	6				S		9	8*	12			2		1	4	11	10					I Hemley	32
	2	3	4	5				14			9•	S	7					1	6	11	8					P Vanes	33
	2	3	4	5	10						8•	S	7		14			1	6	11	9					P Alcock	34
	2	3	4	5	8			14			9•		7		11			1	6	S	10					W Burge	35
	2	3	4*	5	12		8	9			S		7					1	6	11	10					J Parker	36
	2	3	S	5	4		8	9				11	7					1	6	S	10					N Midgley	37
1		3	4	5	6		8*	9		11		7•			12				2	14	10					G Singh	38
1		3	4	5	6			9			10	8	7		S				2		11	S				J Brandwood	39
1	2	3	4	5					10		14	8			12				6	7	9•	11*				A Gunn	40
1	2	3	4	5					10		9*	8	12		7				6		11					M Pierce	41
1	2•	3	11	5	4				10			8	12	14	7*				6				9			J Deakin	42
1	2	3	11	5	4				10			8*			S		7		6			12	9			P Scobie	43
1	2	3	11	5	4				10*						7				6		8•		9	14		S Lodge	44
1	2	3	11	5	4				10			12			7*				6•		8		9	14	12	D Shadwell	45
1	2	3	11	5	4				10•			12			7				6		8		9*	14		R Dilkes	46
1	2	3	11	5	4				14			12			7				6		8*		9	10•		G Poll	47
1	2•	3*	11	5	4				14						7				6		8		9	10†	12	J Carter	48
1	2	3	11	5	4				14						7				6•		8*		9	10	12	P Wright	49
1		3	11	5	4				S						7				6		8		9	10	2	J Martin	50
1	S	3	11	5	4*				14						7•				6		8		9	10	2	G Ashby	51
1	7	3	11	5	4*				10			12			14				6•	14	8		9		2	K Breen	52
	7*	3	11	5	4†				10†			12			14			1	6		8•		9		2†	K Morton	53
26	37	46	44	43	34	18	27	37	13	17	15	12	7		12	9	9	20	30	12	16	1	12	5	4	**League Appearances**	
			1			1		6	5	1	4	8	10	4	4		1		2	1	2	1		3	3	**Substitute Appearances**	
	2	2	2	1	2	1	2	2	0+1	2	2	1+1	0+1	1		1								3	3	**R/lows Appearances**	
	3	4	3	4	4	1	1	2+1	2	2	3				1			4	4	3	2					**FA Cup Appearances**	
	1	1	1	1	0+1	1	1	1	1						1	1		1	1	1						**ZDS Cup Appearances**	

Also Played: Paterson S(41,50)

Players on Loan: Cole (Arsenal)

† = Sent Off

BRISTOL CITY

Club Colours: Red shirts, white shorts, red and white stockings
Change Colours: Purple & green shirts, green shorts
Reserves League: Neville Ovenden Football Combination   **Youth League:** South East Counties League

COMPETITIONS				
Div. 1	Div. 2	Div. 3	Div. 3S	Div. 4
06-11	01-06	60-65	22-23	82-84
76-80	11-22	81-82	24-27	
	23-24	84-90	32-55	
	27-32			
	55-60			
	65-76			
	80-81			
	90-			

HONOURS				
Div. 2	Div. 3s	Ang/Scot	F.R.T.	Welsh
05-06	22-23	77-78	85-86	33-34
	26-27			
	54-55			

MOST GOALS IN A CAREER			
JOHN ATYEO 350 (1951-66)			
Season	League	FA Cup	League Cup
1951-52	12	2	
1952-53	11		
1953-54	22	3	
1954-55	28		
1955-56	30	1	
1956-57	23	5	
1957-58	23	2	
1958-59	26		
1959-60	16	1	
1960-61	19	7	3
1961-62	26	3	
1962-63	16	2	
1963-64	21	4	2
1964-65	23		
1965-66	19		
	315	30	5

MOST APPEARANCES: JOHN ATYEO 643 (1951-66)			
Year	League	FA Cup	League Cup
1951-52	44	2	
1952-53	33		
1953-54	45	3	
1954-55	46	1	
1955-56	39	1	
1956-57	37	3	
1957-58	42	4	
1958-59	40	3	
1959-60	42	1	
1960-61	37	5	3
1961-62	42	5	1
1962-63	30	3	1
1963-64	46	5	1
1964-65	38	4	
1965-66	35	1	
	596	41	6

RECORD TRANSFER FEE RECEIVED			
Amount	Club	Player	Date
£600,000	Norwich City	Rob Newman	7/91
£325,000	Coventry City	Gary Collier	8/79
£110,000	Chelsea	Chris Garland	9/71
£55,000	Leicester City	Bobby Kellard	8/70

RECORD TRANSFER FEE PAID			
Amount	Club	Player	Date
£500,000	Arsenal	Andrew Cole	7/92
£250,000	Everton	Ray Atteveld	3/92
£250,000	Celtic	J. Dziekanowski	1/92
£235,000	St. Mirren	Tony Fitzpatrick	7/79

MANAGERS (*=Caretaker managers)			
Name	Seasons	Best	Worst
Sam Hollis	1901-05	4(2)	6(2)
Harry Thickett	1905-10	2(1)	1(2)
Frank Bacon*	1910-11		
Sam Hollis	1911-13	19(1)	16(2)
George Hedley	1913-15	8(2)	13(2)
Jack Hamilton*	1915-19	War	time
Joe Palmer	1920-21	3(2)	8(2)
A Annan/C Hancock*	1921		
Alex Raisbeck	1921-29	12(2)	1(3s)
Joe Bradshaw	1929-32	16(2)	22(2)
Bob Hewison	1932-38	2(3s)	19(3s)
Clarrie Bourton*	1938-39	8(3s)	8(3s)
Bob Hewison	1940-49	3(3s)	16(3s)
Bob Wright	1949-50	15(3s)	15(3s)
Pat Beasley	1950-58	11(2)	15(3s)
J Seed/L Bardsley*	1958		
Peter Doherty	1958-60	10(2)	22(2)
Les Bardsley*	1960		
Fred Ford	1960-67	5(2)	14(3)
Les Bardsley*	1967		
Alan Dicks	1967-80	13(1)	19(2)
T Collins/K Wimshurst*	1980		
Bob Houghton	1980-82	21(2)	23(3)
R Hodgson/G Sharpe*	1982		
Terry Cooper	1982-88	5(3)	14(4)
Joe Jordan	1988-90	2(3)	11(3)
Jimmy Lumsden	1990-92	9(2)	9(2)
Aizle'd/Osman/Shelton*	1992		
Denis Smith	1992-		

LONGEST LEAGUE RUNS

of undefeated matches:	24 (9.9.1905-10.2.1906)
of undefeated home matches:	25 (24.10.1953-27.11.1954)
without home win:	10 (17.10.1931-5.3.1932)
of league wins:	14 (9.9.1905-2.12.1905)
of league defeats:	7 (5.9.1931-3.10.1931)
	(3.10.1970-7.11.1971)
of league matches w/out a win:	15 (29.4.1933-4.11.1933)
of undefeated away matches:	21 (16.9.1905-22.9.1906)
without an away win:	23 (8.10.1932-28.10.1933)
of home wins:	12 (24.4.1926-29.1.1927)
of away wins:	6 (16.9.1905-25.11.1905)

LOCAL BRANCH
Bristol South Branch
36 East Street
Bedminster
Bristol BS3 4HE Tel: 0272 631166

PREVIOUS NAME
Bristol South End 1894-97

PREVIOUS LEAGUE
Southern League 1897-1901

BIGGEST VICTORIES
League: 9-0 v Aldershot, Division 3S, 28.12.1946
F.A. Cup: 11-0 v Chichester City, Round 1, 5.11.1960
League Cup: 4-0 v Rotherham Utd, Round 2, 15.9.1970
4-0 v Peterborough Utd, Round 3, 2.10.1979

BIGGEST DEFEATS
League: 0-9 v Coventry City, Division 3S, 28.4.1934
F.A. Cup: 0-5 v Preston North End, Rnd 5 replay, 25.2.1935
0-5 v Brentford, Rnd 4 2nd leg, 31.1.1946
1-6 v Sunderland, Round 4, 25.1.1964
League Cup: 0-5 v Everton, Round 2, 13.9.1967
1-6 v West Ham United, Rnd 2 2nd leg, 9.10.1984
1-6 v Sunderland, Round 2 2nd leg, 8.10.1990

MOST POINTS
3 points a win: 91, Division 3, 1989-90
2 points a win: 70, Division 3S, 1954-55

MOST GOALS
104, 1926-27, Division 3S
Walsh 32, Keating 23, Paul 12, Martin 11, Rankin 9, Gilhespy
8, Gray 3, Smailes 2, Drummond 1, Torrance 1, og 2

MOST GOALS IN A MATCH
6, 'Tot' Walsh v Gillingham, Division 3S, 15.1.1927 (9-4)

MOST GOALS IN A SEASON
Don Clark, 41 (League 36, FAC 5), 1946-47
4 goals 3 times = 12, 3 goals 2 times = 6, 2 goals 5 times = 10,
1 goal 13 times = 13

MOST FIRST CLASS MATCHES IN A SEASON
64 (46 League, 6 FA Cup, 9 League Cup, 3 Sherpa Van
Trophy) 1988-89

MOST LEAGUE GOALS CONCEDED
97, Division 2, 1959-60

MOST LEAGUE WINS
30, Division 2, 1905-06;   Div 3S 1954-55

MOST LEAGUE DRAWS
17, Division 2, 1919-20, 1965-66;   Div 4 1982-83

MOST LEAGUE DEFEATS
26, Division 2, 1959-60

OLDEST PLAYER
Terry Cooper, 40 years 86 days, 6.10.1984

YOUNGEST PLAYER
Nyrere Kelly, 16 years 8 months, 16.10.1982

MOST CAPPED PLAYER
Billy Wedlock (England) 26

BEST PERFORMANCES BY BRISTOL CITY

League: 1905-06: Matches played 38, Won 30, Drawn 6, Lost 2, Goals for 83, Goals against 28, Points 66. Champions Div. 2

Highest: 1906-07: Runners-up Division 1.

F.A. Cup: 1908-09: 1st rnd. Southampton 1-1 (h), 2-0 (a); 2nd rnd. Bury 2-2 (h), 1-0 (a); 3rd rnd. Norwich City 2-0 (h); 4th rnd.
Glossop 0-0 (a), 1-0 (h); Semi-Final. Derby County 1-1 (n), 2-1 (n); Final Manchester United 0-1 (n).

League Cup: 1970-71: 2nd rnd. Rotherham Utd 0-0 (a), 4-0 (h); 3rd rnd. Blackpool 1-0 (a); 4th rnd. Leicester City 2-2 (a), 2-1
aet (h); 5th rnd. Fulham 0-0 (a), 1-0 (h); Semi-Final Tottenham Hotspur 1st leg 1-1 (h), 2nd leg 0-2 aet (a).

1988-89: 1st rnd. Exeter City, 1st leg 1-0 (h), 2nd leg 1-0 (a); 2nd rnd Oxford Utd, 1st leg 4-2 (a), 2nd leg 2-0 (h); 3rd rnd.
Crystal Palace 4-1 (h); 4th rnd Tranmere Rovers 1-0 (h); 5th rnd. Bradford City 1-0 (a); Semi-Final Nottingham Forest, 1st leg
1-1 (a), 2nd leg 0-1 aet (h).

DIVISIONAL RECORDS

	Played	Won	Drawn	Lost	For	Against	Points
DIVISION 1	358	114	94	150	428	510	**322**
DIVISION 2	1510	549	379	582	2079	2166	**1510**
DIVISION 3	552	240	138	174	892	716	**747**
DIVISION 3S	860	374	209	277	1411	1207	**957**
DIVISION 4	92	37	27	28	129	114	**138**
TOTALS	**3372**	**1314**	**847**	**1211**	**4939**	**4713**	**3674**

BRISTOL CITY   APPEARANCES   GOALS

PLAYERS NAME / Honours	Ht	Wt	Birthdate	Birthplace / Transfers	Contract Date	Clubs	League	L/Cup	FA Cup	Other	Lg	L/C	FAC	Oth
GOALKEEPERS														
Andy Leaning	6.0	13.0	18.05.63	York		Rowntree Mack								
				f	01.07.85	York City	69	4	8	5				
				f	28.05.87	Sheffield Utd	21	2	2					
				£12,000	09.11.88	Bristol City	74	5	7	2				
Keith Welch	6.2	12.5	01.10.68	Bolton		Bolton W								
				£200,000	03.03.87	Rochdale	205	12	10	12				
					25.07.91	Bristol City	26	2						
DEFENDERS														
Mark Aizlewood	6.1	13.8	01.10.59	Newport	01.10.77	Newport Co	35+3		2		1			
W:17,u21.2,Div.2.82				£50,000	01.04.78	Luton Town	90+8	7	5		3	1		
				£50,000	04.11.82	Charlton Ath	152	10	6	2	9	1	1	
				£200,000	05.02.87	Leeds Utd	65+5	3	1	7	3			1
				£200,000	16.08.89	Bradford City	39	1	2		1			
				£125,000	08.08.90	Bristol City	75+1	5		1+1	3			
Matthew Bryant	6.1	12.4	20.09.70	Bristol	01.07.89	Bristol City (T)	65	2	4	1	3			
				Loan	24.08.90	Walsall	13	4						
Andy Llewellyn	5.7	11.4	26.02.66	Bristol	13.03.84	Bristol City (A)	269+12	20	20	26+2	3			
E:Y5														
Brian Mitchell	6.1	13.1	16.07.63	Stonehaven		King Stree								
S:S; SPD'85; SLC'86					01.07.81	Aberdeen (A)	48+17	7+2	4+1	6+2	1			
				£70,000	13.02.87	Bradford City	170+8	21	7	9	9	1	1	2
				Free	02.07.92	Bristol City								
Russell Osman	6.0	12.0	14.02.59	Repton	01.03.76	Ipswich Town (A)	294	28	30+2	29+1	17	3	1	
E:11,B.2,u21.7,UEFAC'81,FAYC'75				£240,000	31.07.85	Leicester City	108	8	2	2	8			
				£325,000	17.06.88	Southampton	92+4	18	7	3	6			
				£60,000	10.10.91	Bristol City	30+1		4		2			
Martin Scott	5.9	11.0	07.01.68	Sheffield	10.01.86	Rotherham Utd. (A)	93+1	11	7+2	7	3	2		2
Div.4'89				£200,000		Bristol City	73	2	4	1	4			
David Thompson	6.3	12.7	20.11.68	Ashington	26.11.86	Millwall (A)	88+9	4	4	1	6	1		
					18.06.92	Bristol City								
MIDFIELD														
Raymond Atteveld	5.10	12.0	08.09.66	Amsterdam		Haarlem F.C.(Hol)								
				£250,000	22.08.89	Everton	41+10	6+1	6+1	0+3	1	1		
Loan West Ham 07.02.92 1 Lg 2 FAC Apps				£250,000	26.03.92	Bristol City	4+3				1			
Dariusz Dziekanowski				Poland										
via Celtic				£250,000	17.01.92	Bristol City	16+1		2		4		2	
Robert W Edwards	6.0	11.10	01.01.73	Kendal	10.04.90	Carlisle Utd. (T)	48	4	1	2+1	5			
				£135,000	27.03.91	Bristol City	12+8	1+1	2		1			
Gerald Harrison	5.10		15.04.72	Lambeth	18.12.89	Watford	6+3			1				
Loan Cardiff 24.01.92 10 Apps				Free	23.07.91	Bristol City	0+4	1						
Gary Shelton	5.7	10.12	21.03.58	Nottingham	01.03.76	Walsall (A)	12+12	0+1	2+2				1	
E:u21.1				£80,000	18.01.78	Aston Villa	24	2+1			7	1		
Loan Notts Co. 8 Lge				£50,000	28.04.82	Sheffield Wed	195+3	19	23+1	1	18	3	3	
				£150,000	24.07.87	Oxford Utd	60+5	7+1	5	1	1	2		
				P.E	24.08.89	Bristol City	104+1	6	8	4	20			1
FORWARDS														
Wayne Allison	6.1	13.5	16.10.68	Huddersfield	06.07.87	Halifax Town (A)	74+10	3	4+1	8+1	22	2	2	3
£250,000 Watford 26.7.89 6+1 lg				£300,000	09.08.90	Bristol City	55+25	2+3	3+1	2	16	1	1	
Junior Bent	5.5	10.6	01.03.70	Huddersfield	09.12.87	Huddersfield Town	25+11	1	3+1	4	6		1	
Loan Burnley 30.11.89 8 Lge 3 gls				£30,000	22.03.90	Bristol City	22+16	3+1	3+1	1	4		1	
				Loan	26.03.92	Stoke City	1							
Andrew Cole	5.10	11.2	15.10.71	Nottingham	18.10.89	Arsenal (T)	0+1			0+2				
E: Y.,u21				Loan	05.09.91	Fulham								
Loan 13.03.92 then transfer				£500,000	23.03.92	Bristol City	12				8			
Terry Connor	5.7	10.0	09.11.62	Leeds	13.11.79	Leeds Utd	83+13	4+2	6		19	1	2	
E: u21.1, Y.9; UEFA Y'80				PE	25.03.83	Brighton & H.A	153+3	7	10+1	1	51	4	3	
				£200,000	01.07.87	Portsmouth	42+6	5	3+1	0+1	12	1	1	
				£150,000	14.08.90	Swansea City	39	4	4	6	6		2	
				£190,000	21.09.91	Bristol City	9+2			1	1			
Mark Gavin	5.8	10.07	10.12.63	Bailleston		Leeds Utd. (A)	20+10	4+1	0+1		3	1		
Loan Hartlepool 7 Lg				Free		Carlisle Utd	12+1	2		1	1	1		
				Free		Bolton W	48+1	1	5	10	3		1	1
						Rochdale	23	3	1	2	6			
transfer to Hearts 5+4 lg				£30,000	04.10.88	Bristol City	62+7	8	13	6	6		1	1
transfer Watford £100K+P 8+5 Lg 8.90				£60,000	06.12.91	Bristol City	12+2		3					
Nicky Morgan	5.10	13.5	30.10.59	East Ham	03.11.77	West Ham U. (A)	14+7	1		1+3	2			
				£50,000	24.03.83	Portsmouth	79+16	8+1	1+2	2	32	1	1	1
				£30,000	10.12.86	Stoke City	73+15	5	7	3+1	21	3	2	
				£30,000	23.03.90	Bristol City	65+5	6	2		20	6		
Leroy Rosenior	6.0	12.3	24.03.64	Clapton	02.08.82	Fulham	53+1		3		15			
E:S				19.08.85	Q.P.R	27+11	2+3	0+4		7	2		
					19.06.87	Fulham	34	4	1	2	20	1	1	
					25.03.88	West Ham U	44+9	7	4+1	2	15	2	2	4
Loan Fulham 11 Lg & Charlton 3 Lg				Free	19.03.92	Bristol City	5+3				5			

ADDITIONAL CONTRACT PLAYERS

Stephen Benton, Wayne Bessell, Stephen Clifford, Jason Eaton, Andrew Hogg, James McIntrye, Michael Melon, Gerard Mitchell, Shaun Rouse, Deion Vernon

BRISTOL CITY

RECORD WIN & LOSS AGAINST EACH CLUB IN CURRENT DIVISION
(Where score has occured on several occasions the most recent is given)

Club	Rec. Win	Season	Rec. Loss	Season
BARNSLEY	5-0	1957-58	7-1	1912-13
BIRMINGHAM CITY	4-0	1989-90 (away)	4-0	1966-67
BRENTFORD	3-0	1961-62	4-0	1922-23
BRISTOL ROVERS	5-0	1926-27 (away)	5-1	1933-34
CAMBRIDGE UNITED	3-0	1984-85	2-1	1991-92 (home)
CHARLTON ATHLETIC	6-0	1969-70	5-0	1966-67
DERBY COUNTY	4-1	1966-67	8-0	1923-24 (home)
GRIMSBY TOWN	7-0	1914-15	4-0	1905-06
LEICESTER CITY	6-1	1902-03	5-1	1923-24
LUTON TOWN	6-0	1926-27	4-0	1936-37
MILLWALL	5-0	1928-29	4-1	1990-91 (home)
NEWCASTLE UNITED	3-1	1977-78	3-0	1991-92
NOTTS COUNTY	6-0	1961-62	4-0	1985-86
OXFORD UNITED	4-1	1975-76	5-0	1973-74
PETERBOROUGH UTD	3-1	1964-65	4-1	1983-84
PORTSMOUTH	4-1	1990-91	5-0	1961-62
SOUTHEND UNITED	6-0	1951-52	6-0	1934-35
SUNDERLAND	4-1	1958-59	4-0	1909-10
SWINDON TOWN	5-0	1953-54	5-0	1953-54
TRANMERE ROVERS	2-0	1960-61	6-0	1989-90
WATFORD	5-0	1926-27	4-0	1934-35
WEST HAM UNITED	3-1	1955-56	5-0	1980-81
WOLVERHAMPTON WNDRS	4-1	1927-28	4-0	1990-91 (home)

MANAGER: DENIS SMITH

DATE OF BIRTH: 19.11.1947   **PLACE OF BIRTH:** Stoke-on-Trent

DATE OF APPOINTMENT: MARCH 1992

PREVIOUS CLUBS
  as Manager: York City, Sunderland
  as Asst. Man./Coach:
  as Player: Stoke City, York City

HONOURS
  as Manager: York City: Div 4 Championship 1984. Sunderland: Promotion to Div 1 1990
  as Asst. Man./Coach:
  as Player: Stoke City: League Cup Winners 1972

Value Rating: ★ ★ ★

Programme Editor: Phil Tottle

Price of 1992-93 Programme: £1
Number of Pages: 24
Subscriptions: £40 (home), £45 (away), £85 (all programmes)

Local Newspapers: Bristol Evening Post, Western Daily Press, Sunday Independent

Local Radio Stations: Radio Bristol, GWR/Brunel Radio, Galaxy Radio

Additional Publications on Club: 'A Complete Record

LEADING LEAGUE GOALSCORERS
SEASONS 1979-80 – 1991-92

1979-80	**TOM RITCHIE**	13	1980-81	**KEVIN MABBUTT**	9
1981-82	**MICK HARFORD**	11	1982-83	**GLYN RILEY**	16
1983-84	**GLYN RILEY**	16	1984-85	**TERRY CONNOR**	14
1985-86	**STEVE NEVILLE**	19	1986-87	**ALAN WALSH**	16
1987-88	**ALAN WALSH**	12	1988-89	**ALAN WALSH**	11
1989-90	**BOB TAYLOR**	27	1990-91	**NICKY MORGAN**	13

1991-92   **WAYNE ALLISON**   10

ASHTON GATE Bristol BS3 2EJ

Capacity: 23,636   **Uncovered Standing:** 7,304   **Seating:** 16,332

Tel: Ground: 0272 632812   **Clubcall:** 0898 12 11 76

All premium rate calls (0898/0891) cost 36p per minute cheap rate and 48p per minute at all other times. Call costings correct at time of going to press.

GROUNDS
St John's Lane 1894-1904; Ashton Gate 1904-

ATTENDANCES
Highest: (St John's Lane) 17,909 v Sheffield Utd, FA Cup Rnd 1, 6.2.1904
(Ashton Gate) 43,335 v Preston North End, FA Cup Rnd 5, 16.2.1935
N.B. Over 50,000 were judged to be in the ground on 30.1.1935 for the FA Cup Rnd 4 replay, v Portsmouth, when the gates were rushed and the crowd broke in. Official paid attendance was given as 42,885

Lowest: (St John's Lane) 1,700 v Stockport County, Div 2, 13.2.1904
(Ashton Gate) 1,700 v Watford, Division 3S, 25.1.1933.

RECORD RECEIPTS (with previous records)
£107,774 v Bristol Rovers, Division 2, 4.9.91
£97,780 v Chelsea, FA Cup Rnd 4, 27.1.1990
£97,097 v Nottingham Forest, Semi-Final Littlewoods Cup, 26.2.1989
£45,300 v Bristol Rovers, FA Cup Rnd 2, 8.12.1984
£45,000 v Aston Villa, FA Cup Rnd 4, 23.1.1982

ASHTON GATE
First game: v Bolton Wanderers, 3.9.1904
First floodlit game: v Wolverhampton Wndrs, 27.1.1953

Season Tickets:
Stands: £185, Juv/OAP £120
Enclosure: £160, Juv/OAP £120

Cost of Stand Tickets: Grandstand: £9.50, juv/OAP £7; Dolman Stand: £9.50, juv/OAP £7; Covered End £6, £4; Open End £6, £4; Away supporters £6; Dolman Enclosure £6, £4

Match and Ticket Information: Any time before match applications by post (with sae) are accepted.

Car Parking: Winterstoke Road car park £60; Wills £50
There is limited street parking around ground

Nearest Railway Station: Temple Meads (0272 294255)

How to get to the ground

From North and West: Use Motorway M5 until junction 16, leave motorway and follow signs Bristol A38. Follow signs to City Centre then follow signs Taunton A38. In 1.2m cross Cumberland Basin swing bridge, then branch left into Winterstoke Road for Bristol City FC

From East: Use Motorway M4, then M32 and follow signs City Centre, then follow signs Taunton A38. In 1.2m cross Cumberland Basin swing bridge, then branch left into Winterstoke Road for Bristol City FC

From South: Use Motorway M5 until junction 18. Leave motorway and follow signs Bristol A4 along Portway then turn right and follow signs Taunton over Cumberland Basin swing bridge, then branch left into Winterstoke Road for Bristol City FC. To use Bristol City FC park and ride scheme follow AA signs to 'Bristol City FC car park', which is in Anchor Road

BRISTOL ROVERS

Division 1

Formed: 1883   **Turned Professional:** 1897   **Ltd Co:** 1896

SPONSORED BY: Roman Glass of Bristol & Bath Ltd   **NICKNAME:** The Pirates

ROVERS started the season with a new manager, Martin Dobson, the former Bury manager. Dobson selected Dennis Rofe, the former Southampton coach as Rovers chief coach. New players were recruited including Justin Skinner a record club signing at £130,000. Experienced utility player Steve Cross and Richard Evans boosted the playing staff to 28.

New team formations were tried which effected team spirit and early results were disappointing. Rovers recorded just one win but more importantly eight defeats including two in Cup ties in their opening eleven matches. Not surprisingly with the club bottom of the league table Dobson's contract was terminated.

Dennis Rofe was given the opportunity to lead Rovers, initially as caretaker manager. Rofe immediately made his presence felt inspiring Rovers to a sensational Rumbelows Cup victory over fierce rivals Bristol City. Rovers trailing 4-1 on aggregate at Ashton gate before they recovered to score a vital extra-time goal to win the tie on the away goals rule. Rovers succumbed to Nottingham Forest, the eventual finalists in the next round.

Rovers' best performances of the season were saved for the two captivating F.A. Cup ties against Liverpool. Many critics agreed Rovers were most unfortunate not to beat the eventual cup winners at Twerton Park.

Rovers league form improved considerably under Rofe particularly at Twerton, where the club suffered just one home defeat in 21 league and cup matches. Few Rovers supporters would have imagined that following the early season struggle that the club would finish the season in thirteenth position, identical to last season but with four more points.

The prospects for the new season look promising if late signing John Taylor can continue to consistently score goals. Holding on to 'Player of the Season' Brian Parkin and emerging young striker Marcus Stewart could hold the key for a serious challenge for one of the play-off places.

Mike Jay

Back row L-R: Gareth Taylor, Lee Maddison, David Mehew, Andy Gurney, Andy Reece, Carl Saunders, Marcus Stewart, Adie Boothroyd, Vaughan Jones, Richard Evans. **Middle row:** Roy Dolling (Physio), Bill Clark, John Taylor, Gavin Kelly, Marcus Browning, Steve Yates, Brian Parkin, Geoff Twentyman, Justin Skinner, Ray Kendall (kit manager). **Front:** Paul Tovey, Phil Purnell, Paul Chenoweth, Ian Alexander, Steve Cross (coach), Dennis Rofe (Manager), Tony Gill (Youth Team Coach), Tony Pounder, Paul Hardyman, Dave Wilson, Lee Archer.

BRISTOL ROVERS

DIVISION TWO: 13th   **FA CUP:** 4th RND   **RUMBELOWS CUP:** 3rd RND   **ZDS CUP:** 1st RND

M	DATE		COMP.	VEN	OPPONENTS	RESULT		H/T	LGE POS	GOALSCORERS/GOAL TIMES	ATTEN-DANCE
1	A	17	BL	H	Ipswich Town	D	3-3	0-1		Stewart 66, White 73, 82	6,444
2		23	BL	A	Tranmere Rovers	D	2-2	1-1	12	Stewart 44, 89 (pen)	(10,150)
3		31	BL	H	Newcastle United	L	1-2	0-1	20	Skinner 88	6,334
4	S	4	BL	A	Bristol City	L	0-1	0-0	22		(20,183)
5		7	BL	H	Grimsby Town	L	2-3	0-1	22	White 56, Evans 61	4,641
6		14	BL	A	Southend United	L	0-2	0-1	23		(4,670)
7		17	BL	A	Swindon Town	L	0-1	0-1	23		(11,391)
8		21	BL	H	Oxford United	W	2-1	1-1	23	Alexander 37, Cross 67	4,854
9		25	RC 2/1	H	**Bristol City**	L	1-3	1-2		Llewelyn (og) 37	5,155
10		28	BL	A	Brighton & H A	L	1-3	1-1	24	Saunders 26	(6,392)
11	O	2	ZDS 1	H	**Ipswich Town**	L	1-3	1-1		Pounder 28	1,490
12		5	BL	H	Middlesbrough	W	2-1	0-1	21	Reece 65, Twentyman 85	4,936
13		9	RC 2/2	A	**Bristol City**	W	†4-2	2-1		White 15, 17, Mehew 85, 92	(9,880)
14		12	BL	A	Charlton Athletic	L	0-1	0-0	23		(5,685)
15		19	BL	H	Plymouth Argyle	D	0-0	0-0	23		5,049
16		26	BL	A	Sunderland	D	1-1	1-1	22	Reece 15	(14,746)
17		30	RC 3	A	**Nottingham Forest**	L	0-2	0-1			(17,529)
18	N	2	BL	H	Port Vale	D	3-3	2-1	24	Saunders 33, 40, Skinner 72	3,565
19		5	BL	A	Wolverhampton W	W	3-2	1-1	22	Reece 5, Pounder 67, Saunders 75	(8,536)
20		9	BL	A	Barnsley	W	1-0	0-0	22	Reece 65	(6,688)
21		16	BL	H	Watford	D	1-1	1-1	22	Saunders 31	5,064
22		20	BL	A	Leicester City	D	1-1	0-1	22	Mehew 79	(10,950)
23		23	BL	A	Derby County	L	2-3	2-1	22	Cross 12, Mehew 15	6,513
24		30	BL	A	Millwall	W	1-0	1-0	21	Mehew 21	(7,824)
25	D	7	BL	H	Cambridge United	D	2-2	2-1	20	Mehew 19, White 42	5,280
26		14	BL	A	Blackburn Rovers	L	0-3	0-3	22		(12,295)
27		21	BL	H	Bristol City	W	3-2	2-1	18	White 44, Pounder 45, Saunders 81	6,306
28		26	BL	H	Portsmouth	L	0-2	0-1	19		(10,710)
29		28	BL	A	Newcastle United	L	1-2	1-0	21	White 30	(19,329)
30	J	1	BL	H	Leicester City	D	1-1	1-1	21	Saunders 24	6,673
31		5	FAC 3	H	**Plymouth Argyle**	W	5-0	2-0		Alexander 38, Saunders 4 (43, 50, 59, 70)	6,767
32		11	BL	A	Tranmere Rovers	W	1-0	0-0	18	Stewart 57	7,138
33		18	BL	A	Ipswich Town	L	0-1	0-0	20		(10,435)
34		29	BL	H	Portsmouth	W	1-0	1-0	17	White 21	5,330
35	F	1	BL	A	Plymouth Argyle	D	0-0	0-0	15		(6,631)
36		5	FAC 4	H	**Liverpool**	D	1-1	0-1		Saunders 59	9,484
37		8	BL	H	Sunderland	W	2-1	0-0	15	Saunders (pen) 71, 90	6,318
38		11	FAC 4R	A	**Liverpool**	L	1-2	1-0		Saunders 18	(30,142)
39		15	BL	A	Derby County	L	0-1	0-0	15		(11,154)
40		22	BL	H	Millwall	W	3-2	1-1	14	White 3, 90, Mehew 61	5,747
41		28	BL	A	Cambridge United	L	1-6	1-1	14	Heaney (og) 39	(6,164)
42	M	7	BL	H	Blackburn Rovers	W	3-0	2-0	15	Mehew 27, 67, White 40	6,313
43		11	BL	A	Wolverhampton W	D	1-1	0-0	15	White 53	6,968
44		14	BL	A	Port Vale	W	1-0	1-0	14	Saunders 36	(5,861)
45		21	BL	H	Barnsley	D	0-0	0-0	16		5,665
46		28	BL	A	Watford	L	0-1	0-0	16		(7,496)
47	A	1	BL	H	Southend United	W	4-1	0-1	13	Mehew 60, Stewart 62, Taylor 76, 85	5,375
48		4	BL	A	Grimsby Town	W	1-0	0-0	12	Taylor 66	(4,859)
49		12	BL	H	Swindon Town	D	1-1	0-0	14	Clark 78	6,905
50		18	BL	A	Oxford United	D	2-2	0-2	15	Taylor 68, Pounder 72	(6,891)
51		20	BL	H	Brighton & H A	W	4-1	2-0	12	Pounder 35, Taylor 3 (45, 58, 75)	6,092
52		25	BL	A	Middlesbrough	L	1-2	1-0	13	Taylor 5	(14,057)
53	M	2	BL	H	Charlton Athletic	W	1-0	0-0	13	Mehew 79	7,630

Best Home League Attendance: 7,630 v Charlton Athletic   **Smallest:** 3,565 v Port Vale   **Av Home Att:** 5,876

Goal Scorers: **Compared with 90-91: -57**

League (60):   White 11, Saunders 10 (1 pen), Mehew 9, Taylor 8, Stewart 5 (1 pen), Reece 4, Pounder 4, Cross 2, Skinner 2, Clark, Twentyman
                  Alexander, Opponents, Evans

R/lows C (5):   White 2, Mehew 2, Opponents

FA Cup (7):   Saunders 6, Alexander

ZDS Cup (1):   Pounder   † = After extra-time

Parkin B.	Alexander I.	Twentyman G.	Yates S.	Mehew D.	Boothroyd A.	Evans R.	Reece A.	White D.	Stewart W.	Pounder A.	Clark W.	Purnell P.	Willmott I.	Wilson D.	Skinner J.	Archer L.	Maddison L.	Saunders C.	Cross S.	Browning M.	Kelly G.	Moore K. (L)	Bloomer R.	Hopkiss J.	Taylor J.	Referee	
1	2	3	4	5	6	7*	8	9	10	11	S	14														L Shapter	1
1			4	5*	2		8	9	10	11	3	14	6	7												N Midgley	2
1		3	4	5*	2		8	9	10	11		14	6	7*	12											P Taylor	3
1		3	4		2		8	9	10		5	11*		7*	6			S	14							M Bodenham	4
1	2	3	4	5	6*		8	9	10			11*			7			12	14							J Martin	5
1	2	3	4		12	7*	8	9	10	11		5*			6				14							R Wiseman	6
1	2	3	4					9		11	5			7*	6			10	8	12						G Singh	7
1	2	3	4			7		9*		11	5				12			10	8	14						V Callow	8
1	2	3	4			7	S	9		11*	5				6			10	8	12						K Cooper	9
1	2	3	4			7*		9	S	11	5				6			10	5	14						R Lewis	10
1	2	3	4			7*	8	9*	12	11					6			10	5	14						K Barratt	11
1	2	3	4			7	8	9		11	S				6			10*	5	14						M Pierce	12
1	2*	3	4			7*	8	9		11	12	14			6				5	10						J Deakin	13
1	2	3	4			7	8	9		11	S	14			6*				5	10						R Shepherd	14
1	2	3	4			7	8	9*		11	S	14			6				5	10						G Pooley	15
1	2	3	4			7	8	9	14	11	S				6				5	10*						C Trussell	16
1	2	3	4			7*	8	9		11	S	14			6			10	5							B Hill	17
1		3	4		2	7*	8	9		11	S	14			6			10	5							D Frampton	18
1	2	3	4			7	8	9	S	11					6			10	5							K Breen	19
1	2	3	4			7	8	9		11	S	S			6			10	5							R Nixon	20
1	2	3	4			7	8	9	14	11*	S				6			10	5							M Brandwood	21
1	2	3	4			7	8	9	14	11	S				6			10*	5							M Reed	22
1	2	3	4			7*	8	9	14	11	S				6			10	5							T Holbrook	23
1	2	3	4			7*	8	9	S	11		14			6			10	5							I Borrett	24
	2*	3	4			7	8	9	S	11	12				6			10	5				1			D Shadwell	25
	2	3	4		12	7*	8	9	14	11*					6			10	5				1			A Hart	26
	2	3	4			7	S	9	S	11					6			10	5				1			P Durkin	27
1	2	3	4		12	7*	8	9	14	11*					6			10	5							A Ward	28
1	2	3	4		S	7	8	9	14	11					6			10	5*							K Hackett	29
1	2	3	4		S	7	8	9	S	11					6			10	5							K Burge	30
1	2	3*	4				8		S	11		14			6		5	10		7	9					D Elleray	31
1	2		4				8			11		14			6		5	10		7	9*					A Gunn	32
1	2		4				8			11*		14			6		5*	10		7	9	3	12			R Pawley	33
1	2		4			7	8	9*	12	11	5				6*			10		14		3				C Wilkes	34
1	2		4			7	8	9	S	11					6		5	10	S			3				R Gifford	35
1	2		4		S	7	8	9	S	11	3				6			10	5							B Hill	36
1	2				14	7*	8	9	12	11*	4				6			10	5			3				P Don	37
1	2		4		12	7	8	9	14	11*	3				6			10	5*							B Hill	38
1	2					7	8	9	14	11*	4				6		S	10*	5			3				T West	39
1	2					7	8	9	14	11*	4				6		S	10*	5			3				R Poulain	40
1	2					7*	8	9	14	11*	4				6		12	10	5							G Willard	41
1	2					7	8	9	14	11*	4				6		S	10	5				3			P Danson	42
1	2					7	8	9	14	11*	4				6		S	10	5				3			P Jones	43
1	2					7*	8	9	S	11	4	11			6		12	10	5				3			B Coddington	44
1		2						9	14	11	4	7*			6		5	10	8*				12	3		G Ashby	45
1	2		4			7	8		14	11*	3				6		5*	10					12		9	P Foakes	46
1	2		4			7	8		10*	11	3				6			14					5	S	9	A Smith	47
1	2		4			7	8		10*	11*	3				6			14					5	12	9	I Cruikshanks	48
1	2		4			7*	8		12	11*	3				6			10					5	14	9	H King	49
1	2		4			7	8		10	11	3				6*	5			S				12		9	J Carter	50
1	2		4			7	8		10*	11	3				6	5*		14					12		9	P Scoble	51
1	2		4		12	7	8		10*	11*	3				6			14	5						9	J Rushton	52
1	2		4			7	8		10	11	3				6		5		S				S		9	M Bodenham	53
43	41	25	39	37	8	2	42	35	17	38	22	5	2	3	41	3	8	31	31	5	3	7	4	4	8	League Appearances	
				5					16	2	1	7			1	2	2	5	1	6			5	2		Substitute Appearances	
3	3	3	3	2	1		2	3	1	2	1+1	0+2			2	1		2	3	1+1						R/lows Appearances	
3	3	1	3	2	0+1		3	2	1+1	2+1	2				3			1	3	3	1					FA Cup Appearances	
1	1	1	1	1			1	1	0+1	1					1			1	1	1						ZDS Cup Appearances	

Also Played: Posn.(Game): Hazel S(2), G Taylor S(7),3(41), Jones 6*(8)
Players on Loan: Moore (Southampton)

BRISTOL ROVERS

Club Colours: Blue shirts with blue and white quarters and white trim, white shorts and blue stockings
Change Colours: Yellow and green quartered shirts, black shorts, yellow socks
Reserves League: Neville Ovenden Football Combination   **('A' Team):** South East Counties League Div 2

COMPETITIONS		
Div. 2	Div. 3	Div. 3S
53-62	62-74	20-53
74-81	81-90	
90-		

HONOURS	
Division 3	Division 3S
1989-90	1952-53

MOST APPEARANCES: STUART TAYLOR 620 (65-80)			
Year	League	FA Cup	League Cup
1965-66	3		
1966-67	16	2	
1967-68	44	4	1
1968-69	45	7	1
1969-70	46	2	1
1970-71	46	3	7
1971-72	46	3	6
1972-73	41	1	6
1973-74	46	3	1
1974-75	33	2	3
1975-76	39		5
1976-77	40	3	2
1977-78	39	4	1
1978-79	41	3	2
1979-80	21	1	
	546	38	36

MOST GOALS IN A CAREER			
GEOFF BRADFORD 260 (1949-64)			
Season	League	FA Cup	League Cup
1949-50	3		
1950-51	13	3	
1951-52	26	3	
1952-53	33	1	
1953-54	21		
1954-55	26	1	
1955-56	25	1	
1956-57	11	2	
1957-58	20	2	
1958-59	20		
1959-60	12		
1960-61	12		1
1961-62	12		2
1962-63	2		
1963-64	4	2	
	242	15	3

RECORD TRANSFER FEE RECEIVED			
Amount	Club	Player	Date
£1,000,000	C. Palace	Nigel Martyn	11/89
£500,000	Watford	Gary Penrice	11/89
£200,000	Luton Town	Steve White	12/79
£180,000	Stoke City	Paul Randall	12/78

RECORD TRANSFER FEE PAID			
Amount	Club	Player	Date
£160,000	Sunderland	Paul Hardyman	8/92
£125,000	Fulham	Justin Skinner	8/91
£100,000	Birmingham City	S Barrowclough	7/79
£50,000	Birmingham City	Gary Emmanuel	1/79

MANAGERS			
Name	Seasons	Best	Worst
Alf Homer	1899-20	1(s1)	17(3S)
Ben Hall	1920-21	10(3S)	10(3S)
Andrew Wilson	1921-26	9(3S)	19(3S)
Joe Palmer	1926-29	10(3S)	19(3S)
David McLean	1929-30	20(3S)	20(3S)
Albert Prince Cox	1930-36	7(3S)	20(3S)
Percy Smith	1936-37	15(3S)	15(3S)
Brough Fletcher	1938-49	5(3S)	22(3S)
Bert Tann	1950-68	6(2)	19(3)
Fred Ford	1968-69	16(3)	16(3)
Bill Dodgin	1969-72	3(3)	6(3)
Don Megson	1972-77	15(2)	19(3)
Bobby Campbell	1977-79	16(2)	18(3)
Harold Jarman	1979-80	19(3)	19(3)
Terry Cooper	1980-81	7(3)	15(4)
Bobby Gould	1981-83	22(3)	18(3)
Dave Williams	1983-85	5(3)	6(3)
Bobby Gould	1985-87	16(3)	19(3)
Gerry Francis	1987-91	13(3)	8(3)
Martin Dobson	1991	12(2)	24(2)
Dennis Rofe	1991-	13(2)	13(2)

LONGEST LEAGUE RUNS	
of undefeated matches:	32 (7.4.1973-27.1.1974)
of undefeated home matches:	34 (18.2.1989-3.10.1990)
without home win:	10 (19.4.1980-1.11.1980)
of league wins:	12 (18.10.1952-17.1.1953)
of league defeats:	8 (29.4.1961-9.9.1961)
of league matches without a win:	20 (5.4.1980-1.11.1980)
of undefeated away matches:	17 (7.4.1973-27.1.1974)
without an away win:	11 (5.1.1935-2.9.1935)
of home wins:	10 (16.1.1935-23.4.1935)
of away wins:	5 (25.10.1952-17.1.1953)
	(18.1.1964-29.2.1964)

BIGGEST VICTORIES
League: 7-0 v Swansea, 2.10.1954
v Brighton, 29.11.1952
v Shrewsbury, 21.3.1964
F.A. Cup: (Proper): 6-0 v Merthyr Tydfil, Round 1, 14.11.1987
League Cup: 6-2 v Shrewsbury, 23.9.63
4-0 v Brighton, (h), Rnd 2, 5.9.1972
4-0 v Torquay, (a), Rnd 1 2nd leg, 15.9.1982
5-1 v Swindon Town, (a), Rnd 1 1st leg, 27.8.1984

BIGGEST DEFEATS
League: 0-12 v Luton Town, 13.4.1936
F.A. Cup: 1-8 v Q.P.R., 27.11.1937
League Cup: 0-4 v Blackburn R, 16.10.1961
0-4 v Wolves, 31.10.1972
0-4 v Hereford, (a), Rnd 1 2nd leg, 16.8.1978
0-4 v Arsenal, (a), Rnd 2 1st leg, 25.9.1984
0-4 v Reading, Rnd 1 2nd leg, 3.9.1986

MOST POINTS
3 points a win: 93, Division 3, 1989-90
2 points a win: 64, Division 3S, 1952-53

MOST GOALS
92, Division 3S, 1952-53
Bradford 33, Lambden 24, Bush 12, Petherbridge 10,
McIlvenny 3, Roost 2, Warren 2, Bamford 1, Fox 1, Leonard
1, og 3

MOST GOALS IN A MATCH
6. Jack Jones v Weymouth, FA Cup, 15-1, 17.11.1900

MOST GOALS IN A SEASON
Alfie Biggs 37 (League 30, FAC 1, League Cup 6) 1963-64

MOST FIRST CLASS MATCHES IN A SEASON
58 (46 League, 2 FA Cup, 2 League Cup, 4 Sherpa Van
Trophy, 4 Play-Offs) 1988-89

MOST LEAGUE GOALS CONCEDED
95, Division 3S, 1935-36

MOST LEAGUE WINS
26, Division 3S, 1952-53; Division 3, 1989-90

MOST LEAGUE DRAWS
17, Division 3S, 1973-74; Division 3, 1988-89

MOST LEAGUE DEFEATS
24, Division 3S, 1927-28; Division 2, 1980-81

OLDEST PLAYER
Bill Culley, 43 years, 1928

YOUNGEST PLAYER
Ronnie Dix, 15 years 180 days v Norwich City, 3.3.1928 –
Youngest player to score in the Football League (in his
second match)

MOST CAPPED PLAYER
Neil Slatter (Wales) 10, 1983-84

BEST PERFORMANCES BY BRISTOL ROVERS

League: 1952-53: Matches Played 46, Won 26, Drawn 12, Lost 8, Goals for 92, Goals against 46, Points 64. First in Division 3S

Highest: 6th Division 2, 1955-56, 1958-59

F.A. Cup: 1950-51: 1st rnd. Llanelli 1-1 (h), 1-1 (a), 3-1 (n); 2nd rnd. Gillingham 2-2 (h), 1-1 (a), 2-1 (n); 3rd rnd. Aldershot 5-1 (h), 4th rnd. Luton Town 2-1 (a); 5th rnd. Hull 3-0 (h); 6th rnd. Newcastle Utd 0-0 (a), 1-3 (h)

1957-58: 3rd rnd. Mansfield Town 5-0 (h); 4th rnd. Burnley 2-2 (h) 3-2 (a); 5th rnd. Bristol City 3-0 (h); 6th rnd. Fulham 1-3 (a)

League Cup: 1970-71: 2nd rnd. Brighton & Hove Albion 1-0 (h), 2-1 (a); 3rd rnd. Norwich City 1-1 (a), 3-1 (h); 4th rnd. Birmingham City 3-1 (h); 5th rnd. Aston Villa 1-1 (h) 0-1 (a)

1971-72: 1st rnd. Exeter City 3-0 (h); 2nd rnd. Sunderland 3-1 (h); 3rd rnd. Charlton Athletic 2-1 (h); 4th rnd. Queens Park Rangers 1-1 (a) 1-0 (h); 5th rnd. Stoke City 2-4 (h)

DIVISIONAL RECORDS

	Played	Won	Drawn	Lost	For	Against	Points
DIVISION 2	764	262	199	304	1109	1230	**753**
DIVISION 3	966	396	263	307	1466	1276	**1226**
DIVISION 3S	1104	408	253	443	1666	1717	**1069**
TOTALS	**2834**	**1066**	**714**	**1054**	**4241**	**4223**	**3048**

BRISTOL ROVERS

PLAYERS NAME / Honours	Ht	Wt	Birthdate	Birthplace / Transfers	Contract Date	Clubs	League	L/Cup	FA Cup	Other	Lg	L/C	FAC	Oth
GOALKEEPERS														
Gavin Kelly	6.1	13.00	29.09.68	Beverley	09.05.87	Hull City (A)	11	1		1				
				Loan	22.03.90	Bristol Rovers								
				Free	01.07.90	Bristol Rovers	10							
Brian Parkin Div.3'90	6.1	12.0	12.10.65	Birkenhead	31.03.83	Oldham Ath. (A)	6	2						
				Free	22.07.85	Crewe Alexandra	98	7	2	6				
				Free	01.07.88	Crystal Palace	20	3		2				
				Loan	11.11.89	Bristol Rovers								
				Free	11.01.90	Bristol Rovers	112	5	7	10				
DEFENDERS														
Ian Alexander Div.3'90	5.8	10.7	26.01.63	Glasgow	01.10.81	Rotherham Utd	5+6	1+1	1					
					01.09.83	Motherwell	19+5	3	1		2	1		
					01.02.85	Morton	6+1				1			
						Pezoporikos(Cyprus)								
					21.08.86	Bristol Rovers	228+4	12	12	21	5	1	2	
Adrian Boothroyd	5.7	11.0	08.02.71	Bradford	01.07.89	Huddersfield Town (1)	9+1							
				£30,000	20.06.90	Bristol Rovers	10+6	1	0+1					
Billy Clark	6.0	12.3	19.05.67	Bournemouth	25.09.84	Bournemouth	4							
					21.01.88	Bristol Rovers	76+3	3+1	2+1	5	3			1
Paul Hardyman E:u21.2	5.8	11.4	15.09.65	Manchester		Waterloovi								
						Fareham T								
					17.05.84	Portsmouth	113+4	5	6	8	3			1
				£130,000	25.07.89	Sunderland	101+5	11	8+1	3	9	2	1	
				£160,000	03.08.92	Bristol Rovers								
Vaughan Jones W:u21.2; Div.3'90	5.9	12.4	08.09.59	Tonyrefail	10.09.77	Bristol Rovers	93+8	3+2	5		3			
					04.08.82	Newport Co	67+1	6	8	1	4			
					23.07.84	Cardiff City	11	4						
					21.03.85	Bristol Rovers	265+3	14	15	24	9		1	
Lee Maddison	5.11		05.10.72	Bristol	18.07.91	Bristol Rovers (T)	8+2		1					
Geoff Twentyman Div.3'90	6.1	13.12	10.03.59	Liverpool		Chorley								
					25.08.83	Preston N.E	95+3	11	3+1	4+1	4	4		
					22.11.86	Bristol Rovers	241+3	11	13	17	6	1		
Steve Yates Div.3'90	5.11	11.0	29.01.70	Bristol	01.07.88	Bristol Rovers	151+1	7	9	19				
MIDFIELD														
Paul Chenoweth	5.4		05.02.73	Bristol	18.07.91	Bristol Rovers								
Steve Cross Div3 '79; WC '79 '84	5.10	11.5	20.12.59	Wolverhampton	29.12.77	Shrewsbury Town	240+22	15+2	14+1	2	34	3	3	
				£70,000	04.07.86	Derby County	42+31	4+3	3+2	3+5	3			2
				£40,000	12.09.91	Bristol Rovers	31+1	3	3	1	2			
David Mehew Div.3'90	5.11	12.0	29.10.67	Camberley	06.08.84	Leeds Utd								
					11.07.85	Bristol Rovers	181+17	10	8	16+3	60	2	1	4
Andy Reece Div.3'90	5.11	12.0	05.09.62	Shrewsbury		Walsall								
						Worcester								
						Dudley Town								
						Willenhall								
					11.08.87	Bristol Rovers	208+5	10	10+2	21	15		3	3
Justin Skinner	6.0	11.6	30.01.69	London	17.11.86	Fulham (A)	111+24	10+1	5+1	10+1	23	4		1
				£130,000	27.08.91	Bristol Rovers	41+1	2	3	1	2			
David Wilson	5.9	10.10	20.03.69	Burnley	24.03.87	Manchester Utd. (A)	0+4		0+2					
				Loan	01.11.90	Lincoln City	3	1						
				Loan	28.03.91	Charlton Ath	6+1				2			
				Free	29.07.91	Bristol Rovers	3							
FORWARDS														
Marcus Browning	6.1	13.0	22.04.71	Bristol		Bristol Rovers	5+7	1+1	1	0+1				
Phil Purnell Div.3'90	5.7	10.0	16.09.64	Mangotsfield										
				Monthly 7	07.07.86	Bristol Rovers	130+23	6+2	7+1	17+1	22			
				Loan	12.12.91	Swansea City	5				1			
Carl Saunders Div.3'90	5.9	11.5	28.11.64	Marston	12.07.83	Stoke City (A)	130+34	6+2	9+2	6+2	23	1	5	1
				£70,000	02.02.90	Bristol Rovers	86+8	4	4	7	32		6	2
Marcus Stewart E: S	5.10	10.3	07.11.72	Bristol	18.07.91	Bristol Rovers (T)	17+16	1	1+1	0+1	5			
John Taylor Div.3'91	6.1	12.2	24.10.64	Norwich		Sudbury								
					13.09.88	Cambridge Utd	139+21	9+2	21	12+2	46	2	9	2
				Swap	28.03.92	Bristol Rovers	8				8			
ADDITIONAL CONTRACT PLAYERS														
Lee Archer	5.6		06.11.72	Bristol	18.07.91	Bristol Rovers	3+2	1						
Richard Evans						Weymouth								
				£30,000	09.08.91	Bristol Rovers	2		1		1			
(F) Tony Pounder	5.8	11.0	11.03.66	Yeovil		Westland Sports								
						Weymouth								
					24.07.90	Bristol Rovers	78+8	4	3+1	3	7			2
Gareth Taylor					29.07.91	Bristol Rovers	1							
Glenn Thomas					21.06.90	Bristol Rovers								

BRISTOL ROVERS

RECORD WIN & LOSS AGAINST EACH CLUB IN CURRENT DIVISION
(Where a score has occured on several occasions the most recent is given)

Club	Rec. Win	Season	Rec. Loss	Season
BARNSLEY	4-0	1970-71	4-0	1962-63
BIRMINGHAM CITY	1-0	1979-80	2-1	1954-55
BRENTFORD	5-0	1965-66 (away)	5-1	1982-83
BRISTOL CITY	5-1	1933-34	5-0	1926-27 (home)
CAMBRIDGE UNITED	3-1	1980-81	6-1	1991-92
CHARLTON ATHLETIC	4-0	1924-25	4-0	1979-80
DERBY COUNTY	5-2	1957-58	4-1	1961-62
GRIMSBY TOWN	7-3	1958-59	7-0	1957-58 (home)
LEICESTER CITY	3-0	1953-54	7-2	1956-57
LUTON TOWN	5-0	1920-21	12-0	1935-36
MILLWALL	4-0	1982-83	6-1	1927-28 (home)
NEWCASTLE UNITED	2-0	1990-91 (away)	5-2	1961-62
NOTTS COUNTY	5-1	1976-77	6-0	1946-47
OXFORD UNITED	3-1	1965-66	4-1	1966-67
PETERBOROUGH UTD	4-0	1964-65	5-2	1965-66
PORTSMOUTH	5-1	1982-83	3-0	1974-75
SOUTHEND UNITED	5-1	1926-27	6-0	1929-30
SUNDERLAND	4-0	1987-88	6-1	1961-62
SWINDON	5-0	1938-39	5-2	1981-82
TRANMERE ROVERS	3-0	1969-70	5-2	1969-70
WATFORD	3-0	1951-52	5-1	1930-31 (home)
WEST HAM UNITED	3-2	1954-55 (away)	6-1	1957-58
WOLVERHAMPTON WNDRS	4-3	1985-86	5-1	1976-77 (home)

MANAGER: DENNIS ROFE

DATE OF BIRTH: 1.6.1950   **PLACE OF BIRTH:** Fulham

DATE OF APPOINTMENT: October 1991

PREVIOUS CLUBS
  as Manager: None
  as Asst.Man/Coach: Bristol Rovers
  as Player: L Orient, Leicester City, Chelsea, Southampton

HONOURS
  as Manager:
  as Player:
  International: England u-23 1 cap

Value Rating: ★ ★ ★ ★

Programme Editor: Mike Jay

Price of 1992-93 Programme: £1.20

Number of Pages: 48

Subscriptions: £45.50 (Inland), £56.00 (Europe), £90.00 (Overseas)

Local Newspapers: Western Daily Press, Bristol Evening Post, Bath Evening Chronicle, Sunday Independent, Kingswood/North Avon Gazette

Local Radio Stations: Radio Bristol, GWR Radio

Additional Publications on Club: A Complete Record 1883-1987 by Mike Jay. Breedon Books £14.95
Champions & Cup Finalists 1990 by Mike Jay. BRSC £3
The Pirates at Wembley 1990 by Mike Jay. BRFC £2.95

LEADING LEAGUE GOALSCORERS
SEASONS 1979-80 – 1991-92

1979-80	STEWART BARRACLOUGH	12	1980-81	GARRY MABBUTT		5
				AIDAN McCAFFERY		5
1981-82	PAUL RANDELL	12	1982-83	PAUL RANDELL		20
1983-84	ARCHIE STEPHENS	13	1984-85	PAUL RANDELL		18
1985-86	TREVOR MORGAN	16	1986-87	DAVID MEHEW		10
1987-88	GARY PENRICE	18	1988-89	GARY PENRICE		20
1989-90	DAVID MEWHEW	18	1990-91	CARL SAUNDERS		16

1991-92   **DEVON WHITE**   **11**

TWERTON PARK Bath

Capacity: 8,730   **Covered Standing:** 3,165   **Seating:** 1,026 + 14 disabled

Tel: Ground: 0272 352508/352303   **Ticket Sales:** 0272 352508 (Match days only) 0225 312327   **Clubcall:** 0891 66 44 22

All premium rate calls (0898/0891) cost 36p per minute cheap rate and 48p per minute at all other times. Call costings correct at time of going to press.

GROUNDS
Eastville

Club Registered Office: 199 Two Mile Hill Road, Kingswood, Bristol BS15 1AZ. (0272 352508/352303)

ATTENDANCES
Highest: (Eastville): 38,472 v Preston North End, FA Cup Round 4, 30.1.1960
(Twerton Park): 9,813 v Bristol City, Barclays League, 2.5.1990

Lowest: (Eastville): 2,223 v Swansea City, Freight Rover Trophy, 19.3.1985
(Twerton Park): 1,490 v Ipswich Town, ZDS Cup, 2.10.1991

Record Receipts: (Eastville): £31,809 v Bristol City, FA Cup Round 2, 2.12.1983
(Twerton Park): £62,480 v Liverpool, FA Cup Rnd 4, 8.2.1992

TWERTON PARK
First game: v Reading, League Cup, 1986-87
First floodlit game: as above

Season Tickets:
Stands: £239, juv/OAP £166.50, YP £137
Ground: £127, juv/OAP £88, £73

Cost of Stand Tickets: Seats: Grandstand £13, juv/OAP £8.50, Young Pirate £7; Family stand £9, juv/OAP £6, Young Pirate £6; Family enclosure £4, juv/OAP £4, Young Pirate £3.50.
Terraces: £6.50, juv/OAP £4.50, Young Pirates £3.50 Visiting supporters terracing only: £6.50, juv £6.50

Match and Ticket Information: Stand tickets available two weeks before each match. None for visitors

Car Parking: Restricted to permit holders only

Nearest Railway Station: Bath Spa (1 mile from ground)

How to get to the ground

From North, East, South & West: Use M4 & M5. Leave M5 at Junction 18 via A46 to Bath, follow ring road to Twerton for Bristol Rovers FC

BURNLEY

Division 2

Formed: 1882   **Turned Professional:** 1883   **Ltd Co:** 1897

SPONSORED BY: Endsleigh Insurance   **NICKNAME:** The Clarets

Chairman
F J Teasdale

Vice-Chairman
Dr R D Iven (Vice-Chairman)
MRCS(Eng),LRCOP(Lond),MRCGP

Directors
R B Blakeborough
B Dearing
C Holt
B M Rothwell, JP

Secretary
Mark Blackbourne (0282 27777)

Team Manager
Jimmy Mullen

Reserve Team Coach
Harry Wilson

Physiotherapist
J Holland

Marketing Manager
Cynthia Howarth

Groundsman
Arthur Bellamy

Club Statistician for the Directory
Wallace Chadwick

AFTER the previous season's play-off failure, a number of changes were made to the playing staff. Leading scorer Ron Futcher left for Crewe and was replaced by Mike Conroy, bought for £35,000 from Reading (where he had actually been used in defence); the sale of Steve Davis to Barnsley led to the purchase of his namesake for £60,000 from Southampton, Davis II having made a good impression at Turf Moor during a loan spell in 1989-90. Another new arrival was winger Steve Harper from Preston.

Things started badly, with only three wins in the first eight League games and defeat in both legs of the first round Rumbelows Cup tie against Wigan. Manager Frank Casper, often the butt of the crowd when things were going badly, resigned following a particularly poor performance at Scarborough, and his assistant Jimmy Mullen was appointed caretaker. Mullen was given the title of manager after two victories, the second of which was a 6-2 triumph at Wrexham in which teenager striker Graham Lancashire scored a hat-trick.

Few managers can have had a better start than Mullen. The first nine League games under his charge were won, and the unbeaten run in all competitions extended to 16 games before Rotherham won at Turf Moor on Boxing Day. By this time, Burnley led the Fourth Division, and it was a position they rarely relinquished from then to the end of the season.

Motivation seemed to be the key factor in the improvement from the previous season. There were no lost causes, as the number of late goals to clinch victory or a draw proved . . . those were the most crucial points on the run-in to promotion. The team also proved its capabilities in the Cup competitions, with a memorable series of matches against Derby (the first replay was abandoned through fog) bringing out the best not only in the players but also in the ever-swelling ranks of the club's supporters. In the Autoglass Trophy, victory over Third Division Huddersfield earned a place in the Northern Section final, but Stockport's aerial assualt proved too much to handle.

Conroy became the first player to score 20 League goals in a season for Burnley since Willie Irvine in 1965-66, and he was ably assisted up front by Roger Eli, many of whose goals were spectacular efforts. Davis and John Pender were rock-steady at the back, while veteran Joe Jakub had his best season in claret and blue after moving from midfield to left-back.

The season's main hero, though, was undoubtedly Jimmy Mullen, who brought the success the Burnley public have craved for too long. Over 20,000 attended the final home match of the season; support like that deserves a successful team.

Wallace Chadwick

Back row L-R: Andy Farrell, Michael Conroy, Roger Eli, John Pender, Neil Howarth, John Deary, Paul Murray. **Middle row:** Jamalur Rahman, Simon Wallace, Steve Penney, Ian Measham, David Williams, Graham Lancashire, Danny Sonner, Robbie Painter, Adrian Randall, Paul McKenzie. **Front row:** Mark Yates, Steve Davis, Mark Monington, Paul McKay, Jimmy Mullen (Manager), Joe Jakub, Les Thompson, Steve Harper, Brian Welch.

BURNLEY

DIVISION FOUR: CHAMPIONS **FA CUP:** 3rd RND **RUMBELOWS CUP:** 1st RND **AUTOGLASS:** Nth FINAL

M	DATE		COMP.	VEN	OPPONENTS	RESULT		H/T	LGE POS	GOALSCORERS/GOAL TIMES	ATTEN-DANCE
1	A	17	BL	A	Rotherham United	L	1-2	1-0		Conroy 39	(6,042)
2		20	RC 1/1	A	Wigan Athletic	L	1-3	1-1		Conroy 8	(2,826)
3		27	RC 1/2	H	Wigan Athletic	L	2-3	0-0	8	Patterson (og) 47, Davis 79	3,876
4		31	BL	A	Doncaster Rovers	W	4-1	1-1	3	Conroy (pen) 2, 85, Harper 74, Yates 77	(2,940)
5	S	3	BL	H	Chesterfield	W	3-0	1-0	2	Eli 3 (25, 55, 82)	6,647
6		7	BL	H	Crewe Alexandra	D	1-1	0-0	2	Francis 52	9,657
7		14	BL	A	Hereford United	L	0-2	0-1	8		(4,400)
8		21	BL	H	Rochdale	L	0-1	0-0	10		8,633
9		28	BL	A	Scarborough	L	1-3	1-2	11	Lancashire 18	(2,596)
10	O	5	BL	H	Carlisle United	W	2-0	1-0	11	Pender 23, Lancashire 57	6,157
11		12	BL	A	Wrexham	W	6-2	4-2	8	Lancashire 3 (3, 28, 29), Harper 4, Davis 57, Eli 89	(3,181)
12		19	BL	A	Walsall	W	2-0	2-0	7	Davis (pen) 20, Lancashire 24	7,289
13		22	AGT Pre	A	Blackpool	W	3-1	3-1		Francis 32, Eli 36, 41	(2,805)
14		26	BL	A	Lincoln City	W	3-0	1-0	7	Francis 39, Conroy (pen) 75, Lancashire 83	(3,235)
15	N	2	BL	A	Halifax Town	W	2-0	0-0	3	Deary 56, Farrell 87	(4,491)
16		5	BL	H	York City	W	3-1	2-1	3	Conroy 11, Deary 15, Lancashire 82	7,380
17		9	BL	H	Mansfield Town	W	3-2	1-1	3	Conroy (pen) 7, Davis 56, Pender 85	11,848
18		16	FAC 1	H	Doncaster Rovers	D	1-1	0-0		Davis 66	7,976
19		19	AGT Pre	H	Doncaster Rovers	W	2-0	2-0		Francis 29, Eli 44	2,590
20		23	BL	A	Maidstone United	W	1-0	1-0	3	Conroy (pen) 28	(2,375)
21		27	FAC 1R	A	Doncaster Rovers	W	3-1	1-1		Harper 38, 54, Eli 86	(4,207)
22		30	BL	A	Northampton Town	W	2-1	1-0	2	Conroy 20, 86	(4,020)
23	D	7	FAC 2	H	Rotherham United	W	2-0	0-0		Conroy 59, Lancashire 89	9,773
24		14	BL	H	Scunthorpe United	D	1-1	1-0	2	Farrell 33	8,419
25		26	BL	H	Rotherham United	L	1-2	0-0	1	Francis 70	13,812
26		28	BL	H	Doncaster Rovers	W	2-1	2-0	1	Conroy 7, Eli 26	9,605
27	J	1	BL	A	Chesterfield	W	2-0	2-0	1	Deary 3, Francis 25	(7,789)
28		4	FAC 3	H	Derby County	D	2-2	1-1		Harper 6, Eli 83	18,772
29		11	BL	A	Blackpool	L	2-5	0-2	2	Conroy 64, Francis 70	(8,007)
30		18	BL	H	Gillingham	W	4-1	1-1	1	Conroy 3 (8, 65, 83), Randall 66	8,908
31		25	FAC 3R	A	Derby County	L	0-2	0-0			(18,374)
32	F	1	BL	H	Walsall	D	2-2	0-1	1	Eli 69, Conroy 85	(5,287)
33		4	AGT 1	H	Scarborough	W	3-1	0-0		Conroy 55, Deary 62, Eli 90	2,956
34		8	BL	H	Lincoln City	W	1-0	1-0	1	Conroy 45	9,748
35		11	BL	H	Northampton Town	W	5-0	1-0	1	Deary 35, Eli 50, Conroy 56, Harper 68, Francis 78	8,825
36		15	BL	A	Scunthorpe United	D	2-2	0-2	1	Conroy (pen) 46, Davis 90	(5,303)
37		18	AGT 2	A	Rotherham United	D	†1-1	1-0		Francis 10 (Won 4-2 on pens)	(2,578)
38		22	BL	H	Blackpool	D	1-1	1-1	1	Eli 30	18,183
39		29	BL	A	Cardiff City	W	2-0	0-0	1	Randall 85, Conroy 89	(16,030)
40	M	3	BL	A	Gillingham	L	0-3	0-1	3		(3,729)
41		7	BL	H	Barnet	W	3-0	1-0	1	Davis 11, Barnett (og) 52, Deary 62	12,018
42		14	BL	H	Halifax Town	W	1-0	0-0	3	Pender 70	10,903
43		17	AGT NSF	H	Huddersfield Town	W	2-0	2-0		Conroy (pen) 8, Eli 24	10,775
44		21	BL	A	Mansfield Town	W	1-0	0-0	2	Conroy 41	(8,336)
45		24	BL	A	Barnet	D	0-0	0-0	2		(4,881)
46		28	BL	H	Maidstone United	W	2-1	0-0	1	Davis 77, Eli 87	10,986
47		31	BL	H	Hereford United	W	2-0	2-0	1	Monington 26, Conroy 31	10,578
48	A	4	BL	A	Crewe Alexandra	L	0-1	0-0	1		(5,530)
49		7	AGT NF1	H	Stockport County	L	0-1	0-1			13,272
50		15	AGT NF1	A	Stockport County	L	1-2	1-1		Pender 22	(8,329)
51		20	BL	H	Scarborough	D	1-1	1-1	1	Eli 9	12,312
52		22	BL	H	Cardiff City	W	3-1	1-1	1	Painter 1, Farrell 60, Conroy 63	12,408
53		25	BL	A	Carlisle United	D	1-1	1-0	1	Francis 43	(9,051)
54		28	BL	A	York City	W	2-1	0-1	1	Deary 61, Francis 90	(7,620)
55	M	2	BL	H	Wrexham	L	1-2	1-0	1	Conroy 32	21,216
56		5	BL	A	Rochdale	W	3-1	2-1	1	Measham 31, Conroy 41, Painter 67	(8,175)

Best Home League Attendance: 21,216 v Wrexham   **Smallest: 6,157 v Carlisle United**   **Av Home Att: 10,740**

Goal Scorers: Compared with 90-91: +2,862

League (79): Conroy 24 (5 pens), Eli 10, Lancashire 8, Francis 8, Deary 6, Davis 6 (1 pen), Pender 3, Farrell 3, Harper 3, Painter 2, Randall 2, Opponents, Monington, Measham, Yates

R/lows C (3): Davis, Conroy, Opponents

FA Cup (8): Harper 3, Eli 2, Lancashire, Davis, Conroy

Autoglass (12): Eli 5, Francis 3, Conroy 2 (1 pen), Pender, Deary   †=After extra-time

Pearce C.	Measham I.	Jakub Y.	Deary J.	Pender J.	Monington M.	Farrell A.	Davis S.	Francis J.	Conroy M.	Harper S.	Lancashire G.	Hardy J.	Bray I.	Eli R.	Hamilton D.	France M.	Marriott A.	Yates M.	Sonner D.	Randall A.	Kendall M.	Walker J.	Painter P.	McKenzie P.	Williams D.	Referee	
1	2	3	4	5	6	7	8	9*	10	11•	12	14														G Poll	1
1	2	11•	8	5	6	14	4	9	10	12			3	7*												**E Parker**	2
1			8	5	6	12	4	9	10	14			3*	7	11•	2										**P Harrison**	3
			8	5	6		4	9	10	12			3*	11	14	2•	1	7								D Shadwell	4
			8	5	6	S	4	9	10	3			S	7	2		1	11								D Phillips	5
			8*	5	6	12	4	9	10	3			S	7	2		1	11								J Key	6
	12		5	6	11	4	9	10	3				14	7	2*		1	8•								P Jones	7
	11	8	5	6	2		9	10			4		3*	12			1	7•	14							I Hendrick	8
2	10	8	5	14	6	4					9*	3		11			1	12								S Bell	9
2	10•	8	5	6		4				7	9*	3		11			1	14	12							J Kirby	10
	10	8	5	12		6	4			7	9*	3		11	2		1	S								P Vanes	11
	10	8	5	S		6	4	12		7	9	3*		11	2		1									B Coddington	12
	2	3	8	5		6	4	11	12	7	9*			10			1	S								**R Nixon**	13
	2	3	8	5		6	4	9	10	7	12			11*			1	S								R Wiseman	14
	3	8	5			6	4	9	10	7	12			11*	2		1	S								P Danson	15
	3	8	5			6	4	9	10*	7				11	2		1	S	12							J Lloyd	16
	3	8	5			6	4	9*	10	7				11	2	12	1	S								T Holbrook	17
1	3	8	5			6	4	9	10	7				11*	2	12		S								**P Wright**	18
	2	3	8	5		6	4	9*	10•	7	14			11			1	12								**W Burns**	19
	2	3	8	5		6	4	9	10	7	S			11			1	S								G Pooley	20
1	2	3	8	5*		6	4	9	10	7	S			11				12								**P Wright**	21
	2	3	8	5		S	6	4*	9	10	7			11*			1	5								A Flood	22
1	2	3	8	5		6	4	9	10	7	12			11*				S								**J Watson**	23
1	2	3	8*	5		6	4	9	10	7	14			11•				12								A Dawson	24
1	2	3	8	5		6•	4	9	10	7	11*			12					14							J Rushton	25
1	2	3	8	5		6	4	9	10	14				11•				12		7*						K Lupton	26
	2	3	8	5		6	4	9	10*	S	12			11						7	1					I Cruikshanks	27
	2	3	8	5		6	4	9*	10	7	12			11			S				1					**K Redfern**	28
	2	3	8	5		6	4	9	10	7*	S			11					12		1					M Reed	29
1	2	3	8	5		6*	4	9	10	7	11•							14		12						K Hackett	30
1	2	3	8	5		6	4	9	10	7*	11•			12				14								**K Redfern**	31
1	2	3	8	5		6*	4	9	10	12	14			11•				7								P Durkin	32
1	2	3	8	5		6	4	9	10	7	S			11				S								**T Holbrook**	33
1	2	3	8	5		6	4	9	10	7	12			11*					S							D Phillips	34
1	2	3	8	5		6*	4	9	10	7	14			11•					12							A Wilkie	35
1	2	3	8	5		6*	4	9	10	7	S			11					12							J Kirkby	36
1	2	3	8	5		6	4	9	10	7	12			11*					S							**R Nixon**	37
	2	3	8	5		6*	4	9	10	7•	14			11					12		1					J Worrall	38
	2	3	8				5	4	9	10	7			12	S	11*			6		1					J Martin	39
	2	3	8				5	4	9	10	7			12				14	6•		1					B Hill	40
	2	3	8	5		6	4*	9	10	7	S			11					12		1					P Vanes	41
	2	3	8	5	12	4		9	10	7*	11			S				6			1					T West	42
	2	3	8†	5	4	6		9	10	7*	12			11				S			1					**J Watson**	43
	3	8	5		S	2	4	9	10	7	11			S					6		1					R Gifford	44
1	3	8	5		S	2	4	9	10	7	12			11*					6		1					R Pawley	45
1	3	8	5		2	4		9*	10	7•				12				14		6				11		R Poulain	46
1	3		5	6	2	4			10		12			11*				8	7				9		S	W Burns	47
1	3		5	6	2	4			10*		12		10	11				7					9	S		A Dawson	48
1	3		5	6	2	4		9				10*		11				7						12		**G Courtney**	49
1	3	8	5	14	2	4		9	10	7*				11•				6						12		**K Hackett**	50
1	2	3	8	5		6	4	9	10	12				11*				S					7			K Breen	51
	2	3	8	5		6	4	9	10	12				S				11*					7		1	**G Courtney**	52
	2	3	8	5	S	6	4	9	10	11*				S				7					12		1	R Hart	53
	2	3	8	5		6	4	9	10	11*				S				7					12		1	J Brandwood	54
	2	3	8	5	14	6*	4	9	10					12				7					11•*		1	J Watson	55
	2	3	8	5			4	9	10	11				6				7*					12		1	V Callow	56
14	27	38	40	39	8	38	40	36	38	31	10	2	5	28	3	6	15	9		11	2	6	9	1	5	**League Appearances**	
1				4		1		4	16	1	1	4	1				8	3	7					3		**Substitute Appearances**	
2	1	1	2	2		0+2	2	2	2		0+2			2	2	1	1									**R/lows Appearances**	
4	4	5	5	5		5	5	5	5		2+2			3+2		1		0+2			1					**FA Cup Appearances**	
4	5	7	7	7		2+1	7	6	6	5+1	6		2+3	1	7			2	2+1				1	0+2		**Autoglass Appearances**	

Also Played: Posn.(Game): Mumby 7*(9)

† = Sent Off

119

BURNLEY

Club Colours: Claret shirts with light blue sleeves, white shorts and stockings
Change Colours: White shirts, claret shorts
Reserves League: Pontins Central League Div 2

Previous Name: Burnley Rovers 1881-82
Previous Managers: 1945-49 Cliff Britton 1949-54 Frank Hill 1954-57 Alan Brown 1957-58 Billy Dougal 1958-70 Harry Potts 1970-76 Jimmy Adamson 1976-77 Joe Brown 1977-79 Harry Potts 1979-83 Brian Miller 1983 Frank Casper (Caretaker) 1983-84 John Bond 1984-85 John Benson 1985 Martin Buchan 1985-86 Tommy Cavanagh 1986-89 Brian Miller 1989-91 Frank Casper Jimmy Mullen 1991-
Honours: Champions Div 1 1920-21, 1959-60 Champions Div 2 1897-98, 1972-73 Champions Div 3 1981-82 Champions Div 4 1991-92 FA Cup Winners 1913-14 Anglo-Scottish Cup Winners 1978-79 FA Charity Shield Winners 1973, Joint Winners 1960
League Career: Founder Members of the League 1888 Relegated to Div 2 1896-97 Promoted to Div 1 1897-98 Relegated to Div 2 1899-1900 Promoted to Div 1 1912-13 Relegated to Div 2 1929-30 Promoted to Div 1 1946-47 Relegated to Div 2 1970-71 Promoted to Div 1 1972-73 Relegated to Div 2 1975-76 Relegated to Div 3 1979-80 Promoted to Div 2 1981-82 Relegated to Div 3 1982-83 Relegated to Div 4 1984-85 Promoted to Div 3 1991-92

CLUB RECORDS

Most Appearances for Club: Jerry Dawson, 1907-28: League 522 + FA Cup 45 + Charity Shield 1 **Total 568**
Most Capped Player: Jimmy McIlroy, 52 N Ireland **For England:** Bob Kelly 11
Record Goalscorer in a Match: Louis Page 6 v Birmingham City (a), 7-1 Div 1, 10.4.1926
Record League Goalscorer in a Season: George Beel, 35 Div 1, 1927-28 **In All Competitions:** Jimmy Robson 37 (League 25 + FA Cup 5 + League Cup 4 + European Cup 3), 1960-61 Willie Irvine 37 (League 29, FA Cup 5, League Cup 3) 1965-66
Record League Goalscorer in a Career: George Beel, 178, 1923-32 **In All Competitions:** George Beel 187 (League 178 + FA Cup 9)
Record Transfer Fee Received: £325,000 from Everton for Trevor Steven, July 1983
Record Transfer Fee Paid: £165,000 to Queens Park Rangers for Leighton James, Sept 1978
Best Performances: League: Champions 1920-21, 1959-60 **FA Cup:** Winners 1913-14 **League Cup:** Semi-finalists 1960-61, 1968-69, 1982-83 **European Cup:** Quarter-final **European Fairs Cup:** Quarter-final
Most League Points: (3pts for win) 83, Div 4, 1991-92 (2pts for win) 62, Div 2 1972-73
Most League Goals: 102, Div 1, 1960-61
Record League Victory and Most Goals Scored in a League Match: 9-0 v Darwen, Div 1, 9.1.1892
Most Goals Scored in a Cup Tie: 9-0 v Crystal Palace, 2nd Round FA Cup, 10.1.1909 9-0 v New Brighton, 4th Round FA Cup, 26.1.1957 9-0 v Penrith, 1st Round FA Cup, 17.11.1984
Record League Defeat: 0-10 v Aston Villa, Div 1, 29.8.1925 0-10 v Sheffield United, Div 1, 19.1.1929
European Competitions entered: European Cup 1960-61 European Fairs Cup 1966-67
Oldest Player in a League Match: Jerry Dawson (Christmas Day 1928) 40 years 282 days
Youngest Player in a League Match: Tommy Lawton, 16 years 174 days, 28.3.1936

LONGEST LEAGUE RUNS

of undefeated matches: 30 (1920-21)	**of league matches without a win:** 24 (1979)
of undefeated home matches: 34 (1911-13)	**of undefeated away matches:** 15 (1972-73)
without home win: 11 (1979)	**without an away win:** 31 (1901-03)
of league wins: 10 (1912-13)	**of home wins:** 17 (1920-21)
of league defeats: 8 (1889-90, 1895)	**of away wins:** 7 (1991-92)

BARCLAYS

BARCLAYS BUSINESS CENTRE
Burnley Business Centre
72-78 St James Street
Burnley
Lancs BB11 1JQ
Tel: 0282 20211

BARCLAYBANK MACHINE

BURNLEY

PLAYERS NAME Honours	Ht	Wt	Birthdate	Birthplace Transfers	Contract Date	Clubs	League	L/Cup	FA Cup	Other	Lg	L/C	FAC	Oth
GOALKEEPERS														
David P Williams	6.0	12.0	18.09.68	Liverpool		Oldham Ath. (T)								
					23.03.89	Burnley	22			2				
				Loan	02.09.91	Rochdale	6	1						
DEFENDERS														
Stephen M Davis	6.2	12.8	30.10.68	Hexham	06.07.87	Southampton	5+1							
				Loan	21.11.88	Burnley	7+2							
Loan Notts County (28.03.91) 0+2				£60,000	17.08.91	Burnley	40	2	5	6	6	1	1	
Paul McKay			28.01.71	Banbury	29.11.89	Burnley	8+4		1+1					
Ian Measham	5.11	11.1	14.12.64	Barnsley	16.12.82	Huddersfield T (A)	17							
				Loan	18.10.85	Lincoln City	6							
Loan Rochdale (21.03.86) 12lg				M	15.08.88	Cambridge Utd	46	6	3	2				
					05.01.89	Burnley	138+1	4	14	17	2			
Mark Monington	6.1	13.0	21.10.70	Bilsthorpe	23.03.89	Burnley	27+6	4		2+1	2			
John Pender	6.0	12.3	19.11.63	Luton	08.11.81	Wolves (A)	115+2	5	7		3		1	
Ei:u21,1,Y				£35,000	23.07.85	Charlton Ath	41	1	1	2				1
					30.10.87	Bristol City	83	11	8	12	3			
				£70,000	18.10.90	Burnley	79	4	8	14	3			
MIDFIELD														
John Deary	5.10	11.11	18.10.62	Ormskirk	13.03.80	Blackpool (A)	285+18	20	16+2	14	43	5	4	1
				£30,000	18.07.89	Burnley	122+2	7+1	12	14	15		1	1
Roger Eli	5.10	11.4	11.09.65	Bradford	15.09.83	Leeds Utd. (A)	1+1							
					17.01.86	Wolverhampton W	16+2	1+1		1				
				N.C	09.09.87	Crewe Alexandra	20+7		1	2	1			1
				N.C	03.11.88	York City	3+1		1	1	1			
				Free	11.01.89	Bury	0+2							
				Free		Burnley	67+20	4+2	6+3	13	20		5	6
Andy Farrell	5.11	11.0	07.10.65	Colchester	21.09.83	Colchester Utd. (A)	98+7	9	8	6	5			
				£13,000	07.08.87	Burnley	184+9	13+3	13+2	26	14	1		2
Yanek Joe Jakub	5.6	9.6	07.12.56	Falkirk	01.12.73	Burnley (A)	42	2						
				£19,000	08.10.80	Bury	262+3	16	21	6	27	4	2	
via A Z Alkaat				Free	24.08.88	Chester City	42	4	2	2	1			
				£15,000	25.07.89	Burnley	130+1	7	14	16	8			1
Steve Penney	5.9	10.4	16.01.64	Ballymena		Ballymena								
N:17					25.11.83	Brighton & H.A	125+13	9	12	2+1	14	1		
				Free		Hearts	9							
				Free	31.07.92	Burnley								
FORWARDS														
Michael Conroy	6.0	11.0	31.12.65	Glasgow		Coventry City								
						Clyde	92+22	4+1	5+2		38			
						St. Mirren	9+1		0+1		1			
				£50,000	28.07.88	Reading	65+15	3+2	8+2	2+2	7		1	
				£35,000	16.07.91	Burnley	38	2	5	5+1	24	1	1	2
John Francis	5.8	11.2	21.11.63	Leeds		Halifax Town	1+3			2	1			
via Emley				15.09.85	Sheffield Utd	14+28	0+2	0+1	3+2	6			1
				£90,000	24.01.90	Burnley	99+2	5	8	11+1	27		1	5
Steve Harper	5.10	11.5	03.02.69	Stoke	29.06.87	Port Vale (A)	16+12	1+2		1+1	2			
				23.03.89	Preston N.E	57+20	1+1	1+2	6	10			1
				Free	23.07.91	Burnley	31+4	0+2	5	6	3		3	
Graham Lancashire	5.10		19.10.72	Blackpool	01.07.91	Burnley (T)	10+16		2+2	2+3	8		1	
Peter Painter	5.10		26.01.71	Billinge	01.07.88	Chester City	58+27	2+2	7+1	3+4	8		3	
				£30,000	16.08.91	Maidstone Utd	27+3	2	1+1	0+2	5			
				£25,000	27.03.92	Burnley	9				2			
Adrian Randall	5.11	11.0	10.11.68	Amesbury	02.09.86	Bournemouth (A)	3			1+2				
E:Y2				15.09.88	Aldershot	102+5	3	10	8	12		3	2
				£40,000	12.12.91	Burnley	11+7				2			
Les Thompson	5.10	11.0	23.09.68	Cleethorpes		Leek Town								
				27.03.87	Hull City (A)	21+5	4	1	0+1	4			
				Loan	24.12.88	Scarborough	2+1				1			
				Free	16.08.91	Maidstone Utd	38	2	2	2			1	
				Free	10.07.92	Burnley								
Mark Yates	5.11	11.9	24.01.70	Birmingham	08.07.88	Birmingham City (A)	37+16	5	0+2	5	6	1		
AMC'91				Loan		Colchester Utd			3					
				£40,000	30.08.91	Burnley	9+8		0+2	2+1	1			
ADDITIONAL CONTRACT PLAYERS														
Barry Cass					20.09.89	Burnley								
Lee Dixon					29.10.88	Burnley								
Neil Howarth			15.11.71	Farnworth	02.07.90	Burnley (T)	0+1							
Richard Kay					20.09.89	Burnley								
James Leighton					05.08.88	Burnley								
Paul A McKenzie					05.02.92	Burnley	1+3			0+2				
Stephen Mercer					29.10.88	Burnley								
Paul G Murray					04.07.92	Burnley (T)								
Jamalur Rahman					04.07.92	Burnley (T)								
Daniel Sonner					06.08.90	Burnley	1+4			0+2				
Simon P Wallace					04.07.92	Burnley (T)								
Brian J Welch					10.01.92	Burnley								

LEADING LEAGUE GOALSCORERS SEASONS 1985-86 – 1991-92

1985-86	**STEVE TAYLOR**	**16**	1986-87	**LEIGHTON JAMES**	**10**
1987-88	**GEORGE OGHANI**	**14**	1988-89	**BRENDAN O'CONNELL**	**13**
1989-90	**WINSTON WHITE** **RON FUTCHER**	**7**	1990-91	**RON FUTCHER**	**18**
	1991-92	**MICHAEL CONROY**	**24**		

TURF MOOR Brunshaw Road, Burnley, Lancs BB10 4BX

Capacity: 20,912   **Covered Standing:**   **Seating:** 7,437

Tel: Ground: 0282 27777   **Ticket Sales:** As ground number   **Clubcall:** 0898 12 11 53

All premium rate calls (0898/0891) cost 36p per minute cheap rate and 48p per minute at all other times. Call costings correct at time of going to press.

ATTENDANCES
Highest: 54,775 v Huddersfield Town, FA Cup Round 3, 23.2.1924

Lowest: 1,138 v Darlington, Freight Rover Trophy, 13.3.1986

Record Receipts: £63,988 v Sheffield Wednesday, FA Cup Round 6, 12.3.1983

Season Tickets:
Stands: from £117 to £180
Ground: from £55 to £90 (Concessions)

Executive Box Season Tickets: None

Cost of Stand Tickets: Bob Lord Stand: £10, juveniles/OAP £5; Cricket Field Stand (Members only): £8, juveniles/OAP £3.50
Terraces: £6.50, juveniles/OAP £3

Match and Ticket Information: See telephone number above

Car Parking: Parks in Church Street and Fulledge Recreation Ground for approx 500 vehicles each (chargeable). Both are 5 minutes walk from ground

Nearest Railway Station: Burnley Central

How to get to the ground

From North: Follow signs Burnley A56 into Town Centre, at roundabout take 1st exit into Yorkshire Street, shortly over crossroads into Brunshaw Road for Burnley FC

From East: Follow signs Burnley A646 then join A671 enter city centre by Todmorden Road and at end at crossroads turn right into Brunshaw Road for Burnley FC

From South: (or use route from west). Use M62, M66 and A56 signposted Burnley into town centre, then at roundabout take 3rd exit in Yorkshire Street, shortly at crossroads forward into Brunshaw Road for Burnley FC

From West and South: Use M6 to junction 31, then Blackburn bypass and A679 into Burnley town centre and at roundabout take 3rd exit into Yorkshire Street, shortly over crossroads into Brunshaw Road for Burnley FC

Value Rating: ★ ★ ★

Programme Editor: Cynthia Howarth

Price of 1992-93 Programme: £1.20
Number of Pages: 36
Subscriptions: £50 (home) £70 (home/away/cup matches)

Local Newspapers: Lancashire Evening Telegraph, Burnley Express

Local Radio Stations: Radio Lancashire, Red Rose Radio

BURY

Division 3

Formed: 1885   **Turned Professional:** 1885   **Ltd Co:** 1897

SPONSORED BY: MacPherson Paints Ltd   **NICKNAME:** The Shakers

Chairman
T Robinson

Vice-Chairman
Canon J R Smith,MA

Directors
J Smith
I J Pickup,LLB
C H Eaves FCA
F Mason
A M Noonan

Chief Executive
T Robinson (061-764 4881)

Assistant Secretary
S Atkinson

Team Manager
Mike Walsh

Assistant Manager
J Chapman

Physio
Mandy Johnson MCSP, SRP

Commercial Manager
N Neville (061-705 2144)

Groundsmen
G Horrocks/M Curtis

Club Statistician for the Directory
Paul Greenlees

A SEASON long struggle against relegation for the Shakers had largely been expected by the supporters. More of the highly successful squad which had reached the play-offs in consecutive seasons were sold to help meet financial commitments which were threatening the existence of the club. Charlie Bishop joined Barnsley during the summer and with the new season barely a week old, popular winger David Lee joined Southampton in a record breaking £400,000 deal. The major summer signing was Ian Stevens who was brought in on a free transfer and enjoyed a splendid campaign.

The season began well, and after returning from the ill-tempered 2-0 win at Darlington on October 5th, the Shakers found themselves in seventh position. However, the seeds of doubt over the defensive ability of the team had already been sown in two amazing games. Firstly, a 2-1 lead at Reading was turned into a 3-2 defeat in the final minute. But it was the home game with Huddersfield which will never be forgotten. Four goals ahead after half an hour and 4-2 ahead with five minutes to play, Bury hung on in injury time to a 4-4 draw leaving the field shattered!

Thereafter, goals were conceded with alarming regularity and few points gathered, so that by Christmas the club were languishing in the relegation zone. Manager, Mike Walsh, decided to re-arrange the defence to play five at the back. The change and the 1-0 win over Birmingham looked to have saved the season as a six match unbeaten run was enjoyed in mid-February. It included a 3-0 win at Brentford which earned the 'Performance of the Week' award. Just as the light began to shine at the end of the tunnel, the pendulum swung the other way and only one win was recorded in eleven games, amazingly at Stoke 2-1.

The financial problems at the club again surfaced on the transfer deadline day when Colin Greenall was sold to Preston for £50,000. It was a deal which effectively sealed the club's fate as it coincided with the five match ban of fellow defender Peter Valentine who had been stupidly sent-off at Bolton for retaliation.

A brief revival was seen in April following the introduction of on-loan Darren Lyons from Ashton. By the final day of the season, Bury knew that victory on the plastic pitch at Deepdale and failure by Exeter to win at Darlington would bring safety. As it happened, Exeter lost 5-2, but a disappointing display by the Shakers saw a 2-0 defeat and relegation.

First round knock-outs in the three cup competitions brought little financial reward. However, there is optimism around the club with the announcement of a £911,000 grant to upgrade the ground thus ensuring the Shakers continue their 107 year association with Gigg Lane. **Paul Greenlees**

Back row L-R: Mark Kearney, Alan Knill, Matthew Lambert, David Jones, Darren Lyons. **Middle row:** Jack Chapman (Chief Scout), Ian Hughes, Darren Wilson, Gary Kelly, Andy Gorton, Mick Pollitt, Ian Stevens, Lawrence Greenhalgh, John King (Asst. Manager). **Front:** Paul Robertson, Lee Anderson, Kevin Hulme, Mike Walsh (Manager), Peter Valentine, Liam Robinson, Darren Emmett, Ian Scott.

BURY

DIVISION THREE: 21st   **FA CUP:** 1st RND   **RUMBELOWS CUP:** 1st RND   **AUTOGLASS:** 2nd RND

M	DATE		COMP.	VEN	OPPONENTS	RESULT	H/T	LGE POS	GOALSCORERS/GOAL TIMES	ATTEN-DANCE
1	A	17	BL	A	Birmingham City	L 2-3	1-2		Lee (pen) 22, Robinson 65	(9,033)
2		20	RC 1/1	A	Hartlepool United	L 0-1	0-1			(2,833)
3		24	BL	H	Shrewsbury Town	D 0-0	0-0			2,373
4		27	RC 1/2	H	Hartlepool United	D 2-2	0-0		Stanislaus 71, Mauge 85	1,917
5		31	BL	A	Reading	L 2-3	0-1	22	Valentine 65, Smith 81	(2,886)
6	S	3	BL	H	Peterborough Utd	W 3-0	2-0	16	Robinson 10, R Robinson (og) 34, Stevens 89	2,240
7		7	BL	A	Hull City	W 1-0	1-0	9	Stevens 21	(3,679)
8		14	BL	H	Huddersfield Town	D 4-4	4-1	10	Robinson 2, Greenall 21, Stevens 25, Smith 32	4,409
9		17	BL	H	Fulham	W 3-1	2-1	9	Valentine 4, Greenall 37, Robinson 64	2,248
10		21	BL	A	Stockport County	L 0-2	0-0	9		(5,083)
11		28	BL	H	Hartlepool United	D 1-1	0-0	9	Greenall 10	2,600
12	O	5	BL	A	Darlington	W 2-0	1-0	7	Stevens 22, 89	(3,006)
13		12	BL	H	Preston North End	L 2-3	2-1	10	Robinson 3, Greenall 31	4,265
14		19	BL	A	Exeter City	L 2-5	0-3	15	Robinson (pen) 60, 83 (pen)	(3,904)
15		22	AGT Pre	A	Scunthorpe United	W 3-1	1-0		Stevens 38, Hulme 74, D Wilson 78	(1,122)
16		26	BL	H	Brentford	L 0-3	0-2	17		2,280
17	N	2	BL	A	West Bromwich A.	D 1-1	1-0	17	Stevens 20	(8,439)
18		5	BL	H	Stoke City	L 1-3	1-1	18	Stevens 7	3,245
19		9	BL	A	Bolton Wanderers	D 1-1	0-1	19	Robinson 78	5,886
20		16	FAC 1	H	Bradford City	L 0-1	0-0			3,805
21		19	AGT Pre	H	Halifax Town	D 2-2	2-1		Smith 21, Robinson 45	788
22		22	BL	A	Wigan Athletic	L 0-2	0-1	19		(2,268)
23		30	BL	H	Bournemouth	L 0-1	0-1	21		1,886
24	D	21	BL	A	Shrewsbury Town	D 1-1	1-1	21	Robinson 44	(2,573)
25		26	BL	H	Reading	L 0-1	0-0	22		2,333
26		28	BL	H	Birmingham City	W 1-0	0-0	20	Smith 82	4,253
27	J	1	BL	A	Peterborough Utd	D 0-0	0-0	21		(5,567)
28		4	BL	A	Bradford City	D 1-1	0-1	21	Stevens 90	(6,354)
29		11	BL	H	Swansea City	W 1-0	0-0	20	D Wilson 47	2,161
30		14	AGT 1	H	Chesterfield	W 2-1	0-0		Greenall 50, Hulme 85	1,036
31		18	BL	A	Torquay United	W 2-0	1-0	15	Stevens 44, Stanislaus 76	(2,625)
32	F	4	AGT 2	H	Huddersfield Town	L 1-2	1-0		Knill 39	1,789
33		8	BL	A	Brentford	W 3-0	2-0	18	Stanislaus 15, Hulme 30, Stevens 85	(6,789)
34		11	BL	A	Bournemouth	L 0-4	0-1	19		(3,558)
35		15	BL	H	Leyton Orient	W 4-2	3-0	16	Stevens 3 (15, 36, 56), Hulme 24	2,120
36		22	BL	A	Swansea City	L 1-2	1-0	17	Greenall (pen) 10	(2,787)
37		25	BL	H	Chester City	L 1-2	1-2	17	Stanislaus 13	2,283
38		29	BL	H	Bradford City	L 0-1	0-1	19		2,983
39	M	3	BL	H	Torquay United	D 0-0	0-0	18		1,663
40		7	BL	A	Chester City	L 1-3	1-1	22	Valentine 21	(1,228)
41		11	BL	A	Stoke City	W 2-1	0-0	20	Stevens 50, 75	(12,385)
42		14	BL	H	West Bromwich A.	D 1-1	1-1	20	Kearney 2	3,810
43		21	BL	A	Bolton Wanderers	L 1-2	0-1	21	Hulme 49	(7,619)
44		24	BL	A	Leyton Orient	L 0-4	0-1	22		(3,074)
45		28	BL	H	Wigan Athletic	L 1-4	0-1	22	Lyons 52	2,618
46		31	BL	A	Huddersfield Town	L 0-3	0-2	22		(5,890)
47	A	4	BL	H	Hull City	W 3-2	2-0	21	Lyons 18, 30, Robinson 50	2,245
48		11	BL	A	Fulham	L 2-4	0-3	21	Hulme 72, Knill 85	(4,060)
49		14	BL	H	Exeter City	W 3-1	2-1	21	Lyons 29, I Wilson 41, Stevens 76	1,756
50		18	BL	H	Stockport County	D 0-0	0-0	21		4,726
51		20	BL	A	Hartlepool United	D 0-0	0-0	21		(2,503)
52		25	BL	H	Darlington	W 1-0	0-0	21	Stevens 71	2,351
53	M	2	BL	A	Preston North End	L 0-2	0-1	21		(6,932)

Best Home League Attendance: 5,886 v Bolton Wanderers   **Smallest:** 1,663 v Torquay United   **Av Home Att:** 2,901

Goal Scorers: **Compared with 90-91:** -671

League (55): Stevens 17, Robinson 10 (2 pens), Greenall 5 (1 pen), Lyons 4, Hulme 4, Stanislaus 3, Valentine 3, Smith 3, I Wilson, Knill Opponents, Kearney, D Wilson, Lee (1 pen)

R/lows C (2): Stanislaus, Mauge
FA Cup (0):
Autoglass (8): Hulme 2, Robinson, Stevens, Greenall, Smith, Knill, D Wilson

1991-92

Kelly G.	Wilson D.	Stanislaus R.	Robinson S.	Valentine P.	Greenall C.	Lee D.	Hulme K.	Stevens I.	Parkinson P.	Kearney M.	Smith N.	Knill A.	Mauge R.	Wilson I.	Jones D.	Anderson L.	Hughes I.	Robertson P.	Cullen A. (L)	Emmett	Greenhalgh	Flitcroft G. (L)	Lyons D. (L)	Winter	Referee	
1	2	3	4	5	6	7	8*	9	10	11	12	S													P Alcock	1
1	2	3	4	5	6	7	14	9*	10	11	8*		12												R Poulain	2
1	2	3	4	5	6	7	8	9*	10	11	S			12											W Burns	3
1	2	3	8	5	6		9	S	10*	4	7		12	11											R Nixon	4
1	2	3	8	5	6		14	9*	10	4	7		12	11*											K Morton	5
1	2	3	8	5	6		S	9	10	4	7		S	11											K Lupton	6
1	2	3	8	5	6		14	9	10	4	7•		12	11*											J Rushton	7
1	2	3	8	5	6		S	9	10	4	7		12	11*											G Singh	8
1	2	3	8	5	6		12	9*	14	10		7	4	11•											A Dawson	9
1	2	3	8	5	6		14	9•	12	10		7	4	11*											K Cooper	10
1	2	3	8	5	6			9*	10	4	7		12	11*	14										A Smith	11
1	2	3	8	5	6			9	10	4	7•		12	11	S										A Bennett	12
1	2	3	8	5	6			9	10	4	7		S	11*	12										K Breen	13
1		3	8	5*	6			9	12	4	7	10*		11	14	2									K Cooper	14
1	12	3	8*		6		14	9	10	4	7			11		2*	5								M Brandwood	15
1	2	3*	8	5	6		10	9*	14	4	7			11	12										T West	16
1	2		8	5	6			9	S	4	7			11	S			3	10						M Bodenham	17
1	2		8	5	6			9	12	4	7			11*	S			3	10						K Redfearn	18
1			8	5	6			9•	4		7	2		11*	4		12	3	10						K Hackett	19
1		3	8	5	2		12	9	4		7	6		11	10*	S									T Holbrook	20
1	S	3	8	5	2		12		4		7	6		10			9*		11						I Cruikshank	21
1	12	3	8	5	2		14	9	4		7	6*		11			10*								I Hendrick	22
1	12	3	8	5	2		9•	14	4	10	7	6		11*											G Courtney	23
1	3		8	5	2			9	4	10	7	6				S	11	S							G Ashby	24
1	3	12	8	5	2			9	4	10	7	6•	14	11*											J Key	25
1	3	11	8	5	2			9	4	10	7	6				S	S								M Peck	26
1	3	11	8*	5	2			9	4	10	7	6				12	S								J Moules	27
1	3	11*	8	5	2			9	4	10	7	6				12	S								J Watson	28
1	3	11	8*	5	2		12	9	4	10	7	6				S									B Coddington	29
1	3	11	8	5	2		14	9	4	10•	7	6*				12									R Hart	30
1	3	11	8•	5	2		14	9	4		7	6	10*				12								P Scoble	31
1	3•	11	8	5	2		12	9			7	6				4*	14	10							M Reed	32
1	3	11	8	5	2		7	9		10		6				S	4†		S						D Frampton	33
1	3*	11	8	5	2		7	9	4	10	12	6•					14								A Ward	34
1	3	11	8•	5	2		7	9	4*		10	6	12				14								D Shadwell	35
1	3•	11	8	5	2		7	9			10*	14	6	12	4										D Elleray	36
1	3	11	12		2		7	9			10*	8	6	5	4		S								A Bennett	37
1	3	11	8		2		7	9			10		6	4	S	S		5							D Gallagher	38
1	S	11	8	5	2		7	9			10		6	4	12			3*							K Lupton	39
1	S	11		5	2		7	9			10	8	6		S			3				4			J Kirby	40
1	S	11		5	2		7	9			10	8	6		S			3				4			M Peck	41
1	S	11		5	2		7	9			10	8*	6					3				4	12		R Shepherd	42
1		11•	14	5†	2		7	9			10	8	6	12				3*				4			T Holbrook	43
1	3•	11	8	5	2			9			10*	7	6	12			14					4			B Hill	44
1	2	3	8					9	10		7*	6	4	12								5†	11	S	S Lodge	45
1	2*	3	8					9•	10		7	5	4	S			12					6	11		W Flood	46
1	S	3	8				7*	9	10•		12	6	4			2						5	11		B Nixon	47
1		3	8•				7	9	14	10•		6	4	12		2						5	11		G Willard	48
1	S		S				8	9	10	3		6	4	11		2						5	7		R Lewis	49
1		12	14				8	9*	10*	3		6	4	11		2						5	7		M Reed	50
1	12	S		5			8	9	10	3		6	4			2						11*	7		S Bell	51
1	12		8•	5			14	9	10	3		6	4	11*		2							7		M Brandwood	52
1	12		8	5			14	9	10	3*		6	4	11		2							7•		R Dilkes	53
46	30	36	38	38	37	2	21	44	26	43	30	33	15	21	1	3	13	5	4			12	9		**League Appearances**	
2	4	3	1				9	1	6		4	2	7	3	8	2	4						1		**Substitute Appearances**	
2	2	2	2	2	2	1	1+1	1	2	2	2		0+2	1											**R/lows Appearances**	
1	1	1	1	1			1	1	1		1	1		1	1										**FA Cup Appearances**	
4	2+1	4	4	3	4		0+3	3+1	3	2	4	3	0+1	2	1	1+1	3		1						**Autoglass Appearances**	

Players on Loan: Cullen (Sunderland), Flitcroft (Manchester City), Lyons (Ashton Utd)

† = Sent Off

BURY

Club Colours: White shirts, navy blue shorts, navy blue stockings
Change Colours: All purple
Reserves League: Lancashire League Division One

Previous League: Lancashire League
Previous Managers: (Since 1946): Norman Bullock John McNeil Dave Russell Bob Stokoe Bert Head Les Shannon Jack Marshall Les Hart Colin McDonald Tommy McAnearney Allan Brown Bobby Smith Bob Stokoe Dave Hatton Dave Connor Jim Iley Martin Dobson Sam Ellis
Honours: Champions Div 2, 1894-95 Champions Div 3, 1960-61 FA Cup Winners 1900, 1903
League Career: Elected to Div 2 1894 Promoted to Div 1 1894-95 Relegated to Div 2 1911-12
Promoted to Div 1 1923-24 Relegated to Div 2 1928-29 Relegated to Div 3 1956-57 Promoted to Div 2 1960-61
Relegated to Div 3 1966-67 Promoted to Div 2 1967-68 Relegated to Div 3 1968-69 Relegated to Div 4 1970-71
Promoted to Div 3 1973-74 Relegated to Div 4 1979-80 Promoted to Div 3 1984-85 Relegated to Div 4 1991-92

CLUB RECORDS

Most Appearances for Club: Norman Bullock, 1920-35: League 506 + FA Cup 33 **Total 539**
Most Capped Player: Bill Gorman, (Eire) 11
Record Goalscorer in a Match: Ray Pointer 5 v Rotherham United, 6-1, Div 2, 2.10.1965 Eddie Quigley 5 v Millwall (h), 5-2 Div 2, 15.2.1947
Record League Goalscorer in a Season: Craig Madden 35 Div 4, 1981-82 **In All Competitions:** Craig Madden 43 (League 35 + FA Cup 4 + League Cup 3 + Group Cup 1)
Record League Goalscorer in a Career: Craig Madden 129, 1977-86 **In All Competitions:** Craig Madden 153 (League 129 + FA Cup 11 + League Cup 10, Others 3) 1977-86
Record Transfer Fee Received: £400,000 from Southampton for David Lee, August 1991
Record Transfer Fee Paid: £175,000 to Shrewsbury Town for John McGinley, June 1990
Best Performances: League: 4th Div 1, 1925-26 **FA Cup:** Winners 1900, 1903 **League Cup:** Semi-final 1963
Most League Points: (3pts a win) 84, Div 4, 1984-85 (2pts a win) 68, Div 3, 1960-61
Most League Goals: 108 Div 3, 1960-61
Record League Victory: 8-0 v Tranmere Rovers, Div 3, 10.1.1970 (Bury have scored eight goals four times in the League)
Most Goals Scored in a Cup Tie: 12-1 v Stockton, 1st Rnd Replay FA Cup, 2.2.1897
Record League Defeat: 0-8 v Sheffield United, Div 1, 6.4.1896 0-8 v Swindon Town, Div 3, 8.12.1979
Record Cup Defeat: 0-10 v West Ham United, League Cup Round 2, 25.10.1983
Oldest Player in a League Match: Derek Fazackerley, 37 years 182 days, 6.5.1989
Youngest Player in a League Match: Brian Williams, 16 years 133 days, 18.3.1972

LONGEST LEAGUE RUNS	
of undefeated matches: 18 (1961)	of league matches without a win: 19 (1911)
of undefeated home matches: 25 (1967-68)	of undefeated away matches: 8 (1961)
without home win: 13 (1937, 1978)	without an away win: 42 (1910-1912)
of league wins: 9 (1960)	of home wins: 15 (1894-95)
of league defeats: 6 (1953, 1967)	of away wins: 6 (1960)

BURY

PLAYERS NAME Honours	Ht	Wt	Birthdate	Birthplace Transfers	Contract Date	Clubs	APPEARANCES League	L/Cup	FA Cup	Other	GOALS Lg	L/C	FAC	Oth
GOALKEEPERS														
Gary Kelly	5.11	12.3	03.08.66	Fulwood	26.07.82	Newcastle Utd. (A)	53	4	3	2				
Ei: B.1;u21.7. FAYC'85				Loan	07.10.88	Blackpool	5							
				Loan	05.10.89	Bury								
				£60,000	01.12.89	Bury	130	4	4	15				
Michael Pollitt	6.3	14.11	29.02.72	Bolton	01.07.90	Manchester Utd. (T)								
				Loan	05.10.90	Oldham Ath								
				Free	10.07.91	Bury								
				Loan	26.03.92	Lincoln City								
DEFENDERS														
Mark Kearney	5.10	11.0	12.06.62	Ormskirk		Marine								
FRT'87				£23,000	08.10.81	Everton								
				Free	18.03.83	Mansfield Town	248+2	18	9+3	22+1	29	2	2	5
				Loan	24.01.91	Bury	1							
				P.E	28.03.91	Bury	65	2		4	2			
Alan Knill	6.2	11.7	08.10.64	Slough	14.10.82	Southampton (A)								
W: 1; Y; W.C.'89					13.07.84	Halifax Town	118	6	6	6	6			
				£15,000	14.08.87	Swansea City	89	4	5	7	3			
				£95,000 W	18.08.89	Bury	95+3	1	4	10+1	3			1
Ron Mauge	5.10	10.06	10.03.69	London		Charlton Ath. (T)								
					21.09.88	Fulham	47+3	4	1	2	2			
					30.07.90	Bury	41+10	2+2	1	2+2	6	2	1	
				Loan	26.09.91	Manchester City				0+1				
Paul Robertson	5.7	11.06	05.02.72	Stockport		York City (T)								
					29.08.89	Stockport Co	7+3	3		3				
				Free	18.07.91	Bury	5							
Roger Stanislaus	5.9	12.6	02.11.68	Hamersmith		Arsenal (A)								
					15.10.87	Brentford	109+2	8	7	9	4	1		
				£90,000	30.07.90	Bury	76+8	4	2	9	5	1		
Peter Valentine	5.10	12.0	16.04.63	Huddersfield	16.04.81	Huddersfield Town (A)	19	2	1		1			
				Free	18.07.83	Bolton W	66+2	4	4	5	1			
				Free	23.07.85	Bury	279+4	23	15	13+1	19	1	1	
MIDFIELD														
Lee Anderson					16.10.91	Bury (T)	3+2			1+1				
FORWARDS														
Kevin Hulme	5.10	11.9	02.12.67	Bolton		Radcliffe Bor								
				£5,000 Wee	26.05.89	Bury	50+28	1+2		3+8	12			2
				Loan	26.10.89	Chester City	4							
David B Jones	6.3		03.07.64	Harrow		Watford (A)								
					01.08.87	Crystal Palace								
					01.11.97	Chelsea								
					01.09.88	Bury	0+1							
					01.12.88	Leyton Orient	0+2							
					01.02.89	Burnley	4							
					01.10.89	Ipswich Town								
				Free	01.11.89	Doncaster Rovers	34+6	3	2	5	14	1		3
				Free	26.09.91	Bury	1+8		1	1				
Liam Robinson	5.7	11.5	29.12.65	Bradford	05.01.84	Huddersfield Town	17+4			2				
				Loan	18.12.85	Tranmere Rovers	4			3				
					08.07.86	Bury	234+14	12+3	8	22	82	5		4
Ian Stevens	5.9	12.0	21.10.66	Malta	22.11.84	Preston N.E. (T)	9+2			1	2			
SVT'89					27.10.86	Stockport Co	1+1		0+1	0+1				
					25.03.87	Bolton W	26+21	1+2	4	3+1	7		2	
				Free	03.07.91	Bury	44+1	1	1	3+1	17			1
Darren Wilson					05.07.90	Manchester City (T)								
				Free	03.06.91	Bury	30+2	2		2+1	1			1
ADDITIONAL CONTRACT PLAYERS														
Patrick Bradley					20.07.90	Bury (T)				0+1				
Richard Hartford					14.02.91	Bury								
Ian Hughes					19.11.91	Bury (T)	13+4			3				
(M) Matthew Lambert	6.0	12.6	28.09.71	Morecambe	09.07.90	Preston N.E. (T)	11+5			0+1	2			
				Free	19.06.92	Bury								
Darren Lyons					06.03.92	Bury	9+1				4			
Marc Malone					20.09.89	Bury								
Paul McGuinness					22.03.91	Bury								
Philip Murphy					06.08.90	Bury								

LEADING LEAGUE GOALSCORERS SEASONS 1985-86 – 1991-92

1985-86	**CRAIG MADDEN**	14		1986-87	**NIGEL GREENWOOD**	14
1987-88	**LIAM ROBINSON**	19		1988-89	**LIAM ROBINSON**	20
1989-90	**JAMIE HOYLAND**	16		1990-91	**DAVID LEE**	15
			1991-92	**IAN STEVENS**	17	

GIGG LANE Bury, Lancs BL9 9HR

Capacity: 11,614   **Covered Standing:** 4,825   **Seating:** 6,787

Tel: Ground: 061 764 4881   **Clubcall:** 0898 12 11 97

All premium rate calls (0898/0891) cost 36p per minute cheap rate and 48p per minute at all other times. Call costings correct at time of going to press.

ATTENDANCES
Highest: 35,000 v Bolton Wanderers, FA Cup Round 3, 9.1.1960
Lowest: 416 v Tranmere Rovers, Freight Rover Trophy, 26.2.1986

Record Receipts: £37,000 v Bolton Wndrs, League Play-Offs, 19.5.1991

GIGG LANE
First game: v Accrington and Church Clubs, 18.6.1885
First floodlit game: v Wolverhampton Wanderers, 3-1, 6.10.1953

Season Tickets:
Stands: from £94.50 to £136.50, Juv/OAP £60 to £70
Ground: £94, juv/OAP £35

Cost of Stand Tickets: (Members) £5.50, £6.50, £7.50, juv/OAP £3, £4, £4.50; (Non-members) £7, £8, £9; Away supporters £7, £8; Family tickets 1+1: £7-£10.50 + £2.50-£3 per additional child
Reserved Chairs: £7.50

Match and Ticket Information: 500 seats in reserved chair section bookable two weeks before each match Re: Family Tickets: A number of tickets are available on the day of the match only. These tickets are for 'A' stand which is also open to the public. So it is not strictly a family only area

Membership Scheme: Club Membership £12 adults, £7 juniors

Car Parking: First come first served. Ample side-street parking is available

Nearest Railway Station: Bury Metro Interchange

How to get to the ground

From North: Use Motorway M66 until junction 2, then leave motorway and follow signs Bury A58. In 0.5m turn left into Heywood Street and at end forward into Parkhills Road. At end turn left A56 into Manchester Road, then shortly turn left into Gigg Lane for Bury FC
From East, South and West: Use Motorway M62 until junction 17. Leave Motorway and follow signs Bury A56. In 3.1m turn right into Gigg Lane for Bury FC

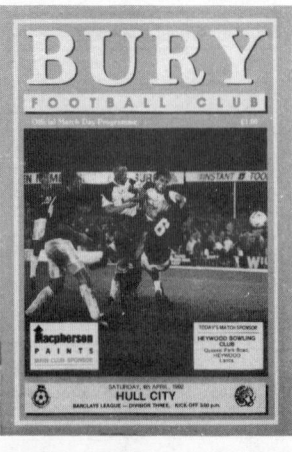

Value Rating: ★ ★ ★

Programme Editor: N Neville

Price of 1992-93 Programme: £1
Number of Pages: 32
Subscriptions: £1 per match +50p P&P or SAE

Local Newspapers:

Local Radio Stations: Piccadilly Radio, G.M.R.

CAMBRIDGE UNITED
Division 1

Formed: 1919   **Turned Professional:** 1946   **Ltd Co:** 1948

SPONSORED BY: FUJITSU   **NICKNAME:** UNITED

CAMBRIDGE UNITED F.C.

Chairman
R H Smart

Life President/Vice Chairman
D A Ruston (0223 241237)

Directors
G G Harwood
J S Howard
R F Hunt
G P Lowe
R J Smith

Company Secretary
Steve Greenall (0223 241237)

Team Manager
John Beck

Assistant Manager
Gary Peters

Youth Team Manager
Gary Johnson

Commercial Manager
John Holmes

Physiotherapist
Ken Steggles

Stadium Manager
Ian Darler

Club Statistician for the Directory
Colin Faiers

ANOTHER exciting season in the history of Cambridge United finished with the club's highest placing in the league – fifth in division two, but with the disappointment of losing in the play-offs and missing out on the chance of premier division football in 1992-93. This should not detract from the team's creditable performance which saw them move from the lower reaches of division four to division two promotion challengers in under three years.

Early season league form was promising and by the end of September, the team were in the top three after an excellent 5-1 victory against Leicester City. The Rumbelows Cup also produced an early bonus when, after beating Reading in Round 1, United were rewarded with a money spinning tie against the then league leaders Manchester United and despite losing the away leg managed a creditable 1-1 draw in the home game. The Zenith Data trophy saw the team beat Charlton on penalties and then lose at West Ham which left the team to concentrate on the league.

The team continued to play well and on November 9 after a well fought victory against local rivals Ipswich Town, United moved to the top of the table and held this position for a month. Unfortunately the team then ran into poor form and were unable to produce a home league victory for nearly four months resulting in a slide down the table out of the automatic promotion places. The game to break the sequence saw a 6-1 win against Bristol Rovers at the end of February.

The F.A. Cup produced another United giantkilling when Coventry City were beaten at the Abbey Stadium in a third round replay – the only goal being a bizarre own goal in the last minute following a penalty save. However the exploits of the previous years were not to be matched as the team lost at home to Swindon in the next round.

United made one transfer deadline move – selling John Taylor to Bristol Rovers and acquiring Devon White from the same club. March and April saw the club only lose three games but they were never able to maintain a place for automatic promotion and a last day of the season draw at Cup Finalists Sunderland guaranteed a play-off place. Opponents Leicester City had beaten United a few weeks earlier and the first leg at the Abbey Stadium produced a 1-1 draw – Danny O'Shea scoring the goal, his first since the opening day of the season. The return leg saw Leicester run out 5-0 winners, and so end the dream of United becoming the first team to move through three divisions in consecutive years.

Can United achieve promotion next season? Much will depend on how many of the players, who are out of contract, stay with the club. The desire to play football at a higher level is understandable but it is hoped that the team which has formed the nucleus of the side that moved from Division Four to Division Two can stay together for another attempt at the Premier League. **Colin Faiers**

Back row L-R: Michael Cheetham, Richard Wilkins, Jamie Smeeth, Danny O'Shea, Gary Rowett, Steve Ball, Lee Philpott, Gary Clayton, Chris Leadbitter. **Middle row:** Roger Parker (Kit Manager), Ken Steggles (Physiotherapist), Liam Daish, Michael Norbury, Mick Heathcote, Jon Sheffield, John Vaughan, Devon White, Warren Patmore, Phil Chapple, John Griffin (Chief Scout), Neil Lanham (Technical adviser), Paul Ashworth (Youth Development Officer). **Front row:** Andy Fensome, Phil Parkhill, Paul Raynor, Gary Peters (Asst. Manager), John Beck (Manager), Gary Johnson (Youth Manager), Gareth Ainsworth, Tony Dennis, Alan Kimble.

CAMBRIDGE UNITED

DIVISION TWO: 5th   **FA CUP:** 4th RND   **RUMBELOWS CUP:** 2nd RND   **ZDS CUP:** 2nd RND

M		DATE	COMP.	VEN	OPPONENTS	RESULT	H/T	LGE POS	GOALSCORERS/GOAL TIMES	ATTEN-DANCE
1	A	17	BL	A	Grimsby Town	W 4-3	1-1		Dublin 31, Taylor 60, Wilkins 76, O'Shea 90	(7,657)
2		21	RC 1/1	H	**Reading**	**W 1-0**	**0-0**		**Claridge 79**	3,701
3		24	BL	H	Swindon Town	W 3-2	1-1	3	Philpott 22, 80, Summerbee (og) 58	6,232
4		28	RC 1/2	A	**Reading**	**W 3-0**	**2-0**		**Taylor 19, Dublin 39, Claridge 45**	(3,578)
5		31	BL	A	Watford	W 3-1	1-0	2	Philpott 45, Claridge 53, Cheetham 74	(8,902)
6	S	3	BL	H	Southend United	L 0-1	0-0	2		6,412
7		7	BL	A	Millwall	W 2-1	1-1	4	Cheetham 33, Rowett 74	(8,232)
8		13	BL	H	Derby County	D 0-0	0-0	2		7,923
9		17	BL	H	Wolverhampton W	W 2-1	2-0	2	Taylor 25, Wilkins 34	6,552
10		20	BL	A	Portsmouth	L 0-3	0-2	4		(7,801)
11		25	RC 2/1	A	**Manchester United**	**L 0-3**	**0-1**			(30,931)
12		29	BL	H	Leicester City	W 5-1	4-0	3	Dublin 11, 34, Claridge 47, 52, Heathcote 72	7,052
13	O	2	ZDS 1	H	**Charlton Athletic**	**W †1-1**	**1-1**		**Taylor 3 (Won 4-2 on pens)**	3,168
14		5	BL	A	Port Vale	L 0-1	0-0	4		(5,991)
15		9	RC 2/2	H	**Manchester United**	**D 1-1**	**0-1**		**Dublin 88**	9,248
16		12	BL	H	Sunderland	W 3-0	2-0	3	Dublin 11, Wilkins 39, Dennis 68	7,857
17		18	BL	A	Tranmere Rovers	W 2-1	2-0	2	Dublin 6, Claridge 17	(7,625)
18		22	ZDS 2	A	**West Ham United**	**L 1-2**	**1-1**		**Rowett 51**	(7,812)
19		26	BL	H	Barnsley	W 2-1	0-0	2	Claridge 71, Dublin 82	5,534
20	N	2	BL	H	Bristol City	D 0-0	0-0	3		4,810
21		6	BL	A	Newcastle United	D 1-1	0-0	2	Claridge 59	(13,077)
22		9	BL	A	Ipswich Town	W 2-1	1-0	1	Rowett 36, Claridge 82	(20,586)
23		16	BL	H	Brighton & H A	D 0-0	0-0	1		7,625
24		23	BL	A	Charlton Athletic	W 2-1	2-0	1	Taylor 26, Dublin 38	(6,350)
25		30	BL	H	Oxford United	D 1-1	0-0	1	Dublin 50	6,496
26	D	7	BL	A	Bristol Rovers	D 2-2	1-2	1	Dublin 35, Taylor 67	(5,280)
27		22	BL	A	Southend United	D 1-1	1-1	2	Philpott 1	(9,353)
28		26	BL	H	Plymouth Argyle	D 1-1	0-0	2	Dublin 79	7,105
29		29	BL	H	Watford	L 0-1	0-0	2		8,439
30	J	1	BL	A	Blackburn Rovers	L 1-2	0-0	5	Chapple 65	(15,001)
31		4	FAC 3	A	**Coventry City**	**D 1-1**	**1-0**		**Dublin 31**	(11,428)
32		11	BL	A	Swindon Town	W 2-0	0-0	4	Heaney 60, Dublin 84	(10,878)
33		14	FAC 3R	H	**Coventry City**	**W 1-0**	**0-0**		**Hurst (og) 90**	9,804
34		18	BL	H	Grimsby Town	L 0-1	0-1	6		6,092
35		25	FAC 4	H	**Swindon Town**	**L 0-3**	**0-1**			7,428
36		31	BL	H	Tranmere Rovers	D 0-0	0-0	4		5,491
37	F	8	BL	A	Barnsley	D 0-0	0-0	7		(6,196)
38		11	BL	A	Plymouth Argyle	W 1-0	1-0	4	Cheetham 14	(4,290)
39		15	BL	H	Charlton Athletic	W 1-0	0-0	3	Dennis 49	6,472
40		22	BL	A	Oxford United	L 0-1	0-1	4		(5,605)
41		25	BL	H	Blackburn Rovers	W 2-1	2-0	3	Chapple 9, May (og) 23	7,857
42		28	BL	H	Bristol Rovers	W 6-1	1-1	2	Fensome (p)12, Dublin 52,63, Leadbitter 55, Heaney 60, Taylor 78	6,164
43	M	7	BL	A	Middlesbrough	D 1-1	0-1	3	Dublin 53	(14,686)
44		10	BL	H	Newcastle United	L 0-2	0-2	3		8,254
45		14	BL	A	Bristol City	W 2-1	0-1	3	Heathcote 69, Norbury 83	(9,579)
46		17	BL	H	Middlesbrough	D 0-0	0-0	2		7,318
47		21	BL	H	Ipswich Town	D 1-1	0-0	2	Heathcote 56	9,766
48		28	BL	A	Brighton & H A	D 1-1	0-1	3	Heathcote 89	(7,702)
49	A	1	BL	A	Derby County	D 0-0	0-0	3		(15,353)
50		4	BL	H	Millwall	W 1-0	0-0	2	Dublin 46	6,385
51		11	BL	A	Wolverhampton W	L 1-2	0-0	2	Norbury 64	(11,188)
52		17	BL	H	Portsmouth	D 2-2	1-0	4	Claridge 4, Wilkins 57	9,225
53		21	BL	A	Leicester City	L 1-2	0-1	5	Claridge 55	(21,894)
54		25	BL	H	Port Vale	W 4-2	0-1	5	Heathcote 49, Claridge (pen) 62, Chapple 71, Philpott 77	7,559
55	M	2	BL	A	Sunderland	D 2-2	1-2	5	Claridge 35, 75	(19,042)
56		10	PO SF1	H	**Leicester City**	**D 1-1**	**0-1**		**O'Shea 76**	9,225
57		13	PO SF2	A	**Leicester City**	**L 0-5**	**0-2**			(21,024)

Best Home League Attendance: 9,766 v Ipswich Town   Smallest: 4,810 v Bristol City   **Av Home Att: 7,082**

Goal Scorers: Compared with 90-91: +1,579

League (65): Dublin 15, Claridge 12 (1 pen), Philpott 5, Taylor 5, Heathcote 5, Wilkins 4, Chapple 3, Cheetham 3, Rowett 2, Dennis 2, Heaney 2, Norbury 2, Opponents 2, Leadbitter, Fensome (1 pen), O'Shea

R/lows C (5): Dublin 2, Claridge 2, Taylor

FA Cup (2): Opponents, Dublin

ZDS Cup (2): Rowett, Taylor

Play-Offs (1): O'Shea

† = After extra-time

Vaughan J.	Fensome A.	Kimble A.	Baillie C.	Clayton G.	O'Shea D.	Cheetham M.	Wilkins R.	Dublin D.	Taylor J.	Phillpott L.	Dennis J.	Rowett G.	Claridge S.	Leadbitter C.	Chapple P.	Heathcote M.	Sheffield J.	Daish L.	Heaney N.	Norbury M.	Raynor P.	White D.	Referee	
1	2	3	4*	5	6	7	8	9	10	11	12	S											V Callow	1
1	2	3	4	5	6	7	8	9†	10	11*			12	S									P Taylor	2
1	2	3	4•	5	6	7	8	9	10*	11	14		12										I Borrett	3
1	2	3	4•	5	6	7	8	9*	10	11	14		12										B Hamer	4
1	2	3	4	5	6	7	8•	9	10*	11			12	14									P Alcock	5
1	2	3	4	5	6	7		9	10	11*	8•		12	14									J Moules	6
1	2	3	4	5		7			10*	11	8	12•	9	14	6								K Morton	7
1	2	3	4	5		7			10	11	8	S	9	9	S	6							M James	8
1	2	3	4	5		7	8		10	11	S		9	S	6								P Jones	9
1	2	3	4	5•		7	8	12	10	11*	14		9		6								R Milford	10
1	2•	3	4	14	6	7	8	9*	10	11			12		5								A Dawson	11
1	2	3	S			7	8	9•	14	11	4		10		6	5							J Worrall	12
	2	3	S			7	8	9	11		14		10	4•	5		1	6					D Elleray	13
1	2	3	12			7	8	9	14	11		4*	10		6	5•							K Hackett	14
1	2	3	12	5			8	9	S	11	4	7*	10					6					D Axcell	15
1	2	3	12	5			8	9	7*	11	4		10*	14				6					R Lewis	16
1	2	3	S	5			8	9	7	11	4		10	S				6					J Brandwood	17
	12	3	2	5			8	9	10•	11	4	7*		14			1	6					R Hemley	18
	2	3	12	5			8	9	7	11	4		10*	14				6					P Foakes	19
1	2	3	8		S		5	9	7	11	4		10	S				6					R Shepherd	20
1	2	3	8	12	5*			9	7	11•	4		10	14				6					T Fitzharris	21
1	2	3	8		5			9	12	11	4	7*	10•				14	6					G Pooley	22
1	2	3	8		5			9	12	11•	4	7*	10					6					D Gallagher	23
1	2	3	8		S	7*		9	10	11		4	12		6	5							L Shapter	24
1	2	3	8		S	7		9	10*	11	12	4			6	5							J Key	25
1	2	3	8•	14	6		12	9	10	11		4*				7	5						D Shadwell	26
1	2	3	4		6		8	9	10	11*	7		12		5		S						G Singh	27
1	2	3	4*		6		8	9	10	11	7		12		5		S						A Buksh	28
1	2	3	4		6		8	9	10	11	S		7		5		S						K Cooper	29
1	2	3	4		6		8	9*	10	11	12		7•		5			14					P Vanes	30
1	2	3	4		6		8	9	10	11	12		7•		5			14*					T Ward	31
1	2	3	12					9	10•	11	7	4			8*	5			6	14			R Lewis	32
1	2	3					8	9	10	11	4	7	S	5*					12	6			T Ward	33
1	2	3	4				8	9	10	11		7*			5	S			6	12			P Danson	34
1	2	3	4			7	8	9•	10				14	12	5				6		11*		W Burns	35
1	2	3					8*	9	10	14	11•	4	7		12	5			6				M Pierce	36
1	2	3	4*	5		7	10	9		11	8				S		6	12					T Holbrook	37
	2	3		5		7*	10•	9		11	4			14	8		1	6	12				K Burge	38
	2	3	12	5				9		11	4		10•	8*			1	6	7	14			M James	39
	2	3		5				9•		11	4		10	8*	12		1	6	7	14			B Coddington	40
	2	3	8					9	12		4	7*	10•		5		1	6		11	14		P Don	41
	2	3	8					9	12		4•	7	10*	14	5		1	6		11			G Willard	42
	2*	3	12				8	9	10			7•	4		5		1	6		11	14		J Key	43
		3	4	2			9		7•	10	8				5		1	6	11	14			P Foakes	44
		3	4•	2*				9		8			10	11	5	12	1	2	6	7	14		J Deakin	45
		3					8	9	12		4		10*	11	5	2	1	6*	7	14			K Breen	46
		3					8	9	12		4		10*	11	5	2	1	6*	7*	14			K Barratt	47
		3				7*	8	9			4			11	5	2	1	6	10	12	S		G Ashby	48
		3				6	7•	8	9		4			11	5	2	1		10*	12	14		A Ward	49
1		3				6	9		12		11	4			8	5	2		14	7*	10*		T Phillips	50
1		3				6	7	8	9•		4		14	11*	5	2			10	12			D Allison	51
1		3				6	11*	8	9		12•	4		10	14	5	2			7			J Kirkby	52
1		3•				6		8	9	11	4		10	14	5	2			14	7			R Milford	53
1		S				6		8	9•	11	4		10	3	5	2			14	7			P Alcock	54
1		3				6		8	12	11	4		10	S	5	2			9*	7			T Fitzharris	55
1		3				6	7	8	9	11*	4•		10		5	2			12	14			J Martin	56
1		3				6*	7	8	9	11	4		10		5	2			12	S			M Bodenham	57
33	34	45	23	9	30	21	30	40	27	29	36	10•	25	14	29	17	13	22	9	4	5	1	League Appearances	
		5	2	1	1	2	3	8	2	4	3	4	11	5					4	10	3	1	Substitute Appearances	
4	4	4	3+1	2+1	4	3	4	4	3	4	1+1		1	1+3	1		1						R/lows Appearances	
3	3	3	2		1	1	3	3	3	2	1+2	2+1		3	0+2	2	1						FA Cup Appearances	
	1+1	2		1		2	2	2	2	1	1	1	1	1+1		1	2	2					ZDS Cup Appearances	
2		2	2	2	2	2	2	2	2	2		2			2	2			0+2	0+1			Play-Offs Appearances	

Players on Loan: N Heaney (Arsenal)

† = Sent Off

CAMBRIDGE UNITED

Club Colours: Amber shirts with black pin stripe, black shorts, amber stockings with black trim
Change Colours: All sky blue
Reserves League: Wendy Fair Capital League   **Youth League:** South East Counties

COMPETITIONS		
Div. 2	Div. 3	Div. 4
78-84	73-74	70-73
91-	77-78	74-77
	84-85	85-90
	90-91	

HONOURS	
Division 3	Division 4
1990-91	1976-77

MOST APPEARANCES: STEVE SPRIGGS 463+5 (75-87)				
Year	League	FA Cup	Lge Cup	AMC
1975-76	45	1	2	
1976-77	41	2	3	
1977-78	37+1	1	3	
1978-79	40	1	2	
1979-80	40	3	2	
1980-81	41	1	5	
1981-82	33	1	2	
1982-83	15+3	2		
1983-84	27+1		1	
1984-85	29	1	2	2
1985-86	29	1	2	2
1986-87	34	3	6	1
	411+5	17	30	5

MOST GOALS IN A CAREER			
ALAN BILEY 82 (1975-87)			
Season	League	FA Cup	League Cup
1975-76	3		1
1976-77	19		1
1977-78	21	2	
1978-79	20	1	1
1979-80	12		
1986-87		1	
	75	4	3

RECORD TRANSFER FEE RECEIVED			
Amount	Club	Player	Date
£1,000,000	Manchester United	Dion Dublin	8/92
£350,000	Derby County	Alan Biley	1/80
£35,000	Bournemouth	Brian Greenhalgh	2/74

MANAGERS			
Name	Seasons	Best	Worst
Bill Whittaker	1951-55		
Gerry Williams	1955		
Bert Johnson	1955-59		
Bill Craig	1959		
Allan Moore	1959-60		
Bill Craig	1960-63		
Roy Kirk	1963-66		
Matt Wynn	1967		
Bill Leivers	1967-74	21(3)	10(4)
Ray Freeman	1974		
Ron Atkinson	1974-78	1(4)	13(4)
John Docherty	1978-83	8(2)	14(2)
John Ryan	1984-85	22(2)	22(2)
John Cozens	1985		
Ken Shellito	1985	24(3)	24(3)
Chris Turner	1986-90	8(4)	22(4)
John Beck	1990-	5(2)	6(4)

RECORD TRANSFER FEE PAID			
Amount	Club	Player	Date
£150,000	Shrewsbury Town	Mickey Heathcote	9/91
£140,000	Northampton T	George Reilly	11/79
£50,000	Northampton T	Derrick Christie	10/78
£22,000	Oxford United	Nigel Cassidy	3/74

LONGEST LEAGUE RUNS	
of undefeated matches:	14 (9.9.1972-10.11.1972)
of undefeated home matches:	22 (10.9.1977-29.4.1978)
without home win:	16 (8.10.1983-21.4.1984)
of league wins:	7 (19.2.1976-1.4.1976)
of league defeats:	7 (11.2.1984-24.3.1984)
	(29.12.1984-26.2.1985) (8.4.1985-30.4.1985)
of league matches without a win:	31 (8.10.1983-23.4.1984)
of undefeated away matches:	12 (7.4.1990-3.11.1990)
without an away win:	32 (14.11.1981-2.4.1983)
of home wins:	10 (27.9.1977-14.1.1978)
of away wins:	3 (1971, 1975, 1977, 1991)

PREVIOUS NAME
Until 1951 Abbey United

PREVIOUS LEAGUE
Southern League

BIGGEST VICTORIES
League: 6-0 v Darlington, Div 4, 18.9.1971
6-0 v Hartlepool, Div 4, 11.2.1989
F.A. Cup: 5-1 v Bristol City, Round 5 2nd replay, 27.2.1990
4-0 v Sheffield Wed., Round 5, 16.2.1991
League Cup: No more than 3 goals

BIGGEST DEFEATS
League: 0-6 v Aldershot, Div 3, 13.4.1974
0-6 v Darlington, Div 4, 28.9.1974
0-6 v Chelsea, Div 2, 15.1.1983
F.A. Cup: 1-5 v Bournemouth, Rnd 1, 18.11.1972
League Cup: 0-5 v Colchester Utd, Rnd 1, 1979-71
0-5 v Derby County, Rnd 2, 4.10.1989

MOST POINTS
3 points a win: 86, Division 3, 1990-91
2 points a win: 65, Division 4, 1976-77

MOST GOALS
87, Division 4, 1976-77
Biley 19, Finney 16, Hall 15, Spriggs 9, Horsfall 6, Watson 6,
Fallon 4, Howard 4, Bowker 1, O'Neil 1, Seddon 1, Streete 1,
Stringer 1, og 3

MOST GOALS IN A MATCH
4. Brian Greenhalgh v Darlington, Div 4, 18.9.1971

MOST GOALS IN A SEASON
David Crown 27, 1977-78
3 goals 1 time = 3; 2 goals 3 times = 6; 1 goal 18 times = 18.
Total 27

MOST FIRST CLASS MATCHES IN A SEASON
65 (46 League, 10 FA Cup, 4 League Cup, 2 Freight Rover
Trophy, 3 Play-Off) 1989-90

MOST LEAGUE GOALS CONCEDED
95, Division 3, 1984-85

MOST LEAGUE WINS
26, Division 4, 1976-77

MOST LEAGUE DRAWS
17, Div 4, 1972-73 & Div 2, 1991-92

MOST LEAGUE DEFEATS
33, Division 3, 1984-85

OLDEST PLAYER
John Ryan, 37 years 134 days v Derby County, 1.12.1984

YOUNGEST PLAYER
Andy Sinton, 16 years 228 days v Wolverhampton Wndrs,
2.11.1982

MOST CAPPED PLAYER
Tom Finney (Northern Ireland) 7

BEST PERFORMANCES BY CAMBRIDGE UNITED

League: 1976-77: Matches Played 46, Won 26, Drawn 13, Lost 7, Goals for 87, Goals against 40, Points 65. First in Division 4

Highest: 5th Division 2, 1991-92

F.A. Cup: 1989-90: 1st rnd. Aldershot (a) 1-0; 2nd rnd. Woking (h) 3-1; 3rd rnd. Darlington (a) 0-0 (h) 3-1; 4th rnd. Millwall (a) 1-1 (h) 1-0; 5th rnd Bristol City (a) 0-0 (h) 1-1 (h) 5-1; 6th rnd. Crystal Palace (h) 0-1

1990-91: 1st rnd. Exeter City (a) 2-1; 2nd rnd. Fulham (a) 0-0 (h) 2-1; 3rd rnd. Wolverhampton Wndrs (a) 1-0; 4th rnd. Middlesbrough (h) 2-0; 5th rnd Sheffield Wednesday (h) 4-0; 6th rnd. Arsenal (a) 1-2

League Cup: 1980-81: 2nd rnd. Wolverhampton Wndrs (h) 3-1 (a) 1-0; 3rd rnd. Aston Villa (h) 2-1; 4th rnd. Coventry City (a) 1-1 (h) 0-1

1986-87: 1st rnd. Orient (a) 2-2 (h) 1-0; 2nd rnd. Wimbledon (h) 1-1 (a) 2-2; 3rd rnd. Ipswich Town (h) 1-1; 4th rnd. Tottenham Hotspur (h) 1-3

DIVISIONAL RECORDS

	Played	Won	Drawn	Lost	For	Against	Points
DIVISION 2	298	92	88	118	341	407	321
DIVISION 3	184	65	41	78	232	272	200
DIVISION 4	506	199	143	164	709	651	643
TOTALS	988	356	272	360	1282	1330	1164

CAMBRIDGE UNITED							APPEARANCES				GOALS			
PLAYERS NAME Honours	Ht	Wt	Birthdate	Birthplace Transfers	Contract Date	Clubs	League	L/Cup	FA Cup	Other	Lg	L/C	FAC	Oth
GOALKEEPERS														
Jonathan Sheffield	6.0	12.0	01.02.69	Bedworth	16.02.87	Norwich City (A)	1							
				Loan	22.09.89	Aldershot	11			1				
				Loan	21.08.90	Aldershot	15			1				
				Loan	18.03.91	Cambridge Utd	2							
				Free	31.07.91	Cambridge Utd	13			2				
John Vaughan	5.10	13.1	26.06.64	Isleworth	30.06.82	West Ham U. (A)								
11.03.85 Loan Charlton A. 6 Lg Apps.				Loan	05.09.85	Bristol Rovers	6							
23.10.85 Loan Wrexham 4 Lg Apps.				Loan	04.03.86	Bristol City	2							
				£20,000	21.08.86	Fulham	44	4	4	3				
21.01.88 Loan Bristol C. 3 Lg Apps.					06.06.88	Cambridge Utd	151	11	23	15				
DEFENDERS														
Colin Bailie	5.11	10.11	31.03.64	Belfast		Swindon Town (A)	105+2	3	7	4	4			
Div.3.86,SC'88				£22,500		Reading	83+1	9	5+2	9	1			1
				£25,000	24.08.88	Cambridge Utd	104+15	10+1	18	9+1	3			
Phil Chapple	6.2	12.7	26.11.66	Norwich	10.07.85	Norwich City								
					29.03.88	Cambridge Utd	167+2	9	23	15	17	1	1	
Michael Heathcote	6.1	12.7	10.09.65	Kelloe		Spennymoor				1				
				£15,000	19.08.87	Sunderland	6+3			0+1				
				Loan	17.12.87	Halifax Town	7		1		1			
				Loan	04.01.90	York City	3			1				
				£55,000	12.07.90	Shrewsbury Town	43+1	6	5	4	6			
				£150,000	12.09.91	Cambridge Utd	17+5		0+2	3	5			
Alan Kimble	5.10	12.4	06.08.66	Poole	08.08.84	Charlton Ath	6				1			
				Loan	23.08.85	Exeter City	1	1						
					22.08.86	Cambridge Utd	249+4	18+1	28	20	19		1	
Danny O'Shea	6.0	12.8	26.03.63	Kennington	23.12.80	Arsenal (A)	6	3						
Div.3'91				Loan	23.02.84	Charlton Ath	9							
				Free	24.08.84	Exeter City	45	2	2	2	2			
				£5,000	09.08.85	Southend Utd	116+2	8	5+1	6	12			
				Free		Cambridge Utd	83+14	9+1	8+3	8+2	1			1
MIDFIELD														
John Beck	5.10	11.9	25.05.54	Edmonton	01.05.72	Q.P.R. (A)	32+8	2	4		1			
AMC'84					01.06.76	Coventry City	60+9	5	3		6			
					12.10.78	Fulham	113+1	6	6		12			
					08.09.82	Bournemouth	132+5	6+1	6+1	12+1	13		2	3
				Free N.C	08.07.86	Cambridge Utd	105+7	8	6	2	11	2		1
Michael Cheetham	5.11	11.05	30.06.67	Amsterdam	10.10.88	Ipswich Town	1+3			0+1				
via loan period October 1989					11.01.90	Cambridge Utd	99+3	5	17	10+1	20	1	1	3
Liam Daish	6.2	13.5	23.09.68	Portsmouth	29.09.86	Portsmouth	1			1+1				
Ei: 1, u21.5				Free	11.07.88	Cambridge Utd	105	5	14	10	2			2
John.A Dennis	5.7	10.11	01.12.63	Tadlow		Plymouth A	7+2	1	0+1			1		
						Exeter City	3+1	1						
via non-league to				£15,000	22.02.89	Cambridge Utd	77+18	5+1	2+4	6+1	9			1
Andrew Fensome	5.7	10.10	18.02.69	Northampton	16.02.87	Norwich City (A)								
					21.11.89	Cambridge Utd	94	6	16+2	8+1	1			
Chris Leadbitter	5.9	10.6	17.10.67	Middlesbrough		Grimsby Town								
Div.3'91						Hereford Utd	32+4	2	2	3	1			
					01.10.88	Cambridge Utd	110+28	8	15+2	9+2	12	3	3	1
Lee Philpott	5.9	11.8	21.02.70	Barnet	17.07.86	Peterborough U	1+3		0+1	0+2				
				Free	31.05.89	Cambridge Utd	102+16	7	19	13	15	3		
Richard Wilkins	6.0	11.6	28.05.65	Haverhill		Haverhill Rov								
					20.11.86	Colchester Utd	150+2	6	7+2	9+3	22		4	3
				£65,000	25.07.90	Cambridge Utd	71+2	6	8+1	9	7			
FORWARDS														
Steve Claridge	5.11	11.8	10.04.66	Portsmouth		Portsmouth								
Div.3'91 via Fareham to						Bournemouth	3+4		1		1			
Via Weymouth (1 FAC App) to				Free	11.10.88	Crystal Palace								
					25.11.88	Aldershot	58+4	2+1	6	5	19		1	2
				£75,000	08.02.90	Cambridge Utd	70+18	2+4	1	6+3	28	2		1
Paul Raynor	5.8	11.12	29.04.66	Nottingham	02.04.84	Nottm. Forest (A)	3	1						
				Loan	28.03.85	Bristol Rovers	7+1							
				Free	15.08.85	Huddersfield Town	38+12	3	2+1	1	9			
				Free	27.03.87	Swansea City	170+21	11+1	8	15+1	27	3	1	3
				Loan	17.10.88	Wrexham	6							
				Free	10.03.92	Cambridge Utd	5+3			0+1				
Devon White	6.3	13.8	02.03.64	Nottingham		Arnold Kingswell								
Div.3'90					14.12.84	Lincoln City	21+8		2+1	4				2
via Boston United to					21.08.87	Bristol Rovers	190+12	9	10	19	54	2	3	2
				£100,000+p	28.03.92	Cambridge Utd	1+1							
ADDITIONAL CONTRACT PLAYERS														
Gareth Ainsworth			From Preston via Northwich Vic.		21.01.92	Preston N.E	2+3			1				1
				Free	01.06.92	Cambridge Utd								
Greg Allen			From Arsenal via Dagenham		N.C.	Cambridge Utd	4	0+1						
Michael Norbury						Ossett Town								
via Scarborough, Ossett & Bridlington T.					13.02.92	Cambridge Utd	4+10			0+2	2			
Gary Rowett					10.09.91	Cambridge Utd. (T)	10+3	1	2+1	1	2			1

Neil Doherty, John A. Fowler, Stephen Lewis, Philip Parkhill, David J. Robinson, Jamie Smeeth, Gary Woolf

CAMBRIDGE UNITED

RECORD WIN & LOSS AGAINST EACH CLUB IN CURRENT DIVISION
(Where a score has occured on several occasions the most recent is given)

Club	Rec. Win	Season	Rec. Loss	Season
BARNSLEY	2-0	1974-75	4-0	1975-76
BIRMINGHAM CITY	3-0	1990-91 (away)	1-0	1990-91 (home)
BRENTFORD	3-0	1990-91 (away)	2-0	1984-85
BRISTOL CITY	2-1	1991-92 (away)	3-0	1984-85
BRISTOL ROVERS	6-1	1991-92	3-1	1980-81
CHARLTON ATHLETIC	4-0	1981-82	5-2	1983-84
DERBY COUNTY	3-0	1980-81	2-0	1984-85 (home)
GRIMSBY TOWN	5-1	1980-81	4-0	1988-89
LEICESTER CITY	5-1	1991-92	4-0	1982-83
LUTON TOWN			3-1	1980-81 (home)
MILLWALL	2-1	1991-92 (away)	2-0	1978-79
NEWCASTLE UNITED	2-1	1980-81	2-0	1991-92 (home)
NOTTS COUNTY	2-1	1970-71	4-1	1970-71
OXFORD UNITED	3-2	1977-78 (away)	1-0	1991-92
PETERBOROUGH UTD	5-1	1988-89 (away)	5-2	1971-72 (home)
PORTSMOUTH	1-0	1977-78	5-0	1983-84
SOUTHEND UNITED	3-2	1973-74	4-1	1990-91
SUNDERLAND	3-0	1991-92	2-0	1979-80
SWINDON	5-2	1977-78	1-0	1985-86
TRANMERE ROVERS	3-1	1990-91	6-2	1985-86
WATFORD	4-0	1976-77	3-0	1973-74
WEST HAM UNITED	2-0	1979-80	5-0	1978-79
WOLVERHAMPTON WNDRS	2-1	1991-92	3-0	1987-88

MANAGER: JOHN BECK

DATE OF BIRTH: 25.5.1954   **PLACE OF BIRTH:** Edmonton

DATE OF APPOINTMENT: January 1990

PREVIOUS CLUBS
  as Manager: None
  as Asst.Man/Coach: None
  as Player: Q.P.R., Coventry, Fulham, AFC Bournemouth, Cambridge Utd

HONOURS
  as Manager: Promotion from 4th to 3rd Div 1989-90, Third Div Champions 1990-91, Third Div Manager of the Year 1990-91, Three times Manager of the Month
  as Player: Full Members Cup with Bournemouth 1984
  International: None

Value Rating: ★ ★ ★ ★

Programme Editor: A Pincher/D Brown

Price of 1992-93 Programme: £1
Number of Pages: 44
Subscriptions: £30.00

Local Newspapers: Cambridge Evening News

Local Radio Stations: BBC Radio Cambridgeshire, CNFM 103

Additional Publications on Club: 'United in Endeavour' the history of Abbey United/Cambridge United Football Club. Cost £10.95 (£12 inc. P+P), Dawn Publications, 84 The Spinney, Bar Hill, Cambridge CB3 8SU 'On The Up' 1988-1991. Available as above.

LEADING LEAGUE GOALSCORERS
SEASONS 1979-80 – 1991-92

1979-80	TOM FINNEY	13		1980-81	STEVE SPRIGGS	9
1981-82	JOE MAYO	8		1982-83	GEORGE REILLY	10
1983-84	ROBBIE COOKE	6		1984-85	ROBBIE COOKE	6
					ANDY SINTON	6
1985-86	MARK COOPER	13		1986-87	DAVID CROWN	23
1987-88	DAVID CROWN	9		1988-89	LAURIE RYAN	12
					JOHN TAYLOR	12
1989-90	JOHN TAYLOR	15		1990-91	DION DUBLIN	17
	DION DUBLIN	15				

1991-92   DION DUBLIN   15

ABBEY STADIUM Newmarket Road, Cambridge CB5 8LL

Capacity: 10,206   **Covered Standing:** 6,790   **Seating:** 3,416

Tel: Ground: 0223 241237   **Clubcall:** 0898 12 11 41

All premium rate calls (0898/0891) cost 36p per minute cheap rate and 48p per minute at all other times. Call costings correct at time of going to press.

ATTENDANCES
Highest: 14,000 v Chelsea (friendly), 1.5.1970

Lowest: 857 v Colchester Utd, Sherpa Van Trophy, 24.11.1987

Record Receipts: £86,308 v Manchester Utd., Rumbelows Cup 2nd Rnd 2nd leg, 9.10.1991

ABBEY STADIUM
First game: v University Press, Friendly, 31.8.1932
First floodlit game: 1964-65

Season Tickets:
Stands: from £175 to £265 (juv £100-£150, OAP £90-£150)
Terraces: £140 (juv/OAP £70)

Cost of Stand Tickets: £9-£13 (juv/OAP £5-£7)
Terraces: £7, OAP/Juvenile £4

Match and Ticket Information: Cambridge 241237
(Postal applications with payment & SAE two weeks in advance)

Car Parking: Limited parking at main entrance. Off-street parking permitted. Also at Coldhams Common for visitors

Nearest Railway Station: Cambridge (0233 311999)

How to get to the ground

From North: Use A1 and A604 S.P. Cambridge into City Centre, then follow signs Newmarket A45 into Newmarket Road for Cambridge United FC

From East: Follow signs Cambridge A45 into Newmarket Road for Cambridge United FC

From South: Use A10 or A130 into Cambridge, then follow signs Newmarket A45 into Newmarket Road for Cambridge United FC

From West: Follow signs Cambridge A422, into Cambridge via A45 then keep forward S.P. Newmarket into Newmarket Road for Cambridge United FC

CARDIFF CITY

Division 3

Formed: 1899   **Turned Professional:** 1910   **Ltd Co:** 1910

SPONSORED BY: The South Wales Echo   **NICKNAME:** The Bluebirds

Directors
David Henderson

Secretary
K D Butler

1st Team Coach
Eddie May

Reserve & Youth Team Coach
Steve McCrae

Youth Development Officer
Gavin Tait

Physiotherapist
Jimmy Goodfellow

Groundsman
Wayne Nash

Club Statistician for the Directory
Alan Jenkins

CARDIFF City began to hit the headlines more for what was going on off the field rather than on it early in the season. A new 'saviour' in millionaire Rick Wright, a revolutionary scheme whereby fans would pay a rising scale of admission prices depending on the clubs position in the table and a bonus of £1,000,000, payable to the players if they secure the Fourth Division championship!

Unfortunately results on the field didn't reflect the goings-on off the field for the first few weeks of the season. An early exit from the Rumbelows Cup and a mid-table position in the League didn't do much for the fans' confidence. Things began to improve slowly and from late October the team lost only once (an F.A. Cup defeat at local rivals Swansea) through to the end of the year. An excellent away record helped hide the fact that the team were dropping a lot of points at home and with only two players (Pike and Dale) carrying the burden of scoring goals it was always going to be an uphill climb to the end of the season.

Another of Rick Wright's schemes, giving free entry to youngsters who joined a Junior Bluebirds section organised by the local evening paper and the opening of the first phase of the development to turn Ninian Park into an all-seater stadium within 12 months, boosted the attendance for the New Years Day game at home to Maidstone, but a disastrous defeat by five goals to nil soon brought everyone back down to earth (with a bump!)

This had the effect of spurring on the players and a marvellous run of eight league games without defeat brought Burnley to Ninian Park at the end of February. Another home defeat made it clear that promotion and even the play-offs looked decidedly unlikely. Even little Maesteg Park, through to the Welsh Cup semi-final for the first time, were to add to Cardiff's woes, holding the Bluebirds to a nil-nil draw at Ninian Park. Luckily the non-league side decided to go back to Ninian Park for the replay. The winners were guaranteed a place in the European Cup Winners Cup as English non-league Hednesford Town won through in the other semi-final.

April was fairly kind to the club as far as their results were concerned but Cardiff had to rely on others if they were to attain a place in the play-offs. In the end all the club had to look forward to was the Welsh Cup Final at rugby's National Stadium. A crowd of over 11,000 created a marvellous atmosphere although the game itself was not a classic. The right result was attained and the club now look forward to the coming season with plenty of confidence. Perhaps this will be Cardiff's year!

Alan Jenkins

Back row L-R: Lee Baddeley, Chris Pike, Gareth Abraham, Paul Millar, Derek Brazil. **Middle:** Jason Donovan, Robbie James, Jason Perry, Gavin Ward, Mark Grew, Allan Lewis, Nick Richardson, Paul Ramsey. **Front:** Cohen Griffith, Damon Searle, Roger Gibbins, Eddie May (Coach), John Williams, Carl Dale, Nathan Blake.

CARDIFF CITY

DIVISION FOUR: 9th   **FA CUP:** 1st RND   **RUMBELOWS CUP:** 1st RND   **AUTOGLASS:** 1st RND

M	DATE		COMP.	VEN	OPPONENTS	RESULT	H/T	LGE POS	GOALSCORERS/GOAL TIMES	ATTEN-DANCE
1	A	17	BL	H	Lincoln City	L 1-2	0-1		Pike (pen) 88	5,137
2		21	RC 1/1	H	**Bournemouth**	W 3-2	1-1		**Miller 44, Gibbins 49, Searle 50**	3,439
3		24	BL	A	Crewe Alexandra	D 1-1	1-0	16	Dale 41	(3,799)
4		27	RC 1/2	A	**Bournemouth**	L 1-4	1-0		**Jones (pen) 31**	(4,849)
5		31	BL	H	Carlisle United	W 1-0	0-0	11	Jones (pen) 66	4,096
6	S	4	BL	A	Maidstone United	D 1-1	1-1	11	Dale 8	(1,019)
7		7	BL	H	Rochdale	L 1-2	0-1	15	Pike 64	4,029
8		14	BL	A	Blackpool	D 1-1	1-1	15	Davies (og) 34	(3,931)
9		17	BL	A	Halifax Town	D 1-1	1-0	15	Dale 30	(1,041)
10		21	BL	H	Scarborough	W 2-1	1-1	12	Heard 2, Dale 85	3,227
11		28	BL	A	Barnet	L 1-3	1-2	14	Dale 34	(4,000)
12	O	5	BL	H	Wrexham	W 5-0	2-0	12	Dale 17, Blake 32, Pike 3 (50, 80, 82)	3,652
13		19	BL	A	Mansfield Town	L 0-3	0-1	12		(3,180)
14		26	BL	H	Doncaster Rovers	W 2-1	1-1	12	Pike (pen) 1, 84 (pen)	2,591
15	N	2	BL	H	Scunthorpe United	D 2-2	0-0	12	Dale 64, Pike 74	2,356
16		5	BL	A	Gillingham	D 0-0	0-0	12		(2,641)
17		16	FAC 1	A	**Swansea City**	L 1-2	1-1		Pike 25	(9,315)
18		19	AGT Pre	A	**Swansea City**	D 0-0	0-0			(2,955)
19		23	BL	H	Northampton Town	W 3-2	1-1	10	Gibbins 40, Dale 47, 65	2,922
20		30	BL	H	Rotherham United	W 1-0	1-0	10	Dale 23	3,551
21	D	10	AGT Pre	H	**Bournemouth**	D 3-3	3-2		**Dale 8, 15, Pike 9**	1,337
22		14	BL	A	York City	W 3-1	1-1	7	Pike 32, Dale 49, 80	(1,904)
23		26	BL	A	Lincoln City	D 0-0	0-0	9		(3,162)
24		28	BL	A	Carlisle United	D 2-2	0-0	9	Pike (pen) 57, Ramsey 62	(3,080)
25	J	1	BL	H	Maidstone United	L 0-5	0-1	10		8,023
26		11	BL	H	Hereford United	W 1-0	0-0	9	Dale 90	5,305
27		14	AGT 1	A	**Stoke City**	L 0-3	0-1			(4,951)
28		18	BL	A	Walsall	D 0-0	0-0	9		(3,654)
29		25	BL	H	Chesterfield	W 4-0	2-0	8	Pike 25, 54, Dale 32, Blake 90	5,131
30		31	BL	H	Mansfield Town	W 3-2	2-1	8	Blake 6, Pike (pen) 41, Newton 58	8,201
31	F	8	BL	A	Doncaster Rovers	W 2-1	1-1	7	Dale 27, Douglas (og) 55	(2,094)
32		11	BL	A	Rotherham United	W 2-1	1-0	6	Newton 38, Blake 50	(3,827)
33		15	BL	H	York City	W 3-0	0-0	5	Pike (pen) 61, 82, Dale 62	8,067
34		22	BL	A	Hereford United	D 2-2	0-1	5	Ramsey 60, Harrison 75	(5,691)
35		29	BL	H	Burnley	L 0-2	0-0	7		16,030
36	M	3	BL	H	Walsall	W 2-1	0-1	6	Dale 55, Searle 86	7,517
37		7	BL	A	Chesterfield	D 2-2	0-2	6	Newton 70, Dale 89	(3,803)
38		10	BL	H	Gillingham	L 2-3	2-1	7	Griffith 23, Dale 41	8,521
39		14	BL	A	Scunthorpe United	L 0-1	0-0	8		(2,766)
40		27	BL	A	Northampton Town	D 0-0	0-0	7		(2,678)
41		31	BL	H	Blackpool	D 1-1	1-1	7	Burgess (og) 16	8,430
42	A	4	BL	A	Rochdale	L 0-2	0-1	9		(2,650)
43		11	BL	H	Halifax Town	W 4-0	1-0	9	Ramsey (pen) 36, Dale 65, 85, Pike 82	5,261
44		14	BL	A	Scarborough	D 2-2	0-1	9	Pike 53, 73	(935)
45		20	BL	H	Barnet	W 3-1	2-0	9	Pike (pen) 5, Dale 23, Newton 79	7,720
46		22	BL	A	Burnley	L 1-3	1-1	9	Blake 31	(12,408)
47		25	BL	A	Wrexham	W 3-0	2-0	9	Pike 16, 19, Gill 76	(4,002)
48		28	BL	H	Crewe Alexandra	D 1-1	1-0	9	Blake 36	10,523

Best Home League Attendance: 16,030 v Burnley   Smallest: 2,356 v Scunthorpe Utd   Av Home Att: 6,204

Goal Scorers: Compared with 90-91: +3,245

League (66):	Dale 22, Pike 21 (7 pens), Blake 6, Newton 4, Ramsey 3 (1 pen), Opponents 3, Heard, Searle, Gill, Harrison, Gibbins, Jones (1 pen), Griffith
R/lows C (4):	Jones (1 pen), Searle, Miller, Gibbins
FA Cup (1):	Pike
Autoglass (3):	Dale 2, Pike

Hansbury R.	Jones M.	Searle D.	Gibbins R.	Abraham G.	Lewis A.	Semark R.	Matthews N.	Griffith C.	Pike C.	Heard T.	Baddeley L.	Unsworth J.	Perry J.	Millar P.	Dale C.	Ramsey P.	Blake N.	Ward G.	Gorman A.	Williams W.	Newton E.	Harrison G.	Gill G.	Bellamy G.	Walsh A.	Referee	
1	2	3	4	5*	6	7	8	9	10	11	12	S														G Singh	1
1	2	3	4	5	14		8*	7	12	11*			6	9	10											**D Shadwell**	2
1	2	3	4	5	14		8*	7*	12				6	9	10	11										P Harrison	3
1	2	3	4	5	S			7*	12	8			6	9	10	11										**J Moules**	4
1	2	3	4	5			S	7*	8				6	9	10	11	12									G Poll	5
1	2	3	4	5			14	12	8				6	9	10*	11	7*									P Alcock	6
1	2	3	4*	5			14	12	8				6	9	10	11	7*									D Frampton	7
	2	3	4	5	8		14	7	S				6	9	10*	11		1								J Lloyd	8
	2	3	4	5*	8		14	7*	12				6	9	10	11		1								K Redfearn	9
	2	3	4	5		7		9*		11*	14		6		10	8		1								D Gallagher	10
	2	3	4		14				8	11	5		6		10	7*	9	1								G Willard	11
	2	3	4*			12	8	9			5		6		10*	7	11	1								M James	12
		3	4	5			8	9				14	6	12	10	7*	11	1								I Borrett	13
		3	4	5		7	8	9				2	6		10		11	1	S							M Scoble	14
1	2	3	4	12	14		8*	9			5*		6		10	7	11									C Wilkes	15
1		3	4	5	8	2	12	9*			S		6		10	7	11									D Axcell	16
1		3	4	S		2	8*	9			5		6	14	10	7	11									**K Cooper**	17
1		3	4*		8	2		9			5		6*	12	10	7†	11		14							A Smith	18
1		3	4	S	6	2	8	9*			5			12	10	7	11									K Cooper	19
		3	4	S	6	2	8	9*			5			12	10	7	11	1								R Lewis	20
		3	4	12		7*	2	8	9		5	S	6		10		11	1								**G Singh**	21
		3	4	S	12	2	8	9*		7			6		10			1	11*	5						T Fitzharris	22
		3	4	S			8	9			5				10	7	12	1			6	11*				B Hill	23
		3	4	S		2	8	9							10	7	11	1			6					R Hart	24
		3	4	S		2*	8	9		12					10	7	11	1			6					J Lloyd	25
	2	3	4	6*	S	12	8	9							10	7	11	1		5						P Vanes	26
	2*	3	4	6			8	9			5		12		10*	7	11	1								**K Breen**	27
		3	4	S			8	9		6	5				10	7	11	1	2							R Poulain	28
		3	4	S			8	9			5				10	7	12	1	2		6	11*				M James	29
		3	4				S	9			5*		14		10	7	11	1	2		6	8				K Barratt	30
		3	4	12			14	10*					6		10	7	11	1	2		5	8*				R Nixon	31
		3	4	12				9*					5		10	7	11	1	2		6	8				J Watson	32
		3	4	5			S	9	S				2		10	7	11	1			6	8				M Reed	33
		3	4	5*				9*	12				2		10	7	11	1	14		6	8				M Brandwood	34
		3	4					9	12		5		2		10	7	11*	1	14		6	8*				J Martin	35
		3	4*	S				9		11	5		2		10	7		1	12		6	8				G Ashby	36
		3	4	12				9		11	5*		2		10	7		1	S		6	8				S Bell	37
		3	4	5*			12	9		11*	14		2		10	7					6	8				V Callow	38
1		3	4					9*		14	5	2			10	7*					12	11	8			T Lunt	39
1		3	4					12		9			2		10	7					6	8		5	11*	A Smith	40
1		3	4					11*		9			2	12	10	7	14				6	8*		5		M Bodenham	41
1	3*		4				8	9		S			2	12	10	7	11				6			5		A Bennett	42
1	3		4							12			6	9*	10	7	11		2*		8		14	5		M Pierce	43
1	3		4					12		9			6		10	7*	11				8		14	5		J Lloyd	44
1	14	3	2*				8	9*		12			6		10	7	11				4			5		J Carter	45
1		3	4				8		S			2	6	9	10	7	11				4		S	5		G Courtney	46
1		3	4*	6			8	9					2	14	10	7*	11						12	5		R Shepherd	47
1		3	4	6			8	9*					2	14	10	7	11						S	5		D Frampton	48
18	13	42	41	13	8	4	12	26	36	7	14	1	35	8	41	39	27	24	7	5	18	10	3	9	1	**League Appearances**	
	2			4	2	3	11	4	1	4	2	1				7		4		4				3		**Substitute Appearances**	
2	2	2	2	2	0+1	1	2	0+2	2				2	2	2	1										**R/lows Appearances**	
1		1	1	1			1	1	1	1			1	0+1	1	1	1									**FA Cup Appearances**	
1		3	3		2	1	2	2	3	3		3	2+1	0+1	3	2	3	2	0+1							**Autoglass Appearances**	

Also Played: Posn.(Game): Marriott 14(12), Donovan S(14), Toshack 12(10)14(27)S(11,24,28,32)

Players on Loan: Harrison (Bristol City), Newton (Chelsea)

† = Sent Off

CARDIFF CITY

Club Colours: Royal blue shirts with white collar, white shorts, blue stockings
Change Colours: All yellow
Reserves League: Neville Ovenden Football Combination

Previous League: Southern League
Previous Name(s): Riverside FC (1899-1908) amalgamated with Riverside Albion (1902); Cardiff City (1908-)
Previous Managers: 1910-11 Davy McDougall 1911-33 Fred Stewart 1933-34 Bartley Wilson 1934-37 B Watts Jones 1937-39 Bill Jennings 1939-46 Cyril Spiers 1946-48 Billy McCandless 1948-54 Cyril Spiers 1954-58 Trevor Morris 1958-62 Bill Jones 1962-64 George Swindin 1964-73 Jimmy Schoular 1973-74 Frank O'Farrell 1974-78 Jimmy Andrews 1978-81 Richie Morgan 1981-82 Graham Williams 1982-84 Len Ashurst 1984 Jimmy Goodfellow & Jimmy Mullen (Caretakers) 1984-86 Alan Durban 1986-89 Frank Burrows 1989-91 Len Ashurst 1991- Eddie May
Honours: Champions Div 3S 1946-47 FA Cup Winners 1926-27 Charity Shield 1927 Welsh FA Cup Winners 21 times
League Career: Elected to Div 2 1920 Promoted to Div 1 1920-21 Relegated to Div 2 1928-29 Relegated to Div 3S 1930-31 Promoted to Div 2 1946-47 Promoted to Div 1 1951-52 Relegated to Div 2 1956-57 Promoted to Div 1 1959-60 Relegated to Div 2 1961-62 Relegated to Div 3 1974-75 Promoted to Div 2 1975-76 Relegated to Div 3 1981-82 Promoted to Div 2 1982-83 Relegated to Div 3 1984-85 Relegated to Div 4 1985-86 Promoted to Div 3 1987-88 Relegated to Div 4 1989-90

CLUB RECORDS

Most Appearances for Club: Phil Dwyer (1972-85): League 471 + FA Cup 23 + League Cup 28 + Welsh Cup 43 + Anglo-Scottish Cup 3 + European Cup Winners Cup 5. **Total 573**
Most Capped Player: Alf Sherwood 39 Wales **For England:** None
Record Goalscorer in a Match: Derek Tapscott 6 v Knighton Town (Welsh FA Cup) 20.01.61.
Record League Goalscorer in a Season: Stan Richards 30 1946-47 **In All Competitions:** John Toshack 31 (League 22 + Cup ties 9) 1968-69
Record League Goalscorer in a Career: Len Davies 127, 1920-31
Record Transfer Fee Received: £215,000 from Portsmouth for Jimmy Gilligan, September 1989
Record Transfer Fee Paid: £200,000 to San Jose Earthquakes for Godfrey Ingram, Sept 1982
Best Performances: League: Runners-Up Div 1, 1923-24 **FA Cup:** Winners 1926-27 **League Cup:** Semi-Final 1965-66 **Welsh Cup:** Winners 20 times **European Cup Winners Cup:** Semi-final 1967-68
Most League Points: (3pts a win) 86, Div 3 1982-83 (2pts a win) 66, Div 3(S), 1946-47
Most League Goals: 93, Division 3(S), 1946-47
Record League Victory and Most Goals Scored in a League Match: 7-0 v Burnley, Div 1, 1.9.1928 9-2 v Thames, Div 3S, 6.2.1932 7-0 v Barnsley, Div 2, 7.12.1957
Most Goals Scored in a Cup Tie: 16 v Knighton, Welsh Cup, 20.1.1961
(First Class Cup Tie) 8-0 v Enfield, FA Cup Rnd 1, 1931-32
Record Cup Victory (Europe): 8-0 v P.O. Larnaca (Cyprus), European Cup Winners Cup Rnd 1, 1970-71
Record League Defeat: 2-11 v Sheffield United, Div 1, 1.1.1926 0-9 v Preston North End, Div 2, 7.5.1966
Cardiff lost 1-9 v Wolves at home on 3.9.1955 which is a joint record for Div 1 and then won the return game at Molyneux 2-0
Record Cup Defeat: 1-6 v Aston Villa, FA Cup Rnd 3, 1928-29 0-5 v Charlton Athletic, FA Cup Rnd 3, 1937-38
European Competitions entered: European Cup Winners Cup 1964-65, 1965-66, 1967-68, 1968-69, 1969-70, 1970-71, 1971-72, 1973-74, 1974-75, 1976-77, 1977-78, 1988-89, 1992-93
Oldest Player in a League Match: George Latham 42 v Blackburn Rovers, Division 1, 2.1.1922.
Youngest Player in a League Match: John Toshack 16 v Leyton Orient, Division 2, 13.11.1965.

LONGEST LEAGUE RUNS

of undefeated matches: 21 (1946-47)	**of league matches without a win:** 15 (1936-37)
of undefeated home matches: 27 (1939/46/47)	**of undefeated away matches:** 10 (1946-47)
without home win: 10 (1986-87)	**without an away win:** 44 (1971-73)
of league wins: 9 (1946)	**of home wins:** 9 (1922-23, 1951-52)
of league defeats: 7 (1933)	**of away wins:** 8 (1946)

CARDIFF CITY

PLAYERS NAME Honours	Ht	Wt	Birthdate	Birthplace Transfers	Contract Date	Clubs	League	L/Cup	FA Cup	Other	Lg	L/C	FAC	Oth
GOALKEEPERS														
Gavin Ward	6.2	12.12	30.06.70	Sutton Coldfield	26.09.88	Shrewsbury Town								
				Free	18.09.89	West Brom A								
				Free	01.10.89	Cardiff City	26+1			4				
DEFENDERS														
Gareth Abraham	6.4	12.12	13.02.69	Merthyr Tydfil	10.07.87	Cardiff City (A)	82+5	7	8	5	4			1
Lee Baddeley					13.08.91	Cardiff City (T)	16+4		1	3				
Alan Lewis	6.2	12.10	31.05.71	Pontypridd	05.07.89	Cardiff City (T)	27+23	1+2	2	5				
Jason Perry W: u21.1	5.11	10.04	02.04.70	Newport	10.08.87	Cardiff City (T)	118+1	11	5	5+2				
William J Williams Div3'87	6.2	14.4	03.10.60	Liverpool	18.10.79	Tranmere Rovers	167+6	13+1	12	2	13	1		
					30.07.85	Port Vale	50	7	1	4	2			
				£30,000	18.12.86	Bournemouth	115+2	9+1	7	5	9			1
				Loan	17.10.91	Wigan Ath	4							
				£15,000	12.11.91	Cardiff City	5							
MIDFIELD														
Nathan Blake W: Y	6.0	12.8	27.01.72	Cardiff	20.08.90	Cardiff City (T)	63+14	2+2	3	4+2	10			
Roger Gibbins E:S,FAYC'74	5.10	11.9	06.09.55	Enfield	01.12.72	Tottenham H. (A)								
					01.08.75	Oxford Utd	16+3				2			
				Free	01.06.76	Norwich City	47+1	1	2		12	1		
				£60,000		New Eng. Teamen								
				Free	27.09.79	Cambridge Utd	97+3	7	2+1		12	3	1	
				Free	01.08.82	Cardiff City	135+4	14	5		17	5	1	
				Free	10.10.85	Swansea City	35		2	4	6			
				Free	22.08.86	Newport County	79	8	3	4	8	1		1
				£5,000	25.03.88	Torquay Utd	32+1	2	3+2	6	5			2
				£10,000		Newport Co								
					23.03.89	Cardiff City	131+3	7	8	6	7	1		
Gary Gill Div4'91	5.10	10.9	28.11.64	Middlesbrough	16.12.82	Middlesbrough (A)	69+8	5+3	4+1	6+1	2			
				Loan	23.12.83	Hull City	0+1							
				£20,000	01.12.89	Darlington	55+1	6	2	4	9		1	1
				Free	12.03.92	Cardiff City	3+3				1			
Paul Ramsey NI: 14	5.10	12.0	03.09.62	Londonderry	11.04.80	Leicester City (A)	278+12	19	9+1	2+1	13	1	1	
				£100,000	23.08.91	Cardiff City	39	1	1	2	3			
FORWARDS														
Carl Dale	6.0	12.00	29.04.66	Deganwy		Bangor City								
				£12,000	19.05.88	Chester City	106+10	7+1	9	6	41		5	2
				£100,000	19.08.91	Cardiff City	41	2	1	3	22			2
Cohen Griffith	5.10	11.7	26.12.62	Guyana		Kettering Town			5				2	
				£70,000	05.10.89	Cardiff City	107+13	6	7	5	20	5		2
Paul Millar YPoY(N.I)'86.IFAC'86	6.2	12.7	16.11.66	Belfast		Portadown								
				£35,000	29.12.88	Port Vale	19+21		0+2	1+1	5			
				£60,000	21.08.91	Cardiff City	8+7	2	0+1	0+1		1		
Chris Pike	6.2	12.7	19.10.61	Cardiff		Barry Town								
					14.03.85	Fulham	32+10	3+1		3	4	1		1
				Loan	12.12.86	Cardiff City	6		3		2		1	
				Free		Cardiff City	114+6	5+2	5+1	6	53	2	2	1
ADDITIONAL CONTRACT PLAYERS														
Paul Marriott						Cardiff City	0+1							
Mario Miethig					15.12.89	Cardiff City								
Jason Roberts						Cardiff City (T)				0+1				
(D) Damon Searle W: Y	5.11	10.5	26.10.71	Cardiff	20.08.90	Cardiff City (T)	76+1	2	3	6	1	1		
Douglas Wile						Cardiff City (T)		1						

1985-86	**NIGEL VAUGHAN**	13	1986-87	**PAUL WIMBLETON**	8
1987-88	**JIMMY GILLIGAN**	20	1988-89	**JIMMY GILLIGAN**	14
1989-90	**CHRIS PIKE**	18	1990-91	**CHRIS PIKE**	14

| | 1991-92 | **CARL DALE** | 22 | |

NINIAN PARK Sloper Road, Cardiff CF1 8SX

Capacity: 21,000   **Covered Standing:** Nil   **Seating:** 14,000

Tel: Ground: 0222 398636   **Bluebirds Call:** 0898 88 86 03

All premium rate calls (0898/0891) cost 36p per minute cheap rate and 48p per minute at all other times. Call costings correct at time of going to press.

ATTENDANCES
Highest: 61,566 Wales v England, 14.10.1961
57,893 v Arsenal, Div 1, 22.4.1953

Lowest: 1,006 v Swansea City, Freight Rover Trophy,
28.1.1986
581 v Taffs Well, Welsh Cup, 25.11.1986

Record Receipts: £50,517.75 v Queens Park Rangers, FA
Cup Rnd 3, 6.1.1990

NINIAN PARK
First game: v Ton Pentre, Southern Lge Div 2, 24.9.1910
First floodlit game:

Season Tickets:
Stands: from £100 to £160, juv/OAP £65 to £95
Ground: £100, juv/OAP £65

Executive Box Season Tickets: None available

Cost of Stand Tickets: Grand Stand C & D: Catagory C
£7, B £8, A £9, juv/OAP C £4, B £5, C £5; Grand Stand
other areas: C £6, B £7, A £8, juv/OAP C £3, B £4, C £4;
Covered Family enclosure, Canton St. Seat, Popular
Bank: C £4, B £5, A £6, juv/OAP C £2, B £3, C £3

Match and Ticket Information: Bookable in Advance

Car Parking: (Shared with the Leckwith athletics
stadium) across the road from Ninian Park

Nearest Railway Station: Cardiff Central (0222 228000)

How to get to the ground

From North: Follow signs Cardiff A470 until junction with
Cardiff bypass. At roundabout take 3rd exit A48 (S.P. Port
Talbot). In 2m at roundabout take 1st exit A4161 into
Cowbridge Road. In 0.5m turn right along Lansdowne
Road. At end at crossroads turn right A4055 into Leckwith
Road. In 0.2m turn left into Sloper Road to Cardiff City FC

From East: Use Motorway M4, then A48 into Cardiff
bypass. Follow Port Talbot then in 2m at roundabout take
1st exit A4161 into Cowbridge Road. In 0.5m turn right
along Lansdowne Road. At end at crossroads turn right
A4055 into Leckwith Road. In 0.2m turn left into Sloper
Road for Cardiff City FC

From West: Use the M4 and leave at Junction 33, taking
the A4232 (traffic from the A48 can also join the A4232 at
the Culverhouse Cross junction). Leave the A4232 at the
exit the City Centre, B4267 for Cardiff City FC

Value Rating: ★ ★

Programme Editor:

Price of 1992-93 Programme:
Number of Pages:
Subscriptions:

Local Newspapers: South Wales Echo, Western Mail

Local Radio Stations: BBC Radio Wales, Red Rose
Radios (ILR), BBC Radio Cymru

CARLISLE UNITED — Division 3

Formed: 1904   **Turned Professional:**   **Ltd Co:** 1921

SPONSORED BY: Lloyd Ltd   **NICKNAME:** The Cumbrians

President
J C Monkhouse JP

Vice-Presidents
T L Sibson
Dr T Gardner, MB ChB MBE

Chairman & Chief Executive
Michael Knighton

Vice-Chairman
B Chaytow

Directors
H A Jenkins   J R Sheffield
T A Bingley   R S Liddell FCA
J B Lloyd   C J Vasey
R McKnight

Secretary
Alison Moore (0228 26237)

Team Manager
Aidan McCaffery

Assistant Manager/Physio
Peter Hampton

Youth Team Coach
David Wilkes

Commercial Manager
Jim Thoburn (0228 24014)

Community Football Officer
John Halpin (0228 512266)

Groundsman
Peter Kemp

Club Statistician for the Directory
Bill Rodger

THE 1991-92 campaign can best be summed up by stating that the most exciting action took place after the end of the playing season.

An opening day success at Doncaster proved to be a false dawn, with more than two months elapsing before the next victory was achieved. By this time, the unsuccessful pattern for the season had been well and truly set, but even the long suffering supporters were less than prepared for the happenings of the closing weeks of the campaign which saw, first, Aldershot resign, and then Doncaster's fortunes improve sufficiently to leave Carlisle bottom of the table for the one and only time on the final day of the season.

Sadly, the cup competitions painted no brighter a picture. First round exits in the Rumbelows and F.A. Cups at the hands of fellow Fourth Division members Rochdale and Crewe did little to sustain interest. The Autoglass Trophy threw up a strange situation, in that having thrashed Third Division Stockport County in a qualifying, the same opponents were drawn to return to Brunton Park in the first knock-out stage, duly took their revenge and eventually went on to make a Wembley appearance in the competition.

As always the lack of success led to dwindling attendances. No fewer than nine of the 21 home league fixtures attracted fewer than 2,000 spectators, and only the good fortune of the fixture list which brought championship chasing Burnley to Carlisle for the last game of the season brought in a crowd more than double the season's previous best.

By this time, the board had announced that the club was up for sale and hopefully the close season news that the new owner was to be ex-Manchester United director, Michael Knighton, will rekindle some of the interest that has undoubtedly drained away as a result of the club's recent conspicuous lack of playing success.

However, the fans will undoubtedly want to see the current confident predictions of the new owner matched by improved performances on the field to be convinced that the depression of recent seasons is to be lifted.

Bill Rodger

Back row L-R: Paul Proudlock, Craig Potts, Andy Watson, Richard Sendall, Mick Holmes, Kelham O'Hanlon, Simon Davey, Ian Dalziel, Andy Barnsley, Jeff, Thorpe, Darren Edmondson, Neil Williams. **Front row:** Peter Hampton (Physio/Asst. Manager), Ian Knight, Derek Walsh, George Oghani, Michael Knighton (Chairman), Ricardo Gabbiadini, Ian Arnold, Dean Walling, Aidan McCaffery (Manager).

CARLISLE UNITED

DIVISION FOUR: 22nd   **FA CUP:** 1st RND   **RUMBELOWS CUP:** 1st RND   **AUTOGLASS:** 1st RND

M	DATE	COMP.	VEN	OPPONENTS	RESULT	H/T	LGE POS	GOALSCORERS/GOAL TIMES	ATTEN-DANCE
1	A 17	BL	A	Doncaster Rovers	W 3-0	1-0	4	Sendall 44, Fyfe 55, Proudlock 67	(2,639)
2	20	RC 1/1	A	Rochdale	L 1-5	1-2		Barnsley 21	(1,650)
3	24	BL	H	Blackpool	L 1-2	1-2	7	Walling 13	4,369
4	27	RC 1/2	H	Rochdale	D 1-1	0-0		Barnsley 79	1,572
5	31	BL	A	Cardiff City	L 0-1	0-0	14		(4,096)
6	S 3	BL	H	Rotherham United	L 1-3	1-1	16	Barnsley (pen) 39	2,346
7	14	BL	H	Lincoln City	L 0-2	0-2	19		2,149
8	17	BL	H	Mansfield Town	L 1-2	0-0	20	Edmondson 60	1,803
9	21	BL	A	Northampton Town	D 2-2	1-1	21	Watson 5, 90	(2,656)
10	28	BL	H	Walsall	D 3-3	1-0	22	Fyfe 20, 67, Barnsley (pen) 55	2,148
11	O 5	BL	A	Burnley	L 0-2	0-1	22		(6,157)
12	12	BL	H	Scunthorpe United	D 0-0	0-0	22		1,988
13	19	BL	A	Wrexham	L 0-3	0-1	22		(1,266)
14	22	AGT P	A	York City	D 1-1	1-0		Fyfe 5	(957)
15	26	BL	H	Crewe Alexandra	W 2-1	0-0	20	Watson 52, Fyfe 76	1,905
16	N 2	BL	H	Gillingham	D 0-0	0-0	21		1,672
17	5	BL	A	Barnet	L 2-4	1-0	21	Bodley (og) 26, Fyfe (pen) 54	(2,983)
18	9	BL	A	Scarborough	D 2-2	0-2	21	Thorpe 54, Graham 61	(1,501)
19	16	FAC 1	H	Crewe Alexandra	D 1-1	0-1		Watson 56	3,106
20	19	AGT P	H	Stockport County	W 4-0	3-0		Thorpe 15, Fyfe 35, Walling 41, 52	894
21	23	BL	H	Hereford United	W 1-0	0-0	20	Walling 54	2,032
22	26	FAC 1R	A	Crewe Alexandra	L †3-5	0-2		Barnsley (pen) 48, 65 (pen), Fyfe 80	(3,733)
23	30	BL	H	Maidstone United	W 3-0	2-0	17	Watson 27, 89, Barnsley (pen) 29	2,146
24	D 21	BL	A	Blackpool	L 0-1	0-0	20		(3,440)
25	26	BL	H	Doncaster Rovers	W 1-0	1-0	17	Jeffels 45	3,106
26	28	BL	H	Cardiff City	D 2-2	0-0	17	Watson 60, Jeffels 90	3,080
27	J 1	BL	A	Rotherham United	L 0-1	0-0	18		(4,856)
28	4	BL	A	Chesterfield	D 0-0	0-0	18		(2,892)
29	11	BL	H	Rochdale	D 0-0	0-0	17		2,494
30	14	AGT 1	H	Stockport County	L 1-3	0-3		Watson 62	1,243
31	18	BL	A	York City	L 0-2	0-0	20		(1,953)
32	25	BL	H	Halifax Town	D 1-1	0-1	18	Watson (pen) 70	2,091
33	F 7	BL	A	Crewe Alexandra	L 1-2	1-1	18	Watson 27	(3,232)
34	12	BL	A	Maidstone United	L 1-5	0-3	21	Watson 89	(944)
35	22	BL	A	Rochdale	L 1-3	1-2	21	Watson 39	(1,691)
36	29	BL	H	Chesterfield	L 1-2	0-2	21	Edmondson 53	2,038
37	M 3	BL	H	York City	D 1-1	1-1	21	Watson 18	1,681
38	7	BL	A	Halifax Town	L 2-3	1-0	21	Walling 39, Watson 74	(1,015)
39	10	BL	H	Barnet	L 1-3	0-2	21	Holmes 60	1,888
40	14	BL	A	Gillingham	W 2-1	1-0	21	Holmes 24, Watson 68	(2,179)
41	21	BL	H	Scarborough	D 2-2	0-0	21	Walling 87, Holmes 89	1,813
42	24	BL	H	Wrexham	L 0-1	0-0	21		1,826
43	28	BL	A	Hereford United	L 0-1	0-1	21		(1,810)
44	A 1	BL	A	Lincoln City	L 0-1	0-0	21		(2,118)
45	11	BL	A	Mansfield Town	L 1-2	1-0	21	Walling 13	(3,085)
46	18	BL	H	Northampton Town	W 2-1	1-0	21	Watson 25, Holmes 85	1,935
47	21	BL	A	Walsall	D 0-0	0-0	21		(2,406)
48	25	BL	H	Burnley	D 1-1	0-1	21	Thomas 79	9,051
49	M 2	BL	A	Scunthorpe United	L 0-4	0-2	22		(3,733)

Best Home League Attendance: 9,051 v Burnley   Smallest: 1,672 v Gillingham   **Av Home Att: 2,554**

Goal Scorers: **Compared with 90-91: -454**

League (41): Watson 14 (1 pen), Walling 5, Fyfe 5 (1 pen), Holmes 4, Barnsley 3 (3 pens), Edmondson 2, Jeffels 2, Sendall, Proudlock, Thorpe, Graham, Opponents, Thomas

R/lows C (2): Barnsley 2

FA Cup (4): Barnsley 2 (2 pens), Fyfe, Watson

Autoglass (6): Walling 2, Fyfe 2, Watson, Thorpe

† = After extra-time

O'Hanlon K.	Armstrong L.	Barnsley A.	Miller D.	Jeffels S.	Graham M.	Thomas G.	Sendall R.	Walling D.	Fyfe T.	Proudlock P.	Thorpe G.	Wilkes D.	Edmondson D.	Potts C.	Deakin J.	Bennett M.	Nevin P.	Watson A.	Gallimore A.	Lowery T.	Holliday J.	Walsh D.	Gorman P.	Holmes M.	Prinz J.	Referee	
1	2	3	4	5	6	7●	8	9	10	11	12	14														R Wiseman	1
1	2	3	4	5	6	7		9	10	8	11*	12	S													S Bell	2
1		3	4	5	6	7		9	10*	8	11●	12	2	14												A Dawson	3
1		3	4	5	6●	7		9	10	8	11*	12	2		14											**I Cruickshank**	4
1	14	3	4	5	6	7		9*	10	8	12		2		11●											G Paul	5
1	S	3	4	5	6	7			10	8	9*	12	2		11											I Hendrick	6
1	12	3	4	5	6	8		9	10	7*		14	11●	2												R Poulain	7
1	12*	2	4	5	6	7			8	11		10			S	3	9									W Burns	8
1		2	4	5	6	7		9		11	12	10*				3†	S	8								M Brandwood	9
1	S	2	4	5	6	7*		12	9	11			10					8	3							P Wright	10
1	2		4	5†	6	7●		12	9*	11			10					8	3	14						J Kirkby	11
1	2		4	5	6	7		9	10	12							S	11*	3	8						R Nixon	12
1	2		4		6	7		9	10	12							S	11*	3	8	5					D Phillips	13
1	12		4		6	7		9	10	11	3		2					S		8*	5					**E Parker**	14
1		2	12	4		7		9	10	S			6					11	3	8	5*					R Shepherd	15
1		2	S	4		7		9*	10	12			6					11	3	8	5					A Wilkie	16
1		2	S	4		7		9	10	12			6					11	3	8	5*					I Hemley	17
1		2	7	4●	14			10	9	12			6					11	3	8	5*					A Bennett	18
1	14		4	5	2	7		12	10	9	3		6					11●		8*						**A Dawson**	19
1	2	12	4	5*		7		9	10	8	11		6		3						S					**T Lunt**	20
1	5	4		2		7		8	10	9	11*		6					S	12	3						C Trussell	21
1	S	3	4	5	2	7		8	10	9			6*					12	11							**A Dawson**	22
1		6	4	5	2	7*		8	10	9	S							12	11	3						T Fitzharris	23
1	S	6	4	5	2			8	10	9	3							S	11			7				P Jones	24
1		6	4	5	2			8	10	9	3							S	11			7	S			K Breen	25
1	S	6*	4	5	2			8		9	3		12						11			7	10			R Hart	26
1	S		4	5	2			8		9	3			S		6			11			7	10			T West	27
1	S		4	5	2	6		8		9	3			S					11			7	10			R Bigger	28
1	2		4	5		6		9		10	11						S	8				7	3			J Lloyd	29
1	2●		4	5	3	6*		9	14	10	11							8				7				**K Lupton**	30
1	S		4	5	2	6		9	10	7	11*							8					3			R Nixon	31
1	12			5	2	7		9	10	11			6*					8		4						E Parker	32
1	2				4	7		9	10*	12	11●		6				14	8		5						G Courtney	33
1	2			5	4	7		9	10●	12	11		6*				14	8								P Don	34
1				2	8			12	10*	7●	11		6				14	9		5				4		W Burns	35
1	6*		5	2	8			10			11		7				12	9	3		S			4		J Watson	36
1	6			5	2	12		10		11			7				9*	8	3		S			4		C Trussell	37
1	S	6			2	9		10		11			7				S	8	3		5			4		I Hendrick	38
1	S	6			2	9		10		11			7				S	8	3		5			4		R Shepherd	39
1		6			4	7		10		S	11		2					9	3		5			8		G Willard	40
1		6	12		4	7		10			11	14	2*					9	3		5●			8		J Kirkby	41
1		6	4	5	2●			10*	12	7	11							9	3			14		8		S Lodge	42
1		6		5	2	4		10		12	11		S					9	3		7*			8		J Pierce	43
1	2	6		5				14	10●	12	11							9		4*	3		7			T Lunt	44
1	2●	6				14	8	4	10	11*								9		5	3		7		12	P Taylor	45
1		6			4	8		10					5	3				12	9		2			7	11*	P Harrison	46
1		6			3*	8		10	11				4	12				9		5	2		7	S		P Alcock	47
1	14	6				8		10			3●		4	12				9		5	2		7	11*		R Hart	48
1	14	6				8		9			3●		4	11				12		5	2		7	10*		P Danson	49
42	**8**	**28**	**25**	**26**	**37**	**35**	**1**	**33**	**25**	**26**	**23**	**1**	**26**	**3**	**3**	**5**	**2**	**34**	**16**	**6**	**16**	**14**	**5**	**15**	**3**	**League Appearances**	
	6		1	1	1	2		4	1	8	3	1	3					2	6	1		1			1	**Substitute Appearances**	
2	1	2	2	2	2	2		2	2	2	2		0+2	1		0+1		2	6	1		1				**R/lows Appearances**	
2	0+1	1	2	2	2	2		1+1	2	2	1		2					0+1	2		1					**FA Cup Appearances**	
3	2+1	0+1	3	3	1	3		3	2+1	3	3		2			0		1		1	1	1	1	1		**Autoglass Appearances**	

Also Played: Posn.(Game): N Cranston 12(30,31)14(32)S(29,40,46), C Freeman 3(32●,33,34,35)

Players on Loan: A Gallimore (2 spells)

†=Sent Off

CARLISLE UNITED

Club Colours: Blue shirts with white pinstripe, white collar with red and blue trim, white shorts and blue stockings
Change Colours: All red
Reserves League: Lancashire League Div 1   **'A' Team:** Lancashire League Div 2

Previous League: North Eastern League
Previous Managers: W Clark Ivor Broadis Bill Shankly Fred Emery Andy Beattie Ivor Powell Alan Ashman Tim Ward Bob Stokoe Ian MacFarlane Alan Ashman Dick Young Bobby Moncur Martin Harvey B S Robson Bob Stokoe Harry Gregg
Honours: Champions Div 3, 1964-65
League Career: Elected to Div 3N 1928   Transferred to Div 4 1958   Promoted to Div 3 1961-62
Relegated to Div 4 1962-63   Promoted to Div 3 1963-64   Promoted to Div 2 1964-65   Promoted to Div 1 1973-74
Relegated to Div 2 1974-75   Relegated to Div 3 1976-77   Promoted to Div 2 1981-82   Relegated to Div 3 1985-86
Relegated to Div 4 1986-87

CLUB RECORDS

Most Appearances for Club: Alan Ross 1963-79: 466
Most Capped Player: Eric Welsh 4, N Ireland   **For England:** None
Record Goalscorer in a Match: H Mills, 5 v Halifax Town, 5-2, Div 3(N), 11.9.1937   Jim Whitehouse, 5 v Scunthorpe United, 8-0, Div 3N, 25.12.1952
Record League Goalscorer in a Season: Jimmy McConnell 42, Div 3N, 1928-29   **In All Competitions:** Hugh McIlmoyle 44 (League 39 + 5 League Cup) 1963-64
Record League Goalscorer in a Career: Jimmy McConnell 126, 1928-32
Record Transfer Fee Received: £275,000 from Vancouver Whitecaps for Peter Beardsley, April 1981
Record Transfer Fee Paid: £120,000 to York City for Gordon Staniforth, October 1979
Best Performances: League: 22nd Div 1, 1974-75   **FA Cup:** 6th Round, 1974-75   **League Cup:** Semi-Final 1969-70
Most League Points: (3pts a win) 80, Div 3, 1981-82   (2pts a win) 62, Div 3(N), 1950-51
Most League Goals: 113, Div 4, 1963-64
Record League Victory: 8-0 v Hartlepool, Div 3N, 1.9.1928   8-0 v Scunthorpe United, Div 3N, 25.12.1952   (Carlisle also won against Nelson, Div 3, 14.3.1931)
Most Goals Scored in a Cup Tie: 6-1 v Billingham Synthonia, FA Cup Rnd 1, 17.11.1956
Record League Defeat: 1-11 v Hull City, Div 3N, 14.1.1939
Record Cup Defeat: 0-5 v West Ham Utd, FA Cup Rnd 1 replay, 1909-10   1-6 v Wigan Athletic, FA Cup Rnd 1, 1934-35   1-6 v Bradford City, FA Cup Rnd 1, 1951-52   0-5 v Bristol City, FA Cup Rnd 4 replay, 28.1.1981
Oldest Player in a League Match: Bryan 'Pop' Robson, 39 years 321 days v Shrewsbury Town, 28.9.1985
Youngest Player in a League Match:

LONGEST RUNS

of undefeated matches: 15 (1950-51, 1983-84)	**of league matches without a win:** 14 (1935)
of undefeated home matches: 22 (1950-51)	**of undefeated away matches:** 12 (1950-51)
without home win: 8 (1954, 1991-92)	**without an away win:** 20 (1970-71)
of league wins: 6 (1937, 1981-82)	**of home wins:** 7 (1930-36)
of league defeats: 8 (1935)	**of away wins:** 4 (1964-65)

CARLISLE UNITED

PLAYERS NAME / Honours	Ht	Wt	Birthdate	Birthplace / Transfers	Contract Date	Clubs	League	L/Cup	FA Cup	Other	Lg	L/C	FAC	Oth
GOALKEEPERS														
Antony Caig					10.07.92	Carlisle Utd. (T)								
Kelham O'Hanlon	6.1	13.6	16.05.62	Saltburn	21.05.80	Middlesbrough (A)	87	4	6					
Ei:1,u21.1; Div.4'89				Free	07.08.85	Rotherham Utd	248	22	18	16				
				£25,000	05.08.91	Carlisle Utd	42	2	2	3				
DEFENDERS														
Andy Barnsley	6.0	11.11	09.06.62	Sheffield		Denaby Utd								
Div.4'89					10.07.85	Rotherham Utd	28		3	3				
				£25,000	17.07.86	Sheffield Utd	73+4	3	5+1	7				
				£30,000	15.12.88	Rotherham Utd	77+6	5+1	5	3+1	3			1
					15.08.91	Carlisle Utd	28	2	1	0+1	3	2	2	
Ian Dalziel	5.8	11.10	24.10.62	Sunderland	31.10.79	Derby County (A)	22	3+1	1+1		4			
					18.05.83	Hereford Utd	137+13	9	9	10	8			
					05.07.88	Carlisle Utd	79	3	3	3+1	2			1
Darren Edmondson	6.0	12.2	04.11.71	Coniston		Hull City (T)								
					17.07.90	Carlisle Utd. (T)	56+2	1	3	4	2			
John Holliday					06.09.89	Carlisle Utd	17		1					
MIDFIELD														
Jeffery Thorpe	5.10	12.8	17.11.72	Whitehaven	02.07.91	Carlisle Utd. (T)	29+12	2	1	3+1	1			1
Derek Walsh	5.9	11.4	24.10.67	Hamilton		Everton (A)	1							
						Hamilton Accies	2							
				Free	05.08.88	Carlisle Utd	90+8	7	6	6	6		1	1
Andrew Watson	5.9	11.02	01.04.67	Huddersfield		Harrogate								
WC'91					12.09.88	Halifax Town	75+8	5+1	6	7	15	2	1	1
				£40,000	31.07.90	Swansea City	9+5	0+1		1+1	1			
				Loan	19.09.91	Carlisle Utd								
				£30,000	01.11.91	Carlisle Utd	34+1		2	1	14		1	1
David Wilkes	5.8	10.02	10.03.64	Barnsley		Barnsley	14+3	2			2			
				Loan		Halifax Town	4							
						Stockport Co	8	4				2		
						Frickley			0+2					
						Hong Kong								
					02.07.91	Carlisle Utd	1+4	0+2						
FORWARDS														
Michael Holmes	5.8	10.8	09.09.65	Blackpool	20.07.84	Bradford City	0+5			3+1				
Div.4'88; SVT'88				Free	28.11.85	Wolverhampton W	74+9	3	3+1	9+5	13			
					08.07.88	Huddersfield Town	3+4	1						
				Free	01.02.89	Torquay Utd	16+6			7	2			
				£15,000	21.02.92	Carlisle Utd	15				4			
Paul Proudlock	5.9	10.5	25.10.65	Hartlepool	13.03.85	Hartlepool Utd	8+7		1					
				Free	14.11.86	Middlesbrough	2+3			1+1	1			2
				£20,000	23.03.89	Carlisle Utd	113+16	8	4	6	18	1	2	1
Richard Sendall	5.10	11.6	10.07.67	Stamford		Watford (A)								
				Free	03.07.85	Blackpool	6+5	2	0+1	1			1	
				Free Month	05.07.88	Carlisle Utd	48+26	2	2+3	1+1	13		1	
				Loan	07.09.89	Cardiff City	3+1							
Dean Walling	6.0	10.8	17.04.69	Leeds		Leeds Utd. (A)								
FA Vase '91.				Free	30.07.87	Rochdale	43+22	3	0+1	1+1	8			
						Guiseley								
					01.07.91	Carlisle Utd	33+4	2	1+1	3	5			2
ADDITIONAL CONTRACT PLAYERS														
Craig Potts						Carlisle Utd	3+3							
Jason Prins						Carlisle Utd	3+1							

LEADING LEAGUE GOALSCORERS SEASONS 1985-86 – 1991-92

1985-86	**ANDY HILL**	8	1986-87	**PAUL BAKER**	9
1987-88	**MALCOLM POSKETT**	12	1988-89	**BRENT HETHERINGTON**	11
1989-90	**KEITH WALWYN**	11	1990-91	**ERIC GATES**	8

1991-92   **ANDY WATSON**   14

BRUNTON PARK Warwick Road, Carlisle, Cumbria CA1 1LL

Capacity: 13,913   **Covered Standing:** 11,762   **Seating:** 2,151

Tel: Ground: 0228 26237   **Clubcall:** 0898 12 16 32

All premium rate calls (0898/0891) cost 36p per minute cheap rate and 48p per minute at all other times. Call costings correct at time of going to press.

ATTENDANCES
Highest: 27,500 v Birmingham City, FA Cup Round 3,
5.1.1957 and v Middlesbrough, FA Cup Round 5, 7.2.1970

Lowest: 894 v Stockport, Autoglass Trophy, 19.11.1991

Record Receipts: £40,382.40 v Burnley, Division 4,
25.4.1992

Season Tickets:
Stands: from £119 to £130 (no reductions); Family
seats: £119 (£66)
Ground: £90, juv/OAP £50

Executive Box Season Tickets: None

Cost of Stand Tickets: Stands: £7.50, £7, OAP/juveniles
£4.50, £4; Family Stand: 1+1 £7, 1+2 £11, 1+3 £15
Terraces: Paddock: £5; OAP/juvenile £3; Family Terrace:
1+1 £7, 1+2 £10, 1+3 £13

Match and Ticket Information: Tickets may be booked 3
weeks in advance by post or phone (0228 26237)

Car Parking: Car park for 1,500 vehicles next to grond.
Entrance in St Aidan's Road. 50p cars, £2.00 coaches.
Limited street parking permitted

Nearest Railway Station: Carlisle Citadel (0228 4471)

How to get to the ground

From North, East, South: Use Motorway M6 until
junction 43. Leave motorway and follow signs Carlisle
A69 into Warwick Road for Carlisle United FC

From West: Follow signs into Carlisle then forward A69
along Warwick Road for Carlisle United FC

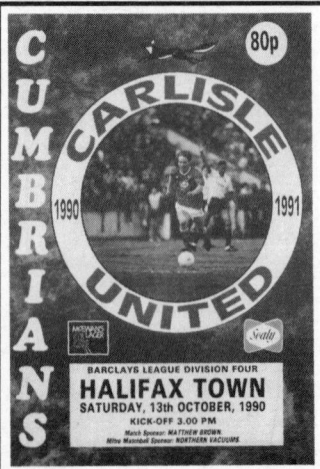

Value Rating: ★ ★

Programme Editor: Jim Thoburn

Price of 1992-93 Programme: £1
Number of Pages: 32
Subscriptions: £28 per season (home), £56 (home &
away)

Local Newspapers: Cumbrian Newspapers

Local Radio Stations: BBC Radio Cumbria

CHARLTON ATHLETIC   Division 1

Formed: 1905   **Turned Professional:** 1920   **Ltd Co:** 1919

SPONSORED BY: **NICKNAME:** The Addicks

President
R D Collins

Chairman
R N Alwen

Directors
R D Collins   R A Murray
M A Simons   M C Stevens
D G Ufton

Assistant General Manager
Jonathan Fuller

Secretary
Chris Parkes

Assistant Secretary
Anne Bligh (081-293 4567)

Player-Managers
Alan Curbishley & Steve Gritt

Reserve Team Coach
Keith Peacock

Youth Team Coach
John Cartwright

Youth Development Officer
Jimmy Hampson

Physiotherapist
Jimmy Hendry

Commercial Manager
Andrew Bryant

Groundsman
Colin Powell

Club Statistician for the Directory
Paul Clayton

CHARLTON started the season at Upton Park, as The Valley was not ready. It soon became apparent that due to financial and contractural difficulties, it was unlikely that football would be played at the former ground at all during the season, and this was indeed the case.

Shortly before commencement of the season, manager Lennie Lawrence had surprised the club by taking on the vacant Middlesbrough job. An even bigger surprise to the supporters was the joint appointment of Steve Gritt and Alan Curbishley to replace him. Changes to the playing staff during the summer were few. Mark Reid had joined St Mirren on a free, and Paul Mortimer had gone to Aston Villa for £350,000. Chelsea's John Bumstead and Brighton's Steve Gatting signed on frees, and Brighton's Garry Nelson was signed for a tribunal set £50,000 fee. In November, captain Andy Peake joined his former manager at Middlesbrough for £150,000, and was replaced by Alan Pardew on a free from Crystal Palace.

Charlton started well, and were to stay with the front runners all season. A final placing of seventh was achieved, with a play-off place being denied them on the last day of the season. A brilliant achievement for the new management team, with a small playing squad and no money to spend. Once again away form was far superior to home, with an all time record of eleven away league wins being equalled. Defensively, Charlton only conceded 48 goals, which was bettered by only two clubs in the division. However, it was their goalscoring record that let them down, with only five teams in the division scoring less, and only bottom club Port Vale scoring less at home. Numerous goalscoring chances were missed during home games when Charlton had dominated the play.

Robert Lee was again leading goalscorer in League matches with 12 goals, but Carl Leaburn who had scored only four goals in 100 previous matches, netted 14 in all games to be leading scorer overall. Injury prevented him from taking part in the final promotion run in and he was undoubtedly missed. Bob Bolder and Darren Pitcher were ever present. Simon Webster, appointed the club captain on Andy Peake's departure, had an outstanding season, and was voted the supporters 'Player of the Year', narrowly beating runner-up Carl Leaburn. Scott Minto and Anthony Barness excelled in defence.

In the cup competitions, Charlton beat Barnet before losing to Sheffield United an F.A. Cup replay at Bramall Lane. Norwich dismissed Charlton from the Rumbelows Cup after Fulham had been beaten and Charlton lost 2-4 on penalties in the ZDS Cup after drawing at Cambridge.

Attendances were slightly up on last season, but support could drop off considerably if a return to The Valley is not forthcoming next season.

Paul Clayton

Back row L-R: Scott Minto, Darren Pitcher, Simon Webster, Tommy Caton, Robert Lee, Colin Walsh. **Middle:** Stuart Balmer, Steve Brown, Carl Leaburn, Bob Bolder, Mike Salmon, Alex Dyer, Anthony Barness, John Bumstead. **Front:** Dean Dye, Paul Gorman, Paul Bacon, Alan Curbishley (1st Team Coach), Andy Peake, Steve Gritt (1st Team Coach), Kim Grant, Mark Tivey, Andy Salako.

CHARLTON ATHLETIC

DIVISION TWO: 7th   **FA CUP:** 4th RND   **RUMBELOWS CUP:** 2nd RND   **ZDS CUP:** 1st RND

M	DATE		COMP.	VEN	OPPONENTS	RESULT		H/T	LGE POS	GOALSCORERS/GOAL TIMES	ATTEN-DANCE
1	A	18	BL	H	Newcastle United	W	2-1	0-0	4	Lee 62, Leaburn 71	9,322
2		21	RC 1/1	H	Fulham	W	4-2	2-0		**Leaburn 11, Minto 22, Walsh 52, Peake 70**	**3,027**
3		24	BL	A	Wolverhampton W	D	1-1	1-1	8	Lee 6	(16,309)
4		27	RC 1/2	A	Fulham	D	1-1	1-1		**Leaburn 25**	(3,543)
5	S	1	BL	H	Derby County	L	0-2	0-0	15		6,606
6		3	BL	A	Tranmere Rovers	D	2-2	0-1	15	Webster 47, Lee 63	(7,609)
7		7	BL	A	Plymouth Argyle	W	2-0	0-0	12	Pitcher (pen) 51, Nelson 74	(5,602)
8		14	BL	H	Portsmouth	W	3-0	2-0	7	Nelson 30, Lee 43, 87	5,707
9		17	BL	H	Sunderland	L	1-4	1-1	11	Webster 14	5,807
10		21	BL	A	Watford	L	0-2	0-2	14		(8,459)
11		25	RC 2/1	H	Norwich City	L	0-2	0-1			2,886
12		28	BL	A	Port Vale	W	2-0	1-0	9	Nelson 12, Leaburn 74	4,049
13	O	2	ZDS 1	A	Cambridge United	D	†1-1	1-1		Gorman 45 (Lost 4-2 on pens)	(3,168)
14		5	BL	A	Leicester City	W	2-0	0-0	7	Nelson 50, Dyer 80	(11,467)
15		9	RC 2/2	A	Norwich City	L	0-3	0-2			(5,507)
16		12	BL	H	Bristol Rovers	W	1-0	0-0	5	Leaburn 71	5,685
17		19	BL	H	Brighton & H A	W	2-0	2-0	5	Nelson 1, Walsh 21	5,598
18		23	BL	A	Oxford United	W	2-1	0-0	2	Pitcher 50, Lee 66	(4,069)
19		26	BL	A	Southend United	D	1-1	0-1	3	Leaburn 53	(7,320)
20		30	BL	H	Ipswich Town	D	1-1	1-1	3	Gatting 35	6,939
21	N	2	BL	A	Grimsby Town	L	0-1	0-1	4		(4,743)
22		6	BL	H	Swindon Town	D	0-0	0-0	4		5,398
23		9	BL	H	Blackburn Rovers	L	0-2	0-1	4		7,114
24		16	BL	A	Middlesbrough	L	0-2	0-0	7		(13,093)
25		23	BL	H	Cambridge United	L	1-2	0-2	10	Gorman 81	6,350
26		30	BL	A	Bristol City	W	2-0	1-0	9	Pardew 22, Gorman 59	(9,123)
27	D	7	BL	H	Barnsley	D	1-1	0-0	9	Pardew (pen) 51	4,581
28		26	BL	A	Ipswich Town	L	0-2	0-1	10		(13,826)
29		28	BL	A	Derby County	W	2-1	1-0	10	Leaburn 33, Nelson 85	(14,367)
30	J	5	FAC 3	H	Barnet	W	3-1	1-1		**Gatting 36, Leaburn 66, Grant 78**	**9,618**
31		8	BL	H	Oxford United	D	2-2	0-2	10	Leaburn 50, Lee 85	4,101
32		15	BL	H	Wolverhampton W	L	0-2	0-1	10		5,703
33		18	BL	A	Newcastle United	W	4-3	1-3	8	Barnes 36, Walsh 73, 76, Pardew 89	(15,663)
34		26	FAC 4	H	Sheffield United	D	0-0	0-0			**11,982**
35	F	1	BL	A	Brighton & H A	W	2-1	1-1	8	Gorman 44, Lee 68	(8,870)
36		5	FAC 4R	A	Sheffield United	L	1-3	0-3		**Gatting 83**	16,242
37		8	BL	H	Southend United	W	2-0	0-0	9	Webster 52, Leaburn 87	9,724
38		15	BL	A	Cambridge United	L	0-1	0-0	9		(7,500)
39		22	BL	H	Bristol City	W	2-1	0-1	8	Walsh 81, Webster 88	5,900
40		26	BL	A	Millwall	L	0-1	0-1	8		(12,882)
41		29	BL	A	Barnsley	L	0-1	0-0	10		(6,208)
42	M	3	BL	H	Grimsby Town	L	1-3	0-3	10	Leaburn 75	3,658
43		7	BL	H	Millwall	W	1-0	0-0	7	Hendry 84	8,177
44		10	BL	A	Swindon Town	W	2-1	1-0	4	Leaburn 25, Webster 77	(7,196)
45		21	BL	A	Blackburn Rovers	W	2-0	0-0	5	Lee 56, Leaburn 62	(14,844)
46		28	BL	H	Middlesbrough	D	0-0	0-0	6		8,250
47		31	BL	A	Portsmouth	W	2-1	0-0	4	Leaburn 67, Whyte 74	(14,539)
48	A	4	BL	H	Plymouth Argyle	D	0-0	0-0	4		6,787
49		11	BL	A	Sunderland	W	2-1	0-0	6	Lee 70, Minto 76	(21,326)
50		18	BL	H	Watford	D	1-1	0-1	6	Lee 46	7,477
51		21	BL	A	Port Vale	D	1-1	0-0	6	Gritt 88	(8,461)
52		25	BL	A	Leicester City	W	2-0	2-0	6	Lee 40, Whyte 45	15,357
53		28	BL	H	Tranmere Rovers	L	0-1	0-1	6		7,645
54	M	2	BL	A	Bristol Rovers	L	0-1	0-0	7		(7,630)

Best Home League Attendance: 15,357 v Leicester City   **Smallest:** 3,658 v Grimsby Town   **Av Home Att:** 6,780

Goal Scorers: **Compared with 90-91: +233**

League (54):	Lee 12, Leaburn 11, Nelson 6, Webster 5, Walsh 4, Gorman 3, Pardew 3 (1 pen), Pitcher 2 (1 pen), Whyte 2, Hendry, Barnes, Gatting, Minto, Gritt, Dyer
R/lows C (5):	Leaburn 2, Walsh, Peake, Minto
FA Cup (4):	Gatting 2, Grant, Leaburn
ZDS Cup (1):	Gorman

† = After extra-time

1991-92

Bolder R.	Pitcher D.	Minto S.	Peake A.	Gritt S.	Gatting S.	Lee R.	Bumstead J.	Leaburn C.	Nelson G.	Walsh C.	Brown S.	Salako	Bacon P.	Webster S.	Dyer A.	Grant K.	Barness A.	Gorman P.	Balmer S.	Pardew A.	Rosenior L.	Wilder C.	Darlington J.	Hendry J.	Whyte D.	Referee	
1	2	3	4	5	6	7	8	9	10	11	S	S														B Hill	1
1	2	3	4	5	6	7		9	10	11*	S	12	8													M James	2
1	2	3	4	S	6	7		9	10	11			8	5	S											H King	3
1	2	3	4	12	6	7		9*	10	11*			8	5		14										M Bailey	4
1	2	3	4	S	6	7		9	10	11			8*	5		12										G Willard	5
1	2	3	4	S	6	7		9	10	11			8	5	S											M Reed	6
1	2	3	4	14	6	7		9	10*	11			8*	5		12										R Groves	7
1	2	3*	4	12	6	7		9	10	11*			8	5		14										A Smith	8
1	2		4	3*	6	7		9	10	11*			8	5		14	12									T Holbrook	9
1	2		4		6	7		9*	10	11	14		8*	5	12		3									P Don	10
1	2		4		6	7		9	10		S		8	5	11*	12	3									M Pierce	11
1	2	3	4		6	7*	8	9	10	11*			14	5		12										A Gunn	12
1			4		6		8		10			14	7*	5	11	12	3	9*								D Elleray	13
1	2		4		6		8		10*		S		7	5	11	12	3	9								D Frampton	14
1	2	10	4		6		8						7*	5	11	9	3	12	S							R Wiseman	15
1	2	3	4		6	7	8	9	10		S			5	11		S									D Shepherd	16
1	2	3	4		6	7	8	9	10	11				5*	S	12										J Martin	17
1	2	3	4		6	7	8	9	10	11				5	S	S										C Wilkes	18
1	2	3	4		6†	7	8	9	10	11				5	S	S										K Morton	19
1	2	3	4		6	7	8	9	10	11				5	S	S										P Jones	20
1	2	3	4		6	7	8	9	10*	11	S			5		12										S Lodge	21
1	2	3	4		6	7	8	9	10*	11†				5		12	S									R Pawley	22
1	2	3	4			7	8	9	10*	11				5		12	S		6*		S					D Axcell	23
1	2	3	4			7	8	9						5		12	S		6							J Worrall	24
1	2	3	4			7	8	9						5	11*	12		10	6*	14						L Shapter	25
1	2	3			6	7	8	12		11				5				10*	4†	9	S					G Ashby	26
1	2	3			6	7	8			11				5		S		10	4	9	S					M Pierce	27
1	4	3*			6	7	8	14	10	11				5†		12			9*			2				P Taylor	28
1	4				6	7	8	9	10	11				5			3	S	S	4						J Bell	29
1	2		14		6	7	8	9	10*	11			4*	5		12	3									P Don	30
1	2		S		6	7	8*	9	10	11				5		12	3			4						R Milford	31
1	2		S		6	7		9	10	11				5		12	3	5		4						M Bodenham	32
1	2		14		6		8		10	11*			7*	5		12	3			4						K Breen	33
1	2		S		6	7	8	9	10	11*				5		12	3			4						J Worrall	34
1	2	11*	14	6	7	8			10					5			3	9*		4			12			P Foakes	35
1	2	12			6	7*	8*	9	10	11				5			3	14		4						R Gifford	36
1	2	14			6	7	8*	9	10	11*				5			3	12		4						K Cooper	37
1	2	14			6	7	8*	9	10*	11				5			3	12		4						M James	38
1	2	S			6	7	8*	9	10	11				5			3	12		4						G Singh	39
1	2				8			9	10	11			12	5*			3		6	4				7*		P Alcock	40
1	2				8	6		9	10	11			7*	5			3		S	4				12		I Hendrick	41
1	2				6*		8*	9	10	11			12	5			3		14	4				7		G Pooley	42
1	2	3				7	8	9	10	11			7*	5			S		6	4				12		G Poll	43
1	2	3				7	8	9	10*	11*				5		12			6	4				14		B Hill	44
1	2*	3		12		7	8	9	10*	11				5					6	4				14		D Gallagher	45
1	2	3				7	8	9	10*	11				5			S		6	4				S		R Groves	46
1	2	3				7	8	9	10*	11				5			S		6	4				12		P Vanes	47
1	2	3		S		7*	8							5		12			6	4				10		A Smith	48
1	2	3	14	12	7	8	9*		11*					5		4			6					10		E Parker	49
1	2	3	S		7	8	9		11					5		S			6	4				10		A Gunn	50
1	2	3	12		8	9*	10	11						5		S			6	4				7		T West	51
1	2	3	12	14	7*	8	10*	11						5					6	4				9		D Axcell	52
1	2	3	12		7	8*	10*	11						5		14			6	4				9		J Carter	53
1	2	S		S	7	8	10	11						5		3			6	4				9		M Bodenham	54
46	46	32	20	4	30	39	36	37	41	42			11	44	3		16	5	16	23	3	2	1	1	7	**League Appearances**	
	1			10	2			2			1						3	3	2	1				1	4	**Substitute Appearances**	
4	4	3		4	1+1	4		3	3	2		1+1	4	3	2	1+2	2	0+1					1	4	1	**R/lows Appearances**	
3	3	0+1		3	3	3	3	3	3			1	3			3			2							**FA Cup Appearances**	
1	1			1	1	1			1			1	1	1	0+1	1	1									**ZDS Cup Appearances**	

Also Played: Posn.(Game): Curbishley 8*(32), Tivey 14(40)

Players on Loan: Hendry (Tottenham), Rosenior (West Ham), Whyte (Crystal Palace), Wilder (Sheff. Utd)

† = Sent Off

CHARLTON ATHLETIC

Club Colours: Red shirts, white shorts, red stockings
Change Colours: Blue & black diagonal striped shirts, black shorts, black stockings
Reserves League: Neville Ovenden Football Combination

COMPETITIONS			
Div. 1	Div. 2	Div. 3	Div. 3S
36-57	29-33	72-75	21-29
86-90	35-36	80-81	33-35
	57-72		
	75-80		
	81-86		
	90-		

HONOURS	
F.A. Cup	Div. 3S
1947	28-29
	34-35

MOST APPEARANCES: SAM BARTRAM 623 (1934-56)		
Year	League	FA Cup
34/35	18	
35/36	39	1
36/37	42	1
37/38	41	5
38/39	42	1
45/46	–	10
46/47	41	6
47/48	42	3
48/49	41	1
49/50	42	4
50/51	37	2
51/52	41	1
52/53	38	1
53/54	40	2
54/55	42	3
55/56	33	3
	579	44
Previous holder: Norman Smith 449 (1922-36)		

MOST GOALS IN A CAREER			
DEREK HALES 168 (1973-76 & 1978-85)			
Season	League	FA Cup	League Cup
1973-74	8	–	–
1974-75	20	–	1
1975-76	28	–	3
1976-77	16	–	2
1978-79	8	–	1
1979-80	8	–	1
1980-81	17	4	2
1981-82	11	–	2
1982-83	14	1	2
1983-84	10	–	1
1984-85	8	–	–
Total	148	5	15
Stuart Leary scored most **league** goals (153) 1951-62 (League 153; FA Cup 8; League Cup 2) Total: 163			

HIGHEST TRANSFER FEE RECEIVED			
Amount	Club	Player	Date
£650,000	Crystal Palace	Mike Flanagan	8/79
£600,000	Sheffield Wed.	Paul Williams	8/90
£500,000	Arsenal	Colin Pates	1/90
£500,000	Sheffield Wed.	Peter Shirtliff	7/89

MANAGERS			
Name	Seasons	Best	Worst
Walter Rayner	1920-25	12(3S)	16(3S)
Alex McFarlane	1925-28	13(3S)	21(3S)
Albert Lindon	1928	11(3S)	11(3S)
Alex McFarlane	1928-32	10(2)	1(3S)
Albert Lindon	1932-33	22(2)	22(2)
Jimmy Seed	1933-56	2(1)	5(3S)
Jimmy Trotter	1956-61	22(1)	10(2)
Frank Hill	1961-65	4(2)	20(2)
Bob Stokoe	1965-67	16(2)	19(2)
Eddie Firmani	1967-70	3(2)	20(2)
Theo Foley	1970-74	20(2)	14(3)
Andy Nelson	1974-80	7(2)	3(3)
Mike Bailey	1980-81	3(3)	3(3)
Alan Mullery	1981-82	13(2)	13(2)
Ken Craggs	1982	17(2)	17(2)
Lennie Lawrence	1982-91	5(1)	17(2)
A Curbishley/S Gritt	1991-	7(2)	7(2)

HIGHEST TRANSFER FEE PAID			
Amount	Club	Player	Date
£600,000	Chelsea	Joe McLaughlin	8/89
£430,000	Chelsea	Colin Pates	10/88
£350,000	Port Vale	Andy Jones	9/87
£324,000	Barcelona	Allan Simonsen	10/82

LONGEST LEAGUE RUNS	
of undefeated matches:	15 (4.10.80-20.12.80)
of undefeated home matches:	28 (13.4.1935-3.10.1936)
without home win:	9 (5.3.1955-20.8.1955)
of league wins:	7 (7.10.1980-1.11.1980)
of league defeats:	10 (11.4.1990-15.9.1990)
of league matches without a win:	16 (26.2.1955-22.8.1955)
of undefeated away matches:	7 (4.10.1980-6.12.1980)
	(29.12.1990-1.4.1990)
without an away win:	33 (29.3.1969-14.11.1970)
of home wins:	11 (4.12.1937-18.4.1938)
of away wins:	5 (26.1.1935-23.3.1935)

PREVIOUS LEAGUE
Southern League

BIGGEST VICTORIES
League: 8-1 v Middlesbrough, Division 1, 12.9.1953.
F.A. Cup: 7-0 v Burton Albion, Round 3, 7.1.1956.
League Cup: 5-0 v Brentford, Round 1, 12.8.1980.

BIGGEST DEFEATS
League: 1-11 v Aston Villa, Division 2, 14.11.1959.
F.A. Cup: 0-6 v Wrexham, Round 3, 5.1.1980.
League Cup: 1-7 v Blackpool, Round 2, 25.9.1963.

MOST POINTS
3 Points a win: 77, Division 2, 1985-86.
2 Points a win: 61, Division 3(S), 1934-35

MOST GOALS
107, 1957-58 (Division 2).
Summers 28, Leary 17, Ayre 11, Ryan 10, Kiernan 8, Hewie 6, Werge 6, Lucas 6, White 2, Firmani 2, Lawrie 2, Jago 1, Allen 1, og 7.
MOST GOALS IN A GAME
5. Wilson Lennox, v Exeter (A), Division 3(S), 2.2.1929 (5-2).
Eddie Firmani, v Aston Villa, Division 1, 5.2.1955 (6-1).
John Summers, v Huddersfield, Division 2, 21.12.1957 (7-6).
John Summers, v Portsmouth, Division 2, 1.10.1960 (7-4).

MOST GOALS IN A SEASON
33. Ralph Allen, 32 League, 1 FA Cup (1934-35).
4 goals once = 4; 3 goals once = 3; 2 goals 6 times = 12; 1 goal 14 times = 14. Total 33.
Previous holder: Cyril Pearce 29, (26 Lge + 3 FAC) 1933-34.

MOST FIRST CLASS MATCHES IN A SEASON
57 (42 League, 1 FA Cup, 4 League Cup, 5 Full Members Cup, 5 Play-Offs) 1986-87

MOST LEAGUE GOALS CONCEDED
120, Division 1, 1956-57

MOST LEAGUE WINS
27, Division 3S, 1934-35

MOST LEAGUE DRAWS
17, Division 2, 1969-70 & 1990-91

MOST LEAGUE DEFEATS
29, Division 1, 1956-57

OLDEST PLAYER
Sam Bartram, 42 years 48 days, v Arsenal (Div 1), 10.3.1956.

YOUNGEST PLAYER
Mark Penfold, 16 years 258 days, v York City (Div 3), 25.8.1973.

MOST CAPPED PLAYER
John Hewie (Scotland) 19

BEST PERFORMANCES BY CHARLTON ATHLETIC

League: 1934-35: Matches played 42, Won 27, Drawn 7, Lost 8, Goals for 103, Goals against 52, Points 61. First in Division 3S.

Highest: 1936-37: Second in Division 1.

F.A. Cup: 1946-47: 3rd rnd. Rochdale, 3-1; 4th rnd. West Bromwich Albion, 2-1; 5th rnd. Blackburn Rovers, 1-0; Sixth rnd. Preston North End, 2-1; Semi-Final Newcastle United, 4-0; Final Burnley, 1-0.

League Cup: 1962-63: 2nd rnd. Leicester City, 4-4, 2-1; 3rd rnd. Bradford P.A., 2-2, 1-0; 4th rnd. Orient, 2-3.

1964-65: 2nd rnd. Middlesbrough, 2-1; 3rd rnd. Orient 2-1; 4th rnd. Bradford City 0-1.

1978-79: 1st rnd. Colchester United 3-2, 0-0; 2nd rnd. Walsall, 2-1; 3rd rnd. Chesterfield, 5-4; 4th rnd. Stoke City 2-3.

1986-87: 2nd rnd. Lincoln City, 3-1, 1-0; 3rd rnd. Queens Park Rangers, 1-0; 4th rnd. Arsenal 0-2.

Full Members Cup: 1986-87: 2nd rnd. Birmingham City 3-2; 3rd rnd. Bradford City, 2-0; 4th rnd. Everton, 2-2 a.e.t., (won on penalties 6-5); Semi-Final Norwich City, 2-1 a.e.t., Final Blackburn Rovers, 0-1.

DIVISIONAL RECORDS

	Played	Won	Drawn	Lost	For	Against	Points
DIVISION 1	746	262	171	313	1082	1209	732
DIVISION 2	1352	466	352	534	2038	2253	1392
DIVISION 3	184	83	39	62	274	245	205
DIVISION 3S	420	165	109	146	622	567	439
TOTALS	2702	976	671	1055	4016	4274	2768

CHARLTON ATHLETIC

							APPEARANCES				GOALS			
PLAYERS NAME Honours	Ht	Wt	Birthdate	Birthplace Transfers	Contract Date	Clubs	League	L/Cup	FA Cup	Other	Lg	L/C	FAC	Oth
GOALKEEPERS														
Bob Bolder	6.1	14.8	02.10.85	Dover	01.03.77	Sheffield Wed	196	16	12					
				£125,000	08.08.83	Liverpool								
					16.10.85	Sunderland	22	2	3	2				
					15.08.86	Charlton Ath	222	14	11	16				
Mick Salmon	6.2	12.12	14.07.64	Leyland	16.10.81	Blackburn Rovers (A)	1							
				Loan	18.10.82	Chester City	16		2					
				Free	03.08.83	Stockport Co	118	10	3	3				
				Free	31.07.86	Bolton W	26	2	4	4				
				£18,000	07.03.87	Wrexham	100	4	4	9				
				£100,000	06.07.89	Charlton Ath	7	1	1					
DEFENDERS														
Tommy Caton	6.2	13.0	06.10.62	Kirby	09.10.79	Manchester City (A)	164+1	21	12		8			
E: u21.14,Y.4,S; UEFA Y'80; UEFA u21'82				£500,000	01.12.83	Arsenal	81	10	4		2			
				£160,000	03.02.87	Oxford Utd	50+3	8	2	2	3			
				£100,000	18.11.88	Charlton Ath	56+1	2	4	1	5			
Stephen Gatting	5.11	11.11	25.09.59	Park Royal	01.03.77	Arsenal (A)	50+8	3+1	9+1	3+1	5		1	
				£200,000	10.09.81	Brighton & H.A	313+3	14	26	13	19	1		1
				Free	16.08.91	Charlton Ath	30+2	4	3	1	1		2	
Scott Minto	5.9	10.7	06.08.71	Wirral	02.02.89	Charlton Ath	95+7	4	1+2	4	4	2		1
E: Y.1														
Darren Pitcher	5.9	12.2	12.10.69	London	12.01.88	Charlton Ath. (A)	88+2	7	4	2	5			
E: S					13.01.89	Galway Utd								
Simon Webster	6.0	11.7	20.01.64	Earl Shilton	01.12.81	Tottenham H	2+1							
				Loan	10.11.83	Exeter City	26			3				
					21.02.85	Huddersfield Town	118	7	7	2	4			
				£35,000	18.03.88	Sheffield Utd	26+11	5	5+1	3+1	3			
via Loan at Charlton to					13.09.90	Charlton Ath	87	5	4	2	5			
MIDFIELD														
John Bumstead	5.8	12.0	27.11.58	Rotherhithe		Fisher Ath								
Div2'84'89; FMC'86; ZDC'90					29.11.76	Chelsea (A)	314+25	29+5	18+1	16	38	1	3	2
				Free	22.07.91	Charlton Ath	36		3	1				
Alan Curbishley	5.10	11.7	08.11.57	Forest Gate	01.07.75	West Ham U. (A)	78+7	3	5		5			
E: u21.1,Y,S				£275,000	11.07.79	Birmingham City	128+2	12	10		11	3		
				£100,000	25.03.83	Aston Villa	34+2	5		2	1			
				£40,000	24.12.84	Charlton Ath	62+1	1	3	2	6			
				£32,000	21.08.87	Brighton & H.A	115+5	4	6	6	13		2	
				Free	03.07.90	Charlton Ath	20+5		1					
Steve Gritt	5.9	10.10	31.10.57	Bournemouth	01.07.76	Bournemouth	4+2	2			3			
				Free	02.07.77	Charlton Ath	320+27	22	16+1	11	24			1
				Free	06.07.89	Walsall	20	2	3	2	1			
				Free	20.02.90	Charlton Ath	11+15	1+1		0+1	1			
Alan Pardew	5.11	11.0	18.07.61	Wimbledon		Yeovil								
				£7,000	17.03.87	Crystal Palace	111+17	9+3	8	20	8	1	1	2
				Free	21.11.91	Charlton Ath	23+1		2		3			
Colin Walsh	5.9	11.0	22.07.62	Hamilton	16.08.79	Nottm. Forest (A)	115+24	8+5	9+2	12	32		2	3
S: u21.5, Y				£125,000	11.09.86	Charlton Ath	121+10	11	7	12	15	4		4
				Loan	02.02.89	Peterborough U	5				1			
				Loan	17.01.91	Middlesbrough	10+3		1		1			
FORWARDS														
Alex Dyer	5.11	12.0	14.11.65	Forest Gate	14.07.82	Watford (A)								
				Free	20.10.83	Blackpool	101+7	8+1	4+1	7	19	1		1
				£37,000	13.02.87	Hull City	59+1	2	4		14		1	
				£250,000	11.11.88	Crystal Palace	16+1	3+1	1+1	3+1	2			3
via Loan at Charlton to				£100,000	30.11.90	Charlton Ath	37+11	2	1	2	6		1	
Paul M Gorman	5.10	12.8	18.09.68	Macclesfield	13.07.87	Doncaster Rovers (A)	1+15	0+2	1+2	1+1	2			
via Fisher Athletic to				£15,000	01.04.91	Charlton Ath	7+9	0+1		1	5			1
Carl Leaburn	6.3	13.0	30.03.69	Lewisham	22.04.87	Charlton Ath. (A)	96+23	5	4+2	1+3	15	2		1
E: Y.1, u19				Loan	22.03.90	Northampton T	9							
Robert Lee	5.10	11.6	01.02.66	Plaistow		Hornchurch								
E:u21.2					12.07.83	Charlton Ath	267+24	16+3	14	9+2	58	1	2	3
Garry Nelson	5.10	11.10	16.01.61	Braintree	09.07.79	Southend Utd	106+23	3+1	6+2		17	1		
Div4'81				£10,000	17.08.83	Swindon Town	78+1	4	5	5	7	1		1
				£15,000	12.07.85	Plymouth A	71+3	4	7	3	20		2	
				£80,000	17.07.87	Brighton & H.A	132+12	7	7	8	48		6	6
				Loan		Notts County	0+2							
				£50,000	16.08.91	Charlton Ath	41	3	3	1	6			
ADDITIONAL CONTRACT PLAYERS														
(M) Paul Bacon	5.8	10.11	20.12.70	London	02.02.89	Charlton Ath	11+4	4		1				
Stuart Balmer						Celtic								
				£120,000	24.08.90	Charlton Ath	35+7			1				
Anthony Barness					06.03.91	Charlton Ath	16+6	2	3	1	1			
Steven Brown					03.07.90	Charlton Ath. (T)	0+1							
Kim Grant					06.03.91	Charlton Ath	11+5	1+2	0+2	0+1	2		1	
(G) Lee Harrison	6.2	11.0	12.09.71	Billericay	03.07.90	Charlton Ath. (T)								
18.11.91 Loan Fulham 1 0th App.				Loan	24.03.92	Gillingham	2							

Jermaine Darlington,   Vernon Lacey,   V Nguyen,   Danny Warden.

CHARLTON ATHLETIC

RECORD WIN & LOSS AGAINST EACH CLUB IN CURRENT DIVISION
(Where a score has occured on several occasions the most recent is given)

Club	Rec. Win	Season	Rec. Loss	Season
BARNSLEY	4-0	1958-59	7-1	1958-59
BIRMINGHAM CITY	3-1	1968-69	4-0	1967-68
BRENTFORD	3-0	1924-25	4-0	1925-26
BRISTOL CITY	5-0	1966-67	6-0	1969-70
BRISTOL ROVERS	4-0	1979-80	4-0	1924-25
CAMBRIDGE UNITED	5-2	1983-84	4-0	1981-82
DERBY COUNTY	6-1	1959-60	5-0	1950-51
GRIMSBY TOWN	5-1	1958-59 (away)	5-0	1973-74
LEICESTER CITY	5-1	1938-39 (away)	5-0	1969-70 (home)
LUTON TOWN	6-1	1961-62 (away)	7-1	1977-78
MILLWALL	3-1	1934-35	6-0	1930-31
NEWCASTLE UNITED	6-3	1949-50	6-0	1951-52
NOTTS COUNTY	6-1	1972-73	4-0	1929-30
OXFORD UNITED	3-0	1971-72	5-0	1984-85
PETERBOROUGH UTD	3-0	1974-75		
PORTSMOUTH	6-1	1959-60	5-1	1969-70
SOUTHEND UNITED	5-0	1925-26	5-0	1926-27
SUNDERLAND	5-0	1946-47	8-1	1956-57
SWINDON TOWN	6-0	1934-35	5-0	1969-70
TRANMERE ROVERS	1-0	1974-75 (away)	4-0	1972-73
WATFORD	5-2	1934-35	4-1	1986-87
WEST HAM UNITED	3-0	1987-88	7-3	1932-33
WOLVERHAMPTON WNDRS	5-1	1947-48	6-1	1936-37

MANAGERS: STEVE GRITT/ALAN CURBISHLEY

DATE OF BIRTH: (Gritt) 31.10.57   (Curbishley) 8.11.57

PLACE OF BIRTH: (Gritt) Bournemouth   (Curbishley) Essex

DATE OF APPOINTMENT: 20.7.1991

PREVIOUS CLUBS
as Manager:
as Player: (Gritt): AFC Bournemouth, Walsall
(Curbishley): West Ham, Aston Villa, Brighton, Birmingham

HONOURS
as Manager:
as Player: (Gritt): Football League XI 1988

Value Rating: * * *

Programme Editor: Steve Dixon

Price of 1992-93 Programme: £1.30
Number of Pages: 36

Subscriptions: £50 home, £45 away, £85 home & away

Local Newspapers: Kentish Times, South East London Mercury, South London Press, Croydon Advertiser, News Shopper, Greenwich Comet Leader

Books available about Club: The Long Good Friday. The Story of Charlton Athletic 1905-1990. Richard Redden (Breedon Books £16.95)

The Valiant 500, by Colin Cameson (£15.95)

LEADING LEAGUE GOALSCORERS
SEASONS 1979-80 – 1991-92

1979-80	DEREK HALES	8	1980-81	DEREK HALES	17
1981-82	PAUL WALSH	13	1982-83	DEREK HALES	14
1983-84	DEREK HALES	10	1984-85	JIM MELROSE	14
1985-86	MIKE FLANAGAN	11	1986-87	JOHN PEARSON	14
1987-88	GARTH CROOKS	10	1988-89	PAUL WILLIAMS	13
1989-90	PAUL WILLIAMS	10	1990-91	ROBERT LEE	13

1991-92	**ROBERT LEE**	**12**

THE VALLEY Floyd Road, London SE7 8BL

Capacity: TBA   **Covered Standing:** TBA   **Seating:** TBA

Charlton Athletic's home games for 1992-93 will be played at Upton Park until work at the Valley is complete

Tel: Ground: 081 293 4567   **Ticket Sales:** As ground Number   **Clubcall:** 0898 12 11 46

All premium rate calls (0898/0891) cost 36p per minute cheap rate and 48p per minute at all other times. Call costings correct at time of going to press.

GROUNDS
Siemens Meadow 1906-07, Woolwich Common 1907-08; Pound Park 1908-13; Horn Lane 1913-19; The Valley 1919-23; The Mount 1923-24; The Valley 1924-85, Selhurst Park 1985-1991

ATTENDANCES
Highest: 28,095 v Liverpool, Div 1, 23.1.1988 (at Selhurst Park)
75,031 v Aston Villa, FA Cup, 12.2.1938 (The Valley)

Lowest: 3,015 v Halifax, Div 3, 6.3.1973 (The Valley)
817 v Bradford City, Full Members Cup 3rd Rnd, 25.11.1986 (Selhurst Park)

RECORD RECEIPTS (with previous records):
£120,000 v Liverpool, Div 1, 23.1.1988 (Selhurst Park)
£52,000 v West Ham United, FA Cup 3rd Round, 5.1.86 (Selhurst Park)
£38,963 v Ipswich Town, FA Cup 3rd Round, 3.1.1983 (The Valley)

Season Tickets:
Stands: £200, juv/OAP £100
Ground: £164, juv/OAP £82

Cost of Stand Tickets: Seats: £10-£12, juv/OAP £5-£6
Terraces: £8-£9, juv/OAP £4-£5

Visitors Parking: Plans are being made to locate visitors coaches in Anchor and Hope Lane, which is five minutes walk from the ground. Car parking in the vicinity of the ground will be restricted and visitors are advised to use organised on public transport

Nearest Railway Station: Charlton

How to get to the ground

By Road: From M25 take Junction 2 (A2 London bound) and follow until road becomes A102(M). Take the turning marked 'Woolwich Ferry' and turn right along A206 Woolwich Road. This route takes you into Charlton.
By Rail: Charlton Station (British Rail main line) can be reached from Charing Cross, Waterloo (East) or London Bridge and is 2 minutes from the ground.

For directions to Upton Park please refer to Page 632

CHELSEA

Formed: 1905

Turned Professional: 1905

Ltd Co: 1905

Premier

SPONSORED BY: Commodore Business Machines

NICKNAME: The Blues

President
G M Thomson

Chairman
K W Bates

Directors
C Hutchinson (Managing)
Y Todd

Match Secretary/Safety Officer
Keith Lacy

Team Manager
Ian Porterfield

Assistant Manager
Gwyn Williams

First Team Coach
Don Howe

Youth Team Coach
Peter Nicholas

Youth Development Manager
Dave Collyer

Commercial Manager
John Shaw

Physiotherapist
Bob Ward

Members Club
Pippa Robinson

Groundsman
John Anstiss

Club Statistician for the Directory
Ron Hockings

THE inconsistency which has too frequently been a notable feature of Chelsea's history was again much in evidence, throughout a season of much frustration for the club's management and supporters.

Never likely to prove serious championship contenders, the team struggled to remain in the top half of the table for much of the time, before an indifferent run-in resulted in a disappointing final standing of 14th.

Highlights in the League programme were few and far between. Pride of place went to the 2-1 victory over Liverpool on Merseyside at the beginning of February; Chelsea's first win in that competition at Anfield since December 1935. Another satisfactory achievement was the 'double' over Tottenham Hotspur. Otherwise, there was little jam on the bread-and-butter diet, with goals in short supply.

In knock-out football fortunes were mixed. Once again, a team from a lower division, this time Tranmere Rovers, expelled Chelsea from the League Cup. Three somewhat unconvincing wins in the Zenith Data Systems Cup were followed by defeat in both legs of the semi-final against Southampton. Only, in the F.A. Cup were hopes raised. First, Hull City were beaten, without alarm, at Boothferry Park. Next Everton were sent on their way back north by a fine Clive Allen goal, followed immediately by Kevin Hitchcock's crucial save from Tony Cottee's penalty kick. Sheffield United were the victims in the fifth round, also by a 1-0 margin at The Bridge. When a similar scoreline saw Sunderland trailing in the quarter-final, hopes of a visit to Wembley in May were beginning to stir. However, John Byrne's late equaliser and an even later 88th minute winning goal from Gordon Armstrong in the replay not only dispelled any such thoughts, but also effectively ended Chelsea's season.

Frequent activity in the transfer market bore mixed fruit. Tommy Boyd, a Scottish international defender from Motherwell, never settled and returned north of the border in February. Vinnie Jones brought steel, and artistry at times, into the midfield department. But, Clive Allen, at £250,000 hailed as one of the season's bargain buys, was unexpectedly, and to most inexplicably, shunted off to West Ham United after less than four months on the payroll, having scored nine times in 22 starts. Also baffling was central defender Jason Cundy's move to Tottenham Hotspur, a loan deal to be made permanent during the summer.

So, as the curtain came down with the future of Stamford Bridge stadium still not finally determined, and with Fulham Football Club's ground-sharing scheme also in limbo, Chelsea's own playing propects pose problems. Neither Dave Beasant nor Kevin Hitchcock appear to fit the goalkeeping bill; rumours continue to circulate about Andy Townsend's future, with several clubs seemingly prepared to sign a seven-figure cheque to obtain his services; and Kerry Dixon, Tony Cascarino and Graham Stuart's striking aggregate of seven goals from 63 League games suggest a strengthening of the attack would not come amiss. This makes Allen's departure seem even more bizarre.

Scott Cheshire

Back row L-R: Graham Stuart, Gareth Hall, Damien Matthew, Kevin Hitchcock, Steve Clarke, Graeme Le Saux, Kevin McAllister (now Falkirk). **Middle row:** Eddie Niedzwiecki, Bob Ward (Physio), David Lee, Kerry Dixon, Paul Elliott, Dave Beasant, Ken Monkou, Erland Johnsen, Alan Dickens, Gwyn Williams (Asst. Manager), Dave Collyer. **Front row:** Jason Cundy, Dennis Wise, Gordon Durie, Ian Porterfield (Manager), Andy Townsend, Tommy Boyd, Kevin Wilson.

CHELSEA

DIVISION ONE: 14th   **FA CUP:** 6th RND   **RUMBELOWS CUP:** 2nd RND   **ZDS CUP:** STH. S/FINALS

M	DATE	COMP.	VEN	OPPONENTS	RESULT	H/T	LGE POS	GOALSCORERS/GOAL TIMES	ATTEN-DANCE
1	A 17	BL	H	Wimbledon	D 2-2	1-1		Elliott 36, Allon 86	22,574
2	21	BL	A	Oldham Athletic	L 0-3	0-2			(14,997)
3	24	BL	A	Tottenham Hotspur	W 3-1	2-0	12	Dixon 2, Wilson 24, Townsend 46	(34,645)
4	28	BL	H	Notts County	D 2-2	0-1	11	Elliott 54, Allon 63	15,847
5	31	BL	H	Luton Town	W 4-1	3-0	7	Le Saux 19, Townsend 32, Dixon 44, Wise 60	17,457
6	S 3	BL	A	Sheffield United	W 1-0	0-0	3	Wise 56	(17,400)
7	7	BL	A	West Ham United	D 1-1	0-0	5	Dixon 56	(18,875)
8	14	BL	H	Leeds United	L 0-1	0-0	9		23,439
9	18	BL	H	Aston Villa	W 2-0	1-0	3	Jones 22, Townsend 58	17,182
10	21	BL	H	Queens Park R.	D 2-2	0-1	5	Townsend 70, Wise 90	(19,579)
11	25	RC 2/1	H	**Tranmere Rovers**	D 1-1	0-0		**Townsend 74**	11,311
12	28	BL	H	Everton	D 2-2	0-1	5	Wilson 51, Wise 75	19,038
13	O 5	BL	A	Arsenal	L 2-3	2-1	7	Le Saux 14, Wilson 19	(42,074)
14	8	RC 2/2	A	**Tranmere Rovers**	L †1-3	0-1		**Wise 61**	(11,165)
15	19	BL	H	Liverpool	D 2-2	1-1	9	Jones 9, Myers 52	30,230
16	23	ZDS 2	H	**Swindon Town**	W 1-0	0-0		**Jones 90**	5,784
17	26	BL	A	Crystal Palace	D 0-0	0-0	10		(21,841)
18	N 2	BL	H	Coventry City	W 1-0	1-0	8	Le Saux 18	(11,343)
19	16	BL	A	Norwich City	L 0-3	0-2			15,755
20	23	BL	A	Southampton	L 0-1	0-1	12		(14,933)
21	26	ZDS 3	H	**Ipswich Town**	W †2-2	1-1		**Jones 34, Allon 85 (Won 4-3 on pens)**	6,325
22	30	BL	H	Nottingham Forest	W 1-0	0-0	11	Dixon 46	19,420
23	D 7	BL	A	Sheffield Wed.	L 0-3	0-1	11		(27,383)
24	10	ZDS S S	A	**Crystal Palace**	W 1-0	1-0		**Dixon 33**	(8,416)
25	15	BL	H	Manchester United	L 1-3	0-1	12	Allen 76	23,120
26	21	BL	H	Oldham Athletic	W 4-3	3-1	9	Wise (pen) 5, Allen 25, 90, Elliott 42	13,136
27	26	BL	A	Notts County	L 0-2	0-1	11		(11,933)
28	28	BL	A	Luton Town	L 0-2	0-2	12		(10,738)
29	J 1	BL	H	Manchester City	D 1-1	0-0	14	Allen 56	18,196
30	4	FAC 3	A	**Hull City**	W 2-0	1-0		**Jones 38, Wise 54**	(13,580)
31	11	BL	H	Tottenham Hotspur	W 2-0	1-0	12	Allen 12, Wise 70	28,628
32	18	BL	A	Wimbledon	W 2-1	1-0	8	Townsend 41, Allen 72	(8,413)
33	21	ZDS S F	A	**Southampton**	L 0-2	0-1			(8,726)
34	26	FAC 4	H	**Everton**	W 1-0	0-0		**Allen 71**	21,152
35	29	ZDS S F	H	**Southampton**	L 1-3	1-2		**Wise (pen) 37**	9,781
36	F 1	BL	A	Liverpool	W 2-1	1-1	7	Jones 21, Wise 75	(38,681)
37	8	BL	H	Crystal Palace	D 1-1	0-1	7	Cascarino 86	17,810
38	12	BL	H	Southampton	D 1-1	1-1	7	Townsend 74	7,148
39	15	FAC 5	H	**Sheffield United**	W 1-0	1-0		**Stuart 25**	34,447
40	22	BL	A	Nottingham Forest	D 1-1	0-1	8	Allen 74	(24,095)
41	26	BL	A	Manchester United	D 1-1	0-0	7	Donaghy (og) 62	(44,872)
42	29	BL	H	Sheffield Wed.	L 0-3	0-3	7		17,538
43	M 9	FAC 6	H	**Sunderland**	D 1-1	1-0		**Allen 36**	33,948
44	11	BL	A	Norwich City	W 1-0	0-0	7	Dixon 84	(13,430)
45	14	BL	H	Coventry City	L 0-1	0-0	9		10,962
46	18	FAC 6R	A	**Sunderland**	L 1-2	0-1		**Wise 85**	(26,039)
47	21	BL	H	Sheffield United	L 1-2	0-1	11	Cundy 50	11,247
48	28	BL	A	Manchester City	D 0-0	0-0	12		(23,633)
49	A 4	BL	H	West Ham United	W 2-1	1-1	9	Wise 26, Cascarino 48	20,684
50	11	BL	A	Leeds United	L 0-3	0-3	9		(31,363)
51	18	BL	H	Queens Park R.	W 2-1	1-0	11	Clarke 44, Wise (pen) 48	18,952
52	20	BL	A	Aston Villa	L 1-3	0-1	11	Sinclair 50	(19,269)
53	25	BL	H	Arsenal	D 1-1	0-0	11	Wise 81	26,003
54	M 2	BL	A	Everton	L 1-2	0-1	14	Newton 72	(20,163)

Best Home League Attendance: 30,230 v Liverpool	Smallest: 7,148 v Southampton	Av Home Att: 18,779

Goal Scorers: Compared with 90-91: -2,223

League (50):   Wise 10 (2 pens), Allen 7, Townsend 6, Dixon 5, Elliott 3, Jones 3, Le Saux 3, Wilson 3, Allon 2, Cascarino 2, Cundy, Newton
Opponents, Myers, Clarke, Sinclair

R/lows C (2):   Wise, Townsend

FA Cup (6):   Wise 2, Allen 2, Stuart, Jones

ZDS Cup (5):   Jones 2, Allon, Wise (1 pen), Dixon   † = After extra-time

1991-92

Beasant D.	Clarke S.	Boyd T.	Townsend A.	Elliot P.	Monkou K.	Le Saux G.	Hall G.	Dixon K.	Wilson K.	Wise D.	Dickens A.	Allon J.	Sinclair F.	Hitchcock K.	Johnsen E.	Myers A.	Jones V.	Matthew D.	Pearce I.	Cundy J.	Burley C.	Stuart G.	Allen C.	Cascarino A.	Barnard D.	Referee	
1	2	3	4	5	6	7	8*	9	10•	11	12	14														T Ward	1
1	2	3	4	5	6	7		9	12	11	8*	14	10•													G Singh	2
	2	3	4	5		7		9	10	11	8	S		1	6	S										P Don	3
	2	3	4	5		7*		9	10	11	8*	12		1	6		4									J Martin	4
	2	3	8	5	6	7		9	10*	11		12		1	S		4									M Pierce	5
	2	3	8	5	6	7		9	10	11		S	S	1			4									W Burns	6
	2	3	8	5	6	7		9	10*	11	S	12		1			4									J Carter	7
	2	3•	8	5	6	7		9	10*	11	14	12		1			4									R Milford	8
1	2	3	8	5	6	7		9	S	11	12	10*					4									B Hill	9
1	2	3*	8	5	6	7		9	10	11	S	12					4									R Hamer	10
1	2	3	8	5*	6	7		9	10	11		12					4									G Pooley	11
1	2	3	8	5	6	7		9	10	11	S						4					S				R Pawley	12
	2	3*	8	5	6	7		9	10	11		12		1			4					S				A Buksh	13
	2	3	8	5	6	7		9*	10•	11		12		1		14	4†									P Harrison	14
	2	3*	8	5	6	7		9•	10	11				1			4					12	14			K Redfern	15
	2	3		5		7		9*	10	11				1			4									J Rushton	16
	2	3	8	5		7*		9	10					1			4			12	S	6	11			D Axcell	17
1	2	3		5		7		9	10	11							4			8	S	6			S	K Lupton	18
1	2			5	6	7		9	10	11			3*				4	8•		14	12					P Foakes	19
	2	S		5	6	7		9	10	11	8	12		1			4									G Willard	20
	2	3*	8	5	6	7		9	10•	11	8	14		1			4					12				M Reed	21
	2	3	8	5	6	7		9		11	S			1			4					S	10			M Bodenham	22
	2	3	8	5	6	7•		9		11*				1†			4				12	14	10			T Holbrook	23
	2	3	8	5	6	7		9		11				1			4				S	S	10			J Martin	24
	2	3*	8	5	6	7		9		11				1			4				S	12	10			G Courtney	25
1	2	S	8	5	6	3		9	S	11							4					7	10			K Morton	26
1	2	14	8	5	6•	3		9	12	11							4					7*	10			I Hemley	27
1	2*	3†	8	5	6	7		9	14	11							4•					12	10			J Deakin	28
1		3	8	5	7*	2		9		11							4			6	S	12	10			J Carter	29
		3	8	5		2		9	S	11				1			4			6	S	7	10			T Fitzharris	30
			8	5	3	2		9	14	11				1			4*			6	12	7•	10			R Hart	31
		3	8	5	S	2		9	S	11				1			4			6		7	10			C Wilkes	32
		3	8	5	6	2		9	12	11				1			4			6		7*	10			R Milford	33
		3	8	5	7	2*		9	S	11				1			4			6		12	10			K Hackett	34
		3	8	5*		7			14	11*				1			4			6†	2	9	10			V Callow	35
		3	8	5	7	2			S	11				1			4			6		9	10			G Peck	36
			8*	5	3•	7			12	11				1			4			6	2	14	10	9		R Gifford	37
		3	8		6	7•			12	11*			3	1			4		5		2		10	9		P Danson	38
			8	5	7	2			14		12		3	1			4*			6		11	10•	9		K Burge	39
				5		2			14	11	12		3	1		8	4*			6		7•	10	9		J Rushton	40
			8	5	7*	2			12	11			3	1			4			6		9	10		S	V Callow	41
			8	5	7	2			12	11•			3	1			4			6		14	10	9*		D Frampton	42
			8	5	S	2		9		11	4		3	1						6		7	10		S	T Holbrook	43
1	2				6	7		9	S	S			3				4		5			11	10			D Axcell	44
1	2		8†	5*	6	7		9•	14				3				4					11	12†	10		J Martin	45
1	2		8	5		7*		9		11			3				4			6•		12	14	10		T Holbrook	46
1	2			5				9•	14	11			3*			12	4			6	8	7	10			I Borrett	47
1	2				6	7		S		11			3		5	8	4					9	10		S	B Nixon	48
1	2			5	6	7				11			3			8	4*					9	10	12		P Jones	49
1	2*		8	5	6	7•			12	11			3				4					9	10	14		N Midgley	50
1	2		8	5*	6	7		9		11			3				4	S					10	12		G Ashby	51
1	2•		8		6	7		9		11			3				4*	12					10		5	D Gallagher	52
1			8		6•	3		9	14	11			2				4	12					7*	10		R Hamer	53
1			8		6†	3		9		11			2				4	12					7*	10		J Deakin	54

Beasant D.	Clarke S.	Boyd T.	Townsend A.	Elliot P.	Monkou K.	Le Saux G.	Hall G.	Dixon K.	Wilson K.	Wise D.	Dickens A.	Allon J.	Sinclair F.	Hitchcock K.	Johnsen E.	Myers A.	Jones V.	Matthew D.	Pearce I.	Cundy J.	Burley C.	Stuart G.	Allen C.	Cascarino A.	Barnard D.		
21	31	22	35	35	31	39	9	32	15	37	6	2	8	21	6	10	35	2		12	6	20	15	11	1	League Appearances	
	1					1	1	3	7	1	4	9		1	1					2	2	7	1		3	Substitute Appearances	
1	2	2	2	2		2	2	2	2	2		0+2		1		0+1	1	1								R/lows Appearances	
1	1	2	5	5		3		4	4+1	1+1	4		1	4		2	4			5		3+2	4+1	2		FA Cup Appearances	
3	5	3	5	3		4+1	1	2+1	4	1		1+1		5		1	5		0+1	2	2	2+1	3			ZDS Cup Appearances	

Also Played: Posn.(Game): D Lee S(16)3*(20), M Gilkes 12(35)S(36)14(38), E Newton 14(54)

Players on Loan: M Gilkes (Reading)

† = Sent Off

CHELSEA

Club Colours: Royal blue shirts with white trim, blue shorts, blue stockings.
Change Colours: Red shirt with red pinstripe and blue band on collar.
Reserves League: Combination

COMPETITIONS				
Div. 1	Div. 2	ECWC	EUFA	A/Scot
07-10	05-07	70-71	65-66	75-76
12-24	10-12	71-72	68-69	76-77
30-62	24-30			77-78
63-75	62-63			
77-79	75-77			
84-87	79-84			
89-	88-89			

HONOURS					
Div. 1	Div. 2	FA Cup	Lge Cup	ECWC	C/shld
54-55	83-84	1970	1965	1971	1955
	88-89				FMC
					1986
					1990

MOST GOALS IN A CAREER				
BOBBY TAMBLING 202 (1958-70)				
Season	League	FA Cup	Lge Cup	EUFA
1958-59	1	–	–	–
1959-60	1	–	–	–
1960-61	9	–	3	–
1961-62	20	2	–	–
1962-63	35	2	–	–
1963-64	17	2	–	–
1964-65	15	4	6	–
1965-66	16	5	–	2
1966-67	21	6	1	–
1967-68	12	3	–	–
1968-69	17	1	–	2
Total	**164**	**25**	**10**	**3**

MOST APPEARANCES: RON HARRIS 791+12 (1961-80)						
Year	League	FAC	Lge C	ECWC	EUFA	A/Scot
61/62	3					
62/63	7					
63/64	41	3	1			
64/65	42	5	6			
65/66	36	6		10		
66/67	42	7	3			
67/68	40	5	1			
68/69	40	5	3		4	
69/70	30	8	3			
70/71	38	3	4	9		
71/72	41	3	9	4		
72/73	42	3	7			
73/74	36	2	1			
74/75	42	2	4			
75/76	38+2	4	1			3
76/77	15+4	2	0+1			2
77/78	37	4	1			2+1
78/79	38+2	1	1			
79/80	38+1	1	1+1			
	646+9	64	46+2	13	14	7+1

Previous holder: P Bonetti 729

MANAGERS			
Name	Seasons	Best	Worst
J T Robertson	1905-06	3(2)	3(2)
David Calderhead	1907-33	8(1)	9(2)
Leslie Knighton	1933-39	8(1)	20(1)
Billy Birrell	1939-52	13(1)	19(1)
Ted Drake	1952-62	1(1)	22(1)
Tommy Docherty	1962-67	3(1)	2(2)
Dave Sexton	1967-74	3(1)	17(1)
Ron Stuart	1974-75	21(1)	21(1)
Eddie McCreadie	1975-77	2(2)	11(1)
Ken Shellitto	1977-78	16(1)	16(1)
Danny Blanchflower	1978-79	22(1)	22(1)
Geoff Hurst	1979-81	4(2)	12(2)
John Neal	1981-85	1(2)	18(2)
John Hollins	1985-88	6(1)	18(1)
Bobby Campbell	1988-91	5(1)	1(2)
Ian Porterfield	1991-		

RECORD TRANSFER FEE RECEIVED			
Amount	Club	Player	Date
£2,200,000	Tottenham H.	Gordon Durie	8/91
£1,700,000	Leeds United	Tony Dorigo	6/91
£925,000	Everton	Pat Nevin	7/88
£825,000	Manchester Utd.	Ray Wilkins	8/79

RECORD TRANSFER FEE PAID			
Amount	Club	Player	Date
£2,100,000	Norwich City	Robert Fleck	8/92
£1,800,000	Wimbledon	Dennis Wise	7/90
£1,200,000	Norwich City	Andy Townsend	7/90
£725,000	Newcastle Utd.	Dave Beasant	1/89

LONGEST LEAGUE RUNS	
of undefeated matches:	27 (29.10.1988-15.4.1989)
of undefeated home matches:	34 (28.4.1910-24.2.1912)
without home win:	11 (30.3.1974-28.9.1974)
of league wins: 8 (5.2.1927-21.3.1927)	(15.3.1989-8.4.1989)
of league defeats:	7 (1.11.1952-20.12.1952)
of league matches without a win:	21 (3.11.1987-2.4.1988)
of undefeated away matches:	13 (5.11.1988-8.4.1989)
without an away win:	22 (1.3.1952-14.3.1953)
of home wins:	13 (12.11.1910-2.9.1911)
of away wins:	7 (4.2.1989-8.4.1989)

BIGGEST VICTORIES
League: 7-0 v Lincoln City, Division 2, 29.10.1910
7-0 v Port Vale, Division 2, 3.3.1906
9-2 v Glossop N.E., Division 2, 1.9.1906
7-0 v Portsmouth, Division 2, 21.5.1963
7-0 v Walsall (A), Division 2, 4.2.1989
F.A. Cup: 9-1 v Worksop, Round 1, 31.1.1908.
League Cup: 7-0 v Doncaster Rovers, Round 3, 16.11.1960
Europe: 13-0 v Jeunesse Hautcharage, ECWC, 29.9.1971.

BIGGEST DEFEATS
League: 1-8 v Wolverhampton Wndrs, Division 1, 26.9.1923.
0-7 v Leeds United, Division 1, 7.10.1967
0-7 v Nott'm Forest, Division 1, 20.4.1991
F.A. Cup: 0-6 v Sheffield Wed, Rnd 2 Replay, 5.2.1913.
1-7 v Crystal Palace, Round 3, 16.11.1960.
League Cup: 2-6 v Stoke City, Round 3, 22.10.1974.
Europe: 0-5 v Barcelona, Semi-Final EUFA, 25.5.1966.

MOST POINTS
3 points a win: 99, Div 2, 1988-89 (Div 2 record, 46 games)
2 points a win: 57, Div 2, 1906-07.

MOST GOALS IN A MATCH
6, George Hilsdon, v Worksop, FA Cup, (9-1), 11.1.1908.

MOST GOALS
98, Division 1, 1960-61.
Greaves 41, Tindall 16, Tambling 9, Brabrook 8, Livesey 8, Bluntstone 5, Sillett 2, Anderton 1, Bradbury 1, Bridges 1, Brooks 1, Gibbs 1, Mortimore 1, Harrison 1, og 2.

MOST GOALS IN A SEASON
Jimmy Greaves, 43, League 41, League Cup 2, 1960-61.
5 goals once = 5, 4 goals twice = 8, 3 goals three times = 9, 2 goals 4 times = 8, 1 goal 12 times = 12. Total 43.
Previous holder: Jimmy Greaves, 31, 1959-60.

MOST FIRST CLASS MATCHES IN A SEASON
60 (42 League, 6 FA Cup, 12 Fairs Cup) 1965-66
60 (42 League, 3 FA Cup, 4 League Cup, 1 Charity Shield, 10 European Cup Winners Cup) 1970-71

MOST LEAGUE GOALS CONCEDED
100, Division 1, 1960-61

MOST LEAGUE WINS
29, Division 2, 1988-89

MOST LEAGUE DRAWS
18, Division 1, 1922-23

MOST LEAGUE DEFEATS
27, Division 1, 1978-79

OLDEST PLAYER
Dick Spence 39 yrs 1 month, 1947-48.

YOUNGEST PLAYER
Ian Hamilton 16 yrs 4 months, 1966-67.

MOST CAPPED PLAYER
Ray Wilkins (England) 24

BEST PERFORMANCES BY CHELSEA

League: 1988-89: Matches played 46, Won 29, Drawn 12, Lost 3, Goals for 96, Goals against 50. Points 99. First in Division 2.

Highest: 1954-55: First in Division 1

F.A. Cup: 1969-70: 3rd rnd. Birmingham City, 3-0; 4th rnd. Burnley, 2-2, 3-1; 5th rnd. Crystal Palace, 4-1; 6th rnd. Queens Park Rangers, 4-2; Semi-Final Watford, 5-1; Final Leeds United 2-2, 2-1.

League Cup: 1964-65: 2nd rnd. Birmingham City, 3-0; 3rd rnd. Notts County, 4-0; 4th rnd. Swansea, 3-2; 5th rnd. Workington, 2-2, 2-0; Semi-Final Aston Villa, 3-2, 1-1; Final Leicester, 0-0, 3-2.

E.C.W.C: 1970-71: 1st rnd. Aris Salonica, 1-1, 5-1; 2nd rnd. CSKA Sofia, 1-0, 1-0; 3rd rnd. Bruges, 0-2, 4-0; Semi-Final Manchester City, 1-0, 1-0; Final Real Madrid, 1-1, 2-1.

EUFA: 1965-66: 1st rnd. A.S. Roma, 0-0, 4-1; 2nd rnd. Wiener S.H., 0-1, 2-0; 3rd rnd. A.C. Milan, 2-1, 1-2, 1-1*; 4th rnd. Munich 1860, 2-2, 1-0; Semi-Final Barcelona 2-0, 0-2, 0-5.
*Won on toss of a coin.

DIVISIONAL RECORDS

	Played	Won	Drawn	Lost	For	Against	Points
DIVISION 1	2360	828	619	913	3439	3754	**2377**
DIVISION 2	786	383	202	201	1323	887	**1018**
TOTALS	**3146**	**1211**	**821**	**1114**	**4762**	**4641**	**3395**

CHELSEA

PLAYERS NAME Honours	Ht	Wt	Birthdate	Birthplace Transfers	Contract Date	Clubs	League	L/Cup	FA Cup	Other	Lg	L/C	FAC	Oth
GOALKEEPERS														
Dave Beasant	6.3	13.0	20.03.59	Willesden		Edgware Town								
Div4'83; Div2'89; FAC'88; ZDC'90				£1,000	07.08.79	Wimbledon	340	21	27	3				
				£800,000	13.06.88	Newcastle Utd	20	2	2	1				
				£725,000	14.01.89	Chelsea	116	11	5	8				
Kevin Hitchcock	6.1	12.2	05.10.62	Custom House		Barking								
FRT'87					04.08.83	Nottm. Forest								
					01.02.84	Mansfield Town	182	12	10	20				
					25.03.88	Chelsea	14	1		4				
				Loan	28.12.90	Northampton T.	17							
DEFENDERS														
Steve Clarke	5.9	11.10	29.08.63	Saltcoats		St. Mirren	151	21	19	6	6		1	
S: 5, B.3, u21.8, Y, S; S.Lge.1; Div2'89				£422,000	19.01.87	Chelsea	161+2	10	8	16	6	1	1	1
Mal Donaghy	5.10	12.7	13.09.57	Belfast		Larne								
NI:56,u21.1,Div2'82,LC'88; ECWC'91				£20,000	23.06.78	Luton Town	410	34	36	3	16	2	3	
				£650,000	28.10.88	Manchester Utd	77+13	9+5	10	3+3				
				Loan	14.12.89	Luton Town	5							
				£150,000	01.08.92	Chelsea								
Paul Elliott	6.2	14.1	18.03.64	London		Charlton Ath. (A)	61+2	5	1+1		1	1		
E:B.1,u21.3,Y.6				£145,000	03.03.83	Luton Town	63+3	5	2		4			
				£400,000	04.12.85	Aston Villa	56+1	7	4	1	7			
					01.07.87	Pisa								
				£600,000	07.07.89	Celtic	52+2	5	8	1	2	3		
				£1,400,000	17.07.91	Chelsea	35	2	5	5	3			
Gareth Hall	5.10	12.0	20.03.69	Croydon	25.04.86	Chelsea	71+12	7	6	9+3	1			1
W: 7, u21.1, Div.2'89; ZDC'90														
Erland Johnsen	6.1	13.5	05.04.67	Frederikstad Norway		Bayern Munich								
ZDC'90				£306,000	01.12.89	Chelsea	30+1		4	4				
Graham Le Saux	5.10	11.2	17.10.68	Harrow	09.12.88	Chelsea (T)	67+9	6+3	6+1	8+1	8	1		
E: u21.4														
David J Lee	6.3	13.12	26.11.69	Bristol	01.07.88	Chelsea (T)	53+19	6+1	1+4	5+1	6	1		1
E: u21.1, Y.1; Div2'89				Loan	30.01.92	Reading	5				5			
				Loan	26.03.92	Plymouth A	9				1			
Frank Sinclair	5.8	11.2	03.12.71	Lambeth	17.05.90	Chelsea (T)	12		1		1			
				Loan	12.12.91	West Brom A								
MIDFIELD														
Craig Burley	6.1	11.07	24.09.71	Ayr	01.09.89	Chelsea (T)	6+3			2				
Alan Dickens	6.1	12.2	03.09.64	Plaistow	14.08.82	West Ham U	173+19	14+3	19+3	3	23	3	3	1
E:u21.1,Y5				£650,000	11.08.89	Chelsea	39+9	3		4	1			3
Vinny Jones	6.0	11.12	05.01.65	Watford		Wealdstone			0+1					
FAC'88; Div.2'90				£10,000	20.11.86	Wimbledon	77	6+2	11+2	3	9		1	
				£650,000	20.06.89	Leeds Utd	44+2	2	1	4	5			
				£700,000	13.09.90	Sheffield Utd	35	4	1	1	2			
				£575,000	30.08.91	Chelsea	35	1	4	5	3		1	2
Damian Matthew	5.11	10.10	23.09.70	Islington	13.06.89	Chelsea (T)	10+7	5		1				
E: u21.3														
Edward Newton	5.11	11.2	13.12.71	Hammersmith	17.05.90	Chelsea	0+1				1			
E: Y				Loan	23.01.92	Cardiff City	18				4			
Andy Townsend	5.11	12.7	27.07.63	Maidstone		Welling								
Ei: 17				£13,500		Weymouth			1					
				£35,000	15.01.85	Southampton	77+6	7+1	2+3	3+2	5			
				£300,000	31.08.88	Norwich City	66+5	3+1	10	3	8		2	
				£1,200,000	05.07.90	Chelsea	69	11	6	4	8	4		
FORWARDS														
Joe Allon	5.11	12.2	12.11.66	Gateshead	16.11.84	Newcastle Utd. (T)	9	1			2			
E:Y1,FAYC'85				Free	06.08.87	Swansea City	27+7	2	2	2	12			1
					29.11.88	Hartlepool Utd	112	5	6+1	7	50	2	5	2
				£200,000	14.08.91	Chelsea	2+9	0+2		1+1	2			1
				Loan	27.02.92	Port Vale	2+4							
Tony Cascarino	6.2	14.2	01.09.62	St. Pauls Cray		Crockenhil								
Ei:7; Div2'88					14.01.82	Gillingham	209+10	18	15+2	15	78	11	9	12
				£200,000	23.06.87	Millwall	105+42	10+1	8+2	5	33		1	1
				£1,500,000	16.03.90	Aston Villa	43+3	2+1	2	3	11	1		
				£1,100,000	19.07.91	Celtic								
				Swap	06.02.92	Chelsea	11		2		2			
Robert Fleck	5.7	10.8	11.08.65	Glasgow		Partick Thistle	1+1				1			
S:3,u21.7, SPD'87, SLC'87'88						Glasgow Rangers	61+24	3+5	1+1	3+4	29	2		3
				£580,000	17.12.87	Norwich City	130+13	13	16+2	7	40	11	11	4
				£2,100,000	01.08.92	Chelsea								
Mick Harford	6.2	12.9	12.02.59	Sunderland	06.07.77	Lincoln City	109+6	8	3		41	5		
E: 2, B1; LC'88				£180,000	24.12.80	Newcastle Utd	18+1				4			
				£160,000	24.08.81	Bristol City	30	5	5		11	1	2	
				£100,000	26.03.82	Birmingham City	92	10	7		25	6	2	
				£250,000	13.12.84	Luton Town	135+4	16	27	4	57	10	11	3
				£450,000	18.01.90	Derby County	58	7	1	2	15	3		
				£325,000	12.09.91	Luton Town	29	1		1	12			
				£300,000	01.08.92	Chelsea								

CHELSEA

PLAYERS NAME Honours	Ht	Wt	Birthdate	Birthplace Transfers	Contract Date	Clubs	League	L/Cup	FA Cup	Other	Lg	L/C	FAC	Oth
							APPEARANCES				**GOALS**			
Forwards cont.														
Graham Stuart	5.8	11.06	24.10.70	Tooting	15.06.89	Chelsea (T)	39+9	5	4+2	3+2	5	1	1	1
E: u21.4, Y.5, S														
Dennis Wise	5.6	9.5	15.12.66	London		Southampton (A)								
E: , B.3, u21.1; FAC'88				Free	28.03.85	Wimbledon	127+8	14	11	5	27		3	
				£1,600,000	03.07.90	Chelsea	70+1	9	5	5	20	3	2	2
ADDITIONAL CONTRACT PLAYERS														
Darren Barnard	5.10	11.0	30.11.71	Rintein (Ger.)		Wokingham Town								
					25.07.90	Chelsea	1+3							
Ian Chatfield	5.10	12.10	10.11.72	Redhill	01.07.91	Chelsea								
Andrew Myers	5.10				25.07.91	Chelsea	10+4	0+1	2	1	1			
E: Y.														
Ian Pearce	6.1		07.05.74	Bury St Edmonds	01.08.91	Chelsea (T)	0+3			0+1				
Zeke Rowe	6.0	12.8	30.10.73	Stoke Newington		Chelsea								
Neil Shipperley	5.11	13.2	30.10.74	Chatham		Chelsea								
Terry Skiverton	5.9	12.8	26.06.75	Mile End, London		Chelsea								
(F) John Spencer						Glasgow Rangers								
				£450,000	01.08.92	Chelsea								

MANAGER: IAN PORTERFIELD

DATE OF BIRTH: 11.02.1947 **PLACE OF BIRTH:** Dunfermline

DATE OF APPOINTMENT: 10.06.1991

PREVIOUS CLUBS
as Manager: Aberdeen, Reading, Rotherham, Sheff. Utd
as Asst. Man./Coach: Chelsea
as Player: Sunderland, Raith Rovers, Sheffield Wednesday

HONOURS
as Manager: Two League Championships with Rotherham & Sheff. Utd;
Aberdeen R/up Skol Cup Final
as Asst. Man./Coach: 2nd Div Championship
as Player: FA Cup Winner & League Championship with Sunderland;
Promotion with Raith Rovers and Sheff. Wed.

Value Rating: ★ ★ ★ ★

Price of 1992-93 Programme: £1.50-£2

Number of Pages: 64

Subscriptions: £42.00 (UK postage) for members per season. £42.00 (UK postage) for non-members per season. All league & any FA Cup, Littlewoods Cup & Zenith Data Cup

Local Newspapers: Fulham Chronicle, West London Observer, Chelsea News.

Local Radio Stations: LBC (away games only). (261 medium wave).

LEADING LEAGUE GOALSCORERS
SEASONS 1979-80 – 1991-92

1979-80	CLIVE WALKER	13		1980-81	COLIN LEE	15
1981-82	CLIVE WALKER	16		1982-83	MIKE FILLERY	9
1983-84	KERRY DIXON	28		1984-85	KERRY DIXON	10
1985-86	KERRY DIXON	24		1986-87	KERRY DIXON	14
					DAVID SPEEDIE	14
1987-88	GORDON DURIE	12		1988-89	KERRY DIXON	25
1989-90	KERRY DIXON	20		1990-91	GORDON DURIE	12
			1991-92	DENNIS WISE	10	

STAMFORD BRIDGE Fulham Road, London SW6 1HS

Capacity: 37,633   **Covered Standing:** 20,708   **Seating:**

Tel: Ground: 071 385 5545   **Ticket Sales:** 0898 12 10 11   **Clubcall:** 0898 12 11 59

All premium rate calls (0898/0891) cost 36p per minute cheap rate and 48p per minute at all other times. Call costings correct at time of going to press.

ATTENDANCES
Highest: 82,905 v Arsenal, Div 1, 12.10.1935

Lowest: 4,767 v Plymouth Argyle, Simod Cup, 9.11.1988

RECORD RECEIPTS (with previous records):
£212,894 v Arsenal, Div 1, 30.9.1989
£170,797 v Liverpool, Div 1, 30.4.1988
£169,326 v Manchester United, Div 1, 26.10.1985
£161,218 v Manchester United, 26.10.1984
£158,227 v Tottenham Hotspur, 6.3.1982
£147,225 Orient v Arsenal, 8.4.1978
£110,000 Southampton v Crystal Palace, 3.4.1976
£72,771 Ipswich v West Ham, 9.4.1975
£34,125 v Manchester City, 14.4.1971

STAMFORD BRIDGE
First game: v Liverpool (friendly) 4-0, 4.9.1905
First floodlit game: v Sparta, 19.3.1951
Internationals: England v Scotland, 1913
England v Wales, 1929
England v Austria, 1932

Season Tickets:
Stands: from £189 to £433, juv/OAP £139 to £210
Ground: £165, juv/OAP £115

Executive Club Season Tickets: Apply to club

Cost of Stand Tickets: (All prices are for catorgory A, B
& C games) East Stand Middle £15, £25, £30; East Stand
Upper £12, £17, £25; East Stand Lower (members only)
£10, £10, £12; West Stand £10, £13, £20; Family Section
(1 adult, 1 child) £10, £10, £12; Terrace £7, £8, £10;
Members Enclosure £7, £8, £8

Match and Ticket Information: Personal & credit card
postal bookings are accepted in advance. Club
membership available only by completing a membership
application form available from club. Membership £22
(£20 juvenile/OAP), Family Membership from £30 (1
adult + 1 juvenile)

Car Parking: Street parking only, very limited

Nearest Tube Station: Fulham Broadway (District Line)

How to get to the ground

From North: From Motorway M1 and A1. Follow signs
Central London to Hyde Park Corner, then follow signs
Guildford (A3) into Knightsbridge A4. In 1m turn left A308
into Fulham Road for Chelsea FC

From East: Via Hyde Park Corner as above or via
Embankment and Cheyne Walk A3212. Follow signs
Chelsea A322C then at crossroads turn left A308 into
Fulham Road for Chelsea FC

From South: Use A13 or A24 then A219 to cross Putney
Bridge. Follow signs West End A304, then join A308 into
Fulham Road for Chelsea FC

From West: From Motorway M4. Follow signs Central
London, then Westminster A3220. In 0.8m at crossroads
turn right A308 into Fulham Road for Chelsea FC

CHESTER CITY

Division 2

Formed: 1884   **Turned Professional:** 1902   **Ltd Co:** 1909

SPONSORED BY: Corbett Bookmakers   **NICKNAME:** The Blues

President
R Rowlands

Chairman
R H Crofts

Directors
P Russell
W D MacDonald
N A MacLennon
H McNally

Secretary
R A Allan (0244 371376/371809)

Team Manager
Harry McNally

Assistant Manager
Graham Barrow

Commercial Manager
Miss A Walker (0244 390243)

Groundsman
Gary Kent

Club Doctors
Dr M Swallow
Dr J Kane

Club Statistician for the Directory
John Martin

CITY ended the season five points clear of the relegation zone, although their fate was not decided until the last game of the campaign, with Bury's defeat at Preston making the victory over Leyton Orient academic.

The fact that City escaped relegation is an amazing achievement in itself as at the turn of the year they were anchored at the foot of the table adrift from their nearest rivals. A remarkable run of just four defeats in the last twenty-two League games is a credit to the hard work and determination that the players put in and is just reward for the loyal fans who made the eighty mile round trip to Macclesfield during the past two seasons.

The season opened with a win against Fulham at The Moss Rose and things looked quite promising as Swansea were also beaten 2-0 in the second League game at home at the end of August. Unfortunately no games were won throughout the month of September and the team slumped towards the bottom of the table, in fact only two other League victories were gained before Christmas, against Stockport away (4-0) and Preston at home (3-2). By the time that Christmas came the team were rooted at the foot of the table before that remarkable run during the second half of the season ensured survival in Division Three.

During that run some notable victories were gained against Preston at Deepdale (3-0) and Stoke at The Victoria ground (1-0) whilst a 3-2 win over Stockport at Moss Rose gave City the 'double' over their Cheshire neighbours who narrowly missed promotion in the play-offs.

Away from the League Lincoln were defeated over two legs in the First Round of the Rumbelows League Cup before Manchester City ended 'The Blues' hopes in Round 2 with a 6-1 aggregate score. In the F.A. Cup F.A. Vase finalists Guiseley were the opponents at Moss Rose. A Graham Barrow goal clinched the tie. However, in Round 2 Crewe won 2-0 at Gresty Road. The Autoglass Trophy did not provide City with any success, as after beating Darlington 2-1 in the Preliminary Round a visit to Rotherham in the First Round proper proved to be a real let down – 3-0 to the Yorkshire club being the final score.

It was the League form that was to be the most important to the club and ensured that City will return from their two year exile at Macclesfield to a new purpose-built ground back in Chester in the new Football League Division Two.

John Martin

Back row L-R: David Pugh, Barry Butler, Graham Abel, Billy Stewart, Barry Siddall, Chris Lightfoot, Spencer Whelan, Gary Bennet, Joe Hinnigan. **Front row:** Albert Albiston, Paul McGuinness, Brian Croft, Harry McNally (Manager), Ray Croft (Chairman), Graham Barrow (Asst. Manager), Roger Preece, Eddie Bishop.

CHESTER CITY

DIVISION THREE: 18th   **FA CUP:** 2nd RND   **RUMBELOWS CUP:** 2nd RND   **AUTOGLASS:** 1st RND

M	DATE		COMP.	VEN	OPPONENTS	RESULT		H/T	LGE POS	GOALSCORERS/GOAL TIMES	ATTEN-DANCE
1	A	17	BL	H	Fulham	W	2-0	1-0		Lightfoot 43, Bennett 79	1,444
2		20	RC 1/1	H	Lincoln City	W	1-0	0-0		Barrow 55	1,018
3		23	BL	A	Wigan Athletic	L	1-2	1-0		Rimmer 11	(2,637)
4		28	RC 1/2	A	Lincoln City	L	†3-4	1-1		Bennett 18, Rimmer 82, 106	(2,170)
5		31	BL	H	Swansea City	W	2-0	0-0	7	Abel 57, Morton 72	1,127
6	S	4	BL	A	Huddersfield Town	L	0-2	0-1	8		(5,321)
7		7	BL	H	Bournemouth	L	0-1	0-0	13		1,117
8		14	BL	A	Bradford City	D	1-1	1-0	14	Bishop 44	(4,843)
9		17	BL	A	Birmingham City	L	2-3	2-2	19	Bishop 10, Rimmer 16	(8,154)
10		21	BL	H	West Bromwich A.	L	1-2	1-1	20	Barrow 44	3,895
11		24	RC 2/1	A	Manchester City	L	1-3	0-0		Bennett 68	(10,987)
12		28	BL	A	Torquay United	L	2-3	1-2	21	Bishop 38, Rimmer 74	(2,062)
13	O	5	BL	H	Stoke City	D	0-0	0-0	21		4,212
14		8	RC 2/2	H	Manchester City	L	0-3	0-1			4,146
15		12	BL	A	Leyton Orient	L	0-1	0-1	21		(4,049)
16		18	BL	A	Stockport County	W	4-0	1-0	19	Bennett 3 (44, 47, 76), Rimmer 87	(4,820)
17		26	BL	H	Bolton Wanderers	L	0-1	0-0	20		1,867
18	N	2	BL	H	Preston North End	W	3-2	1-0	19	Rimmer 38, 68, Bishop 47	1,219
19		5	BL	A	Peterborough Utd	L	0-2	0-2	20		(2,810)
20		9	BL	A	Hull City	L	0-1	0-1	21		(4,305)
21		16	FAC 1	H	Guiseley	W	1-0	1-0		Barrow 24	1,851
22		19	AGT Pre	A	Crewe Alexandra	L	1-2	0-1		Lightfoot 56	(1,779)
23		23	BL	A	Reading	D	2-2	1-1	22	Rimmer 6, Abel 71	1,124
24		30	BL	A	Exeter City	D	0-0	0-0	23		(3,235)
25	D	7	FAC 2	A	Crewe Alexandra	L	0-2	0-0			(5,299)
26		14	BL	H	Shrewsbury Town	L	1-4	1-1	24	Morton 13	1,016
27		26	BL	A	Swansea City	L	0-3	0-2	24		(4,098)
28		28	BL	A	Fulham	D	2-2	0-0	24	Abel 77, 79	(3,708)
29	J	1	BL	H	Huddersfield Town	D	0-0	0-0	24		3,504
30		4	BL	H	Darlington	L	2-5	2-2	24	Cornstive 9, Tait (og) 43	1,020
31		7	AGT Pre	H	Darlington	W	2-1	2-0		Morton 29, Bennett 36	416
32		11	BL	A	Hartlepool United	L	0-1	0-0	24		(3,088)
33		18	BL	H	Brentford	D	1-1	0-1	24	Butler 50	1,447
34		21	AGT 1	A	Rotherham United	L	0-3	0-2			(2,543)
35	F	8	BL	H	Bolton Wanderers	D	0-0	0-0	24		6,609
36		11	BL	H	Exeter City	W	5-2	3-1	24	Butler 9, 18, Rimmer 16, Abel 54, Cornstive 90	871
37		15	BL	A	Shrewsbury Town	D	2-2	2-1	24	Rimmer 4, Lightfoot 10	(2,807)
38		18	BL	A	Wigan Athletic	W	1-0	0-0	22	Rimmer 76	1,065
39		22	BL	H	Hartlepool United	W	2-0	2-0	22	Butler 4, 25	1,072
40		25	BL	A	Bury	W	2-1	2-1	20	Lightfoot 25, Bennett 41	(2,283)
41		29	BL	A	Darlington	D	1-1	0-0	20	Rimmer 85	(2,579)
42	M	3	BL	A	Brentford	L	0-2	0-1	20		(6,869)
43		7	BL	H	Bury	W	3-1	1-1	20	Bennett 45, 78, Abel 70	1,228
44		10	BL	H	Peterborough Utd	L	2-4	1-1	20	Butler 40, Abel 84	1,063
45		14	BL	A	Preston North End	W	3-0	2-0	18	Rimmer 8, Bennett 26, 71	(3,909)
46		21	BL	H	Hull City	D	1-1	1-0	20	Cornstive 39	1,269
47		24	BL	H	Stockport County	W	3-2	1-0	19	Abel 6, 81, Bennett 52	3,747
48		28	BL	A	Reading	D	0-0	0-0	19		(2,813)
49		31	BL	H	Bradford City	D	0-0	0-0	20		1,149
50	A	3	BL	A	Bournemouth	L	0-2	0-1	20		(5,974)
51		11	BL	H	Birmingham City	L	0-1	0-0	19		4,895
52		18	BL	A	West Bromwich A.	D	1-1	1-0	19	Abel 32	(10,137)
53		20	BL	H	Torquay United	W	2-0	1-0	19	Rimmer 42, Lightfoot 58	1,317
54		25	BL	A	Stoke City	W	1-0	0-0	18	Bennett 59	(18,474)
55	M	2	BL	H	Leyton Orient	W	1-0	0-0	18	Barrow 85	2,008

Best Home League Attendance: 4,895 v Birmingham City   **Smallest:** 871 v Exeter City   Av Home Att: 1,855

Goal Scorers: Compared with 90-91: +255

League (56):   Rimmer 13, Bennett 11, Abel 10, Butler 6, Lightfoot 4, Bishop 4, Cornstive 3, Barrow 2, Morton 2, Opponents

R/lows C (5):   Bennett 2, Rimmer 2, Barrow
FA Cup (1):   Barrow
Autoglass (3):   Lightfoot, Bennett, Morton

† = After extra-time

1991-92

Stewart W.	Whelan S.	Albiston A.	Butler B.	Abel G.	Lightfoot C.	Bishop E.	Barrow G.	Rimmer S.	Bennett G.	Pugh D.	Comstive P.	Morton N.	Preece R.	Siddall B.	Croft B.	McGuinness P.	Nolan D.	Limbert	Allen A.	Knop	Referee	#
	2	3	4*	5	6	7	8	9	10	11				1	S	12					R Dilkes	1
	2	3	4	5	6	7	8	9	10	11				1	S	S					J Kirby	2
	2	3	4	5	6	7	8	9	10	11•				1	14	S					T West	3
1	2	3	4*	5	6	7	8	9	10	11•					S	12					W Burns	4
1	2	3	4	5	6	7	8	9	10*	11	14					12					G Singh	5
1	2	3	4*	5	6	7	8	9	12			10•			11	14					T Lunt	6
1	2	3	4*	5	6	7	8	9	12	14		10•			11						M Brandwood	7
1	2	3	4	5	6	7	8	9	10*		S				12	11					R Hart	8
1	2	3	4	5	6	7	8	9	10•			14	S		11						A Bennett	9
1		3	4	5	6	7	8	9	10	2		S			11	S					H King	10
1		3	12	5	6	7*	8	9	10	4		14			11•	2					S Bell	11
1		3	8	5	6		7	9*	10	4	11	12			2		S				M Pierce	12
1	6	3	12	5*		7	8		10	4	9				11	2			S		A Dawson	13
1	6	3	12	5		7	8		10	4	9*				11	2			S		J Rushton	14
1	2	3	6	5		7		9	10	4	12				11*	8			S		P Scoble	15
1	2	3	S	5	6	7	8	9	10	4	S				11						I Cruikshank	16
1	2•	3	14	5	6	7	8	9	10*	4	12				11						R Pawley	17
1	2	3	14	5	6	7	8	9	10*	4•	12				11						D Phillips	18
1	2	3	4*	5*	6	7	8	9				10	12		11	14					I Borrett	19
1	2	3	S	5	6	7	8	9	10•	4					11				14		B Coddington	20
	2	3	4	5	6	7	8	9	10*				12	1	11		S				T West	21
	2	3	4	5	6	7	8	9	S				10	1	11		S				T Fitzharris	22
	2	3	4	5	6	7	8	9	10*				12	1	11		S				M Reid	23
1	2	3	14	5	6	7	8	9	10•	4					11*						J Carter	24
1	2	3		5	6	7	8	9*	10	4	12				11		S				J Kirby	25
1	2	3	12	5	6	7	8		10	4	9		S		11*						K Cooper	26
	2	3	11•	5	6	7*	8	9	10	4	12			1	14						R Groves	27
1	2	3		5	6	S	8	9	10	4	7•				11	14					P Foulkes	28
1	2	3		5	6	S	8	9	10	4	7•		11		14						M Brandwood	29
1	3*	2		5	6		8	9	10	4	7•		11		14	12					P Dawson	30
1			12	5	6		8	9	7		4	10	2		11		3*	S			R Shepherd	31
1			S	5	6		8	9	11	3	4	10•	2		14		7				S Bell	32
1			9	5	6		8	10	7	3	4	12	2		11*		S				V Callow	33
1			9	5	6		8	10	7*	3	4	12	2		11		S				L Dilkes	34
1	S	3	9	5	6		8	10	7*	11	4		2		12						K Redfern	35
1		3	9	6	5		8	10	7		4		S	2	S						P Harrison	36
1	14	3	9	6	5•		8	10	7	11	4				12						G Poll	37
1	5	3	9*		6		8	10	7•	11	4	14	2			12					R Poulain	38
1	5	3	9	S	6		8	10	7		4	11	2			S					K Hackett	39
1	5	3	9*	12	6		8	10	7	11	4		S	2		12					A Bennett	40
1	5•	3	9	14	6		8	10	7*	11	4	12	2								T West	41
1	5	3	9	14	6•		8	10	7*	11	4	12	2								A Pierce	42
1	5	3	9•	12	6		8	10	7	11	4		14	2							J Kirby	43
1	5	3	9*		6		8	10	7	11•	4	12	2			14					D Allison	44
1	2	3	9	5	6			10	7	11	4		12		8*	S					Shadwell	45
	2	3	9	5	6			10		11	4	12	8	1	7*						I Hemley	46
1	2•	3	9	5	6			10	7	11	4	14	8		S						P Wright	47
	S	3	9	5	6			10	7	11	4	12	2	1							P Don	48
	14	3	9*	5	6			10	7•	11	4	12	2	1							E Parker	49
	S	3	9*	5	6			10	7	11	4	12	2	1							M James	50
		3	9*	5	6			10	7*	11	4	12	2	1	14						J Key	51
1	2		9*	5	6			10	7	11	4		8		12	S					D Frampton	52
1		3	9	5	6		8•	10	7	11	4	14	2		S						C Trussell	53
1		3	9	5	6	S	8	10	7	11	4		2		S						K Pawley	54
1		3	9	5	6	7•	8	10		11	4*	14	2		12						V Callow	55
37	30	44	36	40	44	21	40	44	40	33	28	12	26	9	18	3	1				**League Appearances**	
	2			5	4					2	2		22	3		14	4		1		**Substitute Appearances**	
3	3	4	2+2	3	4	4	4	3	4	4		1+1		1	2	2+1					**R/lows Appearances**	
1	2	2	1	2	2	2	2	2	2		1	0+2		1	2						**FA Cup Appearances**	
2	1	1	2+1	3	3	1	3	3	2	1	2	2	2	1	3		1				**Autoglass Appearances**	

CHESTER CITY

Club Colours: Royal blue shirts, white shorts and blue stockings
Change Colours: Gold shirts, black shorts, black stockings
Reserves League: Lancashire League

Previous League: Cheshire League
Previous Name: Chester until 1983
Previous Managers: 1930-36 Charles Hewitt 1936-38 Alex Raisbeck 1938-53 Frank Brown 1953-56 Louis Page 1956-59 John Harris 1959-61 Stan Pearson 1961-63 Bill Lambton 1963-68 Peter Hauser 1968-76 Ken Roberts 1976-82 Alan Oakes 1982 Cliff Sear* 1982-83 John Sainty* 1983-85 John McGrath
* Includes period as caretaker manager
Honours: Welsh Cup Winners (3) Debenhams Cup Winners 1977 Division 3(N) Cup Winners 1935-36, 1936-37
League Career: Elected to Div 3N 1931 Relegated to Div 4 1957-58 Promoted to Div 3 1974-75
Relegated to Div 4 1981-82 Promoted to Div 3 1985-86

CLUB RECORDS

Most Appearances for Club: Trevor Storton (1974-84): League 396, FA Cup 23, League Cup 28, Football League Trophy 3, Group Cup 3 **Total 453**
(League Appearances only): Ray Gill (1951-62), 408
Most Capped Player: Bill Lewis, 7 Wales **For England:** None
Record Goalscorer in a Match: T Jennings, 5 v Walsall, 5-1, Div 3(N), 30.1.1932 Barry Jepson, 5 v York City, 9-2, Div 4, 8.2.1958
Record League Goalscorer in a Season: Dick Yates 36, Div 3N, 1946-47 **In All Competitions:** Dick Yates, 44 (League 36, Others 8) 1946-47
Record League Goalscorer in a Career: Gary Talbot 83, 1963-66 **In All Competitions:** Gary Talbot 100 (League 83, Cups 17) 1963-67 & 1968-70
Record Transfer Fee Received: £300,000 from Liverpool for Ian Rush, May 1980
Record Transfer Fee Paid: £120,000 to Barnsley for Stuart Rimmer, August 1991
Best Performances: League: 5th Div 3, 1977-78 **FA Cup:** 5th Round Replay, 1976-77, 1979-80 **League Cup:** Semi-final 1974-75
Welsh Cup: Winners (3)
Most League Points: (3pts a win) 84, Div 4, 1985-86 (2pts a win) 57, Div 4, 1974-75
Most League Goals: 119, Div 4, 1964-65 (In this season 4 players scored 20 goals or more, the only occasion this has ever happened in the Football League. The 119 goals were shared between just 8 players
Record League Victory and Most Goals Scored in a League Match: 12-0 v York City, Div 3N, 1.2.1936
Record Cup Victory and Most Goals Scored in a Cup Tie: 6-1 v Darlington, FA Cup 1st Round, 1933-34 5-0 v Crew Alex., FA Cup Round 1, 1964-65 5-0 v Runcorn (a), FA Cup Round 1 Replay, 28.11.1978
Record League Defeat: 0-9 v Barrow, Div 3(N), 10.2.1934 2-11 v Oldham Athletic, Div 3N, 19.1.1952
Record Cup Defeat: 0-7 v Blackburn Rovers, FA Cup Round 2, 1890-91 2-9 v Leyton Orient, League Cup Rnd 3, 1962-63
Oldest Player in a League Match: Graham Barrow 37 years 294 days v L. Orient 2.5.1992 (still playing)
Youngest Player in a League Match: Aidan Newhouse, 15 years 350 days v Bury, 7.5.1988

LONGEST LEAGUE RUNS	
of undefeated matches: 18 (1934-35)	of league matches without a win: 26 (1961-62)
of undefeated home matches: 27 (1973-75)	of undefeated away matches: 12 (1939-46)
without home win: 13 (1961-62)	without an away win: 29 (1971-72, 1977-78)
of league wins: 8 (1934, 1936, 1978)	of home wins: 10 (1932, 1963-64)
of league defeats: 7 (1955, 1956, 1982)	of away wins: 4 (1934, 1936)

CHESTER CITY

PLAYERS NAME / Honours	Ht	Wt	Birthdate	Birthplace / Transfers	Contract Date	Clubs	APPEARANCES League	L/Cup	FA Cup	Other	GOALS Lg	L/C	FAC	Oth
GOALKEEPERS														
Billy Stewart	5.11	11.7	01.01.65	Liverpool	05.01.83	Liverpool (A)								
				Free	02.07.84	Wigan Ath	14			1				
				Free	11.08.86	Chester City	223	17	17	18				
DEFENDERS														
Graham Abel	6.2	13.0	17.09.60	Runcorn		Runcorn								
NPL'81, All.Prem'82, FAT'84						Northwich Victoria			3+2					
				£3,000	31.10.85	Chester City	259+4	16	20	23	29	1	2	
Paul Comstive	6.1	12.7	12.11.61	Southport	19.10.79	Blackburn Rovers	3+3							
WC86				Loan	23.09.82	Rochdale	9	1			2			
				Free	03.08.83	Wigan Ath	35	5	4	1	2			
				Free	22.11.84	Wrexham	95+4	3+3	6	11	8			2
				£8,000	07.08.87	Burnley	81+1	8	2	11	17	3		3
				£37,500	20.09.89	Bolton W	42+7	6	3+1	6+2	3	1	1	
				£10,000	27.11.91	Chester City	28		1	2	3			
Joe Hinnigan	6.1	12.7	03.12.55	Liverpool		South Liverpool								
NPL'75				£1,000		Wigan Ath	66	4	10		10			
				£80,000	20.02.80	Sunderland	63	1	1		4			
				£15,000	24.12.82	Preston N.E	51+1	3	1	3	8	2		
				Free	17.08.84	Gillingham	99+4	8	8	8	7		1	1
				Free	05.08.87	Wrexham	28+1	1	2	2	1		1	
				Free	13.08.88	Chester City	52+2	4	2	3	2			1
Chris Lightfoot	6.1	12.00	01.04.70	Warrington	11.07.88	Chester City (T)	161+12	11+2	9+2	6+2	15	1		3
Spencer Whelan						Liverpool (T)								
					03.04.90	Chester City	39+4	3	3	1				
MIDFIELD														
Graham Barrow	6.2	13.7	13.06.54	Chorley		Altrincham				7				
FRT'85; APL'80,81; APL LgC'81				£10,000	27.07.81	Wigan Ath	173+6	11	13	14	36	3		5
				£6,000	04.08.86	Chester City	202	14	15+2	16	15	2	1	2
Eddie Bishop	5.11	12.0	28.11.62	Liverpool		Winsford Utd								
LDC'90						Northwich Victoria								
via Altrincham (1 FAC App + 1 G) & Runcorn to					17.03.88	Tranmere Rovers	46+30	8+3	2+2	2+4	19	3		
				£70,000	28.12.90	Chester City	40	4	2	1	11			
				Loan	19.03.92	Crewe Alexandra	2	1						
Barry Butler	6.2	13.0	04.06.62	Farnworth		Atherstone L.R.								
					20.12.85	Chester City	225+12	10+2	19	23+1	15		1	
Brian Croft	5.9	11.6	27.09.67	Chester	23.07.86	Chester City (T)	36+23	1	2+3	7+3	3		1	
				£10,000	18.11.88	Cambridge Utd	12+5		3	3	2		2	1
				£3,000	17.08.89	Chester City	90+24	7	10	9+1	3	2	3	
Roger Preece	5.9	10.4	09.06.69	Much Wenlock		Coventry City								
				Free	15.08.86	Wrexham	89+21	2+1	5	8+1	12			1
				Free	14.08.90	Chester City	61+3	4		3				
David Pugh	5.10		19.09.64	Liverpool		Runcorn			2+2				1	
				£35,000		Chester City	97+10	9	5+1	6	6			
Dave Thompson	5.9	11.6	27.05.62	Manchester	26.09.81	Rochdale	147+8	7	7+1	6	13			
				22.08.86	Notts County	52+3	3+1	3	2	8			
				£35,000	20.10.87	Wigan Ath	107+1	5	3+1	6	16	2		1
				01.08.90	Preston N.E	39+7	1+1		3	4			
				Free		Chester City								
FORWARDS														
Gary M Bennett	6.1	12.6	20.09.63	Liverpool	09.10.84	Wigan Ath	10+10		1	3+1	3			1
FRT'85				Free	22.08.85	Chester City	109+17	6+4	8+1	10	36	1	5	5
					11.11.88	Southend Utd	36+6	4	1	2+1	6	4		
				£20,000	01.03.90	Chester City	71+9	8	5	4	15	2	1	1
John Kelly	5.10	10.9	20.10.60	Bebbington	10.09.79	Tranmere Rovers	55+9	7	1		9		2	
				08.10.81	Preston N.E	120+10	11	4	3	27	2	1	
				12.08.85	Chester City	85	6	8	6	17		2	1
				24.06.87	Swindon Town	3+4	1			1			
				13.11.87	Oldham Ath	51+1	4	1	1	6			
				£35,000	09.08.89	Walsall	36+3	1+1	4	5+1	1			2
				Loan	22.03.90	Huddersfield Town	9+1				1			
				Free	14.02.91	Huddersfield Town	16+2		1	3+2				
				Free		Chester City								
Niel Morton	5.9	10.7	21.12.68	Congleton	25.09.87	Crewe Alexandra	18+13	0+3	0+1	0+2	1			
via Northwich Vic. (1 FAC App) to				£50,000	05.10.90	Chester City	43+25	2+1	2+3	4	9			2
Stuart Rimmer	5.8	11.0	12.10.64	Southport	15.10.82	Everton (A)	3							
E: Y.3				£10,000	19.03.85	Chester City	110+4	6	4+3	11+1	67	6		3
				£205,000	18.03.88	Watford	10	0+1			1	1		
				£200,000	10.11.88	Notts County	3+1		2	3	2			
				£150,000	02.02.89	Walsall	85+3	6	5	7	31	4	2	7
				£150,000		Barnsley	10+5			1	1			
				£150,000	15.08.91	Chester City	44	3	2	3	13	2		
ADDITIONAL CONTRACT PLAYERS														
Andrew Allen			04.09.74	Liverpool		Chester City	0+1							
Ross Greer			23.09.57	Perth (Aus)	16.11.89	Chester City	2		1	1				
Darren Ryan					23.10.90	Shrewsbury Town	3+1			0+1				
				Free		Chester City								

Richard Callaway, Michael Carroll, Chris Davies, David Edwards, Adrian Jones, Shane Jones.

LEADING LEAGUE GOALSCORERS SEASONS 1985-86 – 1991-92

1985-86	STUART RIMMER	16	1986-87	GARY BENNETT	13
1987-88	STUART RIMMER	25	1988-89	CARL DALE	22
1989-90	CARL DALE	9	1990-91	CARL DALE	10

1991-92	STUART RIMMER	13

DEVA STADIUM Bumpers Lane, Chester, Cheshire

Capacity: 6,000   **Covered Standing:** 2,640   **Seating:** 3,094

Tel: Ground: 0244 371376   **Ticket Sales:** 0244 373829

ATTENDANCES
Highest: 20,500 v Chelsea, FA Cup Round 3 Replay, 16.1.1952 (Sealand Rd)

Lowest: 409 v Bury, Leyland Daf Cup, 27.11.1990

Record Receipts: £26,616 v Sheffield Wednesday, FA Cup Round 4, 31.1.1987 (Sealand Rd)

DEVA STADIUM
First game: v Stockport Co., Rumbelows Cup, 25.8.1992
First floodlit game: As above

Season Tickets:
Stands: £147, juv/OAP £115.50
Ground: £105, juv/OAP £84

Cost of Stand Tickets: £7, juveniles/OAP £5.50
Terraces: £5, juveniles/OAP £4
Family enclosure (seated): 1 adult + 1 juv £10.50, additional juv £3.50

Car Parking: Parking at the ground

Nearest Railway Station: British Rail, Chester (0244 340170)

How to get to the ground

From North: Use motorway M56, A41 or A56 S.P. Chester into Town Centre, then follow signs Queensferry A548 onto Sealand Road, turn into Bumpers lane for Chester City F.C.

From East: Use A54 or A51 S.P. Chester into Town Centre, then follow signs Queensferry A548 into Sealand Road, turn into Bumpers Lane for Chester City F.C.

From South: Use A41 or A483 S.P. Chester Town Centre then follow signs Queensferry A548 into Sealand Road, turn into Bumpers Land for Chester City F.C.

From West: Use A55, A494 or A548 S.P. Chester, then follow signs Queensferry. Follow signs Birkenhead A494 then in 1.2m branch left to join A548 Chester into Sealand Road, turn into Bumpers Lane for Chester City F.C.

Value Rating: ★ ★ ★

Programme Editor: John Martin

Price of 1992-93 Programme: 80p
Number of Pages: 32, Size A
Subscriptions: Available on request (0244 371376)

Local Newspapers: Chester Chronicle, Evening Leader

Local Radio Stations: Radio Merseyside, Marcher Sound Radio

CHESTERFIELD

Division 3

Formed: 1866   **Turned Professional:** 1891   **Ltd Co:** 1871

SPONSORED BY: Coalite   **NICKNAME:** The Spireites

President
His Grace The Duke of Devonshire
MC,DL,JP

Vice-Presidents
P C J T Kirkman OBE

Hon. Life Member
A G Sutherland

Chairman
J Norton Lea

Vice-Chairman
B W Hubbard

Directors
J A Plant, J.P.
R F Pepper   R Brealey

Secretary
Nicola Hodgson (0246 209765)

Manager
Chris McMenemy

Assistant Manager
Dave Rushbury

Physiotherapist
Dave Rushbury

Club Doctors
Dr M Bradley
Dr M Blagden

Commercial Manager
Jim Brown

A quick look at the club's match by match performances last season will immediately show where their weakness lay.

Considering the lack of fire power, the defence must take great credit in keeping Chesterfield in mid-table for the whole season and the consistent performances of Dyche, Brien and McGugan gave the team a certain stability.

Vital goals were scored by leading marksman Steve Norris (10), who had enjoyed such a spectacular season at Halifax Town in the previous campaign, but he couldn't help in the cup ties where a total of three goals spread evenly over the three competitions meant immediate elimination. The fact that Stoke City, Darlington and Bury were the opposition probably made the club's failure even more disappointing for the loyal fans.

The lack of excitement at The Recreation Ground was sadly reflected in the attendances and it's difficult to see where the finance will be obtained to bring about any improvement.

Taking the view that things must get better and accepting that there are a lot more Third Division clubs in real trouble, the Spireites must enter this season's competition with the hope that things will get better and perhaps the family managerial courage and determination will help the club survive a disappointing period in its history.

T.W.

Back row L-R: Mark Preston, Steve Williams, Tony Brien, Stuart Cash, Steve Norris. **Middle row:** Lee Turnbull, Dave Lancaster, Mick Leonard, Andy Morris, Mark Goldring, Paul McGugan, Sean Dyche. **Front row:** Cliff Carr, Lee Rogers, Trevor Hebberd, Steve Hetzke (Coach), Chris McMenemy (Manager), Dave Rushbury (Physio/Asst. Manager), Scott Whitehead, Paul Lemon, Mick Kennedy

CHESTERFIELD

DIVISION FOUR: 13th   **FA CUP:** 1st RND   **RUMBELOWS CUP:** 1st RND   **AUTOGLASS:** 1st RND

M	DATE		COMP.	VEN	OPPONENTS	RESULT	H/T	LGE POS	GOALSCORERS/GOAL TIMES	ATTEN-DANCE
1	A	17	BL	H	Maidstone United	W 3-0	1-0		Williams 38, Hewitt 64, 81	3,466
2		21	RC 1/1	A	Stoke City	L 0-1	0-1			(7,815)
3		27	RC 1/2	H	Stoke City	L 1-2	0-1		Lancaster 58	5,091
4		31	BL	H	Mansfield Town	L 0-2	0-1			4,740
5	S	3	BL	A	Burnley	L 0-3	0-1			(6,647)
6		7	BL	A	York City	W 1-0	1-0	14	Lancaster 37	(2,382)
7		14	BL	H	Scunthorpe United	L 0-1	0-0			3,338
8		17	BL	H	Walsall	L 0-1	0-0			2,690
9		21	BL	A	Lincoln City	W 2-1	2-0	13	Dyche 27, Cooke 40	(2,896)
10	O	5	BL	A	Gillingham	W 1-0	1-0	9	Cooke 28	(2,835)
11		12	BL	H	Rotherham United	D 1-1	1-0		Turnbull 10	6,133
12		15	BL	A	Northampton Town	D 1-1	1-0		Cooke 28	(2,426)
13		19	BL	A	Halifax Town	L 0-2	0-0	11		(1,506)
14		26	BL	H	Hereford United	W 2-0	1-0	9	Hewitt 6, Hawke 68	2,949
15	N	2	BL	A	Rochdale	D 3-3	1-2	9	Turnbull 12, 75, McGugan 60	(1,852)
16		9	BL	H	Blackpool	D 1-1	0-0	11	Francis 88	4,917
17		16	FAC 1	A	Darlington	L 1-2	1-1		Cooke 12	(3,628)
18		23	BL	A	Wrexham	W 1-0	1-0		Turnbull 3	(1,636)
19		30	BL	A	Barnet	W 2-1	1-0	7	Cooke 8, Lancaster 82	(3,725)
20	D	21	BL	H	Northampton Town	L 1-2	1-0		Williams 26	3,048
21		26	BL	A	Maidstone United	W 1-0	1-0		Cooke 10	(1,325)
22		28	BL	A	Mansfield Town	L 1-2	0-2	10	Turnbull 75	(6,503)
23	J	1	BL	H	Burnley	L 0-2	0-2			7,789
24		4	BL	H	Carlisle United	D 0-0	0-0	11		2,892
25		13	AGT 1	A	Bury	L 1-2	0-0		Cooke 82	(1,036)
26		18	BL	H	Doncaster Rovers	D 0-0	0-0	10		3,372
27		25	BL	A	Cardiff City	L 0-4	0-2	11		(5,131)
28	F	8	BL	A	Hereford United	L 0-1	0-1			(2,315)
29		11	BL	H	Barnet	W 3-2	1-1		Lemon 11, Norris 49, 82	3,076
30		15	BL	A	Crewe Alexandra	L 1-3	1-0		Turnbull 3	(3,172)
31		22	BL	H	Scarborough	W 1-0	0-0	11	Norris 70	2,749
32		29	BL	A	Carlisle United	W 2-1	2-0		Dunn 19, Norris 40	(2,038)
33	M	2	BL	A	Doncaster Rovers	W 1-0	1-0		McGugan 21	(2,385)
34		7	BL	H	Cardiff City	D 2-2	2-0		Norris 45, Dyche 45	3,803
35		14	BL	H	Rochdale	L 0-1	0-1	11		3,231
36		17	BL	A	Scarborough	L 2-3	2-2		Norris 16, Turnbull (pen) 46	(1,302)
37		21	BL	A	Blackpool	L 1-3	1-3		Norris 30	(4,447)
38		24	BL	H	Crewe Alexandra	W 2-1	0-1		Dyche 62, Lancaster 90	2,534
39		28	BL	H	Wrexham	D 1-1	0-1	11	McGugan 82	2,961
40		31	BL	A	Scunthorpe United	L 0-2	0-1			(2,224)
41	A	4	BL	H	York City	L 1-3	1-2	13	Lancaster 11	2,461
42		7	BL	H	Halifax Town	W 4-0	0-0		Lancaster 55, 71, Norris 65, Morris 82	1,802
43		11	BL	A	Walsall	D 2-2	1-1	11	Norris 36, Lemon 73	(2,472)
44		18	BL	H	Lincoln City	L 1-5	1-0	12	Cooke 44	2,748
45		25	BL	H	Gillingham	D 3-3	1-1	13	Norris 16, Lancaster 67	2,109
46	M	2	BL	A	Rotherham United	D 1-1	0-1	13	Morris 70	(8,913)

Best Home League Attendance: 7,789 v Burnley   **Smallest:** 1,802 v Halifax Town   **Av Home Att:** 3,467

Goal Scorers: **Compared with 90-91:** -245

League (48):	Norris 10, Turnbull 7 (1 pen), Lancaster 7, Cooke 6, Hewitt 3, McGugan 3, Dyche 3, Lemon 2, Morris 2, Williams 2, Hawke, Francis, Dunn
R/lows C (1):	Lancaster
FA Cup (1):	Cooke
Autoglass (1):	Cooke

Leonard M.	Dyche S.	Williams S.	Rogers L.	Brien A.	McGugan P.	Gunn B.	Hewitt J.	Morris A.	Caldwell D.	Grayson N.	Benjamin C.	Dunn I.	Cooke J.	Evans G.	Lancaster D.	Turnbull L.	Francis L.	Goldring M.	Hawke W.	Hebberd T.	Lemon P.	Norris S.	Whitehead S.	Jones	Referee	
1	2	3	4	5	6	7	8	9	10*	11	12	S													E Parker	1
1	2	3	4	5	6	7	8*	9		11	10*		12	14											H King	2
1	2	3	4	5	6	7		11*	10			8*	14	9	12										T Fitzharris	3
1	2	3	4*	5	6	7			12	10*		11	9	8	14										C Trussell	4
1	2	3		5	6	7		11*	10		S	8	12	9		4									D Phillips	5
1	2	3		5	6	7			10*	12	11	8	14	9*		4									P Harrison	6
	2	3		5	6	7		10*	14	12	11*	8		9		4	1								G Poll	7
1	2	3		5	6	7		10	14	12	11*	8		9*		4									T West	8
1	2	3		5	6	7	11	10*			S	8	12	9		4									K Morton	9
1	2	3		5	6		11		12		S	8		9	7	4				10*					M Bailey	10
1	2	3		5	6		11			S		S	8		9	7	4			10					P Jones	11
1	2	3		5		6	11		12		S	8		9	7	4				10*					M James	12
1	2	3		5		6	11		12	14		8*		9	7	4				10*					T Lunt	13
1	2	3		5	6	S	11			S		8		9	7	4				10					A Dawson	14
1	2	3		5	6	S	11			S		8		9	7	4				10					R Nixon	15
1	2	3*		5	6		11		14			8		9*	7	4				10	12				R Poulain	16
	2	3	S	5	6		11		9		S	8			7	4	1			10					J Parker	17
1	2	3	12	5	6		11		9*	14		8			7	4				10					D Shadwell	18
1	2	3	7	5	6	S	11		9*	12		8			10	4									P Foakes	19
1	2	3*	7	5	6		11	12		14		8			10*	9	4								G Pooley	20
1	2	3	S	5	6		11	12	9*			8			10	7	4								A Gunn	21
1	2	3	S	5	6		11		9			8*			10	7	4			12					K Morton	22
1	2	3*	14	5	6		11			12		8			10*	7	4			9					I Cruikshanks	23
1	2		3	5	6		11*		9		12	8*			14	7	4			10					R Bigger	24
	2	3		6	12			9*				8	14	11	7*	4	1			10	5				R Hart	25
	2		3	6	S	11	12					8			7*	4	1			10	5	9			P Vanes	26
	2	3	14	6			11					8*	14		7	4*	1			10	5	9			M James	27
1	2	12	3	6			11	8*							S	7	4			10	5	9			P Taylor	28
1	2	3		5	6		11	S		S						7	4			10	8	9			T Holbrook	29
1	2	3		5	6		11			12			S	S	9	4				10	7*	8			H King	30
1	2	3		5	6		11			7		S	S		9	4				10		8			K Cooper	31
1	2	3	12	5	6		11			7*		S			9	4				10		8			J Watson	32
1	2	3	12	5	6		11			7		S			9	4				10*		8			P Harrison	33
1	2	3	10	5	6	S	11			7*	12				9	4						8			S Bell	34
1	2	3	12	5	6*		11			7•	14				9	4				10		8			M Reed	35
1	2	3*	6	5		S	11			7					9	4				10	12	8			L Dilkes	36
1	2	S	3	5	6		11			S					9	4				10	7	8			J Rushton	37
1	2	S	3	5	6		11			S					9	4				10	7	8			I Borrett	38
1	2	4*	3	5	6		11			12					9					10	7	8	S		T West	39
1	2	S	3*	5	6		11			4					9		12			10	7	8			D Allison	40
1	2	S		5	6		11			4					9		3			10	7*	8	12		A Wilkie	41
1	2			5	6*			3	14			11		9*		4				10	12	8	7		K Breen	42
	2	S		5	6			3	12			11		9*		4	1			10	6	8	7		G Lloyd	43
	2			5	6			3	12			11		9*	14	4	1			10	6	8•	7		M Brandwood	44
	2	3		5	6		11	9				7		14	10•		1				4*	8	12		M Peck	45
	2			5	6			3	9			7		11		4	1			10		8	S	S	D Gallagher	46
35	42	30	13	40	37	9	37	4	5	9		8	29	1	27	26	37	7	7	22	13	21	3		League Appearances	
	1	5	1			4		4	6	4	5	4		4	2	1	2			2	2		2		Substitute Appearances	
2	2	2	2	2	2	1	2			2	1		1+1	0+2	1		0+1								R/lows Appearances	
1	1		1	1		1				1			1			1	1	1		1					FA Cup Appearances	
1		1		1	0+1		1				1		0+1	1	1	1	1		1	1					Autoglass Appearances	

CHESTERFIELD

Club Colours: Royal blue shirts with white pin stripe, white shorts with blue stripe at sides, blue stockings
Change Colours: Red shirt, black shorts, red stockings
Reserves League: Midland Intermediate

Previous League: Midland League
Previous Names: Chesterfield Municipal until 1915 Chesterfield Town 1919-22
Previous Managers: 1945-49 Bob Brocklebank 1949-52 Bob Marshall 1952-58 Ted Davison 1958-62 Dugald Livingstone 1962-67 Tony McShane 1967-73 Jimmy McGuigan 1973-76 Joe Shaw 1976-80 Arthur Cox 1980-83 Frank Barlow 1983-87 John Duncan 1987-88 Kevin Randall 1988-91 Paul Hart
Honours: Champions Div 3N 1930-31, 1935-36 Champions Div 4 1969-70, 1984-85 Anglo-Scottish Cup Winners 1980-81
League Career: Elected to Div 2 1899 Failed re-election 1908-09 Re-elected to Div 3N 1921-22
Promoted to Div 2 1930-31 Relegated to Div 3N 1932-33 Promoted to Div 2 1935-36 Relegated to Div 3N 1950-51
Transferred to Div 3 1958 Relegated to Div 4 1960-61 Promoted to Div 3 1969-70 Relegated to Div 4 1982-83
Promoted to Div 3 1984-85 Relegated to Div 4 1988-89

CLUB RECORDS

Most Appearances for Club: Dave Blakey (1948-67): League 617 + FA Cup 35 + League Cup 6 **Total 658**
Most Capped Player: Walter McMillan (Northern Ireland) 4 **For England:** None
Record Goalscorer in a Match: No player has ever scored more than 4 goals in a match, but this feat has been achieved on 19 occasions
Record League Goalscorer in a Season: Jimmy Cookson, 44, Div 3N, 1925-26 **In All Competitions:** Jimmy Cookson 46 (League 44 + FA Cup 2) 1925-26
Record League Goalscorer in a Career: Ernie Moss 161, 1968-76, 1979-81, 1984-86 **In All Competitions:** Ernie Moss 184 (League 161 + FA Cup 8 + League Cup 15) 1968-76, 1979-81, 1984-86
Record Transfer Fee Received: £200,000 from Wolverhampton Wanderers for Alan Birch, August 1981
Record Transfer Fee Paid: £150,000 to Carlisle United for Phil Bonnyman, March 1980
Best Performances: League: 4th Div 2, 1946-47 **FA Cup:** 5th Round 1932-33, 1937-38, 1949-50 **League Cup:** 4th Round 1964-65
Most League Points: (2pts a win) 64, Div 4, 1969-70 (3pts a win) 91, Div 4, 1984-85
Most League Goals: 102, Div 3N, 1930-31
Record League Victory: 10-0 v Glossop, Div 2, 17.1.1903
Record Cup Victory: (First Class) 5-0 v Wath Athletic (a), FA Cup Round 1, 1925-26 5-0 v Scunthorpe United, League Cup Round 1 Replay, 1972-73
Record League Defeat: 0-10 v Gillingham (a), Div 3, 5.9.1987
Record Cup Defeat: 1-8 v West Ham United, FA Cup Round 1, 1913-14 0-7 v Burnley, FA Cup Round 3, 1956-57
Oldest Player in a League Match: Billy Kidd, 40 years 232 days v Southampton, Div 2, 20.9.1947
Youngest Player in a League Match: Dennis Thompson, 16 years 160 days v Notts County, Div 2, 26.12.1950

LONGEST RUNS

of undefeated matches: 13 (1984)	**of league matches without a win:** 16 (1960-61, 1983)
of undefeated home matches: 27 (1925-26)	**of undefeated away matches:** 10 (1935, 1969-70)
without home win: 9 (1963)	**without an away win:** 26 (1907-08)
of league wins: 10 (1933)	**of home wins:** 17 (1929-30)
of league defeats: 9 (1960)	**of away wins:** 6 (1933)

BARCLAYS

BARCLAYS BUSINESS CENTRE
Chesterfield Business Centre
PO Box No. 14
37 Rose Hill
Chesterfield
Derbyshire S40 1LS
Tel: 0246 209801

BARCLAYBANK MACHINE

CHESTERFIELD

PLAYERS NAME Honours	Ht	Wt	Birthdate	Birthplace Transfers	Contract Date	Clubs	League	L/Cup	FA Cup	Other	Lg	L/C	FAC	Oth
GOALKEEPERS														
Mark Goldring	6.2		17.09.72	Southampton	14.08.91	Chesterfield (T)								
Michael Leonard	5.11	11.0	09.05.59	Carshalton		Epsom & Ewell								
					01.07.76	Halifax Town	69	6	1					
				£30,000	14.09.79	Notts County	204	15	20	15				
					03.03.89	Chesterfield	92	3	3	5				
				Loan		Halifax Town	3							
DEFENDERS														
Tony Brien	5.11	11.9	10.02.68	Dublin	13.02.87	Leicester City	12+4	1	1	3	1			
				£90,000	16.12.88	Chesterfield	113+2	4	4	9	7			
Paul McGugan	6.2	12.0	17.07.64	Glasgow		Eastercrai								
						Celtic	45+4	7	2+1	3	2			
					15.10.87	Barnsley	47+2	2+1	6	2	2			
				Loan	24.01.91	Chesterfield								
				£15,000	26.02.91	Chesterfield	22				1			
Lee Rogers	5.11	12.1	28.10.66	Doncaster	27.07.84	Doncaster R.(T)								
						Chesterfield	161+8	5+1	6	15+1				
MIDFIELD														
Trevor Hebberd Div3'84, Div2'85, LC'86	6.0	11.4	19.06.58	Winchester	01.07.76	Southampton (A)	69+28	9+1	4+3		7	3		
				Loan	21.09.81	Bolton W	6							
				Loan	27.11.81	Leicester City	4				1			
				P.E	25.03.82	Oxford Utd	260	37	17	9	37	3	1	1
				£150,000	17.08.88	Derby County	70+11	13	5	7	10	2	2	
				Monthly	03.10.91	Portsmouth	1+3							
				Free	07.11.91	Chesterfield								
Paul Lemon Div3'88	5.11	11.6	03.06.66	Middlesbrough	04.05.84	Sunderland (A)	91+16	6+1	2+2	8	15			4
				Loan	20.12.84	Carlisle Utd	2							
				Loan	02.11.89	Walsall	2		1					
				Loan	15.12.89	Reading	3							
				Loan	06.09.90	Chesterfield								
					08.11.90	Chesterfield	39	1	2	2	2			2
Lee Turnbull	6.0	11.9	27.09.67	Stockton	07.09.85	Middlesbrough (A)	8+8	0+1		1+1	4			1
					24.08.87	Aston Villa								
				£17,500	03.11.87	Doncaster Rovers	108+15	3+1	5+1	9+1	21	2		2
				£35,000	14.02.91	Chesterfield	19				9			
FORWARDS														
Kevin Godfrey Div.3'92	5.10	11.2	24.02.60	Kennington		Leyton Orient	255+30	15+2	0+1	6+2	63	4	5	
				Loan		Plymouth A	7				1			
				Free	31.12.88	Brentford	40+16	2	5+3	4+4	10	1		1
					15.03.91	Brentford	92+27	11	14+3	11+8	25	5		3
				Loan		Chesterfield	2							
David Lancaster NPL Div1'89,NPL Prem'90	6.3	14.0	08.09.61	Preston		Colne Dynamoes								
					15.08.90	Blackpool	7+1	2		0+1	1			
				Loan	26.02.91	Chesterfield	12				4			
				£70,000	27.08.91	Chesterfield								
Andrew Morris	6.4	15.7	17.11.67	Sheffield	29.07.85	Rotherham Utd	0+7	0+1						
					12.01.88	Chesterfield	101+9	6	5	9	17	5	3	2
				Loan	04.03.92	Exeter City	4+3				2			
Steve Norris E: SP.1	5.10	10.10	22.09.61	Coventry		V S Rugby			3					
						Telford			2					
				£46,000	25.07.88	Scarborough	35+10	9	1	3+1	13	2		1
				Loan	08.11.89	Notts County	0+1		1					
				Loan	28.12.89	Carlisle Utd								
				£40,000	19.01.90	Carlisle Utd	21+8	0+2			5			
				Swap for F	05.10.90	Halifax Town	56	2	5	3	35	1	2	1
				£33,000	16.01.92	Chesterfield								
Steven B Williams	5.11	10.06	18.07.70	Mansfield		Mansfield Town	4+7							
					11.11.89	Chesterfield	22+14	0+1	3+1	2	5			1
ADDITIONAL CONTRACT PLAYERS														
Scott Cordner						Chesterfield	1+3			0+1	1			
(M) Sean Dyche	6.0	11.7	28.06.71	Kettering	20.05.89	Nottm. Forest (T)								
				Loan	01.02.90	Chesterfield								
				Free	01.03.90	Chesterfield	43+7	1	1	5	4			
Andrew Higginbottom					22.03.90	Chesterfield								
Gavin MacDonald						Chesterfield (T)	5+7			1+1	1			1
Dean Wright					21.09.89	Chesterfield								

LEADING LEAGUE GOALSCORERS SEASONS 1985-86 – 1991-92

1985-86	ERNIE MOSS	14	1986-87	DAVID CALDWELL	14
1987-88	DAVE WALLER	19	1988-89	DAVE WALLER	18
1989-90	DAVE WALLER	16	1990-91	LEE TURNBULL	9
		1991-92	STEVE NORRIS	10	

RECREATION GROUND Chesterfield S40 4SX

Capacity: 11,308   **Covered Standing:**   **Seating:** 2,608

Tel: Ground: 0246 209765   **Ticket Sales:** As ground number   **Clubcall:** 0898 12 15 73

All premium rate calls (0898/0891) cost 36p per minute cheap rate and 48p per minute at all other times. Call costings correct at time of going to press.

ATTENDANCES
Highest: 30,968 v Newcastle United, Div 2, 7.4.1939

Lowest: 1,053 v Burnley, Freight Rover Trophy, 21.1.1986

Record Receipts: £32,410 v Sheffield United, Div 3, 25.3.1989

Season Tickets:
Stands: from £112 to £121, juv/OAP £58 to £70
Ground: £93, juv/OAP £40

Executive Box Season Tickets: Apply to club for details

Cost of Stand Tickets: Seats: £7, juv/OAP £3.50
Terraces: £5, juv/OAP £2.50

Match and Ticket Information: Centre and Wing Stands bookable in advance

Car Parking: Street parking near ground allowed. Car parks 0.5 mile from ground in Saltergate

Nearest Railway Station: Chesterfield (0246 74371)

How to get to the ground

From North: Use Motorway M1 until junction 30, then follow signs Chesterfield A619. In town centre follow signs Old Brampton into Saltergate for Chesterfield FC

From East and South: Follow signs Chesterfield A617 into town centre then follow signs Old Brampton into Saltergate for Chesterfield FC

From West: Follow signs Chesterfield A619 then at roundabout take 1st exit into Foljambe Road at end turn right into Saltergate for Chesterfield FC

Value Rating: ★ ★ ★

Programme Editor: K Barson

Price of 1992-93 Programme: £1
Number of Pages: 32
Subscriptions: £12.50 + £2.50 p&p

Local Newspapers: Derbyshire Times, Sheffield Star, Chesterfield Star

Local Radio Stations: Radio Hallam, Radio BBC Sheffield

COLCHESTER UNITED

Division 3

Formed: 1937 **Turned Professional:** 1937 **Ltd Co:** 1937

SPONSORED BY: Colchester Hippodrome **NICKNAME:** The U's

Chairman
J Bowridge

Vice-Chairman
J H Shultz

Directors
H F Carson
D A Johnson
G H Parker
H R Piper
R Pleydell

Chief Executive
David Barnard

Company Secretary
Mike Tuew

Club Secretary
D Elwood

Lottery Manager
C Harvey

Player/Manager
Roy McDonough

Coach
Ian Phillips

Youth Team Manager
Steve Foley

Physiotherapist
Chris Toulson

Consultant Physio
Charlie Simpson

THREE important dates will live in the memories of all Colchester United supporters. The appointment of Roy McDonough as Player / Coach, the lifting of the Vauxhall Conference Championship and, finally the completion of the double with the winning of the Vauxhall F.A. Trophy.

For years all the Layer Road faithful have had to talk about is that famous F.A. Cup victory over Leeds United in 1971. However, now they have new achievements to celebrate and new heroes to worship.

Pre-season preparations were sent into turmoil when Ian Atkins left to join Birmingham City just over two weeks before the start of the season. A replacement had to be found and although it was at short notice Roy McDonough was the ideal choice. 'Big Roy' as he is affectionately known by the fans led from up front, and while he was rather too frequently in trouble with referees nobody could question his committment or desire to succeed. Many believed that McDonough was past his sell-by date but they have been proved wrong as he finished as the club's top scorer with 29 goals to his credit.

McDonough's partner up front, Steve McGavin was never far behind in the goalscoring stakes with 28 goals. However it was McGavin's eye for the spectacular which really lit up Layer Road. Few will forget his two wonderful goals against Wycombe Wanderers, one a curling left foot shot past a shell-shocked goalkeeper and the other a right foot shot from the opposite side of the 18-yard-box. It was not just his goals which endeared him to the supporters but his superb ball skills and the ability to make something from nothing.

Last season Nicky Smith failed to score in any competition, but this year he has chipped in with 11 goals. Nearly all of those goals have been of some significance, including: the first goal in the away win against Wycombe, a cracking volley to win the home game against Northwich and finally, the second goal at Wembley in that glorious Trophy victory. Quite rightly Smith was awarded the accolade of 'Player of the Year'. He won this with his 100 per cent effort in every game but also his willingness, in even the most tension packed of games, to share a joke with the crowd and above all SMILE!!

Quite obviously I couldn't finish this article without mentioning a certain goalkeeper. Scott Barrett received nationwide acclaim with his exploits appearing on BBC's 'A Question of Sport'. But he should be remembered for crucial saves at crucial times, particularly in the Trophy semi-final and final. There is some doubt about the custodian's future at Layer Road but every effort is being made to persuade him to stay.
Steve Whitney

Back row L-R: Steve Foley (Youth Team Coach), Tony English (Captain), Martin Grainger, Nathan Munson, Steve Munson, Steve McGavin, Paul Roberts, Roy McDonough (Manager). **Middle:** Chris Toulson (Physio), Robbie Deveraux, Nicky Smith, Julian Hazel, James Goodwin, Paul Abrahams, Eamon Mongan, Ian Phillips (Asst. Coach). **Front row:** Gary Bennett, Warren Donald, Jason Cook, Mark Kinsella, Nicky Cropper.

COLCHESTER UNITED

DIVISION GMVC: CHAMPIONS **FA CUP:** 1st RND **FA TROPHY:** WINNERS

M	DATE		COMP.	VEN	OPPONENTS	RESULT		H/T	LGE POS	GOALSCORERS/GOAL TIMES	ATTEN-DANCE
1	A	17	GMVC	H	Macclesfield	W	2-0	-		Bennett, McGavin	2,233
2		24	GMVC	A	Barrow	D	1-1	-		Kinsella	(1,480)
3		26	GMVC	A	Slough Town	W	4-2	-		McDonough (4)	(2,226)
4		31	GMVC	H	Bath City	W	5-0	-		Bennett (3), McGavin (2)	2,416
5	S	7	GMVC	A	Witton Albion	D	2-2	-		Collins, McDonough	(1,045)
6		10	GMVC	H	Farnborough Town	L	2-3	-		Collins, McGavin	2,954
7		13	GMVC	H	Yeovil Town	W	4-0	-		English, Bennett (2), McGavin	2,979
8		21	GMVC	A	Cheltenham Town	D	1-1	-		McDonough	(1,157)
9		28	GMVC	A	Wycombe Wndrs	W	2-1	-		Barrett, Smith	(5,186)
10	O	5	GMVC	H	Altrincham	D	3-3	-		McDonough, McGavin	2,853
11		8	LORD 1	H	Kettering Town	W	4-0	-		Collins, McGavin, Kinsella (2)	1,289
12		12	GMVC	H	Runcorn	W	2-1	-		Bennett, McDonough (pen)	2,617
13		19	GMVC	A	Telford United	W	3-0	-		McDonough (2), Smith	(1,109)
14		26	FAC 4Q	H	Burton Albion	W	5-0	-		Kinsella, McDonough, McGavin, Restarick	2,147
15		30	GMVC	A	Yeovil Town	W	1-0	-		McGavin	(2,385)
16	N	2	GMVC	H	Stafford Rangers	W	2-0	-		McDonough, Smith	2,139
17		9	GMVC	A	Farnborough Town	W	2-0	-		Elliot, Bennett	(3,069)
18		16	FAC 1	H	Exeter City	D	0-0	-			4,965
19		23	GMVC	H	Welling	W	3-1	-		English, Bennett, Cook	2,933
20		27	FAC 1R	A	Exeter City	D	0-0	-		McDonough	(4,066)
21		30	GMVC	A	Northwich Victoria	D	1-1	-			(1,042)
22	D	3	GMVC	A	Stafford Rangers	D	3-3	-		Bennett (2), McGavin	(961)
23		7	GMVC	H	Wycombe Wndrs	W	3-0	-		McGavin (2)	5,086
24		14	GMVC	A	Gateshead	W	2-0	-		Bennett, McDonough	(542)
25		16	LORD 2	H	Wycombe Wndrs	L	2-6	-		Restarick, McGavin	919
26		21	GMVC	H	Witton Albion	W	3-2	-		Bennett, McGavin, English	2,842
27		26	GMVC	A	Redbridge Forest	L	1-2	-		McDonough	(2,327)
28		28	GMVC	A	Runcorn	W	3-1	-		Cook, Bennett, McGavin	(883)
29	J	1	GMVC	H	Redbridge Forest	W	1-0	-		McGavin	4,773
30		4	GMVC	A	Merthyr Tydfil	L	0-2	-			(1,032)
31		11	FAT 1	H	Kingstonian	D	2-2	-		English	2,724
32		14	FAT 1R	A	Kingstonian	W	3-2	-		English, Bennett, McGavin, Smith	(1,642)
33		18	GMVC	H	Cheltenham Town	W	4-0	-		Kinsella, McDonough, McGavin (2), Smith	2,643
34		24	GMVC	A	Kettering Town	D	2-2	-		McGavin	(4,100)
35	F	2	FAT 2	A	Merthyr Tydfil	D	0-0	-			(1,211)
36		4	FAT 2R	H	Merthyr Tydfil	W	1-0	-		McDonough	2,746
37		7	GMVC	A	Kidderminster H	D	2-2	-		Bennett, Smith	(1,828)
38		11	GMVC	H	Boston	W	1-0	-		McGavin	3,229
39		15	GMVC	A	Welling United	L	1-4	-		McDonough (pen)	(1,837)
40		22	FAT 3	H	Morecambe	W	3-1	-		Stewart (2), McGavin	3,206
41		28	GMVC	A	Altrincham	W	2-1	-		McDonough, McGavin	(905)
42	M	7	GMVC	H	Gateshead	W	2-0	-		Roberts, Masters	2,897
43		14	FAT 4	H	Telford Utd	W	4-0	-		Kinsella, Bennett, McGavin, Smith	3,894
44		21	GMVC	H	Northwich Victoria	W	1-0	-		Smith	3,218
45		24	GMVC	A	Bath City	D	0-0	-			(1,101)
46		28	GMVC	H	Kidderminster H	W	3-0	-		English, Stewart	3,073
47	A	4	FAT SF1	H	Macclesfield	W	3-0	-		English, Stewart, McDonough (pen)	5,443
48		10	FAT SF2	A	Macclesfield	D	1-1	-		Cook	(1,650)
49		14	GMVC	H	Slough Town	W	4-0	-		Kinsella, Stewart, McDonough, Masters	3,197
50		18	GMVC	H	Telford United	W	2-0	-		McDonough (2)	3,964
51		20	GMVC	H	Merthyr Tydfil	W	2-0	-		Masters	4,148
52		22	GMVC	A	Boston	W	4-0	-		Masters, McDonough (1), McGavin	(2,305)
53		25	GMVC	A	Macclesfield	D	4-4	-		English (2), McDonough	(886)
54		28	GMVC	H	Kettering Town	W	3-1	-		McDonough (2), McGavin	6,303
55	M	2	GMVC	H	Barrow	W	5-0	-		Masters (3), Smith, McDonough	7,193
56		10	FAT Fin	N	Witton Albion	W	3-1	-		Masters, Smith, McGavin	(27,806)

Best Home League Attendance: 7,193 v Barrow **Smallest:** 2,139 v Stafford R **Av Home Att:** 3,509

Goal Scorers: **Compared with 90-91:** +506

League (91): McDonough 25 (2 pens), McGavin 20, Bennett 15, Masters 7, Smith 7, English 5, Kinsella 3, Stewart 2, Collins 2, Cook 2 Barrett, Roberts, Elliot

FA Trophy (20): McGavin 4, Smith 3, English 3, Stewart 3, Bennett 2, McDonough 2 (1 pen), Cook, Masters, Kinsella

FA Cup (5): McDonough 2, Restarick, McGavin, Kinsella

Bob Lord (6): Kinsella 2, McGavin 2, Restarick, Collins

No.	Barrett S.	Donald W.	Grainger M.	Kinsella M.	English A.	Elliot S.	Collins E.	Bennett G.	McDonough R.	McGavin S.	Smith N.	Walsh M.	Phillips I.	Restarick S.	Goodwin J.	Gray S.	Abrahams P.	Roberts P.	Cook J.	Duffett S.	Partner W.	Hannigan W.	Dart J.	Masters M.	Stewart I.	Martin D.	Referee
1	1	2	3	4	5	6	7	8	9	10*	11	12		S													
2	1	2	3	4	5	6	7	8	9	10	11		S		S												
3	1	2	3	4	5	6	7	8	9	10*	11		12				14										
4	1	2	3	4	5	6	7	8	9•	10	11		S				14										
5	1	2	3	4	5	6	7	8	9	10	11			S				S									
6	1	2	3•	4	5	6	7	8	9	10	11				14			S									
7	1	2	3	4	5	6	7	8	9	10	11			S			14•										
8	1	2	3	4	5	6	7	8	9					S		10		S									
9	1	2	S	4	5	6	7	8	9	10	11							3	S								
10	1	2	S	4	5	6	7	8	9	10	11							3	S								
11	1	2	3	12	5		7*	8		10	11						14	6	4	9*							
12	1	2	S	14	5	6	7	8•	9	10	11							3	4								
13	1	2	14		5	6	7	8	9*	10	11		12					3	4•								
14	1	2		4	5	6	7*	8	9•	10	11		3	12			14										
15	1	2		4	5	6	7	8*	9	10	11		S	12				3									
16	1	2*		4	5	6	7	8	9•	10	11			12	14			3									
17	1	2		4	5	6	7	8*	9•	10	11			12				3	14								
18	1	2	12	4	5	6	7	8	9	10	11*			S				3									
19	1	2		4	5	6*	7	8	9	10	11			S				3	12								
20	1	2	12	4	5		7	8*	9	10	11			14	6•			3									
21	1	2	5	S		6	7		9	10	11		4	S				3	8								
22	1	2	S	4		6	7	8	9	10	11			S				3	5								
23	1	2	S	4		6	7	8	9	10	11			S				3	5								
24	1	2	S	4		6	7	8	9		11					10	14	3	5								
25	1	3			6				9•	10				8	7		11	5*	2		4	12					
26	1	2	4*	S		6	7	8•	9	10	11				14			3	5								
27	1	2		4	5	6	12	8•	9	10	11			14				3	7•								
28	1	2	12		5	6	7	8	9	10	11			S				3	4•								
29	1	2	12		5	6	7	8*	9	10	11			S				3	4								
30	1	14		4	5	6	7	8*	9	10	11			12				3	2•								
31	1	2	14	12	5		7*	8		10	11			9•				3	4								
32	1	2	12	4*	5	6		8		10	11			9•				3	7				14				
33	1	2	S	4	5	6		8*	9	10	11							3	7				12				
34	1	2	14	4	5	6		8*	9	10	11							3	7				12				
35	1	2		4	5	6	S	12	9	10	11							3	7				8*				
36	1	14		4	5*	6	7	8	9	10	11							3	2				S				
37	1	S		4	5	6	7	8	9	10	11							3	2				S				
38	1	14		4	5	6	7	8	9	10	11							3	2*						12		
39	1	14		4	5	6	7	8*	9	10	11							3	2•						12		
40	1	2		4	5		7		9	10	11							3*	6				14	12	8•		
41	1	2		4	5		7	14	9*	10•	11							3	6					12	8		
42	1	2		4	5		7	12	9*	10	11							3	6					14	8•		
43	1	2		4	5	6	14	8	9*	10	11							3	7						12		
44	1	2		4	5	6	14	8•		10	11							3	7*					9	12		
45	1	2		4	5	6	14		10*		11							3	7					9	8	12	
46	1	2		4	5		14		9*	10	11							3•	7					12	8	6	
47	1	2		4	5		12	14	9	10	11							3	7*					8•		6	
48	1	2		4	5		S		9	10	11							3	7					S	8	6	
49	1	2		4	5		S		9	10	11							3	7					12	8	6	
50	1	2*		4	5	6	12		9	10•	11							3						14	8	7	
51	1	2		4	5	14	12		9*	10	11							3	7•					8		6	
52	1	2		4	5	S	12		9	10*	11							3	7					8		6•	
53	1	2		4	5	S	S		9	10	11							3	7					8		6	
54	1	2		4	5	14	12		9	10	11							3	7					8*		6	
55	1	2		4	5	S	10		9		11							3	7					8	S	6	
56	1	2		4	5	S	12		9*	10	11							3	7					8		6	
League Appearances	42	38	9	37	37	33	29	31	40	39	41		1	1		1		34	27					7	6	8	
Substitute Appearances	2	2	4		2	4	6					1	2	4	3	1	4		2				2	5	3	1	
FA Trophy Apps	9	8+1	0+2	8+1	9	5	3+2	4+3	7	9	9			2				9	9				1+2	1+1	3+1	3	
FA Cup Appearances	3	3		3	3	2	3	3	3	3	3			1	0+2	1		0+1	1		1						
Bob Lord Appearances	2	1	2		2		1	1	1	2	1			1	1		1+1	2	2	1	1	0+1					

COLCHESTER UNITED

Club Colours: Royal blue & white striped shirts, royal blue shorts, white stockings
Change Colours: All red
Reserves League: **Youth Team:**

Previous League: Southern League
Previous Managers: (Since joining the Football League)
Ted Fenton   Jimmy Allen   Jack Butler   Benny Fenton   Neil Franklin   Dick Graham   Jim Smith   Bobby Roberts   Allan Hunter
Cyril Lea   Jock Wallace   Ian Atkins
Honours: GMVC Winners 1991-92, FA Trophy Winners 1991-92
League Career: Elected to Div 3S 1950   Transferred to Div 3 1958   Relegated to Div 4 1960-61
Promoted to Div 3 1961-62   Relegated to Div 4 1964-65   Promoted to Div 3 1965-66   Relegated to Div 4 1967-68
Promoted to Div 3 1973-74   Relegated to Div 4 1975-76   Promoted to Div 3 1976-77   Relegated to Div 4 1980-81
Relegated to GM Vauxhall Conference 1989-90   Promote to Div 3 (old 4) 1991-92

CLUB RECORDS

Most Appearances for Club: Mickey Cook: League 609 + 4, FA Cup 46, League Cup 36 **Total 691 + 4 subs**
Most Capped Player: None
Record Goalscorer in a Match: No one has scored more than four
Record League Goalscorer in a Season: Bobby Hunt 37, Div 4, 1961-62   **In All Competitions:** Bobby Hunt 38 (League 37, FA Cup 1)
Record League Goalscorer in a Career: Martyn King 131, 1959-65
Record Transfer Fee Received: £120,000 from Wimbledon for P McGee, February 1989
Record Transfer Fee Paid: £45,000 to Sporting Lochern for D Tempest, August 1987
Best Performances: League: 3rd Div 3S, 1956-57   **FA Cup:** 6th Round (shared record for Div 4), 1970-71   **League Cup:** 5th Round 1974-75
Most League Points: 81, Div 4, 1982-83
Most League Goals: 104, Div 4, 1961-62
Record League Victory and Most Goals Scored in a League Match: 9-1 v Bradford City, Div 4, 30.12.1961
Most Goals Scored in a Cup Tie: 7 v Yeovil, FA Cup 2nd Round, 1958
Record League Defeat: 0-8 v Leyton Orient, 15.10.1988
Oldest Player in a League Match: Benny Fenton 39 years 6 months
Youngest Player in a League Match: Peter Barlow 16 years 10 months

LONGEST RUNS	
of undefeated matches: 20 (1956-57)	**of league matches without a win:** 20 (1968)
of undefeated home matches: 27 (1956-57)	**of undefeated away matches:** 9 (1956-57)
without home win: 11 (1958)	**without an away win:** 19 (1950-51, 1959-60)
of league wins: 7 (1968-69)	**of home wins:** 13 (1976-77)
of league defeats: 8 (1954)	**of away wins:** 5 (1981, 1987)

COLCHESTER UNITED

PLAYERS NAME Honours	Ht	Wt	Birthdate	Birthplace Transfers	Contract Date	Clubs	League	L/Cup	FA Cup	Other	Lg	L/C	FAC	Oth
GOALKEEPERS														
DEFENDERS														
Mark Grainger				Enfield		Colchester Utd								
Paul Roberts			27.04.62	West Ham		Millwall	142+4							
						Brentford	61+1							
						Swindon Town	25+2							
						Southend Utd	38							
						Aldershot	36+3							
						Exeter City	3							
						Southend Utd	54							
				£2,000		Fisher Ath.								
MIDFIELD														
Gary Bennett	5.7	9.13	13.11.70	Enfield	03.11.88	Colchester Utd. (T)	6+3				1			
Warren Donald	5.6	10.10	07.10.64	Uxbridge	08.10.82	West Ham U. (A)	1+1							
E: S(1),Div.4'87				£11,000	04.10.85	Northampton T	180+8	10	8+2	12	13		1	
					01.06.90	Colchester Utd								
Jason Cook	5.7	10.6	29.12.69	Edmonton	16.12.88	Tottenham								
						Southend Utd	30							1
					01.06.90	Colchester Utd								
Tony English	5.11	11.2	19.10.66	Luton		Coventry City (A)								
E:Y5				f	24.12.84	Colchester Utd	176+2	6	13	13+1	33			
					01.06.90	Colchester Utd								
Mark Kinsella						Home Farm								
				Free		Colchester Utd								
Nick Smith	5.8	10.0	28.01.69	Berkeley	09.07.87	Southend Utd	50+11	2+1	0+2	4+2	1			
				Free	01.06.90	Colchester Utd								
FORWARDS														
Roy McDonough	6.1	11.11	16.10.58	Solihull	01.10.76	Birmingham City (A)	2				1			
				£15,000	07.09.78	Walsall	76+6	4	5		15	1		
				£15,000	29.10.80	Chelsea								
				£15,000	12.02.81	Colchester Utd	89+4	9	6		24	2		
				Free	18.08.83	Southend Utd	22	2	2		4			
					20.01.84	Exeter City	19+1	2		2+1	1			
				£5,000	13.10.84	Cambridge Utd	30+2		1	1	5			
					15.08.85	Southend Utd	163+23	12+1	5	11+1	21		3	1
						Southend Utd								
						Colchester Utd								
Steve McGavin				Suffolk		Ipswich (T)					3			
GMVC, FAT						Sudbury Town								
				£10,000		Colchester Utd								

LEADING LEAGUE GOALSCORERS SEASONS 1985-86 – 1991-92

1985-86	**TONY ADCOCK**	**15**		1986-87	**TONY ADCOCK**	**12**
1987-88	**DALE TEMPEST**	**11**		1988-89	**MARIO WALSH**	**9**
1989-90	**Trevor Morgan**	**12**		1990-91	Not in League	
			1991-92	Not in League		

LAYER ROAD GROUND Colchester, Essex CO2 7JJ

Capacity: 7,223 | **Covered Standing:** | **Seating:** 1,169

Tel: Ground: 0206 574042 | **Ticket Sales:** As ground number | **Clubcall:** 0891 66 46 46

All premium rate calls (0898/0891) cost 36p per minute cheap rate and 48p per minute at all other times. Call costings correct at time of going to press.

ATTENDANCES
Highest: 19,073 v Reading, FA Cup Round 1, 27.11.1948
Lowest:

Record Receipts: £22,754 v Manchester United, Milk Cup Round 3, 8.11.1983

Season Tickets
Seats: from £95 to £128, juv £58 to £81
Ground: £81, juveniles/OAP £39

Executive Box Season Tickets: None

Cost of Stand Tickets: Seats £6 to £7.50, juv/OAP £4 to £5.50
Terraces: £5, juveniles/OAP £2.50

Match and Ticket Information: Bookable two weeks in advance and retained if paid for until 48 hours before kick-off

Car Parking: Available in Butts Road and Layer Road (150 yards from ground South side of Colchester, Also in Army Barracks (150 yards from ground)

Nearest Railway Station: Colchester North (0206 64777)

How to get to the ground

From North: Follow signs in Colchester on A133/B1508 or A12, then follow signs Layer B1026 into Layer Road for Colchester United FC

From East: Follow signs into Colchester on A604 or A133 then follow signs Layer B1026 into Layer Road for Colchester United FC

From South and West: Follow signs into Colchester on A604 or A12 then follow signs Layer B1026 into Layer Road for Colchester United FC

Value Rating: ★ ★ ★

Programme Editor: Hal Mason

Price of 1992-93 Programme: £1
Number of Pages: 26
Subscriptions: £80 per season (home & away)

Local Newspapers: Evening Gazette (Mon-Fri evenings), East Anglian Daily Times (Mon-Sat Morning), Essex County Standard (weekly-Fridays)

Local Radio Stations: Radio Orwell (Ipswich), Essex Radio (Southend & Chelmsford) (257 medium wave)

COVENTRY CITY Premier

Formed: 1883 **Turned Professional:** 1893 **Ltd Co:** 1907

SPONSORED BY: Peugeot **NICKNAME:** The Sky Blues

Life President
Derrick H Robins

Chairman
P D H Robins

Vice-Chairman
B A Richardson

Directors
M F French FCA
G W Curtis (Managing Director)
J F W Reason   A M Jepson

Secretary
G P Hover (0203) 223535

Team Manager
Bobby Gould

Assistant Manager
Phil Neal

Reserve Team Coach
Brian Roberts

Youth Team Manager
Bert Edwards

Youth Team Coach
Trevor Gould

Youth Development Officer
Roy Evans

Physiotherapist
George Dalton

Promotions Manager
Arthur Pepper

Business Development Manager
Samantha Clegg

Safety Officer
Tom Meffen, OBE

Club Statistician for the Directory
Rod Dean

AFTER the upheavals of the previous season it would be difficult to envisage a more traumatic season than 1991-92. Both on and off the field the situation reached an all time low. Every single member of the management and coaching team with the exception of the physiotherapist has been dimissed and there are a number of litigation cases outstanding.

The appointment of Terry Butcher was always going to be a huge gamble; a player-manager with no management experience, a suspect knee and a long lucrative contract: it was a gamble that ultimately failed and team spirit gradually declined culminating with the sale of skipper Trevor Peake, one of the final links with the Cup winning team of 1987. With the team sinking towards the relegation zone on the back of some spineless displays changes became inevitable.

A new reconstituted board under Peter Robins, son of 1960s' hero Derrick Robins, had forced some early management changes on Butcher, bringing in ex-England coach Don Howe. With goals in such short supply a wretched F.A. Cup display against Cambridge United forced their hand and after failing to agree to reduced terms, based on his enforced absence from the field of play, Butcher was sacked.

Howe was left to pick up the pieces and managed to steer the club to safety and a place in the Premier League. However, only 8 goals were scored in the last 18 League games (3 against Spurs) and the final tally of 35 was the lowest in the League history of the club. But for Luton's failure at Notts County on the final day of the season their enviable record of 25 years of unbroken First Division membership would have ended.

Since the end of the season old hero Bobby Gould, a Coventry man through and through, rejoined the club as manager with responsibility for the transfer market, but Don Howe then returned to London and Gould has accepted full responsibility with Phil Neal as his assistant. The Board have made encouraging noises about 'this must never happen again' and 'money is available' but after the eighth occasion of final day of the season escape the fans will remain sceptical.

The extra money from TV revenues will be useful but with further expenditure planned on the postponed new stand it will be a difficult equation for the management to solve. At least the age profile of the squad is now much lower but there is an alarming lack of quality in many positions and it will take all of Gould's dealing skills to redress the balance to a position of respectability. Once again they will need 'lady luck' to smile on them. **Rod Dean**

Back row L-R: Terry Fleming, David Smith, Billy Woods, Paul Edwards, Stewart Robson, David Busst, John Williams, Andy Pearce, Robert Rosario, Phil Babb, Chris Greenman, Luke Chadwick, Ray Woods, Martyn Booty. **Middle:** Kevin Gallacher, Stewart Bowen, Barry Crews, Peter Ndlovu, Sean Flynn, Tony Sheridan, Lee Hurst, Martin Davies, Steve Ogrizovic, Jonathan Gould, Peter Billing, Craig Middleton, Gerard Carr, Michael Stephenson, Ricky Smith, Carl Wilson, Brian Borrows. **Front:** Kenny Sansom, Lloyd McGrath, J Gowens (Asst. Physio), T Exeter (Coach), I Cockerill (Psychologist), R Evans (Yth Develop. Officer), P Neil (Asst. Man.), B Gould (Manager), B Roberts (Res. Coach), B Edwards (Yth Man.), P Hill (Kit Man.), G Dalton (Physio), Michael Gynn, Peter Atherton.

COVENTRY CITY

DIVISION ONE: 19th   **FA CUP:** 3rd RND   **RUMBELOWS CUP:** 4th RND   **ZDS CUP:** 2nd RND

M	DATE		COMP.	VEN	OPPONENTS	RESULT		H/T	LGE POS	GOALSCORERS/GOAL TIMES	ATTEN-DANCE
1	A	17	BL	H	Manchester City	L	0-1	0-1			18,013
2		21	BL	H	Luton Town	W	5-0	3-0	4	Gallacher 7, 39, Rosario 45, Smith 68, Furlong 71	10,084
3		24	BL	A	Queens Park R.	D	1-1	0-0	6	Gynn 46	(9,393)
4		28	BL	H	Sheffield United	W	3-1	3-1	3	Smith (pen) 8, Furlong 28, Rosario 35	12,601
5		31	BL	H	Wimbledon	L	0-1	0-1	8		9,469
6	S	3	BL	A	Oldham Athletic	L	1-2	0-1	11	Furlong 73	(12,996)
7		7	BL	A	Arsenal	W	2-1	1-0	6	Dixon (og) 1, Ndlovu 85	(28,142)
8		14	BL	H	Notts County	W	1-0	0-0	4	Furlong 47	10,635
9		18	BL	H	Leeds United	D	0-0	0-0	4		15,488
10		21	BL	A	Everton	L	0-3	0-1	8		(20,542)
11		25	RC 2/1	H	Rochdale	W	4-0	2-0		Rosario 1, 22, Gallacher 75, McGrath 89	5,982
12		28	BL	H	Aston Villa	W	1-0	1-0	6	Ndlovu 40	17,851
13	O	5	BL	A	West Ham United	W	1-0	0-0	5	Gallacher 78	(21,817)
14		8	RC 2/2	A	Rochdale	L	0-1	0-0			(2,288)
15		19	BL	H	Crystal Palace	L	1-2	0-1	6	Gynn (pen) 69	10,591
16		23	ZDS 2	H	Aston Villa	L	0-2	0-1			6,447
17		26	BL	A	Liverpool	L	0-1	0-1	9		(33,339)
18		30	RC 3	H	Arsenal	W	1-0	1-0		Gallacher 33	15,337
19	N	2	BL	H	Chelsea	L	0-1	0-1	10		11,343
20		16	BL	A	Nottingham Forest	L	0-1	0-1	14		(21,154)
21		23	BL	A	Norwich City	L	2-3	1-0	14	Gallacher 28, 47	(12,052)
22		30	BL	A	Southampton	W	2-0	1-0	13	Gallacher 23, Pearce 70	8,585
23	D	4	RC 4	H	Tottenham Hotspur	L	1-2	0-1		Furlong 67	20,095
24		7	BL	A	Manchester United	L	0-4	0-3	16		(42,549)
25		20	BL	A	Luton Town	L	0-1	0-0	17		(7,533)
26		26	BL	A	Sheffield United	W	3-0	1-0	14	Robson 49, Flynn 56, Billing 66	(19,638)
27		28	BL	H	Wimbledon	D	1-1	1-0	13	Robson 38	(3,270)
28	J	1	BL	H	Tottenham Hotspur	L	1-2	1-1	15	Rosario 11	19,639
29		4	FAC 3	H	Cambridge United	D	1-1	0-1		Borrows (pen) 77	11,428
30		11	BL	A	Queens Park R.	D	2-2	1-0	16	Gallacher 9, Rosario 65	11,999
31		14	FAC 3R	A	Cambridge United	L	0-1	0-0			(9,864)
32		18	BL	A	Manchester City	L	0-1	0-0	16		(23,005)
33	F	1	BL	A	Crystal Palace	W	1-0	1-0	15	Smith 30	(13,818)
34		8	BL	H	Liverpool	D	0-0	0-0	17		21,540
35		22	BL	H	Southampton	D	0-0	0-0	17		(13,719)
36		29	BL	H	Manchester United	D	0-0	0-0	17		23,967
37	M	4	BL	H	Norwich City	D	0-0	0-0	17		8,459
38		7	BL	A	Sheffield Wed.	D	1-1	0-0	16	Gallacher 66	(23,959)
39		11	BL	H	Nottingham Forest	L	0-2	0-2	18		11,158
40		14	BL	A	Chelsea	W	1-0	0-0	16	Robson 68	(10,962)
41		21	BL	H	Oldham Athletic	D	1-1	1-1	16	Pearce 10	12,840
42		28	BL	A	Tottenham Hotspur	L	3-4	1-3	17	Flynn 24, Smith 78, McGrath 85	(22,744)
43	A	4	BL	H	Arsenal	L	0-1	0-1	19		14,133
44		8	BL	H	Sheffield Wed.	D	0-0	0-0	19		13,293
45		11	BL	A	Notts County	L	0-1	0-0	19		(6,655)
46		18	BL	H	Everton	L	0-1	0-0	19		14,669
47		20	BL	A	Leeds United	L	0-2	0-0	19		(26,582)
48		25	BL	H	West Ham United	W	1-0	1-0	19	Gynn 44	15,392
49	M	2	BL	A	Aston Villa	L	0-2	0-2	19		(31,984)

Best Home League Attendance: 23,967 v Manchester United   **Smallest:** 8,459 v Norwich City   **Av Home Att:** 13,893

Goal Scorers: **Compared with 90-91:** +6

League (35):   Gallacher 8, Rosario 4, Smith 4 (1 pen), Furlong 4, Gynn 3 (1 pen), Robson 3, Flynn 2, Ndlovu 2, Pearce 2, McGrath, Billing Opponents

R/lows C (6):   Gallacher 2, Rosario 2, McGrath, Furlong
FA Cup (1):   Borrows (1 pen)
ZDS Cup (0):

Ogrizovic S.	Borrows B.	McGrath L.	Robson S.	Pearce A.	Peake T.	Woods R.	Gynn M.	Rosario R.	Gallacher K.	Smith D.	Furlong P.	Billing P.	Ndlovo P.	Edwards P.	Atherton P.	Drinkell K.	Emerson D.	Hurst L.	Baker	Greenman C.	Booty M.	Middleton C.	Sansom K.	Flynn S.	Heald P.	Referee	
1	2	3	4	5	6	7	8	9	10	11	12			S												D Elleray	1
1	2	3	4	5	6	7	8	9	10*	11	12			S												M Bailey	2
1		2	4	5		7	8*	9•		11	10	12	14	3	6											K Morton	3
1	2	8	4	5		7		9		11•	10	12	14	3*	6											R Groves	4
1	2	7	4	5			9*	10	11	8	3	12		6		S										R Dilkes	5
1	2	8	4	5		7		10	11*	9	3	12		6		S										J Lloyd	6
1	2	8	4	5		7*		10	9	3	14		11•	12												R Gifford	7
1	2	7	4	5		8•		10	9	3	12	11*	6		14											J Worrall	8
1	2	7	4	5		8	9	10*	11	3	12		6		S											D Axcell	9
1	2	7	4	5		8*	9		11	3•	10	14	6		12											A Flood	10
1	2	7		5		9*	10		11	6	8	3		4	12			S								M Brandwood	11
1	2	7	4	5		8		10		9	4	11*	3*	6	12			S								P Alcock	12
1	2	7	4	5		8	12	10	9*	3	11•		6		14											P Foakes	13
	2	7	4*	5		8	14	10	9•	6	11	3		12	1											C Trussell	14
1	2	7	4	5		8	9		12	11*	6•	14		3												G Ashby	15
1	2	7	4			9•	10		11	14	3	12		8*												R Wiseman	16
1	2*	3	4	5		7	8	14	10	11	9*		12	6												R Milford	17
1		8	4	5		7		10	11	9	6	S		S	3		2									M Bodenham	18
1		8	4	5		7*		10	11	9	6	12		S	3		2									K Lupton	19
1	2	12	8	5		7	8	10		9*	S	11	6		3											G Courtney	20
1		7	4*	5		S	8	10		9	12		11	3	6	2										R Lewis	21
1	2	7		5		8*	9	10	S	11			6		4	3		12								P Taylor	22
1	2	7		5			9	10	S	11	6				4	3		S	8							R Gifford	23
1	2	7		5		9*		11*	14	12			6		4	3			8							P Wright	24
1	2	7		5		12	10	11	9	S	8*		6		4	3										K A Cooper	25
1	2	7	4			9*	10	11	12	5			6			S							3	8		T Fitzharris	26
1	2	7	4			9	10	11	12	5			6			S							3	8		B Hill	27
1	2	7	4			9	10	11*	12	6						S							3	8		J Key	28
1	2	7	4	5		9	10	11	12	6			S					8*			3					T Ward	29
1	2	7	4	5		11*	9	10		S	6						12			4*	3			8		D Gallagher	30
1	2	7		5		12	8	9		10	6					S	11			4*	3					T Ward	31
1	2*		4	5		8•	9	10		14			6			12	11				3		7			M Peck	32
1		4					9	10	11	S			6		8	2		5		S	3		7			D Axcell	33
1		2	4				9	10	11		5		6	S	8	S					3		7			R Hart	34
1		2	4				9†	10		12	5		6		8					S	3		7*			M Bodenham	35
1		2	4	5		S	9	10	11	S			6		8						3		7			R Hamer	36
1	2	14	4	5			9*	10		11			6	12	8*						3		7			C Trussell	37
1	2	8	4	5				10	11	9			6	S	S						3		7			W Burns	38
1	2	8	4	5			9*	10*	11	12			6		14						3		7			P Durkin	39
1	2	8	4*	5			9		11	10*			6	12	14						3		7			J Martin	40
	2	10	4	5			12	9		11*			S		6	8					3		7		1	P Don	41
	2	10		5				9		11	8	12		S	6	S	4				3*		7		1	G Courtney	42
	2	8*	4	5			12			11	10	14	9		6						3		7*			R Gifford	43
	2	7	4	5			8	9		11*	10•		14		6						3		12			A Buksh	44
1	2	7	4	5			8	9*			10	S	12		6						3		11			W Burge	45
1	2	10•	4	5			8		11	14	9*			12	6						3		7			C Wilkes	46
1	2	11*	4	5			8		10•	9*			12		6		14				3		7			R Nixon	47
1	12	2	4				8		10	11	S	5	9		6						3*		7			P Wright	48
1	2	3	4				8		10	11•	12	5	9*		6			14					7			T Ward	49
38	34	38	37	36	2	9	21	26	33	23	27	17	9	4	35	2	10	8		4	2	1	21	21	2	**League Appearances**	
	1	2					2	3		1		10	5	14	1		2	11	2			1			1	**Substitute Appearances**	
3	3	4	2	4		1	1	2+1	4	1	4	4	2	2			2+1	2+1	1		1	1				**R/lows Appearances**	
2	2	2	1	2		0+1	1	2	1	1	1+1	2		1				1			2			2		**FA Cup Appearances**	
1	1	1	1				1		1	1		1		0+1	1						1					**ZDS Cup Appearances**	

Also Played: Posn.(Game): Butcher 6† (10), Sealey 1(43,44)

† = Sent Off

COVENTRY CITY

Club Colours: All sky blue
Change Colours: All yellow
Reserves League: Pontins Central League Division 1

COMPETITIONS					
Div. 1	Div. 2	Div. 3	Div. 3S	Div. 4	Texaco
67-	20-25	59-64	26-36	58-59	71-72
	36-52		52-58		72-73
	64-67				73-74
			Div. 3N		UEFA
			25-26		70-71

HONOURS			
Div. 2	Div. 3	Div 3S	FA Cup
66-67	63-64	35-36	1987

MOST APPEARANCES: GEORGE CURTIS 534+4 (55-70)			
Year	League	FA Cup	League Cup
1955-56	3		
1956-57	19		
1957-58	15	1	
1958-59	43	2	
1959-60	45	2	
1960-61	46	3	2
1961-62	46	2	1
1962-63	45	9	2
1963-64	46	2	2
1964-65	41	1	4
1965-66	42	4	4
1966-67	42	1	3
1967-68	3+1		
1968-69	28+2	2	3
1969-70	19+1		1
	483+4	29	22
Previous holder: George Mason 350 (1932-52)			

MOST GOALS IN A CAREER		
C BOURTON 180 (1931-37)		
Season	League	FA Cup
1931-32	49	1
1932-33	40	3
1933-34	25	
1934-35	26	3
1935-36	22	2
1936-37	9	
Total	171	9
Previous holder: F Herbert 87 (1922-29)		

MANAGERS			
Name	Seasons	Best	Worst
H Pollitt	1920-21	20(2)	20(2)
A Evans	1921-25	18(2)	22(2)
J Kerr	1926-28	15(3S)	20(3S)
J McIntyre	1928-31	6(3S)	14(3S)
H Storer	1931-45	4(2)	12(3S)
R Bayliss	1946-47	8(2)	8(2)
W Frith	1947-49	10(2)	16(2)
H Storer	1949-54	7(2)	14(3S)
J Fairbrother	1954-55	9(3S)	14(3S)
C Elliott		9(3S)	9(3S)
J Carver	1955-56	9(3S)	9(3S)
G Rayner			
H Warren	1957-58	8(3S)	19(3S)
W Frith	1958-62	4(3)	2(4)
J Hill	1962-68	20(1)	14(3)
N Cantwell	1968-72	6(1)	20(1)
R Dennison	1972		
J Mercer	1972-74	16(1)	19(1)
G Milne	1974-81	7(1)	19(1)
D Sexton	1981-83	14(1)	19(1)
R Gould	1983-84	18(1)	19(1)
D Mackay	1984-86	17(1)	18(1)
G Curtis/J Sillett	1986-87	18(1)	10(1)
J Sillett	1987-90	7(1)	12(1)
T Butcher	1990-91	16(1)	16(1)
D Howe	1991-92	19(1)	19(1)
B Gould	1992-		

RECORD TRANSFER FEE RECEIVED			
Amount	Club	Player	Date
£1,250,000	Nottingham Forest	Ian Wallace	7/80
£365,000	Portland Timbers	Gary Collier	3/80
£200,000	Arsenal	Geoff Blockley	10/72
£90,000	Arsenal	Bobby Gould	2/68

RECORD TRANSFER FEE PAID			
Amount	Club	Player	Date
£900,000	Dundee Utd	Kevin Gallacher	2/90
£800,000	Glasgow Rangers	Kevin Drinkell	10/89
£780,000	Chelsea	David Speedie	7/87
£325,000	Bristol City	Gary Collier	8/79

LONGEST LEAGUE RUNS	
of undefeated matches:	25 (26.11.1966-13.5.1967)
of undefeated home matches:	19 (11.4.1925-13.3.1926)
without home win:	10 (30.8.1919-20.12.1919)
	(1.1.1992-18.4.1992)
of league wins:	6 (24.4.1964-1.9.1964)
of league defeats:	9 (30.8.1919-4.10.1919)
of league matches w/out a win:	19 (30.8.1919-20.12.1919)
of undefeated away matches:	12 (19.11.1966-19.8.1967)
without an away win:	28 (5.1.1924-4.4.1925)
of home wins:	11 (18.10.1952-28.2.1953)
of away wins:	4 (29.8.1963-14.9.1963)

PREVIOUS NAME
Singers F.C. 1883-98

PREVIOUS LEAGUE
Southern League, Birmingham & District League

BIGGEST VICTORIES
League: 9-0 v Bristol City, Division 3S, 28.4.1934
F.A. Cup: 7-0 v Scunthorpe, Round 1, 24.11.1934
League Cup: 7-2 v Chester City, Round 2, 9.10.1985
5-0 v Watford, Rnd 5 replay, 9.12.1980
5-0 v Sunderland, Rnd 5 replay, 24.1.1990
Europe: 4-1 v Trakia Plovdiv, Round 1 (UEFA) 16.9.1970

BIGGEST DEFEATS
League: 2-10 v Norwich, Division 3S, 15.3.1930
1-9 v Millwall, Div 3(S), 19.11.1927
F.A. Cup: 2-11 v Berwick Rangers, 2.11.1901
League Cup: 1-8 v Leicester City (h), 1.12.1964
Europe (UEFA): 1-6 v Bayern Munich, 20.10.1970

MOST POINTS
3 points a win: 63, Division 1, 1986-87
2 points a win: 60, Div 4, 1958-59, Div 3, 1963-64

MOST GOALS
108, 1931-32, (Division 3S).
Bourton 49, Lauderdale 19, Lake 14, Shepperd 7, White 6,
Holmes 5, Cull 3, Baker, Bowden, Heinmann, Johnson 1
each, og 1

MOST GOALS IN A MATCH
5. C Bourton v Bournemouth, 6-1, Div 3S, 17.10.1931
5. A Bacon v Gillingham, 7-3 (a), Div 3S, 30.12.1933
5. C Regis v Chester City, 7-2, Lge Cup, 9.10.1985

MOST GOALS IN A SEASON
Clarrie Bourton 50 (League 49, FAC 1) 1931-32.
5 goals once = 5; 4 goals once = 4; 3 goals 5 times = 15; 2
goals 6 times = 12; 1 goal 14 times = 14.
Previous holder: F Herbert 27 (1926-27).

MOST FIRST CLASS MATCHES IN A SEASON
57 (46 League, 9 FA Cup, 2 League Cup) 1962-63

MOST LEAGUE GOALS CONCEDED
97, Division 3S, 1931-32

MOST LEAGUE WINS
24, Division 3S, 1935-36; Division 4, 1958-59

MOST LEAGUE DRAWS
17, Division 3, 1962-63

MOST LEAGUE DEFEATS
22, Division 2, 1919-20; Division 2, 1924-25; Division 3S,
1927-28; Division 2, 1951-52; Division 1, 1984-85

OLDEST PLAYER
Alf Wood, 44 years 207 days v Plymouth, FAC 2nd Rnd,
7.12.1958.

YOUNGEST PLAYER
Perry Suckling 16 years 321 days, v Southampton, (Div 1),
28.8.1982.

MOST CAPPED PLAYER
David Clements (N. Ireland) 21 & Ronnie Rees (Wales) 21

BEST PERFORMANCES BY COVENTRY CITY

League: 1966-67: Matches played 42, Won 23, Drawn 13, Lost 6, Goals for 74, Goals against 43, Points 59. First in Division 2.

Highest: 1969-70: 6th in Division 1.

F.A. Cup: 1986-87: 3rd rnd. Bolton Wanderers 3-0 (H); 4th rnd. Manchester Utd. 1-0 (A); 5th rnd. Stoke City 1-0 (A); 6th rnd. Sheffield Wednesday 3-1 (A); Semi-Final Leeds Utd 3-2; Final Tottenham Hotspur 3-2.

League Cup: 1980-81: 2nd rnd. Manchester Utd. 1-0, 1-0; 3rd rnd. Brighton & H.A. 2-1; 4th rnd. Cambridge Utd. 1-1, 1-0; 5th rnd. Watford 2-2, 5-0; Semi-Final West Ham 3-2, 0-2.
1989-90: 2nd rnd. Grimsby Town 1-3, 3-0; 3rd rnd. QPR 1-0; 4th rnd. Manchester City 1-0; 5th rnd. Sunderland 0-0, 5-0; Semi-Final Nottingham Forest 1-2, 0-0

Europe (UEFA): 1970-71: 1st rnd. Trakia Plovdiv 4-1, 2-0; 2nd rnd. Bayern Munich 1-6, 2-1.

DIVISIONAL RECORDS

	Played	Won	Drawn	Lost	For	Against	Points
DIVISION 1	1036	331	284	421	1217	1465	**1091**
DIVISION 2	756	279	186	291	1050	1099	**744**
DIVISION 3	230	93	66	71	403	347	**252**
DIVISION 3S	696	282	158	256	1278	1102	**722**
DIVISION 3N	42	16	6	20	73	82	**38**
DIVISION 4	46	24	12	10	84	47	**60**
TOTALS	**2806**	**1025**	**712**	**1069**	**4105**	**4141**	**2907**

COVENTRY CITY

PLAYERS NAME Honours	Ht	Wt	Birthdate	Birthplace Transfers	Contract Date	Clubs	League	L/Cup	FA Cup	Other	Lg	L/C	FAC	Oth
GOALKEEPERS														
Steve Ogrizovic	6.3	14.7	12.09.57	Mansfield	28.07.77	Chesterfield	16	2						
FAC'87				£70,000	18.11.77	Liverpool	4		1					
				P.E	11.08.82	Shrewsbury Town	84	7	5					
				£72,000	22.06.84	Coventry City	316	32	19	11	1			
DEFENDERS														
Peter Atherton	5.11	12.3	06.04.70	Wigan	12.02.88	Wigan Ath	145+4	8	7	12+1	1			
					23.08.91	Coventry City	35							
Peter Billing	6.1	13.11	24.10.64	Liverpool		South Liverpool			1					
					15.01.86	Everton	1			4				
				£12,000	23.12.86	Crewe Alexandra	83+5	1+1	5	9	1			
				£120,000	28.06.89	Coventry City	48+7	9+1	7	2	1			
Brian Borrows	5.10	10.12	20.12.60	Liverpool	23.04.80	Everton	27	2						
E: B.1				£10,000	24.03.83	Bolton W	95	7	4	4				
				£80,000	06.06.85	Coventry City	261+2	31	16	10+1	9		1	
Paul R Edwards	5.11	11.0	25.12.63	Birkenhead		Altrincham			4					
NPL LgC'85					12.01.88	Crewe Alexandra	82+4	6	8	7+1	6			1
				£350,000	16.03.90	Coventry City	32+4	6	2	2				
Kenny Sansom	5.6	11.8	26.09.58	Camberwell	01.12.75	Crystal Palace (A)	172	11	17		3		1	
E:86,B.2,U21.8,Y,S,Div2'79,FAYC'77,LC'87,F.lg				£955,000	14.08.80	Arsenal	314	48	26	6	6			
				£300,000	24.12.88	Newcastle Utd	20	4						
				£300,000	08.06.89	Q.P.R	64	7	10	1			2	
				£100,000	22.03.91	Coventry City	30	2						
MIDFIELD														
Phillip Babb	6.0	11.7	30.11.70	Lambeth	25.04.89	Millwall (T)								
				Free	10.08.90	Bradford City	73+7	5+1	3	3+1	14			
				£500,000	21.07.92	Coventry City								
Michael Gynn	5.5	10.6	19.08.61	Peterborough	04.04.79	Peterborough U. (A)	152+4	10	13		33	1	3	
FAC'87				£60,000	25.08.83	Coventry City	188+33	22+4	15+2	6	30	7	4	2
Lloyd McGrath	5.8	10.6	24.02.65	Birmingham	31.12.82	Coventry City (A)	170+8	19	15	6	4	1		
E:u21.1,Y.4; FAC'87														
Stewart Robson	5.11	11.13	06.01.64	Billericay	12.11.81	Arsenal (A)	150+1	20	13	2	16	3	1	1
E: u21.8, Y.16				£700,000	07.01.87	West Ham U	68+1	8	6	1	4	1	1	
				Loan	07.03.91	Coventry City	3+1							
				Free	23.05.91	Coventry City	37	2	1	1	3			
David Smith	5.8	10.2	29.03.68	Gloucester	07.07.86	Coventry City	138+10	16	6	5+1	18			
E: u21.10														
Raymond Woods	5.11	11.6	07.06.65	Birkenhead		Tranmere Rovers	9+5	1		0+1	2			
						Colne Dynamoes								
					30.08.90	Wigan Ath	25+3	2	4	2	3		1	
				£200,000	30.01.91	Coventry City	21	1	0+1		1			
FORWARDS														
Terrence Fleming	5.9		05.01.73	Meridan	02.07.91	Coventry City (T)	0+2							
Kevin Gallacher	5.8	10.10	23.11.66	Clydebank		Dundee Utd	118+13	13	20+3	15+6	27	5	5	3
S: 12, B.2, u21.7, Y				£900,000	29.01.90	Coventry City	80	9	3	2	22	7		
Peter Ndlovu	5.8		25.02.73	Zimbabwe		H'landers,								
				£10,000	16.08.91	Coventry City	9+14	2		0+1	2			
Robert Rosario	6.3	13.12	04.03.64	Hammersmith		Harrow Borough								
E:u21.4,u19.3				23.12.83	Norwich City	115+11	11	13+1	8+1	18	3	3	5
				Loan	13.12.85	Wolverhampton W	2			2	1			
				£600,000	27.03.91	Coventry City	26+4	2+1	2	1	4	2		
ADDITIONAL CONTRACT PLAYERS														
(D) Martyn Booty	5.8	11.2	30.05.71	Kirby Muxloe	30.05.89	Coventry City (T)	2+1	1	2					
David Busst						Moor Green								
					14.01.92	Coventry City								
Sean M Flynn					03.12.91	Coventry City	21+1				2			
(D) Chris Greenman	6.1		22.12.68	Bristol	04.07.88	Coventry City	4		1					
(M) Lee Hurst	5.10	10.12	21.09.70	Nuneaton	30.05.89	Coventry City (T)	11+3	2+1	1+1					
(D) Lee Middleton	5.11	10.12	10.09.70	Nuneaton	30.05.89	Coventry City (T)	0+2							
				Monthly	08.07.91	Coventry City	1	1						
(F) Craig Middleton	5.11	10.13	10.09.70	Nuneaton	30.05.89	Coventry City (T)	0+1							
(D) Andy Pearce	6.6	14.6	20.04.66	Bradford		Halesowen Town			1					
					14.05.90	Coventry City	47	4	2	1	3			
Jose Perdomo					29.08.90	Coventry City	4	2						
Anthony Sheridan					18.09.91	Coventry City								
(F) John Williams						Cradley Town								
				£5,000	19.08.91	Swansea City	36+3	2+1	3	1	11			
				£250,000	01.07.92	Coventry City								

COVENTRY CITY

RECORD WIN & LOSS AGAINST EACH CLUB IN CURRENT DIVISION
(Where a score has occured on several occasions the most recent is given)

Club	Rec. Win	Season	Rec. Loss	Season
ARSENAL	3-0	1974-75	6-1	1990-91
ASTON VILLA	2-0	1989-90	4-0	1982-83
BLACKBURN ROVERS	6-1	1950-51	2-0	1948-49
CHELSEA	5-1	1977-78	6-2	1984-85
CRYSTAL PALACE	8-0	1931-32	4-1	1924-25 (home)
EVERTON	4-1	1975-76 (away)	6-0	1977-78
IPSWICH TOWN	5-0	1966-67	4-0	1980-81 (home)
LEEDS UNITED	4-0	1981-82	4-0	1949-50 (home)
LIVERPOOL	4-0	1983-84	6-1	1989-90 (home)
MANCHESTER CITY	4-0	1982-83	5-1	1985-86
MANCHESTER UNITED	3-0	1982-83	5-1	1924-25
MIDDLESBROUGH	3-0	1964-65	2-0	1975-76
NORWICH CITY	4-0	1954-55	10-2	1929-30
NOTTINGHAM FOREST	5-1	1938-39	4-0	1971-72
OLDHAM ATHLETIC	5-1	1924-25	5-0	1924-25
QUEENS PARK RANGERS	7-0	1932-33	5-1	1978-79
SHEFFIELD UNITED	3-0 (away)	1991-92	3-0	1938-39 (home)
SHEFFIELD WEDNESDAY	5-0	1988-89	4-0	1967-68
SOUTHAMPTON	5-1	1965-66	8-2	1983-84
TOTTENHAM HOTSPUR	4-0	1938-39	5-0	1919-20 (home)
WIMBLEDON	2-1	1987-88	2-1	1986-87

MANAGER: BOBBY GOULD

DATE OF BIRTH: 12.06.1948   **PLACE OF BIRTH:** Coventry

DATE OF APPOINTMENT: MAY 1992

PREVIOUS CLUBS
as Manager: Bristol Rovers; Coventry City; Bristol City; Wimbledon; West Brom
as Coach: Aldershot; Chelsea
as Player: Coventry; Arsenal; Wolves (twice); Bristol C; WBA; West Ham; Bristol Rov; Hereford; Wimbledon; Aldershot

HONOURS
as Manager: FA Cup 1988 (Wimbledon)
as Player: Coventry: Div 2 Champions 1967; Wolves: Div 2 Champions 1977; West Ham: FA Cup Winners 1975

Value Rating: ★ ★ ★

Price of 1991-92 Programme: £1
Number of Pages: 32, Size B
Subscriptions: Subscriptions on request to club

Local Newspapers: Coventry Evening Telegraph

Local Radio Stations: Mercia Sound

Books available about Club: Singers to Sky Blues – The Story of Coventry City Football Club

LEADING LEAGUE GOALSCORERS
SEASONS 1979-80 – 1991-92

1979-80	IAN WALLACE	13	1980-81	GERRY DALY	8
1981-82	MARK HATELEY	13	1982-83	STEVE WHITTON	12
1983-84	TERRY GIBSON	17	1984-85	TERRY GIBSON	15
1985-86	TERRY GIBSON	12	1986-87	CYRILLE REGIS	12
1987-88	CYRILLE REGIS	10	1988-89	DAVID SPEEDIE	14
1989-90	DAVID SPEEDIE	8	1990-91	KEVIN GALLAGHER	11

1991-92 **KEVIN GALLAGHER** 8

HIGHFIELD ROAD STADIUM King Richard St, Coventry CV2 4FW

Capacity: 25,259   **Covered Standing:**   **Seating:** 17,609

Tel: Ground: 0203 223535   **Ticket Sales:** 0203 225545   **Clubcall:** 0898 12 11 66

All premium rate calls (0898/0891) cost 36p per minute cheap rate and 48p per minute at all other times. Call costings correct at time of going to press.

GROUNDS
Binley Road 1883-87; Stoke Road 1887-99; Highfield Road 1899-

ATTENDANCES
Highest: 51,455 v Wolverhampton W, Div 2, 29.4.1967

Lowest: 1,086 v Millwall, Full Members Cup, 15.10.1985

RECORD RECEIPTS (with previous records):
£177,271 v Nott'm Forest, L/woods Cup S/F 2nd leg, 25.2.1990
£127,056 v Liverpool, Division 1, 22.3.1989
£102,000 v Liverpool, L/woods Cup 4th Rnd, 19.11.1986
£68,029 v West Ham United, League Cup, 27.1.1981
£51,493 v West Bromwich Albion, FA Cup, 9.1.1979
£45,061 v Liverpool, League Cup, 20.12.1977
£29,674 v Newcastle United, FA Cup, 24.1.1976

HIGHFIELD ROAD
First game: v Shrewsbury Town, 9.9.1899
First floodlit game: v San Lorenzo (Argentina), Friendly, 30.1.1956

Season Tickets:
Stands: from £153 to £252, juv/OAP £85.50 to £121.50
Terraces: £135, juv/OAP £76.50

Cost of Stand Tickets: Seats: £8 to £13.50, juv.OAP £3.50 to £6.50
Terraces: £6.50 to £8.50, juv/OAP £3 to £5

Match and Ticket Information: Postal applications for stand tickets accepted (with SAE) 21 days before each match by the Ticket Office Manager at the Stadium, King Richard St., Coventry

Car Parking: Street parking around ground permitted. Special park – for coaches is situated at Gosford Green on Walsgrave Road (A4600) 200 yards from stadium. Visitors coach park is by the railway bridge in Walsgrave Road. Street parking for cars.

Nearest Railway Station: Coventry (0203) 555211
Outside station take No.17 or 27 bus and ask for 'stop' Gosford Green

How to get to the ground

From North, West and South: At M6 motorway Junction 2, take the A4600 and follow signs for City Centre. Follow this road for approximately 3 miles, and just under the railway bridge, turn right at the traffic lights into Swan Lane. Highfield Road Stadium is just on your left hand side

From East and South: Take M45 motorway then A45. Pass the Peugeot Talbot plant, and at next roundabout take the 3rd exit, A423, then in approximately 1 mile at next roundabout, follow B4110 signposted 'Stoke'. Follow this road acroos all traffic lights to T-junction, then turn left into Walsgrave Road and immediately right into Swan Lane

CREWE ALEXANDRA

Division 3

Formed: 1877   **Turned Professional:** 1893   **Ltd Co:** 1892

SPONSORED BY: Boldon James   **NICKNAME:** The Railwaymen

President
N Rowlinson

Chairman
J Bowler, MPS

Directors
J McMillan (Vice-Chairman)
K Potts
D Rowlinson
R Clayton
N Hassall FCCA
D Gradi
E Weetman
R G Holmes

Team Manager
Dario Gradi

Assistant Manager
Kenny Swain

Secretary
Mrs Gill Palin (0270 213014)

Hon.Medical Officer
Dr J M Davies

Commercial Manager
Gill Palin

Club Statistician for the Directory
Harold Finch

EVERYONE at the club had hoped season 1991-92 would see the club make a quick return to Division 3, but hopes of that were ended at Scunthorpe in the second-leg of the Play Off Semi Final, losing 2-0.

The opening day of the season saw them in opposition to League newcomers Barnet and this resulted in a 7-4 victory. That was the best away result by the club, but the irony of the seven goals 'against' conceded by Barnet was the fact that it equalled the total that Crewe themselves conceded when they played their first League fixture in 1892.

A record nine goals against Doncaster in round 1 of the Rumbelows League Cup gave them an attractive second round tie against Newcastle United but they lost 5-3 on aggregate in the two legged tie.

On the transfer front, the club hit the headlines when Rob Jones joined Liverpool in October for a fee of £300,000 with additional payments based on appearances. By the end of the season that total had reached £525,000 leaving just one more payment to come to bring the figure to £600,000. For Rob, it was an amazing season for he was also capped by England and went on to get an F.A. Cup Winners medal in May.

In the Cup itself, the club reached round 3 once more, disposing of Carlisle after a replay, Chester in round 2 and then in round 3 came that magic draw, Crewe v Liverpool. Played in front of a capacity crowd they lost 4-0 but they created another first, the game being screened live on BSkyB Television. That was not the end of their cup exploits for they reached the Semi-final stage in the Northern Area of the Autoglass Trophy before losing narrowly to Stockport County, 2-1.

Along with other clubs in the Division, the Alex had completed the double over Aldershot. After 24 visits to their ground, Crewe won on their 25th visit only to find some time later that that victory was expunged from the official records. They conceded the double to just one club, Mansfield Town but some consolation was gained from the fact that Crewe were the only club to gain a double over Blackpool, later to gain promotion through the play offs.

Several young players made their debuts in the club colours during the season, with Neil Sorvel and Michael Jackson outstanding, The youth team progressed to the 4th round of the F.A. Youth Cup before going out to finalists, Crystal Palace.

Tony Naylor topped the scoring charts, closely followed by Craig Hignett; and out of the 59 games played, a new club record, Gus Wilson, in his first season in League football missed only one of those games. The clubs recruits from non-League circles, Tony Naylor, Phil Clarkson and finally Steve Macauley all made significant contributions during the season.   **Harold Finch**

Back row L-R: Gus Wilson, Ahmed Mettioui, Steve Macauley, Dele Adebola, Anthony Hughes, Michael Jackson, Mark Gardiner. **Middle row:** Dario Gradi (Manager), Jimmy Harvey, Phil Clarkson, Shaun Smith, Dean Greygoose, Dave McKearney, Gareth Whalley, Kenny Swain (Asst. Manager). **Front row:** Rob Edwards, Richard Annan, Craig Hignett, Steve Garvey, Tony Naylor, Steve Walters. *Photo courtesy of Steve Finch L.R.P.S.*

CREWE ALEXANDRA

DIVISION FOUR: 6th   **FA CUP:** 3rd RND   **RUMBELOWS CUP:** 2nd RND   **AUTOGLASS:** Nth S/FINALS

M		DATE	COMP.	VEN	OPPONENTS	RESULT	H/T	LGE POS	GOALSCORERS/GOAL TIMES	ATTEN-DANCE
1	A	17	BL	A	Barnet	W 7-4	3-2		Naylor 17, Futcher 18, Edwards 3(27,70,78), Hignett (p)60,71	(5,090)
2		20	RC 1/1	H	Doncaster Rovers	W 5-2	3-1		Edwards 4, Gardiner 24, Naylor 31, 57, Callaghan 47	2,900
3		24	BL	H	Cardiff City	D 1-1	0-1	5	Murphy 84	3,799
4		27	RC 1/2	A	Doncaster Rovers	W 4-2	0-1		Futcher 60, 73, Naylor 76, Hignett 84	(1,376)
5		31	BL	A	Rotherham United	W 2-1	1-1	2	Naylor 11, Edwards 88	(4,362)
6	S	7	BL	A	Burnley	D 1-1	0-0	1	Hamilton (og) 55	(9,657)
7		13	BL	H	Mansfield Town	L 1-2	1-2	5	Naylor 15 secs	4,667
8		17	BL	H	Northampton Town	D 1-1	1-1	7	Naylor 24	3,597
9		21	BL	A	Scunthorpe United	L 0-1	0-1	9		(3,021)
10		24	RC 2/1	H	Newcastle United	L 3-4	2-2		Evans 3, 14, Gallaghan 22	4,251
11		28	BL	H	Gillingham	W 2-1	1-0	6	Gardiner 29, McKearney 85	3,126
12	O	5	BL	A	Doncaster Rovers	W 3-1	1-0	6	Evans 45, 78, Walters 69	(1,779)
13		9	RC 2/2	A	Newcastle United	L 0-1	0-0			(9,197)
14		11	BL	H	Walsall	L 0-1	0-1	7		4,749
15		19	BL	H	Scarborough	D 3-3	2-0	8	McKearney 19, Hignett 30, Clarkson 67	2,696
16		22	AGT Pre	A	Darlington	D 2-2	0-2		Hignett 47, McPhillips 62	(1,098)
17		26	BL	A	Carlisle United	L 1-2	0-0	10	Edwards 88	(1,905)
18	N	5	BL	H	Maidstone United	D 1-1	1-1	11	Hignett 37	2,476
19		9	BL	H	Wrexham	W 2-1	2-0	10	Gardiner 44, 45	3,596
20		16	FAC 1	A	Carlisle United	D 1-1	1-0		Hignett 33	(3,106)
21		19	AGT Pre	H	Chester City	W 2-0	1-0		Edwards 15, 74	1,779
22		23	BL	A	Blackpool	W 2-0	1-0	7	Carr 21, 58	(4,595)
23		26	FAC 1R	H	Carlisle United	W †5-3	2-0		Walters 13, Naylor 33, 101, Gardiner 47, Barnsley (og) 113	3,733
24		30	BL	H	Hereford United	W 4-2	3-0	5	Naylor 8, Futcher 32, Hignett 36, 74 (pen)	2,990
25	D	7	FAC 2	H	Chester City	W 2-0	0-0		Hignett 54, Naylor 90	5,299
26		26	BL	H	Barnet	W 3-0	2-0	8	Hignett (pen) 10, Edwards 32, Naylor 72	4,736
27		28	BL	H	Rotherham United	L 0-1	0-1	8		4,490
28	J	6	FAC 3	H	Liverpool	L 0-4	0-3			7,457
29		11	BL	H	Lincoln City	W 1-0	0-0	8	Walters 64	3,073
30		14	AGT 1	H	Bolton Wanderers	W 2-0	1-0		Edwards 9, Hignett 64	2,155
31		18	BL	A	Rochdale	L 0-1	0-1	9		(2,965)
32	F	4	AGT 2	H	Hull City	W 1-0	0-0	9	Naylor 48	2,348
33		7	BL	H	Carlisle United	W 2-1	1-1	8	Naylor 5, Hignett 69	3,232
34		12	BL	A	Hereford United	W 2-1	1-1	7	Futcher 13, Gardiner 51	(2,181)
35		15	BL	H	Chesterfield	W 3-1	0-1	7	Gardiner 63, Naylor 70, Walters 77	3,172
36		18	BL	A	Scarborough	L 1-2	1-0	7	Carr 45	(1,352)
37		22	BL	A	Lincoln City	D 2-2	1-2	6	Naylor 35, Hignett (pen) 54	(2,261)
38		25	BL	H	York City	W 1-0	0-0	4	Naylor 44	3,327
39		28	BL	H	Halifax Town	W 3-2	2-1	4	Evans 37, Clarkson 44, Naylor 60	3,514
40	M	3	BL	H	Rochdale	D 1-1	0-0	5	Clarkson 83	3,870
41		7	BL	A	York City	D 1-1	1-1	6	Naylor 14	(2,208)
42		11	BL	A	Maidstone United	L 0-2	0-1	6		(1,174)
43		17	AGT NSF	H	Stockport County	L 1-2	0-2		McKearney 75	5,594
44		21	BL	A	Wrexham	L 0-1	0-0	8		(3,899)
45		24	BL	A	Chesterfield	L 1-2	1-0	9	Clarkson 14	(2,534)
46		28	BL	H	Blackpool	W 1-0	0-0	8	Naylor 65	4,913
47		31	BL	A	Mansfield Town	L 3-4	0-3	8	Clarkson 52, 80, McKearney 66	(3,108)
48	A	4	BL	H	Burnley	W 1-0	0-0	8	Gardiner 85	5,530
49		11	BL	A	Northampton Town	W 1-0	0-0	8	Hignett 60	(3,300)
50		14	BL	A	Halifax Town	L 1-2	1-0	8	McKearney 8	(1,022)
51		18	BL	H	Scunthorpe United	D 1-1	0-0	8	Hignett 84	3,313
52		20	BL	A	Gillingham	W 1-0	0-0	8	Naylor 55	(2,928)
53		24	BL	H	Doncaster Rovers	W 1-0	0-0	8	Futcher 34	3,639
54		28	BL	A	Cardiff City	D 1-1	0-1	6	Macauley 84	(10,523)
55	M	2	BL	A	Walsall	W 3-2	3-0	6	Hignett 13, 19, Naylor 39	(4,997)
56		10	PO SF 1	H	Scunthorpe United	D 2-2	2-2		Hignett 6, Naylor 39	6,083
57		13	PO SF 2	A	Scunthorpe United	L 0-2	0-0			(7,938)

Best Home League Attendance: 5,530 v Burnley   **Smallest: 2,476 v Maidstone Utd**   **Av Home Att: 3,738**

Goal Scorers: **Compared with 90-91: -10**

League (66): Naylor 15, Hignett 13 (4 pens), Clarkson 6, Edwards 6, Gardiner 6, McKearney 4, Futcher 4, Carr 3, Walters 3, Evans 3, Murphy Macauley, Opponents

R/lows C (12): Naylor 3, Callaghan 2, Evans 2, Futcher 2, Edwards, Gardiner, Hignett
FA Cup (8): Naylor 3, Hignett 2, Walters, Gardiner, Opponents
Autoglass (8): Edwards 3, Hignett 2, Naylor, McPhillips, McKearney
Play-Offs (2): Hignett, Naylor

† = After extra-time

Greygoose D.	Wilson E.	Jones R.	Smart J.	Callaghan A.	Walters S.	Hignett C.	Naylor A.	Futcher R.	Gardiner M.	Edwards R.	Garvey S.	Murphy A.	Carr D.	Jasper D.	Rose C.	Evans S.	McPhillips T.	McKearney D.	Sorvel N.	Clarkson P.	Noble D.	Payne R.	Whitehurst W.	Macauley S.	Smith G.	Referee	
1	2	3	4	5	6•	7	8	9*	10	11	12	14														P Jones	1
1	2	3		5	6	7	8*	9	10	11	12	S	4													K A Cooper	2
1	2	3		5	6	7	8*	9•	10	11	12	14	4													P Harrison	3
1	2	3	14	5*		7	8	9	10	11		6*	4	12												I Hendrick	4
1	2	3		5*	6•	7	8	9	10	11	12		4	14												D Allison	5
1	2	3	4	5	6		8	9†	10•	11*	7	14		12												J Key	6
1	2	3	4	5	6		8	9	10	11	7•	14						12								D Shadwell	7
1	2	3*		5	6		8	9	10	11	7•	14	4	S												T Lunt	8
1	2	3		5	6	9	8*		10	11		7•	4	14				12								D Phillips	9
1	2	3		5	6				10	11	7•		4			9	8	14								R Dilkes	10
1	2†	3		5	6			14	10	11			4			9•	8*	7								P Vanes	11
1	2			5	6			S	10	11			4			9	8		14			7•				K Morton	12
1	2			5*				14	10	11			4		12	9	8	6				7•				A Bennett	13
1	2			5	6			12	10	11			4			9*	8•	3				7				I Hemley	14
1		2	5	6	7				10	11			4			9	S	3		8•		14				R Hamer	15
1	2			5		7			10	11			4			9	8	3	6	S						T West	16
1	2			5	6	7			10	11			4			9	8*	3	S	12						R Shepherd	17
	2			5		7			10	14			4			9	8•		6	1	1	12				C Trussell	18
1	2			5	6	7			10	12			4			9		3	S	11•		8				J Parker	19
1	2			5		7	8•	12	10	11*			4			9		3	6*			14				A Dawson	20
1	2				6	7	8•	9*		11			4	10		12		3								T Fitzharris	21
1	2	3			6	7	8	9•	10	11*			4					14		12						G Singh	22
1	2				6	7	8•	9*	10	11			4	14				3		S						A Dawson	23
1	2			5	6	7	8•	9*	10	11			4	14				3		12						P Danson	24
1	2			5	6	7	8	9*	10	11•			4	14				3		12						J Kirkby	25
1	2			5	6	7•	8			11			4			9•		3		12		14				K Hackett	26
1	2			5	6	7*	8			11			4			9•		3		12		10				K Breen	27
1	2			5	6	7	8		10	11			4*	9*	14			3		12						T Holbrook	28
1	2			5	6	7	8•		10	11			4			12		3		9						A Bennett	29
1	2			5		7		12		11			4	10			8*	3	6	9						P Vanes	30
1	2			5	14	7*	8			12			4	10*				3		11		9				S Lodge	31
1	2			5	6	7	8	S	10*	12			4					3		11		9				K Barratt	32
1	2			5*	6	7	8	14	10	12			4					3		11		9•				G Courtney	33
1	2			5	6	7	8*	9	10	11•			4					3		S		12				C Wilkes	34
1	2			5	6	7	8*	9	10	11•			4					3		S		12				H King	35
1	2			5	6	7	8	9•	10	11			4					3		S		14				M Bailey	36
1	2			5		7	8	9	10	11•	12		4					3	6*	14						R Pawley	37
1	2			5		7	8	9*	10•	11			4	12				3	6	14						J Deakin	38
	2		5				8		10	14	7•		4		6	9*		3	12	11	1					I Hemley	39
	2		5	S		12			10		7		4		6	9*		3		11						J Kirkby	40
	2		5	S	6				10		7		4		6	9*		3		11	1					B Coddington	41
	2		5	14	6				10	12	7*		4			9*		3		11	1					J Carter	42
	2		5		6	12	8			7			4	11•	9	14	3	10*		1						J Worrall	43
	2		5		6	7	8		11*			4			14		3		9	1						K Cooper	44
1	2		5	4	6	7	8	12						10		3			9							I Borrett	45
1	2			11*	6•	7	8		10			4				3			9			12	5	14		G Poll	46
1	2			11*		7	8		10			4				3			9			12	5	14		J Brandwood	47
1	2			6		7	8		10			4			S		S	11*			9	5	3			A Dawson	48
1	2			11	6	7	8		10•			4					14	9			12	5*	3			P Alcock	49
1	2			10	6	7	8				S	4				5		11			9		3			M Peck	50
1	2			8	6	7		9	10				14	S•			4		11				5	3•		R Gifford	51
1	2				6	7	8	9•	10				12	11				4*	14				5	3		R Bigger	52
	2			11	6	7	8	9*	10			S						4	14	1		12	5	3		T West	53
	2			11*	6	7	8	9*	10				12					4	14	1			5	3		D Frampton	54
	2		12	11	6	7	8*	9•	10									4	14	1			5	3		R Groves	55
	2			11	6	7	8	9*	10			S						4	12	1			5	3		M Bodenham	56
	2			14	11•		7	8	10			6*					12	4	9				5	3		A Buksh	57
33	41	8	10	36	34	32	34	18	37	22	8	1	33	3	2	13	5	30	5	18	7	3	4	9	8	League Appearances	
	1	1		3			6		3		6	3	4	3	4	1	1		4	10		3	6		2	Substitute Appearances	
4	4	3	0+1	4	2	2	2	2+1	4	4			1+1	1		4		0+1	0+1	2	2	1+1		1		R/lows Appearances	
4	4		3	3	4	4	2	4	4	4			1			1+2	2	4		1+1		0+1				FA Cup Appearances	
4	5		1	3	3	4+1	3	1	2+1	3+1	1		5	2	1	2+1	2+1	5	4	1	1		1			Autoglass Appearances	
	2			0+1	2	1	2	2		1			1+1	1		2		1+1	1				2	2		Play-Offs Appearances	

Also Played: Posn.(Game): Rutherford 5(10)14(11)S(45), Downes 3(12,13)14(14), Swain 3(18), Disley 14(21,29)S(50), P Edwards 1(40,41,57), Bishop 10(44)11*(45)6•(47), Kelly 12*(44), Jackson S(16,30)5(21,22,23)   **Players on Loan:** R Payne (Liverpool), E Bishop (Chester)

CREWE ALEXANDRA

Club Colours: Red shirts, white shorts, red stockings
Change Colours: Blue shirts, white or blue shorts
Reserves & A Team: Lancashire League

Previous League: Central League
Previous Managers: (Since 1946): George Lillycrop   Frank Hill   Arthur Turner   Harry Catterick   Ralph Ward   Maurice Lindley   Harry Ware   Jimmy McGuigan   Ernie Tagg   Dennis Viollet   Jimmy Melia   Ernie Tagg   Harry Gregg   Warwick Rimmer   Tony Waddington   Arfon Griffiths   Peter Morris
Honours: Welsh Cup Winners 1936, 1937
League Career: Original Members of Div 2 1892   Failed to gain re-election 1896   Re-Joined Div 3N 1921   Transferred to Div 4 1958   Promoted to Div 3 1962-63   Relegated to Div 4 1963-64   Promoted to Div 3 1967-68   Relegated to Div 4 1968-69   Promoted to Div 3 1988-89   Relegated to Div 4 1990-91

CLUB RECORDS

Most Appearances for Club: Tommy Lowry, 1966-78: League 436 + FA Cup 20 + League Cup 18 + Watney Cup 1 **Total 475**
Most Capped Player: Bill Lewis 12, Wales   **For England:** J H Pearson 1
Record Goalscorer in a Match: No one has scored more than four goals
Record League Goalscorer in a Season: Terry Harkin 35, Div 4, 1964-65   **In All Competitions:** Terry Harkin 35
Record League Goalscorer in a Career: Bert Swindells 126, 1928-37   **In All Competitions:** Bert Swindells 133 (League 126 + FA Cup 7)
Record Transfer Fee Received: £525,000 from Liverpool for Rob Jones, October 1991. (A third instalment for games played will take the fee to £600,000)
Record Transfer Fee Paid: £50,000 to Barnsley for Darren Foreman, March 1990
Best Performances: League: 10th Div 2 1892-93   **FA Cup:** Semi-Final 1888   **League Cup:** 3rd Round 1974-75, 1975-76, 1978-79 **Welsh Cup:** Winners (2)
Most League Points: (3pts for win) 78, Div 4, 1988-89   (2pts for win) 59, Div 4, 1962-63
Most League Goals: 95, Div 3(N), 1931-32
Record League Victory: 8-0 v Rotherham United, Div 3N, 1.10.1932
Record Cup Victory: 5-0 v Druids, FA Cup First Series Rnd 1, 1887-88   5-0 v Billingham Synthonia, FA Cup Rnd 1, 1948-49
Record League Defeat: 1-11 v Lincoln City, Div 3N, 29.9.1951
Record Cup Defeat: 2-13 v Tottenham Hotspur, FA Cup Rnd 4 Replay, 3.2.1960
Oldest Player in a League Match: Kenny Swain, 39 years 281 days v Maidstone, 5.11.1992
Youngest Player in a League Match: Steve Walters, 16 years 119 days v Peterborough, 6.5.1988

LONGEST LEAGUE RUNS

of undefeated matches: 14 (1990)	**of league matches without a win:** 30 (1956-57)
of undefeated home matches: 28 (1967-68)	**of undefeated away matches:** 7 (1966-67, 1990)
without home win: 15 (1979)	**without an away win:** 56 (1955-57)
of league wins: 7 (1928-29, 1986)	**of home wins:** 16 (1938)
of league defeats: 10 (1923, 1957-58, 1979)	**of away wins:** 5 (1986)

BARCLAYS

CREWE ALEXANDRA

PLAYERS NAME Honours	Ht	Wt	Birthdate	Birthplace Transfers	Contract Date	Clubs	League	L/Cup	FA Cup	Other	Lg	L/C	FAC	Oth
GOALKEEPERS														
Dean Greygoose	5.11	11.5	18.12.64	Thetford	12.11.82	Cambridge Utd. (A)	26	1					·	
E:Y5				Loan	28.03.85	Leyton Orient				2				
				Loan	21.09.85	Lincoln City	6							
					07.12.85	Leyton Orient	1			1				
				Free	29.08.86	Crystal Palace								
					27.08.87	Crewe Alexandra	175	10	15	13				
DEFENDERS														
Richard Annan	5.8	10.0				Guiseley								
FA Vase '91.					15.05.92	Crewe Alexandra								
Aaron Callaghan	5.11	11.2	08.10.66	Dublin	12.10.84	Stoke City (A)	10+5			1				
Ei:u21.2				Loan	28.11.85	Crewe Alexandra	8			2				
				£10,000	31.10.86	Oldham Ath	11+5	4		1	2			
				£15,000	23.05.88	Crewe Alexandra	148+10	11+1	13+1	13	6	2	1	1
Darren J Carr	6.2	13.0	04.09.68	Bristol	20.08.86	Bristol Rovers	26+4	2+2	3	2				
					30.10.87	Newport Co	9							
				£8,000	10.03.88	Sheffield Utd	12+1	1	3+1	1	1			
				Loan	18.09.90	Crewe Alexandra								
					20.12.90	Crewe Alexandra	65+7	5	9	7	3		1	
Jason Smart	6.0	12.10	15.02.69	Rochdale	21.08.86	Rochdale	116+1	9+1	3	6	4			
				£45,000	10.07.89	Crewe Alexandra	87+2	5+3	9	3+2	3			
Neil Sorvel	5.11		02.03.73	Widness	31.07.91	Crewe Alexandra	5+4		1+1	4				
Eugene Wilson			11.04.63	Runcorn	31.07.91	Crewe Alexandra	41	4	4	6				
MIDFIELD														
Philip I Clarkson			13.11.68			Fleetwood Town								
				£22,500	15.10.91	Crewe Alexandra	18+10			2+1	6			
Mark Gardiner	5.11	12.3	25.12.66	Cirencester	01.10.84	Swindon Town (A)	7+3		0+2		1		1	
					06.02.87	Torquay Utd	37+12	3+1	1+1	1+1	4		1	
					22.08.88	Crewe Alexandra	128+7	10+1	12+1	11+1	32	3	4	
Jimmy Harvey	5.9	11.4	02.05.58	Lurgan N.I		Glenavon								
NI: u23.1; LDC'90				£30,000	12.08.77	Arsenal	2+1			1				
				Free	14.03.80	Hereford Utd	276+2	16	15+1	12	39	5	2	1
				£25,000	27.03.87	Bristol City	2+1							
				Loan	11.09.87	Wrexham	6							
				£25,000	08.10.87	Tranmere Rovers	174+10	14+1	11+1	25+5	18			1
				Free	21.07.92	Crewe Alexandra								
Craig Hignett	5.10	11.0	12.01.70	Whiston		Liverpool (T)								
					11.05.88	Crewe Alexandra	94+13	6	10+1	6+1	34	1	4	3
Neil Lennon	5.9	12.4	25.06.71	N.Ireland	26.08.89	Manchester City (T)	1							
NI: u23.1,u21.1				Free	09.08.90	Crewe Alexandra	32+2	1+1	4	2	3			
Steve Macauley						Fleetwood Town								
				£25,000	24.03.92	Crewe Alexandra	9			2	1			
Steve Walters	5.10	11.08	09.01.72	Plymouth	02.03.89	Crewe Alexandra (T)	84+8	7+2	8+1	10	5		2	
E: Y.4, S														
FORWARDS														
Robert Edwards	5.8	11.7	23.02.70	Manchester	07.06.91	Crewe Alexandra (T)	48+23	4	5+5	3+5	18	1	1	3
Stuart J Evans	6.3	11.5	15.11.60	Maltby	17.11.78	Rotherham Utd. (A)								
Div.4'83,'89						Gainsborough T.								
				£6,000	18.11.80	Sheffield Utd								
					15.03.82	Wimbledon	165+10	13	9	1	50	3	2	
					19.08.86	West Brom A	13+1	2		1	1			
					27.03.87	Plymouth A	36+9	2	1	1	10		1	
					11.11.88	Rotherham Utd	45+20	2	7+3	8+1	14		2	
				Loan	13.03.91	Torquay Utd	15			3	5			
				£10,000	19.09.91	Crewe Alexandra	13+4	2+2	1+1	2+1	3	2		
Stephen Garvey					25.10.91	Crewe Alexandra (T)	8+4	1+1		1				
David McKearney	5.10	11.2	20.06.68	Liverpool	23.11.87	Bolton W								
				Free	13.10.89	Crewe Alexandra	67+12	5+1	8	8+2	6		1	1
Tony Naylor	5.5	9.0	29.03.67	Gorton		Droylesden								
				£20,000	22.03.90	Crewe Alexandra	39+11	3+1	4	5	16	3	3	2
ADDITIONAL CONTRACT PLAYERS														
(F) Martin Disley	5.7		24.06.71	Ormskirk	22.09.89	Crewe Alexandra	0+1		0+1					
					20.09.91	Crewe Alexandra	0+1			0+1				
Kevin Donohue					09.02.91	Crewe Alexandra								
Ashley Fothergill					25.03.89	Rochdale	8+1			1				
				N.C	15.11.90	Crewe Alexandra								
(F) Andrew Gunn	6.0	12.1	02.02.71	Barking	10.03.89	Watford (T)								
FAYC'89				Free	26.02.90	Crewe Alexandra	2+2			0+1				
Tony Hughes						Crewe Alexandra								
				Loan	28.02.92	Witton Albion								
Michael J Jackson			04.12.73	W.Cheshire		Crewe Alexandra	1		1	1				
(M) Andrew Kelsey	5.9	10.8		Crewe	08.05.90	Crewe Alexandra								
Ahmed Mettioui						Morroco								
				£6,000	27.07.92	Crewe Alexandra								
(D) Shaun Smith				Leeds	01.07.89	Halifax Town (T)	6+1			1				
				Free		Crewe Alexandra	8+2			2				

Robert Powner, Gareth Whalley, Gus Wilson, Andrew Woodward.

LEADING LEAGUE GOALSCORERS SEASONS 1985-86 – 1991-92

1985-86	DAVE WALLER	12		1986-87	DAVID PLATT	22
1987-88	DAVID PLATT	19		1988-89	PAUL FISHENDEN	17
1989-90	CRAIG HIGNETT	8		1990-91	CRAIG HIGNETT	13
	ANDY SUSSEX	8				
	1991-92	TONY NAYLOR	15			

GRESTY ROAD Crewe, Cheshire CW2 6EB

Capacity: 7,200   **Covered Standing:**   **Seating:** 1,200

Tel: Ground: 0270 213014   **Ticket Sales:** As ground number   **Clubcall:** 0898 12 16 47

All premium rate calls (0898/0891) cost 36p per minute cheap rate and 48p per minute at all other times. Call costings correct at time of going to press.

ATTENDANCES
Highest: 20,000 v Tottenham Hotspur, FA Cup Round 4, 30.1.1960

Lowest: (Post War) 994 v Stockport County, Freight Rover Trophy, 14.1.1986

Record Receipts: £24,556 v Chelsea, FA Cup 3rd Round, 10.1.1990

Season Tickets:
Stands: £125, juv/OAP £85
Ground: from £85 to £90, juv/OAP £60 to £65

Executive Box Season Tickets: None

Cost of Stand Tickets: Seats: £7, juv/OAP £5
Terraces: £5, juv/OAP £3.50

Match and Ticket Information: Advance bookings available for all games

Car Parking: Parking at the ground for 200 cars

Nearest Railway Station: Crewe (5 mins) (0270 255245)

How to get to the ground

From North: Use Motorway M6 until junction 17 and follow signs Crewe A534. At Crewe roundabout follow signs Chester into Nantwich Road. Then take next turning on left into Gresty Road for Crewe Alexandra FC

From East and South: Use A52 then A5020 (S.P. Crewe) then at Crewe roundabout follow signs Chester into Nantwich Road. Then take next turning on left into Gresty Road for Crewe Alexandra FC

From West: Use A534 (S.P. Crewe) and immediately before Crewe Railway Station turn right into Gresty Road for Crewe Alexandra FC

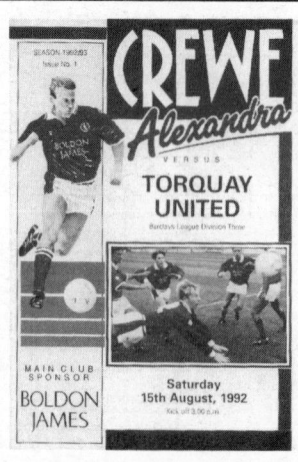

Value Rating: ★ ★ ★

Programme Editor: Harold Finch

Price of 1992-93 Programme: £1
Number of Pages: 32
Subscriptions: Subscription rates on request from the club

Local Newspapers: Crewe Chronicle, Crewe Guardian – Evening Sentinel – Hanley

Local Radio Stations: Radio Stoke (200 medium wave), Signal Radio

CRYSTAL PALACE   Premier

Formed: 1905   **Turned Professional:** 1905   **Ltd Co:** 1905

SPONSORED BY: Tulip Computers   **NICKNAME:** The Eagles

President
S Stephenson

Chairman
R G Noades

Directors
B Coleman O.B.E
A S C De'Souza
G Geraghty   S Hume-Kendall
P H N Norman   R Anderson
V E Murphy

Club Secretary
Mike Hurst

Commercial Manager
Graham Drew

Sales & Marketing Manager
T Willis

Manager
Steve Coppell

Assistant Manager
Alan Smith

Youth Development Officers
Dave Garland/Stuart Scott/Andy Ritchie

Physiotherapist
David West, MCSP, SRP

Groundsman
Bill Harrison

Club Statistician for the Directory
Mike Purkiss

THE 1991-92 campaign was a disappointing season, when more headlines were made off the pitch than on it, although two close season signings, Sinnott and Coleman, made excellent additions to the staff

Following a television programme with the chairman discussing the strength of black players in the winter months, saw Ian Wright go to Arsenal for a club record fee £2,500,000. He was replaced by Marco Gabbiadini for our record buying fee of £1,800,000 only to be sold to Derby County at a loss of £600,000 a few months later. Another sale caused concern when Paul Bodin was sold at a reduced price, this after a loan period at Newcastle, then Andy Gray was loaned to Spurs for the rest of the season, this with long term injuries to John Salako and Richard Shaw, upset the balance of the team. Manager Coppell offered to resign after the defeat at Forest but was given a vote of confidence by the chairman. In the league more goals were scored away than at Selhurst Park. The win against 'champions to be' Leeds (their only one until February) and the double over Liverpool were the bright spots as we reached 10th position and so qualifying for founder members of the Premier League.

Mark Bright was the only ever present and leading scorer, creating a new club record of scoring in 8 consecutive matches. In the cup a last minute goal at Leicester saw our departure from the F.A. Cup, this after Eric Young was sent off in the 30th minute. The Zenith Data Cup was returned after Chelsea beat us. However, the Rumbelows Cup was more successful until we met our cup bogey side Nottingham Forest who, for the third consecutive season, beat us in a cup competition. Our juniors had the honours for this term being Champions in the league and F.A. Youth Cup finalists against Manchester United, they also had a record 8-0 win away at Aldershot only to be cancelled out when Aldershot resigned from all leagues.

The international scene saw Nigel Martyn (England), Andy Gray (England), Eddie McGoldrick (Eire) and Chris Coleman (scoring for Wales) gained their first full caps. For Martyn a mixed season as he became the first Palace keeper to be sent off, this under the new F.A. ruling.

Before the season began Thompson and Witter were sold to Q.P.R. followed by Pardew (Charlton) and Hopkins to Bristol Rovers, but welcome Andy Barnes (who was out injured most of the time) and Mortimore who returned to Selhurst Park, being an ex-Charlton player!

Player of the Year Eddie McGoldrick look's certain to leave after rejecting terms, while Rudi Hedman was given a free transfer. The only loan signing was Neil Sullivan (Wimbledon) for the last game of the season when all four professional goalkeepers were not available.   **Mike Purkiss**

Back row L-R: Mark Holman, Grant Watts, Niall Thompson, Andy Woodman, Nigel Martyn, Jimmy Glass, Mark Hawthorne, Gareth Southgate, Andy Barnes. **Sitting:** Torje Eike (Physio), David West (Physio), Alan Smith (Asst. Manager), Paul Mortimer, John Humphrey, Chris Coleman, Mark Bright, Geoff Thomas, Andy Thorn, Lee Sinnott, Eric Young, Bobby Bowry, Wally Downs (1st Team Coach), Steve Harrison (1st Team Coach), Spike Hill (Kit Man). **Front:** John Budden, Ricky Newman, Dean Gordon, Jamie Moralees, Simon Osborn, Simon Rodger, Stan Collymore, Steve Coppell (Manager), John Salako, David Whyte, Darren Patterson, Stuart Massey, Russell Edwards.

CRYSTAL PALACE

DIVISION ONE: 10th   **FA CUP:** 3rd RND   **RUMBELOWS CUP:** 5th RND   **ZDS CUP:** Sth S/Finals

M	DATE	COMP.	VEN	OPPONENTS	RESULT	H/T	LGE POS	GOALSCORERS/GOAL TIMES	ATTEN-DANCE
1	A 24	BL	A	Manchester City	L 2-3	1-2	22	Thomas 18, Bright 48	(28,023)
2	27	BL	H	Wimbledon	W 3-2	2-1	13	Bright 31, Gray (pen) 44, Wright 63	16,736
3	31	BL	H	Sheffield United	W 2-1	0-0		Thomas 80, Wright 89	15,507
4	S 4	BL	A	Aston Villa	W 1-0	1-0	8	Wright 3	(20,740)
5	7	BL	A	Everton	D 2-2	1-0	9	Gray (pen) 33, Bright 69	(21,065)
6	14	BL	H	Arsenal	L 1-4	0-1	13	Bright 85	24,228
7	17	BL	H	West Ham United	L 2-3	1-0	15	Salako 12, Wright 61	21,363
8	21	BL	A	Oldham Athletic	W 3-2	1-1	12	Salako 14, Wright 51, Bright 70	(13,391)
9	25	RC 2/1	A	**Hartlepool United**	D 1-1	1-0		**Bright 11**	(6,697)
10	28	BL	H	Queens Park R.	D 2-2	0-1	12	Bright 81, Collymore 84	15,372
11	O 1	BL	H	Leeds United	W 1-0	0-0	7	Bright 89	18,298
12	5	BL	A	Sheffield Wed.	L 1-4	1-3	9	Bright 22	(26,230)
13	8	RC 2/2	H	**Hartlepool United**	W 6-1	2-0		**Bright 30,71, Gabbiadini 44, Thom 47, Gray (p) 49, Collymore 78**	9,153
14	19	BL	A	Coventry City	W 2-1	1-0	7	Bright 45, Gabbiadini 80	(10,551)
15	22	ZDS 2	H	**Southend United**	W †4-2	2-2		**McGoldrick 57, Bright 61, Thomas 98, Gray 102**	7,185
16	26	BL	H	Chelsea	D 0-0	0-0	7		21,841
17	29	RC 3	A	**Birmingham City**	D 1-1	0-0		**Gray 87**	(17,270)
18	N 2	BL	A	Liverpool	W 2-1	0-1	7	Gabbiadini 51, Thomas 72	(34,231)
19	16	BL	H	Southampton	W 1-0	0-0	5	Thomas 67	15,861
20	19	RC 3R	H	**Birmingham City**	D †1-1	0-0		**Thomas 117**	10,698
21	23	BL	A	Nottingham Forest	L 1-5	0-2	5	Thomas 84	(22,387)
22	26	ZDS 3	A	**Queens Park R.**	W 3-2	2-0		**Thomas 33, Gabbiadini 45, Young 57**	(4,492)
23	30	BL	H	Manchester United	L 1-3	1-1	6	Mortimore 17	29,017
24	D 3	RC 3R2	H	**Birmingham City**	W 2-1	2-1		**Gray (pen) 18, Thom 43**	11,384
25	7	BL	A	Norwich City	D 3-3	1-1	8	Newman (og) 30, McGoldrick 50, Osborn 52	(12,667)
26	10	ZDS S S	H	**Chelsea**	L 0-1	0-1			8,416
27	17	RC 4	A	**Swindon Town**	W 1-0	1-0		**Gray 33**	(10,044)
28	22	BL	H	Tottenham Hotspur	L 1-2	0-2	10	Fenwick (og) 63	22,491
29	26	BL	A	Wimbledon	D 1-1	0-0	10	Gabbiadini 51	(15,009)
30	28	BL	A	Sheffield United	D 1-1	0-1	11	Gabbiadini 64	(17,969)
31	J 1	BL	H	Notts County	W 1-0	1-0	10	Gabbiadini 7	14,202
32	4	FAC 3	A	**Leicester City**	L 0-1	0-0			(19,613)
33	8	RC 5	H	**Nottingham Forest**	D 1-1	0-0		**Walker (og) 64**	14,941
34	11	BL	H	Manchester City	D 1-1	1-0	9	Bright 43	14,766
35	18	BL	A	Leeds United	D 1-1	1-1	9	Thomas 17	(27,717)
36	F 1	BL	H	Coventry City	L 0-1	0-1	10		13,818
37	5	RC 5R	A	**Nottingham Forest**	L 2-4	1-3		**Bright 34, Whyte 62**	(18,918)
38	8	BL	A	Chelsea	D 1-1	1-0	10	Whyte 36	(17,810)
39	16	BL	A	Tottenham Hotspur	W 1-0	0-0	8	McGoldrick 81	(19,834)
40	22	BL	A	Manchester United	L 0-2	0-1	9		(46,347)
41	25	BL	H	Luton Town	D 1-1	1-0	9	Bright 19	12,109
42	29	BL	H	Norwich City	L 3-4	2-4	10	Osborn 17, Bright 22, 65	14,021
43	M 3	BL	H	Nottingham Forest	D 0-0	0-0	10		12,680
44	7	BL	A	Luton Town	D 1-1	1-0	10	McGoldrick 21	(8,951)
45	11	BL	A	Southampton	L 0-1	0-1	12		(12,926)
46	14	BL	H	Liverpool	W 1-0	1-0	10	Young 40	23,680
47	21	BL	H	Aston Villa	D 0-0	0-0	10		15,445
48	28	BL	A	Notts County	W 3-2	1-2	7	Coleman 45, Bright 54, Mortimore 80	(7,674)
49	A 4	BL	H	Everton	W 2-0	0-0	7	Coleman 65, Bright (pen) 71	14,338
50	11	BL	A	Arsenal	L 1-4	1-3	8	Coleman 8	(36,016)
51	18	BL	H	Oldham Athletic	D 0-0	0-0	9		12,680
52	21	BL	A	West Ham United	W 2-0	1-0	10	Bright 26, Coleman 63	(17,710)
53	25	BL	H	Sheffield Wed.	D 1-1	0-1	10	Bright 88	21,573
54	M 1	BL	A	Queens Park R.	L 0-1	0-1			(14,903)

Best Home League Attendance: 29,017 v Manchester United   **Smallest:** 12,109 v Luton Town   **Av Home Att:** 17,597

Goal Scorers: Compared with 90-91: -1,923

League (53): Bright 17 (1 pen), Thomas 6, Gabbiadini 5, Wright 5, Coleman 4, McGoldrick 3, Opponents 2, Gray 2 (2 pens), Osborn 2, Mortimore 2, Salako 2, Young, Whyte, Collymore

R/lows C (15): Gray 4 (2 pens), Bright 4, Thom 2, Gabbiadini, Whyte, Collymore, Opponents, Thomas

FA Cup (1):

ZDS Cup (7): Thomas 2, McGoldrick, Bright, Gray, Gabbiadini, Young

† = After extra-time

Crystal Palace — 1991-92 Appearances Grid

Martyn N.	Humphrey J.	Bodin P.	Gray A.	Shaw R.	Sinnott L.	Salako J.	Thomas G.	Bright M.	Wright I.	McGoldrick E.	Pardew A.	Southgate G.	Thorn A.	Suckling P.	Young E.	Collymore S.	Osborn S.	Gabbiadini M.	Rodger S.	Gordon D.	Mortimer P.	Coleman C.	Whyte D.	Moralee J.	Hedman R.	Referee	
1	2	3*	4	5	6	7	8	9	10	11	12	S														R Hart	1
1	2	12	4	3*	5	7	8	9	10	11		S	6													D Elleray	2
1	2	S	4	3	5	7	8	9	10	11		S	6													L Shapter	3
1	2		4	3	5	7	8	9	10	11		S	6													T Fitzharris	4
1	2		4	3	5	7	8	9	10*	11	12	S	6													J Kirby	5
	2•		4	3	5	7	8*	9	10	11	12	14	6	1												K Hackett	6
	2		4	3		11		9	10	7*	8	S	6	1	5	12										R Milford	7
	2	3	4		6	7		9	10	11	8	S		1	5		S									M Reed	8
1	2	3	4		6		10	9		11	8	S			5	S	7									J Watson	9
1	2	3	4		6		10	9		11	7	12			5*	14	8•									A Ward	10
1			4	3	11*		8	9		S		2	6		5	12	7	10								J Martin	11
1			4	3			8	9			14	2	6		5	12	7*	10•	11							A Gunn	12
1			4	3			8	9		11	S	2*	6		5		10		12							P Taylor	13
1			4	12	3		8	9		11		2	6		5		S	10	7*							G Ashby	14
1			4	3			8	9*		11		2	6		5		14	10•	12	7						V Callow	15
1	S		4	3			8	9		11		2	6		5		10•		7	12						D Axcell	16
1	12		4	3			8	9		11		2	6*		5		10	7		S						J Lodge	17
1	6	4•		3			8	9		11	14	2			5		10	12	7*							T Holbrook	18
1	6	4		3*			8	9		11		2			5	14	10		7•	12						R Groves	19
1	3	4					8	9		11		2	6•		5	12	10		7*		14					R Hamer	20
1	3	4					8	9		11		2	6		5		10	S	7		S					J Lloyd	21
1	14	4					8	9		11		2•	6		5		12	10*	7		3					R Lewis	22
1	14	4					8•	9		11		2	6		5	12	10		7*		3					P Durkin	23
1	S	4						9		11		2	6		5	12	8	10*	7		3					B Hill	24
1	S	4						9		11		2	6		5		8	10*	12		7	3				G Pooley	25
1		4						9		11		2*	6		5		8	10	12		7	3•	14			J Martin	26
1	12	4						9		11		2	6		5		8*	10*	7		3	14				K Hackett	27
1	6	4						9		11		2					8	10	7	12	5	3*	S			P Foakes	28
1	6	4	3					9		11		2					8	10	7	5*		12				P Don	29
1	2	4	3					9		11					5		8	10	7	6		S	S			A Flood	30
1	2	4	3				8	9		11					5		S	10	7	6		S				K Cooper	31
1	2	4	3				8	9		11			6		5			10*	12	7			S			J Deakin	32
1	2	4	3				8	9		11			6		5		S	10	7*				12			K Barratt	33
1	2	4	3				8	9		11*			6		5			10	7				S			R Wiseman	34
1	2	4	3				8	9		11		5	6				S	10*	7				12			T Fitzharris	35
1	2	4*	3				8	9		11		5	6				12			7		10•	14			D Axcell	36
1	2		3				8*	9		11		5	6				4		7			12	10	S		M Peck	37
1	2		3				8	9		11		5	6				4		7			S	10	S		R Gifford	38
1	2		3				8	9		11		S	6		5		4		7			S	10			J Deakin	39
1	2		3				8	9		11		S	6		5		4		7			S	10			K Redfern	40
1	2	3*					8	9		11		14	6		5		4		7			12	10•			P Danson	41
1	2		3				8•	9		11		14	6		5		4		7			12	10*			R Nixon	42
1	2		3					9		11		8	6		5		4*		7		12	10	S			K Burge	43
1	2		3*	12				9		11		8	6		5				7		4•	14	10•	4*		D Elleray	44
1	2		3					9		11		8	6		5	12			7		14		10•	4*		A Gunn	45
1	2		3					9		11		8	6		5	S			7		4	10	S			G Courtney	46
1	2		3					9				8	6		5	11			7	S	4	10	S			J Worrall	47
1	2		3				8	9				4	6		5	11*			7		12	10	S			T Holbrook	48
1	2		3				8	9				4	6		5	11*			7•		12	10	14			M Bailey	49
1	2		3				8	9				4	6		5	11*			7		10	S	12			R Bigger	50
1	2		3				8	9		11		4•	6		5	12			7*		10		14			P Durkin	51
1	2		3				8	9		11		4	6		5				7*		10	12	S			A Buksh	52
1	2		3				8	9		11		4	6		5				7*		10•	14	12			B Hill	53
	2		3				8	9		11		4	6		5				7*	14	5	10				R Lewis	54

Martyn N.	Humphrey J.	Bodin P.	Gray A.	Shaw R.	Sinnott L.	Salako J.	Thomas G.	Bright M.	Wright I.	McGoldrick E.	Pardew A.	Southgate G.	Thorn A.	Suckling P.	Young E.	Collymore S.	Osborn S.	Gabbiadini M.	Rodger S.	Gordon D.	Mortimer P.	Coleman C.	Whyte D.	Moralee J.	Hedman R.		
38	36	3	25	9	35	10	30	42	8	36	3	26	33	3	30	4	13	15	20	2	17	14	7	2		League Appearances	
	1	1		1	1							5	4				8	1		2	2	4	4	4	3	Substitute Appearances	
8	4+2	1	7		5	1	5	8		8	1	6	7		7	0+2	4	6	6	0+1		2+2	1+2			R/lows Appearances	
1	1		1		1		1	1		1			1		1			1	0+1	1						FA Cup Appearances	
3	0+1		3		1		2	3		3		3	3		3		1+2	3	0+1		3	2	0+1			ZDS Cup Appearances	

Also Played: Posn.(Game): Barnes 12•(54), Sullivan 1(54)

CRYSTAL PALACE

Club Colours: Red and blue wide-striped shirt, red shorts, red socks.
Change Colours: Yellow shirts, blue shorts, white stockings.
Reserves League: Combination

COMPETITIONS					
Div. 1	Div. 2	Div. 3	Div. 3S	Div. 4	Texaco
69-73	21-25	20-21	25-58	58-61	72-73
79-81	64-69	61-64			
89-	73-74	74-76			
	76-79				
	81-89				

HONOURS	
Div. 2	Div. 3
78-79	20-21

MOST APPEARANCES: JIM CANNON 656+4 (1972-86)				
Year	League	FA Cup	L/Cup	Others
72-73	3			
73-74	13+1		1	
74-75	34+2	2	0+1	
75-76	40	8	2	
76-77	46	6	3	
77-78	39	1	4	
78-79	41	4	4	
79-80	42	3	3	
80-81	33	1	4	
81-82	42	5	4	
82-83	41	4	5	
83-84	30	2	2	
84-85	40	2	2	
85-86	42	1	4	1
86-87	42	2	4	1
87-88	40	1	1	1
	568+3	42	43+1	3

MOST GOALS IN A CAREER		
PETER SIMPSON 166 (1929-34)		
Season	League	FA Cup
1929-30	36	1
1930-31	46	8
1931-32	24	1
1932-33	14	1
1933-34	20	1
1934-35	14	
Total	154	12

MANAGERS			
Name	Seasons	Best	Worst
John Robson	1905-07		
Eddie Goodman	1907-25	14(2)	1(3S)
Alec Maley	1925-27	6(3S)	13(3S)
Fred Maven	1927-30	2(3S)	9(3S)
Jack Tresadern	1930-35	2(3S)	12(3S)
Tom Bromilow	1935-36	6(3S)	6(3S)
R. S. Moyse	1936	14(3S)	14(3S)
Tom Bromilow	1937-39	2(3S)	7(3S)
George Irwin	1939-47	13(3S)	22(3S)
Jack Butler	1947-49	3(3S)	3(3S)
Ron Rooke	1949-50	3(3S)	3(3S)
F Dawes/C Slade	1950-51	24(3S)	24(3S)
Laurie Scott	1951-54	13(3S)	22(3S)
Cyril Spiers	1954-58	14(3S)	23(3S)
George Smith	1958-60	7(4)	8(4)
Arthur Rowe	1960-63	11(3)	2(4)
Dick Graham	1963-66	7(2)	2(3)
Arthur Rowe	1966		
Bert Head	1966-72	18(1)	11(2)
Malcolm Allison	1972-76	21(1)	5(3)
Terry Venables	1976-80	13(1)	3(3)
Ernie Walley	1980	20(1)	22(1)
Malcolm Allison	1980-81	22(1)	22(1)
Dario Gradi	1981	22(1)	15(2)
Steve Kember	1981-82	15(2)	15(2)
Alan Mullery	1982-84	15(2)	18(2)
Steve Coppell	1984-		

RECORD TRANSFER FEE RECEIVED			
Amount	Club	Player	Date
£2,500,000	Arsenal	Ian Wright	9/91
£1.35m nett	Arsenal	Kenny Sansom	8/80
£400,000	Derby County	Dave Swindlehurst	4/80
£200,000	Tottenham H	Peter Taylor	9/76

RECORD TRANSFER FEE PAID			
Amount	Club	Player	Date
£1,800,000	Sunderland	Marco Gabbiadini	9/91
£1,000,000	Bristol Rovers	Nigel Martyn	11/89
£1,000,000	Arsenal	Clive Allen	8/80
£650,000	Charlton Athletic	Mike Flanagan	8/79

LONGEST LEAGUE RUNS	
of undefeated matches:	18 (1.3.1969-16.8.1969)
of undefeated home matches:	32 (28.2.1930-8.10.1932)
without home win:	11 (14.4.1973-17.11.1973)
of league wins:	8 (9.2.1921-26.3.1921)
of league defeats:	8 (18.4.1925-19.9.1925)
of league matches w/out a win:	20 (24.2.1962-13.10.1962)
of undefeated away matches:	10 (22.12.1928-1.4.1929)
	(26.12.1968-10.8.1969) (16.8.1975-6.12.1975)
	(18.11.1978-3.4.1979)
without an away win:	31 (15.3.1980-3.10.1981)
of home wins:	12 (19.12.1925-28.8.1926)
of away wins:	4 (1931-32, 1932-33 & 1975-76)

PREVIOUS LEAGUE
Southern League

BIGGEST VICTORIES
League: 9-0 v Barrow, Division 4, 10.10.1959
F.A. Cup: 7-0 v Luton Town, Round 3, 16.1.1929
League Cup: 8-0 v Southend, Round 2, 25.9.1990

BIGGEST DEFEATS
League: 0-9 v Liverpool, Division 1, 12.9.1989
F.A. Cup: 0-9 v Burnley, Rnd 2 Replay, 1908-09
League Cup: 0-5 v Nottingham Forest, Rnd 3 Replay, 1.11.1989

MOST POINTS
3 points a win: 81, Division 2, 1988-89
2 points a win: 64, Division 4, 1960-61

MOST GOALS IN A MATCH
6, Peter Simpson v Exeter, 7-2, Div 3(S), 4.10.1930

MOST GOALS
110, Division 4, 1960-61
Byrne 30, Summersby 25, Heckman 14, Woan 13, Gavin 8,
Petchley 7, Uphill 6, Barnett 2, Lunnis 1, McNicholl 1, Noakes 1,
og 2.

MOST GOALS IN A SEASON
Peter Simpson, 46 League, 8 F.A. Cup = 54. 1930-31.
6 goals once = 6; 4 goals twice = 8; 3 goals 7 times = 21; 2 goals 3
times = 6; 1 goal 13 times = 13.
Previous holder: P. A. Cherrett, 32, 1926-27.

MOST FIRST CLASS MATCHES IN A SEASON
59 (46 League, 1 FA Cup, 3 League Cup, 5 Simod Cup, 4 Play-Offs) 1988-89

MOST LEAGUE GOALS CONCEDED
86, Division 3S, 1953-54

MOST LEAGUE WINS
29, Division 4, 1960-61

MOST LEAGUE DRAWS
19, Division 2, 1978-79

MOST LEAGUE DEFEATS
29, Division 1, 1980-81

OLDEST PLAYER
Wally Betteridge, 41 (Debut – Player/Coach), 27.10.1928 (0-8)

YOUNGEST PLAYER
Phil Hoadley, 16 years 3 months, 27.4.1968

MOST CAPPED PLAYER
Paddy Mulligan (Rep. of Ireland) 14
Ian Walsh (Wales) 14
Peter Nicholas (Wales) 14 + 3 while on loan from Arsenal

BEST PERFORMANCES BY CRYSTAL PALACE

League: 1960-61: Matches played 46, Won 29, Drawn 6, Lost 11, Goals for 110, Goals against 69, Points 64. 2nd in Division 4

Highest: 1990-91: 3rd Division 1.

F.A. Cup: Finalists 1989-90: 3rd rnd. Portsmouth, 2-1; 4th rnd. Huddersfield Town, 4-0; 5th rnd. Rochdale, 1-0; 6th rnd. Cambridge, 1-0; Semi-Final Liverpool, 4-3; Final Manchester United, 3-3 aet, replay 0-1

League Cup: 1968-69: 2nd rnd. Preston North End, 3-1; 3rd rnd. Leyton Orient, 1-0; 4th rnd. Leeds, 2-1; 5th rnd. Burnley, 0-2.
1970-71: 2nd rnd. Rochdale, 3-3, 3-1; 3rd rnd. Lincoln, 4-0; 4th rnd. Arsenal, 0-0, 2-0; 5th rnd. Manchester United, 2-4.
1991-92: 2nd rnd. Hartlepool 1-1 (a), 6-1 (h); 3rd rnd. Birmingham City 1-1 (a), 1-1 (h), 2-1 (h); 4th rnd. Swindon Town 1-0 (a); 5th rnd. Nottingham Forest 1-1 (h), 2-4 (a).

DIVISIONAL RECORDS

	Played	Won	Drawn	Lost	For	Against	Points
DIVISION 1	370	100	107	163	386	549	354
DIVISION 2	846	311	231	304	1053	1047	985
DIVISION 3	276	113	86	77	419	332	312
DIVISION 3S	1166	438	292	436	1831	1853	1168
DIVISION 4	138	68	30	40	284	204	166
TOTALS	2796	1030	746	1020	3973	3985	2985

CRYSTAL PALACE

PLAYERS NAME / Honours	Ht	Wt	Birthdate	Birthplace / Transfers	Contract Date	Clubs	League	L/Cup	FA Cup	Other	Lg	L/C	FAC	Oth
GOALKEEPERS														
Nigel Martyn	6.2	13.10	11.08.66	St. Austell		St.Blazey								
E: 2, B.2,u21.11; Div.3'90					06.08.87	Bristol Rovers	101	6	6	11				
				£1,000,000	21.11.89	Crystal Palace	101	13	11	14				
DEFENDERS														
Chris Coleman	6.2	12.10	10.06.70	Swansea	01.09.87	Swansea City (A)	159+1	8	13	15	2		1	
W: 1, u21.1				£275,000	19.07.91	Crystal Palace	14+4	2+2		2	4			
John Humphrey	5.10	10.13	31.01.61	Paddington	14.02.79	Wolverhampton W (A)	149	8	7		3			
				£60,000	22.07.85	Charlton Ath	194	13	9	15	3			1
				£400,000	18.06.90	Crystal Palace	74+1	9+2	4	6+1	1			
Darren Patterson	6.2	11.10	15.10.69	Belfast	05.07.88	West Brom A. (T)								
NI:Y				Free	17.04.89	Wigan Ath	69+28	7+1	5+4	7	6	3	1	
				£225,000	01.07.92	Crystal Palace								
Richard Shaw	5.9	11.5	11.09.68	Brent	04.09.87	Crystal Palace (A)	75+9	9+2	8	10+1	1			
				Loan	14.12.89	Hull City	4							
Lee Sinnott	6.1	11.9	12.07.65	Pelsall		Rushall Ol								
E:u21.1,Y.4					16.11.82	Walsall (A)	40	3	4		2			
				£100,000	15.09.83	Watford	71+7	6	11		2			
				£130,000	23.07.87	Bradford City	173	19	9	12	6			1
				£300,000	08.08.91	Crystal Palace	35+1	5	1	1				
Andy Thorn	6.0	11.5	12.11.66	Carshalton	13.11.84	Wimbledon	106+1	7	9	1	2			
E:u21.5,FAC'88				£850,000	01.08.88	Newcastle Utd	36	4		3	2	1		
				£650,000	05.12.89	Crystal Palace	84	12	10	11	2	2		
Eric Young	6.3	12.6	25.03.60	Singapore		Staines Town								
W: 10; FAC'88; Isthmian PL'81						Slough Town			2					
				£10,000	01.11.82	Brighton & H.A	126	8	11	2	10		1	
				£70,000	29.07.87	Wimbledon	96+3	12	6+1	7	9		1	
				£850,000	15.08.90	Crystal Palace	64	12	4	8	4	1		1
MIDFIELD														
Eddie McGoldrick	5.10	11.7	30.04.65	London		Kettering Town			2					
Ei: 4; Div.4'87						Nuneaton Borough			1					
				£10,000	23.08.86	Northampton T	97+10	9	6+1	7	9		1	1
				£200,000	10.01.89	Crystal Palace	97+8	13+1	4	13+1	3			3
Paul Mortimer	5.11	11.3	08.05.68	London		Fulham (A)								
E: u21.2					22.09.87	Charlton Ath	108+5	4+1	8	3+1	17			
				£350,000	24.07.91	Aston Villa	10+2	2			1			
				£500,000	18.10.91	Crystal Palace	17+4		1	3	2			
Richard Newman	5.9	10.7	05.08.70	Guildford	22.01.88	Crystal Palace (T)								
				Loan	28.02.92	Maidstone Utd	9+1				1			
Geoff Thomas	6.1	12.0	05.08.64	Manchester	13.08.82	Rochdale	10+1			0+1	1			
E: 9				Free	22.03.84	Crewe Alexandra	120+5	8	2	2+1	21			
				£50,000	08.06.87	Crystal Palace	164+2	20	12+1	15+1	24	3	2	4
FORWARDS														
Mark Bright	6.0	11.0	06.06.62	Stoke	30.03.91	Lincoln City								
FMC'91				Free	04.08.82	Port Vale	18+11	1+1	0+1	2	10		1	
				£33,000	19.07.84	Leicester City	26+16	3+1	1		6			
				£75,000	26.01.87	Crystal Palace	219+3	22	13+1	23	89	11	2	9
Stanley Collymore	6.2	12.2	22.01.71	Stone		Stafford Rangers			1					
				£100,000	04.01.91	Crystal Palace	4+14	0+2			1	1		
John Salako	5.10	11.0	11.02.69	Nigeria	03.11.86	Crystal Palace (A)	87+38	9+2	11	11+3	11	2	2	2
E: 5; FMC'91				Loan	14.08.89	Swansea City	13			2	3			1
ADDITIONAL CONTRACT PLAYERS														
Andrew J Barnes						Sutton Utd								
				£100,000	18.09.91	Crystal Palace	0+1							
Robert Bowry					08.08.90	Q.P.R								
					04.04.92	Crystal Palace								
(G) James Glass	6.1	11.10	01.08.73	Epsom	04.07.91	Crystal Palace (T)								
Dean Gordon	6.0	11.5	10.02.73	Thornton Heath	04.07.91	Crystal Palace (T)	2+2	0+1						
Stuart Massey						Sutton Utd								
				£20,000	17.07.92	Crystal Palace								
Jamie Moralee	5.11	11.0	02.09.71	Steatham	03.07.90	Crystal Palace	2+4							
(M) Simon Osborn	5.10		19.01.72	New Addington	03.01.90	Crystal Palace (T)	15+3	4		1+3	2			
Martyn O'Connor						Bromsgrove R.								
				£225,000	31.07.92	Crystal Palace								
Simon Rodger	5.9	10.13	03.10.71	Sussex		Bognor Regis								
					02.07.90	Crystal Palace	20+2	6	0+1	0+1				
(M) Gareth Southgate	5.10		03.09.70	Watford	17.01.89	Crystal Palace (T)	27+4	6+1		4				
David Whyte	5.8	10.7	03.10.71	Shoreham-by-Sea	01.07.89	Crystal Palace	7+4	1+2		0+1	1	1		
				Loan	26.03.92	Charlton Ath	7+1				2			
(G) Andrew Woodman	6.1	11.10	11.08.71	London	01.07.89	Crystal Palace								

CRYSTAL PALACE

RECORD WIN & LOSS AGAINST EACH CLUB IN CURRENT DIVISION
(Where a score has occured on several occasions the most recent is given)

Club	Rec. Win	Season	Rec. Loss	Season
ARSENAL	1-0	1979-80	5-1	1969-70 (home)
ASTON VILLA	4-2	1968-69	4-1	1987-88
BLACKBURN ROVERS	5-0	1977-78	3-0	1982-83
CHELSEA	2-0	1972-73	5-1	1969-70 (home)
COVENTRY CITY	4-1	1924-25 (away)	8-0	1931-32
EVERTON	2-0	1970-71	5-0	1980-81
IPSWICH TOWN	4-1	1979-80	3-0	1947-48
LEEDS UNITED	3-0	1987-88	4-0	1972-73
LIVERPOOL	1-0	1990-91	9-0	1989-90
MANCHESTER CITY	3-1	1987-88 (away)	4-0	1971-72
MANCHESTER UNITED	5-0	1972-73	5-1	1923-24
MIDDLESBROUGH	5-2	1980-81	4-0	1968-69
NORWICH CITY	7-1	1926-27	5-0	1950-51 (home)
NOTTINGHAM FOREST	4-1	1921-22	6-1	1950-51 (home)
OLDHAM ATHLETIC	4-0	1981-82	3-0	1958-59
QUEENS PARK RANGERS	4-0	1937-38	4-0	1930-31
SHEFFIELD UNITED	5-1	1971-72	3-1	1984-85 (home)
SHEFFIELD WEDNESDAY	4-0	1976-77	6-0	1923-24
SOUTHAMPTON	3-0	1972-73	6-0	1970-71
TOTTENHAM HOTSPUR	1-0	1990-91	3-0	1970-71 (home)
WIMBLEDON	3-0	1990-91 (away)	5-0	1984-85 (home)

MANAGER: STEVE COPPELL

DATE OF BIRTH: 09.07.1955   **PLACE OF BIRTH:** Liverpool

DATE OF APPOINTMENT: JUNE 4th 1984

PREVIOUS CLUBS
  as Manager: None
  as Asst. Man./Coach: None
  as Player: Tranmere Rovers; Manchester United

HONOURS
  as Manager: Promotion to Div 1 (C. Palace); FA Cup Finalists 1989-90; Zenith Data Winners 1991
  as Asst. Man./Coach: None
  as Player: Manchester United: FA Cup Winners 1977; FA Cup Runners-Up 1976, 1979; Milk Cup Finalists 1983

Value Rating: ★ ★ ★ ★

Programme Manager: Pete King

Price of 1992-93 Programme: £1.50
Number of Pages: 48
Subscriptions: £49 (Inland) Homes only

Local Newspapers: Croydon Advertiser, South London Press

Additional Publications on Club: Complete Record 1905-89, Mike Purkiss (Breedon Books)

LEADING LEAGUE GOALSCORERS
SEASONS 1979-80 – 1991-92

1979-80	DAVID SWINDLEHURST	7		1980-81	CLIVE ALLEN	9
1981-82	KEVIN MABBUTT	8		1982-83	KEVIN MABBUTT	10
1983-84	IAN EVANS	7		1984-85	TREVOR AYLOTT	8
1985-86	ANDY GRAY	10		1986-87	KEVIN TAYLOR	8
					MARK BRIGHT	8
					IAN WRIGHT	8
1987-88	MARK BRIGHT	24		1988-89	IAN WRIGHT	24
1989-90	MARK BRIGHT	12		1990-91	IAN WRIGHT	15

1991-92   **MARK BRIGHT**   17

SELHURST PARK London SE25 6PU

Capacity: 30,115   **Covered Standing:**   **Seating:** 15,515

Tel: Ground: 081 653 4462   **Ticket Sales:** 081 771 8841   **Clubcall:** 0898 400 333

All premium rate calls (0898/0891) cost 36p per minute cheap rate and 48p per minute at all other times. Call costings correct at time of going to press.

GROUNDS
Crystal Palace 1905-15, Herne Hill 1915-18, The Nest 1918-24, Selhurst Park 1924-

ATTENDANCES
Highest: 51,482 v Burnley, Division 2, 5.5.1979

Lowest: 2,207 v Brighton & H.A., Full Members Cup, 16.10.1985

RECORD RECEIPTS (with previous records):
£247,684 v Manchester Utd, Div 1, 30.11.1991
£228,000 v Arsenal, Div 1, 10.11.1990
£179,250 v Liverpool, 20.1.1990
£103,173 v West Ham, FA Cup, 28.1.1986
£74,868 v Tottenham Hotspur, Division 1, 6.10.1979

GROUND NAME
First game: v Sheffield Wednesday, Division 2, 30.8.1924
First floodlit game: v Chelsea, 28.9.1953

Season Tickets:
Stands: from £275 to £330, juv/OAP £165 to £220
Ground: £150, juv/OAP £100

Cost of Stand Tickets: Main Stand (Catagory A & B):
Lounges: £20 & £15, £25 & £20; Family Lounge A & J
Block: £8, u18/OAP/Grandparents £5; Arthur Wait Stand:
U,V,W, £18 & £14, juv/OAP £10 & 7; S,T, £15 & £12,
juv/OAP £10 & £7; Family Enclosure R Block: £8,
juv/OAP/Grandparents £5
Terraces: Whitehorse Lane Terrace: £8, juv/OAP £5;
Holmesdale Terrace £9, juv/OAP £5

Match and Ticket Information: All tickets bookable in

advance, one month by post (with sae) and two weeks for personal applications. Cheques should be made payable to Crystal Palace FC (1986) Ltd., and should record the name and address of applicant on reverse. Separate applications for each match. Visa and Access applications may be made by telephone.
Wheelchairs: Contact club re special enclosure

Car Parking: Executive Car Park (220 spaces) by prior arrangement through Club Secretary. Supporters may use Club Car Park (for 468 cars) on 1st come 1st served basis. Street parking is also available

Nearest Railway Station: Thornton Heath/Norwood Junction/Selhurst. Best from London is Victoria/London Bridge to East Croydon (2 stops) then taxi.

How to get to the ground

From North: From Motorway M1 or A1, use A406 North Circular Road to Chiswick. Follow signs South Circular Road A205 to Wandsworth. Then use A3 to A214 and follow signs to Streatham. Join A23. In 1m turn left B273. At end turn left into High Street then forward into Whitehorse Lane for Crystal Palace FC
From East: Use A232 (S.P. Croydon) to Shirley then join A215 (S.P. Norwood). In 2.2m turn left B266 into Whitehorse Lane.
From South: Use A23 (S.P. London) then follow signs Crystal Palace B266 via Thornton Heath into Whitehorse Lane.
From West: Use Motorway M4 to Chiswick then route from North or A232 (S.P. Croydon) to Beddington, then follow signs London A23. After, follow signs Crystal Palace B266 via Thornton Heath into Whitehorse Lane

DARLINGTON

Division 3

Formed: 1883   **Turned Professional:** 1908   **Ltd Co:** 1891

SPONSORED BY: Hutchison Telecom   **NICKNAME:** The Quakers

Chairman
Alan Noble

Deputy Chairman
John Brockbank

Directors
Bernard Lowery
Gordon Hampton
Sean Brockbank
Richard Tonks
Gordon Hodgson
Stephen Weeks

Manager
Billy McEwan

Secretary/Commercial Manager
Brian Anderson

Youth Development Officer
Barry Geldart

Chief Scout
Barry Geldart

Physiotherapist
Nigel Carnell

Youth Team Manager
Clive Middlemass

Club Statistician for the Directory
Frank Tweddle

DARLINGTON created what is possible a unique record by finishing either top or bottom of their league in four successive seasons. Relegation from the Football League in 1989 had been followed by the championship of the Conference in 1990 and Division Four in 1991, but it was back down to earth again as the club suffered its worst ever season for League defeats with twenty nine altogether, thirteen of these at home, to finish bottom of Division Three. The departure of manager Brian Little to Leicester City in the summer of 1991 marked the zenith of the Quakers recent achievements. His replacement, Frank Gray, who had played in the two championship winning sides, looked to have the qualities to ensure continuity at Feethams and build on Little's success.

The season started brightly enough with a win at Bournemouth on the opening day, but by the turn of the year only four more League wins had been secured and the writing was on the wall. In a desperate bid to salvage something from the season the club smashed their transfer record by paying Motherwell £95,000 for former Peterborough striker, Nick Cusack. However, he only managed six goals in twenty-one appearances and as nobody else was scoring regularly it was just not enough. The leading scorer at the end of the season was young Lee Ellison with just ten goals from twenty-seven appearances.

At the end of February, Frank Gray was sacked, along with his assistant, Tony Matthews, and Ray Hankin was promoted from youth team coach to caretaker manager for the remainder of the season. Alas he faired even worse than Gray, with only two wins in his sixteen games in charge. The defence which had been so solid over the previous two seasons, crumbled to concede ninety goals compared to just sixty-three in the last two League campaigns. Mark Prudhoe performed heroics in goal and stalwart centre-back Kevan Smith, approaching four hundred League appearances, set a captain's example, but perhaps the departure of Jimmy Willis to Leicester for £200,000 in November did as much as anything to upset the defence.

So, sadly the Quakers are back in the Fourth Division yet again. The team was virtually the same one that had won the Conference two years before and what was good enough to beat Barnet and Boston was not strong enough for Birmingham and Brentford. The new man in charge at Feethams is former Sheffield United and Rotherham boss, Billy McEwan, who must rebuild not only the team but also the supporters' confidence, which was badly dented by finishing bottom after two consecutive championships.   **Frank Tweddle**

Back row L-R: Anthony Isaacs, Simon Shaw, Mark Prudhoe, Adrian Swan, Stephen Ball, Alan Dowson. **Middle:** Tim Parkin, Steve Tupling, Gary Hinchley, Sean Gregan, Kevan Smith, Steve O'Shaughnessy, Richard Cooper, Nick Pickering, Billy McEwan (Manager). **Front:** Clive Middlemass (Youth Team Coach), Andy Toman, Steve Mardenborough, Steve Gaughan, Mark Sunley, Lee Ellison, Mark Dobie, Nigel Carnell (Physio).

DARLINGTON

DIVISION THREE: 24th **FA CUP:** 2nd RND **RUMBELOWS CUP:** 1st RND **AUTOGLASS:** Prelim.

M		DATE	COMP.	VEN	OPPONENTS	RESULT		H/T	LGE POS	GOALSCORERS/GOAL TIMES	ATTEN-DANCE
1	A	17	BL	A	Bournemouth	W	2-1	0-0	7	Watson (og) 47, Willis 63	(6,210)
2		20	RC 1/1	H	Huddersfield Town	W	1-0	1-0		Cook 23	3,140
3		24	BL	H	West Bromwich A.	L	0-1	0-0	13		5,658
4		28	RC 1/2	A	Huddersfield Town	L	0-4	0-1			(3,907)
5		31	BL	A	Birmingham City	L	0-1	0-1	15		(8,768)
6	S	3	BL	H	Bolton Wanderers	W	3-2	3-0	10	Willis 9, Cook 37, Coatsworth 44	3,384
7		7	BL	H	Stoke City	L	0-1	0-0	17		4,230
8		14	BL	A	Leyton Orient	L	1-2	0-0	20	Toman 65	(3,962)
9		21	BL	H	Brentford	L	1-2	1-2	21	Cook 20	3,900
10		28	BL	A	Wigan Athletic	W	2-1	1-0	19	Cook 9, Borthwick 90	(2,034)
11	O	5	BL	H	Bury	L	0-2	0-1	20		3,006
12		12	BL	A	Exeter City	L	1-4	1-2	20	Ellison (pen) 36	(3,548)
13		19	BL	H	Shrewsbury Town	D	3-3	0-2	21	Ellison 65, 69 (pen), Hamilton 72	2,188
14		22	AGT Pre	H	Crewe Alexandra	D	2-2	2-0		Willis 18, Ellison (pen) 26	1,095
15		26	BL	A	Hull City	L	2-5	2-1	22	Ellison 10, Norton (og) 35	(3,514)
16	N	2	BL	H	Hartlepool United	W	4-0	3-0	22	Ellison 9, 84, MacPhail (og) 13, McCarrison 39	5,041
17		5	BL	A	Reading	D	2-2	0-0	21	Hamilton 46, Toman 81	(2,808)
18		9	BL	A	Preston North End	L	1-2	0-0	21	Cork 52	(4,643)
19		16	FAC 1	H	Chesterfield	W	2-1	1-1		Ellison (pen) 17, Smith 56	3,628
20		23	BL	H	Peterborough Utd	L	1-2	1-0	24	Smith 26	2,815
21		30	BL	H	Fulham	W	3-1	1-0	20	Ellison 20, 59, McCarrison 61	2,655
22	D	14	BL	A	Huddersfield Town	L	1-2	0-1	21	Pickering 79	(5,677)
23		17	FAC 2	H	Hartlepool United	L	1-2	0-2		Toman 86	5,509
24		22	BL	A	West Bromwich A.	L	1-3	0-1	23	Ellison (pen) 73	(13,261)
25		26	BL	H	Birmingham City	D	1-1	1-0	21	Gill 6	4,421
26		28	BL	H	Bournemouth	D	0-0	0-0	22		3,172
27	J	1	BL	A	Bolton Wanderers	L	0-2	0-0	23		(5,851)
28		4	BL	A	Chester City	W	5-2	2-2	22	Pickering 29, Mardenborough 36,55, Ellison 75, Borthwick 79	(1,020)
29		7	AGT Pre	A	Chester City	L	1-2	0-2		Gill 72	(416)
30		11	BL	H	Torquay United	W	3-2	3-1	22	Toman 13, 45, Mardenborough 36	2,493
31		18	BL	A	Stockport County	L	0-2	0-0	22		(4,186)
32		28	BL	A	Swansea City	L	2-4	1-3	22	Dewhurst 32, Cusack 80	(2,743)
33	F	1	BL	A	Shrewsbury Town	W	2-0	1-0	20	Mardenborough 36, 47	(2,657)
34		8	BL	H	Hull City	L	0-1	0-1	21		3,636
35		11	BL	A	Fulham	L	0-4	0-1	21		(2,988)
36		15	BL	H	Huddersfield Town	L	1-3	1-1	22	Pickering 16	3,120
37		22	BL	A	Torquay United	L	0-3	0-2	24		(2,415)
38		29	BL	H	Chester City	D	1-1	0-0	24	Pickering 62	2,579
39	M	3	BL	H	Stockport County	L	1-3	1-1	24	Cusack 43	2,384
40		7	BL	A	Bradford City	W	1-0	1-0	24	O'Shaughnessy 4	(5,579)
41		10	BL	H	Reading	L	2-4	0-1	24	Borthwick 62, Cusack 69	2,388
42		14	BL	A	Hartlepool United	L	0-2	0-2	24		(4,442)
43		21	BL	H	Preston North End	L	0-2	0-2	24		2,270
44		28	BL	A	Peterborough Utd	D	1-1	1-1	24	Cusack 36	(5,218)
45		31	BL	H	Leyton Orient	L	0-1	0-0	24		1,704
46	A	3	BL	A	Stoke City	L	0-3	0-2	24		(13,579)
47		7	BL	H	Bradford City	L	1-3	1-2	24	Mardenborough 43	1,946
48		11	BL	H	Swansea City	D	1-1	0-1	24	Cork 72	1,507
49		18	BL	A	Brentford	L	1-4	0-3	24	Cork 79	(8,383)
50		20	BL	H	Wigan Athletic	L	0-1	0-1	24		1,223
51		25	BL	A	Bury	L	0-1	0-0	24		(2,351)
52	M	2	BL	H	Exeter City	W	5-2	2-1	24	Cusack 28, 89, Pickering 42, Borthwick 68, 84	1,573

Best Home League Attendance: 5,658 v West Bromwich A.   **Smallest:** 1,223 v Wigan Athletic   **Av Home Att:** 2,926

Goal Scorers: **Compared with 90-91:** -1,122

League (56): Ellison 10 (3 pens), Mardenborough 6, Cusack 6, Borthwick 5, Pickering 5, Toman 4, Opponents 3, Cook 3, Cork 3, Hamilton 2, Willis 2, McCarrison 2, Gill, Smith, Dewhurst, Coatsworth, O'Shaughnessy

R/lows C (1): Cook
FA Cup (3): Smith, Ellison (1 pen), Toman
Autoglass (3): Gill, Ellison (1 pen), Willis

1991-92

Prudhoe M.	McJannet W.	Gray F.	Willis J.	Smith K.	Gill G.	Cook M.	Toman J.	Borthwick J.	Cork D.	Tait M.	Coatsworth G.	Trotter M.	Mardenborough S.	Ellison A.	Hamilton G.	Coverdale D.	Sunley M.	Gregan S.	Pickering N.	McCarrison D.	Dewhurst R.	Gaughan S.	O'Shaughnessy S.	Cusack N.	Hinchley G.	Referee	No.
1	2	3	4	5	6	7	8	9	10	11*	12	S														R Pawley	1
1	2	3*	4	5	6	7	8	9	10		11	S	12													C Trussell	2
1	2	3*	4	5	6	7	8	9	10		11	S	12													D Phillips	3
1	2	3*	4	5	6	7	8	9	10		11	S	12													W Flood	4
1	12		4	5		3	8	9	10	11	2	6*		7												P Jones	5
1		3*	4	5		7	8	9		12	11	2	6	10												J Key	6
1		3•	4	5		7	8	9*		12	11	2	6	10	14											M Peck	7
1		3•	4	5		7	8	9*		12		2	6	14	10											P Durkin	8
1			4	5•	6	3	8	9		S	11		14	10	7											T Lunt	9
1			4		6	3	8•	12	10	11	5		14	9*	7											R Hamer	10
1			4		6	3†	8	14	10*	11†	5			9*	7											A Bennett	11
1			4†	5	6	3	8		10*	11	S			9	7											J Deakin	12
1			4	5	6		8		10	11*	S			9	7	3										I Hendrick	13
1			4	5*			8		10		2	6		9	7	3	12	S								T West	14
1			4	5	6		8		10	11*	2		12	9	7	3		S								R Poulain	15
1	2			5	6	3	8	S	S	11				9	7				4	10						A Dawson	16
1	2			5	6	3	8	12	14	11				9*	7*				4	10						G Poll	17
1	2			5	6•	3	8	12	14	11				9*	7				4	10						V Callow	18
1	2			5		3	8	S	7	11		6	S	9					4	10						E Parker	19
1	2			5•			8	12	6	11			14	9	7				4	10						P Harrison	20
1	2		4	5		3	8	12		11		7		9*				S	6	10†						R Nixon	21
1	2			5		3†	8*	9	S	11			12	10	7				4	6						M Bailey	22
1	2			5		3	8	14	S	11			10	9	7				4•	6						M Peck	23
1				5		3	8•	12	14				10	9		7*		2	4	6	11					P Scoble	24
1				5	7	3	8	12					10	9*			S	2	4	6	11					D Phillips	25
1				5	7		8	S		3			10	9			S	2	4	6	11					J Kirkby	26
1				5	7*		8	12		3			10	9			S	2	4	6	11					A Smith	27
1				5	7		8	12		3			10*	9			S	2	4	6	11					P Danson	28
1				5	7		8	10	6*					9			12	2	4	3	11					R Shepherd	29
1				5	7	14	8	12		3			10*	9•				2	4	6	11					K Breen	30
1				5	7	6	8	12	S	3			10	9*				2	4		11					T Lunt	31
1				5			8			3			10	12			S		4*		11	2	7	9		R Hamer	32
1				5			8	S		3		7	10				S		4		11	2	6	9		C Trussell	33
1				5			8	14		3		7*	10*	12					4		11	2	6	9		J Lloyd	34
1		S		5					S	3			10	8					4		11	2	6	9		R Bigger	35
1		3		5	7		8	S		11			10				S		4			2	6	9		I Hendrick	36
1	2			5*	12	3	8		14	11			10•						4			7	6	9		K Burge	37
1	2			5		3	8	S	6				10				S				11	7	4	9		T West	38
1	2			5		3	8*	12	10•				6	14							11	7	4	9		A Dawson	39
1	2			5		3	8	S	10								S				11	7	4	9	6	W Flood	40
1	2			5		3	8	12	10					7•							11		4	9	6*	K Hackett	41
1	2			5•		3	8	12	10				14						4		11	7*	6	9		J Watson	42
1	2					3	8	S	10										4	5*	11	7	6	9		S Bell	43
1							8	S	10	6			12						4	5	3	7		9	2	T Ward	44
1							8	14	10	6				11*					4	5	3	7		9	2	B Coddington	45
1							8•		10	11*	6*			11					4	5	3	7		9	2	P Don	46
1							8	S	10	6				11		3			4	5•		7	6	9	2	W Burns	47
1	2			5			8•	12	10	6				11	14						3	7	4*	9		P Harrison	48
1	2			5			8	S	10	6				11		3	S					7	4	9		M James	49
1	2			5			8	S	10	6				11		3				4		7		9		W Burns	50
1				5					10		4		11			3		2		6		8		9		M Brandwood	51
1				5				14	10*	4			7			3		2		6	11	8		9		J Key	52
46	**19**	**6**	**12**	**39**	**19**	**26**	**43**	**11**	**22**	**34**	**9**	**5**	**21**	**25**	**11**	**10**	**15**	**17**	**29**	**5**	**11**	**20**	**15**	**21**	**6**	League Appearances	
	1								1	1	18	8	1	8	2		4									Substitute Appearances	
2	2	2	2	2	2	2	2	2	2	1	1		0+2		4											R/lows Appearances	
2	2			2	1		2	2		0+1	1		2				1		1	2	1					FA Cup Appearances	
1	2	1		2	1		2	2	0+1	1			2	1			1	1+1	1+1	1		1	2	1		Autoglass Appearances	

Also Played: Posn.(Game): Tucker S(5,6,50)12(11,12,13)11(14)14(41,51), Clark 2(9 to 13), Reed 14(46), Shaw 12(51)
Isaacs S(29)7(35)12(43,45,46,52)11(44)14(14)6(50)   †=Sent Off

Players on Loan: Howard Clark (Coventry City), Gary Hamilton (Middlesbrough), Dugald McCarrison (Celtic), Bob Dewhurst (Blackburn Rov)

DARLINGTON

Club Colours: White shirts with diagonal black stripes, black shorts, white stockings
Change Colours: All pale blue
Reserves League: Midland Senior League

Previous Leagues: Northern League, North Eastern League, G.M. Vauxhall Conference
Previous Name:
Previous Managers: Since 1946: Bill Forrest   George Irwin   Bob Gurney   Dick Duckworth   Eddie Carr   Lol Morgan   Jimmy Greenhalgh   Ray Yeoman   Len Richley   Frank Brennan   Allan Jones   Ralph Brand   Dick Conner   Bill Horner   Peter Madden   Len Walker   Billy Elliott   Cyril Knowles   Paul Ward (Player/Manager)   David Booth   Brian Little   Frank Gray   Ray Hankin
Honours: Div 3N Champions 1924-5, Div 3N Cup 1933-34, G.M.V.C. Champions 1989-90   Division 4 Champions 1991
League Career: Original member of Div 3N 1921   Promoted to Div 2 1924-5   Relegated to Div 3N 1926-7
Tranferred to Div 4 1958   Promoted to Div 3 1965-6   Relegated to Div 4 1966-7   Promoted to Div 3 1984-5
Relegated to Div 4 1986-7   Relegated to G.M.V.C 1988-89   Promoted to Div 4 1989-90   Promoted to Div 3 1990-91
Relegated to Div 4 1991-92

CLUB RECORDS

Most Appearances for Club: Ron Greener, 442, 1955-68
Most Capped Player: None
Record Goalscorer in a Match: Tom Ruddy, 5 v South Shields, Div 2, 23.4.1927;   Maurice Wellock, 5 v Rotherham United, Div 3N, 15.2.1930
Record League Goalscorer in a Season: David Brown, 39, Div 3N, 1924-5   **In All Competitions:** David Brown, 1924-5
Record League Goalscorer in a Career: Alan Walsh, 90, 1978-84   **In All Competitions:** Alan Walsh, 100 (87 League + 6 FA Cup + 7 Milk Cup) 1978-84
Record Transfer Fee Received: £200,000 from Leicester City for Jimmy Willis, December 1991
Record Transfer Fee Paid: £95,000 to Motherwell for Nick Cusack, Jan 1992
Best Performances: League: 15th Div 2, 1925-6   **FA Cup:** 3rd Round 1910-11, 5th Round 1957-58 (both last 16)   **League Cup:** 5th Round, 1967-68
Most League Points: 85 in Div 4, 1984-5   (87 in GMVC 1989-90)
Record League Victory and Most Goals Scored in a League Match: 9-2 v Lincoln City, Div 3N, 7.1.1928
Record Cup Victory and Most Goals Scored in a Cup Tie: 7-2 v Evenwood Town, FAC 1, 17.11.1958;   7-0 v Halifax Town, FRT, 3.3.1985
Record League Defeat: 0-10 v Doncaster Rovers, Div 4, 25.1.1964
Oldest Player in a League Match: John Spuhler, 38 yrs 7 months, 25.4.1956
Youngest Player in a League Match: Dale Anderson, 16 yrs 254 days, 4.5.1987

LONGEST LEAGUE RUNS

of undefeated matches: 17 (1968)	**of league matches without a win:** 19 (1988-89)
of undefeated home matches: 36 (1923-25)	**of undefeated away matches:** 14 (1968-69)
without home win: 18 (1988-89)	**without an away win:** 36 (1952-54)
of league wins: 5 (1922, 1924, 1928, 1975, 1985, 1989 (GMVC))	**of home wins:** 8 (1923-24, 1924, 1935-36)
of league defeats: 8 (1985)	**of away wins:** 4 (1948) 5 (1989 G.M.V.C.)

DARLINGTON							APPEARANCES				GOALS			
PLAYERS NAME Honours	Ht	Wt	Birthdate	Birthplace Transfers	Contract Date	Clubs	League	L/Cup	FA Cup	Other	Lg	L/C	FAC	Oth
GOALKEEPERS														
Mark Prudhoe	6.0	13.0	11.11.63	Washington	11.09.81	Sunderland (A)	7							
GMVC'90,Div4'91,FLgXI				Loan	04.11.83	Hartlepool Utd	3							
				£22,000	24.09.84	Birmingham City	1	4						
				£22,000	27.02.86	Walsall	26	4	1					
				Loan	11.12.86	Doncaster Rovers	5							
				Loan	26.03.87	Grimsby Town	8							
				Loan	29.08.87	Hartlepool Utd	13							
				Loan	06.11.87	Bristol City	3			2				
				£10,000	11.12.87	Carlisle Utd	34	2						
				£10,000	16.03.89	Darlington	105	6	8	5				
Adrian Swan	6.0		31.07.73	Middlesbrough	04.07.91	Darlington								
				Loan	20.05.92	Leicester City								
DEFENDERS														
Sean Gregan					20.12.91	Darlington (T)	17		1	1				
Gary Hinchley						Guisborough Town								
					26.02.92	Darlington	6							
Steve O'Shaughnessy	6.2	13.1	13.10.67	Wrexham	15.10.85	Leeds Utd								
W:Y				f	07.11.85	Bradford City	0+1	0+1		0+1				1
				f	15.08.88	Rochdale	101+8	5	9	7	16	3	2	
				£10,000	25.07.91	Exeter City	1+2	1						
				Free	21.01.92	Darlington	15			1				
Adam Reed			18.02.75	Bishop Auckland		Darlington	0+1							
Kevan Smith	6.3	12.6	13.12.59	Eaglescliff		Stockton								
GMVC'90,Div4'91				f	28.09.79	Darlington	242+3	10+1	18	4	11		1	
				f	31.07.85	Rotherham Utd	59	6	5	2	4		1	
				£60,000	04.12.86	Coventry City	5+1		1					
				£40,000	11.05.88	York City	30+1			2	5			
				£10,000	09.06.89	Darlington	85	6	8	5	5		1	
Mark Sunley					04.10.89	Middlesbrough (T)								
				Free N.C	16.02.91	Millwall								
				Free	01.07.91	Darlington	15		1+1					
MIDFIELD														
Stephen Gaughan	5.11	11.2	14.04.70	Doncaster	08.07.88	Doncaster Rovers (A)	42+25	2+2	4+1	5+1	3			
				Free	01.07.90	Sunderland								
				£10,000	21.01.92	Darlington	20							
Anthony Isaacs	5.8		08.04.73	Middlesbrough	04.07.91	Darlington	3+4			0+1				
Nick Pickering	6.0	12.2	04.08.63	Newcastle	03.08.81	Sunderland (A)	177+2	18	10	2	18			
E:1,U21.15,Y.1; FAC '87; UEFA u21'84				£120,000	30.01.86	Coventry City	76+2	7	6	3	9	1		
				£250,000	15.08.88	Derby County	35+10	7+1	3	3	3			
					31.10.91	Darlington	29		2	1	5			
Simon Shaw	6.0	12.00	21.09.73	Teeside		Darlington	0+1							
Andy Toman	5.10	11.7	07.03.62	Northallerton		Bishop Auckland								
GMVC'90,Div4'91				£10,000	16.08.85	Lincoln City	21+3	2		0+1	4			
						Bishop Auckland								
				£6,000	23.01.87	Hartlepool Utd	112	4	9	7	28		4	
				£40,000	01.08.89	Darlington	86	6	8	5	9		2	3
FORWARDS														
Tony Ellison					08.11.90	Darlington	34+6		3+1	2	13		1	1
Steve Mardenborough	5.7	11.9	19.09.64	Birmingham	06.08.82	Coventry City (A)								
				Free		Birmingham City								
				Free	20.09.83	Wolverhampton W	9	0+1	0+1		1			
				Loan	23.02.84	Cambridge Utd	6							
				Free	30.07.84	Swansea City	32+4	2	2	3+1	7			
				Free	19.07.85	Newport Co	50+14	4+1	5+1	2+1	11		1	1
				Free	27.03.87	Cardiff City	18+14	1	0+1	1+1	1			
				f	28.07.88	Hereford Utd	20+7	2	1	1+1				
				Free	01.07.89	IFK Ostersund (Swe)								
						Cheltenham Town								
				Free	06.07.90	Darlington	38+26	0+5	2+1	2	7			
ADDITIONAL CONTRACT PLAYERS														
James Cousins						Darlington								
Francis Gray					18.07.91	Darlington	6	2						
James Rodwell						Darlington	1							

LEADING LEAGUE GOALSCORERS SEASONS 1985-86 – 1991-92

1985-86	GARY McDONALD	16	1986-87	DAVID CURRIE	12
1987-88	DAVID CURRIE	21	1988-89	GARY WORTHINGTON	12
1989-90	JOHN BORTHWICK	19	1990-91	JOHN BORTHWICK	10
	1991-92	TONY ELLISON	10			

FEETHAMS Darlington, Co. Durham DL1 5JB

Capacity: 9,984   **Covered Standing:** 2,822   **Seating:** 973

Tel: Ground: 0325 465097   **Ticket Sales:** As ground   **Clubcall:** 0898 12 11 49

All premium rate calls (0898/0891) cost 36p per minute cheap rate and 48p per minute at all other times. Call costings correct at time of going to press.

ATTENDANCES
Highest: 21,023 v Bolton Wanderers, League Cup 3rd Rnd, 14.11.1960

Lowest: 657 v Halifax Town, Freight Rover Trophy, 3.3.1985

Record Receipts: £32,300.74 v Rochdale, Div 4, 11.5.1991

FEETHAMS
First game: 1883
First floodlit game: v Millwall, 19.9.1960

Season Tickets:
Stands: from £123.50 to £142.50, juv/OAP £57 to £85.50
Ground: from £104.50 to £123.50, juv/OAP £47.50 to £66.50

Executive Box Season Tickets: None available

Cost of Stand Tickets: Seats: adults £7.50, juv/OAP £4.50; Family seats: £6.50, juv/OAP £3
Terraces: adults £5.50, £6.50, juv/OAP £2.50, £3.50

Match and Ticket Information: Postal and telephone one month in advance

Car Parking: Adequate space in adjacent side streets

Nearest Railway Station: Darlington (0325 55111)

How to get to the ground

From North: Use Motorway A1M then A167 S.P. Darlington into town centre then follow signs Northallerton into Victoria Road for Darlington F.C.

From East: Use A67 S.P. Darlington into town centre, then follow signs Northallerton into Victoria Road for Darlington F.C.

From South: Use Motorway A1M and A66M then A66 S.P. Darlington and at roundabout take 4th exit into Victoria Road for Darlington F.C.

From West: Use A67 S.P. Darlington into town centre and at roundabout take 3rd exit into Victoria Road for Darlington F.C.

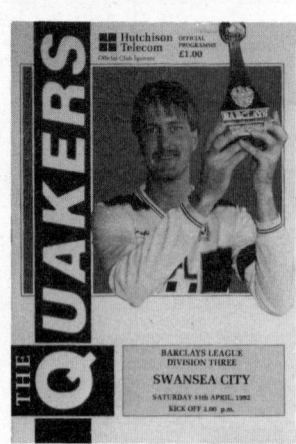

Value Rating: ★ ★

Programme Editor: Brian Anderson

Price of 1992-93 Programme: £1
Number of Pages: 28
Subscriptions: £34 (all home games)

Local Newspapers: Northern Echo, Evening Gazette

Local Radio Stations: BBC Radio Cleveland, T.F.M. Radio

DERBY COUNTY

Division 1

Formed: 1884 **Turned Professional:** 1884 **Ltd Co:** 1896

SPONSORED BY: AUTOWINDSCREENS **NICKNAME:** The Rams

Chairman
B E Fearn

Vice-Chairman
L V Pickering

Directors
J N Kirkland BSc,CEng,MICE
W Hart
C W McKerrow
A Cox
M Mills
S Adams

Manager
Arthur Cox

Assistant Manager
Roy McFarland

General Manager/Secretary
Michael Dunford (0332)40105

Commercial Manager
Colin Tunnicliffe (0332) 40105

Youth Development Officer
Gerry Summers

Chief Scout
Jimmy Sirrel

Physiotherapist
Gordon Guthrie

Youth Team Manager
Richie Williams

Community Officer
John Jarmans

Club Statistician for the Directory
Steven McGhee

AFTER all the traumas of the previous season, including the notorious Robert Maxwell episodes, Derby started 1991-92 with both a new board and money in the bank to allow them, at last, to enter the transfer market.

The new centre-back pairing of Simon Coleman and Andy Comyn settled down well, but the initial lack of goals led to the loan signing of former Rams favourite Bobby Davison from Leeds. While not signing permanently, his return of nine goals in ten games helped push Derby up the table from 15th to 6th. Further attacking options were given by the signing of Ian Ormondroyd from Villa.

Steady progress in the League was not matched in the cups. A 2-0 aggregate win over Ipswich in the Second Round of the Rumbelows Cup preceded a 1-2 defeat at Oldham in the Third Round. Middlesbrough dealt a 2-4 defeat in the Zenith Data Cup, while in the F.A. Cup a replay win over Burnley (2-2, 2-0) brought Aston Villa to the Baseball Ground for the Fourth Round. A classic game saw 'The Rams' go down 3-4.

With only the League left, Arthur Cox entered the transfer market again, paying several million pounds for more firepower up front. Kitson from Leicester, Gabbiadini from Palace, Simpson from Oxford and Johnson from Notts County were all signed while Phil Gee and Ian Ormondroyd headed to Leicester.

A good run-in, with only one defeat in the last 10 games led Derby to a play-off place. Indeed, they were only 11 minutes from promotion on the last day of the season, untill Middlesbrough equalised at Wolves.

In the play-offs, some slack defending in the first leg at Blackburn left too much to do at home, thus the season ended in disappointment.

A club record 12 away League wins was negated by a lamentable eight home defeats and, if the home form can be improved, promotion must be a good bet for 1992-93.

The close season has brought yet more big signings with Mark Pembridge from Luton and Darren Wassell moving down the road from Nottingham Forest to strengthen the squad yet further.

Steve McGhee

Back Row L-R: Roy McParland (Asst. Man.), Phil Gee, Ted McMinn, Michael Forsyth, Andy Comyn, Peter Shilton, Michael Harford, Martin Taylor, Justin Phillips, Simon Coleman, Nick Pickering, Trevor Hebberd, Gordon Guthrie (Physio).
Front Row: Mark Patterson, Jason Kavanagh, Paul Williams, Steve Cross, Geraint Williams, Arthur Cox (Manager), Gary Micklewhite, Criag Ramage, Mel Sage, Steve Hayward, Martyn Chalk.

DERBY COUNTY

DIVISION TWO: 3rd   **FA CUP:** 4th RND   **RUMBELOWS CUP:** 3rd RND   **ZDS CUP:** 2nd RND

M	DATE		COMP.	VEN	OPPONENTS	RESULT	H/T	LGE POS	GOALSCORERS/GOAL TIMES	ATTEN-DANCE
1	A	17	BL	A	Sunderland	D 1-1	0-0		Harford 66	(20,509)
2		21	BL	H	Middlesbrough	W 2-0	0-0		Comyn 62, Harford 88	12,805
3		24	BL	H	Southend United	L 1-2	0-2	7	P Williams 77	12,284
4	S	1	BL	A	Charlton Athletic	W 2-0	0-0	5	P Williams 65, Harford 90	(6,602)
5		4	BL	H	Blackburn Rovers	L 0-2	0-1	9		12,078
6		7	BL	H	Barnsley	D 1-1	1-0	10	P Williams 34	10,559
7		13	BL	A	Cambridge United	D 0-0	0-0	12		(7,923)
8		18	BL	A	Oxford United	L 0-2	0-0	15		(4,319)
9		21	BL	H	Brighton & H A	W 3-1	1-0	11	Davison 42, Patterson 63, P Williams (pen) 79	12,004
10		**25**	**RC 2/1**	**H**	**Ipswich Town**	**D 0-0**	**0-0**			**10,215**
11		28	BL	A	Newcastle United	D 2-2	1-0	13	Davison 31, Ormondroyd 57	(17,581)
12	O	5	BL	H	Bristol City	W 4-1	1-0	8	Aizlewood (og) 18, Micklewhite 48, Davison 63, 80	11,880
13		**8**	**RC 2/2**	**A**	**Ipswich Town**	**W 2-0**	**2-0**		**Gee 23, P Williams (pen) 29**	**(8,957)**
14		12	BL	A	Swindon Town	W 2-1	1-0	6	Taylor (og) 41, Gee 69	(11,883)
15		19	BL	H	Portsmouth	W 2-0	0-0	6	McMinn 52, P Williams 89	13,190
16		**22**	**ZDS 2**	**A**	**Middlesbrough**	**L 2-4**	**2-0**		**Micklewhite 14, Stallard 31**	**(6,385)**
17		26	BL	H	Millwall	W 2-1	1-1	6	Davison 38, Ormondroyd 88	(7,660)
18		**29**	**RC 3**	**A**	**Oldham Athletic**	**L 1-2**	**1-0**		**Forsyth 25**	**(11,219)**
19	N	2	BL	H	Tranmere Rovers	L 0-1	0-1	6		11,500
20		6	BL	A	Port Vale	L 0-1	0-0	7		(8,589)
21		9	BL	A	Wolverhampton W	W 3-2	1-1	6	Davison 11, 89, Ormondroyd 84	(15,672)
22		16	BL	H	Ipswich Town	W 1-0	0-0	3	Davison 57	12,493
23		23	BL	A	Bristol Rovers	W 3-2	1-2	3	Patterson 6, P Williams (pen) 80, Davison 90	(6,513)
24		30	BL	H	Leicester City	L 1-2	0-2	3	Ormondroyd 51	19,306
25	D	7	BL	A	Watford	W 2-1	1-0	4	Ormondroyd 2, 87	(8,302)
26		26	BL	H	Grimsby Town	D 0-0	0-0	6		16,392
27		28	BL	H	Charlton Athletic	L 1-2	0-1	8	Ormondroyd 81	14,367
28	J	1	BL	A	Middlesbrough	D 1-1	0-1	8	Chalk 61	(16,288)
29		**4**	**FAC 3**	**A**	**Burnley**	**D 2-2**	**1-1**		**Chalk 1, Comyn 77**	**(18,793)**
30		11	BL	A	Southend United	L 0-1	0-1	9		(8,295)
31		18	BL	H	Sunderland	L 1-2	0-2	11	G Williams 85	15,384
32		**25**	**FAC 3R**	**H**	**Burnley**	**W 2-0**	**0-0**		**P Williams 54, Ormondroyd 64**	**18,364**
33	F	1	BL	A	Portsmouth	W 1-0	0-0	11	Gabbiadini 59	(12,008)
34		**5**	**FAC 4**	**H**	**Aston Villa**	**L 3-4**	**2-4**		**Gee 6, 38, P Williams 59**	**22,452**
35		8	BL	H	Millwall	L 0-2	0-0	11		12,773
36		11	BL	A	Blackburn Rovers	L 0-2	0-0	11		(15,350)
37		15	BL	A	Bristol Rovers	W 1-0	0-0	10	Coleman 52	11,154
38		22	BL	A	Leicester City	W 2-1	1-0	9	Ormondroyd 3, Simpson 68	(18,148)
39		29	BL	H	Watford	W 3-1	2-0	6	P Williams 3 (7, 22, 47 pen)	14,052
40	M	7	BL	A	Plymouth Argyle	D 1-1	1-1	6	Simpson 17	(8,864)
41		11	BL	H	Port Vale	W 3-1	1-1	4	G Williams 2, Simpson 56, Gabbiadini 63	15,345
42		14	BL	A	Tranmere Rovers	L 3-4	1-1	7	Kitson 1, Coleman 53, Simpson 60	(10,386)
43		21	BL	H	Wolverhampton W	L 1-2	1-0	9	Kitson 44	21,024
44		25	BL	H	Plymouth Argyle	W 2-0	1-0	5	Johnson 17, McMinn 73	13,799
45		28	BL	A	Ipswich Town	L 1-2	0-2	8	Simpson 82	(15,305)
46	A	1	BL	H	Cambridge United	D 0-0	0-0	7		15,353
47		4	BL	A	Barnsley	W 3-0	2-0	5	Simpson 10, Forsyth 31, P Williams (pen) 63	(10,121)
48		7	BL	A	Grimsby Town	W 1-0	1-0	4	Gabbiadini 25	(7,040)
49		11	BL	H	Oxford United	D 2-2	1-1	5	Simpson 40, P Williams (pen) 72	15,555
50		15	BL	A	Brighton & H A	W 2-1	1-0	4	Gabbiadini 36, 81	(8,159)
51		20	BL	H	Newcastle United	W 4-1	2-0	3	P Williams (pen) 4, Kitson 16, Ramage 69, 76	21,364
52		25	BL	A	Bristol City	W 2-1	1-1	4	Gabbiadini 25, Micklewhite 81	(16,658)
53	M	2	BL	H	Swindon Town	W 2-1	1-0	3	Kitson 27, Johnson 56	22,608
54		**10**	**PO SF1**	**A**	**Blackburn Rovers**	**L 2-4**	**2-2**		**Gabbiadini 2, Johnson 14**	**(19,677)**
55		**13**	**PO SF2**	**H**	**Blackburn Rovers**	**W 2-1**	**1-0**		**Comyn 23, McMinn 73**	**22,920**

Best Home League Attendance: 22,608 v Swindon Town   **Smallest:** 10,559 v Barnsley   **Av Home Att:** 14,664

Goal Scorers:

Compared with 90-91: -1,704

League (69):	P Williams 12 (5 pens), Davison 9, Ormondroyd 8, Simpson 7, Gabbiadini 6, Kitson 4, Harford 3, G Williams 2, Johnson 2 Micklewhite 2, Ramage 2, Coleman 2, McMinn 2, Patterson 2, Opponents 2, Forsyth, Chalk, Gee, Comyn
R/lows C (3):	Gee, Forsyth, P Williams (1 pen)
FA Cup (7):	Gee 2, P Williams 2, Comyn, Chalk, Ormondroyd
ZDS Cup (2):	Stallard, Micklewhite
Play-Offs (2):	Gabbiadini, McMinn, Johnson, Comyn

Player columns (left to right): Shilton P., Sage M., Forsyth M., Williams G., Coleman S., Comyn A., Micklewhite G., Gee P., Harford M., Williams P., McMinn T., Cross S., Hayward S., Ramage C., Kavanagh J., Patterson M., Stallard M., Ormondroyd I., Davison B., Chalk M., Gabbiadini M., Simpson P., Round S., Kitson P., Johnson T., Sutton S.

Shi	Sag	For	WiG	Col	Com	Mic	Gee	Har	WiP	McM	Cro	Hay	Ram	Kav	Pat	Sta	Orm	Dav	Cha	Gab	Sim	Rou	Kit	Joh	Sut	Referee	#
1	2	3	4	5	6	7	8*	9	10	11	14															D Allison	1
1	2	3	4	5	6	7	8	9	10	11	S															D Gallagher	2
1	2	3	4	5	6	7	8*	9	10	11	S															D Frampton	3
	2	3	4	5	6	7	8	9	10	11*	14															G Willard	4
1	2	3	4	5	6	7*	8*	9	10	11	14	12														V Callow	5
1	2	3	4	5	6	7	8*	9	10	11	14															K Barratt	6
1	2	3	4	5	6	7	8		10	11		12	9*	S												M James	7
1	2	3	4	5	6	7	8*		10*	11			9		12	14										K Cooper	8
1	2	3	4	5	6	7*			10	11		S			14				8	9						P Foakes	9
1	2	3	4	5	6	7•		9*	10	11		12			14				8							J Kirkby	10
1	2•	3	4	5	6	7	S		10	11					14				8	9						C Trussell	11
1	2*	3	4	5	6	7	S		10	11					12				8	9						L Dilkes	12
1		3	4	5	6	7		9	10	11		S				2			8							J Moules	13
1		3	4	5	6	7		9	10	11		S				2			8							P Wright	14
1	2	3	4	5	6	7		9	10	11		S				S			8							T Fitzharris	15
		3		5	6	7	8		10•	11		4				2	9*		12							I Hendrick	16
1	2	3	4	5	6	7	S		10	11		S							8	9						I Hemley	17
1	2	3	4	5	6	7		9*	10	11		12				S			8							R Lewis	18
1	2	3	4	5	6	7			10	11	S	S							8	9						A Ward	19
1	2	3	4	5	6	7			10	11	S	S							8	9						G Singh	20
1	2	3	4	5	6	7			10	11	S	S							8	9						D Elleray	21
1	2*	3	4	5	6	7	S		10	11		12							8	9						R Milford	22
1	3*		4		6	7	12		10	11		5•	14			2			8	9						T Holbrook	23
1			4	5	6	7	S		10	11		3				2			8	9						J Watson	24
1		3	4	5	6	7	9		10	11						2			S							J Worrall	25
1		3	4	5	6	7	9•		10	11						2			14							M Reed	26
1		3	4	5	6	7*	9•		10	11		12				2			14							S Bell	27
1		3	4	5	6				10	11	S	S				2	9		8	7						S Lodge	28
1		3	4	5	6				10	11	S	S				2	9		8	7						K Redfern	29
1		3*	4	5	6							14	12			2	9		8	7						A Ward	30
1		3	4	5	6	7*		9	10	11						2			12	7						G Pooley	31
1		3	4	5	6			9	10	11						2	S		8	7						K Redfern	32
1		3	4	5	6		S		10	11						2			8	7*		9				M Bodenham	33
1		3	4	5	6		9		10	11						2•			12	8		7*				K Morton	34
1		3	4	5	6	7			10	11						2			8	7*		9				M Peck	35
1		3	4	5	6	7			10	11						2			8	S		9				K Lupton	36
1		3	4	5	6	7	12		10	11						2			8	S		9*				T West	37
1		3	4	5	6	S	S		10	7						2			8	9		11				P Taylor	38
1		3	4	5	6	S	S		10	7						2			8	9		11				P Harrison	39
			4	5	6	12			10	7*						2			8	9		11	3			J Deakin	40
			4	5	6	7			10							2			S	9		11	3	8		H King	41
		3	4	5	6	S			10							2				9	11*		8	7		N Midgley	42
		3	4	5	6	S			10	12						2				9	11*		8	7		M James	43
		3	4	5	6	S			10*	12						2				9	11	S	8	7	1	L Dilkes	44
		3	4	5	6	S			10							2				9	11	S	8	7	1	P Alcock	45
		3	4	5	6	S			10							2				9	11	S	8	7	1	A Ward	46
		3		5	6	S			4	10•						2				9	11	14	8	7	1	R Hart	47
		3		5	6	S			4				10			2				9	11	S	8	7	1	N Midgley	48
		3		5	6	S			4				10			2				9	11	S	8	7	1	T Holbrook	49
		3		5	6	8			4				10			2		S		9	11	S		7	1	D Axcell	50
		3			6	12			4	5			10			2				9	11	S	8	7	1	B Coddington	51
		3		6		12			4	5			10			2				9	11	S	8*	7	1	K Breen	52
		3		5	6	12				4			10			2				9*	11	S	8	7	1	M Reed	53
		3		5	6	12			10	4•			14			2				9*	11		8	7	1	K Hackett	54
		3		5	6	S			10	4			S			2				9	11		8	7	1	M Bullivant	55
31	**17**	**43**	**39**	**43**	**46**	**28**	**17**	**6**	**41**	**35**	**3**	**7**	**22**	**8**	**2**	**25**	**10**	**4**	**20**	**16**	**2**	**12**	**12**	**12**	**10**	League Appearances	
						4	2		2	4	4	4		3	4	1			3				1			Substitute Appearances	
3	2	3	3	3	3	3			3	3			0+2			1+1		3								R/lows Appearances	
3		3	3	3	3				3	3					2	1	1+1	3		3						FA Cup Appearances	
		1		1	1	1			1	1		1				1	1		0+1							ZDS Cup Appearances	
		2		2	2	0+1			2	2		2			0+1	2				2	2		2	2	2	Play-Offs Appearances	

Also Played: Posn.(Game): T Hebberd S(6), N Pickering S(1,2,4)12(3), D Sturridge 11•(30), M. Taylor 1(4,16,40,41,42,43,),
J Davidson S(13,14,31,32,33,36,41)14(16,34)10(30)

Players on Loan: B Davison (Leeds Utd)

DERBY COUNTY

Club Colours: White shirts, black shorts, white stockings with black tops
Change Colours: Sky blue shirts, white shorts, white stockings
Reserves League: Pontins Central League Division 1

COMPETITIONS					
Div. 1	Div. 2	Div. 3	Div. 3N	Euro C	Texaco
89-07	07-12	84-86	55-57	72-73	71-72
12-14	14-15			75-76	
19-21	21-26				**Wat C**
26-53	53-55			**UEFA**	1970
69-80	57-69			74-75	
87-91	80-84			76-77	
	86-87				
	91-				

HONOURS						
Div. 1	Div. 2	Div 3N	FAC	Texaco	Wat C	C/S'ld
71-72	11-12	56-57	45-46	71-72	1970	1975
74-75	14-15					
	68-69					
	86-87					

MOST APPEARANCES: KEVIN HECTOR 581+8 (1966-82)				
Year	League	FA Cup	Lge Cup	Other
1966-67	30	1		
1967-68	41	1	7	
1968-69	41	1	8	
1969-70	41	4	6	
1970-71	42	3	3	
1971-72	42	5	2	6
1972-73	41	5	3	8
1973-74	42	4	3	
1974-75	38	2	2	6
1975-76	29+3	2	2	4
1976-77	28+1	4	2	3
1977-78	11		2	
1980-81	25	2		
1981-82	27+4		2	
	478+8	34	42	27
Previous holder: J Parry 482+1 (1948-65)				

MOST GOALS IN A CAREER		
STEVE BLOOMER 331 (1892-1914)		
Season	League	FA Cup
1892-93	11	
1893-94	19	
1894-95	10	
1895-96	22	5
1896-97	24	7
1897-98	15	5
1898-99	24	6
1899-00	19	
1900-01	24	
1901-02	15	3
1902-03	12	1
1903-04	20	5
1904-05	13	
1905-06	12	
1910-11	20	4
1911-12	18	1
1912-13	13	1
1913-14	2	
Total	293	38

RECORD TRANSFER FEE RECEIVED			
Amount	Club	Player	Date
£2,900,000	Liverpool	Dean Saunders	7/91
£2,200,000	Liverpool	Mark Wright	6/91
£800,000	Millwall	Paul Goddard	12/89
£525,000	Aston Villa	Nigel Callaghan	2/89

RECORD TRANSFER FEE PAID			
Amount	Club	Player	Date
£1,300,000	Notts County	Tommy Johnson	3/92
£1,200,000	Crystal Palace	Marco Gabbiadini	1/92
£1,000,000	Oxford Utd.	Dean Saunders	10/88
£650,000	Southampton	Mark Wright	8/87

MANAGERS			
Name	Seasons	Best	Worst
Harry Newbould	1896-06	3(1)	15(1)
Jimmy Methvan	1906-22	7(1)	14(2)
Cecil Potter	1922-25	3(2)	14(2)
George Jobey	1925-41	2(1)	3(2)
Ted Magner	1941-46		
Stuart McMillan	1946-53	3(1)	22(1)
Jack Barker	1953-55	18(2)	22(2)
Harry Storer	1955-62	7(2)	2(3S)
Tim Ward	1962-67	8(2)	18(2)
Brian Clough	1967-73	1(1)	18(2)
Dave Mackay	1973-76	1(1)	4(1)
Colin Murphy	1976-77	15(1)	15(1)
Tommy Docherty	1977-79	12(1)	19(1)
Colin Addison	1979-81	19(1)	6(2)
John Newman	1981-83	13(2)	16(2)
Peter Taylor	1982-84	20(2)	20(2)
Arthur Cox	1984-	5(1)	7(2)

LONGEST LEAGUE RUNS	
of undefeated matches:	22 (8.3.1969-25.10.1969)
of undefeated home matches:	23 (5.10.1929-11.10.1930)
without home win:	9 (24.11.1990-4.5.1991)
of league wins:	9 (15.3.1969-9.8.1969)
of league defeats:	8 (3.4.1965-15.9.1965)
	(12.12.1987-10.2.1988)
of league matches without a win:	20 (1.12.1990-4.5.1991)
of undefeated away matches:	13 (18.1.1969-27.9.1969)
without an away win:	33 (1.9.1919-2.4.1921)
of home wins:	12 (23.10.1971-1.4.1972)
of away wins:	6 (29.3.1969-16.8.1969)

BARCLAYS

LOCAL BRANCH
PO Box No. 67
St James's Street
Derby DE1 1QU
Tel: 0332 363451

BARCLAYBANK MACHINE

BARCLAYS BUSINESS CENTRE
PO Box No. 202
Sir Frank Whittle Road
Derby DE1 9NT
Tel: 0332 363451

BARCLAYBANK MACHINE

BIGGEST VICTORIES
League: 9-0 v Wolverhampton W., 10.1.1891
9-0 v Sheffield Wednesday, Division 1, 2.1.1899
F.A. Cup: 8-1 v Barnsley, Round 1, 30.1.1897
League Cup: 6-0 v Sunderland, Round 3, 31.10.1991
Europe (UEFA): 12-0 v Finns Harps, Round 3, 15.9.1976

BIGGEST DEFEATS
League: 0-8 v Blackburn Rovers, Div 1, 3.1.1891
0-8 v Sunderland, Div 1, 1.9.1894
F.A. Cup: 2-11 v Everton, Round 1, 18.1.1890
League Cup: 0-5 v Southampton, 8.10.1974
0-5 v West Ham United, Round 3, 1.11.1988
Europe (UEFA): 1-5 v Real Madrid, Rnd 2, 5.11.1975

MOST POINTS
3 points a win: 84, Div 3 1985-86, Div 2 1986-87
2 points a win: 63, Div 3N 1955-56 & 1956-57, Div 2 1968-69

MOST GOALS IN A MATCH
6. Steve Bloomer v Sheffield Wednesday, Division 1,
2.1.1899

MOST GOALS
111, Div 3(N), 1956-57
Straw 37, Woodhead 14, Ryan 12, Brown 9, Parry 7,
Crowshaw 6, Buchanan 5, Barrowcliffe 4, Ackerman 4, Mays
4, Powell 1, Pye 1, Davies 1, Wyer 1, og 5.

MOST GOALS IN A SEASON
Jack Bowers 39 (League 37, FAC 2) 1930-31.
4 goals 3 times = 12; 3 goals twice = 6; 2 goals 6 times = 12; 1
goal 9 times = 9.
(League only): Ray Straw, 37, Div 3(N), 1956-57

MOST FIRST CLASS MATCHES IN A SEASON
60 (46 League, 7 FA Cup, 5 League Cup, 2 Freight Rover
Trophy) 1985-86

MOST LEAGUE GOALS CONCEDED
90, Division 1, 1936-37

MOST LEAGUE WINS
28, Division 3N, 1955-56

MOST LEAGUE DRAWS
19, Division 1, 1976-77; Division 2, 1982-83

MOST LEAGUE DEFEATS
26, Division 2, 1954-55

OLDEST PLAYER
Peter Shilton, 42 years 164 days v Watford, Div 2, 29.2.1992

YOUNGEST PLAYER
Steve Powell, 16 years 33 days v Arsenal, Div 1, 23.10.1971

MOST CAPPED PLAYER
Peter Shilton (England) 34

BEST PERFORMANCES BY DERBY COUNTY

League: 1956-57: Matches played 46, Won 26, Drawn 11, Lost 9, Goals for 111, Goals against 53, Points 63. First in Division 3 North.

Highest: 1971-72, 1974-75: Division 1 Champions.

F.A. Cup: 1945-46: 3rd rnd. Luton Town 6-0, 3-0; 4th rnd. West Bromwich Albion 1-0, 3-1; 5th rnd. Brighton & H.A. 4-1, 6-0; 6th rnd. Aston Villa 4-3, 1-1; Semi-Final Birmingham City 1-1, 4-0; Final Charlton 4-1.

League Cup: 1967-68: 2nd rnd. Hartlepool United 4-0; 3rd rnd. Birmingham City 3-1; 4th rnd. Lincoln City 1-1, 3-1; 5th rnd. Darlington 5-4; Semi-Final Leeds United 0-1, 2-3.

European Cup: 1972-73: 1st rnd. Zelj Znicars 2-0, 2-1; 2nd rnd. Benefica 3-0, 0-0; 3rd rnd. Spartak Trnava 0-1, 2-0; Semi-Final Juventus 1-3, 0-0.

DIVISIONAL RECORDS

	Played	Won	Drawn	Lost	For	Against	Points
DIVISION 1	2202	838	515	849	3493	3490	**2236**
DIVISION 2	1282	520	309	452	2015	1835	**1430**
DIVISION 3	92	42	28	22	145	95	**154**
DIVISION 3N	92	54	18	20	221	108	**126**
TOTALS	**3668**	**1454**	**870**	**1344**	**5874**	**5528**	**3946**

DERBY COUNTY

PLAYERS NAME Honours	Ht	Wt	Birthdate	Birthplace Transfers	Contract Date	Clubs	League	L/Cup	FA Cup	Other	Lg	L/C	FAC	Oth
GOALKEEPERS														
Steve Sutton	6.1	14.0	16.04.61	Hartington	19.09.80	Nottm. Forest	199	33	14	11				
LC'89'90; SC'89				Loan	10.03.81	Mansfield Town	8							
				Loan	01.03.85	Derby County	14							
				Loan	01.02.91	Coventry City	1							
				Loan	28.11.91	Luton Town	14							
				£300,000	06.03.92	Derby County	10			2				
Martin Taylor	5.11	12.4	09.12.66	Tamworth		Mile Oak R								
				Loan	23.09.87	Carlisle Utd	10	1	1	2				
				Loan	17.12.87	Scunthorpe Utd	8							
					02.07.86	Derby County	15	2		2				
DEFENDERS														
Simon Coleman	6.0	10.8	13.06.68	Worksop	29.07.85	Mansfield Town (A)	96	9	7	7	7			1
				£400,000	26.09.89	Middlesbrough	51+4		5	10	2			1
				£300,000	15.08.91	Derby County	43	3	3	3	2			
Andrew Comyn	6.1	11.12	02.06.68	Wakefield		Manchester Utd								
						Alvechurch								
				£34,000	22.08.89	Aston Villa	12+3	2+1	2	1				
				£200,000	08.08.91	Derby County	46	3	3	3	1		1	1
Mick Forsyth	5.11	12.2	20.03.66	Liverpool	16.11.83	West Brom A. (A)	28+1	1	2	1				
E: B.1, u21.1, Y.8; Div2'87				£25,000	28.03.86	Derby County	134	26	9	14	5	1		
Shane Nicholson	5.10	11.0	03.06.70	Newark	19.07.86	Lincoln City (A)	122+11	8+3	6	7+1	7		1	
APL(GMVC)'88					22.04.92	Derby County								
Mark Patterson	5.10	11.5	13.09.68	Leeds	30.08.86	Carlisle Utd. (T)	19+3	4		1				
				£60,000	10.11.87	Derby County	24+9	5+2	1	2+1	3			
Mark Pembridge	5.6	11.01	29.11.70	Merthyr Tydfil	01.07.89	Luton Town (T)	60	2	4	4	6			
W: 5, B,u21					02.06.92	Derby County								
Mel Sage	5.8	10.4	24.03.64	Gillingham	30.03.82	Gillingham (A)	126+6	10	12	5	5		2	
Div2 '87				£60,000	22.08.86	Derby County	137+3	22+1	4	8	4			
Darren Wassall	5.11	12.3	27.06.68	Edgbaston	02.07.87	Nottm. Forest (A)	17+10	6+2	3+1	4+2				1
				Loan	23.10.87	Hereford Utd	5		1	1				
				Loan	02.03.89	Bury	7			1				
				£600,000	15.06.92	Derby County								
MIDFIELD														
Jason Kavanagh	5.9	11.0	23.11.71	Birmingham		Birmingham City								
E: Y.7, S.				£25,000 #	09.12.88	Derby County	22+9		3	4				
Ted McMinn	6.0	12.11	28.09.62	Castle Douglas	01.01.82	Queen of the South	56+6	4+2	1		5			
SLc '86					01.01.84	Glasgow Rangers	37+26	4+2		2+3	4	2		
				£225,000	05.02.88	Seville (Spa)								
				£300,000	05.02.88	Derby County	102+2	10	6	6	7	3	1	1
Gary Micklewhite	5.7	10.4	21.03.61	Southwark	23.03.78	Manchester Utd								
Div 2 '83'87				Free	04.07.79	Q.P.R	97+9	12+1	4+2	1+1	11	5	1	
				£90,000	26.02.85	Derby County	219+15	23+2	8+2	7+1	31	2	4	6
Paul Simpson	5.6	11.3	26.07.66	Carlisle	04.08.83	Manchester City (A)	98+20	10+1	10+2	8+3	18	2	4	
E: u21.5, Y.2				£200,000	31.10.88	Oxford Utd	138+6	10	9	5	43	3	2	2
				£500,000	20.02.92	Derby County	16			2	7			
Paul D Williams	5.11	12.0	26.03.71	Burton	13.07.89	Derby County (T)	67+3	4	3	3	17	1	2	
				Loan	09.11.89	Lincoln City	3		2	1				
FORWARDS														
Marco Gabbiadini	5.10	12.4	20.01.68	Nottingham	05.09.85	York City (A)	42+18	4+3		4	14	1		3
E: B1, u21.2; FLg Xl.2; Div.3'88				£80,000	23.09.87	Sunderland	155+2	14	5	9	74	9		4
				£1,800,000	01.10.91	Crystal Palace	15	6	1	3	5	1		1
				£1,000,000	31.01.92	Derby County	20			2	6			1
Thomas Johnson	5.10	10.6	15.01.71	Newcastle u Tyne	19.01.89	Notts County (T)	100+18	7+2	3+2	14+3	47	5	1	4
E:u21.2				£1,300,000	12.03.92	Derby County	12			2	2			1
Paul Kitson	5.11	10.12	09.01.71	County Durham	15.12.88	Leicester City (T)	39+11	5	1+1	5	6	3	1	1
E: FLg u18(1)				£800,000+2	11.03.92	Derby County	12			2	4			
Craig Ramage	5.9	11.8	30.03.70	Derby		Derby County	30+6	6+1	3	0+3	4	2	FAC	
				Loan	16.02.89	Wigan Ath	10			0+1	2			
Mark Stallard					06.11.91	Derby County (T)	2+1		1+1	1				1
Dean Sturridge					01.07.91	Derby County (T)	1							
ADDITIONAL CONTRACT PLAYERS														
Leonel Alvarez						Derby County								
Lee Carsley					06.07.92	Derby County								
(F) Martyn Chalk	5.6	10.0	30.08.69	Louth		Louth Utd								
				£10,000	23.01.90	Derby County	4+3		3	0+1	1		1	
Mark Clarke					01.07.91	Derby County (T)								
Thomas Curtis					01.07.91	Derby County								
Simon A Dunne					03.03.92	Derby County								
Stewart Hadley						Halesowen								
				Free	06.07.92	Derby County								
(M) Steve Hayward	5.10	11.7	08.09.71	Walsall	17.09.88	Derby County	4+7	0+2		1				
E: Y.5; FLg u18.1														
Jamie Hillyer					08.07.91	Derby County								
Michael T Moore					06.07.92	Derby County								
(D) Justin Phillips	6.3	14.0	17.12.71	Derby	24.07.90	Derby County	3			1				
(D) Stephen Round	5.10	11.0	09.11.70											

DERBY COUNTY

RECORD WIN & LOSS AGAINST EACH CLUB IN CURRENT DIVISION
(Where a score has occured on several occasions the most recent is given)

Club	Rec. Win	Season	Rec. Loss	Season
BARNSLEY	7-0	1914-15	5-0	1922-23
BIRMINGHAM CITY	8-0	1895-96	5-1	1976-77
BRENTFORD	4-1	1953-54	6-0	1935-36
BRISTOL CITY	8-0	1923-24	4-1	1966-67
BRISTOL ROVERS	4-1	1961-62	5-2	1957-58
CAMBRIDGE UNITED	2-0	1984-85 (away)	3-0	1980-81
CHARLTON ATHLETIC	5-0	1950-51	6-1	1959-60
GRIMSBY TOWN	6-0	1909-10	4-1	1935-36
LEICESTER CITY	6-0	1914-15 (away)	6-0	1909-10
LUTON TOWN	5-0	1974-75	4-1	1960-61 (home)
MILLWALL	5-1	1966-67	3-2	1966-67
NEWCASTLE UNITED	5-2	1930-31 (away)	5-1	1930-31 (home)
NOTTS COUNTY	4-1	1902-03	4-0	1906-07
OXFORD UNITED	2-0	1968-69	1-0	1987-88 (home)
PETERBOROUGH UTD	(Never played in League fixture)			
PORTSMOUTH	6-1	1930-31 (away)	5-1	1934-35
SOUTHEND UNITED			1-0	1991-92
SUNDERLAND	7-2	1903-04	8-0	1894-95
SWINDON TOWN	4-1	1964-65	4-2	1964-65
TRANMERE ROVERS	4-0	1956-57	4-3	1991-92
WATFORD	3-2	1981-82	6-1	1981-82
WEST HAM UNITED	6-0	1928-29	3-0	1977-78
WOLVERHAMPTON WNDRS	9-0	1890-91	7-0	1905-06

MANAGER: ARTHUR COX

DATE OF APPOINTMENT: JUNE 1984

PREVIOUS CLUBS
as Manager: Chesterfield; Newcastle United
as Asst. Man./Coach: Asst.: Sunderland; Blackpool; Coach: Coventry (Youth); Walsall; Aston Villa; Preston; Halifax
as Player: Coventry City

HONOURS
as Manager: Sunderland: Div 2 Championship 1976; Derby: Promotion to Div 2 1986; Div 2 Championship 1987
as Asst. Man./Coach: Sunderland: FA Cup Winners 1973
as Player:

Value Rating: ✱ ✱ ✱ ✱ ✱

Programme Editor: M. Dunford

Price of 1992-93 Programme: £1.20
Number of Pages: 32
Subscriptions: £1 plus postage per match

Local Newspapers: Derby Evening Telegraph

Local Radio Stations: BBC Radio Derby, Radio Trent (Commercial)

Books available about Club: The Complete Record 1884-1988 (Breedon Books)
Derby County Quiz Book (1990)
Annual Handbook, Vol 1 1989-90, Vol 2 1990-91, Vol 3 1991-92

LEADING LEAGUE GOALSCORERS
SEASONS 1979-80 – 1991-92

1979-80	ALAN BILEY	9	1980-81	DAVID SWINDLEHURST	11
1981-82	KEVIN WILSON	9	1982-83	DAVID SWINDLEHURST	8
				BOBBY DAVISON	8
1983-84	BOBBY DAVISON	14	1984-85	BOBBY DAVISON	24
1985-86	BOBBY DAVISON	16	1986-87	BOBBY DAVISON	19
1987-88	PHIL GEE	6	1988-89	DEAN SAUNDERS	14
	JOHN GREGORY	6			
1989-90	DEAN SAUNDERS	11	1990-91	DEAN SAUNDERS	17

1991-92	PAUL WILLIAMS	13

BASEBALL GROUND Shaftesbury Crescent, Derby DE3 8NB

Capacity: 23,500   **Covered Standing:** 8,400   **Seating:** 15,100

Tel: Ground: 0332 40105   **Ticket Sales:** As ground number   **Clubcall:** 0898 12 11 87

All premium rate calls (0898/0891) cost 36p per minute cheap rate and 48p per minute at all other times. Call costings correct at time of going to press.

GROUNDS
Race Course Ground 1884-95; Baseball Ground 1895-

ATTENDANCES
Highest: 41,826 v Tottenham Hotspur, Division 1, 20.9.1969

Lowest: 1,990 v West Bromwich Albion, 27.10.1894

RECORD RECEIPTS (with previous records):
£135,000 v Aston Villa, FA Cup 4th Rnd, 5.2.1992
£130,000 v West Ham Utd., Littlewoods Cup 24.1.1990
£108,000 v Manchester United, FA Cup, 19.2.1983
£65,000 v Juventus, European Cup, 25.4.1973
£17,500 v Wolverhampton Wanderers, FA Cup, 23.1.1971

BASEBALL GROUND
First game: v Sunderland, 2-0, 14.9.1885
Internationals: England v Ireland: 9.3.1895

Season Tickets:
Stands: from £160 to £230, juv/OAP £120
Ground: from £130, juv/OAP £70

Cost of Stand Tickets: Seats: £9, £10, £11, juv £6
Terraces: £6

Match and Ticket Information: Available 14 days prior to match

Car Parking: Eight parks within half-a-mile of ground run by club in co-operation with local corporation. Street parking within same distance

Nearest Railway Station: Derby Midland (0332 32051) Ramsline Halt (Specials only)

How to get to the ground

From North: Follow signs Derby A38 into Town Centre, then follow signs Melbourne A514. Then on nearside of Railway Bridge turn right into Shaftsbury Street for Derby County FC

From East, South and West: Use Derby Ring Road from East and South (S.P. Burton) and from West (S.P. Nottingham) as far as junction with A514, then follow signs town centre into Osmaston Road. In 1.3m turn left into Shaftesbury Street for Derby County FC

DONCASTER ROVERS

Division 3

Formed: 1879   **Turned Professional:** 1885   **Ltd Co:** 1905 & 1920

SPONSORED BY: Doncaster Free Press   **NICKNAME:** The Rovers

Chairman
J J Burke

Vice-Chairman
K Chappell

Directors
M Collett
J Ryan
W Turner

Secretary
Mrs K J Oldale
(0302) 539441

Team Manager
Steve Beaglehole

First Team Coach
J Bird

Physiotherapist
E Brailsford

Youth Team Manager
J Golze

Club Statistician for the Directory
Ernest Wiles

ROVERS had to wait until the seventh game of the season before notching their first victory – a 3-1 home League success over Wrexham. This result – their only credit of three points in 1991 – was notable (no pun intended) for two opportunist goals from their eventual top-scorer Kevin Noteman.

Incredibly, the Doncaster players next win bonus was not paid out until 4th January, 1992, when they convincingly overcame Walsall 3-1 (with Noteman's name again on the score-sheet).

An early exit in the Rumbelows Cup at the hands of Crewe Alexandra (4-9 on aggregate) in Round One, hardly helped the team's confidence, and the attendance of 1376 was some 1300 down on the first home match of the season.

The one spark of optimism was lit in the FA Cup. A fighting 1-1 draw in Round One, away to high-flying Burnley on 16th January, in front of nearly 8,000 fans, was in fact the first of three games against the Turf Moor club. Prior to the replay, on 27th January, the Rovers had to travel to Burnley again in the Autoglass Trophy, and were comfortably despatched 2-0.

The replay itself proved to be a complete anti-climax. 4,000 supporters at the Belle Vue Ground undoubtedly generated real atmosphere, but Rovers just could not rise to the occasion. Although the tie was all-square (1-1) at half-time, Burnley increased the pressure in the second period and ran out easy 3-1 victors.

Matters hardly improved in the League – although they received a slight crumb of comfort on 18th February with a 2-0 home win over Hereford.

The Rovers completed the double over Hereford on 7th March (1-0), with Noteman hitting the winner in the 2nd minute. A surprising and much-needed home victory over promotion-seeking Barnet, the only goal coming from Jeffrey, eased their desperate situation just a shade and in fact Doncaster managed to win five of their last seven League games, thus finishing in 22nd position.

Manager Steve Beaglehole will hope 'Lady Luck' goes more in his favour in 1993, but knows that a great deal of work has to be done if Rovers are to make any kind of impression. The fact that the Rovers are well known for their progressive youth policy certainly augurs well for the future.

Greg Tesser

Back row L-R: Mark Hine, Craig Bennett, Grant Morrow, Eddie Gormley, Steve Prindiville, Mike Jeffrey. **Middle:** Steve Beaglehole (Manager), Jamie Hewitt, Jon Cullen, Colin Douglas, Paul Crichton, Peter Heritage, Andy Crosby, John Bird (First Team Coach). **Front:** Shane Reddish, Steve Hodder, Steve Richards, Jamie Roberts, Brian Rowe.

DONCASTER ROVERS

DIVISION FOUR: 22nd   **FA CUP:** 1st RND   **RUMBELOWS CUP:** 1st RND   **AUTOGLASS:** Prelim.

M	DATE		COMP.	VEN	OPPONENTS	RESULT	H/T	LGE POS	GOALSCORERS/GOAL TIMES	ATTEN-DANCE
1	A	17	BL	H	Carlisle United	L 0-3	0-1			2,639
2		20	RC 1/1	A	Crewe Alexandra	L 2-5	1-3		Whitehurst 14, 86	(2,900)
3		24	BL	A	Scunthorpe United	L 2-3	1-2	22	Kerr 14, Tynan 50	(3,505)
4		27	RC 1/2	H	Crewe Alexandra	L 2-4	1-0		Cullen 33, Noteman 62	1,376
5		31	BL	H	Burnley	L 1-4	1-1	22	Noteman 28	2,940
6	S	3	BL	A	Northampton Town	L 1-3	0-1	23	Noteman 90	(2,702)
7		7	BL	H	Wrexham	W 3-1	1-0	19	Noteman 36, 51, Rankine 74	1,474
8		14	BL	A	Barnet	L 0-1	0-1	22		(3,762)
9		18	BL	A	Scarborough	L 0-1	0-1	23		(1,506)
10		20	BL	H	Blackpool	L 0-2	0-2	23		2,428
11		28	BL	A	Rochdale	D 1-1	1-1	23	Milner (og) 72	(2,653)
12	O	5	BL	H	Crewe Alexandra	L 1-3	0-1	23	Rankine 56	1,879
13		12	BL	A	Maidstone United	D 2-2	1-0	23	Rankine 30, McKenzie 85	(1,255)
14		19	BL	H	Gillingham	D 1-1	0-0	23	Limber 88	1,468
15		26	BL	A	Cardiff City	L 1-2	1-1	23	Gormley 32	(2,491)
16	N	2	BL	A	Mansfield Town	D 2-2	2-0	23	Harle 3, Noteman 42	(4,180)
17		5	BL	H	Rotherham United	D 1-1	0-0	23	Gormley 65	3,507
18		8	BL	A	York City	L 0-1	0-1	23		2,144
19		16	FAC 1	A	Burnley	D 1-1	0-0		Rankine 64	(7,976)
20		19	AGT Pre	A	Burnley	L 0-2	0-2			(2,590)
21		27	FAC 1R	H	Burnley	L 1-3	1-1		Whitehurst 45	4,207
22		30	BL	H	Lincoln City	L 1-5	0-3	23	Ormsby 61	1,999
23	D	17	AGT Pre	H	Blackpool	D 2-2	0-0		Rankine 70, Limber 74	613
24		20	BL	H	Scunthorpe United	L 1-2	1-1	23	Gormley 1	1,825
25		26	BL	A	Carlisle United	L 0-1	0-1	23		(3,174)
26		28	BL	A	Burnley	L 1-2	0-2	23	Noteman 77	(9,605)
27	J	1	BL	H	Northampton Town	L 0-3	0-1	23		1,973
28		4	BL	A	Walsall	W 3-1	2-0	23	Muir 22, Gormley 37, Noteman 53	(3,444)
29		11	BL	H	Halifax Town	L 0-2	0-0	23		2,067
30		18	BL	A	Chesterfield	D 0-0	0-0	23		(3,372)
31	F	1	BL	A	Gillingham	L 1-2	0-1	23	Ormsby 68	(2,366)
32		8	BL	H	Cardiff City	L 1-2	1-1	23	Noteman 17	2,094
33		12	BL	A	Lincoln City	L 0-2	0-1	23		(2,011)
34		18	BL	H	Hereford United	W 2-0	2-0	22	Noteman 26, Gormley 36	1,270
35		22	BL	A	Halifax Town	D 0-0	0-0	22		(1,285)
36		29	BL	H	Walsall	L 0-1	0-0			1,919
37	M	3	BL	H	Chesterfield	L 0-1	0-1	22		2,385
38		7	BL	A	Hereford United	W 1-0	0-0		Noteman 2	(1,974)
39		10	BL	A	Rotherham United	L 1-3	0-0		Jeffrey 50	(4,883)
40		14	BL	H	Mansfield Town	L 0-1	0-0			2,846
41		21	BL	A	York City	D 1-1	0-0	22	Jeffrey 70	(2,127)
42		31	BL	H	Barnet	W 1-0	1-0	23	Jeffrey 38	1,247
43	A	3	BL	A	Wrexham	W 2-1	2-1	23	Nicholson 25, Reddish 32	(2,769)
44		11	BL	H	Scarborough	W 3-2	2-0	23	Worboys 25, Jeffrey 40, Nicholson 65	1,638
45		14	BL	A	Blackpool	L 0-1	0-0	23		(4,353)
46		20	BL	H	Rochdale	W 2-0	1-0	23	Worboys 14, Jeffrey 49	2,255
47		23	BL	A	Crewe Alexandra	L 0-1	0-1	23		(3,639)
48	M	2	BL	H	Maidstone United	W 3-0	1-0	22	Reddish 45, Ormsby (pen) 55, Jeffrey 87	1,680

Best Home League Attendance: 3,507 v Rotherham United   **Smallest:** 1,247 v Barnet   **Av Home Att:** 2,080

Goal Scorers: **Compared with 90-91:** -756

League (40): Noteman 10, Jeffrey 6, Gormley 5, Ormsby 3 (1 pen), Rankine 3, Nicholson 2, Reddish 2, Worboys 2, Opponents, Kerr, McKenzie Tynan, Limber, Harle, Muir

R/lows C (4): Whitehurst 2, Noteman, Cullen
FA Cup (2): Whitehurst, Rankine
Autoglass (2): Rankine, Limber

Samways M.	Rankine S.	Limber N.	Cullen D.	Ormsby B.	Crosby A.	Reddish S.	Muir J.	Tynan T.	Whitehurst W.	Gormley E.	Boyle L.	Bennett C.	Noteman K.	Rowe B.	Ashurst J.	Douglas C.	Crichton P.	Harle D.	Morrow G.	McKenzie R.	Stiles J.	Nicholson M.	Raven P.	Prindiville S.	Jeffrey M.	Referee	
1	2	3	4	5*	6	7	8	9	10	11	S	12														R Wiseman	1
1	2		4	S	7	8	9*	10		6	11	3	12													**K A Cooper**	2
1	2	8	5		7*	12	9	10	S				11		4	6										A Wilkie	3
	2	8	5			12	9	10	3*	7•			11	14	4	6	1									**I Hendrick**	4
	2	7*	5			9	12	10†	8		4	11	S	6	1												D Shadwell	5
	2	7	5			9*	12		8	6	10	11	S	4		1										R Bigger	6
	2	12	5			S	9	10	8*			11	4	6	1	7										T Fitzharris	7
	2		5			10	9*	8•			11	14	4	6	1	7	12									D Axcell	8
	2		5			12	10	8		11•	14	4	6	1†	7	9*										I Cruikshanks	9
	2		5			12	9*	10	8		11	S	4	6	1	7										I Borrett	10
	2		5			9		10	8	S	12	11•	6	4	12	1	7									T West	11
1	2		5*					10†	8	S	12	11	9	4	6		7									K Morton	12
	10	3	6	5	2	S			S	11	8	4		1	7		9									J Carter	13
	10	3	8•	5	2	14	12			11	6	4		1	7	9*										J Lloyd	14
1	10	3†	5	2		12		8	S	11	6	4		1	7	9*										M Scoble	15
1	10	3	5		2		S	8	S	11	6	4	9	7												G Pooley	16
1	10	3	5		2	12		8•	14	11	6	4*	9	7												A Dawson	17
1	10		5		2*	14	8	3	4	11	6		9	7•		12										P Jones	18
1	9	S	5	4	S	10	8	3	11	2	6	7														**P Wright**	19
1	9	12	5	4	14	8*	3	11	2	6	7	10*														**W Burns**	20
1	9	12	5	4	2•	10	8	11	12	3	7*	14	6													P Wright	21
1	9		5	4	2•	10	8	11	12	3	7*	14	6													R Pawley	22
1	9	3	6	5		8	11	S	4	2	7	10*	12													**K Redfearn**	23
1	9	6*	5		8	11	12	4	7	10•	14	2														P Harrison	24
1	9	3	5†	14	8	11	12	4	2	7•	10*	6														K Breen	25
1	9	3	5	10	8*	11	6	4	S	7	12	2														K Lupton	26
1	9	3	5	10	11	14	4	6	7*	12	8*	2†														E Parker	27
1	9	3	S	10	6	11	S	4	2	7	8	5														G Poll	28
1	9	3		10	6	11	S	4	2	7*	12	8	5													M Bailey	29
1	9		5	3	10	11	4	2	7	S	8															P Vaines	30
1		5	3	10	12	11	4	2	7	8*																T Ward	31
1		5	10	12	6	11	4	2	7	8	9*															R Nixon	32
1		5	14	9*	10	6•	11	4	2	7	8	12	3													J Rushton	33
1		5	12	10*	6	11	4	2	7	S	8	9	3*													I Hendrick	34
1		5	14	10•	6	11	4	2	7*	12	8	9	3													R Dilkes	35
1		5	S	6	11	10•	4	2	7	8	9	3														W Burns	36
1		5	S	6	11	10*	4	2	7	12	8	9	3													P Harrison	37
1		5	S	6	11	S	4	2	7	8	9	3	10													R Milford	38
1		5	14	6*	11	12	4	2	7	8	9*	3	10													K Redfern	39
1		5	8	12	6	11	4	2	7	S	9*	3	10													A Smith	40
1		5	S	6	11	6	4	2	7*	12	8	9	3	10											T Lunt	41
		5	12	11	6	8	4	2*	1	14	9	3	10													K A Cooper	42
		5	4	11	6*	8	2	1	12	9	3	10														K Cooper	43
		5	S	11	6	8	4	2	1	12	9	3	10													C Trussell	44
		5	S	11	6	8	4	2	1	S	9	3	10													K Barratt	45
		5	14	11	6	8	4	2	1	12	9*	3	10													A Wilkie	46
		5	12	11	6	8	4	2	1	S	9*	3	10													T West	47
	S	5	4	11	6	8	2	1	7	9	3	10														W Flood	48
26	24	12	7	35	15	15	14	5	9	37	2	3	34	18	37	33	16	13	19	7	9	21	7	16	11	League Appearances	
	1	7	2	6	6			1	2		7			1			10	1	3							Substitute Appearances	
1	2	2	1		1	1+1	2	2	1	2		2	0+2	1	1	1										R/lows Appearances	
2	2	0+1	2	2		1		2	2	1		2	1+1	2		2					0+1	1				FA Cup Appearances	
2	2	1+1	1	2		1			2	2	1		2		2					1		2				Autoglass Appearances	

Also Played: Posn.(Game): D Jones 5(2), Penny 3*(32)S(43), N Morris 12(36), Kerr 3(3,5,6,7,8,9,10), Roberts S(30,31,38), Stevenson 9(31)S(43), Warboys 14(32)7(42*,43,44*,45,46*,48)

Players on Loan: P Raven (WBA), M Jeffrey (Bolton W), D Kerr (Leeds Utd), A Stevenson (Scunthorpe) † = Sent Off

DONCASTER ROVERS

Club Colours: Red shirts with white sleeves and red/green trim, white shorts, red stockings with white/green tops
Change Colours: Dark blue shirts, white sleeves/red trim, white shorts with white/red, red stockings, blue/white tops
Reserves League: Central League Division 2

Previous League: Midland League
Previous Managers: (Since 1946): Bill Marsden Jackie Bestall Peter Doherty Jack Hodgson Syd Bycroft Jack Crayston Jack Bestall Norman Curtis Danny Malloy Oscar Hold Bill Leivers Keith Kettleborough George Raynor Lawrie McMenemy Maurice Setters Stan Anderson Billy Bremner
Honours: Champions Div 3N 1934-35, 1946-47, 1949-50 Champions Div 4 1965-66, 1968-69
League Career: Elected to Div 2 1901 Failed to gain re-election 1903 Re-elected to Div 2 1904
Failed to gain re-election 1905 Re-elected to Div 3N 1923 Promoted to Div 2 1934-35 Relegated to Div 3N 1936-37
Promoted to Div 2 1946-47 Relegated to Div 3N 1947-48 Promoted to Div 2 1949-50
Relegated to Div 3 1957-58 Relegated to Div 4 1958-59 Promoted to Div 3 1965-66 Relegated to Div 4 1966-67
Promoted to Div 3 1968-69 Relegated to Div 4 1970-71 Promoted to Div 3 1980-81 Relegated to Div 4 1982-83
Promoted to Div 3 1983-84 Relegated to Div 4 1987-88

CLUB RECORDS

Most Appearances for Club: Fred Emery 1924-36: League 406 + FA Cup 19 **Total 425**
Most Capped Player: Len Graham 14 N Ireland **For England:** I Snodin 4 (under-21)
Record Goalscorer in a Match: Tom Keetley 6 v Ashington (a), 7-4 Div 3N, 16.2.1929
Record League Goalscorer in a Season: Clarrie Jordan 42, Div 3N, 1946-47 **In All Competitions:** Clarrie Jordan 44 (League 42 + FA Cup 2) 1946-47
Record League Goalscorer in a Career: Tom Keetley 180, 1923-29 **In All Competitions:** Tom Keetley 185 (League 180 + FA Cup 5)
Record Transfer Fee Received: £250,000 from Q.P.R. for Rufus Brevett, February 1991
Record Transfer Fee Paid: £60,000 to Stirling Albion for John Philliben, March 1984
Best Performances: League: 7th Div 2 1901-02 **FA Cup:** 5th Round 1951-52, 1953-54, 1954-55, 1955-56 **League Cup:** 5th Round 1975-76
Most League Points: (3pts for win) 85, Div 4 1983-84 (2pts for win) 72, Div 3N, 1946-47
Most League Goals: 123, Div 3N, 1946-47
Record League Victory: 10-0 v Darlington, Div 4, 25.1.1964
Record Cup Victory: 7-0 v Blyth Spartans, FA Cup Rnd 1, 1937-38
Record League Defeat: 0-12 v Small Heath, Div 2, 11.4.1903
Record Cup Defeat: 0-8 v Everton, FA Cup Rnd 4, 1938-39
Oldest Player in a League Match: Mitchell Downie 40 years 252 days
Youngest Player in a League Match: Alick Jeffrey 15 years 229 days

---

LONGEST LEAGUE RUNS

of undefeated matches: 21 (1968-69)	**of league matches without a win:** 16 (1991-92)
of undefeated home matches: 33 (1931-33)	**of undefeated away matches:** 17 (1939, 1946)
without home win: 8 (1954, 1989)	**without an away win:** 44 (1902-03, 1904-05, 1923-24)
of league wins: 10 (1947)	**of home wins:** 11 (1934-35)
of league defeats: 9 (1905)	**of away wins:** 9 (1939, 1946)

DONCASTER ROVERS

PLAYERS NAME / Honours	Ht	Wt	Birthdate	Birthplace / Transfers	Contract Date	Clubs	League	L/Cup	FA Cup	Other	Lg	L/C	FAC	Oth
GOALKEEPERS														
Paul Crichton	6.0	12.1	03.10.68	Pontefract	23.06.86	Nottm. Forest (A)								
				Loan	19.09.86	Notts County	5							
				Loan	30.01.87	Darlington	5							
				Loan	27.03.87	Peterborough U	4							
				Loan	24.12.87	Swindon Town	4							
				Loan	09.03.88	Rotherham Utd	6							
				Loan	25.08.88	Torquay Utd	13	2						
				Loan	29.09.88	Torquay Utd								
					03.11.88	Peterborough U	47		5	3				
					25.08.90	Doncaster Rovers	36	3	2	2				
DEFENDERS														
Colin Douglas	6.1	11.0	09.09.62	Hudlford		Celtic								
					26.11.81	Doncaster Rovers	202+10	13+1	11	6	49	5	4	
				£17,000	18.07.86	Rotherham Utd	82+1	7	6	5+1	4	3		
				£15,000	03.08.88	Doncaster Rovers	170+1	7	7	13	4			
Shane Reddish			05.05.71	Bolsover	16.08.89	Mansfield Town								
				Free N.C	07.02.90	Doncaster Rovers	0+1							
					01.07.90	Doncaster Rovers	24+4	1	1		2			
Steve Richards GMVC'87	6.0	12.0	24.10.61	Dundee	26.10.79	Hull City	55+3	3	4		2			
						Glentoran								
				N.C	22.12.84	York City	6+1			3				
						Goole Town								
					16.08.85	Lincoln City	21	2	1	1		1		
				Free	28.03.86	Cambridge Utd	4				2			
				Free		Scarborough	164	15	5	12	13	3		2
				£40,000	29.07.91	Halifax Town	24+1	2	2	1				
				Free	27.05.92	Doncaster Rovers								
MIDFIELD														
Edward Gormley Ei: u21.3	5.7	10.7	23.10.68	Dublin		Bray Wanderers								
					27.11.87	Tottenham H								
				Loan	24.11.88	Chesterfield	4		2					
				Loan	01.02.89	Motherwell								
				Loan	02.09.89	Shrewsbury Town								
				Free	04.07.90	Doncaster Rovers	69+8	3	4	4	10		1	
Mark Hine GMVC'90	5.8	9.11	18.05.64	Middlesbrough	06.10.83	Grimsby Town	20+2	1	1	2	1			
				Free	03.07.86	Darlington	126+2	10	5	9	8	2		1
				£50,000	05.01.90	Peterborough U	55	3	5	3	7			
				£30,000	28.03.91	Scunthorpe Utd	19+3	2+1		1+1	2			
					22.06.92	Doncaster Rovers								
FORWARDS														
Craig Bennett	6.0		29.08.73	Doncaster	02.07.91	Doncaster Rovers (T)	4+3	2		1				
Michael Jeffrey	5.9	10.06	11.08.71	Liverpool		Bolton W	9+6	1+2	1	2+1				
				Loan	05.03.92	Doncaster Rovers								
					01.06.92	Doncaster Rovers	11				6			
Grant Morrow	5.10		04.10.70	Glasgow		Rowntree Mack								
						Doncaster Rovers	29+12			1+1	3			
Tommy Tynan WC'80	5.10	13.0	17.11.55	Liverpool	01.11.72	Liverpool (A)								
				Loan	01.10.75	Swansea City	6				2			
				£10,000	01.09.76	Sheffield Wed	89+2	12	4		31	5	1	
				£33,000	06.10.78	Lincoln City	9				1			
				£25,000	23.02.79	Newport Co	168+15	11+1	7+1	5	66	5	4	4
				£55,000	08.08.83	Plymouth A	80	8	13	3+1	43	1	4	4
				£30,000	31.07.85	Rotherham Utd	32	4	4	3	13	2	4	
				£25,000	05.09.86	Plymouth A	181+1	9	10	4	82+4	5	3	2
				Free	30.05.90	Torquay Utd	34+1	4	1	6	13	1	1	4
				Free	04.07.91	Doncaster Rovers	5+6	2			1			
ADDITIONAL CONTRACT PLAYERS														
Andrew Beaglehole					10.01.89	Doncaster Rovers								
Andrew Crosby					04.07.91	Doncaster Rovers	15+7		2	2				
David Cullen					16.09.91	Doncaster Rovers	8+1	2	0+1	1		1		
Nicholas Gallacher			28.01.71	Boston	01.06.89	Doncaster Rovers	0+1							
(D) Steven Hodder	5.9	10.12	18.10.71	Sheffield	01.07.90	Nottm. Forest (T)								
					09.03.91	Notts County								
				Free	13.07.92	Doncaster Rovers								
Simon Holland						Doncaster Rovers	1							
Brian Rowe					10.10.90	Doncaster Rovers	21+8	0+2	1+1	1				

LEADING LEAGUE GOALSCORERS SEASONS 1985-86 – 1991-92

1985-86	**COLIN DOUGLAS**	13	1986-87	**NEIL REDFEARN**	14
1987-88	**BRIAN DEANE**	10	1988-89	**MARK RANKINE**	11
1989-90	**DAVID JONES**	12	1990-91	**JOHNNY MUIR**	13
	1991-92	**KEVIN NOTEMAN**	10		

BELLE VUE GROUND Doncaster, South Yorkshire DN4 5HT

Capacity: 7,794   **Covered Standing:** 2,125   **Seating:** 1,259

Tel: Ground: 0302 539441   **Ticket Sales:** As Ground Number

---

ATTENDANCES
Highest: 37,149 v Hull City, Div 3N, 2.10.1948

Lowest: 613 v Blackpool, Autoglass Trophy, 17.12.1991

Record Receipts: £22,000 v Queens Park Rangers, FA Cup Round 3, 5.1.1985

BELLE VUE
First game: v Gainsborough Trinity, August 1922
First floodlit game: v Hibernian, 4.3.1952

Season Tickets:
Stands: £120, juv/OAP £95
Ground: £95, juv/OAP £57

Executive Box Season Tickets: £200

Cost of Stand Tickets: Seats: £7 (no reductions)
Terraces: £5.50, juv/OAP £3.50

Match and Ticket Information: No advance bookings except for Cup matches

Car Parking: Very large car and coach park adjacent to ground; entrance direct from Great North Road

Nearest Railway Station: Doncaster (0302 20191)

How to get to the ground

From North: Use Motorway A1(N) then A638 S.P. Doncaster into Town Centre, then follow signs Bawtry (A368) and in 1.2m at roundabout take 3rd exit into Bawtry Road for Doncaster FC

From East: Use Motorway M18 then A630 S.P. Doncaster. In 2.7m at roundabout take 1st exit A18. In 2.5m at roundabout take 1st exit into Bawtry Road A638 for Doncaster FC

From South: Use Motorway M1 then M18, take junction 3 S.P. Doncaster A6182 in 2m at roundabout take 3rd exit S.P. Racecourse and Scunthorpe A18. In 1.25m at roundabout take 3rd exit A638 into Bawtry Road for Doncaster FC

From West: Use A635 in Doncaster Town Centre then follow signs Bawtry A638 and in 1.2m at roundabout take 3rd exit into Bawtry Road for Doncaster FC

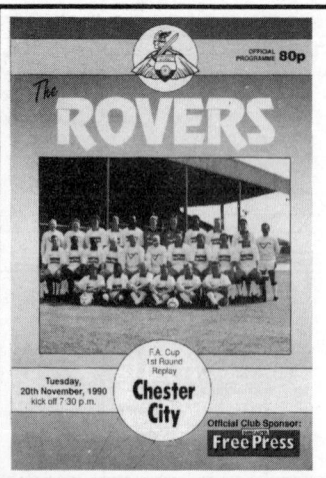

Value Rating: ★ ★

Programme Editor: K Avis

Price of 1992-93 Programme: £1
Number of Pages: 15
Subscriptions: £30

Local Newspapers: Doncaster Star, Yorkshire Post

Local Radio Stations: Radio Hallam, Radio Sheffield

EVERTON
Premier

Formed: 1878   **Turned Professional:** 1885   **Ltd Co:** 1892

SPONSORED BY: N.E.C   **NICKNAME:** The Toffeemen

Chairman
Sir Philip D Carter, CBE

Directors
D M Marsh (Dep. Chairman)
A W Waterworth
K M Tamlin
D A B Newton
D M Marsh
W Kenwright

Chief Executive/Secretary
J Greenwood

Assistant Secretary
B Forsyth

Marketing Manager
D Johnston

Team Manager
Howard Kendall

Chief Coach
Colin Harvey

Youth Development Officer
Ray Hall

Chief Scout
Brian Greenhalgh

Groundsman
D Rose

Club Statistician for the Directory
Richard Swift

AFTER a reasonably active pre-season in the transfer market, where Everton signed Gerry Peyton, Mark Ward, Alan Harper and most notably Peter Beardsley. It was hoped that they would at last deliver a trophy. With these new additions the team had a more balanced look, coupled with creativity in abundance. The only conceivable problem was the lack of a consistent goalscorer. But too many home draws and away losses resulted in a disappointing term for the Merseyside outfit. Also for the first time in years, Everton found no consolation in the different cup competitions and by the 26th January, they were forced to concentrate on the League.

The campaign began with the usual early season optimism. This soon vanished when the team experienced a dodgy patch of form until mid-September, when they found themselves in 19th position in the division. But a mini-revival followed, when six out of seven matches were won in all competitions. The run pushed the team up an amazing nine positions in the table. These lapses dogged the club for the duration of the season and halted promising unbeaten runs. This suggested a mediocre final League placing, which would later become reality.

The T.V. companies appeared to have more faith in Everton than the average fan. They screened four Toffees matches in just over a month early in the new year. Unfortunately the team were unable to rise to the occasion, drawing three, losing one and scoring only twice. These games again revealed the squad's lack of firepower, despite Kendall splashing out £1.5 million for the services of Glasgow Rangers striker Mo Johnston.

Everton, usually such a worthy cup team, appeared rather more subdued than in previous years. Their lethargic manner was especially noticed in the most prestigous of them all, the F.A. Cup. After despatching not too convincingly of Southend in the third round, it came as no surprise when the Toffees cup campaign ground to an inconclusive halt against Chelsea. Clive Allen won the game for the Londoners but Tony Cottee unforgivably missed the late chance of an equalising penalty. They faired no better in the League Cup, after seeing off the threat of Watford and Wolves, Everton fell to high flying Leeds. The match ended 4-1 after the Toffees had taken a 20 minute lead.

Currently Everton are going through a period of transition, but it's obvious that Howard Kendall will not rest, until the ultimate aim of reliving those glory days of his first reign at the club are achieved.   **Richard Swift**

Back row L-R: Andy Hinchcliffe, Eddie Youds, Neville Southall, Martin Keown, Gerry Peyton, Dave Watson, Alan Harper. **Middle row:** Les Helm (Physio), Jimmy Gabriel (Reserve Team Coach), Raymond Atteveld, Robert Warzycha, Neil McDonald, Mike Newell, John Ebbrell, Peter Beagrie, Pat Nevin, Colin Harvey (First Team Coach). **Front row:** Kevin Sheedy, Ian Snodin, Mark Ward, Howard Kendall (Manager), Kevin Ratcliffe, Tony Cottee, Peter Beardsley.

EVERTON

DIVISION ONE: 12th   **FA CUP:** 4th RND   **RUMBELOWS CUP:** 4th RND   **ZDS CUP:** 3rd RND

M	DATE		COMP.	VEN	OPPONENTS	RESULT		H/T	LGE POS	GOALSCORERS/GOAL TIMES	ATTENDANCE
1	A	17	BL	A	Nottingham Forest	L	1-2	1-0		Pearce (og) 37	(24,442)
2		20	BL	H	Arsenal	W	3-1	1-0		Ward 45, 71, Cottee 59	31,200
3		24	BL	H	Manchester United	D	0-0	0-0	9		36,085
4		28	BL	A	Sheffield Wed.	L	1-2	0-0	14	Watson 65	(28,690)
5		31	BL	A	Liverpool	L	1-3	0-2	18	Newell 78	(39,072)
6	S	3	BL	H	Norwich City	D	1-1	0-0	18	Ward 49	19,197
7		7	BL	H	Crystal Palace	D	2-2	0-1	18	Warzycha 54, Beardsley 61	21,065
8		14	BL	A	Sheffield United	L	1-2	1-0	19	Beardsley 7	(19,817)
9		17	BL	A	Manchester City	W	1-0	0-0	17	Beardsley 67	(27,509)
10		21	BL	H	Coventry City	W	3-0	1-0	14	Beardsley 3 (40, 61, 75)	20,542
11		25	RC 2/1	H	Watford	W	1-0	0-0		Beardsley 48	8,284
12		28	BL	A	Chelsea	D	2-2	1-0	14	Ebbrell 32, Beardsley 86	(19,038)
13	O	1	ZDS 2	H	Oldham Athletic	W	3-2	1-1		Newell 25, Watson 68, Cottee 82	4,588
14		5	BL	H	Tottenham Hotspur	W	3-1	3-1	10	Cottee 3 (14, pen 21, 30)	29,505
15		8	RC 2/2	A	Watford	W	2-1	0-0		Newell 81, Beardsley 82	(11,561)
16		19	BL	H	Aston Villa	L	0-2	0-1	14		27,688
17		26	BL	A	Queens Park R.	L	1-3	0-1	15	Cottee 53	(10,002)
18		31	RC 3	H	Wolverhampton W	W	4-1	2-1		Beagrie 17, 23, Cottee 61, Beardsley 88	19,065
19	N	2	BL	A	Luton Town	W	1-0	0-0	12	Warzycha 65	(8,002)
20		16	BL	H	Wimbledon	W	2-0	1-0	9	Cottee (pen) 42, Watson 57	18,762
21		23	BL	H	Notts County	W	1-0	1-0	9	Cottee 37	24,230
22		27	ZDS 3	A	Leicester City	L	1-2	0-2		Beardsley 76	(13,242)
23		30	BL	A	Leeds United	L	0-1	0-0	10		(30,043)
24	D	4	RC 4	H	Leeds United	L	1-4	1-2		Atteveld 20	25,467
25		7	BL	H	West Ham United	W	4-0	3-0	7	Cottee 8, Beagrie 10, Beardsley 37, Johnston 53	21,563
26		14	BL	A	Oldham Athletic	D	2-2	1-1	7	Sheedy 40, Nevin 71	(14,955)
27		21	BL	A	Arsenal	L	2-4	2-3	8	Warzycha 3, Johnston 15	(29,684)
28		26	BL	H	Sheffield Wed.	L	0-1	0-0	9		30,788
29		28	BL	H	Liverpool	D	1-1	0-1	10	Johnston 61	37,681
30	J	1	BL	A	Southampton	W	2-1	1-0	9	Ward 5, Beardsley 69	(16,546)
31		4	FAC 3	H	Southend United	W	1-0	1-0		Beardsley 15	22,606
32		11	BL	A	Manchester United	L	0-1	0-0	9		(46,619)
33		19	BL	H	Nottingham Forest	D	1-1	0-1	10	Watson 85	17,717
34		26	FAC 4	A	Chelsea	L	0-1	0-0			(21,152)
35	F	2	BL	A	Aston Villa	D	0-0	0-0	10		(17,451)
36		8	BL	H	Queens Park R.	D	0-0	0-0	9		18,212
37		23	BL	H	Leeds United	D	1-1	0-0	10	Jackson 66	19,248
38		29	BL	A	West Ham United	W	2-0	1-0	9	Johnston 6, Ablett 64	(20,976)
39	M	7	BL	H	Oldham Athletic	W	2-1	1-1	7	Beardsley 3, 69	21,014
40		10	BL	A	Wimbledon	D	0-0	0-0	7		(3,569)
41		14	BL	H	Luton Town	D	1-1	0-1	7	Johnston 51	16,707
42		17	BL	A	Notts County	D	0-0	0-0	7		(7,480)
43		21	BL	H	Norwich City	L	3-4	2-1	8	Johnston 10, 50, Beardsley 28	(11,900)
44	A	1	BL	H	Southampton	L	0-1	0-1	11		15,201
45		4	BL	A	Crystal Palace	L	0-2	0-0	13		(14,338)
46		11	BL	H	Sheffield United	L	0-2	0-1	16		18,285
47		18	BL	A	Coventry City	W	1-0	0-0	13	Beagrie 76	(14,669)
48		20	BL	H	Manchester City	L	1-2	1-2	15	Nevin 11	21,101
49		24	BL	A	Tottenham Hotspur	D	3-3	0-3	16	Beardsley 64, 78, Unsworth 82	(34,630)
50	M	2	BL	H	Chelsea	W	2-1	1-0	12	Beardsley (pen) 33, Beagrie 69	20,163

Best Home League Attendance: 37,681 v Liverpool   **Smallest:** 15,201 v Southampton   **Av Home Att:** 23,141

Goal Scorers: **Compared with 90-91:** -1,986

League (52):   Beardsley 15 (1 pen), Cottee 8 (1 pen), Johnston 7, Ward 4, Watson 3, Beagrie 3, Warzycha 3, Nevin 2, Opponents, Ebbrell Newell, Unsworth, Jackson, Ablett, Sheedy

R/lows C (8):   Beardsley 3, Beagrie 2, Cottee, Atteveld, Newell

FA Cup (1):   Beardsley

ZDS Cup (4):   Cottee, Watson, Newell, Beardsley

Southall N.	Harper A.	Ebbrel J.	Ratcliffe K.	Watson D.	Keown M.	Warzycha R.	Sheedy K.	Beardsley P.	Cottee A.	Ward M.	McDonald N.	Nevin P.	Newell M.	Hinchcliffe A.	Ateveld R.	Youds E.	Barlow S.	Jackson M.	Beagrie P.	Johnston M.	Peyton G.	Ablett G.	Jenkins I.	Unsworth D.	Kenny	Referee	
1	2	3	4	5	6	7•	8	9	10	11*	12	14														T Holbrook	1
1	2	3	4	5	6	7	8	9	10	11•		14	S													D Phillips	2
1	2	3	4	5	6	7•	8	9	10*	11		14	12													J Key	3
1	2	3	4	5	6	7•	8	9	10*	11		14	12													K Barrett	4
1	2	3	14	5	6•	12	11	8	10*	7	4	9														R Lewis	5
1	2	6	4	5		7	10	8	S	11		S	9	3												S Bell	6
1	2*	3	4	5	6	7•		8	11			14	9	3												J Kirby	7
1			4	5	6		10	8	12	11*	S		9	3	2											A Dawson	8
1			4	5	6	7•	10	8	S	11		14	9	3	2											M Reed	9
1			4	5	6	7	10•	8	S	11		14	9	3	2											A Flood	10
1	6		4	5			10	8	12	11*		7	9	3	2	S										R Hart	11
1			4	5	6	7*	10	8	12				11	9	3	2	S									R Pooley	12
1	2	4		5			11	8	10			7	9*	3	12	6	S									M Peck	13
1	2	4	3	5	6	7	10*	8	9	11•			14	12												R Milford	14
1	2	4	3	5	6*	7•	8	9		11	14		12													R Bigger	15
1	10	4	3•	5	6	7	11*	8	9			14	12					2								S Lodge	16
1		4		5	6	7•	10	8	9	11*			14	3	12			2								H King	17
1		4		5	6	14		8	9*			7•	10	3	2	12			11							J Watson	18
1		4		5	6	12		8	14			7•	9	3	10			2*	11							M Brandwood	19
1	10	4		5	6	S	S	8	9	7				3				2	11							R Shepherd	20
1	12	4		5	6	14		8	10	7				3				2	11•	9*						P Wright	21
1	4			5	6	7•		8	10	11				3	12			2*	14	9						K Cooper	22
1	3	4		5	6	14		8	10	7•		S			9			2	11							T Ward	23
1	12	2	4*	5	6			8	10•	7				3	11			14	9							K Redfern	24
1	S	4		5	6	14		8	10	7•				3				2	11	9						A Wilkie	25
1	12	4		5	6	7•	10*	8					14	3				2	11	9						W Burns	26
1	3	4		5		7	10•	8	14			12			2			6	11*	9						P Vanes	27
1	3	4		5	6	7•		8	10	11					2			14	9	S						J Lloyd	28
1	3	4		5	6	7•		8		10	14					S		2	11	9						V Callow	29
1	3	4		5	6	7•		8	12	10	14				12			2	11*	9						G Ashby	30
1	3*	4		5	6	7•		8	12	10	14							2	11	9						J Key	31
1	3	4		5	6	7*		8	14	10					12			2	11•	9						T Holbrook	32
1	10	4		5	6	7•		8	14	11								2*	12	9		3				D Elleray	33
1	S	4		5	6	14		8	9	10	7•							2	11			3				K Hackett	34
1	S	4		5	6	14		8•	10	11	7							2	9			3				P Don	35
1	10•	4		5	6	14		8		7	12							2	11	9*		3				K Hackett	36
1		4		5	6	7*		8	10*	11				12				2	14	9		3				J Martin	37
1	12	4		5	6			8	10*	7				11				2•	14	9		3				A Smith	38
1	10	4		5	6*	S		8		7				11				2	14	9		3				M Peck	39
1	12	4		5	6	10*		8		7				11				2	14	9•		3				D Gallagher	40
1	10	4		5	6	14		8		7				12				2*	11	9•		3				K Barratt	41
1	10	4	5•	6		12		8		7				11*				2	14	9		3				J Rushton	42
1	10	4			6	7		8		11			5		14			2	S	9•		3				G Willard	43
1	3	4			6	7•		8	14	10								2	11	9•		5	S			K Redfern	44
1	3	4			6	7•		8		10						14		2	11	9		5		S		M Bailey	45
1	2	4		6*				8	10•	7		12				14		5	11	9		3				P Vanes	46
1	10		5	6	S	8		4		7						14		2	11	9•		3		5		C Wilkes	47
1	3	4			6	14		8		10			7•			9		2*	11			5	12			D Allison	48
1	4						2	8		10			7			9	6	11			5	3•	14	S		K Morton	49
1	4*						6	14		8			10			7		9•	2	11		5	12	3		J Deakin	50
42	29	39	8	35	39	26	16	42	17	37	1	7	8	15	8	3		30	20	21		17	1	1		League Appearances	
4			1		11		7		4	10	5	3	5		4			7					2	1		Substitute Appearances	
4	1+1	4	2	4	4	1+1	2	4	3+1	2		3	2+1	3	3+1	0+1		1+1	1							R/lows Appearances	
2	1	2		2	2	1		2	1	2		1+1			0			2	2	1		1				FA Cup Appearances	
2	2	1		2	1	1		2	2	1		1	1	2	0+2	1		1		1						ZDS Cup Appearances	

EVERTON

Club Colours: Blue and white trim shirts, white shorts, blue stockings.
Change Colours: Salmon and navy striped shirts, navy shorts, salmon stockings.
Reserves League: Pontins Central League Division 2

COMPETITIONS					
Div. 1	Div. 2	Euro C	ECWC	UEFA	Texaco
88-30	30-31	63-64	66-67	62-63	73-74
31-51	51-54	70-71	84-85	64-65	
54-				65-66	
				75-76	
				78-79	
				79-80	

HONOURS				
Div. 1	Div. 2	FA Cup	ECWC	C/Sh'ld
90-91	30-31	1906	84-85	1928
14-15		1933		1932
27-28		1966		1963
31-32		1984		1970
38-39				1984
62-63				1985
69-70				1986
84-85				1987
86-87				

MOST APPEARANCES: BRIAN LABONE 530 (1957-71)				
Year	League	FA Cup	Lge Cup	Europe
1959-60	31	1		
1960-61	42	1	4	
1961-62	41	3		
1962-63	40	3		2
1963-64	34	4		2
1964-65	42	4		6
1965-66	37	8		3
1966-67	40	6		4
1967-68	40	6	2	
1968-69	42	5	4	
1969-70	34	1	4	
1970-71	16	3		2
1971-72	4		1	
	451	45	15	19
Previous holder: Ted Sager 465 (1929-53)				

MOST GOALS IN A CAREER		
WILLIAM DEAN 377 (1924-38)		
Season	League	FA Cup
1924-25	2	
1925-26	32	1
1926-27	21	3
1927-28	60	3
1928-29	26	
1929-30	23	2
1930-31	39	9
1931-32	45	1
1932-33	24	5
1933-34	9	
1934-35	26	1
1935-36	17	
1936-37	24	3
1937-38	1	
Total	**349**	**28**
Previous holder: Chadwick 78 (1888-99)		

HIGHEST TRANSFER FEES RECEIVED			
Amount	Club	Player	Date
£2,800,000	Barcelona	Gary Lineker	6/86
£1,500,000	Glasgow Rangers	Trevor Steven	6/89
£1,250,000	Glasgow Rangers	Stuart McCall	8/91
£1,000,000	Glasgow Rangers	Gary Stevens	5/88

HIGHEST TRANSFER FEES PAID			
Amount	Club	Player	Date
£2,300,000	West Ham Utd.	Tony Cottee	8/88
£1,500,000	Glasgow Rangers	Mo Johnston	11/91
£1,000,000	Leicester City	Mike Newell	7/89
£1,000,000	Manchester City	Mark Ward	8/91

MANAGERS			
Name	Seasons	Best	Worst
Theo Kelly	1939-48	1(1)	14(1)
Cliff Britton	1948-56	11(1)	16(2)
Ian Buchan	1956-58	15(1)	16(1)
John Carey	1958-61	5(1)	16(1)
Harry Catterick	1961-73	1(1)	17(1)
Billy Bingham	1973-77	4(1)	11(1)
Steve Burtenshaw	1977		
Gordon Lee	1977-81	3(1)	19(1)
Howard Kendall	1981-87	1(1)	8(1)
Colin Harvey	1987-90	4(1)	8(1)
Howard Kendall	1990-	9(1)	12(1)

LONGEST LEAGUE RUNS	
of undefeated matches:	20 (29.4.1978-16.12.1978)
of undefeated home matches:	39 (6.9.1961-7.9.1963)
without home win:	12 (14.9.1957-22.3.1958)
of league wins:	12 (27.3.1894-6.10.1894)
of league defeats:	6 (5.3.1930-12.4.1930)
	(29.3.1958-19.4.1958) (4.11.1972-9.12.1972)
of league matches without a win:	14 (6.3.1937-4.9.1937)
of undefeated away matches:	11 (21.4.1908-27.9.1909)
without an away win:	35 (19.9.1970-8.4.1972)
of home wins:	15 (4.10.1930-4.4.1931)
of away wins:	6 (2.9.1908-14.11.1908)

BIGGEST VICTORIES
League: 8-0 v Stoke City, Div 1, 2.11.1889
9-1 v Manchester City, Division 1, 3.9.1906
9-1 v Plymouth, Division 2, 27.12.1930
8-0 v Southampton, Div 1, 20.11.1971
F.A. Cup: 11-2 v Derby, Round 1, 18.1.1890
League Cup: 8-0 v Wimbledon, Round 2, 24.8.1978
Europe (UEFA): 5-0 v Finn Harps, Rnd 1 1st leg, 12.9.1978
5-0 v Finn Harps, Rnd 1 2nd leg, 26.9.1978

BIGGEST DEFEATS
League: 0-7 v Sunderland, Division 1, 26.12.1934
0-7 v Wolverhampton Wndrs, Division 1, 22.2.1939
0-7 v Portsmouth, Division 1, 10.9.1949
F.A. Cup: 0-6 v Crystal Palace (h), Round 1, 7.1.1922
League Cup: No more than 3 goal difference
Europe (UEFA): 0-3 v Ujpest Dozsa, Rnd 2 1st leg, 3.11.1965

MOST GOALS
121, Division 1, 1930-31.
Dean 39, Down 14, Critchley 13, Johnson 13, Stein 11, White 10, Martin 7, Rigby 4, Griffith 3, Gee 2, Wilkinson 2, McPherson 1, Mclure 1, og 1.

MOST POINTS
3 points a win: 90, Division 1, 1984-85, (Div 1 record)
2 points a win: 66, Division 1, 1969-70.

MOST GOALS IN A MATCH
6. Jack Southwork v West Bromwich Alb., 7-1, Div 1, 30.12.1893

MOST GOALS IN A SEASON
William 'Dixie' Dean, 63 (League 60, FAC 3) 1927-28
5 goals once = 5; 4 goals once = 4; 3 goals 5 times = 15; 2 goals 15 times = 30; 1 goal 9 times = 9
Previous holder: B Freeman 38 (1908-09)

MOST FIRST CLASS MATCHES IN A SEASON
63 (42 League, 7 FA Cup, 4 League Cup, 1 Charity Shield, 9 European Cup Winners Cup) 1984-85
63 (42 League, 7 FA Cup, 5 League Cup, 1 Charity Shield, 8 Screen Super Cup) 1985-86

MOST LEAGUE GOALS CONCEDED
92, Division 1, 1929-30

MOST LEAGUE WINS
29, Division 1, 1969-70

MOST LEAGUE DRAWS
18, Division 1, 1925-26; Division 1, 1971-72; Division 1, 1974-75

MOST LEAGUE DEFEATS
22, Division 1, 1950-51

OLDEST PLAYER
Ted Sager, 42 years, 1953

YOUNGEST PLAYER
Joe Royle, 16 years, 1966

MOST CAPPED PLAYER
Neville Southall (Wales) 61

BEST PERFORMANCES BY EVERTON

League: 1969-70: Matches played 42, Won 29, Drawn 8, Lost 5, Goals for 72, Goals against 34, Points 72. 1st Division 1.

Highest: Division 1 Champions 9 times.

F.A. Cup: 1905-06: 1st rnd. West Bromwich Albion 3-1; 2nd rnd. Chesterfield 3-0; 4th rnd. Bradford City 1-0; 5th rnd. Sheffield Wednesday 4-3; Semi-Final Liverpool 2-0; Final Newcastle 1-0

1932-33: 3rd rnd. Leicester City 3-2; 4th rnd. Bury 3-1; 5th rnd. Leeds United 2-0; 6th rnd. Luton Town 6-0; Semi-Final West Ham United 2-1; Final Manchester City 3-0.

1965-66: 3rd rnd. Sunderland 3-0; 4th rnd. Bedford 3-0; 5th rnd. Coventry City 3-0 6th rnd. Manchester City 2-0; Semi-Final Manchester United 1-0; Final Sheffield Wednesday 3-2.

1983-84: 3rd rnd. Stoke City 2-0; 4th rnd. Gillingham 0-0, 0-0, 3-0; 5th rnd. Shrewsbury Town 3-1; 6th rnd. Notts County 2-1; Semi-Final Southampton 1-0; Final Watford 2-0.

League Cup: 1976-77: 2nd rnd. Cambridge United 3-0; 3rd rnd. Stockport County 1-0; 4th rnd. Coventry City 3-0; 5th rnd. Manchester United 3-0; Semi-Final Bolton Wanderers 1-1, 1-0; Final Aston Villa 1-1, 2-3.

ECWC: 1984-85: 1st rnd. University of Dublin 0-0, 1-0; 2nd rnd. Inter Bratislav 1-0, 3-0; 3rd rnd. Fortuna S 3-0, 2-0; Semi-Final Bayern Munich 0-0, 3-1; Final Rapid Vienna 3-1.

DIVISIONAL RECORDS

	Played	Won	Drawn	Lost	For	Against	Points
DIVISION 1	3480	1460	839	1181	5670	4944	**3966**
DIVISION 2	168	77	45	46	348	257	**199**
TOTALS	**3648**	**1537**	**884**	**1227**	**6018**	**5201**	**4165**

EVERTON   APPEARANCES   GOALS

PLAYERS NAME / Honours	Ht	Wt	Birthdate	Birthplace / Transfers	Contract Date	Clubs	League	L/Cup	FA Cup	Other	Lg	L/C	FAC	Oth
GOALKEEPERS														
Jason Kearton	6.1	11.10	09.07.69	Ipswich (Aust)	31.10.88	Everton								
				Loan	13.08.91	Stoke City	16		1					
				Loan	09.01.92	Blackpool	14							
Gerry Peyton	6.2	13.11	20.05.56	Birmingham		Atherstone								
Ei:33,Xl.3; Div3'87					01.05.75	Burnley	30	1	1					
				£40,000	01.12.76	Fulham	345	26	20	2				
16.09.83 Loan Southend Utd. 10 Lg Apps.				Free	22.07.86	Bournemouth	202	15	13	8				
				£80,000	11.07.91	Everton								
				Loan	21.02.92	Bolton W	1							
Neville Southall	6.1	12.2	16.09.58	Llandudno		Bangor								
W:61;Div1'85'87;FAC'84;CS'84'85;ECWC'85						Winsford U								
				£6,000	14.06.80	Bury	39		5					
				Loan	27.01.83	Port Vale	9							
				£150,000	13.07.81	Everton	371	48	55	32				
DEFENDERS														
Gary Ablett	6.0	11.4	19.11.65	Liverpool	25.01.85	Derby County	3+3			2				
E:u21.1;Div1'88'90.CS'88.FAC'89				Loan	10.09.86	Hull City	5							
					19.11.83	Liverpool (A)	103+6	10+1	16+2	9	1			
				£750,000	14.01.92	Everton	17		1					
Andy Hinchcliffe	5.10	12.10	05.02.69	Liverpool	17.06.86	Manchester City (A)	107+5	11	12	4	8	1	1	1
E: u21.1,Y.7				£600,00 +P	17.07.90	Everton	36+3	5	5	4	1			
Matthew Jackson	6.0		19.10.71	Leeds	04.07.90	Luton Town (T)	7+2	2		0+1				
E.S.F.A.u18.5				Loan	27.03.91	Preston N.E	3+1							
				£600,000	18.10.91	Everton	30	2	1	1				
Martin Keown	6.1	12.4	24.07.66	Oxford	02.02.84	Arsenal (A)	22	5						
E: 9, u21.8,EY4				Loan		Brighton & H.A	21+2	2		2	1	1		1
				£200,000	09.06.86	Aston Villa	109+3	12+1	6	2	3			
				£750,000	07.08.89	Everton	79+4	7	10+1	6				
Dave Watson	5.11	11.12	20.11.61	Liverpool	25.05.79	Liverpool								
E: 12,u21.7; CS'87; Div1'87; Div2'86;				£100,000	29.11.80	Norwich City	212	21	18		11	3	1	
MC'85; UEFA u21'84				£900,000	22.08.86	Everton	199+1	23	30	14	17	2	3	3
MIDFIELD														
John Ebbrell	5.7	9.12	01.10.69	Bromborough	07.11.86	Everton (A)	87+9	9	10	6+2	4	1	2	1
E: u21.7,u19.2,Y.2,S; GMAFS														
Alan Harper	5.8	9.7	01.11.60	Liverpool	22.04.78	Liverpool (A)								
E: Y.1; Div1'85'87,CS'86'87					01.06.83	Everton	103+24	17+2	10+8	13+1	4		1	
				£275,000	06.07.88	Sheffield Wed	32+3	1+1	1	1				
				£150,000	15.12.89	Manchester City	46+4	3	6	3	1	1		
				£1.3m incl	12.08.91	Everton	29+4	1+1	1	2				
Barry Horne	5.10	12.3	18.05.63	St.Asaph		Rhyl								
W: 30; WC'86					26.06.84	Wrexham	136	10	7	15	17	1	2	3
				£60,000	17.07.87	Portsmouth	66+4	3	6		7			
				£700,000	22.03.89	Southampton	11+1	15+2	15	7	6	3	3	1
				£675,000	01.07.92	Everton								
Ian Snodin	5.7	9.0	15.08.63	Rotherham	18.08.80	Doncaster Rovers (A)	181+7	9	11+1	3	25	1	1	
E:B1,u21.4,Y,Div1'87				£200,000	22.05.85	Leeds Utd	51	3	1	1	6	2		
				£840,000	16.01.87	Everton	93+3	15+1	22	3	2	1	2	
Mark Ward	5.5	10.0	10.10.62	Prescot	05.09.80	Everton (A)								
ESP1. via Northwich Vic.(3 FAC App+2G) to				£10,000	19.07.83	Oldham Ath	84	5	3		12			
				£250,000	15.08.85	West Ham U	163+2	20+1	17	6	12	2		
				£1,000,000	29.12.89	Manchester City	55	3	6	3	14			2
				£1,3m incl		Everton	37	2	2	1	4			
Robert Warzycha						Gorniz Zabrze(Pol).								
					18.03.91	Everton	33+12	1+1	1	4	5			2
FORWARDS														
Peter Beagrie	5.8	9.10	28.11.65	Middlesborough	17.06.86	Middlesbrough	24+9	1		1+1	2			
E: B.2, u21.2				£35,000	16.08.86	Sheffield Utd	81+3	5	5	4	11			
				£215,000	29.06.88	Stoke City	54	4	3		7		1	
				£750,000	02.11.89	Everton	48+15	1+1	5+2	5	5	2		1
				Loan	26.09.91	Sunderland	5				1			
Peter Beardsley	5.8	11.7	18.01.61	Newcastle	09.08.79	Carlisle Utd	93+11	6+1	15		22		7	
E:49;F.Lg.1;Div1'88'90;FAC'89;CS'88				£275,000	01.04.81	Vancouver Wh'caps								
				£300,000	09.09.82	Manchester Utd		1						
01.03.93 Free to Vancouver Whitecaps				£150,000	23.09.83	Newcastle Utd	146+1	10	6	1	61			
				£1,900,000	24.07.87	Liverpool	120+11	13+1	22+3	5	46	1	11	1
				£1,000,000	05.08.91	Everton	42	4	2	2	15	3	1	1
Tony Cottee	5.8	11.5	11.07.65	West Ham	01.09.82	West Ham U. (A)	203+9	19	24	1	92	14	11	1
E: 7, u21.10, Y.3				£2,300,000	02.08.88	Everton	97+19	12+3	13+5	11+2	44	7	4	12
Maurice Johnston			30.04.63	Glasgow		Partick Thistle								
S: 38					01.11.83	Watford	37+1				23			
				£400,000	01.11.84	Celtic								
01.07.88 £373,000 to Nantes (Fra.)				£1,500,000	01.07.89	Glasgow Rangers								
				£1,500,000	20.11.91	Everton	21	1	1	1	7			
David Unsworth			16.10.73	Preston		Everton	1+1				1			

ADDITIONAL CONTRACT PLAYERS

(F) Stuart Barlow (3+6 Lg App); **Iain Jenkins** (2+2 Lg App); **William Kenny**; **Neil Moore**; **Philip Quinlan** (Loan 27.03.91 Huddersfield T. 7+1 Lg App + 2 Lg G)

EVERTON

RECORD WIN & LOSS AGAINST EACH CLUB IN CURRENT DIVISION
(Where a score has occured on several occasions the most recent is given)

Club	Rec. Win	Season	Rec. Loss	Season
ARSENAL	6-1	1985-86	6-0	1963-64
ASTON VILLA	7-0	1889-90	6-2	1989-90
BLACKBURN ROVERS	7-1	1933-34	6-0	1913-14
CHELSEA	6-0	1977-78	6-0	1948-49
COVENTRY CITY	6-0	1977-78	4-1	1975-76 (home)
CRYSTAL PALACE	5-0	1980-81	2-0	1970-71
IPSWICH TOWN	5-2	1961-62	4-0	1980-81
LEEDS UNITED	7-1	1936-37	5-1	1956-57
LIVERPOOL	5-0	1914-15 (away)	6-0	1935-36
MANCHESTER CITY	9-1	1906-07	6-2	1957-58
MANCHESTER UNITED	6-0	1892-93	5-0	1959-60
MIDDLESBROUGH	5-1	1931-32	6-1	1935-36
NORWICH CITY	4-0	1986-87	4-2	1979-80
NOTTINGHAM FOREST	6-0	1961-62	4-0	1909-10 (home)
OLDHAM ATHLETIC	4-0	1953-54 (away)	4-1	1919-20
QUEENS PARK RANGERS	5-1	1977-78 (away)	5-0	1975-76
SHEFFIELD UNITED	5-0	1913-14	5-0	1899-00
SHEFFIELD WEDNESDAY	8-1	1893-94	6-0	1950-51
SOUTHAMPTON	8-0	1971-72	3-0	1980-81
TOTTENHAM HOTSPUR	4-0	1976-77	10-4	1958-59
WIMBLEDON	3-0	1986-87	3-1	1989-90

MANAGER: HOWARD KENDALL

DATE OF BIRTH: 22.5.1946   **PLACE OF BIRTH:** Ryton-on-Tyne, Co. Durham

DATE OF APPOINTMENT: 6.11.1990

PREVIOUS CLUBS
as Manager: Blackburn Rov., Everton, Bilbao, Manchester City
as Chief Coach:
as Player: Preston North End, Everton, Birmingham City, Stoke City

HONOURS
as Manager: FA Cup Winners 1984, European Cup Winners Cup 1984-85, League Champions 1984-85, 1986-87
as Asst. Man./Coach:
as Player: League Championship 1969-79
International:

Value Rating: ★ ★ ★ ★ ★

Programme Editor: Mike Beddow

Price of 1992-93 Programme: £1.30
Number of Pages: 32
Subscriptions: £40 UK. (For overseas rates apply to club)

Local Newspapers: Liverpool Daily Post, Liverpool Echo

Local Radio Stations: Radio Merseyside, Radio City

Books available about Club: 100 Years of Goodison Glory. Ken Rogers

LEADING LEAGUE GOALSCORERS
SEASONS 1979-80 – 1991-92

1979-80	ANDY KING	9	1980-81	PETER EASTOE	15
	BRIAN KIDD	9			
1981-82	GRAEME SHARP	15	1982-83	GRAEME SHARP	15
1983-84	ADRIAN HEATH	12	1984-85	GRAEME SHARP	21
1985-86	GARY LINEKER	30	1986-87	TREVOR STEVEN	14
1987-88	GRAEME SHARP	13	1988-89	TONY COTTEE	13
1989-90	TONY COTTEE	13	1990-91	TONY COTTEE	10

1991-92   **PETER BEARDSLEY   15**

GOODISON PARK Liverpool L4 4EL

Capacity: 38,500   **Covered Standing:**   **Seating:** 36,500

Tel: Ground: 051 521 2020   **Ticket Sales:** As ground number   **Clubcall:** 0898 12 11 99

All premium rate calls (0898/0891) cost 36p per minute cheap rate and 48p per minute at all other times. Call costings correct at time of going to press.

GROUNDS
Stanley Park 1878-82; Priory Road 1882-84; Anfield Road 1884-92; Goodison Park 1892-

ATTENDANCES
Highest: 78,299 v Liverpool, Division 1, 18.9.1948

Lowest: 2,079 v West Bromwich Albion, 23.2.1899

RECORD RECEIPTS (with previous records):
£274,555 Liverpool v Manchester Utd, 13.4.1985
£174,945 Liverpool v Manchester Utd, 4.4.1979
£68,767 v Bolton, 1.1977
£56,462 Arsenal v Stoke, 4.1977

GROUND NAME
First game: v Bolton Wanderers, Division 1, 2.9.1892
First floodlit game: v Liverpool, 9.10.1957
Internationals: England v Scotland: 1895, 1911
England v Ireland: 1907, 1924, 1928, 1935, 1947, 1953, 1973
England v R. of Ireland: 1949
England v Portugal: 1951
England v Poland: 1966
Brazil v Bulgaria: 1966
Brazil v Hungary: 1966
Portugal v Brazil: 1966
Portugal v North Korea: 1966
West Germany v Russia: 1966
Ireland v Wales: 1973

Season Tickets:
Stands: from £145 to £198, juv/OAP £70 to £123
Ground: N/A

Executive Box Season Tickets: £9,000 pa – box for 10 persons with restaurant and waiter service in boxes

Cost of Stand Tickets: Stand: £9.50 to £13, juv/OAP £4.50
No terraces for home supporters

Match and Ticket Information: Box Office open each weekday 0900 to 1700. Except matches v Liverpool reserved stand seats can be purchased for all home fixtures any time during the season by post (with remittance and SAE) or personally from the box office at the Goodison Road side of the ground. Postal applications to the Box Office Manager. (Ticket Office 051-523 6666; 24-hour information 0898 121 599. Diat a Seat service for Access/Visa Card holders 051-525 1231

Car Parking: Extensive parking is available on site at the corner of Prior and Utting Avenue

Nearest Railway Station: Liverpool (Lime Street) 051-709 9696

How to get to the ground

From North: Use Motorway M6 until junction 28 then follow signs Liverpool on A58 then A580 and forward into Walton Hall Avenue for Everton FC
From East, South: Use Motorway M6 then M62 until end of Motorway then turn right A5058 into Queens Drive. In 3.7m turn left A580 into Walton Hall Avenue for Everton FC
From West: Use Mersey Tunnel into Liverpool City Centre, then follow signs Preston A580 into Walton Hall Avenue for Everton FC

EXETER CITY

Division 2

Formed: 1904   **Turned Professional:** 1908   **Ltd Co:** 1908

SPONSORED BY: Carling Black Label (Bass)   **NICKNAME:** The Grecians

President
C Hill

Chairman
L G Vallance

Directors
S W Dawe
A R W Trump
A W Gooch JP
G Vece

Secretary
Michael Holladay (0392 54073)

Team Manager
Alan Ball

Player/Assistant Manager
Steve Williams

Company Secretary
Allen Trump

Commercial & Marketing Manager
Steve Birley

Reserve & Youth Teams Coach
Mike Radford

Groundsman
Colin Wheatcroft

Club Statistician for the Directory
C Lucas

AT the end of June 1991 club president Clifford Hill formed a new board of directors, apparently reneging on a verbal agreement for the return of banned chairman Ivor Doble. With Doble and his allies threatening to reclaim their investment in the club and other creditors unhappy with the new set up Shaun Taylor, Richard Dryden and Murray Jones are sold for £525,000 during July. Terry Cooper signs six new players for a £10,000 outlay but resigns on 1.8.1991 after arguments with the new board. Within a week his assistants Steve Neville leaves for Hong Kong. On 5th August Alan Ball is appointed manager and signs three more players before the start of the season.

After a disastrous start to the campaign seven more players are signed in the space of two weeks and City embark on a ten match unbeaten run that takes them from 24th to 5th. But City lack the quality to sustain a promotion push and slip into mid-table. Almost to the end of March Ball talked of a push for the play-offs, but the season ended with a series of defeats that took City to the brink of relegation, only Bury's failure to win at Preston saving them from disaster.

With the strikers lacking the skill to keep hold of the ball and with a lack of pace in central midfield City struggled to win or keep posession and as a consequence the defence, the strongest part of the team, came under so much pressure that only Darlington conceded more goals. Scott Hiley, the P.F.A's choice as best right-back in the division and central defender Peter Whiston, the supporters' 'Player of the Year', were the only players to perform to a consistently high standard. Most of City's efforts went into setting up chances for Steve Moran and he finished with a commendable tally of goals. He became the first Exeter player in 60 years to score 4 goals in a league game. Keeper Kevin Miller was a mixture of brilliance and mistakes and Steve Williams and Andy Cook were occasionally excellent. Jon Brown once again showed great fighting spirit and his passing improved considerably on the previous season.

Injury problems were not as bad as the previous season but were exacerbated by a disgraceful disciplinary record that caused a succession of suspensions. The management's main excuse for the poor season was the disruption of pre-season training.

In March Ball had said with two or three more players City would be good enough to play in Division Two. By May he was talking of his humiliation and embarrassment at his team's performances and was threatening Wholesale changes for next season.   **G. Lucas**

Back row L-R: Steve Allen, Mark Hutchings, Scott Daniels, Kevin Maloy, Kevin Miller, Eamonn Dolan, Richard Pears, Philip Lafferty. **3rd row:** Mike Chapman, George Kent, Alan Tonge, Gary Chapman, David Cooper, Gary Marshall, Toby Redwood, John Brown, Craig Taylor, Tom Kelly, Eamonn Collins, Mike Radford, Alan Ball. **2nd row:** Andy Cook, Steve Moran, Scott Hiley, Peter Whiston, Steve Williams, Glen Sprod, Andy Harris, John Hodge. **Front row:** Mark Brown, Anthony Thirlby, Martin Phillips, Kevin Darch, Marc Baines, Jimmy Ball, Gary Rice, Mattew Harris.

EXETER CITY

DIVISION THREE: 20th **FA CUP:** 3rd RND **RUMBELOWS CUP:** 1st RND **AUTOGLASS:** 2nd RND

M	DATE		COMP.	VEN	OPPONENTS	RESULT		H/T	LGE POS	GOALSCORERS/GOAL TIMES	ATTEN- DANCE
1	A	17	BL	A	West Bromwich A.	L	3-6	1-2		Cooper 43, Moran 83, Marshall 85	(12,892
2		21	RC 1/1	H	Birmingham City	L	0-1	0-1			4,07
3		24	BL	H	Brentford	L	1-2	0-2	24	Moran 67	3,51
4		27	RC 1/2	A	Birmingham City	L	0-4	0-2			(6,177
5		31	BL	A	Shrewsbury Town	L	1-6	1-3	24	Rowbotham 22	(2,912
6	S	4	BL	H	Torquay United	W	1-0	0-0	22	Kelly 90	5,77
7		7	BL	A	Huddersfield Town	D	0-0	0-0	22		(5,758
8		14	BL	H	Hartlepool United	D	1-1	0-0	22	Daniels 61	2,90
9		17	BL	H	Stockport County	W	2-1	2-1	17	Knowles (og) 17, Whiston 38	3,03
10		21	BL	A	Peterborough Utd	D	1-1	0-1	18	Wimbleton 54	(4,249
11		28	BL	H	Reading	W	2-1	0-0	14	Daniels 58, 77	3,38
12	O	5	BL	A	Hull City	W	2-1	0-1	12	Chapman 58, Moran 61	(3,143
13		12	BL	H	Darlington	W	4-1	2-1	8	Moran 4 (12, 14, 60, 80)	3,54
14		19	BL	H	Bury	W	5-2	3-0	5	Kelly (pen) 12, 58, Chapman 29, 45, Moran 83	3,90
15		23	AGT Pre	H	Torquay United	W	2-1	2-1		Whiston 35, Moran 44	2,95
16		26	BL	A	Wigan Athletic	L	1-4	1-1	8	Hilaire 39	(1,76
17	N	2	BL	A	Leyton Orient	L	0-1	0-0	9		(3,038
18		6	BL	H	Bradford City	W	1-0	0-0	7	Gardner (og) 71	2,62
19		9	BL	H	Stoke City	D	0-0	0-0	6		5,30
20		16	FAC 1	A	Colchester Utd	D	0-0	0-0			(4,965
21		23	BL	A	Birmingham City	L	0-1	0-0	9		(11,319
22		27	FAC 1R	H	Colchester Utd	D	0-0	0-0		(Won 4-2 on pens)	4,06
23		30	BL	H	Chester City	D	0-0	0-0	9		3,23
24	D	7	FAC 2	H	Swansea City	D	0-0	0-0			4,18
25		14	BL	A	Swansea City	L	0-1	0-1	11		(2,848
26		17	FAC 2R	A	Swansea City	W	2-1	1-0		Brown 31, Marshall 86	(3,159
27		22	BL	A	Brentford	L	0-3	0-2	13		(7,226
28		26	BL	H	Shrewsbury Town	W	1-0	0-0	11	Hiley 73	3,85
29		28	BL	H	West Bromwich A.	D	1-1	0-0	11	Moran (pen) 89	5,83
30	J	1	BL	A	Torquay United	L	0-1	0-0	13		(5,696
31		4	FAC 3	H	Portsmouth	L	1-2	0-1		Moran 55	6,76
32		7	AGT Pre	A	Hereford United	L	1-2	0-1		Marshall 47	(1,564
33		11	BL	H	Bolton Wanderers	D	2-2	1-1	14	Moran 31, 82	3,33
34		14	AGT 1	A	West Bromwich A.	W	1-0	1-0		Robson 25	(6,034
35		18	BL	A	Preston North End	W	3-1	2-0	13	Robson 3, Wimbleton 27, Hilaire 78	(3,585
36		25	BL	H	Fulham	D	1-1	1-0	12	Moran (pen) 45	4,00
37	F	8	BL	H	Wigan Athletic	L	0-1	0-0	16		3,03
38		11	BL	A	Chester City	L	2-5	1-3	16	Moran 44, Wimbleton 82	(871
39		15	BL	H	Swansea City	W	2-1	2-0	14	Moran 21, Thompstone 45	2,36
40		22	BL	A	Bolton Wanderers	W	2-1	1-1	13	Kelly 4, Wimbleton 76	(5,631
41		25	AGT 2	A	Peterborough Utd	L	0-1	0-0			(2,321
42		29	BL	H	Bournemouth	L	0-3	0-1	14		4,53
43	M	3	BL	H	Preston North End	W	4-1	2-1	12	Hilaire 3, 66, Moran 5, 63	2,21
44		7	BL	A	Fulham	D	0-0	0-0	12		(3,957
45		10	BL	A	Bradford City	D	1-1	0-0	13	Whiston 89	(4,170
46		14	BL	H	Leyton Orient	W	2-0	0-0	13	Morris 58, Marshall 84	3,07
47		21	BL	A	Stoke City	L	2-5	1-3	14	Whiston 45, Thompstone 72	(13,634
48		24	BL	A	Bournemouth	L	0-1	0-1	14		(4,959
49		28	BL	H	Birmingham City	W	2-1	1-1	13	Moran 15, 84 (pen)	5,47
50		31	BL	A	Hartlepool United	L	1-3	0-1	14	Morris 82	(2,222
51	A	4	BL	H	Huddersfield Town	L	0-1	0-0	14		3,04
52		10	BL	A	Stockport County	L	1-4	1-1	14	Hodge 8	(4,546
53		14	BL	A	Bury	L	1-3	1-2	16	Marshall 36	(1,756
54		18	BL	H	Peterborough Utd	D	2-2	1-1	15	Kelly (pen) 33, Thompstone 69	3,05
55		20	BL	A	Reading	L	0-1	0-1	17		(3,325
56		25	BL	H	Hull City	L	0-3	0-0	20		2,77
57	M	2	BL	A	Darlington	L	2-5	1-2	20	Moran 17, Chapman 61	(1,573

Best Home League Attendance: 5,830 v West Bromwich A.   **Smallest: 2,214 v Preston North**   Av Home Att: 3,64

Goal Scorers: Compared with 90-91: -64

League (57): Moran 19 (3 pens), Kelly 5 (2 pens), Chapman 4, Hilaire 4, Wimbleton 4, Marshall 3, Thompstone 3, Whiston 3, Daniels 3, Morris 2, Opponents 2, Cooper, Hodge, Rowbotham, Robson, Hiley

R/lows C (1):
FA Cup (3): Marshall, Brown, Moran
Autoglass (4): Moran, Whiston, Robson, Marshall   †=After extra-time

1991-92

Maloy K.	Hiley S.	Brown J.	Williams S.	Daniels S.	O'Donnell C.	Rowbotham D.	Cooper M.	Moran S.	Kelly T.	Marshall G.	O'Shaughnessy S.	Miller K.	Redwood T.	Wimbleton P.	Chapman G.	Cook A.	Whiston P.	Dolan E.	Hodge J.	Hilaire V.	Harris A.	Cooper D.	Robson M.	Thompsyone I.	Morris A.	Referee	
1	2	3	4	5	6	7	8	9	10	11	S															K Breen	1
1	2	3	4	6	5	7*	8	9	10	11	S															P Scoble	2
1	2	3	4	6	5*	7	8	9	10	11•	12															B Hamer	3
	2	3	4	6	S		10	9	11	12	8*	1														P Danson	4
	2	12	4•	6		7	8	9	3†	10		1														E Parker	5
	2	8	4	6		7•		9	10	11	14	1			3*											P Vanes	6
	2	3	4	5		7*		9	10	12	6†	1	S	8	11											K Lupton	7
	2	11	4	5		7*					S	1		8	10	3	6		9	12						A Smith	8
	2	S	4	5				S	10			1		8	11	3	6		9	7						A Smith	9
	2	S	4	5				12	10			1		8	11	3	6		9	7*						D Axcell	10
	2		4	5				12	10			1		8	11	3	6		9*	7*	14					R Wiseman	11
	2	S	4	5				12	10			1		8	11	3	6		9*	7						K Redfern	12
	2	S	4	5				9	11			1		8	10	3	6	S		7						J Deakin	13
	2	S	4	5				9	11			1		8	10	3	6	S		7						K Cooper	14
	2	S		5				9	11	12		1		8	10	3	6		4*	7						A Gifford	15
	2	14	4	5				9*	11•			1		8	10	3	6		12	7						I Cruickshanks	16
	2	S	4	5				9	11			1		8*	10	3	6		12	7						P Foakes	17
	2	S	4	5				9	11			1		8	10*	3	6		12	7						K A Cooper	18
	2	3	4	5				9	11			1		8	10*		6	12	14	7•						M Pierce	19
	2	8	4†	5				9	11			1		S	10	3	6	S		7						G Pooley	20
	2	8	4	5				9•	11			1			10*	3	6	14	12	7						A Wilkie	21
		2	4	5					10	9		1	14	8•	11	3	6			7*						G Pooley	22
	2	10		5						14		1		8	11*	3	6		9	7•	4					J Carter	23
	2	14	4	5				9	12			1		8*	11	3	6			7*		10				M Bodenham	24
	2	8	4*	5				9	14			1		12	10•	3	6			7						G Ashby	25
	2	10	4*	5				9	7			1		8		3	6				11	12				M Bodenham	26
	2	11	4	5				S	7			1		8		3	6				12	4*				G Willard	27
	2	11	4	5				9	7			1		8		3	6				12		S			P Durkin	28
	2	11	4	5				9	7			1		8	S	3	6						S			P Alcock	29
	2		4	5				9	7*			1		8	12	3	6		14			11•				J Deakin	30
	2	10	4	5				9	7			1		8	S	3	6		S			11				I Hemley	31
	2		4	5				9	7			1		8	10*	3	6		12			S	11			J Lloyd	32
	2		4	5				9	7			1		8		3	6		12			S	11			J Martin	33
	2			5				9*	7			1		4			6	10•	8		3	11				R Milford	34
	2		4	5				9	10			1		8			6	S		7	3	11				M Brandwood	35
	2		4	5				9	7			1		8		3	6		12		11*		5			C Wilkes	36
			4						7			1		8	12	3	6		10		11*			9		J Rushton	37
			4	5				9	12			1	2			3	6	7*	8*		11			10		P Harrison	38
	2		4	5				9				1		8		3*	6	11•		7	12	14		10		D Frampton	39
	2		4	5				9	10			1		8			6		7*	12	3	11				V Callow	40
	2		4*	5				9	10			1		8			6		12	7	3	11				J Martin	41
		6	4	5				9*	10			1		8		3			12	7		11	2			K Cooper	42
		6	4	5				9	10	11		1		8	S	3				7			2			R Groves	43
	2		4	5					10	11		1		8		3	6	S		7			S	9		K Morton	44
	2			5					10	11		1		8		3	6		7*	4		12		9		T West	45
	2			5					10	7		1		8		3	6		11	4			S	9		P Danson	46
	2		4•	5					10	12		1		8		3	6		11			14	7	9*		V Callow	47
	2	11	4*	5					10			1		8		3	6		7				S	9	12	A Buksh	48
	2	7		5				9	12			1		8*		3	6		11					10	S	J Deakin	49
	2	7		5				9	11	12		1		8•		3	6		4					10*	14	R Nixon	50
	2		4	5				9	10	12		1		8*		3	6		11				7•		14	P Scoble	51
	2		4	5				9	10	12		1†				3	6*		11	8		S	7			S Bell	52
	2		4	5				9*	11	12		1				3	6		7	8		5		10•		C Trussell	53
	2		4	5					10	11		1		S		3	6		7	8		S		9		D Shadwell	54
	2	6	4*	5					10•			1			11	3			7	8*	14	12		9		P Vanes	55
1	2	8	4*	5•					10	12					11	3	6		7			14		9		J Carter	56
1	2*		4	5				9	10					8	12	3	6		7			14		11*		J Key	57
4	33	33	36	43	2	5	3	31	32	17	1	42	1	35	17	38	36	5	16	24	5	9	7	15	4	League Appearances	
		2						3		11	2			1	3			2	7	9	1	4	1		3	Substitute Appearances	
	2	2	2	2	1	2	2	2	2	1+1	1			1											1	R/lows Appearances	
	4	4+1	5	5				4	2	3		5		0+1	4	3	5	5		4	1+1	1				FA Cup Appearances	
	2	3	1	4				4	2	2		4		4	2	2	4	2+2	3		2	3				Autoglass Appearances	

Also Played: Posn.(Game): Cole 5(4)12(22,23)14(5)S(1); Hobson 12(2)14(3), O'Doherty 5(5†,6), Waters 11(5)12(6)14(34), Damerell 11(25)S(26), Humphrey 9(27)10(28*), Edwards 10(27,29,30,33*), Sprod 12(34)S(35,36,37,45), Tonge 2(37)14(38,53), Masefield 5(37)S(40,41,42,43,46).

Players on Loan: O'Doherty (Huddersfield), Humphrey (Millwall), Robson (Tottenham), Morris (Chesterfield).   † = Sent Off

235

EXETER CITY

Club Colours: Red and white striped shirts, black shorts, red stockings
Change Colours: All white
Reserves League: Clifton Stockbrokers South West Counties   **'A' Team:** Devon & Exeter Premier

Previous League: Southern League
Previous Managers: 1908-22 Arthur Chadwick   1923-27 Fred Mavin   1928-29 David Wilson   1929-35 Billy McDevitt   1935-40 Jack English   1945-52 George Roughton   1952-53 Norman Kirkman   1953-57 Norman Dodgin   1957-58 Bill Thompson   1958-60 Frank Broome   1960-62 Glen Wilson   1962-63 Cyril Spiers   1963-65 Jack Edwards   1965-66 Ellis Stuttard   1966-67 Jock Basford   1967-69 Frank Broome   1969-76 John Newman   1977-79 Bobby Saxton   1979-83 Brian Godfrey   1983-84 Gerry Francis   1984-85 Jim Iley   1985-87 Colin Appleton   1988 John Delve (caretaker)   1988-91 Terry Cooper
Honours: Champions Div 4, 1989-90   Division 3 South Cup Winners 1933-34
League Career: Elected to Div 3 1920   Transferred to Div 3S 1921   Relegated to Div 4 1957-58   Promoted to Div 3 1963-64   Relegated to Div 4 1965-66   Promoted to Div 3 1976-77   Relegated to Div 4 1983-84   Promoted to Div 3 1989-90

CLUB RECORDS

Most Appearances for Club: Keith Harvey, 1952-69: League 483 + FA Cup 21 + League Cup 13 **Total 517** (League only): Arnold Mitchell, 495, 1952-66
Most Capped Player: Dermot Curtis 1, Eire   **For England:** None
Record Goalscorer in a Match: James Bell 6 v Weymouth, FA Cup 1st Prelim. Round, 3.10.1908   Fred Whitlow v Crystal Palace, Div 3S Cup, 24.1.1934 (11-6)
Record League Goalscorer in a Season: Fred Whitlow, 33, Div 3S, 1932-3   **In All Competitions:** Rod Williams 37 (League 29, FA Cup 7, Div 3S Cup 1) 1936-37
Record League Goalscorer in a Career: Tony Kellow 129   **In All Competitions:** Tony Kellow 150 (League 129, FA Cup 11, League Cup 10) 1976-78, 1980-83 & 1985-87
Record Transfer Fee Received: £300,000 (Initial £200,000 + £100,000 for completion of 20 first team appearances paid Oct '91) from Glasgow Rangers for Chris Vinnicombe, November 1989. Further £100,000 instalments for 30 & 40 first team appearances, plus £100,000 should he play for England
Record Transfer Fee Paid: £10,000 + £5,000 + £125,000 to Bristol Rovers for Richard Dryden, March 1989, May 1989, July 1991
Best Performances: League: 2nd Div 3(S) 1932-33   **FA Cup:** 6th Round Replay 1930-31   **League Cup:** Never beyond 4th Round
Most League Points: (3pts a win) 89, Div 4, 1989-90   (2pts a win) 62, Div 4, 1976-77
Most League Goals: 88, Div 3S, 1932-33
Record League Victory: 8-1 v Coventry, Div 3S, 4.12.1926   8-1 v Aldershot, Div 3S, 4.5.1935   7-0 v Crystal Palace, Div 3(S), 9.1.1954
Record Cup Victory and Most Goals Scored in a Cup Tie: 9-1 v Aberdare, FA Cup 1st Round, 26.11.1927   11-6 v Crystal Palace, Div 3(S) Cup, 24.1.1934
Record League Defeat: 0-9 v Notts County, Div 3S, 16.10.1948   0-9 v Northampton Town, Div 3S, 12.4.1958
Record Cup Defeat: 1-8 v Aston Villa, League Cup Rnd 2, 7.10.1985
Oldest Player in a League Match:
Youngest Player in a League Match: Cliff Bastin, 16 years 31 days v Coventry City, 14.4.1928

LONGEST LEAGUE RUNS	
of undefeated matches: 13 (1986)	of league matches without a win: 18 (1984)
of undefeated home matches: 23 (1989-90)	of undefeated away matches: 8 (1964)
without home win: 9 (1984)	without an away win: 27 (1986-87)
of league wins: 7 (1977)	of home wins: 13 (1932-33)
of league defeats: 7 (1921, 1923, 1925, 1936, 1984)	of away wins: 6 (1977)

EXETER CITY | APPEARANCES | GOALS

PLAYERS NAME / Honours	Ht	Wt	Birthdate	Birthplace / Transfers	Contract Date	Clubs	League	L/Cup	FA Cup	Other	Lg	L/C	FAC	Oth
GOALKEEPERS														
Kevin Maloy	6.1		12.11.66	Aldershot	30.07.91	Exeter City	4	1						
Kevin Miller	6.1	13.0	15.03.69	Falmouth		Newquay								
Div.4'90					01.07.89	Exeter City	119	3	10	11				
DEFENDERS														
Johnathon Brown	5.10	11.3	08.09.66	Barnsley		Denaby Utd								
				£1,500	01.07.90	Exeter City	59+5	2	5+1	7			1	
Andy Cook	5.9	10.12	10.08.69	Romsey	06.07.87	Southampton	11+5	4	1	1	1			
				£50,000	13.09.91	Exeter City	38		5	2				
David B E Cooper						Luton Town								
				Free	06.08.91	Exeter City	9+4		1	2				
Scott Daniels	6.1	11.9	22.11.69	Benfleet	01.07.88	Colchester Utd. (T)	64+9	2	10	4+1				
				£50,000	16.08.91	Exeter City	43	2	5	4	3			
Tom Kelly	5.10	11.10	28.03.64	Bellshill		Hibernian								
					14.08.85	Hartlepool Utd	14+1	2		1				
				Free	16.07.86	Torquay Utd	116+4	7+1	7+1	16				
				Free	22.03.90	York City	35	4	1	3	2			1
				£15,000	22.03.90	Exeter City	56+10	2	3	4	8			
Toby Redwood					01.07.92	Exeter City (T)	1		0+1					
Alan Tonge	5.8	11.11	25.02.72	Bury	09.07.90	Manchester Utd. (T)								
Flg u18.1				N.C.	19.12.91	Exeter City	1+2							
Peter Whiston	6.0	11.6	04.01.68	Widnes		Plymouth A	4+6		1	1				
				Loan	21.03.90	Torquay Utd	8				1			
				Free	01.06.90	Torquay Utd	31+1	5	1	6		1		
				£25,000	13.09.91	Exeter City	36		5	4	3			1
MIDFIELD														
Eamonn Collins	5.8	8.13	22.10.65	Dublin		Blackpool				2				
Ei:Y,E1,u21.4,Y				Free	25.09.83	Southampton	1+2	1+1						
				Free	21.06.86	Portsmouth	4+1	0+1	0+1	1+2				
				Loan	19.11.87	Exeter City	8+1			1				
				Loan	19.11.88	Gillingham				1				
				Free	20.05.89	Colchester Utd	39	2	7	2	2	1		
				Free	20.06.92	Exeter City								
Scott Hiley	5.9	10.4	27.09.68	Plymouth	04.08.86	Exeter City (T)	172+5	13	12	11+2	9			
Div.4'90														
Craig Taylor					10.07.92	Exeter City (T)								
Steven C Williams	5.11	10.11	12.07.58	London	01.09.74	Southampton (A)	277+1	28+1	27	12	18	3	3	2
E:6,B4,u21.14,LC'87				£550,000	31.12.84	Arsenal	93+2	15	11		4	1		
				£300,000	05.08.88	Luton Town	39+1	5	2	2	1			
				Free	14.08.91	Exeter City	36	2	5	1				
FORWARDS														
Gary Chapman	5.8	11.0	01.05.64	Leeds		Frickley Athletic								
					27.09.88	Bradford City	2+3	0+1						
				Loan	13.09.89	Notts County								
				£15,000	23.02.90	Notts County	13+12			2+1	4			
				Loan	04.10.90	Mansfield Town	6							
				£10,000	05.09.91	Exeter City	17+3		3	2	4			
Eammon Dolan	5.10	12.1	20.09.67	Dagenham	01.04.85	West Ham U	9+6	4		1+1	3			1
Ei: u21.5				Loan	09.02.89	Bristol City	3							
				£30,000	31.12.90	Birmingham City	6+6	2		2	1			
				Swap	06.09.91	Exeter City	5+2							
Andrew Harris	6.0	12.0	17.11.69	Birmingham		Birmingham City (A)	0+1			0+1				
				Loan	17.10.91	Oxford Utd	1							
				Free	28.11.91	Exeter City	5+1		1+1					
John Hodge					12.09.91	Exeter City	16+7			2+2	1			
Gary Marshall	5.11	10.10	20.04.64	Shepton Mallet	11.07.83	Bristol City	48+20	3+3	3+4	6+4	7		2	
				Loan	21.01.84	Torquay Utd	7			2	1			
					13.07.88	Carlisle Utd	18+3	2	3	2	2			
				£50,000	20.07.89	Scunthorpe Utd	38+3	4	4	2	3			
				£22,000	19.10.90	Exeter City	48+11	1+1	3	2	6		1	2
Steve Moran	5.8	11.0	10.01.61	Croydon	24.08.79	Southampton (A)	173+7	17+3	18	10+1	78	6	12	3
E:u21.2				£300,000	11.09.86	Leicester City	35+8	5+2	1	0+1	14	3		
				£220,000	13.11.87	Reading	91+25	6	10+4	7	30	2	3	3
				Free	14.08.91	Exeter City	31+3	2	4	4	19		1	1
ADDITIONAL CONTRACT PLAYERS														
(M) Phil Lock	6.1	12.11	13.07.71	Launceston	21.07.89	Exeter City (T)				1				
Stephen Nute					24.07.89	Plymouth A								
				N.C.	26.03.91	Exeter City								
Martin Parker						Exeter City (T)	0+1							
Stuart Smith						Exeter City (T)								

LEADING LEAGUE GOALSCORERS SEASONS 1985-86 – 1991-92

1985-86	TONY KELLOW	9	1986-87	TONY KELLOW	15
1987-88	DEAN EDWARDS	12	1988-89	DARREN ROWBOTHAM	20
1989-90	DARREN ROWBOTHAM	20	1990-91	STEVE NEVILLE	12
			1991-92	STEVE MORAN	19

ST. JAMES PARK Well Street, Exeter, Devon EX4 6PX

Capacity: 8,960   **Covered Standing:** 3,200   **Seating:** 1,664

Tel: Ground: 0392 54073   **Ticket Sales:** As ground number   **Clubcall:** 0898 12 16 34

All premium rate calls (0898/0891) cost 36p per minute cheap rate and 48p per minute at all other times. Call costings correct at time of going to press.

ATTENDANCES
Highest: 20,984 v Sunderland, FA Cup 6th Round Replay, 4.3.1931

Lowest:

Record Receipts: £35,504 v Norwich City, FA Cup 3rd Round, 6.1.1990

Season Tickets:
Stands: £180, juv/OAP £115
Ground: from £115 to £138, juv/OAP £69

Executive Box Season Tickets: None

Cost of Stand Tickets: £8, OAP/Juv £5
Terraces: £5, £6, OAP/Juv £3

Match and Ticket Information: Tickets usually bookable up to two weeks prior to each match at 'The Near Post' (Tel: 0392 540073). Clubhouse 'Centre Spot' behind goal at opposite end to St James Road, refreshments in all areas

Car Parking: Use City car parks

Nearest Railway Station: Exeter St. Davids (0392 33551)

How to get to the ground

From North: Use Motorway M5 until junction 30. Leave Motorway and follow signs City Centre along Sidmouth Road for Heavitree Road, then at roundabout take 4th exit into Western Way and at roundabout take 2nd exit into Old Tiverton Road, then take next turning left into St. James Road for Exeter FC

From East: Use A30 (S.P. Exeter) into Heavitree Road, than at roundabout take 4th exit into Western Way and at Roundabout take 2nd exit into Old Tiverton Road, then take next turning left into St James Road for Exeter FC

From South and West: Use A38 and follow signs City Centre into Western Way and at roundabout take 3rd exit passing Coach Station, then at next roundabout take 2nd into Old Tiverton Road, and turn left into St. James Road for Exeter City

Value Rating: ★ ★ ★ ★

Programme Editor:

Price of 1992-93 Programme: £1
Number of Pages: 32
Subscriptions: £25 for full seasons League programmes (Cups not included)

Local Newspapers: Express & Echo, Western Morning News, Sunday Independent

Local Radio Stations: BBC Radio Devon, Devon Air

FULHAM

Division 2

Formed: 1879   **Turned Professional:** 1898   **Ltd Co:** 1903

SPONSORED BY: **NICKNAME:** The Cottagers

Chairman
Jimmy Hill

Directors
W F Muddyman (Vice-Chairman)
D E Shrimpton
C A Swain
A M Muddyman

Secretary
Mrs Janice O'Doherty (071-736 6561)

Chief Executive
Brian Naysmith

Manager
Don Mackay

Club Coach
Ray Lewington

Club Statistician for the Directory
Dennis Turner

FOR Fulham, 1991-92 was very much a 'season of two halves'. Until Christmas, it seemed that they had started where they had left off each of the two previous seasons, flirting with relegation to Division Four. A change of manager and one new signing, however, raised morale, and the Cottagers fought back to come within touching distance of the promotion play-off places. In the end, they failed to make the top six in the closing weeks, but it was, nevertheless, the Cottagers best placing for three years.

There was little to cheer in the opening weeks of the season. Early elimination from the Rumbelows League Cup was followed by the humiliation of a 0-2 home defeat by non-league Hayes in the First Round of the F.A. Cup. In the League, most of the best performances were reserved for away games. Impressive victories came at Bradford City and Bolton in October, once Arsenal's on loan striker Andrew Cole had settled in alongside Gary Brazil.

With the team out of both major Cup competitions and in the bottom third of the table, Fulham parted company with manager Alan Dicks in November 1991. His 18 months back in English football had not been a conspicuous success. Ray Lewington briefly resumed the reins, but in December he made way for Scotsman Don Mackay, recently displaced at Blackburn, but whose CV included spells at Bristol City and Coventry.

A top priority for the manager was a striker, and he brought in Sean Farrell from Luton, initially on loan. When he scored a hat-trick in Fulham's surprise win at promotion chasing West Brom on New Years Day, the move was made permanent. During 1992, the Cottagers form improved, and they picked up 44 of their 70 league points from the 26 matches played after January. There were still some nasty surprises, however, such as a home defeat by Fourth Division Wrexham in the Autoglass Trophy.

With two games to go, Fulham were in seventh place, their hopes relying more on mathematics than realism. Even these were crushed, when eventual champions Brentford ran out comfortable 4-0 winners at Griffin Park on a Sunday morning. In spite of this, it had been a relatively good season, even though results seemed to be more important than performances. With more encouraging news during the summer on the future of Craven Cottage, Fulham fans will start 1992-93 in good heart.
Dennis Turner

Back row L-R: Stacey North, Kelly Haag, Gavin Nebbeling, Glen Thomas, Martin Pike, Sean Farrell. **Second row:** Junior Lewis, Alan Gough, Jim Stannard, Gus Hurdle, Terry Bullivant (Youth Coach). **Third row:** Ray Lewington (Coach), Julian Hails, Paul Sheldrick, John Marshall, Leon Lewis, Jeff Eckhardt, Peter Baah, Martin Ferney, Jimmy Sugrue, Mark Tucker, Eric Deanus (Kit Manager). **Front row:** Mark Newsom, Lee Tierling, Udo Onwere, Don Mackay (Team Manager), Simon Morgan, Paul Kelly, Gary Brazil.

FULHAM

DIVISION THREE: 9th **FA CUP:** 1st RND **RUMBELOWS CUP:** 1st RND **AUTOGLASS:** Sth Q/FINALS

M	DATE		COMP.	VEN	OPPONENTS	RESULT	H/T	LGE POS	GOALSCORERS/GOAL TIMES	ATTEN- DANCE
1	A	17	BL	A	Chester City	L 0-2	0-1			(1,444)
2		21	RC 1/1	A	**Charlton Athletic**	L 2-4	0-2		Brazil 51, 55	(3,027)
3		24	BL	H	Birmingham City	L 0-1	0-1	22		4,762
4		27	RC 1/2	H	**Charlton Athletic**	D 1-1	1-1		Browne 16	3,543
5		31	BL	A	Torquay United	W 1-0	0-0	18	Onwere 70	(3,299)
6	S	3	BL	H	West Bromwich A.	D 0-0	0-0	19		4,523
7		7	BL	H	Swansea City	W 3-0	1-0	10	Pike 43, 47, Brazil 88	3,426
8		14	BL	A	Stoke City	D 2-2	0-1	11	Cole 56, Newsom 75	(10,567)
9		17	BL	A	Bury	L 1-3	1-2	16	Thomas 9	(2,248)
10		21	BL	H	Leyton Orient	W 2-1	1-1	12	Eckhardt 40, Haag 80	4,934
11		27	BL	A	Bournemouth	D 0-0	0-0	13		(6,450)
12	O	5	BL	H	Brentford	L 0-1	0-1	15		7,710
13		12	BL	A	Bradford City	W 4-3	3-1	13	Newsom 2, Onwere 6, Brazil 18, Haag 74	(5,142)
14		19	BL	A	Bolton Wanderers	W 3-0	1-0	9	Brazil 33, 70, Cole 72	(5,152)
15		23	AGT Pre	A	**Maidstone United**	W 6-2	2-1		Brazil 3 (12, 48, 66), Pike 44, Haag 88, 89	(937)
16		26	BL	H	Preston North End	W 1-0	1-0	7	Morgan 41	4,022
17	N	2	BL	H	Hull City	D 0-0	0-0	6		3,365
18		6	BL	A	Huddersfield Town	L 1-3	1-1	9	Onwere 16	(5,064)
19		9	BL	A	Hartlepool United	L 0-2	0-1	12		(2,999)
20		15	FAC 1	H	**Hayes**	L 0-2	0-0			6,404
21		20	AGT Pre	H	**Gillingham**	W 2-0	1-0		Morgan 12, Cole 67	1,108
22		23	BL	H	Stockport County	L 1-2	0-0	13	Cole 79	3,680
23		30	BL	A	Darlington	L 1-3	0-1	15	Brazil 49	(2,655)
24	D	21	BL	A	Birmingham City	L 1-3	0-1	16	Brazil 73	(5,877)
25		26	BL	H	Torquay United	W 2-1	2-1	15	Farrell 12, Morgan 43	4,186
26		28	BL	H	Chester City	D 2-2	0-0	17	Thomas 54, Scott 73	3,708
27	J	1	BL	A	West Bromwich A.	W 3-2	2-1	15	Farrell 3 (3, 20, 67)	(16,442)
28		11	BL	A	Peterborough Utd	L 1-4	0-1	15	Newsom (pen) 82	(4,975)
29		14	AGT 1	H	**Gillingham**	W 2-0	1-0		Marshall 36, Morgan 48	1,483
30		18	BL	H	Shrewsbury Town	L 0-1	0-0	16		3,440
31		25	BL	A	Exeter City	D 1-1	0-1	15	Brazil 64	(4,002)
32		28	BL	H	Wigan Athletic	D 1-1	0-1	15	Morgan 64	2,465
33	F	1	BL	H	Bolton Wanderers	D 1-1	1-0	16	M Kelly 43	3,804
34		8	BL	A	Preston North End	W 2-1	2-0	13	Brazil 16, Farrell 29	(2,988)
35		11	BL	H	Darlington	W **4-0**	1-0	12	Brazil 43, 78, Farrell 57, Eckhardt 77	3,878
36		15	BL	A	Reading	W 2-0	0-0	12	Eckhardt 60, Farrell 61	(4,388)
37		22	BL	H	Peterborough Utd	L 0-1	0-1	12		5,233
38		25	AGT SQF	H	**Wrexham**	L 0-2	0-0			2,236
39		28	BL	A	Wigan Athletic	W 2-0	1-0	10	Eckhardt 5, Farrell 75	(2,202)
40	M	3	BL	A	Shrewsbury Town	D 0-0	0-0	10		(2,137)
41		7	BL	H	Exeter City	D 0-0	0-0	10		3,957
42		10	BL	H	Huddersfield Town	W 1-0	0-0	10	Eckhardt 55	3,134
43		14	BL	A	Hull City	D 0-0	0-0	11		(3,742)
44		20	BL	H	Hartlepool United	W 1-0	1-0	10	Haag 8	4,359
45		27	BL	A	Stockport County	L 0-2	0-1	11		(4,654)
46		31	BL	H	Stoke City	D 1-1	1-0	11	Haag 20	5,779
47	A	4	BL	A	Swansea City	D 2-2	0-1	11	Hails 49, Eckhardt 68	(3,307)
48		7	BL	H	Reading	W 1-0	0-0	10	Eckhardt 70	3,499
49		11	BL	H	Bury	W 4-2	3-0	10	Brazil 17, 35, Thomas 33, Haag 52	4,060
50		18	BL	A	Leyton Orient	W 1-0	0-0	10	Farrell 72	(7,094)
51		20	BL	H	Bournemouth	W 2-0	0-0	7	Brazil 74, Farrell 84	7,619
52		26	BL	A	Brentford	L **0-4**	0-4	8		(12,071)
53	M	2	BL	H	Bradford City	W 2-1	2-1	9	Brazil 5, Haag 32	8,671

Best Home League Attendance: 8,671 v Bradford City   **Smallest: 2,465 v Wigan Athletic**   **Av Home Att: 4,531**

Goal Scorers: **Compared with 90-91: +474**

League (57): Brazil 14, Farrell 10, Eckhardt 7, Haag 6, Cole 3, Morgan 3, Newsom 3 (1 pen), Thomas 3, Onwere 3, Pike 2, Hails, Scott, M Kelly

R/lows C (3): Brazil 2, Browne

FA Cup (0):

Other (10): Brazil 3, Morgan 2, Haag 2, Pike, Marshall, Cole

Stannard J.	Marshall J.	Pike M.	Newson M.	Eckhardt J.	Thomas G.	Scott P.	Onwere U.	Haag K.	Brazil G.	Morgan S.	Milton S.	Cobb G.	Georgiou G.	Baker G.	Browne C.	Kelly P.	Cole A. (L)	Nebbeling G.	Kelly M.	Harrison (L)	Finch J.	Farrell S.	Byrne D. (L)	Hails J.	Tucker M.	Referee	
1	2	3	4	5	6	7	8•	9*	10	11	12	14														L Dilkes	1
1	2	3•	4	5	6	7	8	9*	10	11	12	14														M James	2
1	2	3		5	6	7	8•	9*	10	11		4	12	14												D Axcell	3
1	2	3		5	6		8	S	10	11				9	7*	4	12									M Bailey	4
1	2	3	4	5	6	14	8		10				12	9*	7	11•										K Cooper	5
1	2	3	4	5	6	11	8•	9	10	S		14		7												M Pierce	6
1	2	3	4	5	6•	11	8	12	10	14				7*				9								I Borrett	7
1	2	3	4	5	6	11	8		10	S			12					9	7*							R Shepherd	8
1	2	3	4	5	6	11	8		10	S			12					9	7*							A Dawson	9
1	2	3	4	5	6	11	8	12	10	S		7*						9								M Bodenham	10
1	2	3	4	5	6	11	8	S	10	14		7•						9								P Scoble	11
1	2	3	4	5	6	11	8	12	10			7*						9	S							B Hill	12
1	2	3	4	5	6	11	8	12	10		7	S						9*								G Courtney	13
1	2	3	4	5	6	11	8	S	10		7	S						9								J Kirkby	14
1		3	4		6	11	8	14	10•	7*		2						9	12	5						R Bigger	15
1	2	3	4	5	6	11	8*	14	10		7	12						9•								G Willard	16
1	2	3	4	5	6	11	8	12	10		7							9	S	5*						D Shadwell	17
1	2	3	4		6	11	8	S	10		7	14						9	5•							I Hendrick	18
1	2	3	4		6	11	8	5	10		7	14						9•	S							M Peck	19
1	2	3	4		6	11	8	9	10		7	5						S	S							P Alcock	20
		3	4				8			12	10*	7	2			11•		9	5	14	1	6				I Hemley	21
1	2	S	4	5	6	11	8*		10		7	12						9	3							G Poll	22
1	2	3	4•	5	6	11	8	9	10		7	S									14					R Nixon	23
1	8	3*	2	4	6	11•	12	14	10		7										5	9				W Flood	24
1	2*	3	4	5	6	11	12	S	10		7										8	9				P Danson	25
1	2	3	4	5	6	11	S	S	10		7										8	9				P Foakes	26
1	8	3	2	4	6	11	12	S	10		7										5*	9				P Harrison	27
1	8•	3	2	4*	6	11	12	14	10		7										5	9				D Frampton	28
1	2	3	4*	5	6	11	8•	14	10		7										12	9				R Hamer	29
1	2	3	5•		6		8*	14	10		7								4		9			11	12	M Reed	30
1	2	3	8		6		S	S	10		5					4			11		9			7		C Wilkes	31
1	2	3	5*		6		12	14	10		7					8			4		9•			11		P Durkin	32
1	2	3	5		6	4	12		10		7								11		9*	8		S		B Gunn	33
1	2	3	5		6	4	12		10		7								11•		9*	8		14		A Dawson	34
1	2	3	5		6	4	12		10		7								11		9*	8•		14		R Bigger	35
1	2	3	5		6	4	S		10		7					S			11		9	8				K Cooper	36
1	2	3	5		6	4	12		10		7					S			11*		9	8				R Gifford	37
1		3	5		6	4	12		10		7					14			11*	2•	9	8				B Gunn	38
1	2	3	8		6	4	12		10		S					S		5	11		9			7*		S Bell	39
1	2	3	8		6	4	12		10		S					S		5	11		9*			7		R Poulain	40
1	2	3	8		6	4	11		10		7					S		5			9*			12		K Morton	41
1	2	3	8		6	4	11		10		7					S		5			9			S		G Poll	42
1	2	3	8		6	14	11		10		7					4•		5			9			S		A Bennett	43
1	4	3	7		6		11		10							S		5	8		9			S	2	J Deakin	44
1	2	3•	7		6	14	11		10	4						5*			8		9			12		D Phillips	45
1	4	3	7		6	S	11		10	2						5			8		9			S		G Singh	46
1	4	3	7		6	S	11		10	2						5			8		9*			12		J Rushton	47
1	4	3	7		6	9	11		10	2						5			8*					12	S	R Pawley	48
1•		3	7		6	9	12		11	10						2		5	8				4*	14		G Willard	49
1		3	5	7	6	4	12		11	10						2			9*			8		S		K Cooper	50
1		3	6	7	8	S	11		10	2								5			9	4				P Foakes	51
1		3	12	7	6*	4•	11		10									5	14		9	8				I Borrett	52
1	S	3	2	7	6	4	11•		10									5	14		9	8				G Ashby	53
46	41	45	25	43	45	37	19	18	46		34	4	1	3	1	3	13	16	19		5	25	5	11	1	League Appearances	
	1				2	8	16		2		1		7	3		1			2		1			7	1	Substitute Appearances	
2	2	2	1	2	2	1	2	1	2	2	0+1	0+1	1			1	1	1	0+1							R/lows Appearances	
1	1	1	1		1	1	1	1	1	1	1					1										FA Cup Appearances	
3	1	4	3	2	3	3	0+4	4	4	2		2				1	2	1+1	2+1		2+1	2		1		Autoglass Appearances	

Players on Loan: A Cole (Arsenal), L Harrison (Charlton), D Byrne (Reading)

FULHAM

Club Colours: White shirts with black trim, white shorts and white stockings with black trim
Change Colours: All red
Reserves League: Football Combination   **Youth League:** S E Counties

Previous Name: Fulham St. Andrews 1879-98
Previous League: Southern League
Previous Managers: 1904-09 Harry Bradshaw   1909-24 Phil Kelso   1924-26 Andy Ducat   1926-29 Joe Bradshaw   1929-31 Ned Liddell   1931-34 James McIntyre   1934-35 Jimmy Hogan   1935 Joe Edelston (acting)   1935-48 Jack Peart   1948-49 Frank Osborne   1949-53 Bill Dodgin   1956-58 Dug Livingstone   1958-64 Bedford Jezzard   1964-65 Arthur Stevens (acting)   1965-68 Vic Buckingham   1968 Bobby Robson   1968 Johnny Haynes (acting)   1968-72 Bill Dodgin (jnr)   1972-76 Alec Stock   1976-80 Bobby Campbell   1980-84 Malcolm Macdonald   1984-86 Ray Harford   1986-90 Ray Lewington   1990-91 Alan Dicks   1991 Ray Lewington (caretaker)   1991- Don Mackay
Honours: Champions Div 2, 1948-49   Champions Div 3S 1931-32
League Career: Elected to Div 2 1907   Relegated to Div 3S 1927-28   Promoted to Div 2 1931-32   Promoted to Div 1 1948-49   Relegated to Div 2 1951-52   Promoted to Div 1 1958-59   Relegated to Div 2 1967-68   Relegated to Div 3 1968-69   Promoted to Div 2 1970-71   Relegated to Div 3 1979-80   Promoted to Div 2 1981-82   Relegated to Div 3 1985-86

CLUB RECORDS

Most Appearances for Club: Johnny Haynes 1952-70: 594
Most Capped Player: Johnny Haynes 56, England
Record Goalscorer in a Match: Ronnie Rooke 6 v Bury, 6-0, FA Cup Round 3, 7.1.1939
Record League Goalscorer in a Season: Frank Newton 43, Div 3S, 1931-32
Record League Goalscorer in a Career: Gordon Davies, 158, 1978-84, 1986-91   **In All Competitions:** Gordon Davies, 178 (League 158, F.A. Cup 8, Lge Cup 11, AMC 1) 1978-84, 1986-91
Record Transfer Fee Received: £333,333 from Liverpool for Richard Money, May 1980
Record Transfer Fee Paid: £150,000 to Orient for Peter Kitchen, February 1979   £150,000 to Brighton for Teddy Maybank, December 1979
Best Performances: League: 10th Div 1 1959-60   **FA Cup:** Finalists 1974-75   **League Cup:** 5th Round 1967-68, 1970-71
Most League Points: (3pts a win) 78, Div 3, 1981-82   (2pts a win) 60, Div 2, 1958-59   60, Div 3, 1970-71
Most League Goals: 111, Div 3S, 1931-32
Record League Victory and Most Goals Scored in a League Match: 10-1 v Ipswich Town, Div 1, 26.9.1963   (Fulham also beat Torquay 10-2, Div 3, 10.9.1931)
Record Cup Victory and Most Goals Scored in a Cup Tie: 6-0 v Wimbledon, FA Cup Rnd 1 Replay, 1930-31   6-0 v Bury, FA Cup Round 3, 7.1.1939   8-3 v Luton Town (a), 1st Round FA Cup, 1907-08
Record League Defeat: 0-9 v Wolverhampton Wanderers, Div 1, 16.9.1959
Record Cup Defeat: 0-10 v Liverpool, Littlewoods Cup, 2nd Round, 23.9.1986
Oldest Player in a League Match: Jimmy Sharpe 40 years, April 1920 (Played in an emergency and scored his only goal for the club many years after officially retiring!)
Youngest Player in a League Match: Tony Mahoney, 16 years, 1976

LONGEST RUNS

of undefeated matches: 15 (1957, 1970)	**of league matches without a win:** 15 (1950)
of undefeated home matches: 28 (1921-22)	**of undefeated away matches:** 9 (1958, 1970)
without home win: 8 (1950, 1951-52, 1961-62, 1980)	**without an away win:** 31 (1964-66)
of league wins: 8 (1963)	**of home wins:** 12 (1959)
of league defeats: 11 (1961-62)	**of away wins:** 5 (1966, 1981)

FULHAM

PLAYERS NAME / Honours	Ht	Wt	Birthdate	Birthplace / Transfers	Contract Date	Clubs	League	L/Cup	FA Cup	Other	Lg	L/C	FAC	Oth
GOALKEEPERS														
Alan Gough	5.10		10.03.71	Watford	01.01.01	Shelbourne								
Ei:u21.3					13.10.88	Portsmouth								
				Loan	26.03.92	Fulham								
				Free	25.06.92	Fulham								
Jim Stannard	6.0	13.6	06.10.62	Harold Hill	05.06.80	Fulham	41	3	1					
				Loan	17.09.84	Southend Utd	6							
				Loan	01.02.85	Charlton Ath	1							
				Loan	28.03.85	Southend Utd	11							
					08.07.85	Southend Utd	92	6	4	5				
				£50,000	14.08.87	Fulham	223	12	8	12	1			
DEFENDERS														
Jeff Eckhardt	6.0	11.7	07.10.65	Sheffield	23.08.84	Sheffield Utd	73+1	7	2	5	2			
					20.11.87	Fulham	183+2	9	3+1	9	14			
Simon Morgan	5.10	11.7	05.09.66	Birmingham	15.11.84	Leicester City	147+13	14	4+1	3	2	1		
E: u21.2				£100,000	12.10.90	Fulham	66+2	2	4	6	4			2
Gavin Nebbeling	6.0	12.4	15.05.63	Johannesburg		Arcadia Sh								
					05.08.81	Crystal Palace	145+6	8+1	5	8	8			
				Loan	23.10.85	Northampton T	11			1				
				£80,000	31.07.89	Fulham	57+1	2	3	3+1				
				Loan	12.12.91	Hereford Utd	3		1					
Mark Newson	5.11	12.0	07.12.60	Stepney	15.12.78	Charlton Ath								
E: SP.5; Div3'87						Maidstone Utd			12				3	
				Free	24.05.85	Bournemouth	172+5	12	11	4+1	23	2	2	
				£125,000	28.02.90	Fulham	72+1	3	4	5	4			
Stacey North	6.2	12.6	25.11.64	Luton	05.08.82	Luton Town (A)	24+1	1						
E: Y.1				Loan	22.11.85	Wolverhampton W	3							
				£100,000	06.01.87	West Brom A	96+2	5	6	1				
				£135,000	04.10.90	Fulham	38		3	2				
Martin Pike	5.10	11.7	21.10.64	South Shields	26.10.82	West Brom A. (A)								
				Free	18.08.83	Peterborough U	119+7	8	10	5	8			1
				£20,000	22.08.86	Sheffield Utd	127+2	10	12	5+1	5			
				Loan	10.11.89	Tranmere Rovers	2	2	1					
				Loan	14.12.89	Bolton W	5			1	1			
				£65,000	08.02.90	Fulham	110+1	4	4	7	7		1	1
Glen Thomas	6.1	11.0	06.10.67	London	09.10.85	Fulham (A)	159+5	13	6	9+1	6			
MIDFIELD														
Mark Kelly	5.8	10.4	07.10.66	Blackpool	07.12.85	Shrewsbury Town								
WC'88				Free	01.07.87	Cardiff City	93+12	7	6+1	9	2			
				£31,000	02.07.90	Fulham	36+3	2	2	2+1	1			
John Marshall	5.9	11.4	18.08.64	Balham	20.08.82	Fulham (A)	293+13	25	12+1	15	23	2	3	2
FORWARDS														
Peter Baah	5.9	10.4	01.05.73	Littleborough	14.06.91	Blackburn Rovers (T)	1							
				Loan	08.04.92	Rotherham Utd								
				Free	03.07.92	Fulham								
Gary Brazil	5.11	9.13	19.09.62	Tunbridge Wells		Crystal Palace (A)								
				f	11.08.80	Sheffield Utd	39+23	4+1	4+5	1+1	9		1	
				Loan	24.08.84	Port Vale	6				3			
				£12,500	15.02.85	Preston N.E	163+3	13	10	13	58	6	3	5
				£50,000+P	09.02.89	Newcastle Utd	7+16	1+1	0+1	0+1	2	1		
				Loan	06.09.90	Fulham								
				£110,000	02.11.90	Fulham	87+1	2	4	7	18	2	1	3
Gary Cobb	5.8	11.5	06.08.68	Luton	05.08.86	Luton Town (A)	6+3			1				
				Loan	13.10.88	Northampton T	1							
				Loan	14.08.89	Swansea City	5	2		1				
					19.10.90	Fulham	8+14	0+1	2	2				
Sean Farrell	6.1	12.08	28.02.69	Watford	01.07.87	Luton Town (T)	14+11		2+1	1+2	1		1	2
				Loan	01.03.88	Colchester Utd	4+5				1			
				Loan	13.09.91	Northampton T	4				1			
				£100,000	19.12.91	Fulham	25			2	10			
ADDITIONAL CONTRACT PLAYERS														
(M) Martin Fearney	5.11		08.11.71	Lambeth	11.07.90	Fulham (T)	12+2		0+1	1+2				
Kelly Haag	6.0	12.3	06.10.70	Middlesex		Brentford (T)	1+4	0+1	0+1					
				Free	21.08.90	Fulham	30+27	1+1	2	0+5	9			3
Julian Hails					29.08.90	Fulham	11	7		1	1			
Agustus Hurdle					17.07.92	Fulham								
Paul L M Kelly					02.07.92	Fulham (T)	3	0+1		1				
Karl J Lewis					03.07.92	Fulham (T)								
Leon Lewis					03.07.92	Fulham (T)								
(M) Udo Onwere	5.10		09.11.71	Hammersmith	11.07.90	Fulham (T)	24+10	2	1	3	4			
Paul Sheldrick					02.07.92	Fulham (T)								
Lee Tierling					22.07.91	Portsmouth (T)								
				Free	22.05.92	Fulham								
(D) Mark Tucker	6.0		27.04.72	Woking	11.07.90	Fulham (T)	1+1							
Terence Victory					28.12.90	Fulham								

LEADING LEAGUE GOALSCORERS SEASONS 1985-86 – 1991-92

1985-86	**DEAN CONEY**	12	1986-87	**DEAN CONEY**	10
1987-88	**LEROY ROSENIOR**	20	1988-89	**GORDON DAVIES**	14
1989-90	**CLIVE WALKER**	13	1990-91	**GORDON DAVIES**	6

1991-92 **GARY BRAZIL** **14**

CRAVEN COTTAGE Stevenage Road, Fulham, London SW6 6HH

Capacity: 17,304   **Covered Standing:** 1,500   **Seating:** 7,214

Tel: Ground: 071 736 6561   **Ticket Sales:** As ground number   **Call-line:** 0891 660 222

All premium rate calls (0898/0891) cost 36p per minute cheap rate and 48p per minute at all other times. Call costings correct at time of going to press.

ATTENDANCES
Highest: 49,335 v Millwall, Div 2, 8.10.1938

Lowest: 1,317 v Notts County, Leyland Daf Cup, 28.11.1989

Record Receipts: £80,247 v Chelsea, Div 2, 8.10.1983

CRAVEN COTTAGE
First game: v Minerva, 5-0, Middx Snr Cup, 10.10.1896
First floodlit game: v Sheff. Wed, 4-1, League, Sept 1962

Season Tickets:
Stands: £168.30 to £184.80, juv/OAP £56.10 to £61.60
Ground: £105.60 to £118.80, juv/OAP £35.20 to £39.60
Family Enclosure: £168.30

Executive Box Season Tickets: Riversides' Club £250.80

Cost of Stand Tickets: Stevenage Road & Eric Miller: £9, juv/OAP £3; Family Enclosure: £9, juv/OAP £2.50
Terraces: Hammersmith Terrace: £6, juv/OAP £2; Putney Terrace: £7, juv/OAP £4; Stevenage Road Enclosure: £6.50, juv/OAP £2.50

Match and Ticket Information: Computerised. Bookable daily during season 9.30-4.30

Car Parking: Ample in adjacent streets

Nearest Railway Station: Putney

Nearest Tube Station: Putney Bridge

How to get to the ground

From North: Use Motorway M1 S.P. London then take North Circular Road A406 S.P. West to Neasden follow signs Harlesden A404, then Hammersmith A219 and at Broadway follow sign Fulham and in 1m turn right into Harbord Street and at end turn left for Fulham FC
From East & South: Use South Circular Road A205 and take sign Putney Bridge A219. Cross bridge and follow sign Hammersmith and in 0.5m turn left into Bishops Park Road and at end turn right for Fulham FC
From West: Use Motorway M4 then A4 and in 2m branch left S.P. other routes into Hammersmith Broadway, follow sign Fulham A219 and in 1m turn right into Harbord Street and at end turn left for Fulham FC

Value Rating: ★ ★ ★ ★

Programme Editor: David Gore

Price of 1992-93 Programme: £1.30
Number of Pages: 32
Subscriptions: All League & Cup matches £38.00

Local Newspapers: Fulham Chronicle, Hammersmith & Fulham Times

Local Radio Stations: LBC, Capital Radio

Additional Publications on Club: A Complete Record 1879-1987. By Dennis Turner and Alex White, Breedon Books £14.95

GILLINGHAM

Division 3

Formed: 1893   **Turned Professional:** 1894   **Ltd Co:** 1893

SPONSORED BY: Medway Toyota   **NICKNAME:** The Gills

President
J W Leech

Vice-Presidents
G C Goodere
G V W Lukehurst
G V Kemsley
M Bradley
A Taylor

Chairman
B R Baker

Vice-Chairman
Rt Hon Earl Henry Sondes

Directors
A Smith (Managing)
P H Giles (Financial)
G T Carney (Legal)
M G Lukehurst

Chief Executive/Secretary
Barry W Bright (0634 851854/576828)

Team Manager
Damien Richardson

Assistant Manager
Ron Hillyard

Physiotherapist
Javed Mughal

General Manager
Bill Williams

Community Officer
Phil Attfield

Club Statistician for the Directory
Roger Triggs

GILLINGHAM finished in a disappointing 11th place in Division Four this season after much had been expected from the team. It was the goals against which contributed to the club not being amongst the front-runners. As manager Damien Richardson expressed at the end of the season, "We have to stop making silly errors at the back. The more clean sheets we keep the brighter our chances of succcess".

Richardson was busy in the close season searching for players to strengthen the squad but made only major signing – defender Paul Clark from Southend United. He went onto to become a large influence on the side and it was no surprise when he walked away with the 'Player of the Year' awards.

The cup competitions also brought little cheer; in the Rumbelows Cup Portsmouth overcome us 6-4 on aggregate in the First Round. In the FA Cup Gillingham put up a supreme effort at Third Division leaders Brentford to gain a 3-3 draw in front of the Sky cameras, only to disappoint in the replay at Priestfield in front of the highest gate of the season. A 2-0 defeat at Fulham accounted for us in the First Round of the Autoglass Trophy.

Although the club has a loyal following of supporters, our average League attendance for the season was only 3,185, the lowest in the club's history. As with all lower Division clubs, money is tight and the sale of forward Peter Beadle to Tottenham for in excess of £350,000 has certainly helped the club's budget. It's these younger players that the club is looking to and during the season, many of them were blooded in the first team and certainty did not let the side down.

Other arrivals during the season were Neil Smith (Tottenham), Lawrence Osborne (Maidstone), and Richard Green (Swindon), whilst Karl Elsey, Tim O'Shea and Mike Trusson all left the club for pastures new. Season 1992-93 is Gillingham's centenary and the mood around Priestfield is being accompanied by an air of expectancy unsurpassed in recent years. Damien Richardson has made a number of important signings during the summer of 1992 to mount a determined promotion challenge.

Roger Triggs

Back row L-R: Richard Carpenter, Nick Forster, Mark Dempsey, Neil Smith, Eliot Martin, Mark O'Connor, Joe Dunne, David Crown. **Middle row:** Pat Hilton (Youth Team Manager), Richard Green, Tony Butler, Scott Barrett, Trevor Aylott, Harvey Lim, Brian Clarke, Gary Breen, Javed Mughal (Physio). **Front row:** Lawrence Osbourne, Steve Lovell, Liburd Henry, Damien Richardson (First Team Manager), Paul Clark (Captain), Ron Hillyard, Tony Eeles, Lee Palmer.

GILLINGHAM

DIVISION FOUR: 11th   **FA CUP:** 1st RND   **RUMBELOWS CUP:** 1st RND   **AUTOGLASS:** 1st RND

M	DATE		COMP.	VEN	OPPONENTS	RESULT		H/T	LGE POS	GOALSCORERS/GOAL TIMES	ATTEN-DANCE
1	A	17	BL	H	Scunthorpe United	W	4-0	1-0	1	Elsey 23, Crown 50, O'Connor 59, Beadle 87	3,480
2		20	RC 1/1	A	Portsmouth	L	1-2	0-1		Beadle 76	(4,801)
3		24	BL	A	York City	D	1-1	0-1	4	Crown 52	(2,324)
4		27	RC 1/2	H	Portsmouth	L	3-4	1-2		Crown 38, Walker 46, Beadle 85	5,114
5	S	4	BL	A	Hereford United	L	0-2	0-1	12		(2,544)
6		7	BL	H	Scarborough	W	2-0	0-0	10	Arnott 84, Lovell 87	3,375
7		14	BL	A	Wrexham	L	1-2	1-2	11	Elsey 40	(1,602)
8		17	BL	A	Blackpool	L	0-2	0-1	14		(3,035)
9		21	BL	H	Barnet	D	3-3	2-2	15	Eeles 1, Crown 30, 64	4,864
10		28	BL	A	Crewe Alexandra	L	1-2	0-1	16	Trusson (pen) 72	(3,126)
11	O	5	BL	H	Chesterfield	L	0-1	0-1	19		2,835
12		12	BL	A	Halifax Town	W	3-0	1-0	13	Crown 3, 63, Beadle 46	(1,435)
13		19	BL	A	Doncaster Rovers	D	1-1	0-0	14	Lovell 50	(1,468)
14		26	BL	H	Northampton Town	W	3-1	0-0	13	Crown 3 (58, 60, 80)	2,544
15	N	2	BL	A	Carlisle United	D	0-0	0-0	13		(1,672)
16		5	BL	H	Cardiff City	D	0-0	0-0	13		2,641
17		9	BL	H	Maidstone United	D	1-1	0-0	13	O'Connor 80	6,716
18		18	FAC 1	A	Brentford	D	3-3	1-2		Walker 45, 73, Smith 83	(5,830)
19		20	AGT Pre	A	Fulham	L	0-2	0-1			(1,108)
20		23	BL	A	Mansfield Town	L	3-4	2-2	14	Lovell 9, Crown 26, Arnott 48	(3,287)
21		26	FAC 1R	H	Brentford	L	1-3	0-1		Walker 88	7,328
22	D	10	AGT Pre	H	Maidstone United	W	4-2	2-0	13	Smith 23, 90, Crown 41, Haylock (og) 51	2,300
23		14	BL	A	Rotherham United	D	1-1	1-0	13	Crown 35	(3,137)
24		21	BL	H	York City	D	1-1	0-0	15	Crown 89	2,711
25		26	BL	A	Scunthorpe United	L	0-2	0-1	15		(3,883)
26	J	1	BL	H	Hereford United	W	2-1	2-1	15	Lovell 18, Smith 19	3,392
27		4	BL	A	Lincoln City	L	0-1	0-0	15		(2,169)
28		11	BL	H	Walsall	W	4-0	4-0	12	Crown 3 (1, 26, 44), Elsey 12	2,715
29		14	AGT 1	A	Fulham	L	0-2	0-1			(1,483)
30		18	BL	A	Burnley	L	1-4	1-1	14	Walker 19	(8,908)
31	F	1	BL	H	Doncaster Rovers	W	2-1	1-0	13	Smith 7, O'Connor 58	2,366
32		8	BL	A	Northampton Town	D	0-0	0-0	11		(3,007)
33		15	BL	H	Rotherham United	W	5-1	4-1	10	Lovell 3 (9, 11, 62), Dempsey 19, Crown 30	2,486
34		22	BL	A	Walsall	W	1-0	1-0	10	Dempsey 4	(2,987)
35		29	BL	H	Lincoln City	L	1-3	1-0	10	Lovell 30	3,160
36	M	3	BL	H	Burnley	W	3-0	1-0	10	Crown 42 secs, Beadle 64, Lovell 70	3,729
37		7	BL	A	Rochdale	L	1-2	1-0	12	Crown 6	(1,941)
38		10	BL	A	Cardiff City	W	3-2	1-2	10	Green 11, 48, Crown 79	(8,521)
39		14	BL	H	Carlisle United	L	1-2	0-1	10	Crown 86	2,789
40		17	BL	H	Rochdale	D	0-0	0-0	10		2,300
41		21	BL	A	Maidstone United	D	1-1	0-1	10	Lovell 88	(3,264)
42		28	BL	H	Mansfield Town	W	2-0	2-0	10	Lovell 6, Beadle 36	2,682
43		31	BL	A	Wrexham	W	2-1	2-0	10	Lovell (pen) 17, Green 35	3,078
44	A	4	BL	A	Scarborough	L	1-2	0-0	10	Crown 70	(1,174)
45		11	BL	H	Blackpool	W	3-2	1-1	10	Lovell 14, Crown 48, Beadle 69	3,684
46		18	BL	A	Barnet	L	0-2	0-1	10		(4,049)
47		20	BL	A	Crewe Alexandra	L	0-1	0-0	11		2,928
48		25	BL	A	Chesterfield	D	3-3	1-1	11	Thomas 40, Lovell 59, Green 75	(2,109)
49	M	2	BL	H	Halifax Town	W	2-0	0-0	11	Lovell 83, 88 (pen)	2,413

Best Home League Attendance: 6,716 v Maidstone United	Smallest: 2,300 v Rochdale	Av Home Att: 3,185
Goal Scorers:		**Compared with 90-91: -322**

League (63):	Crown 22, Lovell 16 (2 pens), Beadle 5, Green 4, O'Connor 3, Elsey 3, Arnott 2, Dempsey 2, Smith 2, Trusson (1 pen), Eeles Walker, Thomas
R/lows C (4):	Beadle 2, Crown, Walker
FA Cup (4):	Walker 3, Smith
Autoglass (4):	Smith 2, Crown, Opponents

1991-92

Lim H.	O'Shea T.	Palmer L.	Elsey K.	Walker A.	Butler P.	Clark P.	Lovell S.	Crown D.	O'Connor M.	Eeles A.	Trusson M.	Beadle P.	Martin E.	Arnott A.	Clarke B.	Dempsey M.	Carpenter R.	Branagan K. (L)	Smith N.	Polston A. (L)	Berkley A.	Thomas R.	Osborne L.	Dunne J.	Green R. (L)	Referee	
1	2	3	4	5	6	7	8	9•	10	11	12	14														P Scoble	1
1	2		4	5	6	7	8	9•	10	11*	12	14	3													J Carter	2
1	2		4	5	6	7	8•	9	10	11*	12	14	3													P Danson	3
1	2	3	4*	5	6	7	8	9	10•	11	12	14														G Pooley	4
1	2	3†	4*	5	6	7	8	9	10*	11	12	14														A Bennett	5
1	2	3	4*	5		7	8		10	11	12	9•		14	6											M James	6
1	2		4*	5		7	8		10	11	3•	9		14	6	12										R Gifford	7
1	2		4	5		7	9	12	10*	11	3	8•			6	14										J Kirkby	8
1	2		4	5		7	14	8	10	11		9•			6	12	3*									M Pierce	9
1	2		3*	5		7	14	8	10•	11	4	9			6	12										P Vanes	10
1	2		3•	5		7	10	8	14	11	4		9*		6	12										M Bailey	11
	2		3	5		7	10	8	11		4	6	9*		12		S		1							J Watson	12
	2*		3	5		7	10	8	11	4		6	9				S		12							J Lloyd	13
	2		3	5		7	8	10	11	6*		9			12		S		4							P Taylor	14
	2		3	5		7	10	8	11*	6		9			S		12		4							A Wilkie	15
	2		3	5		7	10	8	11	6*		9•		14		12			4							D Axcell	16
	2		3*	5		7	10	8	11	S		12	9			6			4							R Pawley	17
1	2		3	5		7	10	8	11	14		9*			12	6			4•							J Carter	18
1				12		7	10		11				3	9*	5	6*	8	4		2		14				I Hemley	19
1	2		3•	5*		7	10	8	11	14			9			6	12		4							R Hart	20
1	2		3•	5		7	10	8	11	14			9*			6			4							J Carter	21
	2		S	5		7	10	8	11			9				6•			4	3		14				R Wiseman	22
1	2			5		7	10	8	11			14		9•		S			4	3			6			R Nixon	23
1	2		3	5		7	10	8	11			14		12		9•			4				6•			R Lewis	24
1	2		3•	5		7	10	8	11*	12		9		14		6			4							W Burns	25
1	2					7	10	8	11			9*	3	12	5	6			4•			14				K Morton	26
1	2	14	12			7	10	8*	11				3	9•	5	6*	8		4							D Shadwell	27
1	2	9	5*			7	8	10	11				3		12	6•			4			14				I Borrett	28
1	2	9*				7	8	10	11				3	12	5	6*			4			14				R Hamer	29
1	2	9	5•			7	10	8*	11				3	14		6			4				12			K Hackett	30
1	2	14	8*	5		7	10		11				9*	3	12	6			4							T Ward	31
1	2	S	8	5		7	10		11				9*	3	12	6			4							G Poll	32
1	2	14	8	5		7	10	9*	11				3	12		6•			4							P Alcock	33
1	2	14	8	5•		7	10	9	11			12	3		6				4				4*			R Milford	34
1	2	12	8*	5		7	10	9	11•			14†	3			6*			4							J Carter	35
1	2	12	S	5		7	10	9	11			8	3			6*			4							B Hill	36
1	2	12	S	5		7	10	9	11			8	3*			6			4							I Cruikshank	37
1		3	S	5		7	10	9	11			8			6				4•					14	2	V Callow	38
1		3•		5		7	10	9	11			14			6				4			8*		12	2	G Willard	39
1			S	5		7	10	9					3	12	6				4†			8*		11	2	P Foakes	40
1		S	12	5		7	10	9				8	3		6				4			11*			2	P Durkin	41
1		S		5		7	10	9		4		8	3		S	12						11		6*	2	D Elleray	42
1		S		5		7	10	9		4		8	3		S							11		6	2	J Martin	43
1			5	S		7	10	9		4		8	3•		14							11		6	2	I Hendrick	44
1†			5			7	10	9†	4			8	3		S		S		6			11		6	2	G Pooley	45
1			5			7	10	9	4			8	3•		S	6						11		6	2	A Bennett	46
1			5†			7	10	9*	4			8	3			6						11•		12	2	R Bigger	47
			5			7	10	4				9	3		6*	S	8					11		12	2	M Peck	48
			5	9		7	10	4				8*	3	12		6						11*		14	2	C Wilkes	49
39	30	5	25	39	5	42	40	35	38	14	6	25	22	7	9	18	2	1	26	1		8	4	7	12	**League Appearances**	
	6	2	1			2	1	1		3	4	8		12	2	12	1				1	3		1	4	**Substitute Appearances**	
2	2	1	2	2	2	2	2	2	2	2	0+2	0+2	1													**R/lows Appearances**	
2	2		2	2		2	2	2	0+2		1+1		1+1		2				2							**FA Cup Appearances**	
										2	1+1	2	3	1		3	2	0+3	2							**Autoglass Appearances**	

Also Played: Posn.(Game): Dalton 1(22), Harrison 1(48,49)

Players on Loan: Branagan (Millwall), Polston (Tottenham), Green (Swindon), Thomas (Watford), Harrison (Charlton)   † = Sent Off

GILLINGHAM

Club Colours: Blue shirts, white shorts, blue stockings
Change Colours: Black and white striped shirts, black shorts, white stockings
Reserves League: Kent Midweek   **Youth League:** S E Counties

Previous League: Southern League
Previous Name: New Brompton 1893-1913
Previous Managers: (Since 1920): John McMillan 1920-23   Harry Curtis 1923-26   Albert Hoskins 1926-30   Dick Hendrie 1930-32
Fred Mavern 1932-37   Alan Ure 1937-38   Bill Harvey 1938-39   Archie Clark 1939-58   Harry Barratt 1958-62   Freddie Cox 1962-66
Basil Hayward 1966-71   Andy Nelson 1971-74   Len Ashurst 1974-75   Gerry Summers 1975-81   Keith Peacock 1981-87   Paul
Taylor 1987-88   Keith Burkinshaw 1988-89   Damien Richardson 1989-
Honours: Champions Div 4 1963-64
League Career: Original Members of Div 3 1920   Transferred to Div 3S 1921   Failed to gain re-election 1938
Southern League 1938-44   Kent League 1944-46   Southern League 1946-50   Re-elected to Div 3S 1949
Transferred to Div 4 1958   Promoted to Div 3 1963-64   Relegated to Div 4 1970-71   Promoted to Div 3 1973-74
Relegated to Div 4 1988-89

CLUB RECORDS

Most Appearances for Club: Ron Hillyard (1974-90): League 559 + FA Cup 35 + League Cup 44 **Total 638**
(League only): John Simpson, 571, 1957-72
Most Capped Player: Tony Cascarino 3 Eire
Record Goalscorer in a Match: Fred Cheesmuir 6 v Merthyr Tydfil (h), 6-0 Div 3S 26.4.1930
Record League Goalscorer in a Season: Ernie Morgan, 31 Div 3S, 1954-55   Brian Yeo, 31 Div 4, 1973-74   **In All Competitions:**
Ernie Morgan 33 (League 31 + FA Cup 2) 1954-55
Record League Goalscorer in a Career: Brian Yeo, 135, 1963-75   **In All Competitions:** Brian Yeo, 148 (League 135 + FA Cup 9 +
League Cup 4) 1963-75
Record Transfer Fee Received: £285,000 from Oxford United for Colin Greenall, Feb 1988
Record Transfer Fee Paid: £102,500 to Tottenham Hotspur for Mark Cooper, Oct 1987
Best Performances: League: 4th Div 3 1978-79, 1984-85   FA Cup: 5th Round 1969-70   League Cup: 4th Round 1963-64
Most League Points: (3pts for win) 83, Div 3, 1984-85   (2pts for win) 62, Div 4, 1973-74
Most League Goals: 90, Div 4, 1973-74
Record League Victory and Most Goals Scored in a League Match: 10-0 v Chesterfield, Div 3, 5.9.1987 (Div 3 record)
Most Goals Scored in a Cup Tie: 10-1 v Gorleston (h), FA Cup 1st Round, 16.11.1957
Record League Defeat: 0-8 v Luton Town, Div 3S, 14.4.1929
Record Cup Defeat: 0-6 v Oxford United, League Cup Rnd 2, 24.9.1986
Oldest Player in a League Match: John Simpson, 39 years 137 days
Youngest Player in a League Match: Billy Hughes, 15 years 275 days v Southend, 13.4.1976

LONGEST LEAGUE RUNS

of undefeated matches: 20 (1973-74)	**of league matches without a win:** 15 (1972)
of undefeated home matches: 48 (1963-65)	**of undefeated away matches:** 10 (1973-74)
without home win: 9 (1961)	**without an away win:** 26 (1937-38-50)
of league wins: 7 (1954-55)	**of home wins:** 10 (1963)
of league defeats: 10 (1988-89)	**of away wins:** 4 (1953-1981)

Missing seasons in aways without a win between 1938-50 was when they were a non-league club

GILLINGHAM

PLAYERS NAME Honours	Ht	Wt	Birthdate	Birthplace Transfers	Contract Date	Clubs	League	L/Cup	FA Cup	Other	Lg	L/C	FAC	Oth
GOALKEEPERS														
Harvey Lim	6.0	13.07	30.08.67	Halesworth		Norwich City (A)								
					Loan	Plymouth A								
via Kettering Town 3FAC, via Ornskolsbik (Swe)					09.11.89	Gillingham	82	2	3	7				
DEFENDERS														
Philip A Butler	6.2	10.10	28.09.72	Stockport	13.05.91	Gillingham (T)	11	2		0+1				
Paul P Clark	5.10	12.13	14.09.58	Benfleet	01.07.76	Southend Utd. (A)	29+4	0+1	1		1			
E:Y				£55,000	16.11.77	Brighton & H.A	69+10	7+2	4+1		9			
Loan Reading (01.10.81) 2lg				Free	13.08.82	Southend Utd	269+7	15+1	12+1	14+1	3	1	1	1
				Free	18.07.91	Gillingham	42	2	2	3				
Brian Clarke	6.3	13.2	10.10.68	Eastbourne		Gillingham	33	2	1	3				
					27.02.92	Gillingham	9+2			2				
Paul Hague	6.2	13.3	16.09.72	Shotley Bridge	13.05.91	Gillingham (T)	6+1							
Michael Harle	6.0	12.0	31.10.72			Gillingham (T)	1+1			1				
Eliot Martin	5.8		27.09.72	Plumstead	13.05.91	Gillingham (T)	22	1		2				
Lee Palmer	6.0	12.04	19.09.70	Gillingham	28.07.89	Gillingham (T)	62+10	4+1	2	3	4			
Lawrence Osborne	5.11	12.7	23.10.67	London		Dagenham								
						Arsenal (A)								
						Newport Co	15		1	1				
via Wycombe Wanderers and Bedford					02.08.90	Maidstone Utd	49+4	2	4	5	8		1	2
				£40,000	12.12.91	Gillingham	4+1							
Neil J Smith	5.7	11.10	30.09.71	London	24.07.90	Tottenham H. (T)								
FAYC'90				£40,000	17.10.91	Gillingham	26		2	3	2		1	2
Alan Walker	6.1	12.2	17.12.59	Ashton-U-Lyme	23.08.78	Stockport Co								
FAT'83; Div2'88						Telford			4				1	
				£50,000	14.10.83	Lincoln City	74+1	2	5	4	4		1	2
				£32,500	30.07.85	Millwall	92	7	9	6	8	3	1	1
				£50,000	25.03.88	Gillingham	150+1	8	5	6	7	2	3	3
MIDFIELD														
Richard Carpenter	6.0	12.0	30.09.72	Minster	13.05.91	Gillingham (T)	8+4			1	1			
Anthony Eeles	5.7	11.0	15.11.70	Chatham		Gillingham (T)	42+17	4	1+2	3+2	3			
FORWARDS														
Andrew Arnott	6.1		18.10.73	Chatham	13.05.91	Gillingham	7+12		1+1	1+1	2			
					Loan 20.05.92	Manchester Utd								
Trevor Aylott	6.1	14.0	26.11.57	London		Fisher Athletic								
Div3'87					01.07.76	Chelsea (A)	26+3	2	1		2			
				£60,000	12.11.79	Barnsley	93+3	10	9		26	4	4	
				£150,000	14.08.82	Millwall	32	2	1		5			
				£65,000	24.03.83	Luton Town	32	2	1		10	1		
				PE	18.07.84	Crystal Palace	50+3	3+1	2	2	12		1	1
Loan Barnsley (21.03.86) 9lg				£15,000	22.08.86	Bournemouth	137+10	13	7	2+1	27	4	2	
				£40,000	23.10.90	Birmingham City	25+2		0+1	4+1			1	
				Free	12.09.91	Oxford Utd	35+2		2	1	6			
				Free	13.07.92	Gillingham								
David Crown	5.10	11.4	16.02.58	Enfield		Waltham Avenue								
				£13,000	23.07.80	Brentford	44+2	4	3		8	1	1	
					27.10.81	Portsmouth	25+3		2		2			
				Loan	24.03.83	Exeter City	6+1				3			
				Free	04.08.83	Reading	87+1	4	6	2+1	15	2	1	
				Free	26.07.85	Cambridge Utd	106	12	3	4	45	6	2	2
					07.11.87	Southend Utd	113	8	4	7	61	4	1	4
				£50,000	27.06.90	Gillingham	64+2	2	3	5	34	1	1	2
Mark Dempsey	5.7		10.12.72	Dublin	09.08.90	Gillingham (T)	18+14		2	3	2			
Joseph Dunne	5.9		25.05.73	Dublin	09.08.90	Gillingham (T)	32+5	2	1	2+1				
Liburd Henry	5.11	11.0	29.08.67	Dominica		Colchester Utd								
						Rainham Town								
						Millwall								
						LOri								
				£20,000	20.11.87	Watford	8+2	1	3	1	1			
				Loan	01.09.88	Halifax Town	1+4							
				£40,000	01.07.90	Maidstone Utd	61+6		3+1	3	9		1	
				Free	11.06.92	Gillingham								
Stephen Lovell	5.9	11.2	16.07.60	Swansea	04.08.77	Crystal Palace (A)	68+6	9+1	2+1		3	1	1	
W:6				Loan	03.10.79	Stockport Co	12		1					
				f	10.03.83	Millwall	143+3	12	14	6	42	5	6	3
				Loan	04.02.87	Swansea City	2				1			
				£20,000	19.02.87	Gillingham	211+9	13	10	13+2	90	4	2	3
Mark O'Connor	5.7	10.2	10.03.63	Rochdale	01.06.80	Q.P.R. (A)	2+1							
Div3'87				Loan	07.10.83	Exeter City	38		2	3	2		1	1
				£20,000	13.08.84	Bristol Rovers	79+1	8	7	4	10	1	1	1
				£25,000	27.03.86	Bournemouth	115+13	5+3	7	4+1	12			
				£70,000	15.12.89	Gillingham	91+4	4	3	5	7			
ADDITIONAL CONTRACT PLAYERS														
Stuart Barton					22.03.91	Gillingham								
Nicholas Forster					22.05.92	Gillingham								
Lyndon Guscott			29.03.72	London		Gillingham (T)	0+2							

LEADING LEAGUE GOALSCORERS SEASONS 1985-86 – 1991-92

1985-86	TONY CASCARINO	14		1986-87	DAVID SHEARER	16
					TONY CASCARINO	16
1987-88	STEVE LOVELL	25		1988-89	STEVE LOVELL	14
1989-90	STEVE LOVELL	16		1990-91	STEVE LOVELL	19
	1991-92	DAVID CROWN	22			

PRIESTFIELD STADIUM Redfern Avenue, Gillingham, Kent ME7 4DD

Capacity: 10,422   **Covered Standing:** 4,823   **Seating:** 1,225

Tel: Ground: 0634 851854   **Ticket Sales:** As ground number   **Clubcall:** 0898 800 676

All premium rate calls (0898/0891) cost 36p per minute cheap rate and 48p per minute at all other times. Call costings correct at time of going to press.

ATTENDANCES
Highest: 23,002 v Queens Park Rangers, FA Cup Round 3, 10.1.1948

Lowest: 963 v Colchester United, Freight Rover Trophy, 23.1.1985

Record Receipts: £49,377 v Swindon Town, League Play-offs, 22.5.1987

PRIESTFIELD STADIUM
First game: v Woolwich Arsenal, Friendly, 2.9.1893
First floodlit game: v Bury, Lge Cup, 25.9.1963

Season Tickets:
Stands: from £165 to £190, juv/OAP £120 to £175
Ground: £115, juv/OAP £85

Executive Box Season Tickets: Information from Commercial Office

Cost of Stand Tickets: Main Stand: £10; Enclosure Seats: £6 (juveniles/OAP £6)
Terraces: £6 (juveniles/OAP £4)

Match and Ticket Information: Can reserved by postal application with payment and SAE

Car Parking: Season Tickets: £100. Plenty of parking in nearby roads

Nearest Railway Station: Gillingham (10 minutes walk from ground)

Social Club: Situated alongside club offices in Redfern Avenue. Open every night of the week and lunchtimes at weekends. Telephone number (0634 51385)

How to get to the ground

Use Motorway M2 until junction 4, leave Motorway and follow signs Gillingham, straight over 2 roundabouts, at 3rd roundabout A2 turn left, in 500yds straight over roundabout. T.R. traffic lights in 200 yds Woodlands Road – straight over until next traffic lights – stadium on left, 1 block street parking

Value Rating: ★ ★ ★

Programme Editors: Andy Bradley

Price of 1992-93 Programme: £1
Number of Pages: 32
Subscriptions: £25 including postage

Local Newspapers: Kent Evening Post, Chatham News and Standard

Local Radio Stations: BBC Radio Kent, Invicta Radio

GRIMSBY TOWN

Division 1

Formed: 1878   **Turned Professional:** 1890   **Ltd Co:** 1890

SPONSORED BY: CIBA-GEIGY CHEMICALS LTD   **NICKNAME:** The Mariners

Life President
T J Lindley
T Wilkinson

Chairman
P W Furneaux

Vice-Chairman
W H Carr

Directors
T Aspinall   G W Duffield
G Lamming   J Mager

Secretary
Ian Fleming (0472 697111)

Team Manager
Alan Buckley

Reserve Team Manager
Arthur Mann

Youth Coach
Richard O'Kelly

Physiotherapist
Ken Reed

Groundsman
Frank Bridge

Lottery Manager
Tim Harvey

Commercial Manager
Tony Richardson

Club Statistician for the Directory
Les Triggs

LIFE for a Grimsby Town supporter is often frustrating but seldom dull. In forty-six seasons of post-war football the Mariners have been either promoted or relegated no fewer than fifteen times, with many more close run seasons.

1991-92 was no exception when interest was kept alive until the last day of the season when a seventh minute Tommy Watson goal against Port Vale not only ensured the Mariners' Second Division survival, but also condemned the Potteries club to relegation.

Examination of the scorelines tells its own story. Despite playing some attractive football the Mariners failed to find the net on 16 occasions and scored but one goal on 18 others, indeed during March and April they failed to score in 9 out of 14 league games.

In fairness it must be said that Grimsby Town have had more than their fair share of injuries with key players missing for long periods. As a result Alan Buckley has not been able to field a settled side and during the last few weeks of the season was hard pushed to find thirteen fit players.

The one bright feature of the season was in The Rumbelows League Cup when after holding Aston Villa to a goalless draw at Blundell Park the Mariners won the second round tie on away goals after a 1-1 draw in the second leg at Villa Park.

Despite a sterling performance in the next round at Blundell Park, the Mariners lost 0-3 to Tottenham Hotspur, a scoreline that failed to reflect the balance of play.

So what of the coming season. Hopefully the close season will provide an opportunity for all the long term injuries to clear up. There have also been calls for Buckley to sign a 'proven striker', but is there any such a being? How often in the past has a large investment on such a player proved a failure when that player fails to live up to expectations at his new club.

With a full squad to call on and with such team strengthening as Buckley may deem neccessary, Mariners supporters will be looking forward to a more rewarding period, for there is no doubt that there is enough talent in the Mariners squad to more than hold their own in the new First Division of the Football League.

Les Triggs

Back row L-R: P Agnew, T Rees, T Ford, P Futcher, P Reece, N Woods, M Smith, J Dobbin. **Middle:** K Reed (Physio), I Baraclough, G Rodger, R Wilmot, S Sherwood, M Lever, J Cockerill, A Mann (Reserve Team Coach). **Front:** C Hargreaves, K Jobling, J McDermott, G Childs, A Buckley (Manager), D Gilbert, T Watson, S Burns, G Croft.

GRIMSBY TOWN

DIVISION TWO: 19th   **FA CUP:** 1st RND   **RUMBELOWS CUP:** 3rd RND   **ZDS CUP:** 2nd RND

M	DATE		COMP.	VEN	OPPONENTS	RESULT	H/T	LGE POS	GOALSCORERS/GOAL TIMES	ATTEN-DANCE
1	A	17	BL	H	Cambridge United	L 3-4	1-1	19	Watson 45, Rees 68, 77	7,657
2		20	RC 1/1	A	Rotherham United	W 3-1	2-0		Dobbin 22, Jones 44, Rees 66	(3,839)
3		24	BL	A	Oxford United	W 2-1	2-1	13	Cockerill 11, McDermott 20	(4,411)
4		27	RC 1/2	H	Rotherham United	W 1-0	1-0		Birtles 7	3,637
5		31	BL	H	Tranmere Rovers	D 2-2	0-1	14	Woods 77, 85	7,018
6	S	4	BL	A	Leicester City	L 0-2	0-1	20		(16,242)
7		7	BL	A	Bristol Rovers	W 3-2	1-0	16	Jobling 39, Jones 58, Gilbert 90	(4,641)
8		14	BL	H	Plymouth Argyle	W 2-1	1-0	11	Jobling 7, Jones 58	5,432
9		17	BL	H	Portsmouth	D 1-1	1-0	12	Woods 39	5,348
10		21	BL	A	Sunderland	W 2-1	1-0	8	Dobbin 11, Cunnington 82	(16,535)
11		24	RC 2/1	H	Aston Villa	D 0-0	0-0			13,835
12		28	BL	A	Ipswich Town	L 1-2	1-1	11	Gilbert 40	6,621
13	O	1	ZDS 1	H	Wolverhampton W	W 1-0	1-0		Rees 29	1,593
14		5	BL	A	Watford	L 0-2	0-2	15		(6,930)
15		9	RC 2/2	A	Aston Villa	D †1-1	0-0		Gilbert (pen) 52 (Won on away goals)	(15,338)
16		12	BL	H	Port Vale	L 1-2	1-1	18	Childs 25	8,218
17		19	BL	H	Middlesbrough	W 1-0	0-0	13	Woods 82	10,285
18		23	ZDS 2	A	Tranmere Rovers	L 1-5	1-2		Vickers (og) 13	(4,653)
19		26	BL	A	Blackburn Rovers	L 1-2	1-1	13	Childs 6	(11,096)
20		29	RC 3	H	Tottenham Hotspur	L 0-3	0-1			17,017
21	N	2	BL	H	Charlton Athletic	W 1-0	1-0	12	Childs 12	4,743
22		6	BL	A	Brighton & H A	L 0-3	0-3	15		(4,420)
23		9	BL	A	Newcastle United	L 0-2	0-2	16		(16,955)
24		16	FAC 1	A	Blackpool	L 1-2	0-1	18	Cunnington 67	(4,074)
25		23	BL	H	Millwall	D 1-1	0-0	18	Cunnington 62	5,701
26		26	BL	A	Wolverhampton W	L 1-2	0-1	19	Dobbin 76	(9,378)
27		30	BL	A	Swindon Town	D 1-1	1-1	22	Dobbin 34	(8,397)
28	D	7	BL	H	Bristol City	W 3-1	1-1	16	Woods 2, Jones 69, Smith 88	4,866
29		14	BL	A	Barnsley	L 1-4	0-2	19	Smith 89	(6,856)
30		26	BL	A	Derby County	D 0-0	0-0	20		(16,392)
31		28	BL	A	Tranmere Rovers	D 1-1	0-1	20	Ford 69	(7,900)
32	J	1	BL	H	Wolverhampton W	L 0-2	0-1	22		9,158
33		11	BL	H	Oxford United	W 1-0	1-0	20	Rees 30	5,117
34		18	BL	A	Cambridge United	W 1-0	1-0	16	Dobbin 17	(6,092)
35	F	8	BL	H	Blackburn Rovers	L 2-3	1-3	19	Mendonca 38, Cunnington 68	10,174
36		15	BL	A	Millwall	D 1-1	1-1	18	Rees 31 secs	(6,807)
37		18	BL	H	Southend United	W 3-2	1-0	16	Smith 22, Cunnington 61, Dobbin 63	5,337
38		22	BL	H	Swindon Town	D 0-0	0-0	16		6,817
39		29	BL	A	Bristol City	D 1-1	0-1	17	Woods 79	8,992
40	M	3	BL	A	Charlton Athletic	W 3-1	3-0	14	Smith 16, Barness (og) 17, Rees 19	(3,658)
41		7	BL	H	Barnsley	L 0-1	0-1	17		6,913
42		10	BL	H	Brighton & H A	L 0-1	0-0	17		4,583
43		17	BL	H	Leicester City	L 0-1	0-0	18		6,377
44		21	BL	H	Newcastle United	D 1-1	1-1	18	Cunnington 1	11,613
45		28	BL	A	Southend United	L 1-3	1-2	19	Woods 17	(4,591)
46		31	BL	A	Plymouth Argyle	W 2-1	1-0	17	Mendonca 16, Woods 76	(6,274)
47	A	4	BL	H	Bristol Rovers	L 0-1	0-0	18		4,859
48		7	BL	H	Derby County	L 0-1	0-1	18		7,040
49		11	BL	A	Portsmouth	L 0-2	0-1	19		(10,576)
50		18	BL	H	Sunderland	W 2-0	0-0	18	Dobbin 65, Mendonca 80	8,864
51		21	BL	A	Ipswich Town	D 0-0	0-0	18		(22,393)
52		25	BL	H	Watford	L 0-1	0-1	19		6,483
53		28	BL	A	Middlesbrough	L 0-2	0-2	19		(18,570)
54	M	2	BL	A	Port Vale	W 1-0	1-0	19	Watson 7	(8,678)

Best Home League Attendance: 11,613 v Newcastle United   **Smallest:** 4,583 v Brighton & Hove Alb.   **Av Home Att:** 6,923

Goal Scorers: **Compared with 90-91:** -314

League (47): Woods 8, Dobbin 6, Cunnington 5, Rees 5, Smith 4, Mendonca 3, Childs 3, Jones 3, Watson 2, Gilbert 2, Jobling 2, Opponents Ford, Cockerill, McDermott

R/lows C (5): Dobbin, Jones, Birtles, Rees, Gilbert (1 pen)

FA Cup (1): Cunnington

ZDS Cup (2): Opponents, Rees

† = After extra-time

Sherwood S.	McDermott J.	Jobling K.	Futcher P.	Lever M.	Dobbin J.	Watson T.	Gilbert D.	Rees A.	Smith M.	Woods N.	Jones M.	Agnew P.	Birtles G.	Cockerill J.	Hargreaves C.	North M.	Childs G.	Cunnington S.	Reece P.	Ford T.	Rodger G.	Mendonca C.	Knight I.	Baraclough	Referee	
1	2	3	4	5	6•	7	8	9	10*	11	12		14												V Callow	1
1	2	10	4	5•	6	7	8	9		11	12	3	14												T Lunt	2
1	2	3	4	5	6	7	8		12	11*	9*		14	10											R Gifford	3
1	2	3	4	5	6	7	8*		12	11			9*	10	14										R A Hart	4
1	2	3	4	5	6	7*	8		12	11	9•		14	10											G Courtney	5
1	2	3	4	5	6	7	8		12	11	9*		14	10*											A Flood	6
1	2	3	4	5	6	7	8		12	11	9*			10	14										J Martin	7
1	2	3	4	5	6	7*	8		12	11•	9			10											R Pawley	8
1	2	3	4	5	6		8		12	11	9	10		S			7*							S	J Rushton	9
1	2		4	5	10		8			11	9	3			12		7*	6						S	J Key	10
1	2		4	5	10		8	14	12	11	9*	3*					7	6							D Phillips	11
1	2		4	5	10		8		12	3	11	9			14		7	6							D Allison	12
1	2		4	5	10		8		9*	3	11	12		S			7	6							B Hill	13
1	2		4	5	10*		8		9	3	11	12	14				7*	6							G Ashby	14
1	2		4	5	10		8		9*	3	11	12		S			7	6							J Lloyd	15
1	2•		4		10*	14	8	9	3	11	12			5			7	6							K Lupton	16
1	2	3	4	5	10		8		9	S	11			S			7	6							G Singh	17
1	2	3•	4	5*	10		8		9	14	11		12				7	6							T Holbrook	18
1	2	3	4	5	10*		8		9		11		14	12			7*	6							M Peck	19
1	2	3•	4*	5	12		8		9	14	11			10			7	6							K Barratt	20
1	2			5	12		8		14	11	3	4•	10*	9			7	6							S Lodge	21
1	2		4	5			S		8*		11	3	12	10†	9		7	6							R Hamer	22
1	2*			5	10		8			11	9	3	4	12	S		7	6							P Wright	23
1	2		4					9	8	11	12•	3	5*	10	14		7	6							A Wilkie	24
		3	4				10	S		9	8	11*	12	5			7	6	1	2					J Worrall	25
		3	4				8	S	9	12				5	10		7	6*	1	2					J Moules	26
		3	4		6	8*		S	9	12	11			5	10*		7		1	2					P Don	27
S		3	4		6		8		9	11	12			5	10*		7		1	2					R Poulain	28
		3	4*	12	10		8			9	11		14	5			7*	6	1	2					I Cruickshanks	29
	2	10	4	5			8			11	9	3		S			S	6	1	7					M Reed	30
	2	4†	5	6		S	8	10	9		3			12			11		1*	7					B Coddington	31
1	2		5	6	14	8		9		3	10*			12			11			7					S Bell	32
	2	3		5	6		8		9*	S	12						7		1	11	4	10			J Watson	33
	2	3		5	6		8		9		12						7		1	11	4	10*			P Danson	34
	2•	3		5	11		8		9		12						7*	6		14	4	10			M Bailey	35
	2	3		5	11		8*		9	10	12						7	6	1	S	4				M Pierce	36
	2	3		5	11		8*		9	10	12						7•	6	1	14	4				D Phillips	37
	2	3		5	11		8		9	10*	12						7	6	1	S	4				R Hart	38
	2	3		5	11•		8		9	10	12		14				7*	6	1				4		M Brandwood	39
	2	3		5	11*		8		9	10	S		12				7	6	1				4		G Pooley	40
	2	3		5*	11		8		9	10	12			S			7	6	1				4		I Hemley	41
	2			5	11		8		9	10	12	3					7*	6		14			4•		A Dawson	42
	2	3		5•	8				9*	10	11		12				7	6	1	14	4				J Kirkby	43
	2	3	4	5	9		8*			11	12	S						6	1	7		10			M Brandwood	44
1	2	3	4•	5	9*		8			11	12		14					6		7		10			P Scobie	45
1	2	S		5			8		9	11	S	3						6		7	4	10			R Hamer	46
1	2	14		5			8		9*	11	12	3						6		7	4	10			I Cruickshanks	47
1	2	3		5			8•		12	11	9*		14					6		7*	4	10			N Midgley	48
	2			5	12		8		3	11	9*		14					6		7	4	10•			D Shadwell	49
	2	3	4		10		8		S	11							7*	6	1	12	5	9			R Poulain	50
	2	3	4			7	8		9	11	S	10		S				6	1			5			G Willard	51
	2	3	4			7	8*		9	11•	12		14					6	1	10		5			I Hendrick	52
	2	3	4	S		7	8	9	S	11		10						6	1			5			L Dilkes	53
	2	3	4			7	8	9*	11	12		10		S				6	1			5			G Singh	54
21	39	35	29	35	32	13	41	22	28	30	14	20	3	8	2		29	33	25	17	16	10	4		**League Appearances**	
	1		1		4		1	11	7	14	4	5	2	8	1				5						**Substitute Appearances**	
5	5	3	5	5	4	2+1	5	3+1	1+3	5	1+2	2	1+1	2			3	3							**R/lows Appearances**	
1	1		1		1	1	1	0+1	1	1	1			1			1	1							**FA Cup Appearances**	
2	2	1	2	2	1	1	2	2	1+1	2	0+1						2	2							**ZDS Cup Appearances**	

Players on Loan: Mendonca (Sheffield Utd)

† = Sent Off

GRIMSBY TOWN

Club Colours: Black and white striped shirts, black shorts and white stockings
Change Colours: Yellow shirts, red shorts, red stockings
Reserves League: Pontins Central League   **Youth:** Midland Purity League

COMPETITION				
Div. 1	Div. 2	Div. 3	Div. 3N	Div. 4
01-03	92-01	20-21	21-26	68-72
29-32	03-10	59-62	51-56	77-79
34-48	11-20	64-68		88-90
	26-29	72-77		
	32-34	79-80		
	48-51	87-88		
	56-59	90-91		
	62-64			
	80-87			
	91-			

HONOURS			
Div. 2	Div. 3N	Div. 3	Div. 4
00-01	25-26	79-80	71-72
33-34	55-56		

MOST GOALS IN A CAREER		
PAT GLOVER 197 (1930-39)		
Season	League	FA Cup
1930-31	2	
1931-32	12	4
1932-33	22	2
1933-34	42	1
1934-35	34	2
1935-36	31	4
1936-37	29	4
1937-38	4	
1938-39	4	
Total	180	17

MOST APPEARANCES: KEITH JOBLING 493 (1953-66)			
Year	League	FA Cup	Lge Cup
1953-54	9		
1954-55	6	1	
1956-57	6		
1957-58	13		
1958-59	42	3	
1959-60	42	2	
1960-61	36	1	1
1961-62	46	1	1
1962-63	41	1	1
1963-64	41	1	1
1964-65	46	4	2
1965-66	42	6	5
1966-67	21	2	4
1967-68	18	1	
1968-69	41	1	4
	450	24	19

MANAGERS			
Name	Seasons	Best	Worst
Haydn Price	1920		
George Fraser	1921-24	3(3N)	14(3N)
Wilf Gillow	1924-32	13(1)	12(3N)
Frank Womack	1932-36	5(1)	13(2)
Charles Spencer	1937-51	16(1)	22(2)
Bill Shankly	1951-54	2(3N)	17(3N)
Bill Walsh	1954-55	17(3N)	23(3N)
Allenby Chilton	1955-59	13(2)	23(3N)
Tim Ward	1960-62	2(3)	6(3)
Tom Johnston	1962-64	19(2)	21(2)
Jimmy McGuigan	1964-67	10(3)	17(3)
Don McEvoy	1967-68	22(3)	22(3)
Bill Harvey	1968-69	22(3)	23(4)
Bobby Kennedy	1969-71	16(4)	23(4)
Lawrie McMenemy	1971-73	9(3)	19(4)
Ron Ashman	1973-75	6(3)	16(3)
Tommy Casey	1975-76	16(3)	18(3)
John Newman	1977-79	2(4)	6(4)
George Kerr	1979-82	7(2)	1(3)
Dave Booth	1982-85	5(2)	19(2)
Mick Lyons	1985-87	15(2)	21(2)
Bobby Roberts	1987-88	22(3)	22(3)
Alan Buckley	1988-	19(2)	9(4)

RECORD TRANSFER FEE RECEIVED			
Amount	Club	Player	Date
£650,000	Sunderland	Shaun Cunnington	7/92
£500,000	Q.P.R.	Andy Tillson	12/90
£300,000	Everton	Paul Wilkinson	8/85
£125,000	Aston Villa	Terry Donovan	7/79

RECORD TRANSFER FEE PAID			
Amount	Club	Player	Date
£135,000	Luton Town	Graham Rodger	2/92
£110,000	Watford	Jimmy Gilligan	7/85
£105,000	Leicester City	Andy Peake	7/85
£80,000	Vancouver W'caps	Trevor Whymark	12/80

LONGEST LEAGUE RUNS	
of undefeated matches:	19 (16.2.1980-30.8.1980)
of undefeated home matches:	33 (8.10.1974-28.2.1976)
without home win:	12 (27.9.1947-17.3.1948)
of league wins:	11 (19.1.1952-29.3.1952)
of league defeats:	9 (30.11.1907-18.1.1908)
of league matches w/out a win:	18 (10.10.1981-16.3.1982)
of undefeated away matches:	9 (23.2.1980-30.8.1980)
	(19.11.1983-10.3.1984)
without an away win:	23 (2.10.1982-28.10.1983)
of home wins:	17 (9.3.1894-28.3.1895)
of away wins:	5 (26.1.1952-22.3.1952)

PREVIOUS NAME
Grimsby Pelham

PREVIOUS LEAGUE
Football Alliance; Midland League (1910)

BIGGEST VICTORIES
League: 9-2 v Darwen, Div 2, 15.4.1899
7-0 v Bristol Rovers (a), Div 2, 1957-58
F.A. Cup: 10-0 v Boston, Round 2, 24.10.1891
League Cup: 6-1 v Rotherham Utd, Round 2, 6.11.1984

BIGGEST DEFEATS
League: 1-9 v Arsenal, Div 1, 28.1.1931
F.A. Cup: 1-9 v Phoenix Bessemer, Rnd 2, 25.11.1982
League Cup: 0-6 v Burnley, Rnd 2, 10.9.1968

MOST POINTS
3 points a win: 83, Division 3, 1990-91
2 points a win: 68, Division 3N, 1955-56

MOST GOALS
103, Division 2, 1933-34
Glover 42, Craven 18, Jennings 13, Bestall 11, Holmes 7,
Kelly 3, Dyson 3, Ponting 2, Moralee 2, Dodds 1, Lewis 1

MOST GOALS IN A MATCH
6. Tommy McCairns v Leicester Fosse, Div 2, 11.4.1896

MOST GOALS IN A SEASON
Pat Glover 43 (League 42, FAC 1) 1933-34
3 goals 3 times = 9; 2 goals 8 times = 16; 1 goal 18 times = 18.
Total 43

MOST FIRST CLASS MATCHES IN A SEASON
59 (46 League, 4 FA Cup, 9 League Cup) 1979-80

MOST LEAGUE GOALS CONCEDED
111, Division 1, 1947-48

MOST LEAGUE WINS
31, Division 3N, 1955-56

MOST LEAGUE DRAWS
17, Division 3, 1964-65

MOST LEAGUE DEFEATS
28, Division 1, 1947-48

OLDEST PLAYER
George Tweedy, 40 years 84 days v York City, 3.4.1953

YOUNGEST PLAYER
Tony Ford, 16 years 143 days (sub) v Walsall, 4.10.1975

MOST CAPPED PLAYER
Pat Glover (Wales) 7

BEST PERFORMANCES BY GRIMSBY TOWN

League: 1925-26: Matches Played 42, Won 26, Drawn 9, Lost 7, Goals for 93, Goals against 40, Points 61. First in Division 3N

Highest: 5th Division 1, 1934-35

F.A. Cup: 1935-36: 3rd rnd. Hartlepool (a) 0-0, (h) 4-1; 4th rnd. Port Vale (a) 4-0; 5th rnd. Manchester City (h) 3-2; 6th rnd. Middlesborough (h) 3-1; Semi-Final Arsenal 0-1
1938-39: 3rd rnd. Tranmere Rovers (h) 6-0; 4th rnd. Millwall (a) 2-2, (h) 3-2; 5th rnd. Sheffield Utd (a) 0-0, (h) 1-0; 6th rnd. Chelsea (a) 1-0; Semi-Final Wolverhampton W 0-5

League Cup: 1979-80: 1st rnd. Scunthorpe Utd (h) 2-0, (a) 0-0; 2nd rnd. Huddersfield Town (h) 1-0 (a) 4-1; 3rd rnd. Notts County (h) 3-1; 4th rnd. Everton (h) 2-1; 5th rnd. Wolverhampton W. (h) 0-0, (a) 1-1 (n) 0-2
1984-85: 2nd rnd. Barnsley (h) 3-0 (a) 1-1; 3rd rnd. Rotherham Utd (a) 0-0, (h) 6-1; 4th rnd. Everton (a) 1-0; 5th rnd. Norwich City (h) 0-1

DIVISIONAL RECORDS

	Played	Won	Drawn	Lost	For	Against	Points
DIVISION 1	488	167	97	224	756	940	431
DIVISION 2	1610	602	345	663	2476	2623	1644
DIVISION 3	690	272	170	248	976	913	750
DIVISION 3S	42	15	9	18	49	59	39
DIVISION 3N	432	200	85	147	672	534	485
DIVISION 4	368	155	92	121	520	460	441
TOTALS	3630	1411	798	1421	5449	5529	3790

GRIMSBY TOWN

PLAYERS NAME / Honours	Ht	Wt	Birthdate	Birthplace / Transfers	Contract Date	Clubs	League	L/Cup	FA Cup	Other	Lg	L/C	FAC	Oth
GOALKEEPERS														
Paul Reece	5.10	12.7	16.07.68	Nottingham		Stoke City	2							
via Kettering Town				£10,000	18.07.88	Grimsby Town	54	3	5	4				
Steve Sherwood	6.4	14.7	10.12.53	Selby	01.07.71	Chelsea (A)	16	1						
Div.4.78				Loan		Brighton & H.A								
Loan Millwall (01.10.73) 1lg				Loan	01.01.74	Brentford	62	2	2					
				£4,000	01.11.76	Watford	211	23	23	6	1			
				Free	06.07.87	Grimsby Town	176	12	9	8				
Rhys Wilmot	6.1	12.0	21.02.60	Newport	25.01.84	Arsenal (A)	8	1						
W:u21.6				Loan	18.03.83	Hereford Utd	9							
				Loan		Leyton Orient	46	4	4	3				
Loan Swansea City (26.08.88) 16lg				Loan	23.02.89	Plymouth A	17							
				£100,000	20.07.89	Plymouth A	116	8	2	4				
				tribunal	01.07.92	Grimsby Town								
DEFENDERS														
Paul Agnew	5.9	10.7	15.08.65	Lisburn		Cliftonville								
NI: u23.1, Y ,S				£4,000	15.02.84	Grimsby Town	171+14	12	19	11+1	3			
John Cockerill	6.0	12.7	12.07.61	Cleethorpes		Stafford Rangers								
				£18,500	19.08.88	Grimsby Town	99+8	6	11	6	19		2	2
Paul Futcher	6.0	12.3	25.09.56	Chester	01.01.74	Chester City (A)	20		1					
E:u21.11				£100,000	01.06.74	Luton Town	131	4	6		1			
				£350,000	02.06.78	Manchester City	36+1	3+1	3	2				
				£150,000	01.08.80	Oldham Ath	98	10	3		1			
				£44,000	28.01.83	Derby County	35	1	4					
				£30,000	22.03.84	Barnsley	229+1	13	20	4				
				Free	24.07.90	Halifax Town	15	4	3					
				£10,000	21.02.91	Grimsby Town	51	5		2				
Mark Lever	6.3	12.8	29.03.70	Beverly	09.08.88	Grimsby Town (T)	147+5	11	10	9	6			
John McDermott	5.7	10.0	03.01.69	Middlesbrough	01.06.87	Grimsby Town (A)	191+9	11+1	11+1	8	2			
Graham Rodger	6.2	11.13	01.04.67	Glasgow		Wolves (A)	1							
E:u21.4,FAC'87				Free	18.02.85	Coventry City	31+5	3+1	1+1	0+1	2			
				£150,000	01.08.89	Luton Town	27+1	2			2			
				£135,000	08.01.92	Grimsby Town	16							
MIDFIELD														
Jim Dobbin	5.9	10.7	17.09.61	Dunfermline		Celtic	1+1	4				1		
S:Y				Loan	01.02.84	Motherwell	1+1							
				£25,000	19.03.84	Doncaster Rovers	56+8	5	2	3	13	1		
				£35,000	19.09.86	Barnsley	116+13	3+1	11	4	12			1
				£200,000	15.07.91	Grimsby Town	32	4		1	6	1		
Tony Ford	5.9	12.2	14.05.59	Grimsby	01.05.77	Grimsby Town (A)	321+33	31+3	14+4	2	54	4	2	
E: B.2; Div.3'80; LC'82				Loan	27.03.86	Sunderland	8+1				1			
				£35,000	08.07.86	Stoke City	112	8	9	6	13			1
					24.03.89	West Brom A	114	7	4	2+1	14	1		
				£50,000	21.11.91	Grimsby Town	17+5				1			
Dave Gilbert	5.4	10.4	22.06.63	Lincoln	29.06.81	Lincoln City (A)	15+15	5	3		1			
Div.4'87				Free	18.08.82	Scunthorpe Utd	1	1						
via Boston United (Free) 4FAC, 2gl				30.06.86	Northampton T	120	10	6	9	21	2	3	1
				£55,000	23.03.89	Grimsby Town	141	11	4	6	27	3	1	
Kevin Jobling	5.9	10.11	01.01.68	Sunderland	09.01.86	Leicester City (A)	4+5		0+1	3				2
				P.E	19.02.88	Grimsby Town	155+6	8	4+2	4+4	8		1	
Tommy Watson	5.8	10.10	29.09.69	Liverpool	12.07.88	Grimsby Town (A)	84+30	4+3	2	6+2	16	1		
FORWARDS														
Ian Baraclough	6.1	11.10	04.12.70	Leicester	15.12.88	Leicester City (T)		1		0+1				
E: FLg u18(1)				Loan	22.03.90	Wigan Ath	8+1				2			
Loan Grimsby Town (21.03.90) 1+3lg				Free	13.08.91	Grimsby Town								
Gary Childs	5.7	10.8	19.04.64	Birmingham	13.02.82	West Brom A. (A)	2+1							
E:Y4				£15,000	07.10.83	Walsall	120+11	14+2	9+1	7	17	2	2	2
				£50,000	08.07.87	Birmingham City	39+16	0+2	3	2	2			
				Free		Grimsby Town	93+5	9	4	5	12	1		
Christian Hargreaves	5.11	11.0	12.05.72	Cleethorpes	06.12.89	Grimsby Town (T)	15+32	2+1	1+1	2+2	5	1	2	
Tony Rees		5.9	11.13	01.08.64	Merthyr Tydfil	01.08.82	Aston Villa								
W: 1, u21.1, Y; FAYC'80				Free	07.03.83	Birmingham City	75+20	7+1	5	1+2	12	2	2	
				Loan	01.10.85	Peterborough U	5				2			
Loan Shrewsbury (01.03.86) 1+1lg				01.03.88	Barnsley	27+4	2	0+1	1	3			
					17.08.89	Grimsby Town	93+1	9+1	3+1	4	28	2		2
Mark Smith	5.9	12.2	16.12.61	Sheffield		Sheffield Utd								
via Worksop Town, Gainsborough T. and Kettering Town				15.07.88	Rochdale	26+1	2	2	2	7			
				£50,000	10.02.89	Huddersfield Town	85+11	5	5+1	5	11		1	1
				£55,000	21.03.91	Grimsby Town	29+21	1+3	1	1+1	4			
Neil Woods	6.0	12.11	30.07.66	York	31.08.83	Doncaster Rovers	55+10	4	5	5+2	16	1	2	3
				£120,000	22.12.86	Glasgow Rangers	0+3							
				£120,000	03.08.87	Ipswich Town	15+12			4	5			1
					01.03.90	Bradford City	13+1				2			
				£82,000	27.09.90	Grimsby Town	72+9	5	2	4	20			
ADDITIONAL CONTRACT PLAYERS														
Stuart I Burns					07.07.92	Grimsby Town (T)								
Gary Croft			17.02.74	Burton-on-Trent	07.07.92	Grimsby Town (T)	0+1							

GRIMSBY TOWN

RECORD WIN & LOSS AGAINST EACH CLUB IN CURRENT DIVISION
(Where a score has occured on several occasions the most recent is given)

Club	Rec. Win	Season	Rec. Loss	Season
BARNSLEY	8-1	1899-00	7-2	1949-50
BIRMINGHAM CITY	4-0	1937-38	6-0	1901-02
BRENTFORD	7-2	1950-51	6-1	1937-38
BRISTOL CITY	4-0	1904-05	7-0	1914-15
BRISTOL ROVERS	7-0	1957-58 (away)	7-3	1958-59
CAMBRIDGE UNITED	4-0	1988-89	5-1	1980-81
CHARLTON ATHLETIC	5-0	1973-74	5-1	1958-59 (home)
DERBY COUNTY	4-1	1935-36 (away)	6-0	1909-10
LEICESTER CITY	8-2	1930-31	5-1	1904-05
LUTON TOWN	6-1	1949-50	6-0	1981-82
MILLWALL	5-1	1985-86	4-1	1928-29
NEWCASTLE UNITED	4-0	1929-30	5-1	1901-02
NOTTS COUNTY	3-0	1895-96	4-0	1972-73
OXFORD UNITED	2-0	1979-80	5-2	1976-77
PETERBOROUGH UTD	3-0	1965-66	4-2	1975-76
PORTSMOUTH	3-0	1934-35	4-0	1983-84
SOUTHEND UNITED	4-1	1971-72	4-0	1964-65
SUNDERLAND	6-0	1936-37	6-2	1962-63
SWINDON TOWN	3-0	1959-60	5-0	1967-68
TRANMERE ROVERS	8-0	1925-26	3-1	1974-75
WATFORD	3-0	1920-21	7-1	1967-68
WEST HAM UNITED	4-0	1930-31	5-1	1980-81 (home)
WOLVERHAMPTON WNDRS	6-0	1926-27	8-1	1909-10

MANAGER: ALAN BUCKLEY

DATE OF BIRTH: 20.4.1951   **PLACE OF BIRTH:** Eastwood

DATE OF APPOINTMENT: JUNE 1988

PREVIOUS CLUBS
  as Manager:
  as Asst.Man/Coach:
  as Player: Nottingham Forest, Walsall (2 spells), Birmingham City

HONOURS
  as Manager: (Grimsby): Div 4 Runners-up 1989-90; Promotion to Div 2 (3rd place) 1990-91
  as Player:

Value Rating: ★ ★ ★

Programme Editor:

Price of 1992-93 Programme: £1
Number of Pages: 32
Subscriptions: £40 per season

Local Newspapers: Grimsby Evening Telegraph, Grimsby Gazette, Grimsby Target

Local Radio Stations: Radio Humberside, Viking Radio

Additional Publications on Club: Who's Who of Grimsby Town Football Club
(Douglas Lamming); Paperback £4.95

LEADING LEAGUE GOALSCORERS
SEASONS 1979-80 – 1991-92

Season	Player	Goals	Season	Player	Goals
1979-80			1980-81		
1981-82			1982-83		
1983-84			1984-85		
1985-86	GORDON HOBSON	16	1986-87	IAN WALSH	9
1987-88	MARC NORTH	11	1988-89	KEITH ALEXANDER	14
1989-90	TONY REES	13	1990-91	DAVE GILBERT	12

1991-92 **NEIL WOOD** 8

BLUNDELL PARK Cleethorpes, South Humberside DN35 7PY

Capacity: 17,526   **Standing:** 12,505   **Seating:** 5,021

Tel: Ground: 0472 697111   **Ticket Sales:** 0472 697111   **Clubcall:** 0898 12 15 76

All premium rate calls (0898/0891) cost 36p per minute cheap rate and 48p per minute at all other times. Call costings correct at time of going to press.

ATTENDANCES
Highest: 31,657 v Wolverhampton Wanderers, FA Cup Round 5, 20.2.1937

Lowest: 970 v Scunthorpe Utd, Sherpa Van Trophy, 15.12.1987

Record Receipts:
£96,636.10 v Tottenham H., League Cup, 29.10.1991
£55,480.00 v Newcastle Utd, Div 2, 21.3.1992
£53,958.40 v Exeter City, BL Div 3, 11.5.1991
£44,137 v Norwich City, Milk Cup 5th Round, 16.1.1985

BLUNDELL PARK
First game: v Luton Town, 3-3, 2.9.1899
First floodlit game: v Gainsborough T, 9.3.1953

Season Tickets:
Stands: from £152 to £184, juv/OAP £85.50 to £103.50
Ground: from £104.50 to £126.50, juv/OAP £66.50 to £80.50

Executive Box Season Tickets: Consult Commercial Manager

Cost of Stand Tickets: Seats £8, juv/OAP £4.50
Terraces: adults £5.50, juniors/OAP £3.50
*Concessionary tickets for juniors/OAPs available only from office 24 hours prior to fixture

Match and Ticket Information: Seats bookable two weeks in advance of each match

Car Parking: Street parking available

Nearest Railway Station: Cleethorpes, Grimsby (0472 353556)

How to get to the ground

From North and West: Use Motorway M18 then A180 (S.P. Grimsby) then follow signs to Cleethorpes A1098

From South: Use A1 then A16 and follow signs to Cleethorpes and at roundabout take 1st exit into Grimsby Road A1098 for Grimsby Town FC

HALIFAX TOWN
Division 3

Formed: 1911 **Turned Professional:** 1911 **Ltd Co:** 1911

SPONSORED BY: Paraglas **NICKNAME:** The Shaymen

Chairman
Jim Brown

Vice-Chairman
David Greenwood

Director
B J Boulton

Ass. Directors
I R Stewart   J Hallet
G H Butler   G Bastow
P Reynolds   G Swift
D A Newiss

Secretary
Angie Harrison (0422 353423)

Manager
John McGrath

Promotion & Marketing Exec.
Nick Beaumont

Physiotherapist
Mick Rathbone

Club Statistician for the Directory
Gavin Dimmock

HALIFAX Town had a disappointing season. Poor league form, combined with first round cup exits, pay testament to this. Never, in their 71 year history, had they scored so few goals – only 34. Just seven home League wins and an end of season run of ten consecutive away defeats saw Town finish in twentieth position.

October 2nd saw McCalliog dismissed as manager. Ex-Preston boss John McGrath was appointed the following day. He immediately brought in Oshor Williams as his assistant, and ex-England international Frank Worthington as part-time coach.

Restricted by existing contracts and no available funds, McGrath made several loan signings. The Huddersfield duo of Kevin Donovan and Dudley Lewis arrived, as did Jason Hardy of Burnley and Swansea's goalkeeper Lee Bracey. After protracted dealings the directors paid £47,500 of their own cash to make Bracey a permanent signing. A fee of £30,000 captured the skills of Paul Wilson from Northampton whilst Ronnie Hildersley was a free signing from Canadian football.

The problem of scoring goals was a constant headache throughout the season. Nick Richardson converted from midfield into a striker, and top scored with ten goals. Ian Juryeff, who returned a paltry five goals from 43 appearances, made the opposite switch into midfield, where he acquited himself capably.

Last season's leading marksman, Steve Norris, failed to re-capture his form. He appeared hesitant and lacking confidence in front of goal. With the fans and management discouraged, he found himself on loan to Chesterfield, who bought him for £30,000. Ironically, he has since found his eye for the net!

January saw the retirements through injury of Tommy Graham and ex-Bradford player Mark Ellis. Former England youth international, Tony Gregory, had to be released by the club due to a long-term injury that saw him play only 21 times in 21 months at the Shay. Also released were Jonathan Gould to West Bromwich Albion, Paul Donnelly to Northwich Victoria, Ian Hutchinson and Graham Cooper.

The Rumbelows Cup provided spectators with a thrilling tie. Town lost both legs 3-4, but put up a tremendous performance against Second Division Tranmere, forcing the second leg into extra-time.

A stunning late equaliser in the F.A. Cup first round salvaged a replay against Witton Albion. However, optimistic hopes turned to abject despair and humiliation as the non-league part-times took the tie into extra-time before winning through. From that point on the season was effectively finished, as Town also failed to qualify for the knockout stages of the Autoglass Trophy.

Attendances fell as fans become dis-illusioned. Only 881 saw the Shaymen manage their biggest score of the season, 4-3 against Wrexham. It is to be hoped that McGrath and Williams can assemble a winning team capable of drawing the crowds and the subsequent revenue. Otherwise, Halifax Town might travel the same road as that of Aldershot.

Gavin R Dimmock

Back row L-R: Paul Wilson, Ian Juryeff, Nigel Greenwood, Chris Lucketti, Nick Richardson, Lee Bracey, Ian Thompstone, Russell Bradley, Neil Griffiths, Scott Longley, Billy Barr. **Front row:** Jamie Paterson, John Thomas, Greg Abbott, Kevin Megson, Alan Kamara, M Rathbone (Physio), Jimmy Case, David German, Jason Hardy, Ron Hildersley.

HALIFAX TOWN

DIVISION FOUR: 20th   **FA CUP:** 1st RND   **RUMBELOWS CUP:** 1st RND   **AUTOGLASS:** Prelim.

M	DATE		COMP.	VEN	OPPONENTS	RESULT		H/T	LGE POS	GOALSCORERS/GOAL TIMES	ATTEN-DANCE
1	A	17	BL	H	Northampton Town	L	0-1	0-0			1,834
2		20	RC 1/1	H	Tranmere Rovers	L	3-4	3-2		Norris (pen) 5, Richardson 16, Juryeff 45	1,910
3		24	BL	A	Maidstone United	W	1-0	0-0	10	Juryeff 67	(1,216)
4		27	RC 1/2	A	Tranmere Rovers	L	†3-4	2-1		Barr 5, 13, Cooper 51	(4,285)
5		30	BL	H	York City	D	0-0	0-0	10		2,167
6	S	7	BL	A	Walsall	L	0-3	0-1	17		(2,981)
7		13	BL	H	Rotherham United	L	0-4	0-0	17		2,653
8		17	BL	H	Cardiff City	D	1-1	0-1	19	Bradley 58	1,041
9		27	BL	H	Mansfield Town	L	1-3	0-1	19	Norris 76	2,026
10	O	5	BL	A	Lincoln City	D	0-0	0-0	18		(2,092)
11		12	BL	H	Gillingham	L	0-3	0-1	20		1,435
12		19	BL	H	Chesterfield	W	2-0	0-0	17	Norris (pen) 52, 62	1,506
13		26	BL	A	Rochdale	L	0-1	0-1	16		(2,323)
14	N	2	BL	H	Burnley	L	0-2	0-0	19		4,491
15		6	BL	A	Hereford United	W	2-0	1-0	17	Juryeff 34, Norris 80	(2,207)
16		9	BL	A	Barnet	L	0-3	0-1	19		(4,837)
17		16	FAC 1	A	Witton Albion	D	1-1	0-1		Hildersley 88	(2,002)
18		19	AGT Pre	A	Bury	D	2-2	1-2		Cooper 31, 53	(788)
19		22	BL	H	Scarborough	W	1-0	1-0	15	Richardson 31	1,395
20		27	FAC 1R	H	Witton Albion	L	†1-2	0-0		Richardson 115	2,172
21		30	BL	A	Blackpool	L	0-3	0-3	18		(3,118)
22	D	13	BL	H	Wrexham	W	4-3	1-1	14	Patterson 22, Richardson 59, 62, Juryeff 76	881
23		21	BL	H	Maidstone United	D	1-1	0-1	15	Cooper 73	1,040
24		26	BL	A	Northampton Town	L	0-4	0-4	16		(3,147)
25		28	BL	A	York City	D	1-1	0-0	16	Wilson 56	(2,396)
26	J	7	AGT Pre	H	Scunthorpe United	L	0-2	0-0			646
27		11	BL	A	Doncaster Rovers	W	2-0	0-0	16	Norris 49, Hutchinson 76	(2,067)
28		18	BL	H	Scunthorpe United	L	1-4	0-1	17	Patterson 88	1,232
29		25	BL	A	Carlisle United	D	1-1	1-1	16	Richardson 41	(2,091)
30	F	8	BL	H	Rochdale	D	1-1	1-0	16	Cooper 41	2,213
31		12	BL	H	Blackpool	L	1-2	0-2	19	Barr (pen) 80	2,158
32		15	BL	A	Wrexham	L	0-2	0-0	19		(2,076)
33		22	BL	H	Doncaster Rovers	D	0-0	0-0	19		1,285
34		28	BL	A	Crewe Alexandra	L	2-3	1-2	19	Wilson 4, Richardson 83	(3,514)
35	M	3	BL	A	Scunthorpe United	L	0-1	0-0	19		(2,448)
36		6	BL	H	Carlisle United	W	3-2	0-1	18	Bradley 69, Cooper 82, Wilson 85	1,015
37		11	BL	H	Hereford United	L	0-2	0-0	19		918
38		14	BL	A	Burnley	L	0-1	0-0	20		(10,003)
39		21	BL	H	Barnet	W	3-1	0-0	20	Richardson 46, 62, Wilson (pen) 71	1,756
40		28	BL	A	Scarborough	L	0-3	0-3	20		(1,363)
41		31	BL	A	Rotherham United	L	0-1	0-0	20		(4,517)
42	A	3	BL	H	Walsall	W	1-0	1-0	20	Wilson 28	1,006
43		7	BL	A	Chesterfield	L	0-4	0-0	20		(1,802)
44		11	BL	A	Cardiff City	L	0-4	0-1	20		(5,261)
45		14	BL	H	Crewe Alexandra	W	2-1	0-1	20	Barr 85, 89	1,022
46		21	BL	A	Mansfield Town	L	2-3	0-1	20	Juryeff 57, Abbott 76	(3,936)
47		25	BL	H	Lincoln City	L	1-4	1-1	20	Richardson 12	1,296
48	M	2	BL	A	Gillingham	L	0-2	0-0	20		(2,413)

Best Home League Attendance: 4,491 v Burnley   **Smallest: 881 v Wrexham**   **Av Home Att: 1,637**

Goal Scorers: **Compared with 90-91: -64**

League (34): Richardson 8, Wilson 5 (1 pen), Norris 5 (1 pen), Juryeff 4, Barr 3 (1 pen), Cooper 3, Patterson 2, Bradley 2, Abbott Hutchinson

R/lows C (6): Barr 2, Norris (1 pen), Cooper, Richardson, Juryeff
FA Cup (2): Richardson, Hildersley
Autoglass (2): Cooper 2

† = After extra-time

Gould J.	Evans D.	Kamara A.	Abbott G.	Richards S.	Graham T.	Megson K.	Cooper G.	Juryeff I.	Richardson N.	Paterson J.	Barr W.	Ellis M.	Norris S.	Lucketti C.	Bradley R.	Griffiths N.	Bracey L.	Hutchinson I.	Lewis D.	Hildersley R.	Gregory A.	Wilson P.	Hardy J.	German D.	Donovan K.	Referee	
1	2	3	4	5	6	7	8	9	10	11	S	S														D Shadwell	1
1		3	4	5	6	7*	11	9	10	12	2		8	S												A Flood	2
1	2	3	4	5	6	S	11	9	10		7		8	S												G Pooley	3
1	2	3	4	5	6	12	11*	9	10		7		8	S												G Singh	4
1	2	3	4	5	6	S	11	9	10		7		8	S												A Wilkie	5
1	2	3	4	12	14	11•		9	10		7*		8		6											K Cooper	6
1	2	3	4	12	14	11*		9†	10	7•			8		6											P Harrison	7
1		3	12	5	4*		11		10	7*	2		8	S	6											K Redfearn	8
1		3	12	5	4*		11		10	7•	2		8	14	6											J Lloyd	9
1	4	3	11*	5	S				10	7	2		8	12	6†											J Brandwood	10
1	4•	3	11	5	14				10*	7	2		8	12	6											J Watson	11
	4	3		5	10			9	7	S	2	11	8	6			1	S								T Lunt	12
	4	3	12•	5	10			9	7*		2	11	8	14	6		1									K A Cooper	13
	4	3*		5	7†			9	10	S	2	11	8	6†	S		1									P Dawson	14
	4	3*		5	7			9	10	S	2	11	8	12			1	6	S							L Shapter	15
	4			5	7*			9	10	2	11	8	3	S			1	6	12							P Alcock	16
1	4	7*	5					9	10	2	11	8		3			1	6	12						S	I Hendrick	17
1	14	7	5•			8*		9	10	2	11		4	3		1		6	12							I Cruikshanks	18
	14	7	5					9	10	2	11*	8	4	3•		1		6	12							T West	19
1	6	7	5					9	10	2	11*	8	4	3				12							S	I Hendrick	20
	12	7*	5					9	10	14	2		8•	4	3		1		6	11						W Burns	21
		7	5				12	9	10	11•	2	14	8*	4	3		1		6							C Trussell	22
	S	7	5				8	9	10		2		4	5			1		6	11		3				P Wright	23
11	12	7	14				8	9	10	2*			4	5•			1		6			3				D Elleray	24
11*		7	S				8	9	10	2			4	5			1		6	12		3				D Allison	25
1	8	7						9*	10	2			4	5	12			3	6	11•						R Hart	26
	7						S	8	S	10	2	9	4	5			1	3	6			11				M Bailey	27
	12	7					8	9	10	14	2*		4	5•			1		6	11		3				P Jones	28
	6	7	5		S	8		9	10	11*	2		4				1	12				3				E Parker	29
	6	7	S	5		9	8	10	2			4			1					11*	3	12				A Flood	30
	6	7*	14	5		9	8	10	2			4			1					11*	3	12				K Lupton	31
	6	7*		5		8•	9	10	2			4			1			14		3	12		11			A Smith	32
	6	S		5		9	8	10	2			4			1			11		3	S		7			R Dilkes	33
	6			5		8	10	9•	2*			4	12		1			11		3	14		7			I Hemley	34
	6	14		5		8	10	9•	S			2	4		1			11		3			7			D Gallagher	35
	6	S		5		9	8	10			4		2	4	S		1			11		3			7	I Hendrick	36
	6	10					9	8	2•				4	5	S		1			11	7*	3				T West	38
	14	6					8	9	2*				4	5	S		1			11	7	3				R Hart	39
	7	6	10		S		8	9	2				4	5	S		1			11		3				P Jones	40
	7	6	10		S		8	9	2				4	5			1	S		11		3				J Rushton	41
	14	6	10			2	8	9	11	S			4	5			1				7•	3				P Wright	42
	7	6	10			2	8	9	11				4	5	S		1	S				3				K Breen	43
	7	6	10			2	8	9	11†				4	5†	S		1	S				3				M Pierce	44
	7	6	10			2	8		12				4	5	S		1	9*		11		3				M Peck	45
	S	6	10			2	8	9	7•				4	5	S		1			11		3		14		T Lunt	46
	5	6	10			2		9	8				4		12		1	3						11		M Reed	47
	5	6	10			2		9	8	11*			4		12		1	3						7		C Wilkes	48

Gould J.	Evans D.	Kamara A.	Abbott G.	Richards S.	Graham T.	Megson K.	Cooper G.	Juryeff I.	Richardson N.	Paterson J.	Barr W.	Ellis M.	Norris S.	Lucketti C.	Bradley R.	Griffiths N.	Bracey L.	Hutchinson I.	Lewis D.	Hildersley R.	Gregory A.	Wilson P.	Hardy J.	German D.	Donovan K.		
9	26	34	24	24	12	8	19	37	41	13	34	6	17	31	25		32	4	11	14	5	23		2	6	League Appearances	
5	1	4	1	2	2	3			2	1	1		5	1	2		1			4			4	1		Substitute Appearances	
2	1	2	2	2	1+1	2	2	2	0+1	2		2														R/lows Appearances	
2	2		2	2				2	2	2	2	2	1	2			1				2					FA Cup Appearances	
2	0+1	1	1	2	1			1	2		2	1	2	1	2		0+1		1	2	1+1					Autoglass Appearances	

Also Played: Posn.(Game): Matthews 9(9,10,11), Brown 1(33), Donnelly 14(26), Longley 7*(47)S(48), Armstrong S(47)

Players on Loan: Donovan (Huddersfield), Matthews (Stockport), Lewis (Huddersfield), Hardy (Burnley)   † = Sent Off

HALIFAX TOWN

Club Colours: Royal blue and white striped shirts, white shorts, white stockings
Change Colours: All red
Reserves League:

Previous League: North Eastern League
Previous Managers: (Since 1946) Jack Breedon W Wooton Jimmy Thompson Gerald Henry Bobby Browne Willie Watson Billy Burnicle Harry Hooper Willie Watson Vic Metcalfe Alan Ball (snr) George Kirby Ray Henderson George Mulhall John Quinn Alan Ball (snr) Jimmy Lawson **George Kirby** Micky Bullock Mick Jones Bill Ayre Jim McCaliog John McGrath
Honours: None
League Career: Original Members of Div 3N 1921 Transferred to Div 3 1958 Relegated to Div 4 1962-63 Promoted to Div 3 1968-69 Relegated to Div 4 1975-76

CLUB RECORDS

Most Appearances for Club: John Pickering 1965-74: 367
Most Capped Player: None
Record Goalscorer in a Match: William Chambers 5 v Hartlepool United, 6-2, Div 3N, 7.4.1934 (6-2) Albert Valentine 5 v New Brighton, 6-2, Div 3N, 9.3.1935 (6-2)
Record League Goalscorer in a Season: Albert Valentine 34, Div 3N, 1934-35
Record League Goalscorer in a Career: Ernest Dixon, 129, 1922-30
Record Transfer Fee Received: £250,000 from Watford for Wayne Allison, August 1989
Record Transfer Fee Paid: £50,000 to Hereford Utd for Ian Juryeff, Sept 1990
Best Performances: League: 2nd Div 3(N), 1934-35 **FA Cup:** 5th Round 1932-33, 1952-53 **League Cup:** 4th Round 1964
Most League Points: (2pts for win) 57, Div 4, 1968-69 (3pts for win) 60, Div 4, 1982-83
Most League Goals: 83, Division 3N, 1957-58
Record League Victory: 6-0 v Bradford (P.A.), Div 3N, 3.12.1955 6-0 v Doncaster Rovers, Div 4, Nov 1976
Most Goals Scored in a League Match: (6 on 9 occasions): 6-1 v Ashington (h), Div 3N, 5.9.1927
6-2 v Southport (h), Div 3N, 24.3.1934
6-2 v Hartlepool (h), Div 3N, 7.4.1934
6-2 v New Brighton (h), Div 3N, 9.3.1935
6-1 v Carlisle United (h), Div 3N, 2.1.1937
6-0 v Bradford (h), Div 3N, 3.12.1955
6-2 v Southend United (h), Div 3, 24.12.1960
6-0 v Doncaster Rovers (h), Div 4, 2.11.1976
6-1 v Workington (h), Div 4, 5.2.1977
Most Goals Scored in a Cup Tie: 7-0 v Bishop Auckland (h), FA Cup 2nd Round Replay, 1966
Record League Defeat: 0-13 v Stockport County, Div 3N, 6.1.1934
Record Cup Defeat: 0-7 v Darlington, Frieght Rover Trophy, 3.3.1985
Oldest Player in a League Match:
Youngest Player in a League Match: Paul Willis, 17 years 80 days, 14.4.1987

LONGEST LEAGUE RUNS	
of undefeated matches: 17 (1969)	**of league matches without a win:** 22 (1978-79)
of undefeated home matches: 19 (1974-75)	**of undefeated away matches:** 11 (1970-71)
without home win: 13 (1990)	**without an away win:** 40 (1950-52)
of league wins: 7 (1964)	**of home wins:** 8 (1935)
of league defeats: 8 (1946-47)	**of away wins:** 4 (1927)

HALIFAX TOWN

PLAYERS NAME / Honours	Ht	Wt	Birthdate	Birthplace / Transfers	Contract Date	Clubs	League	L/Cup	FA Cup	Other	Lg	L/C	FAC	Oth
GOALKEEPERS														
Lee Bracey	6.1	12.08	11.09.68	Ashford		West Ham U. (T)								
					17.10.88	Swansea City	99	8	11	10				
				£47,500	16.01.92	Halifax Town	32							
Nicholas Brown					05.07.91	Halifax Town	1							
DEFENDERS														
Russell Bradley	6.2		28.03.66	Birmingham		Nottm. Forest								
WC'90				Loan	13.11.88	Hereford Utd	12		1	3	1			
				£15,000	26.07.89	Hereford Utd	75+2	8		5+1	3			
				£45,000	06.09.91	Halifax Town	25+1		2	2	2			
David Evans	5.11	12.5	20.05.58	Solihull	01.02.76	Aston Villa (A)	2			1				
Div3'85				£22,500	21.06.79	Halifax Town	218	10	10	1	9	1	1	
				Free	21.06.84	Bradford City	222+1	23	14	14	3		1	
				Free	09.08.90	Halifax Town	68+5	5	5	3+1	1	1		
David German					14.07.92	Halifax Town (T)	2+2							
Neil Griffiths	6.0	12.3	04.09.72	Halifax	05.07.91	Halifax Town (T)	1+2			0+1				
Jason Hardy	5.10	11.04	14.12.69	Burnley	20.07.88	Burnley (T)	38+5		3+2	2	1		1	
Loan Halifax (30.01.92) 0+4lg				Free	01.07.92	Halifax Town								
Alan Kamara	5.6	11.2	15.07.88	Sheffield		Barnsley								
via Kiverton Park					03.07.79	York City	10							
				Free	13.06.80	Darlington	134	6	4		1			
via York Railway Inst., Retford and Burton Albion					05.11.87	Scarborough	158+1	13	5	10+1	2			
				Free	09.08.91	Halifax Town	34+1	2	1					
Chris Lucketti			28.09.71	Littleborough		Rochdale (T)	1							
				Monthly	24.11.90	Stockport Co								
				Free	12.07.91	Halifax Town	31+5		1	2				
Paul Wilson	5.10	10.6	02.08.68	Bradford	12.06.86	Huddersfield Town	15	1						
				£30,000	23.07.87	Norwich City								
				£30,000	12.02.88	Northampton T	132+9	10	7	6+3	6	1		
					19.12.91	Halifax Town	23				5			
MIDFIELD														
Greg Abbott	5.9	10.7	14.12.63	Coventry	05.01.82	Coventry City (A)								
Div3'85				Free	10.09.82	Bradford City	256+25	22+3	15+1	19+2	38	6	3	5
				£25,000	22.07.91	Halifax Town	24+4	2	2	2	1			
Jimmy Case	5.9	12.5	18.05.54	Liverpool		S Liverpool								
E:u23.1,ESC'77,LC'81,Div1'76'77'79'80,EC'77'78'81,UEFAC'76					01.05.73	Liverpool	170+16	21+1	20+1	28+3	23	3	7	13
				£350,000	19.08.81	Brighton & H.A	124+3	8	13+1		10		5	
				£30,000	20.03.85	Southampton	213+2	34	15	7	10	2	1	1
				Free	25.07.91	Bournemouth	38+2	3	5	1	1			
				Free	16.05.92	Halifax Town								
Ron Hildersley	5.5	10.0	06.04.65	Kirkcaldy	13.04.83	Manchester City (A)	1							
ScS					05.07.84	Chester City	14+4		1	1				
				Free	24.08.85	Rochdale	12+4							
				Free	16.06.86	Preston N.E	54+4	5	7	4	3	1	1	
Loan Cambridge United (21.01.88) 9lg, 3gl				Free	18.07.88	Blackburn Rovers	25+5	0+1	3	3	4		1	
				Free	17.08.90	Wigan Ath	4	1						
				Free	05.11.91	Halifax Town	14+4		0+2	1+1			1	
Nicholas Richardson	6.1		11.04.67	Halifax	15.11.88	Halifax Town	89+12	6+4	2+1	6	17	2	1	1
Ian Thompstone	6.0	11.3	17.01.71	Manchester	01.09.89	Manchester City (T)	0+1				1			
via Oldham Athletic (Free)				Free	23.01.92	Exeter City	15				3			
				Free	14.07.92	Halifax Town								
FORWARDS														
William Barr	5.11	11.7	21.06.69	Halifax	06.07.87	Halifax Town (A)	150+18	8+1	11+1	13+2	10	2	2	
Nigel Greenwood	5.11	12.0	27.11.66	Preston	15.09.84	Preston N.E. (A)	36+9	2+3	0+1	1+1	14			1
				£15,000	14.08.86	Bury	78+32	11+1	4+1	5+5	25	2		1
				£20,000	02.02.90	Preston N.E	24+6		1+1	1+1	4		1	
				Free	07.07.92	Halifax Town								
Ian Juryeff	5.11	12.0	24.11.62	Gosport	28.11.80	Southampton (A)	0+2							
				Loan	22.03.84	Mansfield Town	12				5			
Loan Reading (12.11.84) 7lg 1gl, 3L/Cup 2gls £5,000					15.02.85	Leyton Orient	106+5	9	10	9+1	44	3	7	6
Loan Ipswich Town (09.02.89) 0+2lg				£40,000	10.08.89	Halifax Town	15+2	3	2	1	7			1
				£50,000	14.12.89	Hereford Utd	25+3	2			4			
				£50,000	14.09.90	Halifax Town	71	2	5	4	13	1	2	
Kevin Megson	5.10	11.0	01.02.71	Bradford	01.07.89	Bradford City (T)	24+3	3	1	1		1		
				£5,000	28.03.91	Halifax Town	13+2	1+1						
Jamie Paterson	5.5	9.7	26.04.73	Dumfries	05.07.91	Halifax Town (T)	3+3	0+1			1			
John W Thomas	5.8	11.3	05.08.58	Wednesbury	18.08.77	Everton								
SVT'89				Loan	30.03.79	Tranmere Rovers	10+1				2			
Loan Halifax (05.10.79) 5lg				Free	17.06.80	Bolton W	18+4	1			6	1		
				Free	04.08.82	Chester City	44	2	2		20	1		
				£22,000	26.08.83	Lincoln City	56+11	3+1	0+1	4+1	18	2		
				£15,000	25.06.85	Preston N.E	69+9	8	5+1	3	38		7	1
				£30,000	29.07.87	Bolton W	71+2	4	2	6+2	33	1	3	2
				£30,000	27.07.89	West Brom A	8+10	2		0+1	7	3		
				£50,000	23.02.90	Preston N.E	16	2			4			
				Monthly	21.09.91	Preston N.E	8+3		3	3	2		1	2
				Free	26.03.92	Hartlepool Utd	5+2				1			
				Free	01.07.92	Halifax Town								

LEADING LEAGUE GOALSCORERS SEASONS 1985-86 – 1991-92

1985-86	BILLY KELLOCK	17	1986-87	PHIL BROWN	12
1987-88	RICK HOLDEN	10	1988-89	TERRY McPHILLIPS	23
1989-90	NEIL MATTHEWS	12	1990-91	STEVE NORRIS	30

| | 1991-92 | **NICK RICHARDSON** | **8** |

THE SHAY GROUND Halifax, West Yorkshire, HX1 2YS

Capacity: 8,049　　　　**Covered Standing:** 3,802　　　　**Seating:** 1,878

Tel: Ground: 0422 361582　　　　**Ticket Sales:** 0422 353423　　　　**Clubcall:** 0898 12 11 06

All premium rate calls (0898/0891) cost 36p per minute cheap rate and 48p per minute at all other times. Call costings correct at time of going to press.

ATTENDANCES
Highest: 36,885 v Tottenham Hotspur, FA Cup Round 5, 14.2.1953

Lowest: 150 v Lincoln City, Frieght Rover Trophy, 11.2.1986
(Lowest ever crowd for a first class match in England)

Record Receipts: £27,000 v Manchester Utd, Rumbelows Cup 2nd Rnd, 26.9.1990

THE SHAY GROUND
First game: v Darlington, 3.9.1921
First floodlit game: v Belgrade, 1961

Season Tickets:
Stands: from £140, £80 juv/OAP
Ground: from £100, £60 juv/OAP
Family Stand: 1 adult + 1 juv £190

Cost of Stand Tickets: Seating: £7, OAP/juveniles £4;
Family Stand: £10 for 1 adult + 1 child
Terraces: £5, OAP/juveniles £3 (home)
(Away) £5 (no concessions)

Match and Ticket Information: Applications in advance may be sent to secretary

Car Parking: Car park available with entrance in Shaw Hill

Nearest Railway Station: Halifax

How to get to the ground

From North: Use A629 into Halifax Town Centre, then at roundabout take 2nd exit into Broad Street and follow signs Huddersfield A629 into Skircoat Road for Halifax Town FC

From East, South and West: Use Motorway M62 until junction 24, leave Motorway and follow signs Halifax A629, then follow signs to town centre into Skircoat Road for Halifax Town FC

Value Rating: ✶ ✶ ✶

Programme Editor: Nick Beaumont

Price of 1992-93 Programme: £1
Number of Pages: approx 34
Subscriptions: Apply to club for details with an S.A.E.

Local Newspapers: Halifax Courier, Yorkshire Post, Telegraph Argus

Local Radio Stations: Pennine Radio, Radio Leeds

HARTLEPOOL UNITED　　Division **2**

Formed: 1908　　　**Turned Professional:** 1908　　　**Ltd Co:** 1908

SPONSORED BY: Yuills – Heritage Homes　　　**NICKNAME:** The Pool

President
E Leadbitter, MP

Chairman
G Gibson

Vice-Chairman
A Bamford

Directors
D Jukes
A Elliot

Team Manager
Alan Murray

Assistant Manager
Eddie Kyle

Coach
Tony McAndrew

Physiotherapist
Gary Henderson

Club Statistician for the Directory
Gordon Small

SEASON 1991-92 was another important campaign for Hartlepool United as they attempt to work their way up the Barclays League ladder. After winning promotion in 1990-91 it was understandable that there be optimism at the club for the new season. In the event Hartlepool did acquit themselves well and achieved a final position in the top half of Division Three.

Manager Alan Murray can be happy with his teams performance over the season, although consistency wasn't really one of the strong points. The early results proved Hartlepool were quite capable of holding their own and in mid-season 'Pool were the match of any team in the division and for a time were looking good for a play-off position. Then came a second spell when nothing went right, and relegation began to look a distinct possibility, but another recovery ensured safety.

Hartlepool had their moments in all three cup competitions. In the Rumbelows Cup they reached the Second Round to earn some money and a hammering from First Division Crystal Palace. In the F.A. Cup they reached the Third Round and were then desparately unlucky not to defeat Second Division Ipswich Town at Portman Road. Finally in the Autoglass Trophy Hartlepool made one of their rare ventures into the competition proper before going down to an in-form Stockport County.

For most of 1991-92 Alan Murray was able to field a settled side. New goalkeeper Martin Hodge made an uncertain start, then gained the respect of the supporters as the season progressed. John MacPhail, as captain, was outstanding at the centre of the defence – his best partner was Keith Nobbs, who was rewarded for his consistency by being named 'Player of the Year'. Brian Honour had another excellent season (but this can be taken for granted) and Paul Olsson was the only ever present. David McCreery was another player to make a slow start, but his experience was welcome towards the end of the season. Early on Paul Baker was on form as 'Pools major goalscorer – he was ably assisted by Paul Dalton, who had his best season yet scoring a number of spectacular goals. Steve Fletcher and Nicky Southall are young players who will have benefitted from being regular first team squad members, while big money signings Lenny Johnrose and Andy Saville, and youngsters Ian McGuckin and Steven Jones, are others who are expected to make their mark next season.　　　　**Gordon Small**

Back row L-R: K Nobbs, P Dalton, I McGucklin, S Tupling. **Middle row:** E Kyle (Youth Team Coach), A Davies, J Tinkler, J MacPhail, M Hodge, I Bennyworth, N Southall, N Nesbitt, G Henderson (Physio). **Front row:** R Gabbiadini, P Olsson, B Honour, D McCreery (Asst. Manager), R McKinnon, M Smith, S Fletcher.

HARTLEPOOL UNITED

DIVISION THREE: 11th   **FA CUP:** 3rd RND   **RUMBELOWS CUP:** 2nd RND   **AUTOGLASS:** 2nd RND

M	DATE		COMP.	VEN	OPPONENTS	RESULT	H/T	LGE POS	GOALSCORERS/GOAL TIMES	ATTEN-DANCE
1	A	17	BL	A	Torquay United	L 1-3	0-2		Baker 74	(4,163)
2		20	RC 1/1	H	Bury	W 1-0	1-0		Baker 19	2,833
3		24	BL	H	Reading	W 2-0	1-0	10	Baker 20, Olsson 83	2,858
4		27	RC 1/2	A	Bury	D 2-2	0-0		Gabbiadini 61, Fletcher 86	(1,917)
5		31	BL	A	Bradford City	D 1-1	0-0	10	Rush 67	(5,872)
6	S	3	BL	H	Brentford	W 1-0	0-0	6	Gabbiadini 74	3,660
7		7	BL	A	Leyton Orient	L 2-3	1-1	11	Dalton 7, Rush 55	3,581
8		14	BL	A	Exeter City	D 1-1	0-0	13	Baker (pen) 66	(2,906)
9		17	BL	A	Stoke City	L 2-3	0-2	15	Baker 50, Olsson 65	(9,394)
10		21	BL	H	Birmingham City	W 1-0	1-0	11	Baker 2	4,643
11		25	RC 2/1	H	Crystal Palace	D 1-1	0-1		Honour 52	6,697
12		28	BL	A	Bury	D 1-1	0-1	12	Gabbiadini 80	(2,600)
13	O	5	BL	H	Wigan Athletic	W 4-3	3-1	11	Honour 4, Dalton 7, 12, McKinnon 88	3,047
14		8	RC 2/2	A	Crystal Palace	L 1-6	0-2		Tinkler 49	(9,153)
15		12	BL	A	Bournemouth	L 0-2	0-1	14		(4,817)
16		19	BL	H	Hull City	L 2-3	1-2	16	Southall 40, 60	2,868
17		26	BL	A	Peterborough Utd	L 2-3	0-2	18	Bennyworth 72, Honour 77	(3,385)
18	N	2	BL	A	Darlington	L 0-4	0-3	18		(5,041)
19		5	BL	A	West Bromwich A.	D 0-0	0-0	19		2,970
20		9	BL	H	Fulham	W 2-0	0-0	17	Honour 61, Morgan (og) 68	2,999
21		16	FAC 1	H	Shrewsbury Town	W 3-2	1-1		Tinkler 26, Johnson 57, Baker (pen) 76	2,864
22		19	AGT Pre	A	Bradford City	D 3-3	1-2		Tinkler 20, Fletcher 42, Fletcher 84	(1,562)
23		23	BL	A	Shrewsbury Town	W 4-1	3-0	14	Olsson 19, 70, Dalton 27, Baker 39	(2,368)
24		30	BL	H	Huddersfield Town	D 0-0	0-0	14		4,017
25	D	14	BL	A	Preston North End	W 4-1	2-0	9	Baker 11, 46, Dalton 18, Johnson 49	(5,032)
26		17	FAC 2	A	Darlington	W 2-1	2-0		Dalton 14, Honour 30	(5,509)
27		20	BL	A	Reading	W 1-0	0-0	8	Baker 50	(2,535)
28		26	BL	H	Bradford City	W 1-0	1-0	7	Baker 45	5,412
29		28	BL	H	Torquay United	D 1-1	1-1	8	Johnson 16	3,812
30	J	1	BL	A	Brentford	L 0-1	0-0	9		(7,103)
31		4	FAC 3	A	Ipswich Town	D 1-1	1-0		Baker 38	(12,507)
32		7	AGT Pre	H	Hull City	W 2-0	2-0		Dalton 18, Baker 36	1,550
33		11	BL	H	Chester City	W 1-0	0-0	7	Honour 53	3,088
34		15	FAC 3R	H	Ipswich Town	L 0-2	0-1			6,700
35		18	BL	A	Bolton Wanderers	D 2-2	1-0	7	Olsson 5, Kelly (og) 84	(6,129)
36		21	AGT 1	H	Scunthorpe United	W 2-1	1-1		Honour 33, Tinkler 74	1,351
37	F	1	BL	A	Hull City	W 2-0	1-0	8	Dalton 20, Baker 61	(3,483)
38		4	AGT 2	A	Stockport County	L 0-3	0-1			(2,255)
39		8	BL	H	Peterborough Utd	L 0-1	0-0	8		2,481
40		11	BL	A	Huddersfield Town	L 0-1	0-1	9		(5,559)
41		15	BL	H	Preston North End	W 2-0	0-0	8	Peake 63, Baker 79	2,140
42		18	BL	H	Stockport County	L 0-1	0-0	8		2,473
43		22	BL	H	Chester City	L 0-2	0-2	10		(1,072)
44		29	BL	H	Swansea City	L 0-1	0-0	11		2,669
45	M	3	BL	H	Bolton Wanderers	L 0-4	0-3	13		2,244
46		6	BL	A	Stockport County	W 1-0	0-0	11	Baker 57	(4,473)
47		11	BL	A	West Bromwich A.	W 2-1	1-0	11	Dalton 4, 26	(10,307)
48		14	BL	H	Darlington	W 2-0	2-0	9	Saville 15, Dalton 16	4,442
49		20	BL	A	Fulham	L 0-1	0-1	11		(4,359)
50		28	BL	H	Shrewsbury Town	W 4-2	2-1	10	Thomas 33, Dalton 45, Fletcher 85, Johnrose (pen) 86	2,515
51		31	BL	H	Exeter City	W 3-1	1-0	10	Dalton 45, 49, Southall 61	2,222
52	A	4	BL	A	Leyton Orient	L 0-4	0-1	10		(4,245)
53		11	BL	H	Stoke City	D 1-1	1-1	11	Olsson 39	4,360
54		18	BL	A	Birmingham City	L 1-2	0-0	11	Fletcher 89	(13,698)
55		20	BL	H	Bury	D 0-0	0-0	11		2,503
56		24	BL	A	Wigan Athletic	D 1-1	0-0	11	MacPhail 89	(2,002)
57		28	BL	A	Swansea City	D 1-1	1-1	11	Dalton 36	(2,167)
58	M	2	BL	H	Bournemouth	W 1-0	0-0	11	Johnrose 90	2,612

Best Home League Attendance: 5,412 v Bradford City   **Smallest:** 2,140 v Preston North End   **Av Home Att:** 3,201

Goal Scorers: **Compared with 90-91: +35**

League (57): Dalton 13, Baker 13 (1 pen), Olsson 6, Honour 4, Southall 3, Fletcher 2, Gabbiadini 2, Johnson 2, Rush 2, Opponents 2, Johnrose 2 (1pen) MacPhail, Peake, Thomas, McKinnon, Bennyworth, Saville

R/lows C (5): Fletcher, Honour, Baker, Tinkler, Gabbiadini

FA Cup (6): Baker 2 (1 pen), Johnson, Dalton, Tinkler, Honour

Autoglass (7): Tinkler 2, Baker 2, Fletcher, Dalton, Honour

Hodge M.	Nesbitt M.	McKinnon R.	McCreery D.	Nobbs A.	Bennyworth I.	Rush D.	Olsson P.	Baker D.	Honour B.	Dalton P.	MacPhail J.	Tinkler J.	Gabbiadini H.	Southall N.	Tupling S.	Fletcher S.	Smith M.	Johnson D.	Smith A.	Cross P.	McGuckin T.	Peake J.	Johnrose L.	Thomas J.	Referee	
1	2*	3	4	5	6	7	8	9	10	11	12	S													P Durkin	1
1		3	4*	2	6		8	9	10	11	5	12	7	S											R Poulain	2
1		3	4*	2	6	7	8	9	10	11	5	12	S												J Kirkby	3
1		3	4•	2	6		8	9	10	11		14	7*		5	12									R Nixon	4
1		3	4*	2	6	7	8	9	10	11	5	12	S												P Vanes	5
1		3		2	6	7	8		10	11	5	4	12	S			9*								L Dilkes	6
1		3		2	6	7	8		10	11	5	4	12		S		9*								E Parker	7
1		3		2	6	7	8	9	10	11	5	4		S	S										A Smith	8
1		3	12	2	6	7*	8	9	10*	11	5	4			14										I Hendrick	9
1		3	S	2	6	7	8	9	10	11	5	4		S											T Fitzharris	10
1		3	12	2	6		8	9	10	11	5	4	7*	S											J Watson	11
1		3	7*	2	6		8	9	10	11	5	4	12	S											A Smith	12
1		3		2	6		8	9	10	11	5	4*	7*		14	12									J Key	13
1		3		2	6*		8	9	10	11	5	4	7*		14	12									P Taylor	14
1		3		2			8	9	10	11	5	4	12	7*	S	6									D Axcell	15
1		3		2			8	9	10	11	5	4	S	7	6										W Burns	16
1		3	4	2	6		8	9	10	11	5	S	12	7*											P Alcock	17
1		3	14	2	6•		8		10	11	5	4	12	7*				9							A Dawson	18
1		3	4*	2			8		10	11	5	7	S	12	6			9							P Wright	19
1		3	4*	2			8		10	11	5	7	S	12	6			9							M Peck	20
1		3	S	2			8	9	10	11	5*	4		12	6	7									D Allinson	21
1		3	S	2			8	9	10	11		4	7*		6	12	5								A Flood	22
1		3		2			8	9	10	11	5	4	12	S	6				7*						B Coddington	23
1		3	2*				8	9	10	11	5	4	12		6	14			7*						K Breen	24
1		3	4	S			8	9	10	11	5			S	6	2			7						J Lloyd	25
1		3	4*	2			8	9	10	11	5			S	6	S			7						M Peck	26
1		3	4	2			8	9	10	11	5			S	6				7						A Buksh	27
1		3	4	2			8	9	10		5			S	6				11	7					A Wilkie	28
1		3	4*	2			8	9	10	11	5		12		6	S			7						A Bennett	29
1		3	4	2			8	9	10	11	5	12	7*		6	S									R Pawley	30
1		3	4	2			8	9		11	5	10*	7		6	12	S								T West	31
1				2			8	9		11	5	4	7		6	10	S			3					D Philips	32
1			4*	2			8	9	10	11	5		12	S	6	7	S			3					S Bell	33
1			4*	2			8	9	10	11	5	3	12		6	7	S								T West	34
1			S	2			8	9	10	11*	5	4	12		6	7	S			3					D Shadwell	35
1				2			8	9*	10	11	5	4	12		6	7	S			3					I Hendrick	36
1			S	2			8	9	10	11	5	4	12		6	7*				3					P Danson	37
1				2			8	9	10	11	5	4	12	3	6						S				V Callow	38
1			4*	2			8	9	10	11	5	12	14	7*	6					3					N Midgley	39
1				2			8	9	10	11	5	4	12	7*	6	S				3					D Allison	40
1				2			8	9	10	11	5	4	S	6	S					3		7			A Flood	41
1				2			8	9	10	11	5	4	S	6	12					3		7*			J Rushton	42
1				2			8	9	10	11	5	4	12	14	6*					3		7•			K Hackett	43
1				2			8	9	10		5	4	S	12	6					3	11*	7			R Shepherd	44
1		12					8	9	10		5	4	2	S	6					3*	11	7			M Peck	45
1		2					8	9	10	11	5	4	12		6*					3•	14	7			J Lloyd	46
1		2					8		10	11		4		S		9				3		S	7		A Ward	47
1		2					8		10	11		4		S		3	5	S	9						J Watson	48
1		2			6		8		10	11		4		S		7				3	5*		9		J Deakin	49
1		2			6		8		10	11		4		S		12				3	5	9	7*		J Key	50
1		2*			6		8		10	11		4	12			S				3	5	9	7		R Nixon	51
1		2			6		8		10	11		4		S		12				3	5	9	7*		D Frampton	52
		2			6		8			11		4	7*			10				3	5	9	12	1	S Lodge	53
		2			6		8			11		4	7*			10				3	5	9	12	1	R Lewis	54
		2			6		8			11	5		S	4		10				3		9	7	1	S Bell	55
		2			6		8			11	5	12	4			10				3		9	7*	1	K Cooper	56
		2			6		8			11	5	4	7			10				3		9	S	1	J Gallagher	57
		2*			6		8			11	5	4	7			10	12			3		9	S	1	C Trussell	58
40	1	23	27	41	12	8	46	29	40	43	40	31	1	13	17	14	7	7	4	21	7	5	15	6	**League Appearances**	
		3											1	8	8	9	4	4	1		1		1	2	**Substitute Appearances**	
4		4	2+1	4	4		4	4	4	4	3	2+2	4		1+1	0+2									**R/lows Appearances**	
4		3	3	4			4	4	3	4	4	3		1+2	4	1+1		2							**FA Cup Appearances**	
4		1		4			4	4	3	4	3	4		0+1	3+1	2+1	1		2						**Autoglass Appearances**	

Also Played: Posn.(Game): Thompson S(22) 7*(38), Davies 6(47,48)12(49), Saville 7(48)

Players on Loan: Rush (Sunderland), Johnson (Sheff Wed), A Smith (Sunderland), Peake (Leicester City)

HARTLEPOOL UNITED

Club Colours: White shirts with blue trimmings, dark blue shorts
Change Colours: All yellow or all silver grey
Reserves League: Midland Senior   **Youth Team:** Northern Intermediate

Previous League: North Eastern League
Previous Name: Until 1968 Hartlepools United: 1968-77 Hartlepool
Previous Managers: 1908-12 Fred Priest   1912-13 Percy Humphreys   1913-20 Jack Manners   1920-22 Cecil Potter   1922-24 David Gordon   1924-27 Jack Manners   1927-31 Bill Norman   1931-35 Jackie Carr   1935-39 Jimmy Hamilton   1943-57 Fred Westgarth   1957-59 Ray Middleton   1959-62 Bill Robinson   1962-63 Allenby Chilton   1963-64 Bob Gurney   1964-65 Alvan Williams   1965 Geoff Twentyman   1965-67 Brian Clough   1967-70 Angus McLean   1970-71 John Simpson   1971-74 Len Ashurst   1974-76 Ken Hale   1976-83 Billy Horner   1983 John Duncan   1983 Mick Docherty   1983-86 Billy Horner   1986-88 John Bird   1988-89 Bobby Moncur   1989-91 Cyril Knowles
Honours: None
League Career: Original Members of Div 3N 1921   Transferred to Div 4 1958   Promoted to Div 3 1967-68   Relegated to Div 4 1968-69   Promoted to Div 3 1990-91

CLUB RECORDS

Most Appearances for Club: Watty Moore 1948-60: Football League 447 + FA Cup 25 **Total 472**
Most Capped Player: Amby Fogarty 1 Eire   **For England:** None
Record Goalscorer in a Match: Billy Smith 7 v St Peters Albion (10-1), FAC, 17.11.1923   Harry Simmons 5 v Wigan Borough (6-1), Div 3N 1 Jan 1931   Bobby Folland 5 v Oldham Athletic (5-1), Div 3N, 15.4.1961
Record League Goalscorer in a Season: Billy Robinson, 28, Div 3N, 1927-28 & Joe Allon, 28, Div 4, 1990-91   **In All Competitions:** Joe Allon, 35, 1990-91
Record League Goalscorer in a Career: Ken Johnson, 98, 1949-64   **In All Competitions:** Ken Johnson 106 (League 98 + FA Cup 6 + League Cup 2)
Record Transfer Fee Received: £250,000 from Plymouth Argyle for Paul Dalton, May 1992
Record Transfer Fee Paid: £60,000 to Barnsley for Andy Saville, March 1992
Best Performances: League: 2nd Div 3N 1956-57   **FA Cup:** 4th Round 1954-55, 1977-78, 1988-89   **League Cup:** 4th Round 1974-75
Most League Points: (3pts a win) 82, Div 4, 1990-91   (2pts a win) 60, Div 4, 1967-68
Most League Goals: 90, Div 3N, 1956-57
Record League Victory and Most Goals Scored in a League Match: 10-1 v Barrow, Div 4, 4.4.1959
Most Goals Scored in a First Class Cup Tie: 6-0 v North Shields, FA Cup Rnd 1, 30.10.1946   6-1 v Scarborough, FA Cup Rnd 1, 20.11.1971   6-3 v Marine, FA Cup Rnd 2 replay, 15.12.1975
Record League Defeat: 1-10 v Wrexham, Division 4, 3.3.1962
Record Cup Defeat: 0-6 v Manchester City, FA Cup Rnd 3, 1975-76   1-7 v York City, Leyland Daf Cup, 7.11.1989
Oldest Player in a League Match: Jackie Carr 39 years 360 days, 21.11.1931
Youngest Player in a League Match: John McGovern, 16 years 205 days, 21.5.1966

LONGEST LEAGUE RUNS

of undefeated matches: 17 (1968)	**of league matches without a win:** 18 (1962-63)
of undefeated home matches: 27 (1967-68)	**of undefeated away matches:** 7 (1968, 1991)
without home win: 8 (1977, 1984, 1986)	**without an away win:** 31 (1937-38)
of league wins: 7 (1956, 1968)	**of home wins:** 12 (1933, 1951)
of league defeats: 8 (1950)	**of away wins:** 4 (1921-22, 1979, 1991)

HARTLEPOOL UNITED

PLAYERS NAME Honours	Ht	Wt	Birthdate	Birthplace Transfers	Contract Date	Clubs	League	L/Cup	FA Cup	Other	Lg	L/C	FAC	Oth
GOALKEEPERS														
Martin Hodge	6.2	14.2	04.02.59	Southport	01.02.77	Plymouth A (A)	43	1	1					
				£135,000	01.07.79	Everton	25		6					
				Loan		Preston N.E	28							
Loan Oldham Athletic 4lg				Loan		Gillingham	4							
Loan Preston N.E 16lg				£50,000	01.08.83	Sheffield Wed	197	24	25	3				
				£250,000	31.08.88	Leicester City	75	4	1	1				
				Free	07.08.91	Hartlepool Utd	40	4	4	4				
Steven Jones					07.05.92	Hartlepool Utd. (T)	6							
DEFENDERS														
Paul Cross	5.8	10.0	31.10.65	Barnsley	01.11.83	Barnsley (A)	114+4	8	11+1	3+1				
				Loan	26.09.91	Preston N.E	5			1				
				£20,000	24.01.92	Hartlepool Utd	21							
Ryan Cross	6.0	11.08	11.10.72	Plymouth	30.03.91	Plymouth A	18+1	2		1				
					11.06.92	Hartlepool Utd								
John MacPhail	6.0	12.3	07.12.55	Dundee		St.Columbu								
Div.4 '82 '84; Div.3'88						Dundee	64+4	11	5					
				£30,000	18.01.79	Sheffield Utd	135	9	8		7		1	
				Free	30.03.83	York City	141+1	10	16	5	24	3	1	1
				£14,000	18.07.86	Bristol City	26		5	6	1			
				£23,000	31.07.87	Sunderland	130	10	5	8	22			
				Loan	16.09.90	Hartlepool Utd	14		2	1				
					13.12.90	Hartlepool Utd	68+1	3	4	5	2			
Keith Nobbs	5.10	11.10	18.09.61	Bishop Auckland	22.09.79	Middlesbrough (A)	1							
Northern Lg'85					05.08.82	Halifax Town	87	4	2	1	1			
						Bishop Auckland								
					09.08.85	Hartlepool Utd	247+6	13+1	12+1	16	1			
MIDFIELD														
Dean Emerson	5.8	10.8	27.12.62	Salford	01.07.82	Stockport Co	156	10	3	3	7	3		1
						Rotherham Utd	55	6	4	3	8	1		1
					16.10.88	Coventry City	98+16	4+4	6	3				
				Free	16.05.92	Hartlepool Utd								
Brian Honour	5.7	12.5	16.02.64	Hurdern	26.02.82	Darlington (A)	59+15	5	5	2	4	1		2
						Peterlee								
					06.02.85	Hartlepool Utd	248+17	13+3	16	15	18	2	2	4
Lennie Johnrose	5.10	11.5	29.11.69	Preston	16.06.88	Blackburn Rovers (T)	20+22	2+1	10+3	2	11	1		
				Loan	21.01.92	Preston N.E	1+2				1			
				£50,000	28.02.92	Hartlepool Utd	15				2			
Paul Olsson	5.8	10.11	24.12.65	Hull		Hull City (A)				1+1				1
				Free		Exeter City	38+5	2	0+1		2			
					25.10.88	Scarborough	34+14	5+1	2	8	5			
				£5,000	26.12.89	Hartlepool Utd	94+6	7+1	6	6+1	6			1
Mick Tait	5.11	12.5	30.09.56	Wallsend		Oxford Utd	61+3	2+1	2		23	1		
Div.3'83; SC'88.Div4'91				£65,000		Carlisle Utd	101+5	7	7		20		2	
				£150,000		Hull City	29+4		1		3		1	
				£100,000		Portsmouth	228+12	23+1	13	2+1	30	1	1	
				£50,000		Reading	98+1	9	16	9	9	2		3
				Free	03.08.90	Darlington	79	5	4	3	2			
				Free	31.07.92	Hartlepool Utd								
FORWARDS														
Paul Baker	6.1	12.10	05.01.63	Newcastle		Bishop Auckland								
				£4,000	01.07.84	Southampton								
				f	02.07.85	Carlisle Utd	66+5	4	3	2+1	11	1		
					31.07.87	Hartlepool Utd	192+5	12	16	16	65	4	6	5
John Gallacher	5.10	10.08	26.01.69	Glasgow		Falkirk	9+9		0+1		5			
				£100,000		Newcastle Utd	22+7	3	2	3	6	1		1
				Free	16.05.92	Hartlepool Utd								
Andy Saville	6.0	12.0	12.12.64	Hull	17.06.85	Hull City	74+26	6	3+2	4+2	18	1	1	
				£100,000	23.03.89	Walsall	28+10	2		1+1	5			
				£80,000	09.03.90	Barnsley	71+11	5+1	2	4	22			1
				£60,000	13.03.92	Hartlepool Utd	1				1			
Nicholas Southall					21.02.91	Hartlepool Utd	13+9		1+2	3+1	3			
ADDITIONAL CONTRACT PLAYERS														
Scott Garrett					15.10.90	Lincoln City								
				Free	07.05.92	Hartlepool Utd								
Anthony Harrison					24.09.88	Hartlepool Utd								
David J Hughes					10.07.92	Hartlepool Utd								
Stephen Locker						Hartlepool Utd	0+1							
Simon McBeth					10.07.92	Hartlepool Utd								
Thomas McGuckin					20.06.91	Hartlepool Utd	7							
Christopher Pollock					23.08.88	Hartlepool Utd								
Lee Roxby					24.01.90	Middlesbrough (T)								
				N.C	11.03.91	Hartlepool Utd								
John Shotton					02.08.90	Manchester Utd								
				Monthly	14.09.90	Stockport Co								
				Monthly	12.10.90	Hartlepool Utd	0+1							
Paul D Thompson					22.10.91	Hartlepool Utd								

LEADING LEAGUE GOALSCORERS SEASONS 1985-86 – 1991-92

1985-86	ALAN SHOULDER	17		1986-87	ANDY DIXON	9
1987-88	PAUL BAKER	20		1988-89	SIMON GRAYSON	12
1989-90	JOE ALLON	18		1990-91	JOE ALLON	28
			1991-92	PAUL DALTON	13	

THE VICTORIA GROUND Hartlepool, Cleveland TS24 8BZ

Capacity: 9,607   **Covered Standing:**   **Seating:** 1,500

Tel: Ground: 0429 272584   **Ticket Sales:** 0429 222077   **Clubcall:** 0898 12 11 47

All premium rate calls (0898/0891) cost 36p per minute cheap rate and 48p per minute at all other times. Call costings correct at time of going to press.

ATTENDANCES
Highest: 17,426 v Manchester United, FA Cup Round 3, 18.1.1957

Lowest: 655 v Bradford City, Football League Trophy, 18.8.1982
790 v Stockport County, Div 4, 5.5.1984

Record Receipts: £45,000 v Tottenham, Rumbelows Cup, 9.10.1990

Season Tickets:
Stands: from £161 to £184, juv/OAP £92 to £115
Ground: £138, juv/OAP £98

Executive Box Season Tickets: Apply to club for details

Cost of Stand Tickets: Grandstand: adults £8, £7, juniors/OAP £4, £5
Terraces: adults £6, juniors/OAP £4

Match and Ticket Information: No pre-booking of tickets

Car Parking: Side street parking is ample

Nearest Railway Station: Hartlepool Church Street (0429) 74039

How to get to the ground

From North: Use A1, A19 then A179 S.P. Hartlepool to Hart. In 2.5m at traffic signals forward, then at crossroads turn right into Clarence Road for Hartlepool United FC

From South and West: Use A1, A19 and A689 into Hartlepool town centre, then bear right into Clarence Road for Hartlepool United FC

Value Rating: ✱ ✱ ✱

Programme Editor: Lisa Charlton & Brian Hewitson

Price of 1992-93 Programme: £1
Number of Pages: 32
Subscriptions: Please apply to club

Local Newspapers: Hartlepool Mail, Northern Echo

Local Radio Stations: Radio Tees, Radio Cleveland

HEREFORD UNITED   Division 3

Formed: 1924   **Turned Professional:** 1924   **Ltd Co:** 1939

SPONSORED BY: Sun Valley   **NICKNAME:** United

Life Vice-Presidents
A Bush

Chairman
P S Hill,FRICS

Directors
M B Roberts(Vice-Chairman)
D H Vaughan
D Jones
J Duggan

Company Secretary/Director
D H Vaughan (0432 276666)

Assistant Secretary
Mrs J Fennessey

Player/Coach
Greg Downs

Commercial Manager
(0432 273155)

Physiotherapist
Colin Taylor

Club Statistician for the Directory
Lawerence Appleby

SINCE the exciting days when Hereford United campaigned successfully to join The Football League following some historic Cup runs, the little club enjoyed initial success and then settled down quietly in the Fourth Division.

An loyal band of supporters occassionally have their hopes raised as a better than average squad emerges and so it was at the beginning of the 1991-92 campaign that six victories in the first nine matches put United into the top three and the potential of Peter Heritage looked certain to provide the goals to keep Hereford in a challenging position.

Indeed the diminutive Brain, a bargain buy from Cheltenham Town started and ended the season with a goal, was one of the club's most consistent performers and finished top scorer with thirteen goals. The experience of popular Greg Downs was a great help, but Heritage found scoring more difficult as the season developed, so John Narbett's contribution, mainly from the penalty spot was vital and memories were stirred as John Sillett plotted an unspectacular but worthwhile FA Cup run getting through to the Fourth Round.

The club won few new friends by the dour manner in which Woking were eliminated, but with the Cup reputation the Surrey club had and the importance of survival, the result certainly supported the tactics used. The reward was an exciting visit to The City Ground and a test at Nottingham Forest.

A good FA Cup atmosphere failed to bring the fairytale result and in hindsight Hereford's season seemed to fall away from then on. There was an early exit in the Autoglass Trophy, and with goals becoming more and more difficult to find, Hereford sank to seventeenth position, and on the last day of the season the lowest attendance of the campaign, 1,297, saw United lose 1-2 to a stressful Northampton Town who were struggling for survival themselves.

Greg Downs who is now in charge at Edgar Street will need to change the club's fortunes very quickly to reassure the loyal hardcore of support that there is a future at Hereford for full-time League football. **T.W.**

Back row: Youth and Trainee contract players. **3rd row:** Peter Isaac (Trainer), Meshach Wade, Gareth Davies, Paul Robinson, Alan Judge, Andy Theodosiou, Owen Pickard, David Titterton, Richard Jones, John Layton (Youth team manager). **2nd row:** Chris Fry, Jed Jennings, Max Nicholson, Greg Downs (Player-coach), Simon Brain, Derek Hall, Colin Anderson. **Front row:** Youth and Trainee contract players.

HEREFORD UNITED

DIVISION FOUR: 17th   **FA CUP:** 4th RND   **RUMBELOWS CUP:** 1st RND   **AUTOGLASS:** 1st RND

M		DATE	COMP.	VEN	OPPONENTS	RESULT	H/T	LGE POS	GOALSCORERS/GOAL TIMES	ATTEN-DANCE
1	A	17	BL	A	Wrexham	W 1-0	1-0		Brain 18	(3,225)
2		20	RC 1/1	A	**Torquay United**	L 0-2	0-0			(2,410)
3		24	BL	H	Scarborough	W 4-1	4-1	4	Theodosiou 2, Narbett 3 (15, 30 pen, 45 pen)	2,600
4		28	RC 1/2	H	**Torquay United**	W 2-1	1-1		**Narbett (pen) 16, Theodosiou 60**	2,333
5		31	BL	A	Barnet	L 0-1	0-0	4		(2,860)
6	S	4	BL	H	Gillingham	W 2-0	1-0		Heritage 19, Narbett (pen) 53	2,554
7		6	BL	A	Rotherham United	D 0-0	0-0	4		(3,778)
8		14	BL	H	Burnley	W 2-0	1-0	4	Lowndes 26, Heritage 58	4,400
9		18	BL	H	York City	W 2-1	2-0	4	Brain 12, Heritage 45	3,540
10		21	BL	A	Walsall	L 0-3	0-2	4		(4,509)
11		28	BL	H	Lincoln City	W 3-0	1-0	3	Heritage 1, Narbett (pen) 13, Lowndes 38	2,081
12	O	5	BL	A	Scunthorpe United	D 1-1	0-0	3	Martin (og) 72	(2,384)
13		26	BL	A	Chesterfield	L 0-1	0-1	4		(2,949)
14	N	2	BL	A	Maidstone United	L 2-3	1-2	7	Lowndes 2, Downs (pen) 18	(846)
15		6	BL	H	Halifax Town	L 0-2	0-1			2,207
16		9	BL	H	Rochdale	D 1-1	1-0	8	Brain 45	2,959
17		16	FAC 1	A	**Atherstone**	D 0-0	0-0			(2,589)
18		19	AGT Pre	A	**Torquay United**	W 1-0	1-0		**Russell 34**	(2,138)
19		23	BL	A	Carlisle United	L 0-1	0-0	8		(2,032)
20		26	FAC 1R	H	**Atherstone**	W 3-0	0-0		**Lowndes 31, Brain 72, 84**	3,479
21		30	BL	A	Crewe Alexandra	L 2-4	0-3	11	Russell 47, Vaughan 61	(2,550)
22	D	7	FAC 2	A	**Aylesbury**	W 3-2	2-1		**Fry 7, Heritage 10, Tomlinson (og) 63**	(3,200)
23		26	BL	H	Wrexham	W 3-1	1-0		Fry 6, Brain 51, Narbett 68	3,542
24		28	BL	H	Barnet	D 2-2	2-1		Heritage 5, Pejic 40	4,654
25	J	1	BL	A	Gillingham	L 1-2	1-2		Caffrey 48	(3,392)
26		4	FAC 3	A	**Woking**	D 0-0	0-0			(4,500)
27		7	AGT Pre	H	**Exeter City**	W 2-1	1-0		**Brain 4, 76**	1,564
28		11	BL	A	Cardiff City	L 0-1	0-0	13		(5,305)
29		13	FAC 3R	H	**Woking**	W †2-1	1-0		**Narbett 42, Brain 101**	8,679
30		18	BL	H	Blackpool	L 1-2	1-0	15	Narbett (pen) 28	3,008
31		21	AGT 1	H	**Walsall**	L †0-1	0-0			1,503
32		26	FAC 4	A	**Nottingham Forest**	L 0-2	0-1			(24,259)
33	F	8	BL	H	Chesterfield	W 1-0	1-0	15	Brain 12	2,315
34		12	BL	H	Crewe Alexandra	L 1-2	1-1		Heritage 39	2,181
35		15	BL	A	Mansfield Town	D 1-1	1-1		Heritage 34	(2,550)
36		18	BL	A	Doncaster Rovers	L 0-2	0-2			(1,270)
37		22	BL	H	Cardiff City	D 2-2	1-0	15	Brain 45, Fry 59	5,691
38		25	BL	H	Mansfield Town	L 0-1	0-1			2,122
39		29	BL	A	Northampton Town	W 1-0	1-0	15	Downs 12	(2,468)
40	M	3	BL	A	Blackpool	L 0-2	0-0			(3,560)
41		7	BL	H	Doncaster Rovers	L 0-1	0-1	17		1,974
42		10	BL	A	Halifax Town	W 2-0	0-0		Narbett (pen) 56, Brain 58	(961)
43		14	BL	H	Maidstone United	D 2-2	0-1	17	Brain 61, Titterton 66	1,910
44		21	BL	A	Rochdale	L 1-3	0-1		Jones 48	(2,122)
45		28	BL	H	Carlisle United	W 1-0	1-0	16	Heritage 13	1,810
46		31	BL	A	Burnley	L 0-2	0-2			(10,578)
47	A	4	BL	H	Rotherham United	W 1-0	0-0	16	Fry 77	1,868
48		7	BL	A	Scarborough	D 1-1	0-0		Brain 66	(1,008)
49		11	BL	A	York City	L 0-1	0-1	16		(1,614)
50		18	BL	H	Walsall	L 1-2	1-1	17	Caffrey 28	2,291
51		20	BL	A	Lincoln City	L 0-3	0-1			(2,358)
52		24	BL	H	Scunthorpe United	L 1-2	1-1	17	Devine 34	1,583
53		28	BL	H	Northampton Town	L 1-2	0-2	17	Brain 74	1,297

Best Home League Attendance: 5,691 v Cardiff City   **Smallest:** 1,297 v Northampton   **Av Home Att:** 2,695

Goal Scorers: | | **Compared with 90-91:** +118

League (44): Brain 10, Narbett 8 (4 pens), Heritage 8, Lowndes 3, Fry 3, Downs 2 (1 pen), Caffrey 2, Theodosiou, Vaughan, Devine Pejic, Titterton, Jones, Opponents, Russell

R/lows C (2): Theodosiou, Narbett (1 pen)

FA Cup (8): Brain 3, Lowndes, Opponents, Heritage, Fry, Narbett

Autoglass (3): Brain 2, Russell

† = After extra-time

Elliott A.	Fry C.	Downs G.	Theodosiou A.	Bradley R.	Lowndes S.	Hall D.	Caffrey H.	Brain S.	Robinson P.	Narbett J.	Heritage P.	Pejic M.	Devine S.	Vaughan N.	Titterton D.	Jones R.	Jennings K.	Wade P.	Judge A.	McIntyre S.	Russell K.	Moran O.	Nebbeling G.	Davies G.	Jones S.	Referee	
1	12	3	4		6	7	11*	9	10†	S	8		5	2												B Coddington	1
1	2	3	4	5	6	7	11	9	10	8																J Deakin	2
1	2	3	4	5*	6	7	8	9	10	11	12	S														A Smith	3
1	11	3	4	5	2	6	7*	9•	14	8	10	12														M Brandwood	4
1	2	3	4	5	6	7*		9			10	8	12	11												P Scoble	5
1	7	3	4	5*	6	8		9		11	10	2	12	S												A Bennett	6
1	2	3	4		6	7		9			10	8	5	11	S					S						N Midgley	7
1	2	3	4		6	7	S	9		11	10	8	5		S											P Jones	8
1	2	3	4		6	7	12	9*		11	10	8	5		S											V Callow	9
1	2	3	4		6		12	8	10	9	7		5*		11•											D Frampton	10
1	2	3	4		6		S	9		11	10	8	5		7											R Nixon	11
1	2*	3	4		6			9		11	10	7	5		8	12				S						E Parker	12
1		3	4		6	14	2	9		11	10	7*	5		8•	12										A Dawson	13
1		3	4		6	7*	11	14	9		10	2	5*		12	8										G Willard	14
	3•		4		6	12	11	9		14	10	2*	5		7	8		1								L Shapter	15
	2	3	4		6	11	S	8		10		5	S			1	7	9								J Rushton	16
	2	3	4		6	7	8*	12	10		5	9	S			1		11								R Nixon	17
10		3	4			7	S		9	2	5	11			S	6	1		8							W Burge	18
	2	3	4		14	7		9	6	5*	10•					11	1		8	12						C Trussell	19
	9		4		8	6	S	10		11	3	5	7	S			2	1							12	R Nixon	20
	2				3	7	8•		10	4	6*	5		12		11	1		9	14						P Danson	21
	2	3	4		11	7	S	8		10	9	6	5	S		1										K Cooper	22
	2	3			7		S	8		10	9	5		6	12			1	11		4*					R Hamer	23
	11	3			7		S	8		10	9	6*	12				1	2		5						R Gifford	24
1	2	3			7	6	8		10	9*		5		S		11	4								12	K Morton	25
	2	3	S		7			10	9		5	6*	12	8		11	1						4			P Durkin	26
		3			7	11	10•	8	4	5	6*	9		2	1							14				J Lloyd	27
	2	3	4		S	7		8	10	9	5	S	6			11	1									P Vanes	28
1	9*	3	4		8	6		10		7	11	5	S	12		2										P Durkin	29
1	11	3*	4		6	7	8•		10	9	5	12	14		2											P Alcock	30
1	9*	3	4		6	8		10	S		11	5	12		7		2									R Groves	31
1	12	3	4		6	7	8	9	5	10*	S		11	2												D Axcell	32
1	12	3	4		6	7*	8	9	5	S	10		11	2												P Taylor	33
1	12	3	4		6*	7	8	9	5	10	S		11	2												C Wilkes	34
1	7	3	4		S	S	11	8	6	9	5	10	2													I Cruikshank	35
1	7*	3*	4		14	12	11	8	6	9	5	10	2													I Hendrick	36
	7	3	4		11	S	8	6	9	5	S	10	2	1												M Brandwood	37
	7•	3	4		11	14	8	6	9	5	10	12	2*	1												M Bodenham	38
		3			7*	S	8	10	6	9	5	12	11			4		1	2							A Bennett	39
	14	3			12		8•	10	6	9	5		11			4		1	2							K Breen	40
		3	8		7*		9		6		5		11	12	4		1	2							10•	R Milford	41
	7	3	4			10	9	8			5	S	6	11	2		1						S			R Nixon	42
	7	3	4		S		9		8	10	5	S	6	11	2		1									H King	43
	7•	3*	4		12		14	10	8	9	5		6	11	2		1	4								P Vanes	44
	7	3	4		2	12	9	S	8	10	5		6	11*		1										W Pierce	45
	7	3	4		2	14	10*	12	8	9	5		6	11•		1										W Burns	46
	7	3	4		11		9	S	8	10	5	S	6		2		1									J Worrall	47
	7	3	4		11		9	S	8	10	5	S	6		1		2						12	R Bigger	48
	7	3	4*		11		9	12•	8	10	5	14	6		1		2								K Lupton	49
	7	3			2		11	9	8	10	5	S	6	S		1		4								J Deakin	50
	7*	3	4			11•	10	12	8	9		14	6	5			1	2					7	I Hemley	51
	11					9	10	8		5	3		6			1	2*		4			7	M Bailey	52
	7	3	4			10		8	9		5		6	2		1	S		S			11	T Fitzharris	53
18	33	40	33	3	29	15	12	40	7	33	38	15	35	8	20	14	9	10	24	12	3		3	3	4	League Appearances	
	4				3	5	5	1	4		1		2	4	5	2	2				2				2	Substitute Appearances	
2	2	2	2	2	2	2	2	1+1	2	1	0+1															R/lows Appearances	
2	5+1	5	5		5	6		5		3	6	2	6	4	0+2	1		4	4	2				1		FA Cup Appearances	
1	2	2	3		1	3		2	1	1	3	1	3	2	1+1		3	2	1	1					0+1	Autoglass Appearances	

Also Played: Posn.(Game): Goddard S(5,11)14(10), Harris S(52), Burton 12(27,52), Culpin 7*(40)14(41)

Players on Loan: G Nebbling, P Culpin, K Russell, A Morah

† = Sent Off

HEREFORD UNITED

Club Colours: White shirts with red and black trim, black shorts, white stockings with red and black tops
Change Colours: All red
Reserves League: No Reserve Team

Previous League: Southern League
Previous Managers: Since joining the Football League
Colin Addison 1971-74   John Sillett 1974-78   Tony Ford 1978   Mike Bailey 1978-79   Frank Lord 1979-82   Tommy Hughes 1982-83   John Newman 1983-87   Ian Bowyer 1987-1990   Colin Addison 1990-91   John Sillett 1991-92   Greg Downs 1992-
Honours: Div 3, 1975-76   Welsh FA Cup 1989-90
League Career: Elected to Div 4 1972   Promoted to Div 3 1972-73   Promoted to Div 2 1975-76
Relegated to Div 3 1976-77   Relegated to Div 4 1977-78

CLUB RECORDS

Most Appearances for Club: Mel Pejic, 1980-91: League 404+8, FA Cup 20+1, League Cup 23+2, Other Competitions 26+1 **Total 473+12**
Most Capped Player: Brian Evans, 1 Wales   **For England:** None
Record Goalscorer in a Match: 'Dixie' McNeil 4 v Chester, Div 3, 10.3.1976
Record League Goalscorer in a Season: 'Dixie' McNeil 35, Div 3, 1975-76   **In All Competitions:** 'Dixie' McNeil, 37 (League 35, FA Cup 2), 1975-76
Record League Goalscorer in a Career: Stewart Phillips, 93, 1978-88 & 1990-91   **In All Compeititions:** Stewart Phillips, 111, (League 93, FA Cup 5, Lge Cup 9, Other 4) 1978-88 & 1990-91
Record Transfer Fee Received: £250,000 from Queens Park Rangers for Darren Peacock, March 1991
Record Transfer Fee Paid: £50,000 to Halifax Town for Ian Juryeff, 14.12.1989
Best Performances: League: 22nd Div 2, 1976-77   **FA Cup:** 4th Round 1971-72, 1976-77, 1981-82, 1989-90, 1991-92   **League Cup:** 3rd Round, 1974-75   **Welsh Cup:** Finalists (4 times)   Winners 1989-90
Most League Points: (3pts a win): 77, Div 4, 1984-85   (2pts a win): 63, Div 3, 1974-75
Most League Goals: 86, Div 3, 1975-76
Record League Victory: 6-0 v Burnley (a), Div 4, 24.1.1987
Record Cup Victory: 6-1 v Queens Park Rangers, FA Cup Rnd 2, 7.12.1957
Record League Defeat: 0-6 v Rotherham United (a), Div 4, 29.4.1989
Record Cup Defeat: 0-5 v Newport County, League Cup Rnd 1, 11.8.1981   2-7 v Arsenal, FA Cup Rnd 3 Replay, 21.1.1985   0-5 v Nottingham Forest, League Cup Rnd 2, 7.10.1987
Oldest Player in a League Match: John Jackson 40 years 6 days
Youngest Player in a League Match: Stuart Phillips 16 years 112 days

LONGEST LEAGUE RUNS	
of undefeated matches: 14 (1972-73, 1984)	of league matches without a win: 13 (1977-78, 1978)
of undefeated home matches: 21 (1972-73)	of undefeated away matches: 6 (1972-73, 1984)
without home win: 11 (1981-82)	without an away win: 28 (1977-78)
of league wins: 5 (1984)	of home wins: 12 (1973)
of league defeats: 8 (1986-87)	of away wins: 3 (1975-76, 1976-77, 1984-85, 1987-88)

HEREFORD UNITED

PLAYERS NAME Honours	Ht	Wt	Birthdate	Birthplace Transfers	Contract Date	Clubs	APPEARANCES				GOALS			
							League	L/Cup	FA Cup	Other	Lg	L/C	FAC	Oth
GOALKEEPERS														
Alan Judge	5.11	11.5	21.06.59	Kinsbury	03.01.78	Luton Town (A)	11	1						
LgC86				Loan	02.09.82	Reading	33							
				Free	14.07.83	Reading	44	4	3	1				
				£10,000	24.12.84	Oxford Utd	80	11	5	4				
				Loan	06.11.85	Lincoln City	2							
				Loan	01.11.88	Cardiff City	8			1				
				Free	25.07.91	Hereford Utd	24		4	2				
DEFENDERS														
Steve Devine	5.9	10.7	11.12.64	Strablane	31.12.82	Wolves (A)								
NI:Y; Welsh Cup'90				f	17.03.83	Derby County	10+1							
				N.C	22.08.85	Stockport Co	2							
				f	09.10.85	Hereford Utd	235+10	12+1	15	20	4			
Greg Downs	5.9	10.7	13.12.58	Carlton	01.12.76	Norwich City (A)	162+7	16	20		7		1	
FAC'87				Loan	29.11.77	Torquay Utd	1				1			
				£40,000	16.07.85	Coventry City	142+4	19+1	9	7	4	2	1	
				Free	02.08.90	Birmingham City	16+1	2	2	2		1		
				Free	18.07.91	Hereford Utd	40	2	5	2	2			
Richard Jones	5.11	11.01	26.04.69	Pontypool		Newport Co	31+10		0+1	2	1			
					24.08.88	Hereford Utd	108+5	6	6+1	10+2	6	3		1
Andrew Theodosiou	6.1	12.8	30.10.70	Stoke Newington		Tottenham H. (T)								
				Free	04.07.89	Norwich City								
				Free	18.07.91	Hereford Utd	33	2	5	3	1			
David Titterton	5.11	12.9	25.09.71	Hatton, nr Warwick	24.05.90	Coventry City (T)	0+2	1						
E: Y.1				£8,000	12.09.91	Hereford Utd	20+5		0+2	1+1	1			
MIDFIELD														
Chris Fry	5.9	9.06	23.10.69	Cardiff	03.08.88	Cardiff City	22+33	1+2	0+2	0+2	1			
				Free	02.08.91	Hereford Utd	33+4	2	5+1	2	3	1		
Derek Hall	5.8	11.2	05.01.65	Ashton-U-Lyme	08.10.82	Coventry City (A)	1							
				f	23.03.84	Torquay Utd	55	2	2	3	6			1
				f	29.07.85	Swindon Town	9+1	2	1+1					
				f	21.08.86	Southend Utd	120+3	13	6	8	15	1	2	1
				Free		Halifax Town	48+1	5	2	5	4	1		1
				Free	18.07.91	Hereford Utd	15+5	2	6	3				
FORWARDS														
Simon Brain						Cheltenham		1						
				£10,000	20.12.90	Hereford Utd	60+3	2	5	3	18		3	2
Paul Culpin	5.10	10.8	08.02.62	Kirby Muxloe		Leicester City (A)		2				1		
						Nuneaton Borough		2				1		
				£50,000	10.06.85	Coventry City	5+4	1		2	2			
				£55,000	10.10.87	Northampton T	52+11	4+1	2+1	6	23	2		1
				£40,000	06.10.89	Peterborough U	30+17	3+2	4+5	3	14	1	3	1
				Monthly	28.02.92	Hereford Utd	1+1							
Owen Pickard	5.10	11.03	18.11.69	North Devon		Plymouth A	6+10	0+1		0+2	1			
				Free	16.07.92	Hereford Utd								
Paul Robinson	6.2	11.8	21.02.71	Nottingham		Bury (T)								
				Free	22.05.89	Scarborough	13+7	2	1	0+1	3	1		
				£15,000		Plymouth A	7+1			1	3			
				£15,000	18.06.91	Hereford Utd	7+4	1+1		1				
ADDITIONAL CONTRACT PLAYERS														
Michael Campbell					24.08.88	Hereford Utd	1							
Gareth M Davies					10.04.92	Hereford Utd	3							
William Foley					17.03.90	Hereford Utd								
Darren Goodall						West Brom A. (A)								
					07.09.89	Hereford Utd								
William Green					30.11.88	Hereford Utd								
Kentione Jennings						P'broke Be								
				Free	19.10.91	Hereford Utd	9+2							
Sean Kimberley					11.11.88	Hereford Utd								
Darren Lush						Bournemouth (A)								
					03.08.89	Hereford Utd								
Adam Moore			11.12.70	Cardiff		Newport Co. (A)								
					21.07.89	Hereford Utd								
Maximilian Nicholson			03.10.71	Leeds	13.02.91	Doncaster Rovers	2+1			0+1				
				Free	16.05.92	Hereford Utd								
James O'Donnel	5.9	11.10		Manchester	01.07.87	Manchester Utd								
				Loan	06.12.88	Charlton Ath								
				Loan	21.03.89	Swindon Town								
				Free	22.03.90	Hereford Utd								
Ian Rock					23.09.88	Hereford Utd								
Meshach Wade						P'broke Be								
				Free	19.10.91	Hereford Utd	10		4	3				
Richard D Walker					24.09.90	Hereford Utd								

LEADING LEAGUE GOALSCORERS SEASONS 1985-86 – 1991-92

1985-86	**OLLIE KEARNS**	**13**		1986-87	**OLLIE KEARNS**	**16**	
1987-88	**STEVE SPOONER**	**8**		1988-89	**PHIL STANT**	**23**	
	PHIL STANT	**8**					
1989-90	**MARK JONES**	**9**		1990-91	**STEWART PHILLIPS**	**11**	
	1991-92	**SIMON BRAIN**	**10**				

EDGAR STREET   Hereford, HR4 9JU

Capacity: 13,752   **Covered Standing:** 10,855   **Seating:** 2,897

Tel: Ground: 0432 276666   **Ticket Sales:** As ground number   **Clubcall:** 0898 12 16 45

All premium rate calls (0898/0891) cost 36p per minute cheap rate and 48p per minute at all other times. Call costings correct at time of going to press.

ATTENDANCES
Highest: 18,114 v Sheffield Wednesday, FA Cup Round 3, 4.1.1958

Lowest: 1,194 v Aldershot, Leyland Daf Cup, 8.11.1989

Record Receipts: £51,234 v Arsenal, FA Cup Round 3, 5.1.1975

Season Tickets:
Stands: £139, juv/OAP £99
Ground: £99, juv/OAP £80

Executive Box Season Tickets: None

Cost of Stand Tickets: adult £7, child/OAP £5
Terraces: Adults £5, £4 juveniles/OAP

Match and Ticket Information: Bookable in advance

Car Parking: Available near ground for 1,000 cars (approx)

Nearest Railway Station: Hereford (0432 266534)

How to get to the ground

From North: Use A49 (S.P. Hereford) into Edgar Street for Hereford United FC

From East: Use A465 or A438 (S.P. Hereford) into town centre, then follow signs Leominster A49 into Edgar Street for Hereford United FC

From South: Use A49 or A465 (S.P. Hereford) into town centre, then follow signs Leominster A49 into Edgar Street for Hereford United FC

From West: Use A438 (S.P. Hereford) into town centre, then follow signs Leominster A49 into Edgar Street for Hereford United FC

Value Rating: ★ ★

Programme Editor: Dave Bradley

Price of 1992-93 Programme: £1
Number of Pages: 28
Subscriptions: £28 (All home programmes)

Local Newspapers: Herefordshire Times, Evening News

Local Radio Stations: Radio Wyvern

© 1973

HUDDERSFIELD TOWN Division 2

Formed: 1908   **Turned Professional:** 1908   **Ltd Co:** 1908

SPONSORED BY: GOLA Plc   **NICKNAME:** The Terriers

Chairman
K S Longbottom

Directors
F L Thewlis
C Hodgkinson
B Buckley
G A Leslie
D G Headey (Vice-Chairman)
C Senior (Vice-President)

Associate Directors
T Fisher
T Cherry

Chief Executive
Paul Fletcher

Secretary
C D Patzelt (0484 420335/6)

Assistant Secretary
Mrs M Baldwin

Commercial Manager
Tony Flynn (0484 534867)

Manager
Ian Ross

Physiotherapist
Wayne Jones

Chief Scout/Youth Development
George Mulhall

Groundsman
Raymond Chappell

Club Statistician for the Directory
Richard Stead

HUDDERSFIELD Town began the season in optimistic mood believing they had a side capable of achieving promotion. This was reflected in pre-season transfer activity with the only moves of note being goalkeeper Tim Clarke from Coventry for £30,000 and Phil Starbuck from Nottingham Forest for an undisclosed fee.

The first eight games brought four wins and four draws followed by Town's first defeat, although it was another month before Town conceded their first goal at home, resulting in the first home defeat.

Progress was also made in the Rumbelows Cup at the expense of Darlington and Sunderland, the latter on a 6-1 aggregate.

In the other cup competitions Town faired equally well progressing in the Autoglass Trophy and the F.A. Cup. The 7-0 win over Lincoln United equalling Town's record score in a first class F.A. Cup tie.

Over Christmas and New Year Town consolidated their 4th position with two wins and a draw including completion of the 'double' over eventual third division champions, Brentford.

Town then followed this with an inexplicable loss of form with only two wins from the next 11 league games. Part of the problem was a long term injury to midfielder Chris Marsden and although a number of loan deals were set up the team failed to recover their early season form.

Despite this run the team slipped only as low as 6th but the pursuing pack were fast gaining ground. As a result manager Eoin Hand left the club by 'mutual agreement', to be replaced by coach Ian Ross.

Initially results didn't improve and Town slipped to 8th, their lowest league position of the season.

With all looking lost, Town's fortunes were rekindled first, by the return of Chris Marsden and secondly the signing, on loan, of ex-Town apprentice Peter Butler. During the last eight games Town achieved seven wins and a draw which catapulted them into a final position of 3rd, only three points behind promoted Birmingham. Town entered the play-offs with optimism but lost the services of Marsden again to injury and Southends refusal to extend Butler's loan period.

Despite achieving a 2-2 draw in the away leg and taking the lead in the second after only two minutes they were unable to hold on and lost 4-3 on aggregate to eventual play-off winners Peterborough United.

Although this result left the club despondent, if the team remains together, then, barring injures Town should be able to make an even greater challenge for promotion next season. On an individual note, Town provided three players for the P.F.A. Third Division team of the season in Charlton, Marsden and Roberts. Striker Roberts also finished second highest scorer in the Third Division with a post war club record of 34 goals in a season and was also capped by Wales.

Richard Stead

Back row L-R: Wright, Roberts, Elliott, Clarke, Onoura, Trevitt. **Middle row:** Donovan, Mitchell, O'Regan, Billy, Lampkin, Mooney, Dyson, Ireland, Dysart, Barnett. **Front row:** Collins, Marsden, Charlton, Jackson, Ross, Starbuck, Booth, Brennan, Parsley

HUDDERSFIELD TOWN

DIVISION THREE: 3rd **FA CUP:** 3rd RND **RUMBELOWS CUP:** 3rd RND **AUTOGLASS:** S/FINALS

M	DATE		COMP.	VEN	OPPONENTS	RESULT	H/T	LGE POS	GOALSCORERS/GOAL TIMES	ATTEN-DANCE
1	A	17	BL	A	Bolton Wanderers	D 1-1	1-0	13	Marsden 12	(7,606)
2		20	RC 1/1	A	Darlington	L 0-1	0-1			(3,140)
3		25	BL	H	Bradford City	W 1-0	1-0	6	O'Regan (pen) 4	9,234
4		28	RC 1/2	H	Darlington	W 4-0	1-0		Roberts 18, Starbuck 75, 87, Onuora 80	3,907
5		31	BL	A	Brentford	W 3-2	1-1	5	O'Regan (pen) 26, Roberts 63, Starbuck 66	(5,459)
6	S	4	BL	H	Chester City	W 2-0	1-0	3	Onuora 45, Barnett 54	5,321
7		7	BL	H	Exeter City	D 0-0	0-0	3		5,758
8		14	BL	A	Bury	D 4-4	1-4	4	Roberts 41, 89, Starbuck 62, 86	(4,409)
9		17	BL	A	Wigan Athletic	W 3-1	2-1	2	Starbuck 2, 33, Roberts 54	(3,531)
10		21	BL	H	Bournemouth	D 0-0	0-0	4		6,802
11		24	RC 2/1	A	Sunderland	W 2-1	1-0		Charlton 10, Starbuck 71	(8,161)
12		28	BL	H	Leyton Orient	L 0-1	0-1	5		(3,741)
13	O	5	BL	H	Swansea City	W 1-0	0-0	5	Roberts 55	5,578
14		9	RC 2/2	H	Sunderland	W 4-0	0-0		Onuora 47, Roberts 62, 71, Barnett 70	11,177
15		12	BL	A	Torquay United	W 1-0	0-0	4	Barnett 74	(2,936)
16		19	BL	A	Preston North End	L 0-1	0-0	4		(6,866)
17		22	AGT Pre	A	Wigan Athletic	W 1-0	1-0		Roberts 45	(1,214)
18		25	BL	H	Stockport County	L 0-1	0-0	5		9,229
19		29	RC 3	H	Swindon Town	L 1-4	0-2		Barnett 56	10,088
20	N	2	BL	A	Stoke City	W 2-0	2-0	4	Roberts 12, 15	(10,116)
21		6	BL	H	Fulham	W 3-1	1-1	3	O'Regan 28, Starbuck 76, Jackson 90	5,064
22		9	BL	H	Birmingham City	W 3-2	1-0	3	Roberts 8, 49, Onuora 77	11,688
23		16	FAC 1	H	Lincoln City	W 7-0	3-0		O'Regan17, Donovan23,87, Staplt'n40, Rob'ts53,62, Onuora 59	6,763
24		19	AGT Pre	H	Scarborough	D 1-1	0-0		Roberts 76	1,134
25		23	BL	A	West Bromwich A.	L 1-2	1-2	4	Roberts 19	(14,029)
26		30	BL	A	Hartlepool United	D 0-0	0-0	4		(4,017)
27	D	7	FAC 2	A	Rochdale	W 2-1	0-1		Roberts 74, Onuora 81	(5,776)
28		14	BL	H	Darlington	W 2-1	1-0	4	Starbuck (pen) 32, Roberts 46	5,677
29		22	BL	A	Bradford City	D 1-1	0-1	4	Roberts 58	(10,050)
30		26	BL	H	Brentford	W 2-1	1-0	4	Roberts 34, O'Regan 80	10,605
31		28	BL	H	Bolton Wanderers	W 1-0	1-0	4	Roberts 15	11,884
32	J	1	BL	A	Chester City	D 0-0	0-0	4		(3,504)
33		4	FAC 3	H	Millwall	L 0-4	0-4			10,879
34		11	BL	A	Reading	L 0-1	0-0	4		(4,732)
35		18	BL	H	Peterborough Utd	D 0-0	0-0	5		8,763
36		21	AGT 1	H	Blackpool	D †1-1	1-1		Roberts 16 (Won 3-1 on pens)	1,585
37		25	BL	A	Shrewsbury Town	D 1-1	0-1	5	Onuora 88	(3,688)
38	F	1	BL	H	Preston North End	L 1-2	0-0	5	Roberts 83	6,700
39		4	AGT QF	A	Bury	W 2-1	0-1		Onuora 47, Roberts 55	(1,786)
40		7	BL	A	Stockport County	D 0-0	0-0	5		(7,519)
41		11	BL	H	Hartlepool United	W 1-0	1-0	5	Roberts 39	5,559
42		15	BL	A	Darlington	W 3-1	1-1	4	Onuora 40, 85, Starbuck (pen) 49	(3,120)
43		22	BL	A	Reading	L 1-2	0-1	5	Roberts 78	6,259
44		25	BL	H	Hull City	D 1-1	0-0	4	Roberts 70	6,003
45		29	BL	A	Hull City	L 0-1	0-1	4		(5,310)
46	M	3	BL	A	Peterborough Utd	L 0-2	0-1	6		(6,257)
47		7	BL	H	Shrewsbury Town	W 2-1	1-1	4	Onuora 35, Roberts 71	4,674
48		10	BL	A	Fulham	L 0-1	0-0	7		(3,134)
49		14	BL	H	Stoke City	L 1-2	0-2	7	Starbuck (pen) 55	10,156
50		17	AGT SF	A	Burnley	L 0-2	0-2			(10,775)
51		21	BL	A	Birmingham City	L 0-2	0-1	8		(12,482)
52		28	BL	H	West Bromwich A.	W 3-0	1-0	8	Starbuck 26, Billy 50, Strodder (og) 73	7,428
53		31	BL	H	Bury	W 3-0	2-0	6	Starbuck 18, Billy 24, Roberts 67	5,890
54	A	4	BL	A	Exeter City	W 1-0	0-0	6	Roberts 52	(3,047)
55		11	BL	H	Wigan Athletic	W 3-1	2-0	5	Roberts 13, Trevitt 24, Starbuck 84	7,058
56		14	BL	A	Bournemouth	D 1-1	0-1	5	Roberts 72	(7,655)
57		20	BL	H	Leyton Orient	W 1-0	1-0	5	Onuora 10	10,011
58		25	BL	H	Swansea City	W 1-0	1-0	4	Roberts 30	(3,964)
59	M	2	BL	H	Torquay United	W 4-0	2-0	3	Starbuck 34, 45, Onuora 49, Barnett 81	7,961
60		11	PO SF 1	A	Peterborough Utd	D 2-2	1-0		Onuora 28, Robinson (og) 67	(11,751)
61		14	PO SF 2	H	Peterborough Utd	L 1-2	1-0		Starbuck 2	16,167

Best Home League Attendance: 11,884 v Bolton Wanderers   **Smallest:** 4,674 v Shrewsbury Town   **Av Home Att:** 7,535

Goal Scorers:

                                                  Compared with 90-91: +2,184

League (59): Roberts 24, Starbuck 14 (3 pens), Onuora 8, O'Regan 4 (2 pens), Barnett 3, Billy 2, Trevitt, Jackson, Opponents, Marsden

R/lows C(11): Roberts 3, Starbuck 3, Onuora 2, Barnett 2, Charlton

FA Cup (9): Roberts 3, Donovan 2, Onuora 2, O'Regan, Stapleton

Autoglass (5): Roberts 4, Onuora

Play-offs (3): Onuora, Starbuck, Opponents

† = After extra-time

Clarke T.	Trevitt S.	Charlton S.	Marsden C.	Mitchell G.	Jackson P.	O'Regan P.	Onuora I.	Roberts I.	Haylock G.	Barnett G.	Wright M.	Donovan K.	Starbuck P.	Ireland S.	Parsley N.	Stapleton F.	O'Doherty K.	Walsh A. (N.C.)	Kelly J.	Callaghan N. (L)	McNab N.	Martin L.	Billy C.	Campbell D.	Butler P. (L)	Referee	
1	2	3	4	5	6	7	8	9	10	11	S	S														P Wright	1
1	2	3	4	5	6	7	8	9		11*	S	14	10													**C Trussell**	2
1	2	3	4	5	6	7	8	9		11	S	S	10													I Cruikshanks	3
1	2	3	4	5	6	7	8	9		11	S	S	10													**A Flood**	4
1	2	3	4	5	6	7	8	9		11	S	S	10													P Foakes	5
1	2	3	4	5	6	7	8	9		11	S	14	10													T Lunt	6
1	2	3	4	5	6	7	8*	9		11	S	14	10													K Lupton	7
1	2	3*	4	5	6	7		9		11	12	8*	10	14												G Singh	8
1		3	4	5	6	7		9		11	S	8	10	S	2											B Nixon	9
1	2	3	4	5	6	7	14	9		11	S	8*	10													N Midgley	10
1	2	3	4	5	6	7	8	9		11	S	S	10													**E Parker**	11
1	2	3	4	5	6	7	8	9		11*	S	14	10													I Hemley	12
1	2	3	4	5	6	7	8	9		11	S	14	10													A Wilkie	13
1	2	3	4	5	6	7	8	9		11	S	S	10													**T West**	14
1	2	3	4	5	6	7	8	9		11	S	S	10													K Cooper	15
1	2	3	4	5	6	7	8*	9		11	S	14	10													P Danson	16
1	2	3	4	5	6	7	S	9		11	S	8	10													**A Dawson**	17
1	2	3	4	5	6	7	8*	9		11	S	14	10													W Burns	18
1	2	3	4	5	6	7	8*	9		11	S		10			14										**T Holbrook**	19
1	2	3	4	5	6†	7	S	9		11	S		10			8										K Burge	20
1	2	3	4	5	6	7	S	9		11	S		10			8										I Hendrick	21
1	2	3	4	5	6	7	14	9		11	S		10*			8										J Worrall	22
1	2	3		5		7	10	9		11*	12	4		14		8*	6									**A Flood**	23
1	2	3		5	6	7	10	9		11*		4		14		8	12									P Vanes	24
1	2	3		5	6	7	10	9		11	S	14				8			4*							J Martin	25
1	2	3		5	6	7	10	9		11	4		14		S	8*										K Breen	26
1	2	3		5	6	7	8	9		11	4		10*		S	14										**K Lupton**	27
1	2	3		5	6	7	8	9		11	4	S	10*	14												M Bailey	28
1	2			5	6	7	8	9		11	3		10*		S			14	4							V Callow	29
1	2	3		5	6	7	8	9		11	S		10					S	4							D Shadwell	30
1	2	3		5	6	7	8	9		11	S		10					S	4							G Courtney	31
1	2	3		5	6	7	8	9*		11*	12		10					14	4							J Brandwood	32
1	2			5	6	7	8	9		11	3		10		S			14*	4							**J Rushton**	33
1	2	3		5	6	7	8	9			S		10*		11			14	4							R Groves	34
1	2	3		5		7	8*	9			S				11		6	14*	4							I Cruikshanks	35
1	2	3		5		7	8*	9		12	4*		10	11			6	14								**P Wright**	36
1	2	3		5		7	14	9			S		10*	11					4	8						R Lewis	37
1	2*	3		5	6	7	10	9		12	11*							14	4	8						G Singh	38
		3		5	6	7	11	9		12			10		2				4	8		1	S			**M Reed**	39
		3		5	6	7	11	9			S		10		2				4		8*	1	14			R Dilkes	40
		3		5*	6	7	11	9			S		10		2				4		8	1	S			D Allison	41
		3			6	7*	11	9			S		10		2				4		8	1	S	5		I Hendrick	42
		3			6	7*	11	9		12			10	14	2				4		8*	1		5		M Peck	43
	2	3		5	6	7	11	9					10		14				4		8*	1	7	5		M Reed	44
	2	3		5	6	12	11	9					10		14				4		8*	1	7*			A Dawson	45
	2	3			6	12	11	9*		8	S		10	14					4			1				M James	46
1	2	3		5	6	7	11	9		8	S		10						4				S			T Fitzharris	47
1	2	3		5	6	7	11	9		8*	S		10						4							G Poll	48
1	2	3		5	6	7	11	9			S		10				8*		4*							J Parker	49
1	2	3		5	6	7*	11	9					10	8	12				4*		14					**J Watson**	50
1	2	3		5	6	7*	11†	9					10*						4				12			P Alcock	51
1	2	3	4	5	6		S	9					10										7		8	N Midgley	52
1	2	3	4*	5	6	12	11	9					10										7		8	A Flood	53
1	2	3	4	5	6		S	9		11			10										7		8	P Scoble	54
1	2	3	4	5	6		S	9		11		14	10										7*		8	P Jones	55
1	2	3	4	5	6		S	9		11			10										7		8	R Pawley	56
1	2	3	4	5	6		S	9		11			10*										7		8	A Smith	57
1	2	3	4	5	6		S	9		11		14	10										7*		8	D Shadwell	58
1	2	3		5	6	7	11	9				14	10*						4				8*			T Holbrook	59
1	2	3		5	6	7	11	9			12	14	10						4				8			**D Elleray**	60
1	2	3		5	6	7	11	9			12	14	10						4				8			**G Courtney**	61
39	41	45	23	43	45	37	38	46	1	27	4	4	42	3	5	5	1		13	8	11	7	8	3	7	**League Appearances**	
							2		3		4	4	6	2	6			1	4	1			2			**Substitute Appearances**	
5	5	5	5	5	5	5	5	5		5		0+1	5					0+1								**R/lows Appearances**	
3	3	2		3	2	3	3	3		3	2+1	1	2	0+1		1			1		0+1	1				**FA Cup Appearances**	
4	4	5	1	5	4	5	4	5	2	1+2	4	3+1	1+1	1		1	1+1		1+2	1	1	1				**Autoglass Appearances**	
2	2	2	2	2	2	2	2	2		2			2						2				2			**Play-offs Appearances**	

Also Played: A Booth 14(48,49)12(59)

Players on Loan: N Callaghan (Aston Villa), N McNab (Tranmere), P Butler (Southend)

†=Sent Off

HUDDERSFIELD TOWN

Club Colours: Blue/white striped shirts, white shorts and black with royal blue/white hoop on turnover stockings
Change Colours: Red/black striped shirts, black shorts, black with blue/white hoop on turnover stockings
Reserves League: Pontins Central League   **Youth Team:** Northern Intermediate League

Previous League: Midland League
Previous Managers: F Walker 1908-10   D Puden 1910-12   A Fairclough 1912-19   A Langley 1919-1921   H Chapman 1921-25
C Potter 1925-26   J Chaplin 1926-29   C Stephenson 1929-42   T Magner 1942-43   D Steele 1943-47   G Stephenson 1947-52   A
Beattie 1952-56   W Shankly 1956-60   E Boot 1960-64   T Johnston 1964-68   I Greaves 1968-74   R Collins 1974-75   T Johnston
1975-77   J Haselden 1977-78   M Buxton 1978-86   S Smith 1986-87   M Macdonald 1987-88   O Hand 1988-92   I Ross 1992-
Honours: Champions Division 1 1923-24, 1924-25, 1925-26 (first of only three clubs to win the Championship three years in
succession)   Champions Division 2 1969-70   Champions Division 4 1979-80   FA Cup Winners 1922
League Career: Elected to Div 2 1910   Promoted to Div 1 1919-20   Relegated to Div 2 1951-52
Promoted to Div 1 1952-53   Relegated to Div 2 1955-56   Promoted to Div 1 1969-70   Relegated to Div 2 1971-72
Relegated to Div 3 1972-73   Relegated to Div 4 1974-75   Promoted to Div 3 1979-80   Promoted to Div 2 1982-83
Relegated to Div 3 1987-88

CLUB RECORDS

Most Appearances for Club: W H Smith, 1913-34: League 521 + FA Cup 53 **Total 574**
Most Capped Player: Jimmy Nicholson 31, N Ireland   **For England:** Ray Wilson 30
Record Goalscorer in a Match: D Mangnall 5 v Derby County (h), 6-0, Div 1, 21.11.1931   A P Lythgoe 5 v Blackburn Rovers (h), 6-0,
Div 1, 13.4.1935
Record League Goalscorer in a Season: Sam Taylor 35, Div 2, 1919-20   George Brown, 35, Div 1, 1925-26   **In All Competitions:**
Dave Mangnall 42 (League 33, FA Cup 9) 1931-32
Record League Goalscorer in a Career: Jimmy Glazzard 141, 1946-56   George Brown 142, 1921-29   **In All Competitions:**
George Brown 159 (League 142, FA Cup 17)
Record Transfer Fee Received: £250,000 from Swindon for Duncan Shearer, June 1988   £250,000 from Reading for Craig
Maskell, August 1990
Record Transfer Fee Paid: £275,000 to Watford for Iwan Roberts, August 1990
Best Performances: League: Champions Division 1 (3)   **FA Cup:** Winners (1)   **League Cup:** Semi-Final 1967-68
Most League Points: (3pts for win) 82, Div 3, 1982-83   (2pts for win) 66, Div 4, 1979-80
Most League Goals: 101, Division 4, 1979-80
Record League Victory and Most Goals Scored in a League Match: 10-1 v Blackpool, Div 1, 13.12.1930
Most Goals Scored in a First Class Cup Tie: 7-1 v Chesterfield (a), FA Cup 3rd Rnd, 12.1.1929   7-0 v Lincoln United, F.A. Cup 1st
Rnd, 16.11.1991
Record League Defeat: 1-10 v Manchester City, Div 2, 7.11.1987
Record Cup Defeat: 0-6 v Sunderland, FA Cup 3rd Rnd., 1949-50
Oldest Player in a League Match: W H Smith, 39 years, 1934
Youngest Player in a League Match: Dennis Law, 15 years 10 months, 1956

LONGEST LEAGUE RUNS

of undefeated matches: 27 (1924-25)	**of league matches without a win:** 22 (1971-72)
of undefeated home matches: 28 (1982-83)	**of undefeated away matches:** 18 (1924-25)
without home win: 11 (1971-72)	**without an away win:** 31 (1936-37)
of league wins: 11 (1919-21)	**of home wins:** 11 (1925-26)
of league defeats: 7 (1913-14, 1955-56)	**of away wins:** 5 (1924-25)

BARCLAYS

BARCLAYS BUSINESS CENTRE
Huddersfield Business Centre
PO Box B71
17 Market Place
Huddersfield HD1 2AB

Tel: 0484 533231

HUDDERSFIELD TOWN

PLAYERS NAME / Honours	Ht	Wt	Birthdate	Birthplace / Transfers	Contract Date	Clubs	APPEARANCES League	L/Cup	FA Cup	Other	GOALS Lg	L/C	FAC	Oth
GOALKEEPERS														
Tim Clarke	6.3	13.7	19.09.68	Stourbridge	22.10.90	Coventry City								
				£15,000	22.07.91	Huddersfield Town	39	5	3	6				
Anthony Elliott	6.0	12.12	30.11.69	Nuneaton		Birmingham City (A)		1						
E:Y2;Welsh Cup'90					22.12.88	Hereford Utd	75	5	6	9				
				Free	29.07.92	Huddersfield Town								
DEFENDERS														
Peter Jackson	6.1	12.6	06.04.61	Bradford	07.04.79	Bradford City	267+11	27	10+1	4	24	1		
Div3'85				£250,000	23.10.86	Newcastle Utd	60	3	6	3	3			
					15.09.88	Bradford City	55+3	7	4	2	5			
						Huddersfield Town	83	5	4	7	2			
Tony Kenworthy	5.10	10.10	30.10.58	Leeds	01.07.76	Sheffield Utd. (A)	281+5	21	17	1	34	1	1	
E:Y,Div.4'82,FRT'87				f	11.03.86	Mansfield Town	98+2	5	6	12+1				
				Monthly	30.08.90	Huddersfield Town								
Graham Mitchell	6.1	11.4	16.02.68	Shipley	16.06.86	Huddersfield Town (T)	201+5	12+1	18	14	2	1		
Neil Parsley	5.9	10.12	25.04.66	Liverpool		Witton Albion								
				£20,000	08.11.88	Leeds Utd								
				Loan	13.12.89	Chester City	6			1				
				Free	25.07.90	Huddersfield Town	11+2	2		1				
				Loan	20.02.91	Doncaster Rovers	2+1							
Simon Trevitt	5.11	11.10	20.12.67	Dewsbury	16.06.86	Huddersfield Town	161+12	15	8	10	2	1		
Mark Wright	5.11	10.12	29.01.70	Manchester	10.06.88	Everton (T)	1							
				Loan	23.08.90	Blackpool	3							
				Loan	21.03.91	Huddersfield Town	10				1			
				Free	01.07.91	Huddersfield Town	4+4		2+1	1+4				
MIDFIELD														
Gary Barnett	5.6	9.13	11.03.63	Stratford	22.01.81	Coventry City (A)								
Div.3'84				f	07.07.82	Oxford Utd	37+8	6+2	5	1	9	1		
				Loan	24.02.83	Wimbledon	5				1			
					19.12.84	Fulham	167+15	17	8+1	8+2	30	3	1	1
				£30,000	20.07.90	Huddersfield Town	46+7	7	4	2+3	4	2		
Kevin Donovan	5.9		17.12.71	Halifax	11.10.89	Huddersfield Town (T)	9+8	0+1	1	4	1		2	
				Loan	13.02.92	Halifax Town	6							
Simon Ireland	5.10	10.7	23.11.71	Halifax	01.07.90	Huddersfield Town	6+9		0+1	1+1				
E: S				Loan	11.03.92	Wrexham	2+3			1				
Kevin Lampkin	5.10	11.8	20.12.72	Liverpool	17.05.91	Liverpool								
				Free	03.07.92	Huddersfield Town								
Carl Madrick	5.9	9.11	20.09.68	Bolton	01.07.87	Huddersfield Town	3+5			1				
Chris Marsden	5.11	10.12	03.01.69	Sheffield	06.01.87	Sheffield Utd. (A)	13+3	1		1	1			
					15.07.88	Huddersfield Town	105+7	12+1	6+2	9	9			
Kieran O'Regan	5.8	10.12	09.11.63	Cork	09.04.83	Brighton & H.A	69+17	6+1	3	2+1	2			1
Ei:4					12.08.87	Swindon Town	23+3	5+1	2+1	3	1			1
					04.08.88	Huddersfield Town	150+8	11+1	12+1	15+1	20	1	2	2
Richard Shelton	5.8	10.11	08.06.88	Sheffield		Huddersfield Town								
FORWARDS														
Iwan Roberts	6.3	12.6	26.06.68	Bangor	04.07.86	Watford (A)	40+23	6+2	1+6	5	9	3		
W:1,Y				£275,000	02.08.90	Huddersfield Town	90	7	5	9	38	3	4	4
Phil Starbuck	5.11	12.4	24.11.68	Nottingham	19.08.86	Nottm. Forest	9+27	1+3	2+5	0+4	2			
				Loan	07.03.88	Birmingham City	3							
				Loan	19.02.90	Hereford Utd	6			1				
				Loan	06.09.90	Blackburn Rovers	5+1			1				
				Free	17.08.91	Huddersfield Town	42+2	5	2	5+1	14	3		1
ADDITIONAL CONTRACT PLAYERS														
Chris Billy	6.0	10.9	02.01.73	Huddersfield	01.07.91	Huddersfield T (T)	8+2			2	2			
Andrew D Booth					01.07.92	Huddersfield T (T)	0+3							
Anthony Brennan					01.07.92	Huddersfield T (T)								
(D) Simon Charlton	5.6	11.1	25.10.71	Huddersfield	01.07.89	Huddersfield T (T)	75+3	5	4	9		1		
E: Y														
Simon Collins					01.07.92	Huddersfield T (T)								
John Dysart					13.07.92	Huddersfield T (T)								
Jonathan P. Dyson					29.12.90	Huddersfield Town								
Richard Gledhill					05.06.90	Huddersfield Town								
Richard Gledhill					28.05.91	Huddersfield Town								
Thomas Mooney					01.07.92	Huddersfield T (T)								
Ifem Onuora	6.0		28.07.67	Glasgow	28.07.89	Huddersfield Town	73+31	5+4	7+1	10+1	18	3	3	3

LEADING LEAGUE GOALSCORERS SEASONS 1985-86 – 1991-92

1985-86	DAVE TEMPEST	12	1986-87	DUNCAN SHEARER	21
1987-88	DUNCAN SHEARER	10	1988-89	CRAIG MASKELL	27
1989-90	CRAIG MASKELL	15	1990-91	IWAN ROBERTS	14

1991-92	**IWAN ROBERTS**	**24**

LEEDS ROAD Huddersfield, West Yorks HD1 6PE

Capacity: 17,010   **Covered Standing:** 11,470   **Seating:** 5,340

Tel: Ground: 0484 420335   **Ticket Sales:** As ground number   **Clubcall:** 0898 12 16 35

All premium rate calls (0898/0891) cost 36p per minute cheap rate and 48p per minute at all other times. Call costings correct at time of going to press.

ATTENDANCES
Highest: 67,037 v Arsenal, FA Cup Round 6, 27.2.1932

Lowest: 1,134 v Scarborough, Autoglass Trophy, 19.11.1991

Record Receipts: £65,485 v Manchester City, FA Cup 3rd Rnd Replay, 25.1.88

LEEDS ROAD
First game: 1908
First floodlit game: v Wolves, FA Cup, Jan 1961

Season Tickets:
Stands: from £125 to £160, juv/OAP £63 to £80
Ground: £97, juv/OAP £49

Executive Box Season Tickets: Consult Secretary

Cost of Stand Tickets: £8.50 (£5 juniors/OAP)
Terraces: £6 (£4 juniors/OAP)

Match and Ticket Information: Advance reservations only for special matches, otherwise admission to ground and stands on day of matches (0484 420335)

Car Parking: Ample parking on all sides of the ground for 1,500 cars approx. All within 200 yards of ground

Nearest Railway Station: Huddersfield (0484 531226)

How to get to the ground

From East and M1 (Junction 38): Use A642 (S.P. Huddersfield) into town centre, then follow signs Leeds A62 into Leeds Road for Huddersfield Town FC

From South: Use A616 (S.P. Huddersfield) into town centre, then follow signs Leeds A62 into Leeds Road for Huddersfield Town FC

From West: Use Motorway M62 until junction 23 then A640 or A62 into Leeds Road for Huddersfield Town FC

Value Rating: ★ ★ ★

Programme Editor: Chris Patzelt

Price of 1992-93 Programme: £1.20
Number of Pages: 32
Subscriptions: Inland £40, Abroad £45.

Local Newspapers: Huddersfield Examiner

Local Radio Stations: Radio Leeds, Pennine Radio, Radio Aire

HULL CITY

Division 2

Formed: 1904   **Turned Professional:** 1904   **Ltd Co:** 1904

SPONSORED BY: Bonus Accessories   **NICKNAME:** The Tigers

President
T C Waite, FIMI, MIRTE

Vice Presidents
J Johnson, BA, DPA
D Robinson
C M Thorpe, LLB
H Bermitz

Chairman
M W Fish

Vice-Chairman
R M Chetham

Directors
G H C Needler BA, FCA
M St. Quinton, BA (Hon.)

Company Secretary
Tom Wilson

Commercial Department
Simon Cawkill

Team Manager
Terry Dolan

Assistant Team Manager
Jeff Lee

Youth Team Manager
Bernard Ellison

Physiotherapist
Jeff Ratcliffe, MCSP, SRP

Club Statistician for the Directory
Richard Stakes

IN what was always likely to prove to be a difficult season, the Tigers retained their third division status. However, from any point of view, the campaign can best be described as patchy. After an initially difficult period, making adjustments after relegation the previous term, the team seemingly settled down well. A good run from mid-October until early December saw only one defeat in eleven games.

The sale of Andy Payton to Middlesbrough in mid-November was perhaps a turning point. After his departure scoring goals became a real problem. In the eleven league games from mid-December only three goals were scored, one point gained and the team were firmly trapped in the danger zone. Despite much hard work, and another good run in February and March, it was a position from which City were only able to escape during an excellent run in the last couple of weeks of the season.

The cup competitions provided some interest until shortly after the turn of the year. The Rumbelows saw a first round victory against Blackburn, but round two ended in a comprehensive defeat by Q.P.R. The F.A. Cup draw sent the team for successive rounds to the Lancashire seaside. Interest ended in a home defeat by Chelsea. The games in the preliminary round of the Autoglass Trophy were also successfully negotiated, but Crewe Alexandra then put a stop to any further progress.

On the positive side many of the youngsters introduced to the first team during the season made good progress; while Windass and France (imports from local non-league football) showed both enthusiasm and commitment. Alan Fettis is to be congratulated on his recognition at full international level by Northern Ireland. Congratulations also to Russ Wilcox for taking the Player of the Year award and to Steve Wilson on his selection as Young Player of the Year.

Off the field money problems continued to trouble the club. None of the large fee received for Payton could be spent on team strengthening. Crowds were well down on the previous season and local people seemed generally indifferent about the team, despite considerable exortations from the Board of Directors. Nevertheless, in a clear indication of their commitment, a group of supporters raised in the latter part of the season some £16,000. This total, which was doubled by one of the directors, will be used to strengthen the side.

The past campaign indicates that without team strengthening, particularly in the attack, there can be little hope of a sustained promotion challenge next season. With apparently so little money to spend on players it may well be a season of consolidation, some experimentation and for allowing some of the youngsters to gain greater experience in League football.   **Richard Stakes**

Back row: Leigh Jenkinson, Neil Allison, Darren France, Gary Hobson, Lee Warren, David Mail. **Middle:** David Hockaday, Mark Calvert, Stuart Young, Steve Wilson, Alan Fettis, Wayne Jacobs, Darren Cairns, Jeff Radcliffe (Physio). **Front row:** Graeme Atkinson, Mick Matthews, Dean Windass, Jeff Lee (Asst. Manager), Martin Fish (Chairman), Terry Dolan (Manager), Russ Wilcox, Paul Hunter, Gareth Stoker, David Norton.

HULL CITY

DIVISION THREE: 14th   **FA CUP:** 3rd RND   **RUMBELOWS CUP:** 2nd RND   **AUTOGLASS:** 2nd RND

M	DATE		COMP.	VEN	OPPONENTS	RESULT		H/T	LGE POS	GOALSCORERS/GOAL TIMES	ATTEN-DANCE
1	A	17	BL	A	Reading	W	1-0	0-0		Jenkinson 63	(4,639)
2		20	RC 1/1	A	**Blackburn Rovers**	D	1-1	1-0		**Payton 67**	(6,300)
3		24	BL	H	Peterborough Utd	L	1-2	0-0	11	Payton 71	4,806
4		27	RC 1/2	H	**Blackburn Rovers**	W	1-0	0-0		**Jenkinson 60**	3,227
5		31	BL	A	Bournemouth	D	0-0	0-0	13		(5,015)
6	S	3	BL	H	Birmingham City	L	1-2	0-0	16	Palin 59	4,801
7		7	BL	H	Bury	L	0-1	0-1	21		3,679
8		14	BL	A	Wigan Athletic	W	1-0	1-0	16	Young 27	(2,445)
9		17	BL	A	Brentford	L	1-4	0-4	20	Jenkinson (pen) 69	(4,586)
10		21	BL	H	Torquay United	W	4-1	2-1	14	Young 18, Walmsley 36, 84, Norton 67	3,093
11		24	RC 2/1	H	**Queens Park R.**	L	0-3	0-2			4,979
12		28	BL	A	West Bromwich A.	L	0-1	0-1	16		(11,932)
13	O	5	BL	H	Exeter City	L	1-2	1-0	18	Jenkinson 38	3,143
14		9	RC 2/2	A	**Queens Park R.**	L	1-5	1-3		**Young 37**	(5,251)
15		12	BL	A	Swansea City	D	0-0	0-0	18		(2,725)
16		19	BL	A	Hartlepool United	W	3-2	2-1	17	Payton 25, 30, Calvert 84	(2,868)
17		22	AGT Pre	H	**Bradford City**	W	2-1	2-1		**Matthews 18, Windass 22**	1,218
18		26	BL	H	Darlington	W	5-2	1-2	12	Payton 30, 70, Stoker 53, 75, Windass 66	3,514
19	N	2	BL	H	Fulham	D	0-0	0-0	14		(3,365)
20		5	BL	H	Shrewsbury Town	W	4-0	3-0	9	Payton 15, Norton 22, Windass 27, Warren 89	5,025
21		9	BL	H	Chester City	W	1-0	1-0	8	Payton 1	4,305
22		16	FAC 1	A	**Morecambe**	W	1-0	1-0		**Wilcox 38**	(2,853)
23		23	BL	A	Leyton Orient	L	0-1	0-1	10		(3,510)
24		30	BL	H	Preston North End	D	2-2	1-0	10	Brown 15, Walmsley 60	4,280
25	D	7	FAC 2	A	**Blackpool**	W	1-0	0-0		**Hunter 55**	(4,554)
26		14	BL	A	Bolton Wanderers	L	0-1	0-0	12		(5,273)
27		20	BL	A	Peterborough Utd	L	0-3	0-2	14		(7,994)
28		26	BL	H	Bournemouth	L	0-1	0-0	15		4,460
29		28	BL	H	Reading	L	0-1	0-1	18		3,600
30	J	1	BL	A	Birmingham City	D	2-2	1-1	17	Francis 5, 75	(12,983)
31		4	FAC 3	H	**Chelsea**	L	0-2	0-1			13,580
32		7	AGT Pre	A	**Hartlepool United**	L	0-2	0-2			(1,5_?)
33		11	BL	H	Stockport County	L	0-2	0-0	18		3,982
34		14	AGT 1	A	**Preston North End**	W	†3-2	1-1		**Windass 38, Palin 89, Pearson 103**	(2,152)
35		18	BL	A	Bradford City	L	1-2	0-0	20	Mail 49	(6,369)
36		25	BL	H	Stoke City	L	0-1	0-1	21		4,996
37	F	1	BL	H	Hartlepool United	L	0-2	0-1	22		3,483
38		4	AGT 2	A	**Crewe Alexandra**	L	0-1	0-0			(2,348)
39		8	BL	A	Darlington	W	1-0	0-0	20	Windass 65	(3,636)
40		12	BL	A	Preston North End	L	1-3	1-1	23	Wilcox 24	(2,932)
41		22	BL	A	Stockport County	D	1-1	0-0	23	Wilcox 55	(4,490)
42		25	BL	A	Huddersfield Town	D	1-1	0-0	21	Atkinson 82	(6,003)
43		29	BL	H	Huddersfield Town	W	1-0	1-0	21	Kelly 22	5,310
44	M	3	BL	H	Bradford City	D	0-0	0-0	21		4,244
45		7	BL	A	Stoke City	W	3-2	1-0	19	Jenkinson 4, 55, Atkinson 49	(13,563)
46		10	BL	A	Shrewsbury Town	W	3-2	2-0	16	Wilcox 37, Atkinson 42, Jenkinson 51	(1,956)
47		14	BL	H	Fulham	D	0-0	0-0	17		3,742
48		21	BL	A	Chester City	D	1-1	0-1	17	Windass 56	(1,269)
49		28	BL	H	Leyton Orient	W	1-0	0-0	17	Atkinson 55	3,802
50		31	BL	H	Wigan Athletic	D	1-1	0-1	16	Atkinson 63	3,389
51	A	4	BL	A	Bury	L	2-3	0-2	18	France 82, Windass 84	(2,245)
52		11	BL	H	Brentford	L	0-3	0-1	19		3,770
53		14	BL	A	Torquay United	L	1-2	1-0	19	Windass 42	(2,239)
54		20	BL	H	West Bromwich A.	W	1-0	1-0	20	Jenkinson 20	4,818
55		25	BL	A	Exeter City	W	3-0	1-0	19	Atkinson 56, France 76, Jenkinson 82	(2,772)
56		28	BL	H	Bolton Wanderers	W	2-0	1-0	16	Wilcox 22, Matthews 82	3,997
57	M	1	BL	H	Swansea City	W	3-0	1-0	14	Atkinson 14, 47, Matthews 75	4,070

Best Home League Attendance: 5,310 v Huddersfield Town   **Smallest:** 3,093 v Torquay United   **Av Home Att:** 4,100

Goal Scorers: **Compared with 90-91:** -2,065

League (54): Jenkinson 8 (1 pen), Atkinson 8, Payton 7, Windass 6, Wilcox 4, Walmsley 3, France 2, Matthews 2, Norton 2, Stoker 2, Young 2, Francis 2, Mail, Warren, Calvert, Palin, Kelly, Brown

R/lows C (3): Payton, Jenkinson, Young
FA Cup (2): Wilcox, Hunter
Autoglass (5): Windass 2, Matthews, Pearson, Palin   † = Sent Off

Fettis A.	Mail D.	Jacobs W.	Wilcox R.	Buckley N.	Calvert M.	Matthews M.	Payton A.	Hunter P.	Norton D.	Jenkinson L.	Hobson G.	Walmsley D.	Atkinson G.	Palin L.	Warren L.	Allison N.	Ngata H.	Brown N.	Windass D.	Shotton M.	Stoker G.	Young S.	Pearson J.	Hockaday D.	France D.	Referee	
1	2	3	4	5	6	7*	8	9•	10	11	12	14														K Burge	1
1	2	3	4	5	6		8	9	10	11	7	S	S													A Wilkie	2
1	2	3	4		6•		8	9	10	11			14			7	S									I Hendrick	3
1		3	4				S	8	9	7	11	6		S		10	2	5								J Key	4
1		3	4				8	9*	7	11	6		S			10	2	5							12	G Ashby	5
1		3	4				S	8	9*	7	11	6				10	2	5							12	J Watson	6
1	4•	3						9*	7	11	6		14	12	10	5	8	2								J Rushton	7
1		3	4*						10	11	12		14	5	7			8•	2		6		9			A Flood	8
1		3*	4•	5					10	11	12		14		7			8	2		6		9			G Pooley	9
1			4					14	10	11	6*				7	3	12	5	2		8		9•			K Lupton	10
1			4					14	10	11	6	8•			7	3	S	S	2		9					T Lunt	11
1	5	12							10	11	6			7*	3	4	S		2		8†		9			G Poll	12
	5	12							10	11	6	14		3*	4		7•		2		8		9			K Redfern	13
	5	3							10	11	6*	14	12		4				2		8		9			J Carter	14
1	5	3			6		8		10	11			12		4				2	14	7•		9*			P Durkin	15
1	5	3			7	12	8		10	11			14		4*				2	6			9•			W Burns	16
1	5	3	14		7*	4	8		10	11		9•							2	6	12					P Harrison	17
1	12	3	5		4*	8	9•		10	11							14		2	6	7					R Poulain	18
1	4	3	5			8			10	11					S	9*			2	6	7	12				D Shadwell	19
1	4	3	5			8			10	11					14	9•			2	6	7*	12				M Hart	20
1	4•	3	5			8			10	11					14	9*			2	6	7	12				B Coddington	21
1	4	3	5						10	11		S	12		2			8	9	6	7*					I Cruikshanks	22
1	4	3	5	9					10	11				12	14			8	2*	6	7*					D Axcell	23
1	4	3	5			12			10	11		8			S			9	2	6	7*					S Lodge	24
1*	4	3	5					14	10	11		8•			7	2		9		6	12					C Trussell	25
1	4	3	5				8		10	11				7	2*			9	12	6	S					T Holbrook	26
1	4	3	5		S		8		10	11				7	S			9	2	6						P Don	27
1	4	3	5			12	9		10	11		8•			7				2	6*					14	R Shepherd	28
1	4•	3	5			8*		14	10	11				7					2	6	12		9			L Dilkes	29
1		3	5			8			10	11		S			7			2†		6	4*	12	9			J Kirkby	30
1		3	5			8			10	11	12				7				6	4•	2*		14	9		T Fitzharris	31
1	4	3				8			10	11	S				5				2	6			12	7*	9	D Phillips	32
1	S	3				8		10*	4	11	5				7				2	6			12	9		J Key	33
1	4	3				12	8*		2	11	6				7		5			10	6	S		9		J Rushton	34
1	4	3*	5			8			2	11	S				7					6	10	S	9			G Singh	35
1	4	3*	5			S			2	11					7					10	6	8	9		12	P Harrison	36
1			5						2	11†	3				7		S			10	6*	4	9		12	P Danson	37
1	12		5					14	8	11	6		3*		4					10		7•	9	2		K Barrett	38
1	4	5•						14	7	11*	3				6					10		9	2	12		J Lloyd	39
1	4	5*						11•	7		3				6					10	14	9	2	S		G Ashby	40
1	4	5							7	11	6							3		10	S	9	2	S		D Allison	41
1	4	5							7	11	6		12	3						10	14	9	2•	8*		M Reed	42
1	4	5							7	11	6			S	3					10	S	9	2			A Danson	43
1	4	5							7	12	11*				6			3		10	S	9	2			M Bailey	44
1	4	5							7	11	8				6			3		10	S	9	2	S		J Worrall	45
1	4	5							7	11	8				6			3		10	12	9	2*	S		C Wilkes	46
1	4	5							7	11	S			8	6			3		10		9	2			A Bennett	47
	4	5							7	11	S			8	6			3*		10		9	2	12		I Hemley	48
1	4	5				10•	14		7	11				8	6			3			9*	2	12			C Trussell	49
1	4	5					14		7	11	S			8	6			3		10		9	2*			I Cruikshanks	50
1	4•	5					14		7	11*	2			8	6			3		10		12		9		R Nixon	51
1	4	5					14		7	11	3			8	6			2*		10		12		9•		K Hackett	52
1	4	5					2		7	11	3			8*	6	S				10		12		9		J Martin	53
1	4	5					2*	14	7	11				8	6			3		10		12		9•		B Hill	54
1	4	5					2	14	7	11				8	6	12		3		10*	7			9•		J Carter	55
1	4•	5					2	14	7	11				8	6	12		3		10				9		R Pawley	56
1		5				S	2	9	7	11	3			8	6	4				10	S					E Parker	57
43	36	23	40	4	7	10	10	11	45	41	15	4	22	13	26	6	7	25	31	16	19	7	15	12	10	League Appearances	
	1	2		1	4	6		4			1	1	5	3		5	2	4		1	1	5	8		7	Substitute Appearances	
3	2	3	3	1	1+1		3	2	4	4		1+1	1+1	1	2	2		1	1		2		1			R/lows Appearances	
3	2	3	3		1		3	0+1	3	0+1	1			2	2		1	1	3	2+1	1			0+1	1	FA Cup Appearances	
1	3+1	3	1+1		1		3	0+1	4	4	2	1	2	1	1		4	3		0+1	1+1	2	2	1		Autoglass Appearances	

Also Played: Posn.(Game): De Mange 7•14), Wilson 1(13†,14,48,53), Kelly (L) 8(37,39,40,41,43,44)

Players on Loan: Pearson (Barnsley), Kelly (Stoke City)

† = Sent Off

HULL CITY

Club Colours: Amber and black striped shirts, black shorts, black and amber stockings
Change Colours: Green shirts, white shorts, white stockings
Reserves League: Pontins Central League Division 2

Previous Managers: Ambrose Langley 1905-13   Harry Chapman 1913-14   Fred G Stringer 1914-16   David M Menzies 1916-21   Harry P Lewis 1921-23   Bill McCracken 1923-31   Hayden Green 1931-34   Jack Hill 1934-36   David Menzies 1936   Ernie Blackburn 1936-46   Major Buckley 1946-48   Raich Carter 1948-51   Bob Jackson 1952-55   Bob Brocklebank 1955-61   Cliff Britton 1961-70   Terry Neill 1970-74   John Kaye 1974-77   Bobby Collins 1977-78   Ken Houghton 1978-79   Mike Smith 1980-82   Colin Appleton 1982-84   Brian Horton 1984-88   Eddie Gray 1988-90   Colin Appleton 1990   Stan Ternant 1990-91   Terry Dolan 1991
Honours: Division 3 1965-66   Division 3N 1932-33, 1948-49
League Career: Elected to Div 2 1905   Relegated to Div 3N 1930-31   Promoted to Div 2 1933-34   Relegated to Div 3N 1936-37   Promoted to Div 2 1948-49   Relegated to Div 3N 1956-57   Transferred to Div 3 1958-59   Promoted to Div 2 1959-60   Relegated to Div 3 1960-61   Promoted to Div 2 1966-67   Relegated to Div 3 1978-79   Relegated to Div 4 1981-82   Promoted to Div 3 1983-84   Promoted to Div 2 1985-86   Relegated to Div 3 1990-91

CLUB RECORDS

Most Appearances for Club: Andy Davidson 1952-67: League 520 + FA Cup 43 + League Cup 16 **Total 579**
Most Capped Player: Terry Neill, 15, N. Ireland
Record Goalscorer in a Match: Ken McDonald 5 v Bristol City, 5-1, Div 2, 17.11.1928   Slim Raleigh 5 v Halifax Town, 10-0, Div 3N, 26.12.1930
Record League Goalscorer in a Season: Bill McNaughton, 39, Div 3N 1932-33   **In All Competitions:** Bill McNaughton, 42 (League 39 + FA Cup 3) 1932-33
Record League Goalscorer in a Career: Chris Chilton, 195, 1960-71   **In All Competitions:** Chris Chilton, 221, (League 195 + FA Cup 16 + League Cup 10)
Record Transfer Fee Received: £750,000 from Middlesbrough for Andy Payton, November 1991. (Instalments could take fee to £1,000,000)
Record Transfer Fee Paid: £200,000 to Leeds United for Peter Swan, March 1989
Best Performances: League: 3rd Division 2, 1909-10   **FA Cup:** Semi-Finalists, 1929-30   **League Cup:** 4th Round, 1973-74, 1975-76, 1977-78
Most League Points: (3pts for win) 90, Division 4, 1982-83   (2pts for win) 69, Division 3, 1965-66
Record League Victory and Most Goals Scored in a League Match: 10-0 v Halifax Town, Div 3N, 26.12.1930   11-1 v Carlisle Utd, Div 3N, 14.1.1939
Most Goals Scored in a First Class Cup Tie: 8-2 v Stalybridge Celtic, Round 1, 26.11.1932
Record League Defeat: 0-8 v Wolverhampton Wndrs, Div 2, 4.11.1911
Record Cup Defeat: 0-5 v Fulham, FA Cup Rnd 3, 9.1.1960   0-5 v Lincoln City, League Cup Rnd 1, 9.8.1980   0-5 v Manchester Utd, League Cup Rnd 2/1, 23.9.1987
Oldest Player in a League Match: Eddie Burbanks, 40 years 15 days, 16.4.1953
Youngest Player in a League Match: Ellis Hall, 16 years 180 days, 1906   (Post War) Andy Flounders, 16 years 296 days, 4.10.1980

LONGEST LEAGUE RUNS	
of undefeated matches: 15 (1964-65, 1983)	of league matches without a win: 27 (1990)
of undefeated home matches: 25 (1932-33, 1965-66)	of undefeated away matches: 13 (1948-49)
without home win: 15 (1990)	without an away win: 35 (1979-81)
of league wins: 10 (1948, 1966)	of home wins: 19 (1965-66)
of league defeats: 8 (1934)	of away wins: 5 (Several occasions)

HULL CITY							APPEARANCES				GOALS			
PLAYERS NAME Honours	Ht	Wt	Birthdate	Birthplace Transfers	Contract Date	Clubs	League	L/Cup	FA Cup	Other	Lg	L/C	FAC	Oth
GOALKEEPERS														
Alan Fettis						Ards.W.I.								
				£50,000	14.08.91	Hull City	43	3	3	4				
Stephen L Wilson	5.10	11.0			13.07.92	Hull City (T)	2							
Hull														
DEFENDERS														
Neil Allison	6.2	11.10	20.10.73	Hull	13.07.92	Hull City (T)	7+2	2	2	1				
Gary Hobson	6.1		12.11.71	Hull	17.07.91	Hull City (T)	19	4	0+1	2				
David Hockaday	5.10	10.9	09.11.57	Billingham	01.06.75	Blackpool	131+16	18+1	10+2		24		2	
Div.4'86				Free	02.08.83	Swindon Town	227+18	21	18+2	22	7	2		2
				£50,000	13.09.90	Hull City	47	2	0+1	2	1			
Wayne Jacobs	5.9	10.2	03.02.69	Sheffield		Sheffield Wed. (A)	5+1	3		1				
				£27,000	25.03.88	Hull City	127+2	7	8	6	4			
David Mail	5.11	11.12	12.09.62	Bristol	15.07.80	Aston Villa (A)								
FMC'87				Free	04.01.82	Blackburn Rovers	200+6	12+1	12	17	4			
				£160,000	03.08.90	Hull City	71+2	3	2	4+1	2			
David Norton	5.7	11.3	03.03.65	Cannock	23.03.83	Aston Villa (A)	42+2	8	2+1	2	2			
E:Y7				£30,000	24.08.88	Notts County	22+5	3+1		4+1	1			
				Loan	18.10.90	Rochdale	9			2				
				Loan	10.01.91	Hull City	15							
				£80,000	16.08.91	Hull City	45	4	3	4	2			
Russell Wilcox	6.0	11.10	25.03.64	Hemsworth	28.05.80	Doncaster R. (A)	1							
E: S-P,Div.4'87;ESP.3						Frickley Athletic			7				1	
				£15,000	30.06.86	Northampton T	137+1	6	10	8	9			1
				£120,000	06.08.90	Hull City	64+7	5	3	2+1	5		1	
MIDFIELD														
Graeme Atkinson	5.7		11.11.71	Hull	06.05.90	Hull City (T)	42+12	2+1		1	9			
Michael Matthews	5.8	10.12	25.09.60	Hull	10.10.78	Wolves (A)	72+4	5	2		7			
				£5,000	24.02.84	Scunthorpe Utd	56+2	4	5	8	5			3
				f	26.09.86	Halifax Town	98+1	3	5	8	8		1	2
				£25,000	14.12.88	Scarborough	7			2	1			
				£36,000	02.02.89	Stockport Co	35	4	2		3	1		
				£15,000	07.12.89	Scarborough	64+2	2	0+1	2	4	1		1
						North Ferriby Utd								
					14.08.91	Hull City	10		1	3	2			1
Leigh Palin	5.9	10.3	12.09.65	Worcester	20.09.83	Aston Villa (A)								
E:u19.3				Loan	12.12.84	Shrewsbury Town	2							
				£20,000	02.11.85	Nottm. Forest								
				£25,000	31.10.86	Bradford City	65+6	7+3	6	5+3	10	1		2
				Loan	15.09.89	Stoke City								
				£95,000	26.09.89	Stoke City	17+2	2		2	3			
				£100,000	22.03.90	Hull City	57	4	3	3	7			1
				Loan	24.10.91	Rochdale	3							
Gareth Stoker	5.9	10.12	22.02.73			Leeds Utd								
B.Auckland					13.09.91	Hull City	19+5	2	2+1	0+1	2			
Dean Windass						North Ferriby Utd								
				Free	24.10.91	Hull City	31+1	1	1	4	6			2
FORWARDS														
Darren Cairns	5.0	10.4	01.09.74		30.07.92	Hull City								
Kilmarnock														
Darren France	6.0	11.10	08.08.67			Nth Ferriby U.								
Hull					07.11.91	Hull City	10+7		1	1	2			
Paul Hunter	6.0	12.09	30.08.68	Kirkcaldy		East Fife	133+31	4+2	6+2		56	3	5	
				£150,000	15.03.90	Hull City	18+24	2	0+2	0+2	5		1	
Lee Warren	6.0	11.10	28.02.69	Manchester	27.07.87	Leeds Utd. (A)								
					28.10.87	Rochdale	31		1	2	1			
				£100,000	25.08.88	Hull City	78+6	2	2	1	1			1
				Loan	20.09.90	Lincoln City	2+1			1				
Stuart Young						Arsenal								
					11.07.91	Hull City	7+8	1	1	1+1	2	1		
ADDITIONAL CONTRACT PLAYERS														
Mark Calvert	5.9	11.8	11.09.70	Newcastle	01.07.89	Hull City (T)	19+4	1+1		1	1			

LEADING LEAGUE GOALSCORERS SEASONS 1985-86 — 1991-92

1985-86	FRANK BUNN	14	1986-87	ANDY SAVILLE	9
1987-88	GARY PARKER	8	1988-89	KEITH EDWARDS	26
	ALEX DYER	8			
1989-90	ANDY PAYTON	16	1990-91	ANDY PAYTON	25
		1991-92	LEIGH JENKINSON	8	

BOOTHFERRY PARK Boothferry Road, Hull, Nth Humberside HU4 6EU

Capacity: 17,528   **Covered Standing:** 9,203   **Seating:** 5,515

Tel: Ground: 0482 51119   **Ticket Sales:** As ground number   **Clubcall:** 0898 88 86 88

All premium rate calls (0898/0891) cost 36p per minute cheap rate and 48p per minute at all other times. Call costings correct at time of going to press.

GROUNDS

ATTENDANCES
Highest: 55,019 v Manchester United, FA Cup Round 6, 26.2.1949

Lowest: 1,218 v Bradford C, Autoglass Trophy, 20.10.1991

RECORD RECEIPTS:
£90,000 v Liverpool, FA Cup Round 5, 18.2.1989

BOOTHFERRY PARK
First game: 31st August 1946
First floodlit game:

Season Tickets:
Stands: from £95 to £138, juv/OAP £44 to £50
Ground: £75, juv/OAP £40

Executive Box Season Tickets: None avialable

Cost of Stand Tickets: Best Stand: £8, £3 OAP/Juv; South Stand: £7, OAP/Juv £3; Family: adult £7, child £3 Ground: £6, OAP/Juv £2

Match and Ticket Information: Contact club for details

Car Parking: Limited parking in front of ground

Nearest Railway Station: Hull Paragon (0482 26033) or Boothferry Halt by the ground

How to get to the ground

From North: Use A1 or A19 then A1079 S.P. Hull into town centre, then follow signs Leeds A63 into Anlaby Road, then at roundabout take 1st exit into Boothferry Road for Hull City FC

From West: Use Motorway M62 then A63 S.P. Hull into Boothferry Road for Hull City FC

From South: Use Motorway M1, M18 then M62 and A63 S.P. Hull in Boothferry Road for Hull City FC

Value Rating: ★ ★ ★

Price of 1992-93 Programme: £1
Number of Pages: 32
Subscriptions: £35.00

Local Newspapers: Hull Daily Mail

Local Radio Stations: BBC Radio Humberside (95.5 FM MW1485KHZ), Viking Radio (96.9 FM)

Books available about Club: Who's Who of Hull City Football Club. Douglas Lamming £2.95.
Hull City – A Complete Record (1904-1989), Chris Elton, Breedon Books (1989) £14.95

IPSWICH TOWN   Premier

Formed: 1887   **Turned Professional:** 1936   **Ltd Co:** 1936

SPONSORED BY: FISONS   **NICKNAME:** The Blues,The Town

Chairman
John Kerr MBE

Directors
Kenneth Brightwell
Patrick Cobbold (President)
John Kerridge
J.Murray Sangster (Vice-President)
Harold Smith
David Sheepshanks

Secretary
David Rose(0473-219211)

Sales & Promotions Manager
Mike Noye (0473 212202)

Development Manager
Richard Powell

Manager
John Lyall

Team Manager
Mick McGiven

Assistant Manager
Charlie Woods

Coach
Bryan Klug

Youth Team Coach
Peter Trevivian

Physiotherapist
David Bingham

Groundsman
Winston Chapman

Football in the Community
Jackie Tye

Club Statistician for the Directory
Paul Voller

THERE was an air of despondancy amongst Ipswich supporters prior to the season because no new players had been signed and there was no prospect of an improved performance in the coming months.

The opening game at Bristol Rovers did little to dispel these fears for after establishing a three goal lead they preceeded to let Rovers back into the game and by the end were hanging on for a point. It was against this background that only 8,937 turned up for the first home game of the season against Port Vale – Town's lowest ever opening home crowd.

However, successive victories over Port Vale, Middlesbrough and Blackburn saw Ipswich at the top of the table by the end of August. They soon came down to earth though, losing 1-4 at home to Swindon while a Thompson penalty was enough to secure the points against local rivals Southend. During the month John Wark rejoined the club for a third spell.

Ipswich lost to Derby over two legs in the Rumbelows Cup but in the ZDS Cup there was success at Bristol Rovers and Luton were beaten on penalties. They dropped to fifth place in the League, mainly due to five successive draws and then suffered two home defeats in the same week, to Sunderland and Cambridge. The Cambridge game produced the best attendance of the season thus far.

Eddie Youds joined the club in mid-November and made his debut at Derby but was injured after an hour and never played again during the season. The team got back to winning ways at Wolverhampton and then acquitted themselves well at Chelsea in the ZDS Cup, but lost on penalties. A 0-1 defeat at Plymouth in early December was a low point, which was compounded by the dismissal of Whitton.

A maximum points haul over Christmas and The New Year saw the club restored to second place before taking on Hartlepool in the F.A. Cup. A Dozzell goal in the 84th minute salvaged a replay which they won easily and then they brushed aside Bournemouth in the next round to gain a home tie with Liverpool in the fifth round. The match was marred by a strong wind but many felt that Ipswich had done enough to win. The replay was an excellent game with Town playing superbly but losing out in extra-time to two inspired Liverpool goals.

Their League form did not suffer as a result of the cup run and six successive League wins consolidated second place and won John Lyall the Manager of the Month award for February. The crunch game against Derby, won with two Dozzell goals in the first quarter of an hour, was the springboard for five consecutive victories which saw Ipswich ten points clear at the top with five games remaining. A point from both Grimsby and Oxford gave them the Championship and a place in the Premier League.

John Lyall was deservedly named the Second Division Manager of the Year for the squad that won the Championship was virtually the one he inherited.

Paul Voller

Back row L-R: Geraint Williams, Simon Milton, Gavin Johnson, Neil Thompson, Steve Whitton, Eddie Youds, Adam Tanner, David Lowe (now Leicester City), Lee Honeywood. **Middle:** Gary Thompson, Steve Palmer, Phil Whelan, Craig Forrest, Declan Devine, Jason Winters, David Gregory, Neil Gregory, Lee Durrant. **Front:** Mick Stockwell, Frank Yallop, Paul Goddard, David Linighan, Jason Dozzell, Chris Kiwomya, Glenn Pennyfather.

IPSWICH TOWN

DIVISION TWO: CHAMPIONS **FA CUP:** 5th RND **RUMBELOWS CUP:** 2nd RND **ZDS CUP:** 5th Q/FINALS

M	DATE	COMP.	VEN	OPPONENTS	RESULT	H/T	LGE POS	GOALSCORERS/GOAL TIMES	ATTEN-DANCE
1	A 17	BL	A	Bristol Rovers	D 3-3	1-0		Dozzell 12, Goddard 55, Stockwell 65	(6,444)
2	20	BL	H	Port Vale	W 2-1	1-1	2	Kiwomya 23, Thompson (pen) 51	8,937
3	24	BL	H	Middlesbrough	W 2-1	0-0	1	Dozzell 48, Goddard 67	9,822
4	31	BL	A	Blackburn Rovers	W 2-1	1-0	1	Kiwomya 30, Goddard 46	(8,898)
5	S 3	BL	H	Swindon Town	L 1-4	1-2	4	Kiwomya 13	11,002
6	7	BL	H	Southend United	W 1-0	0-0	3	Thompson (pen) 49	12,732
7	14	BL	A	Barnsley	L 0-1	0-0	4		(6,786)
8	17	BL	A	Newcastle United	D 1-1	1-0	4	Kiwomya 36	(16,336)
9	21	BL	H	Bristol City	W 4-2	1-1	2	Thompson 37, Linighan 65, Kiwomya 88, Goddard 90	9,692
10	25	RC 2/1	A	Derby County	D 0-0	0-0			(10,215)
11	28	BL	A	Grimsby Town	W 2-1	1-1	2	Lowe 28, Johnson 55	(6,621)
12	O 2	ZDS 1	A	Bristol Rovers	W 3-1	1-1		Dozzell 44, Lowe 70, 81	(1,490)
13	5	BL	H	Oxford United	W 2-1	2-0	2	Milton 29, Whitton 32	9,922
14	8	RC 2/2	H	Derby County	L 0-2	0-2			8,982
15	12	BL	A	Brighton & H A	D 2-2	1-0	2	Milton 15, Dozzell 63	(9,010)
16	19	BL	H	Millwall	D 0-0	0-0	3		11,175
17	22	ZDS 2	H	Luton Town	D †1-1	0-0		Lowe 90 (Won 2-1 on pens)	5,750
18	26	BL	A	Portsmouth	D 1-1	1-1	5	Milton 17	(8,007)
19	30	BL	A	Charlton Athletic	D 1-1	1-1	5	Whitton 35	(6,939)
20	N 2	BL	A	Leicester City	D 2-2	0-0	5	Wark 48, Johnson 76	(11,331)
21	5	BL	H	Sunderland	L 0-1	0-1	5		9,768
22	9	BL	H	Cambridge United	L 1-2	0-1	7	Stockwell 80	20,586
23	16	BL	A	Derby County	L 0-1	0-0	9		(12,493)
24	23	BL	A	Wolverhampton W	W 2-1	0-1	6	Linighan 55, Dozzell 61	(11,915)
25	26	ZDS SQF	A	Chelsea	D †2-2	1-1		Kiwomya 13, 68 (Lost 4-3 on pens)	(6,325)
26	30	BL	H	Tranmere Rovers	W 4-0	2-0	5	Milton 5, Thompson 30, Linighan 71, Wark (pen) 90	11,072
27	D 7	BL	A	Plymouth Argyle	L 0-1	0-0	6		(4,986)
28	20	BL	A	Swindon Town	D 0-0	0-0	6		(7,404)
29	26	BL	H	Charlton Athletic	W 2-0	1-0	6	Kiwomya 37, 58	13,826
30	28	BL	H	Blackburn Rovers	W 2-1	0-1	3	Johnson 48, Dozzell 86	17,657
31	J 1	BL	A	Port Vale	W 2-1	1-0	2	Kiwomya 41, 53	(8,075)
32	4	FAC 3	H	Hartlepool United	D 1-1	0-1		Dozzell 84	12,507
33	11	BL	A	Middlesbrough	L 0-1	0-0	5		(15,104)
34	15	FAC 3R	H	Hartlepool United	W 2-0	1-0		Dozzell 40, Milton 79	(8,500)
35	18	BL	H	Bristol Rovers	W 1-0	0-0	3	Milton 55	10,435
36	F 1	BL	A	Millwall	W 3-2	1-0	3	Dozzell 33, Thompson 49, Kiwomya 62	(8,847)
37	5	FAC 4	H	Bournemouth	W 3-0	2-0		Dozzell 19, Whitton 32, Kiwomya 59	17,193
38	8	BL	A	Portsmouth	W 5-2	3-1	2	Dozzell 7, 19, Kiwomya 10, 52, Awford (og) 63	13,494
39	16	FAC 5	H	Liverpool	D 0-0	0-0			26,104
40	21	BL	A	Tranmere Rovers	W 1-0	0-0	2	Milton 63	(9,161)
41	26	FAC 5R	A	Liverpool	L †2-3	0-1		Johnson 82, Dozzell 95	(27,355)
42	29	BL	H	Plymouth Argyle	W 2-0	0-0	2	Kiwomya 49, Whitton 88	12,852
43	M 7	BL	A	Watford	W 1-0	0-0	2	Whitton 86	(9,199)
44	14	BL	H	Leicester City	D 0-0	0-0	2		16,174
45	17	BL	H	Watford	L 1-2	0-0	3	Dozzell 88	12,484
46	21	BL	A	Cambridge United	D 1-1	0-0	3	Milton 53	(9,766)
47	28	BL	H	Derby County	W 2-1	2-0	1	Dozzell 3, 15	15,305
48	31	BL	H	Barnsley	W 2-0	1-0	1	Kiwomya 35, 49	14,148
49	A 4	BL	A	Southend United	W 2-1	0-0	1	Whelan 53, Thompson 89	(10,003)
50	7	BL	A	Wolverhampton W	W 2-1	0-0	1	Whelan 58, Whitton (pen) 90	17,379
51	11	BL	H	Newcastle United	W 3-2	1-2	1	Whitton (pen) 32, Wark 69, Kiwomya 72	20,673
52	14	BL	A	Sunderland	L 0-3	0-0	1		(22,131)
53	18	BL	A	Bristol City	L 1-2	0-1	1	Whitton (pen) 83	(16,931)
54	21	BL	H	Grimsby Town	D 0-0	0-0	1		22,393
55	25	BL	A	Oxford United	D 1-1	1-1	1	Johnson 9	(10,525)
56	M 2	BL	H	Brighton & H A	W 3-1	2-1	1	Whitton (pen) 8, 83, Johnson 45	26,803

Best Home League Attendance: 26,803 v Brighton & H Alb. **Smallest:** 8,937 v Port Vale **Av Home Att:** 14,275

Goal Scorers: **Compared with 90-91: +2,456**

League (70): Kiwomya 16, Dozzell 11, Whitton 9 (4 pens), Milton 7, Thompson 6 (2 pens), Johnson 5, Goddard 4, Wark 3 (1 pen), Linighan 3, Stockwell 2, Whelan 2, Opponents, Lowe

R/lows C (0):
FA Cup (8): Dozzell 4, Milton, Johnson, Whitton, Kiwomya
ZDS Cup (6): Lowe 3, Kiwomya 2, Dozzell

† = After extra-time

1991-92

Forrest C.	Yallop F.	Thompson N.	Zondervan R.	Gayle B.	Humes A.	Stockwell M.	Goddard P.	Johnson G.	Dozzell J.	Kiwomya C.	Lowe D.	Whitton S.	Linighan D.	Milton S.	Wark J.	Whelan P.	Gregory D.	Palmer S.	Durrant	Edmonds D.	Moncur J.	Youds E.	Pennyfather G.	Referee	
1	2	3	4	5	6	7	8*	9	10	11	12	S												L Shapter	1
1	12	3	7	5	6	4*	8	2	10	11	S	9												G Willard	2
1	12	3	7	5		4*	8	2	10	11•	14	9	6											M Brandwood	3
1	S	3	7	5		4	8	2	10	11	S	9	6											R Shepherd	4
1	14	3	7•	5		4	8	2	10	11	12	9*	6											P Danson	5
1	S	3	7		5	4	8*	2	10	11	12	9	6											A Gunn	6
1	S	3	7		5	4	8	2*	10	11	12	9	6											P Wright	7
1	12	3	7		5*	4	8	2	10	11	S	9	6											E Parker	8
1	5	3	7			4•	8	2*	10	11	14	9	6	12										A Buksh	9
1	5	3	7			4	8	2	10	11		9	6	S	S									J Kirkby	10
1	5	3	7			4*		2	10	11	8	9	6	S	12									D Allison	11
1	5	3				4			10		7	9		11	6	2	8	S	S					K Barratt	12
1	5	3	8			4				11	7	9	6	10	2			S	S					R Bigger	13
1	5	3	8			4				11	7	9	6	10*	2			12	S					J Moules	14
1	S	3	5			4			10	11*	7	9	6	8	2			12						R Wiseman	15
1	2	3	8			4			10		7	9	6	11*	5			S		12				J Key	16
1	2*	3	8			4			10		7	9	6	11	5•			14		12				B Hill	17
1	2	3•	8			4		14	10		7*	9	6	11	5						12			P Durkin	18
1	2	3				4		7	10			9	6	11	5			S		S	8			P Jones	19
1	2	3				4		12	10	11	7*	9	6	8	5			S						P Vanes	20
1	2*	3				4		12	10	11		9	6	7•	5					14	8			M Bailey	21
1	12	3				4		2	10	11		9*	6	7	5					S	8			G Pooley	22
1	12	3				4		9	10	11	7		6	S	5					8	2*			R Milford	23
1	S	3				4		2	10	11	S	9	6		5					7				R Groves	24
1	12	3				4	8•	2	10*	11	14		6	9	5			7						M Reid	25
1		3				4		2	10	11	12	9*	6	7	5			8		S				I Hemley	26
1	12	3				4		2	10	11	S	9†	6	7	5			8*						D Frampton	27
1	S	3				4		2	10	11		9	6	7	5			8				S		M James	28
1	S	3				4		2	10	11		9	6	7	5		S	8				7		P Taylor	29
1	S	3				4		2	10	11*		9	6	7	5			8				12		R Hamer	30
1	S	3				4		2	10	11		9	6	7	5			8				S		W Flood	31
1	12	3				4		2	10	11		9	6	7	5			8				S		T West	32
1	12	3				4		2	10	11		9	6	7	5		S	8*				3		T Fitzharris	33
1		3	S			4		2	10	11	S	9	6	7	5			8*						T West	34
1		3	12			4		2	10	11	S	9	6	7	5			8*						R Pawley	35
1		3	12			4		2	10	11	S	9	6	7	5*			8						K Lupton	36
1		3	S			4		2	10	11	S	9	6	7	5			8						K Barratt	37
1		3	S			4		2	10	11	S	9	6	7	5			8						V Callow	38
1		3	S			4		2	10	11	S	9	6	7	5			8						A Buksh	39
1		3	S			4		2	10	11*	12	9	6	7	5			8						I Cruikshanks	40
1		3	14			4		2	10	11	12	9	6	7	5•			8*						A Buksh	41
1		3	14			4		2	10*	11	12•	9	6	7	5			8						T Ward	42
1		3	S			4	S	2	10	11		9	6	7	5			8						J Rushton	43
1		3	S			4		2	10	11	12	9	6	7	5			8*						K Hackett	44
1		3*	S			4		2	10	11	12	9	6	7	5			8						A Gunn	45
1		3	2			4	8	S	10	11		9	6	7	5			S						K Barratt	46
1		3	2			4	8	12	10	11		9	6	7*	5			S						P Alcock	47
1		3	2			4	8	12	10	11		9•	6*	7	5			14						P Danson	48
1		3	2			4	8•	14	10	11		9		7*	5	6		12						G Ashby	49
1		3	2			4	8•	14	10	11		9		7*	5	6		12						D Axcell	50
1		3	2			4	8•	14	10	11		9		7*	5	6		12						A Buksh	51
1		3	2			4	S	7*	10	11		9		12	5	6		8						P Harrison	52
1		3	2			4•	8	14	10	11		9		7	5*	6		12						J Martin	53
1		3	2*			4	8	14	10	11		9		7•	5	6		12						G Willard	54
1		3	2			4	8	7	10	11		9		S	5	6						S		J Worrall	55
1		3	2•			4*	8	7	10	11		9		14	5	6		12						P Vanes	56
46	9	45	25	5	5	46	19	33	45	43	7	43	36	31	36	8		16			5	1	2	**League Appearances**	
	8		3		5		9				7			3	1		1	7		2	1		1	**Substitute Appearances**	
2	2	2	2		2	1	1	1	2	1		2	2	1	1				0+1					**R/lows Appearances**	
5	0+1	5	0+1			5	0+1	5	5	5		5	5	5	5			5						**FA Cup Appearances**	
3	2+1	3	2			2	1	1	3	1	2+1	2	2	3	3	1	1	1+1		0+1				**ZDS Cup Appearances**	

Players on Loan: Moncur (Tottenham)

† = Sent Off

IPSWICH TOWN

Club Colours: Royal blue shirts with white collars & sleeves, white with blue trim shorts, blue stockings
Change Colours: White & royal blue or black & red
Reserves League: Neville Ovenden Football Combination

COMPETITIONS					
Div. 1	Div. 2	Div. 3S	Euro. C	EUFA	Texaco
61-64	54-55	38-54	62-63	73-74	72-73
68-86	57-61	55-57		74-75	
92-	64-68		**ECWC**	75-76	
	86-92		78-79	77-78	
				79-80	
				80-81	
				81-82	
				82-83	

HONOURS					
Div. 1	Div. 2	Div. 3S	FA Cup	EUFA C	Texaco
61-62	60-61	53-54	77-78	80-81	72-73
	67-68	56-57			
	91-92				

MOST APPEARANCES: MICK MILLS 737+4 (1966-82)				
Year	League	FA Cup	Lge Cup	Europe
1965-66	2			
1966-67	21+1	1	2	
1967-68	9+1	1	1+1	
1968-69	35+1	1		
1969-70	40	1	3	
1970-71	42	6	2	
1971-72	35	2	1	
1972-73	42	2	2	
1973-74	42	3	4	8
1974-75	42	9	5	
1975-76	42	3	1	4
1976-77	37	3	2	
1977-78	34	7	2	5
1978-79	42	5	1	6
1979-80	37	4	2	3
1980-81	33	6	5	10
1981-82	42	3	8	2
1982-83	11		2	2
	588+3	57	43+1	40
Plus 8 Texaco Cup 1972-73 & 1 Charity Shield 1978-79				

MOST GOALS IN A CAREER				
RAY CRAWFORD 227 (1958-69)				
Season	League	FA Cup	League C	Europe
1958-59	25	1		
1959-60	18			
1960-61	40			
1961-62	33	1	3	
1962-63	25			8
1963-64	2			
1965-66	8			
1966-67	21	3	1	
1967-68	16		5	
1968-69	16		1	
Total	204	5	10	8

MANAGERS			
Name	Seasons	Best	Worst
Michael O'Brien	1936-37		
Adam Scott Duncan	1937-55	1(1)	3(3S)
Alf Ramsey	1955-63	1(1)	3(3S)
Jackie Milburn	1963-64	22(1)	22(1)
Bill McGarry	1964-68	1(2)	15(2)
Bobby Robson	1968-82	2(1)	19(1)
Bobby Ferguson	1982-87	9(1)	5(2)
John Duncan	1987-90	8(2)	9(2)
John Lyall	1990-	1(2)	14(2)

RECORD TRANSFER FEE RECEIVED			
Amount	Club	Player	Date
£800,000	Sheffield Utd	Brian Gayle	9/91
£750,000	Glasgow Rangers	Terry Butcher	8/86
£500,000	Tottenham H.	Alan Brazil	3/83
£450,000	Arsenal	Brian Talbot	1/79

RECORD TRANSFER FEE PAID			
Amount	Club	Player	Date
£650,000	Derby County	Geraint Williams	5/92
£330,000	Manchester City	Brian Gayle	1/90
£300,000	Shrewsbury Town	David Linighan	5/88
£250,000	Millwall	Kevin O'Callaghan	1/80

BARCLAYS BUSINESS CENTRE
Ipswich: Princes Street
PO Box No. 3
1 Princes Street
Ipswich IP1 1PB
Tel: 0473 217017

BARCLAYBANK MACHINE

LONGEST LEAGUE RUNS	
of undefeated matches:	23 (8.12.1979-26.4.1980)
of undefeated home matches:	33 (27.10.1979-28.3.1981)
without home win:	9 (24.8.1963-28.12.1963)
of league wins:	8 (19.8.1953-16.9.1953)
of league defeats:	10 (9.9.1954-16.10.1954)
of league matches w/out a win:	21 (28.8.1963-20.12.1963)
of undefeated away matches:	11 (15.12.1979-18.4.1980)
without an away win:	27 (10.5.1963-29.9.1964)
of home wins:	14 (19.9.1956-9.3.1957)
of away wins:	5 (10.9.1976-27.12.1976)

PREVIOUS LEAGUE
Southern League

BIGGEST VICTORIES
League: 7-0 v Portsmouth, Division 2, 7.11.1964
7-0 v Southampton, Division 1, 2.2.1974
7-0 v West Bromwich Albion, Division 1, 6.11.1976
F.A. Cup: 11-0 v Cromer, Qual. Rnd, 31.10.1936
League Cup: 5-0 v Northampton, Round 2, 30.8.1977
6-1 v Swindon, Round 4, 26.11.1985
Europe: 10-0 v Floriana, 25.9.1962

BIGGEST DEFEATS
League: 1-10 v Fulham, Division 1, 16.12.1983
F.A. Cup: 1-7 v Southampton, Round 3, 2.2.1974
League Cup: 0-4 v Arsenal, Round 2, 9.9.1971
2-6 v Aston Villa, Round 4, 30.11.1988
Europe: 0-4 v Bruges, Round 2, 5.11.1975

MOST POINTS
3 points a win: 83, Division 1, 1981-82.
2 points a win: 64, Division 3S, 1953-54, 1955-56

MOST GOALS
106, Division 3S, 1955-56.
Parker 30, Garneys 19, Grant 16, Reed 12, Blackman 8,
McLuckie 6, Elsworthy 3, Leadbetter 4, Acres 2, Brown 2,
Myles 1, Snell 1, og 2

MOST GOALS IN A MATCH
5. Ray Crawford v Floriana, 10-0, European Cup, 25.9.1962
5. Alan Brazil v Southampton, 5-2, Division 1, 16.2.1982

MOST GOALS IN A SEASON
Ted Phillips 46, League 41, FAC 5) 1956-57.
Previous holder: 31, T Parker, 30 League, 1 FAC, 1955-56.

MOST FIRST CLASS MATCHES IN A SEASON
66 (42 League, 7 FA Cup, 5 League Cup, 12 UEFA Cup)
1980-81

MOST LEAGUE GOALS CONCEDED
121, Division 1, 1963-64

MOST LEAGUE WINS
27, Division 3S, 1953-54

MOST LEAGUE DRAWS
18, Division 2, 1990-91

MOST LEAGUE DEFEATS
26, Division 1, 1963-64

OLDEST PLAYER
Mick Burns, 43 years 219 days v Gateshead, FA Cup,
12.1.1952.

YOUNGEST PLAYER
Jason Dozzell 16 years 56 days v Coventry City, 4.2.1984.

MOST CAPPED PLAYER
Allan Hunter (Northern Ireland) 47

BEST PERFORMANCES BY IPSWICH TOWN

League: 1955-56: Matches played 46, Won 25, Drawn 14, Lost 7, Goals for 106, Goals against 64, Points 64. Third in Division 3S.

Highest: 1961-62: First in Division 1.

F.A. Cup: 1977-78: 3rd rnd. Cardiff 2-0; 4th rnd. Hartlepool 4-1; 5th rnd. Bristol Rovers 2-2, 3-0; 6th rnd. Millwall 6-1; Semi-Final West Bromwich Albion 3-1; Arsenal 1-0.

League Cup: 1981-82: 2nd rnd. Leeds United 1-0, 3-0; 3rd rnd. Bradford City 1-1, 3-2; 4th rnd. Everton 2-0; 5th rnd. Watford 2-1; Semi-Final Liverpool 0-2, 2-2.

1984-85: 2nd rnd. Derby County 4-2, 1-1; 3rd rnd. Newcastle Utd 1-1, 2-1; 4th rnd. Oxford Utd 2-1; 5th rnd. Q.P.R. 0-0, 2-1; Semi-Final Norwich City 1-0, 0-2

UEFA Cup: 1980-81: 1st rnd. Aris Salonika 5-1, 1-3; 2nd rnd. Bohemians 0-2, 3-0; 3rd rnd. Widzew Lodz 5-0, 0-1; 4th rnd. St Ettiene 4-1, 3-1; Semi-Final Cologne 1-0, 1-0; Final AZ67 Alkmaar 3-0, 2-4.

DIVISIONAL RECORDS

	Played	Won	Drawn	Lost	For	Against	Points
DIVISION 1	882	345	212	325	1223	1188	**982**
DIVISION 2	648	272	175	211	1034	932	**823**
DIVISION 3S	486	214	112	160	806	695	**540**
TOTALS	**2016**	**831**	**489**	**696**	**3063**	**2815**	**2345**

IPSWICH TOWN

PLAYERS NAME Honours	Ht	Wt	Birthdate	Birthplace Transfers	Contract Date	Clubs	APPEARANCES League	L/Cup	FA Cup	Other	GOALS Lg	L/C	FAC	Oth
GOALKEEPERS														
Craig Forrest	6.4	14.4	20.09.67	Vancouver	31.08.85	Ipswich Town (A)	162	11	8	11				
				Loan	01.03.88	Colchester Utd	11							
Jason Winters	6.0	11.8	15.09.71	Rutland, Leics	17.05.90	Chelsea (T)								
E: Y				Free	24.12.91	Ipswich Town								
DEFENDERS														
David Gregory	5.11	11.6	23.01.70	Colchester	31.03.87	Ipswich Town (T)	15+13	3+1	1	3+2	1			4
Gavin Johnson	5.11	11.7	10.10.70	Stowmarket	01.03.89	Ipswich Town	45+14	1+1	5	3+1	5		1	1
David Linighan	6.2	12.6	09.01.65	Hartlepool	03.03.82	Hartlepool Utd	84+7	3+1	4	2	5	1		
				Loan	01.04.85	Leeds Utd								
					11.08.86	Derby County								
				£30,000	04.12.86	Shrewsbury Town	65	5	3	1	2			
				£300,000	23.06.88	Ipswich Town	162+1	9	9	10	8			
Neil Thompson	6.0	13.7	02.10.63	Beverley		Nottm. Forest (A)								
ESP4,BLT84,GMVC'87					28.11.81	Hull City	29+2							
						Scarborough	87	8	4	9	15	1		1
					09.06.89	Ipswich Town	122+6	4+1	8	8	15			1
Frank Yallop	5.10	10.3	04.04.64	Watford	05.07.82	Ipswich Town (A)	238+17	18+1	12+2	21+2	4	1		
E:Y5														
Edward Youds	6.0	10.10	03.05.70	Liverpool	10.06.88	Everton	5+3	0+1		0+1				
				Loan	29.12.89	Cardiff City	0+1		0+1					
				Loan	08.02.90	Wrexham	20				2			
				£250,000	15.11.91	Ipswich Town	1							
MIDFIELD														
Jason Dozzell	6.2	12.0	09.12.67	Ipswich	20.12.84	Ipswich Town (A)	271+20	22+1	18	22	45	3	10	4
E:u21.6,Y5														
Simon Milton	5.10	11.0	23.08.63	Fulham		Bury								
				£5,500	17.07.87	Ipswich Town	131+18	8+2	8	10+1	34	1	1	3
				Loan	01.11.87	Exeter City	2			1	3			
				Loan	01.03.88	Torquay Utd	4				1			
Glenn Pennyfather	5.8	10.10	11.02.63	Billericay	17.02.81	Southend Utd	231+7	12+1	14+3	5+1	36	2	1	3
				£150,000	03.12.87	Crystal Palace	31+3		1	4+2	1			
				£80,000	25.10.89	Ipswich Town	9+2		0+1	0+1	1			
Michael Stockwell	5.6	10.13	14.02.65	Malden	17.12.82	Ipswich Town (A)	205+14	15+2	10+3	16+2	15	2		1
Geraint Williams	5.7	10.6	05.01.62	Treorchy	12.01.80	Bristol Rovers	138+3	14	9+2	5	8		2	
W: 11, u21.2; Div2'87				£40,000	29.03.85	Derby County	276+1	26+3	17	11	9	1		
				£650,000	01.07.92	Ipswich Town								
Romeo Zondervan	5.7	11.2	03.03.59	Paramaribo		F.C. Twente								
Hol:6,u21,S				£225,000	09.03.82	West Brom A	82+2	6	5		5			
				£70,000	22.03.84	Ipswich Town	270+4	24	11+2	14	13	3	2	2
FORWARDS														
Paul Goddard	5.8	11.8	12.10.59	Harlington	06.07.77	Q.P.R. (A)	63+7	4+1			23			
E: 1,u21.8;Div2'81;UEFA u21.82				£800,000	13.08.80	West Ham U	159+11	26	10+1	6	54	12	3	2
				£415,000	07.11.86	Newcastle Utd	61	3	6		19	1	3	
				£450,000	02.08.88	Derby County	49	7	1+1	5	15	2		1
				£800,000	29.12.89	Millwall	17+3		4+1		1		1	
				Free	29.01.91	Ipswich Town	37+6	1	0+1	2	10			
Chris Kiwomya	5.9	10.7	02.12.69	Huddersfield	31.03.87	Ipswich Town (T)	112+23	6	8	5+1	33	1	1	3
Gary M Thompson	6.0	11.5	07.09.72	Ipswich	01.07.90	Ipswich Town								
E: u17.1														
Steve Whitton	6.0	12.7	04.12.60	East Ham	15.09.78	Coventry City (A)	64+10	3+2	3		21		2	
				£175,000	11.07.83	West Ham U	35+4	6	1		6	2		
				£60,000	31.01.86	Birmingham City	102+1	7+1	5	3	30	4		1
				£275,000	03.03.89	Sheffield Wed	22+10	3	0+1	0+1	4	4		
				£150,000	11.01.91	Ipswich Town	53	2	5	4	11		1	
ADDITIONAL CONTRACT PLAYERS														
Andrew Bernall						Ipswich Town	4+5			0+2				
(D) Lee Honeywood	5.9	10.3	03.08.71	Chelmsford	31.05.89	Ipswich Town (T)								
E: Y.1														
Robert Mayes					10.11.88	Ipswich Town				0+1				
Bruce Murray					29.08.90	Ipswich Town								
(M) Steve Palmer	6.1	12.7	31.03.68	Brighton	01.08.89	Ipswich Town	37+14	2	6	3+2	1			
(D) Phil Whelan	6.4	14.1			02.07.90	Ipswich Town	8		1		2			

IPSWICH TOWN

RECORD WIN & LOSS AGAINST EACH CLUB IN CURRENT DIVISION
(Where a score has occured on several occasions the most recent is given)

Club	Rec. Win	Season	Rec. Loss	Season
ARSENAL	4-1	1976-77 (away)	6-0	1963-64
ASTON VILLA	3-0	1984-85	6-1	1977-78
BLACKBURN ROVERS	3-1	1989-90	4-1	1954-55
CHELSEA	5-1	1978-79	4-0	1963-64
COVENTRY CITY	4-0	1980-81 (away)	5-0	1966-67
CRYSTAL PALACE	3-0	1947-48	4-1	1979-80
EVERTON	4-0	1980-81	5-2	1961-62
LEEDS UNITED	4-0	1960-61	4-0	1969-70
LIVERPOOL	3-0	1959-60	6-0	1963-64
MANCHESTER CITY	4-0	1979-80	4-0	1988-89
MANCHESTER UNITED	6-0	1979-80	7-2	1963-64 (home)
MIDDLESBROUGH	6-1	1954-55	5-2	1957-58
NORWICH CITY	5-0	1976-77	2-0	1984-85
NOTTINGHAM FOREST	2-0	1982-83	4-0	1977-78
OLDHAM ATHLETIC	2-0	1987-88	4-0	1988-89
QUEENS PARK RANGERS	4-0	1956-57	3-0	1984-85
SHEFFIELD UNITED	4-0	1961-62	7-0	1971-72
SHEFFIELD WEDNESDAY	4-1	1961-62 (away)	4-1	1963-64 (home)
SOUTHAMPTON	7-0	1973-74	3-0	1984-85
TOTTENHAM HOTSPUR	4-0	1974-75	5-0	1962-63
WIMBLEDON				

MANAGER: JOHN LYALL

DATE OF BIRTH: 24.02.1940 **PLACE OF BIRTH:** Ilford

DATE OF APPOINTMENT: 11.05.1990

PREVIOUS CLUBS
as Manager: West Ham United
as Player Manager: West Ham United
as Player: West Ham United

HONOURS
as Manager: FA Cup Winners 1975, 1980; League Cup Runners-Up 1981; Division Two Champions 1981.
as Asst. Man./Coach:
as Player:
International: England Youth

Value Rating: ★ ★ ★ ★

Programme Editor: N Manning & E King

Price of 1992-93 Programme: £1.20
Number of Pages: 32

Local Newspapers: East Anglian Daily Times, Evening Star.

Local Radio Stations: Radio Orwell, Saxon Radio.

Additional Publications on Club: The Men Who Made The Town, The Official History of the Club. (John Eastwood and Tony Moyse) £14.95.

LEADING LEAGUE GOALSCORERS
SEASONS 1979-80 – 1991-92

1979-80	PAUL MARINER	17		1980-81	JOHN WARK	18
1981-82	ALAN BRAZIL	22		1982-83	JOHN WARK	20
1983-84	ERIC GATES	13		1984-85	ERIC GATES	13
1985-86	KEVIN WILSON	7		1986-87	KEVIN WILSON	20
1987-88	DAVID LOWE	17		1988-89	JOHN WARK	13
1989-90	DAVID LOWE	13		1990-91	CHRIS KIWOMYA	10

1991-92   **CHRIS KIWOMYA**   16

PORTMAN ROAD Ipswich, Suffolk IP1 2DA

Capacity: 22,500   **Covered Standing:** n/a   **Seating:** 22,500

Tel: Ground: 0473 219211   **Ticket Sales:** As ground number   **Clubcall:** 0898 66 44 88

All premium rate calls (0898/0891) cost 36p per minute cheap rate and 48p per minute at all other times. Call costings correct at time of going to press.

GROUNDS

ATTENDANCES
Highest: 38,010 v Leeds United, FAC 6th Round, 8.3.1975
34,635 v Arsenal, Division 1, 10.3.1973
30,857 v Manchester United, Division 1, 1.2.1969

Lowest: 3,116 v Leyton Orient, 25.3.1953

RECORD RECEIPTS (with previous records):
£105,950 v AZ Alkmaar, European Cup, 6.5.1981
£46,009 v Liverpool, FA Cup 6th Round, 10.3.1979
£32,000 v Wolverhampton W, FA Cup 4th Round, 29.1.1977
£23,500 v Leeds United, FA Cup 6th Round, 8.3.1975
£11,518 v Arsenal, Division 1, 10.3.1973

PORTMAN ROAD
First game: v V Beccles Caxton, Suffolk Challenge Cup, 7-1, 2.3.1889
First floodlit game: v Arsenal, Friendly, 16.2.1960

Season Tickets:
Stands: from £130 to £375, juv/OAP £75 to £250

Executive Box Season Tickets: Apply to club for details

Cost of Stand Tickets: Portman Stand Z: £18, juv/OAP £12; A: £15, £10 juv/OAP; B: £12.50, £8 juv/OAP; E: £10, £6 juv/OAP; Pioneer Stand Y: £15, £10; H/N/O: £15, £10 juv/OAP; G/I/M/P/: £12.50, £8 juv/OAP; F/J/Q/R: £10, £6 juv/OAP; Lower: £7, £4 juv/OAP; Family Seating (Pioneer Stand) £9, £5 juv/OAP; Portman lower: £7, £4 juv/OAP; Churchmans, North £7, £4 juv/OAP

Match and Ticket Information: On sale 12 days prior to match. Postal, Access, Visa bookings accepted

Centre Spot Restaurant: (Manager Raf Zaza 0473 213201)

Car Parking: Large parks in Portman Road, Portman's Walk & West End Road

Nearest Railway Station: Ipswich (0473 57373)

How to get to the ground

From North and West: Use A45 signposted to Ipwich West. Proceed straight through Post House traffic lights, at the second roundabout turn right into West End Road. The ground is 400m along on the left.

From South: Follow signs for Ipswich West, then proceed as above.

LEEDS UNITED   Premier

Formed: 1919(as United)   **Turned Professional:** 1919   **Ltd Co:** 1920

SPONSORED BY: Admiral Sportswear   **NICKNAME:** The Whites

President
Rt Hon Earl of Harewood

Chairman
L Silver OBE

Vice-Chairman
P J Gilman

Directors
R Barker MCIT,MBIM
W J Fotherby (Managing Director)
G M Holmes B Sc(Econ)
J W G Marjason (Dep. Chairman)
M J Bedford
E Carlile
A Hudson
R Feldman
P Ridsdale
K Woolmer

Company Secretary
Nigel Pleasants (0532 716037)

Commercial Manager
Bob Baldwin(0532 716037)

Team Manager
Howard Wilkinson

Assistant Manager
Michael Hennigan

Chief Scout
Ian MacFarlane

Physiotherapist
Alan Sutton

Administration Manager
A Roberts

Club Statistician for the Directory
Mark Evans

IN order to attain 'greater success' than on their return to the top flight, had to finish higher than fourth place. This was attained in style and the 'Champions' tag has returned to the club after a gap of eighteen years.

Before the season kicked-off Howard Wilkinson, again proved successful in the transfer market, and strengthened his squad by signing: Rod Wallace for £1,600,000 from Southampton, the club's new record signing eventually finished as second top scorer; Tony Dorigo arrived from Chelsea for £1,300,000 and deservedly won the 'Supporters Player of the Season' award. Steve Hodge cost £900,000 from Nottingham Forest and the joint signing of Jon Newsome and David Weatherall for £275,000 proved to be inspired investments. In February, the brilliantly skilled Frenchman, Eric Cantona arrived on a three month loan, and immediately proved his popularity with the supporters. He scored what was probably one of the finest goals scored at Elland Road against Chelsea, and completed his £1 million transfer in May. Chris Kamara was the first departure of the season to Luton (£150,000), and was followed by Andy Williams (£175,000 to Notts County), Simon Grayson and Mike Whitlow (£50,000 and £250,000 to Leicester) and Glyn Snodin (free to Hearts).

The nucleus of the side though remained the same, with inspirational skipper Gordon Strachan leading consistent performers, Lukic, Sterland, Fairclough, Whyte and McClelland who were as ever dependable in defence, Batty, Speed and MacAllister joined him to prove arguably the best midfield in the Division and Lee Chapman, who was once again the top scorer (twenty goals in all including two hat-tricks).

The Rumbelows Cup and F.A. Cup brought defeats against Manchester United, but in the League, Leeds were never out of the top two from September, along with Manchester United. Always considered second favourites in the media, but when it comes to belief in themselves and their team mates Leeds were second to none. Notable performances included the 'live TV' victories at Sheffield Wednesday (6-1) and Aston Villa (4-1), both superb footballing performances. Indeed a major factor of the success was the number of goals scored, four on four occasions, five against Wimbledon (5-1) leaving Leeds as top divisional scorers away from home and second overall.

The two horse race ran from September, but on Sunday 26 April following the 3-2 victory at Sheffield United and Manchester United's defeat at Liverpool, the race was over and the League Championship was on its way to Elland Road. Howard Wilkinson had achieved his finest domestic achievement to date and deservedly brought glory back to the club.

The future now looks excellent, Leeds are back in Europe, and will have a new £5.5m stand ready for 1993-94 to provide an all-seater capacity of 40,000. Howard Wilkinson has already turned this great club around and certainly looks the man to lead them to further glories.   **Mark Evans**

Back row: Chris Whyte, Gary McAllister, John Lukic, Lee Chapman, Mervyn Day, Jon Newsome, David Wetherall. **Middle row:** Alan Sutton (Physio), Mel Sterland, Steve Hodge, David Rocastle, Chris Fairclough, Carl Shutt, Eric Cantona, Michael Hennigan (Assistant Manager). **Front row:** Scott Sellars, Gary Speed, Tony Dorigo, Howard Wilkinson (Manager), Gordon Strachan, David Batty, Rod Wallace. *Copyright Leeds United AFC*

LEEDS UNITED

DIVISION ONE: CHAMPIONS **FA CUP:** 3rd RND **RUMBELOWS CUP:** 5th RND **ZDS CUP:** 2nd RND

M	DATE		COMP.	VEN	OPPONENTS	RESULT	H/T	LGE POS	GOALSCORERS/GOAL TIMES	ATTEN-DANCE
1	A	20	BL	H	Nottingham Forest	W 1-0	1-0		McAllister 13	29,457
2		24	BL	H	Sheffield Wed.	D 1-1	0-0	10	Hodge 87	30,260
3		28	BL	A	Southampton	W 4-0	2-0	4	Speed 24, 89, Strachan (pen) 59, 69 (pen)	(15,862)
4		31	BL	A	Manchester United	D 1-1	1-0	6	Chapman 7	(43,778)
5	S	3	BL	H	Arsenal	D 2-2	0-1	6	Strachan (pen) 66, Chapman 86	29,396
6		7	BL	H	Manchester City	W 3-0	2-0	4	Dorigo 18, Batty 34, Strachan (pen) 79	29,986
7		14	BL	A	Chelsea	W 1-0	0-0	2	Shutt 61	(23,439)
8		18	BL	A	Coventry City	D 0-0	0-0	2		(15,488)
9		21	BL	H	Liverpool	W 1-0	1-0	2	Hodge 25	32,917
10		24	RC 2/1	A	**Scunthorpe United**	D 0-0	0-0			(8,392)
11		28	BL	A	Norwich City	D 2-2	0-0	2	Dorigo 62, Speed 72	(15,828)
12	O	1	BL	A	Crystal Palace	L 0-1	0-0	2		(18,250)
13		5	BL	H	Sheffield United	W 4-3	3-0	2	Hodge 5, 47, Sterland 29, 38 (pen)	28,362
14		8	RC 2/2	H	**Scunthorpe United**	W 3-0	0-0		Sterland (pen) 70, Chapman 80, Speed 81	14,558
15		19	BL	A	Notts County	W 4-2	2-1	2	Chapman 19, Hodge 29, Whyte 48, McAllister 55	(12,964)
16		22	ZDC 2	H	**Nottingham Forest**	L 1-3	0-2		**Rod Wallace 55**	6,145
17		26	BL	H	Oldham Athletic	W 1-0	0-0	1	Kilcline (og) 54	28,109
18		29	RC 3	H	**Tranmere Rovers**	W 3-1	0-0		**Chapman 68, 80, Shutt 90**	18,265
19	N	2	BL	A	Wimbledon	D 0-0	0-0	2		(7,025)
20		16	BL	H	Queens Park R.	W 2-0	0-0	1	Sterland 59, Rod Wallace 62	27,087
21		24	BL	A	Aston Villa	W 4-1	1-0	1	Rod Wallace 41, Sterland 47, Chapman 56, 90	(23,713)
22		30	BL	H	Everton	W 1-0	0-0	1	Rod Wallace 87	30,043
23	D	4	RC 4	A	**Everton**	W 4-1	2-1		**Speed 27, Chapman 39, Rod Wallace 54, 55**	(25,467)
24		7	BL	A	Luton Town	W 2-0	0-0	1	Rod Wallace 68, Speed 70	(11,550)
25		14	BL	H	Tottenham Hotspur	D 1-1	1-1	1	Speed 38	31,404
26		22	BL	A	Nottingham Forest	D 0-0	0-0	2		(27,170)
27		26	BL	H	Southampton	D 3-3	2-0	2	Hodge 27, 30, Speed 73	29,053
28		29	BL	H	Manchester United	D 1-1	0-0	2	Sterland (pen) 80	32,638
29	J	1	BL	A	West Ham United	W 3-1	2-1	1	Chapman 11, 85, McAllister 38	(21,766)
30		8	RC 5	H	**Manchester United**	L 1-3	1-1		**Speed 16**	28,886
31		12	BL	A	Sheffield Wed.	W **6-1**	3-1	1	Chapman 3 (9,43,66), Dorigo 32, Whitlow 70, Rod Wallace 86	(32,228)
32		15	FAC 3	H	**Manchester United**	L 0-1	0-1			31,819
33		18	BL	H	Crystal Palace	D 1-1	1-1	2	Fairclough 32	27,717
34	F	1	BL	H	Notts County	W 3-0	1-0	1	Sterland 12, Batty 57, Rod Wallace 77	27,224
35		8	BL	A	Oldham Athletic	L 0-2	0-1	2		(18,409)
36		23	BL	A	Everton	D 1-1	0-0	2	Shutt 61	(19,248)
37		29	BL	H	Luton Town	W 2-0	0-0	2	Cantona 57, Chapman 85	28,231
38	M	3	BL	H	Aston Villa	D 0-0	0-0	2		28,886
39		7	BL	A	Tottenham Hotspur	W 3-1	1-0	1	Rod Wallace 37, Newsome 76, McAllister 78	(27,622)
40		11	BL	A	Queens Park R.	L 1-4	1-1	1	Speed 10	(14,641)
41		14	BL	H	Wimbledon	W 5-1	3-0	1	Rod Wallace 20, Chapman 3 (23, 27, 80), Cantona 74	26,760
42		22	BL	A	Arsenal	D 1-1	0-0	1	Chapman 73	(27,844)
43		28	BL	H	West Ham United	D 0-0	0-0	1		31,101
44	A	4	BL	A	Manchester City	L **0-4**	0-2	2		(30,239)
45		11	BL	H	Chelsea	W 3-0	0-0	1	Rod Wallace 55, Chapman 86, Cantona 88	31,363
46		18	BL	A	Liverpool	D 0-0	0-0	2		(37,186)
47		20	BL	H	Coventry City	W 2-0	0-0	1	Fairclough 53, McAllister (pen) 81	26,582
48		26	BL	A	Sheffield United	W 3-2	1-1	1	Rod Wallace 44, Newsome 64, Gayle (og) 77	(31,082)
49	M	2	BL	H	Norwich City	W 1-0	1-0	1	Rod Wallace 25	32,673

Best Home League Attendance: 32,917 v Liverpool **Smallest:** 26,582 v Coventry City **Av Home Att:** 29,488

Goal Scorers: **Compared with 90-91: +516**

League (74): Chapman 16, Rod Wallace 11, Speed 7, Hodge 7, Sterland 6 (2 pens), McAllister 5 (1 pen), Strachan 4 (4 pens), Dorigo 3, Cantona 3, Newsome 2, Opponents 2, Batty 2, Shutt 2, Fairclough 2, Whyte, Whitlow

R/lows C (11): Chapman 4, Speed 3, Rod Wallace 2, Sterland (1 pen), Shutt
FA Cup (0):
ZDS Cup (1): Rod Wallace

Lukic J.	McClelland J.	Dorigo A.	Batty D.	Fairclough C.	Whyte C.	Strachan G.	Wallace Rod	Chapman L.	McAllister G.	Speed D.	Sterland M.	Hodge S.	Wetherall D.	Shutt C.	Whitlow M.	Varadi I.	Newsome J.	Kelly G.	Snodin G.	Kamara C.	Grayson S.	Williams A.	Davison R.	Cantona E.	Agana P.	Referee	
1	2	3*	4	5	6	7	8	9	10	11	S	S														N Midgeley	1
1	2*	3	4	5	6	7	8	9	10	11*	12	14														C Trussell	2
1	2	3	4	5*	6	7	8	9	10*	11	12	14														G Ashby	3
1	5	3	4		6	7	8	9	10*	11	2	12	S													K Redfern	4
1	5	3*	4		6	7	8	9	10	11	2*	12	14													B Nixon	5
1	5	3	4		6	7	8*	9	10	11	2	12	S													I Cruikshanks	6
1	5	3	4		6	7*		9	10	11	2	12	S	8												R Milford	7
1	5	3	4		6	7		9	10	11	2	12	S	8*												D Axcell	8
1	5	3	4		6	7		9	10	11*	2	8		12	S											G Courtney	9
1	5	3	4		6	7*		9	10	11	2	8		12	S											I Hendrick	10
1	5	3	4		6			9	10	11	2	8*		12	14	7*										P Jones	11
1	5	3	4		6			9	10*	11	2	8		12	14	7*										J Martin	12
1	5	3	4	12	6			9	10*	11	2	7		8	14											K Barratt	13
1	5	3	4	12	6			9		11	2	7		8•			14					10*				P Danson	14
1		3	4	5	6	7		9•	12•	11	2	10		8			14									B Hill	15
1		3	4	5	6		12			11	2•			8		7•		9	10	14						J Worrall	16
1		3	4	5	6	7*	8	9	10	11*	2			12			14									D Allison	17
1		3		5	6	7	11•	9	10		2	4*		8				12	14							V Callow	18
1		3		5	6	7	8•	9	10	11	2			4				12	S							A Gunn	19
1	S	3	4	5	6	7	8	9	10	11*	2					12										K Breen	20
1	11	3	4	5	6	7	8	9	10		2	S		S												A Buksh	21
1	14	3	4	5†	6	7	8	9	10		2	11*		12•												A Ward	22
1	S	3	4	5	6	7*	8	9	10	11	2	12														K Redfern	23
1	S	3	4	5	6	7	8	9	10	11	2	S														P Vanes	24
1	5	3	4		6	7	8	9	10	11	2	S		S												M Peck	25
1	5	3	4		6	7*	8	9	10	11	2	S				12										M Reed	26
1	5	3	4		6		8	9	10	11	2	7		S	S											J Watson	27
1	S	3	4*	5	6	7	8	9	10	11	2	12														B Nixon	28
1		3	4	5	6	7	8	9	10	11	2	S		S												R Groves	29
1	14	3•	4	5	6	7	8	9*	10	11	2	12														G Courtney	30
1		3		5	6		8	9	10	11	2	4*		7•	14							12				P Don	31
1		3		5	6		8	9	10	11	2	4*		14							7•	12	14			R Lewis	32
1		3	4	5	6	7	8		10•	11	2	9*		12	14											T Fitzharris	33
1		3	4	5	6	7•	8		10	11	2*	9		12			14									D Allison	34
1		3	4	5	6	7	8		10	11	2•	9*		14								12				A Wilkie	35
1	S	3	4	5	6	7	8*	9	10	11	2	12											9			B Hill	36
1		3*	4	5	6	7	8•	9	10	11	2													12	14	A Flood	37
1	12		4	5*	6	7			10	11	2				3							14		8•		P Wright	38
1			4	5	6	7	8	9	10	11	2*			12	3•									14		R Gifford	39
1			4	5	6	7	8	9	10•	11					3		2		S					12		K Cooper	40
1			4	5	6	7*	8	9	10	11				12			2					3				K Morton	41
1		3	4	5	6	7	8*	9	10	11		S		S			2									M Bodenham	42
1		3	4	5		7	8*	9	10	11	12				6		2									K Barratt	43
1		3	4	5	6	7	8	9	10	11		S		S			2									J Watson	44
1		3	4	5	6	7	8•	9	10	11	2*				12									14		N Midgley	45
1		3	4	5	6		8•	9	10	11		7•	14				2							12		K Redfearn	46
1		3	4	5	6	7*	8	9	10•	11							2							12		B Nixon	47
1		3	4	5	6	7*	8	9	10*	11							2							14		G Courtney	48
1		3	4	5	6	12	8	9•	10	11		14					2							7*		R Milford	49
42	16	38	40	30	41	35	34	38	41	41	29	12		6	3	2	7							6	1	**League Appearances**	
2			1		1			1		2	11	1		9	7	1	3	2		2		2		9	1	**Substitute Appearances**	
5	2+1	5	4	3+1	5	4	3	5	4	4	5	3+2		2+1				0+1		0+1		1+1				**R/lows Appearances**	
1		1	1	1	1	1	1	1	1	1	1	0+1										1	0+1			**FA Cup Appearances**	
1	1	1	1	1	1	0+1		1	1	1		1		1			1		1	1	1	0+1				**ZDS Cup Appearances**	

Also Played: Mauchlen S(41,43)

Players on Loan: Agana (Notts Co.), Mauchlen (Leicester City)

† = Sent Off

LEEDS UNITED

Club Colours: White/blue and yellow trim shirts, white shorts & stockings with yellow/blue trim.
Change Colours: All blue with yellow/white trim.
Reserves League: Pontins Central League Division 1

COMPETITIONS

Div. 1	Div. 2	Euro C	ECWC	UEFA
24-27	20-24	69-70	72-73	65-66
28-31	27-28	74-75		66-67
32-47	31-32	92-93		67-68
56-60	47-56			68-69
64-82	60-64			70-71
90-	82-90			71-72
				73-74
				79-80

HONOURS

Div. 1	Div. 2	FAC	Lge C	UEFA	C/S'ld
68-69	23-24	1972	67-68	67-68	1969
73-74	63-64			70-71	1974
91-92	89-90				

MOST APPEARANCES: JACK CHARLTON 772 (1952-73)

Year	League	FAC	Lge C	Euro	C/S'ld
1952-53	1				
1953-54					
1954-55	1				
1955-56	34	1			
1956-57	21	1			
1957-58	40	1			
1958-59	39	1			
1959-60	41	1			
1960-61	41	1	4		
1961-62	34	2	3		
1962-63	38	3	1		
1963-64	25		2		
1964-65	39	8	2		
1965-66	40	2	1	11	
1966-67	29	6	4	7	
1967-68	34	4	5	11	
1968-69	41	2	2	7	
1969-70	32	9	2	7	1
1970-71	40	4	1	10	
1971-72	41	5	4		
1972-73	18	1	4	2	
	629	52	35	55	1

MOST GOALS IN A CAREER

PETER LORIMER 238 (1962-79 & 1983-85)

Season	League	FA Cup	Lge Cup	Europe	FMC
1965-66	13	3		3	
1966-67	9	2	2	1	
1967-68	17	2	4	8	
1968-69	8	1		3	
1969-70	14	2		3	
1970-71	12	2		5	
1971-72	23	3	2	1	
1972-73	15	3	3	2	
1973-74	12	2			
1974-75	9		3	4	
1975-76	10		1		
1976-77	3				
1977-78	6		3		
1983-84	4				
1984-85	9		1		
1985-86	4				1
Total	168	20	19	30	1

Previous holder: John Charles 154 lge, 4 FAC (1948-57 & 62)

HIGHEST TRANSFER FEES RECEIVED

Amount	Club	Player	Date
£850,000	Everton	Ian Snodin	1/87
£700,000	Sheffield Utd	Vinny Jones	9/90
£650,000	Nottingham Forest	John Sheridan	8/89
£550,000	Middlesbrough	John Hendrie	2/90

HIGHEST TRANSFER FEES PAID

Amount	Club	Player	Date
£2,000,000	Arsenal	David Rocastle	7/92
£1,600,000	Southampton	Rod Wallace	7/91
£1,300,000	Chelsea	Tony Dorigo	7/91
£1,000,000	Leicester City	Gary McAllister	7/90
£1,000,000	Arsenal	John Lukic	6/90
£1,000,000	Nimes (France)	Eric Cantona	5/92

MANAGERS

Name	Seasons	Best	Worst
Arthur Fairclough	1920-27	18(1)	14(2)
Dick Ray	1927-35	5(1)	2(2)
Billy Hampson	1935-47	9(1)	22(1)
Willis Edwards	1947-48	18(2)	18(2)
Frank Buckley	1948-53	5(2)	15(2)
Raich Carter	1953-58	8(1)	10(2)
Bill Lambton	1958-59	15(1)	15(1)
Jack Taylor	1959-61	21(1)	14(2)
Don Revie	1961-74	1(1)	19(2)
Brian Clough	1974		
Jimmy Armfield	1974-78	5(1)	10(1)
Jock Stein	1978		
Jimmy Adamson	1978-80	5(1)	11(1)
Allan Clarke	1980-82	9(1)	20(1)
Eddie Gray	1982-85	7(2)	10(2)
Billy Bremner	1985-88	4(2)	14(2)
Howard Wilkinson	1988-	1(1)	10(2)

LONGEST LEAGUE RUNS

of undefeated matches:	34 (26.10.1968-26.8.1969)
of undefeated home matches:	39 (14.8.1968-28.2.1970)
without home win:	10 (6.2.1982-12.5.1982)
of league wins:	9 (26.9.1931-21.11.1931)
of league defeats:	6 (26.4.1947-26.5.1947)
of league matches without a win:	17 (1.2.1947-26.5.1947)
of undefeated away matches:	17 (2.11.1968-26.8.1969)
without an away win:	27 (29.4.1938-30.8.1947)
of home wins:	13 (23.11.1968-9.8.1969)
of away wins:	8 (1.10.1963-21.12.1963)

PREVIOUS NAMES: Leeds United were formed in October 1919 after Leeds City (formed 1904) had been suspended 'sine die' by the F.A. earlier that same month

PREVIOUS LEAGUE: Leeds City: West Yorkshire League 1904-05 prior to becoming a Football League Club. Leeds United: gained admission to the Midland League in November 1919 and the first team competed in this League prior to gaining Football League status in summer 1920

BIGGEST VICTORIES
League: 8-0 v Leicester City, Division 1, 7.4.1934
F.A. Cup: 8-1 v Crystal Palace, Round 3, 11.1.1930
7-0 v Leeds Steelworks, Prelim. Rnd, 25.9.1920
League Cup: 5-1 v Mansfield, Round 2, 26.9.1963
4-0 v Chesterfield, Round 2, 23.11.1960
4-0 v Burnley, Round 2, 6.9.1972
4-0 v Colchester, Round 3, 26.11.1977
4-0 v York City, Round 2, 6.10.1987
Europe: 10-0 v Lyn Oslo, European Cup Round 1 1st leg, 17.9.1969

BIGGEST DEFEATS
League: 1-8 v Stoke City, Division 1, 27.8.1934
F.A. Cup: 2-7 v Middlesbrough, Round 3 2nd leg, 9.11.1946
League Cup: 0-7 v Arsenal, Round 2 2nd leg, 4.9.1979
0-7 v West Ham United, Round 4, 7.11.1966
Europe: 0-4 v Lierse, Round 1 2nd leg UEFA, 29.9.1971

MOST POINTS
3 points a win: 85, Division 2, 1989-90
2 points a win: 67, Division 1, 1968-69

MOST GOALS
98, Division 2, 1927-28.
Jennings 21, White 21, Keetley 18, Wainscoat 18, Mitchell 8, Turnbull 8, Armand 2, Hart 1, Townsley 1.

MOST GOALS IN A MATCH
5. Gordon Hodgson v Leicester City, 8-2, Div 1, 1.10.1938

MOST GOALS IN A SEASON
John Charles 43 (League 42, FAC 1) 1953-54.
4 goals once = 4; 3 goals 4 times = 12; 2 goals six times = 12; 1 goal 15 times = 15
Previous holder: T Jennings 35 League, 2 FA Cup, 1926-27

MOST FIRST CLASS MATCHES IN A SEASON
66 (42 League, 5 FA Cup, 7 League Cup, 12 UEFA Cup) 1967-68

MOST LEAGUE GOALS CONCEDED
92, Division 1, 1959-60

MOST LEAGUE WINS
27, Division 1, 1968-69; Division 1, 1970-71

MOST LEAGUE DRAWS
21, Division 2, 1982-83

MOST LEAGUE DEFEATS
30, Division 1, 1946-47

OLDEST PLAYER
Peter Lorimer, 38 years 317 days v Barnsley, 27.10.1985

YOUNGEST PLAYER
Peter Lorimer, 15 years 289 days v Southampton, 29.9.1962

MOST CAPPED PLAYER
Billy Bremmner (Scotland) 54

BEST PERFORMANCES BY LEEDS UNITED

League: 1968-69: Matches played 42, Won 27, Drawn 13, Lost 2, Goals for 66, Goals against 27, Points 67. 1st in Division 1.

Highest: 1968-69, 1973-74, 1991-92: Division 1 Champions.

F.A. Cup: 1971-72: 3rd rnd. Bristol Rovers 4-1; 4th rnd. Liverpool 0-0, 2-0; 5th rnd. Cardiff City 2-0; 6th rnd. Tottenham Hotspur 2-1; Semi-Final Birmingham City 3-0; Final Arsenal 1-0.

League Cup: 1967-68: 2nd rnd. Luton Town 3-1; 3rd rnd. Bury 3-0, 4th rnd. Sunderland 2-0; 5th rnd. Stoke City 2-0; Semi-Final Derby County 1-0, 3-2; Final Arsenal 1-0

UEFA: 1967-68: 1st rnd. Spora Luxembourg 9-0, 7-0; 2nd rnd. Partizan Belgrade 2-1, 1-1; 3rd rnd. Hibernian 1-0, 1-1; 4th rnd. Rangers 0-0, 2-0; Semi-Final Dundee 1-1, 1-0; Final Ferencvaros 1-0, 0-0.

1970-71: 1st rnd. Sarpsborg 1-0, 5-0; 2nd rnd. Dynamo Dresden 1-0, 1-2; 3rd rnd. Sparta Prague 6-0, 3-2; 4th rnd. Vitoria Setubal 2-1, 1-1; Semi-Final Liverpool 1-0, 0-0; Final Juventus 2-2, 1-1 (Leeds won on away goals).

DIVISIONAL RECORDS

	Played	Won	Drawn	Lost	For	Against	Points
DIVISION 1	1592	657	398	537	2438	2211	1763
DIVISION 2	1144	483	309	352	1731	1451	1369
TOTALS	**2736**	**1140**	**707**	**889**	**4169**	**3662**	**3132**

LEEDS UNITED

PLAYERS NAME Honours	Ht	Wt	Birthdate	Birthplace Transfers	Contract Date	Clubs	League	L/Cup	FA Cup	Other	Lg	L/C	FAC	Oth
GOALKEEPERS														
Mervyn Day	6.2	15.1	26.06.55	Chelmsford	01.03.73	West Ham U	194	14	14	10				
E:u23.5,Y; FAC'75; Div2.'90				£100,000	01.07.79	Leyton Orient	170	8	10					
				£15,000	12.08.83	Aston Villa	30	3						
				£30,000	01.02.85	Leeds Utd	225	14	10	16				
Loan Coventry City (28.03.91)				Loan	05.03.92	Luton Town	4							
				Loan	01.05.92	Sheffield Utd	1							
John Lukic	6.4	13.7	11.12.60	Chesterfield	16.12.78	Leeds Utd. (A)	146	7	9	3				
E: u21.7,Y.10; Div.1'89'92; LC'87				£50,000	25.07.83	Arsenal	223	32	21	4				
				£1,000,000	14.06.90	Leeds Utd	80	11	7	5				
DEFENDERS														
Tony Dorigo	5.8	10.7	31.12.65	Melbourne, Aus	14.01.82	Aston Villa	106+5	14+1	7	2	1			
E:10, B.4, u21.11; Div2'89; ZDC'90; Div1'92				£475,000	04.06.87	Chelsea	146	14	4	16	11			1
				£1,300,000	06.06.91	Leeds Utd	38	5	1	1	3			
Chris Fairclough	5.11	11.2	12.04.64	Nottingham	12.10.81	Nottm. Forest	102+5	9+1	6	9+2	1	1		
E: B.1, u21.7; Div.2'90; Div1'92				£387,000	03.07.87	Tottenham H	60	7	3		5			
				£500,000	23.03.89	Leeds Utd	117+1	11+2	8	8	14	2		
Peter Haddock	5.11	11.5	09.12.61	Newcastle	01.12.79	Newcastle Utd	53+4	5	3					
Div.2'90				Loan	01.03.86	Burnley	7							
				£40,000	16.07.86	Leeds Utd	106+12	9+2	5+2	9+1	1			
Dylan Kerr	5.9	11.4	14.01.67	Valetta (Malta)		Arcadia Shepherds								
						Sweden								
					08.02.89	Leeds Utd	3+5		1	0+4				
				Loan	22.08.91	Doncaster Rovers	7				1			
				Loan	31.12.91	Blackpool	12			1	1			
Mel Sterland	5.11	13.2	01.10.61	Sheffield	03.10.79	Sheffield Wed. (A)	271+8	30	34+1	3	37	7	5	
E: B.1,u21.7; Flg.1; Div.2'90; UEFA u21'84 Div1'92				£800,000	03.03.89	Glasgow Rangers	7+2		4		3			
				£600,000	28.07.89	Leeds Utd	108+3	13	8	9	16	1	1	2
Raymond Wallace	5.6	10.2	02.10.69	Lewisham	21.04.88	Southampton (T)	33+2	8	2	2				
E: u21.4				£100,000	08.07.91	Leeds Utd								
				Loan		Swansea City	2							
Chris Whyte	6.1	13.0	02.09.61	London		Arsenal (A)	86+4	14	5	3+1	8			
E: u21.4 Div1'92				Loan		Crystal Palace	13	4						
				via L.A.Ra		Holland								
						West Brom A	83+1	5	5	2	7	2		
				£400,000		Leeds Utd	79	12	5	5	4	1		
MIDFIELD														
David Batty	5.5	10.0	02.12.68	Leeds	03.08.87	Leeds Utd	163+9	15	9	12	3			
E:10,u21.1; Div.2'90 Div1'92														
Steve Hodge	5.8	9.11	25.10.62	Nottingham	25.10.80	Nottm. Forest (A)	122+1	10	6	11	30	2		4
E:24,U21.8,B1; UEFA.u21'84; LC'89'90; SC'89 Div1'92				£450,000	27.08.85	Aston Villa	53	12	4	1	12	3	1	
				£650,000	23.12.86	Tottenham H	44+1	2	7		7		2	
				£550,000	17.08.88	Nottm. Forest	79+3	20+1	11+1	9	20	6	2	2
				£900,000	25.07.91	Leeds Utd	12+11	3+2	1		7			
Gary McAllister	6.1	11.5	25.12.64	Motherwell		Motherwell	52+7	3+1	7		6		2	
S:18, B.2, u21.1, S; Div1'85'92				£125,000	15.08.85	Leicester City	199+2	14+1	5	4	47	3	2	
				£1,000,000	02.07.90	Leeds Utd	79+1	11	7	4	7	2	1	1
David Rocastle	5.9	11.1	02.05.67	Lewisham	31.12.84	Arsenal (A)	204+14	32+1	18+2	9	24	6	4	
E:14;u21.14; LC'87; Div1'89; CT'89				£2,000,000	01.07.92	Leeds Utd								
Scott Sellars	5.8	10.0	27.11.65	Sheffield	25.07.83	Leeds Utd	72+4	4	4	2	12	1		1
E:u21.3,FMC'87				£20,000	28.07.86	Blackburn Rovers	194+8	12	11	20	35	3	1	2
				£800,000	01.07.92	Leeds Utd								
Gary Speed	5.11	10.12	08.09.69	Mancot	13.06.88	Leeds Utd. (T)	89+16	11+1	7	4+3	17	6		
W:14, u21.1, Y; Div.2'90 Div1'92														
Gordon Strachan	5.6	10.8	09.02.57	Edinburgh		DunU	56+13	10+1	7		13	1	1	
S:50,u21.1,Y;SPD'80'84;SC'82'83'84;ECWC'83;FAC'85;Div.2'90.E Div1'92						Aberdeen	165+6	43+3	25	34	53	20	7	7
				£500,000	13.08.84	Manchester Utd	155+5	12+1	22	10+2	33	1	2	3
				£300,000	23.03.89	Leeds Utd	126+1	13	7	9	30	2	1	2
FORWARDS														
Eric Cantona						Auxerre								
Div1'92						Marseilles (Fra)								
						Bordeaux (Fra)								
						Montrose								
						Nimes								
				£1,000,000	06.02.92	Leeds Utd	6+9				3			
Lee Chapman	6.2	13.0	05.02.59	Lincoln	22.06.78	Stoke City (A)	95+4	5	3		34	3	1	
E:u21.1; LC'89; SC'89; Div.2'90 Div1'92				Loan	05.12.78	Plymouth A	3+1							
				£500,000	25.08.82	Arsenal	15+8	0+2	0+1	2	4			2
				£200,000	29.12.83	Sunderland	14+1		2		3		1	
				£100,000	24.08.84	Sweden	147+2	17	17+1	2+1	63	6	10	
				£350,000	01.06.88	Niort (Fra)								
				£350,000	17.10.88	Nottm. Forest	48	12	5	6	15	6	3	3
				£400,000	11.01.90	Leeds Utd	97	11	7	4	49	8	3	3
Carl Shutt	5.10	11.13	10.10.61	Sheffield		Spalding U								
Div.2'90 Div1'92					13.05.85	Sheffield Wed	36+4	3	4+1		16	1	4	
				£55,000	30.10.87	Bristol City	39+7	5+2	7+1	10+1	10	4	4	4
					23.03.89	Leeds Utd	40+26	5+2	6	4+3	18	1		3

302

PLAYERS NAME Honours	Ht	Wt	Birthdate	Birthplace Transfers	Contract Date	Clubs	APPEARANCES League	L/Cup	FA Cup	Other	GOALS Lg	L/C	FAC	Oth
Imre Varadi	5.8	11.2	08.07.59	Paddington		Letchworth								
Div.2'90				Free	01.04.78	Sheffield Utd	6+4		2		4			
				£80,000	01.03.79	Everton	22+4		6+1	0+2	6		1	
				£100,000	27.08.81	Newcastle Utd	81	4	5		39	1	2	
				£150,000	26.08.83	Sheffield Wed	72+4	11	7		33	2	5	
				£285,000	19.07.85	West Brom A	30+2	5	2	2	9	4		
					17.10.86	Manchester City	56+9	4+2	6+1	2+1	26	2	1	2
				P.E	30.09.88	Sheffield Wed	14+8	1+1	2	1	3	1	2	
				£50,000	08.02.90	Leeds Utd	19+3	1		1+1	4			1
				Loan	26.03.92	Luton Town	5+1				1			
Rodney Wallace	5.7	10.1	02.10.69	Lewisham	19.04.88	Southampton (T)	111+17	18+1	10	3+1	44	6	3	2
E:B.1,u21.3 Div1'92				£1,600,000	07.06.91	Leeds Utd	34	3	1	0+1	11	2		1
ADDITIONAL CONTRACT PLAYERS														
Scott Cousin					06.02.92	Leeds Utd								
Damian Henderson					05.07.91	Leeds Utd								
Nikolai Iliev					24.11.90	Leeds Utd								
Garry Kelly					24.09.91	Leeds Utd	0+2	0+1						
(D) Jon Newsome	6.2	13.11	06.09.70	Sheffield	01.07.89	Sheffield Wed. (T)	6+1	3						
				£250th com	11.06.91	Leeds Utd	7+3		1		2			
Ryan Nicholls					05.07.91	Leeds Utd								
Patrick O'Connell					06.08.91	Leeds Utd								
Michael Thomas					31.07.90	Leeds Utd								
Mark Tinkler					29.11.91	Leeds Utd. (T)								
Esa Viitanen					22.03.90	Leeds Utd								
(D) David Wetherall	6.2	13.8	14.03.71	Sheffield	01.07.89	Sheffield Wed. (T)								
E.S.F.A.u18.3				£250th com	15.07.91	Leeds Utd	0+1							
Russell Wigley					01.08.90	Leeds Utd. (T)								

MANAGER: HOWARD WILKINSON

DATE OF BIRTH: 13.11.1943   **PLACE OF BIRTH:** Sheffield

DATE OF APPOINTMENT: OCTOBER 1988

PREVIOUS CLUBS
as Manager: Boston Utd (Player/Man.); England Semi-Pro; Notts Co.; Sheffield Wed
as Asst. Man.: Notts County; England Under-21 Team
as Player: Sheffield Wednesday; Brighton & Hove Albion; Boston United
HONOURS
as Manager: Notts County: Promotion to Div 1 1981; Sheffield Wednesday: Division 2 Runners-Up 1984; Leeds United: Division Two Champions
as Asst. Man./Coach:
as Player:
International: England: Youth International

Value Rating: ★ ★ ★ ★ ★

Editor: John Curtis

Price of 1992-93 Programme: £1.50
Number of Pages: 32
Subscriptions: £46 UK

Local Newspapers: Yorkshire Post, Yorkshire Evening Post, Bradford Telegraph & Argus

Local Radio Stations: BBC Radio Leeds, Radio Aire (Leeds), Pennine Radio (Bradford)

Books available about Club: Leeds United 'A Complete Record 1919-1989' (Martin Jarred, Malcolm MacDonald) £13.95.

LEADING LEAGUE GOALSCORERS
SEASONS 1979-80 – 1991-92

1979-80	KEVIN HIRD	8	1980-81	CARL HARRIS	10
1981-82	FRANK WORTHINGTON	9	1982-83	AIDAN BUTTERWORTH	11
	ARTHUR GRAHAM	9			
1983-84	GEORGE McCLUSKEY	8	1984-85	TOMMY WRIGHT	14
	TOMMY WRIGHT	8			
1985-86	IAN BAIRD	12	1986-87	JOHN SHERIDAN	15
				IAN BAIRD	15
1987-88	JOHN SHERIDAN	12	1988-89	BOBBY DAVISON	14
1989-90	GORDON STRACHAN	16	1990-91	LEE CHAPMAN	21

1991-92   **LEE CHAPMAN**   **16**

ELLAND ROAD Leeds, West Yorkshire LS11 0ES

Capacity: 30,937   **Covered Standing:** 9,276   **Uncoverd Standing:** 5,739   **Seating:** 15,922

Tel: Ground: 0532 716037   **Ticket Sales:** 0532 710710   **Clubcall:** 0898 12 11 80

All premium rate calls (0898/0891) cost 36p per minute cheap rate and 48p per minute at all other times. Call costings correct at time of going to press.

ATTENDANCES
Highest: 57,892 v Sunderland, FA Cup Round 5 Replay, 15.3.1967

Lowest: 2,274 v Sheffield Utd, Full Members Cup, 16.10.1985

RECORD RECEIPTS:
£146,483 Everton v West Ham United, FA Cup Semi-Final Replay, 16.4.1980

ELLAND ROAD
First game: 1920
First floodlit game: v Hibernian, 9.11.1953

Season Tickets:
Stands: from £265 to £340 (juv/OAP £132.50 to £170)
Ground: £140 (juv/OAP £70)

Executive Box Season Tickets: Contact club for information

Executive Suite Membership: Contact club

Cost of Stand Tickets: West Stand & Paddock: £18;
South Stand, North East, South East Upper, Stand F,
Stand B: £14; Family Stand: adult £13, child £6.50
Terraces: Kop/Lowfields: £7.50

Car Parking: Wesley Street Corner has park for 1,000 cars (approx), one minute walk from ground

Nearest Railway Station: Leeds City (0532 448133)

How to get to the ground

From North: Use A58 or A61 into Leeds City Centre, then follow signs Motorway M621 to join motorway. In 1.6m leave motorway and at roundabout join A643 into Elland Road for Leeds United FC

From East: Use A63 or A64 into Leeds city centre, then follow signs motorway M621 to join motorway. In 1.6m leave motorway and at roundabout join A643 into Elland Road for Leeds United FC

From South: Use Motorway M1 then M621 until junction with A643, leave motorway and at roundabout join A643 into Elland Road for Leeds United FC

From West: Use Motorway M62 then M621 until junction with A643. Leave motorway and at roundabout join A643 into Elland Road for Leeds United FC

LEICESTER CITY

Division 1

Formed: 1884 **Turned Professional:** 1888 **Ltd Co:** 1897

SPONSORED BY: Walkers Crisps **NICKNAME:** The Foxes

President
K R Brigstock

Chairman
M F George

Vice-Chairman
T Smeaton

Directors
J M Elsom FCA
R W Parker
J E Sharp
T W Shipman
W K Shooter FCA

General Secretary
A K Bennett (0533 555000)

Team Manager
Brian Little

Coaches
John Gregory
Allan Evans   Steve Hunt

Physiotherapist
Alan Smith

Directory of Marketing
Barrie Pierpoint

Press Officer
Paul Mace

Assistant Secretary
Ian Silvester

Club Statistician for the Directory
Dave Smith

AFTER the near disaster of the previous season there was a new broom sweeping the corridors of power at Filbert Street during the summer. Martin George had taken over as chairman and had quickly appointed Brian Little as the new manager. Little immediately began to reshape his first team squad with an initial target of consolidation and respectability.

As the season progressed the targets began to be revised, as a serious promotion challenge began to unfold. It was a challenge that resulted in the clubs first trip to Wembley for 23 years and ultimately was doomed to failure in a brave but controversial defeat beneath the twin towers.

Long before that, the highlights had started to come thick and fast as the league campaign was supplemented by the first cup tie victories for three years. Eventually Filbert Street would throb with ten near-capacity crowds as Little restored pride and self-belief to players and supporters alike.

An early season run of six successive victories rocketed the Foxes into the promotion contest and set up a glamour League Cup tie with champions Arsenal, but it was in the much maligned Zenith Data competition that dreams of Wembley were first nurtured.

A staggering display to see off Everton, followed by a performance of character beyond belief to snatch an extra-time victory at Notts County on a foul January evening led to a pulsating two-legged Northern Final against neighbours Nottingham Forest.

In the meantime, the first F.A. Cup victory for seven years, thanks to a dramatic injury-time winner, had seen the Filbert Street roof nearly lifted off.

In the league campaign there were several highlights, but none greater than the sensational 5-0 drubbing of Cambridge in the Play-Off Semi-Final to set up that Wembley finale.

On the individual front, Paul Kitson made a huge impact during the early months, but by March he had become the club's record outgoing transfer in a £1.35m deal that took him to the Baseball Ground. Tommy Wright enjoyed his most prolific season since joining City, David Oldfield proved to be a revelation in midfield and Kevin Poole, skipper Steve Walsh and ever-present Player-of-the-Year Gary Mills were all models of consistency throughout.

Brian Little continued to be an inspirational figure throughout and also a brave manager, refusing to settle for respectability and launching into a late spending spree in an effort to clinch promotion.

As a result of the season's exploits, optimism is definitely back in fashion in Leicester. The question now is whether Little can deliver the goods in 1992-93.

Dave Smith

Back row L-R: Ashley Ward, Jimmy Willis, Colin Gordon, Steve Walsh, Carl Muggleton, Kevin Poole, Russell Hoult, Tony James, Michael Trotter, Gary Coatsworth, Richard Smith. **Middle:** Neil Lewis, Colin Gibson, Lewis Mogg, Gary Mills, Paul Fitzpatrick, Ian Ormondroyd, David Oldfield, Steve Thompson, Nicky Platnauer, Colin Hill. **Front:** David Lowe, Simon Grayson, Warren Haughton, Allan Evans (Coach), Brian Little (Manager), John Gregory (Coach), Steve Holden, Mike Whitlow, Phil Gee.

LEICESTER CITY

DIVISION TWO: 4th   **FA CUP:** 3rd RND   **RUMBELOWS CUP:** 2nd RND   **ZDS CUP:** Nth FINALISTS

M	DATE		COMP.	VEN	OPPONENTS	RESULT	H/T	LGE POS	GOALSCORERS/GOAL TIMES	ATTEN-DANCE
1	A	17	BL	A	Swindon Town	D 0-0	0-0			(12,426)
2		21	RC 1/1	H	Maidstone United	W 3-0	1-0		Kitson 30, Kelly 47, Mills 79	9,610
3		24	BL	H	Plymouth Argyle	W 2-0	1-0	6	Gibson 14, Kitson 61	11,852
4		28	RC 1/2	A	Maidstone United	W 1-0	0-0		Kitson 57	(1,638)
5		31	BL	A	Southend United	W 2-1	0-0	5	Wright 85, Walsh 89	(6,944)
6	S	4	BL	H	Grimsby Town	W 2-0	1-0	3	Fitzpatrick 29, Gibson 65	16,242
7		7	BL	H	Bristol City	W 2-1	2-1	2	Gibson 16, Fitzpatrick 37	17,815
8		14	BL	A	Middlesbrough	L 0-3	0-0	3		(16,633)
9		17	BL	A	Barnsley	L 1-3	1-1	7	Kitson 11	(9,318)
10		21	BL	H	Blackburn Rovers	W 3-0	2-0	3	Walsh 20, Kitson 23, Gordon 60	13,278
11		25	RC 2/1	H	Arsenal	D 1-1	0-1		Walsh 89	20,679
12		29	BL	A	Cambridge United	L 1-5	0-2	6	Gordon 67	(7,052)
13	O	2	ZDS 1	H	Barnsley	W †4-3	3-0		Wright 4, 25, Kelly 30, Walsh 108	3,995
14		5	BL	A	Charlton Athletic	L 0-2	0-0	9		11,467
15		8	RC 2/2	A	Arsenal	L 0-2	0-0			(28,580)
16		12	BL	A	Newcastle United	L 0-2	0-0	12		(16,966)
17		19	BL	H	Wolverhampton W	W 3-0	2-0	7	Gordon 5, 48, Wright 39	14,428
18		23	ZDS 2	H	Port Vale	W 4-0	0-0		Wright 66, 89, Kitson 72, Gordon 86	4,858
19		26	BL	A	Oxford United	W 2-1	1-0	7	Wright 25, Thompson 72	(5,206)
20		30	BL	A	Brighton & H A	W 2-1	1-0	7	Walsh 13, Kitson 48	(6,424)
21	N	2	BL	H	Ipswich Town	D 2-2	0-0	6	Kitson 53, Oldfield 58	11,331
22		5	BL	A	Portsmouth	L 0-1	0-1	6		(7,147)
23		9	BL	A	Watford	W 1-0	0-0	5	Kitson 2	(9,271)
24		20	BL	H	Bristol Rovers	D 1-1	1-0	6	Wright 16	10,950
25		23	BL	H	Port Vale	L 0-1	0-1	7		11,450
26		27	ZDS 3	H	Everton	W 2-1	2-0		Oldfield 3, Thompson 37	13,242
27		30	BL	A	Derby County	W 2-1	2-0	6	Fitzpatrick 21, Walsh 38	(19,306)
28	D	7	BL	H	Millwall	D 1-1	0-0	7	Gordon 84	12,127
29		14	BL	A	Sunderland	L 0-1	0-0	7		(15,094)
30		26	BL	H	Brighton & H A	W 2-1	1-0	7	Mauchlen 44, Thompson 89	16,767
31		28	BL	H	Southend United	W 2-0	0-0	6	Oldfield 53, Smith 63	15,635
32	J	1	BL	A	Bristol Rovers	D 1-1	1-1	6	Oldfield 7	(6,673)
33		4	FAC 3	H	Crystal Palace	W 1-0	0-0		Smith 90	19,613
34		8	ZDS NSF	A	Notts County	W †2-1	0-1		Wright 82, Fitzpatrick 92	(11,559)
35		11	BL	A	Plymouth Argyle	D 2-2	0-2	7	Turner (og) 51, Thompson 64	(5,846)
36		18	BL	H	Swindon Town	W 3-1	1-0	5	Fitzpatrick 35, Wright 51, 58	14,226
37		25	FAC 4	H	Bristol City	L 1-2	0-1		Kitson 87	19,313
38	F	1	BL	A	Wolverhampton W	L 0-1	0-1	6		(18,574)
39		8	BL	H	Oxford United	W 2-1	1-0	6	Kitson 28, Wright 77	12,178
40		12	ZDS NF1	H	Nottingham Forest	D 1-1	0-0		Gordon 81	19,537
41		15	BL	A	Port Vale	W 2-1	1-1	4	Russell 11, 68	(8,084)
42		22	BL	A	Derby County	L 1-2	0-1	5	Mills (pen) 77	18,148
43		26	ZDS NF1	A	Nottingham Forest	L 0-2	0-1			(21,562)
44		29	BL	A	Millwall	L 0-2	0-2	7		(7,562)
45	M	11	BL	H	Portsmouth	D 2-2	0-1	8	Mills 76, Russell 78	14,207
46		14	BL	A	Ipswich Town	D 0-0	0-0	9		(16,174)
47		17	BL	A	Grimsby Town	W 1-0	0-0	6	Wright 58	(6,377)
48		21	BL	H	Watford	L 1-2	0-2	7	Walsh 57	14,519
49		27	BL	A	Tranmere Rovers	W 2-1	0-1	5	Ormondroyd 61, Gee 66	(9,061)
50	A	1	BL	H	Middlesbrough	W 2-1	1-0	4	Mills (pen) 4, Wright 79	19,352
51		4	BL	A	Bristol City	L 1-2	1-1	6	Oldfield 18	(13,020)
52		8	BL	H	Sunderland	W 3-2	3-2	5	Wright 8, Mills 30, 34 (pen)	16,533
53		11	BL	A	Barnsley	W 3-1	0-1	3	Walsh 50, Mills (pen) 65, Wright 83	14,438
54		15	BL	H	Tranmere Rovers	W 1-0	0-0	2	Russell 90	18,555
55		18	BL	A	Blackburn Rovers	W 1-0	0-0	2	Russell 76	(18,075)
56		21	BL	H	Cambridge United	W 2-1	1-0	2	Wright 42, Gee 52	21,894
57		25	BL	H	Charlton Athletic	L 0-2	0-2	2		(15,537)
58	M	2	BL	H	Newcastle United	L 1-2	0-1	4	Walsh 89	21,844
59		10	PO SF 1	A	Cambridge United	D 1-1	1-0		Russell 40	(9,225)
60		13	PO SF 2	H	Cambridge United	W 5-0	2-0		Wright 29, 60, Thompson 35, Russell 59, Ormondroyd 64	21,024
61		25	PO Fin	N	Blackburn Rovers	L 0-1	0-1			(68,147)

Best Home League Attendance: 21,894 v Cambridge Utd	**Smallest:** 10,950 v Bristol Rovers	**Av Home Att:** 15,184

Goal Scorers: **Compared with 90-91: +3,638**

League (62):	Wright 12, Walsh 7, Mills 6 (4 pens), Kitson 6, Gordon 5, Russell 5, Fitzpatrick 4, Oldfield 4, Thompson 3, Gibson 3, Gee 2 Mauchlen, Smith, Kelly, Opponents, Ormondroyd
R/lows C (5):	Kitson 2, Walsh, Mills, Kelly
FA Cup (2):	Smith, Kitson
ZDS Cup (13):	Wright 5, Gordon 2, Thompson, Kitson, Fitzpatrick, Oldfield, Kelly, Walsh
Play-Offs (6):	Wright 2, Russell 2, Ormondroyd, Thompson

† = Sent Off

Poole K.	Mills G.	Platnauer N.	Fitzpatrick P.	Smith R.	James A.	Gibson C.	Reid P.	Ward A.	Kelly D.	Kitson P.	Wright T.	Oldfield D.	Walsh S.	Russell K.	Gordon C.	Ormondroyd I.	Mauchlen A.	Gee P.	Thompson S.	Coatsworth G.	Hill C.	Muggleton C.	Willis J.	Grayson S.	Whitlow M.	Referee	
1	2	3	4	5	6	7	8	9•	10	11*	12	14														M Pierce	1
1	2	3	4		6	7	8•	9*	10	11	12	14	5													A Smith	2
1	2	3	4		6	8	12		10*	11	9•	7	5	14												D Gallagher	3
1	2	3	4		6	8•			12	11*	9	7	5	14												D Axcell	4
1	2	3*	4*	14	6	8			10	11	9	7	5	12												A Ward	5
1	2	3	4		6	8			10	11	9	7	5	S												A Flood	6
1	2	3	4		6	8			10	11*	9•	7	5	12	14											P Don	7
1	2	3•	4		6	8*			10	11	9	7	5	12												B Nixon	8
1	2	3	4*		6		8	12	10	11†	9	7	5		S											K Lupton	9
1	2	3			6	8		12	10	11	9•	7	5	4*	14											K Hackett	10
1	2	3	S		6	8			10	11	9	7	5	4*	12											N Midgley	11
1	2	3	12		6	8*			10	11	9	7•	5	4	14											J Worrall	12
1	2		4			8	12	14	10		9	7	5	11*												R Groves	13
1	2	3•	4*		6	8	S	12	10		9	7	5	11												D Frampton	14
1	2	12	S	4	6	8			11	10	9	7	5	3*												J Barrett	15
1	2			4	6	8		11*	10	12	9	7	5													S Lodge	16
1	2	14	4	6•	3		12		10		9	7	5				11*		8							R Dilkes	17
1	2	6	4	3			S			10	9	7	5		11				8	S						M Bodenham	18
1	2	6	4	3			S			10	9	7	5		11		8*			12						A Buksh	19
1	2	6	4	3			S			10	9*	7	5		11		12		8							D Elleray	20
1	2	6	4	3						10	9	7	5		11		S		8	S						P Vanes	21
1	2	6•	4	3*						10	9	7	5		11		14		8	12						J Deakin	22
1	2	6	4	3			S			10	9	7	5		11		12		8*							K Morton	23
1	2	6	4	3•			12			10	9	7	5		11*		14		8							M Reed	24
1	2	3	6	4						10	9	7	5		11		S		8	S						K Redfern	25
1	2	3	6	4*			14			10		7	5		11	9			8•	12						K Cooper	26
1	2	3	6	12			S			10		7	5	4	11	9			8*							J Watson	27
1	2	3	6	12			14			10•		7	5	4*	11	9			8							V Callow	28
1	2	3•	6	4		8	14			10*		7	5		11	9	12									D Allinson	29
1	2	12	4	3					10	11*		7	5		6	9			8							R Pawley	30
1	2	9	4	3			S		10	11		7	5		6				8							T Holbrook	31
	2	12	4	3						11		7	5		6	9•			8			1	10*			K Burge	32
	2	S	4	3			12			11		7	5		6	9			8			1	10*			J Deakin	33
	2	14	4	3						11	9	7•	5	12	6*				8			1	10			K Hackett	34
	2	S	4	3						11	9	7	5		6				8			1	10			K Cooper	35
	2	6	4	3			S			11	9	7	5						8			1	10*			P Wright	36
	2	S	6*	4	3		12			11	9	7	5						8			1	10			P Vanes	37
1	2	14	4	3			12			11	9	7*	5		10•				8				6			I Cruikshanks	38
1	2	3	4				S			11	9	7	5	12	10				8*				6			T Lunt	39
1	2	3	4							11	9	7	5	8	6*		10		12				S			I Borrett	40
1	2	3	S	4						11	9	7*		8	6		10		12				5			S Bell	41
1	2	14	4	3•						11	9		8	12			10		7				5			P Taylor	42
1	2	12	4*	3						11	9		5	8	6*		10		7				14			R Lewis	43
1	2	6			3					11	9		5	8			10*		7				4			G Pooley	44
1	2	3	4				S			9		5	8	10	6		11	7					S			M Reed	45
1	2	3	4				S			9		5	8	10			11	7					S	6		K Hackett	46
1	2	3	4*				S			9		5	8	10			11	7					12	6		J Kirkby	47
1	2	3	S							9	12	5	8	10			11	7					4*	6		W Burns	48
1	2	3								9		8	5	S	S		10	11	7		4			6		K Lupton	49
1	2	14								9*		8	5	12			10	11	7		4			6	3•	J Lloyd	50
1	2	S								9		8	5	12			10	11	7*		4			6	3	G Poll	51
1	2*	S								9		8	5	12			10	11	7		4			6	3	T Holbrook	52
1	2	3								9		8	5	S	S		10	11	7		4			6		P Scoble	53
1	2	3								9	8*	5		12	14	10•		11	7		4			6		T West	54
1	2	3								9	8	5		12	S		10	11*	7		4			6		P Wright	55
1	2	3•								9	8	5		12			10	11*	7		4			6	14	R Milford	56
1	2	14								9	8*	5		12			10	11•	7		4			6	3	D Axcell	57
1	2	3	14							9	8	5		12			10*	11•	7		4	1		6		D Elleray	58
	2	3				6				9	S	5		11			10		S	7	4	1		8	3	J Martin	59
	2	3				6				9	12	5		11			10		S	7	4	1		8	3*	M Bodenham	60
	2					6*				9	S	5		11			10		12	7	4	1		8	3	G Courtney	61
42	**46**	**26**	**21**	**23**	**12**	**17**	**10**	**2**	**12**	**29**	**42**	**39**	**43**	**7**	**18**	**14**	**14**	**14**	**31**	**2**	**10**	**4**	**9**	**13**	**4**	**League Appearances**	
	3	5	2	1	2	8		1	2	2				13	3		6		3	1			1		1	**Substitute Appearances**	
4	4	3+1	2	1	4	4	1	2+1	4	3	3+1	3+1	4	0+1		1+1										**R/lows Appearances**	
	2			1	2			2		1+1	2	2	2		1		1		2			2	2			**FA Cup Appearances**	
5	6	2	3+2	5		2	2+2	1	5	5	6	2	4+1		6		3+1	0+1			1	1				**ZDS Cup Appearances**	
	3			3				3		0+1	3	3	3		0+1	3			3		0+1	3		3	3	**Play-Offs Appearances**	

Also Played: Posn.(Game): Linton 14(8)6(13)S(16), Oakes 3(13•,16)· Holden 6*(42), Trotter S(30,31,35,44)14(32)12(36)

Players on Loan: C Hill (Sheffield Utd)

† = Sent Off

LEICESTER CITY

Club Colours: All royal blue
Change Colours: All white
Reserves League: Pontins Central League Division 1

<table>
<tr><th colspan="6">COMPETITIONS</th></tr>
<tr><th>Div. 1</th><th>Div. 2</th><th>ECWC</th><th>Texaco</th><th>A/Scot</th><th>A/Ital</th></tr>
<tr><td>08-09</td><td>94-08</td><td>61-62</td><td>72-73</td><td>75-76</td><td>71-72</td></tr>
<tr><td>25-35</td><td>09-25</td><td></td><td>73-74</td><td></td><td></td></tr>
<tr><td>37-39</td><td>35-37</td><td></td><td></td><td></td><td></td></tr>
<tr><td>54-55</td><td>39-54</td><td></td><td></td><td></td><td></td></tr>
<tr><td>57-69</td><td>55-57</td><td></td><td></td><td></td><td></td></tr>
<tr><td>71-78</td><td>69-71</td><td></td><td></td><td></td><td></td></tr>
<tr><td>80-81</td><td>78-80</td><td></td><td></td><td></td><td></td></tr>
<tr><td>83-87</td><td>81-83</td><td></td><td></td><td></td><td></td></tr>
<tr><td></td><td>87-</td><td></td><td></td><td></td><td></td></tr>
</table>

<table>
<tr><th colspan="3">HONOURS</th></tr>
<tr><th>Div. 2</th><th>League Cup</th><th>C/Shield</th></tr>
<tr><td>24-25</td><td>63-64</td><td>1971</td></tr>
<tr><td>36-37</td><td></td><td></td></tr>
<tr><td>53-54</td><td></td><td></td></tr>
<tr><td>56-57</td><td></td><td></td></tr>
<tr><td>70-71</td><td></td><td></td></tr>
<tr><td>79-80</td><td></td><td></td></tr>
</table>

<table>
<tr><th colspan="5">MOST APPEARANCES: GRAHAM CROSS 596＋3
(1960-75)</th></tr>
<tr><th>Year</th><th>League</th><th>FA Cup</th><th>Lge Cup</th><th>Europe</th></tr>
<tr><td>60-61</td><td>1</td><td></td><td></td><td></td></tr>
<tr><td>61-62</td><td>6</td><td></td><td></td><td>2</td></tr>
<tr><td>62-63</td><td>29</td><td>6</td><td>2</td><td></td></tr>
<tr><td>63-64</td><td>39</td><td>1</td><td>6</td><td></td></tr>
<tr><td>64-65</td><td>35</td><td>5</td><td>9</td><td></td></tr>
<tr><td>65-66</td><td>38</td><td>4</td><td>1</td><td></td></tr>
<tr><td>66-67</td><td>41</td><td>1</td><td>3</td><td></td></tr>
<tr><td>67-68</td><td>29</td><td>6</td><td>1</td><td></td></tr>
<tr><td>68-69</td><td>37</td><td>8</td><td>2</td><td></td></tr>
<tr><td>69-70</td><td>42</td><td>5</td><td>6</td><td></td></tr>
<tr><td>70-71</td><td>42</td><td>6</td><td>5</td><td></td></tr>
<tr><td>71-72</td><td>39</td><td>3</td><td>1</td><td></td></tr>
<tr><td>72-73</td><td>38</td><td>2</td><td>1</td><td></td></tr>
<tr><td>73-74</td><td>40</td><td>7</td><td>1</td><td></td></tr>
<tr><td>74-75</td><td>38＋2</td><td>5</td><td>2</td><td></td></tr>
<tr><td>75-76</td><td>1＋1</td><td></td><td></td><td></td></tr>
<tr><td></td><td>495＋3</td><td>59</td><td>40</td><td>2</td></tr>
<tr><td colspan="5">Previous holder: A Black 557 (League 528), 1919-34</td></tr>
</table>

<table>
<tr><th colspan="3">MOST GOALS IN A CAREER</th></tr>
<tr><th colspan="3">ARTHUR CHANDLER 273 (1923-34)</th></tr>
<tr><th>Season</th><th>League</th><th>FA Cup</th></tr>
<tr><td>1923-24</td><td>24</td><td></td></tr>
<tr><td>1924-25</td><td>32</td><td>6</td></tr>
<tr><td>1925-26</td><td>26</td><td></td></tr>
<tr><td>1926-27</td><td>28</td><td>1</td></tr>
<tr><td>1927-28</td><td>34</td><td></td></tr>
<tr><td>1928-29</td><td>34</td><td></td></tr>
<tr><td>1929-30</td><td>32</td><td></td></tr>
<tr><td>1930-31</td><td>18</td><td></td></tr>
<tr><td>1931-32</td><td>12</td><td>2</td></tr>
<tr><td>1932-33</td><td>4</td><td></td></tr>
<tr><td>1933-34</td><td>6</td><td>5</td></tr>
<tr><td>1934-35</td><td>9</td><td></td></tr>
<tr><td>Total</td><td>259</td><td>14</td></tr>
</table>

<table>
<tr><th colspan="4">HIGHEST TRANSFER FEES RECEIVED</th></tr>
<tr><th>Amount</th><th>Club</th><th>Player</th><th>Date</th></tr>
<tr><td>£1,350,000</td><td>Derby County</td><td>Paul Kitson</td><td>3/92</td></tr>
<tr><td>£.8＋.25m</td><td>Everton</td><td>Gary Lineker</td><td>7/85＋86</td></tr>
<tr><td>£1,000,000</td><td>Leeds United</td><td>Gary McAllister</td><td>7/90</td></tr>
<tr><td>£850,000</td><td>Everton</td><td>Mike Newell</td><td>6/89</td></tr>
</table>

<table>
<tr><th colspan="4">HIGHEST TRANSFER FEES PAID</th></tr>
<tr><th>Amount</th><th>Club</th><th>Player</th><th>Date</th></tr>
<tr><td>£350,000</td><td>Luton Town</td><td>Mike Newell</td><td>9/87</td></tr>
<tr><td>£350,000</td><td>Derby County</td><td>Ian Ormondroyd</td><td>3/92</td></tr>
<tr><td>£300,000</td><td>Southampton</td><td>Steve Moran</td><td>9/86</td></tr>
<tr><td>£300,000</td><td>Oldham Athletic</td><td>Tommy Wright</td><td>8/89</td></tr>
</table>

<table>
<tr><th colspan="5">MANAGERS</th></tr>
<tr><th>Name</th><th>Seasons</th><th>Best</th><th>Worst</th></tr>
<tr><td>Peter Hodge</td><td>1919-26</td><td>17(1)</td><td>14(2)</td></tr>
<tr><td>Willie Orr</td><td>1926-32</td><td>2(1)</td><td>19(1)</td></tr>
<tr><td>Peter Hodge</td><td>1932-34</td><td>17(1)</td><td>19(1)</td></tr>
<tr><td>Arthur Lochhead</td><td>1934-36</td><td>21(1)</td><td>6(2)</td></tr>
<tr><td>Frank Womack</td><td>1936-39</td><td>16(1)</td><td>1(2)</td></tr>
<tr><td>Tom Bromilow</td><td>1939-45</td><td></td><td></td></tr>
<tr><td>Tom Mather</td><td>1945-46</td><td></td><td></td></tr>
<tr><td>John Duncan</td><td>1946-49</td><td>9(2)</td><td>19(2)</td></tr>
<tr><td>Norman Bullock</td><td>1949-55</td><td>21(1)</td><td>15(2)</td></tr>
<tr><td>David Halliday</td><td>1955-58</td><td>18(1)</td><td>5(2)</td></tr>
<tr><td>Matt Gillies</td><td>1959-68</td><td>4(1)</td><td>14(1)</td></tr>
<tr><td>Frank O'Farrell</td><td>1968-71</td><td>21(1)</td><td>3(2)</td></tr>
<tr><td>Jimmy Bloomfield</td><td>1971-77</td><td>7(1)</td><td>18(1)</td></tr>
<tr><td>Frank McLintock</td><td>1977-78</td><td>22(1)</td><td>22(1)</td></tr>
<tr><td>Jock Wallace</td><td>1978-82</td><td>21(1)</td><td>17(2)</td></tr>
<tr><td>Gordon Milne</td><td>1982-86</td><td>15(1)</td><td>3(2)</td></tr>
<tr><td>Bryan Hamilton</td><td>1986-87</td><td>20(1)</td><td>13(2)</td></tr>
<tr><td>David Pleat</td><td>1987-91</td><td>13(2)</td><td>22(2)</td></tr>
<tr><td>Gordon Lee</td><td>1991</td><td>22(2)</td><td>22(2)</td></tr>
<tr><td>Brian Little</td><td>1991-</td><td>4(2)</td><td>4(2)</td></tr>
</table>

<table>
<tr><th colspan="2">LONGEST LEAGUE RUNS</th></tr>
<tr><td>of undefeated matches:</td><td>19 (6.2.1971-18.8.1971)</td></tr>
<tr><td>of undefeated home matches:</td><td>40 (12.2.1898-17.4.1900)</td></tr>
<tr><td>without home win:</td><td>8 (19.4.1975-25.10.1975)</td></tr>
<tr><td>of league wins:</td><td>7 (15.2.1908-28.3.1908)</td></tr>
<tr><td></td><td>(24.1.1925-17.3.1925) (26.12.1962-9.3.1963)</td></tr>
<tr><td>of league defeats:</td><td>7 (28.11.1931-16.1.1932)</td></tr>
<tr><td></td><td>(28.8.90-29.9.90)</td></tr>
<tr><td>of league matches without a win:</td><td>18 (12.4.1975-1.11.1975)</td></tr>
<tr><td>of undefeated away matches:</td><td>10 (27.2.1971-14.8.1971)</td></tr>
<tr><td>without an away win:</td><td>22 (2.4.1977-14.3.1978)</td></tr>
<tr><td>of home wins:</td><td>13 (3.9.1906-29.12.1906)</td></tr>
<tr><td>of away wins:</td><td>4 (13.3.1971-12.4.1971)</td></tr>
</table>

PREVIOUS NAME
Leicester Fosse 1884-1919

PREVIOUS LEAGUE
Midland League

BIGGEST VICTORIES
League: 10-0 v Portsmouth, (h), Div 1, 20.10.1928
F.A. Cup: 7-0 v Crook Town, (h), Rnd 3, 1931-32
League Cup: 8-1 v Coventry City, (a), 5th rnd., 1.12.1964
Europe: 4-1 v Glenavon, (a), 1st rnd., 13.9.1961

BIGGEST DEFEATS
League: 0-12 v Nottingham Forest, (a), Div 1, 21.4.1909.
F.A. Cup: No more than 4 clear goals. (7 instances)
League Cup: 0-4 v Burnley, (a), 4th rnd., 16.10.1968.
0-4 v Manchester City, (a), 2nd Rnd, 13.9.1967.
Europe: 0-2 v Atletico Madrid, (a), 2nd rnd., 15.11.1961.

MOST POINTS
3 points a win: 77, Division 2, 1991-92.
2 points a win: 61, Division 2, 1956-57.

MOST GOALS
109, Division 2, 1956-57.
Rowley 44, McNeil 18, Hines 14, Wright 10, McDonald 7, Hogg 5, Gardiner 4, Appleton 1, Morris 1, Moran 1, Milburn 1, og 3.

MOST GOALS IN A MATCH
6. John Duncan v Port Vale 7-0, Div. 2, 25.12.1924.
6. Arthur Chandler v Portsmouth 10-0, Div. 1, 20.10.1928.

MOST GOALS IN A SEASON
Arthur Rowley 44 League (5 pens), 1956-57.
3 goals 4 times = 12; 2 goals 6 times = 12; 1 goal 20 times = 20.

MOST FIRST CLASS MATCHES IN A SEASON
61 (46 League, 2 FA Cup, 4 League Cup, 6 Zenith Data, 3 Play-Offs) 1991-92

MOST LEAGUE GOALS CONCEDED
112, Division 1, 1957-58

MOST LEAGUE WINS
25, Division 2, 1956-57

MOST LEAGUE DRAWS
19, Division 1, 1975-76

MOST LEAGUE DEFEATS
25, Division 1, 1977-78

OLDEST PLAYER
Joe Calvert: 40 years 313 days, 13.12.1947.

YOUNGEST PLAYER
Dave Buchanan: 16 years 192 days, 1.1.1979.

MOST CAPPED PLAYER
John O'Neill (Northern Ireland) 39

BEST PERFORMANCES BY LEICESTER CITY

League: 1956-57: Matches played 42, Won 25, Drawn 11, Lost 6, Goals for 109, Goals against 67, Points 61. First in Division 2.

Highest: 1928-29: 2nd in Division 1.

F.A. Cup: 1948-49: 3rd rnd. Birmingham City 1-1, 1-1, 2-1; 4th rnd. Preston North End 2-0; 5th rnd. Luton Town 5-5, 5-3; 6th rnd. Brentford 2-0; Semi-Final Portsmouth 3-1; Final Wolverhampton Wanderers 1-3.

1960-61: 3rd rnd. Oxford United 3-1; 4th rnd. Bristol City 5-1; 5th rnd. Birmingham City 1-1, 2-1; 6th rnd. Barnsley 0-0, 2-1; Semi-Final Sheffield United 0-0, 0-0, 2-0; Final Tottenham Hotspur 0-2

1962-63: 3rd rnd. Grimsby Town 3-1; 4th rnd. Ipswich Town 3-1; 5th rnd. Leyton Orient 1-0; 6th rnd. Norwich City 2-0; Semi-Final Liverpool 1-0; Final Manchester United 1-3.

1968-69: 3rd rnd. Barnsley 1-1, 2-1; 4th rnd. Millwall 1-0; 5th rnd. Liverpool 0-0, 1-0; 6th rnd. Mansfield Town 1-0; Semi-Final West Bromwich Albion 1-0; Final Manchester City 0-1.

League Cup: 1963-64: 2nd rnd. Aldershot 2-0; 3rd rnd. Tranmere Rovers 2-1; 4th rnd. Gillingham 3-1; 5th rnd. Norwich 1-1, 2-1; Semi-Final West Ham United 4-3, 2-0; Final Stoke City 1-1, 3-2.

Cup Winners Cup: 1961-62: 1st rnd. Glenavon 4-1, 3-1; 2nd rnd. Atletico Madrid 1-1, 0-2.

DIVISIONAL RECORDS

	Played	Won	Drawn	Lost	For	Against	Points
DIVISION 1	1592	519	410	663	2442	2791	**1497**
DIVISION 2	1936	794	474	668	3003	2749	**2181**
TOTALS	**3528**	**1313**	**984**	**1331**	**5445**	**5540**	**3678**

LEICESTER CITY

PLAYERS NAME Honours	Ht	Wt	Birthdate	Birthplace Transfers	Contract Date	Clubs	League	L/Cup	FA Cup	Other	Lg	L/C	FAC	Oth
GOALKEEPERS														
Russell Hoult	6.4	13.2	22.11.72	Leicester	28.03.91	Leicester City								
				Loan	27.08.91	Lincoln City	2	1						
				Loan	25.03.92	Blackpool								
Carl Muggleton	6.0	11.13	13.09.68	Leicester	17.09.86	Leicester City (A)	29		3	4				
E: u21.1				Loan	01.08.87	Chesterfield	17			2				
				Loan	01.02.88	Blackpool	2							
				Loan	28.10.88	Hartlepool Utd	8			2				
				Loan	01.03.90	Stockport Co	4							
				Loan	21.09.90	Liverpool								
Kevin Poole	5.10	11.11	21.07.63	Bromsgrove	26.08.81	Aston Villa (A)	28	2	1	1				
Loan Northampton 08.11.84 3 Lg apps					27.08.87	Middlesbrough	34	4	2	2				
				Loan	27.03.91	Hartlepool Utd	12							
					30.07.91	Leicester City	42	4		5				
DEFENDERS														
Steven Holden	6.0	11.13	04.09.72	Luton	28.03.91	Leicester City	1							
Anthony James	6.3	13.08	27.06.67	Sheffield	22.08.88	Lincoln City	24+5	2		0+1				
				£150,000	23.08.89	Leicester City	73+9	6	2	3+1	9		1	
Richard Smith	5.11	12.4	03.10.70	Leicester	15.12.88	Leicester City (T)	25+8	1	2	5	1		1	
				Loan	06.09.89	Cambridge Utd	4	1						
Michael Trotter	6.1	11.11	27.10.69	Hartlepool	14.11.87	Middlesbrough (A)								
				Loan	19.11.88	Doncaster Rovers	3		1	2				
				Free	26.06.90	Darlington	16+13	1	2	1+2	2			
				£100,000	20.12.91	Leicester City	0+2							
Steve Walsh	6.2	11.10	03.11.64	Fulwood	11.09.82	Wigan Ath	123+3	7	6	10+2	4			
FRT'85				£100,000	24.06.86	Leicester City	194+1	17	5	13	22	2		1
Jimmy Willis	6.2	12.4	12.07.68	Liverpool			Blackburn Rovers (A)							
GMVC'90		Transfer Halifax Town 21.08.86 0 apps			30.12.87	Stockport Co	10							
				£12,000	24.03.88	Darlington	78	3	5	5	4			
				£100,000	20.12.91	Leicester City	9+1		2	1				
				Loan	26.03.92	Bradford City	9							
MIDFIELD														
Gary Coatsworth	6.1	11.6	07.10.68	Sunderland	10.04.87	Barnsley	3+3							
Div4'91				Free	01.07.89	Darlington	15+7	1+1		2+1	2			
				£15,000	31.10.91	Leicester City	2+1			0+1				
Paul Fitzpatrick	6.4	11.10	05.10.65	Liverpool			Tranmere Rovers							
						Liverpool (A)								
	via Preston N.E.				12.03.85	Bolton W	13+1	3	1	1				
				Free	20.08.86	Bristol City	40+4	3+1	5	6+1	7			
				£40,000	01.10.88	Carlisle Utd	106+3	5	5	5	4	1	1	
				Loan	02.12.88	Preston N.E	2							
					04.07.91	Leicester City	21+5	2	1	3+2	4			1
Colin Gibson	5.8	10.10	06.04.60	Bridport	13.04.78	Aston Villa (A)	181+4	26	12	14+1	10	4	1	2
E:B1,u21.1,ESC'82,Div1'81,FAC'90				£275,000	29.11.85	Manchester Utd	74+5	7	8+1	2	9			1
				Loan	27.09.90	Port Vale	5+1				2			
				£100,000	21.12.90	Leicester City	34+1	4	1	2	4			
Nicky Platnauer	5.11	12.10	10.06.61	Leicester			Bedford Town			1				
Welsh Cup'88				Free	04.08.82	Bristol Rovers	21+3	1	0+1		7	1		
				£50,000	26.08.83	Coventry City	38+6	5	4		6			
				£60,000	14.12.84	Birmingham City	23+5	3	5		2			
Loan Reading 7Lg 1oth				Free	26.09.86	Cardiff City	110+5	6	9	12	6	2		
				£50,000	01.08.89	Notts County	57	6	1	10	1			
				Loan	18.01.91	Port Vale	14		1					
				Free	19.07.91	Leicester City	26+3	3+1		2				
Steven J Thompson	5.9	11.0	02.11.64	Oldham	04.11.82	Bolton W (A)	329+6	27	21	39	49	2	4	2
SVT'89				£180,000	13.08.91	Luton Town	5	2						
				Swap	22.10.91	Leicester City	31+3		2	6+1	3			2
Peter Weir	5.11	11.2	18.01.58	Johnstone			Leicester City	8+2	1						
S:6,SP2,SLC3,ECWC83														
Michael Whitlow	6.1	11.6	13.01.68	Liverpool			Witton Albion							
Div.2'90				£10,000	11.11.88	Leeds Utd	62+15	4+1	1+4	9	4			
				£250,000	27.03.92	Leicester City	4+1			3				
Darren Williams	5.10	10.5	15.02.68	Birmingham	03.01.87	Leicester City (T)	7+3	3		1	2			
Loan Lincoln 23.11.89 0 apps				Loan	23.03.90	Lincoln City	7+2			1				
				Loan	17.09.90	Chesterfield	4+1				1			
FORWARDS														
Phil Gee	5.9	10.0	19.12.64	Pelsall			Gresley Ro							
Div2 '87				£5,000	02.09.85	Derby County	106+17	11+2	6+1	7+1	26	3	2	
				P.E	11.03.92	Leicester City	14			0+1	2			
Colin Gordon	6.1	12.12	17.01.63	Stourbridge	01.11.84	Swindon Town	70+2	6	2	3	33			
				£80,000	03.07.86	Wimbledon	2+1	2		1		1		
				Loan	15.02.87	Gillingham	4				2			
				£80,000	17.07.87	Reading	23+1	6	0+1	1	9	2		
				Loan	24.03.88	Bristol City	8			2	4			
				£90,000	07.10.88	Fulham	12+5		1		2			
				£80,000	29.06.89	Birmingham City	17+9	2+1	0+1		3			
				Loan	19.12.90	Walsall	6				1			
Loan Bristol Rov. 23.01.91 3+1 Lg				Free	19.07.91	Leicester City	18+3	1	1	4+1	5			2

LEICESTER CITY CONTINUED

PLAYERS NAME / Honours	Ht	Wt	Birthdate	Birthplace / Transfers	Contract Date	Clubs	League	L/Cup	FA Cup	Other	Lg	L/C	FAC	Oth
David Lowe	5.10	11.4	30.08.65	Liverpool	01.06.83	Wigan Ath. (A)	179+9	8	16+1	18	40		4	9
E:u21.2,Y7,FRT85				£80,000	26.06.87	Ipswich Town	21+13	10	3	10+2	37	2		6
				Loan	19.03.92	Port Vale	8+1				2			
				£250,000	13.07.92	Leicester City								
Gary Mills	5.8	11.1	11.11.61	Northampton	13.07.78	Nottm. Forest (A)	50+8	7+3	3	4+2	8	2		
E: u21.2, Y, S; E.Cup'80						Seattle Sounders								
					13.10.82	Derby County	18	2	3		1			
via Seattle Sounders to					02.12.83	Nottm. Forest	63+16	9+2	2	3+1	4	1		
					14.08.87	Notts County	75	6	5	10	8	1		
				£150,000+P	02.03.89	Leicester City	131+2	6	4	10	15	1		
David Oldfield	6.0	12.2	30.05.68	Perth, Aus	16.05.86	Luton Town (A)	21+8	4+2	0+1	2+1	4	2		2
E: u21.1				£600,000	14.03.89	Manchester City	18+8	2+1		0+1	6	2		1
				£150,000	12.01.90	Leicester City	87+16	5+1	3	5+2	16			1
Ian Ormondroyd	6.5	13.9	22.09.64	Bradford			Thackley							
					06.09.85	Bradford City	72+15	12+2	7	7+2	20	4	2	1
				Loan	27.03.87	Oldham Ath	8+2				1			
				£600,000	02.02.89	Aston Villa	41+15	4+2	5	6	6	2	2	
				£350,000	19.09.91	Derby County	25	3	3		8		1	
				P.E	11.03.92	Leicester City	14			3	1			1
Ashley Ward	6.1	12.4	24.11.70	Manchester	05.08.89	Manchester City (T)	0+1		0+2					
				Loan	10.01.91	Wrexham	4			1	2			
				£80,000	30.07.91	Leicester City	2+8	2+1						
ADDITIONAL CONTRACT PLAYERS														
Ian Blyth					08.11.91	Leicester City (T)								
Darren Cameron					21.09.90	Leicester City								
(M) Simon N Grayson	5.11	10.7	16.12.69	Ripon	13.06.88	Leeds Utd. (T)	2			1+1				
				£50,000	13.03.92	Leicester City	13			3				
Warren Haughton					07.07.92	Leicester City (T)								
Godfrey Ingram					13.09.89	Leicester City								
Jamie Ireland					27.10.89	Leicester City								
(D) Andrew Jeffrey	5.10	11.0	15.01.72	Scotland	13.02.90	Leicester City (T)								
				Monthly	23.07.91	Leicester City								
Neil A Lewis					09.07.92	Leicester City (T)								
Lewis Mogg					09.07.92	Leicester City (T)								

MANAGER: BRIAN LITTLE

DATE OF BIRTH: 25.11.1953   **PLACE OF BIRTH:** Newcastle upon Tyne

DATE OF APPOINTMENT: 1.6.1991

PREVIOUS CLUBS
as Manager: Darlington, Wolverhampton Wanderers
as Coach: Wolverhampton Wanderers
as Player: Aston Villa

HONOURS
as Manager: GM Vauxhall Conference Championship 1989-90; Division Four Championship 1990-91
as Player: Promotion to Div 1 1975, League Cup Winners 1975 & 1977, FA Youth Cup Winners 1972
International: England: Full and Youth

Value Rating: ★ ★ ★ ★

Programme Editor: David Callaghan

Price of 1991-92 Programme: £1.20
Number of Pages: 32

Local Newspapers: Leicester Mercury, Leicester Trader.

Local Radio Stations: Leicester Sound, Radio Leicester.

Additional Publications on Club: Of Fossils & Foxes, (Dave Smith & Paul Taylor) £19.95.
Club Handbook, £2.95

LEADING LEAGUE GOALSCORERS
SEASONS 1979-80 – 1991-92

1979-80	ALAN YOUNG	14		1980-81	JIM MELROSE	9
1981-82	GARY LINEKER	17		1982-83	GARY LINEKER	26
1983-84	GARY LINEKER	22		1984-85	GARY LINEKER	24
1985-86	ALAN SMITH	19		1986-87	ALAN SMITH	17
1987-88	GARY McALLISTER	9		1988-89	MIKE NEWELL	13
1989-90	GARY McALLISTER	10		1990-91	DAVID KELLY	14
1991-92	**TOMMY WRIGHT**	**12**				

FILBERT STREET Leicester LE2 7EL

Capacity: 22,181   **Covered Standing:** 9,348   **Seating:** 12,833

Tel: Ground: 0533 555000   **Ticket Line:** 0898 12 10 28   **Clubcall:** 0898 12 11 85

All premium rate calls (0898/0891) cost 36p per minute cheap rate and 48p per minute at all other times. Call costings correct at time of going to press.

GROUNDS
Fosse Road/Racecourse 1884-85; Victoria Park 1985-87; Belgrave Road 1887-88; Victoria Park 1888-89; Mill Lane 1889-91; Aylestone Road 1891; Filbert Street 1891-Present Day

ATTENDANCES
Highest: 47,298 v Tottenham, FA Cup 5th rnd, 18.2.1928

Lowest: 3,440 v Huddersfield Town, Simod Cup 1st rnd, 10.11.1987

RECORD RECEIPTS:
£179,912 v Nott'm Forest, ZDS Cup, 12.2.1992
£123,695 v Nott'm Forest, Littlewoods Cup, 30.11.1988

CITY STADIUM
First game: v Nottingham Forest 'A' (Friendly), 7.11.1891
First floodlit game: v Borussia Dortmund (Friendly), 23.10.1957

Season Tickets:
Stands: from £140 to £190
Ground: £115
(Reductions for juniors/OAP)

Executive Box Season Tickets: Apply to club for details

Cost of Stand Tickets (Standard Matches): £11, £10, £9, £8, £7.50; Family Club £7.50, juveniles £4
Terraces: £5.50, Family Club £4.50, Juveniles £3

Match and Ticket Information: Applications with SAE are accepted two months prior to each match

Car Parking: Parking adjacent to stadium for season ticket holders only. Street parking is available and there is also a public car park five minutes walk from the ground

Nearest Railway Station: Leicester (0533 29811)

How to get to the ground

From North: Use Motorway M1 until junction 22 or A46/A607 into Leicester city centre. Follow signs Rugby into Almond Road, then at end turn right into Aylestone Road. Shortly turn left into Walnut Street, then turn left into Filbert Street for Leicester FC

From East: Use A47 into Leicester city centre. Follow signs Rugby into Almond Road, then at end turn right into Aylestone Road. Shortly turn left into Walnut Street, then turn left into Filbert Street for Leicester City FC

From South: Use Motorway M1 or M69 until junction 21 then A46 (S.P. Leicester). Under railway bridge and in 0.2m turn right into Upperton Road, then turn right into Filbert Street for Leicester City FC

From West: Use Motorway M69 or A50 into Leicester city centre and follow signs Rugby into Almond Road, then at end turn into Aylestone Road. Shortly turn left into Walnut Street, then left into Filbert Street for Leicester City FC

LEYTON ORIENT

Division 2

Formed: 1881   **Turned Professional:** 1903   **Ltd Co:** 1906

SPONSORED BY: Independent Transport Co. Ltd   **NICKNAME:** The O's

Chairman
A Wood

Directors
A Pincus
D L Weinrabe
H Linney
M Pears

Secretary
Miss Carol Stokes (01-539 2223/4)

Assistant Secretary
Mrs Sue Tilling

Managing Director
Frank Clark

Team Manager
Peter Eustace

Physiotherapist
Andy Taylor

Commercial Manager
F Woolf

Head Groundsman
Charlie Hasler

Club Statistician for the Directory
Don Hales

AFTER 13th position in 1990-91 Orient hoped to mount a serious promotion challenge. However a slow start – the first win did not come until league matche number five – ensured that a play-off position was the most that they could hope for throughout the season.

Indeed when they faced First Division Sheffield Wednesday at home in the Rumbelows Cup in late September they occupied 17th position. A gritty 0-0 draw seemed to inspire them and they began climbing the table with a series of good results.

The Wednesday tie ended in a brave 4-1 defeat in the 2nd leg and a few weeks later Youth International Chris Bart-Williams (O's youngest ever league player) joined Wednesday to ease the club's strained financial resources. A few weeks earlier Orient signed goalie Chris Turner from the Owls. With Turner going on to be voted No. 1 in the P.F.A. awards, the Wednesday connection proved extremely valuable to the club.

In addition to the Rumbelows Cup the O's enjoyed good runs in the other cups. First Division Oldham Athletic were accounted for in the F.A. Cup before going out in the 4th Round to Portsmouth. Wembley beckoned briefly in the Autoglass Trophy before defeat at Stoke City in the Southern semi-final.

Highlights of the League campaign included a 4-2 home win over eventual champions Brentford and an outstanding 3-1 away victory at fellow promotion contenders West Bromwich Albion.

The season's biggest League win – 4-0 at home to Hartlepool United at the beginning of April – hoisted the O's to 5th position and expectation ran high. However all the remaining six League matches were lost by the odd goal and the club had to settle for 10th place, well out of contention for a place in the play-offs.

Despite continuing financial problems and the departure of several members of the first team squad there is still plenty of talent remaining at Brisbane Road. With more youngsters waiting eagerly for the opportunity for first team football together with the signing Simon Livett (West Ham) and Vaughan Ryan (Wimbledon) the squad still looks good for the division. With a better start , more consistency and just a little luck the Orient could find themselves in the new Division One next term.

Don Hales

Back row L-R: Robert Taylor, Mark Cooper, Paul Heald, Chris Turner, Keith Day, Sam Kitchen. **Middle:** Geoff Pike (Coach), Bernie Dixon (Chief Scout/Youth Development Officer), Mark Warren, Simon Livett, Chris Zoricich, Warren Hackett, Adrian Whitbread, Greg Berry (now Wimbledon), Andy Jones, Barry Lakin, Mick Pentney (Kit Manager), Andy Taylor (Physoptherapist). **Front:** Mickey Tomlinson, Danny Carter, Kenny Achampong, Peter Eustace (Manager), Frank Clark (Managing Director), Kevin Hales, Steve Okai, Dominic Ludden.

LEYTON ORIENT

DIVISION THREE: 10th **FA CUP:** 4th RND **RUMBELOWS CUP:** 2nd RND **AUTOGLASS:** Sth S/FINALS

M	DATE	COMP.	VEN	OPPONENTS	RESULT	H/T	LGE POS	GOALSCORERS/GOAL TIMES	ATTEN-DANCE
1	A 17	BL	A	Brentford	L 3-4	1-1		Burnett 45, Nugent 60, Sayer 75	(6,156)
2	20	RC 1/1	H	Northampton Town	W 5-0	3-0		Burnett 3, Nugent 23, 89, Sayer 42, Berry 62	2,954
3	24	BL	H	Stockport County	D 3-3	2-2		Sayer 20, Nugent 23, 86	3,650
4	31	BL	A	Bolton Wanderers	L 0-1	0-0			(5,058)
5	S 3	BL	H	Bradford City	D 1-1	1-0		Sayer 36	3,435
6	7	BL	A	Hartlepool United	W 3-2	1-1	19	Otto 39, Castle 58, Carter 83	(3,581)
7	10	RC 1/2	A	Northampton Town	L 0-2	0-1			(1,437)
8	14	BL	H	Darlington	W 2-1	0-0		Otto 75, 79	3,962
9	17	BL	H	Preston North End	D 0-0	0-0			3,296
10	21	BL	A	Fulham	L 1-2	1-1	17	Nugent 41	(4,934)
11	24	RC 2/1	H	Sheffield Wed.	D 0-0	0-0			6,431
12	28	BL	H	Huddersfield Town	W 1-0	1-0		Day 41	3,738
13	O 5	BL	A	Peterborough Utd	W 2-0	1-0	9	Nugent 30, 88	(4,291)
14	9	RC 2/2	A	Sheffield Wed.	L 1-4	0-2		Nugent 72	(14,398)
15	12	BL	H	Chester City	W 1-0	1-0		Jones 10	4,049
16	19	BL	H	Bournemouth	D 1-1	0-1	7	Castle 60	3,876
17	22	AGT Pre	H	Reading	W 1-0	1-0		Otto 22	1,054
18	26	BL	A	Stoke City	L 0-2	0-1	10		(9,555)
19	N 2	BL	H	Exeter City	W 1-0	0-0	7	Castle 50	3,021
20	5	BL	A	Swansea City	D 2-2	2-2		Otto 11, Howard 45	(2,081)
21	9	BL	A	Torquay United	L 0-1	0-1	16		(2,388)
22	16	FAC 1	H	Welling United	W 2-1	0-1		Howard 78, Cooper 81	4,858
23	23	BL	A	Hull City	W 1-0	1-0		Howard 30	3,936
24	30	BL	A	Wigan Athletic	D 1-1	0-1	8	Berry 46	(2,066)
25	D 3	AGT Pre	A	Northampton Town	W 2-1	1-1		Richardson (og) 26, Berry 64	(1,153)
26	9	FAC 2	H	West Bromwich A.	W 2-1	1-0		Berry 1, 88	6,189
27	20	BL	A	Stockport County	L 0-1	0-0			(2,745)
28	26	BL	H	Bolton Wanderers	W 2-1	0-1		Cooper 47, 89	4,896
29	28	BL	H	Brentford	W 4-2	2-2	7	Berry 7, 20, Castle 47, Jones 78	7,333
30	J 1	BL	A	Bradford City	D 1-1	1-1	8	Castle 41	(6,810)
31	4	FAC 3	A	Oldham Athletic	D 1-1	0-0		Day 20	(10,764)
32	11	BL	A	Birmingham City	D 2-2	1-0	9	Nugent 37, Castle 88	(10,445)
33	15	FAC 3R	H	Oldham Athletic	W †4-2	0-1		Harvey 58, Nugent 77, 108, Castle (pen) 95	10,056
34	18	BL	A	West Bromwich A.	D 1-1	1-1	9	Jones 17	6,328
35	21	AGT 1	H	Brentford	W 3-2	2-0		Otto 14, Jones 35, Day 76	1,856
36	25	FAC 4	A	Portsmouth	L 0-2	0-0			(16,138)
37	28	BL	H	Sheffield United	W 2-0	1-0	7	Castle 21, Achampong 84	3,197
38	F 1	BL	H	Bournemouth	W 1-0	1-0	7	Nugent 24	(6,544)
39	4	AGT 2	A	Barnet	W 1-0	1-0		Jones 9	(2,969)
40	8	BL	H	Stoke City	L 0-1	0-1	7		7,153
41	11	BL	H	Wigan Athletic	W 3-1	0-1	7	Berry 58, Whitbread 63, Jones 70	3,142
42	15	BL	A	Bury	L 2-4	0-3	7	Taylor 68, Carter 71	(2,120)
43	22	BL	A	Birmingham City	D 0-0	0-0	7		6,025
44	29	BL	A	Shrewsbury Town	W 1-0	1-0	7	Howard 4	(2,873)
45	M 3	BL	A	West Bromwich A.	W 3-1	3-0	7	Howard 11, Berry 16, Nugent 20	(11,165)
46	7	BL	H	Reading	D 1-1	1-1	8	Nugent 17	4,436
47	10	BL	H	Swansea City	L 1-2	0-0	8	Castle 79	3,328
48	14	BL	A	Exeter City	L 0-2	0-0	8		(3,070)
49	17	AGT SSF	H	Stoke City	L 0-1	0-1			3,792
50	21	BL	H	Torquay United	W 2-0	0-0	7	Otto 53, Nugent 69	3,636
51	24	BL	H	Bury	W 4-0	1-0	7	Berry 3 (41, 65, 85), Wilder 78	3,074
52	28	BL	A	Hull City	L 0-1	0-0	7		(3,802)
53	31	BL	A	Darlington	W 1-0	0-0	6	Cooper 64	(1,704)
54	A 4	BL	H	Hartlepool United	W 4-0	1-0	5	Cooper 30, Achampong 62, Jones 83, Castle 85	4,245
55	11	BL	A	Preston North End	L 1-2	0-0	8	Castle 65	(3,926)
56	18	BL	H	Fulham	L 0-1	0-0	10		7,094
57	20	BL	A	Huddersfield Town	L 0-1	0-1	10		(10,011)
58	25	BL	H	Peterborough Utd	L 1-2	1-0	10	Cooper 21	5,996
59	29	BL	A	Reading	L 2-3	0-1	10	Okai 59, Cooper 82	(2,690)
60	M 2	BL	A	Chester City	L 0-1	0-0	10		(2,008)

Best Home League Attendance: 7,333 v Brentford   **Smallest: 3,021 v Exeter City**   **Av Home Att: 4,472**

Goal Scorers: **Compared with 90-91: +277**

League (62): Nugent 11, Castle 10, Berry 8, Cooper 6, Jones 5, Otto 5, Howard 4, Sayer 3, Carter 2, Achampong 2, Taylor, Wilder, Day Whitbread, Okai, Burnett

R/lows C (6): Nugent 3, Berry, Sayer, Burnett

FA Cup (9): Nugent 2, Berry 2, Howard, Cooper, Harvey, Day, Castle (1 pen)

Autoglass (7): Jones 2, Otto 2, Day, Berry, Opponents

†=After extra-time

Player columns (left → right): Heald P. · Howard T. · Dickenson K. · Whitbread A. · Day K. · Bart-Williams C. · Berry G. · Burnett W. · Nugent K. · Sayer A. · Otto R. · Zoricich C. · Carter D. · Castle S. · Newell P. · Harvey L. · Hackett W. · Jones A. · Achampong K. · Turner C. · Hales K. · Cooper M. · Roeder G. · Taylor R. · Wilder C. · Hendon I.

Heald P.	Howard T.	Dickenson K.	Whitbread A.	Day K.	Bart-Williams C.	Berry G.	Burnett W.	Nugent K.	Sayer A.	Otto R.	Zoricich C.	Carter D.	Castle S.	Newell P.	Harvey L.	Hackett W.	Jones A.	Achampong K.	Turner C.	Hales K.	Cooper M.	Roeder G.	Taylor R.	Wilder C.	Hendon I.	Referee	#
1	2	3	4*	5	6	7*	8	9	10	11	12	14														K Morton	1
1	2	3	S	5	6	7*	8	9	10	11	4	14														**G Poll**	2
1	2	3	S	5	6	7*	8	9	10	11	4		12													M Bailey	3
	2*	3	5	12	6	14	8*	9	10	11	4		7	1												J Watson	4
	2	3	5	S	6	7	14	9	10	11	4		8*	1												R Pawley	5
	2	3	5*	12	6	7	9		10*	11	4	14	8	1												E Parker	6
	2	3	4	S	6	12	9		10	11*	5	7	8	1												**R Wiseman**	7
	2	3	5	4	6*	12	14	9	10	11		7*	8	1												P Durkin	8
	2	3	5	4	6	14	S	9	10*	11		7	8	1												I Borrett	9
	2		5	4	6	11	3	9	10*			14	7	8	1	12*										M Bodenham	10
	2	S	4	5	6	10	9		11	12	7		1	8		3										**P Alcock**	11
	2	3	4	5	6		9	11*		7	8	1	12	10		S										I Hemley	12
	2		4	5	6*		9		3	7	10	1	12	8	11*	14										G Singh	13
	2	S	4	5	6		3*	9		7	8	1	12	10		11										**I Cruikshank**	14
	2	S	4	5		6	9		11	7*	10	1	12	3	8											P Scoble	15
	2		4	5	6	7*	9		11*		10	1	12	3	8	14										R Bigger	16
	2		4	5	6	S	9		11*		10	1	12	3	8	7										**M James**	17
	2			5	7		9		11	S		10	12	3	8	4	1	6*								A Wilkie	18
	2		4		6	14	9		11*	5		10	7*	3	8		1	12								P Foakes	19
	2		4	7	12		9		11	5		10	6*	3	8		1	S								P Danson	20
	2		4	5	6	14	9		11			10	7*	3*	8		1	12								R Hamer	21
	2		4	5	12	14	11*					8			3	9	7	1	6*	10						**G Poll**	22
	2		4	5	11	6†	10					8			3	9*	7	1	S	12						D Axcell	23
	2		4	5	11	6	10					8*	12	3	9*	7	1	14								J Kirby	24
	2		4	5	11		10					8*	12	3	9		1	7	S							**C Wilkes**	25
	2		4	5	11		10					8		6	3	9*	7	1	S	12						**K Morton**	26
	2		4	5		11	10				14	8	6*	3		7	1	S	9							S Bell	27
	2		4	5		11	10			6*		8		3	12	7	1	S	9							D Gallagher	28
	2	4*	5		11	14	10*	6				8		3	12	7†	1		9							D Elleray	29
	2		5		11	4*	10	6*				8		3	12	7	1	14	9*							J Worrall	30
	2		6	5	11	4	10					8		3	12	7*	1	14	9*							**S Lodge**	31
	2		6	5	11	4*	10					8	14	3	12		1	9*	7							D Allison	32
	2		6	5	11	4	10	S				8	7*	3	9		1		14							**S Lodge**	33
	2		6	5	11	4	10	12				8		3	9		1		S	7*						J Carter	34
	2		5			4	10	11				8*		3	9*	12	1	7	14	6						**M Bailey**	35
	2		4	5		6	10	11*				8		3	9*	12	1	14	7							**M Bodenham**	36
	2		6	5	11	4	10	7				8*		3	9*	12	1	14								M Pierce	37
	2		6	5	11*	4	10	12		7				3	9*	8	1	S	S							P Scoble	38
	2		6	5	11	4	10			7				3	9	8	1	S	S							**P Foakes**	39
	2*		6	5	11	4	10			7	12			3	9*	8	1	14								G Willard	40
	2		6	5	11	4	10*				12	8		3	9	7*	1	14								A Gunn	41
	2		5*	11	4	10				7	8			3*	9		1		14	12						D Shadwell	42
	2		6		11	4	10				7*	3*	9				1		5	14						M James	43
	2		6		11	4	10				12	8			9*	7*	1		5	14	3					T Lunt	44
	2		6		11	4	10			5	14	8			12		1	7*		9*	3					J Lloyd	45
	2		5		11	4	10			7	8				12	1		S	9*	3						D Axcell	46
	2		6	5		11*	4	9		14	7	8*					1		10	12	3					R Pawley	47
	2		6	5		11*	4	9		14	7				10		1			12	3*					P Danson	48
	2		6	5		11	4*	10		9	8	7*			14		1			12	3					**B Hill**	49
	2		6	5		11*	4	9		10	8	7					S	14	1			3					R Bigger	50
	2		6	5		11	4			12	8	7*			10*	9	1		14		3					P Jones	51
	2		6	5		11	4			14	8	7*			10*	9	1				3	12				C Trussell	52
	2		6	5		11	4			S	8				S	9	1		10		3	7				B Coddington	53
	2		6			11*	4			12	8				14	9	1	5	10*		3					D Frampton	54
	2		6				4			11	8				12	9	1	5*		14	10*	3				W Burns	55
	2		6	5			4			11	8				12	9	1	5*		S	10	3				K Cooper	56
	2		6			10				11*	8		7*			12	9	1	14	5		3		4		A Smith	57
	2		6			11	5		12		8					9	1	S	10		7*	3	4			K Cooper	58
	2		6			4				12	8					9	1	S	10	5	3	7			P Durkin	59
			6			5				11	8					1	7*	10	2		3	4*			V Callow	60

2	45	8	43	31	15	30	33	36	8	23	19	15	35	10	5	22	20	20	34	6	11	6	6	16	5	**League Appearances**	
			2			6	3		1	9	3	5	2		8		10	4		4	7	2	5		1	**Substitute Appearances**	
1	4	2	3	3	4	1	3+1	4		2	3	2+1	3+1	2		3	0+1	2	2							**R/lows Appearances**	
5		5	5		3+1	3	4		2			5		2	5	4+1	3+1	5	1+1	2+2	1		0+1			**FA Cup Appearances**	
5		5	1	5	1	3	4	5		3	1	2	3	1	0+2	4	4+1	2+1	4	2	0+1	1	0+1	1		**Autoglass Appearances**	

Also Played: Posn.(Game): Okai 11*(59), Cobb 9(60), Warren 12(60), Tomlinson 14(60)

† = Sent Off

LEYTON ORIENT

Club Colours: Red with white shirts, white shorts, red stockings
Change Colours: Yellow with blue shirts, blue shorts, yellow stockings
Reserves League: Capital League   **Youth Team:** S E Counties

Previous League: Southern League Division 2
Previous Names: 1981-86 Glyn Cricket and Football Club   1886-88 Eagle Football Club   1988-98 Orient Football Club   1898-1946 Clapton Orient   1946-67 Leyton Orient   1967-87 Orient   1987- Leyton Orient
Previous Managers: 1905-07 S Ormerod   1907-22 W Holmes   1923-28 P Proudfoot   1929-30 A Grimsdell   1930-31 P Proudfoot   1931-33 J Seed   1933-35 D Pratt   1935-39 P Proudfoot   1939-40 W Wright   1945 W Hall   1945-46 W Wright   1946-48 C Hewitt   1948-49 N McBain   1949-56 A Stock   1956 L Gore (Caretaker)   1956-57 A Stock   1957-58 L Gore (Caretaker)   1958-59 A Stock   1961-63 J Carey   1963 L Gore (Caretaker)   1963-64 B Fenton   1964-65 L Gore (Caretaker)   1965 D Sexton   1965-66 L Gore (Caretaker)   1966-68 R Graham   1968-71 J Bloomfield   1971 G Petchey   1971-81 J Bloomfield   1981 P Went   1981-83 K Knighton   1983-91 Frank Clark   1991- Peter Eustace
Honours: Champions Div 3 1969-70   Champions Div 3S 1955-56
League Career: Elected to Div 2 1905   Relegated to Div 3S 1928-29   Promoted to Div 2 1955-56   Promoted to Div 1 1961-62   Relegated to Div 2 1962-63   Relegated to Div 3 1965-66   Promoted to Div 2 1969-70   Relegated to Div 3 1981-82   Relegated to Div 4 1984-85   Promoted to Div 3 1988-89

CLUB RECORDS

Most Appearances for Club: Peter Allen: 1965-78, League 432 + FA Cup 25 + League Cup 24 **Total 481**
Most Capped Player: John Chiedozie (Nigeria) 8   **For England:** J Townrow 2 & O Williams 2
Record Goalscorer in a Match: R Heckman 5 v Lovells Athletic (h), 7-1, FA Cup 1st Round, 19.8.1955
Record League Goalscorer in a Season: Tom Johnston 35, Div 2, 1957-58   **In All Competitions:** Tom Johnston 36 (League 35 + FA Cup 1)
Record League Goalscorer in a Career: Tom Johnston 121   **In All Competitions:** Tom Johnston 123 (League 121 + FA Cup 2) 1956-58, 1959-61
Record Transfer Fee Received: £600,000 from Notts County for John Chiedozie, August 1981
Record Transfer Fee Paid: £175,000 to Wigan Athletic for Paul Beesley, October 1989
Best Performances: League: 22nd Div 1, 1962-63   **FA Cup:** Semi-Final 1977-78   **League Cup:** 5th Round 1963
Most League Points: (2pts a win) 66, Div 3, 1955-56   (3pts a win) 75, Div 4, 1988-89
Most League Goals: 106, Div 3S, 1955-56
Record League Victory: 8-0 v Crystal Palace, Div 3, 12.11.1955   v Rochdale, Div 4, 20.10.1987,   v Colchester Utd, Div 4 15.10.1988
Most Goals Scored in a League Match: 9-2 v Aldershot, Div 3S, 10.2.1934
Most Goals Scored in a Cup Tie: 9-2 v Chester, 3rd Round League Cup, 15.10.1962
Record League Defeat: 1-7 v Torquay (A), Div 3S, 16.4.1949   1-7 v Stoke City (a), Div 2, 7.9.1956, also 0-6 (on seven occasions)
Record Cup Defeat: 0-8 v Aston Villa, FA Cup 4th Rnd., 30.1.1929
Oldest Player in a League Match: John Rutherford 42 years v Portsmouth (h), Div 2, 2.4.1927
Youngest Player in a League Match: Chris Bart-Williams 16 years 232 days v Tranmere Rovers (h), Div 3, 2.2.1991

LONGEST LEAGUE RUNS	
of undefeated matches: 14 (1954-55)	**of league matches without a win:** 23 (1962-23)
of undefeated home matches: 25 (1913-14)	**of undefeated away matches:** 9 (1954-55)
without home win: 14 (1962-63)	**without an away win:** 34 (1938-47)
of league wins: 10 (1956)	**of home wins:** 12 (1954)
of league defeats: 8 (1927-28)	**of away wins:** 6 (1956)

BARCLAYS

LOCAL BRANCH
Leyton Branch
267 High Road
Leyton
London E10 5QL
Tel: 081-519 7100

BARCLAYBANK MACHINE

BARCLAYS BUSINESS CENTRE
Stratford Broadway
20-22 The Mall
Stratford
London E15 1XJ
Tel: 081-519 7100

BARCLAYBANK MACHINE

LEYTON ORIENT

PLAYERS NAME Honours	Ht	Wt	Birthdate	Birthplace Transfers	Contract Date	Clubs	League	L/Cup	FA Cup	Other	Lg	L/C	FAC	Oth
GOALKEEPERS														
Paul Heald	6.2	12.5	20.09.68	Wath on Dearne		Sheffield Utd. (T)								
					02.12.88	Leyton Orient	105	11	6	10				
				Loan	10.03.92	Coventry City	2							
Paul Newell	6.1	12.8	23.02.69	Woolwich	17.06.87	Southend Utd	15		2	1				
				£5,000	06.08.90	Leyton Orient	18	3		1				
Chris Turner	5.10	11.11	15.09.58	Sheffield	01.08.76	Sheffield Wed. (A)	91	11	13					
E:Y;LC'91				Loan	06.10.78	Lincoln City	5							
				£80,000	04.07.79	Sunderland	195	21	7					
				£275,000	15.08.85	Manchester Utd	64	7	8	2				
				£175,000	12.09.88	Sheffield Wed	75	6	8	1				
				Loan	15.11.89	Leeds Utd	2							
				Loan	25.10.91	Leyton Orient								
				£75,000	21.11.91	Leyton Orient	34		5	4				
DEFENDERS														
Keith Day	6.1	11.6	29.11.62	Grays		Aveley								
					23.08.84	Colchester Utd	113	5	6	6	12			
					21.07.87	Leyton Orient	177+5	15	13	17	8	1	1	1
Warren Hackett				Tottenham H. (T)										
FAYC'90				Free	03.07.90	Leyton Orient	26	2	5	4				
Kevin Hales	5.7	10.4	13.01.61	Dartford	12.01.79	Chelsea (A)	18+2		7		2			
				Free	25.08.83	Leyton Orient	256+15	21	22+1	20	22	2		1
Terry Howard	6.1	11.7	26.02.66	Stepney	01.03.84	Chelsea (A)	6							
E: u19.3				Loan	09.01.86	Crystal Palace	4							
				Loan	23.01.87	Chester City	2		2					
				£10,000	19.03.87	Leyton Orient	235	21	18	19	23	1	2	
Adrian Whitbread	6.2	11.13	22.10.71	Essex	13.11.89	Leyton Orient (A)	89	8+1	10	6	1			
MIDFIELD														
Kenny Achampong	5.10	10.13	26.06.66	Kilburn	03.06.84	Fulham (A)	68+13	8+1	1+1	5	15	1		4
				Loan	14.01.89	West Ham U								
					30.08.89	Charlton Ath	2+8	0+1		2				
				Loan	23.08.90	Leyton Orient	0+2							
				£25,000	24.09.90	Leyton Orient	45+11	4+1	5+1	4+1	6			
Wayne Burnett	6.0	12.6	04.09.71	London	13.11.89	Leyton Orient (T)	34+6	3	3	4	1	1		
Lee Harvey	5.11	11.7	27.12.66	Harlow	05.12.84	Leyton Orient (A)	116+47	13+3	10+4	18+4	19	3	2	2
E: Y.5														
FORWARDS														
Greg Berry	5.8		05.03.71	Essex		East Thurrock								
				Free	03.07.89	Leyton Orient	68+12	6	8+2	5+3	14	3	2	1
Danny Carter			29.06.69		04.07.88	Leyton Orient	82+12	11+2	6	6+1	12	2	1	
Paul Cobb					26.11.90	Leyton Orient	3+2							
Mark D Cooper	6.1	13.0	05.04.67	Watford	16.10.84	Cambridge Utd	61+10	7	4	4	17	3		
					02.04.87	Tottenham H								
				Loan	10.09.87	Shrewsbury Town	6				2			
				£105,000	09.10.87	Gillingham	38+11	2+1	3+1	4	11			
					02.02.89	Leyton Orient	77+16	4	3+2	6	28	1	1	3
Andy M Jones	5.10	12.7	09.01.63	Wrexham		Rhyl								
W: 6; S.P.'84,'85				£5,000	03.06.85	Port Vale	87+3	9+1	3+1	8	49	6		6
				£350,000	26.09.87	Charlton Ath	51+15	4+3	4	2	15	3	2	
				Loan	02.02.89	Port Vale	8+9				3			
				Loan	30.11.89	Bristol City	2+2			1	1			1
				£80,000	26.10.90	Bournemouth	36+4	2	4	2	8	2	3	1
				£90,000	01.10.91	Leyton Orient	20+10		4+1	4+1	5			2
Stephen Okai					06.07.92	Leyton Orient (T)	1				1			
Ricky Otto					06.02.91	Leyton Orient	23+11	3	2	3	5			2
Robert A Taylor	6.0	11.6	26.03.71	Watton, Norfolk	26.03.90	Norwich City (T)								
				Loan	28.03.91	Leyton Orient	0+3				1			
				Monthly	31.08.91	Birmingham City								
					21.10.91	Leyton Orient	6+5		0+1	0+1	1			
Michael Tomlinson			15.09.72	London	05.07.91	Leyton Orient (T)	0+2				1			
ADDITIONAL CONTRACT PLAYERS														
Barry Lakin					06.07.92	Leyton Orient (T)								
Dominic Ludden					06.07.92	Leyton Orient (T)								
Mark A. O'Neill					12.03.91	Leyton Orient								
Brett Patience					27.03.92	Leyton Orient (T)								
Keith Sharman	6.2	12.0	08.11.71	London	03.07.90	Leyton Orient (T)								
David C Thompson					06.07.92	Leyton Orient (T)								
Mark Warren					06.07.92	Leyton Orient (T)	0+1							

LEADING LEAGUE GOALSCORERS SEASONS 1985-86 – 1991-92

1985-86	PAUL SHINNERS	15		1986-87	ALAN COMFORT	11
1987-88	IAN JURYEFF	16		1988-89	ALAN COMFORT	19
1989-90	MARK COOPER	11		1990-91	STEVE CASTLE	12
		1991-92	KEVIN NUGENT	11		

BRISBANE ROAD Leyton, London E10 5NE

Capacity: 18,869   **Covered Standing:**   **Seating:** 7,171

Tel: Ground: 081 539 2223   **Ticket Sales:** As ground number   **Clubcall:** 0898 12 11 50

All premium rate calls (0898/0891) cost 36p per minute cheap rate and 48p per minute at all other times. Call costings correct at time of going to press.

ATTENDANCES
Highest: 34,345 v West Ham United, FA Cup Round 4, 25.1.1964
Lowest: 749 v Brentford, Freight Rover Trophy, 15.12.1986

Record Receipts: £87,867.92 v West Ham United, FA Cup Round 3, 10.1.1987

BRISBANE ROAD
First game: v Cardiff City, 28.8.1937
First floodlit game: v Brighton, 10.9.1959

Season Tickets:
Stands: from £115 to £160, juv/OAP £60 to £110
Ground: £100, juv/OAP £50

Executive Box Season Tickets: Apply to club for details

Cost of Stand Tickets: Main Centre: £9.50*; Main Wings: £7.50*; West Stand: adults £6.00, child/OAP £3; **Terrace:** North/Enclosure: adults £5.00; child/OAP £3 (*Includes programme)

Match and Ticket Information: Bookable at least two weeks in advance

Car Parking: Street parking around the ground.

Nearest Railway Station: Leyton Central

Nearest Tube Station: Leyton (Central Line)

How to get to the ground

From North and West: Use A406 North Circular Road (S.P. Chelmsford) to Edmonton, then in 2.6m at roundabout take 3rd exit A112 (S.P. Leyton). Pass Leyton Midland Road Station and in 0.5m turn right into Windsor Road, then turn left into Brisbane Road for Leyton Stadium
From East: Use A12 (S.P. London then City) to Leytonstone and follow signs Hackney into Grove Road. A Leyton cross main road and forward into Ruckholt Road, then turn right then left into Leyton High Road and in 0.2m turn left into Buckingham Road then right into Brisbane Road for Leyton Orient FC
From South: Use A120M through Blackwall Tunnel and follow signs Newmarket A102 to join A11 to Stratford. Follow signs Stratford Station into Leyton Road A112, to Leyton Station then keep forward. In 0.4m keep left then turn right then left into Leyton High Road and proceed as from East

Value Rating: ★ ★ ★

Programme Editor: Tim Reder

Price of 1992-93 Programme: £1
Number of Pages: 32
Subscriptions: Rates obtainable from shop manager

Local Newspapers: Waltham Forest Guardian, Ilford Recorder, Hackney Gazette, East London Advertiser, Stratford Express

Local Radio Stations: Radio Goodmayes, Whipps Cross Hospital Radio

LINCOLN CITY

Division 3

Formed: 1884   **Turned Professional:** 1885   **Ltd Co:** 1895

SPONSORED BY: Lincolnshire Echo   **NICKNAME:** The Red Imps

President
H Dove

Chairman
K J Reames

Vice-Chairman
M B Pryor

Directors
G R Davey (Managing Director)
H C Sills
J Hicks

Hon Life Vice-Presidents
D W Bocock
V C Withers

Managing Director
G R Davey

Team Manager
Steve Thompson

Commercial Manager
Suzanne Smith

Lotteries Manager
B Baldam

Physiotherapist
Neil McDiarmid, GRAD.DIP (Phys)
M.C.S.P., S.R.P.

Club Doctor
Dr N Huntley

Hon. Consultant Surgeon
B D Smith FRCS

Club Statistician for the Directory
Ian Nannestad

LINCOLN City's 1991-92 campaign can best be described by that overworked cliche 'a season of two halves'. The bare statistics suggest a very ordinary season – 10th position for the third time in four seasons, elimination from all three cups at the first hurdle for the second year in a row and the continuing weakness in front of goal – but reality was slightly different.

The season began with a 2-1 victory at Cardiff but a record home defeat (0-6) at the hands of newcomers Barnet had a shattering effect on the side. Injuries and suspensions also contributed to the club's woes and the first-half of the season was very much an uphill struggle. Away performances remained creditable but the players seemed to have no confidence at Sincil Bank following the Barnet debacle and only one of the next nine home games was won. Goals were a rarity apart from consecutive victories over Scunthorpe (4-2 and Doncaster (5-1) in November, but to the surprise of most fans these were to be the first signs of a revival of fortunes.

Confidence returned in the second half of the season and the side finished with a magnificent run which saw just one defeat in the final 18 matches. All five of the games played in April were won, earning Steve Thompson the Manager of the Month award (the first for a City manager in the Football League since 1982) and victory over promotion-seeking Blackpool on the final day of the season extended the sequence to seven wins on the trot – surely championship form.

There were some inspired performances particularly in the second half of the campaign when the whole of the defence played well throughout, conceding just 11 goals in the last 22 games. Ian Bowling,the fans' player of the year, Matt Carmichael and David Puttnam all showed consistent quality. New faces during the season included Jason Kabia (a signing from Central Midlands League side Oakham United), Sean Dunphy (who finally made his debut after a lengthy injury) and YTS lads Ben Dixon and Darren Chapman. Apart from the lack of goals the other main concern was the appalling disciplinary record – eight players were dismissed during the season.

Off the field the club struggled financially with gates below 3,000 until the sale of 'keeper Matt Dickins to Blackburn for a club record £250,000 and Shane Nicholson to Derby for £80,000 brought a return to stability. This allowed the directors to commence the construction of a new stand at the South Park end of the ground which when completed will mean the board have redeveloped three sides of the ground in a five year period. As well as increasing capacity this should eliminate the 'wind tunnel' effect which has affected matches for the last two and a half seasons.

Manager Steve Thompson will be aware that form approaching that already shown in 1992 will be sufficient to achieve promotion is spread over a whole season. Barring serious injuries and suspensions he already has a good enough defence, if midfield and attack are strengthened with new signings then 1992-93 could see a determined and successful bid for higher status. **Ian Nannestad**

Back row L-R: Paul Dobson, Paul Ward, Jason Kabia, John Schofield, David Puttnam, Dean West, David Clarke. **Middle row:** Graham Bressington, Sean Dunphy, Gary West, Ian Bowling, Jason Lee, Matt Carmichael, Kevin Finney, Grant Brown, Anthony Lormor. **Front row:** Keith Alexander (Youth Team Coach), J Hicks (Dir), S Sills (Dir), K J Reames (Chairman), Steve Thompson (Manager), M Pryor (Vice-Chairman), G R Davey (Managing Director), Neil McDiarmid (Physio).

LINCOLN CITY

DIVISION FOUR: 10th　　**FA CUP:** 1st RND　　**RUMBELOWS CUP:** 1st RND　　**AUTOGLASS:** Prelim.

M	DATE	COMP.	VEN	OPPONENTS	RESULT	H/T	LGE POS	GOALSCORERS/GOAL TIMES	ATTEN-DANCE
1	A 17	BL	A	Cardiff City	W 2-1	2-0		Carmichael (pen) 25, Dobson 44	(5,137)
2	20	RC 1/1	A	Chester City	L 0-1	0-0			(1,018)
3	24	BL	H	Rotherham United	L 0-2	0-0	11		4,134
4	28	RC 1/2	H	Chester City	W †4-3	1-1		Schofield 32, 63, Dobson 88, Ward 118	2,170
5	31	BL	A	Rochdale	L 0-1	0-1			(2,086)
6	S 4	BL	H	Barnet	L 0-6	0-2	19		3,067
7	14	BL	A	Carlisle United	W 2-0	2-0	17	Lee 16, 30	(2,149)
8	17	BL	A	Maidstone United	W 2-0	1-0	12	P Smith 24, Puttnam 69	(1,113)
9	21	BL	H	Chesterfield	L 1-2	0-2	14	Dobson 90	2,896
10	28	BL	A	Hereford United	L 0-3	0-3	15		(2,801)
11	O 5	BL	H	Halifax Town	D 0-0	0-0	16		2,092
12	13	BL	A	Blackpool	L 0-3	0-1	18		(5,086)
13	19	BL	A	York City	D 1-1	0-0	19	P Smith 54	(1,893)
14	26	BL	H	Burnley	L 0-3	0-1	19		3,235
15	N 5	BL	A	Walsall	D 0-0	0-0	18		(2,555)
16	9	BL	A	Northampton Town	L 0-1	0-0	20		(2,575)
17	16	FAC 1	H	Stockport County	L 1-3	0-0		Lee 66	(3,864)
18	19	AGT Pre	A	Shrewsbury Town	L 0-1	0-0			(615)
19	23	BL	H	Scunthorpe United	W 4-2	1-1	17	Finney 17, Lormor 3 (55, 76, 85)	3,078
20	30	BL	A	Doncaster Rovers	W 5-1	3-0	16	Lormor 21, Puttnam 35, Finney 45, Lee 63, Carmichael 90	(1,999)
21	D 4	AGT Pre	H	West Bromwich A.	L 1-2	0-0		G West 87	1,861
22	17	BL	H	Scarborough	L 0-2	0-2	17		1,752
23	21	BL	A	Rotherham United	D 1-1	1-0	18	G West 40	(3,293)
24	26	BL	H	Cardiff City	D 0-0	0-0	19		3,162
25	28	BL	H	Rochdale	L 0-3	0-3	19		2,916
26	J 1	BL	A	Barnet	L 0-1	0-1	20		(3,739)
27	4	BL	H	Gillingham	W 1-0	0-0	16	Dobson 67	2,169
28	11	BL	A	Crewe Alexandra	L 0-1	0-0	18		(3,060)
29	18	BL	H	Wrexham	D 0-0	0-0	18		2,213
30	F 8	BL	A	Burnley	L 0-1	0-1	20		(9,748)
31	12	BL	H	Doncaster Rovers	W 2-0	1-0	17	Lee 12, Dobson 90	2,011
32	15	BL	A	Scarborough	D 1-1	1-0	18	P Smith 15	(1,614)
33	22	BL	H	Crewe Alexandra	D 2-2	2-1	18	Lormor 6, Lee 34	2,261
34	29	BL	A	Gillingham	W 3-1	1-1	17	Puttnam 29, Kabia 67, 77	(3,160)
35	M 3	BL	A	Wrexham	D 1-1	0-0	17	Puttnam 88	(2,716)
36	7	BL	H	Mansfield Town	W 2-0	1-0	15	Nicholson 35, Lormor 55	4,387
37	11	BL	H	Walsall	W 1-0	0-0	14	Puttnam 85	2,021
38	18	BL	H	York City	D 0-0	0-0	14		1,875
39	21	BL	H	Northampton Town	L 1-2	0-2	14	Brown 81	2,486
40	24	BL	A	Mansfield Town	D 0-0	0-0	13		(3,604)
41	28	BL	A	Scunthorpe United	W 2-0	1-0	14	Schofield 43, D West 52	(3,297)
42	A 1	BL	H	Carlisle United	W 1-0	0-0	11	D West 68	2,118
43	11	BL	H	Maidstone United	W 1-0	1-0	12	Carmichael 3	2,241
44	18	BL	A	Chesterfield	W 5-1	0-1	11	Lormor 49, Dunphy 58, Puttnam 63, Carmichael (p) 75, Kabin 78	(2,748)
45	20	BL	H	Hereford United	W 3-0	0-0	10	D West 39, Carmichael 55, Lee 73	2,358
46	25	BL	A	Halifax Town	W 4-1	1-1	10	Lormor 26, 52, Abbott (og) 87, Alexander 90	(1,296)
47	M 2	BL	H	Blackpool	W 2-0	1-0	10	Carmichael (pen) 26, 90 (pen)	7,884

Best Home League Attendance: 7,884 v Blackpool　　　　Smallest: 1,752 v Scarborough　　　　**Av Home Att: 2,874**

Goal Scorers:　　　　　　　　　　　　　　　　　　　　　　　　　　　　　　　　　　**Compared with 90-91: -93**

League (50):　　Lormor 9, Carmichael 7 (4 pens), Puttnam 6, Lee 6, Dobson 4, Kabia 3, P Smith 3, D West 3, Finney 2, Dunphy, Nicholson
　　　　　　　　　　Opponents, Brown, Schofield, G West, Alexander

R/lows C (4):　　Schofield 2, Dobson, Ward
FA Cup (1):　　Lee
Autoglass (1):　　G West

† = After extra-time

320

1991-92

Dickins M.	Smith P.	Clarke D.	West D.	Carmichael M.	Brown G.	Finney K.	Ward P.	Lee J.	Dobson P.	Putnam D.	Alexander K.	Smith N.	West G.	Nicholson S.	Hoult R. (L)	Schofield J.	Bowling I.	Costello P. (L)	Lormor A.	Dye D. (N.C.)	Dunphy S.	Bressington G.	Kabia J.	Dixon B.	Chapman D.	Referee	
1	2	3	4	5	6	7	8	9	10*	11	12	S														G Singh	1
1	2*	3	4		6	7	8	9	10*	11	12		5	14												J Kirkby	2
1	2	3*	4•		6	7	8	9	10	11	14		5	12												B Hill	3
		14*	4		6	2	8	9	12	10	11		5*	3	1	7										B Burns	4
	4	12	14	5	6†	2•	8		9*	10	11			3	1	7										B Coddington	5
	2		4		6	12	8†	9	10*	11		S	5	3	1	7										M Bailey	6
	2	6	4	5		10	8*	S			12			3		7	1	11								R Poulain	7
	2	8*	4	5	6	10		9•			12		14	3		7	1	11								P Foakes	8
	2		4	5	6		8*	9	14	11				3		7	1		10•		12					K Morton	9
	2	8	4*	5	6	S		9	10		12			3		7	1	11								R Nixon	10
1	12	2	4		6*		8	9	14	11•			5	3		7			10							J Brandwood	11
1	4	12	2		6	S	8	9†		11*			5	3†		7			10							C Trussell	12
1	2	S		5	6	4	8	9*		11	12			3		7			10							A Bennett	13
1	2		4		6	S	8	9		11			5	3		7			10*		12					R Wiseman	14
1	2	3	14		6	4	8	9*	10	11•			5			7			12							A Flood	15
1	2	3	S		6	4	8	12	9*	11			5			7			10							P Don	16
1	3*	2•	12		6†	4	8	14	9	11			5			7			10							M Reed	17
1	14	12			6	4	8*	9	2	11			5*	3		7			10							K Cooper	18
1	11*	12	2		6	4	8	9					5	3		7			10		S					M Bullivant	19
1	2	3	S		6	4	8*	9		11			5			7			10		12					R Pawley	20
1	2	3	12		6	4*	8	9		11		S	5			7			10							G Pooley	21
1	2	3	12	14	6	4	8*	9		11			5*			7			10							I Hendrick	22
1	2	3	12	14	6	4•	8	9†		11*			5†			7			10							J Parker	23
1	2	3	S		6	4	8	9*		11	12		5			7			10							B Hill	24
1	2	3	12		6	4	8	9•		11	14		5*			7			10							P Taylor	25
1	2	3	4	5	6		8			11	12		9			7			10*		S					G Willard	26
1	2	3*	12	5	6		8	14	9	11•				4		7			10							D Shadwell	27
1	2	3*	4	5	6		8	12		11		S	9			7			10							A Bennett	28
1	2	3	4*	5	6		8	12	14	11			9			7			10•							G Poll	29
	2	3	12	5•	6		8	9*		11	14			4		7	1		10							D Phillips	30
	2		4	5	6		8*	9	14	11•				3		7	1		10			12†				J Rushton	31
	2	3	S	5	6		8	9	12	11						7	1		10*			4				J Worrall	32
	2	3	12	5	6			9•		11			8			7	1		10			4*	14			R Pawley	33
	2	3	4	5*	6					11			12	8•		7	1		10				9	14		J Carter	34
	2	3	4*	5	6					11			12			7	1		10				9	S		P Danson	35
	2	3*		5	6		8	9		11		S		4		7	1		10			12				R Dilkes	36
	2	3		5	6		8*	9		11		14		4		7•	1		10			12				K Morton	37
	2	12		5	6		8*	9		11		S		3		7	1		10			4				J Key	38
1	3	12	2		6			9		11			5*	4		7			10		S		8			A Dawson	39
1	2	3	12	5	6			9		11		S		4		7			10				8*			K Cooper	40
1	2	3*	12	5	6			9		11		S		4		7			10				8			K Breen	41
	2		4	5	6	12		9		11				3		7			10*				8	S		T Lunt	42
	2		4	5		7		9•		11	12			3			1		10		6		8*	14		J Kirkby	43
	2	3•	4		6			9*		11	12					7	1		10		5		8	14		J Brandwood	44
	2	3	4		6		8*	9		11		S				7	1		10		5		12			I Hemley	45
	2	3	4		6		8*	9•		11	14					7	1		10		5		12			M Reed	46
	2	3	4		6		8*	9	12	11						7	1				5		10•	14		B Hamer	47
20	39	27	19	36	37	21	28	33	4	37	5		14	28	2	39	20	3	33		5	2	10			League Appearances	
	1	13	4		2	1	2	7	2	10	1		4	1					2	2		1	5	3	1	Substitute Appearances	
1	1	1+1	2		2	2	2	1+1	2	1+1			2	1+1	1		1		1							R/lows Appearances	
1	1	1		2	0+1	1	1	0+1	1	1			1			1			1							FA Cup Appearances	
2	1	1	0+1	1+1	2	2	2	2	1	2			1			2			2							Autoglass Appearances	

Players on Loan: Hoult (Leicester City), Costello (Peterborough Utd) | † = Sent Off

LINCOLN CITY

Club Colours: Red and white striped shirts, black shorts, red stockings
Change Colours: All royal blue
Youth League: (Juniors) Midland Purity Youth League;   (U-16s & U-15s) Yorkshire Conference

Previous Managers: (Secretary Managers): Jimmy West 1897-1900   David Calderhead Snr. 1900-07   Jack Strawson 1907-19   George Fraser 1919-21   David Calderhead Jnr. 1921-24   Horace Henshall 1924-27   Harry Parkes 1927-36   Joe McClelland 1936-47   (Managers): Bill Anderson 1947-64   Con Moulson (coach) 1965   Roy Chapman (player/coach) 1965-66   Ron Gray 1966-70   Bert Loxley 1970-71   David Herd 1971-72   Graham Taylor 1972-77   George Kerr 1977   Willie Bell 1977-78   Colin Murphy 1978-85   John Pickering 1985   George Kerr 1985-87   Peter Daniel (caretaker) 1987   Colin Murphy 1987-90   Alan Clarke 1990
note: Bill Anderson was relieved of his duties in September 1964 but a replacement manager was not appointed until October 1966. In the intervening period the club employed a coach to take charge of team affairs
Honours: Champions Div 3N 1931-32, 1947-48, 1951-52   Champions Div 4, 1975-76   GMVC 1987-88
League Career: Original Members of Div 2 1892   Not re-elected to Div 2 1908   Re-elected to Div 2 1909   Not re-elected 1911   Re-elected to Div 2 1912   Not re-elected 1920   Elected to Div 3N 1921
Promoted to Div 2 1931-32   Relegated to Div 3N 1933-34   Promoted to Div 2 1947-48   Relegated to Div 3N 1948-49
Promoted to Div 2 1951-52   Relegated to Div 3 1960-61   Relegated to Div 4 1961-62   Promoted to Div 3 1975-76
Relegated to Div 4 1978-79   Promoted to Div 3 1980-81   Relegated to Div 4 1985-86   Relegated to Vauxhall Conference 1986-87
Promoted to Div 4 1987-88

CLUB RECORDS

Most Appearances for Club: Tony Emery (1945-59): League 402, FA Cup 22 **Total 424**
Most Capped Player: David Pugh 3, Wales   George Moulson 3, Eire
Record Goalscorer in a Match: Andy Graver 6 v Crewe Alexandra (h), 11-1, Div 3N, 29.9.1951   Frank Keetley 6 v Halifax Town (h), 9-1 Div 3N, 16.1.1932
Record League Goalscorer in a Season: Allan Hall 42, Div 3N, 1931-32
Record League Goalscorer in a Career: Andy Graver 144, 1950-54, 1955, 1958-61
Record Transfer Fee Received: £250,000 from Blackburn Rovers for Matt Dickins, March 1992 (+£150,000 after a set number of games)
Record Transfer Fee Paid: £60,000 to Southampton for Gordon Hobson, Sept 1988;   £60,000 to Sheffield Utd for Alan Roberts, Oct 1989;   £60,000 to Leicester City for Grant Brown, Jan 1990
Best Performances: League: 5th Div 2, 1901-02   **FA Cup:** Equivalent 5th Round 1886-87, 1889-90, 1901-02   **League Cup:** 4th Round 1967-68
Most League Points: (3pts for win) 77, Div 3, 1981-82   (2pts for win) 74, Div 4, 1975-76
Most League Goals: 121, Div 3N, 1951-52
Record League Victory and Most Goals Scored in a League Match: 11-1 v Crewe Alexandra, Div 3N, 29.9.1951
Most Goals Scored in a Cup Tie: 13-0 v Peterborough (a), FA Cup 1st Qualifying Round, 12.10.1895
(First Class): 8-1 v Bromley, FA Cup Round 2, 10.12.1938
Record League Defeat: 3-11 v Manchester City, Div 2, 23.3.1895   0-8 v Notts County, Div 2, 23.1.1897   0-8 v Preston North End, Div 2, 28.12.1901   1-9 v Wigan Borough, Div 3N, 3.3.1923   0-8 v Stoke City, Div 2, 23.2.1957
Record Cup Defeat: 0-5 v Grimsby Town, FA Cup 4th Qual Rnd, 10.12.1892   0-5 v Stoke City, FA Cup 1st rnd. 11.01.1907   0-5 v Leicester City, League Cup 3rd Rnd., 05.10.1966   2-7 v Doncaster Rov., Div 3 North Cup Rnd 1, 28.10.1937
Oldest Player in a League Match: (since 1945) Mark Wallington, 38 years 201 days v Blackpool (h) 6.4.1991
Youngest Player in a League Match: (since 1945) League: Shane Nicholson, 16 years, 172 days v Burnley 22.11.1986
Cup: Shane Nicholson, 16 years 112 days, Lge Cup v Charlton, 23.9.1986

LONGEST LEAGUE RUNS

of undefeated matches: 18 (1980)	**of league matches without a win:** 19 (1978)
of undefeated home matches: 35 (1975-76)	**of undefeated away matches:** 12 (1980)
without home win: 11 (1978-79)	**without an away win:** 35 (1896-98)
of league wins: 10 (1930)	**of home wins:** 14 (1982)
of league defeats: 12 (1896-97)	**of away wins:** 5 (1968, 1975, 1989)

 **BARCLAYS**

LOCAL BRANCH
PO Box No. 41
316/318 High Street
Lincoln LN5 7DP
Tel: 0522 532311
BARCLAYBANK MACHINE

BARCLAYS BUSINESS CENTRE
City Office Park
Tritton Road
Lincoln LN6 7AR
Tel: 0522 532311
BARCLAYBANK MACHINE

LINCOLN CITY

PLAYERS NAME Honours	Ht	Wt	Birthdate	Birthplace Transfers	Contract Date	Clubs	APPEARANCES				GOALS			
							League	L/Cup	FA Cup	Other	Lg	L/C	FAC	Oth
GOALKEEPERS														
Ian Bowling	6.4	14.0	27.07.65	Sheffield		Gainsborough T								
						Lincoln City	44			2				
				Loan	17.07.89	Hartlepool Utd	1							
DEFENDERS														
Grant Brown	6.0	11.12	19.11.69	Sunderland	01.07.88	Leicester City	14	2						
				Loan	20.08.89	Lincoln City								
				£60,000	04.01.90	Lincoln City	103	4	2	5	4			
Sean Dunphy	6.3	13.5	05.11.70	Rotherham	19.06.89	Barnsley (T)	5+1							
				£30,000	12.07.90	Lincoln City								
				Free	30.11.91	Goole Town								
					30.12.91	Lincoln City	5				1			
Gary West	6.1	12.2	25.08.64	Scunthorpe	26.08.82	Sheffield Utd. (A)	75	3	7	2	1			
E:Y				£35,000	16.08.85	Lincoln City	83	5	2	4	4			
				£50,000	15.07.87	Gillingham	51+1	5+1	3	2	3			
				£70,000	13.02.89	Port Vale	14+3			2+1	1			
				Loan	01.11.90	Gillingham	1			1				
				Loan	31.01.91	Lincoln City	3							
				£25,000	16.08.91	Lincoln City	17+4	2	1	2	1			1
MIDFIELD														
Graham Bressington	6.0		08.07.66	Eton		Wycombe Wands								
Isthmian LgP'87				£10,000		Lincoln City	111+2	6	4	5	3			
Kevin Finney	6.0	12.0	19.10.69	Newcastle-U-Lyme	29.06.87	Port Vale (A)	20+17	2+2	3+1	3+1	1		1	
				Free	17.08.91	Lincoln City	20+2	2	1	2	2			
John Schofield	5.11	11.03	16.05.65	Barnsley		Gainsborough T								
					10.11.88	Lincoln City	137+2	3	1+2	7	8	2		
Paul Ward	5.11	12.5	15.09.63	Sedgefield	07.08.81	Chelsea (A)								
					08.09.82	Middlesbrough	69+7	5	3+1		1			
					13.09.85	Darlington	124	6	4	9	9		1	1
				£10,000	06.07.88	Leyton Orient	30+1	5	3	3+3	1		1	1
				£45,000	20.10.89	Scunthorpe Utd	24+1		3	1	4			
						Lincoln City	37+1	2	1	2		1		
FORWARDS														
Keith Alexander	6.4	12.7	14.11.58	Nottingham		Kettering Town			2				1	
						Barnet			1					
				£11,500	11.07.88	Grimsby Town	64+19	4+2	8	4+1	26	1	1	1
				£8,500	10.09.90	Stockport Co	9+2		1	0+1				
				£7,000	12.12.90	Lincoln City	47+14	1	1	1	7			
Matthew Carmichael	6.2	11.07	13.05.64	Singapore		Basingstok								
					08.08.89	Lincoln City	72+20	5+1	2+1	5+1	14			1
Tony Lormor	6.0	11.5	24.10.70	Wallsend	25.02.88	Newcastle Utd. (A)	6+2				3			
				Loan	14.11.88	Norwich City								
				£25,000	29.01.90	Lincoln City	85+5	1	2	4	29		1	
David Puttnam	5.10	11.9	03.02.67	Leicester		Leicester Utd								
				£8,000	09.02.89	Leicester City	4+3	0+1						
				£35,000	21.03.90	Lincoln City	98+7	4	2	3+1	13			
ADDITIONAL CONTRACT PLAYERS														
Jason Kabia					08.01.92	Lincoln City	10+5			3				
(F) Jason Lee	6.3	15.10	09.05.71	London	02.06.89	Charlton Ath	0+1			0+2				
				Loan		Fisher Athletic								
				Loan	06.02.91	Stockport Co	2							
				£35,000	01.03.91	Lincoln City	50+2	2	0+1	2	9		1	
Dean West		11.7	05.12.72	Wakefield	17.08.91	Lincoln City (T)	20+13	2	1	0+1	4			

LEADING LEAGUE GOALSCORERS SEASONS 1985-86 – 1991-92

1985-86	NEIL REDFEARN	8	1986-87	GARY LUND	13
1987-88	PHIL BROWN	16	1988-89	GORDON HOBSON	15
1989-90	GORDON HOBSON	8	1990-91	TONY LORMOR	12
			1991-92	TONY LORMOR	9

SINCIL BANK Lincoln LN5 8LD

Capacity: 12,548   **Covered Standing:** 1,882   **Seating:** 3,301

Tel: Ground: 0522 510263   **Ticket Sales:** As ground number   **Clubcall:** 0898 12 18 89

All premium rate calls (0898/0891) cost 36p per minute cheap rate and 48p per minute at all other times. Call costings correct at time of going to press.

ATTENDANCES
Highest: 23,196 v Derby County, League Cup 4th Round, 15.11.1967

Lowest: 1,003 v Scunthorpe, Freight Rover Trophy, 25.11.1986

Record Receipts: £34,843.30 v Tottenham Hotspur, Milk Cup, 26.10.1983

Season Tickets:
Stands: from £69.30 to £135.00
Ground: from £80.20, juv/OAP £53.50

Executive Season Tickets: £310.00

Cost of Stand Tickets: Stand: adults £5, £6.80, juveniles/OAP £5, £3.50; Family Tickets from £6.50-£13.50
Terraces: £4.50, £3, juveniles/OAP
Prices will go up 50p per match if Lincoln are in the top three.

Match and Ticket Information: Contact Club

Car Parking: Club Car Park plus street parking available

Nearest Railway Station: Lincoln Central (0522 39502)

How to get to the ground

From North, East and West: Use A15, A57, A46 or A158 into Lincoln city centre then follow Newark (A46) in High Street. Under railway bridge then take next turning left into Queen Street for Lincoln City FC

From South: Use A1 then A46 (S.P. Lincoln) then following signs city centre into High Street and on nearside or railway bridge turn right into Queen Street for Lincoln City FC

Value Rating: ★ ★ ★

Programme Editor: G. R. Davey

Price of 1992-93 Programme: £1
Number of Pages: 32
Subscriptions: £30 for home; £30 for aways

Local Newspapers: Lincolnshire Echo, Adscene

Local Radio Stations: BBC Radio Lincolnshire

LIVERPOOL | Premier

Formed: 1892   **Turned Professional:** 1892   **Ltd Co:** 1892

SPONSORED BY: Carlsberg   **NICKNAME:** The Reds, The Pool

TWENTY-EIGHT players used; sixth-place in the League; sixth-lowest scorers in the First Division; Rumbelows Cup defeat at the hands of lowly Peterborough; an ever-changing team; two-legged defeat in the UEFA Cup; the manager reprimanded for his behaviour; and an inordinate number of injuries – an unusual season for Liverpool FC, which even the winning of the F.A. Cup could not completely overshadow.

Manager Souness was aware when he arrived that there was much work to be done and there is still a mountain to climb in order to put Liverpool at the top of English and European football. The defence had its problems, particularly with the absence of Mark Wright; the midfield lacked urgency and determination; whilst the attack scored the lowest total of goals for twenty years. Much has changed at Anfield since the retirement of Joe Fagan, and Souness would be wise to concentrate on restoring the basic Anfield philosophies. He should consider, too, that as manager he is the foremost representative of the club, but not greater than the club. His maverick personality enables him to be a winner, but supporters expect it to be harnessed to the good name of the club.

There were occasions when the team showed flashes of their old brilliance, but the swagger and the arrogance will take some time to restore. Teams are no longer afraid to travel to Anfield, but that might change next season. Young players were blooded and performed extremely well under the circumstances – time will tell whether they deserve the epithet of greatness.

The stadium, too, is undergoing change. It is indeed a period of great change as Liverpool FC move towards the next century, but change can only be successful if set against firm foundations. As Liverpool FC enter their centenary season, they would do well to consider the basic tenets instigated by Shankly and upheld by Paisley. As a protegé of the most successful manager in English football, Souness learned a lot. He would be wise to put those lessons into practice. Liverpool FC would undoubtedly be the more fulfilled because of it . . .

Brian Pead

Club Statistician for the Directory
Brian Pead

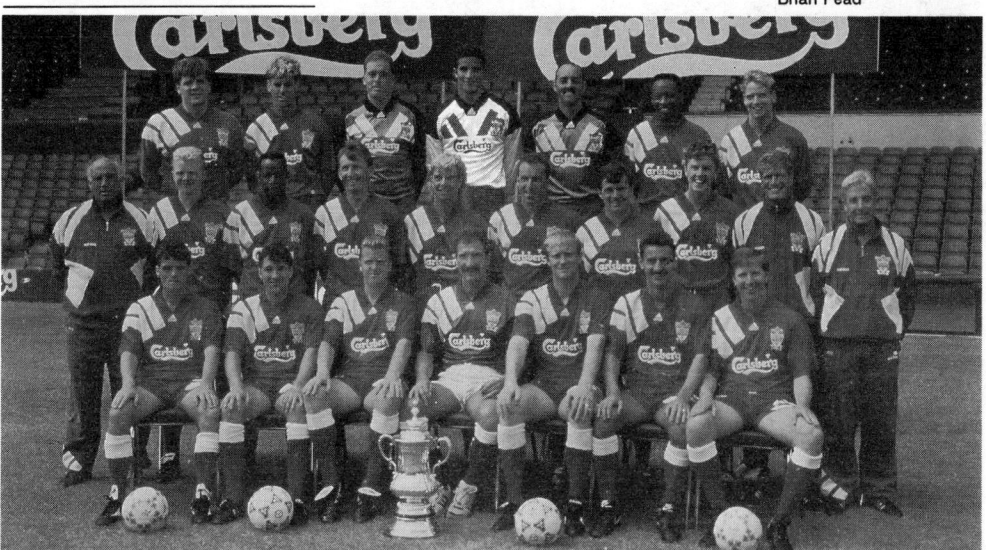

Back row: Jan Molby, Nicky Tanner, Mike Hooper, David James, Bruce Grobbelaar, Mark Walters, Rob Jones. **Middle:** Ronnie Moran, David Burrows, Michael Thomas, Istvan Kozma, Barry Venison (now Newcastle Utd), Ronny Rosenthal, Ray Houghton, Steve McManaman, Phil Boersma, Roy Evans. **Front row:** Mike Marsh, Dean Saunders, Steve Nicol, Graeme Souness (Manager), Mark Wright (Capt.), Ian Rush, Ronnie Whelan.

LIVERPOOL

DIVISION ONE: 6th   **FA CUP:** WINNERS   **RUMBELOWS CUP:** 4th RND   **UEFA CUP:** Q/FINALS

M	DATE		COMP.	VEN	OPPONENTS	RESULT		H/T	LGE POS	GOALSCORERS/GOAL TIMES	ATTEN-DANCE
1	A	17	BL	H	Oldham Athletic	W	2-1	0-1		Houghton 52, Barnes 77	38,841
2		21	BL	A	Manchester City	L	1-2	0-1		McManaman 75	(37,332)
3		24	BL	A	Luton Town	D	0-0	0-0	11		(11,132)
4		27	BL	H	Queens Park R.	W	1-0	0-0	3	Saunders 62	32,700
5		31	BL	H	Everton	W	3-1	2-0	2	Burrows 48 secs, Saunders 15, Houghton 62	39,072
6	S	7	BL	A	Notts County	W	2-1	0-1	2	Rosenthal 70, Walters (pen) 88	(16,051)
7		14	BL	H	Aston Villa	D	1-1	1-1	3	Walters (pen) 39	38,400
8		21	BL	A	Leeds United	L	0-1	0-1	9		(32,917)
9		28	BL	H	Sheffield Wed.	D	1-1	1-0	9	Houghton 17	37,071
10	O	6	BL	A	Manchester United	D	0-0	0-0			(44,997)
11		19	BL	A	Chelsea	D	2-2	1-1	10	McManaman 4, Rush 60	(30,230)
12		26	BL	H	Coventry City	W	1-0	1-0	8	Houghton 34	33,339
13	N	2	BL	H	Crystal Palace	L	1-2	1-0	9	Hysen 43	34,231
14		17	BL	A	West Ham United	D	0-0	0-0	11		(23,569)
15		23	BL	A	Wimbledon	D	0-0	0-0	11		(13,373)
16		30	BL	H	Norwich City	W	2-1	2-1	9	Molby 3, Houghton 30	34,881
17	D	7	BL	A	Southampton	D	1-1	0-0	10	Redknapp 75	(19,503)
18		14	BL	H	Nottingham Forest	W	2-0	1-0	8	McMahon 16, Molby 80	35,285
19		18	BL	A	Tottenham Hotspur	W	2-1	1-1	4	Saunders 29, Houghton 80	(27,434)
20		21	BL	H	Manchester City	D	2-2	1-0	4	Saunders 9, Nicol 82	36,743
21		26	BL	A	Queens Park R.	D	0-0	0-0	5		(21,693)
22		28	BL	A	Everton	D	1-1	1-0	6	Tanner 41	(37,681)
23	J	1	BL	H	Sheffield United	W	2-1	0-1	5	Houghton 52, Saunders 79	35,993
24		11	BL	H	Luton Town	W	2-1	0-1	3	McManaman 85, Saunders 90	35,095
25		18	BL	A	Oldham Athletic	W	3-2	2-1	3	McManaman 17, Saunders 42, Thomas 73	(18,952)
26		29	BL	H	Arsenal	W	2-0	1-0	3	Molby (pen) 45, Houghton 69	37,353
27	F	1	BL	H	Chelsea	L	1-2	1-1	3	Rosenthal 31	38,681
28		8	BL	A	Coventry City	D	0-0	0-0	3		(21,540)
29		22	BL	A	Norwich City	L	0-3	0-0	5		(20,411)
30		29	BL	H	Southampton	D	0-0	0-0	5		34,449
31	M	11	BL	H	West Ham United	W	1-0	1-0	5	Saunders 3	30,821
32		14	BL	A	Crystal Palace	L	0-1	0-1	5		(23,680)
33		21	BL	H	Tottenham Hotspur	W	2-1	0-0	4	Saunders 48, 81	36,968
34		28	BL	A	Sheffield United	L	0-2	0-1	4		(26,943)
35		31	BL	H	Notts County	W	4-0	2-0	4	Thomas 13, McManaman 34, Rush 58, Venison 76	25,457
36	A	8	BL	H	Wimbledon	L	2-3	2-1	5	Thomas 6, Rosenthal 44	26,134
37		11	BL	A	Aston Villa	L	0-1	0-0	5		(37,755)
38		18	BL	H	Leeds United	D	0-0	0-0	6		37,186
39		20	BL	A	Arsenal	L	0-4	0-3	6		(38,517)
40		22	BL	A	Nottingham Forest	D	1-1	1-1	6	Rush 44	(23,787)
41		26	BL	H	Manchester United	W	2-0	1-0	6	Rush 12, Walters 87	38,669
42	M	2	BL	A	Sheffield Wed.	D	0-0	0-0	6		(34,861)

Best Home League Attendance: 39,072 v Everton   **Smallest:** 25,457 v Notts County   **Av Home Att:** 35,113

Goal Scorers: **Compared with 90-91:** -908

League (47):   Saunders 10, Houghton 8, McManaman 5, Rush 4, Thomas 3, Walters 3 (2 pens), Molby 3 (1 pen), Rosenthal 3, Redknapp, Venison Burrows, McMahon, Tanner, Hysen, Barnes, Nicol

(Liverpool Cup games shown on page 668)

Grobbelaar B.	Ablett G.	Burrows D.	Nicol S.	Whelan R.	Wright M.	Saunders D.	Houghton R.	McManaman S.	Barnes J.	McMahon S.	Walters M.	Marsh M.	Tanner N.	Rosenthal R.	Harkness S.	Rush I.	Hooper M.	Jones R.	Redknapp J.	Hysen G.	Molby J.	Venison B.	Thomas M.	Kozma I.	Hutchison D.	Referee	
1	2	3	4	5	6	7	8	9	10	11*	12	S														K Hackett	1
1	2	3	4	5	6•	7	8	9	10*	11	12	14														P Vanes	2
1	2	3	4	5•		7	8	9		11†	10*	14	6	12												J Moules	3
1		3	4			7	8	9		11	10*	5	2	12	6										S	S Lodge	4
1	2	3	4	5•		7	8	9		11	10*	14	6	12												R Lewis	5
1	2	3	4			7	8	9		10		5	6	12	11*										S	A Buksh	6
1	2	3	4			7•	8	9		10		5	6	11*	14	12										M Peck	7
1	2	3	4			7	8	11		10*		5	6•	12	14	9										G Courtney	8
1	14	3	4			7	8	10		11	12	5*	6•		2	9										P Danson	9
	2†	3	4			7•	8	14	11	10	12		6			9	1				5*					M Reed	10
1	S	3	4			7	8	11	10			5			6	9		2								K Redfearn	11
1		3				7*	8	11	10		12			14	6	9		2	4	5•						R Milford	12
1	10	3				7	8	11		S	12				6	9		2	4	5*						T Holbrook	13
1	S	3	4			7	8	S	10	11		5			6	9		2								G Ashby	14
1	10	3	4			7	8	11			12	5			6	9*		2	S							R Pawley	15
1	2	3	4	5		7	8	9		11*	12				6			S			10					B Hill	16
1		3	4	5		7	8	9		11					6			2•	12	14	10*					R Lewis	17
1	S	3	4	5		7	8	9		11				S	6			2			10					K Hackett	18
1		3	4	5		7	8	9		11•				14	6			2			10*		12			J Martin	19
1		3	4	5		7	8	9•		11*	12			14	6			2			10					D Phillips	20
1		3*	4	5		7	8	9							6			2	S		10	12	11			I Borrett	21
1		3	4	5*		7	8	12		9					6			2	S		10		11			V Callow	22
1		3	4	5		7	8	12		9*					6			2	S		10		11			P Wright	23
1			4	5		7	8	9		10	S		6	14				2				3•	11			W Burns	24
1			4	5		7	8	9		10*	12		6					2	S			3	11			K Redfern	25
1			4	5		7	8	S		9	12		6					2			10	3	11*			M Reed	26
1		3		5*		7	8	11		9•				14	6			2	4		10			12		M Peck	27
1		3		5		7	8	11		9*	12			14	6•			2	4		10					R Hart	28
1				5		7•	8	11			12			14	6*	9		2	4		10	3				M Bailey	29
1		3	4	5		7		11*			12				6	9		2•			10		8	14		S Lodge	30
1			4		6	7	8*	11		10•	12			14		9		2	5			3				J Rushton	31
1			4	5		7*		11	10		12			14	6•	9		2				3	8			G Courtney	32
1		3	4	12		7			10	8•				14	6	9		2			5*		11			R Milford	33
1		3	4	5		7	8	S						14	6	9		2			10		11•			A Wilkie	34
1		3		5		7*	8	9•							6			2	4		10		11	12	14	D Phillips	35
1				5		7	8	9			12				6*			2	4		10	3	11		S	J Key	36
1			4	5		7	8	9•			12				6			2*			10	3	11	14		R Pawley	37
1		3	4			7	8		10		12			S		9		2		6	5		11*			K Redfern	38
			4			7•	8	11	10		12					9	1	2•		6	5	3		14		K Hackett	39
			4			7	8	11	10							9	1	2		6	5	3	S		S	A Flood	40
		3			6	7	8	9•	10					14		9	1	2	4*		5		11	12		R Gifford	41
		3	4	5•	6	7	8	9	10*		12						1	2					11	14		J Martin	42
37	13	30	34	9	21	36	36	26	12	15	18	19	32	7	7	16	5	28	5	3	25	9	16	3		League Appearances	
	1			1	1			4			7	15		13	4	2		1	2	1	4	1	2	3		Substitute Appearances	

LIVERPOOL

Club Colours: All red with white trim
Change Colours: Green shirts with white trim, white shorts with green trim, green socks with white tops
Reserves League: Pontins Central League Division 1

COMPETITIONS

Div. 1	Div. 2	Euro C	ECWC	UEFA	Sup. C	WCC
94-95	93-94	64-65	65-66	67-68	1977	1981
96-04	95-96	66-67	71-72	68-69	1978	1984
05-54	04-05	73-74	74-75	69-70		
62-	54-62	76-77	92-93	70-71		Sc Sp
		77-78		72-73		Sup C
		78-79		75-76		1986
		79-80		91-92		
		80-81				
		81-82				
		82-83				
		83-84				
		84-85				

HONOURS

Div. 1	Div. 2	FAC	Lge C	Euro C	UEFA	C/Sh'd
1900-01	93-94	64-65	80-81	76-77	72-73	1964
05-06	95-96	73-74	81-82	77-78	75-76	1965
21-22	04-05	85-86	82-83	80-81		1966
22-23	61-62	88-89	83-84	83-84		1974
46-47	91-92	91-92			ESC	1976
63-64					1977	1977
65-66						1979
72-73			Sc Sp			1980
75-76			Sup C			1982
76-77			1986			1986
78-79						1988
79-80						1989
81-82						
83-84						
85-86						
87-88						
89-90						

MOST GOALS IN A CAREER
ROGER HUNT 285 (1959-70)

Season	League	FA Cup	Lge Cup	Europe
1959-60	21	2		
1960-61	15	1	3	
1961-62	41	1		
1962-63	24	2		
1963-64	31	2		
1964-65	25	5		7
1965-66	30	1		2
1966-67	14	1		3
1967-68	25	2		3
1968-69	13	1	2	1
1969-70	6			1
Total	**245**	**18**	**5**	**17**
Previous holder: Billy Liddell, 216 (1939-60)				

RECORD TRANSFER FEE RECEIVED

Amount	Club	Player	Date
£3,200,000	Juventus	Ian Rush	6/87
£650,000	Sampdoria	Graham Souness	6/84
£500,000	S V Hamburg	Kevin Keegan	6/77
£240,000	Coventry City	Larry Lloyd	8/74

RECORD TRANSFER FEE PAID

Amount	Club	Player	Date
£2,900,000	Derby Co.	Dean Saunders	7/91
£2,800,000	Juventus	Ian Rush	8/88
£1,900,000	Newcastle Utd	Peter Beardsley	7/87
£900,000	Brighton & H A	Mark Lawrenson	8/81

LONGEST RUNS

of undefeated matches:	31 (4.5.1987-16.3.1988)
of undefeated home matches:	63 (25.2.1978-31.1.1981)
without home win:	10 (13.10.1951-22.3.1952)
of league wins:	12 (21.4.1990-6.10.1990)
of league defeats:	9 (29.4.1899-14.10.1899)
of league matches without a win:	14 (5.12.1953-3.4.1954)
of undefeated away matches:	16 (2.9.1893-3.9.1894)
without an away win:	24 (21.2.1953-7.4.1954)
of home wins:	21 (29.1.1972-30.12.1972)
of away wins:	6 (24.9.1904-19.11.1904)
	(31.12.1904-11.3.1905) (27.2.1982-24.4.1982)

MOST APPEARANCES: IAN CALLAGHAN 839+7 (59-78)

Year	League	FA Cup	Lge Cup	Europe
1959-60	4			
1960-61	3		2	
1961-62	24	5		
1962-63	37	6		
1963-64	42	5		
1964-65	37	8		9
1965-66	42	1		9
1966-67	40	4		5
1967-68	41	9	2	6
1968-69	42	4	3	2
1969-70	41	6	2	3+1
1970-71	21+1	4	1	5
1971-72	41	3	3	4
1972-73	42	4	8	12
1973-74	42	9	6	4
1974-75	41	2	3	4
1975-76	40	2	3	12
1976-77	32+1	4+1	2	7
1977-78	25+1	1	7	5
	637+3	**77+1**	**42**	**87+1**
Previous holder: Billy Liddell 492 (1946-61)				

MANAGERS

Name	Seasons	Best	Worst
John McKenna	1892-96	16(1)	1(2)
Tom Watson	1896-15	1(1)	1(2)
Dave Ashworth	1920-23	1(1)	4(1)
Matt McQueen	1923-28	4(1)	16(1)
George Patterson	1928-36	7(1)	18(1)
George Kay	1936-51	1(1)	19(1)
Don Welsh	1951-56	9(1)	11(1)
Phil Taylor	1956-59	3(2)	4(2)
Bill Shankly	1959-74	1(1)	3(2)
Bob Paisley	1974-83	1(1)	5(1)
Joe Fagan	1983-85	1(1)	2(1)
Kenny Dalglish	1985-91	1(1)	2(1)
Graeme Souness	1991-	6(1)	6(1)

LOCAL BRANCH
Liverpool: Breck Road Branch
304 Breck Road, Liverpool L5 6QD
Tel: 051-260 6070
BARCLAYBANK MACHINE

BARCLAYS BUSINESS CENTRE
City Office, PO Box No.107, 4 Water Street
Liverpool L69 2DU Tel: 051-236 5428
BARCLAYBANK MACHINE

PREVIOUS LEAGUE
Lancashire League

BIGGEST VICTORIES
League: 10-1 v Rotherham United, Division 2, 18.2.1896
9-0 v Crystal Palace, Division 1, 12.9.1989
F.A. Cup: 8-0 v Swansea City, Round 3 Replay, 9.1.1990
League Cup: 10-0 v Fulham, Round 2 1st leg, 23.9.1986
Europe: 11-0 v Stromsgodset Gwc, ECWC, 17.9.1974

BIGGEST DEFEATS
League: 1-9 v Birmingham City, Division 2, 11.12.1954
0-8 v Huddersfield Town, Division 1, 10.11.1934
F.A. Cup: 0-5 v Bolton Wndrs, Round 4, 1945-46
League Cup: 1-4 v West Ham, Round 4, 30.11.1988
Europe (UEFA): 1-5 v Ajax, Round 2, 7.12.1966

MOST POINTS
3 points a win: 90, Division 1, 1987-88 (equalled record)
2 points a win: 68, Division 1 1978-79 (Division 1 record)

MOST GOALS
106, 1895-6.
Allan 25, Ross 23, Becton 17, Bradshaw 12, Geary 11,
McVean 7, McQue 5, Hannah 3, Wilkie 1, Bull 1, McCartney 1

MOST GOALS IN A MATCH
5. Andy McGuigan v Stoke City, Division 1, 4.1.1902 (7-0 h)
5. John Evans v Bristol Rovers, Division 2, 15.9.1954 (5-3 h)
5. Ian Rush v Luton Town, Division 1, 29.10.1983 (6-0 h)

MOST GOALS IN A SEASON
Ian Rush 47 (Lge 32, FAC 2, Lge Cup 8, Euro Cup 5) 1983-84
5 goals once = 5; 4 goals once = 4; 3 goals twice = 6; 2 goals 5
times = 10; 1 goal 22 times = 22.
Previous holder: Roger Hunt 41, 1961-62.

MOST FIRST CLASS MATCHES IN A SEASON
67 (42 League, 2 FA Cup, 13 League Cup, 1 Charity Shield, 9
European Cup) 1983-84

MOST LEAGUE GOALS CONCEDED
97, Division 1, 1953-54

MOST LEAGUE WINS
30, Division 1, 1978-79

MOST LEAGUE DRAWS
19, Division 1, 1951-52

MOST LEAGUE DEFEATS
23, Division 1, 1953-54

OLDEST PLAYER
Kenny Dalglish, 39 years 58 days v Derby County, 1.5.1990

MOST CAPPED PLAYER
Emlyn Hughes (England) 59

BEST PERFORMANCES BY LIVERPOOL

League: 1978-79: Matches played 42, Won 30, Drawn 8, Lost 4, Goals for 85, Goals against 16, Points 68. First in Division 1.
Highest: Division 1 Champions 18 times.
F.A. Cup: 1964-65: 3rd rnd. West Bromwich Albion 2-1; 4th rnd. Stockport County 1-1, 2-0; 5th rnd. Bolton Wanderers 1-0; 6th rnd. Leicester City 0-0, 1-0; Semi-Final Chelsea 2-0; Final Leeds United 2-1.
1973-74: 3rd rnd. Doncaster Rovers 2-2, 2-0; 4th rnd. Carlisle United 0-0, 2-0; 5th rnd. Ipswich Town 2-0; 6th rnd. Bristol City 2-0; Semi-Final Leicester City 0-0, 3-1; Final Newcastle 3-0.
1985-86: 3rd rnd. Norwich City 5-0; 4th rnd. Chelsea 2-1; 5th rnd. York City 1-1, 3-1; 6th rnd. Watford 0-0, 2-1; Semi-Final Southampton 2-0; Final Everton 3-1.
1988-89: 3rd rnd. Carlisle Utd 3-0; 4th rnd. Millwall 2-0; 5th rnd. Hull 3-2; 6th rnd. Brentford 4-0; Semi-Final Nottingham Forest 3-1; Final Everton 3-2 aet.
1991-92: 3rd rnd. Crewe Alex. 4-0; 4th rnd. Bristol Rovers 1-1, 2-1; 5th rnd. Ipswich Town 0-0, 3-2; 6th rnd. Aston Villa 1-0; Semi-Final Portsmouth 1-1, 0-0 (won 3-1 on pens); Final Sunderland 2-0
League Cup: 1980-81: 2nd rnd. Bradford City 0-1, 4-0; 3rd rnd. Swindon 5-0; 4th rnd. Portsmouth 4-1; 5th rnd. Birmingham City 3-1; Semi-Final Manchester City 1-0, 1-1; Final West Ham United 1-1, 2-1.
1981-82: 2nd rnd. Exeter City 5-0, 6-0; 3rd rnd. Middlesbrough 4-1; 4th rnd. Arsenal 0-0, 3-0; 5th rnd. Barnsley 0-0, 3-1; Semi-Final Ipswich 2-0, 2-2; Final Tottenham Hotspur 3-1 (aet).
1982-83: 2nd rnd. Ipswich Town 2-1, 2-0; 3rd rnd Rotherham United 1-0; 4th rnd. Norwich City 2-0; 5th rnd. West Ham United 2-1; Semi-Final Burnley 3-0, 0-1; Final Manchester United 2-1.
1983-84: 2nd rnd. Brentford 4-1, 4-0; 3rd rnd. Fulham 1-1, 1-1, 1-0; 4th rnd Birmingham City 1-1, 3-0; 5th rnd. Sheffield Wednesday 2-2, 3-0; Semi-Final Walsall 2-2, 2-0; Final Everton 0-0, 1-0.
European Cup: 1976-77: Prelim rnd. Crusaders 2-0, 5-0; 1st rnd. Trabzonspor 0-1, 3-0; 2nd rnd. St. Etienne 0-1, 3-1; Semi-Final Zurich 3-1, 3-0; Final B Munchengladbach 3-1.
1977-78: 1st rnd. Dyn. Dresden 5-1, 1-2; 2nd rnd. Benfica 2-1, 4-1; Semi-Final B Munchen'bach 1-2, 3-0; Final FC Bruges 1-0.
1980-81: 1st rnd. Ops Oula 1-1, 10-1; 2nd rnd. Aberdeen 1-0, 4-0; 3rd rnd. CSK Sofia 5-1, 1-0; 4th rnd. Bayern M 0-0, 1-1; Final Real Madrid 1-0.
1983-84: 1st rnd. Odense 1-0, 5-0; 2nd rnd. Athletico Bilbao 0-0, 1-0; 3rd rnd. Benfica 1-0, 4-1; Semi-Final Dynamo Bucharest 1-0, 2-1; Final Roma 1-1 (Won on penalties).
UEFA Cup: 1972-73: 1st rnd. Eintracht Frankfurt 2-0, 0-0; 2nd rnd AEK Athens 3-0, 3-1; 3rd rnd. Dynamo Berlin 0-0, 3-1; 4th rnd. Dynamo Dresden 2-0, 1-0; Semi-Final Tottenham Hotspur 1-0, 1-2; Final Borrusia Munchengladbach 3-0, 0-2.
1975-76: 1st rnd. Hibernian 0-1, 3-1; 2nd rnd. Real Sociedad 3-1, 6-0; 3rd rnd. Slask Wroclaw 2-1, 3-0; 4th rnd. Dynamo Dresden 0-0, 2-1; Semi-Final Barcelona 1-0, 1-1; Final Bruges 3-2, 1-1.

DIVISIONAL RECORDS

	Played	Won	Drawn	Lost	For	Against	Points
DIVISION 1	3096	1407	769	920	5094	3956	3836
DIVISION 2	428	243	82	103	977	571	568
TOTALS	3524	1650	851	1023	6071	4527	4404

LIVERPOOL

PLAYERS NAME / Honours	Ht	Wt	Birthdate	Birthplace / Transfers	Contract Date	Clubs	League	L/Cup	FA Cup	Other	Lg	L/C	FAC	Oth
GOALKEEPERS														
Bruce Grobbelaar	6.1	12.0	06.10.57	Zimbabwe		Vancouver W'caps								
Zimbabwe;Div1'82'83'84'86'88'90;LC'82'83'84;				N.C		Crewe Alexandra	24				1			
FAC'86'89'92;CS'82'86'88;EC'						Vancouver W'caps								
					£250,000	12.03.81	Liverpool	406	63	60	53				
Mike Hooper	6.3	13.0	10.02.64	Bristol	08.11.83	Bristol City	1		1	1				
CS'86				Free	08.02.85	Wrexham	34	4						
				£40,000	25.10.85	Liverpool	42	7	3	5+1				
				Loan	21.09.90	Leicester City	14			1				
David James	6.5	15.0	01.08.70	Welwyn Garden C.	01.07.88	Watford (T)	89	6	2	1				
E: Y, u21, FAYC'89. Div 2'92				£1,000,000	01.07.92	Liverpool								
DEFENDERS														
David Burrows	5.8	11.0	25.10.68	West Bromwich	08.11.86	West Brom A. (A)	37+9	3+1	2	1	1			
E: U21.7,B.1.CS'89.Div1'90; FAC'92				£550,000	20.10.88	Liverpool	103+9	11	16+1	9	1			
Steven Harkness	5.10	10.11	27.08.71	Carlisle	23.03.89	Carlisle Utd. (T)	12+1							
E:Y.5,S				£75,000	17.07.89	Liverpool	7+4	2+1	1	3				
Rob Jones	5.11	11.0	05.11.71	Wrexham	20.12.88	Crewe Alexandra (T)	59+16	9	0+3	3	2			
E:1, Y.2; FAC'92				£300,000	04.10.91	Liverpool	28		9	2				
Steve Nicol	5.10	11.2	11.12.61	Irvine		Ayr Utd	68+2	16	3		7	1		
S:27,U21.;Div1'84'86'88'90.FAC'86'89'92,EC'84				£300,000	26.10.81	Liverpool	265+11	35	47	30+2	35	4	3	3
Nick Tanner	6.2	13.7	24.05.65	Bristol		Mangotsfield								
						Bristol Rovers	104+2	5	10	5	3			
				£20,000		Liverpool	34+2	5	2	5+1	1			
				Loan	01.03.90	Norwich City								
				Loan	28.09.90	Swindon Town	7							
Mark Wright	6.3	12.11	01.08.63	Dorchester, Oxon	26.08.80	Oxford Utd	8+2		1					
E: 42, u21.4; FAC'92				P.E	25.03.82	Southampton	170	25	17	10	7	2	1	1
				£760,000	27.08.87	Derby County	144	15	5	7	10			
				£2,200,000	15.07.91	Liverpool	21+1	1	9	4				
MIDFIELD														
Istvan Kozma						Dunfermline								
				£300,000	08.02.92	Liverpool	3+2		0+2					
Mike Marsh	5.8	10.14	21.07.69	Liverpool		Kirby Town								
					23.03.88	Liverpool	20+19	4+1	4+2	7				1
Jan Molby	6.1	13.8	04.07.63	Kolding,Jutland		Ajax (Amsterdam)								
Denmark; Div.1'86'90; FAC'86'92; CS'86				£575,000	24.08.84	Liverpool	164+19	20+3	24+4	14+2	36	8	4	4
Jamie Redknapp	5.11	11.08	25.06.73	Barton	27.06.90	Bournemouth (T)	6+7	3	3	2				
E:Y.2				£350,000		Liverpool	5+1		2	1+1	1			
Paul Stewart	5.11	11.10	07.10.64	Manchester	13.10.81	Blackpool	188+13	11	7	6	55	3	2	1
E:3, B.3, u21.1, Y.2					19.03.87	Manchester City	51	6	4	2	26	2	1	1
				£1,700,000	21.06.88	Tottenham H	126+5	23	9	9	28	7	2	
				£2,300,000	29.07.92	Liverpool								
Michael Thomas	5.10	12.4	24.08.67	Lambeth	31.12.84	Arsenal (A)	149+14	22+2	14+3	4+2	24	5	1	1
E:2;B.4,u21.12,u19.6,Y.14,S;LC'87;				Loan	01.01.87	Portsmouth	3							
Div1'89;CT'89;Eb'2;FAC'92				£1,500,000	16.12.91	Liverpool	16+1		5		3		2	
Ronnie Whelan	5.9	10.13	25.09.61	Dublin		Home Farm								
Ei:42,u21.1Div1'82'83'84'86'88'90.FAC'86'89'92;EC'84.LC'82'83'84					01.10.79	Liverpool	311+11	46+4	40+1	37+2	44	14	7	6
FORWARDS														
John Barnes	5.11	11.10	07.09.63	Jamaica		Sunbury Co								
E:67, u-21(3);FAYC'82;Div1'88'90;CS'88;FAC'89;PoY'88;FoY'88				14.07.81	Watford	232+1	21	31	7	65	7	11	
				£900,000	19.06.87	Liverpool	152	10	32	5	60	3	14	2
Donald Hutchison	6.2	11.04	09.05.71	Gateshead	20.03.90	Hartlepool Utd	19+5	1+1	2	1	3			
				£175,000	27.11.90	Liverpool	0+3							
Lee Jones	5.9	10.10	29.05.73	Wrexham	05.07.91	Wrexham (T)	24+15	2	1+2	4+1	9		1	2
				£300,000	12.03.92	Liverpool								
Steven McManaman	5.11	10.4	11.02.72	Liverpool (T)	19.02.90		26+6	5	8+1	8	5	3	3	
E: Y,S; FAC'92														
Ronny Rosenthal	5.11	12.00	11.10.63	Haifa		Maccabi Haifa								
Israel. CS'90				via FC Brugge		Standard Liege								
Loan Luton Town				N.C	22.03.90	Liverpool	5+3				7			
				£1,000,000	29.06.90	Liverpool	11+25	0+6	4+2	1+1	8			
Ian Rush	6.0	12.6	25.10.61	St.Asaph	25.09.79	Chester City (A)	33+1		5		14		3	
W:54,u21.2,S;Div1'82'83'84'86'90;				£300,000	01.05.80	Liverpool	182	38	22	31+1	109	21	20	17
LC'81'82'83'84;FAC'86'89'92;EC				£3,500,000	01.07.86	Juventus (Italy)								
				Loan	01.07.86	Liverpool	42	9	3	3	30	4		6
				£2,800,000	23.08.88	Liverpool	105+10	13	20+2	9	45	11	15	1
Dean Saunders	5.8	10.6	21.06.64	Swansea	24.06.82	Swansea City (A)	42+7	2+1	1	1+1	12			
W:34,F.LgXl,FAC'92				Loan	01.04.85	Cardiff City	3+1							
				Free	07.08.85	Brighton & H.A	66+6	4	7	3	21		5	
				£60,000	12.03.87	Oxford Utd	57+2	9+1	2	2	22	8	2	1
				£1,000,000	28.10.88	Derby County	106	12	6	7	42	10		5
				£2,900,000	19.07.91	Liverpool	36	5	8	5	10	2	2	9
Mark Walters	5.9	11.5	02.06.64	Birmingham	18.05.82	Aston Villa (A)	168+13	20+1	11+1	7+3	39	6	1	2
E:1,u21.9,Y.10,FAYC'80,ESC'82,SPD'89'90'91.				£550,000	31.12.87	Glasgow Rangers	101+5	13	14	10	32	11	6	2
SLC'89'91				£1,250,000	13.08.91	Liverpool	18+7	4	2+1	5	3	2		1

ADDITIONAL CONTRACT PLAYERS

Phil Charnock, Tony Cousins, Robert Fowler, Stuart Gelling, Marc Kenny, Dominic Matteo, Rodney McAree, Scott Pateson, John Scott, Andrew Taylor, Tom White.

LIVERPOOL

RECORD WIN & LOSS AGAINST EACH CLUB IN CURRENT DIVISION

(Where a score has occured on several occasions the most recent is given)

Club	Rec. Win	Season	Rec. Loss	Season
ARSENAL	5-0	1893-94 (away)	8-1	1934-35
ASTON VILLA	6-1	1953-54	6-1	1931-32
BLACKBURN ROVERS	4-0	1933-34	6-2	1913-14
CHELSEA	6-0	1934-35	6-1	1937-38
COVENTRY CITY	6-1	1989-90 (away)	4-0	1982-83
CRYSTAL PALACE	9-0	1989-90 (away)	2-1	1991-92 (home)
EVERTON	6-0	1935-36	5-0	1914-15 (home)
IPSWICH TOWN	6-0	1963-64	3-0	1959-60
LEEDS UNITED	5-0	1966-67	5-0	1932-33
MANCHESTER CITY	5-0	1981-82 (away)	6-0	1935-36
MANCHESTER UNITED	7-1	1895-96	6-1	1927-28
MIDDLESBROUGH	7-2	1931-32	5-0	1929-30
NORWICH CITY	6-0	1978-79	3-0	1991-92 (home)
NOTTINGHAM FOREST	6-1	1967-68	5-1	1908-09
OLDHAM ATHLETIC	5-2	1920-21	4-0	1921-22
QUEENS PARK RANGERS	4-0	1987-88	3-1	1990-91 (home)
SHEFFIELD UNITED	6-1	1963-64	6-2	1932-33
SHEFFIELD WEDNESDAY	5-1	1988-89	5-0	1894-95
SOUTHAMPTON	5-0	1982-83	4-1	1989-90
TOTTENHAM HOTSPUR	7-0	1978-79	7-2	1962-63
WIMBLEDON	3-1	1986-87 (away)	2-1	1986-87 (home)

MANAGER: GRAEME SOUNESS

DATE OF BIRTH: 6.5.1953   **PLACE OF BIRTH:** Edinburgh

DATE OF APPOINTMENT: 27.3.1991

PREVIOUS CLUBS
as Manager: Glasgow Rangers
as Player: Tottenham Hotspur, Middlesbrough, Liverpool, Sampdoria, Glasgow Rangers (player/manager)

HONOURS
as Manager: League Champions (Scotland) 4 times; Liverpool: FA Cup (1)
as Asst. Man./Coach:
as Player: Liverpool: Champions (5), League Cup (1), European Cup (3), Milk Cup (3). Rangers: Champions (2), League Cup (4). Sampdoria: Italian Cup (1)
International: 54 caps (Scotland)

Value Rating: ★ ★ ★ ★

Programme Editor: Vince Wilson

Price of 1992-93 Programme: £1.10
Number of Pages: 32

Subscriptions: £44 inc. postage UK/Ireland, £50 inc. postage overseas

Local Newspapers: Liverpool Daily Post, Liverpool Echo

Local Radio Stations: Radio Merseyside, Radio City

Additional Publications on Club: A Complete Record 1892-1990, by Brian Pead, Breedon Books £16.95. You'll Never Walk Alone, Official Illustrated History of Club (Stephen Kelly £12.95).

LEADING LEAGUE GOALSCORERS
SEASONS 1979-80 – 1991-92

1979-80	DAVID JOHNSON	21		1980-81	TERRY McDERMOTT	13
1981-82	IAN RUSH	17		1982-83	IAN RUSH	24
1983-84	IAN RUSH	32		1984-85	JOHN WARK	18
1985-86	IAN RUSH	23		1986-87	IAN RUSH	30
1987-88	JOHN ALDRIDGE	26		1988-89	JOHN ALDRIDGE	21
1989-90	JOHN BARNES	20		1990-91	IAN RUSH	16
					DEAN SAUNDERS	16
1991-92	DEAN SAUNDERS	10				

ANFIELD ROAD Anfield, Liverpool L4 OTH

Capacity: 44,631   **Covered Standing:** 16,480   **Seating:** 28,151

Tel: Ground: 051 263 2361   **Ticket Sales:** 051 260 8680   **Clubcall:** 0898 121 184

All premium rate calls (0898/0891) cost 36p per minute cheap rate and 48p per minute at all other times. Call costings correct at time of going to press.

ATTENDANCES
Highest: 61,905 v Wolverhampton W., FA Cup 4th Round, 2.2.1952

Lowest: 1,000 v Loughborough, Division 2, 7.12.1895

RECORD RECEIPTS (with previous records):
£342,000 v Genoa, UEFA Cup, 18.3.1992
£227,351 v Q.P.R., FA Cup 6th Rnd Replay, 14.3.1990
£164,000 v Panathanaikos, European Cup, 10.4.1985
£154,000 Wales v Scotland, 12.10.1977
£79,000 v F.C. Bruges (UEFA), 28.4.1972

ANFIELD
First game: v Rotherham, 1.9.1892
First floodlit game: v Everton, 30.10.1957
Internationals: England v Ireland: 1899, 1926
England v Wales: 1905, 1922, 1931
Wales v Scotland: 1977

Season Tickets:
Stands: £240, juv/OAP £215
Ground: £145 (no reductions)

Executive Box Season Tickets:

Cost of Stand Tickets: Main Stand: £12, (Premium matches) £13; Main Stand (Extreme Wing section) £8.50 (Premium) £9
Terraces: Spion Kop: £7 (Premium) £8, juv/OAP £4 (Premium) £4.50

Match and Ticket Information: All seats available 26 in advance

Car Parking: Limited street parking. Mainly privately-owned car park in Priory Road (5 minutes walk from ground)

Nearest Railway Station: Kirkdale or Lime Street (051-709 9696)

How to get to the ground

From North: Use Motorway M6 until Junction 28 then follow signs Liverpool on A58 and forward into Walton Hall Avenue past Stanley Park and turn left into Anfield Road for Liverpool FC

From East and South: Use Motorway M6 the M62 until end of motorway then turn right A5058 into Queens Drive. In 3m turn left into Utting Avenue. In 1m turn right into Anfield Road for Liverpool FC

From West: Use Mersey tunnel into Liverpool City Centre then follow signs Preston A580 into Walton Hall Avenue, then on nearside of Stanley Park turn right into Anfield Road for Liverpool FC

LUTON TOWN

Division 1

Formed: 1885   **Turned Professional:** 1890   **Ltd Co:** 1897

SPONSORED BY: **NICKNAME:** The Hatters

President
Ed Pearson

Chairman
Roger J Smith

Directors
E S Pearson
P Collins
N Terry
H Richardson
D A Kohler B.Sc(Hons)ARICS Managing

Secretary
John K Smylie

Commercial Executive
John Buttle

Manager
David Pleat

Reserve Team Coach
John Moore

Youth Team Coach
Terry Westley

Physiotherapist
Brian Owen

Groundsman
Dave Chapman

Club Statistician for the Directory
Roger Wash

MANY neutral football followers all over England have a soft spot for 'The Hatters' of Luton. The club always appear to be attempting to play a cultured style of football and in their manager David Pleat, they have a true lover of the game who talks a lot of sense when working with the media.

Sadly, modern financial trends are such that little clubs like Luton find it difficult to challenge successfully in the transfer market and it is also a great temptation to cash in by selling their young talent.

Although old favourite Mick Harford returned to top the goalscoring charts with twelve league goals, the club never managed more than two goals in any first team competitive match and indeed registered just six league goals in the first twelve Barclays matches, as they sunk into the bottom two places. Unfortunately, despite a really good battle throughout the last two months of the season when they once again gave themselves a chance of survival, Luton never climbed higher than nineteenth and after a defeat in the last match the club were relegated.

It was good to see Brian Stein back at the club and playing in his 400th league match for The Hatters but the younger players who certainly showed good form and excellent potential were not helped by the constant pressure at the foot of the table. The long suffering Kenilworth Road fans will have to accept that the club may have to sell some of their favourites.

Cup football brought no respite last season but the high standards that David Pleat demands from his players will see the club through its disappointments and I am sure they will be back at the top of the First Division fighting for a Premier place at the end of the season.

T.W.

Back row L-R: Julian James, Sean Farrell, David Baumont, Graham Rodger, Alec Chamberlain, Darron McDonough, Marvin Johnson, John Dreyer, Richard Harvey. **Front row:** Kurt Nogan, Ceri Hughes, Jason Rees, David Preece, Mark Pembridge, Kingsley Black.

LUTON TOWN

DIVISION ONE: 20th   **FA CUP:** 3rd RND   **RUMBELOWS CUP:** 2nd RND   **ZDS CUP:** 2nd RND

M	DATE	COMP.	VEN	OPPONENTS	RESULT	H/T	LGE POS	GOALSCORERS/GOAL TIMES	ATTEN-DANCE
1	A 17	BL	A	West Ham United	D 0-0	0-0			(25,079)
2	21	BL	A	Coventry City	L 0-5	0-3			(10,084)
3	24	BL	H	Liverpool	D 0-0	0-0	19		11,132
4	27	BL	A	Arsenal	L 0-2	0-1	22		(25,898)
5	31	BL	A	Chelsea	L 1-4	0-3	22	Gray 47	(17,457)
6	S 4	BL	H	Southampton	W 2-1	2-1	19	Gray 32, Harvey 40	8,055
7	7	BL	A	Wimbledon	L 0-3	0-1	20		(3,231)
8	14	BL	H	Oldham Athletic	W 2-1	0-0	17	Harford 85, 89	9,005
9	17	BL	H	Queens Park R.	L 0-1	0-0	20		9,085
10	21	BL	A	Manchester United	L 0-5	0-1	21		(46,491)
11	25	RC 2/1	H	**Birmingham City**	D 2-2	0-1		**Gray 48, Nogan 83**	6,315
12	28	BL	A	Notts County	D 1-1	0-0	20	Gray 68	7,629
13	O 5	BL	A	Aston Villa	L 0-4	0-1	21		(18,722)
14	8	RC 2/2	A	**Birmingham City**	L 2-3	0-1		**Gray 61, 63**	(13,252)
15	19	BL	H	Sheffield Wed.	D 2-2	1-1	21	Harford 28, Nogan 80	9,401
16	22	ZDS 2	A	**Ipswich Town**	D †1-1	0-0		**Telfer 79 (Lost 1-2 on pens)**	(7,750)
17	26	BL	A	Norwich City	L 0-1	0-1	21		(10,514)
18	N 2	BL	H	Everton	L 0-1	0-1	21		8,022
19	16	BL	A	Tottenham Hotspur	L 1-4	1-0	22	Harford 43	(27,543)
20	23	BL	H	Manchester City	D 2-2	1-0	22	Harford 17, Dreyer 56	10,031
21	30	BL	A	Sheffield United	D 1-1	0-0	22	Telfer 79	(21,804)
22	D 7	BL	H	Leeds United	L 0-2	0-0	22		11,550
23	20	BL	H	Coventry City	W 1-0	0-0	22	Harford 55	7,533
24	26	BL	H	Arsenal	W 1-0	0-0	22	Harford 79	12,665
25	28	BL	H	Chelsea	W 2-0	2-0	20	Harvey 38, Dreyer 41	10,738
26	J 1	BL	A	Nottingham Forest	D 1-1	1-0	19	Pembridge 1	(23,809)
27	4	FAC 3	A	**Sheffield United**	L 0-4	0-1			(12,201)
28	11	BL	A	Liverpool	L 1-2	1-0	20	Tanner (og) 31	(35,095)
29	18	BL	H	West Ham United	L 0-1	0-0	22		11,088
30	F 1	BL	A	Sheffield Wed.	L 2-3	2-1	22	Preece 21, Oakes 35	(22,291)
31	8	BL	H	Norwich City	W 2-0	0-1	21	Preece 67, Harford 88	8,554
32	15	BL	A	Manchester City	L 0-4	0-1	21		(22,137)
33	22	BL	H	Sheffield United	W 2-1	2-1	20	Stein 6, Harford 23	9,003
34	25	BL	A	Crystal Palace	D 1-1	0-1	20	Pembridge (pen) 50	(12,109)
35	29	BL	A	Leeds United	L 0-2	0-0	20		(28,231)
36	M 7	BL	H	Crystal Palace	D 1-1	0-1	19	Oakes 68	8,591
37	11	BL	H	Tottenham Hotspur	D 0-0	0-0	19		11,494
38	14	BL	H	Everton	D 1-1	1-0	19	Stein 7	(16,707)
39	21	BL	A	Southampton	L 1-2	1-0	20	Pembridge 1	(15,313)
40	A 4	BL	H	Wimbledon	W 2-1	1-1	20	Varadi 27, Preece 64	7,754
41	11	BL	A	Oldham Athletic	L 1-5	1-2	20	Harford 25	(13,210)
42	14	BL	H	Nottingham Forest	W 2-1	2-1	20	Harford 12, James 24	8,014
43	18	BL	H	Manchester United	D 1-1	0-1	20	Harford 50	13,410
44	20	BL	A	Queens Park R.	L 1-2	0-0	20	Pembridge (pen) 64	(10,749)
45	25	BL	H	Aston Villa	W 2-0	1-0	20	Stein 10, Pembridge 48	11,178
46	M 2	BL	A	Notts County	L 1-2	1-1	20	James 18	(11,380)

Best Home League Attendance: 13,410 v Manchester Utd   **Smallest:** 7,533 v Coventry City   **Av Home Att:** 9,711

Goal Scorers: **Compared with 90-91:** -564

League (38):	Harford 12, Pembridge 5 (2 pens), Preece 3, Gray 3, Stein 3, Oakes 2, Dreyer 2, Harvey 2, James 2, Varadi, Nogan, Opponents Telfer
R/lows C (4):	Gray 3, Nogan
FA Cup (0):	
ZDS Cup (1):	Telfer

† = Sent Off

Chamberlain A.	Beaumont D.	Harvey R.	McDonough D.	Ridger G.	Dreyer J.	Preece D.	Stein B.	Pembridge M.	Black K.	Gray P.	Harford M.	Campbell J.	Day M.	Hughes C.	Jackson M.	James J.	Kamara C.	Nogan K.	Oakes S.	Peake T.	Rees J.	Salton D.	Sutton S.	Telfer P.	Thompson S.	Referee	
1	2	3	4	5	6		8	9	10	11	12					S										M Bodenham	1
1	2	3	4	5	6		8	9*	10	11	12					S										M Bailey	2
1	2	3	4	5	6		8	9	10	11	7				S											J Moules	3
1	2*		4●		4	5	3	8	9	10	11	7				12				6						P Foakes	4
1	2*			4	5	3	8	9	10		7					12			14	6						M Pierce	5
1	12	3	4		5		8	11	10		7					2*			14	6						A Smith	6
1		3●	4	14	5		8		10		7					2			9	6				12		A Bennett	7
1			4*	5	3	7	8●		10		9					2			14	6				12	11	P Alcock	8
1			4	5	3	7	8●		10		9					2			14	6				12	11*	P Durkin	9
1	14			5	3	7	8*		10		9					2●			12	6			4	11		A Gunn	10
1	6			5	3	7	8*	10			9●					2			12				14	4	11	R Pawley	11
1	6			5	3	7		10			8	9●				12	2		14				4*	11		J Rushton	12
1	14			5●	3		12	10			8					11*	2		9	6			7	4		P Don	13
1	5	3			11	14	10	8		9●						2			12	6			7	4*		K Burge	14
1	3*			5	11●	14	10	8	9					12	2	4				6				7		D Elleray	15
1			6					11			9●	14	4	8		10			12	5			2			B Hill	16
1	14		6*	3			10				4	8		9	11	5	7●			2						K Hackett	17
1				5		14	3	10*	9			8	2*	4	12	11	6						7			M Brandwood	18
1	3			5			8	10	9				S	4	12	11	6						7			D Frampton	19
1	3			5		12	8	10	9						4		11	6		S			7			J Key	20
1		3		5		12	8	10	9*	11						2	4			6	S	1	7			M Reed	21
		3		5		14	8*	10	9	12						2●	4		11	6		1	7			P Vanes	22
		3		5		12	8	10	9							2	4	S	11*	6		1	7			K Cooper	23
		3		5		11*	8	10	9	S						2	4		12	6		1	7			R Wiseman	24
		3		5		11*	8*	10	9	14						2	4		12	6		1	7			J Deakin	25
		3		5		11●	8*	10	9	14						2	4		12	6		1	7			D Allison	26
1		3		5		11	8	10			12					2*	4		9	6		S	7			K Barratt	27
		3		5		11*	8	10		S						2	4	9	12	6			7			W Burns	28
		3		5		11	8	10			12					2	4	9●	14	6		1	7*			R Bigger	29
		3		5		11	8*	10		9					12	2	4		7	6		S	1			P Harrison	30
		3		5		11	12	10		9		8			2	4*	S	7		6			1			P Jones	31
		3		5		11	8	10		9			14		12	2*	4		12	6		1	7*			K Breen	32
		3		5		11*	8*	10		9	14				12	2	4		7	6		1				T Holbrook	33
		3		5		11	8●	10		9	14				12	2	4		7*	6		1				P Danson	34
		3		5		11	12	10		9	8*			7●		2	4			6		14	1			A Flood	35
		3		5		11	8*	10			9	1	12			2	4		7	6						D Elleray	36
		3		5		11	8	10		9	1	7			2	4			6	S						R Hamer	37
		3		5		11*	8●	10		9	14	1	12			2	4		6	7*						K Barratt	38
		3		5		11	8*	10		9		1	12		2*	4			6	7						C Wilkes	39
1		3		5		11	8	10		9	S		S			2	4			6						B Hill	40
1		3●		5		11*	8	10		9			12			2	4			6	14					R Hart	41
1		3		5		11*	8	10		12	9		14			2	4			6						T Fitzharris	42
1		3*		5		11	14	10		12	9					2	4		8●	6						M Bodenham	43
1		3		5		11	14	10			9		12			2	4		8	6						D Axcell	44
1				3		11	8	10		S	9					2	4		7*	6			5			G Pooley	45
1				3		11	8	10		12	9					2	4		7	6	14		5*			R Nixon	46
24	**6**	**31**	**9**	**11**	**42**	**34**	**32**	**42**	**4**	**9**	**29**	**4**	**4**	**6**	**7**	**28**	**28**	**6**	**15**	**38**	**3**	**2**	**14**	**17**	**5**	**League Appearances**	
3	2	1		1				5		7		12	2			8	6		2	1			3			**Substitute Appearances**	
2	2	1		1		1		2		1+1	2		2	1			2		0+2	1		0+1	2	2		**R/lows Appearances**	
1		1			1	1	1	1			0+1				1	1			1	1				1		**FA Cup Appearances**	
1		1		1	1	1	1				0+1		1	1			0+1	1				1		1		**Other Competitions**	

Also Played: Posn.(Game): Farrell 7*(1)7†(2)S(3)14(4)11(5), Glover 9●(6), Holsgrove 11*(7), Allpress 3(16), Williams 7*(16)14(39), Linton 12(17)2*(20)S(36)S(37), Varadi 7(40)7(41,42,43*,44)12(45)

Players on Loan: L Glover (Nott'm Forest), S Sutton (Nott'm Forest), M Day (Leeds Utd), I Varadi (Leeds Utd)

LUTON TOWN

Club Colours: White with navy/orange trim, navy blue shorts, white stockings with orange/blue trim.
Change Colours: Navy blue/white trim, navy blue shorts, orange stockings/white and navy trim.
Reserves League: Neville Ovenden Football Combination

COMPETITIONS

Div. 1	Div. 2	Div. 3	Div. 3S	Div. 4	Texaco
55-60	97-00	20-21	21-37	65-68	74-75
74-75	37-55	63-65			
82-92	60-63	68-70			**Wat Cup**
	70-74				1971
	75-82				
	92-				

HONOURS

Div. 2	Div. 3S	Div. 4	League Cup
81-82	36-37	67-68	87-88

MOST APPEARANCES: BOB MORTON 550 (1948-64)

Year	League	FA Cup	League Cup
1948-49	17	3	
1949-50	10	0	
1950-51	24	2	
1951-52	28	6	
1952-53	42	4	
1953-54	40	4	
1954-55	39	3	
1955-56	39	1	
1956-57	40	2	
1957-58	27	1	
1958-59	35	9	
1959-60	33	3	
1960-61	27	3	
1961-62	27	3	3
1962-63	34	1	3
1963-64	33	3	1
	495	**48**	**7**
Previous holder: Gordon Turner 406 (1950-64)			

MOST GOALS IN A CAREER
GORDON TURNER 265 (1949-64)

Season	League	FA Cup	League Cup
1951-52	4	2	
1952-53	13	3	
1953-54	16		
1954-55	32	5	
1955-56	19		
1956-57	30	1	
1957-58	33		
1958-59	14		
1959-60	6	3	
1960-61	26	2	1
1961-62	20		1
1962-63	14		2
1963-64	16	2	
Total	**243**	**18**	**4**
Previous holder: A Rennie 147 (1927-35)			

HIGHEST TRANSFER FEE RECEIVED

Amount	Club	Player	Date
£1,500,000	Nott'm Forest	Kingsley Black	8/91
£1,300,000	Derby County	Mark Pembridge	5/92
£1,000,000	Queens Park R	Roy Wegerle	12/89
£750,000	Liverpool	Paul Walsh	5/84

RECORD TRANSFER FEE PAID

Amount	Club	Player	Date
£650,000	Odense	Lars Elstrup	8/89
£300,000	Arsenal	Steve Williams	8/88
£250,000	Birmingham City	Mike Harford	12/84
£200,000	Bristol Rovers	Steve White	12/79

MANAGERS

Name	Seasons	Best	Worst
George Thomson	1925-27	7(3S)	8(3S)
John McCartney	1927-29	7(3S)	13(3S)
George Kay	1929-31	7(3S)	13(3S)
Harold Wightman	1931-35	4(3S)	14(3S)
Edwin Liddell	1935-38	12(2)	2(3S)
Neil McBain	1938-39	7(2)	7(2)
George Martin	1939-47	13(2)	13(2)
Dally Duncan	1947-58	8(1)	19(2)
Syd Owen	1959-60	22(1)	22(1)
Sam Bartram	1960-62	13(2)	13(2)
Jack Crompton	1962		
Bill Harvey	1962-64	22(2)	18(3)
George Martin	1964-66	21(3)	6(4)
Allan Brown	1966-68	1(4)	17(4)
Alec Stock	1968-72	6(2)	3(3)
Harry Haslam	1972-78	20(1)	13(2)
David Pleat	1978-86	9(1)	18(2)
John Moore	1986-87	7(1)	7(1)
Ray Harford	1987-90	9(1)	16(1)
Jim Ryan	1990-91	17(1)	18(1)
David Pleat	1991-		

LONGEST RUNS

of undefeated matches:	19 (13.1.1968-27.4.1968)
	(7.4.1969-11.10.1969)
of undefeated home matches:	39 (24.1.1925-30.4.1927)
without home win:	10 (26.10.1964-25.1.1965)
	(16.9.1972-6.1.1973)
of league wins:	9 (22.1.1977-8.3.1977)
of league defeats:	8 (11.11.1899-6.1.1900)
of league matches without a win:	16 (1964)
of undefeated away matches:	10 (20.4.1981-14.11.1981)
without an away win:	32 (26.11.1898-28.4.1900)
of home wins:	15 (1.4.1967-26.12.1967)
of away wins:	5 (2.5.1981-3.10.1981)

PREVIOUS LEAGUES
United League,   Southern League

BIGGEST VICTORIES
League: 12-0 v Bristol Rovers, Division 3S, 13.4.1936.
(Divisional record)
F.A. Cup: 9-0 v Clapton, Round 1, 30.11.1927
League Cup: 7-2 v Mansfield, 2nd Rnd, 3.10.1989

BIGGEST DEFEATS
League: 0-9 v Birmingham City, Division 2, 12.11.1898
F.A. Cup: 0-7 v Crystal Palace, Round 1, 16.1.1929
League Cup: 1-5 v Everton, Round 3, 1968-69

MOST POINTS
3 points a win: 88, Division 2, 1981-82.
2 points a win: 66, Division 4, 1967-68.

MOST GOALS
103, 1936-37.
Payne 55, Stephenson 17, Ball 8, Dawes 8, Roberts 8, Rich 2,
Finlayson 2, Fellowes 1, Hancock 1, Hodge 1.

MOST GOALS IN A MATCH
10. Joe Payne v Bristol Rovers, 12-0, Division 3S, 13.4.1936,
(League record)

MOST GOALS IN A SEASON
Joe Payne 58, 55 League, 3 FAC (1936-37).
4 goals twice = 8, 3 goals 5 times = 15, 2 goals 8 times = 16, 1 goal
19 times = 19.

MOST FIRST CLASS MATCHES IN A SEASON
58 (40 League, 6 FA Cup, 8 League Cup, 4 Simod Cup) 1987-88

MOST LEAGUE GOALS CONCEDED
95, Division 2, 1898-99

MOST LEAGUE WINS
27, Division 3S, 1936-37; Division 4, 1967-68

MOST LEAGUE DRAWS
18, Division 2, 1949-50; Division 2, 1971-72

MOST LEAGUE DEFEATS
24, Division 2, 1962-63; Division 3, 1964-65

OLDEST PLAYER
Dally Duncan, 39 years, 11 days, 25.10.1947.

YOUNGEST PLAYER
Mike O'Hara, 16 years, 32 days, 1.10.1960.

MOST CAPPED PLAYER
Mal Donaghy (Northern Ireland) 58

BEST PERFORMANCES BY LUTON TOWN

League: 1981-82: Matches played 42, Won 25, Drawn 13, Lost 4, Goals for 86, Goals against 46, Points 88. First in Division 2.

Highest: 1986-87: 7th in Division 1.

F.A. Cup: 1958-59: 3rd rnd. Leeds United 5-1; 4th rnd. Leicester City 1-1, 4-1; 5th rnd. Ipswich 5-2; 6th rnd. Blackpool 1-1, 1-0; Semi-Final Norwich City 1-1, 1-0; Final Nottingham Forest 1-2.

League Cup: 1987-88: 2nd rnd. Wigan 1-0, 4-2; 3rd rnd. Coventry City 3-1; 4th rnd. Ipswich 1-0; 5th rnd. Bradford City 2-0; Semi-Final Oxford United 1-1, 2-0; Final Arsenal 3-2

DIVISIONAL RECORDS

	Played	Won	Drawn	Lost	For	Against	Points
DIVISION 1	658	213	168	277	863	1011	**725**
DIVISION 2	1148	438	286	424	1792	1695	**1187**
DIVISION 3	184	75	46	63	266	255	**196**
DIVISION 3S	714	308	175	231	1295	1038	**791**
DIVISION 4	138	67	29	42	236	187	**163**
TOTALS	2842	1101	704	1037	4452	4186	**3062**

LUTON TOWN

PLAYERS NAME / Honours	Ht	Wt	Birthdate	Birthplace / Transfers	Contract Date	Clubs	League	L/Cup	FA Cup	Other	Lg	L/C	FAC	Oth
GOALKEEPERS														
Alec Chamberlain	6.2	11.11	20.06.64	Ely		Ramsey Tow								
				Free	27.07.81	Ipswich Town								
				Free	03.08.82	Colchester Utd	188	11	10	12				
				£80,000	28.07.87	Everton								
				Loan	01.11.87	Tranmere Rovers	15							
				£150,000	27.07.88	Luton Town	106	7	5	7				
Andrew Petterson	6.2	14.12	26.09.69	Freemantle (Aus)	30.12.88	Luton Town								
				Loan	30.12.88	Swindon Town								
				Loan	20.10.89	Swindon Town								
				Loan	26.03.92	Ipswich Town								
DEFENDERS														
Jamie Campbell	6.1		21.10.72	Birmingham	01.07.91	Luton Town	4+7		0+1	0+1				
John Dreyer	6.0	11.6	11.06.63	Alnwick		Wallingfor								
						Oxford Utd	57+3	10+1	2	3	2			
				Loan		Torquay Utd	5							
				Loan		Fulham	12				2			
				£140,000	27.07.88	Luton Town	134+2	11	5	5	8	1		1
Ken Gillard	5.9	11.08	30.04.72	Dublin	01.07.89	Luton Town								
Richard Harvey	5.9	11.10	17.04.69	Letchworth	10.01.87	Luton Town (A)	90+14	6	6	5	2	1		
EY:3,u19.3														
Julian James	5.10	11.11	22.03.70	Tring	01.07.88	Luton Town (A)	58+11	2+1	5+1	5	4			
E:u21.2				Loan	12.09.91	Preston N.E	6							
Marvin Johnson	5.11	11.6	29.10.68	Wembley	12.11.86	Luton Town (A)	54+9	2+2	2+1	5				
Trevor Peake	6.0	12.9	10.02.57	Nuneaton		Nuneaton B								
E: SP.2; FAC'87				£27,750	15.06.79	Lincoln City	171	16	7		7	2		
				£100,000	06.07.83	Coventry City	277+1	30	17	10	6		1	
				£100,000	27.08.91	Luton Town	38	1	1					
Darren Salton	6.1	13.08	16.03.72	Edinburgh	23.03.89	Luton Town	2+1	0+1		1				
MIDFIELD														
Ceri Hughes	5.9	11.06	26.02.71	Pontypridd	01.07.89	Luton Town (T)	24+12	2		1	1			
W:1														
Chris Kamara	6.1	12.0	25.12.57	Middlesborough	01.01.76	Portsmouth (A)	56+7	1	4		7		1	
Div.4.86				£20,000	10.08.77	Swindon Town	133+14	18+4	14		21	1	4	
				£50,000	25.08.81	Portsmouth	11	3				1		
				PE	28.10.81	Brentford	150+2	15	13	7	28	1	2	1
				£14,500	21.08.85	Swindon Town	86+1	9	5	12+1	6			
				£27,500	04.07.88	Stoke City	60	4	4	3	5	1		1
				£150,000	29.01.90	Leeds Utd	15+5	1+2		1	1			
				£150,000	01.11.91	Luton Town	28		1					
David Preece	5.6	10.0	28.05.63	Bridgnorth	22.07.80	Walsall (A)	107+4	18	6	1	5	5	1	
E:B.3;LC'88				PE£150,000	06.12.84	Luton Town	215+10	16	14	5	9	2	1	
Jason Rees	5.5	9.08	22.12.69	Aberdare	01.07.88	Luton Town (T)	22+18	1+1	0+1	3+1				2
W:u21.3,B.1														
Ian Scott	6.1	11.05	25.11.68	Luton	01.07.89	Luton Town								
Paul Telfer	5.9	10.02	21.10.71	Edinburgh	07.11.88	Luton Town (T)	17+4	2	1	1	1			1
FORWARDS														
Steve Claridge	5.11	11.8	10.04.66	Portsmouth		Portsmouth								
						Bournemouth	3+4			1	1			
via Weymouth (£10,000) to				Free	11.10.88	Crystal Palace								
				Free	25.11.88	Aldershot	58+4	2+1	6	5	19		1	2
				£75,000	08.02.90	Cambridge Utd	45+14	2	5	5+2	16			1
					17.07.92	Luton Town								1
Phil Gray	5.10	11.7	02.10.68	Belfast	21.08.86	Tottenham H. (T)	4+5		0+1					
NI: u23.1, u21.1				Loan	17.01.90	Barnsley	3	1						
				Loan	08.11.90	Fulham	3			2				1
				£275,000	16.08.91	Luton Town	9+5	2			3	3		
Kurt Nogan	5.10	11.01	09.09.70	Cardiff	11.07.89	Luton Town (T)	17+16	1+3		1+1	3	1		
W:u21.2														
ADDITIONAL CONTRACT PLAYERS														
Chris Brooks					03.07.92	Luton Town								
David M Greene					03.09.91	Luton Town								
(D) Desmond Linton	6.1	11.13	05.09.71	Birmingham	09.01.90	Leicester City (T)	6+5	0+1		1				
				Swap	22.10.91	Luton Town	1+1							
Paul A Murray					02.07.92	Luton Town (T)								
(F) Scott Oakes	5.10	9.12	05.08.72	Leicester	09.05.90	Leicester City (T)	1+2			1				
				Swap	22.10.91	Luton Town	15+6		1		2			
Juergen Sommer					05.09.91	Luton Town								
				Loan	13.11.91	Brighton & H.A	1							
Martin K Williams					13.09.91	Luton Town	0+1		1					

LUTON TOWN

RECORD WIN & LOSS AGAINST EACH CLUB IN CURRENT DIVISION
(Where a score has occured on several occasions the most recent is given)

Club	Rec. Win	Season	Rec. Loss	Season
BARNSLEY	6-0	1952-53	6-1	1950-51
BIRMINGHAM CITY	4-1	1974-75 (away)	9-0	1898-99
BRENTFORD	6-2	1963-64 (away)	3-0	1924-25
BRISTOL CITY	4-0	1936-37	6-0	1926-27
BRISTOL ROVERS	12-0	1935-36	5-0	1920-21
CAMBRIDGE UNITED	3-1	1980-81 (away)	1-1	1981-82
CHARLTON ATHLETIC	7-1	1977-78	6-1	1961-62 (home)
DERBY COUNTY	4-1	1960-61 (away)	5-0	1974-75
GRIMSBY TOWN	6-0	1981-82	6-1	1949-50
LEICESTER CITY	4-0	1984-85	6-1	1898-99
MILLWALL	6-0	1926-27	7-0	1926-27
NEWCASTLE UNITED	4-0	1987-88	7-2	1946-47
NOTTS COUNTY	6-0	1978-79	5-2	1966-67
OXFORD UNITED	4-0	1970-71	4-2	1986-87
PETERBOROUGH UTD	1-1	1964-65	2-0	1964-65
PORTSMOUTH	4-1	1987-88	5-0	1957-58
SOUTHEND UNITED	4-0	1924-25	5-0	1964-65
SUNDERLAND	8-2	1955-56	7-1	1960-61
SWINDON TOWN	6-0	1931-32	9-1	1920-21
TRANMERE ROVERS	3-0	1938-39	2-0	1965-66
WATFORD	5-0	1925-26	3-0	1984-85
WEST HAM UNITED	6-1	1951-52	4-1	1978-79 (home)
WOLVERHAMPTON WNDRS	4-0	1983-84	5-0	1958-59

MANAGER: DAVID PLEAT

DATE OF BIRTH: 15.1.1945   **PLACE OF BIRTH:** Nottingham

DATE OF APPOINTMENT: July 1991

PREVIOUS CLUBS
as Manager: Nuneaton, Luton Town, Tottenham Hotspur, Leicester City
as Asst. Man.: Luton Town
as Player: Nott'm Forest, Luton Town, Shrewsbury, Exeter, Peterborough

HONOURS
as Manager: Div 2 Championship 1981-82, FA Cup Final 1986-87, League Cup Semi-Final 1986-87, FA Cup Semi-Final 1984-85, 1986-87
as Asst. Man./Coach:
as Player:
International: England Schoolboy 1961, England Youth 1962, 1963, 1964

Value Rating: ★ ★ ★

Programme Editor: Robert Alexander

Price of 1992-93 Programme: £1.50
Number of Pages: 32

Local Newspapers: Luton News, The Herald

Local Radio Stations: Chiltern Radio, BBC Radio Bedfordshire

LEADING LEAGUE GOALSCORERS
SEASONS 1979-80 – 1991-92

1979-80	DAVID MOSS	24	1980-81	BRIAN STEIN	18
1981-82	BRIAN STEIN	21	1982-83	PAUL WALSH	14
				BRIAN STEIN	14
1983-84	PAUL WALSH	11	1984-85	MICK HARFORD	15
1985-86	MICK HARFORD	22	1986-87	BRIAN STEIN	12
				MIKE NEWELL	12
1987-88	MARK STEIN	11	1988-89	DANNY WILSON	9
				KINGSLEY BLACK	9
1989-90	KINGSLEY BLACK	11	1990-91	LARS ELSTRUP	15
	1991-92	**MICK HARFORD**	**12**		

KENILWORTH ROAD 1 Maple Road, Luton, Beds LU4 8AW

Capacity: 13,410   **Covered Standing:** 4,350   **Seating:** 8,956

Tel: Ground: 0582 411622   **Ticket Sales:** 0582 416976   **Clubcall:** 0898 12 11 23

All premium rate calls (0898/0891) cost 36p per minute cheap rate and 48p per minute at all other times. Call costings correct at time of going to press.

GROUNDS
Excelsior Dallow Lane 1885-97; Dunstable Road 1897-05; Kenilworth Road 1905-

ATTENDANCES
Highest: 30,069 v Blackpool, FA Cup 6th Round Replay, 4.3.1959

Lowest: 2,272 v Bristol Rovers, Div 3S, 13.3.1933

RECORD RECEIPTS (with previous records):
£80,588 v West Ham Utd, FA Cup, 5.1.1991
£65,183 v West Ham Utd, L/woods Cup S-Final, 1.3.1989
£55,906 v Manchester United, FA Cup, 29.1.1983
£42,870 v Ipswich Town, FA Cup, 23.1.1982
£31,233 v West Ham United, Division 2, 1.3.1980

KENILWORTH ROAD
First game: v Plymouth, 4.9.1905
First floodlit game: v Fenerbahce, 7.10.1957

Season Tickets:
Stands: from £124 to £248.50, juv/OAP £72.50 to £124
Ground: from £113.50, juv/OAP £62

Executive Members Tickets: Apply to club for details

Executive Boxes: North Stand match day hire, 8 and 14 seater boxes. Unique choice of viewing. Personal open balcony, 12 feet from the action. Prices contact Commercial Department

Cost of Stand Tickets: Mainstand A-E & New Stand: £12 & £13, junior/OAP £6, £6.50, F £9 & £10, G £6 & £6.50; Enclosure C & G: £9 & £10, junior/OAP £4 & £4.50; Kenilworth Stand (seats) £9 & £10, junior/OAP £4 & £4.50; (standing) £5.50 & £6, junior/OAP £3 & £3.30

Match and Ticket Information: Entry by membership only

Car Parking: Street parking near ground only available

Nearest Railway Station: Luton Midland Road (0582 27612)

How to get to the ground

From North and West: Use Motorway M1 until Junction 11 then follow signs Luton A505 into Dunstable Road. Forward through one-way system and then turn right into Kenilworth Road for Luton Town FC

From South and East: Use Motorway M1 until Junction 10 or A6/A612 into Luton town centre, then follow signs Dunstable into Dunstable Road A505. Under railway bridge then turn left into Kenilworth Road for Luton Town FC

MAIDSTONE UNITED

Division 3

Formed: 1897   **Turned Professional:** 1989   **Ltd Co:** Yes

SPONSORED BY: Prosperity Financial Services Group   **NICKNAME:** The Stones

Chairman & Managing Director
J C Thompson

Directors
G Pearson
D Berry
R J Gilbert

Company Secretary
D Twiddy

Club Chaplain
Rev. N Gallagher

Secretary
M K Mercer (0622 754403)

Team Manager
C Walker

Assistant Manager
D Madden

Groundsman
M Maytum

Physiotherapist
F D Brooks

Office Manager
Mrs B Legg

Lottery Managers
Mrs M & B L Holden (0622 670474)

Kit Manager
R Gee

IT is very difficult to report positive news from Maidstone. A very tough season was survived with great difficulty, and certainly trying to establish club identity away from your home town is virtually impossible, as support dwindles away and credibility becomes difficult.

On the field 'The Stones' main goalscoring hope, Mark Gall, left for Brighton, where he was voted 'Player of the Year', and subsequently goalscoring for Maidstone became a problem. Five goals were scored twice in a mid-season run of six unbeaten games but by the end of the campaign the supply had virtually dried up and it was Liburd Henry who finished the season as top scorer with eight goals.

Iain Hesford was the club's only ever-present but consistent seasons were also contributed by Oxbrow, Sandeman, Thompson and Stebbling, while Breen played well in central defence for the second-half of the season.

Since the excitement of gaining a Football League place wore off amidst dwindling attendances, lack of local council encouragement and the struggle for life itself, the whole cause became a desperate disappointment to those who love the club. The great days in non-League football when, as a top club, Maidstone challenged for all honours with star players at the top of their particular level of football, are sadly missed.

The club feels let down by the local council. The supporters feel let down by council and club. The Football League aren't too happy with development either.

Everyone is completely confused by the idea of a Maidstone club playing in the North East, and Wycombe Wanderers, a club with ground, playing staff and finance capable of being a valuable asset to the Football League feel even more aggrieved than anyone, as their chance of taking Maidstones' place has now been lost.

The club didn't win a cup tie last season and as the average home attendance was 1,428 it is difficult to find any positive viewpoints for the club.

Different rumours and counter rumours find their way into the press by the day, so all we can do is wish those dedicated Maidstone United supporters who helped their club gain the treasured Football League place as happy a conclusion as possible to this very depressing story.

T.W.

Back row L-R: L Henry, M Smalley, P Rumble, L Osbourne, T Sorrell. **Third row:** S Parris, K Steggles (Physio), M Chaplin (Yth Development Officer), D Davis, J Roast, D Oxbrow, N Johns, I Marshall, I Hesford, S Cuggy, B Sandeman, N Elli, C Walker (Asst. Manager), M Chaplin. **Second row:** J Lillis, A Tutton, P Haylock, B Legg (Office Manager), B Williams (Gen. Manager), J Thompson (Chairman), G Carr (Team Manager), M Mercer (Secretary), L Thompson, M Gall, R Painter. **Front row:** J Means, D Heath, R Sinclair, D Johnson, T Addlington, G Breem, A Davies, G Porter, C Older, T Mas, R Head.

MAIDSTONE UNITED

DIVISION FOUR: 18th **FA CUP:** 2nd RND **RUMBELOWS CUP:** 1st RND **AUTOGLASS:** Prelim.

M	DATE	COMP.	VEN	OPPONENTS	RESULT	H/T	LGE POS	GOALSCORERS/GOAL TIMES	ATTEN-DANCE
1	A 17	BL	A	Chesterfield	L 0-3	0-1			(3,466)
2	21	RC 1/1	A	Leicester City	L 0-3	0-1			(9,610)
3	24	BL	H	Halifax Town	L 0-1	0-1	23		1,216
4	28	RC 1/2	H	Leicester City	L 0-1	0-0			1,638
5	S 4	BL	H	Cardiff City	D 1-1	1-1	23	Cuggy 13	1,019
6	7	BL	A	Scunthorpe United	L 0-2	0-0	23		(2,738)
7	14	BL	H	Walsall	W 2-1	2-1		Donegal 17, Osborne 42	1,139
8	17	BL	H	Lincoln City	L 0-2	0-1			1,113
9	21	BL	A	Rotherham United	D 3-3	1-1	22	Osborne 35, Henry 57, Gall 90	(3,870)
10	28	BL	H	York City	W 1-0	1-0		Nethercott 25	1,037
11	O 5	BL	A	Mansfield Town	L 0-2	0-1	21		(3,207)
12	12	BL	H	Doncaster Rovers	D 2-2	0-1		Gall 55, Osborne 86	1,255
13	19	BL	H	Rochdale	D 1-1	0-0	20	Sandeman 48	1,016
14	23	AGT Pre	H	Fulham	L 2-6	1-2		Gall 14, Owers 55	937
15	N 2	BL	H	Hereford United	W 3-2	1-2	16	Stebbing 44, Richards 47, Hesford 71	846
16	5	BL	A	Crewe Alexandra	D 1-1	1-1		Richards 5	(2,476)
17	9	BL	A	Gillingham	D 1-1	0-0	18	Osborne 69	(6,716)
18	16	FAC 1	H	Sutton United	W 1-0	1-0		Thompson 9	2,008
19	23	BL	H	Burnley	L 0-1	0-1			2,375
20	30	BL	A	Carlisle United	L 0-3	0-2	21		(2,146)
21	D 7	FAC 2	H	Kettering Town	L 1-2	1-1		Henry 14	2,750
22	10	AGT Pre	A	Gillingham	L 2-4	0-2		Ellis 57, Osborne 82	(2,300)
23	21	BL	A	Halifax Town	D 1-1	1-0		Painter 34	(1,040)
24	26	BL	H	Chesterfield	L 0-1	0-1			1,325
25	J 1	BL	A	Cardiff City	W 5-0	1-0	21	Henry 44, Painter 50, Stebbing 53, Sandeman 66, Smalley 70	(8,023)
26	4	BL	H	Blackpool	D 0-0	0-0	21		1,774
27	8	BL	H	Barnet	D 1-1	1-0		Davis 2	1,988
28	11	BL	A	Wrexham	D 0-0	0-0			(3,167)
29	18	BL	H	Northampton Town	D 1-1	0-0	21	Henry 51	1,364
30	F 12	BL	H	Carlisle United	W 5-1	3-0		Sandeman 3 (2, 38, 67), Henry 39, Lillis 47	994
31	15	BL	A	Barnet	L 2-3	0-2		Painter 78, Davis 89	(2,871)
32	22	BL	H	Wrexham	L 2-4	1-2	20	Lillis 18, Stebbing 51	1,491
33	29	BL	A	Blackpool	D 1-1	1-1		Lillis 10	(4,136)
34	M 3	BL	A	Northampton Town	L 0-1	0-0			(1,677)
35	7	BL	H	Scarborough	W 2-1	0-0		Smalley 50, Painter 53	1,019
36	11	BL	H	Crewe Alexandra	W 2-0	1-0		Henry 21, Painter 88	1,174
37	14	BL	A	Hereford United	D 2-2	1-0		Haylock 29, Henry 47	(1,910)
38	21	BL	H	Gillingham	D 1-1	1-0		Henry 36	3,264
39	28	BL	A	Burnley	L 1-2	0-0	18	Newman 46	(10,896)
40	31	BL	A	Walsall	D 1-1	1-1		Oxbrow 7	(2,045)
41	A 4	BL	H	Scunthorpe United	L 0-1	0-0	18		1,237
42	7	BL	A	Rochdale	W 2-1	0-1		Stebbing 53, Lillis 72	(2,248)
43	11	BL	A	Lincoln City	L 0-1	0-1	18		(2,241)
44	18	BL	H	Rotherham United	D 0-0	0-0	18		1,744
45	20	BL	A	York City	D 1-1	0-1		Sandeman 76	(1,638)
46	25	BL	H	Mansfield Town	D 0-0	0-0	18		1,602
47	29	BL	A	Scarborough	L 0-2	0-0			(939)
48	M 2	BL	A	Doncaster Rovers	L 0-3	0-1	18		(1,680)

Best Home League Attendance: 3,264 v Gillingham   **Smallest:** 846 v Hereford Utd   **Av Home Att:** 1,428

Goal Scorers: **Compared with 90-91:** -416

League (45): Henry 7, Sandeman 6, Painter 5, Stebbing 4, Lillis 4, Osborne 4, Gall 2, Richards 2, Smalley 2, Davis 2, Haylock, Nethercott, Oxbrow, Donegal, Newman, Hesford, Cuggy

R/lows C (0):

FA Cup (2): Thompson, Henry

Autoglass (4): Gall, Owers, Osborne, Ellis

Hesford I.	Haylock P.	Rumble P.	Oxbrow D.	Davis D.	Osborne L.	Gall M.	Painter P.	Henry L.	Sandeman B.	Ellis N.	Lillis J.	Cuggy M.	Thompson L.	Donegal G.	Smalley M.	Nethercott S.	Stebbing G.	Owers A.	Richards C.	Tutton A.	Breen G.	Rutter S.	Newman R.	Hazel I.	Sinclair R.	Referee	
1	2	3	4	5	6	7	8	9	10*	11•	12		14													E Parker	1
1	2	11	4	5	6	7*	8		10		12		14	3	9*											**A Smith**	2
1	2	11	4	5	6	7*	8		10*		12		14	3	9											G Pooley	3
1	2		4	5	6	12	8			11	10		7*	3	9	S										**D Axcell**	4
1	12		4	5*	6	14	8			11	10•		7	3	9	2										P Alcock	5
1	2•	11*			6		8	7	10	12			14	3	9	4	5									P Vanes	6
1	4	12		2	10	14	8*	7					3		9•	6	5	11								P Scoble	7
1	2*			5	8•	14	7	10	12		9			6	4		11									P Foakes	8
1	S	12	2		6	10	8	9	7				3*		4		5	11								J Lloyd	9
1	2		6		10		8	9*	7	S	12		3		4		5	11								P Taylor	10
1	2		6•		10		8*	9	7	14	12		3		4		5	11								T West	11
1	5		4*		10		7	9	12	2	11		3			6	8	S								J Carter	12
1	4		5		10		7	S	11	2			3			6	8	S	9							G Poll	13
1	4		5		10		7	14	11	2*			3•			6	8	12	9							**R Bigger**	14
1	4		5		10			14	11	2			3	S		6	8	7•	9							G Willard	15
1	4		5		10		7		11	2			3	S		6	8	S	9							C Trussell	16
1	4		5		10		7		11	2		S	3	S		6	8		9							R Pawley	17
1	4		5	6	10		7		11	2*		14	3		9•	12	8									**M James**	18
1	4		5		10		7		11	2		9*	12	S		6	8									G Pooley	19
1	4		5		10*		7•		11	2		14	3	9	12	6	8									T Fitzharris	20
1	4		5	6	10	12			11	2		S	3		9*	7	8									P Foakes	21
1	4		6	5*	10	12	7			2	9		3	S	11		8									**R Wiseman**	22
1	2		5	6			7	11	9	10			3	S	4		8		S							P Wright	23
1	2		5	6			7	3	9	10	12				4	11*	8		S							A Gunn	24
1	2		5	6			7	11	9	10		S	3		4		8		S							J Lloyd	25
1	2		5	6			7*	3	9	10		S			4	11	8		12							B Hill	26
1	2*		5	6			7	11•	9	10	12		3	14	4		8									J Deakin	27
1	2			6			7	11	9	10		S	3	14	4		8				5•					K Cooper	28
1	2			6			7	11	9	10		S	3	S	4		8				5					M Pierce	29
1	2			6			S	11	9	10	7	S	3		4		8				5					P Don	30
1	2			6			12	11	9	10*	7	S	3		4		8				5					J Martin	31
1	2			6*			12	11	9	10•	7	14	3		4		8				5					P Jones	32
1	2			6	10			11	9		7*	12•	3		4		8				5		14			D Shadwell	33
1	2			6			7	11*	9		12		3	S	4		8				5		10			P Scoble	34
1	2			6	10			11	S		7		3		4		8				5		S			P Taylor	35
1	2			6	10			11•	9*	14	7		3		4		8				5		12			J Carter	36
1	2			6	10			11•	14		7	S	3		4		8				5		9			H King	37
1	2			6	10			11	9	S	7		3		4		8				5		S			P Durkin	38
1	2			6				11	9	10	7		S	12	4		8				5			3*		R Poulain	39
1	2			6				11*	9	10	7		12	S	4		8				5			3		P Harrison	40
1				6				9	10	7		12	3	14	4		8				5			2•	11*	I Borrett	41
1	2			6				11	9	10	7		3	S	4		8	S			5		S			S Bell	42
1	2*			6				9	10	7			3		4	8•		14	5		5		11	12		J Kirkby	43
1				6*				9	10	7			3	2	4		8		S		5		11	12		K Morton	44
1	S							9	10	7			3	6•	4		8		14		5		11	2		G Singh	45
1	S					11		9	10	7			3	S	4		8				5		6	2		R Bigger	46
1	5			6•				9	10	7*			3	12	4				14				11	2		R Hart	47
1	8					11		9	10	7		12	3	6*	4		S				5			2		W Flood	48
42	31	3	31	20	16	7	27	36	35	22	21	1	38	9	33	13	37	1	4		19		9	6	1	League Appearances	
	1	2				3	3	1	2	6	2	12			5	1			4		1		1	2		Substitute Appearances	
2	2	1	2	2	2		1+1	2		1	1	1+1	1+1	2	2											R/lows Appearances	
2	2		2	2	2		1+1	2		2		1	2	1	1+1		2									FA Cup Appearances	
2	2		2	1	2	1	0+2	2		2		1	2	1		1	2		0+1	1						Autoglass Appearances	

† = Sent Off

MAIDSTONE UNITED

Club Colours: Gold shirts, black shorts, black stockings with gold trim
Change Colours: White shirts, navy blue shorts, white stockings with blue and red trim
Reserves League: No Reserve Side

Previous Leagues: East Kent   Thames & Medway Combination   Kent League   Corinthian   Isthmian   Southern Alliance   Gola   G.M.V.C.
Previous Name: Maidstone Invicta
Previous Managers: 1921 J G Coleman   1936 G Beel   1946 W Wood   1948 G Beel   1951 E Fright   1954 C Martin   1957 J Mills   1960 G Bailey   1962 H Hill   1967 L Henson   1967 D Wiltshire   1969 H Hill   1971 K Spurgeon   1971 R Houghton   1972 E Morgan   1973 R Stepney   1975 T Adlington   1977 B Watling   1980 W Williams   1985 B Fry   1986 W Williams   1987 J L Still   1991 G Carr
Honours: K L Champions 1898-99, 1899-00, 1900-01, 1921-22, 1922-23   Corinthian Champions 1955-56   S L 1st Div(S) Champions 1972-73   Alliance Champions 1983-84   G.M.V.C. Champions 1988-89   T.M.C. Champions 5 times   Kent Senior Cup Winners 15 times
League Career: Promoted to Div 4 1988-89

CLUB RECORDS

Most Appearances for Club: Mark Gall (1988-91): League 69 + 16 + League Cup 3 + 2 + FA Cup 7 + 1 + AMC 7 + 1 + Play-offs 2. **Total 88 + 20.**
Most Capped Player: None. (Brian Thompson won 13 caps for England semi-professional)
Record Goalscorer in a Match: Hat-tricks have been scored in League games by Steve Butler (twice), Mark Gall, Jason Lillis, Ken Charlery and Bradley Sandeman
Record League Goalscorer in a Season: Steve Butler, 21, Division 4, 1989-90   **In All Competitions:** Mark Gall, 27 (18 League + 2 FA Cup + 6 Ley. Daf Cup + 1 Play-Off) 1989-90
Record League Goalscorer in a Career: Steve Butler, 41, 1986-91   **In All Competitions:** Steve Butler, 55, 1986-91 (League 41 + League Cup 3 + FA Cup 7 + AMC 4)
Record Transfer Fee Received: £300,000 from Wimbledon for Warren Barton, May 1990
Record Transfer Fee Paid: £40,000 to Watford for Liburd Henry, July 1990
Best Performances: League: 5th Division 4, 1989-90   **FA Cup:** 3rd Round 1978-79, 1980-81, 1983-84, 1986-87, 1987-88
Most League Points: 73, Division 4, 1989-90
Most League Goals: 77, Division 4, 1989-90
Record League Victory and Most Goals Scored in a League Match: 5-0 v Cardiff City (a), Division 4, 1.1.1992   6-1 v Scunthorpe United, Division Four, 15.9.1990
Most Goals Scored in a Cup Tie: 8 v Callender Athletic, FA Amateur, 13.9.1969
Record League Defeat: 0-4 v Hereford United, Division 4, 23.2.1991
Oldest Player in a League Match: Les Berry, 34 years 267 days, v Scunthorpe United, Division 4, 26.1.1991
Youngest Player in a League Match: Gary Breen, 18 years 30 days v Wrexham, Division 4, 11.1.1992

LONGEST LEAGUE RUNS	
of undefeated matches: 6 (1990, 1992)	of league matches without a win: 10 (1991)
of undefeated home matches: 9 (1989-90)	of undefeated away matches: 4 (1991)
without home win: 5 (1991, 1991-92)	without an away win: 12 (1990-91)
of league wins: 5 (1989)	of home wins: 6 (1989-90)
of league defeats: 5 (1990)	of away wins: 2 (1989-90 twice)

BARCLAYS

MAIDSTONE UNITED

PLAYERS NAME Honours	Ht	Wt	Birthdate	Birthplace Transfers	Contract Date	Clubs	League	L/Cup	FA Cup	Other	Lg	L/C	FAC	Oth
GOALKEEPERS														
Mel Gwinnett	6.1	11.8	14.05.63	Worcester	27.05.81	Peterborough U. (A)								
					14.09.82	Hereford Utd								
						Bralaniza (Swe)	1							
					19.06.84	Bradford City				3				
					23.08.85	Exeter City	46	2	1	1				
						Maidstone Utd	33 + 8	1	3	5 + 1	18		2	7
Iain Hesford	6.2	14.10	04.03.60	Zambia	27.08.77	Blackpool (A)	202	14	13					
E:Y,u21.7,UEFA u21'82,Div.3.88					10.08.83	Sheffield Wed								
				Loan	10.01.85	Fulham	3							
				Loan	29.11.86	Notts County	10			1				
					20.09.86	Sunderland	97	4	3	8				
				P.E	29.12.88	Hull City	91	4	5	2				
				Free	16.08.91	Maidstone Utd	42	2	2	2	1			
DEFENDERS														
Darren Davis	6.0	11.0	05.02.67	Nottingham	05.02.85	Notts County (A)	90 + 2	6	6	7	1		1	
E: Y.2					25.08.88	Lincoln City	97 + 5	8	4	6	4	1	1	1
				£27,500	28.03.91	Maidstone Utd	31	2	2	1	2			
Mark Smalley	5.11	11.6	02.01.65	Newark	25.01.83	Nottm. Forest (A)	1 + 2	1		1				
E:Y1				Loan	28.03.86	Birmingham City	7							
				Loan	19.08.86	Bristol Rovers	10							
					05.02.87	Leyton Orient	59 + 5	2	4	4	4			
				Loan	29.11.89	Mansfield Town								
				£15,000	22.01.90	Mansfield Town	49	1		2	2			
				Free	31.05.91	Maidstone Utd	33 + 1		1 + 1	1	2			
MIDFIELD														
Bradley Sandeman			24.02.70	Northants	14.07.88	Northampton T	28 + 30	2 + 3	2	6 + 1	3			
				£10,000	22.02.91	Maidstone Utd	55 + 2	1	2	2	7			
Gary Stebbing	5.8	11.0	11.08.56	Croydon		K.V. Ostend								
E:Y.12,u19.7					02.08.83	Crystal Palace (A)	95 + 7	7 + 1	6	1 + 1	3			
				Loan	10.01.86	Southend Utd	5			1				
					01.10.90	Maidstone Utd	69 + 7		4	6	5			
FORWARDS														
Glenville Donegal	6.1	12.0	20.06.69	Northampton	14.08.87	Northampton T	7 + 13	2 + 1	0 + 1	0 + 2	3	1		
					01.09.89	Aylesbury								
				£35,000	19.08.91	Maidstone Utd	9 + 5	2	1		1			
Neil Ellis	5.11		30.04.69	Wirral		Bangor City								
				£7,500	01.07.90	Chester City	13 + 8	2 + 2	1 + 1	1	1	1		
				£10,000	15.07.91	Maidstone Utd	22 + 6	1		1				1
ADDITIONAL CONTRACT PLAYERS														
Gary Breen					06.03.91	Maidstone Utd	19							
Paul Haylock					28.03.91	Walsall								
				Free		Maidstone Utd	47 + 1	2	2	2	1			
Mark McCutcheon					29.12.89	Maidstone Utd								
Gary Moore					28.03.91	Maidstone Utd	0 + 5				1			

LEADING LEAGUE GOALSCORERS SEASONS 1985-86 – 1991-92

1985-86	Not in League		1986-87	Not in League	
1987-88	Not in League		1988-89	Not in League	
1989-90	**STEVE BUTLER**	**21**	1990-91	**STEVE BUTLER**	**21**

1991-92   **LIBURD HENRY**   7

WATLING STREET Dartford, Kent

Capacity: 5,327   **Covered Standing:** 2,400   **Seating:** 680

Tel: Ground: 0322 288371   **Ticket Sales:** 0622 754403   **Clubcall:** 0898 800 691

All premium rate calls (0898/0891) cost 36p per minute cheap rate and 48p per minute at all other times. Call costings correct at time of going to press.

ATTENDANCES
Highest: 10,951 v Charlton Athletic, FA Cup 3rd Rnd Replay, 1979

Lowest: Not recorded

Record Receipts: Not available

WATLING STREET
First game: v Altrincham, 27.8.1988
First floodlit game: v Welling United, 7.5.1988

Season Tickets:
Details not available at the time of going to Press

Executive Box Season Tickets: N/A

Cost of Stand Tickets:
Details not available at the time of going to Press

Match and Ticket Information: Match days 0332-288371 – Hotline 0898 800691 (club information) Match enquiries (during week) 0622 754403

Car Parking: Limited inner but ample parking near ground

Nearest Railway Station: Dartford (bus 10 mins), walking 25 minutes

How to get to the ground

Leave Dartford Tunnel approach road, following signs to Dartford

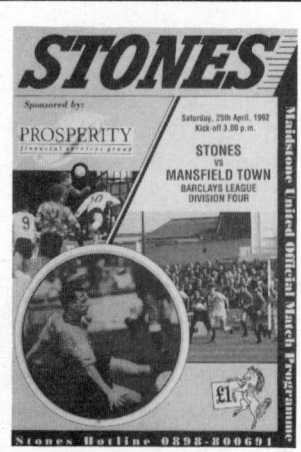

Value Rating: ★ ★

Programme Editor: M Evans

Price of 1992-93 Programme: £1
Number of Pages: 32
Subscriptions: All home games (Tel: 0622 754403)

Local Newspapers: Kent Messenger, Kentish Times, Maidstone Star, Adscene

Local Radio Stations: Invicta Sound, Radio Kent, R.T.M.

Chairman
P J Swales

Vice-Chairman
F Pye

Directors
I L G Niven, FBII
C B Muir OBE   M T Horwich
A Thomas   G Doyle MBI.I
W A Miles,   B Turnbull
J Greibach

Honorary Presidents
S S Rose
A E Alexander

Secretary
J B Halford(061-226 1191/2/3)

Commercial Manager
Phil Critchley (061-2261191)

Manager
Peter Reid

Assistant Manager
Sam Ellis

Youth & Reserve Team Coaches
Tony Book/Terry Darracott/Colin Bell

Youth Development Officer
Ken Barnes/Terr Farrell

Physiotherapist
Eamon Salmon

Groundsman
S Gibson

Club Statistician for the Directory
Ray Goble

PETER Reid can look back with pride over the first full season in charge of a First Division soccer club.

The Maine Road boss may have been plunged in at the deep end when he picked up the reins from Howard Kendall around seventeen months ago.

But there was never any danger of Reid sinking. In fact the Blues manager has visibly grown in stature and authority this season during which time his reputation as being one of the most astute young bosses in the country has risen with every passing week.

And that's hardly surprising when you consider how Reid has coaxed and cajoled his players through a season in which the Blues have been confirmed – on merit – as a major force in the First Division once again.

The Maine Road fans will be understandably disappointed that a European place next season has slipped through City's fingers when it was there for the taking less than two months ago.

A glance at the current season as a whole shows how close Reid has already come to building a team which can compete realistically with the best in the land. After a barn-storming start to the campaign which took the Blues to top spot by the end of August, a run of three successive defeats against Leeds, Sheffield Wednesday and Everton saw Reid's side tumble to 10th place and bring out the cynics with their prediction that the slide would lead to a battle against relegation.

That slide never materialised. In fact Reid galvanised his troops to the extent that his side were back in third place by the middle of November.

It speaks volumes for the way in which the City boss has utilised his limited resources that four months later only Leeds United and Manchester United were keeping the Blues off top spot in the First Division. The fortunes of Reid's side slumped during miserable March . . . that cannot be denied. But City's season was alive and kicking right up to the last match at Oldham Athletic.

At no stage has there been a threat of relegation so at the very least they have consolidated their position in the First Division and given themselves a solid base from which to build upon.

It's in the Cup competitions that City have been most disappointing, going out in the early rounds.

The Reserves and Youth teams both had a reasonably good season.

Ray Goble

Back row L-R: David White, David Brightwell, Martyn Margetson, Tony Coton, Andy Hill, Mark Brennan. **Middle row:** Eamonn Salmon (Physiotherapist), Tony Book (First Team Coach), Rick Holden, Garry Flitcroft, Michael Vonk, Niall Quinn, Paul Lake, Adrian Mike, Sam Ellis (Asst. Manager). **Front row:** Ian Brightwell, Steve McMahon, Keith Curle, Peter Reid (player/manager), Fitzroy Simpson, Michael Quigley, Mike Sheron.

MANCHESTER CITY

DIVISION ONE: 5th   **FA CUP:** 3rd RND   **RUMBELOWS CUP:** 4th RND   **ZDS CUP:** 2nd RND

M	DATE		COMP.	VEN	OPPONENTS	RESULT		H/T	LGE POS	GOALSCORERS/GOAL TIMES	ATTEN-DANCE
1	A	17	BL	A	Coventry City	W	1-0	1-0		Quinn 16	(18,013)
2		21	BL	H	Liverpool	W	2-1	1-0		White 29, 65	37,322
3		24	BL	H	Crystal Palace	W	3-2	2-1	1	Brennan 40, 85, White 45	28,028
4		28	BL	A	Norwich City	D	0-0	0-0	2		(15,376)
5		31	BL	A	Arsenal	L	1-2	1-0	3	I Brightwell 31	(35,009)
6	S	4	BL	H	Nottingham Forest	W	2-1	1-0	2	Quinn 39, Hill 85	29,146
7		7	BL	A	Leeds United	L	0-3	0-2	3		(29,986)
8		14	BL	H	Sheffield Wed.	L	0-1	0-0	7		29,453
9		17	BL	H	Everton	L	0-1	0-0	10		27,509
10		21	BL	A	West Ham United	W	2-1	0-0	6	Redmond 76, Hendry 90	(25,588)
11		25	RC 2/1	H	**Chester City**	W	3-1	0-0		**Quinn 57, White 74, 78**	10,987
12		28	BL	H	Oldham Athletic	L	1-2	1-0	8	White 19	31,271
13	O	6	BL	A	Notts County	W	3-1	0-0	6	Sheron 52, Allen 69, 71	(11,878)
14		8	RC 2/2	A	**Chester City**	W	3-0	1-0		**Allen 41, Sheron 60, Brennan 68**	(4,146)
15		19	BL	A	Tottenham Hotspur	W	1-0	0-0	3	Quinn 77	(30,502)
16		23	ZDS 2	A	**Sheffield Wed.**	L	2-3	1-1		**Hendry 26, 79**	(7,951)
17		26	BL	H	Sheffield United	W	3-2	2-2	3	Sheron 22, Quinn 37, Hughes 76	24,495
18		29	RC 3	H	**Queens Park R.**	D	0-0	0-0			15,512
19	N	2	BL	A	Southampton	W	3-0	1-0	3	Quinn 10, Sheron 47, Gittens (og) 59	(13,933)
20		16	BL	H	Manchester United	D	0-0	0-0	3		38,180
21		20	RC 3R	A	**Queens Park R.**	W	3-1	1-1		**Heath 10, 63, Quinn 74**	(11,033)
22		23	BL	A	Luton Town	D	2-2	0-1	3	Curle 46, Quinn 60	(10,031)
23		30	BL	H	Wimbledon	D	0-0	0-0	3		22,429
24	D	3	RC 4	A	**Middlesbrough**	L	1-2	0-0		**White 88**	(17,286)
25		7	BL	A	Aston Villa	L	1-3	0-2	4	White 65	(26,265)
26		14	BL	H	Queens Park R.	D	2-2	2-0	4	White 13, Curle 25	21,437
27		21	BL	A	Liverpool	D	2-2	0-1	5	White 48, 55	(36,743)
28		26	BL	H	Norwich City	W	2-1	2-1	4	Quinn 28, White 45	28,164
29		28	BL	H	Arsenal	W	1-0	0-0	4	White 70	32,325
30	J	1	BL	A	Chelsea	D	1-1	0-0	4	Sheron 90	(18,196)
31		4	FAC 3	A	**Middlesbrough**	L	1-2	1-0		**Reid 25**	(21,174)
32		11	BL	A	Crystal Palace	D	1-1	0-0	4	Curle 76	(14,766)
33		18	BL	H	Coventry City	W	1-0	0-0	4	White 51	23,005
34	F	1	BL	A	Tottenham Hotspur	W	1-0	1-0	4	White 28	30,123
35		8	BL	A	Sheffield United	L	2-4	1-3	5	Curle 21, Hill 47	(25,893)
36		15	BL	H	Luton Town	W	*4-0*	1-0	3	White 13, 48, Hill 47, Heath 77	22,137
37		22	BL	A	Wimbledon	L	1-2	0-2	3	Sheron 56	(5,082)
38		29	BL	H	Aston Villa	W	2-0	1-0	3	Quinn 3, White 75	28,288
39	M	7	BL	A	Queens Park R.	L	*0-4*	0-2	4		(10,779)
40		15	BL	H	Southampton	L	0-1	0-1	4		24,265
41		21	BL	A	Nottingham Forest	L	0-2	0-0	5		(24,115)
42		28	BL	H	Chelsea	D	0-0	0-0	6		23,663
43	A	4	BL	H	Leeds United	W	*4-0*	2-0	6	Hill 11, Sheron 34, Quinn 61, Brennan 88	30,239
44		7	BL	A	Manchester United	D	1-1	0-1	6	Curle 61	(46,781)
45		11	BL	A	Sheffield Wed.	L	0-2	0-0	6		(32,138)
46		18	BL	H	West Ham United	W	2-0	1-0	5	Pointon 1, Clarke 77	25,601
47		20	BL	A	Everton	W	2-1	2-1	5	Quinn 1, 23	(21,101)
48		25	BL	H	Notts County	W	2-0	1-0	5	Simpson 33, Quinn 57	23,426
49	M	2	BL	A	Oldham Athletic	W	5-2	2-1	5	Mike 16, White 3 (31, 62, 68), Sheron 67	(18,588)

Best Home League Attendance: 38,180 v Manchester United   **Smallest:** 21,437 v Queens Park Rangers   **Av Home Att:** 27,643

Goal Scorers: **Compared with 90-91:** -230

League (61): White 18, Quinn 12, Sheron 7, Curle 5, Hill 4, Brennan 3, Allen 2, Hughes, Mike, Redmond, Opponents, Heath, I Brightwell
Simpson, Hendry, Clarke, Pointon

R/lows C (10): White 3, Heath 2, Quinn 2, Allen, Sheron, Brennan
FA Cup (1): Reid
ZDS Cup (2): Hendry 2

Margetson M.	Hill A.	Pointon N.	Reid P.	Curle K.	Redmond S.	White D.	Brightwell I.	Quinn N.	Megson G.	Brennan M.	Heath A.	Coton A.	Hendry E.	Hughes M.	Sheron M.	Dibble A.	Allen C.	McMahon S.	Brightwell D.	Simpson F.	Quigley M.	Hoekman D.	Vonk M.	Clarke W.	Mike A.	Referee	
1	2	3	4	5	6	7	8	9	10	11	12		S													D Elleray	1
	2	3	4*	5	6	7	8	9	10	11	12	1	S													P Vanes	2
	2	3	4	5	6*	7	8	9	10*	11	12	1	14													R Hart	3
	2	3	4	5	6	7	8		10	11	9	1			S											A Buksh	4
	2	3	4*	5	6	7	8	9	10	11•	12	1	14													B Hill	5
	2	3	4	5	6	7	8	9	10	11	S	1	S													K Cooper	6
	2	3	4	5	6	7	8	9	10	11*	12	1	S													I Cruikshanks	7
	2	3	4	5	6	7	8	9	10	11*	12	1	S													J Watson	8
	2•	3	4*	5	6	7		9	10		8	1	14	11	12											M Reed	9
	2	3		5	6	7	4	9	10		8	1	14	11•	S											K Barrett	10
	2	3		5	6	7	4	9	10		8	1	S	11	S											S Bell	11
	2*	3		5•	6	7	4	9	10		8		14	11	12	1										S Lodge	12
		3	4		6	7		9	10	2*	8	1		11•	5	12	14									A Ward	13
	2	3		6	5	7	4	9	10•		8	1		11	S		14									J Rushton	14
	2	3	4	5	6	7		9	10		8	1		11	S											M Bodenham	15
1		3		5	6	7	4	9	10	2*	8			11	S											P Wright	16
	2	3	4	5	6	7		9	10		8	1		11	S											R Lewis	17
	2	3	4	5	6			9	10		8•	1	14	11	7*											G Ashby	18
	2	3	4	5	6			9•	10		8	1	14	11	7	S										R Gifford	19
	2	3	4•	5	6	7*		9	10		8	1		11	12		14									K Hackett	20
	2	3		5	6	7	4	9	10		8	1		11	S		S									D Axcell	21
1	2	3		5	6†	7*	4	9	10		8			11	12		S									J Key	22
	2•	3		5	6	7	4*	9	10		8	1		11	12		14									K Lupton	23
	2	3		5	6	7	4•	9	10		8	1		11*	12		14									W Burns	24
	2	3		5		7	4	9	10		8	1		11*	6		12									R Groves	25
	2	3		5	6	7	4	9	10		8	1		11	S		S									K Cooper	26
		3	4	5	6	7		9	10	2	8	1		11				S								D Phillips	27
		3	4	5	6	7		9	12	2	8	1		11	S			10*								K Redfern	28
	2	3	4	5	6	7		9	10	12	8	1		11	S											J Rushton	29
		3	4•	5	6	7		9	10	2	8*			11	12	1	14									J Carter	30
		3	4	5	6	7		9	12	2•	8	1		11			14	10*								M Reed	31
		3	4•	5	6	7		9	10	2	8	1		11•	12		14									R Wiseman	32
	2	3*	4	5	6	7	8	S				1		11	9			10	12							M Peck	33
	2	3	4*	5	6	7	8	S				1		11	9			10	12							V Callow	34
	2	3	4	5	6*	7	8	9			14	1		11*	12			10								A Buksh	35
	2	3	4•	5	6	7	8	9			14	1		11*	12			10								K Breen	36
	2	3	4	5	6•	7	8*	9				1		11	12			10	14							G Courtney	37
	2	3	4	5		7	12	9			8	1		11*	S			10	6							C Wilkes	38
	2	3	4	5		7	S	9			8•	1		11				10	6	14						L James	39
	2	3	4•	5		7	12	9			8	1		11				10	6*	14						R Hart	40
1	2		4*	5•	6	7	3	9			8			11				10		14	12					A Wilkie	41
	2	3	S		6	7	4*	9			8	1		11				10					5		12	R Nixon	42
	2	3	S	5	12	7	4	9*			8	1		11				10					6			J Watson	43
	2	3	14	5	12	7	4*	9			8	1		11				10•					6			J Worrall	44
	2	3	14	5		7	4•	9			8	1		11				10*					6		12	D Elleray	45
	2*	3	S	5		7	4	9			8	1		11				10					6		12	M Peck	46
		3	4•	5		7	8*	9		2	14	1		11				10					6		12	D Allison	47
	2	3		5	S	7	S	9			8	1		11						4			6		10	J Key	48
	2	3		5	S	7	S	9			8	1		11						4			6		10	A Gunn	49
3	36	39	29	40	31	39	36	35	18	13	20	37		24	20	2		18	3	9			8		2	**League Appearances**	
		2				4		4		8		6		9		3		1	2	5	1	1			5	**Substitute Appearances**	
5	5	1	4	5	3	5	4	3	2	5	5	0+1	5	2+1		1+1		1		0+2						**R/lows Appearances**	
1	1	1	1	1	1	1	1	0+1		1	1	1		1				1								**FA Cup Appearances**	
1	1	1	1	1	1	1	1		1	1		1		1				1					1			**ZDS Cup Appearances**	

Also Played: Posn.(Game): Mauge 12(16), G Flitcroft S(25)

Players on Loan: Mauge (Bury)

† = Sent Off

MANCHESTER CITY

Club Colours: Sky blue shirts, white shorts, sky blue stockings.
Change Colours: Red/black small squared shirts, black/red trim shorts, black stockings.
Reserves League: Pontins Central League Division 1

COMPETITIONS

Div. 1	Div. 2	Eur Cup	ECWC	EUFA	Texaco
99-02	92-99	68-69	69-70	72-73	71-72
03-09	02-03		70-71	76-77	74-75
10-26	09-10			77-78	
28-38	26-28			78-79	**A/Ital**
47-50	38-47				70-71
51-63	50-51				
66-83	63-66				**A/Scot**
85-87	83-85				75-76
89-	87-89				

HONOURS

Div. 1	Div. 2	FA Cup	Lge Cup	ECWC	C/Sh'ld
36-37	98-99	03-04	69-70	69-70	1937
67-68	02-03	33-34	75-76		1968
	09-10	55-56			1972
	27-28	68-69			
	46-47				
	65-66				

MOST APPEARANCES: ALAN OAKES 672+4 (1959-76)

Year	League	FAC	Lge C	Eur C	ECWC	EUFA
59-60	18	1				
60-61	22					
61-62	25					
62-63	34	2	4			
63-64	41	1	6			
64-65	41	2	1			
65-66	41	8	2			
66-67	39	6	2			
67-68	41	4	4			
68-69	39	7	3	2		
69-70	40	2	7		9	
70-71	30	3	1		4	
71-72	31+1	2				
72-73	13+1		0+1			2
73-74	28		5			
74-75	40	1	2			
75-76	38+1	2	9			
	561+3	41	46+1	2	13	2

Also: 2 A/Ital Cup 70-71; 3 Texaco 74-75; 3 A/Scot 75-76

Previous holder: Bert Trautmann 508 (1949-63)

MOST GOALS IN A CAREER: ERIC BROOK 177 (27-39)

Season	League	FA Cup
1927-28	2	
1928-29	14	
1929-30	16	1
1930-31	16	
1931-32	10	3
1932-33	15	6
1933-34	8	3
1934-35	17	
1935-36	13	3
1936-37	20	2
1937-38	16	1
1938-39	11	
Total	**158**	**19**

Previous holder: Tom Johnson, 158 Lge, 6 FAC (1919-29)

MANAGERS

Name	Seasons	Best	Worst
W Furniss	1892-93	5(2)	5(2)
J Parlby	1893-95	9(2)	13(2)
S Ormrod	1895-02	7(1)	6(2)
T Maley	1902-06	2(1)	1(2)
H W Newbould	1906-12	3(1)	1(2)
J Magnell	1912-24	2(1)	21(1)
D Ashworth	1924-26	10(1)	21(1)
P Hodge	1926-32	3(1)	3(2)
W Wild	1932-46	1(1)	5(2)
S Cowan	1946-47	1(2)	1(2)
J Thompson	1947-50	7(1)	21(1)
L McDowell	1950-63	4(1)	2(2)
G Poyser	1963-65	6(2)	11(2)
J Mercer	1965-72	1(1)	1(2)
M Allison	1972-73	4(1)	11(1)
J Hart	1973		
R Saunders	1973-74	14(1)	14(1)
T Book	1974-79	2(1)	15(1)
M Allison	1979-80	17(1)	17(1)
J Bond	1980-83	10(1)	20(1)
J Benson	1983		
W McNeill	1983-86	15(1)	4(2)
J Frizzell	1986-87	21(1)	21(1)
M Machin	1987-89	2(2)	9(2)
H Kendall	1989-90	14(1)	14(1)
P Reid	1990-	5(1)	5(1)

HIGHEST TRANSFER FEE RECEIVED

Amount	Club	Player	Date
£1,700,000	Tottenham H.	Paul Stewart	6/88
£900,000	Everton	Mark Ward	6/91
£800,000	Sampdoria	Trevor Francis	7/82
£750,000	Blackburn Rovers	Colin Hendry	10/91

HIGHEST TRANSFER FEE PAID

Amount	Club	Player	Date
£2,500,000	Wimbledon	Keith Curle	8/91
£1,150,000	Wolverhampton W	Steve Daley	9/79
£1,000,000	Bordeaux	Clive Allen	7/89
£750,000	Bournemouth	Ian Bishop	7/89

LONGEST LEAGUE RUNS

of undefeated matches:	22 (9.11.1946-3.5.1947)
	(26.12.1936-1.5.1937)
of undefeated home matches:	41 (1.1.1920-3.12.1921)
without home win:	9 (26.12.1979-7.4.1980)
of league wins:	9 (13.4.1912-28.9.1912)
of league defeats:	6 (10.9.1910-8.10.1910)
	(16.4.1960-24.8.1960)
of league matches without a win:	17 (26.12.1979-7.4.1980)
of undefeated away matches:	12 (7.12.1946-26.5.1947)
without an away win:	34 (11.2.1986-17.10.1987)
of home wins:	16 (13.11.1920-27.8.1921)
of away wins:	6 (27.12.1902-14.4.1903)

PREVIOUS NAME
Ardwick F.C. 1887-95 (an amalgamation of West Gorton and Gorton Athletic)

PREVIOUS LEAGUES
Football Alliance

BIGGEST VICTORIES
League: 10-0 v Darwen, Division 2, 1.4.1899
F.A. Cup: 10-1 v Swindon Town, Round 4, 21.9.1930
9-0 v Gateshead, Round 3, 1932-33
League Cup: 6-0 v Scunthorpe, Round 2, 10.9.1974
6-0 v Torquay, Round 2, 25.10.1983.
Europe: 5-0 v Lierske, Round 2, 1969-70.

BIGGEST DEFEATS
League: 1-9 v Everton, Division 1, 3.9.1908
0-8 v Wolverhampton Wndrs, Division 1, 23.12.1933
F.A. Cup: 0-6 v Preston North End, 30.1.1897
2-8 v Bradford Park Avenue (h), Round 4, 30.1.1946
League Cup: 0-6 v Birmingham City, Round 5, 1962-63
Europe: No more than 2 goals

MOST POINTS
3 points a win: 82, Division 2, 1988-89
2 points a win: 62, Division 2, 1946-47

MOST GOALS
108, 1926-27, Division 2.
Johnson 25, Hicks 21, Roberts 14, W Cowan 11, Austin 10, Barrass 7, Broadhurst 7, Bell 4, McMullan 3, S Cowan 2, Gibson 2, Pringle 1, og 1.

MOST GOALS IN A MATCH
6. Dennis Law v Luton, FA Cup 4th Round, 28.1.1961 (match abandoned when score was 6-2)
5. Tom Johnson v Everton (a), 6-2, Division 1, 15.9.1928
5. R.S. Marshall v Swindon T, 10-1, FA Cup Rnd 4, 29.1.1930
5. George Smith v Newport, 5-1, Division 2, 14.6.1947

MOST GOALS IN A SEASON
Tom Johnson, 38, Division 2, 1928-29.
5 goals once = 5, 3 goals once = 3, 2 goals 8 times = 16, 1 goal 14 times = 14.
Previous holder: F Roberts 31.

MOST FIRST CLASS MATCHES IN A SEASON
62 (42 League, 2 FA Cup, 7 League Cup, 1 Charity Shield, 10 European Cup Winners Cup) 1969-70

MOST LEAGUE GOALS CONCEDED
102, Division 1, 1962-63

MOST LEAGUE WINS
26, Division 2, 1946-47; Div 1, 1967-68

MOST LEAGUE DRAWS
17, Division 1, 1970-71

MOST LEAGUE DEFEATS
22, Division 1, 1958-59; Div 1, 1959-60

OLDEST PLAYER
Billy Meredith, 49 years, 245 days v Newcastle Utd., FAC S/Final, 29.3.1924.

YOUNGEST PLAYER
Glyn Pardoe, 15 years 314 days v Birmingham City, Division 1. 11.4.1961.

MOST CAPPED PLAYER
Colin Bell (England) 48

BEST PERFORMANCES BY MANCHESTER CITY

League: 1902-03: Matches played 34, Won 25, Drawn 4, Lost 5, Goals for 95, Goals against 29, Points 54. First in Division 2.

Highest: 1936-37, 1937-38: 1st in Division 1.

F.A. Cup: 1968-69: 3rd rnd. Luton Town 1-0; 4th rnd. Newcastle Utd. 0-0, 2-0; 5th rnd. Blackburn Rovers 4-1; 6th rnd. Tottenham Hotspur 1-0; Semi-Final Everton 1-0; Final Leicester City 1-0.

League Cup: 1969-70: 2nd rnd. Southport 3-0; 3rd rnd. Liverpool 3-2; 4th rnd Everton 2-0; 5th rnd. Queens Park Rangers 3-0; Semi-Final Manchester Utd. 2-1, 2-2; Final West Bromwich Albion 2-1.

1975-76: 2nd rnd. Norwich City 1-1, 2-2, 6-1; 3rd rnd. Nottingham Forest 2-1; 4th rnd. Manchester Utd. 4-0; 5th rnd. Mansfield Town 4-2; Semi-Final Middlesbrough 0-1, 4-0; Final Newcastle Utd. 2-1.

Europe ECWC: 1969-70: 1st rnd. Athletico Bilbao 3-3, 3-0; 2nd rnd. Lierske 3-0, 5-0; 3rd rnd. Academica Colmbra 0-0, 1-0; Semi-Final Schalke 04 0-1, 5-1; Final Gornick Zagrze 2-1.

DIVISIONAL RECORDS

	Played	Won	Drawn	Lost	For	Against	Points
DIVISION 1	2772	1061	677	1034	4277	4242	2895
DIVISION 2	786	402	173	211	1652	1072	1060
TOTALS	**3558**	**1463**	**850**	**1245**	**5929**	**5314**	**3955**

MANCHESTER CITY

PLAYERS NAME / Honours	Ht	Wt	Birthdate	Birthplace / Transfers	Contract Date	Clubs	League	L/Cup	FA Cup	Other	Lg	L/C	FAC	Oth
GOALKEEPERS														
Tony Coton	6.2	13.7	19.05.61	Tamworth		Nato								
					13.10.78	Birmingham City	94	10	10					
Loan Hereford United (01.10.79)				£300,000	27.09.84	Watford	233	18	32	8				
				£1,000,000	20.07.90	Manchester City	70	8	4	3				
Andy Dibble	6.2	13.7	08.05.65	Cwmbran	27.08.82	Cardiff City (A)	62	4	4					
W:3,u21.3,Y,S; LC'88					16.07.84	Luton Town	30	4	1	1				
Loan Sunderland 12lg				Loan	26.03.87	Huddersfield Town	5							
				£240,000	01.07.88	Manchester City	74	6	5	2				
				Loan	20.02.91	Middlesbrough	19			2				
Loan Bolton W. (06.09.91) 13lg 1gl				Loan	27.02.92	West Brom A	9							
Martyn Margetson					05.07.90	Manchester City (T)	5	0+1		1				
DEFENDERS														
David Brightwell	6.2	12.7	07.01.71	Lutterworth	11.04.88	Manchester City (T)	3+1							
				Loan	22.03.91	Chester City	6							
Keith Curle	6.0	12.0	14.11.63	Bristol	20.11.81	Bristol Rovers (A)	21+11	3	1		4			
E:3, B. ; FRT'86; SC'88				£5,000	04.11.83	Torquay Utd	16		1	1	5		1	
				£10,000	03.03.84	Bristol City	113+8	7+1	5	14+1	1			
				£150,000	23.10.87	Reading	40	8	5					
				£500,000	21.10.88	Wimbledon	91+2	7	5	6	3			1
				£2,500,000	14.08.91	Manchester City	40	4	1	1	5			
Andy Hill	5.11	12.0	20.01.65	Maltby	26.01.83	Manchester Utd. (A)								
E: Y.2				Free	04.07.84	Bury	264	22	12	19	10	1		1
				£200,000	21.12.90	Manchester City	43+1	5		1	5			
Nicholas Limber	5.10	10.10	23.01.74			Doncaster Rovers (T)	13			1+1	1			1
Doncaster				£75,000	24.01.92	Manchester City								
MIDFIELD														
Mark Brennan	5.9	11.1	04.10.65	Rossendale	07.04.83	Ipswich Town (A)	165+3	21+1	12	11	19	2	3	1
E:Y4,u21.5				£375,000	27.07.88	Middlesbrough	61+4	6	4	8	6			1
				£500,000	25.07.90	Manchester City	25+4	4	1	2	6	1		
Ian Brightwell	5.10	11.7	09.04.68	Lutterworth		Congleton								
E;u21.4,u19.3				Free	07.05.86	Manchester City	148+28	16+2	8+4	4+3	15		1	
Gary Flitcroft	5.10		06.11.72		02.07.91	Manchester City								
				Loan	05.03.92	Bury	12							
David W Kerr	5.11	11.2	06.09.74		10.09.91	Manchester City (T)								
Dumfris														
Paul Lake	6.0	12.2	28.10.68	Manchester	02.06.87	Manchester City (T)	104+4	10	9	5	7	1	2	1
E:B.1,u21.5														
Stephen Lomas	6.0	11.10	18.01.74		22.01.91	Manchester City								
Hanover (Ger)														
Steve McMahon	5.9	12.1	20.08.61	Liverpool	29.08.79	Everton (A)	99+1	11	9		11	3		
E:17,u21.6,B.2; Div1'86'88'90;FAC'86'89				£175,000	20.05.83	Aston Villa	74+1	9	3	4	7			
CS'86'88'89				£375,000	12.09.85	Liverpool	202+2	27	30	16	29	13	7	1
				£900,000	24.12.91	Manchester City	18		1					
Peter Reid	5.8	10.8	20.06.56	Liverpool	01.05.74	Bour (A)	222+3	18+1	17		22	1	1	
E:13,u21.6,Div2'78,CS'84'85'87,Div1'85'87,FAC'86,CWC'85				£22,188	Everton	155+4	23+2	35	15	8	1	3	1
				Free	09.02.89	Q.P.R	29	2+1			1			
				Free	15.12.89	Manchester City	75+4	3	5		1		1	
FORWARDS														
Sean Harkin	5.2	9.10	09.12.75		03.01.91	Manchester City								
Londondery														
Richard Holden	5.11	12.0	09.09.64	Skipton		Burnley	0+1							
				f	24.09.86	Halifax Town	66+1	2	7	8	12			
				£125,000	24.03.88	Watford	42	2	6	3+1	8		1	1
				£165,000	18.08.89	Oldham Ath	87	12	11	2	14	3	2	
				£900,000	10.07.92	Manchester City								
Niall Quinn	6.4	12.4	06.10.66	Dublin	30.11.83	Arsenal	59+8	14+2	8+1	0+1	14	4	2	
Ei:32,B.1,u23.1,u21.5,Y,Lc'87				£800,000	21.03.90	Manchester City	82	7	3	3	36	2	1	1
Fitzroy Simpson	5.6	10.4	26.02.70	Bradford-on-Avon	06.07.88	Swindon Town (T)	49+26	9+2		1+2	5	1		
				£500,000	06.03.92	Manchester City	38+3	6	2+1	2	5			
David White	6.1	12.9	30.10.67	Manchester	07.11.85	Manchester City (A)	215+12	17+2	17	9	62	9	1	2
E:u19.1,u21.6,B.1														
ADDITIONAL CONTRACT PLAYERS														
Ian McGinty					16.09.89	Manchester City								
(F) Adrian Mike	6.0	11.00	16.11.73	Manchester		Manchester City	2				1			
(M) Michael Quigley	5.7	9.13	02.10.70	Manchester	01.07.89	Manchester City (T)	0+5			1				
(F) Michael Sheron	5.9	10.10	11.01.72		05.07.90	Manchester City (T)	20+9	2+1		1	7	1		
Liverpool				Loan	28.03.91	Bury	1+4			4	1			
(D) Garry Sliney	5.10	10.10	02.09.73		12.12.90	Manchester City								
Dublin														
(F) Scott L Thomas	5.11	11.4	30.10.74		26.03.92	Manchester City (T)								
Bury														
(MF) Michael Vonk	6.2	12.2	28.10.68			SVV Dordrecht								
Alkmar (Hol)				£500,000	11.03.92	Manchester City	8+1							
(F) Michael Wallace	5.8	11.10	05.10.70	Bolton	01.07.89	Manchester City (T)								

MANCHESTER CITY

RECORD WIN & LOSS AGAINST EACH CLUB IN CURRENT DIVISION
(Where a score has occured on several occasions the most recent is given)

Club	Rec. Win	Season	Rec. Loss	Season
ARSENAL	4-0	1912-13 (away)	7-3	1956-57
ASTON VILLA	5-0	1935-36	7-1	1900-01
BLACKBURN ROVERS	8-2	1919-20	4-0	1988-89
CHELSEA	6-2	1977-78	6-3	1960-61
COVENTRY CITY	5-1	1985-86	4-0	1982-83
CRYSTAL PALACE	4-0	1971-72	3-1	1987-88 (home)
EVERTON	6-2	1957-58	9-1	1906-07
IPSWICH TOWN	4-0	1988-89	4-0	1979-80
LEEDS UNITED	6-2	1937-38	4-1	1928-29
LIVERPOOL	6-0	1935-36	5-0	1981-82 (home)
MANCHESTER UNITED	6-1	1925-26 (away)	5-1	1960-61
MIDDLESBROUGH	6-0	1935-36	6-1	1937-38 (home)
NORWICH CITY	5-0	1963-64	4-1	1964-65
NOTTINGHAM FOREST	5-0	1905-06	4-0	1979-80
OLDHAM ATHLETIC	5-2	1991-92 (away)	4-1	1911-12
QUEENS PARK RANGERS	5-2	1950-51	4-0	1991-92
SHEFFIELD UNITED	5-0	1924-25 (away)	8-3	1925-26
SHEFFIELD WEDNESDAY	4-0	1911-12	5-1	1936-37
SOUTHAMPTON	6-1	1927-28	4-1	1982-83
TOTTENHAM HOTSPUR	5-0	1976-77	5-1	1957-58
WIMBLEDON	3-0	1984-85	2-1	1991-92

MANAGER: PETER REID

DATE OF BIRTH: 20.06.56   **PLACE OF BIRTH:** Liverpool

DATE OF APPOINTMENT: 15.11.1990

PREVIOUS CLUBS
as Manager:
as Coach:
as Player: Bolton W, Everton, Q.P.R., Manchester City

HONOURS
as Manager:
as Asst. Man./Coach:
as Player: (Everton): FA Cup, 2 League Championships, European Cup Winners Cup
International: 13 England Caps

Value Rating: ★ ★ ★ ★

Programme Editor: Mike Beddow

Price of 1992-93 Programme: £1.20
Number of Pages: 32
Subscriptions: £19 (postage): (£3 extra abroad and Eire)

Local Newspapers: Manchester Evening News, Sunday Pink.

Local Radio Stations: BBC Radio Manchester, Piccadilly Radio.

Additional Publications on Club: A Complete Record 1887-1987 by Ray Goble, Breedon Books £14.95. City Handbook (released each season since 1987-88)

LEADING LEAGUE GOALSCORERS
SEASONS 1979-80 – 1991-92

1979-80	MICK ROBINSON	8		1980-81	KEVIN REEVES	12
1981-82	KEVIN REEVES	13		1982-83	DAVID CROSS	12
1983-84	DEREK PARLANE	16		1984-85	DAVID PHILLIPS	12
1985-86	MARK LILLIS	11		1986-87	IMRE VARADI	9
1987-88	PAUL STEWART	24		1988-89	PAUL MOULDEN	13
1989-90	CLIVE ALLEN	10		1990-91	NIALL QUINN	20

1991-92	**DAVID WHITE**	**18**

MAINE ROAD Moss Side, Manchester M14 7WN

Capacity: 34,400   **Covered Standing:** 16,388   **Seating:** 15,595

Tel: Ground: 061 226 1191   **Ticket Sales:** 061 226 2224   **Clubcall:** 0898 12 11 91

All premium rate calls (0898/0891) cost 36p per minute cheap rate and 48p per minute at all other times. Call costings correct at time of going to press.

GROUNDS
Clownes Street 1880-81; Kirkmanshulme C.C. 1881-82; Queens Road 1882-84; Pink Bank Lane 1884-87; Hyde Road 1887-1923; Maine Road 1923-

ATTENDANCES
Highest: 84,569 v Stoke City, FA Cup 6th Round, 3.3.1934 (Record outside London)

Lowest: 4,029 v Leeds Utd, Full Members Cup, 14.10.1985

RECORD RECEIPTS (with previous records):
£274,281 Liverpool v Manchester United, FA Cup Semi-Final Replay, 17.4.1985
£240,000 Liverpool v Everton, League Cup Final replay, March 1984
£165,000 Liverpool v Manchester United, FA Cup Semi-Final replay, 31.3.1979
£140,000 Everton v Liverpool, FA Cup Semi-Final, 23.4.1977
£70,000 Leeds United v Wolverhampton W., FA Cup Semi-Final, 7.4.1973

MAINE ROAD
First game: v Sheffield United, 2-1, 25.8.1923
First floodlit game: v Hearts, 14.10.1953

Season Tickets:
Stands: from £165 to £230, juv/OAP £140 to £170
Ground: £125, juv/OAP £85

Executive Box Season Tickets: Contact Club

Cost of Stand Tickets: Seats £10-£11 (no reductions)
Terraces: £7, juv/OAP £4

Match and Ticket Information: Advance booking 14 days prior to matches. Ticketcall – 0898 12 15 91

Car Parking: Kippax Street car park holds 400 vehicles (approx.) Some street parking is permitted, parking at local schools

Nearest Railway Station: Manchester Piccadilly (061-832 8353)

How to get to the ground

From North: Use Motorway M61 then M63 until Junction 9. Leave Motorway and follow signs Manchester A5103. In 2.8m at crossroads turn right in Claremont Road. In 0.4m turn right into Maine Road for Manchester City FC
From East: Use Motorway M61 until Junction 17 then A56 into Manchester. Follow signs Manchester Airport then turn left to join Motorway A57(M). Follow signs Birmingham to join A5103. Then in 1.3 miles turn left into Claremont Road. In 0.4m turn right into Maine Road for Manchester City FC
From South: Use Motorway M6 until Junction 19 then A556 and M56 until Junction 3. Keep forward A5103 S.P. Manchester. In 2.8m at crossroads turn right into Claremont Road. In 0.4m turn right into Maine Road for Manchester City FC
From West: Use Motorway M62 then M63 and route as from north. Or use M56 and route as from south

MANCHESTER UNITED   Premier

Formed: 1878   **Turned Professional:** 1885   **Ltd Co:** 1907

SPONSORED BY: Sharp Electronics (UK) Ltd   **NICKNAME:** The Red Devils

President
Sir Matt Busby CBE

Vice-Presidents
J A Gibson, W A Young
R L Edwards, J G Gulliver

Chairman
C M Edwards

Directors
J M Edelson, R Charlton CBE
E M Watkins, A M Midani
R L Olive, R P Launders

Secretary
Kenneth R Merrett (061-872 1661/2)

Assistant Secretary
K Ramsden

Commercial Manager
D A McGregor (061-872 3488)

Team Manager
Alex Ferguson

Reserve Team Coaches
Bryan 'Pop' Robson / Jimmy Ryan

Youth Team Coach
E Harrison

Cheif Scout
L Kershaw

Physiotherapist
J McGregor

Club Statistician for the Directory
Richard Facer

A superb start to the league campaign – 26 points won out of a possible 30 – and this, together with the fact that United sailed past the first hurdle in the Rumbelows and European Cup Winners Cup, comfortably beating Cambridge and Athinaikos respectively, made United firm favourites for their first title in 25 years.

The first trophy won was the European Super Cup with Brian McClair's goal sealing victory against Red Star Belgrade. Unfortunately for United they were knocked out in their other European competition, losing 4-1 on aggregate to Spanish giants, Athletico Madrid, but a run of five consecutive league wins just before Christmas and victories over Oldham (2-0) and Leeds (3-1) in the Rumbelows Cup fuelled speculation of further trophies to come.

United suffered a demoralising defeat at home to Q.R.R. (4-1) to start 1992 on a bad note, but another victory over Leeds, this time in the F.A. Cup, healed the wounds.

United also had the dubious honour of being the first Division One club to be knocked out of the F.A. Cup on penalties. The defeat, at the hands of Southampton, came after drawing 0-0 and 2-2. However, United still marched on in the Rumbelows Cup, reaching the final after beating Middlesbrough 2-1 on aggregate with goals coming from Lee Sharpe and the P.F.A. Young Player of the Year, Ryan Giggs, but United did stumble in the league, winning only two out of a possible nine games and Leeds took over at the top of the table.

United regained top spot, only 2 weeks later, by beating Norwich while Leeds stuttered, before going into the final of the Rumbelows Cup for the second consecutive year. Brian McClair, again the clubs top scorer, scored the only goal, enabling Steve Bruce (influential captain Bryan Robson was injured) to lift the trophy for the first time in the club's history and this, followed by a win against Southampton, sent morale sky high but a punishing schedule of five games in 10 days proved too much for United with only 4 points gained out of a possible 15. This, coupled with Leeds' winning took the championship to the penultimate game. United battled hard, but didn't have any luck and a Liverpool victory gave Leeds the title. To add insult to injury, Gary Pallister, the P.F.A. Player of the Year, injured his foot ruling him out of the European Championships.

Richard Facer

Back row L-R: Russell Beardsmore, Lee Martin, Lee Sharpe, Darren Ferguson, Ryan Giggs, Andrei Kanchelskis, Mike Phelan, Neil Webb. **Middle row:** Jim McGregor (Physio), Mark Robins, Brian McClair, Peter Schmeichel, Brian Kidd (Asst. Manager), Gary Walsh, Clayton Blackmore, Mark Hughes, Norman Davies (Kit Manager). **Front row:** Paul Parker, Denis Irwin, Paul Ince, Alex Ferguson (Manager), Bryan Robson, Gary Pallister, Steve Bruce, Danny Wallace.

MANCHESTER UNITED

DIVISION ONE: RUNNERS-UP **FA CUP:** 4th RND **RUMBELOWS CUP:** WINNERS **ECWC:** 2nd RND

M	DATE		COMP.	VEN	OPPONENTS	RESULT		H/T	LGE POS	GOALSCORERS/GOAL TIMES	ATTEN-DANCE
1	A	17	BL	H	Notts County	W	2-0	1-0	1	Hughes 40, Robson 57	46,278
2		21	BL	A	Aston Villa	W	1-0	1-0	1	Bruce (pen) 38	(39,995)
3		24	BL	A	Everton	D	0-0	0-0	2		(36,085)
4		27	BL	H	Oldham Athletic	W	1-0	0-0	1	McClair 85	42,078
5		31	BL	H	Leeds United	D	1-1	0-1	1	Robson 88	43,778
6	S	3	BL	A	Wimbledon	W	2-1	2-0	1	Blackmore 25, Pallister 43	(13,824)
7		7	BL	H	Norwich City	W	3-0	3-0	1	Irwin 20, McClair 23, Giggs 28	44,946
8		14	BL	A	Southampton	W	1-0	0-0	1	Hughes 48	(19,264)
9		18	ECWC1/1	A	**Athinaikos**	D	0-0	0-0			(11,000)
10		21	BL	H	Luton Town	W	5-0	1-0	1	Ince 23, Bruce (pen) 63, McClair 76, 80, Hughes 87	46,491
11		25	RC 1/2	H	**Cambridge United**	W	3-0	1-0		**Giggs 44, McClair 48, Bruce 66**	30,934
12		28	BL	A	Tottenham Hotspur	W	2-1	1-1	1	Hughes 21, Robson 85	(35,087)
13	O	2	ECWC1/2	H	**Athinaikos**	W	†2-0	0-0		**Hughes 109, McClair 111**	35,023
14		6	BL	H	Liverpool	D	0-0	0-0	1		44,946
15		9	RC 2/2	A	**Cambridge United**	D	1-1	1-0		**McClair 2**	(9,248)
16		19	BL	H	Arsenal	D	1-1	1-1	1	Bruce 44	46,594
17		23	ECWC2/1	A	**Athletico Madrid**	L	0-3	0-1			(50,000)
18		26	BL	A	Sheffield Wed.	L	2-3	2-1	2	McClair 17, 22	(38,260)
19		30	RC 3	H	**Portsmouth**	W	3-1	0-0		**Robins 59, 89, Robson 74**	29,543
20	N	2	BL	H	Sheffield United	W	2-0	1-0	1	Hoyland (og) 35, Kanchelskis 78	42,942
21		6	ECWC2/2	H	**Athletico Madrid**	D	1-1	1-0		**Hughes 4**	39,654
22		16	BL	A	Manchester City	D	0-0	0-0	2		(38,180)
23		19	ESC	H	**Red Star Belgrade**	W	1-0	0-0		**McClair 67**	22,110
24		23	BL	H	West Ham United	W	2-1	2-0	1	Giggs 15, Robson 42	47,185
25		30	BL	A	Crystal Palace	W	3-1	1-1	2	Webb 26, McClair 57, Kanchelskis 58	(29,017)
26	D	4	RC 4	H	**Oldham Athletic**	W	2-0	2-0		**McClair 10, Kanchelskis 25**	38,550
27		7	BL	A	Coventry City	W	4-0	3-0	1	Bruce 14, Webb 21, McClair 27, Hughes 81	42,549
28		15	BL	A	Chelsea	W	3-1	1-0	1	Irwin 19, McClair 57, Bruce (pen) 61	(23,120)
29		26	BL	A	Oldham Athletic	W	6-3	2-0	1	Irwin 2, 54, Kanchelskis 43, McClair 56, 59, Giggs 78	(18,947)
30		29	BL	A	Leeds United	D	1-1	0-0	1	Webb 46	(32,638)
31	J	1	BL	H	Queens Park R.	L	1-4	0-2	2	McClair 83	38,554
32		8	RC QF	A	**Leeds United**	W	3-1	1-1		**Blackmore 30, Kanchelskis 51, Giggs 55**	(28,886)
33		11	BL	H	Everton	W	1-0	0-0	1	Kanchelskis 56	46,619
34		15	FAC 3	A	**Leeds United**	W	1-0	1-0		**Hughes 44**	(31,819)
35		18	BL	A	Notts County	D	1-1	0-1	2	Blackmore (pen) 70	(21,055)
36		22	BL	H	Aston Villa	W	1-0	0-0	1	Hughes 48	45,022
37		27	FAC 4	A	**Southampton**	D	0-0	0-0			(19,506)
38	F	1	BL	A	Arsenal	D	1-1	1-1	2	McClair 27	(41,703)
39		5	FAC 4R	H	**Southampton**	D	†2-2	1-2		**Kanchelskis 42, McClair 89** (Lost 2-4 on pens)	33,414
40		8	BL	H	Sheffield Wed.	D	1-1	1-1	1	McClair 12	47,074
41		22	BL	H	Crystal Palace	W	2-0	1-0	1	Hughes 10, 49	46,347
42		26	BL	H	Chelsea	D	1-1	0-0	1	Hughes 87	44,872
43		29	BL	A	Coventry City	D	0-0	0-0	1		(23,967)
44	M	4	RC SF 1	A	**Middlesbrough**	D	0-0	0-0			(25,572)
45		11	RC SF 2	H	**Middlesbrough**	W	†2-1	1-0		**Sharpe 29, Giggs 106**	45,875
46		14	BL	A	Sheffield United	W	2-1	0-1	2	McClair 63, Blackmore 82	(30,183)
47		17	BL	A	Nottingham Forest	L	0-1	0-0	2		(28,062)
48		21	BL	H	Wimbledon	D	0-0	0-0	2		45,428
49		28	BL	A	Queens Park R.	D	0-0	0-0	2		(22,630)
50		31	BL	A	Norwich City	W	3-1	1-0	1	Ince 41, 59, McClair 66	(17,489)
51	A	7	BL	H	Manchester City	D	1-1	1-0	1	Giggs 20	46,781
52		12	RC Fin	N	**Nottingham Forest**	W	1-0	1-0		**McClair 15**	(76,810)
53		16	BL	H	Southampton	W	1-0	0-0	1	Kanchelskis 65	43,972
54		18	BL	A	Luton Town	D	1-1	1-0	1	Sharpe 24	(13,410)
55		20	BL	A	Nottingham Forest	L	1-2	1-1	1	McClair 36	47,567
56		22	BL	A	West Ham United	L	0-1	0-0	2		(24,197)
57		26	BL	A	Liverpool	L	0-2	0-1	2		(38,669)
58	M	2	BL	H	Tottenham Hotspur	W	3-1	1-0	2	McClair 38, Hughes 56, 58	44,595

Best Home League Attendance: 47,567 v Nottingham Forest **Smallest: 38,554 v Queens Park Rangers** **Av Home Att: 44,982**

Goal Scorers: **Compared with 90-91: +1,740**

League (63): McClair 18, Hughes 11, Bruce 5 (3 pens), Kanchelskis 5, Irwin 4, Robson 4, Giggs 4, Blackmore 3 (1 pen), Webb 3, Ince 3, Sharpe, Pallister, Opponents

R/lows C (15): McClair 4, Giggs 3, Kanchelskis 2, Robins 2, Sharpe, Bruce, Blackmore, Robson

FA Cup (3): Kanchelskis, Hughes, McClair

ECWC (3): Hughes 2, McClair

Euro Sup Cup (1): McClair

† = After extra-time

1991-92

Schmeichel P.	Irwin D.	Blackmore C.	Bruce S.	Parker P.	Pallister G.	Robson B.	Ince P.	McClair B.	Hughes M.	Giggs R.	Kanchelskis A.	Ferguson D.	Donaghy M.	Webb N.	Phelan M.	Robins M.	Beardsmore R.	Wallace D.	Walsh G.	Wratten P.	Sixsmith P.	Whitworth N.	Martin L.	Wilkinson I.	Sharpe L.	Referee	
1	2	3	4	6	12	7	8*	9	10	14	11			5•												G Courtney	1
1	2	3	4	6	S	7	8	9	10	S	11			5												K Cooper	2
1	2*	3•	4	6	12	7	8*	9	10	11	14			5•												J Key	3
1	3	12	4	2	6	7	8*	9	10	11			14	5•												J Worrall	4
1	3	11	4*	2	6	7	8•	9	10	14				5	12											K Redfern	5
1	12	11	4	2	6	7		9	10	S		3	8	5*												M James	6
1	3	12	4	2	6	7	8	9	10	11	8*			5•	14											V Callow	7
1	3	S	4		6	7	12	9	10	11	8*			5	2											G Pooley	8
1	3		4		6		8	9	10					5	2	7	11•	14	S	S	S	S				A Schmidhuber	9
1	3	9*	4		6	7	8	12	10	11			S	5	2											A Gunn	10
1		11	4		6	7	8	9	10	14			S	5*	2											A Dawson	11
1	3	14	4		6	7	8	9	10	11	5•			S	2											G Ashby	12
1			4		6	7	8	9	10		5			2	12	14	11*	S	S		S		3•			Lo Bello	13
1	3	5	4		6	7	8•	9	10	11	12		14	2*												M Reed	14
1	3	5	4		6*	7	8	9	10	12		2		14								11*	1			D Axcell	15
1	3	2	4		6	7	8	9	10	11	14			5•												T Holbrook	16
1	3		5	2	4	8*	7	9	10					6	11•	S	14		S	S			12			B Heinemann	17
1	3	10	4*	2	6	7		9		11	8		S	5	2								12			K Breen	18
1	3•	10	4	2	6	12		9		11	8		7	5*				14								R Groves	19
1		3	4	2	14	12	8*	9			11•	7		6	5			10								C Trussell	20
1		3	4	2	12	7		9	10	11				5	6•	8*	S	S	1				14	S		G Goethals	21
1	3	8	4		6	7	14	9	10	11	S			5*												K Hackett	22
1	2•	11	4		6		8	9	10	14	7			5	S	S	S						3			M Van der Ende	23
1	3	14	4	2•	6	7	S	9	10	11	8			5												M Peck	24
1	3•	14	4	2	6	7	S	9	10	11	8			5												P Durkin	25
1	3	14	4	2	6	7*	12	9	10	11•	8			5												P Don	26
1	3	14	4	2•	6		8	9	10	11	7		S	5												P Wright	27
1	3	14	4	2	6		8	9	10	11•	7			5	S											G Courtney	28
1	3•	14	4	2	6	7*	8	9	10	12	11			5												I Hendrick	29
1		3•	4	2	6		8	9	10	11	7*		12	5									14			R Nixon	30
1		3	4	2	6		8	9	10	14			S	5	7•								11			K Barratt	31
1		3	4	2	6		8	9	10	11*	7•		12	5									14			G Courtney	32
1		3*	4	2	6		8	9	10	11	7		12	5									S			T Holbrook	33
1	3	S	4	2	6	S	8	9	10	11	7			5												R Lewis	34
1	3	14•	4	2	6		8	9	10	11*	7			5		12										K Morton	35
1	3	S	4		6	7	8	9	10	S	11		2	5												D Allison	36
1	3	11*		2	6	7	8	9	10	12			4	5	S											D Elleray	37
1	3			2	6	7	8*	9	10	12	11		4	5	S											R Groves	38
1	3			2	6	7	8	9	12	10	11*	4•		5				14								D Elleray	39
1	3			2	6	7	8	9	10	2*	11	4		5*		12		14								R Milford	40
1	3		12		6	7	8	9	10	4	11•	2	5*			12										K Redfern	41
	3	14		12	6	7*	8	9	10	4	2	5							1							V Callow	42
	3	14			2	6		8	9	10	11•	7		4	5	S			1							R Hamer	43
1	3				2	6	7	8•	9	10	11		4*	5	12								14			B Nixon	44
1	3		4		2	6	7	8	9				5	S	14								10•			J Martin	45
1	3	14•	4	2	6	7	8	9			11		S	5									10			M Bailey	46
1	3	2	4		6		8	9	10*	14	12			5•	7								11			I Borrett	47
1	3	2	4		6		8	9	10	11	7			5•	S								14			M Peck	48
1	3		4		6	7		9	10	11	8•		2	5									14			J Martin	49
1	3	14			6		7•	9	10	S	5		2										11			M James	50
1	3	5*			6			9	10	7	12		2										11			J Worrall	51
1	3		4	2	6		8	9	10	11	7•			S	5								14			G Courtney	52
1	3		4	2	6		8*	9	10	11	7		12	5									S			K Cooper	53
1	3	14	4	2•				9	10*	7	12		2	5									11			M Bodenham	54
1	3	2	4		6			9	14	10	7		12	8•	5								11*			J Key	55
1	2	8*	4		6			9	10	7	12	14	3•		5								11			J Deakin	56
1	3	S	4		6*	7	8	9	10	11	5		2		12											R Gifford	57
1	3		4				8*	9	10	11	7	2	6	S	5								12			K Hackett	58
40	37	19	37	24	37	26	31	41	38	32	28	2	16	29	14	1		2							8	League Appearances	
1	14		2	3	1	2	1	1	6	6	2	4	2	4	1								1		6	Substitute Appearances	
6	7	4+1	7	6	8	5+1	6+1	8	6	6+2	4		3+1	6	2+1	0+3			1				1	1	1+3	R/lows Appearances	
3	3	1	3	1	3	3	2	2+1	2+1	2	2		2	3											0+1	FA Cup Appearances	
3	2	1	4	2	3+1	3	3	4	4	1	1		3	4		2+1	1+2	1+1	1				1+2			ECWC Appearances	
1	1	1	1		1		1	1	1	0+1	1		1										1			Euro Super Cup Apps.	

MANCHESTER UNITED

Club Colours: Red shirts with white trim, white shorts with red trim, black stockings
Change Colours: Blue shirts with black streaks, blue shorts, blue stockings
Reserves League: Pontins Central League Division 1

COMPETITIONS						
Div. 1	Div. 2	Euro C	ECWC	UEFA	Wat C	C/S'ld
92-94	94-06	56-57	63-64	64-65	1970	1908
06-22	22-25	57-58	77-78	76-77	1971	1911
25-31	31-36	65-66	83-84	80-81		1952
36-37	37-38	67-68	90-91	82-83		1956
38-74	74-75	68-69	91-92	84-85		1957
75-				92-93		1965
						1967
					1985	1977
					1990	1983

HONOURS					
Div. 1	Div. 2	FA Cup	Lge Cup	Euro C	C Shield
07-08	35-36	08-09	91-92	67-68	1908
10-11	74-75	47-48			1911
51-52		62-63			1952
55-56		76-77		ECWC	1956
56-57		82-83		1991	1957
64-65		84-85			1965*
66-67		89-90			1977*
				ESC	1983
				1991	1990*
					*shared

MOST APPEARANCES: BOBBY CHARLTON 756					
Year	League	FAC	Lge C	Europe	C/Sh'ld
1956-57	14	2		1	
1957-58	21	8		2	
1958-59	38	1			
1959-60	37	3			
1960-61	39	3			
1961-62	37	7			
1962-63	28	6			
1963-64	40	7		6	1
1964-65	41	7		11	
1965-66	38	7		8	1
1966-67	42	2			
1967-68	41	2		9	1
1968-69	32	6		8	
1969-70	40	9	8		
1970-71	42	2	6		
1971-72	40	7	6		
1972-73	34 + 2	1	4		
	604 + 2	80	24	45	3

MOST GOALS IN A CAREER					
BOBBY CHARLTON 248 (1956-73)					
Season	League	FAC	Lge C	Europe	C/Sh'ld
1956-57	10	1		1	
1957-58	8	5		3	
1958-59	29				
1959-60	17	3			
1960-61	21				
1961-62	8	2			
1962-63	7	2			
1963-64	9	2		4	
1964-65	10			8	
1965-66	16			2	1
1966-67	12				
1967-68	15	1		2	1
1968-69	5			2	
1969-70	12	1	1		
1970-71	5		3		
1971-72	8	2	2		
1972-73	6		1		
Total	198	19	7	22	2

HIGHEST TRANSFER FEE RECEIVED			
Amount	Club	Player	Date
£2,500,000	Barcelona	Mark Hughes	6/86
£1,500,000	A C Milan	Ray Wilkins	6/84
£800,000	Norwich City	Mark Robins	8/92
£750,000	Middlesbrough	Peter Davenport	11/88
£750,000	Everton	Norman Whiteside	8/89

HIGHEST TRANSFER FEE PAID			
Amount	Club	Player	Date
£2,300,000	Middlesbrough	Gary Pallister	8/89
£2,000,000	Queens Park R.	Paul Parker	8/91
£1,500,000	Barcelona	Mark Hughes	6/88
£1,500,000	Nott'm Forest	Neil Webb	7/89

LONGEST LEAGUE RUNS	
of undefeated matches:	26 (21.1.1956-20.10.1956)
of undefeated home matches:	37 (27.4.1966-27.3.1968)
without home win:	7 (30.3.1920-6.9.1920)
	(19.4.1930-1.10.1930) (9.12.1933-3.3.1934)
	(22.2.1958-21.4.1958) (5.2.1978-29.3.1978)
of league wins:	14 (8.10.1904-1.2.1905)
of league defeats:	14 (26.4.1930-25.10.1930)
of league matches without a win	16 (19.3.1930-25.10.1930)
of undefeated away matches:	14 (21.1.1956-20.10.1956)
without an away win:	26 (15.2.1930-3.4.1931)
of home wins:	18 (15.10.1904-30.4.1904)
of away wins:	6 (3.12.1904-11.2.1905)

MANAGERS			
Name	Seasons	Best	Worst
E Magnall	1903-12	1(1)	3(2)
J R Robson	1914-21	12(1)	18(1)
J Chapman	1921-26	9(1)	14(2)
C Hilditch	1926-27	15(1)	15(1)
H Bamlett	1927-31	12(1)	22(1)
W Crickner	1931-32	12(1)	12(1)
A Scott Duncan	1932-37	21(1)	20(2)
M Busby	1945-69	1(1)	19(1)
J Murphy	1958		
W McGuiness	1969-70	8(1)	8(1)
M Busby	1970-71	8(1)	8(1)
F O'Farrell	1971-72	8(1)	8(1)
T Docherty	1972-77	3(1)	1(2)
D Sexton	1977-81	2(1)	10(1)
R Atkinson	1981-86	3(1)	8(1)
A Ferguson	1986-	2(1)	13(1)

LOCAL BRANCH
Anchorage Quays
Salford Quays
Manchester M5 2XE
Tel: 061-877 48977

BARCLAYBANK MACHINE

BARCLAYS BUSINESS CENTRE
St Ann's Square
Manchester M60 2PX
Tel: 061-835 3555

BARCLAYBANK MACHINE

BARCLAYS

PREVIOUS NAME: Newton Heath 1878-1902

PREVIOUS LEAGUE: Football Alliance

BIGGEST VICTORIES
League: 10-1 v Wolverhampton Wanderers, Division 2, 15.10.1892
9-0 v Walsall, Division 2, 3.4.1895
9-0 v Darwen, Division 2, 24.12.1898
F.A. Cup: 8-0 v Yeovil, Round 5, 12.2.1949
League Cup: 7-2 v Newcastle United, Round 4, 1976-77
5-0 v Tranmere Rovers, Round 2, 1976-77
5-0 v Rotherham, Round 2, 12.10.1988
5-0 v Hull City, Round 2, 23.9.1987
Europe: 10-0 v Anderlecht, European Cup, 26.9.1956

BIGGEST DEFEATS
League: 0-7 v Wolverhampton W, Division 2, 26.12.1931
0-7 v Aston Villa, Division 1, 27.12.1930
0-7 v Blackburn Rovers, Division 1, 10.4.1926
F.A. Cup: 1-7 v Burnley, Round 1, 1901
0-6 v Sheffield Wednesday, Round 2, 1904
League Cup: 1-5 v Blackpool, Round 2, 1966-67
0-4 v Manchester City, Round 4, 12.11.1975
Europe (ECWC): 0-5 v Sporting Lisbon, Q-Final, 18.3.1964

MOST POINTS
3 points a win: 81, Division 1, 1987-88
2 points a win: 64, Division 1, 1956-57

MOST GOALS
103, Division 1, 1956-57
Whelen 26, Taylor 22, Violett 16, Charlton 10, Berry 8, Pegg 6, Edwards 5, Webster 3, Dawson 3, Scanlon 2, Coleman 1, og 1.
1958-59: Charlton 29, Violett 21, Scanlon 16, Bradley 12, Goodwin 6, Webster 5, Dawson 4, Quixhall 4, Cope 2, McGuinness 1, Pearson 1, og 2.

MOST GOALS IN A MATCH
6, Joe Cassidy v Walsall Town Swifts, 9-0, Div 2, 3.4.1895
6, Harold Halse v Swindon Town, 8-4, Charity Shield, 1911
6, George Best v Northampton Town (a), 8-2, FA Cup Rnd 5, 7.2.1970

MOST GOALS IN A SEASON
Dennis Law, 46 (League 30, FA Cup 10, ECWC 6) 1963-64
(League only): Dennis Violet, 32, Div 1, 1959-60

MOST FIRST CLASS MATCHES IN A SEASON
60 (42 League, 7 FA Cup, 11 UEFA Cup) 1964-65
60 (42 League, 7 FA Cup, 9 Lge Cup, 2 UEFA Cup) 1982-83
60 (42 League, 7 FA Cup, 3 Lge Cup, 8 UEFA Cup) 1984-85
60 (38 League, 3 FA Cup, 9 Lge Cup, 9 ECWC, 1 Charity Shield) 1990-91

MOST LEAGUE GOALS CONCEDED
115, Division 1, 1930-31

MOST LEAGUE WINS
28, Division 2, 1905-06; Division 1, 1956-57

MOST LEAGUE DRAWS
18, Division 1, 1980-81

MOST LEAGUE DEFEATS
27, Division 1, 1930-31

OLDEST PLAYER
Billy Meredith, 46 years 285 days v Derby County, 7.5.1921.

YOUNGEST PLAYER
Duncan Edwards, 16 years 182 days v Cardiff City, 4.4.1953.

MOST CAPPED PLAYER
Bobby Charlton (England) 106

BEST PERFORMANCES BY MANCHESTER UNITED

League: 1956-57: Matches played 42, Won 28, Drawn 8, Lost 6, Goals for 103, Goals against 54, Points 64. First in Division 1.
Highest: Division 1 Champions on 7 occasions.

F.A. Cup: 1908-09: 3rd rnd. Brighton & H.A. 1-0; 4th rnd. Everton 1-0; 5th rnd. Blackburn Rovers 6-1; 6th rnd. Burnley 3-2; Semi-Final Newcastle United 1-0; Final Bristol City 1-0.
1947-48: 3rd rnd. Aston Villa 6-4; 4th rnd. Liverpool 3-0; 5th rnd. Charlton Athletic 2-0; 6th rnd. Preston North End 4-1; Semi-Final Derby County 3-1; Final Blackpool 4-2.
1962-63: 3rd rnd. Huddersfield Town 5-0; 4th rnd. Aston Villa 1-0; 5th rnd. Chelsea 2-1; 6th rnd. Coventry City 3-1; Semi-Final Southampton 1-0; Final Leicester City 3-1.
1976-77: 3rd rnd. Walsall 1-0; 4th rnd. Queens Park R. 1-0; 5th rnd. Southampton 2-2, 2-1; 6th rnd. Aston Villa 2-1; Semi-Final Leeds United 2-1; Liverpool 2-1.
1982-83: 3rd rnd. West Ham United 2-0; 4th rnd. Luton Town 2-0; 5th rnd. Derby County 1-0; 6th rnd. Everton 1-0; Semi-Final Arsenal 2-1; Final Brighton & H.A. 2-2, 4-0.
1984-85: 3rd rnd. Bournemouth 3-0; 4th rnd. Coventry City 2-1; 5th rnd. Blackburn Rovers 2-0; 6th rnd. West Ham United, 4-2; Semi-Final Liverpool 2-2, 2-1; Final Everton 1-0.
1989-90: 3rd rnd. Nott'm Forest (a) 1-0; 4th rnd. Hereford Utd 1-0; 5th rnd. Newcastle Utd 3-2; 6th rnd. Sheffiel Utd 1-0; Semi-Final Oldham Ath 3-3, 2-1; Final Crystal Palace 3-3, 1-0

League Cup: 1991-92: 2nd rnd. Cambridge Utd 3-0, 1-1; 3rd rnd. Portsmouth 3-1; 4th rnd. Oldham Athletic 2-0; 5th rnd. Leeds United 3-1; Semi-Final Middlesbrough 0-0, 2-1; Final Nottingham Forest 1-0

European Cup: 1967-68: 1st rnd. Hibernians Valletta 4-0, 0-0; 2nd rnd. Sarajevo 0-0, 2-1; 3rd rnd. Gornik Zabrze 2-0, 0-1; Semi-Final Real Madrid 1-0, 3-3; Final Benfica 4-1 (aet).

European Cup Winners Cup: 1990-91: 1st rnd. Pecsi Munkas 2-1, 1-0; 2nd rnd. Wrexham 3-0, 2-0; 3rd rnd. Montpellier 1-1, 2-0; Semi-Final Legia Warsaw 3-1, 1-1; Final Barcelona 2-1

DIVISIONAL RECORDS

	Played	Won	Drawn	Lost	For	Against	Points
DIVISION 1	2740	1162	704	874	4523	3875	3233
DIVISION 2	816	406	168	242	1433	966	980
TOTALS	3556	1568	872	1116	5956	4841	4213

MANCHESTER UNITED							APPEARANCES				GOALS			
PLAYERS NAME Honours	Ht	Wt	Birthdate	Birthplace Transfers	Contract Date	Clubs	League	L/Cup	FA Cup	Other	Lg	L/C	FAC	Oth
GOALKEEPERS														
Peter Schmeichel						Brondy								
				£550,000	12.08.91	Manchester Utd	40	6	3	4				
Gary Walsh	6.3	14.0	21.03.68	Wigan	25.04.85	Manchester Utd	37	3		2				
E:u21.2; ECWC'91				Loan	11.08.88	Airdrie	3	1						
DEFENDERS														
Derek Brazil	6.0	12.1	14.12.68	Dublin	12.03.86	Manchester Utd	0+2							
Ei:B1,u23.1,u21.7				Loan	20.11.90	Oldham Ath	1			1				
				Loan	12.09.91	Swansea City	12	2	1	2	1			
Steve Bruce	6.0	12.6	31.12.60	Corbridge	27.10.78	Gillingham	203+2	15	14		29	6	1	
E:B.1,Y.8;Div2'86;LC'85;FAC'90;ECWC'91				£125,000	24.08.84	Norwich City	141	20	9	10	14	5	1	
				£800,000	18.12.87	Manchester Utd	161	18	23	14	25	4	1	5
Brian Carey	6.3	11.13	31.05.68	Cork		Cork City								
				£100,000	02.09.89	Manchester Utd								
				Loan	17.01.91	Wrexham	3							
				Loan	24.12.91	Wrexham	13		3	3	1			
Dennis Irwin	5.8	10.10	31.10.65	Cork	03.11.83	Leeds Utd	72	5	3	2	1			
Ei:B.1,Y,S,u21.3;ECWC'91						Oldham Ath	166+1	19	13	5	4	3		
				£700,000	20.06.90	Manchester Utd	70+1	14+1	6	10	4			
Lee Martin	5.10	11.18	05.02.68	Hyde	14.05.86	Manchester Utd	55+17	4+2	13+1	5+5	1		1	
E:u21.2;FAC'90														
Gary Pallister	6.4	13.0	30.06.65	Ramsgate		Bilkingham								
E:5,B.6; FAC'90; ECWC'91					02.04.85	Middlesbrough	156	10	10	13	5		1	
				Loan	18.10.85	Darlington	7							
				£2,300,000	29.08.89	Manchester Utd	108+3	20	14	14+1	4			1
Paul Parker	5.7	10.8	04.04.64	Essex	15.04.82	Fulham (A)	140+13	16	11	2	2	1		
E:17,B.3,u21.8,Y3				£300,000	18.06.87	Q.P.R	121+4	14	16	5	1			
				£2,000,000	08.08.91	Manchester Utd	24+2	6	3	2				
Mike Phelan	5.10	11.2	24.09.62	Nelson	29.07.80	Burnley (A)	166+2	16	16	8	9	2		2
E:1,Y.5;Div3'82,Div2'86;FAC'90;ECWC'91					13.07.85	Norwich City	155+1	14	11	13	9		1	
				£750,000	01.07.89	Manchester Utd	82+7	12+2	8	13	2			
Neil Whitworth	6.1	12.6	12.04.72	Wigan		Wigan Ath	1+1							
				£45,000	01.07.90	Manchester Utd	1							
				Loan	16.01.92	Preston N.E	6							
				Loan	20.02.92	Barnsley	11							
MIDFIELD														
Russell Beardsmore	5.6	9.0	28.09.68	Wigan	02.10.86	Manchester Utd. (A)	30+26	3+1	4+4	2+5	4			
E:u21.5				Loan	19.12.91	Blackburn Rovers	1+1							
Darren Ferguson	5.10	10.9	09.02.72	Glasgow	11.07.90	Manchester Utd. (T)	4+5							
Paul Ince	5.10	11.7	21.10.67	Essex	18.05.85	West Ham U. (T)	66+6	9	8+2	4	7	3	1	1
E:u19.3,U21.2,CS'90,; FAC'90; ECWC'91				£800,000	14.09.89	Manchester Utd	87+3	15+1	11+1	12	6	2		
Giuliano Maiorana	5.9	11.08	18.04.69	Cambridge		Histon								
				£30,000	01.12.88	Manchester Utd	2+5	0+1						
Bryan Robson	5.10	12.12	11.01.57	Chester-le-Street	01.08.74	West Brom A. (A)	193+4	17+1	10+2	12	39	2	2	3
E:90,U21.7,B.3,Y;S: F.Lg:3, CS'83; FAC'83'85'90;ECWC'91				£1,500,000	05.10.81	Manchester Utd	311+5	44+1	32	28	72	5	9	10
Neil Webb	6.1	13.7	30.07.63	Reading	14.11.80	Reading (A)	65+7	2+2	2		22			
E:26,u21.3,Y.10;Div3'83;LC'89;SC'89;				£83,000	29.07.82	Portsmouth	123	9	6		34	3	1	
FAC'90;ECWC'91				£250,000	03.06.85	Nottm. Forest	146	21	13	6	47	4	2	4
				£1,500,000	24.07.89	Manchester Utd	70+4	13	9	10	8	1	1	1
FORWARDS														
Clayton Blackmore	5.9	11.3	23.09.64	Neath		Manchester Utd. (A)								
W:33,u21.3,Y,S; FAC'90'ECWC'91					28.09.82	Manchester Utd	138+34	22+1	15+5	18	19	3	1	4
Dion Dublin	6.0	12.04	22.04.69	Leicester		Norwich City								
Div.3'91					25.01.89	Cambridge Utd	133+23	8+2	21	14	53	5	11	5
				£1,000,000	01.07.92	Manchester Utd								
Ryan Giggs	5.11	10.0	29.11.73	Cardiff	01.12.90	Manchester Utd. (T)	33+7	6+2	2+1	1+1	5	3		
W: U21.1, Y														
Mark Hughes	5.9	11.2	01.11.62	Wrexham		Manchester Utd. (A)	85+4	5+1	10	14+2	37	4	4	2
W:43,u21.5,Y,FAC'85'90;ECWC'91				£2,500,000	01.07.86	Barcelona (Spa)								
				£1,500,000	20.07.88	Manchester Utd	141+4	21	20+1	16+1	47	6	7	5
Andrei Kanchelskis	5.10	12.04	23.01.69	Kirowograd (USSR)		Shakhtyor								
USSR				£650,000	20.05.91	Manchester Utd	29+6	4	2	2	5	2	1	
Brian McClair	5.10	12.13	08.12.63	Belshill	28.07.80	Aston Villa (A)								
S:26,B.1,u21.8; SPD'86; SC'85; FAC'90; CS'90; ECWC'91				£	01.08.81	Motherwell	33+7	9+1	2		15	4	1	
				£	01.07.83	Celtic	129+16	19+1	14+4	13+2	99	9	11	3
				£850,000	30.07.87	Manchester Utd	190+3	28	24	18	70	14	11	6
Lee Sharpe	5.11	11.04	25.07.71	Halesowen		Torquay Utd. (T)	9+5			2+3	3			
E:1,u21.5; ECWC'91				£185,000	10.06.88	Manchester Utd	60+17	11+4	8+2	8+2	4	7		1
Danny Wallace	5.4	10.4	21.01.64	London		Southampton (A)	240+15	36	21+1	10+2	64	6	4	5
E:.1,u21.14,Y.9;UEFA.u21'84'; ECWC'91				£1,200,000	18.09.89	Manchester Utd	36+9	3+3	6+2	4+2	6	2	2	
ADDITIONAL CONTRACT PLAYERS														
Wu Chongwen, Adrian Doherty, Craig Lawton, Su Maozhen, Kieran Toal, Ian Wilkinson.														

MANCHESTER UNITED

RECORD WIN & LOSS AGAINST EACH CLUB IN CURRENT DIVISION

(Where a score has occured on several occasions the most recent is given)

Club	Rec. Win	Season	Rec. Loss	Season
ARSENAL	6-1	1951-52	6-2	1946-47
ASTON VILLA	7-0	1964-65	7-0	1930-31
BLACKBURN ROVERS	6-1	1961-62	7-0	1925-26
CHELSEA	6-0	1960-61	6-2	1930-31
COVENTRY CITY	5-1	1924-25	3-0	1982-83
CRYSTAL PALACE	5-1	1923-24	5-0	1972-73
EVERTON	5-0	1959-60	6-0	1892-93
IPSWICH TOWN	7-2	1963-64 (away)	6-0	1979-80
LEEDS UNITED	6-0	1959-60	5-0	1930-31
LIVERPOOL	6-1	1927-28	7-1	1895-96
MANCHESTER CITY	5-1	1960-61	6-1	1925-26 (home)
MIDDLESBROUGH	4-0	1900-01	5-0	1952-53
NORWICH CITY	5-0	1979-80	2-0	1989-90
NOTTINGHAM FOREST	5-0	1935-36	6-2	1909-10
OLDHAM ATHLETIC	5-1	1931-32	3-0	1920-21 (home)
QUEENS PARK RANGERS	8-1	1968-69	4-0	1976-77
SHEFFIELD UNITED	5-0	1954-55	6-1	1928-29
SHEFFIELD WEDNESDAY	5-0	1906-07	7-2	1929-30
SOUTHAMPTON	5-1	1986-87	4-1	1968-70 (home)
TOTTENHAM HOTSPUR	5-0	1909-10	6-1	1932-33
WIMBLEDON	3-1	1990-91 (away)	2-1	1986-87

MANAGER: ALEX FERGUSON

DATE OF BIRTH: 31.12.1941   **PLACE OF BIRTH:** GOVAN, GLASGOW

DATE OF APPOINTMENT: 05.11.1986

PREVIOUS CLUBS
as Manager: East Stirling; St Mirren; Aberdeen
as Player: Rangers; Queens Park; Dunfermline

HONOURS
as Manager: Aberdeen: Scottish Champions 1980, 1984, 1985; Scottish Cup Winners 1982, 1983, 1984, 1986; Scottish League Cup Winners 1986; European Cup Winners Cup Winners 1983; Alex was appointed Caretaker Manager of Scotland in 1985 on the death of Jock Stein until Andy Roxburgh was made manager in July 1986.
Manchester Utd: FA Cup Winners 1990; European Cup Winners Cup 1991; League Cup Winners 1992

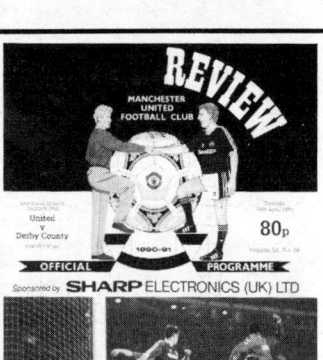

Value Rating: ★ ★ ★ ★

Programme Editor: Cliff Butler

Price of 1992-93 Programme: £1

Number of Pages: 40

Subscriptions: UK £39, Ir Rep £39, Europe £49, Overseas £85

Local Newspapers: Manchester Evening News, Sunday Pink

Local Radio Stations: BBC Radio Manchester, Piccadilly Radio

Books available about Club: The Complete Record 1878-1986 by Ian Morrison and Alan Shury, Breedon Books £13.95; A Pictorial History and Club Record £15.

LEADING LEAGUE GOALSCORERS
SEASONS 1979-80 – 1991-92

1979-80	**JOE JORDAN**	13	1980-81	**JOE JORDAN**	15
1981-82	**FRANK STAPLETON**	13	1982-83	**FRANK STAPLETON**	14
1983-84	**FRANK STAPLETON**	13	1984-85	**MARK HUGHES**	16
1985-86	**MARK HUGHES**	17	1986-87	**PETER DAVENPORT**	15
1987-88	**BRIAN McCLAIR**	25	1988-89	**MARK HUGHES**	14
1989-90	**MARK HUGHES**	12	1990-91	**BRIAN McCLAIR**	13
				STEVE BRUCE	13
1991-92	**BRIAN McCLAIR**	**18**			

OLD TRAFFORD Manchester M16 ORA

Capacity: 34,298   **Covered Standing:** 3,566   **Seating:** 28,395

Tel: Ground: 061 872 1661   **Ticket Sales:** 061 872 0199   **Clubcall:** 0898 12 11 61

All premium rate calls (0898/0891) cost 36p per minute cheap rate and 48p per minute at all other times. Call costings correct at time of going to press.

GROUNDS
North Road, Monsall Road 1880-1893; Bank St. 1983-1910; Old Trafford 1910-1941; Maine Road 1941-49; Old Trafford 1949-

ATTENDANCES
Highest: 82,950 v Arsenal, FA Cup Round 1, 1.1.1949 (at Maine Road)
76,962 Wolves v Grimsby, FA Cup, 25.3.1939

Lowest: 7,800 v Stoke City, 5.2.1947 (at Maine Road)

RECORD RECEIPTS (with previous records):
£237,175.70 v Nottingham Forest, FA Cup 6th Rnd., 18.3.1989
£221,399 v Juventus, UEFA, 11.4.1984
£110,000 Liverpool v Nottingham Forest, 22.3.1978
£102,457 v Tottenham H., Lge Cup 2nd Rnd, 28.12.1981

OLD TRAFFORD
First game: v Liverpool, 19.2.1910
First floodlit game: v Bolton Wanderers 25.03.1957

Season Tickets:
Stands: from £228 to £266 (no reductions)
Ground: £156, juv/OAP £76

Executive Box Season Tickets: Apply to club for details

Cost of Stand Tickets: Seats: £14
Terraces: £8, juv/OAP £4

Match and Ticket Information: Seats can be reserved one calendar month before a match, by post only

Car Parking: Several large parks: 1 Lancashire County Cricket Ground, Talbot Road and Great Stone Road (1,200)

Nearest Railway Station: Manchster Piccadilly (061-832 8353)

Manchester United FC Museum: Situated at the Warwick Road End of Old Trafford. Open everyday except Saturday. Admission £1.50, £1.00 for Children & OAPs

---

How to get to the ground

From North: Use Motorway M61 then M63 until Junction 4. Leave motorway and follow signs Manchester A5081. In 2.5m turn right into Warwick Road, then turn right into United Road for Manchester United FC

From East: Use Motorway M62 until Junction 17 then A56 into Manchestr. Follow signs South then Chester into Chester Road. Un 2m turn right into Warwick Road, then turn left into United Road for Manchester United FC

From South: Use Motorway M6 until Junction 19 then follow signs Stockport A556 then Altrincham A56. From Altrincham follow signs Manchestr. In 6m turn left into warwick Road, then turn left into United Road for Manchester United FC

From West: Use Motorway M62 then M63 and route from north or as route from south

MANSFIELD TOWN

Division 2

Formed: 1910   **Turned Professional:** 1910   **Ltd Co:** 1921

SPONSORED BY: Gunthorpe Textile Company Ltd   **NICKNAME:** The Stags

Chairman
J W Pratt

Directors
G Hall (Managing Director)
J A Brown

Secretary
J D Eaton (0623 23567)

Player Manager
George Foster

Assistant Manager
Bill Dearden

Commercial Manager
John Slater (0623 658070)

Groundsman
David Bennett

Physiotherapist
Dennis Pettitt

Football Community Officer
Dave Bentley

Youth Development Officer
Kevin Rendall

Chief Scout
John Newman

Club Statistician for the Directory
Pete Stevenson

MANSFIELD attained promotion in dramatic fashion on the last day of the season. The Stags needed to beat Rochdale and either Blackpool or Rotherham had to lose. Mansfield had to rely on other clubs results, despite the fact they had been in the top three virtually all season. Mansfield duly won and Blackpool lost and the Stags secured promotion the season after suffering relegation.

The season though, started off badly for Mansfield with three defeats and a draw in the first four games, including an early exit from the Rumbelows Cup. Indeed, before the match with local rivals Chesterfield, a section of the fans were after the head of the manager! These were the same fans that eight months later, were saluting George Foster and his teams achievements. In fact, it was the Chesterfield match which was the turning point. It started a twelve match unbeaten run in the league, which took the club to the top of the table. During this sequence, two of the club records were equalled: the number of consecutive league victories (7) and the number of consecutive away wins (7). In addition, player/manager George Foster deservedly obtained October's 'Manager of the Month' award.

For the remainder of the season the Stags never reached the same heights again but still managed to keep picking up points until late March/early April when they embarked on a disastrous run, collecting only four points from a possible fifteen and appeared to be falling out of the automatic promotion places. But, by collecting ten points from the last twelve, the Stags were able to grab promotion.

The cup competitions brought little relief as Mansfield crashed out in the first round in all the cups. The visit and televising of the Preston F.A. Cup tie by Sky TV created a lot of interest, though, and generated some much needed cash.

Foster's two pre-season signings, Paul Fleming and Phil Stant, both proved great successes and were both selected in the P.F.A. Division Four representative side. Stant in particular, proved to be a massive success, despite not scoring in his first five games and getting sent off on his home debut. He became a cult hero on the terraces (earning the nickname 'Psycho') with his clinical finishing and eye for the spectacular. He scored twenty-six league goals and was deservedly named the clubs' 'Player of the Year'. Paul Holland deserves a special mention. The nineteen-year-old had an outstanding first season. His arrival added another dimension to the midfield. He showed a maturity that belied his age and clearly has a big future ahead of him.

Next year, Mansfield must look solely to consolidate their position in Division Two. Once they have achieved this, only then can they challenge for promotion. Anything above mid-table must be looked upon as a successful season.

Stefan Guy

Back row L-R: Gregg Fee, Steve Wilkinson, Nicky Clarke, Darren Ward, Andy Beasley, Jason Pearcey, Kevin Gray, Paul Holland. **Middle row:** Dennis Pettitt (Club Sports Injury Therapist), Kevin Randall (Youth Development Officer), Paul McLoughlin, Chris Withe, Ian Stringfellow, Gary Castledine, Alex Sykes, Wayne Davidson, Nicky Roddis, Paul Fleming, Steve Parkin, John Newman (Chief Scout). **Front row:** Kevin Noteman, Phil Stant, Steve Charles, George Foster (Manager), Bill Dearden (Asst. Manager), Gary Ford, Wayne Fairclough, Steve Spooner.

MANSFIELD TOWN

DIVISION THREE: 3rd   **FA CUP:** 1st RND   **RUMBELOWS CUP:** 1st RND   **AUTOGLASS:** Prelim.

M	DATE	COMP.	VEN	OPPONENTS	RESULT	H/T	LGE POS	GOALSCORERS/GOAL TIMES	ATTEN-DANCE
1	A 17	BL	A	Scarborough	D 0-0	0-0			(2,343)
2	20	RC 1/1	H	**Blackpool**	L 0-3	0-2			2,124
3	24	BL	H	Barnet	L 1-2	1-2	18	Charles (pen) 34	2,668
4	27	RC 1/2	A	**Blackpool**	L 2-4	1-1		**Gray 45, Spooner 70**	(2,155)
5	31	BL	A	Chesterfield	W 2-0	1-0	8	Ford 36, Holland 54	(4,740)
6	S 3	BL	H	Wrexham	W 3-0	0-0		Stringfellow 73, Wilkinson 81, 87	1,965
7	7	BL	H	Blackpool	D 1-1	1-0	8	Wilkinson 33	2,629
8	13	BL	A	Crewe Alexandra	W 2-1	2-1		Stant 34, Charles (pen) 36	(4,667)
9	17	BL	A	Carlisle United	W 2-1	0-0		Stant 61, Charles 85	(1,803)
10	27	BL	A	Halifax Town	W 3-1	1-0		Stant 18, Fee 68, Wilkinson 87	(2,026)
11	O 5	BL	H	Maidstone United	W 2-0	1-0	2	Wilkinson 3, Stant 81	3,207
12	12	BL	A	Rochdale	W 2-0	0-0	1	Holland 60, Stant 88	(3,871)
13	15	AGT Pre	A	**Wrexham**	L 0-1	0-0			(627)
14	19	BL	H	Cardiff City	W 3-0	1-0	1	Fee 38, Wilkinson 50, Charles 89	3,180
15	26	BL	A	Scunthorpe United	W 4-1	1-0	1	Wilkinson 9, 78, Charles (pen) 87, Stant 90	(3,610)
16	N 2	BL	H	Doncaster Rovers	D 2-2	0-2	1	Stant 82, 84	4,180
17	5	BL	A	Northampton Town	W 2-1	1-1		Angus (og) 35, Fee 67	(2,181)
18	9	BL	A	Burnley	L 2-3	1-1	2	Wilkinson 30, 61	(11,848)
19	23	BL	H	Gillingham	W 4-3	2-2	1	Stant 1, 71, Withe 32, Holland 65	3,287
20	27	FAC 1	H	**Preston North End**	L 0-1	0-0			7,509
21	30	BL	H	Walsall	W 3-1	2-0	1	Stant 25, 28, Ford 47	3,398
22	D 21	BL	A	Barnet	L 0-2	0-1	2		(4,209)
23	26	BL	H	Scarborough	L 1-2	0-0		Clarke 87	4,012
24	28	BL	H	Chesterfield	W 2-1	2-0	2	Stant 15, Holland 38	6,503
25	J 1	BL	A	Wrexham	L 2-3	1-2		Wilkinson 24, 81	(2,422)
26	4	BL	A	York City	W 2-1	2-0	2	Holland 30, Wilkinson 34	(2,660)
27	18	BL	A	Rotherham United	D 1-1	1-0	2	McLoughlin 2	(6,454)
28	31	BL	A	Cardiff City	L 2-3	1-2		McLoughlin 25, Stant 69	(8,201)
29	F 4	AGT Pre	H	**Peterborough Utd**	L 0-3	0-2			2,578
30	8	BL	A	Scunthorpe United	L 1-3	0-2	4	Spooner 51	3,496
31	11	BL	A	Walsall	D 3-3	1-0		O'Hara (og) 34, Fairclough 49, Stant 81	(2,963)
32	15	BL	H	Hereford United	D 1-1	1-1	4	Spooner 20	2,550
33	25	BL	A	Hereford United	W 1-0	1-0		McLoughlin 33	(2,122)
34	29	BL	H	York City	W 5-2	3-1	3	Tutill (og) 2, Fee 14, Fairclough 25, Stant 51, 73	3,290
35	M 3	BL	A	Rotherham United	W 1-0	0-0		Stant 89	5,713
36	7	BL	A	Lincoln City	L 0-2	0-1	3		(4,387)
37	10	BL	H	Northampton Town	W 2-0	1-0		Stant 15, Ford 71	2,852
38	14	BL	A	Doncaster Rovers	W 1-0	0-0	2	Ford 59	(2,846)
39	21	BL	H	Burnley	L 0-1	0-1	3		8,336
40	24	BL	H	Lincoln City	D 0-0	0-0			3,604
41	28	BL	A	Gillingham	L 0-2	0-2	3		(2,682)
42	31	BL	H	Crewe Alexandra	W 4-3	3-0		Wilkinson 10, Stant 40, 64, Fairclough 44	3,108
43	A 4	BL	A	Blackpool	L 1-2	1-1	3	Stant 20	(6,055)
44	11	BL	H	Carlisle United	W 2-1	0-1	3	Holland 75, Charles (pen) 83	3,085
45	21	BL	H	Halifax Town	W 3-2	1-0		Stant 3 (42, 65, 82)	3,996
46	25	BL	A	Maidstone United	D 0-0	0-0	3		(1,602)
47	M 2	BL	H	Rochdale	W 2-1	0-0	3	Stringfellow 48, Stant 73	5,671

Best Home League Attendance: 8,336 v Burnley   Smallest: 1,965 v Wrexham   **Av Home Att: 3,844**

Goal Scorers: Compared with 90-91: +1,147

League (75):   Stant 26, Wilkinson 14, Charles 6 (4 pens), Holland 6, Ford 4, Fee 4, Fairclough 3, McLoughlin 3, Opponents 3, Spooner 2, Stringfellow 2, Clarke, Withe

R/lows C (2):   Spooner, Gray

FA Cup (0):

Autoglass (0):

1991-92

Beasley A.	Fleming P.	Withe C.	Spooner S.	Fee G.	Gray K.	Ford G.	Holland P.	Stant P.	Wilkinson S.	Charles S.	Stringfellow I.	Foster G.	Murray M.	Pearcey J.	Clark M.	Davidson	Carr C.	Fairclough W.	Kite P. (L)	Clarke N.	McLoughlin P.	Castledine G.	Noteman K.	Referee	
1	2	3	4	5	6	7	8	9	10	11	S	S												R Poulain	1
1	2	3	4	5	6	7	8	9†	10*	11	12	S												B Coddington	2
1	2	3	4		6	7	8•	9*	10	11	12	5	14											A Flood	3
	2	3	4		6*	7	8	9	10	11	12	5	S	1										D Phillips	4
1	2	3	4	5		7	8	9	10	11	S	6	S											C Trussell	5
1	2	3	4	5		7	8		10	11	9	6	S		S									I Hemley	6
1	2	3	4	5	S	7	8	12	10	11	9*	6												J Deakin	7
1	2	3	4	5	S	7	8	9*	10	11	12	6												D Shadwell	8
1	2	3	4	5	S	7	8	9	10	11	S	6												W Burns	9
1	2	3*	4	5	12	7	8	9	10	11		6				S								J Lloyd	10
1	2		4	5		7	8	9	10	11		6												T West	11
	2		4	5		7	8	9	10	11	S	6		1	S		3							M Peck	12
	2		4	5	S	7	8	9	10	11	S	6		1			3							S Lodge	13
	2		4	5		7	8	9	10	11	S	6		1	S		3							I Borrett	14
	2		4	5		7	8	9	10	11	S	6		1			3	S						S Bell	15
	2		4	5		7	8	9	10	11*	S	6		1			3	12						G Pooley	16
	2		4	5		7	8	9	10	11	S	6		1			3	S						J Moules	17
	2		4	5		7	8	9	10	11	S	6		1			3	S						T Holbrook	18
	2	3	4	5		7	8	9	10	11	S	6						S	1					R Hart	19
	2	3	4	5		7	8	9	10	11	S	6		1			S							J Key	20
	2	3	4	5		7	8*	9	10	11	S	6												C Trussell	21
	2		4	S		7*	8	9	10	11		6					3	12	1	5				D Axcell	22
2*					S		8	9	10	11	7	6			12		3	4	1	5				G Singh	23
			4	5	S	7	8	9	10	11	S	6					3	2	1					K Morton	24
			4	5	14	7	8	9*	10	11•	12	6					3	2	1					T Lunt	25
	2		4	5		7	8	9	10	11*	S	6					3	12	1					I Hendrick	26
	2		4	5		7	8†	9		11*	S	6					3	12	1		10			K Lupton	27
	2		4	5		7	8	9		11*	S	3					6	12	1		10			K Barratt	28
	2		4	5		7		9		11	S	6*					3	8	1	12	10			A Bennett	29
2*			4	5		7		9		11	14	6			12		3*	8	1		10			B Coddington	30
	2		4	5		7		9		11	S						3	8	1	6	10			A Buksh	31
	2		4	5	S	7	8	9		11	S			1			3			6	10			I Cruickshanks	32
	2		4	5	S	7	8			11	9			1	S		3			6	10			M Bodenham	33
	2		4	5	14	7	8	9		11	12			1			3			6*	10•			P Wright	34
	2		4	5	S	7	8	9		11	12			1			3			6	10*			D Allison	35
	2		4	5	14	7	8	9		11	12			1			3			6	10*			R Dilkes	36
	2		4*	5		7	8	9		11	10			1			3			6	S	12		I Hemley	37
	2			5	S	7	8	9		11	10*			1			3			6	12	4		A Smith	38
	2			5	12	7		9	10*	11				1	4		3			6	14	8*		R Gifford	39
	2			5	S	7		9	10	11				1	4		3			6	8	S		K Cooper	40
	2			5	S	7	8	9	10	11				1			3			6		12	4	D Elleray	41
	2		12	5			8*	9	10					1	7		11*	3		6		14	4	J Brandwood	42
2*				5	12		8	9	10					1	7		3	11		6		S	4	G Courtney	43
	2			5	12	7	8	9	10*	3	14			1	4			6*				11		P Taylor	44
2*				5	6	7	8	9	10	3	14			1	4							12	11•	T Lunt	45
				5	6	7	8	9	10•	3	14			1	4		2	12				11*		R Bigger	46
				5	6	7	8	9	S	3	10			1	S		2	11					4	R Shepherd	47
9	38	10	31	33	11	39	38	39	30	40	7	24		22	7		20	18	11	16	10	3	6	League Appearances	
			1		7			1			10		1		2			7				2	4	Substitute Appearances	
1	2	2	2	1	2	2	2	2	2	0+2	1			1										R/lows Appearances	
	1	1	1	1		1	1	1	1	1	1			1										FA Cup Appearances	
	2		2	1	2	1	2			2		1					2	1	1	0+1	1			Autoglass Appearances	

Players on Loan: Kite (Sheffield Utd)

† = Sent Off

365

MANSFIELD TOWN

Club Colours: Amber shirts with dark blue trim, amber shorts with dark blue trim, amber stockings
Change Colours: White shirts with green trim, green shorts with white trim, black with green socks with white trim
Reserves League: Central League Division 2   **'A' Team:** Midland Purity Youth League

Previous League: Midland League
Previous Managers: 1931-33 J Hickling   1933-35 H Martin   1935 C Bell   1936 H Wightman   1936-38 H Parkes   1938-44 J Poole   1944-45 C Barke   1945-49 R Goodall   1949-51 F Steele   1952-53 G Jobey   1953-56 S Mercer   1956-58 C Mitten   1958-60 S Weaver   1960-63 R Carter   1963-67 T Cummings   1967-70 T Eggleston   1970-71 J Basford   1971-74 D Williams   1974-76 D Smith   1976-78 P Morris   1978-79 B Bingham   1979-81 M Jones   1981-83 S Boam   1983-89 I Greaves
Honours: Champions Div 3, 1976-77   Champions Div 4, 1974-75   Freight Rover Trophy Winners 1986-87
League Career: Elected to Div 3S 1931   Transferred to Div 3N 1932   Transferred to Div 3S 1937
Transferred to Div 3N 1947   Transferred to Div 3 1958   Relegated to Div 4 1959-60   Promoted to Div 3 1962-63
Relegated to Div 4 1971-72   Promoted to Div 3 1974-75   Promoted to Div 2 1976-77   Relegated to Div 3 1977-78
Relegated to Div 4 1979-80   Promoted to Div 3 1985-86   Relegated to Div 4 1990-91   Promoted to Div 3 1991-92

CLUB RECORDS

Most Appearances for Club: Rod Arnold (1973-84): League 440 + FA Cup 29 + League Cup 26 **Total 495**
Most Capped Player: John McClelland 6, N Ireland   **For England:** None
Record Goalscorer in a Match: Ted Harston 7 v Hartlepool United, Div 3N, 8-2, 23-1-1937
Record League Goalscorer in a Season: Ted Harston 55, Division 3N   **In All Competitions:** Ted Harston 58, (League 55, FA Cup 3) 1936-37
Record League Goalscorer in a Career: Harold Johnston 104, 1931-36
Record Transfer Fee Received: £400,000 from Middlesbrough for Simon Coleman, September 1989
Record Transfer Fee Paid: £80,000 to Leicester City for Steve Wilkinson and to Notts County for Wayne Fairclough
Best Performances: League: 21st Div 2 1977-78   **FA Cup:** 6th Round, 1968-69   **League Cup:** 5th Round 1975-76
Most League Points: (2pts a win) 68, Div 4, 1974-75   (3pts a win) 81, Div 4, 1985-86
Most League Goals: 108, Div 4, 1962-63
Record League Victory and Most Goals Scored in a League Match: 9-2 v Rotherham United, Div 3N, 27.12.1932   8-1 v Q.P.R., Div 3, 15.3.1965   7-0 v Scunthorpe United, Div 4, 21.4.1975
Record Cup Victory and Most Goals Scored in a Cup Tie: 8-0 v Scarborough (a), FA Cup Round 1, 22.11.1952   9-2 v Hounslow, FA Cup 1st Replay, 5.11.62
Record League Defeat: 1-8 v Walsall, Div 3N, 19 Jan 1933
Record Cup Defeat: 0-5 v Sheffield Wednesday, (a), FA Cup Rnd 3, 10.1.1946   0-5 v Bristol Rovers, (a), FA Cup Round 3, 4.1.1958   0-5 v Chesterfield (h), League Cup Rnd 1 replay, 23.8.1971   0-5 v Notts County, (a), League Cup Round 1, 30.8.1988   2-7 v Luton Town, (a), League Cup Round 2, 3.10.1989
Oldest Player in a League Match:
Youngest Player in a League Match:

LONGEST LEAGUE RUNS

of undefeated matches: 20 (1976)	**of league matches without a win:** 12 (1959, 1974, 1979-80)
of undefeated home matches: 38 (1976-77)	**of undefeated away matches:** 8 (1976, 1991)
without home win: 11 (1959)	**without an away win:** 37 (1931-33)
of league wins: 7 (1962, 1991)	**of home wins:** 10 (1949)
of league defeats: 7 (1947)	**of away wins:** 7 (1976, 1991)

MANSFIELD TOWN

PLAYERS NAME Honours	Ht	Wt	Birthdate	Birthplace Transfers	Contract Date	Clubs	League	L/Cup	FA Cup	Other	Lg	L/C	FAC	Oth
GOALKEEPERS														
Andy Beasley	6.2	12.2	05.02.64	Sedgley	23.02.82	Luton Town (A)								
					06.07.84	Mansfield Town	94	5	3	7				
Loan Peterborough U. (28.07.86)				Loan	01.03.88	Scarborough	4							
Jason Pearcey	6.1		02.07.71	Leamington		Mansfield Town (T)	32	1	1	3				
DEFENDERS														
Nick Clarke	5.11	11.10	20.08.67	Walsall	15.02.85	Wolvers (A)	73+8	5	2+2	8	1			
					05.12.91	Mansfield Town	16			0+1	1			
Wayne Fairclough	5.10	9.12	27.04.68	Nottingham	28.04.86	Notts County (A)	39+32	1+2	3	10+3				
				£80,000	05.03.90	Mansfield Town	72+7	1	3	5	9			
Greg Fee	6.0	12.0	24.04.64	Halifax	09.05.83	Bradford City	6+1							
via Kettering Town 2FAC and Boston U 2FAC				£20,000	10.08.87	Sheffield Wed	16+10	3+1		1		1		
Loan Northampton Town 1lg, 2FAC				Loan	04.01.91	Preston N.E	15			2				
Loan Leyton Orient 4+1lg 4gls, 1L/Cup, 1oth				£20,000	29.03.91	Mansfield Town	43+1	1	1	1	4			
Paul Fleming	5.7	10.0	06.09.67	Halifax	10.09.85	Halifax Town (A)	135+4	7+1	7	13+1	1		1	
					04.07.91	Mansfield Town	38	2	1	2				
George Foster	5.10	11.2	26.09.56	Plymouth	01.09.74	Plymouth A (A)	201+11	19	10		6			
FRT'87					01.10.76	Torquay Utd	6				3			
Loan Exeter City (17.12.87) 28lg				£40,000	21.06.82	Derby County	30	5	3					
					25.08.83	Mansfield Town	363	22	19	34		'	2	1
Steve Parkin	5.6	10.7	07.11.65	Mansfield	12.11.83	Stoke City (A)	104+9	9	9	6	5			
E: u21.5, Y.6				£190,000	16.06.89	West Brom A	44+4	3		2+1	2			
				Free	16.07.92	Mansfield Town								
Christopher Withe	5.10	11.3	25.09.62	Speke	10.10.80	Newcastle Utd. (A)	2							
Div.3'85				Free	01.06.83	Bradford City	141+2	14	7	6	2			
				£50,000	02.10.87	Notts County	80	4	5	12	3			1
				£40,000	31.07.89	Bury	22+9	2+2		0+3	1			
Loan Chester City (18.10.90) 2lg				P.E	29.03.91	Mansfield Town	31	2	1		1			
MIDFIELD														
Gary Castledine	5.10	10.6	27.03.70	Mansfield	01.02.91	Mansfield Town	3+4							
Steve Charles	5.9	10.7	10.05.60	Sheffield	16.01.80	Sheffield Utd	112+11	12	9+1	3	10	1	1	1
Div.4'82,WC'86					02.09.84	Wrexham	111+2	8	4+1	11+1	37		1	5
					03.08.87	Mansfield Town	209+5	14	12	12+1	36	1	4	4
Gary Ford	5.8	11.10	08.02.61	York	07.02.79	York City (A)	359+7	24	36	9	52	4	7	
Div.4'84				£25,000	19.07.87	Leicester City	15+1	1+1		2	2			1
					06.01.88	Port Vale	66+9	6	7	3	12			1
Loan Walsall (22.03.90) 13lg 2gls				P.E	22.03.91	Mansfield Town	51	2	1	2	5			
Kevin Gray	6.0		07.01.72	Sheffield	01.07.90	Mansfield Town (T)	56+10	4	4+1	7+1	1	1		1
Paul Holland					04.07.91	Mansfield Town	39	2	1	1	6			
Steve Spooner	5.11	12.0	25.01.61	London	05.12.78	Derby County (A)	7+1							
Div.4'85				Free	04.12.81	Halifax Town	71+1	2	1		13			
				Free	14.07.83	Chesterfield	89+4	7+1	3+2	3	14			1
				£7,000	01.08.86	Hereford Utd	84	5	4	8	19	1	1	1
				£29,000	12.07.88	York City	72	6	1	4	11	3		1
					18.07.90	Rotherham Utd	15+4	4	3	2	1			
				P.E	22.03.91	Mansfield Town	43	2	1	2	2	1		
FORWARDS														
Keith Cassells	5.10	11.12	10.07.57	London		Wembley								
FRT'87				£500	07.11.77	Watford	6+6	2	1+1					
Loan Peterborough U. (17.01.80) 8lg				£5,000	10.11.80	Oxford Utd	43+2	5	8		13	4	7	
				£115,000	26.03.82	Southampton	13+6	5	1	2	4	1		
				£25,000	11.02.83	Brentford	80+6	4	5	5+2	28		5	2
				£17,000	16.08.85	Mansfield Town	162+1	11	7	14	52	3	3	3
Paul McLoughlin	5.10	10.7	23.12.63	Bristol		Bristol City								
via Gisborne City					09.01.85	Cardiff City	40+9	2	0+1	2	4			
via Bristol City					03.07.87	Hereford Utd	72+2	5	1	6	14	1		
				£45,000	13.07.89	Wolverhampton W	12+16	0+1			4			
				Loan	05.09.91	Walsall	9				4			
				£35,000	17.01.92	Mansfield Town	10+2			1	3			
				Loan		York City								
Kevin Noteman	5.10	11.0	15.10.69	Preston	13.06.88	Leeds Utd. (T)	0+1			1				
				£10,000	10.11.89	Doncaster Rovers	105+1	4	5+1	11	20	1	2	1
				£25,000	27.03.92	Mansfield Town	6							
Phil Stant	6.1	12.7	13.10.62	Bolton	19.08.82	Reading	3+1		1		2			
via the Army					25.11.86	Hereford Utd	83+6	3	3	11	38	2	2	7
				£175,000	18.07.89	Notts County	14+8	2	0+1	3+2	6	1		
Loan Blackpool (05.09.90) 12lg				Loan	03.01.91	Huddersfield Town	5				1			
Loan Lincoln City 4lg				£60,000	08.02.91	Fulham	19			1	5			
				£50,000	01.08.91	Mansfield Town	39+1	2	1	2	26			
Ian Stringfellow	5.9	10.4	08.05.69	Kirby-in-Ashford	29.08.86	Mansfield Town (A)	73+50	13+2	5+4	7+4	20	5	1	2
FRT'87														
Steve Wilkinson	5.10	10.9	01.09.68	Lincoln	06.09.86	Leicester City (A)	5+4		1		1			
				Loan	09.08.88	Rochdale								
Loan Crewe Alexandra (08.09.88) 3+2lg 2gls				£80,000	02.10.89	Mansfield Town	102+4	4	4+1	8	40	1	1	1
Steve Williams	5.11	10.6	18.07.70	Mansfield	11.07.88	Mansfield Town	4+7							
ADDITIONAL CONTRACT PLAYERS														

Wayne Davidson, Damien O'Brien, Nicholas Roddis, Alexander Sykes, Darren Ward.

LEADING LEAGUE GOALSCORERS SEASONS 1985-86 – 1991-92

1985-86	**NEVILLE CHAMBERLAIN**	16	1986-87	**KEITH CASSELLS**	16
1987-88	**STEVE CHARLES**	12	1988-89	**KEITH CASSELLS**	14
1989-90	**STEVE WILKINSON**	15	1990-91	**STEVE WILKINSON**	11

1991-92   **PHIL STANT**   **26**

FIELD MILL GROUND Quarry Lane, Mansfield, Nottingham NG18 5DA

Capacity: 10,315   **Covered Standing:** 1,638   **Seating:** 3,329

Tel: Ground: 0623 23567   **Ticket Sales:** As ground number   **Clubcall:** 0898 888 656

All premium rate calls (0898/0891) cost 36p per minute cheap rate and 48p per minute at all other times. Call costings correct at time of going to press.

ATTENDANCES
Highest: 24,467 v Nottingham Forest, FA Cup Round 3, 10.1.1963

Lowest: 1,086 v Darlington, Associate Members Cup, 22.2.1984

Record Receipts: £33,321.00 v Wimbledon, FA Cup, Jan. 1988

FIELD MILL GROUND
First game: v Swindon Town, Aug 1931
First floodlit game: v Cardiff City, 5.10.1951

Season Tickets:
Stands: £108.50, jnr/OAP £78.50
Ground: £72.50, jnr/OAP £36.50

Executive Box Season Tickets: None

Cost of Stand Tickets: Stand £8, juveniles/OAP £4
Terraces: £6, juveniles/OAP £3
Family Stand (Members Only): Adults £6, juveniles/OAP £4

Match and Ticket Information: Advance booking for five days prior to match

Car Parking: Space for 500 cars at the ground

Nearest Railway Station: Mansfield Alfreton Parkway

How to get to the ground

From North: Use Motorway M1 until junction 29. Leave Motorway and follow signs Mansfield A617. In 6.3m turn right into Rosemary Street B6030. In 1m turn right into Quarry Lane for Mansfield Town FC

From East: Use A617 to Rainworth. In 3m at crossroads turn left B6030 into Windsor Road. At end turn right into Nottingham Road. Shortly turn left into Portland Street, then turn left into Quarry Lane for Mansfield Town FC

From South and West: Use Motorway M1 until junction 28 then follow signs Mansfield A38. In 6.4m at crossroads turn right into Belvedere Street B6030. In 0.4m turn right into Quarry Lane for Mansfield Town FC

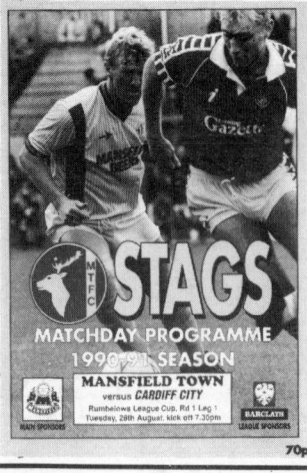

Value Rating: ★ ★ ★

Programme Editor: Jeremy Hall

Price of 1992-93 Programme: £1
Number of Pages: 32
Subscriptions: £32 per season

Local Newspapers: Chronicle Advertiser, Nottingham Evening Post

Local Radio Stations: Radio Trent, Radio Nottingham

Additional Publications on Club: 'Road to Wembley' £2.50 + 50p postage
MTFC Complete History 1910-1990, £16.95 (Available

MIDDLESBROUGH   Premier

Formed: 1892   **Turned Professional:** 1899   **Ltd Co:** 1899(Amateur 1892-99)

SPONSORED BY: ICI   **NICKNAME:** The Boro

Chairman
Mr M C Henderson

Directors
R M Corbidge
S Gibson
G Fordy

Chief Executive/Secretary
K Lamb, F.C.A.

Marketing Manager
M Hatfield

Manager
R M 'Lennie' Lawrence

First Team Coach
J Pickering

Reserve Team Coach
R Train

Youth Development Officer
R Bone

Groundsman
D Rigg

Press & P R Consultant
C Armitage

Physiotherapist
T Johnson / M Nile

Club Statistician for the Directory
David Grey

WITH twenty minutes of the season left, Middlesbrough had just gone a goal down, and were reduced to ten men away at Wolves. Somehow the team managed to fight back to a deserved victory, securing an automatic promotion place, rather than face another tense battle in the play-offs. It was a dream finish to an eventful season.

The close season had been turbulent to say the least, with the departure of manager Colin Todd, along with seven of the previous year's first team squad, and only three additions to the playing staff. Supporters were unsure what to expect from the Boro in the months to come.

1991-92 started well enough, with the team in first place until early November, but they lost this position primarily because of some poor away results. They began to drift down the table, but always had games in hand over their rivals. Away form improved and the unbeaten home record was maintained until April, but these games in hand were not used to their full advantage. Luckily other teams slipped up and Boro managed to sneak into second place during the final week of the season.

The cup competitions brought their own success, notably the Rumbelows Cup, where a record-equalling run was brought to an end in an epic semi-final at Old Trafford, a match which will be long remembered by all who were there. The F.A. Cup was not quite the same success, but wins over Manchester City and away at Sheffield Wednesday did have the fans thinking for a short time of a possible double Wembley appearance.

There were many plus points throughout the year, most notably the success of new manager Lennie Lawrence, and the introduction to the team of Jamie Pollock, who seems to be the battling midfielder we have missed for so long.

On the negative side, Tony Mowbray's departure for Celtic was disappointing, as was Gary Hamilton's inevitable retirement after a long battle against a knee injury, which was fittingly announced before the home game against Manchester United. On the whole, crowds were rather low, probably due to price increases of 50% imposed at the start of the season. Don't be surprised if another similar increase brings even lower gates, even with the prospect of Premier League Football at Ayresome Park.

It is often cited that an F.A. Cup defeat at Molineux was the start of Middlesbrough's decline during the 1980s. Could it be that this win at the same ground symbolises the start of a new period of success for the club? We can only wait and see, though one or two additional players will be necessary if Premier League status is to be consolidated in 1992-93.   **David Grey**

Back row L-R: Jimmy Phillips, Jon Gittens, Paul Wilkinson, Nicky Mohan, Willie Falconer, Jamie Pollock, Robbie Mustoe. **Middle row:** Tommy Johnson (Physio), Andy Payton, Curtis Fleming, Ian Ironside, Steve Pears, Andy Peake, Tommy Wright, Mark Nile (Physio). **Seated:** Gary Parkinson, Mark Proctor, Lennie Lawrence (Manager), Alan Kernaghan, John Pickering (First Team Coach), Bernie Slaven, John Hendrie.

MIDDLESBROUGH

DIVISION TWO: RUNNERS-UP **FA CUP:** 5th RND **RUMBELOWS CUP:** SEMI-FINALS **ZDS CUP:** 3rd RND

M	DATE	COMP.	VEN	OPPONENTS	RESULT	H/T	LGE POS	GOALSCORERS/GOAL TIMES	ATTEN-DANCE
1	A 17	BL	H	Millwall	W 1-0	1-0		Mustoe 45	16,234
2	21	BL	A	Derby County	L 0-2	0-0			(12,805)
3	24	BL	A	Ipswich Town	L 1-2	0-0	17	Wilkinson 81	(9,822)
4	27	BL	H	Newcastle United	W 3-0	1-0	4	Wilkinson 29, Proctor 67, Falconer 82	16,970
5	31	BL	H	Portsmouth	W 2-0	0-0	3	Falconer 70, Slaven 90	12,320
6	S 4	BL	A	Oxford United	W 2-1	0-0	1	Slaven 87, 90	(4,229)
7	7	BL	A	Watford	W 2-1	2-0	1	Wilkinson 25, Falconer 35	(8,715)
8	14	BL	H	Leicester City	W 3-0	0-0	1	Slaven 72, Wilkinson 79, 88	16,633
9	17	BL	H	Tranmere Rovers	W 1-0	0-0	1	Falconer 50	16,550
10	21	BL	A	Plymouth Argyle	D 1-1	0-1	1	Wilkinson 68	(5,280)
11	25	RC 2/1	H	Bournemouth	D 1-1	0-0		Wilkinson 81	10,577
12	28	BL	H	Sunderland	W 2-1	2-0	1	Slaven 1, Wilkinson 36	19,424
13	O 5	BL	A	Bristol Rovers	L 1-2	1-0	1	Yates (og) 24	(4,936)
14	9	RC 2/2	A	Bournemouth	W †2-1	1-0		Hendrie 23, Parkinson (pen) 117	(5,528)
15	12	BL	H	Wolverhampton W	D 0-0	0-0	1		15,253
16	19	BL	A	Grimsby Town	L 0-1	0-0	1		(10,265)
17	22	ZDS 2	H	Derby County	W †4-2	0-2		Wilkinson 75, 87, Phillips 104, Slaven 113	6,385
18	26	BL	A	Port Vale	W 1-0	1-0	1	Kernaghan 25	11,403
19	29	RC 3	H	Barnsley	W 1-0	1-0		Wilkinson 43	9,381
20	N 2	BL	H	Southend United	D 1-1	0-1	1	Ripley 55	9,664
21	5	BL	A	Barnsley	L 1-2	0-2	1	Slaven 57	(6,525)
22	9	BL	A	Brighton & H A	D 1-1	0-1	2	Slaven (pen) 71	(8,270)
23	16	BL	H	Charlton Athletic	W 2-0	0-0	2	Mohan 62, Slaven 71	13,093
24	23	BL	H	Bristol City	W 3-1	2-1	2	Payton 4, Slaven 30, 59	12,928
25	26	ZDS 3	H	Tranmere Rovers	L 0-1	0-0			6,952
26	30	BL	A	Blackburn Rovers	L 1-2	1-1	2	Slaven (pen) 43	(15,541)
27	D 3	RC 4	H	Manchester City	W 2-1	0-0		Mustoe 57, Wilkinson 69	17,286
28	7	BL	H	Swindon Town	D 2-2	1-0	2	Wilkinson 39, Slaven 50	13,300
29	26	BL	A	Newcastle United	W 1-0	0-0	3	Wilkinson 54	(26,563)
30	28	BL	A	Portsmouth	L 0-4	0-3	4		(12,324)
31	J 1	BL	H	Derby County	D 1-1	1-0	4	Mohan 34	16,288
32	4	FAC 3	H	Manchester City	W 2-1	0-1		Kernaghan 80, Wilkinson 81	21,174
33	8	RC 5	A	Peterborough Utd	D 0-0	0-0			(15,302)
34	11	BL	H	Ipswich Town	W 1-0	0-0	3	Payton 79	15,104
35	18	BL	A	Millwall	L 0-2	0-1	4		(8,125)
36	F 4	FAC 4	A	Sheffield Wed.	W 2-1	1-1		Hendrie 39, Wilkinson 69	(29,772)
37	8	BL	A	Port Vale	W 2-1	1-0	5	Hendrie 11, Mustoe 60	(7,019)
38	11	RC 5R	H	Peterborough Utd	W 1-0	0-0		Ripley 80	21,973
39	15	FAC 5	A	Portsmouth	D 1-1	0-0		Kernaghan 87	(18,138)
40	22	BL	H	Blackburn Rovers	D 0-0	0-0	7		19,353
41	26	FAC 5R	H	Portsmouth	L 2-4	2-2		Wilkinson 18, 27	19,479
42	29	BL	A	Swindon Town	D 1-1	0-0	5	Kernaghan 46	(10,379)
43	M 4	RC SF1	H	Manchester United	D 0-0	0-0			25,572
44	7	BL	H	Cambridge United	D 1-1	0-0	4	Wilkinson 64	14,686
45	11	RC SF2	A	Manchester United	L †1-2	0-1		Slaven 50	(45,875)
46	14	BL	A	Southend United	W 1-0	0-0	4	Slaven (pen) 60	(7,272)
47	17	BL	A	Cambridge United	D 0-0	0-0	5		(7,318)
48	21	BL	H	Brighton & H A	W 4-0	2-0	4	Slaven 3 (37, 45, pen 56), Hendrie 51	13,054
49	28	BL	H	Charlton Athletic	D 0-0	0-0	4		(8,250)
50	A 1	BL	A	Leicester City	L 1-2	0-1	6	Pollock 52	(19,352)
51	4	BL	H	Watford	L 1-2	0-0	7	Wilkinson 47	13,699
52	7	BL	A	Bristol City	D 1-1	1-0	6	Hendrie 18	(12,814)
53	10	BL	A	Tranmere Rovers	W 2-1	1-0	4	Proctor 14, Phillips 89	(8,842)
54	13	BL	H	Barnsley	L 0-1	0-0	7		12,743
55	15	BL	H	Oxford United	W 2-1	0-0	5	Ripley 71, Payton 74	11,928
56	18	BL	H	Plymouth Argyle	W 2-1	1-1	3	Ripley 28, Falconer 66	15,086
57	20	BL	A	Sunderland	L 0-1	0-1	4		(25,093)
58	25	BL	H	Bristol Rovers	W 2-1	0-0	4	Wilkinson 60, 74	14,057
59	28	BL	H	Grimsby Town	W 2-0	2-0	2	Phillips (pen) 32, Wilkinson 36	18,570
60	M 2	BL	A	Wolverhampton W	W 2-1	0-0	2	Gittens 72, Wilkinson 77	(19,123)

Best Home League Attendance: 19,424 v Sunderland   **Smallest:** 9,664 v Southend Utd   **Av Home Att:** 14,710

Goal Scorers: **Compared with 90-91:** -2,313

League (58): Slaven 16 (3 pens), Wilkinson 15, Falconer 5, Hendrie 3, Payton 3, Ripley 3, Proctor 2, Kernaghan 2, Mustoe 2, Mohan 2, Phillips 2 (1 pen), Opponents (pen), Pollock, Gittens

R/lows C (8): Wilkinson 3, Ripley, Hendrie, Parkinson (1 pen), Mustoe, Slaven

FA Cup (7): Wilkinson 4, Kernaghan 2, Hendrie

ZDS Cup (4): Wilkinson 2, Slaven, Phillips

† = After extra-time

370

1991-92

Pears S.	Parkinson G.	Phillips J.	Mowbray A.	Kernaghan A.	Falconer N.	Mustoe R.	Proctor M.	Wilkinson P.	Ripley S.	Hendrie J.	Mohan N.	Kavanagh	Fleming C.	Slaven B.	Shannon R.	Hewitt J.	Pollock J.	Arnold I.	Marwood B.	Young M.	Payton A.	Peake A.	Moore	Gittens J.	Ironside I.	Referee	
1	2	3	4	5	6	7	8	9	10	11			S	S												S Lodge	1
1	2	3	4	5	6	7*	8	9	10	11			S	14												D Gallagher	2
1	2*	3	4	5	6	7	8*	9	10	11			12	14												J Brandwood	3
1	2	3	4	5	6	7	8	9	10	11			S	S												K Hackett	4
1	2	3	4	5	6	7*	8	9	10	11			S	14												J Worrall	5
1	2	3	4	5	6	7	8	9	10*	11			S	14												R Groves	6
1	2	3	4	5	6	10	8	9		11		S	S	7												C Wilkes	7
1	2	3	4	5	6	10*	8	9	12	11			S	7												B Nixon	8
1	2	3	4	5	6	12	8	9	10	11*			S	7												S Bell	9
1	2•	3	4	5	6	12	8*	9	10	11			14	7												J Martin	10
1	2	3	4	5	6*	12	8	9	10	11			S	7												J Key	11
1	2	3	4	5		6	8	9	10	11†				7	S	S										R Hart	12
1	2	3	4	5		6•	8	9	10†	11				7*	12	14										M Pierce	13
1	2	3	4	5		6	8	9	10*	11				12	7*		14									R Hamer	14
1	2	3	4	5		6	8	9	10*				12	7			11*	14								D Allison	15
1	2	3	4	5		6	8	9					S	7			10	S	11							G Singh	16
1	2*	3	4	5		6	8	9					12	7			10*	14	11							I Hendrick	17
1	2	3	4	5		6	8*	9		11				7			12	S	10							J Watson	18
1	2	3	4	5		6		9		11			14	7			8	S	10*							M Peck	19
1	2*	3	4	5		6		9	10*	11			12	7			8			14						J Kirkby	20
1	2*	3	4	5		6	8	9	10	11			12	7			S									M Reed	21
1		3		5		6	12	9	10*	11	4		2	14			8*	7*								P Durkin	22
1		3		4		6	8	9	10*	11	5		2	7	12	S										J Worrall	23
1		3		4		6	8	9	11		5		2	7			14			S	10•					P Jones	24
1	S	3		4		6	8	9	10		5		2	7			11*									T Fitzharris	25
1	14	3		4		6*	8	9	11		5		2•	7			12				10					K Barratt	26
1		3		4		6	8	9	10		5		2	7			11	S	S							W Burns	27
1		3		4		6	8	9	10		5		2	7			11•	S		14						R Shepherd	28
1		3		4		6	8	9	10		5		2	7			11*		S	12	10					G Courtney	29
1	14	3		4		6	8	9	12		5		2•	7			10*			8	11					R Milford	30
1	2	3		4		6*	11*	9	10					7			12			14	8					S Lodge	31
1	2	3		4		6•		9	11	14	5		7*				8			12	10					M Reed	32
1	2	3		4		6		9	11	8	5		S	7			10	S								D Elleray	33
1	2	3		4		6		9	11	10*	5			7			8			12	S					C Trussell	34
1	2	3		4		6		9	11	10	5			7•							8*	12				D Frampton	35
1	2	3		4		6		9	14	11*	10	5		7•							12	8				D Allison	36
1	2	3		4		6		9	14	11*	10	5		7•							S	8				R Hamer	37
1	2	3		4		6	7	9	11	10*	5		S				8							S		K Hackett	38
1	2	3		4		6		9	14	11	10*	5		7•							12	8				B Hill	39
1	2	3				6•	14	9	11	10*	5		12				8	7				4				D Phillips	40
1	2	3				6	S	9	11	10*	5		12				4				8*	7				B Hill	41
1		3		4		6		9	11	7			2	S			10				8		5			P Vanes	42
1	2	3		4		6*	12	9	11	10	5		S	7			8									R Nixon	43
1	2•	3		4			12	9	11	10	5			7			8*					6		14		J Key	44
1		3		4	14	6*	12	9	11•	10	5		2	7			8									J Martin	45
1		3†		4		11			9				2	7			8					6	S	S		V Callow	46
1		3		4		11			9				2	7			8•					6	S	14		K Breen	47
1		3		4		11		9*		14	10•	5		2	7			8				12	6		S	P Wright	48
1		3	4				8	9	12	11*	10			2	7			8*					6			R Groves	49
1		3	4				12	9	11*	10	5		2	7			8*					14	6			J Lloyd	50
1		3	4				12	9	11	10	5*		2	7•			8					14	6			M Peck	51
1		3	4	11				9	12	10	5		2				7				8*	6		S		J Carter	52
1		3	4*	8		7		9	11•	10	5		2							14	6		12			R Poulain	53
1	14	3			8			12	9	11	10	5		2•	12		8*					6		5		T Lunt	54
1		3			8		12	9	11	10*	5		2	7							14	6*	4			A Bennett	55
1	14	3			8		6	9	11*	7•	5		2	12			10						4			N Midgley	56
1		3			8		7•	9	11	10	5*		2	12			14					6	4			G Courtney	57
1		3			8			9	11•	7	5		2	14			12				10	6*	4			J Rushton	58
1		3			8			9	11	7	5		2	S			6				10	S	4			L Dilkes	59
1		3			8			9	11•	10	5†		2	7*			6				12	14	4		1	P Don	60
45	23	43	17	38	25	28	27	46	36	38	27		23	28			21	3		8	20	9		1		**League Appearances**	
	4					2	9		3				5	10	1		2	5	1	1	11	3		3		**Substitute Appearances**	
8	6	8	3	8	1+1	7+1	4+2	8	7	7	5		2+1	6+1	1		6+1	1								**R/lows Appearances**	
4	4	4		3		4		4	3+1	4				1			4				1+3	4				**FA Cup Appearances**	
2	1	2	1	2		2	2	2	1		1		1	2			2	0+1	1		0+1					**ZDS Cup Appearances**	

Players on Loan: R Shannon (Dundee), J Hewitt (Celtic), B Marwood (Sheffield Utd), J Gittens (Southampton)   † = Sent Off

MIDDLESBROUGH

Club Colours: Red shirts/white trim, white shorts/red trim, red stockings/white trim.
Change Colours: White & black
Reserves League: Pontins Central League Division 2

COMPETITIONS		
Div. 1	Div. 2	Div. 3
02-24	99-02	66-67
27-28	24-27	86-87
29-54	28-29	
74-82	54-66	
88-89	67-74	
92-	82-86	
	87-88	
	89-92	

HONOURS		
Div. 2	Anglo/Scot	Amateur Cup
26-27	75-76	1895
28-29		1898
73-74		

MOST APPEARANCES: TIM WILLIAMSON 602 (02-23)		
Year	League	FA Cup
1901-02	2	
1902-03	16	
1903-04	34	4
1904-05	33	2
1905-06	34	5
1906-07	38	2
1907-08	37	1
1908-09	38	1
1909-10	38	2
1910-11	36	4
1911-12	36	4
1912-13	37	4
1913-14	29	1
1914-15	20	2
1919-20	37	2
1920-21	42	1
1921-22	26	1
1922-23	30	3
	563	39

MOST GOALS IN A CAREER		
GEORGE CAMSELL 345 (1925-39)		
Season	League	FA Cup
1925-26	3	
1926-27	59	4
1927-28	33	4
1928-29	30	3
1929-30	29	2
1930-31	32	
1931-32	20	
1932-33	17	1
1933-34	23	1
1934-35	14	
1935-36	28	4
1936-37	18	
1937-38	9	1
1938-39	10	
Total	325	20

MANAGERS			
Name	Seasons	Best	Worst
P McWilliam	1931-34	6(1)	19(1)
W Gillow	1934-39	4(1)	20(1)
D Jack	1946-51	6(1)	19(1)
W Rowley	1951-53	13(1)	12(2)
R Dennison	1953-61	5(2)	14(2)
R Carter	1961-65	4(2)	17(2)
S Anderson	1965-70	4(2)	2(3)
J Charlton	1970-77	7(1)	9(2)
J Neal	1977-81	9(1)	14(1)
R Murdoch	1981-82	22(1)	22(1)
M Allison	1982-83	16(2)	16(2)
W Maddren	1983-86	17(2)	21(2)
B Rioch	1986-90	18(1)	2(3)
C Todd	1990-91	7(1)	21(2)
L Lawrence	1991-	2(2)	

RECORD TRANSFER FEE RECEIVED			
Amount	Club	Player	Date
£2,300,000	Manchester Utd	Gary Pallister	8/89
£600,000	Southampton	David Armstrong	8/81
£575,000	Liverpool	Craig Johnston	4/81
£482,322	West Bromwich A	David Mills	1/79

RECORD TRANSFER FEE PAID			
Amount	Club	Player	Date
£900,000	Celtic	Derek Whyte	8/92
£750,000	Hull City	Andy Payton	11/91
£750,000	Manchester Utd	Peter Davenport	11/88
£475,000	Newcastle Utd.	Irving Natrass	8/79

LONGEST RUNS	
of undefeated matches:	24 (8.9.1973-9.1.1974)
of undefeated home matches:	27 (8.2.1935-10.4.1937)
without home win:	10 (10.11.1984-2.3.1985)
of league wins:	9 (16.2.1974-6.4.1974)
of league defeats:	8 (25.8.1954-2.10.1954)
of league matches without a win:	19 (3.10.1981-6.3.1982)
of undefeated away matches:	14 (14.4.1973-12.1.1974)
without an away win:	33 (7.3.1903-7.9.1907)
of home wins:	11 (22.11.1913-22.4.1914)
of away wins:	5 (18.2.1974-30.3.1974) (21.3.87-9.5.87)

BIGGEST VICTORIES
League: 9-0 v Brighton & H.A., Division 2, 23.8.1980.
F.A. Cup: 9-3 v Goole Town, Round 3, 1914-15.
League Cup: 4-0 v Tottenham Hotspur, Round 2, 1974-75.
4-0 v Halifax Town, Round 2, 20.9.1989

BIGGEST DEFEATS
League: 0-9 v Blackburn Rovers, Division 2, 6.11.1954
F.A. Cup: 1-6 v Southampton, Round 3, 1905-06
1-6 v Sheffield Wed., Round 2, 1894-95
1-6 v Wolverhampton W., Round 3, 1936-37
League Cup: 0-4 v Manchester City, Semi-Final, 21.1.1976

MOST POINTS
3 points a win: 94, Division 3, 1986-87.
2 points a win: 65, Division 2, 1973-74.

MOST GOALS
122, Division 2, 1926-27.
Camsell 59, Pease 23, Birrell 16, Williams 9, Carr 6,
McClelland 5, McKay 1, Ashman 1, J Williams 1, og 1.

MOST GOALS IN A MATCH
5. Andy Wilson v Nottingham Forest, 6.10.1923.
5. George Camsell v Manchester City 5-3 (a), 25.12.1926.
5. George Camsell v Aston Villa 7-2 (a), 9.9.1935.
5. Brian Clough v Brighton & H.A. 9-0, Div 2, 22.8.1958.

MOST GOALS IN A SEASON
George Camsell 64 (League 59, FAC 5) 1926-27
(English record and League goals (59) is a Div 2 record)
5 goals once = 5; 4 goals three times = 12; 3 goals six
times = 18; 2 goals seven times = 14; 1 goal 15 times = 15.

MOST FIRST CLASS MATCHES IN A SEASON
60 (46 League, 4 FA Cup, 8 League Cup, 2 Zenith Data Cup)
1991-92

MOST LEAGUE GOALS CONCEDED
91, Division 1, 1953-54

MOST LEAGUE WINS
28, Division 3, 1986-87

MOST LEAGUE DRAWS
19, Division 2, 1924-25

MOST LEAGUE DEFEATS
27, Division 1, 1923-24

OLDEST PLAYER
Tim Williamson 36 years 201 days v Cardiff City, Div 1,
24.3.1923

YOUNGEST PLAYER
Stephen Bell, 16 years 323 days v Southampton, Div 1,
30.1.1982.
Sam Lawrie, 16 years 323 days v Arsenal, Div 1, 3.11.1951.

MOST CAPPED PLAYER
Wilf Mannion (England) 26, 1946-51.

BEST PERFORMANCES BY MIDDLESBROUGH

League: 1986-87: Matches played 46; Won 28; Drawn 11, Lost 8; Goals for 67, Goals against 30; Points 94. Second in Div 3

Highest: 1913-14: Third in Division 1.

F.A. Cup: 1935-36: 3rd rnd. Southampton 1-0; 4th rnd. Orient 3-0; 5th rnd. Leicester City 2-1; 6th rnd. Grimsby 1-3.

1946-47: 3rd rnd. Queens Park Rangers 1-1, 3-0; 4th rnd. Chesterfield 2-1; 5th rnd. Nottingham Forest 2-2, 6-2; 6th rnd. Burnley 1-1, 0-1.

1969-70: 3rd rnd. West Ham Utd. 2-1; 4th rnd. York City 4-1; 5th rnd. Carlisle United 2-1; 6th rnd. Manchester United 1-1, 1-2.

1976-77: 3rd rnd. Wimbledon 0-0, 1-0; 4th rnd. Hereford 4-0; 5th rnd. Bolton Wanderers 2-0; 6th rnd. Orient 0-0, 2-1.

1980-81: 3rd rnd. Swansea City 5-0; 4th rnd. West Bromwich Albion 1-0; 5th rnd. Barnsley 2-1; 6th rnd. Wolverhampton Wanderers 1-1, 1-3.

League Cup: 1975-76: 2nd rnd. Bury 2-1; 3rd rnd. Derby County 1-0; 4th rnd. Peterborough United 3-0; 5th rnd. Burnley 2-0; Semi-Final Manchester Utd 1-0, 0-4.

1991-92: 2nd rnd. Bournemouth 1-1, 2-1; 3rd rnd. Barnsley 1-0; 4th rnd. Manchester City 2-1; 5th rnd. Peterborough Utd 0-0, 1-0; Semi-Final Manchester City 0-0, 1-2.

DIVISIONAL RECORDS

	Played	Won	Drawn	Lost	For	Against	Points
DIVISION 1	1864	653	445	766	2778	2972	**1768**
DIVISION 2	1418	583	341	494	2256	1959	**1630**
DIVISION 3	92	51	19	22	154	94	**149**
TOTALS	**3374**	**1287**	**805**	**1282**	**5188**	**5025**	**3547**

MIDDLESBROUGH

PLAYERS NAME Honours	Ht	Wt	Birthdate	Birthplace Transfers	Contract Date	Clubs	League	L/Cup	FA Cup	Other	Lg	L/C	FAC	Oth
GOALKEEPERS														
Ian Ironside	6.1	11.9	08.03.64	Sheffield	17.09.82	Barnsley (A)								
						North Ferriby Utd								
				N.C	08.03.88	Scarborough	88	2	2	10				
				£80,000	15.08.91	Middlesbrough	1							
				Loan	05.03.92	Scarborough	7							
Stephen Pears	6.0	12.0	22.01.62	Brandon	25.01.79	Manchester Utd. (A)	4	1						
				Loan	01.11.83	Middlesbrough	12		2					
					09.07.85	Middlesbrough	250	26	18	24				
DEFENDERS														
Willie Falconer S:Y	6.1	11.9	05.04.66	Aberdeen		Aberdeen	49+28	5+5	3+2	5+5	14	1	1	2
				£300,000	17.06.88	Watford	85+13	5	6	4+3	12		1	
					16.08.91	Middlesbrough	25	1+1			5			
Philip Gilchrist	6.0	11.12	25.08.73	Stockton-on-Tees	05.12.90	Nottm. Forest								
					10.01.92	Middlesbrough								
Jon Gittens	5.11	12.6	22.01.64	Moseley		Paget Rangers								
				£10,000	16.10.85	Southampton	18	4	1					
				£45,000	22.07.87	Swindon Town	124+2	15+1	9	13+1	6			1
				£400,000	28.03.91	Southampton	16+3	4		1				
				Loan	19.02.92	Middlesbrough	9+3							
				£200,000	27.07.92	Middlesbrough								
Alan Kernaghan	6.1	12.13	25.04.67	Otley	08.03.85	Middlesbrough (A)	144+40	20+7	7+4	14+2	13	1	3	2
				Loan	17.01.91	Charlton Ath	13							
Nicholas Mohan	6.0	11.10	06.10.70	Middlesbrough	18.11.87	Middlesbrough (A)	53+2	7	4+1	5	2			
Gary Parkinson	5.10	11.6	10.01.68	Middlesbrough		Everton								
					12.05.86	Middlesbrough	190+8	20	17	19	5	1		
James Phillips	6.0	12.0	08.02.66	Bolton		Bolton W	103+5	8	7	14	2			
				£75,000		Glasgow Rangers	19+6	4		4				
				£150,000	26.08.88	Oxford Utd	79	3	4	2	6			1
				£250,000	15.03.90	Middlesbrough	99	14	7	5	4			2
MIDFIELD														
Graham Kavanagh	5.9	11.5	02.12.73	Dublin		Home Farm								
					16.08.91	Middlesbrough								
Robbie Mustoe	5.11	11.6	28.08.68	Oxford	02.07.86	Oxford Utd. (A)	78+13	2	2	3	10			
				£375,000	05.07.90	Middlesbrough	67+4	13+1	6	5+1	6	4		
Andy Peake E: u21.1, Y.13; Div.2'80; UEFA Y'80	5.9	11.2	01.11.61	Market Harboro'	22.01.79	Leicester City (A)	141+6	5+1	9		13			
					13.08.85	Grimsby Town	39	5	1	1	4		1	
					11.09.86	Charlton Ath	174+3	12	8	14+1	5	1		
				£150,000	28.11.91	Middlesbrough	20+3		4					
Mark Proctor E:u21.4,Y8	5.10	11.9	30.01.61	Middlesbrough	14.09.78	Middlesbrough (A)	107+2	6	10		12	1	1	
				£425,000	04.08.81	Nottm. Forest	60+4	10	2		5	3	1	
				£115,000	05.08.83	Sunderland	115+2	13	6	2	19	2		2
				£250,000	03.09.87	Sheffield Wed	59	1	6	3	4		1	
				£300,000	23.03.89	Middlesbrough	95+14	7+2	4	11+1	6			
FORWARDS														
John Hendrie S: Y; Div.3'85; Div.2'90	5.7	11.12	24.10.63	Lennoxtown	18.05.81	Coventry City (A)	15+6	2			2			
				Loan	10.01.84	Hereford Utd	6							
				Free	02.07.84	Bradford City	173	17	11	11	46	3	6	4
				£500,000	17.06.88	Newcastle Utd	34	2	4	3	4	1		
				£600,000	20.06.89	Leeds Utd	22+5	1	1	2	5			
				£500,000	05.07.90	Middlesbrough	78+1	13	5+2	3	6	2	1	1
Andy Payton	5.9	10.6	23.10.69	Burnley	29.07.85	Hull City (A)	116+28	9+2	8	3	48	1		1
				£750,000	22.11.91	Middlesbrough	8+11		1+3		3			
Bernie Slaven Ei:6, FLgXl.1	5.10	10.10	13.11.60	Paisley		Morton	11+11		2		1			
						Airdrie	2	3+1						
						Queen of the South	2							
						Albion Rovers	42	2	1		27	3		
					10.10.85	Middlesbrough	273+16	25+1	16+1	27	114	10	4	14
Paul Wilkinson E: u21.4; CS'86; Div1'87	6.0	11.9	30.10.64	Louth	08.11.82	Grimsby Town	69+2	10	4+2		27	5	1	
				£250,000	28.03.85	Everton	19+12	3+1	3	6+2	7	7	1	1
				£200,000	26.03.87	Nottm. Forest	32+2	3	4+1	1	5	1	2	
				£300,000	16.08.88	Watford	133+1	4	8+1	8	53	1		3
				£550,000	16.08.91	Middlesbrough	46	8	4	2	15	3	4	2
Tommy Wright S: u21	5.7	9.9	10.01.66	Dunfermline	15.01.83	Leeds Utd	73+8	3+2	4		24	1	3	
					24.10.86	Oldham Ath	110+2	7+1	3	3	23	2	2	
				£350,000	14.08.89	Leicester City	122+7	7+1	4	10	22			7
				£650,000	01.07.92	Middlesbrough								
ADDITIONAL CONTRACT PLAYERS														
Curtis Fleming				St. Patricks										
				£50,000	16.08.91	Middlesbrough	23+5	2+1		1				
Jamie Pollock					18.12.91	Middlesbrough (T)	21+6	6+1	4	2	1			

Peter Collett, Scott Green, Robert Lake, Alan Moore, Chris Morris, Nick Peverall, Andrew Todd, Derek Whyte, Michael Young.

MIDDLESBROUGH

RECORD WIN & LOSS AGAINST EACH CLUB IN CURRENT DIVISION

(Where a score has occured on several occasions the most recent is given)

Club	Rec. Win	Season	Rec. Loss	Season
ARSENAL	5-0	1979-80	8-0	1934-35
ASTON VILLA	6-0	1948-49	8-1	1930-31
BLACKBURN ROVERS	7-1	1947-48 (away)	9-0	1954-55
CHELSEA	7-2	1978-79	5-0	1951-52
COVENTRY CITY	2-0	1975-76	3-0	1964-65
CRYSTAL PALACE	4-0	1968-69	5-2	1980-81
EVERTON	6-1	1935-36	5-1	1931-32
IPSWICH TOWN	5-2	1957-58	6-1	1954-55
LEEDS UNITED	5-0	1930-31	7-0	1930-31
LIVERPOOL	5-0	1929-30	7-2	1931-32
MANCHESTER CITY	6-1	1937-38 (away)	6-0	1935-36
MANCHESTER UNITED	5-0	1952-53	4-0	1900-01
NORWICH CITY	6-1	1980-81	2-0	1985-86
NOTTINGHAM FOREST	4-0	1922-23	5-1	1973-74
OLDHAM ATHLETIC	4-1	1914-15	5-1	1914-15
QUEENS PARK RANGERS	6-2	1970-71	6-1	1982-83
SHEFFIELD UNITED	10-3	1933-34	6-1	1921-22
SHEFFIELD WEDNESDAY	8-0	1973-74	5-0	1904-05
SOUTHAMPTON	5-0	1960-61	6-0	1962-63
TOTTENHAM HOTSPUR	4-1	1980-81	7-1	1952-53
WIMBLEDON	1-0	1988-89	3-0	1985-86

MANAGER: LENNIE LAWRENCE

DATE OF BIRTH: 14.12.1947   **PLACE OF BIRTH:** Brighton, Sussex

DATE OF APPOINTMENT: July 1991

PREVIOUS CLUBS
as Player/Manager: Plymouth Argyle, Charlton Athletic
as Asst. Manager: Plymouth Argyle, Lincoln City
as Player: Non-League

HONOURS
as Manager: (Charlton): Runners-up Div 2 1985-86, Simod Cup Runners-Up 1987
as Asst. Man.: Promotion to Div 3 1980-81
as Player:
International:

Value Rating: ★ ★ ★ ★

Programme Editor: Clive Armitage

Price of 1992-93 Programme: £1

Number of Pages: 32

Subscriptions: £27 home, £45 home & away (League only)

Local Newspapers: Evening Gazette, Northern Echo, Hartlepool Mail, Yorkshire Post, Journal, Sunday Sun.

Local Radio Stations: BBC Radio Cleveland, TFM (Formerly Radio Tees).

Publications on Club: Middlesbrough – A Complete Record 1876-1989 by Harry Glasper (Breedon Books £14.95)
Middlesbrough F.C. by Eric Paylor (Archive Publications £7.95)

LEADING LEAGUE GOALSCORERS
SEASONS 1979-80 – 1991-92

1979-80	DAVID ARMSTRONG	11		1980-81	BOZO JANKOVIC	12
1981-82	BILLY ASHCROFT	4		1982-83	HEINE OTTO	9
	TONY McANDREW	4			DAVID SHEARER	9
	HEINE OTTO	4				
1983-84	DAVID CURRIE	15		1984-85	DAVID MILLS	14
1985-86	GARY ROWELL	10		1986-87	BERNIE SLAVEN	17
1987-88	BERNIE SLAVEN	21		1988-89	BERNIE SLAVEN	15
1989-90	BERNIE SLAVEN	21		1990-91	BERNIE SLAVEN	16

1991-92 BERNIE SLAVEN 16

AYRESOME PARK Middlesbrough, Cleveland TS1 4PB

Capacity: 26,500   **Standing:** 13,500   **Seating:** 13,000

Tel: Ground: 0642 819659   **Ticket Sales:** 0642 815996   **Clubcall:** 0898 12 11 81

All premium rate calls (0898/0891) cost 36p per minute cheap rate and 48p per minute at all other times. Call costings correct at time of going to press.

GROUNDS
Old Archery Ground 1876-79; Breckon Hill Road 1879-80; Linthorpe Road 1880-1903; Ayresome Park 1903-

ATTENDANCES
Highest: 53,803 v Newcastle United, Division 1, 27.12.1949

Lowest: 2,177 v Carlisle Utd, Full Members Cup, 8.10.1985

RECORD RECEIPTS (with previous records):
£178,977 v Manchester Utd, Lge Cup 5th Rnd, 4.3.1992
£146,300 v Peterborough Utd, Lge Cup S/F, 12.2.1992
£102,530 v Notts Co., Div 2 P/Off, 19.5.1991
£96,985 v Everton, FA Cup 3rd Rnd, 6.1.1990
£57,710 v Barnsley, FA Cup 5th Round, 14.2.1981
£39,596 v Nottingham Forest, Lge Cup Rnd 3, 26.9.1979

AYRESOME PARK
First game: v Sunderland, Div 1, 12.9.1903
First floodlit game: v Sunderland, (Friendly), 16.10.1957
Internationals: England v Ireland, 1914
England v Wales, 1937
USSR v North Korea, 1966
Chile v North Korea, 1966
Italy v North Korea, 1966

Season Tickets:
Stands: from £230 to £250, juv/OAP £84 to £168
Ground: £168 no reductions

Executive Box Season Tickets: None

Cost of Stand Tickets: Seats £11-£12, juv/OAP £4-£8
Terraces: £8

Match and Ticket Information: Postal or personal applications two weeks prior to any match

Car Parking: Off-street near the ground; on-street around the ground

Nearest Railway Station: Middlesbrough (0624 243208)

How to get to the ground

From North: Use A19 (S.P. Middlesbrough), cross Tees Bridge and in 0.2m join A66. In 1.5m at roundabout, take third exit into Heywood Street. At end turn left into Ayresome Street for Middlesbrough FC

From South: Use A1 and A19 to Junction with A1130. In 1m join A66. 1m further at roundabout take fourth exit into Heywood Street, at end turn left into Ayresome Street to Middlesbrough FC

From West: Use A66 (S.P. Middlesbrough). 1.6m after Teeside Park Race Course at roundabout take fourth exit in Heywood Street, at end turn left into Ayresome Street for Middlesbrough FC

MILLWALL

Division 1

Formed: 1885   **Turned Professional:** 1893   **Ltd Co:** 1894

SPONSORED BY: Fairview New Homes   **NICKNAME:** The Lions

President
Lord Melish of Bermondsey

Chairman
R I Burr

Vice-Chairman
Peter Mead

Directors
B E Mitchell   J D Burnige
Councillor D Sullivan

Chief Executive/Secretary
G I S Hortop (071-639 3143)

Player/Manager
Mick McCarthy

First Team Coach
Ian Evans

Youth Coach
Tom Walley

Reserve Team Coach
Ian McDonald

Commercial Director
Mike Ryan

Commercial Manager
Billy Neill (071-639 4590)

Physiotherapist
Peter Melville/Keith Johnstone

Groundsman
John Plummer

Club Statistician for the Directory
Richard Lindsay

TEDDY Sheringham's £2 million departure to Nottingham Forest left a huge void for Bruce Rioch to fill, consequently seven new players appeared for The Lions at Middlesbrough in the first game of the season. The first match at The Den saw the best win of the season, 4-1 v Sunderland. Bruce Rioch's brand of entertaining football was initially well recieved by the fans, but lacked Millwall's traditional fighting spirit, subsequently results were erratic. These inconsistent displays ultimately led to Mr Rioch's resignation during March 1992. Mick McCarthy was at first appointed caretaker-manager, then player-manager a month later.

Seven away wins was a reasonable return but nine home defeats led to a dismal final place of 15th.

Millwall suffered early exits from both the Rumbelows and Zenith Data Cups at the hands of Swindon and Plymouth respectively.

The only break from the diet of second division fare was a brilliant 4-0 win at Huddersfield in the F.A. Cup, with all the goals coming in the first-half. A trip to Norwich saw an equally good performance in round four where a missed penalty contributed to a 2-1 defeat.

The bulk of the goalscoring came from midfield men Paul Kerr and Millwall's first scottish international Alex Rae with 13 goals each.

For a season with many highs and lows The Lions had six men on international duty, Malcolm Allen, who had made a marvellous recovery from a long injury, Ken Cunningham, Mick McCarthy, Paul Kerr, Alex Rae and the latest, Kasey Keller the American goalie.

Richard Lindsay

Back row L-R: Paul Holsgrove, Etienne Verveer, Keith Stevens, Chris Armstrong, Mark Foran, John McGlashan, Tony McCarthy, Paul Stephenson, Tony Dolby. **Middle:** Keith Johnstone (Physio), Paul Manning, John McGinlay, Jon Goodman, Brian Horne, Aidan Davison, John Donegan, Kasey Keller, Carl Emberson, Ken Cunningham, Brian Lee, John Humphrey, Peter Melville (Physio). **Front:** Andy May, Andy Roberts, Ian Bogie, Alex Rae, Mick McCarthy (Player/Manager), Ian Evans (First Team Coach), Phil Barber, Colin Cooper, Ian Dawes, Malcolm Allen.

MILLWALL

DIVISION TWO: 15th   **FA CUP:** 4th RND   **RUMBELOWS CUP:** 2nd RND   **ZDS CUP:** 2nd RND

M	DATE		COMP.	VEN	OPPONENTS	RESULT	H/T	LGE POS	GOALSCORERS/GOAL TIMES	ATTEN-DANCE
1	A	17	BL	A	Middlesbrough	L 0-1	0-1	19		(16,234)
2		24	BL	H	Sunderland	W *4-1*	3-1	12	Barber 14, 70, Falco 20, Kerr 31	10,016
3		31	BL	A	Plymouth Argyle	L 2-3	1-2	19	Rae 45, Burrows (og) 85	(5,369)
4	S	4	BL	H	Brighton & H A	L 1-2	1-1	20	Falco 35	9,266
5		7	BL	H	Cambridge United	L 1-2	1-1	21	Kerr (pen) 4	8,459
6		14	BL	A	Oxford United	D 2-2	2-1	22	Colquhoun 27, Rae 36	(4,347)
7		17	BL	A	Bristol City	D 2-2	2-1	22	McCarthy 34, Colquhoun 35	(10,862)
8		21	BL	H	Newcastle United	W 2-1	1-1	19	Kerr 13, 90	9,156
9		25	RC 2/1	H	**Swindon Town**	D 2-2	1-2		Stephenson 43, Armstrong 55	6,048
10		28	BL	A	Barnsley	W 2-0	1-0	16	Rae 35, 47	(6,544)
11	O	5	BL	H	Blackburn Rovers	L 1-3	0-1	19	Cooper 80	8,026
12		8	RC 2/2	A	**Swindon Town**	L 1-3	1-0		Colquhoun 11	(7,134)
13		12	BL	A	Southend United	W 3-2	2-1	16	Rae 31, Stephenson 37, Colquhoun 89	(7,266)
14		19	BL	A	Ipswich Town	D 0-0	0-0	15		(11,175)
15		22	ZDS 2	A	**Plymouth Argyle**	L 0-4	0-2			(2,021)
16		26	BL	H	Derby County	L 1-2	1-1	18	Kerr 44	7,660
17		29	BL	A	Watford	W 2-0	0-0	13	Rae 57, Kerr 76	(7,333)
18	N	2	BL	H	Portsmouth	D 1-1	1-0	13	Armstrong 27	6,060
19		5	BL	A	Tranmere Rovers	L 1-2	0-1	13	Kerr (pen) 72	(6,108)
20		9	BL	A	Port Vale	W 2-0	0-0	13	Falco 47, 90	(8,944)
21		16	BL	H	Wolverhampton W	W 2-1	2-1	12	Barber 31, McGinlay 34	9,469
22		23	BL	A	Grimsby Town	D 1-1	0-0	12	McGinlay 88	(5,701)
23		30	BL	H	Bristol Rovers	L 0-1	0-1	13		7,824
24	D	7	BL	A	Leicester City	D 1-1	0-0	13	Kerr 66	(12,127)
25		21	BL	A	Brighton & H A	W 4-3	1-0	11	McGinlay 8, 65, Kerr (pen) 56, Verveer 75	(7,598)
26		26	BL	H	Watford	L 0-4	0-2	13		9,237
27		28	BL	H	Plymouth Argyle	W 2-1	1-1	11	McCarthy 40, McGinlay 52	6,980
28	J	1	BL	A	Swindon Town	L 1-3	0-3	12	McGinlay 53	(9,746)
29		4	FAC 3	A	**Huddersfield Town**	W 4-0	4-0		Thompson 7, Verveer 25, Rae 30, 45	(10,879)
30		11	BL	A	Sunderland	L 2-6	1-1	13	Rae 32, Kerr 81	(16,536)
31		18	BL	H	Middlesbrough	W 2-0	1-0	13	McGinlay 40, Rae 89	8,125
32	F	1	BL	H	Ipswich Town	L 2-3	0-1	13	Rae 67, Kerr (pen) 85	8,847
33		5	FAC 4	A	**Norwich City**	L 1-2	0-1		Kerr 84	(17,050)
34		8	BL	A	Derby County	W 2-0	0-0	13	McGinlay 50, Rae 82	(12,773)
35		15	BL	H	Grimsby Town	D 1-1	1-1	13	Rae 30	6,807
36		22	BL	A	Bristol Rovers	L 2-3	1-1	13	Goodman 26, Armstrong 80	(5,747)
37		26	BL	H	Charlton Athletic	W 1-0	0-0	12	Kerr (pen) 19	12,882
38		29	BL	H	Leicester City	W 2-0	2-0	11	Cooper 6, Goodman 25	7,562
39	M	7	BL	A	Charlton Athletic	L 0-1	0-0	11		(8,177)
40		11	BL	H	Tranmere Rovers	L 0-3	0-2	11		6,456
41		14	BL	A	Portsmouth	L *1-6*	0-3	15	Verveer 85	(14,944)
42		21	BL	H	Port Vale	W 1-0	0-0	12	Allen 52	6,148
43		28	BL	A	Wolverhampton W	D 0-0	0-0	14		(11,880)
44	A	1	BL	H	Oxford United	W 2-1	0-1	12	Stephenson 55, Goodman 75	5,850
45		4	BL	A	Cambridge United	L 0-1	0-0	14		(6,385)
46		8	BL	H	Swindon Town	D 1-1	1-1	14	Allen 11	6,722
47		11	BL	H	Bristol City	L 2-3	1-0	15	Barber 21, Atteveld (og) 88	6,989
48		18	BL	A	Newcastle United	W 1-0	0-0	13	Allen 77	(23,821)
49		22	BL	H	Barnsley	D 1-1	1-1	14	Allen (pen) 23	5,703
50		25	BL	A	Blackburn Rovers	L 1-2	0-0	16	Armstrong 47	(12,820)
51	M	2	BL	H	Southend United	W 2-0	0-0	15	Armstrong 73, Allen 81	7,574

Best Home League Attendance: 12,882 v Charlton Athletic   **Smallest:** 5,703 v Barnsley   **Av Home Att:** 7,905

Goal Scorers: **Compared with 90-91:** -2,932

League (64): Kerr 12 (5 pens), Rae 11, McGinlay 8, Allen 5 (1 pen), Barber 4, Falco 4, Armstrong 4, Colquhoun 3, Goodman 3, McCarthy 2, Verveer 2, Cooper 2, Opponents 2, Stephenson 2

R/lows C (3): Colquhoun, Armstrong, Stephenson
FA Cup (5): Rae 2, Verveer, Thompson, Kerr
ZDS Cup (0):

1991-92

Davison H.	Dawes I.	Cooper C.	McGlashan J.	Thompson D.	Wood S.	Kerr P.	Colquhoun J.	Falco M.	Rae A.	Barber P.	Armstrong C.	Bogle I.	McLeary A.	Cunningham K.	Stephenson P.	McCarthy M.	Stevens K.	Branagan K.	Goodman J.	McGinlay J.	Verveer E.	Witter	Allen M.	Roberts A.	Keller K.	Referee	
1	2	3	4	5	6	7*	8	9	10*	11	12	14														S Lodge	1
1	2	3	4	5		7*	8*	9	10	11	12	14	6													J Carter	2
1	2	3	4	5	14	7	10	9	8	11	S				6*											P Durkin	3
1	2	3	4*	5		7	8	9	10	11*	12	14	6													K Barratt	4
1		3		5*	2	7	8	9		11*	10	4	6	12	14											K Morton	5
1	2	3			6	7	8	9	10		12		4*			11•	5	14								B Hill	6
1	2	3			6	7	8	9*	10		12		4			11	5	S								C Wilkes	7
1	2	3			6	7	8	9*	10		12		4			11•	5	14								T Holbrook	8
1	2	3			6	7	8	14	10		9•		S			11	5	4								**D Gallagher**	9
1	2	3	S		6	7	8	9*	10		12		4			11	5									G Courtney	10
1	2	3			6	7	8	9	10		S		4			11	5	S								M Bodenham	11
1	2	3			6	7	8	9*	10		12		4			11•	5		14							**H King**	12
1		3			6	7	8	9	10	14			4			11•	5	2	S							R Pawley	13
1		3			6	7	8	9*	10	12			4	5		11•		2								J Key	14
1		3			6	7*	8	9	10	12			4	5		11•		2								**P Vanes**	15
1•		3		5		7	8	9	10	11		4		6	14		2		S							I Hemley	16
		3		5		7	8	9	10	11	4*			6		S	2	1	12							D Phillips	17
		3		5		7	8	9*	10	11	4			6		S	2	1	12							M James	18
		3		5		7	8		10	11	9*	4		6		S	2	1	12							D Allison	19
		3•		5		7	8	9	10	11		4		6	14		2	1	S							R Milford	20
		3		5		4*	8	9•	10	11			14	6		12	2	1	7							J Martin	21
		3		5		4*	8•		10	11	14	9		6		12	2	1	7							J Worrall	22
		3		5		4			10*	11	8	9		6		S	2	1	7							I Borrett	23
		3		5		4			10	11	12	9		6		8	2	1	7*		S					V Callow	24
		3		5		4			10	11•	12	14		6	S	8	2	1	7*	9						J Brandwood	25
		3		5		4			10	11•	12	14		6	S	8	2	1	7*	9						D Axcell	26
		3		5		4				11		9	4	6	7		2	1		10	8					G Willard	27
		3				4*				11	12	9	14	6	7	5	2	1		10*	8					A Bennett	28
1	3	S		4						11•	6		14		7	9	2		5	10	8					**J Rushton**	29
1	3	S	4							11	6•		14	6	7	9	2		5	10	8					W Flood	30
1	3	2	12							11•	6	12	4		7	9	5	S		10	8					D Frampton	31
1	3	2	12	5						11•	6		4		7	9•	14			10	8					K Lupton	32
1	2	3	5			9	7			11•	6		4		14	S				10	8					**T Holbrook**	33
1	2	3	5			9	7				6		4		S	S			11	10	8					M Peck	34
1	2	3	5			7					6		4			9			11•	10	8					M Pierce	35
1	2	3•	14*			7		6	9	12			4			5			11	10	8•					R Poulain	36
1	2	3	9			7		6		14			4			5	S		11	10	8•					P Alcock	37
1	2	3				7		6		14			4		S	5	S		11	10*	8					G Pooley	38
1	2	3				7		6		14			4		S	5	S		11	10*	8					G Poll	39
1	2	3				7		6		12			4			5	S		11	10	8					A Smith	40
1	3					7		6		9•			11	14		4*	5	2		10	8		12			K Burge	41
1	3								10*	11	14	6		2	7*	4			8•	12			9			K Morton	42
1	3		14						10†	11	6•			2	7*	4			8	12	5		9			M Bailey	43
1	3	6	S						10	11				2	7*	4			8	S	5		9			R Pawley	44
1	3	6	10							11•				2	7*	4			8	12	5		9	14		D Phillips	45
1	3	6						S		11				2	7	4			8	S	5		9	10		P Foakes	46
1	3	6•	12							11				2	7	4			8•	14	5		9	10		P Wright	47
1		6	12						10*	11				3	7•	4			8	14	5		9	2		T Lunt	48
1	3	6	12							11•				2	7•	4			8	14	5		9	10		R Hamer	49
1	3	6	12						10•	11	8			2*	7	4					5		9	14		B Coddington	50
	3	6	12						10		8			2	7	4*			S		5		9	11	1	I Borrett	51
33	36	36	5	29	6	32	27	19	36	26	8	20	28	15	26	14	24	12	15	19	24		10	5	1	**League Appearances**	
		3	4	1	2		2	2	3	17	5		2	2	3	3		2	6	1			1	2		**Substitute Appearances**	
2	2	2		1	1	2	2	1+1	2		1+1	1			2	2	1		0+1							**R/lows Appearances**	
2	2	1		2		2	1	1	2			1		1	1	1	1		2	2						**FA Cup Appearances**	
1		1		1		1	1	1	1	0+1		1	1		1		1	1								**ZDS Cup Appearances**	

Players on Loan: Witter (Q.P.R.)

† = Sent Off

MILLWALL

Club Colours: Blue shirts, white shorts, blue stockings.
Change Colours: Yellow shirts, black shorts, yellow stockings.
Reserves League: Neville Ovenden Football Combination

COMPETITIONS					
Div. 1	Div. 2	Div. 3	Div. 3S	Div. 4	FLT
88-90	28-34	62-64	20-28	58-62	82-83
	38-48	65-66	34-38	64-65	
	66-75	75-76	48-58		
	76-79	79-85			
	85-88				
	90-				

HONOURS				
Div. 2	Div. 3S	Div 3S KO	Div. 4	FLT
87-88	27-28	36-37	61-62	82-83
	37-38			

MOST GOALS IN A CAREER				
TEDDY SHERINGHAM 111 (1983-91)				
Season	League	FA Cup	Lge Cup	AM & FMC
1983-84	1			1
1984-85				
1985-86	4			
1986-87	13		2	1
1987-88	22			2
1988-89	11	1	3	
1989-90	9	2	1	
1990-91	33	2	2	1
Total	**93**	**5**	**8**	**5**

Previous holder: D Possee 87 (Lge 79, FAC 4, LC 4) 1967-73

MOST APPEARANCES: BARRY KITCHENER 589+7			
Year	League	FA Cup	League Cup
1966-67	3+2		
1967-68	42	1	4
1968-69	42	3	2
1969-70	42	1	2
1970-71	42	1	3
1971-72	42	3	1
1972-73	40	3	3
1973-74	41		7
1974-75	39	3	1
1975-76	45	5	2
1976-77	38	1	9
1977-78	31	5	3
1978-79	40	1	3
1979-80	10+2	1+2	
1980-81	18+1	1	2
1981-82	3		
	518+5	**29+2**	**42**

Previous holder: Harry Cripps 390+10 (1961-74)

MANAGERS			
Name	Seasons	Best	Worst
F B Kidd	1894-99	1(SL)	9(SL)
E R Stopher	1899-1900	7(SL)	7(SL)
G A Saunders	1900-11	3(SL)	15(SL)
H Lipsham	1911-18	6(3S)	7(3S)
R Hunter	1918-33	7(2)	13(3S)
W McCracken	1933-36	21(2)	12(3S)
C Hewitt	1936-40	13(2)	8(3S)
W Voisey	1940-44		
J Cock	1944-48	18(2)	22(2)
C Hewitt	1948-56	2(3S)	22(3S)
R Gray	1956-58	23(3S)	23(3S)
J Seed	1958-59	9(3S)	9(3S)
J Smith	1959-61	5(4)	6(4)
R Gray	1961-63	16(3)	1(4)
W Gray	1963-66	2(3)	2(4)
B Fenton	1966-74	3(2)	12(2)
G Jago	1974-77	10(2)	3(3)
G Petchley	1978-80	21(2)	12(3)
P Anderson	1980-82	15(3)	16(3)
G Graham	1982-86	9(2)	17(3)
J Docherty	1986-90	10(1)	16(2)
B Rioch	1990-92	5(2)	5(2)
M McCarthy (p/man.)	1992-		

HIGHEST TRANSFER FEE RECEIVED			
Amount	Club	Player	Date
£2,000,000	Nott'm Forest	Teddy Sheringham	7/91
£1,500,000	Aston Villa	Tony Cascarino	3/90
£800,000	Liverpool	Jimmy Carter	1/91
£400,000	Southampton	Steve Wood	10/91

HIGHEST TRANSFER FEE PAID			
Amount	Club	Player	Date
£800,000	Derby County	Paul Goddard	12/89
£500,000	Lyon	Mick McCarthy	5/90
£400,000	Norwich City	Malcolm Allen	3/90
£300,000	Tottenham H.	Neil Ruddock	6/88

LONGEST LEAGUE RUNS	
of undefeated matches:	19 (27.4.1959-7.11.1959)
of undefeated home matches:	59 (20.4.1964-14.1.1967)
without home win:	9 (1.1.1990-1.9.1990)
of league wins:	10 (10.3.1928-26.4.1928)
of league defeats:	11 (10.4.1929-21.9.1929)
of league matches w/out a win:	20 (26.12.1989-5.5.1990)
of undefeated away matches:	10 (5.3.1921-17.9.1921)
	(13.2.1988-15.10.1988)
without an away win:	26 (7.11.1979-26.12.1980)
of home wins:	13 (15.12.1923-30.8.1924)
of away wins:	5 (17.3.1928-25.4.1928)

PREVIOUS NAMES
Millwall Rovers 1885, Millwall Athletic 1889

PREVIOUS LEAGUES
United London Western Lge's; Southern District Comb.; Southern League

BIGGEST VICTORIES
League: 9-1 v Torquay United, Division 3S, 29.8.1927.
9-1 v Coventry, Division 3S, 19.11.1927.
F.A. Cup: 7-0 v Gateshead, Round 2, 12.12.1936.
League Cup: 5-1 v Northampton, Round 3 replay, 16.10.1967.

BIGGEST DEFEATS
League: 1-8 v Plymouth, Division 2, 16.1.1932.
F.A. Cup: 1-9 v Aston Villa, Round 4, 28.1.1946.
League Cup: 1-7 v Chelsea, Round 1, 10.10.1960.

MOST POINTS
3 points a win: 90, Division 3, 1984-85.
2 points a win: 65, Division 3S, 1927-28 & Division 3, 1965-66.

MOST GOALS
127, 1927-28 (Division 3S record).
Landells 33, Phillips 26, Cock 25, Bryant 12, Black 8, Hawkins 7, Chance 6, Parker 4, Amos 2, Collins 2, Page 1, og 1.

MOST GOALS IN A MATCH
5. Richard Parker v Norwich City, 6-1, Division 3S, 28.8.1926

MOST GOALS IN A SEASON
R Parker (1926-27): League 37, FA Cup 1. Total 38
Peter Burridge (1960-61): League 35, FA Cup 2, League Cup 1. Total 38
E. Sheringham (1990-91): League 33, FA Cup 2, League Cup 2, FMC 1. Total 38

MOST FIRST CLASS MATCHES IN A SEASON
61 (46 League, 7 FA Cup, 4 League Cup, 4 Freight Rover Trophy) 1984-85

MOST LEAGUE GOALS CONCEDED
100, Division 3S, 1955-56

MOST LEAGUE WINS
30, Division 3S, 1927-28

MOST LEAGUE DRAWS
18, Division 3S, 1921-22; Division 3S, 1922-23

MOST LEAGUE DEFEATS
26, Division 3S, 1957-58

OLDEST PLAYER
Jack Fort, 41 years 8 months

YOUNGEST PLAYER
David Mehmet, 16 years 5 months.

MOST CAPPED PLAYER
Eamonn Dunphy (Eire) 22 (23 in all)

BEST PERFORMANCES BY MILLWALL

League: 1927-28: Matches played 42, Won 30, Drawn 5, Lost 7, Goals for 127, Goals against 50, Points 65. First in Division 3S.
Millwall are the only Football League Club to be unbeaten at home in four different Divisions: Div 3S 1927-28; Div 4 1964-65; Div 3 1965-66 & 1984-85; Div 2, 1971-72

Highest: 1988-89: 10th in Division 1.

F.A. Cup: 1899-00: 1st rnd. Jarrow 2-0; 2nd rnd. Queens Park Rangers 2-0; 3rd rnd. Aston Villa 1-1, 0-0, 2-1; Semi-Final Southampton 0-0, 0-3.

1902-03: 1st rnd. Luton 3-0; 2nd rnd. Preston North End 4-1; 3rd rnd. Everton 1-0; Semi-Final Derby 0-3.

1936-37: 1st rnd. Aldershot 6-1; 2nd rnd. Gateshead 7-0; 3rd rnd. Fulham 2-0; 4th rnd. Chelsea 3-0; 5th rnd. Derby County 2-1; 6th rnd. Manchester City 2-0; Semi-Final Sunderland 1-2.

League Cup: 1973-74: 2nd rnd. Nottingham Forest 0-0, 3-1; 3rd rnd. Bolton Wanderers 1-1, 2-1; 4th rnd. Luton Town 3-1; 5th rnd. Norwich City 1-1, 1-2.

1976-77: 1st rnd. Colchester 2-1, 1-2, 4-4; 2nd rnd. Rotherham 2-1; 3rd rnd. Orient 0-0 (2), 3-0; 4th rnd. Sheffield Wednesday 3-0; 5th rnd. Aston Villa 0-2.

DIVISIONAL RECORDS

	Played	Won	Drawn	Lost	For	Against	Points
DIVISION 1	76	19	22	35	86	117	79
DIVISION 2	1102	398	288	416	1476	1541	1177
DIVISION 3	460	182	128	150	643	605	586
DIVISION 3S	956	410	233	313	1508	1253	1053
DIVISION 4	228	105	61	62	422	323	271
TOTALS	2822	1114	732	976	4145	3839	3166

MILLWALL

PLAYERS NAME Honours	Ht	Wt	Birthdate	Birthplace Transfers	Contract Date	Clubs	League	L/Cup	FA Cup	Other	Lg	L/C	FAC	Oth
GOALKEEPERS														
Aidan Davison	6.1	13.2	11.05.68	Sedgefield		Spennymoor Utd		1						
						Billingham Synth.		1						
					25.03.88	Notts County	1							
Loan Leyton Orient (07.09.88)				Loan	07.10.89	Bury								
				£6,000	17.11.89	Bury								
Loan Chester City (21.03.91)				Loan	28.03.91	Blackpool								
					14.08.91	Millwall	33	2	2	1				
John Donegan						Kilkline								
				£30,000		Millwall								
Carl Emberson			13.07.91	Surrey	04.05.91	Millwall								
Brian Horne	5.11	12.4	05.10.67	Billericay	10.10.85	Millwall (A)	163	14	9	10				
E: u21.5, u19.2,Y.8; Div2'88				Loan	26.03.92	Watford								
Kasey Keller						Portland Timbers								
				Free	20.02.92	Millwall	1							
DEFENDERS														
Colin Cooper	5.8	9.4	28.02.67	Durham	17.07.84	Middlesbrough	183+5	18	13	19+1	6			2
E:u21.8				£300,000	25.07.91	Millwall	36	2	1	1	2			
Kenneth Cunningham			28.06.71	Dublin	18.09.89	Millwall	41+4	1	1					
Ian Dawes	5.8	10.2	22.02.63	Croydon	24.12.80	Q.P.R. (A)	229	28	8	5	3	1		
ES,Div2'83				£150,000	26.08.88	Millwall	141+3	10	11	5+1	5			
Mick McCarthy	6.2	13.7	07.02.59	Barnsley	28.07.77	Barnsley (A)	272	27	16		7	3		
Ei:57; SPD'88,SFA'88'89				£200,000	15.12.83	Manchester City	140	10	7	6	2	1		
					31.05.87	Celtic	48	3	8+1	5			1	
via Lyon (France)				£500,000	21.03.90	Millwall	31+4	2	1	0+1	2			
Alan McLeary	5.10	10.9	06.10.64	Lambeth	12.10.81	Millwall (A)	285+16	16+1	24+1	21+1	5		2	2
E:B.2,u21.1,Y6,FLT'83,Div2'88														
Keith Stevens	6.0	12.5	21.06.64	Merton	23.06.81	Millwall (A)	308+7	22	23	20	4			
Div2'88,FLT'83														
MIDFIELD														
Ian Bogie	5.7	10.2	06.12.67	Newcastle	18.12.85	Newcastle Utd. (A)	7+7	0+1	1+2	3				1
				P.E	09.02.89	Preston N.E	67+12	3+1	3	4+1	12			
				£145,000	16.08.91	Millwall	20+5	1	1	1				
John M. Humphrey			02.07.69	Guildford	20.02.91	Millwall								
				Loan	19.12.91	Exeter City	2							
Andrew May	5.8	11.1	26.02.64	Bury	01.03.82	Manchester City (A)	141+9	10	6	7+1	8			
E:u21.1				£36,000	13.07.87	Huddersfield Town	112+2	5	10	8	5	1		
				Loan	24.03.88	Bolton W	9+1				2			
				£90,000	07.08.90	Bristol City	88+2	5	4	2	4		1	1
					18.06.92	Millwall								
John McGlashan	6.1	13.3	03.06.67	Dundee		Montrose	67+1	2	4		11			
					22.08.90	Millwall	9+7		0+1	1				
Alex Rae	5.8	11.8	30.09.69	Glasgow		Falkirk	71+12	5	2+1		20	1		
S:U21.4				£100,000	20.08.90	Millwall	73+4	2+1	5	4	21		4	
Andrew J Roberts			29.10.71			Millwall (T)	5+2							
Etienne Verveer						Chur (Swit								
				£100,000	13.12.91	Millwall	24+1		2		2		1	
FORWARDS														
Malcolm Allen	5.8	11.2	21.03.67	Deinhiolen	19.07.83	Watford (A)								
W:12,Y					23.03.85	Watford	27+12	4+1	6+8		5	2	6	
Loan Aston Villa (03.09.87) 4lg				£175,000	12.08.88	Norwich City	24+11	0+3	5	2+1	8		7	
				£400,000	20.03.90	Millwall	34+6	3		1	14			
Christopher Armstrong	6.0	11.0	19.06.71	Newcastle	03.03.89	Wrexham	40+20	2+1	0+1	5+1	13			3
				£50,000	16.08.91	Millwall	8+17	1+1			4	1		
Phillip Barber	5.11	12.6	10.06.65	Tring		Aylesbury								
				£7,500	14.02.84	Crystal Palace	207+27	13+6	14	19+2	35	3	1	2
				£100,000	25.07.91	Millwall	26+3			0+1	4			
Mark Falco	6.0	11.5	12.07.56	Hackney	14.07.78	Tottenham H. (A)	162+12	19+3	15	27+5	67	3	5	18
E:4,Y,CS'81,UEFAC'84				Loan	25.11.82	Chelsea	3							
					09.10.86	Watford	33		7	1	14		2	
					17.07.87	Brec	9+5	2+1		2	5	3		2
				£350,000	11.01.88	Q.P.R	65+22	5+1	8+2	3	27	4	2	
				£175,000	16.08.91	Millwall	19+2	1+1	1	1	4			
Jonathon Goodman	6.0	12.3	02.06.71	Walthamstow		Wham								
					20.08.90	Millwall	35+5	0+1	3	1	8			
Paul Kerr	5.8	11.11	09.06.64	Portsmouth	18.05.82	Aston Villa (A)	16+8	5+1	2	0+2	3	2	1	
				£50,000	07.01.86	Middlesbrough	114+11	10	9+2	13+3	13	1	3	1
				£100,000	28.03.91	Millwall	42+2	2	2	1	12		1	
John McGinlay	5.9	11.06	08.04.64	Inverness		Yeovil Town			5				2	
Isthmian Lge Prem.'88						Elgin City			1				1	
					22.02.89	Shrewsbury Town	58+2	4	1	3	27		2	2
				£175,000	11.07.90	Bury	16+9	1	1	1+1	9			
				£80,000	28.03.91	Millwall	21+6		2	1	8			1
Paul Stephenson	5.10	10.0	02.01.68	Wallsend	02.01.86	Newcastle Utd. (A)	58+3	3+1	2	2	1			
E:Y2				£300,000	10.11.88	Millwall	81+12	3	9	6	6	1	2	1

ADDITIONAL CONTRACT PLAYERS

Tony Dolby, Mark Foran, Brian Lee, Mark Madden, Paul Manning, Tony McCarhty, Joeseph Okyere-Darkoh

MILLWALL

RECORD WIN & LOSS AGAINST EACH CLUB IN CURRENT DIVISION
(Where a score has occured on several occasions the most recent is given)

Club	Rec. Win	Season	Rec. Loss	Season
BARNSLEY	4-1	1962-63	4-1	1962-63
BIRMINGHAM CITY	6-2	1969-70	4-0	1946-47
BRENTFORD	4-0	1955-56	6-1	1927-28
BRISTOL CITY	4-1	1931-32	5-0	1928-29
BRISTOL ROVERS	6-1	1927-28 (away)	4-0	1982-83
CAMBRIDGE UNITED	2-0	1978-79	2-1	1978-79
CHARLTON ATHLETIC	6-0	1930-31	3-1	1934-35
DERBY COUNTY	2-0	1991-92	5-1	1966-67
GRIMSBY TOWN	4-1	1928-29	5-1	1985-86
LEICESTER CITY	2-0	1991-92	5-0	1946-47
LUTON TOWN	7-0	1926-27	6-0	1926-27
NEWCASTLE UNITED	4-0	1988-89	4-1	1946-47 (home)
NOTTS COUNTY	6-1	1963-64	5-2	1976-77
OXFORD UNITED	3-0	1979-80	4-2	1983-84
PETERBOROUGH UTD	4-1	1965-66	6-0	1962-63
PORTSMOUTH	3-1	1969-70	6-1	1991-92
SOUTHEND UNITED	8-1	1925-26	6-0	1935-36
SUNDERLAND	4-1	1991-92	2-6	1991-92
SWINDON TOWN	6-1	1953-54	4-1	1920-21
TRANMERE ROVERS	3-0	1961-62	5-1	1961-62
WATFORD	6-0	1962-63	4-0	1991-92 (home)
WEST HAM UNITED	2-1	1978-79	3-0	1988-89
WOLVERHAMPTON WNDRS	4-0	1929-30	5-0	1931-32

MANAGER: MICK McCARTHY

DATE OF BIRTH: 07.02.1959　　　　**PLACE OF BIRTH:** Barnsley

DATE OF APPOINTMENT: March 1992

PREVIOUS CLUBS
as Manager:
as Player: Barnsley; Manchester City; Celtic; Lyon (Fra); Millwall

HONOURS
as Manager:
as Asst. Man./Coach:
as Player:
International: Eire: 57 Full Caps

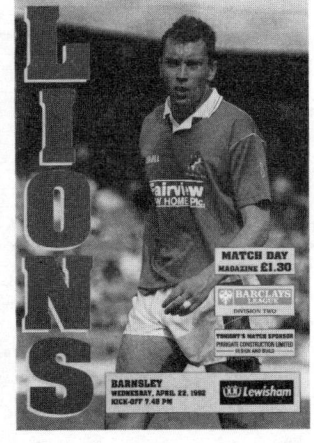

Value Rating: ★ ★ ★

Programme Editor: Deano Standing/Rob Bowden

Price of 1992-93 Programme: £1.40

Number of Pages: 36

Subscriptions: Home League £40, All home games £53, Every game home & away £91

Local Newspapers: South London Press, South East London Mercury, Southwark & Bermondsey News

Local Radio Stations: LBC, Capital

Additional Publications on Club: Lions of the South, (James Murray), Indispensable Publications, £12.95 softback
Millwall – a Complete Record, (Richard Lindsay), Breedon Books, £16.95 hardback
Lions Through the Lens, (Ted Wilding), Temple Printing, £6.95 softback

LEADING LEAGUE GOALSCORERS
SEASONS 1979-80 – 1991-92

1979-80	JOHN LYONS	18		1980-81	MICK CHATTERTON	8
1981-82	DEAN HORRIX	15		1982-83	DEAN NEAL	18
1983-84	KEVIN BREMNER	15		1984-85	STEVE LOVELL	21
1985-86	STEVE LOVELL	14		1986-87	TEDDY SHERINGHAM	13
1987-88	TEDDY SHERINGHAM	22		1988-89	TONY CASCARINO	13
1989-90	TEDDY SHERINGHAM	9		1990-91	TEDDY SHERINGHAM	33
	TONY CASCARINO	9				

1991-92 **PAUL KERR** 12

THE DEN Cold Blow Lane, New Cross, London SE14 5RH

Capacity: 19,922 **Covered Standing:** 16,772 **Seating:** 3,150

Tel: Ground: 071 639 3143 **Ticket Sales:** As ground number **Clubcall:** 0898 400 300

All premium rate calls (0898/0891) cost 36p per minute cheap rate and 48p per minute at all other times. Call costings correct at time of going to press.

GROUNDS
Glengall Road 1885-86; Back of Lord Nelson 1886-90; East Ferry Road 1890-01; North Greenwich 1901-10; The Den 1910-

ATTENDANCES
Highest: 48,672 v Derby County, FA Cup 5th Round, 20.2.1937

Lowest: 967 v West Bromwich Albion, Full Members Cup, 21.10.1986

RECORD RECEIPTS (with previous records):
£110,804 v Liverpool, FA Cup Round 4, 29.1.1989
£75,195 v Arsenal, Div 1, 11.2.1989
£52,637 v Leicester, FA Cup Round 5, 19.2.1985
£26,872 v West Bromwich Albion, League Cup Round 2, 4.10.1983

THE DEN
First game: v Brighton, 0-1, 22.10.1910
First floodlit game: v Manchester United, 1953
International: England v Wales: 1911

Season Tickets:
Stands: from £180 to £216, juv/OAP £99 to £218
Ground: from £125, juv/OAP £98

Executive Box Season Tickets: Executive Club £575 per annum (usual VIP facilities and car park)

Cost of Stand Tickets: Stand: £9.20-£11 (no concessions)
Terraces: £7 adults; £6 members; £6 juveniles/OAP; £4.50 members; Junior Lions £3

Match and Ticket Information: Seats bookable 21 days in advance from club office (Members only)

Car Parking: Good street parking. Also car park near the ground (Ilderton Road)

Nearest Railway Station: New Cross Gate BR & Tube, New Cross BR & Tube, Queens Road (Peckham) BR, South Bermondsey BR (nearest for Away End), all within 15 mins from ground

---

How to get to the ground

From North: From Motorway M1 and A1 follow signs London A1 then City, then follow signs Shoreditch, Whitechapel. Then follos signs Ring Road, Dover to cross Tower Bridge. In 1.8m at roundabout turn left into Old Kent Road, after Railway Bridge take 2nd left (Cassella Rd), 1st left and follow on to Cold Blow Lane for Millwall FC
From East: Use A2 S.P. London. At New Cross follow signs, City, Westminster, into, into Kendar Street and at end turn right then 1st left (Cassell Rd), then 1st left and follow into Cold Blow Lane for Millwall FC
From South: Use A20 and A21 S.P. London. At New Cross follow signs City, Westminster, into Kendar Street and at end turn right, then 1st left (Cassella Rd), then 1st left and follow into Cold Blow Lane for Millwall FC
From West: From Motorway M4 and M3 take South Circular Road A205. Then follow signs Clapham, City A3 then signs Camberwell, New Cross and later Rochester A202 and in 0.8m turn left into Kender Street and at end turn right, then 1st left (Cassella Rd), then 1st left and follow into Cold Blow Lane for Millwall FC

NEWCASTLE UNITED

Division 1

Formed: 1892   **Turned Professional:** 1889   **Ltd Co:** 1890

SPONSORED BY: Newcastle Breweries Ltd   **NICKNAME:** The Magpies

---

Chairman
Sir John Hall

Directors
Douglas Hall
R S Jones
Freddie Shepherd (Vice-Chairman)

Chief Executive
Freddie Fletcher (091-232 8361)

General Manager/Secretary
Russell Cushing (091-232 8361)

Commercial Consultant
Grahame McDonnell (091-232 2285)

Team Manager
Kevin Keegan

Assistant Manager
Terry McDermott

Coaches
Colin Suggett/Derek Fazackerley
John Carver

Youth Development Officer
John Murray

Physiotherapist
Derek Wright

Assistant Secretary
Ken Slater

Community Scheme Organiser
Jeff Clarke (091-261 9715)

Club Statistician for the Directory
Dave Graham & David Stewart

THE 1991-92 season was eagerly anticipated by Newcastle United supporters, in fact the team was installed by the bookies as favourites to claim one of the two automatic promotion places available, what was to follow was a centenary season of total disappointment. The season started with only one league win in the first eleven matches, that being at Bristol Rovers where the side triumphed by 2-1, but the amount of goals being conceded was already a major problem. The loss of defenders Ranson and Kristensen, both with long term injuries, did not help the cause, with the talented but inexperienced youngsters missing the experience both players would have provided. The side continued to impress going forward with wins against Oxford United in the league and Crewe Alexandra in the Rumbelows Cup, both by 4-3. There was also an amazing 6-6 draw against Tranmere Rovers in the Zenith Data Cup which was finally won on penalties by Rovers. Interest in the Rumbelows Cup ended at Peterborough where the third division side triumphed by 1-0. The injuries showed no signs of easing with Quinn suffering a serious ligament injury at Portsmouth and Carr and Clark also missing parts of the season.

The gloom was occasionally lifted with the odd good result, namely home victories over Leicester and Grimsby by 2-0 and Southend 3-2. There was also a 1-1 draw at Sunderland where a very young side helped salvage some local pride.

The end of the year arrived with the team situated in 18th position in the league and the possibility of relegation to the Third Division for the first time in their history a real threat. The performances at the beginning of January did little to improve the situation with a 4-0 defeat at Southend followed by an early F.A. Cup exit at the hands of Third Division Bournemouth, and an amazing 4-3 home defeat by Charlton Athletic, where a 3-0 lead was squandered.

A further defeat by 5-2 at fellow strugglers Oxford United lead to the dismissal of manager Ossie Ardiles. The choice of Kevin Keegan to succeed Ardiles took the fans completely by surprise. Keegan, who although once idolised as a player at the club, had been out of the game for eight years. The appointment though created instant results with Bristol City being defeated 3-0, watched by a crowd of 29,263. Further wins were achieved against Port Vale, 1-0, Cambridge United 2-0, Swindon Town 3-1 and Sunderland 1-0, all of which gave the fans great hope that the dreaded drop to the Third Division could be avoided.

It is now hoped that with Keegan signing a three year contract the club can move forward with more confidence.

The two main highlights of the season were the performances of Gavin Peacock and the usual great loyalty shown by the fans, where a top league average of 21,024 was achieved despite the club never being higher than 15th place in the league. They deserve better.   **David Stewart**

Back row L-R: David Roche, Andy Hunt, Alan Neilson, Darron McDonough, Rob Elliott, Matty Appleby, Barry Venison, David Kelly, Mick Quinn, Peter Garland, John Watson, Phil Mason. **Middle:** Derek Fazackerley (First Team Coach), Colin Suggett (Youth Team Coach), Pavel Srnicek, Bjorn Kristensen, Peter Cormack, Liam O'Brien, Stephen Howey, Stephen Watson, Kevin Scott, Alan Thompson, Tommy Wright, Derek Wright (Physio), Chris Guthrie (Kit Manager). **Front:** Mark Stimson, Kevin Sheedy, Franz Carr, Kevin Brock, Lee Clark, Terry McDermott (Asst. Manager), Kevin Keegan (Manager), Brian Kilcline, Gavin Peacock, Ray Ranson, Paul Bracewell, John Beresford.

NEWCASTLE UNITED

DIVISION TWO: 20th   **FA CUP:** 3rd RND   **RUMBELOWS CUP:** 3rd RND   **ZDS CUP:** 1st RND

M	DATE	COMP.	VEN	OPPONENTS	RESULT	H/T	LGE POS	GOALSCORERS/GOAL TIMES	ATTEN-DANCE
1	A 18	BL	A	Charlton Athletic	L 1-2	0-0		Carr 81	(9,322)
2	24	BL	H	Watford	D 2-2	1-1	19	Hunt 10, Clark 57	22,440
3	27	BL	A	Middlesbrough	L 0-3	0-1	22		(16,970)
4	31	BL	A	Bristol Rovers	W 2-1	1-0	18	O'Brien 44, Quinn 54	(6,334)
5	S 4	BL	H	Plymouth Argyle	D 2-2	0-1	17	Carr 81, Quinn 85	19,543
6	7	BL	A	Tranmere Rovers	L 2-3	2-1	19	O'Brien 42, Clark 45	(11,465)
7	14	BL	H	Wolverhampton W	L 1-2	0-0	20	Madden (og) 83	20,195
8	17	BL	H	Ipswich Town	D 1-1	0-1	21	Quinn (pen) 68	16,336
9	21	BL	A	Millwall	L 1-2	1-1	22	Neilson 8	(9,156)
10	24	RC 2/1	A	Crewe Alexandra	W 4-3	2-3		Peacock 3 (42, 74, 84), Hunt 31	(4,251)
11	28	BL	H	Derby County	D 2-2	0-1	23	Hunt 76, Quinn 77	17,581
12	O 1	ZDS 1	A	Tranmere Rovers	D †6-6	2-2		Quinn 3 (4, 24, 118), Peacock 65, 110, Clark 104 (††)	(4,056)
13	5	BL	A	Portsmouth	L 1-3	0-2	24	Quinn 68	(10,175)
14	9	RC 2/2	H	Crewe Alexandra	W 1-0	0-0		Howey 88	9,197
15	12	BL	H	Leicester City	W 2-0	0-0	22	Hunt 66, Clark 78	16,966
16	19	BL	H	Oxford United	W 4-3	2-1	21	Peacock 3 (33, 48, 90), Hunt 14	16,454
17	26	BL	A	Bristol City	D 1-1	1-0	20	Clark 13	(8,613)
18	29	RC 3	A	Peterborough Utd	**L 0-1**	0-0			(10,382)
19	N 2	BL	A	Swindon Town	L 1-2	0-1	21	Peacock 90	(10,731)
20	6	BL	H	Cambridge United	D 1-1	0-0	21	Hunt 90	13,077
21	9	BL	H	Grimsby Town	W 2-0	2-0	21	Hunt 17, Howey 29	16,959
22	17	BL	A	Sunderland	D 1-1	0-1	21	O'Brien 59	(29,224)
23	20	BL	A	Southend United	W 3-2	3-1	15	Peacock (pen) 10, 15, Hunt 33	14,740
24	23	BL	H	Blackburn Rovers	D 0-0	0-0	16		23,639
25	30	BL	A	Barnsley	L 0-3	0-3	17		(9,648)
26	D 7	BL	H	Port Vale	D 2-2	1-1	17	Makel 40, Peacock (pen) 61	18,162
27	14	BL	A	Brighton & H A	D 2-2	2-1	18	Peacock 33, Kelly 41	(7,658)
28	20	BL	A	Plymouth Argyle	L 0-2	0-1	18		(5,048)
29	26	BL	H	Middlesbrough	L 0-1	0-0	21		26,563
30	28	BL	H	Bristol Rovers	W 2-1	0-0	18	Brock 64, Kelly 81	19,329
31	J 1	BL	A	Southend United	L 0-4	0-2	20		(9,458)
32	4	FAC 3	A	Bournemouth	D 0-0	0-0			(10,639)
33	11	BL	A	Watford	D 2-2	1-2	22	Kelly 23, Hunt 58	(9,811)
34	18	BL	H	Charlton Athletic	L 3-4	3-1	23	Clark 25, Hunt 31, Brock 34	15,663
35	22	FAC 3R	H	Bournemouth	D †2-2	1-0		Hunt 14, 91 (Lost 4-3 on pens)	25,954
36	F 1	BL	A	Oxford United	L 2-5	0-1	23	Scott 62, Peacock (pen) 67	(5,872)
37	8	BL	H	Bristol City	W **3-0**	0-0	22	Kelly 53, 61, O'Brien 55	29,263
38	15	BL	A	Blackburn Rovers	L 1-3	1-1	22	Kelly 12	(19,511)
39	22	BL	A	Barnsley	D 1-1	0-0	22	Kelly 70	27,670
40	29	BL	A	Port Vale	W 1-0	1-0	19	Watson 18	(10,321)
41	M 7	BL	H	Brighton & H A	L 0-1	0-0	21		24,597
42	10	BL	H	Cambridge United	W 2-0	1-0	19	Peacock 38, Kelly 44	(8,254)
43	14	BL	H	Swindon Town	W 3-1	1-0	18	Kelly 30, Peacock 70, Quinn 82	23,138
44	21	BL	A	Grimsby Town	D 1-1	1-1	19	Sheedy 41	(11,613)
45	29	BL	H	Sunderland	W 1-0	1-0	17	Kelly 33	30,306
46	31	BL	A	Wolverhampton W	L **2-6**	1-3	22	Quinn 12, Peacock 77	(14,480)
47	A 4	BL	H	Tranmere Rovers	L 2-3	1-2	19	Brock 30, 86	21,125
48	11	BL	A	Ipswich Town	L 2-3	2-1	19	Peacock 17, 42	(20,673)
49	18	BL	H	Millwall	L 0-1	0-0	21		23,821
50	20	BL	A	Derby County	L 1-4	0-2	22	Peacock 49	(21,363)
51	25	BL	H	Portsmouth	W 1-0	0-0	20	Kelly 85	25,989
52	M 2	BL	A	Leicester City	W 2-1	1-0	20	Peacock 45, Walsh (og) 90	(21,861)

Best Home League Attendance: 30,306 v Sunderland   **Smallest:** 13,077 v Cambridge Utd   **Av Home Att:** 21,024

Goal Scorers: **Compared with 90-91: +4,145**

League (66): Peacock 16 (3 pens), Kelly 11, Hunt 9, Quinn 7 (1 pen), Clark 5, O'Brien 4, Brock 4, Carr 2, Opponents 2, Sheedy, Howey, Neilson, Watson, Scott, Makel

R/lows C (5): Peacock 3, Hunt, Howey

FA Cup (2): Hunt 2

ZDS Cup (6): Quinn 3, Peacock 2, Clark   (†† = Lost 3-2 on pens)   † = After extra-time

Smicek P.	Watson S.	Elliott R.	O'Brien L.	Scott K.	Bradshaw D.	Clark L.	Peacock G.	Quinn M.	Carr F.	Brock K.	Kelly D.	Roche D.	Hunt A.	Makel L.	Neilson A.	Howey S.	Stimson M.	Kristensen B.	Appleby M.	Wright T.	Thompson A.	Kilcline B.	Sheedy K.	Ransom R.	McDonough D.	Referee	
1	2*	3	4	5	6	7	8	9	10	11•			14													B Hill	1
1	2	3	4	5	6	7	8	9	10			S		11	S											R Shepherd	2
1	14	3	4*	5	6	7	8	9	10			12	11•					2								K Hackett	3
1		3	4	5	6	7	8	9	10			11•	S	14	2											P Taylor	4
1		3	4	5	6	7	8*	9	10			11•	12	14	2											M Peck	5
1	2	3	4	5	6	7	8	9	10	11*		12	S													I Hendrick	6
1		3	4	5	6	7	2	9	10	8		S	11			S										W Burns	7
1			4	5	6	7	2	9	10•	8		14	11*					12	3							E Parker	8
1			4	5	6	7	8	9		11		S	14		2			3								T Holbrook	9
1		3	4	5	6	7	8	9				11*	10•		2	14		12								**R Dilkes**	10
1		3	4	5	6•	7	8	9		11		14	12		2											C Trussell	11
1		3	4	5	6	7	8	9		11*		12	10		2											**J Key**	12
1			4	5	6†	7	8	9	12			11•	10*		2		3		14							L Shapter	13
1			4	5		7	8	11				S	10		2	12	3	6								**A Bennett**	14
1			4	5		7	8		11*	14		9•	10		2	12	3									S Lodge	15
			4	5		7	8			S		11	10•		2	9	3		1							R Nixon	16
			4	5		7	8•					11	10	12*	2	9	3		1							D Gallagher	17
			4	5	2	7						11	10*	8•		9	3	6	1		14					**P Durkin**	18
			4	5	2	7	8					11	10•			9	3	6	1	14						A Buksh	19
			4	5	2•	7	8		10			11	12			9	3*	6	1	14						T Fitzharris	20
	14		4	5			8		10•			2	11			9	3	6	1	7						P Wright	21
	14		4	5	2•		8					7	11	12		9	3	6	1	10*						J Lloyd	22
	2		4	5	14		8		12			7	10*			9	3•	6	1	11						P Harrison	23
	2	3	4	5	S		8					14	7	10		9		6	1	11•						I Cruikshanks	24
	2		4	5	12		8					14	7	10		9	3	6*	1	11•						V Callow	25
	S		4	5			8					11	9	2	10	7	S	6	1							D Phillips	26
	14		4•	5			8					11	9	2	10	7	S	6	1							C Wilkes	27
	14			5	2•		8					11	9	4	10	7*		12	6	1						W Burge	28
	2			5			14	8				11	9	4•	10	7*		12	6	1						G Courtney	29
	2			5			7	8				11	9		10*	S		12	6	1	4					K Hackett	30
	2			5	S		7	8				9*		12	11	10			6	1	4					R Wiseman	31
	2		4	5	3		7	8				11	9		10*			12	6	1	S					**V Callow**	32
	2		4	5	3*		7	8					9	10	12		S		6	1	11					J Deakin	33
	2		4	5			7	8				11	9•	14	10*			12	6	1	3					K Breen	34
	2		4	5			7	8				11	9•	10	S			12	6	1	3†					**V Callow**	35
			4	5			7	8				11	9		10•		2	12	3*	14	1					I Hemley	36
	7		4	5			S	8				11	9	14			6		3	1				2		J Parker	37
	7		4		5	10	8		12	11	9	S					6		3	1				2*		P Jones	38
	2		4			10•	8		12	11	9	14					6		3	1			5	7•		N Midgley	39
	7		4	6			14	8	10•	11	9	S					2		3	1			5			R Pawley	40
	7*		4	6			8	12		11	9						S		3	1	2	1	5	10		D Allison	41
	2		4	6			8	7		11	9						S		3	1	3	5	10			P Foakes	42
	2		4	6			8	7		11	9						S	14	3•	1	5	10				A Flood	43
	2			6			8	7		11	9						S	3		1	5	10	14•	4		M Brandwood	44
	2		4	6			S	8	7	11	9						S	3		1	5	10			S	I Hendrick	45
	2		4	6			S	8	7	11	9							3		1	5*	10		12		R Gifford	46
1	2			6			14	8	7	11	9						5	3		1	5	10	S	4•		S Lodge	47
			4	6			7•	8	14	11	9						5	3	12	1		10	2*			A Buksh	48
			4	6			7•	8	14	11	9						3		2*	1		5	10			T Lunt	49
	2		4†	6†			8	S	7•	11	9					3			14	1	3	5	10			B Coddington	50
	S		4	6			8	14	7	11•	9					3				1	5	10	2			S Bell	51
			4	6			12	8		7	11•	9					3•			1	5	10	2			D Elleray	52
13	**23**	**9**	**40**	**44**	**17**	**25**	**46**	**18**	**12**	**31**	**25**	**18**	**21**	**5**	**16**	**13**	**23**	**1**	**16**	**33**	**12**	**13**	**13**	**5**	**2**	**League Appearances**	
	5			2	4		4	3	4		8	6	4		8	1	1		2		2			1	1	**Substitute Appearances**	
2		1	3	3	2	3	2	1	1		2	3	1	2	1+2	2		2+1	1		0+1					**R/lows Appearances**	
	2		2	2	1	2	2				2	1	1					2	2	1						**FA Cup Appearances**	
1		1	1	1	1	1	1			2	1	0+1	1		1											**ZDS Cup Appearances**	

Also Played: Posn.(Game): Fashanu 12(18), Bodin 3(26,27,28,29,30,31), Walker 10(9•,10*)5(12)9*(14), Maguire 6(15,16,17), Robinson 12(1)14(16,17), Gourlay 14(18)5(19), Gallacher S(21), Wilson 6(36)10•(37), Garland 12(49)14(52)   †=Sent Off

Players on Loan: G Maguire (Portsmouth), P Bodin (C. Palace), T Wilson (Nott'm Forest), A Walker (Celtic), B Kilcline (Oldham Ath)

NEWCASTLE UNITED

Club Colours: Black/white striped shirts, black shorts, black stockings/white tops
Change Colours: Yellow shirts, green shorts, yellow stockings/green tops
Reserves League: Pontins Central League Division 1

COMPETITIONS					
Div. 1	Div. 2	UEFA	A/Ital	A/Scot	Texaco
98-34	93-98	68-69	72-73	75-76	71-72
48-61	34-48	69-70		76-77	72-73
65-78	61-65	70-71			73-74
84-89	78-84	77-78			74-75
	89-				

HONOURS							
Div. 1	Div. 2	FAC	UEFA	A/Ital	Texaco	C/S'ld	
04-05	64-65	09-10	68-69	72-73	73-74	1907	
06-07		23-24			74-75	1909	
08-09		31-32					
26-27		50-51					
		51-52					
		54-55					

MOST APPEARANCES: JIM LAWRENCE 496 (1904-22)		
Year	League	FA Cup
1904-05	29	8
1905-06	33	8
1906-07	33	1
1907-08	38	6
1908-09	38	7
1909-10	34	8
1910-11	36	8
1911-12	27	
1912-13	34	8
1913-14	21	
1914-15	31	5
1919-20	20	1
1920-21	42	4
1921-22	16	
	432	**64**
Previous holder: Andrew Aitken 349 (1895-1907)		

MOST GOALS IN A CAREER		
JACKIE MILBURN 200 (1946-57)		
Season	League	FA Cup
1945-46		2
1946-47	7	1
1947-48	20	
1948-49	19	
1949-50	18	3
1950-51	17	8
1951-52	25	3
1952-53	5	
1953-54	16	2
1954-55	19	2
1955-56	19	2
1956-57	12	
Total	**177**	**23**
Previous holder: H Gallagher 143 (1925-30)		

RECORD TRANSFER FEE RECEIVED			
Amount	Club	Player	Date
£2,300,000	Tottenham H	Paul Gascoigne	7/88
£1,900,000	Liverpool	Peter Beardsley	7/87
£750,000	Chelsea	Dave Beasant	1/89
£590,000	Tottenham H	Chris Waddle	7/85

RECORD TRANSFER FEE PAID			
Amount	Club	Player	Date
£850,000	Wimbledon	Andy Thorn	7/88
£850,000	Wimbledon	Dave Beasant	6/88
£750,000	Hearts	John Robertson	4/88
£680,000	Portsmouth	Mick Quinn	7/89

MANAGERS			
Name	Seasons	Best	Worst
A Cunningham	1930-35	5(1)	6(2)
T Mather	1935-39	4(2)	19(2)
S Seymour	1939-47	5(2)	5(2)
G Martin	1947-50	*3(1)	2(2)
S Seymour	1950-54	4(1)	16(1)
D Livingstone	1954-56	*5(1)	8(1)
C Mitten	1958-61	8(1)	21(1)
N Smith	1961-62	11(2)	11(2)
J Harvey	1962-75	7(1)	8(2)
G Lee	1975-77	*7(1)	15(1)
R Dinnis	1977	5(1)	*22(1)
W McGarry	1977-80	21(1)	*22(2)
A Cox	1980-84	*3(2)	11(2)
J Charlton	1984-85	14(1)	14(1)
W McFaul	1985-88	11(1)	*19(1)
J Smith	1988-91	20(1)	*11(2)
O Ardiles	1991-92	11(2)	*23(2)
K Keegan	1992-	20(2)	20(2)
* = Indicates position when manager left club			

LONGEST LEAGUE RUNS	
of undefeated matches:	14 (22.4.1950-30.9.1950)
of undefeated home matches:	31 (9.12.1905-12.10.1907)
without home win:	12 (28.12.1977-26.8.1978)
of league wins:	7 (5.11.1904-17.12.1904)
	(1.1.1909-27.2.1909) (28.11.1964-2.1.1965)
of league defeats:	10 (23.8.1977-15.10.1977)
of league matches without a win:	21 (14.1.1978-23.8.1978)
of undefeated away matches:	10 (16.11.1907-23.3.1908)
without an away win:	18 (4.9.1984-20.4.1985)
of home wins:	20 (24.4.1906-1.4.1907)
of away wins:	5 (1.1.1909-27.2.1909)

PREVIOUS NAME
Newcastle East End 1882-92

PREVIOUS LEAGUES
Northern League

BIGGEST VICTORIES
League: 13-0 v Newport Co., Div 2, 5.10.1946 (Joint record)
F.A. Cup: 9-0 v Southport, Round 4, 1.2.1932
League Cup: 6-0 v Doncaster Rovers, Round 2, 8.10.1973
6-0 v Southport, Round 2, 10.9.1975
Europe: 5-1 v Vittoria Setubal (UEFA), 12.3.1969
4-0 v Bohemians (UEFA), 28.9.77
4-0 v Feyenoord (UEFA) Rnd 1, 11.9.68

BIGGEST DEFEATS
League: 0-9 v Burton Wanderers, Division 2, 15.4.1895
F.A. Cup: 1-7 v Aston Villa, Round 2, 16.2.1895
League Cup: 2-7 v Manchester United, Round 4, 27.10.1976
Europe: No more than 2 goals difference

MOST GOALS IN A MATCH
6. L Shackleton v Newport, Div 2, 13-0, 5.10.1946

MOST POINTS
3 points a win: 80, Division 2, 1983-84 (42 games), 1989-90
(46 games)
2 points a win: 57, Division 2, 1964-65

MOST GOALS
98, Division 1, 1951-52. (League Only)
G. Robledo 33, Milburn 25, Mitchell 9, Foulkes 6, Davies 5,
Hannah 5, Duncan 3, Keeble 3, Prior 2, Walker 2, Brennan 1,
Crowe 1, Harvey 1, Taylor 1, og 1.

MOST GOALS IN A SEASON
Hughie Gallacher 39, (League 36, FAC 3) 1926-27.
4 goals once = 4; 3 goals four times = 12; 2 goals 5 times = 10,
1 goal 13 times = 13.
George Robledo 39, (League 33, FAC 6) 1951-52
4 goals once = 4; 3 goals once = 3; 2 goals 8 times = 16, 1
goal 16 times = 16.

MOST FIRST CLASS MATCHES IN A SEASON
63 (42 League, 10 FA Cup, 3 League Cup, 8 Texaco Cup)
1973-74

MOST LEAGUE GOALS CONCEDED
109, Division 1, 1960-61

MOST LEAGUE WINS
25, Division 1, 1926-27

MOST LEAGUE DRAWS
17, Division 2, 1990-91

MOST LEAGUE DEFEATS
26, Division 1, 1977-78

OLDEST PLAYER
William Hampson, 44 years 225 days, 1927

YOUNGEST PLAYER
Stephen Watson, 16 years 223 days, v Wolves, Div 2,
10.11.90

MOST CAPPED PLAYER
Alf McMichael (Northern Ireland) 40

BEST PERFORMANCES BY NEWCASTLE UNITED

League: 1964-65: Matches played 42, Won 24, Drawn 9, Lost 9, Goals for 81, Goals against 45, Points 57. First in Division 2.

Highest: Division 1 Champions 4 times.

F.A. Cup: 1909-10: 1st rnd. Stoke City 1-1, 2-1; 2nd rnd. Fulham 4-0; 3rd rnd. Blackburn Rovers 3-1; 4th rnd. Leicester City 3-0; Semi-Final Swindon Town 2-0; Final Barnsley 1-1, 2-0.
1923-24: 1st rnd. Portsmouth 4-2; 2nd rnd. Derby County 2-2 (3), 5-3; 3rd rnd. Watford 1-0; 4th rnd. Liverpool 1-0; Semi-Final Manchester City 2-0; Final Aston Villa 2-0.
1931-32: 3rd rnd. Blackpool 1-1, 1-0; 4th rnd. Southport 1-1 (2), 9-0; 5th rnd. Leicester 3-1; 6th rnd. Watford 5-0; Semi-Final Chelsea 2-1; Final Arsenal 2-1.
1950-51: 3rd rnd. Bury 4-1; 4th rnd. Bolton Wanderers 3-2; 5th rnd. Stoke City 4-2; 6th rnd. Bristol Rov 0-0, 3-1; Semi-final Wolverhampton W. 0-0, 2-1; Final Blackpool 2-0.
1951-52: 3rd rnd. Aston Villa 4-2; 4th rnd. Tottenham Hotspur 3-0; 5th rnd. Swansea 1-0; 6th rnd. Portsmouth 4-2; Semi-final Blackburn Rovers 0-0, 2-1; Final Arsenal 1-0.
1954-55: 3rd rnd. Plymouth 1-0; 4th rnd. Brentford 3-2; 5th rnd. Nottingham Forest 1-1, 2-2, 2-1; 6th rnd. Huddersfield 1-1, 2-0; Semi-final York City 1-1, 2-0; Final Manchester City 3-1.

League Cup: 1975-76: 2nd rnd. Southport 6-0; 3rd rnd. Bristol Rovers 1-1, 2-0; 4th rnd. Queens Park Rangers 3-1; 5th rnd. Notts County 1-0; Semi-final Tottenham 0-1, 3-1; Final Manchester City 1-2.

Europe (UEFA): 1968-69: 1st rnd. Feyenoord 4-0, 0-2; 2nd rnd. Sporting Lisbon 1-1, 1-0; 3rd rnd. Real Zaragossa 2-3, 2-1; 4th rnd. Vittoria Setubal 5-1, 1-3; Semi-final Rangers 0-0, 2-0; Final Ujpest Dozsa 3-0, 3-2.

DIVISIONAL RECORDS

	Played	Won	Drawn	Lost	For	Against	Points
DIVISION 1	2544	991	606	947	3955	3774	2651
DIVISION 2	1000	452	209	339	1706	1400	1222
TOTALS	3544	1443	815	1286	5661	5174	3873

NEWCASTLE UNITED

PLAYERS NAME Honours	Ht	Wt	Birthdate	Birthplace Transfers	Contract Date	Clubs	League	L/Cup	FA Cup	Other	Lg	L/C	FAC	Oth
GOALKEEPERS														
Pavel Srnicek					05.02.91	Newcastle Utd	20	2		1				
Thomas J Wright	6.1	12.13	29.08.63	Belfast		Linfield								
NI:8				£30,000	24.03.88	Newcastle Utd	56	1	4					
				Loan	14.02.91	Hull City	6							
DEFENDERS														
Matthew Appleby	5.10	11.0	16.04.72	Middlesbrough	04.05.90	Newcastle Utd. (T)	17+2	2+1	2	0+1				
Robert Elliot	5.10	11.6	25.12.73		03.04.91	Newcastle Utd	14+1	1		1				
Newcastle														
Brian Kilcline	6.2	12.0	07.05.62	Nottingham	01.05.80	Notts County (A)	156+2	16	10		9	1	2	
E:u21.2; FAC'87				£60,000	11.06.84	Coventry City	173	16+1	15	8	28	4	3	
				£400,000	01.08.91	Oldham Ath	8	2						
				£250,000	19.02.92	Newcastle Utd	13	0+1						
Bjorn Kristensen	6.1	12.05	10.10.63	Malling		Aarhus (Den)								
				£250,000	21.03.89	Newcastle Utd	69+11	3	6	5	4			
Philip Mason	5.6	10.7	08.06.71	Consett	04.05.90	Newcastle Utd. (T)								
Alan Neilson	5.11	12.4	26.09.72		11.02.91	Newcastle Utd	18+1	2		1	1			
Webberg (Ger)														
Ray Ranson	5.9	12.1	12.06.60	St Helens	01.06.77	Manchester City (A)	181+2	22	12		1			
E:u21.10,YS				£15,000	16.11.84	Birmingham City	136+1	9	10	2				
				£175,000	23.12.88	Newcastle Utd	75+5	3	10	4	1			
Kevin Scott	6.2	11.6	17.12.66	Easington	19.12.84	Newcastle Utd	164	11	3+1	10+1	6		1	2
FAYC'85														
Mark Stimson	5.11	11.0	27.12.67	Plaistow	15.07.85	Tottenham H. (T)	1+1							
				Loan	15.03.88	Leyton Orient	10							
				Loan	19.01.89	Gillingham	18							
				£200,000	16.06.89	Newcastle Utd	81+3	5	7	4	2		1	
Barry Venison	5.10	11.12	16.08.64	Consett	20.01.82	Sunderland	169+4	21	7+1	3	2			1
E:u21.6,Y; CS'88,Div1'90,FAC'89				£200,000	31.07.86	Liverpool	103+7	14+3	16+5	6+4	1			2
				£250,000	31.07.92	Newcastle Utd								
Stephen Watson	6.1	13.0	01.04.74	Wallsend	06.04.91	Newcastle Utd	45+7		5	1	1			
E: u17.2, u19.4														
MIDFIELD														
John Beresford	5.6	10.12	04.09.66	Sheffield	16.09.83	Manchester City (A)								
E:Y.10,u19.3,S				Free	04.08.86	Barnsley	79+9	5+2	5		5	2	1	
					23.03.89	Portsmouth	102+5	12	11	2	8	2		
				£650,000	01.07.92	Newcastle Utd								
Paul Bracewell	5.8	10.9	19.07.62	Heswall	06.02.80	Stoke City (A)	123+6	6	6		5	1		
E: 3, u21.13; CS'84'85; Div1'85; ECWC'85;				£250,000	01.07.83	Sunderland	38	4	2		4			
UEFA u21'84				£425,000	25.05.84	Everton	95	11	19+2	17+2	7	2		1
				Loan	23.08.89	Sunderland								
				£250,000	29.09.89	Sunderland	112+1	9	10	6	2			
					16.06.92	Newcastle Utd								
Kevin Brock	5.9	10.12	09.09.62	Middleton Stoney	01.09.79	Oxford Utd	229+17	30+2	17+1	3	26	5	1	
E:u21.4,UEFA.u21'84,Div3'84,Div2'85,LC'86				£260,000	13.08.87	Q.P.R.	38+2	6	4	1	2		1	
				£300,000	08.12.88	Newcastle Utd	131+7	5	11	7	13	1	1	
Lee Clark	5.7	11.7	27.10.72	Wallsend	09.12.89	Newcastle Utd. (T)	38+10	3	2	1	7			1
E: Y.2														
Tony Galvin	5.9	11.5	12.07.56	Huddersfield		Goole Town								
Ei: 29; FAC'81'82; EUFA'84				£30,000	26.01.78	Tottenham H	194+7	20+3	22+1	29	20	3	2	6
				£140,000	29.08.87	Sheffield Wed	21+15	4+2		1+1	1			1
				Free	18.08.89	Swindon Town	6+5	0+3						
				Free	04.07.91	Newcastle Utd								
Peter Garland	5.10	12.0	20.01.71	Croydon	01.07.89	Tottenham H. (T)	0+1							
E: Y.6				£35,000	24.03.92	Newcastle Utd	0+2							
Darron McDonough	5.11	11.0	07.11.62	Antwerp	08.01.80	Oldham Ath. (A)	178+5	12	5		14	3		
				£87,500	11.09.86	Luton Town	88+17	8+1	9+1	3	5	1	1	
				£90,000	20.03.92	Newcastle Utd	2+1							
Liam O'Brien	6.1	11.10	05.09.64	Dublin		Shamrock R								
Ei:9;Ei Lg'84'85'86,Ei Cup'85'86				£60,000	14.10.86	Manchester Utd	16+15	1+2	0+2		2			
				£250,000	15.11.88	Newcastle Utd	94+18	6	8+2	6+2	13		1	1
Gavin Peacock	5.7	10.10	18.11.67	Barnehurst	19.11.84	Q.P.R.	7+10		0+1		1			
E:Y3,S,U19.3				£40,000	05.10.87	Gillingham	69+1	4	2	5	11			1
				£250,000	16.08.89	Bournemouth	56	6	2	2	8			
				£150,000	30.11.90	Newcastle Utd	73	2	2	1	23	3		2
David Roche	5.11	12.01	13.12.70	Newcastle	30.08.88	Newcastle Utd. (T)	23+13	2	1	1+1				
Kevin Sheedy	5.7	10.11	21.10.59	Builth Wells	01.10.76	Hereford Utd. (A)	47+4	2+1	2		4		1	
Ei:16,u21.1,Y,CS'84-'87,Div1'85'87,ECWC'85				£80,000	01.07.78	Liverpool	1+2	2				2		
				£100,000	10.08.82	Everton	263+11	31+1	38	24	67	7	15	6
				Free	20.02.92	Newcastle Utd	13				1			
John I Watson	5.9	10.10	14.04.74	South Shields	06.04.92	Newcastle Utd. (T)	0+1							

PLAYERS NAME Honours	Ht	Wt	Birthdate	Birthplace Transfers	Contract Date	Clubs	APPEARANCES League	L/Cup	FA Cup	Other	GOALS Lg	L/C	FAC	Oth
FORWARDS														
Franz Carr	5.7	10.12	24.09.66	Preston	30.07.84	Blackburn R (A)								
E:u21.9,S,Y4,u19.1; LC'90; SC'89				£100,000	02.08.84	Nottm. Forest	122+9	16+2	4+2	5+2	17	5		1
				Loan	22.12.89	Sheffield Wed	9+3		2					
				Loan	11.03.91	West Ham U	1+2							
				£250,000	13.06.91	Newcastle Utd	12+3	1			2			
Stephen Howey	6.1	10.9	26.10.71	Sunderland	11.12.89	Newcastle Utd. (T)	16+17	1+2		1	1	1		
Andrew Hunt	6.0	11.11	09.06.70			Kettering Town								
Thurrock				£150,000	29.01.91	Newcastle Utd	34+9	3	2	1	11	1	2	
David Kelly	5.11	11.3	25.11.65	Birmingham		Alvechurch								
Ei:13, B.1, u23.1, u21.3					21.12.83	Walsall	115+32	11+1	12+2	14+3	63	4	3	10
				£600,000	01.08.88	West Ham U	29+12	11+3	6	2+1	7	5		2
				£300,000	22.03.90	Leicester City	63+3	6	1	2	22	1		1
				£250,000	04.12.91	Newcastle Utd	25		1		11			
Mike Quinn	5.9	10.0	02.06.62	Liverpool		Derby County (A)								
				Free	27.09.79	Wigan Ath	56+13	5	3		19	1	1	
				Free	06.07.82	Stockport Co	62+1	5	2		39	2		
				£52,000	31.01.84	Oldham Ath	78+2	4	2		34	2	1	
					14.03.86	Portsmouth	115+6	7	7	4	54+2	6	7	1
				£680,000	18.08.89	Newcastle Utd	106+4	5	7	6	57		4	5
ADDITIONAL CONTRACT PLAYERS														
Alan Thompson					11.03.91	Newcastle Utd	12+2		1					

MANAGER: KEVIN KEEGAN

DATE OF BIRTH: 14.2.1951   **PLACE OF BIRTH:** Doncaster

DATE OF APPOINTMENT: February 1992

PREVIOUS CLUBS
as Manager: None
as Player: Scunthorpe, Liverpool, SV Hamburg, Southampton, Newcastle Utd
HONOURS
as Manager: None
as Asst. Man./Coach:
as Player: Liverpool: Div 1 Championship 3 times; FA Cup; European Cup (twice); UEFA (twice)
International: E: 63, U23 5

Value Rating: ★ ★

Programme Editor:

Price of 1991-92 Programme: £1
Number of Pages: 32
Subscriptions:

Local Newspapers: Newcastle Chronicle, Newcastle Journal, Sunday Sun, Northern Echo, South Shields Gazette

Local Radio Stations: Metro Radio, Radio Newcastle, Radio Tees

Additional Publications on Club: A Complete Record 1882-1990 (Paul Joannou (£16.95). A History of Newcastle United 1882-1984 (Paul Joannou £3.50). Complete Who's Who (as others £2.50).

LEADING LEAGUE GOALSCORERS
SEASONS 1979-80 – 1991-92

1979-80	ALAN SHOULDER	20	1980-81	BOBBY SINTON	7
1981-82	IMRE VARADI	18	1982-83	KEVIN KEEGAN	21
1983-84	KEVIN KEEGAN	27	1984-85	PETER BEARDSLEY	17
1985-86	PETER BEARDSLEY	19	1986-87	PAUL GODDARD	11
1987-88	MIKE O'NEILL	12	1988-89	MIRANDINHA	9
1989-90	MIKE QUINN	32	1990-91	MIKE QUINN	18

1991-92	GAVIN PEACOCK	16

ST. JAMES PARK Newcastle-upon-Tyne NE1 4ST

Capacity: 30,348   **Covered Standing:**   **Seating:** 11,725

Tel: Ground: 091 232 8361   **Ticket Sales:** 091 261 1571   **Clubcall:** 0898 12 15 90

All premium rate calls (0898/0891) cost 36p per minute cheap rate and 48p per minute at all other times. Call costings correct at time of going to press.

GROUNDS
Chillingham Road, Heaton 1882-1892; St. James Park 1892-

ATTENDANCES
Highest: 68,386 v Chelsea, Division 1, 3.9.1930

Lowest: 6,167 v Oldham Ath., ZDC, 28.15.1989

RECORD RECEIPTS (with previous records):
£157,153 v Sunderland, Div 2 Play-Off Semi-Final 2nd leg, 16.5.1990
£135,173 v Watford, FA Cup 3 Rnd 2nd Replay, 16.1.1989
£83,000 v Liverpool (Kevin Keegan Testimonial), 17.5.1984
£53,462 v Queens Park Rangers, Division 2, 28.8.1982
£42,415 v Ujpest Dosza, UEFA, 29.5.1969

ST JAMES PARK
First game: v Corbridge, Nov 1880
First floodlit game: v Celtic, Feb 1953

Season Tickets:
Stands: from £110 to £270, juv/OAP £55 to £154
Ground: £127, juv/OAP £63

Executive Box Season Tickets: Limited number available. For details contact commercial manager

Cost of Stand Tickets: Milburn Stand £12.50, £10.50, £8.50 (juv £8.50, £7.50, £6.50); East Stand: £12.50, £10.50, £8.50, (juv £8.50, £7.50, £6.50); East Paddock Seat: £8 (juv £5); Family Enclosure Seat: £7 (juv £3.50); Standing £7 (juv £3.50)

Match and Ticket Information: Postal applications 14 days before each match, personal ten days before each.

Car Parking: Parking on the north side of the ground. Also street parking is permitted

Nearest Railway Station: Central Station (091-232 6262)

How to get to the ground

From North: Use A1 into Newcastle then follow sign Hexham into Percy Street, then turn right into Leazes Park Road (or turn left then right into St James' Street) for Newcastle United FC

From South: Use A1, A68 and then A6127, cross River Tyne and at roundabout take 1st exit into Mosley Street. One-way keep to left hand lane into Neville Street. At end turn right into Clayton Street for Newgate Street. Then turn left into Leazes Park Road (one-way) turn left then right into St James' Street for Newcastle United FC

From West: Use A69 (S.P. Newcastle) enter city centre then turn left into Clayton Street for Newgate Street. Then turn into Leazes Park Road (one-way) turn left then right into St James' Street for Newcastle United FC

NORTHAMPTON TOWN   Division 3

Formed: 1897   **Turned Professional:** 1901   **Ltd Co:** 1901

SPONSORED BY: Carpet Supacentre   **NICKNAME:** The Cobblers

Joint Administrators
B J Ward & P J Long

Directors
B Hancock
B Stonhill
P Frost
M Deane
B Lomax
M Church

Secretary/Commercial Manager
P M Hough (0604 234100)

Player/Manager
Phil Chard

Assistant Manager
Stuart Beavon

Youth Team Coach
Paul Curtis

Physiotherapist
Dennis Casey

Commercial Office
All enquiries to Secretary

Club Statistician for the Directory
Frank Grande

THIS has been a season for Northampton where more has happened off the field than on it.

The season started much as the previous season finished with the club holding a mid-table place, there were no new faces, manager Theo Foley relying on the side that missed out on promotion last season, only loan players Marlon Beresford, a keeper from Sheffield Wednesday and Sean Farrell a striker from Luton joined the squad for a spell, then Barry Richardson was signed on permanent terms from Scarborough.

Before Christmas a rift between the Chairman and the rest of the board saw the former running the club on his own, this led to money problems and when wages were not paid the P.F.A. stepped in to help out for two months, slowly key players were sold off, Paul Wilson (Halifax), Tony Adcock and Bobby Barnes (Peterborough), and replacements were non-contract players Christian Mclean and Dean Edwards.

Things could not have been blacker, a winding up order followed by a first round knock-out in the F.A. Cup by non-league Crawley seemed the last straw, but despite all this things were not going too badly in the League and a nine match unbeaten run actually put the club in a possible play-off position. That bubble burst at Burnley in a 0-5 defeat, and only one of the following nine games were won.

April saw action at the County Ground, a team of administrators were brought in attempting to save the club's mounting debts, and winding up threats, they acted quickly, 10 players were sacked, along with the management team of Theo Foley, Joe Kiernan and Billy Best. They were followed by chairman Michael McRitchie who resigned, and a shadow board was made up of ex-directors and members of a newly formed trust. Phil Chard was promoted to player/manager, Stuart Beavon as his assistant, and he was to play out the last six games of the season with what professionals they had left plus youth team players. They did not win many games, just the last one at Hereford, but won lots of admirers with their whole hearted play.

The club start the 1992-93 season with a new spirit and with the supporters getting behind them and a new stadium within the next few seasons, last season will go on record as one of the club's low spots in their history.

Frank Grande

Back row L-R: Michael Bell, David Scope, Sean Parker, Jason Burnham, Greg Campbell, Kevin Wilkin, Tony Adcock, Paul Wilson.
Middle row: Dennis Casey (Physio), David Johnson, Steve Terry, Terry Angus, Peter Gleasure, Steve Brown, Darren Wood, Irvin Gernon, Billy Best (Youth Team Manager). **Front row:** Theo Foley (Manager), Trevor Quow, Stuart Beavon, Phil Chard, Adrian Thorpe, Bobby Barnes, Joe Kiernan (Asst. Manager).

NORTHAMPTON TOWN

DIVISION FOUR: 16th   **FA CUP:** 1st RND   **RUMBELOWS CUP:** 1st RND   **AUTOGLASS:** 1st RND

M	DATE		COMP.	VEN	OPPONENTS	RESULT	H/T	LGE POS	GOALSCORERS/GOAL TIMES	ATTEN-DANCE
1	A	17	BL	A	Halifax Town	W 1-0	0-0		Chard 62	(1,834)
2		20	RC 1/1	A	Leyton Orient	L 0-5	0-3			(2,954)
3		30	BL	A	Wrexham	D 2-2	1-1		Angus 24, Thorpe 49	(2,196)
4	S	3	BL	H	Doncaster Rovers	W 3-1	1-0	9	Ormsby (og) 14, Brown 49, Thorpe 82	2,702
5		7	BL	H	Barnet	D 1-1	1-0	9	Barnes 7	4,339
6		10	RC 1/2	H	Leyton Orient	W 2-0	1-0		Barnes 22, 68	1,437
7		14	BL	A	Rochdale	L 0-1	0-0			(2,631)
8		18	BL	A	Crewe Alexandra	D 1-1	1-1		Farrell (pen) 44	(3,597)
9		21	BL	H	Carlisle United	D 2-2	1-1	11	Wilson 21, Barnes 75	2,656
10	O	5	BL	H	Blackpool	D 1-1	0-1	12	Barnes 64	3,357
11		12	BL	A	Scarborough	L 1-2	0-0		Adcock 54	(2,023)
12		15	BL	H	Chesterfield	D 1-1	0-1		Adcock 64	2,426
13		19	BL	H	Scunthorpe United	L 0-1	0-1	14		2,575
14		26	BL	A	Gillingham	L 1-3	0-1	15	Campbell 65	(2,544)
15	N	2	BL	A	Rotherham United	L 0-1	0-0	18		(3,146)
16		5	BL	H	Mansfield Town	L 1-2	1-1		Adcock 19	2,181
17		9	BL	H	Lincoln City	W 1-0	0-0	17	Adcock 85	2,575
18		16	FAC 1	A	Crawley Town	L 2-4	2-2		Chard 18, Adcock 45	(3,370)
19		20	AGT Pre	A	Reading	W 2-0	2-0		Adcock 19, McLean 39	(1,151)
20		23	BL	A	Cardiff City	L 2-3	1-1		Burnham 4, 86	(2,922)
21		30	BL	H	Burnley	L 1-2	0-1	20	Campbell 85	4,020
22	D	3	AGT Pre	H	Leyton Orient	L 1-2	1-1		Chard 41	1,153
23		7	BL	A	Scarborough	W 3-2	0-0	19	Barnes 50, Adcock 53, Bell 64	1,815
24		21	BL	A	Chesterfield	W 2-1	0-1		McLean 46, Terry 70	(3,048)
25		26	BL	H	Halifax Town	W 4-0	4-0		Adcock 33, 37, Chard 45, Barnes 45	3,147
26		28	BL	H	Wrexham	D 1-1	1-0	14	Angus 38	3,209
27	J	1	BL	A	Doncaster Rovers	W 3-0	1-0	13	Chard 43, Campbell 51, Scope 90	(1,973)
28		11	BL	H	York City	D 2-2	2-2		Terry 4, Barnes 33	3,355
29		14	AGT 1	A	Barnet	L 2-3	1-2		Thorpe 44, 67	(1,422)
30		18	BL	A	Maidstone United	D 1-1	0-0	12	Terry 49	(1,364)
31		28	BL	A	Walsall	W 2-1	2-1		Beavon 9, 25	(2,399)
32	F	8	BL	A	Gillingham	D 0-0	0-0			(3,007)
33		11	BL	A	Burnley	L 0-5	0-1			(8,825)
34		15	BL	H	Walsall	L 0-1	0-1			2,480
35		22	BL	A	York City	D 0-0	0-0	12		(2,044)
36		29	BL	H	Hereford United	L 0-1	0-1			2,428
37	M	3	BL	H	Maidstone United	W 1-0	0-0		Brown 82	1,677
38		10	BL	A	Mansfield Town	L 0-2	0-1			(2,852)
39		14	BL	H	Rotherham United	L 1-2	0-2	12	Brown 64	2,561
40		21	BL	A	Lincoln City	W 2-1	2-0		Bell 14, Beavon (pen) 22	(2,486)
41		28	BL	H	Cardiff City	D 0-0	0-0	15		2,678
42		31	BL	H	Rochdale	D 2-2	1-1		McLean 41, 61	2,010
43	A	4	BL	A	Barnet	L 0-3	0-1	15		(2,816)
44		11	BL	H	Crewe Alexandra	L 0-1	0-0	16		3,300
45		14	BL	A	Scunthorpe United	L 0-3	0-2			(2,286)
46		18	BL	A	Carlisle United	L 1-2	0-1	17		(1,935)
47		25	BL	A	Blackpool	L 0-1	0-0	17		(5,915)
48		28	BL	A	Hereford United	W 2-1	2-0	16	Bell 19, 35	(1,297)

Best Home League Attendance: 4,339 v Barnet   **Smallest: 1,677 v Maidstone Utd**   **Av Home Att: 2,775**

Goal Scorers: **Compared with 90-91: -922**

League (45): Adcock 7, Barnes 6, Bell 4, McLean 3, Terry 3, Beavon 3 (1 pen), Brown 3, Campbell 3, Chard 3, Angus 2, Burnham 2, Thorpe 2, Wilson, Farrell (1 pen), Opponents (pen), Scope

R/lows C (2): Barnes 2
FA Cup (2): Chard, Adcock
Autoglass (5): Thorpe 2, Adcock, McLean, Chard

Edwards D. (N.C.)	Parker S.	Kiernan D.	McClean C.	Beavon M.	Scope D.	Farrell S. (L)	Richardson B.	Thorpe A.	Barnes D.	Johnson D.	Campbell G.	Gernon F.	Bell M.	Adcock A.	Quow T.	Burnham J.	Brown S.	Angus T.	Terry S.	Wilson P.	Chard P.	Beresford M.	Parsons M.	Aldridge M.	Benton J.	Referee	
1	2	3	4	5	6	7	8	9	10*	11	12	S														D Shadwell	1
	2	3*	4	5	6	7*	8	9	10	11	12	14														K Cooper	2
1	2	S	4	5	6	7	8			3	9	S	10	11												R Poulain	3
1	2	9	4	5	6	7	8		S	3*		12	10	11												R Bigger	4
1	2	3	4	5	6	7	8		12	9		S	10	11*												D Bell	5
	2	3	4	5	6	7	8		S	9		S	10	11	1											R Wiseman	6
1	2	3	4	5	6	7*	8		14	9		12	10	11*												J Kirkby	7
1	2	3	4	5†	6	14	8			9		12*	10	11*		7										T Lunt	8
1	2	3	4		6	5	8		11•	9			10			7	14									M Brandwood	9
1	2	3	4		6	5	8		12	9		14	10			7*	11•									P Vanes	10
1	2	3	4	5	6		S	7	11*	9	12	8	10													R Hart	11
1	2	12	4	5	6	3			11	S	9		10			7*	8									M James	12
1	2	3	4	5	6	S	8*	11		9			10			12	7									G Willard	13
1	2	3*	4	5	6*	14	8	11	12	9	10					7										P Taylor	14
1	2	3	4•	5	14	12	8	11		9	10					7										I Cruikshanks	15
1	2	3	4*		5	12	6	8	11	14	9	10•				7										J Moules	16
1	2	3		5	4	6	8	11		9	S	12				7*	10									P Don	17
	2	3	4	5*	6	7•	8	11		12	14		10		1				9							D Elleray	18
	2			5	S	6	12	11	10	4	7*	3		1				8	9							J Carter	19
	2*			5	14	6	12	11	10*	4	7	3		1				8	9•							K Cooper	20
	2	14		5	6	12	11	10•	4*	7	3			1				8	9•							W Flood	21
	2	14		5	12	6	4	11	10•	8	3			1				7	9							C Wilkes	22
	2	3		5	12	6*	4	11	10	14				1				7	9•							K Burge	23
	2		3	5	10	6	4	11*		12	S	8		1				7	9							G Pooley	24
	2		3	5	10	6	4	11		12	S	8		1				7	9*							D Elleray	25
	2		3	5	10	6*	4	11		12	S	8		1				7	9							D Gallagher	26
	2*		3	5	6		4		12	11	10	8		1		14	7	9*								E Parker	27
	2		3	5	10	6	4		9*	11	S	8		1		12	7									G Willard	28
		3	5	10	6*	4		12	14	11	2•	8	9	1			7									M Reed	29
	2•	3	5	10	6	4*		12		14		8	9	1			7	11								M Pierce	30
		3	5	10	6	4		2	12	S	8	9*	1				7	11								J Rushton	31
		3	5		6	4	8	2	9	10			1		S	7	11	S								G Poll	32
		3	5		6	4*	8	2	9	10			1		S	7	11†	12								A Wilkie	33
		3	5		6		8	2		10			1			7	11	12	4•	9						P Foakes	34
		3	5	10	6		12	2		4			1			7	11	S	8*							S Lodge	35
		3†	5	10	6	4	8*			11			9	1		7*		12	14			2				A Bennett	36
		3	5	10	6	S	8			11			9	1		7		S			4	2				P Scoble	37
		3	5	10	6		8*	9	S	12				1		7	11				4	2				I Hemley	38
			5	10	6	14	8•	9	12	3				1		7	11				4	2				R Pawley	39
		3	5	10	6		8	9	12	S				1		7	11				4*	2				A Dawson	40
		3	5	10	6		8	9	S			12	1			7	11				4*	2				A Smith	41
		3	5†	10	6		8	9	S		4	1			7	11	S				2					A Buksh	42
11		3	5	10	6		8					1			7		9	4		2*	12					M Pierce	43
11		3	5	10	6		8					1			7		9	S		2	4*					P Alcock	44
		3		10	6		8					1			7		9	4*		2	14	12				J Watson	45
11		4		10	5		8					1			7		9			2	12	6				P Harrison	46
11*		3		5			8					1			7		9	4		2	10	6				V Callow	47
11		3		5			8					1			7		9	4		2	10	6				T Fitzharris	48
15	29	14	37	37	31	36	24	14	23	27	12	9	18	11	27	4	1	33	19	6	5	7	13	2	4	League Appearances	
	2			4	4	3		7	1	10	6		1				4		3	1			3		1	Substitute Appearances	
2	2	2	2	2	2	2	1	2	0+1	0+1	1	1	1	1												R/lows Appearances	
1	1	1	1	1	1	1	1			0+1			1		1			1								FA Cup Appearances	
2	0+1	1	3	1	3	1+1	3	2+1	2	2+1	1+1	3	3	1	1			3	2							Autoglass Appearances	

Also Played: Posn.(Game): Colkin 14(34)5(45)3*(46), Bultis 14(43,46)11*(45)S(47), Adams 12(47)S(48), Gleasure 1(2), Wood 6*(15), Lamb S(48)

Players on Loan: Beresford (Sheff. Wed.), Farrell (Luton Town)

† = Sent Off

NORTHAMPTON TOWN

Club Colours: Claret with white sleeves, white shorts, claret socks
Change Colours: Yellow shirts, claret shorts, yellow socks
Youth Team: South East Counties League

Previous League: Southern League
Previous Managers: 1903-12 Herbert Chapman 1912-13 Walter Bull 1913-19 Fred Lessons 1920-25 Bob Hewison 1925-31
Jack Tresadern 1931-36 Jack English Snr 1936-37 Sid Puddefoot 1937-War Warney Cresswell War-1949 Tom Smith 1949-
55 Bob Dennison 1955-59 Dave Smith 1959-63 Dave Bowen 1963 Jack Jennings (caretaker) 1963-67 Dave Bowen 1967-68
Tony Marchi 1968-69 Ron Flowers 1969-72 Dave Bowen 1972-73 Bill Baxter 1973-76 Bill Dodgin 1976-77 Pat Crerand
1977 Committee* 1977-78 John Petts 1978-79 Mike Keen 1979-80 Clive Walker 1980-81 Bill Dodgin 1981-84 Clive Walker
1984-85 Tony Barton 1985-90 Graham Carr 1990-92 Theo Foley
*Committee: 1 director, 1 coach, 2 senior players
Honours: Champions Div 3 1962-63 Champions Div 4 1986-87
League Career: Original Members of Div 3 1920 Transferred to Div 3S 1921 Relegated to Div 4 1957-58
Promoted to Div 3 1960-61 Promoted to Div 2 1962-63 Promoted to Div 1 1964-65 Relegated to Div 2 1965-66
Relegated to Div 3 1966-67 Relegated to Div 4 1968-69 Promoted to Div 3 1975-76 Relegated to Div 4 1976-77
Promoted to Div 3 1986-87 Relegated to Div 4 1989-90

CLUB RECORDS

Most Appearances for Club: Tommy Fowler (1946-61): League 521 + FA Cup 31 + League Wartime 31 **Total 583**
Most Capped Player: E Lloyd-Davies, 12 Wales **For England:** None
Record Goalscorer in a Match: R Hoten, 5 v Crystal Palace (h), 8-1, Div 3S, 27.10.1928 A Dawes 5 v Lloyds Bank (h), 8-1, FA Cup
1st Round, 26.11.1932
Record League Goalscorer in a Season: Cliff Holton, 36, Division 3, 1961-62 **In All Competitions:** Cliff Holton 39 (League 36 +
FA Cup 3), 1961-62)
Record League Goalscorer in a Career: Jack English, 135, 1948-60 **In All Competitions:** Jack English, 143 (League 135 + FA
Cup 8)
Record Transfer Fee Received: £265,000 from Watford for Richard Hill, March 1987
Record Transfer Fee Paid: £85,000 to Manchester City for Tony Adcock, January 1988
Best Performances: League: 21st Div 1, 1965-66 **FA Cup:** 5th Round 1911-12, 1933-34, 1949-50, 1969-70 **League Cup:** 5th
Round 1964-65, 1966-67
Most League Points: (3pts for win) 99, Div 4, 1986-87 (2pts for win) 68, Div 4, 1975-76
Most League Goals: 109, Division 3S, 1952-53 109, Division 3, 1962-63
Record League Victory: 10-0 v Walsall, Div 3S, 5.11.1927
Most Goals Scored in a Cup Tie: 10 v Sutton, FA Cup, 7.12.1907
Record League Defeat: 0-10 v Bournemouth, Div 3S, 2.9.1939
Record Cup Defeat: 2-8 v Manchester United (h), FA Cup Round 5, 7.2.1970
Oldest Player in a League Match: Alf Wood, 39 years 351 days v Walsall, 30.4.1955
Youngest Player in a League Match: Adrian Mann, 16 years 297 days v Bury, 5.5.1984

LONGEST LEAGUE RUNS

of undefeated matches: 21 (1986-87)	**of league matches without a win:** 18 (1969)
of undefeated home matches: 29 (1932-33, 1975-76)	**of undefeated away matches:** 12 (1986-87)
without home win: 12 (1989-90)	**without an away win:** 33 (1921-23)
of league wins: 8 (1960)	**of home wins:** 12 (1927)
of league defeats: 8 (1935)	**of away wins:** 5 (1978)

BARCLAYS

LOCAL BRANCH
Wellingborough Road Branch
267 Wellingborough Road
Northampton NN1 4EN
Tel: 0604 26941

BARCLAYBANK MACHINE

BARCLAYS BUSINESS CENTRE
Northampton: St Giles Square
PO Box No. 23
St Giles Square
Northampton NN1 1DB
Tel: 0604 29677

BARCLAYBANK MACHINE

NORTHAMPTON TOWN

PLAYERS NAME Honours	Ht	Wt	Birthdate	Birthplace Transfers	Contract Date	Clubs	League	L/Cup	FA Cup	Other	Lg	L/C	FAC	Oth
GOALKEEPERS														
Barry Richardson	6.1	12.1	05.08.69	Willington Quay	20.05.88	Sunderland (T)								
					21.03.89	Scunthorpe Utd								
				Free	03.08.89	Scarborough	30	1		1				
				Monthly	16.08.91	Stockport Co								
				Free	10.09.91	Northampton T	27	1	1	3				
DEFENDERS														
Terence Angus	5.10	11.00	14.01.66			V S Rugby								
Coventry					22.08.90	Northampton T	79	5	1+1	5	4			
James Benton						Northampton T. (T)	4+1							
Jason Burnham	5.10	10.10	08.05.73		23.07.91	Northampton T. (T)	36+4	2	1	3	2			
Nottingham														
Lee Colkin	5.11	11.01	15.07.74			Northampton T. (T)	2+1							
Hinckley														
Sean Parker	5.10	10.8	23.08.73		23.07.91	Northampton T. (T)	5+1							
Newcastle														
Mark Parsons						Northampton T. (T)	13							
Steve Terry	6.1	13.3	14.06.62	Clapton	08.01.80	Watford (A)	160	20	20+1	4+1	14	4	1	
				£100,000	08.06.88	Hull City	62	4	1	2	4			
				£75,000	12.03.90	Northampton T	100	2	4	4	11			
MIDFIELD														
Stuart Beavon	5.7	10.6	30.11.58	Wolverhampton	01.07.76	Tottenham H. (A)	3+1	0+1						
Div.3'86, SC'88				Loan	07.12.79	Notts County	6							
				£40,000	18.07.80	Reading	380+16	26+2	31+1	16+1	44	2	3	4
				Free	21.08.90	Northampton T	74	4	3	5	13		1	2
Stephen F Brown	5.10		06.07.66	Northampton		Irthlingborough D								
				Free	13.08.89	Northampton T	83+13	6	8	4+1	6	1		
Riccardo Bulzis						Northampton T. (T)	1+2							
Phillip Chard	5.8	11.2	16.10.60	Corby		Corby Town								
Div.4'87; Div.3'89				N.C		Nottm. Forest								
				Free	18.01.79	Peterborough U	153+19	13+2	9	1	18	2	1	
				£10,000	19.08.85	Northampton T	113+2	9	6	5	27	1	1	1
					23.03.88	Wolverhampton W	26+8	3+1		1+1	5			
				£50,000	26.10.89	Northampton T	101	6	9	7	12		1	2
Daniel Kiernan						Northampton T. (T)	6+3							
FORWARDS														
Craig Adams						Northampton T. (T)	0+1							
Martin Aldridge						Northampton T. (T)	2+3							
Michael Bell			15.11.71	Newcastle	01.07.90	Northampton T. (T)	50+14	1+1		3+1	4			

LEADING LEAGUE GOALSCORERS SEASONS 1985-86 – 1991-92

1985-86	IAN BENJAMIN 21	1986-87	RICHARD HILL 29
1987-88	PAUL CULPIN, TONY MORLEY TONY ADCOCK 10	1988-89	TONY ADCOCK 17
1989-90	BOBBY BARNES 18	1990-91	BOBBY BARNES 13
	1991-92	TONY ADCOCK 7	

COUNTY GROUND Northampton NN1 4PS

Capacity: 9,443   **Covered Standing:** 3,250   **Seating:** 357

Tel: Ground: 0604 234100   **Ticket Sales:** 0604 234100   **Clubcall:** 0839 66 44 77

All premium rate calls (0898/0891) cost 36p per minute cheap rate and 48p per minute at all other times. Call costings correct at time of going to press.

ATTENDANCES
Highest: 24,523 v Fulham, Div 1, 23.4.1966

Lowest: 942 v Chester City, 9.3.1985

Record Receipts: £47,292.40 v Coventry City, FA Cup Rnd 3, 6.1.90

Season Tickets:
Stands: from £95 to £157, juv/OAP £66.50
Ground: from £95, juv/OAP £45

Executive Box Season Tickets: None on Sale

Cost of Stand Tickets: Main Stand £7.50; Hotel End £5, juv/OAP £3.50; Cricket Side £5, Juv/OAP £3.50; Family Enclosure £5, Juv/OAP £3;

Match and Ticket Information: No pre-match bookings

Car Parking: Ample street parking

Nearest Railway Station: Northampton Castle (0788 60116)

How to get to the ground

From North and West: Use A45 into Northampton. Follow signs Kettering A43 into Kettering Road. In 0.9m turn right into Abington Avenue for Northampton Town FC

From East: Use A45 S.P. Nothampton to Wilby. In 5.2m at roundabout forward. In 2.5m turn right then over crossroads into Abington Avenue for Northampton Town FC

From South: Use Motorway M1 until junction 15. Leave Motorway and follow signs Northampton A508. Follow signs Kettering A43 into Kettering Road. In 0.9m turn right into Abington Avenue for Northampton Town FC

Value Rating: ★ ★ ★

Programme Editor: Brian Barrow

Price of 1992-93 Programme: £1
Number of Pages: 32
Subscriptions:

Local Newspapers: Chronicle and Echo, Evening Telegraph, Northants Post

Local Radio Stations: Hereward Radio, Radio Northampton

NORWICH CITY   Premier

Formed: 1902   **Turned Professional:** 1905   **Ltd Co:** 1905

SPONSORED BY: Norwich & Peterborough Building Society   **NICKNAME:** The Canaries

NORWICH CITY FC

President
G C Watling

Hon.Senior Life Vice-President
Sir Arthur South J.P.

Chairman
R T Chase,JP

Vice-Chairman
J A Jones

Directors
B W Lockwood   G A Paterson
A Scholes, DMS IPFA

Secretary
Andrew Neville(0603 612131)

Commercial Manager
Ray Cossey

Marketing and Promotions Manager
Trevor Bond

Team Manager
Mike Walker

Assistant Manager
John Deehan

Coaches
John Faulkner / Keith Webb

Physiotherapist
Tim Sheppard MCSP,SRP

Grounds Supervisor
Brian Saunders

Club Statistician for the Directory
John Brock & Andrew Matthews

HOW soon ecstasy turned to agony! At the beginning of April the Canaries were heading for an F.A. Cup semi-final at Hillsborough, filling their supporters with hopes of a first appearance in the final; by the end of April the Canaries had missed out on Wembley and looked like being relegated after a terrible run of defeats. In the end the Canaries gained a life-saving point in their final home game against Wimbledon, but their supporters were made to suffer in a state of high anxiety as the team hung on grimly after Wimbledon's equalizer early in the second half.

Despite a disappointing end to the season, Dave Stringer has had a successful time as the club's manager. He achieved Norwich's highest ever league placing (4th in 1988-89), and has led the club to two F.A. Cup semi-finals. Indeed it came as a shock when he announced his resignation on 1st May.

There was good news before the season started, when Norwich bought two new players (Darren Beckford for a record-breaking £925,000, and Rob Newman for £600,000); and no players were sold. But it was the same old story at the beginning of November, when Norfolk-born Dale Gordon was sold to Glasgow Rangers for a record-equalling £1,200,000. This sale was immediately followed by the team's adoption of a 'diamond formation', which proved an instant success as the Canaries beat a bemused Chelsea 3-0 at Stamford Bridge. The Canaries' next three home matches had exciting climaxes as they scored injury-time goals in each of them. The diamond formation had been abandoned by the time Norwich were knocked out of the Rumbelows League Cup at White Hart Lane in a quarter-final that they had led until near the end.

In mid-February Norwich changed their tactics again. The latest change was to get the ball into the opponents' half of the pitch as quickly as possible and then apply their normal controlled football, not forsaking their passing game altogether. This change of tactics, like the last, worked well initially, with a draw at Highbury and two 3-0 home wins, the second against Liverpool. When good League results were followed by progress to an F.A. Cup semi-final, a fine end to the season appeared in prospect. But it was not to be.

Norwich's attendances slumped for the second season running, and look likely to fall again next year now that Carrow Road has been converted to an all-seater stadium and that 'Player of the Year' Robert Fleck has been sold. It is a shame that some of the massive income generated by the Premier League could not have been used to improve his contract and keep him at Carrow Road. He will be missed.   **John Brock**

Back row L-R: Darren Beckford, Colin Woodthorpe, Ian Culverhouse, Bryan Gunn, Chris Sutton, Mark Walton, Rob Newman, John Polston, Andy Johnson. **Middle row:** Tim Sheppard (Physiotherapist), Sean Collins, Tim Wooding, Jason Minett, Daryl Sutch, Paul Blades, Gary Megson, David Smith, David Phillips, Lee Power, John Faulkner (Reserve Team Manager). **Front row:** Ian Crook, Jeremy Goss, Ian Butterworth, Mike Walker (Manager), John Deehan (Asst. Manager), Ruel Fox, Mark Bowen, Robert Ullathorne.

NORWICH CITY

DIVISION ONE: 18th   **FA CUP:** SEMI-FINALS   **RUMBELOWS CUP:** 5th RND   **ZDS CUP:** 2nd RND

M	DATE		COMP.	VEN	OPPONENTS	RESULT	H/T	LGE POS	GOALSCORERS/GOAL TIMES	ATTEN-DANCE
1	A	17	BL	H	Sheffield United	D 2-2	0-1		Fleck 76, 89	16,380
2		21	BL	A	Queens Park R.	W 2-0	1-0	3	Gordon 29, Newman 76	(10,626)
3		24	BL	A	Oldham Athletic	D 2-2	1-2	5	Crook 22, Newman 50	(13,548)
4		28	BL	H	Manchester City	D 0-0	0-0	7		15,376
5		31	BL	H	Tottenham Hotspur	L 0-1	0-1	15		19,460
6	S	3	BL	A	Everton	D 1-1	0-0	13	Phillips 85	(19,197)
7		7	BL	A	Manchester United	L 0-3	0-3	16		(44,946)
8		14	BL	H	West Ham United	W 2-1	2-1	14	Fox 13, Gordon 39	15,348
9		18	BL	H	Sheffield Wed.	W 1-0	1-0	8	Fleck (pen) 25	12,503
10		21	BL	A	Notts County	D 2-2	0-1	10	Ullathorne 62, Bowen (pen) 90	(9,488)
11		25	RC 2/1	A	**Charlton Athletic**	W 2-0	1-0		**Gordon 41, Newman 57**	(2,886)
12		28	BL	H	Leeds United	D 2-2	0-0	10	Gordon 59, 75	15,828
13	O	5	BL	A	Wimbledon	L 1-3	0-1	15	Beckford 69	(3,531)
14		9	RC 2/2	H	**Charlton Athletic**	W 3-0	2-0		**Fleck 10, 35, Beckford 69**	5,507
15		19	BL	A	Southampton	D 0-0	0-0	15		(12,516)
16		23	ZDS 2	H	**Queens Park R.**	L 1-2	1-1		**Beckford 42**	4,436
17		26	BL	H	Luton Town	W 1-0	1-0	11	Newman 42	10,514
18		30	RC 3	H	**Brentford**	W 4-1	0-0		**Fox 51, Fleck 52, Beckford 74, 84**	7,394
19	N	2	BL	A	Nottingham Forest	D 0-0	0-0	11		13,014
20		16	BL	A	Chelsea	W 3-0	2-0	8	Fleck 12, 64, Bowden 27	(15,755)
21		23	BL	H	Coventry City	W 3-2	0-1	8	Bowen 46, Fleck 84, Sutton 89	12,056
22		30	BL	A	Manchester City	L 1-2	1-2	8	Beckford 35	(34,881)
23	D	4	RC 4	H	**West Ham United**	W 2-1	0-0		**Fleck 65, 89 (pen)**	16,325
24		7	BL	H	Crystal Palace	D 3-3	1-1	9	Thorn (og) 19, Beckford 49, Newman 88	12,667
25		21	BL	H	Queens Park R.	L 0-1	0-0	11		11,436
26		26	BL	A	Manchester City	L 1-2	1-2	14	Newman 6	(28,164)
27		28	BL	A	Tottenham Hotspur	L 0-3	0-1	14		(27,969)
28	J	1	BL	H	Aston Villa	W 2-1	0-0	12	Fleck (pen) 56, Ullathorne 78	15,318
29		4	FAC 3	H	**Barnsley**	W 1-0	0-0		**Fleck (pen) 86**	12,189
30		8	RC 5	A	**Tottenham Hotspur**	L 1-2	1-0		**Fleck 32**	(29,471)
31		11	BL	H	Oldham Athletic	L 1-2	1-0	14	Beckford 38	10,986
32		18	BL	A	Sheffield United	L 0-1	0-0	14		(17,549)
33	F	1	BL	H	Southampton	W 2-1	0-0	13	Ullathorne 50, Fleck 73	10,660
34		5	FAC 4	H	**Millwall**	W 2-1	1-0		**Bowen 4, Fleck 64**	17,010
35		8	BL	A	Luton Town	L 0-2	0-0	16		(8,554)
36		11	BL	A	Arsenal	D 1-1	0-0	13	Fox 58	(22,352)
37		15	FAC 5	H	**Notts County**	W 3-0	2-0		**Sutton 19, 57, Phillips 39**	14,511
38		22	BL	H	Liverpool	W 3-0	1-0		Woodthorpe 66, Fleck 70, 90	20,411
39		29	BL	A	Crystal Palace	W 4-3	4-2	10	Sutton 14, Newman 32, Polston 43, Goss 45	(14,021)
40	M	4	BL	A	Coventry City	D 0-0	0-0	9		(8,459)
41		7	FAC 6	A	**Southampton**	D 0-0	0-0			(20,088)
42		11	BL	H	Chelsea	L 0-1	0-0	13		13,430
43		14	BL	A	Nottingham Forest	L 0-2	0-2	14		(20,271)
44		18	FAC 6R	H	**Southampton**	W †2-1	0-1		**Newman 54, Sutton 116**	21,017
45		21	BL	H	Everton	W 4-3	1-2	13	Beckford 3 (3, 82, 85), Newman 47	11,900
46		28	BL	A	Aston Villa	L 0-1	0-0	14		(16,985)
47		31	BL	H	Manchester United	L 1-3	0-1	15	Power 61	17,489
48	A	5	FAC SF	N	**Sunderland**	L 0-1	0-1			(40,462)
49		8	BL	H	Arsenal	L 1-3	0-1	17	Butterworth 60	12,971
50		11	BL	A	West Ham United	L 0-4	0-2	17		(16,896)
51		18	BL	H	Notts County	L 0-1	0-0	18		12,100
52		20	BL	A	Sheffield Wed.	L 0-2	0-2	18		(27,362)
53		25	BL	H	Wimbledon	D 1-1	1-0	18	Fleck 20	11,061
54	M	2	BL	A	Leeds United	L 0-1	0-1	18		(32,673)

Best Home League Attendance: 20,411 v Liverpool   **Smallest:** 10,514 v Luton Town   **Av Home Att:** 13,853

Goal Scorers: **Compared with 90-91: -1,674**

League (47):   Fleck 11 (2 pens), Newman 7, Beckford 7, Gordon 4, Ullathorne 3, Sutton 2, Bowen 2 (1 pen), Fox 2, Power, Opponents, Butterworth Goss, Polston, Bowden, Phillips, Crook, Woodthorpe

R/lows C (12):   Fleck 6 (1 pen), Beckford 3, Fox, Newman, Gordon

FA Cup (8):   Sutton 3, Fleck 2 (1 pen), Newman, Bowen, Phillips

ZDS Cup (1):   Beckford   † = After extra-time

1991-92

Gunn B.	Culverhouse I.	Bowen M.	Butterworth I.	Blades P.	Crook I.	Gordon D.	Fleck R.	Newman R.	Beckford D.	Phillips D.	Fox R.	Goss J.	Sutton C.	Ullathorne R.	Ball S.	Woodthorpe C.	Power L.	Mortensen H.	Polston J.	Sherwood T.	Sutch D.	Walton M.	Smith D.	Johnson A.	Peyton (L)	Referee	
1	2	3	4	5	6	7	8	9	10*	11	12	S														P Don	1
1	2	3	4	5	6	7	8	9	10*	11	12	S														D Axcell	2
1	2	3	4	5	6	7	8	9	10	11	S	S														K Lupton	3
1	2	3	4	5	6	7	8	9	10*	11	12		S													A Buksh	4
1	2*	3	4	5	6	7	8	9	10	11	12		S													I Hemley	5
1	2	3	4	5	6	7	8	9	10*	11	12	S														S Bell	6
1	2	3	4	5	6	7	8	9	10*	11•	12	14														V Callow	7
1	2	3	4	5	6	7	8	9	S		10	14		11•												T West	8
1		3	4	5	6	7	8	9	S	2	10	14		11•												A Ward	9
1		3	4	5	6	7*	8†	9	12	2	10			11•	14											R Dilkes	10
1		3	4	5	6	7	8*	9	12•	2	10			11		14										**M Pierce**	11
1		3	4	5	6		8	9	S	2	10	S		11												P Jones	12
1		3	4	5	6*	7		9	8	2	10	12.		11		S										R Groves	13
1		3*	4	5		7	6•	9	8		10	2		11	14	12										**R Wiseman**	14
1		3	4	5		7*	8	9	12	2	10	6		11		S										L Shapter	15
1		3	4	5•		7		9	8	2	10	6			S	14	11									**M Bailey**	16
1		3	4	5		7	8	9	12	2	10	6		11*							S					K Hackett	17
1		3	4	5*		7	8	9	11	2	10	6•			14						12					**A Gunn**	18
1		3	4	5		7	8	9	11	2	10	6		S							S					D Gallagher	19
1		3	4	5			8	9		11	2	6		S		7			S	10						P Foakes	20
1		3	4	5	12		8	9	11•	2	6		14	7						10*						R Lewis	21
1		3	4•	5	S		8	9	11	2	6		14	7						10						B Hill	22
1		3		5*	12		8	9	11•	2	14	6	4	7						10						**K Morton**	23
1		3		5			8	9	11	2	12	6	4	7*					S	10						G Pooley	24
1		3		5			8	9	11	2	12	6	4	7					S	10*						A Smith	25
1		3		5			8	9	11•	2	14	6	4	7*					12	10						K Redfern	26
1		3		5			8	9	12	2	11	6	4			7*			S	10						K Burge	27
1		3		5	S		8	9	10	2	7	6	4*	11					12							J Martin	28
1		3		5*	14		8	9	10*	2	7	6	4	11					S							**A Buksh**	29
1		3		5	10*		8	9	12	2	7	6	4	11					S							**M Bodenham**	30
1		3		5	6		8	9	10*	2	7			4		11			S			14				J Rushton	31
1*		3	S		10		8	9	12			6	4	11		2			5	7						R Hamer	32
		3	S		10*		8	9	7	2	12	6	4	11					5				1			P Vanes	33
		3	S		10		8	9	7	2	S	6	4	11					5				1			**T Holbrook**	34
	2	3	4				8	9		11	7	6							5		14	1				P Jones	35
	2	S	4				8	9		11	7	6	10			3			5		S	1				J Key	36
	2		4				8	9		11	7	6	10	S		3			5		S	1				**D Gallagher**	37
	2		4				8	9		11	7	6	10	S		3			5		S	1				M Bailey	38
	2		4				8	9		11	7	6	10	S		3			5		S	1				R Nixon	39
	2		4				12	9		11	7*	6	10•		14	3			5		8	1				C Trussell	40
	2		4	S			8	9		11	7	6	10			3			5		S	1				**G Ashby**	41
	2		4				8	9		11	7	6	12	S		3			5		10*	1				D Axcell	42
	2	12	4	S			8	9		11*	7	6	10			3			5			1				R Dilkes	43
	2	11	4	12			8•	9	14		7	6	10			3*			5			1				**G Ashby**	44
	2	3•	4	11				9	8		7	6	10			12			5*		14	1				G Willard	45
	2	3	4	S	11			9			7	6	10			5			8			1		S		A Buksh	46
	2	3	4	11*				9	8•		7	6	10			5			14		12	1				M James	47
	2	11	4				8	9			7	6	10*	S		3			5		12	1				**N Midgley**	48
	2	3	4					9	10		7	6	14	11			8•		5		S	1				P Wright	49
	2		4					9	10		7	6	14*	3			8•		5		12	1		11		P Foakes	50
	2		4	S				9	10		7	6				3			5		11	1		S		P Don	51
	2		4				8	9	10*		7	6				3	12		5			1	S	11		J Worrall	52
	2	3	4				8	9	10*	11	7	6							12			1		S		I Hemley	53
	2		4				8	9		11	7	6		3*					12			1		10	S	R Milford	54
25	21	35	31	26	20	15	35	41	25	34	27	29	16	20		12	2		16	7	5	17	1	2		**League Appearances**	
	1			1		1		5		10	4	5		2	3	2			3			4				**Substitute Appearances**	
5		5	3	5	2+1	3	5	5	3+2	4	4+1	4	2	4		0+2	0+2		0+1	1						**R/lows Appearances**	
1	4	4	4	1	1+2		6	6	2+1	4	5	6	6	2		4			5			0+1	5			**FA Cup Appearances**	
1		1	1	1		1		1	1	1	1	1							0+1		1					**ZDS Cup Appearances**	

† = Sent Off

NORWICH CITY

Club Colours: Yellow shirts with green splashes, green shorts, yellow stockings
Change Colours: White shirts with purple sleeves, white shorts, white stockings
Reserves League: Neville Ovenden Football Combination

COMPETITIONS					
Div. 1	Div. 2	Div. 3	Div. 3S	A/Scot	Texaco
72-74	34-39	58-60	20-34	75-76	72-73
75-81	60-72		39-58	76-77	73-74
82-85	74-75			77-78	74-75
86-	81-82			78-79	
	85-86				

HONOURS		
Div. 2	Div. 3S	League Cup
71-72	33-34	61-62
85-86		84-85

MOST APPEARANCES: KEVIN KEELAN 680 (1963-80)				
Year	League	FA Cup	Lge Cup	Others
1963-64	16		1	
1964-65	23	1		
1965-66	42	4	1	
1966-67	39	3	1	
1967-68	30	3	3	
1968-69	32	1	3	
1969-70	33		1	
1970-71	38	1	4	
1971-72	42	1	5	
1972-73	42	3	7	7
1973-74	42	1	7	4
1974-75	38	1	9	3
1975-76	42	5	3	3
1976-77	38	1	2	3
1977-78	26	2	1	1
1978-79	22	1	3	
1979-80	26	3	6	
	571	31	57	21
Previous holder: Ron Ashman 662 (1947-63)				

MOST GOALS IN A CAREER		
JOHN GAVIN 132 (1949-58)		
Season	League	FA Cup
1949-50	1	
1950-51	17	1
1951-52	19	1
1952-53	20	
1953-54	13	1
1954-55	6	
1955-56	13	2
1956-57	16	
1957-58	17	5
Total	122	10

MANAGERS			
Name	Seasons	Best	Worst
A Turner	1902-05		
J Bowman	1905-07		
J McEwen	1907-09		
A Turner	1909-10		
J Stansfield	1910-15		
F Buckley	1919-20		
C O'Hagan	1920		
A Gosnell	1921-26	11(3S)	18(3S)
J Stansfield	1926		
C Potter	1926-29	16(3S)	17(3S)
J Kerr	1929-33	3(3S)	22(3S)
T Parker	1933-37	11(2)	1(3S)
R Young	1937-39	14(2)	14(2)
A Jewell	1939	21(2)	21(2)
R Young	1939-45		
D Lochhead	1945-46		
C Spiers	1946-47	21(3S)	21(3S)
D Lochhead	1947-50	10(3S)	21(3S)
N Low	1950-55	2(3S)	11(3S)
T Parker	1955-57	7(3S)	24(3S)
A Macaulay	1957-61	4(2)	8(3S)
W Reid	1961-62	17(2)	17(2)
G Swindin	1962		
R Ashman	1962-66	6(2)	17(2)
L Morgan	1966-69	9(2)	13(2)
R Saunders	1969-73	20(1)	11(2)
J Bond	1973-80	10(1)	3(2)
K Brown	1980-87	5(1)	3(2)
D Stringer	1987-92	4(1)	18(1)
Mike Walker	1992-		

RECORD TRANSFER FEE RECEIVED			
Amount	Club	Player	Date
£2,100,000	Chelsea	Robert Fleck	8/92
£1,200,000	Glasgow Rangers	Dale Gordon	11/91
£1,200,000	Chelsea	Andy Townsend	7/90
£1,200,000	Arsenal	Andy Linighan	7/90
£1,000,000	Everton	Dave Watson	8/86
£1,000,000	Nottingham Forest	Justin Fashanu	8/81

RECORD TRANSFER FEE PAID			
Amount	Club	Player	Date
£925,000	Port Vale	Darren Beckford	6/91
£700,000	Derby County	Paul Blades	7/90
£580,000	Glasgow Rangers	Robert Fleck	12/87
£300,000	Hajduk Split	Drazen Muzinic	9/80

LONGEST LEAGUE RUNS	
of undefeated matches:	20 (31.8.1950-11.1.1951)
of undefeated home matches:	31 (21.8.1971-2.12.1972)
without home win:	12 (29.9.1956-2.3.1957)
of league wins:	10 (23.11.1985-1.2.1986)
of league defeats:	7 (4.9.1935-5.10.1935)
	(12.1.1957-2.3.1957)
of league matches without a win:	25 (22.9.1956-2.3.1957)
of undefeated away matches:	12 (14.9.1985-8.3.1986)
without an away win:	41 (3.9.1977-18.8.1979)
of home wins:	12 (15.3.1952-4.10.1952)
of away wins:	5 (3.9.1988-19.11.1988)

PREVIOUS LEAGUE
Southern League

BIGGEST VICTORIES
League: 10-2 v Coventry City, Division 3S, 15.3.1930.
8-0 v Walsall, Div 3S, 29.12.1951
F.A. Cup: 8-0 v Sutton United, Round 4, 28.1.1989.
League Cup: 7-1 v Halifax Town, Round 4, 27.11.1963.

BIGGEST DEFEATS
League: 0-7 v Walsall, Division 3S, 13.9.1930.
0-7 v Sheffield Wed., Div 2, 19.11.1938
F.A. Cup: 0-6 v Luton Town, Round 2, 10.12.1927.
0-6 v Manchester City, Round 4, 24.1.1981.
League Cup: 1-6 v Manchester City, Rnd 2 (2R), 29.9.1975

MOST POINTS
3 points a win: 84, Division 2, 1985-86
2 points a win: 64, Division 3S, 1950-51.

MOST GOALS
99, 1952-53, Division 3S.
Ackerman 20, Gavin 20, Johnston 15, Summers 10, Ashman 9, Kinsey 7, McCrohan 7, Rattray 5, Adams 3, Coxon 2, og 1.

MOST GOALS IN A MATCH
5. Roy Hollis v Walsall, Division 3S, 29.12.1951
5. T Hunt v Coventry City, 10-2, Div 3S, 15.3.1930

MOST GOALS IN A SEASON
Terry Alcock 37 (League 26, FAC 6, League Cup 5) 1962-63.
4 goals once = 4; 3 goals twice = 6; 2 goals 7 times = 14; 1 goal 13 times = 13

MOST LEAGUE GOALS IN A SEASON
Ralph Hunt 31 (Division 3S) 1955-56

MOST FIRST CLASS MATCHES IN A SEASON
60 (42 League, 3 FA Cup, 7 League Cup, 8 Texaco Cup) 1972-73

MOST LEAGUE GOALS CONCEDED
100, Division 3S, 1946-47

MOST LEAGUE WINS
26, Division 3S, 1951-52

MOST LEAGUE DRAWS
23, Division 1, 1978-79

MOST LEAGUE DEFEATS
24, Division 3S, 1930-31; Div 2, 1938-39; Div 3S, 1946-47

OLDEST PLAYER
Albert Sturgess, 42 years 249 days v Millwall Ath., Div 3S, 14.2.1925

YOUNGEST PLAYER
Ian Davies, 17 years 29 days (sub) v Birmingham City, Div 1, 27.4.1974.

MOST CAPPED PLAYER
Martin O'Neill (N. Ireland) 18

BEST PERFORMANCES BY NORWICH CITY

League: 1950-51: Matches played 46, Won 25, Drawn 14, Lost 7, Goals for 82, Goals against 45, Points 64. Second in Div. 3S.

Highest: 4th in Division 1, 1988-89.

F.A. Cup: 1958-59: 1st rnd. Ilford 3-1; 2nd rnd. Swindon Town 1-1, 1-0; 3rd rnd. Manchester United 3-0; 4th rnd. Cardiff City 3-2; 5th rnd. Tottenham Hotspur 1-1, 1-0; 6th Sheffield United 1-1, 3-2; Semi-final Luton Town 1-1, 0-1.

1988-89: 3rd rnd. Port Vale 3-1; 4th rnd. Sutton United 8-0; 5th rnd. Sheffield United 3-2; 6th rnd. West Ham Utd. 0-0, 3-1; Semi-finals Everton 0-1.

1991-92: 3rd rnd. Barnsley 1-0; 4th rnd. Millwall 2-1; 5th rnd. Notts County 3-0; 6th rnd. Southampton. 0-0, 2-1 (aet); Semi-finals Sunderland 0-1

League Cup: 1961-62: 1st rnd. Chesterfield 3-2; 2nd rnd. Lincoln City 3-2; 3rd rnd. Middlesbrough 3-2; 4th rnd. Sunderland 4-1; Semi-final Blackpool 4-1, 0-2; Final Rochdale 3-0, 1-0.

1984-85: 2nd rnd. Preston N. E. 3-3, 6-1; 3rd rnd. Aldershot 0-0, 4-0; 4th rnd. Notts County 3-0; 5th rnd. Grimsby Town 1-0; Semi-final Ipswich Town 0-1, 2-0; Final Sunderland 1-0.

DIVISIONAL RECORDS

	Played	Won	Drawn	Lost	For	Against	Points
DIVISION 1	700	214	212	274	807	997	762
DIVISION 2	840	329	209	302	1231	1188	914
DIVISION 3	92	46	24	22	171	116	116
DIVISION 3S	1124	423	291	410	1779	1725	1137
TOTALS	2756	1012	736	1008	3988	4026	2929

NORWICH CITY

PLAYERS NAME / Honours	Ht	Wt	Birthdate	Birthplace / Transfers	Contract Date	Clubs	APPEARANCES League	L/Cup	FA Cup	Other	GOALS Lg	L/C	FAC	Oth
GOALKEEPERS														
Bryan Gunn	6.2	12.5	22.12.63	Thurso		Aberdeen	15	4	1	1				
S:1,u21.9,Y,SB3				£150,000	23.10.86	Norwich City	200	18	20	16				
Mark Walton	6.2	14.7	01.06.69	Merthyr Tydfil	21.02.87	Luton Town								
					05.11.87	Colchester Utd	40	3	8	5				
				£75,000	15.08.89	Norwich City	22		5					
DEFENDERS														
Paul Blades	6.0	11.0	05.01.65	Peterborough	29.12.82	Derby County (A)	157+9	9+3	12	8+2	1			
E:Y 3;Div2'87				£700,000	18.07.90	Norwich City	47	8	2	5				
Mark Bowen	5.8	11.6	07.12.63	Neath	01.12.81	Tottenham H. (A)	14+3		3	0+1	2			
W:19,u21.3,Y,S				£90,000	23.07.87	Norwich City	168+2	6	20	11	14	1	1	
Ian Butterworth	6.1	12.6	25.01.65	Crewe	05.08.81	Coventry City (A)	80+10	5	5+1					
E:u21.8					03.06.85	Nottm. Forest	26+1	6	1					
				£160,000	05.12.86	Norwich City	181+3	13+1	22	10+1	3			
Ian Culverhouse	5.10	11.2	22.09.64	Bishop's Stortford	24.09.82	Tottenham H. (A)	1+1							
E:Y6;Div2'86				£50,000	08.10.85	Norwich City	212+1	16	24	17				1
Rob Newman	6.2	12.0	13.12.63	Bradford-on-Avon	05.10.81	Bristol City (A)	382+12	29+1	27	33	52	2	2	5
FRT86				£600,000	15.07.91	Norwich City	41	5	6	1	7		1	
John Polston	5.11	11.3	10.06.68	Walthamstow	16.07.85	Tottenham H. (T)	17+7	3+1		1	1			
E:u19.3,Y3					24.07.90	Norwich City	43+3	0+1	9	5	5			
Robert Ullathorne	5.8	10.7	11.10.71	Wakefield	06.07.90	Norwich City (T)	22	4	2		3			
E:Y.1														
Timothy Wooding	6.0	12.0	05.07.73	Wellingborough	29.08.91	Norwich City (T)								
Colin Woodthorpe	6.0	11.10	13.01.69	Ellesmere Port	23.08.86	Chester City (T)	154+1	10	8+1	18	6			1
				£225,000	17.07.90	Norwich City	13+3	0+2	4	0+1	1			
MIDFIELD														
Ian Crook	5.8	10.6	18.01.63	Romford	01.08.80	Tottenham H. (A)	10+10	1	0+1	1+1	1			
				£80,000	13.06.86	Norwich City	151+19	14+3	13+5	11+1	11	2		1
Ruel Fox	5.6	10.0	14.01.68	Ipswich	20.01.86	Norwich City (A)	91+22	9+2	7+4	6+4	11	1		
Jeremy Goss	5.9	10.9	11.05.65	Cyprus	19.08.87	Norwich City	68+20	5	10+1	9	4	2		3
W:3 E:u19														
Gary Megson	5.10	11.6	02.05.59	Manchester	01.05.77	Plymouth A (A)	78	9	5		10			
				£200,000	18.12.79	Everton	20+2		3		2		1	
				£130,000	24.07.81	Sheffield Wed	123	13	12		13	2	5	
				£175,000	28.08.84	Nottm. Forest								
				£130,000	21.11.84	Newcastle Utd	21+3	1+1	2		1		1	
				£60,000	23.01.86	Sheffield Wed	107+3	10	15	3	12		1	
				£250,000	12.01.89	Manchester City	78+4	5	7+1	2	2			
				Free	01.07.92	Norwich City								
David Phillips	5.10	11.2	24.07.63	Welburg (Ger)	03.08.81	Plymouth A	65+8	2+1	12+1	4	15			1
W:39,u21.4,Y,FAC'87				£65,000	23.08.84	Manchester City	81	8	5	5	13			3
				£150,000	05.06.86	Coventry City	93+7	8	9	5+1	8		1	2
				£550,000	31.07.89	Norwich City	110	10	12	8	9		1	1
David Smith	5.8	11.2	26.12.70	Liverpool	04.07.89	Norwich City (T)	3+2		2	1+1				
Daryl Sutch	5.11	10.12	11.09.71	Lowestoft	06.07.90	Norwich City (T)	7+6	0+1	0+1	1				
E:Y.2														
FORWARDS														
Darren Beckford	6.1	11.1	12.05.67	Manchester	21.08.84	Manchester City (A)	7+4	0+1						
E:Y3					Loan	10.10.85	Bury	12				5			
				£15,000	25.06.87	Port Vale	169+9	12	14	9+1	71	3	4	3
				£925,000	14.06.91	Norwich City	25+5	3+2	2+1	1	7	3		1
Mark Robins	5.7	10.1	22.12.69	Ashton-u-Lyme	23.12.86	Manchester Utd. (A)	19+29	0+7	4+4	4+3	11	2	3	1
FAC'90; ECWC'91				£800,000		Norwich City								
(F) Christopher Sutton	6.3		10.03.73	Nottingham	02.07.91	Norwich City (T)	16+7	2	6		2		3	
Lee Power	5.10	10.10	30.06.72	London	06.07.90	Norwich City (T)	15+6	1			4			
Ei:u21.6														
ADDITIONAL CONTRACT PLAYERS														
Andrew J Johnson					04.03.92	Norwich City (T)	2							
(M) Jason Minett	5.9	10.4	12.08.71	Peterborough	04.07.89	Norwich City (T)	0+2							
(D) Adrian Pennock	5.11	12.1	27.03.71	Ipswich	04.07.89	Norwich City (T)	1							

NORWICH CITY

Club	Rec. Win	Season	Rec. Loss	Season
ARSENAL	3-1	1982-83	5-0	1988-89
ASTON VILLA	5-1	1936-37	4-1	1974-75
BLACKBURN ROVERS	4-0	1938-39	6-0	1938-39
CHELSEA	4-1	1962-63	3-0	1973-74
COVENTRY CITY	10-2	1929-30	4-0	1954-55
CRYSTAL PALACE	5-0	1950-51 (away)	7-1	1926-27
EVERTON	4-2	1984-85	4-0	1986-87
IPSWICH TOWN	2-0	1984-85	5-0	1976-77
LEEDS UNITED	4-0	1985-86	3-0	1990-91
LIVERPOOL	3-0	1991-92	6-0	1978-79
MANCHESTER CITY	4-1	1964-65	5-0	1963-64
MANCHESTER UNITED	2-0	1989-90	5-0	1979-80
MIDDLESBROUGH	2-0	1985-86	6-1	1980-81
NOTTINGHAM FOREST	4-0	1936-37	5-0	1990-91
OLDHAM ATHLETIC	3-1	1985-86 (away)	4-2	1935-36
QUEENS PARK RANGERS	5-0	1924-25	4-0	1969-70
SHEFFIELD UNITED	4-0	1985-86	4-0	1938-39
SHEFFIELD WEDNESDAY	3-1	1937-38	7-0	1938-39
SOUTHAMPTON	5-0	1960-61	7-3	1957-58
TOTTENHAM HOTSPUR	4-0	1979-80	4-0	1989-90
WIMBLEDON	2-0	1988-89 (away)	4-0	1990-91 (home)

MANAGER: MIKE WALKER

DATE OF BIRTH: 28.11.1945 **PLACE OF BIRTH:** Colwyn Bay

DATE OF APPOINTMENT: JUNE 1992

PREVIOUS CLUBS
    as Manager: Colchester Utd (May 1986 to Nov. 1987)
    as Reserve Team Man: Norwich City (Nov. 1987 to June 1992)
    as Player: Reading, Shrewsbury Town, York City, Watford, Charlton Ath. (on loan), Colchester Utd

HONOURS
    as Manager: None
    as Reserve Team Man: None
    as Player: Promotion from Div. 4 1973-74 and 1976-77
    International: Wales under-23

Value Rating: ★ ★ ★ ★ ★

Programme Editor: Kevan Platt

Price of 1992-93 Programme: £1.50
Number of Pages: 36
Subscriptions: £38 inclusive all games; £44 Europe

Local Newspapers: Eastern Counties Newspapers

Local Radio Stations: Radio Norfolk, Radio Broadland

Additional Publications on Club: Canary Citizens Official History of the Club (John Eastwood and Mike Davage £14.95)
Official Handbook, £2.95

LEADING LEAGUE GOALSCORERS
SEASONS 1979-80 – 1991-92

1979-80	JUSTIN FASHANU	11	1980-81	JUSTIN FASHANU	19
1981-82	KEITH BERTSCHIN	12	1982-83	JOHN DEEHAN	20
1983-84	JOHN DEEHAN	15	1984-85	JOHN DEEHAN	13
1985-86	KEVIN DRINKELL	22	1986-87	KEVIN DRINKELL	16
1987-88	KEVIN DRINKELL	12	1988-89	ROBERT FLECK	10
1989-90	ROBERT FLECK	7	1990-91	TIM SHERWOOD	7
	MARK BOWEN	7		DALE GORDON	7

1991-92	ROBERT FLECK	11

CARROW ROAD Norwich NR1 1JE

Capacity: 20,559   **Covered Standing:** 0   **Seating:** 20,559

Tel: Ground: 0603 612131   **Ticket Sales:** 0603 761661   **Clubcall:** 0898 12 11 44

All premium rate calls (0898/0891) cost 36p per minute cheap rate and 48p per minute at all other times. Call costings correct at time of going to press.

GROUNDS
Newmarket Road 1905-08; The Nest, Rosary Road 1908-35; Carrow Road 1935-

ATTENDANCES
Highest: 43,984 v Leicester City, FA Cup 6th Round, 30.3.1963

Lowest: 1,801 v Northampton Town, Football League Trophy, 14.8.1982

RECORD RECEIPTS (with previous records):
£173,570.00 v Nott'm Forest, FA Cup Round 6, 9.3.1991
£109,908.69 v West Ham United, FA Cup Rnd 6 Replay, 22.3.1989
£71,948 v Tottenham Hotspur, FA Cup Round 4, 1.2.1984
£56,894 v Ipswich Town, League Cup Round 3, 8.10.1980
£26,845 v Leyton Orient, FA Cup Round 3, 11.1.1978
£20,853 v Manchester United, League Cup Semi-Final, 22.1.1975

CARROW ROAD
First game: v West Ham United, Division 2, 31.8.1935
First floodlit game: v Sunderland, 17.10.1956

Season Tickets:
Stands: from £140 to £285, juv/OAP £75 to £95

Executive Box Season Tickets: Variable according to match

Cost of Stand Tickets: (Cat A, B, C) Lounges £18, £15, £13; Reserved £13 (juv/OAP £9), £10 (juv/OAP £6), £8 (juv/OAP £4); Unreserved: £11 (£8), £8 (£5), £6 (£3)

Match and Ticket Information: Applications to Box Office 28 days before match with payment and SAE

Car Parking: Numerous private parks nearby. Multi-storey parks in Malt House Road and St. Andrews Street. Street parking nearby in Rose Lane, Carrow Hill and side streets of King Street. Coaches must park at Lower Clarence Road Car Park.

Nearest Railway Station: Norwich (0603 632055)

How to get to the ground

From North: Use A140 to junction with Ring Road, then follow signs Yarmouth A47. In 3.5m at T road turn right. In 0.5m turn left into Carrow Road for Norwich City FC

From East: Use A47 S.P. Norwich; on entering city, keep left into Ring Road for Carrow Road for Norwich City FC

From South and West: Use A11, A140 into Norwich and follow signs Yarmouth A47 into Ring Road, Carrow Road for Norwich City FC

NOTTINGHAM FOREST   Premier

Formed: 1865   **Turned Professional:** 1889   **Ltd Co:** 1982

SPONSORED BY: Labatts/Shipstones (Joint Sponsors)   **NICKNAME:** 'Reds'

Chairman
F Reacher

Directors
G E McPherson JP
J F Hickling (Jt. Vice-Chairman)
I I Korn (Jt. Vice-Chairman)
J M Smith
C Wootton
G W Waterhouse

Secretary
Paul White (0602 822202)

Team Manager
Brian Clough, O.B.E., M.A.

Assistant Manager
Ron Fenton

Coaches
Liam O'Kane
Archie Gemmill

Physiotherapist
Graham Lyas

Groundsman
Steve Mulloy

Commercial Manager
Dave Pullan (0602 820444)

Ground Safety Consultant
Michael Holford, Q.P.M.

Club Statistician for the Directory
Matthew Osbourne

IF Forest had failed to reach Wembley twice they might have looked upon the season as being a touch disappointing, finishing 8th in the league and going out of the F.A. Cup to second division Portsmouth in the quarter-finals.

In the league Forest weren't consistent enough to mount a championship challenge despite having three of Britain's top players, Walker, Pearce and the ever progressing Irish star, Roy Keane. Without these three players Forest could well have been struggling.

The cup competitions were a different kettle of fish altogether. Yet again Forest proved that they are currently the best cup team in Britain.

The F.A. Cup was the only real disappointment. After the dispatching of Wolves, Hereford and Bristol City the Reds fell to Portsmouth 1-0. It was a disappointing way to depart from the competition as the goal was due to an early blunder by Forest keeper, Crossley. Mr Clough must wait another year for another crack at the only competition he's yet to win.

In the Rumbelows Cup Bolton, Bristol Rovers, Southampton and Crystal Palace were all beaten before Forest scraped through against Spurs in the semi-final, 3-2 on aggregate. In the final Nottingham never really got going and Manchester United deservedly won 1-0.

The one major trophy to be won was the Zenith Data Systems Cup. Good wins at Leeds, Villa and Tranmere put them on the road to Wembley. Leicester put up a brave fight but lost 3-1 on aggregate. Forest played Southampton at Wembley in a thrilling final. Young Scot Gemmill scored two superb goals to take the cup back to Nottingham after a 3-2 extra-time win.

On the playing side Walker, Pearce and Keane were outstanding. Others that impressed were Clough, young Scott Gemmill and Teddy Sheringham whose 22 goals made hime easily the top scorer. Big money signings Kingsley Black and Carl Tiler failed to live up to their price tags. The average age of the squad is still about the lowest in the division so they can only improve. Forest reserves easily won the Pontins 1st Division with a blend of youth and experience.

The biggest disappointment of the season was the departure of Des Walker to Sampdoria for a ludicrously small fee of £1.5 million, due to an outrageous clause in his contract. Forest will find him irreplaceable.

The club have built a reputation for fair play and discipline that is admired throughout the country. If only more clubs would realise that concentrating on the game brings results compared with running battles with the opposition, referee and the 'world in general'. Full marks to Mr Clough for setting standards that are never lowered. Let's hope he can erase his F.A. Cup bogie and carry Forest into Europe where their entertaining style of play can be appreciated worldwide.

Matthew Osborne

Back row L-R: Roy Keane, Ian Woan, Steve Chettle, Carl Tiler, Terry Wilson, Roy McKinnon, Tommy Gaynor, Gary Charles. **Middle:** Ron Fenton (Asst. Manager), Archie Gemmill, Liam O'Kane, Andrew Marriott, Teddy Sheringham, Kingsley Black, Mark Crossley, Graham Lyas (Physio), Alan Hill. **Front:** Nigel Clough, Scot Gemmill, Lee Glover, Brian Clough (Manager), Stuart Pearce (Captain), Brian Laws, Gary Crosby.

NOTTINGHAM FOREST

DIVISION ONE: 8th   **FA CUP:** Q-FINALISTS   **RUMBELOWS CUP:** FINALISTS   **ZDS CUP:** WINNERS

M	DATE		COMP.	VEN	OPPONENTS	RESULT	H/T	LGE POS	GOALSCORERS/GOAL TIMES	ATTEN-DANCE
1	A	17	BL	H	Everton	W 2-1	0-1	4	Clough 60, Jemson 87	24,442
2		20	BL	A	Leeds United	L 0-1	0-1	6		(29,447)
3		24	BL	A	Notts County	W 4-0	0-0	4	Crosby 55, Charles 64, Sheringham 70, Keane 73	(21,044)
4		28	BL	H	Tottenham Hotspur	L 1-3	1-1	7	Stewart (og) 10	24,018
5		31	BL	H	Oldham Athletic	W 3-1	2-0	5	Gemmill 28, Keane 41, Pearce 63	23,244
6	S	4	BL	A	Manchester City	L 1-2	0-1	9	Sheringham 65	(29,146)
7		7	BL	A	Sheffield Wed.	L 1-2	0-1	13	Crosby 48	(31,289)
8		14	BL	H	Wimbledon	W 4-2	2-1	10	Keane 11, 47, Black 45, Elkins (og) 62	19,707
9		21	BL	A	Aston Villa	L 1-3	1-0	13	Teale (og) 20 secs	(28,506)
10		25	RC 2/1	H	Bolton Wanderers	W 4-0	2-0		Keane 17, Gaynor 28, 78, Black 64	19,936
11		28	BL	H	West Ham United	D 2-2	1-2	14	Woan 4, Sheringham 77	25,613
12	O	5	BL	A	Queens Park R.	W 2-0	1-0	9	Sheringham 27, 68	(13,508)
13		8	RC 2/2	H	Bolton Wanderers	W 5-2	3-2		Sheringham 14, Keane 17, 70, Gaynor 44, Black 89	(5,469)
14		19	BL	A	Sheffield United	L 2-4	1-2	12	Parker 28, Chettle 80	(23,080)
15		22	ZDS 2	A	Leeds United	W 3-1	2-0		Crosby 15, Sheringham 19, 58	(6,145)
16		26	BL	H	Southampton	L 1-3	0-1	14	Black 84	20,026
17		31	RC 3	H	Bristol Rovers	W 2-0	1-0		Glover 26, Gemmill 56	17,529
18	N	2	BL	A	Norwich City	D 0-0	0-0	17		(13,014)
19		16	BL	H	Coventry City	W 1-0	1-0	13	Sheringham 20	21,154
20		19	ZDS 3	A	Aston Villa	W 2-0	1-0		Pearce 38, Woan 53	(7,859)
21		23	BL	H	Crystal Palace	W 5-1	2-0	10	Sheringham 6, 89 (pen), Pearce 14, Gemmill 49, Woan 64	22,387
22		30	BL	A	Chelsea	L 0-1	0-0	12		(19,420)
23	D	4	RC 4	H	Southampton	D 0-0	0-0			17,939
24		8	BL	H	Arsenal	W 3-2	1-0	10	Woan 44, Sheringham 58, Gemmill 70	22,095
25		10	ZDS N S	A	Tranmere Rovers	W 2-0	1-0		Keane 34, 53	(8,034)
26		14	BL	A	Liverpool	L 0-2	0-1	11		(35,285)
27		17	RC 4R	A	Southampton	W 1-0	1-0		Gemmill 18	(10,861)
28		22	BL	H	Leeds United	D 0-0	0-0	9		27,170
29		26	BL	A	Tottenham Hotspur	W 2-1	1-1	7	Clough 11, Pearce 90	(31,079)
30		28	BL	A	Oldham Athletic	L 1-2	1-0	9	Pearce 28	(16,496)
31	J	1	BL	H	Luton Town	D 1-1	0-1	11	Walker 90	23,809
32		4	FAC 3	H	Wolverhampton W	W 1-0	0-0		Clough 84	27,068
33		8	RC QF	A	Crystal Palace	D 1-1	0-0		Clough 86	(14,941)
34		11	BL	H	Notts County	D 1-1	1-0	11	Black 3	30,168
35		18	BL	A	Everton	D 1-1	1-0	12	Gemmill 37	(17,717)
36		26	FAC 4	H	Hereford United	W 2-0	1-0		Pearce 37, Sheringham 90	24,259
37	F	1	BL	H	Sheffield United	L 2-5	1-3	14	Keane 17, Pearce (pen) 73	22,412
38		5	RC QFR	H	Crystal Palace	W 4-2	3-1		Sheringham 3 (38, 43, pen 72), Pearce 42	18,918
39		9	RC SF1	H	Tottenham Hotspur	D 1-1	0-1		Sheringham 61	21,402
40		12	ZDC N F	A	Leicester City	D 1-1	0-0		Gemmill 74	(19,537)
41		15	FAC 5	H	Bristol City	W 4-1	1-0		Llewellyn (og) 5, Clough 48, Pearce 66, Sheringham (p) 77	24,615
42		22	BL	A	Chelsea	D 1-1	1-0	15	Sheringham 1	24,095
43		26	ZDC N F	H	Leicester City	W 2-0	1-0		Crosby 11, Wassall 53	21,562
44	M	1	RC SF2	A	Tottenham Hotspur	W †2-1	1-1		Glover 10, Keane 100	(28,216)
45		3	BL	A	Crystal Palace	D 0-0	0-0	16		(12,680)
46		7	FAC QF	A	Portsmouth	L 0-1	0-1			(25,402)
47		11	BL	A	Coventry City	W 2-0	2-0	14	Smith (og) 11, Sheringham 41	(11,158)
48		14	BL	H	Norwich City	W 2-0	2-0	13	Keane 38, Gemmill 41	20,721
49		16	BL	H	Manchester United	W 1-0	0-0	11	Clough 59	28,062
50		21	BL	H	Manchester City	W 2-0	0-0	10	Grosby 64, Keane 87	24,115
51		29	ZDC Fin	N	Southampton	W †3-2	2-0		Gemmill 16, 110, Black 45	(67,688)
52		31	BL	A	Arsenal	D 3-3	2-1	11	Woan 40, Clough 44, Keane 69	(27,036)
53	A	2	BL	A	Wimbledon	L 0-3	0-2	12		(3,542)
54		4	BL	H	Sheffield Wed.	L 0-2	0-2	10		26,105
55		8	BL	A	Southampton	W 1-0	1-0	9	Tiler 77	(14,905)
56		12	RC Fin	N	Manchester United	L 0-1	0-1			(76,810)
57		14	BL	A	Luton Town	L 1-2	1-2	8	Black 2	(8,014)
58		18	BL	H	Aston Villa	W 2-0	1-0	8	Gemmill 14, Sheringham 60	22,800
59		20	BL	A	Manchester United	W 2-1	1-1	7	Woan 33, Gemmill 80	(47,576)
60		22	BL	H	Liverpool	D 1-1	1-1	7	Sheringham (pen) 27	23,787
61		24	BL	H	Queens Park R.	D 1-1	0-0	7	Gemmill 77	22,228
62	M	2	BL	A	West Ham United	L 0-3	0-0	8		(20,629)

Best Home League Attendance: 30,168 v Notts County	Smallest: 19,707 v Wimbledon	Av Home Att: 23,722
Goal Scorers:		Compared with 90-91: +1,584

League (60): Sheringham 13 (2 pens), Keane 8, Gemmill 8, Woan 5, Pearce 5 (1 pen), Clough 4, Opponents 4, Black 4, Crosby 2, Charles Grosby, Parker, Walker, Jemson, Chettle, Tiler

R/lows C (20): Sheringham 5, Keane 4, Gaynor 3, Gemmill 2, Black 2, Glover 2, Clough, Pearce

FA Cup (7): Pearce 2, Clough 2, Sheringham 2 (1 pen), Opponents (pen)

ZDS Cup (13): Gemmill 3, Sheringham 2, Crosby 2, Keane 2, Wassall, Black, Woan, Pearce   † = After extra-time

Crossley M.	Charles G.	Pearce S.	Walker D.	Tiler C.	Keane R.	Crosby G.	Gemmill S.	Clough N.	Sheringham E.	Jemson N.	Parker G.	Chettle S.	Laws B.	Woan I.	Glover E.	Black K.	Gaynor T.	Williams B.	Boardman C.	Wassal D.	Marriot A.	Orlygsson T.	Kaminsky J.	Warner	Wilson T.	Referee	
1	2	3	4•	5	6	7	28	9	10	11	S		14													T Holbrook	1
1	2	3		5	6	7	8	9	10	11	S	4	S													N Midgley	2
1	2	3		5	6	7	8	9	10	11•		4	14	S												M Peck	3
1	2	3†		5	6	7	8	9	10	11		4	S	S												V Callow	4
1	2	3		5	6	7	8	9	10	11		4	S	S												R Pawley	5
1	2	3		5	6	7	8	9	10	11•		4	14			S										K Cooper	6
1	2	3		5	6	7	8	9	10			4	S			11	S									A Wilkie	7
1	2			5	6	7	8	9	10		S	4	14			11		3								T Lunt	8
1	2			5	6	7	8*	9•	10		12	4	14			11		3								K Breen	9
1	2•	3		5	6*				10		8	4	14	11		7	9•		12							M Bailey	10
1	2	3	12	5	6				10		8	4	S	11		7	9*									J Watson	11
1	2	3	4		6	7	S		10		8	14				11	9•									J Martin	12
1	2•	3	4	5	6	7	12		10		8*	14				11	9									W Burns	13
1	2	3	4	5	6•	7			10*		8	14		12		11*	9									A Ward	14
1		3	4	5		7	8	9*		11•	2	14				10	12		6							J Worrall	15
1		3	4•	5†		7	8	9		10	2	14	S			11			6							P Don	16
1	2	3	4			7	6		9•		8	5	S	12	10	11										B Hill	17
1	2	3	4*	12		7	6		10		8	5		S	9	11										D Gallagher	18
1	2	3	4		6	7	8	S	10			5	S	11	9											G Courtney	19
1	2	3	4		6•	7	8	12	10			5		11*	9							14				G Ashby	20
1	2	3	4		6•	7*	8	12	10			5		11	9							14				J Lloyd	21
1	2	3	4		6•		8	9	10			5		11	7							14				M Bodenham	22
1	2	3	4	14		7	8	9	10			5•		11					6							A Buksh	23
1	2	3	4	5	6	7	8	9	10					11	S	S										R Milford	24
1	2	3	4•		6*	7	8	9	10			5		11					12							K Barratt	25
1	2	3	4	14	6	7	8	9	10•			5		11					S							K Hackett	26
1	2•	3	4*	5	6		8	9	10					11	12	7						14				T Holbrook	27
1	2	3	4	5	6		8	9	10					11	12	7*										M Reed	28
1	2	3	4	5	6		8	9†	10					11	S							14				R Bigger	29
1	2	3	4	5	6		8	9	10*					11	12	7										I Cruikshanks	30
1	2	3	4	5	6	7	8	9	10				S			11				S						D Allison	31
1	2	3	4	5	6	7	8	9	10				S			11				S						G Ashby	32
1	2	3	4	5	6	7	8	9	10*				12			11				S						K Barratt	33
1	2*	3	4	5•	6	12	8		10					11	9	7			14							R Nixon	34
1		3	4		6	S	8		10		14	2		11	9	7				5•						D Elleray	35
1	2*	3	4		6	12	8		10			S		11	9	7				5						D Axcell	36
1		3	4	5	6	12	8	9			2			11	10	7*				S						J Martin	37
1		3	4	5	6	7	8	9	10		2		S			11				5						M Peck	38
1		3	4	S	6	7	8	9	10		2		S			11				5						D Allison	39
1	S		4		6	7	8	9	10		2	S	3			11				5						I Borrett	40
1	14	3	4		6	7	8	9*	10•		2	12				11				5						N Midgley	41
1	S	3	4		6	7	8	9	10		2	S				11				5						J Rushden	42
1	14	3	4		6	7*	8	9	10		2	12		11•						5						R Lewis	43
1		3	4	S	6	7	8	9	10		S	2		11						5						J Worrall	44
1	2	3	4	5	6		8	9	10		S			11	S					7						K Burge	45
1		3	4	S	6	7	8	9	10*		12	2†		11						5						S Lodge	46
1	2	3	4		6	7	8	9	10			S	11	S						5						P Durkin	47
1	2	3	4	5	6	7	8	9	10			S		S	11					5						R Dilkes	48
	2	3	4		6	7	8	9	10			S		S	11				1	5						I Borrett	49
	2•	3	4		6	7	8	9	10		14			S	11				1	5						A Wilkie	50
	2	3•	4		6	7	8	9	10		14			S	11				1	5						K Hackett	51
	2		4	S	6		8	9	10		3		11	S	7				1	5						P Foakes	52
	2		4	S	6		8	9	10		3	14	11	10	7				1	5						M Bailey	53
			4	5	6	7	8	9			2	11	10	S		3				1		S				K Cooper	54
			4*	11	6		8	9	10		2	S	12			3				1	5					D Elleray	55
	2•		4		6	7	8	9	10		14		S	11		3				1	5					G Courtney	56
1			4*		6	7	8	9	10			5	11			3			2	12	S					T Fitzharris	57
1				6	5	8	9	10			2	11	S	7	S	3				4						W Burns	58
1			4	6	5	8	9	10			2	11		S	S	3				7						J Key	59
1			4	6	5	8	9	10			2	11		S	S	3				7						A Flood	60
1			4	6	5	8	9	10			2	3		S	11	14				7•						K Barratt	61
1			4		5	8	6	9	10		2		11•	14	7		3								6*	N Midgley	62
36	30	30	32	24	39	31	38	33	39	6	5	17	10	20	12	25	3	9		10	6	5			1	**League Appearances**	
	1	1			2	1	1			1	5	5	1	4		1			1		4		1			**Substitute Appearances**	
9	7	9	9	5+1	8	8	8+1	7	10	3	3+1	3+2	3+1	1+2	9	2	1		0+1	4+1	1					**R/lows Appearances**	
4	2+1	4	4	1	4	3+1	4	3	4			2	1	2+1	3					3						**FA Cup Appearances**	
5	3+1	5	5	1	5	6	6	4+1	6		1	3	2+1	2	2+1	4+1	0+1			4+2	1					**ZDS Cup Appearances**	

Also Played: Posn.(Game): Stone 12(62)

† = Sent Off

NOTTINGHAM FOREST

Club Colours: Red shirts, white shorts, red stocking
Change Colours: White shirts, red shorts, white stockings
Reserves League: Pontins Central League Division 1

COMPETITIONS						
Div. 1	Div. 2	Div. 3S	Euro C	UEFA	Sup C	Texaco
92-06	06-07	49-51	78-79	61-62	79-80	70-71
07-11	11-22		79-80	67-68	80-81	
22-25	25-49		80-81	83-84		A/Scot
57-72	51-57			84-85	W.C.C	76-77
77-	72-77				1982	

HONOURS						
Div. 1	Div. 2	Div. 3S	FAC	Lge C	Euro C	A/Scot
77-78	06-07	50-51	1898	77-78	78-79	76-77
	21-22		1959	78-79	79-80	
				88-89		Sup C
			C/Sl'd	89-90		79-80
			1978	Sim C		
				88-89		
				91-92		

MOST APPEARANCES: BOBBY McKINLAY 681+3 (51-70)				
Year	League	FA Cup	Lge Cup	Europe
1951-52	1	1		
1952-53	3			
1953-54	1			
1954-55	37	6		
1955-56	39	1		
1956-57	39	5		
1957-58	40	3		
1958-59	39	9		
1959-60	42	2		
1960-61	42	1	3	
1961-62	42	2	3	2
1962-63	42	7		
1963-64	42	2		
1964-65	42	3		
1965-66	41	1		
1966-67	42	7	2	
1967-68	42	2	2	4
1968-69	30+2	1	1	
1969-70	5+1			
	611+3	53	11	6
Previous holder: J Burkitt 464 (1948-61)				

MOST GOALS IN A CAREER		
GRENVILLE MORRIS 225 (1898-1913)		
Season	League	FA Cup
1898-99	7	8
1899-00	8	3
1900-01	14	1
1901-02	7	2
1902-03	24	2
1903-04	12	2
1904-05	12	1
1905-06	19	3
1906-07	21	1
1907-08	7	
1908-09	12	
1909-10	19	1
1910-11	11	1
1911-12	10	
1912-13	16	1
Total	199	26
Previous holder: McInnes 36 (1892-97)		

HIGHEST TRANSFER FEE RECEIVED			
Amount	Club	Player	Date
£1,500,000	Manchester Utd	Neil Webb	7/89
£1,500,000	Sampdoria	Des Walker	5/92
£1,250,000	Manchester Utd	Gary Birtles	10/81
£1,200,000	Manchester City	Trevor Francis	9/81

HIGHEST TRANSFER FEE PAID			
Amount	Club	Player	Date
£2,000,000	Millwall	Teddy Sheringham	7/91
£1,500,000	Luton Town	Kingsley Black	8/91
£1,400,000	Barnsley	Carl Tiler	5/91
£1,250,000	Coventry City	Ian Wallace	7/80

MANAGERS			
Name	Seasons	Best	Worst
Harry Radford	1889-97	7(1)	13(1)
Harry Haslam	1897-09	4(1)	1(2)
F W Earp	1909-12	14(1)	15(2)
Bob Masters	1912-25	20(1)	20(2)
Jack Baynes	1925-29	5(2)	17(2)
Stan Hardy	1930-31	17(2)	17(2)
Noel Watson	1931-36	5(2)	19(2)
Harold Wightman	1936-39	18(2)	20(2)
Billy Walker	1939-60	10(1)	4(3S)
Andy Beattie	1960-63	9(1)	19(1)
John Carey	1963-68	2(1)	18(1)
Matt Gillies	1969-72	15(1)	21(1)
Dave Mackay	1972-73	14(2)	14(1)
Allan Brown	1973-75	7(2)	16(2)
Brian Clough	1975-	1(1)	8(2)

LONGEST LEAGUE RUNS	
of undefeated matches:	42 (26.11.1977-25.11.1978)
of undefeated home matches:	51 (27.4.1977-17.11.1979)
without home win:	10 (20.11.1909-9.4.1910)
of league wins:	7 (24.12.1892-25.2.1893)
	(29.8.1921-1.10.1921)
of league defeats:	14 (8.2.1913-18.11.1913)
of league matches without a win:	16 (15.3.1913-8.10.1913)
of undefeated away matches:	21 (3.12.1977-9.12.1978)
without an away win:	37 (25.1.1913-23.1.1915)
of home wins:	12 (23.2.1980-20.9.1980)
of away wins: 5 (5.4.1983-29.8.1983)(31.12.1988-25.3.1989)	

PREVIOUS LEAGUE
Football Alliance

BIGGEST VICTORIES
League: 12-0 v Leicester City, Division 1, 12.4.1909 (Joint Div 1 record)
F.A. Cup: 14-0 v Clapton, Round 1, 17.1.1891 (a)
League Cup: 7-0 v Bury, Round 3, 23.9.1980
Europe: 5-1 v AEK Athens, Round 2 (Euro Cup), 15.11.1978
4-0 v Eintracht Frankfurt, Round 1, (UEFA Cup), 17.10.1967

BIGGEST DEFEATS
League: 1-9 v Blackburn Rovers, Division 2, 10.4.1937
0-8 v West Brom. Alb., Division 1, 16.4.1900
0-8 v Leeds City, Division 2, 29.11.1913
0-8 v Birmingham City, Division 2, 10.3.1920
0-8 v Burnley, Div 1, 21.11.1959
F.A. Cup: 0-5 v Southampton, Round 6, 1962-63
League Cup: 0-4 v Manchester United, Round 5, 19.1.1983
Europe: 1-5 v Valencia, Round 1, 14.10.1961

MOST POINTS
3 points a win: 74, Division 1, 1983-84.
2 points a win: 70, Division 3(S), 1950-51. (Division 3S record).

MOST GOALS
110, 1950-51 (Division 3S).
Ardon 36, Capel 23, Collindridge 16, Johnson 15, Scott 9, Leverton 6, Gager 2, Love 1, Burkitt 1, og 1.

MOST GOALS IN A MATCH
A Higgins, 5 v Clapton (a), 14-0, FA Cup 1st rnd, 17.1.1891

MOST GOALS IN A SEASON
Wally Ardron, 36 League goals, Div 3(S), 1950-51
3 goals 3 times = 9; 2 goals 8 times = 16; 1 goal 11 times = 11

MOST FIRST CLASS MATCHES IN A SEASON
65 (42 League, 2 FA Cup, 10 League Cup, 9 European Cup, 2 European Super Cup) 1979-80

MOST LEAGUE GOALS CONCEDED
90, Division 2, 1936-37

MOST LEAGUE WINS
30, Division 3S, 1950-51

MOST LEAGUE DRAWS
18, Division 1, 1969-70;   Division 1, 1978-79

MOST LEAGUE DEFEATS
25, Division 1, 1971-72

OLDEST PLAYER
Sam Hardy, 41 v Newcastle United, 4.10.1924.

YOUNGEST PLAYER
S J Burke 16 years 22 days v Ayr United, Anglo-Scot Cup, 20.10.1976.

MOST CAPPED PLAYER
Stuart Pearce (England) 50

BEST PERFORMANCES BY NOTTINGHAM FOREST

League: 1950-51: Matches played 46, Won 30, Drawn 10, Lost 6, Goals for 110, Goals against 40, Points 70. First in Division 3 South
Highest: 1977-78: Division 1 Champions.

F.A. Cup: 1897-98: 4th rnd. Grimsby Town 4-0; 5th rnd. Gainsborough 4-0; 6th rnd. West Bromwich Albion 3-2; Semi-final Southampton 1-1, 2-0; Final Derby County 3-1.
1958-59: 3rd rnd. Tooting 2-2, 3-0; 4th rnd. Grimsby 4-1; 5th rnd. Birmingham 1-1 (2); 6th rnd. Bolton Wanderers 2-1; Semi-final Aston Villa 1-0; Final Luton Town 2-1.

League Cup: 1977-78: 2nd rnd. West Ham United 5-0; 3rd rnd. Notts County 4-0; 4th rnd. Aston Villa 4-2; 5th rnd. Bury 3-0; Semi-final Leeds United 3-1; Final Liverpool 0-0, 1-0.
1978-79: 2nd rnd. Oldham Athletic 0-0, 4-2; 3rd rnd. Oxford United 5-0; 4th rnd. Everton 3-2; 5th rnd. Brighton & H.A. 3-1; Semi-final Watford 3-1, 0-0; Final Southampton 3-2.
1988-89: 2nd rnd. Chester City 6-0, 4-0; 3rd rnd. Coventry City 3-2; 4th rnd. Leicester City 0-0, 2-1; 5th rnd. Q.P.R. 5-2; Semi-final Bristol City 1-1, 1-0; Final Luton Town 3-1
1989-90: 2nd rnd. Huddersfield Town 1-1, 3-3; 3rd rnd. Crystal Palace 0-0, 5-0; 4th rnd. Everton 1-0; 5th rnd. Spurs 2-2, 3-2; Semi-final Coventry City 2-1, 0-0; Final Oldham Athletic 1-0

European Cup: 1978-79: 1st rnd. Liverpool 2-0, 0-0; 2nd rnd. AEK Athens 2-1, 5-1; 3rd rnd. Grasshoppers 4-1, 1-1; Semi-final Cologne 3-3, 1-0; Final Malmo 1-0.
1979-80: 1st rnd. Oester Vakjo 2-0, 1-0; 2nd rnd. Agres Pitesti 2-1, 2-0; 3rd rnd. Dynamo Berlin 0-1, 3-1; Semi-final Real Madrid 2-0, 0-1; Final S V Hamburg 1-0.

DIVISIONAL RECORDS

	Played	Won	Drawn	Lost	For	Against	Points
DIVISION 1	1980	740	490	750	2840	2886	**2165**
DIVISION 2	1492	548	370	574	2258	2262	**1466**
DIVISION 3S	88	50	19	19	177	79	**119**
TOTALS	**3560**	**1338**	**879**	**1343**	**5275**	**5227**	**3750**

NOTTINGHAM FOREST

PLAYERS NAME Honours	Ht	Wt	Birthdate	Birthplace Transfers	Contract Date	Clubs	League	L/Cup	FA Cup	Other	Lg	L/C	FAC	Oth
GOALKEEPERS														
Mark Crossley	6.0	15.0	16.06.69	Barnsley	02.07.85	Nottm. Forest	84	15	14	8				
E:u21.3				Loan	15.01.90	Manchester Utd								
Andrew Marriott	6.1	13.7	11.10.70	Nottingham	22.10.88	Arsenal (T)								
E:Y2					20.06.89	Nottm. Forest	6	1		1				
				Loan	06.09.89	West Brom A	3							
				Loan	29.12.89	Blackburn Rovers	2							
				Loan	21.03.90	Colchester Utd	10							
				Loan	29.08.91	Burnley	15			2				
DEFENDERS														
Gary Charles	5.9	11.2	13.04.70	London	07.11.87	Nottm. Forest (T)	40+2	8	8+2	4+2	1		1	
E:2,u21.2					16.03.89	Leicester City	5+3							
Steve Chettle	6.1	13.3	27.09.68	Nottingham	28.08.86	Nottm. Forest	126+13	22+2	16	11+1	6	1		1
E:u21.12; LC'90; SC'89														
Brian Laws	5.8	11.0	14.10.61	Wallsend	19.10.79	Burnley	125	14	15		12	2	1	
Div3'82; LC'89'90; SC'89				£10,000	26.08.83	Huddersfield Town	56	7	3		1			
				£30,000	15.03.85	Middlesbrough	103+4	6+1	8+1	6+1	12	2		
				£120,000	07.07.88	Nottm. Forest	98+9	22+3	12+2	9	4		1	
Stuart Pearce	5.10	13.0	24.04.62	Shepherds Bush		Wealdstone			2					
E:50,U21.1; Sthn Lg Challenge Cup'82; LC'89'90; SC'89					20.10.83	Coventry City	51		2		4			
				£450,000	03.06.85	Nottm. Forest	236	43	25	15	39	7	7	6
Carl Tiler	6.2	13.0	11.02.70	Sheffield	02.08.88	Barnsley	67+4	4	4+1	3+1	3			
E: u21.3				£1,400,000	30.05.91	Nottm. Forest	24+1	5+1	1	1	1			
Brett Williams	5.11	12.7	19.03.68	Dudley	31.12.85	Nottm. Forest (A)	34	3	3					
				Loan	13.03.87	Stockport Co	2							
				Loan	14.01.88	Northampton T	3+1							
				Loan	06.09.89	Hereford Utd	14	1	1	1				
				Loan	27.02.92	Oxford Utd	7							
Terry Wilson	6.0	12.9	08.02.69	Broxburn	03.04.86	Nottm. Forest (A)	89+11	11+2	17+1	8	9		2	
S:u21.4; LC'89; SC'89				Loan	30.01.92	Newcastle Utd	2							
MIDFIELD														
Gary Bowyer	6.0	12.13	26.06.71	Manchester	02.12.89	Hereford Utd	12+2				2			
WC'90					15.09.90	Nottm. Forest								
Scot Gemmill	5.10	11.0	02.01.70	Paisley	05.01.90	Nottm. Forest (T)	40+1	8+1	4	6	8	2		3
S:u21														
Roy Keane	5.10	11.3	10.08.71	Cork		CPal								
Ei:7, u21,Y				£10,000	12.06.90	Nottm. Forest	74	12	14	5	16	5	2	2
Thorvaldur Orlygsson	5.11	10.13	02.08.66	Odense (Iceland)		KA Akureyri								
				£150,000	09.12.89	Nottm. Forest	16+1	3	1	0+1	1	1		
FORWARDS														
Gary Bannister	5.8	11.3	22.07.60	Warrington	10.05.78	Coventry City (A)	17+5	2	2		3			
E: u21.1				£100,000	03.08.81	Sheffield Wed	117+1	13	12		55	6	4	
				£200,000	13.08.84	Q.P.R	136	23	9	4	56	9	1	6
				£300,000	10.03.88	Coventry City	39+4	5			11	2		
				£250,000	09.03.90	West Brom A	62+10	3	1	2	18	1		1
				Loan	19.03.92	Oxford Utd	7+3				2			
					01.08.92	Nottm. Forest								
Kingsley Black	5.8	10.11	22.06.68	Luton	07.07.86	Luton Town (A)	123+4	16+2	5+1	3+2	27	1	2	1
NI:2,u21.1; LC'88				£1,500,000	02.09.91	Nottm. Forest	25	9	3	4+1	4	2		1
Nigel Clough	5.9	11.8	19.03.66	Sunderland	01.07.85	Nottm. Forest (A)	232+3	34	21	7+2	86	20	3	1
E:7,B.1,u21.15; LC'89'90; SC'89														
Gary Crosby	5.7	9.13	08.05.64	Sleaford		Lincoln City	6+1	2						
LC'90						Grantham								
				£20,000	21.12.87	Nottm. Forest	115+2	24+1	17+1	10+1	10	5	3	4
Tommy Gaynor	6.1	13.5	29.01.63	Limerick		Limerick								
LC'89; SC'89					19.12.86	Doncaster Rovers	28+5	2+1			7	1		
				£25,000	08.10.87	Nottm. Forest	43+14	10	5+1	3+2	10	8	1	1
				Loan		Newcastle Utd	4				1			
Lee Glover	5.10	12.1	24.04.70	Kettering	02.05.87	Nottm. Forest (A)	37+7	1+3	6+2	3+1	4	2	1	
S:u21.3				Loan	14.09.89	Leicester City	3+2				1			
				Loan	18.01.90	Barnsley	8		4					
				Loan	02.09.91	Luton Town	1							
Teddy Sheringham	5.11	10.9	29.10.61	Highams Park	01.02.85	Aldershot	4+1			1				
E:U21.1,Y.11;Div2'88					19.01.84	Millwall (A)	205+15	16+1	12	11+2	93	8	4	5
				£2,000,000	23.07.91	Nottm. Forest	39	10	4	6	13	5	2	2
Ian Woan	5.10	12.4	14.12.67	Clatterbridge		Runcorn								
				£70,000	14.03.90	Nottm. Forest	29+4	3+1	3+1	3	8			1

ADDITIONAL CONTRACT PLAYERS

Craig Armstrong, Craig Boardman, Raymond Byrne, Christian Davies, Cuan Forrest, Neil Glasser, (D) Chris Hope, Stephen Howe, Jason Kaminsky, Ian Kilford, Paul McGregor, Ray McKinnon, (G) Mark Smith, (M) Steve Stone, Mark Telford, Vance Warner, Dale Wright.

NOTTINGHAM FOREST

RECORD WIN & LOSS AGAINST EACH CLUB IN CURRENT DIVISION
(Where a score has occured on several occasions the most recent is given)

Club	Rec. Win	Season	Rec. Loss	Season
ARSENAL	4-0	1957-58	7-0	1914-15
ASTON VILLA	6-0	1986-87	7-3	1903-04 (home)
BLACKBURN ROVERS	5-2	1962-63 (away)	9-1	1936-37
CHELSEA	7-0	1990-91	5-1	1925-26 (home)
COVENTRY CITY	4-0	1971-72	5-1	1938-39
CRYSTAL PALACE	6-1	1950-51 (away)	4-1	1921-22
EVERTON	4-0	1990-10 (away)	6-0	1961-62
IPSWICH TOWN	4-0	1977-78	2-0	1982-83
LEEDS UNITED	4-0	1924-25	6-1	1971-72
LIVERPOOL	5-1	1908-09	6-1	1967-68
MANCHESTER CITY	4-0	1979-80	5-0	1905-06
MANCHESTER UNITED	6-2	1909-10 (away)	5-0	1935-36
MIDDLESBROUGH	5-1	1973-74	4-0	1922-23
NORWICH CITY	5-0	1990-91	4-0	1936-37
OLDHAM ATHLETIC	5-0	1934-35 (away)	8-3	1925-26
QUEENS PARK RANGERS	4-0	1985-86	3-0	1984-85
SHEFFIELD UNITED	6-1	1976-77	4-0	1904-05
SHEFFIELD WEDNESDAY	4-0	1921-22 (away)	6-0	1909-10 (home)
SOUTHAMPTON	6-0	1946-47	7-2	1935-36
TOTTENHAM HOTSPUR	4-0	1979-80	9-2	1963-64
WIMBLEDON	4-2	1991-92	4-1	1988-89

MANAGER: BRIAN CLOUGH

DATE OF BIRTH: 21.03.1935   **PLACE OF BIRTH:** Middlesbrough

DATE OF APPOINTMENT: 06.01.1975

PREVIOUS CLUBS
as Manager: Hartlepool; Derby County; Brighton; Leeds United
as Player: Middlesbrough; Sunderland

HONOURS
as Manager: Derby County: Div 2 Championship 1969; Div 1 Championship 1972; Nottingham Forest: Promotion to Div 1 1977; Div 1 Championship 1978; Runners-Up 1979; League Cup Winners 1978, 1979, 1989, 1990; European Cup Winners 1979, 1980; Simod Cup 1989, 1992; FA Cup Runners-Up 1991
as Player:
International: England: U-23 3 caps; 2 Full Caps

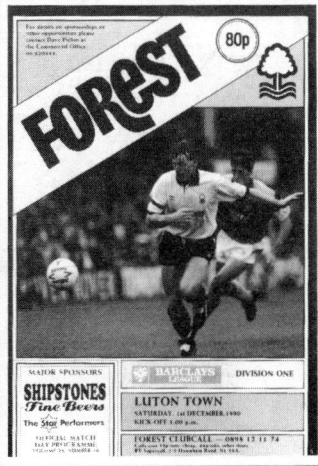

Value Rating: ★ ★ ★

Programme Editor: John Lawson

Price of 1992-93 Programme: £1
Number of Pages: 32
Subscriptions: Contact 'Temple Printers' 0602 868304

Local Newspapers: Nottingham Evening Post, Derby Telegraph

Local Radio Stations: Radio Nottingham, Radio Trent

Additional Publications on Club: Forest Road Pictorial, Milestones of Garibaldi (Keith Mellor £4.95)

LEADING LEAGUE GOALSCORERS
SEASONS 1979-80 – 1991-92

1979-80	TREVOR FRANCIS	14		1980-81	IAN WALLACE	11
1981-82	IAN WALLACE	9		1982-83	IAN WALLACE	13
1983-84	GARY BIRTLES	15		1984-85	PETER DAVENPORT	16
1985-86	NIGEL CLOUGH	15		1986-87	NIGEL CLOUGH	14
					GARY BIRTLES	14
1987-88	NIGEL CLOUGH	19		1988-89	NIGEL CLOUGH	14
1989-90	STEVE HODGE	10		1990-91	NIGEL CLOUGH	14
	1991-92	**TEDDY SHERINGHAM**	**13**			

CITY GROUND City Road, Nottingham NG2 5FJ

Capacity: 28,214   **Covered Standing:** 5,333   **Seating:** 22,881

Tel: Ground: 0602 822202   **Ticket Sales:** 0602 813801   **Clubcall:** 0898 12 11 74

All premium rate calls (0898/0891) cost 36p per minute cheap rate and 48p per minute at all other times. Call costings correct at time of going to press.

GROUNDS
Forest Racecourse 1865-79, The Meadows 1879-80, Trent Bridge 1880-82, Parkside Lenton 1882-85, Gregory Lenton 1885-90, Town Ground 1890-98, City Ground 1898-

ATTENDANCES
Highest: 44,946 v Manchester United, Div 1, 28.10.1967

Lowest: 2,624 v West Bromwich Albion, 30.3.1904

RECORD RECEIPTS (with previous records):
£222,954 v Wolverhampton Wndrs, FA Cup 3rd Rnd, 4.1.1992
£203,206 v Newcastle Utd, FA Cup, 18.2.1991
£163,334 v Bristol City, Littlewoods Cup, 15.2.1989
£152,334 v Ajax, European Cup, 9.4.1979
£120,470 v Cologne, European Cup, 11.4.1979
£50,000 v Manchester City, FA Cup, 31.1.1978
£34,257 v Southampton, FA Cup, 29.1.1977

CITY GROUND
First game: v Blackburn Rovers, 0-1, 3.9.1898
First floodlit game: v Gillingham, 11.9.1961
Internationals: England v Wales, 1909

Season Tickets:
Stands: from £140 to £185 (no reductions)
Ground: £100, juv/OAP £55

Executive Box Season Tickets: Phone Commercial Office for details (0602 820444)

Cost of Stand Tickets: Stand: £13, £12, £11
Terraces: £8, £5, Junior Reds £6

Match and Ticket Information: 14 days in advance (personal); 12 days (postal)

Car Parking: Space for 300 cars in East Stand car park plus street parking off Loughborough and Radcliffe Roads

Nearest Railway Station: Nottingham Midland (0602 46151)

How to get to the ground

From North: Use Motorway M1 until Junction 26, leave motorway and follow signs into Nottingham A610. Follow signs Melton Mowbray, Trent Bridge A606. Cross river and turn left into Radcliffe Road, then turn left into Colwick Road for Nottingham Forest FC

From East: Use A52 S.P. Nottingham into West Bridgeford, then turn left into Colwick Road for Nottingham Forest FC

From South: Use Motorway M1 until Junction 24, leave motorway and follow signs Nottingham (South) to Trent Bridge, turn right into Radcliffe Road, then turn left into Colwick Road for Nottingham FC

From West: Use A52 into Nottingham, then follow signs Melton Mowbray, Trent Bridge A606, cross river and turn left into Radcliffe Road, then turn left into Colwick Road for Nottingham Forest FC

NOTTS COUNTY
Formed: 1862 (Oldest league club) **Turned Professional:** 1885

SPONSORED BY: Home Bitter

Division 1
Ltd Co: 1890

NICKNAME: The Magpies

President
F Sherwood

Chairman
D C Pavis

Vice-Chairman
J Mounteney

Directors
W Hopcroft
D Ward
P Jackson

Chief Executive/Company Secretary
Neal Hook, M Inst M (0602 861155)

Team Manager
Neil Warnock

Assistant Manager
Michael Jones

Coach
Michael Walker

Youth Coach
Russell Slade

Physiotherapist
David Lawson

Commercial Manager
Shuna Shaw

Lottery & Promotions Manager
Les Bradd

FOLLOWING an opening day defeat at Old Trafford, County enjoyed their best spell in the First Division in their next five matches. Three victories and a draw brought them a top ten position, but the initial excitement of a place amongst the elite seemed to wear off and the club found it well neigh impossible to pull away from the danger zone.

Neil Warnock continued to impress as a young manager with an excellent attitude and his standards had obviously been instrumental in achieving a First Division place but his squad were, realistically, not quite strong enough to keep it.

Tommy Johnson finished top scorer with 12 goals, despite leaving to join Derby County in March, but he lacked regular support although twenty different players featured amongst the goalscorers during the season.

The club reached the Firth Round of the F.A. Cup following victories over Wigan Athletic and Blackburn Rovers but Norwich City, on one of their better days, beat them 3-0 at Carrow Road. The Rumbelows and Zenith Data Cups brought little cheer, although Sheffield Wednesday were beaten in the latter competition.

Steve Cherry and Charlie Palmer proved to be the most consistent players but one or two of Warnock's very shrewd signings from the lower leagues, who had done so well to gain the club promotion, sadly found the very top flight a little difficult to master.

However, the club is in good hands and with the experience gained from their season with the big names, The Magpies may well be better prepared for another challenge at the very top, if they can bounce right back this season.

T.W.

Back row L-R: Gavin Warboys, Richard Walker, Andy Williams, Mineert Dijkstra, Kevin Wilson, Michael Johnson, Robert Matthews, Chris Short, Paul Harding, Paul Cox, Steve Slawson, Mark Wells. **Middle:** Dave Lawson (Physio), Paul Devlin, Richard Dryden, Charlie Palmer, Dean Yates, James Walker, Bob Catlin, Steve Cherry, Craig Short, Alan Paris, Don O'Riordan, Tommy Gallagher, Mick Jones (Asst. Manager). **Front:** David Smith, Tony Agana, Phil Turner, Derek Pavis (Chairman), Neil Warnock (Manager), Mark Draper, Kevin Bartlett, Dean Thomas.

NOTTS COUNTY

DIVISION ONE: 21st   **FA CUP:** 5th RND   **RUMBELOWS CUP:** 2nd RND   **ZDS CUP:** Nth S/FINAL

M	DATE		COMP	VEN	OPPONENTS	RESULT		H/T	LGE POS	GOALSCORERS/GOAL TIMES	ATTEN-DANCE
1	A	17	BL	A	Manchester United	L	0-2	0-1			(46,278)
2		20	BL	H	Southampton	W	1-0	1-0		Yates 38	9,653
3		24	BL	H	Nottingham Forest	L	0-4	0-0			21,044
4		28	BL	A	Chelsea	D	2-2	1-0		Johnson 4, Regis 49	(15,846)
5		31	BL	A	West Ham United	W	2-0	0-0		Bartlett 64, 67	(20,093)
6	S	3	BL	H	Sheffield Wed.	W	2-1	1-1		Johnson (pen) 7, 85	12,297
7		7	BL	H	Liverpool	L	1-2	1-0	12	Johnson 42	16,051
8		14	BL	A	Coventry City	L	0-1	0-0			(10,635)
9		17	BL	A	Sheffield United	W	3-1	0-0		Bartlett 73, 77, Rideout 81	(19,375)
10		21	BL	H	Norwich City	D	2-2	1-0	11	Rideout 21, Bowen (og) 72	9,448
11		24	RC 2/1	A	Port Vale	L	1-2	0-1		Johnson 87	(4,722)
12		28	BL	A	Luton Town	D	1-1	0-0		Johnson (pen) 88	(7,692)
13	O	6	BL	H	Manchester City	L	1-3	0-0	16	Thomas 49	11,878
14		9	RC 2/2	H	Port Vale	W	†3-2	0-1		Bartlett 63, 69, Johnson (pen) 77	4,419
15		19	BL	H	Leeds United	L	2-4	1-2	17	Lund 12, Johnson 62	12,964
16		22	ZDS 2	A	Sheffield United	D	†3-3	1-1	19	Draper 19, Bartlett 54, Slawson 117 (Won 2-1 on pens)	(3,291)
17		26	BL	A	Arsenal	L	0-2	0-0	19		(30,011)
18	N	2	BL	H	Oldham Athletic	W	2-0	2-0	15	Rideout 6, Johnson 45	7,634
19		16	BL	A	Aston Villa	L	0-1	0-1	17		(23,020)
20		23	BL	A	Everton	L	0-1	0-1			(24,230)
21		26	ZDS NQF	H	Sheffield Wed.	W	1-0	0-0		Harding 87	4,118
22		30	BL	H	Queens Park R.	L	0-1	0-0	18		7,901
23	D	7	BL	A	Tottenham Hotspur	L	1-2	1-1	19	Craig Short 35	(23,364)
24		20	BL	A	Southampton	D	1-1	0-1		Slawson 81	(11,054)
25		26	BL	H	Chelsea	W	2-0	1-0		Yates 24, Johnson 47	11,867
26		28	BL	H	West Ham United	W	3-0	0-0	18	Turner 51, Harding 62, Agana 69	11,163
27	J	1	BL	A	Crystal Palace	L	0-1	0-1	18		(14,202)
28		5	FAC 3	H	Wigan Athletic	W	2-0	0-0		Johnson 57, Turner 76	5,913
29		8	ZDS NSF	H	Leicester City	L	†1-2	1-0		Chris Short 38	11,559
30		11	BL	A	Nottingham Forest	D	1-1	0-1	18	Dryden 51	(30,168)
31		18	BL	H	Manchester United	D	1-1	1-0	18	Johnson (pen) 10	21,055
32	F	1	BL	A	Leeds United	L	0-3	0-1	19		(27,244)
33		4	FAC 4	H	Blackburn Rovers	W	2-1	1-0		Lund 22, Draper 80	12,173
34		8	BL	A	Arsenal	L	0-1	0-1	19		11,221
35		15	FAC 5	A	Norwich City	L	0-3	0-2			(14,511)
36		22	BL	A	Queens Park R.	D	1-1	0-0	19	Bartlett 48	(8,300)
37		25	BL	H	Wimbledon	D	1-1	1-0		Craig Short 20	6,198
38	M	7	BL	H	Wimbledon	L	0-2	0-1			(4,196)
39		10	BL	H	Aston Villa	D	0-0	0-0			8,389
40		14	BL	A	Oldham Athletic	L	3-4	1-3	21	Draper 11, Williams 50, Lund 84	(12,125)
41		17	BL	H	Everton	D	0-0	0-0			7,480
42		21	BL	A	Sheffield Wed.	L	0-1	0-0			(23,910)
43		28	BL	H	Crystal Palace	L	2-3	2-1	21	Craig Short 10, Wilson 40	7,674
44		31	BL	A	Liverpool	L	0-4	0-2	21		(25,457)
45	A	7	BL	H	Tottenham Hotspur	L	0-2	0-1	21		9,205
46		11	BL	H	Coventry City	W	1-0	0-0	21	Thomas 89	6,655
47		18	BL	A	Norwich City	W	1-0	0-0	21	Matthews 86	(12,100)
48		20	BL	H	Sheffield United	L	1-3	1-1	21	Bartlett 6	12,605
49		24	BL	A	Manchester City	L	0-2	0-1	21		(23,426)
50	M	2	BL	H	Luton Town	W	2-1	1-1	21	Matthews 34, 70	11,380

Best Home League Attendance: 21,055 v Manchester United   **Smallest: 6,198 v Wimbledon**   **Av Home Att: 11,133**

Goal Scorers: **Compared with 90-91: +2,939**

League (40):   Johnson 9 (3 pens), Bartlett 6, Rideout 3, Craig Short 3, Matthews 3, Lund 2, Thomas 2, Yates 2, Slawson, Williams, Opponents
Draper, Harding, Turner, Agana, Regis, Dryden, Wilson

R/lows C (4):   Johnson 2 (1 pen), Bartlett 2

FA Cup (4):   Johnson, Turner, Lund, Draper

Autoglass (5):   Chris Short, Harding, Bartlett, Slawson, Draper   † = After extra-time

Cherry S.	Palmer C.	Paris A.	Short,Craig	Yates D.	O'Riordan D.	Thomas D.	Turner P.	Regis D.	Draper M.	Johnson T.	Bartlett K.	Short,Chris	Harding P.	Dryden R.	Rideout P.	Lund G.	Johnson M.	Slawson S.	Agana P.	Williams A.	McClelland J.	Wilson K.	Farina F.	Devlin P.	Matthews R.	Referee	
1	2	3	4	5	6*	7	8	9	10	11•	12	14														G Courtney	1
1	2	3	4	5		7	8	9	10	11	S	S	6													R Bigger	2
1	2	3•	4	5		7	8	9	10	11	12	14	6*													M Peck	3
1	2	3	4	5		7	8	9•	10	11•	12	14	6†													J Martin	4
1	2	3	4	5		7	12	9*	6	11	10			S	8											J Deakin	5
1	2	3	4	5		7	8	S	6	11	10*		12	9												H King	6
1	2	3	4	5		7	8	12	6	11	10*		S	9												A Buksh	7
1	2•	3*	4	5		7	8	12	6	11	10	14		9												J Worrall	8
1	S	3	4	5		7	S		6	11	10	2		8	9											D Allison	9
1	14	3	4	5		7	12		6*	11•	10	2		8	9											L Dilkes	10
1	S	3	4	5		7	12			11	10*	2	6	8	9											P Vanes	11
1	8	3	4*	5		7	12		14	11	10*	2	6		9											J Rushton	12
1	2	3	4	5		7†	12	14		11	10*		6*	8	9											A Ward	13
1	2	3	4	5		7	8	14	6*	11•	10			12	9											K Breen	14
1	2	3	4*	5		7	8	14	6	11	10			12	9•											B Hill	15
1	2	3		5				9*	6	11	10•		8	7			4		12							T Fitzharris	16
1	2	3		5*		7	8		6	11•	14		12	10		9	4									A Gunn	17
1	2•	3	4			7	14		6	11	10*		8	5		9	12									D Elleray	18
1	2	3	4	5		7	S		6	11		S		8	9					10						K Barratt	19
1	2	3	4	5		7	14		6	11•	12			8	9					10						P Wright	20
1	2		4		6*	7	14			11	S	5	8	3					9	10						K Redfern	21
1	2		4			7	14			11	5*		8	3					9	10						R Milford	22
1	2	3	4			7	8		12	11		5	6	9					S	10						D Axcell	23
1	2	3	4	5		7	8			11		6	9					S	12	10*						P Alcock	24
1	2	3	4	5		7	8			11		6	9					S	S	10						I Hemley	25
1	2	3	4	5		7	8			11•		6	9•					12	14	10						J Worrall	26
1	2	3	4	5		7*	8			11		6	9•					12	14	10						K Cooper	27
1	2	3	4	5			8			11		6	9*	7				12	14	10•						R Pawley	28
1	2	3	4	5			8		12	11		6*	9*	7					14	10						K Hackett	29
1	2	3	4			7	8		12	11•		6	9	5					14	10*						R Nixon	30
1	2	3	4			7	8		6	11	10	5	9	S		S										K Morton	31
1	2	3	4			7	8		6	11•	10		5*	9			14									D Allison	32
1	2	3	4			7	8		6	11	10		5	9•			14									R Nixon	33
1	2	3	4			7*	8		6	11•	10		5	9					12	14						W Burns	34
1	2	3	4			7	8		6	14	10		5	9*				12	11*							D Gallagher	35
1	2		4			7				11	10	5	6	3		9		S	8							M Reed	36
1	2		4			7				11•	10	5	6	3	S	9	12	8								S Lodge	37
1	2						10*		6	11	12	5	8	3	14	9•				7	4					M Bodenham	38
1	2						8		6	11•	10	5	9*	3	14		12			7	4					D Elleray	39
1	2		4	11			8•		6	10			14	3		9	12		7	5*						K Breen	40
1	2		4	12			8*		6	10	5		3			9	14		7	11•						J Rushton	41
1	2		4	5		7*			6	10•	8	14	3			9	12		7	11						N Midgley	42
1	2		4	5			S		6	8			3	9*					7	11•	10	12				T Holbrook	43
1	2		4	5			8		6*			14	3	9					7		10	12				D Phillips	44
1	2		4				14		6			5	8	3	9*			12	7•		11	10				I Borrett	45
1	2		4				14		6			8*	3		5				7		11		9*		12	W Burge	46
1	2		4				9		6			10*	14	3		5			7*		11				12	P Don	47
1	2		4				9		6			10	S	3		5			7*		11				12	V Callow	48
1	2								6			10•		8	3		4	5		9	7	11*			12	J Key	49
1	2		4				3		6				5	8					S	9	7	11*		12	10	R Nixon	50
42	40	26	38	24	1	34	22	5	32	31	24	20	25	28	9	10	5	3	11	14	6	8	1	1	1	League Appearances	
	1	1	1	1		2	7	4	3		5	7	4	1	2	3			10	2	1		2	1	4	Substitute Appearances	
2	1	2	2	2		2	1+1	0+1	1	2	2	1	1	1+1	2											R/lows Appearances	
3	3	3	1	3		3	2	2+1	2	2	2	1	1	2	3											FA Cup Appearances	
3	3	2	2	2	1	1	1	1	1+1	3	1	2	3	2	2		1	0+2	2							Autoglass Appearances	

Also Played: Posn.(Game): Wells 14(16)12(32)S(33), Cox S(36)14(49), Robinson 11•(44)

† = Sent Off

NOTTS COUNTY

Club Colours: Black and white striped shirts, black shorts, black stockings
Change Colours: Amber shirts, black shorts, black stockings
Reserves League: Pontins Central League Div 2 **'A' Team:** Midland Intermediate

COMPETITIONS

Div. 1	Div. 2	Div. 3	Div. 3S	Div. 4
88-93	93-97	58-59	30-31	59-60
97-12	12-14	60-64	35-50	64-71
14-20	20-23	71-73		
23-26	26-30	85-90		
81-84	31-35			
91-92	50-58			
	73-81			
	84-85			
	90-91			
	92-			

HONOURS

Div. 2	Div. 3S	Div 4	FAC
96-97	30-31	70-71	93-94
13-14	49-50		
22-23			

MOST APPEARANCES: ALBERT IREMONGER 602 (1904-26)

Year	League	FA Cup
1904-05	2	
1905-06	22	
1906-07	33	N
1907-08	38	O
1908-09	38	T
1909-10	38	
1910-11	38	A
1911-12	38	V
1912-13	34	A
1913-14	38	I
1914-15	38	L
1919-20	21	A
1920-21	32	B
1921-22	35	L
1922-23	19	E
1923-24	34	
1924-25	32	
1925-26	34	
	565	37

MOST GOALS IN A CAREER LES BRAD 138 (1967-78)

Season	League	FA Cup	Lge Cup
1967-68	10		
1968-69	10	1	
1969-70	8	1	
1970-71	11		
1971-72	21	2	2
1972-73	9	2	2
1973-74	10		
1974-75	6		
1975-76	16		3
1976-77	12		
1977-78	12		
Total	125	6	7

RECORD TRANSFER FEE RECEIVED

Amount	Club	Player	Date
£1,300,000	Derby County	Tommy Johnson	3/92
£350,000	Tottenham H	John Chiedozie	8/84
£150,000	Wrexham	Mark Vinter	6/79

RECORD TRANSFER FEE PAID

Amount	Club	Player	Date
£750,000	Sheffield Utd	Tony Agana	11/91
£600,000	Leyton Orient	John Chiedozie	8/81
£200,000	N K Rijeka	Rad Avramovic	8/79

MANAGERS

Name	Seasons	Best	Worst
Albert Fisher	1913-27	9(1)	16(2)
Horace Henshall	1927-34	5(2)	1(3S)
Charles Jones	1934		
David Platt	1934		
Percy Smith	1935-36	9(3S)	9(3S)
Jim McMullen	1936-37	2(3S)	2(3S)
Harry Parkes	1938-39	11(3S)	11(3S)
Tony Towe	1939-42		
Frank Womack	1942-43		
Frank Buckley	1944-46		
Arthur Strolley	1946-49	6(3S)	11(3S)
Eric Houghton	1949-53	15(2)	11(3S)
George Dryser	1953-57	7(2)	20(2)
Tommy Lawton	1957-58	21(2)	21(2)
Frank Hill	1958-61	5(3)	2(4)
Tim Coleman	1961-63	7(3)	13(3)
Eddie Lowe	1963-65	24(3)	13(4)
Tim Coleman	1965-66	8(4)	8(4)
Jack Burkitt	1966-67	20(4)	20(4)
Andy Beattie	1967		
Bill Gray	1967-68	17(4)	17(4)
Jack Wheeler	1968-69	19(4)	19(4)
Jimmy Sirrell	1969-75	10(2)	8(4)
Ronnie Fenton	1975-77	5(2)	8(2)
Jimmy Sirrell	1977-82	15(2)	15(2)
Howard Wilkinson	1982-83	15(1)	15(1)
Larry Lloyd	1983-84	21(1)	21(1)
Ritchie Barker	1984-85	20(2)	20(2)
Jimmy Sirrell	1985-87	7(3)	7(3)
John Barnwell	1987-88	8(3)	8(1)
Neil Warnock	1988-90	3(3)	9(3)

LONGEST LEAGUE RUNS

of undefeated matches:	19 (26.4.1930-6.12.1930)
of undefeated home matches:	25 (17.8.1970-14.8.1971)
without home win:	13 (3.12.1904-23.9.1905)
	(24.11.1979-26.4.1980)
of league wins:	8 (17.1.1914-14.3.1914)
of league matches without a win:	18 (26.11.1904-8.4.1905)
of undefeated away matches:	10 (24.7.1971-30.10.1971)
without an away win:	24 (23.12.1933-30.1.1935)
of home wins:	14 (17.9.1959-13.2.1960)
of away wins:	5 (15.9.1896-31.10.1896)

BIGGEST VICTORIES
League: 10-0 v Port Vale, Division 2, 1894-95
11-1 v Newport County, 15.1.1949
F.A. Cup: 15-0 v Thornhill (now Rotherham), 24.10.1885
League Cup: 5-0 v Mansfield, 30.8.1988
5-0 v Swindon Town, 17.10.1962

BIGGEST DEFEATS
League: 1-9 v Blackburn Rovers, Division 1, 16.11.1889
1-9 v Aston Villa, Division 3S, 29.9.1930
1-9 v Portsmouth, Division 2, 9.4.1927
0-8 v West Brom. Alb., Division 1, 25.10.1919
0-8 v Newcastle Utd, Division 1, 26.10.1901
F.A. Cup: 1-8 v Newcastle Utd, Rnd 3, 8.1.1927
League Cup: 1-5 v Manchester City, 29.10.1980

MOST POINTS
3 points a win: 87, Division 3, 1989-90
2 points a win: 69, Division 4, 1970-71

MOST GOALS
107, 1959-60 (Division 4)
Newsham 24, Forrest 19, Bircumshaw 17, Roby 11, Joyce 10, Withers 8, Hateley 8, Harabin 7, Carver 2, og 1

MOST GOALS IN A MATCH
9, Harry Curshaw v Wednesbury Strollers, FA Cup, 10.12.1891

MOST GOALS IN A SEASON
Tom Keetley, 41 (League 39, FA Cup 2) 1930-31
4 goals once = 4, 3 goals twice = 6, 2 goals 9 times = 18, 1 goals 13 times = 13

MOST FIRST CLASS MATCHES IN A SEASON
60 (46 League, 3 FA Cup, 2 League Cup, 7 Sherpa Van Trophy, 2 Play-offs) 1987-88

MOST LEAGUE GOALS CONCEDED
97, Division 2, 1934-35

MOST LEAGUE WINS
30, Division 4, 1970-71

MOST LEAGUE DRAWS
18, Division 4, 1968-69

MOST LEAGUE DEFEATS
28, Division 3, 1963-64

OLDEST PLAYER
Albert Iremonger, 41 years 320 days

YOUNGEST PLAYER
Tony Bircumshaw, 16 years 54 days

MOST CAPPED PLAYER
Harry Curshaw (England) 8   Martin O'Neill (N. Ireland) 8

BEST PERFORMANCES BY NOTTS COUNTY

League: 1970-71: Matches played 46, Won 30, Drawn 9, Lost 7, Goals for 89, Goals against, Points 69. First in Div 4

Highest: 1890-91, 1900-01: 3rd in Division 1

F.A. Cup: 1893-94: 1st rnd. Burnley (h) 1-0; 2nd rnd. Burton (a) 2-1; 3rd rnd. Nottingham Forest (a) 1-1 (h) 4-1; Semi-Final Blackburn Rovers 1-0; Final Bolton Wanderers 4-1

League Cup: 1963-64: 2nd rnd. Blackburn (h) 1-3; 3rd rnd. Bradford (a) 3-2; 4th rnd. Portsmouth (h) 3-2; 5th rnd. Manchester City (h) 0-1

1972-73: 1st rnd. York City (h) 3-1; 2nd rnd. Southport (h) 3-2; 3rd rnd. Southampton (a) 3-1; 4th rnd. Stoke City (h) 3-1; 5th rnd. Chelsea (a) 1-3

1975-76: 2nd rnd. Sunderland (h) 2-1; 3rd rnd. Leeds United (a) 1-0, 4th rnd. Everton (a) 2-2 (h) 2-0; 5th rnd. Newcastle United (a) 0-1

DIVISIONAL RECORDS

	Played	Won	Drawn	Lost	For	Against	Points
DIVISION 1	1068	341	253	474	1403	1712	983
DIVISION 2	1378	508	341	529	2059	2120	1390
DIVISION 3	552	228	140	184	830	776	702
DIVISION 3S	378	173	82	123	668	499	428
DIVISION 4	368	152	91	125	545	501	395
TOTALS	3744	1402	907	1435	5505	5608	3898

NOTTS COUNTY

PLAYERS NAME Honours	Ht	Wt	Birthdate	Birthplace Transfers	Contract Date	Clubs	League	L/Cup	FA Cup	Other	Lg	L/C	FAC	Oth
GOALKEEPERS														
Kevin Blackwell	5.11	12.10	21.12.58	Luton		Boston Utd			9					
GMVC'87						Barnet								
						Scarborough	44	11	2	2				
				Loan	08.11.89	Notts County								
				£15,000	14.12.89	Notts County								
Steve Cherry	5.11	11.0	05.08.60	Nottingham	22.03.78	Derby County	77	5	8					
E:Y4				Loan	26.11.80	Port Vale	4		4					
				£25,000	10.08.84	Walsall	71	10	7	6				
				£17,000	22.11.86	Plymouth A	73	4	5	1				
				Loan	01.12.88	Chesterfield	10			3				
				£70,000	16.02.89	Notts County	152	8	8	18				
DEFENDERS														
Richard Dryden	6.0	12.0	14.06.69	Stroud	14.07.87	Bristol Rovers	12+1	2+1	0+2	2				
Div.4'90				Loan	22.09.88	Exeter City								
				£15,000+	08.03.89	Exeter City	92	7	2	4	13	2		
				£250,000	09.08.91	Notts County	28+1	1	1	2	1			
Charlie Palmer	5.11	12.5	10.07.63	Aylesbury	13.07.81	Watford (A)	10	2		4	1			
				Free	12.07.84	Derby County	51	7	1	2	2			
				£32,000	13.02.87	Hull City	69+1	3	3	2	1			
				Loan	15.02.89	Notts County								
				£25,000	23.03.89	Notts County	126+3	7	7	14	6			1
Alan Paris	5.11	10.12	15.08.64	Slough		Slough								
					03.11.82	Watford								
					09.09.85	Peterborough U	135+2	12	10	8	2			
					29.07.88	Leicester City	80+8	7+2	2	3	3	1	1	
				£80,000	18.01.91	Notts County	39+3	2	4	5	1			
Christain Short	5.10	12.02	09.05.70	Munster	11.07.88	Scarborough	42+1	5	1	3+1	1			
				Loan	25.05.90	Manchester Utd								
				£100,000	05.09.90	Notts County	31+11	1	3+1	4	2			
J. Craig Short	6.0	11.4	25.06.68	Bridlington		Pickering Town								
E:S					15.10.87	Scarborough	61+2	6	2	7	7			1
				£100,000	27.07.89	Notts County	125+1	6	8	15	5	1	1	1
Dean Yates	6.1	11.0	26.10.67	Leicester	14.06.85	Notts County (A)	291+1	20	20	32	33			4
E:u21.5														
MIDFIELD														
Mark Draper	5.10	11.0	11.11.70	Derbys	12.12.88	Notts County (T)	118+16	7+1	7	11+2	16		1	3
E:u21.1														
Paul Harding						Barnet								
				£60,000	28.09.90	Notts County	45+8	1	6	7+1	1			2
Donal O'Riordan	5.11	12.0	14.05.57	Dublin	01.05.75	Derby County (A)	2+4	0+1			1			
Ei:u21.1				Loan	21.01.78	Doncaster Rovers	2							
				£30,000		Tulsa Roughnecks								
				£30,000	13.10.78	Preston N.E	153+5	10	8		8			
				£30,000	08.08.83	Carlisle Utd	84	4	4		18			
				£55,000	08.08.85	Middlesbrough	41	2	1	2	2		1	1
				Free	22.08.86	Grimsby Town	86	6	6	3	14			
				£16,000	13.07.88	Notts County	87+5	3+1	6	14+2	4	2		
				Loan	28.09.89	Mansfield Town	6							
Phil Robinson	5.9	10.10	06.01.67	Stafford	08.01.85	Aston Villa (A)	2+1				1			
Div.4'88; Div.3'89; SVT'88; AMC(LDC)'91					03.07.87	Wolverhampton W	63+8	6	3	8+2	8	1		
				£67,500	18.08.89	Notts County	65+1	6	1+1	9+1	5	1		
				Loan	18.03.91	Birmingham City	9			2+1				
Dean Thomas	5.9	11.8	19.12.61	Bedworth		Nuneaton Borough								
				£7,000	20.07.81	Wimbledon	57	2		1	8			
						Aachen (Ger)								
						Fort								
				£50,000	04.08.88	Northampton T	74	6	6	5	11		1	
				£175,000	21.03.90	Notts County	88+2	6	5	7+2	6			
Phil Turner	5.8	10.7	12.02.62	Sheffield	05.02.80	Lincoln City (A)	239+2	19	12	5	19	1		
				PE	22.08.86	Grimsby Town	62	6	6	3	9		1	
				£42,000	19.02.88	Leicester City	18+6	1+1	1		2			
				P.E	03.03.89	Notts County	117+10	4+2	8	16	10		3	2
Andy Williams	6.0	11.10	29.07.62	Birmingham		Solihull B								
Div.2'90				£20,000	24.07.85	Coventry City	3+6			0+1				
				P.E	16.10.86	Rotherham Utd	87	8	6	5	13			2
				£175,000	11.11.88	Leeds Utd	25+21	3+3	2	5+2	3			2
				Loan	11.12.91	Port Vale	5							
				£115,000	04.02.92	Notts County	14+1				1			
FORWARDS														
Tony Agana	5.11	12.0	02.10.63	London		Weymouth			2					
ESP.1				£35,000	13.08.87	Watford	12+3	1+1	2	1	1	2		
				£45,000	19.02.88	Sheffield Utd	105+13	12	14	4+1	42	3	5	1
				£750,000	12.11.91	Notts County	11+2				1			
				Loan	27.02.92	Leeds Utd	1+1							

NOTTS COUNTY

PLAYERS NAME Honours	Ht	Wt	Birthdate	Birthplace Transfers	Contract Date	Clubs	League	L/Cup	FA Cup	Other	Lg	L/C	FAC	Oth
Kevin Bartlett WC'88	5.8	11.5	12.10.62	Portsmouth	06.C9.80	Portsmouth	0+3							
						Fareham								
				Free	23.09.86	Cardiff City	60+22	2+2	8	9+2	25		3	
				£125,000	16.02.89	West Brom A	25+12	2	3	1	10		1	
				£100,000	13.03.90	Notts County	75+8	6	6	9+2	27	3	1	3
Paul J Devlin						Stafford Rangers								
				£40,000	22.02.92	Notts County	1+1							
Gary Lund E:u21.1	5.11	11.0	13.09.64	Grimsby	27.07.83	Grimsby Town	47+13	6+2	4	2	24	1	5	1
				Free	22.08.86	Lincoln City	41+3	4	1	3	13	1	1	1
				£40,000	17.06.87	Notts County	128+16	7+2	10+1	16+5	42		3	3
Kevin Wilson NI: 16; Div2'89; ZDC'90	5.7	10.7	18.04.61	Banbury		Banbury Ut								
				£20,000	21.12.79	Derby County	105+16	8+3	8		30	8	3	
				£100,000	05.01.85	Ipswich Town	94+4	8	10	7	34	8	3	4
				£335,000	25.06.87	Chelsea	124+28	10+2	7+1	14+5	42	4	1	8
				£225,000	27.03.92	Notts County	8				1			
ADDITIONAL CONTRACT PLAYERS														
Kenneth Dolan						Notts County								
Thomas D Gallagher					01.06.92	Notts County (T)								
Philip W Hill					01.07.92	Notts County (T)								
Michael Johnson					09.07.91	Notts County	5			1				
Robert Matthews					26.03.92	Notts County	1+4				3			
Gary Patterson					17.07.91	Notts County								
Darren D Saunders					01.07.92	Notts County (T)								
Paul Sherlock					01.07.92	Notts County (T)								
Michael Simpson					01.07.92	Notts County (T)								
Stephen Slawson					09.07.91	Notts County	3+10		0+2	0+2	1			1
Edward Snook						Notts County								
James Walker					09.07.91	Notts County (T)								
(D) Richard Walker	5.11	10.12	09.11.71	Derby	03.07.90	Notts County (T)								
				Loan	15.10.91	Kettering Town								
Richard Ward					01.07.92	Notts County (T)								
(M) Mark Wells		10.1	15.10.71	Leicester	03.07.90	Notts County (T)	0+1			0+1				
Gavin Worboys			14.07.74	Doncaster		Doncaster Rovers	6+1				2			
				£100,000	01.05.92	Notts County								

MANAGER: NEIL WARNOCK

DATE OF BIRTH: 01.12.48   **PLACE OF BIRTH:** Sheffield

DATE OF APPOINTMENT: Jan 1989

PREVIOUS CLUBS
as Manager: Gainsborough Trinity; Burton Albion; Scarborough
as Asst.Man/Coach:
as Player: Chesterfield, Rotherham Utd, Hartlepool Utd, Scunthorpe Utd, Aldershot, Barnsley, York City, Crewe Alexandra.

HONOURS
as Manager: GMVC '87 (with Scarborough), Promotion to 2nd Division (with Notts County)
as Player:
International:

Value Rating: ★ ★ ★

Programme Editor:

Price of 1992-93 Programme: £1.20
Number of Pages: 36
Subscriptions:

Local Newspapers: Nottingham Evening Post

Local Radio Stations: Radio Nottingham, Radio Trent

Additional Publications on Club: Yearbook 1990-91, £3.99
Notts County Thru' the 80's, £3.95

LEADING LEAGUE GOALSCORERS
SEASONS 1979-80 – 1991-92

1979-80	RAY O'BRIEN	10		1980-81	TREVOR CHRISTIE	14
1981-82	IAIN McCULLOCH	16		1982-83	IAIN McCULLOCH	10
1983-84	TREVOR CHRISTIE	19		1984-85	RACHID HARKOUK	15
1985-86	IAN McPARLAND	15		1986-87	IAN McPARLAND	24
1987-88	IAN McPARLAND	21		1988-89	GARY LUND	8
1989-90	GARY LUND	9		1990-91	TOMMY JOHNSON	16

1991-92 **TOMMY JOHNSON 9**

MEADOW LANE Nottingham NG2 3HJ

Capacity: 19,147   **Covered Standing:** 2,620   **Seating:** 16,527

Tel: Ground: 0602 861155   **Ticket Sales:** 0602 850632   **Clubcall:** 0898 88 86 84

All premium rate calls (0898/0891) cost 36p per minute cheap rate and 48p per minute at all other times. Call costings correct at time of going to press.

ATTENDANCES
Highest: 47,310 v York City, FA Cup Round 6, 10.3.1955

Lowest: 1,616 v Peterborough Utd, Leyland Daf Cup, 12.12.1989

Record Receipts:
£124,539 v Manchester City, FA Cup Round 5, 16.2.1991

MEADOW LANE
First game: v Nott'm Forest, Sept 1910
First floodlit game: v Derby County, 23.3.1953

Season Tickets:
Stands: from £150 to £190
Ground: £120, juv/OAP £60

Executive Box Season Tickets: Consult Commercial Manager

Cost of Stand Tickets: Main Stand: A, B, C, D, E, VP £11; County Road: X, Y £9, Z £8
Terraces: Adult £7, Juvenile, Junior Magpie, OAP £5

Match and Ticket Information: Applications by post (with remittance and SAE) or in person 14 days before each match

Car Parking: No street parking near ground but ample space in the City of Nottingham Corporation car park on the Cattle Market, Meadow Lane, 400 yards from the main entrances

Nearest Railway Station: Nottingham Midland (0602 46151)

How to get to the ground

From North: Use Motorway M1 until junction 26, leave motorway and follow signs into Nottingham A610. Follow signs Melton Mowbray, Trent Bridge A606. On nearside of River Trent turn left into Meadow Lane for Notts County FC

From East: Use A52 S.P. Nottingham to Trent Bridge, cross River and then turn right into Meadow Lane for Notts County FC

From South: Use Motorway M1 until junction 24, leave motorway and follow signs Nottingham (South) to Trent Bridge, cross river and then right into Meadow Lane for Notts County FC

From West: Use A52 into Nottingham, then follow signs Melton Mowbray, Trent Bridge A606 on nearside of River Trent turn left into Meadow Lane for Notts County FC

OLDHAM ATHLETIC   Premier

Formed: 1894   **Turned Professional:** 1899   **Ltd Co:** 1906

SPONSORED BY: **NICKNAME:** The Latics

President
R Schofield

Chairman
I H Stott

Directors
D A Brierley (Vice-Chairman)
R Adams
G T Butterworth
P Chadwick,   J C Slevin
D R Taylor,   N Holden

Secretary
J T Cale (061-624 4972)

Commercial Manager
A Hardy (061-652 0966)

Manager
Joe Royle

Youth Coach
W Urmson

Player/Coach
Willie Donachie

Chief Scout
James Cassell

Physiotherapist
I D Liversedge

Blue Bond Club Manager
G A Lawton

Club Statistician for the Directory
G A Lawton

JOE Royle described the 1991-92 season as the most satisfying of his decade in the Boundary Park hot seat, even though he admitted it had not been as 'romantic' as the two previous campaigns.

The objective was survival and this was achieved with comparative ease as Oldham became founder members of the new Premier League.

What is more Oldham established themselves in the top flight without being forced to sacrifice the positive attacking football which won the nations' hearts over the two previous campaigns.

In that time Oldham won the Second Division championship, reached the final of the Littlewoods Cup and appeared in two epic F.A. Cup semi-finals against Manchester United.

While there was no silverware this time, Oldham still had plenty to applaud as they finished fourth equal top scorers in the First Division with 63 goals.

Their downfall, sadly, was their defensive record with only relegated Luton Town conceding more.

Surprisingly Oldham fared well against the top teams. They were only one of four teams to defeat champions Leeds United – comprehensively too! Third placed Sheffield Wednesday were also blitzed in arguably Oldham's most convincing display of the season.

Royle again operated shrewdly in the transfer-market assembling a team and also showing a near £1 million surplus – mainly through the £1.7m sale of Earl Barrett to Aston Villa.

Graeme Sharp proved an astute signing at £400,000 (previously quoted at half a million). He was the only ever-present in the 49 league and cup games and he finished top scorer with 15 goals.

Royal also re-signed Mike Milligan from Everton and showed a £250,000 profit after only one year away at Everton from whom he also signed Neil McDonald. Brian Kilcline quickly came and went, but the find of the season was undoubtedly young defender Craig Fleming, from Fourth Division Halifax Town, who made 33 full appearances after only initially expecting to be an understudy.

One of the most intriguing moves involved switching Ian Marshall, last season's leading goalscorer, to the centre of defence after 10 goals were leaked in December games against Chelsea and Manchester United.

Had they accumulated another three points, Oldham would have finished above Chelsea, Everton and Tottenham – and not many would have imagined them being so close to a trio of such illustrious names when the season got under way nine months earlier.   **Tony Bugby**

Back row L-R: Paul Moulden, Gunnar Halle, Ian Olney, John Keeley, Neil Tolson, Jon Hallworth, Andy Holden (Player/Coach), Rick Holden, Willie Donachie (Player/Coach). **Middle row:** Billy Urmson (Coach), Jim Cassell (Chief Scout), Graeme Sharp, Neil McDonald, Craig Fleming, Paul Bernard, Andy Barlow, Neil Adams, Ronnie Evans (Kit Manager), Ian Liversedge (Physiotherapist). **Front row:** Roger Palmer, Ian Marshall, Richard Jobson, Joe Royle (Manager), Andy Ritchie, Nick Henry, Mike Milligan.

OLDHAM ATHLETIC

DIVISION ONE: 17th   **FA CUP:** 3rd RND   **RUMBELOWS CUP:** 4th RND   **ZDS CUP:** 2nd RND

M	DATE	COMP.	VEN	OPPONENTS	RESULT	H/T	LGE POS	GOALSCORERS/GOAL TIMES	ATTEN-DANCE
1	A 17	BL	A	Liverpool	L 1-2	1-0		Barrett 8	(38,841)
2	21	BL	H	Chelsea	W 3-0	2-0	5	Marshall 16, Holden 41, Currie 90	14,997
3	24	BL	H	Norwich City	D 2-2	2-1	8	Marshall 3, Barrett 25	13,584
4	28	BL	A	Manchester United	L 0-1	0-0	13		(42,078)
5	31	BL	A	Nottingham Forest	L 1-3	0-2	17	Marshall 50	(23,244)
6	S 3	BL	H	Coventry City	W 2-1	1-0	14	Adams 31, Henry 62	12,996
7	7	BL	H	Sheffield United	W 2-1	2-0	11	Snodin 13, Marshall 33	15,064
8	14	BL	A	Luton Town	L 1-2	0-0	12	Marshall 52	(9,005)
9	21	BL	H	Crystal Palace	L 2-3	1-1	17	Marshall 45, Holden 64	13,391
10	24	RC 2/1	H	Torquay United	W 7-1	1-0		Ritchie 4 (32, 54, 74, 80), Sharp 51, Henry 68, Milligan 71	7,250
11	28	BL	A	Manchester City	W 2-1	0-1	15	Sharp 55, 64	(31,271)
12	O 1	ZDS 2	A	Everton	L 2-3	1-1		Holden 41, Milligan 73	(4,588)
13	5	BL	H	Southampton	D 1-1	0-1	17	Henry 67	13,133
14	9	RC 2/2	A	Torquay United	W 2-0	1-0		Jobson 12	(1,955)
15	19	BL	H	West Ham United	D 2-2	2-1	16	McDonald 6, Breacker (og) 40	14,365
16	26	BL	A	Leeds United	L 0-1	0-0	16		(28,199)
17	29	RC 3	H	Derby County	W 2-1	0-1		Palmer 62, Sharp 86	11,219
18	N 2	BL	A	Notts County	L 0-2	0-2	18		(7,634)
19	16	BL	H	Arsenal	D 1-1	0-0	18	Barlow 67	15,681
20	23	BL	A	Queens Park R.	W 3-1	3-1	15	Henry 25, Palmer 27, Sharp 31	(8,947)
21	30	BL	H	Aston Villa	W 3-2	1-1	14	Sharp (pen) 34, 82, Palmer 65	15,370
22	D 4	RC 4	A	Manchester United	L 0-2	0-2			(38,550)
23	7	BL	A	Wimbledon	L 1-2	0-1	16	Marshall (pen) 70	(4,011)
24	14	BL	H	Everton	D 2-2	1-1	14	Palmer 24, Milligan 65	14,955
25	21	BL	A	Chelsea	L 2-4	1-3	15	Marshall 32, 62	(13,136)
26	26	BL	H	Manchester United	L 3-6	1-0	17	Sharp 48, Milligan 52, Bernard 69	18,947
27	28	BL	H	Nottingham Forest	W 2-1	1-1	16	Sharp 44, Bernard 48	16,496
28	J 1	BL	A	Sheffield Wed.	D 1-1	0-0	16	Adams 71	(32,679)
29	4	FAC 3	H	Leyton Orient	D 1-1	0-1		Sharp 73	10,764
30	11	BL	A	Norwich City	W 2-1	1-0	15	Holden 45, Bernard 65	(10,986)
31	15	FAC 3R	A	Leyton Orient	L †2-4	1-0		Adams 20, Palmer 80	(10,056)
32	18	BL	H	Liverpool	L 2-3	1-2	15	Adams 4, Bernard 86	18,952
33	25	BL	A	Tottenham Hotspur	D 0-0	0-0	14		(20,843)
34	F 1	BL	A	West Ham United	L 0-1	0-1	16		(19,012)
35	8	BL	H	Leeds United	W 2-0	1-0	12	Bernard 18, Barlow 87	18,409
36	15	BL	H	Queens Park R.	W 2-1	1-0	9	Holden 27, Jobson 65	13,092
37	22	BL	A	Aston Villa	L 0-1	0-0	11		(20,509)
38	29	BL	H	Wimbledon	L 0-1	0-1	13		12,166
39	M 7	BL	A	Everton	L 1-2	1-1	14	Fleming 21	(21,004)
40	10	BL	A	Arsenal	L 1-2	0-1	14	Ritchie 84	(22,096)
41	14	BL	H	Notts County	W 4-3	3-1	15	Ritchie 38, 42, Holden 44, Marshall 86	12,125
42	21	BL	A	Coventry City	D 1-1	1-1	13	Henry 29	(12,840)
43	28	BL	H	Sheffield Wed.	W 3-0	1-0	13	Sharp 3, Jobson 55, Adams 65	15,897
44	A 4	BL	A	Sheffield United	L 0-2	0-1	15		(19,843)
45	11	BL	H	Luton Town	W 5-1	2-1	15	Sharp 4 (11, 26, 80, 87)	13,210
46	18	BL	A	Crystal Palace	D 0-0	0-0	14		(12,267)
47	20	BL	H	Tottenham Hotspur	W 1-0	1-0	12	Henry 40	15,443
48	25	BL	A	Southampton	L 0-1	0-0	15		(15,857)
49	M 2	BL	H	Manchester City	L 2-5	1-2	16	Henry 11, Moulden 87	18,558

Best Home League Attendance: 18,952 v Liverpool   **Smallest:** 12,125 v Notts County   **Av Home Att:** 15,087

Goal Scorers: **Compared with 90-91: +1,853**

League (62):	Sharp 12 (1 pen), Marshall 10 (1 pen), Henry 6, Holden 5, Bernard 5, Adams 4, Palmer 3, Ritchie 3, Barlow 2, Barrett 2 Jobson 2, Milligan 2, Snodin, Currie, McDonald, Opponents, Moulden, Fleming
R/lows C (10):	Ritchie 4, Sharp 2, Jobson, Palmer, Milligan, Henry
FA Cup (3):	Palmer, Adams, Sharp
ZDS Cup (2):	Milligan, Holden

† = After extra-time

Hallworth J.	Halle G.	Snodin G.	Henry N.	Barrett E.	Jobson R.	Bernard P.	Marshall I.	Sharp G.	Milligan M.	Holden R.	Currie D.	Kane P.	Adams N.	Fleming C.	Kilcline B.	Ritchie A.	Barlow A.	Keeley J.	McDonald N.	Palmer R.	Donachie W.	Moulden P.	Referee	
1	2	3	4	5	6	7•	8	9	10	11	12	14											K Hackett	1
1	2	3*	4	5	6		8	9	10	11	12	S	7										G Singh	2
1	2	3	4	5	6*		8	9	10	11	14			7•	12								K Lupton	3
1		3	4	5		S		9	10	11	8	S	7	2	6								J Worrall	4
1	2	3	4	5		7*	8	9	10	11	S		12	6									R Pawley	5
1	2	3	4	5			8	9	10	11		7	S	6	S								J Lloyd	6
1	2	3*	4	5			8	9	10	11		7•	12	6	14								T Holbrook	7
1	2		4	5		8*		9	10	11		14	7•	3	6	12							P Alcock	8
1	7•	3*	4	5			8	9	10	11		14	2	6	12								M Reed	9
1	2*	3•	4	5		14		9	10	11		7		12	6	8							A Wilkie	10
1			4	5	2	14	8	9	10	11		12		3	6*	7•							S Lodge	11
			4	5	6	14	12	9	10	11		7		2•		8*	3	1					M Peck	12
1			4	5	6	12	8	9	10	11		2*		S			3		7				V Callow	13
1			4	5	6	S	8	9	10	11		7	S	2			3						C Wilkes	14
1			4	5	6		8	9	10	11		S	2		S		3		7				P Vanes	15
1			4	5	6	S	8	9	10	11				2*			3		7	12			D Allison	16
1		2	6		4*		8	9	10	11			12		5•		3		7	14			R Lewis	17
1			4	5*	6		8	9	10	11			12		5		3		7•	14			D Elleray	18
1			4	5	6		8	9	10	11*		S		12			3		2	7			J Watson	19
1			4	5	6		S	9	10	12				11			3		2*	7			M Pierce	20
1			4	5	6	S	8	9	10	12				11*			3		2	7			R Hart	21
1			4	5	6	S	8	9	10	12				11			3		2*	7			P Don	22
1			4	5	6		8	9	10	11			2			12	3*		S	7			G Ashby	23
1			4	5	6	S	8	9	10	11			2		S		3		7				W Burns	24
1			4	5	6	S	8	9	10	12			2*	11			3		7				K Morton	25
1			4	5	6	14	8	9	10	12			2*	11•			3		7				I Hendrick	26
1	2		4	5	6	3	8	9	10	11			7	S					S				I Cruikshanks	27
1	2*		4	5	6		8	9		11			7				3	S	10	12			R Nixon	28
1			4	5	6	3	8	9		11			7	2				S	10	S			J Rushton	29
1			4	5	6	3	8	9		11			7	2				S	10	S			S Lodge	30
1			4	5	6	3	8	9	S	11			7	2				S	10				S Lodge	31
1			4	3	5	8	6	9	10	11			7	2*		12			S				K Redfearn	32
1			4	2	5	8	6	9	10	11			7	S			3		S				G Willard	33
1			4	2	5	8	6	9	10*	11•			7	12			3		14				K Cooper	34
1			4	2	5	8	6	9		11			S	S			3		10	7			A Wilkie	35
1			4	2	5	8	6	9		11			S	S			3		10	7			A Dawson	36
1			4		5	8	6	9	S	11*			12	2			3		10	7			J Carter	37
1			4		5	8	6	9	7	11*			12	2			3		10	S			J Lloyd	38
1			4	S	5		6	9	10	11				2		12	3		8	7*			M Peck	39
1			4	S	5		6	9	10	11			7	2		12	3		8*				I Borrett	40
1			4		5	S	6	9	10	11			7	2		8*	3			12			K Breen	41
1			4		5	S	6	9	10	11			7	2		8*	3			12			P Don	42
1			4		5	12	6	9	10	11*			7	2		8	3			S			V Callow	43
1			4		5	10*	6	9		11			7	2			3		S	8		12	M Reed	44
1			4		5	12	6	9	10	11			7*	2		8•	3		14				R Hart	45
1			4		5	8	6	9	10	11			7*	2			3		12	S			P Durkin	46
1			4		5	8	6	9	10	11			7	2			3		S	S			T Holbrook	47
1			4		5	8	6	9	10	11				2			3		12	7*	S		M James	48
			4		5•	8	6	9	10	11			7	2			3*	1	14			12	A Gunn	49
41	10	8	42	29	36	16	41	42	36	38	1	1	21	28	8	7	28	1	14	14			League Appearances	
					5				4	3	3		5	4			7		3	7		2	Substitute Appearances	
4	1	1	3	4	3	1+1	3	4	4	3+1		2	0+1	2+1	2	1	3		2	1+1			R/lows Appearances	
2		2	2	2	2	2		2					2	2					2				FA Cup Appearances	
		1	1	1		0+1	1	1	1			1		1		1	1	1					ZDS Cup Appearances	

OLDHAM ATHLETIC

Club Colours: Royal blue shirts, blue shorts, blue stockings
Change Colours: All red or green & white shirts, green shorts, green socks
Reserves League: Pontins Central League Division 2

COMPETITIONS						
Div. 1	Div. 2	Div. 3	Div. 3N	Div. 4	Texaco	A/Scot
10-23	07-10	63-69	35-53	58-63	74-75	77-78
91-	23-35	71-74	54-58	69-71		78-79
	53-54					79-80
	74-91					80-81

HONOURS		
Div. 2	Div. 3	Div. 3N
1990-91	1973-74	1952-53

MOST APPEARANCES: IAN T WOOD 562+8 (65-80)			
Year	League	FA Cup	League Cup
1965-66	1		
1966-67	14		
1967-68	25+3	1+1	1
1968-69	40	1	
1969-70	46	3	1
1970-71	45	1	2
1971-72	46	1	2
1972-73	46	2	1
1973-74	44	6	2
1974-75	40	1	1
1975-76	35+2	1	2
1976-77	30+1	3	2
1977-78	33	2	2
1978-79	36	3	
1979-80	36+1	1	2
	517+7	27+1	18
Previous holder: D Wilson 369 (1907-12)			

MOST GOALS IN A CAREER			
ROGER PALMER 152 (1980-91)			
Season	League	Lge Cup	FA Cup
1980-81	6		
1981-82	7	3	
1982-83	15		
1983-84	13	1	
1984-85	9		
1985-86	15	1	1
1986-87	16	1	
1987-88	17	3	
1988-89	15		
1989-90	16	1	3
1990-91	9		
	138	10	4
Previous holder: Eric Gemmill 110 (1947-54)			

RECORD TRANSFER FEE RECEIVED			
Amount	Club	Player	Date
£1,700,000	Aston Villa	Earl Barrett	2/92
£1,000,000	Everton	Mike Milligan	8/90
£700,000	Manchester Utd	Dennis Irwin	7/90
£350,000	Leicester City	Tommy Wright	7/89

HIGHEST TRANSFER FEE PAID			
Amount	Club	Player	Date
£600,000	Everton	Mike Milligan	7/91
£500,000	Everton	Graham Sharp	7/91
£500,000	Everton	Neil McDonald	11/91
£480,000	Nottingham Forest	David Currie	7/90

MANAGERS			
Name	Seasons	Best	Worst
David Ashworth	1906-14	4(1)	6(2)
Herbert Bamlett	1914-21	2(1)	19(1)
Charles Roberts	1921-22	19(1)	19(1)
David Ashworth	1923-24	7(2)	7(2)
Robert Mellor	1924-27	7(2)	18(2)
Andrew Wilson	1927-32	3(2)	18(2)
Robert Mellor	1932-33	16(2)	16(2)
Jim McMullen	1933-34	9(2)	9(2)
Robert Mellor	1934-45	21(2)	7(3)
Frank Womack	1945-47	6(3N)	19(3N)
Bill Wooton	1947-50	6(3N)	11(3N)
George Hardwick	1950-56	22(2)	15(3N)
Ted Goodier	1956-58	15(3N)	19(3N)
Norman Dodgin	1958-60	21(4)	23(3N)
Danny McLennan	1960		
Jack Rowley	1960-63	2(4)	12(4)
Les McDowell	1963-65	9(3)	20(3)
Gordon Hurst	1965-66	20(3)	20(3)
Jimmy McIlroy	1966-68	10(3)	16(3)
Jack Rowley	1968-69	24(3)	24(3)
Jimmy Frizzell	1970-82	8(2)	3(4)
Joe Royle	1982-	17(1)	16(2)

LONGEST LEAGUE RUNS	
of undefeated matches:	20 (1.5.1990-10.11.1990)
of undefeated home matches:	28 (3.2.1923-18.4.1924)
	(14.1.1989-28.3.1990)
without home win:	9 (4.9.1920-18.12.1920)
of league wins:	10 (12.1.1974-12.3.1974)
of league defeats:	8 (27.12.1932-18.2.1933)
	(15.12.1934-2.2.1935)
of league matches without a win:	17 (4.9.1920-18.12.1920)
of undefeated away matches:	11 (14.4.1973-10.11.1973)
without an away win:	31 (24.4.1974-15.11.1975)
of home wins:	14 (11.1.1903-25.11.1903)
of away wins:	5 (12.1.1973-5.3.1973)

PREVIOUS NAME
Pine Villa

PREVIOUS LEAGUE
Lancashire League

BIGGEST VICTORIES
League: 11-0 v Southport, Division 4, 26.12.1962
F.A. Cup: 11-1 v Lytham, Round 1, 18.11.1925
League Cup: 7-0 v Scarborough, Round 3, 25.10.1989

BIGGEST DEFEATS
League: 4-13 v Tranmere Rovers, Division 3N, 26.12.1935
0-9 v Hull City, Division 3N, 5.4.1958
F.A. Cup: 0-6 v Huddersfield Town, Round 3, 13.1.1932
0-6 v Tottenham H, Round 3, 14.1.1933 (h)
League Cup: 1-7 v Sunderland, Round 2, 24.9.1962

MOST POINTS
3 points a win: 88, Division 2, 1990-91
2 points a win: 62, Division 3, 1973-74

MOST GOALS
95, 1962-63, Division 4.
Lister 30, Whittaker 17, Colquhoun 13, Ledger 8, Frizzell 5, Johnstone 5, Bowie 5, Williams 5, McCall 4, og 3

MOST GOALS IN A MATCH
7. Eric Gemmill v Chester, Division 3N, 19.1.1953 (11-2)
7. Bert Lister v Southport, Division 4, 20.12.1962
Frank Bunn scored 6 goals against Scarborough, Lge Cup, 25.10.1989, thus setting a record for the competition

MOST GOALS IN A SEASON
Tom Davis 35 (League 33, FAC 2) Div 3N, 1936-37

3 goals four times = 12, 2 goals 3 times = 6, 1 goal 17 times = 17
Previous holder: W Walsh 32 (1935-36)

MOST FIRST CLASS MATCHES IN A SEASON
65 (46 League, 9 FA Cup, 9 League Cup, 1 Zenith Data) 1989-90

MOST LEAGUE GOALS CONCEDED
95, Division 2, 1934-35

MOST LEAGUE WINS
25, Division 3, 1973-74

MOST LEAGUE DRAWS
21, Division 2, 1988-89

MOST LEAGUE DEFEATS
26, Division 2, 1934-35; Division 4, 1958-59; Division 4, 1959-60

OLDEST PLAYER
Willie Donachie, 39 years 92 days, v Brentford, FA Cup 3rd Rnd, 5.1.1991

YOUNGEST PLAYER
Wayne Harrison, 15 years 11 months, v Notts County, 27.10.1984.

MOST CAPPED PLAYER
Albert Gray (Wales) 9

BEST PERFORMANCES BY OLDHAM ATHLETIC

League: 1990-91: Matches played 46, Won 25, Drawn 13, Lost 8, Goals for 83, Goals against 53, Points 88. First in Division 2

Highest: 1914-15: Second in Division 1

F.A. Cup: 1912-13: 3rd rnd. Bolton Wanderers 2-0, 4th rnd. Nottingham Forest 5-1; 5th rnd. Manchester City 0-0, 2-1; 6th rnd. Everton 1-0; Semi-final Aston Villa 0-1.
1989-90: 3rd rnd. Birmingham City 1-1, 1-0; 4th rnd. Brighton & H.A. 2-1; 5th rnd. Everton 2-2, 1-1, 2-1; 6th rnd. Aston Villa 3-0; Semi-Final Manchester Utd 3-3, 1-2

League Cup: 1989-90: 2nd rnd. Leeds Utd 2-1, 2-1; 3rd rnd. Scarborough 7-0; 4th rnd. Arsenal 3-1; 5th rnd. Southampton 2-2, 2-0; Semi-Final West Ham United 6-0, 0-3; Final Nottingham Forest 0-1

DIVISIONAL RECORDS

	Played	Won	Drawn	Lost	For	Against	Points
DIVISION 1	400	137	106	157	499	571	**394**
DIVISION 2	1388	521	356	511	1995	2019	**1567**
DIVISION 3	414	156	96	162	593	609	**408**
DIVISION 3N	658	256	171	231	1085	1002	**683**
DIVISION 4	320	121	70	129	499	513	**312**
TOTALS	3180	1191	799	1190	4671	4714	**3364**

OLDHAM ATHLETIC

							APPEARANCES				GOALS			
PLAYERS NAME Honours	Ht	Wt	Birthdate	Birthplace Transfers	Contract Date	Clubs	League	L/Cup	FA Cup	Other	Lg	L/C	FAC	Oth
GOALKEEPERS														
Jon Hallworth	6.2	12.10	26.10.65	Stockport	01.06.83	Ipswich Town (A)	45	4	1	6				
01.01.85 Loan Bristol Rov. 2 Lg Apps.				£125,000	03.02.89	Oldham Ath	118	12	13	1				
John Keeley	6.1	14.4	27.07.61	Plaistow	13.08.79	Southend Utd. (A)	63	4	5	3				
via Chelmsford C. (2 FAC Apps) to					23.08.86	Brighton & H.A	138	6	9	7				
				£250,000	13.08.90	Oldham Ath	1			1				
05.11.91 Loan Oxford Utd. No Apps.				Loan	06.02.92	Reading	6							
DEFENDERS														
Craig Fleming	6.0	11.7	06.10.71	Halifax	21.03.90	Halifax Town (T)	56+1	4	3	3+2				
				£80,000	15.08.91	Oldham Ath	28+4	2+1	2	1	1			
Gunner Halle	5.11	11.2	11.08.65	Oslo		Lillestrom								
				£350,000	15.02.91	Oldham Ath	27	1						
Andy Holden	6.1	13.2	14.09.62	Flint		Rhyl								
W:1,u21.1					18.08.83	Chester City	100	8	2	4	17	1	2	2
				£45,000	30.10.86	Wigan Ath	48+1	3	7	7	4			
				£125,000	12.01.89	Oldham Ath	59+4	3+1	4	1	9			
Richard Jobson	6.1	12.10	09.05.63	Burton Alb										
Div2'91				£22,000	05.11.82	Watford	26+2	2	0+1	5+1	4			
				£40,000	07.02.85	Hull City	219+2	12	13	9	17		1	
				£465,000	30.08.90	Oldham Ath	79+1	5	4	2	3	1		
Ian Marshall	6.1	12.12	20.03.66	Oxford		Everton (A)	9+6	1+1		7	1	1		
				£100,000	24.03.88	Oldham Ath	139+4	14	13	2+1	34		3	1
Neil McDonald	5.11	11.40	02.11.65	Wallsend	19.02.83	Newcastle Utd. (A)	163+17	12	10+1	3	24	3	1	
E: u21.5, Y.7, S				£525,000	03.08.88	Everton	76+14	7	17	10+1	4	3		
				£500,000	01.10.91	Oldham Ath	14+3	2			1			
Neil Pointon	5.10	12.10	28.11.64	Warslip Vale	10.08.82	Scunthorpe Utd. (A)	159	9	13	4	2	1		
CS'87					08.11.85	Everton	95+7	6+2	16+2	9+3	5			
				P.E.	17.07.90	Manchester City	74	8	4	4	2			
				P.E.	10.07.92	Oldham Ath								
Steve Redmond	5.10	11.2	02.11.67	Liverpool	03.12.84	Manchester City (A)	231+4	24	17	11	7			
E:Y,u21.14,u19.2,Y.5; FAYC'86				P.E.	10.07.92	Oldham Ath								
MIDFIELD														
Andrew Barlow	5.9	11.1	24.11.65	Oldham		Oldham Ath	234+13	20	17	6	5			
Div2'91														
Paul Bernard	5.11	11.8	30.12.72	Edinburgh	16.07.91	Oldham Ath. (T)	18+5	1+1	2		6			
Nicholas Henry	5.6	10.8	21.02.69	Liverpool	06.07.87	Oldham Ath. (T)	142+7	16+3	14	4	10	2		
Michael Milligan	5.8	11.0	20.02.67	Manchester	02.03.85	Oldham Ath	161+1	19+1	12	4	17	1	1	
Ei: B.1, u21.1				£925,000	24.08.90	Everton	16+1	0+1	1	4+1	1			1
				£600,000	17.07.91	Oldham Ath	36	4		1	2	1		1
FORWARDS														
Neil Adams	5.8	10.8	23.11.65	Stoke	01.07.85	Stoke City	31+1	3	1	3	4			
E: u21(1);Div.1'87;CS'86				£150,000	07.07.86	Everton	17+3	4+1		5+1		1		
via Oldham 11.01.89 Oldham A. 9 Lg Apps.				£100,000	16.08.89	Oldham Ath	69+24	7+1	8+2	1+1	14	1	2	
Frankie Bunn	5.11	11.6	06.11.62	Birmingham	16.05.80	Luton Town (A)	52+7	6+1	3		9	3		
						Hull City	89+6	5+1	5	5+1	23	2	1	4
				£95,000	03.12.87	Oldham Ath	75+3	8	2		26	8	1	
Paul Moulden	5.7	10.9	06.09.67	Farnworth	07.09.84	Manchester City (A)	48+16	5+1	2+3	3+1	18	4	1	3
E:Y15,u19.2				£160,000	02.08.89	Bournemouth	32	4	0+1	1	13			
				£225,000	23.03.90	Oldham Ath	16+18	2+1			4	1		
Ian Olney	6.1	12.4	17.12.69	Luton	25.07.88	Aston Villa (T)	62+26	8+2	5+1	8+2	16	1	2	2
E: u21.9				£700,000	01.07.92	Oldham Ath								
Roger Palmer	5.10	11.0	30.01.59	Manchester	01.03.77	Manchester City (A)	22+9	3+3		4	9	1		1
				£70,000	20.11.80	Oldham Ath	413+21	34+2	19+4	5+2	141	10	5	1
Andy Ritchie	5.10	11.10	28.11.60	Manchester	05.12.77	Manchester Utd	26+7	3+2	3+1		13			
E:u21.1,Y.4,S; Div2'91				£500,000	17.10.80	Brighton & H.A	82+7	3+1	9		23	1	2	
				P.E.	25.03.83	Leeds Utd	127+9	11	9	2+1	40	3	1	
				£55,000	14.08.87	Oldham Ath	139+11	15	6	3	66	17	3	
Graham Sharp	6.1	11.8	16.10.60	Dumbarton		Dumbarton	37+3	2	3		17		2	
S:12,u21.1,CS'84-'87,FAC'84,Div1'85'87,				£125,000	04.04.80	Everton	306+16	46+2	52+2	21+1	111	15	20	11
ECWC'85				£500,000	17.07.91	Oldham Ath	42	4	2	1	12	2	1	
Neil Tolson					17.12.91	Walsall (T)	3+5		0+1	1+2	1		1	
				£150,000	24.03.92	Oldham Ath								
ADDITIONAL CONTRACT PLAYERS														
(D) Jason Fisk	5.9	10.7	18.09.71	Hull	15.08.90	Oldham Ath. (T)								
W: Y; S														
(G) Paul Gerrard	6.2	13.1	22.01.73	Heywood	02.11.91	Oldham Ath. (T)								
(M) Chris Halstead	5.8	11.7	23.12.71	Burnley	15.08.90	Oldham Ath. (T)								
E: Y; S														
Marvin Harriott						West Ham U. (T)								
					03.04.92	Oldham Ath								
(M) Chris Makin	5.10	10.6	08.05.73	Manchester	02.11.91	Oldham Ath. (T)								
(D) Robert J Miller	6.0	11.11	03.11.72	Wythenshawe	02.11.91	Oldham Ath. (T)								
(F) John Smith	6.0	12.0	29.10.71	Wigan	15.08.90	Oldham Ath. (T)								
(M) Greg J Wilson	5.10	11.6	11.11.72	Ashton	02.11.91	Oldham Ath. (T)								
(D) Willie Donachie (ex Manchester City, Portland Timbers, Norwich City, Portland Timbers and Burnley.)														

OLDHAM ATHLETIC

RECORD WIN & LOSS AGAINST EACH CLUB IN CURRENT DIVISION
(Where a score has occured on several occasions the most recent is given)

Club	Rec. Win	Season	Rec. Loss	Season
ARSENAL	3-0	1919-20	2-0	1922-23
ASTON VILLA	3-1	1921-22	7-1	1912-13
BLACKBURN ROVERS	5-0	1978-79	7-1	1912-13
CHELSEA	3-0	1975-76 (away)	5-0	1924-25 (home)
COVENTRY CITY	5-0	1924-25	5-1	1924-25
CRYSTAL PALACE	3-0	1958-59	4-0	1958-59
EVERTON	4-1	1919-20	4-0	1953-54 (home)
IPSWICH TOWN	4-0	1988-89	2-0	1987-88
LEEDS UNITED	4-2	1953-54	6-0	1984-85
LIVERPOOL	4-0	1921-22	5-2	1920-21
MANCHESTER CITY	4-1	1988-89 (away)	3-0	1926-27
MANCHESTER UNITED	3-0	1920-21 (away)	5-1	1931-32
MIDDLESBROUGH	5-1	1914-15	4-1	1914-15
NORWICH CITY	4-2	1934-35	3-1	1985-86 (home)
NOTTINGHAM FOREST	8-3	1925-26	5-0	1934-35 (home)
QUEENS PARK RANGERS	5-3	1964-65	2-0	1980-81
SHEFFIELD UNITED	5-0	1987-88 (away)	5-1	1985-86 (home)
SHEFFIELD WEDNESDAY	5-2	1914-15	5-0	1912-13
SOUTHAMPTON	3-1	1928-29	4-0	1976-77
TOTTENHAM HOTSPUR	4-1	1914-15	5-1	1977-78
WIMBLEDON	2-1	1985-86	1-0	1984-85

MANAGER: JOE ROYLE

DATE OF BIRTH: 08.04.1949 **PLACE OF BIRTH:** Liverpool

DATE OF APPOINTMENT: JULY 1982

PREVIOUS CLUBS
as Manager: None
as Asst. Man./Coach: None
as Player: Everton; Manchester City; Bristol City; Norwich City

HONOURS
as Manager: Littlewoods Cup Finalists 1990; 2nd Div Champions 1990-91
as Asst. Man./Coach:
as Player: Everton: League Championship 1970; Manchester City: League Cup Winners 1976
International: England 6 Full Caps, U23 (10), Football League XI

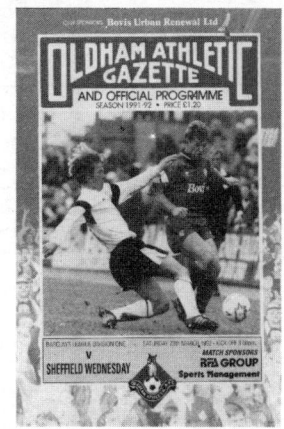

Value Rating: ★ ★ ★ ★

Programme Editor: Alan Hardy

Price of 1992-93 Programme: £1.20
Number of Pages: 44
Subscriptions: £1.60 per programme U.K. Subscription

Local Newspapers: Oldham Chronicle, Manchester Evening News (Saturday Pink), Oldham Advertiser

Local Radio Stations: Radio Piccadilly, Radio Manchester, Radio Cavell (Hospital), Key 103, Sunset Radio

Additional Publications on Club: A Complete Record 1894-1987. Breedon Books.
'Team from a Town of Chimneys', History of the Club. £3.75 (224 pages)

LEADING LEAGUE GOALSCORERS
SEASONS 1979-80 – 1991-92

1979-80	SIMON STAINROD	11		1980-81	RODGER WYLDE	12
1981-82	RODGER WYLDE	16		1982-83	ROGER WYLDE	19
1983-84	ROGER PALMER	13		1984-85	MIKE QUINN	18
1985-86	RON FUTCHER	17		1986-87	ROGER PALMER	16
1987-88	ANDY RITCHIE	19		1988-89	ROGER PALMER	15
1989-90	ANDY RITCHIE	17		1990-91	IAN MARSHALL	17

1991-92 **GRAEME SHARP 12**

BOUNDARY PARK Oldham, Lancs OL1 2PA

Capacity: 16,800   **Covered Standing:** 5,500   **Seating:** 11,300

Tel: Ground: 061 624 4972   **Ticket Sales:** As ground number   **Clubcall:** 0898 12 11 42

All premium rate calls (0898/0891) cost 36p per minute cheap rate and 48p per minute at all other times. Call costings correct at time of going to press.

GROUNDS
Sheepfoot Lane 1894-1905; Boundary Park 1905-
In 1986 En Tout Cas Sporturf laid an artificial surface
1991 New grass surface

ATTENDANCES
Highest: 47,671 v Sheffield Wednesday, FA Cup 4th Round, 25.1.1930

Lowest: 1,841 v West Bromwich Albion, Simod Cup, 10.11.1987

RECORD RECEIPTS (with previous records):
£72,119 v West Ham United, Littlewoods Cup Semi-final 1st leg, 14.2.1990
£65,785 v Everton, FA Cup Round 5, 17.2.1990
£65,387 v Everton, FA Cup Round 5 2nd Replay, 10.3.1990

BOUNDARY PARK
First game: v Colne (Lancs Comb.), 1.9.1906
First floodlit game: v Burnley, 1961-62

Season Tickets:
Stands: from £140 to £240, juv/OAP £90 to £150
Ground: £140, juv/OAP £90

Executive Box Season Tickets: VP Box £370, VP Stand £270

Cost of Stand Tickets: Seats: £12, £11, £9.50, juv/OAP £6 to £7.50

Match and Ticket Information: 12 days in advance postal or personal

Junior Supporters: Secretary: Mrs B Pascall, Junior Latics Club, Boundary Park, Oldham.
Oldham Athletic Supporters in the South (O.A.S.I.S), David Ogden, 3 Warner Street, Chatham, Kent

Car Parking: Parking for 1200 cars on site adjacent to ground

Nearest Railway Station: Werneth

How to get to the ground

From North, East, South and West: Use Motorway M62 until junction 20, then A627 to junction A664. Leave motorway and at roundabout take 1st exit onto Broadway. 1st right off Broadway into Hilbre Avenue, which leads to car park

OXFORD UNITED   Division 1

Formed: 1893   **Turned Professional:** 1949   **Ltd Co:** 1949

SPONSORED BY: UNIPART   **NICKNAME:** The U's

President
The Duke of Marlborough

Chairman
P D McGeough

Managing Director
Keith Cox

Directors
P Lowe
M Clitheroe
T Midgley (Environmental Director)

Secretary
Mick Brown (0865-61503)

Team Manager
Brian Horton

General Manager
Maurice Evans

Physiotherapist
John Clinkard

Groundsman
Mick Moore

Club Statistician for the Directory
Stephen Bradbury

A traumatic season for both the club and the supporters finished on a high note both on and off the pitch. It had promised so much, after the fantastic second-half of the previous campaign, but instead it became a dour struggle against relegation after the worst start in the history of the club of five straight defeats.

Predictably, it became a dogged struggle for the rest of the season with United unable to climb clear of the relegation zone, except briefly in mid-October, until March. Thus, the final Saturday of the campaign found United needing a victory at Tranmere to stand any chance of avoiding the dreaded drop. This they achieved and with Plymouth losing, United secured themselves a place in the new First Division this season.

Considering the aforementioned start, the well publicised financial difficulties, compounded by the death of the major shareholder Robert Maxwell and the forced sale of some of the club's best players, Brian Horton and the team did a magnificent job in defying the odds to stay in the Division. It arguably equalled many of Uniteds triumphs and achievements of the mid-eighties.

The few plusses of the campaign were the emergence of some of the younger players, namely Joey Beauchamp and Chris Allen, undoubtedly thrust into the side sooner than Brian Horton would have liked, and the magnificent team spirit which carried the club forward when all else seemed lost. The icing on the cake, however, was surely the Club's future being assured at the end of the season, by the takeover of the club by Biomass Recycling Ltd. Hopefully with the uncertainty of the Maxwell involvement a thing of the past, the club will go forward and build a solid future. Manager Brian Horton has already been able to make three new signings, free of the financial constraints placed on him for well over a year, and, presumably, will not have to sell the better players for cut price fees!

The new signings will hopefully 'gel' with the good nucleus of players already at the Manor, to ensure an exciting future in the new First Division.

The only sour notes were the recent refusal of planning permission, once again, for the proposed new Stadium. The new owners, however, have already identified a couple of possible new sites but there will obviously be a great deal of work to do before either of these come to fruition. Secondly, the supporters, understandably perhaps, continued to stay away until the last half dozen or so games but, with a new era dawning those that came back will hopefully continue to support the club and give them a firm foundation on which to build.   **Steve Bradbury**

Back row L-R: Matthew Keeble, Paul Simpson, Garry Smart, John Durnin, Paul Byrne, Stuart Fisher, Joey Beauchamp, Matthew McDonnell, Paul Evans, Les Robinson, Paul Harwood. **Middle row:** John Clinkard (Physio), Maurice Evans (Gen. Manager), Darren Jackson, Ceri Evans, Ken Veysey, Andrew Melville, Paul Kee, Jon Muttock, Chris Allen, David Moss (Coach), Steve McClaren (Youth Coach). **Front row:** Mark Stein, Mickey Lewis, Michael Ford, Jimmy Magilton, Brian Horton (Manager), Steve Foster, Lee Nogan, David Penney, Les Phillips

OXFORD UNITED

DIVISION TWO: 21st   **FA CUP:** 4th RND   **RUMBELOWS CUP:** 2nd RND   **ZDS CUP:** 1st RND

M	DATE		COMP.	VEN	OPPONENTS	RESULT	H/T	LGE POS	GOALSCORERS/GOAL TIMES	ATTEN-DANCE
1	A	17	BL	A	Port Vale	L 1-2	1-0		Magilton 12	(6,984)
2		24	BL	H	Grimsby Town	L 1-2	1-2	23	Magilton 26	4,416
3		31	BL	A	Sunderland	L 0-2	0-1	24		(16,151)
4	S	4	BL	H	Middlesbrough	L 1-2	0-0	24	Nogan 90	4,229
5		7	BL	A	Wolverhampton W	L *1-3*	0-3	24	Nogan 80	(12,549)
6		14	BL	H	Millwall	D 2-2	1-2	24	Aylott 42, Melville 90	4,731
7		18	BL	H	Derby County	W 2-0	0-0	23	Aylott 55, Penney 76	4,420
8		21	BL	A	Bristol Rovers	L 1-2	1-1	24	Penney 35	(4,868)
9		24	RC 2/1	A	Portsmouth	D 0-0	0-0			(4,682)
10		28	BL	H	Plymouth Argyle	W 3-2	1-0	22	Nogan 15, Simpson 87, Penney 88	3,724
11	O	1	ZDS 1	A	Swindon Town	D †3-3	0-0		Simpson 56, 117, Melville 82	(6,026)
12		5	BL	A	Ipswich Town	L 1-2	0-2	23	Magilton 80	(9,922)
13		9	RC 2/2	H	Portsmouth	L 0-1	0-1			4,114
14		12	BL	H	Tranmere Rovers	W 1-0	0-0	21	Aylott 63	5,759
15		19	BL	A	Newcastle United	L 3-4	1-2	22	Durnin 3, Ford 47, Lewis 72	(16,454)
16		23	BL	H	Charlton Athletic	L 1-2	0-0	22	Magilton 55	4,069
17		26	BL	H	Leicester City	L 1-2	0-1	23	Simpson 78	5,780
18		30	BL	A	Southend United	W 3-2	3-1	22	Stein 26, Simpson 32, 37	(4,873)
19	N	2	BL	H	Barnsley	L 0-1	0-1	22		3,420
20		6	BL	A	Watford	L 0-2	0-1	23		(4,789)
21		9	BL	A	Portsmouth	L 1-2	0-1	23	Magilton 76	(7,557)
22		16	BL	H	Bristol City	D 1-1	0-0	24	Simpson 60	5,780
23		23	BL	H	Brighton & H A	W 3-1	1-0	24	Simpson 2, Magilton 47, Nogan 50	4,563
24		30	BL	A	Cambridge United	D 1-1	0-0	23	Nogan 65	(6,496)
25	D	7	BL	H	Blackburn Rovers	L *1-3*	0-2	24	Melville 89	5,922
26		26	BL	H	Southend United	L 0-1	0-0	24		5,602
27		28	BL	H	Sunderland	W 3-0	0-0	24	Durnin 49, Aylott 54, Beauchamp 62	6,140
28	J	4	FAC 3	H	Tranmere Rovers	W 3-1	2-0		Beauchamp 20, Magilton 43, Vickers (og) 88	6,025
29		8	BL	A	Charlton Athletic	D 2-2	2-0	24	Durnin 15, Beauchamp 24	(4,101)
30		11	BL	A	Grimsby Town	L 0-1	0-1	24		(5,117)
31		18	BL	H	Port Vale	D 2-2	1-1	24	Beauchamp 30, Lewis 89	4,199
32		28	BL	A	Swindon Town	L 1-2	0-1	24	Magilton 88	(9,707)
33	F	1	BL	H	Newcastle United	W *5-2*	1-0	24	Foster 41, 86, Durnin 61, Simpson 75, Aylott 76	5,865
34		5	FAC 4	H	Sunderland	L 2-3	0-2		Simpson 89, Penney 90	9,954
35		8	BL	A	Leicester City	L 1-2	0-0	24	Melville 75	(12,178)
36		15	BL	A	Brighton & H A	W 2-1	2-1	23	Simpson 28, 35	(6,350)
37		22	BL	H	Cambridge United	W 1-0	1-0	23	Melville 41	5,606
38		29	BL	A	Blackburn Rovers	D 1-1	1-1	23	Durnin 34	(13,917)
39	M	7	BL	H	Swindon Town	W 5-3	3-2	19	Durnin 25, 47, Magilton (pen) 38, Beauchamp 41, 64	7,995
40		11	BL	H	Watford	D 0-0	0-0	22		5,798
41		14	BL	A	Barnsley	L 0-1	0-0	22		(5,436)
42		21	BL	H	Portsmouth	W 2-1	0-0	21	Beauchamp 71, Aylott 80	8,428
43		28	BL	A	Bristol City	D 1-1	0-0	21	Bannister 72	(12,402)
44	A	1	BL	A	Millwall	L 1-2	1-0	22	Allen 9	(5,946)
45		4	BL	H	Wolverhampton W	W 1-0	0-0	20	Penney 87	7,159
46		11	BL	A	Derby County	D 2-2	1-1	20	Magilton (pen) 45, Lewis 60	(15,555)
47		15	BL	A	Middlesbrough	L 1-2	0-0	21	Magilton 62	(11,928)
48		18	BL	H	Bristol Rovers	D 2-2	2-0	20	Magilton 23, Lewis 42	6,891
49		20	BL	A	Plymouth Argyle	L *1-3*	1-2	21	Bannister 25	(9,735)
50		25	BL	H	Ipswich Town	D 1-1	1-1	22	Magilton 8	10,525
51	M	2	BL	A	Tranmere Rovers	W 2-1	0-0	21	Durnin 58, Beauchamp 62	(9,173)

Best Home League Attendance: 10,525 v Ipswich Town   **Smallest: 3,420 v Barnsley**   **Av Home Att: 5,672**

Goal Scorers: **Compared with 90-91: -107**

League (66): Magilton 12 (2 pens), Simpson 9, Durnin 8, Beauchamp 7, Aylott 6, Nogan 5, Melville 4, Lewis 4, Penney 4, Bannister 2, Foster 2, Allen, Stein, Ford

R/lows C (0):
FA Cup (5): Magilton, Simpson, Beauchamp, Opponents, Penney
ZDS Cup (3): Simpson 2, Melville   † = After extra-time

Veysey K.	Robinson L.	Ford M.	Jackson D.	Foster S.	Melville A.	Magilton J.	Steain E.	Nogan L.	Penney D.	Simpson P.	Durnin J.	Evans C.	Phillips L.	Lewis M.	Smart G.	Kee P.	Aylott T.	McClaren S.	Beauchamp J.	Wanless P.	Druce M.	Keeley J.	Allen C.	Williams B.	Bannister G.	Referee	
1	2	3	4	5	6†	7	8	9	10*	11	12	S														K Barratt	1
1	2	3		5	6	7	8*	4	10	11•	9	14														R Gifford	2
1	2	3		5		7	8*	9	10	11	12	6	4	S												K Breen	3
1	2	3		5	6	7		9	S	11	10		4	8	S											R Groves	4
1	2•	3		5	6	7		9	12	11	10		4	8*	14											D Axcell	5
	2		S	5	6	7		10	12	11			4	8*	3	1	9									B Hill	6
	2			5	6	7		10	8	11	S		4	S	3	1	9									K Cooper	7
	2			5	6	7		10	8	11*	12		4	S	3	1	9									V Callow	8
	2			5	6	7		10	8	11	S		4	9	3	1		S								J Moules	9
1	2			5	6	7		10	8	11			S	4*	3		9									J Deakin	10
1	2				6	7		10•	8	11		5		4	14		9		3*				12			P Durkin	11
1	2			5	6	7		10	8*	11			S	4	3		9		12							R Bigger	12
1	2			5	6	7		10		11	9	8*		4•	3				12	14						P Wright	13
1	2			5	6	7		10		11	8	S		4	3		9		S							P Alcock	14
1		2		5	6	7		10		11	8	S		4	3		9									R Nixon	15
1		3		5	6	7	12	10*		11	8	S		4	2		9									C Wilkes	16
		3		5	6	7	8	10		12		S		4	2	1	9									A Buksh	17
	2			5	6	7	8*	10		11				4	3	1	9				12					P Danson	18
	2			5	6	7	8•	10*		11		14		4	3	1	9				12					J Worrall	19
	2			5	6	7		10		11		8		4	3		9	S				S	1			J Martin	20
	2			5	6	7		10		11	12	S		4	3		9		8*				1			G Willard	21
	2			5	6	7		10		11				4	3		9		8			S	1			P Taylor	22
	2			5	6	7		10		11	12	S		4	3		9		8*				1			P Don	23
	2			5	6	7		10		11	12	S		4	3		9*				8		1			J Key	24
	2				6	7		10		11	12	5		4	3		9*		14	8*			1			G Poll	25
1	2				6	7				11	10	5		4	3		9		8	S						R Lewis	26
1	2				6	7				11	10	5		4	3		9		8	S						G Ashby	27
1		3			6	7				11	10	5		4	2		9		8	S						P Jones	28
1	2				6	7				11	10	5		4	3		9		8	S						R Milford	29
1	2				6	7				11	10	5		4	3		9		8*	14						J Watson	30
1	2•				6	7			12	11	10•	5		4	3		9		8	14						R Shepherd	31
1			12		6	7		2		11	10•	5		4	3*		9		8	14						K Barrett	32
1			3	2	6	7				11	10	5		4			9		8	S			S			I Hemley	33
1	14		3	2	6	7				11	10•	5		4			9		8•				12			R Dilkes	34
1	2		3		6					11	10	5		4				7	8	9*			12			T Lunt	35
1	2		3		6	7			S	11	10	5		4			9		8				S			I Borrett	36
1	2		S		6	7			S		10	5		4	3		9		8				11			B Coddington	37
1					6	7			S		10	5		4	2		9		8	S			11	3		K Breen	38
1					6	7			12		10	5		4	2		9*		8	S			11	3		B Phillips	39
1					6	7			12		10	5		4	2		9*		8	S			11	3		G Singh	40
1					6	7			12		10	5		4	2		9		8	S			11*	3		C Trussell	41
1					6	7			S		10	5		4	2		9		8				11•	3	14	D Frampton	42
1					6	7			11		10*	5		4	2		9		8				S	3	14	D Shadwell	43
1					6	7			10*		12	5		4	2		9		8				11*	3	14	R Pawley	44
1	S		S		6	7			3		10	5		4	2				8				11		9	J King	45
1	S		S		6	7			3		10	5		4	2				8	S			11		9	T Holbrook	46
1	S		S		6	7			3†		10	5		4	2				8	S			11		9	A Bennett	47
1	S		S		6	7			10*		12	5		4	2				8	12			11*		9	J Carter	48
1	S				6	7†			3		12	5		4	2		9		8				11*	10		A Ward	49
	S				6	7			3		9	5		4	2	1		12	8				11*	10		J Worrall	50
		3			6	7					10	5		4	2	1	9		8	S			11			A Wilkie	51
32	27	9	4	22	45	44	6	22	17	30	28	27	7	40	38	8	35	4	24	3	6		13	7	7	League Appearances	
		1				1			6	1	9	2			1				2	3	3	2	1		3	Substitute Appearances	
1	2			2	2	2		2	1	2	1	1	1	2	2	1			0+1	0+1			1			R/lows Appearances	
2	0+1	1	1	1	2	1		1		1	1	2		2	2		1		2				0+1			FA Cup Appearances	
1	1			1	1			1		1	1			1	0+1	1		1					0+1			ZDS Cup Appearances	

Also Played: Posn.(Game): Harris S(15)11*(17), Byrne 12(2), McDonnell S(26,27,28,29,30), Muttock S(35)

Players on Loan: G Bannister (WBA), A Harris (Birmingham), J Keeley (Oldham), B Williams (Nott'm Forest)   † = Sent Off

OXFORD UNITED

Club Colours: Yellow shirts, navy blue shorts, navy blue stockings
Change Colours: All red
Reserves League: Neville Ovenden Football Combination

COMPETITIONS			
Div. 1	Div. 2	Div. 3	Div. 4
85-88	68-76 84-85 88-	65-68 76-84	62-65

HONOURS		
Div. 2	Div. 3	League Cup
84-85	67-68 83-84	85-86

MOST APPEARANCES: JOHN SHUKER 529+5 (1962-77)				
Year	League	FA Cup	Lge Cup	Ang/Ital
1962-63	18			
1963-64	12	4		
1964-65	11			
1965-66	33+1	2	1	
1966-67	24+2	3	1	
1967-68	36+1	3	2	
1968-69	34	2	1	
1969-70	34	2	5	
1970-71	42	5	2	
1971-72	41	1	3	
1972-73	36	2	3	3
1973-74	41	1	1	
1974-75	42	1	1	
1975-76	40	1	3	
1976-77	29+1	2	1	
	473+5	29	24	3
Previous holder: Ron Atkinson 425+1 (1962-71)				

MOST GOALS IN A CAREER				
JOHN ALDRIDGE 90 (1983-87)				
Season	League	FA Cup	Lge Cup	FMC
1983-84	4			
1984-85	30	1	3	
1985-86	23	1	5	2
1986-87	15		6	
	72	2	14	2
Previous holder: Peter Foley 88 (1975-83)				

MANAGERS			
Name	Seasons	Best	Worst
A Turner	1959-69	22(2)	18(4)
R Saunders	1969	20(2)	20(2)
G Summers	1969-75	8(2)	17(2)
M Brown	1975-79	20(2)	18(3)
W Asprey	1979-80	17(3)	17(3)
R Barry	1980		
I Greaves	1980-82	5(3)	14(3)
J Smith	1982-85	1(2)	5(3)
M Evans	1985-88	18(1)	18(1)
M Lawrenson	1988		
B Horton	1988-	10(2)	21(2)

HIGHEST TRANSFER FEE RECEIVED			
Amount	Club	Player	Date
£1,000,000	Derby County	Dean Saunders	10/88
£825,000	Liverpool	Ray Houghton	10/87
£775,000	Liverpool	John Aldridge	1/87
£500,000	Derby County	Paul Simpson	2/92

RECORD TRANSFER FEE PAID			
Amount	Club	Player	Date
£275,000	Swansea	Andrew Melville	7/90
£265,000	Watford	David Bardsley	9/87
£235,000	Watford	Richard Hill	9/87
£200,000	Tottenham H.	David Leworthy	12/85

LONGEST LEAGUE RUNS	
of undefeated matches:	20 (17.3.1984-29.9.1984)
of undefeated home matches:	20 (3.10.1964-25.8.1965)
without home win:	13 (21.11.1987-2.5.1988)
of league wins:	6 (14.1.1967-25.2.1967)
	(16.3.1968-6.4.1968) (4.12.1982-3.1.1983)
of league defeats:	7 (4.5.1991-7.9.1991)
of league matches without a win:	27 (14.11.1987-27.8.1988)
of undefeated away matches:	12 (28.2.1984-22.9.1984)
without an away win:	24 (14.9.1974-27.9.1975)
of home wins:	10 (15.9.1984-29.12.1984)
of away wins:	4 (4.12.1982-3.1.1983) (7.5.1984-22.9.1984)

PREVIOUS NAME
Headington United

PREVIOUS LEAGUE
Southern League

BIGGEST VICTORIES
League: 7-0 v Barrow, Division 4, 19.12.1964.
F.A. Cup: 4-0 v Worthing, Round 2, 11.12.1982.
League Cup: 6-0 v Gillingham, Round 2, 24.9.1986

BIGGEST DEFEATS
League: 0-6 v Liverpool, Division 1, 22.3.1986.
F.A. Cup: 1-5 v Arsenal, Round 3, 30.1.1963
League Cup: 0-5 v Nottingham Forest, Round 3, 4.10.1978.

MOST POINTS
3 points a win: 95, Division 3, 1983-84.
2 points a win: 61, Division 4, 1964-65.

MOST GOALS
91, Division 3, 1983-84

MOST GOALS IN A MATCH
4, Tony Jones v Newport County (5-1), Div 4, 22.9.1962
4, Arthur Longbottom v Darlington (5-0), Div 4, 26.10.1963
4, Bill Calder v Walsall (6-1), League Cup Rnd. 1 replay, 7.9.1964
4, John Aldridge v Gillingham (6-0), League Cup Rnd. 2, 24.9.1986
4, Richard Hill v Walsall (a) (5-1), Div 2, 26.12.1988

MOST GOALS IN A SEASON
John Aldridge 34 (League 30, League Cup 3, FAC 1) 1984-85
3 goals twice = 6; 2 goals 8 times = 16; 1 goal 12 times = 12

MOST FIRST CLASS MATCHES IN A SEASON
65 (46 League, 7 FA Cup, 11 League Cup, 1 Associate Members Cup) 1983-84

MOST LEAGUE GOALS CONCEDED
80, Division 1, 1985-86; Division 1, 1987-88

MOST LEAGUE WINS
28, Division 3, 1983-84

MOST LEAGUE DRAWS
19, Division 2, 1990-91

MOST LEAGUE DEFEATS
22, Division 2, 1989-90; Division 2, 1991-92

OLDEST PLAYER
Colin Todd, 35 years 4 months

YOUNGEST PLAYER
Jason Seacole, 16 years 5 months.

MOST CAPPED PLAYER
Ray Houghton (Eire) 12 & Neil Slatter (Wales) 12

BEST PERFORMANCES BY OXFORD UNITED

League: 1983-84: Matches played 46, Won 28, Drawn 11, Lost 7, Goals for 91, Goals against 50, Points 95. First in Division 3.

Highest: 1985-86, 1986-87: 18th in Division 1.

F.A. Cup: 1963-64: 1st rnd. Folkestone 2-0; 2nd rnd. Kettering 2-1; 3rd rnd. Chesterfield 1-0; 4th rnd. Brentford 2-2, 2-1; 5th rnd. Blackburn Rovers 3-1; 6th rnd. Preston North End 1-2.

League Cup: 1985-86: Northampton 2-1, 2-0; 2nd rnd. Newcastle United 3-1; 4th rnd. Norwich City 3-1; 5th rnd. Portsmouth 3-1; Semi-final Aston Villa 2-2, 2-1; Final Queens Park Rangers 3-0.

DIVISIONAL RECORDS

	Played	Won	Drawn	Lost	For	Against	Points
DIVISION 1	124	27	38	59	150	229	**119**
DIVISION 2	562	186	158	218	658	710	**611**
DIVISION 3	506	191	148	167	684	630	**599**
DIVISION 4	138	50	43	45	216	178	**143**
TOTALS	**1330**	**454**	**387**	**489**	**1708**	**1747**	**1472**

OXFORD UNITED

PLAYERS NAME Honours	Ht	Wt	Birthdate	Birthplace Transfers	Contract Date	Clubs	League	L/Cup	FA Cup	Other	Lg	L/C	FAC	Oth
GOALKEEPERS														
Paul Kee	6.3	12.5	08.11.69	Belfast		Ards								
NI: u21.1					01.06.88	Oxford Utd	42	4	2					
Kenneth Veysey	5.11	11.8	08.06.67	Hackney		Dawlish To								
					19.11.87	Torquay Utd	72	2	10	9				
				Loan	29.10.90	Oxford Utd	8	1	1	3				
				£110,000	23.01.91	Oxford Utd	49	1	3	1				
DEFENDERS														
Ceri Evans						Oxford Utd	72+3	4	4	3	3			
Michael Ford	6.0	11.6	09.02.66	Bristol	11.02.84	Leicester City (A)								
S: S					01.08.84	Devizes Town								
				Free	09.01.85	Cardiff City	144+1	6	9	7	13			
				£150,000	10.06.88	Oxford Utd	67+11	4+1	1+1	1	5			
Darren Jackson	6.0	11.8	24.09.71	Bristol	09.05.90	Oxford Utd. (T)	9+2	2	1					
Andrew Melville	6.1	12.6	29.11.68	Swansea	25.07.86	Swansea City (A)	165+10	10	14+1	13	22		5	2
W: 4, u21.1					23.07.90	Oxford Utd	91	8	4	4	7	1		1
Garry Smart	5.7	11.5	29.04.64	Totnes		Wokingham Town								
					11.07.88	Oxford Utd	107+4	4+1	7	2+2				
MIDFIELD														
Michael Lewis	5.6	10.6	25.02.65	Birmingham	18.02.82	West Brom A. (A)	22+2	4+1	4					
E: Y.7				£25,000	16.11.84	Derby County	37+6	2	0+1	4	1			
				PE	25.08.88	Oxford Utd	155	9	7	4+1	6			
John Magilton	5.10	12.7	06.05.69	Belfast	14.05.86	Liverpool								
NI:u21.1u23.1				£100,000	03.10.90	Oxford Utd	81	5	3	4	18	1	2	2
Steve McClaren	5.7	9.4	03.05.61	Fulford		Hull City (A)	171+7	7+2	16	7	16		3	1
						Derby County	23+2	4				1		
				Loan		Lincoln City	8							
					19.02.88	Bristol City	60+1	9	4	7+1	2	1		
				P.E	25.08.89	Oxford Utd	27+6	2	3	1+1				
John Narbett	5.10	10.8	21.11.68	Shrewsbury	19.09.86	Shrewsbury Town (A	20+6	4	1		3			
				£30,000	15.12.88	Hereford Utd	148+1	8	10	14	23		1	3
				Loan	06.11.91	Leicester City								
				£65,000	07.07.92	Oxford Utd								
David Penney	5.8	10.7	17.08.64	Wakefield		Pontefract								
WC'91				£1,500	26.09.85	Derby County	6+13	2+3	1	1+3		1	1	1
				£175,000	23.06.89	Oxford Utd	40+21	4+1	2	1+1	7		1	
				Loan	28.03.91	Swansea City	12				3			
Les Phillips	5.8	10.6	07.01.63	Lambeth	05.08.80	Birmingham City (A)	36+8	8+1	1		3	1		
LgC'86				£5,000	22.03.84	Oxford Utd	156+12	25+2	8	8	11	4		
Leslie Robinson	5.8	11.1	01.03.67	Shirebrook	06.10.84	Mansfield Town (A)	11+4			1				
				27.11.86	Stockport Co	67	2	4	4	3			
				£10,000	24.03.88	Doncaster Rovers	82	4	5	5	12			1
				£150,000	19.03.90	Oxford Utd	71	8	2+1	4				
FORWARDS														
Chris A Allen	5.11	11.0	18.11.72	Oxford	14.05.91	Oxford Utd	13+1		0+1	0+1	1			
Joseph Beauchamp	5.10	11.1	13.03.71	Oxford		Oxford Utd	32+5	1+1	2	1+1	7		1	
Flg.u18.1				Loan	30.10.91	Swansea City	5		1		2			
John Durnin	5.10	11.4	18.08.65	Bootle		Liverpool		1+1						
				Loan	20.10.88	West Brom A	5				2			
				£225,000	10.02.89	Oxford Utd	106+18	4	5	2+1	33	1	1	1
Matthew Keeble	5.9	10.0	08.09.72	Chipping Norton	14.05.91	Oxford Utd								
ADDITIONAL CONTRACT PLAYERS														
(D) **David Collins**	6.1	12.10	30.10.71	Dublin	03.11.88	Liverpool (T)								
Eire:u21.1				Loan	09.01.92	Wigan Ath	9							
				Free	30.07.92	Oxford Utd								
(M) **Tristan Didcock**	5.9	10.0	19.09.73	Chipping Norton	03.07.92	Oxford Utd. (T)								
(F) **Mark Druce**	5.11	11.0	03.03.74	Oxford	03.12.91	Oxford Utd. (T)	0+2							
(F) **Keith N Holmes**	5.10	10.10	04.03.74	Oxford	03.07.92	Oxford Utd. (T)								
(D) **Robert Mutchell**	5.10	11.2	02.01.74	Solihull	03.07.92	Oxford Utd. (T)								
(D) **Stephen Tavinor**	5.11	11.6	28.01.74	Oxford	03.07.92	Oxford Utd. (T)								
(D) **Andrew Wallbridge**	6.0	12.0	14.11.73	Croydon	03.07.92	Oxford Utd. (T)								
(M) **Paul Wanless**	6.0	12.0	14.12.73	Banbury	03.12.91	Oxford Utd. (T)	3+3	0+1						

OXFORD UNITED

RECORD WIN & LOSS AGAINST EACH CLUB IN CURRENT DIVISION
(Where a score has occured on several occasions the most recent is given)

Club	Rec. Win	Season	Rec. Loss	Season
BARNSLEY	4-0	1984-85	3-0	1990-91
BIRMINGHAM CITY	3-0	1988-89	3-1	1985-86
BRENTFORD	2-0	1965-66	5-1	1965-66
BRISTOL CITY	5-0	1973-74	4-1	1975-76
BRISTOL ROVERS	4-1	1966-67	3-1	1965-66
CAMBRIDGE UNITED	1-0	1991-92	3-2	1977-78 (home)
CHARLTON ATHLETIC	5-0	1984-85	3-0	1971-72
DERBY COUNTY	2-0	1991-92	2-0	1968-69
GRIMSBY TOWN	5-2	1976-77	2-0	1979-80
LEICESTER CITY	5-0	1985-86	2-0	1986-87
LUTON TOWN	4-2	1986-87	4-0	1970-71
MILLWALL	4-2	1983-84	3-0	1979-80
NEWCASTLE UNITED	5-2	1991-92	3-0	1985-86
NOTTS COUNTY	4-0	1964-65	4-1	1974-75
PETERBOROUGH UTD	3-1	1967-68	3-0	1966-67 (home)
PORTSMOUTH	3-0	1973-74	3-0	1968-69
SOUTHEND UNITED	3-2	1991-92 (away)	2-0	1981-82 (home)
SUNDERLAND	5-1	1972-73	3-0	1971-72
SWINDON TOWN	5-0	1981-82	4-0	1971-72
TRANMERE ROVERS	4-2	1964-65 (away)	4-1	1977-78
WATFORD	2-1	1970-71	4-0	1988-89 (home)
WEST HAM UNITED	2-1	1990-91	3-1	1985-86
WOLVERHAMPTON WNDRS	3-1	1970-71	3-1	1991-92

MANAGER: BRIAN HORTON

DATE OF BIRTH: 04.02.1949   **PLACE OF BIRTH:** Hednesford

DATE OF APPOINTMENT: 25.10.1988

PREVIOUS CLUBS
   as Player/Manager: Hull City
   as Asst. Man./Coach: Oxford United
   as Player: Walsall, Hednesford Town, Port Vale; Brighton H&A; Luton Town, Hull City

HONOURS
   as Manager: (Hull) Promotion to Div 2
   as Asst. Man./Coach: None
   as Player: (Brighton) Promotion to 2nd & 1st Divs; (Luton) Promotion to 1st Div
   International: None

Value Rating: ★ ★ ★

Programme Editor: Roy Grant

Price of 1992-93 Programme: £1.20
Number of Pages: 32 (sometimes 36)
Subscriptions: £37 per season

Local Newspapers: Oxford Mail, Oxford Times

Local Radio Stations: Radio Oxford

LEADING LEAGUE GOALSCORERS
SEASONS 1979-80 – 1991-92

1979-80	**PAUL BERRY**	14	1980-81	**JOE COOKE**	6
1981-82	**ANDY THOMAS**	14	1982-83	**NEIL WHATMORE**	12
1983-84	**STEVE BIGGINS**	19	1984-85	**JOHN ALDRIDGE**	30
1985-86	**JOHN ALDRIDGE**	23	1986-87	**JOHN ALDRIDGE**	15
1987-88	**DEAN SAUNDERS**	11	1988-89	**MARTIN FOYLE**	14
1989-90	**JOHN DURNIN**	13	1990-91	**PAUL SIMPSON**	17

1991-92 **JIM MAGILTON** 12

MANOR GROUND London Road, Headington, Oxford OX3 7RS

Capacity: 11,071   **Covered Standing:**   **Seating:** 2,777

Tel: Ground: 0865 61503   **Ticket Sales:** As ground number   **Clubcall:** 0898 12 11 72

All premium rate calls (0898/0891) cost 36p per minute cheap rate and 48p per minute at all other times. Call costings correct at time of going to press.

ATTENDANCES
Highest: 22,750 v Preston North End, FA Cup 6th Round, 29.2.1964

Lowest: 1,055 v Portsmouth, ZDS Cup, 12.12.1990

RECORD RECEIPTS (with previous records):
£71,304 v Aston Villa, Milk Cup Semi-Final 2nd Leg, 12.3.1986
£68,091 v Arsenal, League Cup, 3.10.1984
£56,528 v Manchester United, League Cup, 19.12.1984
£17,740 v Portsmouth, Division 3, 18.9.1982
£14,156 v Burnley, Division 3, 17.4.1982
£13,825 v Nottingham Forest, League Cup 3rd Round, 6.10.1978

MANOR GROUND
First game:
First floodlit game:

Season Tickets:
Stands: from £166 to £208, juv/OAP £114
Ground: £120, juv/OAP £128

Cost of Stand Tickets: Seats: £8 to £10, juv/OAP £4.50 to £6.50,
Terraces: £7, juv/OAP £3

Match and Ticket Information: Oxford United's membership scheme incorporates the two sides of the Manor Ground, the Beech Road and the Osler Road. Entry to either of these areas, which includes all home seating, is for members and their guests only. For Oxford United supporters who are not members the only area available in the London Road Terrace. Membership costs £3. Away supporters can normally purchase seats in The Cuckoo Lane East Stand.

Car Parking: Street parking near ground

Nearest Railway Station: Oxford (0865) 722333

How to get to the ground

From North: Follow signs Ring Road, London A40, then a roundabout take 4th exit A420 S.P. Headington. In 0.8m turn right into Sandfield Road, then turn right into Beech Road to Oxford United FC

From East: Use Motorway M40 then A40 and at roundabout take 2nd exit A420 S.P. Headington. In 0.8m turn right into Sandfield Road, then turn right into Beech Road for Oxford United FC

From South: Use A34 then follow signs bypass, London A4142, then at roundabout take 1st Exit A420 S.P. Headington. In 0.8m turn right into Sandfield Road then turn right into Beech Road for Oxford United FC

From West: Use A420 into Oxford, then follow signs London along Headington Road. In 2m turn left into Sandfield Road then turn right into Beech Road for Oxford United FC

PETERBOROUGH UNITED Division 1

Formed: 1934   **Turned Professional:** 1934   **Ltd Co:** 1934

SPONSORED BY: Thomas Cook   **NICKNAME:** The Posh

President
G W Swift OBE

Chairman
J F Devaney

Vice-Chairman
M C Lewis

Finance Director
M G Cook

Directors
J T Dykes
A M Devaney MRPharmS
A Palkovich
P J A Sucik

Secretary/Managing Director
Arnold V Blades

Team Manager
Chris Turner

Assistant Manager
Lil Fuccillo

Youth Team Manager
Gerry McElhinney

Chief Executive
M B Devaney

Commercial Manager
M Vincent

Youth Development Officer
Gerry McElhinney

Physiotherapist
Keith Oakes

Club Statistician for the Directory
Mick Robinson

PETERBOROUGH United went into the 1991-92 season looking for consolidation in Division 3 after gaining promotion by the skin of their teeth.

Things started well enough with four straight victories, home to Preston North End and away to Hull in the League and a double over ill-fated Aldershot in the Rumbelows Cup. The next dozen games saw only one victory, away to first division Wimbledon in the Rumbelows Cup. A home draw with Wimbledon saw a safe passage into the third round, but with only five points picked up in ten league games the club nosedived to 20th in the league. During this run 'Posh' suffered their worst defeat of the season, 0-4 at West Bromwich Albion, a game that also saw the Posh fans proclaiming that Ken Charlery couldn't score in a brothel!

The next three games, all at home in the space of a week, saw an Autoglass victory over Wrexham, a league victory over Hartlepool and a Rumbelows Cup victory over Newcastle. All games in which Ken Charlery scored!

The next 30 games saw the whole season turn around as 20 wins, 7 draws and only 3 defeats saw Posh move into third position and become the bookies favourite for the championship. This run saw Posh beat Liverpool, far more convincingly than the 1-0 result showed, in the fourth round of the Rumbelows Cup before going out in a replay to Middlesbrough. The F.A. Cup only lasted two rounds, a first round trouncing of Harlow 7-0 and a second round replay defeat by Reading. The Autoglass Trophy area final was also reached after victories over Mansfield, Shrewsbury, Exeter and Wrexham. In a season of records Posh also won nine consecutive games to rewrite that particular record during this 30 game run.

The bubble burst, one point out of fifteen saw Posh drop out of even the play-off places, a fighting 3-3 draw away to Stoke live in front of the TV cameras in the area final of the Autoglass Trophy, after being 2-0 down in only four minutes, gave hope of a Wembley appearance.

Two home games yielded four points before Stoke put paid to Posh hopes in the Autoglass Trophy. Eight points out of twelve saw Posh going into the last game of the season with their fate in their hands, a win or draw and a play-off place was theirs. Posh lost to champions Brentford. A tense few minutes passed before the result from Hartlepool came and Posh were in the play-offs.

A late equaliser from captain Mick Halsall gave Posh a 2-2 draw in the home leg with Huddersfield and things looked bleak when Huddersfield went into a second minute lead of the away leg, but slowly Posh took over and possibly the best half of the season saw them push forward, Sterling equalised halfway through the second half and victory was won with a goal four minutes from time from loanee S Cooper.

The big day dawned and around 24,000 in the blue and white army headed south down the A1. Two goals from Ken Charlery the second in the last minute saw Posh achieve promotion to the Second Division for the first time in their history. The season can be summed up as simply the greatest in the clubs history.

Mick Robinson

Back row L-R: Darren Bradshaw, Tony Adcock, Pat Gavin, David Robinson, Lee Howarth, Steve Walsh, Marcus Ebdon. **Middle:** Gerry McElhinney (Youth Team Manager), Hamish Curtis, Peter Costello, Ken Charlery, Fred Barber, Ian Bennett, Ronnie Robinson, Chris White, Noel Luke, Keith Oakes (Team Physio). **Front:** Worrell Sterling, Gary Cooper, Bill Harvey (Club Physio), Lil Fuccillo (Asst. Manager), Chris Turner (Manager), Mick Halsall, Jason O'Connor, Bobby Barnes.

PETERBOROUGH UNITED

DIVISION THREE: 6th **FA CUP:** 2nd RND **RUMBELOWS CUP:** 5th RND **AUTOGLASS:** Sth FINALISTS

M		DATE	COMP.	VEN	OPPONENTS	RESULT	H/T	LGE POS	GOALSCORERS/GOAL TIMES	ATTEN-DANCE
1	A	17	BL	H	Preston North End	W 1-0	0-0	10	Riley 86	6,036
2		24	BL	A	Hull City	W 2-1	0-0	4	Kimble 70, McInerney 89	(4,806)
3		31	BL	H	Stoke City	D 1-1	1-1	6	Kimble 16	7,174
4	S	3	BL	A	Bury	L 0-3	0-2	7		(2,240)
5		7	BL	H	Wigan Athletic	D 0-0	0-0	8		4,488
6		14	BL	A	Birmingham City	D 1-1	0-0	9	Hicks (og) 74	(9,408)
7		17	BL	A	West Bromwich A.	L 0-4	0-2	13		(10,037)
8		21	BL	H	Exeter City	D 1-1	1-0	16	Halsall (pen) 21	4,249
9		28	BL	A	Swansea City	L 0-1	0-0	18		(2,685)
10	O	5	BL	H	Leyton Orient	L 0-2	0-1	19		4,291
11		12	BL	A	Brentford	L 1-2	0-1	19	Culpin 75	(7,705)
12		19	BL	A	Reading	D 1-1	1-0	20	Charlery 30	(2,954)
13		26	BL	H	Hartlepool United	W 3-2	2-0	19	Riley 10, 35, Charlery 76	3,385
14	N	2	BL	A	Shrewsbury Town	L 0-2	0-0	21		(1,866)
15		5	BL	A	Chester City	W 2-0	2-0	17	Charlery 14, 28	2,810
16		9	BL	H	Bradford City	W 2-1	1-0	14	Riley 7, Sterling 74	9,224
17		23	BL	A	Darlington	W 2-1	0-1	12	Riley 57, Charlery 77	(2,815)
18		30	BL	H	Torquay United	D 1-1	0-0	12	Culpin 78	4,007
19	D	14	BL	A	Stockport County	L 0-3	0-1	15		(2,768)
20		20	BL	H	Hull City	W 3-0	2-0	10	D Robinson 29, Riley 44, Charlery 63	7,904
21		26	BL	A	Stoke City	D 3-3	2-2	12	D Robinson 17, Halsall 33, Sterling 81	(14,733)
22		28	BL	A	Preston North End	D 1-1	1-0	12	Charlery 36	(5,200)
23	J	1	BL	H	Bury	D 0-0	0-0	12		5,567
24		11	BL	H	Fulham	W 4-1	1-0	11	Ebdon 32, Adcock 48, 55, Sterling 84	4,975
25		18	BL	A	Huddersfield Town	D 0-0	0-0	12		(8,763)
26	F	1	BL	H	Reading	W 5-3	2-2	10	Lee (og) 17, Halsall 32, 66, Kimble 48, Charlery 58	3,792
27		8	BL	A	Hartlepool United	W 1-0	0-0	9	Charlery 65	(2,481)
28		15	BL	H	Stockport County	W 3-2	1-1	9	Adcock 44, 47, G Cooper (pen) 78	5,301
29		22	BL	A	Fulham	W 1-0	1-0	8	Adcock 38	(5,233)
30		29	BL	H	Bolton Wanderers	W 1-0	0-0	8	Adcock 51	6,270
31	M	4	BL	H	Huddersfield Town	W 2-0	1-0	8	Riley 24, Barnes 77	6,257
32		7	BL	A	Bournemouth	W 2-1	1-1	6	Barnes 6, Riley 73	(5,379)
33		10	BL	A	Chester City	W 4-2	1-1	4	G Cooper 43, 57 (pen), Adcock 60, Barnes 69	(1,063)
34		14	BL	H	Shrewsbury Town	W 1-0	0-0	3	Halsall 79	7,377
35		21	BL	A	Bradford City	L 1-2	0-2	5	Riley 81	(6,896)
36		24	BL	A	Bolton Wanderers	L 1-2	1-2	6	Charlery 20	(5,421)
37		28	BL	H	Darlington	D 1-1	1-1	6	D Robinson 44	5,218
38		31	BL	H	Birmingham City	L 2-3	1-1	8	Barnes 5, 67	12,081
39	A	3	BL	A	Wigan Athletic	L 0-3	0-1	9		(2,485)
40		8	BL	H	Bournemouth	W 2-0	2-0	7	Charlery 8, G Cooper (pen) 29	4,910
41		11	BL	H	West Bromwich A.	D 0-0	0-0	7		9,040
42		18	BL	H	Exeter City	D 2-2	1-1	7	Charlery 28, Butterworth 86	(3,057)
43		21	BL	H	Swansea City	W 3-1	1-0	6	Charlery 20, Kimble 64, Sterling 69	5,526
44		25	BL	A	Leyton Orient	W 2-1	0-1	6	Charlery 51, Ebdon 80	(5,996)
45		28	BL	A	Torquay United	D 2-2	1-1	5	Charlery 33, 64 (pen)	(1,934)
46	M	2	BL	H	Brentford	L 0-1	0-0	6		14,539
47		11	PO SF 1	H	Huddersfield Town	D 2-2	0-1		Charlery 46, Halsall 88	11,751
48		14	PO SF 2	A	Huddersfield Town	W 2-1	0-1		Sterling 69, S Cooper 86	(16,167)
49		24	PO Fin	N	Stockport County	W 2-1	0-0		Charlery 52, 89	(35,087)

Best Home League Attendance: 14,539 v Brentford   **Smallest:** 2,810 v Chester City   **Av Home Att:** 6,279

Goal Scorers: **Compared with 90-91:** +1,079

League (65): Charlery 16 (1 pen), Riley 9, Adcock 7, Barnes 5, Halsall 5 (1 pen), Kimble 4, Sterling 4, G Cooper 4 (3 pens), D Robinson 3 Culpin 2, Opponents 2, Ebdon 2, Butterworth, McInerney

Play-Offs (6): Charlery 3, Sterling, S Cooper, Halsall

(Peterborough's Cup details are on page 668)

(Peterborough's Cup details are on page 668)

1991-92

Barber F.	White C.	Butterworth G.	Halsall M.	Robinson D.	Welsh S.	Sterling W.	Ebdon M.	Gavin P.	Riley D.	Kimble G.	Luke N.	McInerney I.	Cooper G.	Charlery K.	Costello P.	Culpin P.	Johnson P.	Howarth L.	Robinson R.	Adcock A.	Barnes D.	Cooper S.	Salmon D.	Bennett I.	Edwards	Referee	
1	2	3	4	5	6	7	8	9•	10	11	12	14														J Key	1
1	2	3	4	5	6		8	9	10*	11	7	12														I Hendrick	2
1	2	3	4	5	6	14	8	9	10*	11	7	12														J Moules	3
1	2	3	4	5	6	14	8•	9	10*	11	7	12														K Lupton	4
1	S	3	4	5	6	7			10	11	2		8	9•	14											D Gallagher	5
1	S	3	4	5	6	7		9	10	11	2		8	S												J Rushton	6
1	12	3	4	5	6	7		9	10•	11*	2		8	14												A Dawson	7
1		3	4	5	6	7	12	9	10	11*	2	14	8*													D Axcell	8
1	S	3	4	5	6	7		9•	10	11	2	14	8													M Brandwood	9
1		3	4	5†	6	7		12	10•	11	2	14	8*													G Singh	10
1	2	3	4	5	6	7	12		10	11			8*	9•	14											G Poll	11
1	2	S	4		6	7			10	11	2		8	9*	12	3	5									D Shapwell	12
1	S	2	4		6	7			10	11			8	9	S	3	5									P Alcock	13
1	8*	12	4	5	6	7•			10		2			9	14				3							R Groves	14
1	14		4	5	6	7			10	11•	2		8*	9	12				3							I Borrett	15
1	11		4	5	6	7		S	10		2		8	9	S				3							L Dilkes	16
1	S		4	5	6	7			10	11*	2		8	9	12				3							P Harrison	17
1	S		4	5	6	7			10	11*	2		8	9	S				3							A Buksh	18
1			4	5	6	7			10	11	2		8	9•	14				3*			12				B Coddington	19
1			4	5	6	7	12		10	11	2		8*	9	S				3							P Don	20
1			4	5	6	7			10	11•	2		8	9	14				3*			12				T Lunt	21
1			4	5	6	7			10	11•	2		8	9	S				3			12				P Vanes	22
1			4	5	6	7	8		10	11	2			9•	S				3		14					T Phillips	23
1	12		4	5	6	7	8		S	11*	2			9					3•	10						D Frampton	24
1	S		4	5	6	7	8	S		11	2			9					3	10						I Cruikshanks	25
1	S		4	5	6	7		12		11*	2		8	9					3	10						A Smith	26
1	S		4	5	6	7		S		11	2		8	9					3	10						N Midgeley	27
1	S		4	5	6	7		12			2		8	9					3	10	11*					B Hamer	28
1	S		4	5	6	7		S			2		8	10†					3	9	11					R Gifford	29
1	S		4	5	6	7			10		2		8			S			3	9	11					D Axcell	30
1	S		4	5	6	7			10		2		8			S			3	9	11					M James	31
1	S		4	5	6	7			10		2		8			S			3	9	11					R Groves	32
1	S		4	5	6	7			10		2		8		S				3	9	11					D Allison	33
1	14		4	5	6	7			10*		2		8	12					3•	9	11					P Scoble	34
1	S		4	5	6	7			12		2		8	10					3	9	11*					T Fitzharris	35
1	12		4	5	6	7			14		2		8*	10					3	9	11•					R Poulain	36
1			4	5	6	7					2		8	10					3	9	11*	12	S			A Ward	37
1			4	5	6	7					2			12		8			3	9	11	10*	S			G Willard	38
1	S		4	5		7					2			12		8			3	9*	11	10†	6			B Coddington	39
			4	5	6	7			12		2		8	10•					3	9*	11	14		1		P Taylor	40
			4	5	6	7			12		2		8	10					3	9•	11*	14		1		A Flood	41
	4			5	6	7			12		2			10		14			3	9•	11*			1		D Shadwell	42
	S	4			6	7	8			11	2			10		5	3		9•			14		1		D Phillips	43
	S	4		5		7	8			11•	2			10		6	3		9•			14		1		K Cooper	44
	S	4		5		7	8			11	2			10		6	3		9•			14		1		M Pierce	45
	S	4		5		7	8			11•	2			10		6	3		9			14		1		G Ashby	46
1	S		4	5		7	8				2			10			3		9	11	12				11•	D Elleray	47
1			4	5	6	7*	8				2			10		S	3		9	11	12					G Courtney	48
1			4	5	6•	7	8				2			10		14	3		9	11	S					M Bodenham	49
39	7	14	45	43	42	43	12	8	23	30	42	3	33	33			11	6	24	23	15	2	1	7		League Appearances	
	1	5			2	3	3	5		1	7		4	1	7			1	3	1				7		Substitute Appearances	
3			3	3	2	3	3				3			3			1+1	3	3	2	0+2			1		Play-Offs Appearances	

Also Played: Posn.(Game): Turner S(2)

Players on Loan: S Cooper (Tranmere R), Salmon (Plymouth)

† = Sent Off

PETERBOROUGH UNITED

Club Colours: Royal blue shirts, white shorts, blue stockings
Change Colours: All green
Reserves League: Midland Intermediate

COMPETITIONS		
Div. 2	Div. 3	Div. 4
92-	61-68	60-61
	74-79	68-74
	91-92	79-90

HONOURS
Division 4
1960-61
1973-74

MOST APPEARANCES: TOMMY ROBSON 517+45 (68-81)			
Year	League	FA Cup	League Cup
1968-69	28		
1969-70	46	4	2
1970-71	40+3	2	
1971-72	40+2	4	1
1972-73	35+1	4	1
1973-74	46	4	2
1974-75	36+3	8	1
1975-76	39+3	5	5
1976-77	23+3	2	3
1977-78	31+6	3+1	3
1978-79	29+7	1	8
1979-80	29+11	0+1	3+1
1980-81	18+3	6	2
	440+42	43+2	31+1
	+3 Texaco Cup 1974-75		

MOST GOALS IN A CAREER			
JIM HALL 137 (1967-75)			
Season	League	FA Cup	League Cup
1967-68	13		
1968-69	20	2	4
1969-70	24	1	
1970-71	10	1	
1971-72	16	4	
1972-73	21	2	
1973-74	13	1	
1974-75	5		
	122	11	4

RECORD TRANSFER FEE RECEIVED			
Amount	Club	Player	Date
£110,000	Blackpool	Bobby Doyle	7/79
£100,000	Luton Town	Chris Turner	7/78
£55,000	Stoke City	Dave Gregory	7/79

RECORD TRANSFER FEE PAID			
Amount	Club	Player	Date
£100,000	Halifax Town	Dave Robinson	7/89
£72,500	Chester City	Milton Graham	6/89
£70,000	Watford	Worrell Sterling	3/89

MANAGERS			
Name	Seasons	Best	Worst
Jock Porter	1934-36	10	10
Fred Taylor	1936-37	16	10
Vic Poulter	1937-38	19	19
Sam Madden	1938-48	9	10
Jack Blood	1948-50	16	16
Bob Gurney	1950-52	4	9
Jack Fairbrother	1952-54	8	8
George Swindin	1954-58	1	3
Jimmy Hagan	1958-62	5(3)	1(4)
Jack Fairbrother	1962-64	6(3)	10(3)
Gordon Clark	1964-67	8(3)	15(3)
Norman Rigby	1967-69	9(3)	18(4)
Jim Iley	1969-72	8(4)	16(4)
Noel Cantwell	1972-77	7(3)	14(4)
John Barnwell	1977-78	4(3)	4(3)
Billy Hails	1978-79	21(3)	21(3)
Peter Morris	1979-82	5(3)	8(3)
Martin Wilkinson	1982-83	9(4)	9(4)
John Wile	1983-86	7(4)	17(4)
Noel Cantwell	1986-88	7(4)	10(4)
Mick Jones	1988-89	17(4)	17(4)
Mark Lawrenson	1989-90	9(4)	9(4)
Dave Booth	1990-91		
Chris Turner	1991-92	6(3)	4(4)

LONGEST LEAGUE RUNS	
of undefeated matches:	17 (17.12.1960-15.4.1961)
of undefeated home matches:	32 (21.4.1973-9.11.1974)
without home win:	9 (2.2.1985-24.8.1985)
of league wins:	9 (1.2.1992-14.3.1992)
of league defeats:	5 (26.12.1988-21.1.1989)
of league matches without a win:	17 (28.9.1978-30.12.1978)
of undefeated away matches:	8 (28.1.1969-19.4.1969)
without an away win:	26 (7.1.1976-22.3.1977)
of home wins:	15 (3.12.1960-19.8.1960)
of away wins:	5 (22.3.1988-7.5.1988)

BIGGEST VICTORIES
League: 8-1 v Oldham Ath., Div 4, 26.11.1969
7-0 v Barrow, Div 4, 9.10.1971
F.A. Cup: (Proper): 7-0 v Harlow, Rnd 1, 16.11.1991
League Cup: 4-0 v Burnley, Rnd 5, 17.11.1965

BIGGEST DEFEATS
League: 0-7 v Tranmere Rov, Div 4, 29.10.1985
F.A. Cup: 1-8 v Northampton, Rnd 2 Replay, 18.12.1946 (at Coventry)
League Cup: 0-6 v Barnsley, Rnd 1, 18.9.1981

MOST POINTS
3 points a win: 82, Division 4, 1981-82
2 points a win: 66, Division 4, 1960-61

MOST GOALS
134, Division 4, 1960-61
Bly 52, Hails 23, Smith 17, Emery 15, McNamee 15, Ripley 5, Dunne 1, Raymor 1, og 5

MOST GOALS IN A MATCH
6. J Laxton v Rushden, FA Cup, 6.10.1945

MOST GOALS IN A SEASON
Terry Bly 54 (League 52, FAC 2) 1960-61
4 goals 2 times = 8; 3 goals 5 times = 15; 2 goals 6 times = 12; 1 goal 17 times = 17

MOST FIRST CLASS MATCHES IN A SEASON
67 (46 League, 3 FA Cup, 8 League Cup, 7 Autoglass, 3 Play-offs) 1991-92

MOST LEAGUE GOALS CONCEDED
82 Division 3, 1961-62

MOST LEAGUE WINS
28, Division 4, 1960-61

MOST LEAGUE DRAWS
18, Div 3, 1975-76 & Div 4, 1980-81

MOST LEAGUE DEFEATS
21, Division 3, 1978-79

OLDEST PLAYER
Norman Rigby, 33 years 333 days, 21.4.1962

YOUNGEST PLAYER
Mark Heeley, 16 years 229 days, 24.4.1976

MOST CAPPED PLAYER
A Millington (Wales) 8

BEST PERFORMANCES BY PETERBOROUGH UNITED

League: 1960-61: Matches Played 46, Won 28, Drawn 10, Lost 8, Goals for 134, Goals against 65, Points 66. First in Division 4

Highest: 4th Division 3, 1977-78

F.A. Cup: 1964-65: 1st rnd. Salisbury 5-1 (h); 2nd rnd. Q.P.R. 3-3 (a), 2-1 (h); 3rd rnd. Chesterfield 3-0 (a), 4th rnd. Arsenal 2-1 (h); 5th rnd. Swansea 0-0 (h), 2-0 (a); 6th rnd. Chelsea 1-5 (a)

League Cup: 1965-66: 2nd rnd. Newcastle United 4-3 (a); 3rd rnd. Charlton 4-3 (h); 4th rnd. Millwall 4-1 (a); 5th rnd. Burnley 4-0 (h); Semi-Final West Bromwich Albion 1-2 (a), 2-4 (h)

DIVISIONAL RECORDS

	Played	Won	Drawn	Lost	For	Against	Points
DIVISION 3	598	235	161	202	906	840	**651**
DIVISION 4	874	349	253	272	1289	1083	1128
TOTALS	**1472**	**584**	**414**	**474**	**2195**	**1923**	**1779**

PETERBOROUGH UNITED

PLAYERS NAME Honours	Ht	Wt	Birthdate	Birthplace Transfers	Contract Date	Clubs	League	L/Cup	FA Cup	Other	Lg	L/C	FAC	Oth
GOALKEEPERS														
Fred Barber	5.10	12.10	26.08.63	Ferryhill	27.08.81	Darlington (A)	135	9	12	7				
				£50,000	08.04.86	Everton								
				£100,000	05.12.86	Walsall	153	9	12	15				
16.10.89 Loan Peterborough U. 6 Lg App.				Loan	18.10.90	Chester City	3							
29.11.90 Loan Blackpool 2 Lg Apps.				Loan	28.03.91	Chester City	5							
					15.08.91	Peterborough U	39	8	3	8				
Ian Bennett	5.11	12.0	10.10.70	Worksop	19.07.89	Newcastle Utd.								
					02.07.91	Peterborough U	7							
DEFENDERS														
Gary Cooper	5.8	11.3	20.11.64	Edgware		Q.P.R	1	1+1		0+1				
E:Y.11,Southern Prem'87				Loan	01.09.85	Brentford	9+1							
via Fisher Ath. (0+1 FAC Apps) to				£20,000	28.07.89	Maidstone Utd	53+7	3	3+1	10	7			1
					28.03.91	Peterborough U	35+4	6	3	7	5	2		
David A Robinson	6.0	12.3	14.01.65	Cleveland		Billingham								
				Free	21.08.86	Hartlepool Utd	64+2	2	3	3	1			
				Free	21.08.86	Halifax Town	72	3	6	6	1		1	1
				£100,000	28.07.89	Peterborough U	94	11	6	12	9		1	
Ronald Robinson	5.9	11.0	22.10.66	Sunderland	06.11.84	Ipswich Town								
				22.11.85	Leeds Utd	27								
				25.02.87	Doncaster Rovers	76+2	6	5	3	5			
				£80,000	22.03.89	West Brom A	1							
				£40,000	18.08.89	Rotherham Utd	86	9	6	7	2	1		1
				Free	20.03.92	Peterborough U	24+3			8				
Chris White	6.0	12.0	13.07.68	Basingstoke		Portsmouth								
					31.05.91	Peterborough U	7+1	1+1		1+0				
Stephen Welsh	6.0		19.04.68	Glasgow	22.06.90	Cambridge Utd	0+1			2				
				Free	08.08.91	Peterborough U	42	8	3	9				
MIDFIELD														
Marcus Edbon	5.9	11.3	17.10.70	Pontypool	16.08.89	Everton (T)								
				Free	15.07.91	Peterborough U	12+3	2+1		4	2			
Mick Halsall	5.10	11.6	21.07.61	Bootle	01.05.79	Liverpool (A)								
					18.03.83	Birmingham City	35+1	6+1	3		3			
				£5,000	01.11.84	Carlisle Utd	92	3	6	4	11			
					27.02.87	Grimsby Town	12							
				£25,000	27.07.87	Peterborough U	223	24	17	19	26	3	4	2
FORWARDS														
Tony Adcock	5.11	11.9	27.02.63	Bethnal Green	31.03.81	Colchester Utd. (A)	192+18	16+1	12+2	9	98	5	3	6
				£75,000	01.06.87	Manchester City	12+3	2+1	2	2	5	1		3
				£85,000	25.01.88	Northampton T	72	6	1	4	30	3		1
				£190,000	06.10.89	Bradford City	33+5	1	0+1	2	6			
				£75,000	11.01.91	Northampton T	34+1	1	1	2	10		1	1
				£35,000	07.02.92	Peterborough U	23+1			3	7			
Bobby Barnes	5.7	11.0	17.12.62	Kingston	23.09.80	West Ham U. (A)	31+12	2+1	5+1	0+1	5		1	
E:Y;FAYC'81				Loan	28.11.85	Scunthorpe Utd	6							
				Free	14.03.86	Aldershot	49	2	5	11	26		1	5
				£5,000+P	16.10.87	Swindon Town	43+2	2	1	4	13			
				£100,000	23.03.89	Bournemouth	11+3	1						
				£70,000	13.10.89	Northampton T	97+1	5	9	6	37	3	3	1
				£35,000	07.02.92	Peterborough U	15			2	5			
Ken Charlery	6.1	12.7	28.11.64	Stepney		Beckton								
via Basildon and Fisher Ath. (1 FAC App) to				£35,000	28.07.89	Maidstone Utd	41+18	1+3	0+3	5+4	11	1		
				£20,000	28.03.91	Peterborough U	35+6	6	3	10	16	2	1	7
Peter Costello	6.0	11.3	31.10.69	Bradford	28.07.88	Bradford City (T)	11+9	0+1	1	1	2			
				£10,000	09.07.90	Rochdale	31+3	4	2	3	10	1	2	
				£30,000	28.03.91	Peterborough U	3+3	0+1		2+2				2
				Loan	12.09.91	Lincoln City	3							
Pat Gavin	6.0	12.2	05.06.67	Hammersmith	09.03.89	Gillingham	13				7			
					16.06.89	Leicester City	1+2							
				Loan	01.09.89	Gillingham	18+16		0+2	2+1	1			
				£15,000	29.03.91	Peterborough U.	19+4	4+1		2	5	4		1
Noel Luke	5.11	10.11	28.12.64	Birmingham	06.04.82	West Brom A. (A)	8+1	1	2+2		1		1	
				Free	30.07.84	Mansfield Town	41+9	3+1	2	5+5	9			2
					21.08.86	Peterborough U	248+1	25	17	19+1	27	1		3
David Riley	5.7	10.10	08.12.60	Northampton		Keyworth Utd								
					04.01.84	Nottm. Forest	7+5	1			2			
27.02.92 Loan Darlington (6Lg App + 2G)				Loan	28.07.87	Peterborough U	12	4			2	1		
				£20,000	19.10.87	Port Vale	75+1	2+1	11	5+1	11		2	1
				£40,000 N	01.03.90	Peterborough U	73+11	8+1	8	5+1	21	1	3	2
Worrell Sterling	5.7	10.11	08.06.65	Bethnal Green	10.06.83	Watford (A)	82+12	7+2	18	0+1	14	1	2	
FAYC82					23.03.89	Peterborough U	147	12	11	13	20	3	3	2
ADDITIONAL CONTRACT PLAYERS														
(F) Michael Danzey	6.1	12.12	08.02.71	Widnes	20.05.89	Nottm. Forest (T)								
27.02.90 Loan Chester C. 0+2 Lg Apps.				Free	30.01.91	Peterborough U	0+1							
Paul J Hill						Peterborough U	1							
Dale Watkins					23.08.90	Peterborough U	5+5	0+1	1					
Darren Clarke, Adam Heaslewood, Joseph Whibley.														

PETERBOROUGH UNITED

RECORD WIN & LOSS AGAINST EACH CLUB IN CURRENT DIVISION
(Where a score has occured on several occasions the most recent is given)

Club	Rec. Win	Season	Rec. Loss	Season
BARNSLEY	6-3	1972-73	3-2	1964-65
BIRMINGHAM CITY	1-1	1991-92 (away)	3-2	1991-92 (home)
BRENTFORD	6-0	1961-62	5-1	1971-72
BRISTOL CITY	4-1	1983-84	3-1	1964-65
BRISTOL ROVERS	5-2	1965-66	4-0	1964-65
CAMBRIDGE UNITED	5-2	1971-72 (away)	5-1	1988-89 (home)
CHARLTON ATHLETIC	1-1	1974-75	3-0	1974-75
DERBY COUNTY				
GRIMSBY TOWN	4-2	1975-76	3-0	1965-66
LEICESTER CITY				
LUTON TOWN	2-0	1964-65	1-1	1964-65
MILLWALL	6-0	1962-63	4-1	1965-66
NEWCASTLE UNITED				
NOTTS COUNTY	5-1	1963-64	6-0	1970-71
OXFORD UNITED	3-0	1966-67 (away)	3-1	1967-68
PORTSMOUTH	3-0	1961-62 (away)	4-0	1979-80
SOUTHEND UNITED	4-0	1970-71	4-1	1984-85 (home)
SUNDERLAND				
SWINDON TOWN	4-0	1976-77 (away)	4-1	1966-67
TRANMERE ROVERS	4-1	1980-81	7-0	1985-86
WATFORD	5-1	1967-68	4-1	1967-68
WEST HAM UNITED				
WOLVERHAMPTON WNDRS	3-0	1986-87 (away)	1-0	1986-87 (home)

MANAGER: CHRIS TURNER

DATE OF BIRTH: 3.4.1951 **PLACE OF BIRTH:** St. Neots

DATE OF APPOINTMENT: JANUARY 1991

PREVIOUS CLUBS
  as Manager: Cambridge United
  as Asst. Man./Coach:
  as Player: Peterborough, Luton, New England Teamen, Cambridge Utd (twice), Swindon, Southend

HONOURS
  as Manager: (Peterborough): Promotion to Div 2 1991-92 (New Div 1)
  as Asst. Man./Coach:
  as Player: (Peterborough): Div 4 Champions 1973-74

Value Rating: ★ ★ ★

Programme Editor: Melvyn Beck

Price of 1992-93 Programme: £1
Number of Pages: 32
Subscriptions: Please apply to club

Local Newspapers: Herald & Post, Evening Telegraph

Local Radio Stations: Cambridgeshire Radio, Hereward Radio

LEADING LEAGUE GOALSCORERS
SEASONS 1979-80 – 1991-92

1979-80	**BILLY KELLOCK**	19	1980-81	**ROBBIE COOKE**	22
1981-82	**ROBBIE COOKE**	24	1982-83	**MICKEY GYNN**	17
1983-84	**ALAN WADDLE**	12	1984-85	**ERRINGTON KELLY**	11
1985-86	**JACKIE GALLAGHER**	11	1986-87	**STEVE PHILLIPS**	11
1987-88	**MICK GOODING**	18	1988-89	**NICK CUSACK**	10
1989-90	**MICK HALSALL**	11	1990-91	**PAUL CULPIN**	10

1991-92 **KEN CHARLERY 17**

LONDON ROAD GROUND Peterborough PE2 8AL

Capacity: 16,414   **Covered Standing:**   **Seating:** 3,500

Tel: Ground: 0733 63947   **Ticket Sales:** As ground number   **Clubcall:** 0898 12 16 54

All premium rate calls (0898/0891) cost 36p per minute cheap rate and 48p per minute at all other times. Call costings correct at time of going to press.

ATTENDANCES
Highest: 30,096 v Swansea, FA Cup Round 5, 20.2.1965

Lowest: 279 v Aldershot, Frieght Rover, 17.4.1986

Record Receipts: £51,315 v Brighton & Hove Albion, FA Cup 5th Round, 15.2.1986

Season Tickets:
Stands: £216, juv/OAP £108
Ground: from £144 to £153, juv/OAP £72

Executive Box Season Tickets: Apply to club for details

Cost of Stand Tickets: Seats £12, juv/OAP £6
Terrace: £8 to £8.50, juv/OAP £4

Match and Ticket Information: Tickets bookable 14 days in advance

Car Parking: Ample parking available at ground

Nearest Railway Station: Peterborough (0733 68181)

How to get to the ground

From North and West: Use A1 then A47 S.P. Peterborough into town centre. Follow signs Whittlesey and cross river bridge into London Road for Peterborough United FC

From East: Use A47 into Peterborough town centre and follow signs Whittlesey and cross river bridge into London Road for Peterborough United FC

From South: Use A1 Then A15 S.P. Peterborough into London Road for Peterborough United FC

PLYMOUTH ARGYLE

Division 2

Formed: 1886   **Turned Professional:** 1903   **Ltd Co:** 1903

SPONSORED BY: Rotolok   **NICKNAME:** The Pilgrims

President
S Rendell

Chairman
D McCauley

Directors
Mr P Bloom
Mr G Jasper
Mr D Angilley
Mr I Jones

Chief Executive
Liz Baker (0752 562561/2/3)

Team Manager
Peter Shilton

Assistant Manager
John McGovern

Reserve Team Manager
Gordon Nisbet

Youth Development Officer
Peter Distin

Sales Manager
Ray Bond

Groundsman
Mark Lewis

Club Statistician for the Directory
Jonathan Brewer

THE last day of the season came with a victory required over Blackburn Rovers. The game resulted in a 3-1 defeat and relegation. In a season dominated by headlines off the field, Argyle achieved a new chairman, a new manager, a new style and a new challenge in a lower division.

Thursday 13th February proved to be David Kemp's final day at the club. After receiving the customary backing of the chairman he was dismissed due to dropping attendances caused allegedly by his ideas of how to play football. The chairman promised a big name replacement and on this occasion he was as good as his word. Two years and a day after Kemp was brought in to save Argyle from division three Peter Shilton was asked to carry out the same task as well as change the style of play and increase numbers through the turnstiles. The wisdom of trying to change the style with just fourteen games to go and also win matches is open to discussion.

Shilton's job of saving Argyle had been delt a telling blow before he had set foot inside Home Park. The ever reliable centre-forward/centre-back Robbie Turner had broken his shin at Ipswich in the game prior to Shiltons' arrival. In retrospect, maybe Argyle's chance went with Turner's shin. With transfer deadline day drawing near Shilton and his newly appointed assistant John McGovern felt the need for new blood and equalled the club's record transfer by signing striker Kevin Nugent from Leyton Orient for £200,000 but following his second full appearance he followed Turner to the physio's table with a broken foot to return only as substitute for the last game. Other moves saw the experienced Steve McCall (Sheffield Wednesday) sign for £25,000 and England U-21 Dave Lee loaned from Chelsea. Their introduction failed to save Argyle and this summer is likely to see mass changes. Nine players have already left the club and a further eight are likely to follow them to pastures new. Shilton has already invested £160,000 by introducing goalscoring midfielder Warren Joyce from Preston North End and it is almost certain that more new faces will arrive at Home Park before the new season kicks off.

One of the few successes this year was striker Dwight Marshall. A £35,000 bargain from Grays Athletic in his first professional season. His fourteen league goals helped stave off relegation until the final day and also helped him collect a well deserved 'Player of the Year' award. If he continues to find the back of the net maybe Plymouth Argyle will achieve their aim of promotion at the first attempt.

Jonathan Brewer

Back row L-R: Adrian Burrows, Kevin Nugent, Michael Evans, Dave Regis, Ray Newland, Robbie Turner, Andy Morrison, Steve Morgan. **Middle:** Paul Adcock, Steve Jones, Tony Spearing, Kevin Hodges, Mark Fiore, Mark Clode, Marc Edworthy, Darren Garner, Martin Barlow. **Seated:** Warren Joyce, Dwight Marshall, Gary Poole, John McGovern (Asst. Manager), Peter Shilton (Player-manager), Gordon Nesbet (Youth team manager), Steve McCall, Steve Castle, Nicky Marker

PLYMOUTH ARGYLE

DIVISION TWO: 22nd **FA CUP:** 3rd RND **RUMBELOWS CUP:** 1st RND **ZDS CUP:** 5th Q/FINALS

M	DATE	COMP.	VEN	OPPONENTS	RESULT	H/T	LGE POS	GOALSCORERS/GOAL TIMES	ATTEN-DANCE
1	A 17	BL	H	Barnsley	W 2-1	1-0		Marshall 19, Turner 46	6,352
2	20	RC 1/1	A	Shrewsbury Town	D 1-1	0-1		Morrison 88	(2,152)
3	24	BL	A	Leicester City	L 0-2	0-1			(11,852)
4	27	RC 1/2	H	Shrewsbury Town	D †2-2	1-0		Barlow 23, Turner 59	3,580
5	31	BL	H	Millwall	W 3-2	2-1	7	Marshall 28, Burrows 42, Wood (og) 90	5,369
6	S 4	BL	A	Newcastle United	D 2-2	1-0	11	Salman 41, Marshall 61	(19,543)
7	7	BL	H	Charlton Athletic	L 0-2	0-0	17		5,000
8	14	BL	A	Grimsby Town	L 1-2	0-1		Burrows 68	(5,432)
9	17	BL	A	Southend United	L 1-2	0-1	20	Marshall 71	(4,585)
10	21	BL	H	Middlesbrough	D 1-1	1-0	20	Burrows 35	5,280
11	28	BL	A	Oxford United	L 2-3	0-1		Fiore 63, Barlow 84	(3,726)
12	O 1	ZDS 1	H	Portsmouth	W 1-0	1-0		Turner 27	2,303
13	5	BL	H	Swindon Town	L 0-4	0-2	22		6,208
14	12	BL	H	Blackburn Rovers	L 2-5	0-2	24	Marshall 53, Barlow 86	(10,830)
15	19	BL	A	Bristol Rovers	D 0-0	0-0	24		(5,049)
16	22	ZDS 2	H	Millwall	W 4-0	2-0		Fiore 35, Marker 43, Evans 52, Marshall 61	2,022
17	26	BL	H	Watford	L 0-1	0-1	24		4,090
18	N 2	BL	H	Wolverhampton W	W 1-0	1-0	23	Marshall 35	4,200
19	5	BL	A	Bristol City	L 0-2	0-2	24		(7,735)
20	8	BL	A	Tranmere Rovers	L 0-1	0-0	24		(7,490)
21	16	BL	H	Port Vale	W 1-0	0-0	23	Marshall 87	4,363
22	23	BL	H	Sunderland	W 1-0	0-0	23	Fiore 72	6,007
23	26	ZDS SQF	H	Southampton	L 0-1	0-0			5,578
24	30	BL	A	Brighton & H A	L 0-1	0-0	24		(6,713)
25	D 7	BL	A	Ipswich Town	W 1-0	1-0	23	Fiore 26	4,986
26	20	BL	H	Newcastle United	W 2-0	1-0	21	Regis 23, Barlow 77	5,048
27	26	BL	A	Cambridge United	D 1-1	0-0	22	Turner (pen) 86	(7,105)
28	28	BL	A	Millwall	L 1-2	1-1	22	Morgan 28	(6,980)
29	J 1	BL	H	Portsmouth	W 3-2	1-0	19	Turner 7, Morrison 11, Marshall 73	8,887
30	5	FAC 3	A	Bristol Rovers	L 0-5	0-2			(6,767)
31	11	BL	H	Leicester City	D 2-2	2-0	21	Witter 2, Fiore 20	5,846
32	18	BL	A	Barnsley	W 3-1	3-0	18	Marshall 3 (16, 19, 38)	(5,322)
33	F 1	BL	H	Bristol Rovers	D 0-0	0-0	19		6,631
34	4	BL	A	Portsmouth	L 1-4	0-2	21	Regis 86	(10,467)
35	8	BL	A	Watford	L 0-1	0-0	21		(7,260)
36	11	BL	H	Cambridge United	L 0-1	0-1	21		4,290
37	22	BL	H	Brighton & H A	D 1-1	1-0	20	Smith 33	5,259
38	29	BL	A	Ipswich Town	L 0-2	0-0	22		(12,852)
39	M 7	BL	H	Derby County	D 1-1	1-1	23	Morrison 25	8,864
40	10	BL	H	Bristol City	W 1-0	0-0	20	Marshall 49	9,734
41	14	BL	A	Wolverhampton W	L 0-1	0-0	21		(11,556)
42	21	BL	H	Tranmere Rovers	W 1-0	0-0	21	Morgan 79	7,447
43	25	BL	A	Derby County	L 0-2	0-1	21		(13,799)
44	28	BL	A	Port Vale	L 0-1	0-1	22		(5,310)
45	31	BL	H	Grimsby Town	L 1-2	0-1	23	McCall 61	6,274
46	A 4	BL	A	Charlton Athletic	D 0-0	0-0	23		(6,787)
47	11	BL	H	Southend United	L 0-2	0-1	24		7,060
48	16	BL	A	Sunderland	W 1-0	0-0	22	Marshall 67	(23,813)
49	18	BL	A	Middlesbrough	L 1-2	1-0	22	Marshall 27	(15,086)
50	20	BL	H	Oxford United	W 3-1	2-1	20	Morrison 16, Marker 27, Lee 51	9,735
51	25	BL	A	Swindon Town	L 0-1	0-1	21		(10,463)
52	M 2	BL	H	Blackburn Rovers	L 1-3	1-2	22	Smith 12	17,459

Best Home League Attendance: 17,459 v Blackburn Rovers   **Smallest: 4,090 v Watford**   **Av Home Att: 6,713**

Goal Scorers: **Compared with 90-91: -138**

League (42): Marshall 14, Fiore 4, Turner 3 (1 pen), Barlow 3, Burrows 3, Morrison 3, Regis 2, Smith 2, Morgan 2, Marker, Salman, Opponents McCall, Lee, Witter

R/lows C (3): Morrison, Barlow, Turner
FA Cup (0):
ZDS Cup (5): Fiore, Marshall, Evans, Turner, Marker

†=After extra=time

Wilmot R.	Salman D.	Spearing A.	Marker N.	Cross R.	Morgan S.	Barlow M.	Marshall D.	Turner R.	Morrison A.	Fiore M.	Clement A.	Evans M.	Quamina M.	Scott M.	Burrows A.	Edworthy M.	Walter D.	Garner D.	Hodges K.	Hopkins J.	Smith D.	Regis D.	Van Rossum J.	Lee D.	McCall S.	Referee	
1	2	3	4	5	6	7	8	9	10	11*	12	S														G Ashby	1
1	2	3	4	5	6	7	8	9	10	11*	12	S														**P Danson**	2
1	2	3	4	5	6	12	8	9	10	14	11•		7*													D Gallagher	3
1	2*	3	4	5	6	7	8	9†	10	11*	12			14												**D Frampton**	4
1		3	4		6	7	8	9	10*		2	11•		14	5	12										P Durkin	5
1*	12		4		6	7	8	9	10		2			S	5	11										M Peck	6
		3•	4		6	7	8	9	10		2	11•		14	5	12	1									R Groves	7
	2	3	4		6	7	8		10	14	12		9*			11•	1									R Pawley	8
	2	3	4		6	7	8		10	S	11	9		S	5		1									M James	9
	2	3	4		6	7	8			11*	12	10		9	5		1									J Martin	10
		3	4	S	6	7	8	9			11	2	10		5		1									J Deakin	11
		3	4	S	6	7	8	9			11	2	10		5		1									**R Hamer**	12
1	2	3*	4		6	7	8	9			11	S	10		5											K Cooper	13
1	2		4	10*	6	7	8	9†		11*	3	14	12		5											T Holbrook	14
1	2		4	11	6	7	8	9	10*			3		5	12			S								G Pooley	15
1	2		4	11	6	7*	8	9	10			3		5		S		12								**P Vanes**	16
1	2		4	11	6	7*	8		10			3	9		S			12	5							A Smith	17
1	2		4	11	6		8		10			3	14	9•		12		7*	5							M Pierce	18
1	2		4	11•	6	14	8		10			3	9*			12		7	5							K Barrett	19
1	2	S	4		6	7	8		10			3		S	11				5			9				D Phillips	20
1	2		4		6	7*	8		11		10	3			12				5			9				C Wilkes	21
1	2		4		6	S	8		11		10	3		S					5			9				K Cooper	22
1	2		4		6	12	8		11		10	3	9		S				5							**J Deakin**	23
1	2		4		6	12	8		11		10*	3		S					5			9				D Axcell	24
1	2		4		6	S	8		11	14	10	3							5•			9				D Frampton	25
1	3	2	4		6	12	8		11	5	10			S								9				K Burge	26
1	3	2	4		6	7*	8		11	5	10	14								12*		9				A Buksh	27
1	3	2	4		6	7•	8		11	5	10*	12				14						9				G Willard	28
1	3	2	4		6	7	8		11	5	10*					12						9				G Singh	29
1	3*	2			6	7	8		11	5	10		S	4	12							9				**D Elleray**	30
1	12	2			6	7	8		11	5	10*	3	S									9				K Cooper	31
1	10	2	4		6		8		11	5	12	3						S				9*				A Dawson	32
1	10	2†	4		6	7	8		11	5•		3				14						9				R Gifford	33
1	10	2	4		6		8		11	S		3*				5		12				9				K Morton	34
1	10	2	4		6		8	11	6	14		5				7•			3		9					I Borrett	35
1	3	2	4		6		8	11	7	10*		S						9	12	5						K Burge	36
1	2		4		6	7	10	11	8	3			5	S				9	S							H King	37
1		2	4		6	12		11•	3			14				8*	7		10	9	5					T Ward	38
1	2	3	6		11		10	5	4*	8•						4*	8•	12	14	9	7					J Deakin	39
1	2	3	5		11		10	6					S				8	7	S	9	4					M Pierce	40
1	2	3	6		11		10*	4		8			12				14	7*	9		5					R Poulain	41
1	S	S			11	7	10	6		S			2						8	9	4					K Cooper	42
1	S	3	5		11	7	10*	6		8•								2	14	9	4					W Flood	43
1		3	5		11	7•	10*			6	8•							2	14	12	6	4	8			M Reed	44
1			5			3	S	10			S		4				2		11		6	7	8			R Hamer	45
		5				3		10			4	12	S	6			2		11	9	7	7	8*			A Smith	46
		5				3		10			4	12	S	6			2*		11•	9	7	7	8			D Gallagher	47
		5	2			3		10			4	S	9				7		11	S	6	8				A Bennett	48
			5		2	3		10			6		9		5		7		11		6	8				N Midgley	49
		5	2		3		10*			4		9					7	S	11		6	8				A Ward	50
		5	2		3*				4	10	9					7*	14		11	12	6	8				S Lodge	51
		5	2		3		10•			4	14	9*				7			11		6	8				K Burge	52

Wilmot R.	Salman D.	Spearing A.	Marker N.	Cross R.	Morgan S.	Barlow M.	Marshall D.	Turner R.	Morrison A.	Fiore M.	Clement A.	Evans M.	Quamina M.	Scott M.	Burrows A.	Edworthy M.	Walter D.	Garner D.	Hodges K.	Hopkins J.	Smith D.	Regis D.	Van Rossum J.	Lee D.	McCall S.		
34	26	30	44	12	45	23	44	25	29	25	20	11	4	3	14	7	5	8	11	8	14	21	9	9	9	League Appearances	
	2				5			1	7	6	2	1	3	1	8		2	3			4	3				Substitute Appearances	
2	2	2	2	2	2	2	2	2	2	0+2			0+1													R/lows Appearances	
1	1	1			1	1	1	1	1	1						1	0+1				1					FA Cup Appearances	
2	1	2	3	1	3		3	3	2+1	3		3		3	1	1		1		0+1	1					ZDS Cup Appearances	

Also Played: Posn.(Game): S Jones 14(21)S(29), Damerell S(10,11,12)12(13), Meaker 7(22,23*,24,25,26*), Witter 4(31)7(32,34)S(33), Nugent 12(43,52),9(44,45), Shilton 1(46,47,48,49,50,51,52), Pickard 14(47)S(49)12(50)

Players on Loan: Hopkins (Brist Rov), Meaker (QPR), Witter (QPR), Van Rossum (Ekeren), Lee (Chelsea)

† = Sent Off

PLYMOUTH ARGYLE

Club Colours: Green/white striped shirts, black shorts, white stockings with 2 green hoops
Change Colours: Yellow shirts, green shorts, yellow stockings with 2 green hoops
Reserves League: Neville Ovenden Football Combinaton Div 2

Previous Name: Argyle Athletic Club 1886-1903
Previous Managers: 1903-05 Frank Brettall 1905-06 Bob Jack 1906-07 Will Fullerton 1910-38 Bob Jack 1938-48 Jack Tresadern 1948-55 Jim Rae 1955-60 Jack Rowley 1960-61 George Taylor/Neil Dougall 1961-63 Ellis Stuttard 1963 Vic Buckingham 1963-64 Andy Beattie 1964-65 Malcolm Allison 1965-68 Derek Ufton 1968-70 Billy Bingham 1970-72 Ellis Stuttard 1972-77 Tony Waiters 1977-78 Mike Kelly 1978 Lennie Lawrence 1978-79 Malcolm Allison 1979-81 Bobby Saxton 1981-83 Bobby Moncur 1983-84 John Hore 1984-88 Dave Smith 1988-90 Ken Brown 1990-92 David Kemp
Honours: Champions Division 3S 1929-30, 1951-52 Champions Division 3 1958-59
League Career: Founder Members of Division 3 1920 Transfered to Division 3S 1921-22 Promoted to Div 2 1929-30 Relegated to Div 3S 1949-50 Promoted to Div 2 1951-52 Relegated to Div 3S 1955-56 Transfered to Div 3 1958-59 Promoted to Div 2 1958-59 Relegated to Div 3 1967-68 Promoted to Div 2 1974-75 Relegated to Div 3 1976-77 Promoted to Div 2 1985-86 Relegated to Div 3 1991-92

CLUB RECORDS

Most Appearances for Club: Kevin Hodges (1978-92): League 499 + 26, FA Cup 40, League Cup 31 + 2, Other 2 + 1 **Total 572 + 29**
Most Capped Player: Moses Russell (Wales) 20, 1920-28 **For England:**
Record Goalscorer in a Match: Wilf Carter, 5 v Charlton Athletic, 6-4, Div 2, 27.12.1960
Record League Goalscorer in a Season: Jack Cock, 32, 1926-27 **In All Competitions:** Jack Cock, 32 (all league) 1926-27 W Carter 32 (League 26, FA Cup 6) 1957-58 Tommy Tynan, 32 (League 31, FA Cup 1) 1984-85
Record League Goalscorer in a Career: Sam Black, 176, 1924-37 **In All Competitions:** Sam Black, 185 (League 176, FA Cup 9) 1924-37
Record Transfer Fee Received: £250,0000 from Everton for Gary Megson, Feb 1980 £250,000 from Bradford City for Sean McCarthy, June 1990
Record Transfer Fee Paid: £250,000 to Hartlepool for Paul Dalton, June 1992
Best Performances: League: Third in Div 2 1931-32, 1952-53 **FA Cup:** Semi-Finalists 1983-84 **League Cup:** Semi-Finalists 1964-65, 1973-74
Most League Points: (3pts for win) 87, Division 3, 1986-87 (2pts for win) 68, Division 3S, 1929-30
Most League Goals: 107, Division 3S, 1925-26 (42 games) 107, Division 3S, 1951-52 (46 games)
Record League Victory and Most Goals Scored in a League Match: 8-1 v Millwall, Division 2, 16.1.1932 7-0 v Doncaster Rovers, Division 2, 5.9.1936
Record Victory and Most Goals Scored in a Cup Tie: 6-0 v Corby, FA Cup Round 3, 22.1.1966
Record League Defeat: 0-9 v Stoke City, Division 2, 17.12.1960
Record Cup Defeat: 1-7 v Tottenham Hotspur, FA Cup Rnd 4, 1966-67 0-6 v West Ham United, League Cup Rnd 2, 26.9.1962
Oldest Player in a League Match: Peter Shilton, 42 years 8 months (Still playing)
Youngest Player in a League Match: Colin Sullivan, 16 years 8 months 23 days

---

LONGEST LEAGUE RUNS

of undefeated matches: 22 (1929)	**of league matches without a win:** 13 (1962-63)
of undefeated home matches: 47 (1921-23)	**of undefeated away matches:** 9 (1929)
without home win: 8 (1989-90)	**without an away win:** 27 (1975-76)
of league wins: 9 (1930, 1986)	**of home wins:** 17 (1922)
of league defeats: 9 (1947)	**of away wins:** 6 (1929)

BARCLAYS

BARCLAYS BUSINESS CENTRE
Plymouth: Princess Street
PO Box No. 16
19 Princess Street
Plymouth
PL1 2HA
Tel: 0752 263333

BARCLAYBANK MACHINE

PLYMOUTH ARGYLE

PLAYERS NAME Honours	Ht	Wt	Birthdate	Birthplace Transfers	Contract Date	Clubs	League	L/Cup	FA Cup	Other	Lg	L/C	FAC	Oth
GOALKEEPERS														
Ray Newlands			12.09.91		12.09.91	Everton								
				Free	03.07.92	Plymouth A								
Peter Shilton	6.0	14.0	18.09.49	Leicester	01.09.66	Leicester City	286	20	30		1			
E:125,U23.3,Y,S;Div1'78,Div2'71,LC'79,				£300,000	01.11.74	Stoke City	110	4	7					
EC'79'80,ESC'79,FLg.1				£270,000	15.09.77	Nottm. Forest	202	26	18	26				
				£325,000	26.08.82	Southampton	188	28	17	9				
				£90,000	07.07.87	Derby County	175	18	10	8				
				N.C	05.03.92	Plymouth A	7							
DEFENDERS														
Adrian Burrows	5.11	11.12	16.01.59	Sutton	29.05.79	Mansfield Town	77+1	6	1+2		5			
				Free	02.08.82	Northampton T	88	5	10	1	4		1	
				£10,000	20.09.84	Plymouth A	232+3	16+1	16+1	4+1	13			
				Loan	17.10.87	Southend Utd	6	2		1				
Nick Marker	6.0	12.11	03.06.65	Budleigh Salterton	04.05.83	Exeter City	196+6	11	8	8	3	1		3
				Free	06.11.87	Plymouth A	194+1	13	9	7	11	2	1	2
Steve McCall	5.11	11.3	15.10.60	Carlisle	05.10.78	Ipswich Town (A)	249+8	29	23+1	18+1	7		1	3
E:B1,u21.6,Y6,UEFAC'81,UEFA.u21'82				£300,000	03.06.87	Sheffield Wed	21+8	2+3	1	0+1	2			
				Loan	08.02.90	Carlisle Utd	6							
				Nominal	26.03.92	Plymouth A	9				1			
Stephen Morgan	5.11	12.0	19.09.68	Manchester	12.08.86	Blackpool (A)	135+9	13	16	10+1	10	2	1	1
E:u19.2				£115,000	16.07.90	Plymouth A	85	5	3	4	5			
Andy Morrison				Scotland		Plymouth A	76+8	4+1	4	0+1	6	1		
Gary Poole	6.0	11.0	11.09.67	Stratford	15.07.85	Tottenham H. (T)								
					14.08.87	Cambridge Utd	42+1	2	2	3				
via Barnet to				Free	05.06.92	Plymouth A								
Tony Spearing	5.9	10.2	07.10.64	Romford	11.10.82	Norwich City (A)	67+2	5	4	4				
E: Y.6; FAYC'83				Loan	01.11.84	Stoke City	9							
				Loan	01.02.85	Oxford Utd	5							
				£100,000	12.07.68	Leicester City	71+2	2+1	1	2	1			
				Free	01.07.91	Plymouth A	30	2	1	2				
MIDFIELD														
Martin Barlow	5.7		26.06.71	Plymouth	01.07.89	Plymouth A (T)	48+12	3	3	3+1	4	1		
Steve Castle	5.11	12.5	17.05.66	Ilford	18.05.84	Leyton Orient (A)	232+11	15+1	23+1	28+2	55	5	6	
				£195,000	30.06.92	Plymouth A								
Paul Dalton	5.11	12.00	25.04.67	Middlesborough		Brandon Utd								
				£35,000	03.05.88	Manchester Utd								
				£20,000	04.03.89	Hartlepool Utd	140+11	10	7	9	37	2	1	3
					11.06.92	Plymouth A								
Marc Edworthy					30.03.91	Plymouth A	7+8		0+1					
Mark Fiore	5.10	11.10	18.11.69	London	26.07.88	Wimbledon (T)	1	0+1		1				
				£30,000	16.03.90	Plymouth A	74+8	5	1+1	4	8	1		1
Darren Garner			10.12.71	Plymouth	15.03.89	Plymouth A (T)	14+3				1			
Kevin Hodges	5.8	10.0	12.06.60	Bridport	02.03.78	Plymouth A (A)	500+26	32+3	39	9+2	81		3	2
				Loan	21.01.92	Torquay Utd	3							
Warren Joyce	5.9	11.11	20.01.65	Oldham	23.06.82	Bolton W (A)	180+4	14+1	11	11	17	1	1	2
				£35,000	16.10.87	Preston N.E	170+7	8	6	19	35	2	1	7
					19.05.92	Plymouth A								
FORWARDS														
Michael Evans	6.0	11.5	11.11.73	Plymouth	30.03.91	Plymouth A	12+5			1				1
Dwight Marshall	5.11	11.8	03.10.65	Jamaica		Grays Athletic								
				£35,000	09.08.91	Plymouth A	44	2	1	3	14			
Kevin Nugent	6.1	12.4	10.04.69	Edmonton	08.07.87	Leyton Orient	86+8	9+3	9	9+1	19	6	3	
				£200,000	23.03.92	Plymouth A	2+2							
David Regis	6.0		03.03.64	London		Fisher Athletic								
Clubcall Cup						Dunstable								
via Windsor & Eton to Barnet (£8,000) to				£25,000	28.09.90	Notts County	31+15	0+2		6	16			2
				£200,000	07.11.91	Plymouth A	21+3		1		2			
David A Smith	5.11	11.12	25.06.61	Sidcup		Welling								
Southern Lg Prem'86				£3,000	23.08.86	Gillingham	90+14	7	4+1	11+4	10		1	3
					03.08.89	Bristol City	94+3	8	8	2+2	10	4		
				£200,000	19.12.91	Plymouth A	14+4				2			
Robbie Turner	6.3	14.1	18.09.66	Peterlee	19.09.84	Huddersfield T. (A)	0+1	1						
				Loan	10.10.85	Cardiff City	34+5	3	1	1	8	1		
				Loan	02.10.86	Hartlepool Utd	7				1			
02.10.86 Loan Hartlepool U. (7 Lg App + 1 G)Free					29.01.87	Bristol Rovers	19+7	2		0+1	2			
				£15,000	17.12.87	Wimbledon	2+8	1+1	0+1	3+1			1	1
				£45,000	27.01.89	Bristol City	45+7		7	2	12		3	
				£150,000	08.08.90	Plymouth A	64	5	3	3	17	1		2
ADDITIONAL CONTRACT PLAYERS														
(F) Paul Adcock	5.8	10.2	02.05.72	Ilminster	07.08.90	Plymouth A (T)	9+3	1	2					
Stephen A Jones					13.07.92	Plymouth A (T)	0+1							

Lee Cansfield, Mark Clode, Ryan Cross, Peter Shepherd.

LEADING LEAGUE GOALSCORERS SEASONS 1985-86 – 1991-92

1985-86	**KEVIN HODGES**	16	1986-87	**TOMMY TYNAN**	18
1987-88	**TOMMY TYNAN**	16	1988-89	**TOMMY TYNAN**	24
1989-90	**TOMMY TYNAN**	15	1990-91	**ROBBIE TURNER**	14

1991-92   **DWIGHT MARSHALL**   **14**

HOME PARK Plymouth, Devon PL2 3DQ

Capacity: 19,700   **Covered Standing:** 7,000   **Seating:** 6,400

Tel: Ground: 0752 562561   **Ticket Sales:** As ground number   **Clubcall:** 0898 12 16 88

All premium rate calls (0898/0891) cost 36p per minute cheap rate and 48p per minute at all other times. Call costings correct at time of going to press.

ATTENDANCES
Highest: 43,596 v Aston Villa, Division 2, 10.10.1936

Lowest: 1,875 v Hull, 11.5.1979

RECORD RECEIPTS:
£118,000 v Derby County, FA Cup Round 6, 3.3.1984

HOME PARK
First game: v Northampton Town, Southern League, 2-0,
5.9.1903
First floodlit game: v Exeter, 26.10.1953

Season Tickets:
Stands: from £130 to £170, juv/OAP £95 to £150
Ground: from £90 to £105, juv/OAP £60 to £75

Executive Box Season Tickets: None free

Cost of Stand Tickets: Grandstand Centre: £9, OAP £7; Grandstand Wing: £8, OAP £6, Juv £5; Mayflower Stand: £8, OAP £6; Lyndhurst Seating: £7, £5 Juv/OAP; Mayflower Standing: £5.50, Juv/OAP £4; Lyndhurst Road & Devonport End (Standing): £5, Juv/OAP £3

Match and Ticket Information: Grandstand and Mayflower stand tickets are available 2 to 3 weeks before each first team game

Car Parking: Free car park (1,000 cars) adjoining ground

Nearest Railway Station: Plymouth (0752) 21300

How to get to the ground

From all directions: Use A38 Plymouth bypass as far as the Tavistock Road A386, then branch left and follow signs Plymouth A386. In 0.7m turn right then left A3041 into Outland Road for Plymouth Argyle FC

Value Rating: ★ ★ ★ ★

Programme Editor: Stewart Soutter

Price of 1992-93 Programme: £1.20
Number of Pages: 32
Subscriptions:

Local Newspapers: Sunday Independent

Local Radio Stations: Devonair, BBC Radio Devon, Plymouth Sound.

PORTSMOUTH

Division 1

Formed: 1898

Turned Professional: 1898

Ltd Co: 1898

SPONSORED BY: Goodmans

NICKNAME: The Pompey

Chairman
J A Gregory

Vice-Chairman
D K Deacon

Directors
M H Gregory
J Prevost
B Henson
P Britten

Secretary
P A Weld (0705 731204)

Marketing Manager
Julie Baker

Team Manager
Jim Smith

Assistant Manager
G Paddon

Youth Team Coach
K Todd

Physiotherapist
N Sillett

Club Statistician for the Directory
Peter Macey

THE 1991-92 season had initially promised so little for Portsmouth Football Club, as, after the three previous seasons when performances were not as good as they should have been, the fans were expecting more of the same, but what actually happened surprised everyone.

During the pre-season training Jim Smith had threatened that if the older players didn't perform to their true potential then he would have no hesitation in putting the youngsters into the side, and as it was Smith kept to his word and put players like Andy Awford, Kit Symons, Daryll Powell, Darren Anderton and Stuart Doling into the first team with only a few games between them.

Pompey played fifty-nine competitive games, the most the first team have ever played in a season and only Kit Symons played in all of them, but his most impressive statistic is that he was not spoken to by a referee once during the entire campaign. Kit also went from reserve team football to a Welsh full international in six months and made his debut against Eire at Lansdown Road.

To be pushing for promotion was good, but to be in the Semi-finals of the F.A. Cup was beyond anyones wildest dreams. That mis-timed challenge by Andy Awford undoubtedly cost us dear, but as all Pompey fans will tell you, Andy made very few mistakes all season and he will surely go on to greater things.

The prospects for 1992-93 look promising and with the best group of youngsters in the football league, Pompey can feel proud. It was sad to see Darren Anderton's departure to Tottenham but Pompey would have been foolish to turn down £1.7 million for a player who has only played second division football.   If Pompey sell Andy Awford or Kit Symons then it would be a complete sell out as they must be the best pair of centre-half's of their age in the country, and they are the jewels in Pompey's crown.

Pompey were the winners of the PFA fair play award and it was just reward for the improved disciplinary record, which, over the last three seasons has got gradually better from the depths of the mid 1980's when Pompey were pulled up to the disciplinary panel year after year for being one of the most ill disciplined teams in the league. Things look good for Pompey in the future, if only they can keep hold of the youngsters.   **Peter Macey**

Back row L-R: Mark Chamberlain, Guy Whittingham, Darryl Powell, Mark Kelly, Warren Aspinal, Ray Daniel. **Middle row:** Mike Bailey (Reserve Team Coach), Gordon Neave (Kit Man), Lee Russell, Chris Burns, Colin Clarke, Alan Knight, Guy Butters, Kit Symons, Shaun Gale, Neil Sillett (Physio), Kenny Todd (Youth Team Manager). **Front row:** Warren Neill, Steve Wigley, Alan McLoughlin, Andy Awford, Gavin Maguire, Graham Paddon (Asst. Manager), Jim Smith (Manager), Martin Kuhl, Stuart Doling. Micky Ross, Shaun Murray, Paul Walsh.

PORTSMOUTH

DIVISION TWO: 9th　　**FA CUP:** SEMI-FINALISTS　　**RUMBELOWS CUP:** 3rd RND　　**ZDS CUP:** 1st RND

M	DATE	COMP.	VEN	OPPONENTS	RESULT	H/T	LGE POS	GOALSCORERS/GOAL TIMES	ATTEN-DANCE
1	A 17	BL	A	Blackburn Rovers	D 1-1	0-0		Anderton 49	(11,118)
2	20	RC 1/1	H	Gillingham	W 2-1	1-0		Clarke 22, Kuhl 88	4,801
3	24	BL	H	Port Vale	W 1-0	1-0		Clarke 29	8,083
4	27	RC 1/2	A	Gillingham	W 4-3	2-1		Anderton 18, Beresford (pen) 30, Butters 53, Aspinall 87	(5,114)
5	31	BL	A	Middlesbrough	L 0-2	0-0			(12,300)
6	S 3	BL	H	Sunderland	W 1-0	0-0		Burns 68	9,621
7	7	BL	H	Brighton & H A	D 0-0	0-0	13		10,567
8	14	BL	A	Charlton Athletic	L 0-3	0-2			(5,707)
9	17	BL	A	Grimsby Town	D 1-1	0-1		Wigley 78	(5,348)
10	21	BL	H	Cambridge United	W 3-0	2-0	12	Wigley 12, Burns 27, Kimble (og) 53	7,801
11	24	RC 2/1	H	Oxford United	D 0-0	0-0			4,682
12	28	BL	A	Bristol City	W 2-0	2-0		Beresford 34, 43 (pen)	(9,830)
13	O 1	ZDS 1	A	Plymouth Argyle	L 0-1	0-1			(2,303)
14	5	BL	H	Newcastle United	W 3-1	2-0	5	Beresford (pen) 19, Stimson (og) 40, Butters 55	10,175
15	9	RC 2/2	A	Oxford United	W 1-0	1-0		Burns 30	(4,114)
16	12	BL	A	Barnsley	L 0-2	0-1			(6,579)
17	19	BL	A	Derby County	L 0-2	0-0			(13,190)
18	26	BL	H	Ipswich Town	D 1-1	1-1	12	Burns 43	8,007
19	30	RC 3	A	Manchester United	L 1-3	0-0		Beresford 61	(29,543)
20	N 2	BL	A	Millwall	D 1-1	0-1		Anderton 74	(6,060)
21	5	BL	H	Leicester City	W 1-0	1-0		Whittingham 5	7,147
22	9	BL	H	Oxford United	W 2-1	1-0		Butters 30, 63	7,557
23	16	BL	A	Swindon Town	W 3-2	0-0	6	Whittingham 57, Anderton 85, Powell 90	(10,738)
24	23	BL	A	Watford	L 1-2	0-1		Doling 83	(8,135)
25	30	BL	H	Wolverhampton W	W 1-0	1-0	10	Burns 13	11,101
26	D 14	BL	H	Southend United	D 1-1	1-1	10	Anderton 25	9,006
27	21	BL	A	Sunderland	L 0-1	0-1			(14,432)
28	26	BL	H	Bristol Rovers	W 2-0	1-0		Cross (og) 24, Burns 80	10,710
29	28	BL	H	Middlesbrough	W 4-0	3-0	7	Whittingham 9, Powell 34, Beresford (pen) 39, Kuhl 68	12,324
30	J 1	BL	A	Plymouth Argyle	L 2-3	1-2	9	Powell 13, Chamberlain 81	(8,887)
31	4	FAC 3	A	Exeter City	W 2-1	1-0		Whittingham 44, Aspinall 89	(6,765)
32	11	BL	A	Port Vale	W 2-0	2-0		Powell 15, Anderton 18	5,925
33	18	BL	H	Blackburn Rovers	D 2-2	0-1	7	Beresford 79, Whittingham 89	20,106
34	25	FAC 4	A	Leyton Orient	W 2-0	0-0		Anderton 53, 79	16,138
35	29	BL	A	Bristol Rovers	L 0-1	0-1			(5,330)
36	F 1	BL	H	Derby County	L 0-1	0-0	7		12,008
37	4	BL	H	Plymouth Argyle	W 4-1	2-0		Powell 24, Whittingham 41, 74, Marker (og) 67	10,467
38	8	BL	H	Ipswich Town	L 2-5	1-3	8	Anderton 10, Powell 53	(13,494)
39	15	FAC 5	H	Middlesbrough	D 1-1	0-0		Whittingham 59	18,138
40	22	BL	A	Wolverhampton W	D 0-0	0-0	10		(15,770)
41	26	FAC 5R	A	Middlesbrough	W 4-2	2-2		Clarke 25, 38, Anderton 59, 72	(19,479)
42	29	BL	H	Tranmere Rovers	W 1-0	1-0		Burns 6, McLoughlin 11	16,644
43	F 7	FAC 6	H	Nottingham Forest	W 1-0	1-0		McLoughlin 2	25,402
44	11	BL	A	Leicester City	D 2-2	1-0		Burns 29, Clarke 86	(14,207)
45	14	BL	H	Millwall	W 6-1	3-0	7	Kuhl 3, Whittingham 3 (6, 44, 55), McLoughlin 52, Burns 70	14,944
46	17	BL	H	Southend United	W 3-2	2-2		Whittingham 9, Clarke 36, Aspinall 84	(6,832)
47	21	BL	A	Oxford United	L 1-2	0-0		Anderton 49	(8,432)
48	28	BL	H	Swindon Town	D 1-1	0-0	7	Beresford (pen) 72	16,007
49	31	BL	H	Charlton Athletic	L 1-2	0-0		Minto (og) 64	14,539
50	M 5	FAC SF	N	Liverpool	D †1-1	0-0		Anderton 110	(41,869)
51	7	BL	A	Tranmere Rovers	L 0-2	0-1			(6,692)
52	11	BL	H	Grimsby Town	W 2-0	1-0	8	Doling 28, Aspinall 76	10,576
53	13	FAC SFR	N	Liverpool	D †0-0	0-0		(Lost 3-1 on pens)	(40,077)
54	17	BL	A	Cambridge United	D 2-2	0-1	9	Kuhl 67, Aspinall 77	(9,497)
55	20	BL	H	Bristol City	W 1-0	1-0		Wigley 15	17,151
56	22	BL	H	Watford	D 0-0	0-0			14,417
57	25	BL	A	Newcastle United	L 0-1	0-0	9		(25,989)
58	29	BL	A	Brighton & H A	L 1-2	0-1		Aspinall 90	(11,647)
59	M 2	BL	H	Barnsley	W 2-0	0-0	9	Symons 48, Whittingham 67	11,169

Best Home League Attendance: 20,106 v Blackburn Rovers　　**Smallest: 5,925 v Port Vale**　　**Av Home Att: 11,502**

Goal Scorers:　　**Compared with 90-91: +1,812**

League (65): Whittingham 11, Burns 8, Anderton 7, Powell 6, Beresford 6 (4 pens), Aspinall 4, Opponents 5, Wigley 3, Butters 3, Clarke 3, Kuhl 3, McLoughlin 2, Doling 2, Symons, Chamberlain

R/lows C (8): Beresford 2 (1 pen), Butters, Kuhl, Aspinall, Clarke, Burns, Anderton

FA Cup (11): Anderton 5, Whittingham 2, Clarke 2, Aspinall, McLoughlin

ZDS Cup (0):　　† = After extra-time

Knight A.	Awford A.	Beresford J.	Burns C.	Symmons C.	Butters G.	anderton D.	Kuhl M.	Clarke C.	Whittingham G.	Powell D.	Russell L.	Chamberlain M.	Doling S.	Aspinall W.	Wigley S.	Neill W.	Murray S.	Gosney A.	Maguire G.	Ross M.	Hebberd T.	Daniel R.	Hendon I.	McLoughlin A.	McFarlane A.	Referee	
1	2	3	4	5	6	7	8	9	10•	11*	12	14														M Reed	1
1	2	3	4	5	6	7	8	9	10•	11	S	14														J Carter	2
1	2	3	4	5	6	7	8	9		11	S	14	10•													I Hemley	3
1	2	3	4	5	6	7		9		11	S	10	8•	14												G Pooley	4
1	2	3	4	5	6	7	8	9		11	12•	10*		14												J Worrall	5
1	2	3	4	5	6	7	8	9	10	11			S		S											A Buksh	6
1	2	3	4	5	6*	7	8	9	10	11•		12		14												G Ashby	7
1	2	3•	4	5		7	8	9	10•	11	6		12	14												A Smith	8
1	2	3	12	5		7	8		10•		6		4*	9	14	11										J Rushton	9
1	2		4	5	6		8	9*		14	3		S	10	7	11										R Milford	10
1	2	3	4	5	6	12	8	9*		S			10	7	11											J Moules	11
1	2	3	4	5	6	11		9•		14		8		10	7	S										D Elleray	12
		4	5	6		11		9†	3	8*	14			7	10•	1	2	12								R Hamer	13
1	2	3	4	5	6	11		9•		12		8*		10	7						14					L Shapter	14
1	2	3	4	5	6		8	9		12		11*		10	7						S					P Wright	15
1	2	3	4	5	6	11•	8†	9	12				14		7						10*					N Midgley	16
1	2*	3	4•	5	6	11	8		9			10		12	7						14					T Fitzharris	17
1	2	3	4	5	6	11		10*	9			8•		12	7						14					P Durkin	18
1	2	3	4	5	6	11	8	9*	12			10•		14	7											R Groves	19
1	2	3*	4	5	6	11	8		9			12		10•	7					14						M James	20
1	2		4	5	6	11	8	12	9		3			10•	7					14*						P Foakes	21
1	2		4	5	6	11*	8	10•	9		3		12		7					14						G Willard	22
1	2	10•	4	5	6	11	8		9		14	3*	12		7	1										A Gunn	23
1	2	3	4	5	6	11	8	12	9	10*			14		7•											R Gifford	24
1	2	3	4	5	6	11	8	S	9	14				10•	7											R Wiseman	25
1	2	3	4*	5	6	11	8	12	9			14		10•	7											P Don	26
1	2	3	4*	5	6	11	8		9		10•	14		12	7											T Lunt	27
1	2	3	4	5	6	11	8		9*	14		10•		12	7											A Ward	28
1	2	3	4	5		11	8		9*	6		10•		12	7								14			R Milford	29
1	2	3	4*	5		11•	8		9			10		14	12	7										G Singh	30
1	2	3		5	6	11	8		9*	4		10•		14	12	7										I Hemley	31
1	2	3	14	5	6	11•	8		9*	4		10			12	7										J Worrall	32
1	2	3	9•	5	6	11	8		14	4		10*			12	7										P Durkin	33
1	2	3	10	5	6	11	8		9	4*				S	12	7										M Bodenham	34
1	2	3	10	5	6•	11	8		9	4					12	7*							14			C Wilkes	35
1	2	3	10•	5	6	11	8		12	4					9*	7							14			M Bodenham	36
	3	3	10	5	6	11	8	S	9	4	S					7							2			K Morton	37
1	2	3	10	5	6*	11	8	12	9	4					7•								14			V Callow	38
1	2	3	10	5		11	8	S	9	4		12				7	6*									B Hill	39
1	2	3	12	5	6	11	8	14	9•	4*						7								10		G Poll	40
1	2	3	10*	5	6	11	8	9	S	4				12		7										B Hill	41
1	2	3	6	5			11•	8	9	14*	4			12		7								10		R Groves	42
1	2	3	6	5			11	8	9•	14*	4			12		7								10		S Lodge	43
1	2	3	6	5		7•	11	8	9	14*	4			12										10		M Reed	44
1	2	3	6	5			11	8•	9*	10				12	14	7										K Burge	45
1	2	3	6	5	S		8	9	10	11*				12		7							4			J Carter	46
1	2		6	5	3•		11	8	9	10*	14			12		7							4			D Frampton	47
1	2	3	6*	5			11	8*	9	10	14			12		7							4			D Axcell	48
1	2*	3	6	5			11		10	9		14		8*	12	7							4			P Vanes	49
1	2	3	6	5			11	8	14			10*		12		7							4*			M Bodenham	50
1	2	3•	6	5		10	11	8	14					12		7							4*			A Dawson	51
1	2		6	5			14	8	10•	11*			4	9	12	7					3					D Shadwell	52
1	2	3	6	5			11	8	9•	14				12		7					10			4*		M Bodenham	53
1	2		6*	5	9*	11	8		14					10	12	7					3			4		J Kirkby	54
1	2*		12	5			8		9				6	10	11•	7					3			4	14	G Ashby	55
1	2		6	5			11	8*		9•			10	12	14	7					3			4		R Lewis	56
1	2		6	5			11*			9			8	10•	12	7					3			4	14	S Bell	57
1	2		6	5			14	8†		10	9*		4*	12	11	7					3					P Alcock	58
1	2•		6	5	14			8		10	11*			9	12	7					3			4		P Foakes	59
45	45	35	42	46	32	40	41	19	30	26	7	10	7	9	8	38	2	1			1	7	1	14		League Appearances	
	4		1	2		5	5	10	2	6	6	15	15				3	3	1	3				2		Substitute Appearances	
5	5	5	5	5	5	3+1	4	5	1+1	2+1		3+1	1	0+2	2	3	1									R/lows Appearances	
7	7	7	6	7	3	7	7	4	3+3	5		2		0+5	0+2	7	1				1		1	3		FA Cup Appearances	
	1	1	1	1		1	1	1	0+1			1	1	1	1	1	0+1									ZDS Cup Appearances	

† = Sent Off

PORTSMOUTH

Club Colours: Royal blue shirts, white shorts, red stockings.
Change Colours: Red shirts, black shorts, black socks
Reserves League: Neville Ovenden Football Combination

COMPETITIONS				
Div. 1	Div. 2	Div. 3	Div. 3S	Div. 4
27-59	24-27	20-21	21-24	78-80
87-88	59-61	61-62		
	62-76	76-78		
	83-87	80-83		
	88-			

HONOURS				
Div. 1	Div. 3	Div. 3S	FA Cup	C/Shield
48-49	61-62	23-24	38-39	1949
49-50	82-83			

MOST APPEARANCES: JIMMY DICKINSON 829 (46-65)				
Year	Leauge	FA Cup	Lge Cup	C/Shield
1946-47	40	2		
1947-48	42	2		
1948-49	41	5		
1949-50	40	5		1
1950-51	41	1		
1951-52	40	4		
1952-53	40	2		
1953-54	40	7		
1954-55	25			
1955-56	39	2		
1956-57	42	2		
1957-58	42	2		
1958-59	39	4		
1959-60	42	1		
1960-61	40	1	4	
1961-62	46	1	4	
1962-63	42	5	3	
1963-64	42	1	2	
1964-65	41	2	2	
	764	49	15	1

Jimmy also made 26 lge & 5 cup apps. in 1945-46

Previous holder: John Weddle 368 (1928-1938)

MOST GOALS IN A CAREER		
PETER HARRIS 208 (1946-60)		
Season	League	FA Cup
1946-47	1	
1947-48	13	.1
1948-49	17	5
1949-50	16	1
1950-51	5	
1951-52	9	1
1952-53	23	
1953-54	20	4
1954-55	23	
1955-56	23	1
1956-57	12	2
1957-58	18	
1958-59	13	
1959-60	1	
Total	193	15

Previous holder: John Weddle 173 (1928-38)

MANAGERS			
Name	Seasons	Best	Worst
Since joining League			
John McCartney	1920-27	2(2)	12(3S)
John Tinn	1927-47	4(1)	20(1)
J R Jackson	1947-52	1(1)	8(1)
Eddie Lever	1952-58	3(1)	20(1)
Freddie Cox	1958-61	22(1)	21(2)
Bill Thompson	1961		
George Smith	1961-70	5(2)	1(3)
Ron Tindall	1970-73	16(2)	17(2)
John Mortimore	1973-74	15(2)	15(2)
Ron Tindall	1974		
Ian St. John	1974-77	17(2)	20(3)
Jimmy Dickinson	1977-79	24(3)	7(4)
Frank Burrows	1979-82	6(3)	4(4)
Bobby Campbell	1982-84	16(2)	1(3)
Alan Ball	1984-89	20(1)	4(2)
John Gregory	1989-90		
Frank Burrows	1990-91		
Jim Smith	1991-		

RECORD TRANSFER FEE RECEIVED			
Amount	Club	Player	Date
£1,700,000	Tottenham H.	Darren Anderton	6/92
£1,000,000	Inter Milan	Mark Hateley	6/84
£130,000	Brighton & HA	Steve Foster	6/79
£75,000	Carlisle Utd.	David Kemp	3/78

RECORD TRANSFER FEE PAID			
Amount	Club	Player	Date
£450,000	Queens Park R.	Colin Clarke	5/90
£315,000	Aston Villa	Warren Aspinall	8/88
£300,000	Barnsley	John Beresford	3/89
£200,000	Sheffield Wed	Mark Chamberlain	8/88

LONGEST LEAGUE RUNS	
of undefeated matches:	15 (18.4.1924-18.10.1924)
of undefeated home matches:	32 (3.1.1948-27.8.1949)
without home win:	16 (6.2.1958-17.10.1959)
of league wins:	7 (19.4.1980-30.8.1980) (22.1.1983-1.4.1983)
of league defeats:	9 (22.11.1959-17.1.1960)
	(21.3.1959-29.8.1959) (3.11.1963-22.12.1963)
	(21.10.1975-6.12.1975)
of league matches w/out a win:	25 (22.1.1958-17.10.1959)
of undefeated away matches:	14 (1.3.1924-18.10.1924)
without an away win:	24 (26.1.1938-11.3.1939)
of home wins:	14 (13.9.1986-28.2.1987)
of away wins:	6 (1.4.1980-30.8.1980)

PREVIOUS LEAGUE
Southern League

BIGGEST VICTORIES
League: 9-1 v Notts County, Division 2, 9.4.1927
F.A. Cup: 7-0 v Stockport (h), Rnd 3, 8.1.1949
League Cup: 5-1 v Brighton & HA, Round 2, 25.9.1962
5-1 v Coventry, Round 3, 20.10.1962

BIGGEST DEFEATS
League: 0-10 v Leicester City, Division 1, 20.10.1928
F.A. Cup: 0-5 v Everton, Round 1, 1902-03
0-5 v Tottenham H, Round 3, 16.1.1937
0-5 v Blackburn Rov, Rnd 1 2nd Replay, 1899-90
League Cup: 0-5 v Queens Park Rangers, Round 2,
6.10.1981

MOST POINTS
3 points a win: 91, Division 3, 1982-83
2 points a win: 65, Division 3, 1961-62

MOST GOALS
91, 1979-80 (Division 4)
Garwood 17, Laidlaw 16, Hemmerman 13, Brisley 12, Rogers
9, Gregory 5, Ashworth 4, Aizelwood 2, Bryant 2, Perrin 2,
Davey 1, McLaughlin 1, Purdie 1, Todd 1, Showers 1, og 4

MOST GOALS IN A MATCH
5. Alf Strange v Gillingham, Division 3, 27.1.1923 (6-1)
5. Peter Harris v Aston Villa, Division 1, 3.9.1958 (5-2)
(Peter Harris's 5th goal was his 200th league & cup goal for
Portsmouth)

MOST GOALS IN A SEASON
Billy Haines 43 (League 40, FAC 3) 1926-27
4 goals once = 4, 3 goals four times = 12, 2 goals 6 times = 12,
1 goal 15 times = 15
Previous holder: B Haines 31 (1923-24)

MOST FIRST CLASS MATCHES IN A SEASON
59 (46 League, 7 FA Cup, 5 League Cup, 1 ZDS) 1991-92

MOST LEAGUE GOALS CONCEDED
112, Division 1, 1958-59

MOST LEAGUE WINS
27, Division 3, 1961-62; Division 3, 1982-83

MOST LEAGUE DRAWS
19, Division 3, 1981-82

MOST LEAGUE DEFEATS
27, Division 1, 1958-59

OLDEST PLAYER
Jimmy Dickinson MBE, 40 exactly v Northampton, 24.4.1965

YOUNGEST PLAYER
Clive Green, 16 years 259 days v Wrexham, 21.8.1976
(also youngest goalscorer when 16 yrs 280 days v Lincoln
City, 11.9.1976)

MOST CAPPED PLAYER
Jimmy Dickenson (England) 48

BEST PERFORMANCES BY PORTSMOUTH

League: 1961-62: Matches played 46, Won 27, Drawn 11, Lost 8, Goals for 87, Goals against 47, Points 65. 1st in Division 3.

Highest: 1948-49, 1949-50: 1st in Division 1.

F.A. Cup: 1938-39: 3rd rnd. Lincoln 4-0; 4th rnd. West Bromwich Albion 2-0; 5th rnd. West Ham United 2-0; 6th rnd. Preston North End 1-0; Semi-final Huddersfield 2-1; Final Wolves 4-1.

League Cup: 1960-61: 2nd rnd. Coventry 2-0; 3rd rnd. Manchester City 2-0; 4th rnd. Chelsea 1-0; 5th rnd. Rotherham 0-3.

DIVISIONAL RECORDS

	Played	Won	Drawn	Lost	For	Against	Points
DIVISION 1	1090	405	257	428	1729	1828	1074
DIVISION 2	1150	398	306	446	1640	1704	1242
DIVISION 3	318	120	95	103	412	379	376
DIVISION 3S	126	61	36	29	207	121	158
DIVISION 4	92	44	24	24	153	97	112
TOTALS	2776	1028	718	1030	4141	4129	2962

PORTSMOUTH

PLAYERS NAME Honours	Ht	Wt	Birthdate	Birthplace Transfers	Contract Date	Clubs	League	L/Cup	FA Cup	Other	Lg	L/C	FAC	Oth
GOALKEEPERS														
Alan Knight	6.1	13.1	03.07.61	Balham	12.03.79	Portsmouth (A)	446	35	29	9				
E:u21.2,Y3,Div.3.83														
DEFENDERS														
Andrew Awford	5.9		14.07.72	Worcester		Portsmouth (T)	56+7	5+1	7	1				
E:Y.4														
Guy Butters			30.10.69	Hillingdon	05.08.88	Tottenham H. (T)	34+1	2+1	1		1			
E: u21.3				Loan	13.01.90	Southend Utd	16			2	3			
				£375,000	28.09.90	Portsmouth	55+1	8	3	2	3	1		
Shaun Gale	6.0		04.09.66	Sheffield	12.07.88	Portsmouth	2+1			0+1				
Warren Neill	5.10	12.5	21.11.62	Acton	03.09.80	Q.P.R. (A)	177+4	18+1	11+1	3	3	1	2	1
E:S,Div.2.83				£110,000	28.07.88	Portsmouth	146+2	11	13	3	1	1		
Lee Russell	5.10	11.04	03.09.69	Southampton	12.07.88	Portsmouth	25+8	2	1+1	1+1	1			
Christopher Symons	6.1	10.10	05.03.71	Basingstoke	30.12.88	Portsmouth (T)	50	5	6	1+1	1			
MIDFIELD														
Chris Burns					15.03.91	Portsmouth	42+4	5	6	1	8	1		
Ray Daniel	5.10	11.0	10.12.64	Luton	07.09.82	Luton Town (A)	14+8	2	5+1		4			
				Loan	01.09.83	Gillingham	5							
				Free	30.06.86	Hull City	55+3	1	1+1	0+1	3			
				Tribunal	22.08.89	Cardiff City	56	5	5	1	1			
				£80,000	09.11.90	Portsmouth	20+2		1	1				
Stuart Doling					25.06.90	Portsmouth (T)	7+6	1		0+1	2			
Martin Kuhl	5.11	11.13	10.01.65	Frimley	13.01.83	Birmingham City (A)	103+8	13	8	1+1	5		1	
				P.E	20.03.87	Sheffield Utd	38	2	1	1	4			
				£300,000+P	19.02.88	Watford	4							
				£125,000	30.09.88	Portsmouth	143+11	11	13	2	26	1		
Gavin Maguire	5.10	11.8	24.11.67	Hammersmith	08.10.85	Q.P.R. (A)	33+7	1+2	5+1					
				£225,000	04.01.89	Portsmouth	69+1	7	3	2				
				Loan	10.10.91	Newcastle Utd	3							
Alan McLoughlin	5.8	10.0	20.04.67	Manchester	25.04.85	Manchester Utd. (A)								
Ei: 3, B.1				Free	12.08.87	Swindon Town	101+5	11+3	4+2	10	19	5		
				Loan	13.03.87	Torquay Utd	21+3				4			
				£1,000,000	13.12.90	Southampton	22+2	0+1	4	1	1			
				Loan	30.09.91	Aston Villa	1							
				£400,000	17.02.92	Portsmouth	14		3		2		1	
FORWARDS														
Warren Aspinall	5.9	11.12	13.09.67	Wigan	31.08.85	Wigan Ath	39+12	1	2+3	3+5	22		2	4
E:u19.1,Y.2,FRT85				£150,000	04.02.86	Everton	0+7	0+1		0+2				
				£300,000	19.02.87	Aston Villa	40+4	4	1+1		14	2		
				£315,000	26.08.88	Portsmouth	78+22	5+2	3+5	1	19	3	2	
Mark Chamberlin	5.8	9.8	19.11.61	Stoke	01.05.79	Port Vale (A)	90+6	4	10		17		2	
E:8,u21.4,UEFA.u21'84				£135,000	24.08.82	Stoke City	110+2	9	4		17		1	
				£300,000	13.09.85	Sheffield Wed	32+34	5+2	1+11	2+1	8	1	1	
				£200,000	02.08.88	Portsmouth	94+13	7+1	6	4	15	1	1	
Colin Clarke	5.11	12.10	30.10.62	Newry	28.10.80	Ipswich Town (A)								
NI:24				Free	21.07.81	Peterborough U	76+6	7	4	1	18	2	2	
				Loan	22.03.84	Gillingham	8				1			
				Free	03.07.84	Tranmere Rovers	45	2	2	4	22	1	3	3
				£22,500	01.07.85	Bournemouth	46	4	4	2	26	3	2	4
				£400,000	07.07.86	Southampton	82	12	3	1	36	2	1	
				Loan	01.12.88	Bournemouth	3+1				2			
				£800,000	09.03.89	Q.P.R	39+7	3	7		11	1	2	
				£450,000	05.06.90	Portsmouth	57+9	9	7	1	16	3	4	
Mark Kelly	5.8	10.4	27.11.69	Sutton	01.12.86	Portsmouth (A)	24+25	4	0+2	1+1	2			
Ei:B.1,u23.1,u21.1				Loan	18.10.90	Tottenham H								
Shaun Murray	5.7	10.5	17.10.70	Newcastle	10.12.87	Tottenham H. (T)								
E:Y.7				£100,000	12.06.89	Portsmouth	19+8	1+1	1+2	1	1			
Daryl Powell	6.0	12.03	15.11.71	London	22.12.88	Portsmouth (T)	28+19	3+1	5	2+1	6			1
Michael Ross	5.7	9.13	02.09.71	Southampton	30.12.88	Portsmouth (T)	0+4			2+1				
Paul Walsh	5.8	10.4	01.10.62	Plumstead	02.10.79	Charlton Ath	85+2	9	4		24	6	1	
E: 5, u21.7, Y.10; Div1'86; SC'86				£400,000	26.07.82	Luton Town	80				24	1	3	
				£700,000	21.05.84	Liverpool	63+14	10+2	6+2	13+2	25	4	3	5
				£500,000	16.02.88	Tottenham H	84+44	9+6	4+1	1+3	19	2		
16.09.91 Loan Q.P.R. 2 Lg Apps.				£400,000	03.06.92	Portsmouth								
Guy Whittingham	5.10	11.12	10.11.64	Evesham		Waterlooville		1					1	
						Yeovil								
					09.06.89	Portsmouth	103+11	4+2	7+3	2	46	1	10	
Steven Wigley	5.9	10.12	15.10.61	Ashton-under-Lyme		Curzon Ash								
				£2,000	24.03.81	Nottm. Forest	69+13	8+1	5	10	2	1		
					25.10.85	Sheffield Utd	21+7	1+1	1	1	1			
				PE	20.03.87	Birmingham City	87	6	4	2	4		1	
				£300,000	23.09.89	Portsmouth	103+17	9+1	4+2	1+1	12			

ADDITIONAL CONTRACT PLAYERS: Christian Owen, Roy Young.

PORTSMOUTH

RECORD WIN & LOSS AGAINST EACH CLUB IN CURRENT DIVISION
(Where a score has occured on several occasions the most recent is given)

Club	Rec. Win	Season	Rec. Loss	Season
BARNSLEY	4-1	1924-25 (away)	4-0	1990-91
BIRMINGHAM CITY	3-0	1949-50 (away)	5-0	1955-56
BRENTFORD	4-0	1961-62	4-0	1936-37
BRISTOL CITY	5-0	1961-62	4-1	1990-91
BRISTOL ROVERS	3-0	1974-75	5-1	1982-83
CAMBRIDGE UNITED	5-0	1983-84	1-0	1977-78
CHARLTON ATHLETIC	5-1	1969-70	6-1	1959-60
DERBY COUNTY	5-1	1934-35	6-1	1924-25
GRIMSBY TOWN	4-0	1983-84	3-0	1934-35
LEICESTER CITY	5-0	1929-30 (away)	10-0	1928-29
LUTON TOWN	5-0	1957-58	4-1	1987-88
MILLWALL	6-1	1991-92	3-1	1969-70
NEWCASTLE UNITED	6-0	1931-32	5-1	1958-59 (home)
NOTTS COUNTY	9-1	1926-27	4-0	1973-74
OXFORD UNITED	3-0	1968-69	3-0	1973-74
PETERBOROUGH UTD	4-0	1979-80	3-0	1961-62 (home)
SOUTHEND UNITED	6-0	1921-22	4-0	1982-83
SUNDERLAND	4-0	1928-29	5-0	1935-36
SWINDON TOWN	5-0	1964-65	6-2	1920-21
TRANMERE ROVERS	2-0	1991-92	5-2	1977-78 (home)
WATFORD	6-0	1970-71	4-0	1969-70
WEST HAM UNITED	3-0	1931-32	6-0	1958-59
WOLVERHAMPTON WNDRS	5-0	1948-49	7-0	1958-59

MANAGER: JIM SMITH

DATE OF BIRTH: 17.10.1940   **PLACE OF BIRTH:** Sheffield

DATE OF APPOINTMENT: May 1991

PREVIOUS CLUBS
as Manager: Boston Utd, Colchester Utd, Blackburn Rov, Birmingham City, Oxford Utd, Q.P.R.
as Player: Sheffield Utd; Aldershot, Halifax Town, Lincoln City, Boston Utd; Colchester Utd

HONOURS
as Manager: (Colchester): Promotion to Div 3 1974; (Birmingham) Promotion to Div 1 1980; (Oxford) Div 3 Championship 1984, Div 2 Championship 1983
as Player:
International:

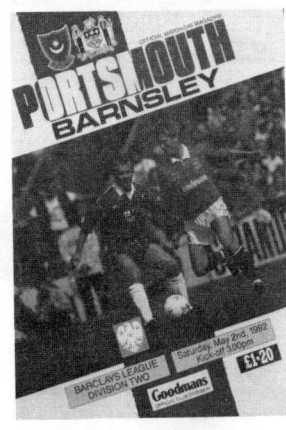

Value Rating: ★ ★ ★ ★

Programme Editor: Julie Baker

Price of 1992-93 Programme: £1.20
Number of Pages: 32
Subscriptions: Available from Club

Local Newspapers: Portsmouth Evening News

Local Radio Stations: Radio Victory, Radio Solent

Additional Publications on Club: Pompey – The History of Portsmouth Football Club, (Mike Neason, Mick Cooper and Doug Robinson, hardback £9.95).

LEADING LEAGUE GOALSCORERS
SEASONS 1979-80 – 1991-92

1979-80	CHRIS GARWOOD	17		1980-81	DAVID GREGORY	13
1981-82	BILLY RAFFERTY	17		1982-83	ALAN BILEY	22
1983-84	MARK HATELEY	21		1984-85	NEIL WEBB	16
1985-86	NICKY MORGAN	14		1986-87	MIKE QUINN	22
1987-88	KEVIN DILLON	9		1988-89	MIKE QUINN	18
1989-90	NEIL WHITTINGHAM	22		1990-91	MARTIN KUHL	13
					COLIN CLARKE	13

1991-92   **GUY WHITTINGHAM**   11

FRATTON PARK Frogmore Road, Portsmouth PO4 8RA

Capacity: 26,452   **Covered Standing:** 2,700   **Seating:** 6,652

Tel: Ground: 0705 731204   **Ticket Sales:** 0705 750825

GROUNDS

ATTENDANCES
Highest: 51,385 v Derby County, FA Cup 6th Round, 20.2.1949

Lowest: 2,499 v Wimbledon, Zenith Data, 1st Rnd, 5.12.1989

RECORD RECEIPTS (with previous records):
£208,000 v Nott'm Forest, FA Cup 6th Rnd, 7.3.1992
£174,000 v Tottenham H. FA Cup 5th Round, 18.2.1991
£122,000 v Southampton, FA Cup 4th Round, 28.1.1984
£59,042.50 v Cardiff City, Division 3, 12.3.1983
£39,521 v Middlesbrough, FA Cup 3rd Round, 9.1.1980
£18,002 v Arsenal, FA Cup 4th Round, 23.1.1971

FRATTON PARK
First game: v Southampton (Friendly), 2-0, 6.9.1899
First floodlit game: v Newcastle, 2.3.1953
2nd Set: v Burnley, 10.10.1962

Season Tickets:
Stands: from £175 to £245, juv/OAP £70 to £150
Ground: £125, juc/OAP £90

Executive Box Season Tickets: None

Cost of Stand Tickets: £12, £10, juv/OAP £6, £7
Terraces: £7, juv/OAP £3 to £5

Match and Ticket Information: All sections bookable 14 days in advance

Car Parking: Side-street parking only

Nearest Railway Station: Fratton (by Fratton Park), Portsmouth 0705 825711

How to get to the ground

From North and West: Use Motorway M27 and M275 and at end at roundabout take 2nd exit and in 0.2m at T road turn right A2047 into London Road. In 1.3m over railway bridge and turn left into Goldsmith Avenue. In 0.6m turn left into Frogmore Road for Portsmouth FC

From East: Use A27 then follow signs Southsea A2030. In 3m at roundabout turn left A288. Then turn right into Priory Crescent then take next turning right into Carisbrooke Road for Portsmouth FC

PORT VALE
Division 2

Formed: 1876   **Turned Professional:** 1885   **Ltd Co:** 1911

SPONSORED BY: Kalamazoo Business Systems   **NICKNAME:** The Valiants

President
J Burgess

Chairman
W T Bell MIMI

Directors
A Belfield (Vice-Chairman)
I McPherson
N C Tizley

Secretary
Eddie Harrison (0782 814134)

Team Manager
John Rudge

Coach
Bobby Downes

Youth Team Coach
Ian Miller

Physiotherapist
J Joyce

Stadium Manager
F W Lodey

Groundsman
R Fairbanks

Commercial Executive
D Hinde (0782-835524)

Club Statistician for the Directory
Philip Sherwin

So Port Vale's three year stay in the heady heights of the Second Division came to an end, but they can have no complaints as the team won the least matches, scored the fewest goals (joint with Plymouth) and gained the fewest points. Just why the club plummetted from a relatively safe mid-table position at Christmas to the foot of the table is harder to fathom.

The first half of the campaign gave no hint of what was to come even though goals were harder to come by as had been expected from the pre-season sales of Darren Beckford and Robbie Earle. Victory over first division Notts County to secure a first ever place in the Rumbelows Cup Third Round preceded a 2-2 draw at Liverpool in what was the club's best performance of the season. Unfortunately Liverpool were not caught again in the replay and just two weeks later it all began to go wrong.

Two unwanted club records, 17 league games without a win and 6 consecutive home defeats, dug a hole too deep to climb out of and something had to be done. Unusually for a club in this position, the manager's head was not called for by the fans, no doubt in view of the previous eight years of success, but coach Mike Pejic lost his job with youth coach Bobby Downes being promoted. Three wins in the next four games gave cause for optimism but they had left themselves too much to do even though they did not finally go down until the last day of the season.

Overall the defence wasn't to bad, only one team conceded less in the bottom ten, but by scoring so few goals the side was always under pressure, never more so than at home, conceeding the first goal on 15 out of 26 occasions. A reflection of the defensive record was born out by goalkeeper Mark Grew winning the supporters 'Player of the Year' award.

Record signing, Martin Foyle, did his best up front with 16 goals in all competitions but he had little support and the club's miserly total of 42 in the league was the lowest since 1965.

Attendances held up well in the circumstances and a good start to the following campaign could even see them increase despite the lower status. That's easier said than done though and there needs to be plenty of comings and goings in the summer months to inject some hope into the proceedings.

Phil Sherwin

Back row L-R: Robin van der Laan, Michael Harrison, Neil Aspin, Richard Clark, Ian Taylor, Keith Houchen, Peter Swan, Chris Gillard, Simon Mills, Dean Glover. **Middle row:** John Rudge (Manager), Jim Joyce (Physio), Nicky Cross, Ray Walker, Bradley Sandeman, Martin Foyle, Ian Miller (Youth Team Coach), Bobby Downes (First Team Coach). **Front row:** Trevor Wood, Chris Sulley, Andy Porter, John Jeffers, Kevin Kent, Paul Kerr, Paul Musselwhite.

PORT VALE

DIVISION TWO: 24th   **FA CUP:** 3rd RND   **RUMBELOWS CUP:** 3rd RND   **ZDS CUP:** 2nd RND

M	DATE	COMP.	VEN	OPPONENTS	RESULT	H/T	LGE POS	GOALSCORERS/GOAL TIMES	ATTEN-DANCE
1	A 17	BL	H	Oxford United	W 2-1	0-1		Foyle 51, 82	6,984
2	20	BL	A	Ipswich Town	L 1-2	1-1	10	Walker (pen) 35	(8,937)
3	24	BL	A	Portsmouth	L 0-1	0-1	10		(8,083)
4	27	BL	H	Barnsley	D 0-0	0-0	13		6,299
5	31	BL	H	Bristol City	D 1-1	1-0	11	Mills S 44	7,057
6	S 3	BL	A	Wolverhampton W	W 2-0	0-0	6	Houchen 61, 78	(16,115)
7	7	BL	H	Swindon Town	D 2-2	0-0	7	Foyle 69, 88	7,168
8	14	BL	A	Blackburn Rovers	L 0-1	0-1	13		(10,225)
9	18	BL	A	Brighton & H A	L 1-3	0-3	13	Houchen 90	(5,790)
10	21	BL	H	Southend United	D 0-0	0-0	18		5,988
11	24	RC 2/1	H	Notts County	W 2-1	1-0		Foyle 33, Mills B 61	4,722
12	28	BL	A	Charlton Athletic	L 0-2	0-1	19		(4,049)
13	O 1	ZDS 1	H	Blackburn Rovers	W 1-0	1-0		Foyle 39	2,355
14	5	BL	A	Cambridge United	W 1-0	0-0	17	Porter 85	5,991
15	9	RC 2/2	A	Notts County	L †2-3	1-0		Foyle 43, Houchen 55	(4,419)
16	12	BL	A	Grimsby Town	W 2-1	1-1	10	Mills S 32, Beckford 62	(8,218)
17	19	BL	H	Sunderland	D 3-3	1-0	14	Swan 1, Foyle 52, Van der Laan 56	7,525
18	23	ZDS 2	A	Leicester City	L 0-4	0-0			(4,853)
19	26	BL	A	Middlesbrough	L 0-1	0-1	14		(11,403)
20	29	RC 3	A	Liverpool	D 2-2	1-1		Van der Laan 7, Foyle 73	(21,553)
21	N 2	BL	A	Bristol Rovers	D 3-3	1-2	17	Foyle 35, 46, Van der Laan 60	(3,565)
22	6	BL	H	Derby County	W 1-0	0-0	14	Jalink 67	8,589
23	9	BL	H	Millwall	L 0-2	0-0	15		8,944
24	16	BL	A	Plymouth Argyle	L 0-1	0-0	15		(4,363)
25	20	RC 3R	H	Liverpool	L 1-4	1-3		Foyle 24	18,725
26	23	BL	A	Leicester City	W 1-0	1-0	14	Jeffers 1	(11,450)
27	30	BL	H	Watford	W 2-1	0-0	12	Foyle 68, Van der Laan 85	5,777
28	D 7	BL	A	Newcastle United	D 2-2	1-1	11	Hughes 43, Glover (pen) 63	(18,162)
29	13	BL	H	Tranmere Rovers	D 1-1	1-1	11	West 38	6,426
30	21	BL	H	Wolverhampton W	D 1-1	0-1	12	Van der Laan 87	8,480
31	26	BL	A	Barnsley	D 0-0	0-0	11		(8,843)
32	28	BL	A	Bristol City	L 0-3	0-2	14		(9,235)
33	J 1	BL	H	Ipswich Town	L 1-2	0-1	17	Hughes 55	8,075
34	4	FAC 3	A	Sunderland	L 0-3	0-2			(15,564)
35	11	BL	H	Portsmouth	L 0-2	0-2	17		5,925
36	18	BL	A	Oxford United	D 2-2	1-1	19	Houchen 19, Swan 80	(4,199)
37	F 1	BL	A	Sunderland	D 1-1	1-1	20	Foyle 1	(19,488)
38	8	BL	H	Middlesbrough	L 1-2	0-1	20	Mohan (og) 77	7,019
39	15	BL	H	Leicester City	L 1-2	1-1	20	Foyle 13	8,084
40	22	BL	A	Watford	D 0-0	0-0	19		(6,602)
41	29	BL	H	Newcastle United	L 0-1	0-1	21		10,321
42	M 6	BL	A	Tranmere Rovers	L 1-2	0-0	24	Jeffers 60	(8,477)
43	11	BL	A	Derby County	L 1-3	1-1	24	Jeffers 12	(14,983)
44	14	BL	H	Bristol Rovers	L 0-1	0-1	24		5,861
45	21	BL	A	Millwall	L 0-1	0-0	24		(6,148)
46	28	BL	H	Plymouth Argyle	W 1-0	1-0	24	Walker (pen) 33	5,310
47	31	BL	H	Blackburn Rovers	W 2-0	1-0	24	Van der Laan 27, Foyle 73	10,384
48	A 4	BL	A	Swindon Town	L 0-1	0-1	24		(8,014)
49	11	BL	H	Brighton & H A	W 2-1	0-0	22	Swan 71, Lowe 84	6,441
50	15	BL	A	Southend United	D 0-0	0-0	22		(4,462)
51	21	BL	H	Charlton Athletic	D 1-1	0-0	23	B Mills 52	8,461
52	25	BL	A	Cambridge United	L 2-4	1-0	23	B Mills 45, Lowe 74	(7,559)
53	M 2	BL	H	Grimsby Town	L 0-1	0-1	24		8,678

Best Home League Attendance: 10,384 v Blackburn Rovers   **Smallest:** 5,310 v Plymouth Argyle   **Av Home Att:** 7,382

Goal Scorers: **Compared with 90-91:** -693

League (42): Foyle 11, Van der Laan 5, Houchen 4, Swan 3, Jeffers 3, B Mills 2, Hughes 2, Lowe 2, Walker 2 (2 pens), Mills S 2, Glover (1 pen) Porter, Opponents, Jalink, Beckford, West

R/lows C (7): Foyle 4, Van der Laan, Mills B, Houchen

FA Cup (0):

ZDS Cup (1): Foyle

† = After extra-time

462

Grew M.	Mills S.	Hughes D.	Walker R.	Aspin N.	Glover D.	Jalink N.	Van der Laan R.	Houchen K.	Foyle M.	Kent K.	Swan P.	Mills B.	Webb A.	Jeffers J.	Porter A.	Parkin T.	Beckford J.	Kidd D.	Rushton D.	West C.	Williams A.	Cross N.	Allon J.	Lowe D.	Referee	
1	2	3	4	5	6	7	8	9	10	11	S	S													K Barratt	1
1	2	3	4	5	6	7	8	9	10	11*	12	S													G Willard	2
1	2	3	4	5	6	7	8	9*	10	11*	12	14													I Hemsley	3
1	2	3	4	5	6	7*	8	9	10		11		S	14											T Holbrook	4
1	2	3	4	5	6		8	9•	10		11	14			7	S									M Reed	5
1	2	3	4	5	6		8	9	10	S	S			11	7										R Lewis	6
1	2	3	4	5	6		8	9*	10		14	12		11	7*										L Dilkes	7
1	2	3	4	5	6	14	8	9*	10		12			11•	7										S Lodge	8
1	S	3•	4	5	6	7	8	9	10		14	2		11											M Pierce	9
1	2	3	4	5*	6	7•	8	9	10		14	12		11											R Groves	10
1	**2**	**3**	**4**		**6**	S	**8**	**9•**	**10**	**11**	**5**		**14**		**7**										**P Vanes**	**11**
1			4*		6	12	8		10	11	5	9	2	3	7•	14									A Gunn	12
1	**4**	**3**			**6**		**8**		**10**	**11**	**5**	**9**	**2***		**7**					**12**	S				**H King**	**13**
1	2	3			6		8		10	11*	5	9		12	4	7	S								K Hackett	14
1	**2**	**3**			**6**		**8**	**9**	**10**	**7***	**5**	**12**		**11•**	**4**		**14**								**K Breen**	**15**
1	2	3	11	6			8	9*	10		5	12			4	7	S								K Lupton	16
1	2	3	11	6		S	8		10		5	9		12	4	7*									V Callow	17
1	**2**	**3**	**11**	**6•**	**8**				**10**		**5***	**12**		**9**	**4**	**14**			**7**						**M Bodenham**	**18**
1	2	3		5	6	8			10	S		9		7	4	S	11								J Watson	19
1	**2**	**3**		**5**	**6**	**7**	**8•**		**10**		**9**	S		**11**	**4**		**14**								**A Ward**	**20**
1	2	3	S	5	6	7	8		10		9			11	4	S									D Frampton	21
1	2	3	S	5	6	7	8		10		9			11	4	S									G Singh	22
1	2	3		5	6	7	8		10•	12	9			11	4*	14									R Milford	23
1	2	3		5	6	7	8*		10	14		12		11	4•	9									C Wilkes	24
1	**2**	**3**		**5**	**6**	**7**	**8**		**10**		**9**	**12**	S	**11**	**4***										**L Shapter**	**25**
1		3		5	6	7	8		10	14	12•	2		11	4					9*					K Redfern	26
1		3		5	6	7	8		10	14	S			11	4•	2				9					D Allison	27
1	2	3		5	6	7	8	14	10					11	4	S				9•					D Phillips	28
1	2	3		5	6	7	8		10			S		11		S				9	4				D Gallagher	29
1	2	3		5	6	7	8		10			12	S	11						9*	4				T West	30
1	2	3		5	6	7	8	12	10		9*	S		11							4				E Parker	31
1	2	3		5	6	7	8	10*			9•	14		11	12						4				A Smith	32
1	2	3		5	6	7*	8	9	10	S		12		11							4				W Flood	33
1	**2**	**3**		**5**	**6**	**7***	**8**	**9**	**10**			**12**	**14**	**11***	**4**										**M Peck**	**34**
1	2	3		5	6	12	8	9	10		7	11*	4•		14										J Worrall	35
1	2	3	4		6	S	8	9	10	11	5			12	7*										R Shepherd	36
1	2	3	7		6	14	8	9•	10	S	5			11	4										J Kirby	37
1	2	3	7		6	12	8		10	14	5	9•		11	4*										R Hamer	38
1	S	3	4	2	6		8	9	10	7	5			11•							14				S Bell	39
1		3	4	9	6		8	S	10	7	5			11	2	S									P Scoble	40
1		3	4	2	6	14		9*	10	7	5			11	8•							12			R Pawley	41
1		3	4	2	12				10	S	5			11	8					7	9*				J Watson	42
1		3	4	2	6*	14*	8		10		5			11	7					9	12				H King	43
1		3	4	2	6		8		10	7	9			S	5					11*	12				B Coddington	44
1			4	2	6		8		10	12	9			3*	7	5					11*	12			K Morton	45
1		3	4	2	6		8		10	11	5						S				9*	12	7		M Reed	46
1		3	4	2	6		8		10		5	12		11			S				9*		7		T Holbrook	47
1	12	3	4	2	6		8		10	11	5						S				9*		7		R Milford	48
1	12	3	4	2	6		8				5	10•	14	11							9*		7		V Callow	49
1	2	3	4	5	6		8		S	10•	9			11	14								7		G Poll	50
1	2	3•	4	5	6		8		S	10		9		11	14								7		T West	51
1	2		4		6		8		S	10	5	9•		11	14	3							7		P Alcock	52
1	2		4	3	6		8		12	10	14	5		9*	11•								7		G Singh	53
46	31	42	26	42	46	20	43	18	43	13	27	13	3	27	30	4	4	1		5	5	7	2	8	League Appearances	
	2							8	3		10	6	8		6	2	3	1			1	4		1	Substitute Appearances	
4	4	4	1	2	4	2	4	2	4	2	4	0+3		3	4				0+2						R/lows Appearances	
1	1	1		1	1	1	1	1	1			0+1	0+1	1	1										FA Cup Appearances	
2	2	2		1	2	1	1	1	2	1+1	1		1	2	0+1		0+1	1							ZDS Cup Appearances	

Players on Loan: Beckford (Manchester City), West (West Brom A.), Williams (Leeds Utd), Allon (Chelsea), Lowe (Ipswich Town)

PORT VALE

Club Colours: White shirts with black flashes, black shorts, black & white stockings
Change Colours: All yellow
Reserves League: Pontins Central League Division 2   **Youth League:** Midland Purity Youth League

Previous Name: Burslem Port Vale 1884-1909
Previous Managers: T Clare 1905-06   S Gleaves 1906-07   A Walker 1911-13   H Myatt 1913-14   T Holford 1914-17   J Cameron 1918-19   J Schofield 1919-29   T Morgan 1929-32   T Holford 1932-36   W Cresswell 1936-37   T Morgan 1937-39   W Frith 1944-46   G Hodgson 1946-51   I Powell 1951   F Steele 1951-57   N Low 1957-62   F Steele 1962-65   J Mudie 1965-67   S Matthews 1967-68   G Lee 1968-74   R Sproson 1974-77   C Harper 1977   R Smith 1977-78   D Butler 1978-79   A Bloor 1979   J McGrath 1979-83
Honours: Champions Division 3N 1929-30, 1953-54   Champions Division 4 1958-59
League Career: Original Member Division 2 1892   Not re-elected to Division 2 1896   Re-elected to Division 2 1898   Resigned from Division 2 1907   **Returned to Division 2 1919   Relegated to Div 3N 1928-29   Promoted to Div 2 1929-30   Relegated to Div 3N 1935-36   Transfered to Div 3S 1938   Transfered to Div 3N 1952   Promoted to Div 2 1953-54   Relegated to Div 3S 1956-57   Original Members of Division 4 1958   Promoted to Div 3 1958-59   Relegated to Div 4 1964-65   Promoted to Div 3 1969-70   Relegated to Div 4 1977-78   Promoted to Div 3 1982-83   Relegated to Div 4 1983-84   Promoted to Div 3 1985-86   Promoted to Div 2 1988-89   Relegated to Div 3 1991-92

CLUB RECORDS

Most Appearances for Club: Roy Sproson 1950-72: League 755+5, FA Cup 65, League Cup 11   **Total 831+5**
Most Capped Player: Sammy Morgan (Northern Ireland) 7, 1972-73
Record Goalscorer in a Match: Stewart Littlewood 6 v Chesterfield, 9-1, Div 2, 24.9.1932
Record League Goalscorer in a Season: Wilf Kirkham, 38, Div 2, 1926-27   **In All Competitions:** Wilf Kirkham, 41 (League 38, FA Cup 3) 1926-27
Record League Goalscorer in a Career: Wilf Kirkham, 154, 1923-29 & 1931-33   **In All Competitions:** Wilf Kirkham, 165, (League 154, FA Cup 11) 1923-29 & 1931-33
Record Transfer Fee Received: £925,000 from Norwich City for Darren Beckford, June 1991
Record Transfer Fee Paid: £375,000 to Oxford United for Martin Foyle, June 1991
Best Performances: League: 5th Division 2, 1930-31   **FA Cup:** Semi-Finalists 1953-54   **League Cup:** 3rd Round replay 1991-92
Most League Points: (3pts for win) 88, Division 4, 1982-83   (2pts for win) 69, Division 3N, 1953-54
Record League Victory and Most Goals Scored in a League Match: 9-1 v Chesterfield, Div 2, 24.9.1932   8-0 v Gateshead, Div 4, 1958-59
Most Goals Scored in a First Class Cup Tie: 8-2 v Alfreton (a), 6th Qual. Rnd, 13.12.1924
Record League Defeat: 0-10 v Sheffield United, Div 2, 10.12.1892   0-10 v Notts County, Div 2, 26.2.1895
Record Cup Defeat: 0-7 v Small Heath, FA Cup 5th Qual., 10.12.1898
Oldest Player in a League Match: Tom Holford, 46 years 3 months, 5.4.1924
Youngest Player in a League Match: Malcolm McKenzie, 15 years 347 days, 12.4.1965

LONGEST LEAGUE RUNS	
of undefeated matches: 19 (1969)	**of league matches without a win:** 17 (1991-92)
of undefeated home matches: 42 (1952-54)	**of undefeated away matches:** 10 (1969)
without home win: 12 (1978)	**without an away win:** 29 (1903-04)
of league wins: 8 (1893)	**of home wins:** 12 (1952, 1953)
of league defeats: 9 (1957)	**of away wins:** 4 (1930)

PORT VALE

PLAYERS NAME Honours	Ht	Wt	Birthdate	Birthplace Transfers	Contract Date	Clubs	League	L/Cup	FA Cup	Other	Lg	L/C	FAC	Oth
GOALKEEPERS														
Paul Musselwhite	6.2	12.9	22.12.68	Portsmouth		Portsmouth								
				f	28.06.88	Scunthorpe Utd	132	11	7	13				
				£20,000	30.07.92	Port Vale								
Trevor Wood	6.0	12.6	03.11.68	Jersey	30.12.87	Brighton & H.A. (A)								
					08.07.88	Port Vale	37	2	2	2				
DEFENDERS														
Neil Aspin	6.0	12.6	12.04.65	Gateshead	06.10.82	Leeds Utd. (A)	203+4	9	17	11	5	1		
				£200,000	28.07.89	Port Vale	123+2	8	6	4				
Dean Glover	5.9	11.2	29.12.63	West Bromwich	30.12.81	Aston Villa	25+3	7	3	1		1		
				Loan	17.10.86	Sheffield Utd	5							
					17.06.87	Middlesbrough	44+6	4	5	7	5			2
				£200,000	03.02.89	Port Vale	153	10	6	8	6			
Darren Hughes	5.11	10.11	06.10.65	Prescot	08.10.83	Everton (A)	3							
FAYC'84				Free	13.06.85	Shrewsbury Town	34+3	5+1	1	2	1			
				£35,000	30.09.86	Brighton & H.A	26		2	1	2			
				£10,000	02.10.87	Port Vale	183+1	12	14	12	4			
Chris Sulley	5.9	11.0	03.12.59	Camberwell	07.08.78	Chelsea (A)								
AMC'84; FMC'87.					12.03.81	Bournemouth	205+1	14	18	10	3			
				£15,000	07.07.86	Dundee Utd.	7			1				
				£15,000	10.04.87	Blackburn Rovers	134+1	5	6	9	3			
				Free	31.07.92	Port Vale								
Peter Swan	6.2	12.0	28.09.66	Leeds	06.08.84	Leeds Utd. (A)	43+6	3	3	1+2	11	2		
				£200,000	23.03.89	Hull City	76+4	2+3	2	1	24	1		
				£300,000	16.08.91	Port Vale	27+6	4		2	3			
MIDFIELD														
John Jeffers	5.10	10.10			13.10.86	Liverpool								
				Loan	11.12.88	Port Vale	4+1		1					
				£30,000	23.03.89	Port Vale	101+13	7	5	8	6			1
Simon Mills	5.8	11.4	16.08.64	Sheffield	18.08.82	Sheffield Wed. (A)	1+4		1					
E:Y.7					13.06.85	York City	97+2	8	13	6	5	1	2	1
				£35,000	24.12.87	Port Vale	177+4	13	8	10+1	8			
Andy Porter	5.9	11.2	17.09.68	Holmes Chapel	29.06.87	Port Vale (A)	114+15	10	4+2	11	3			
Robin Van der Laan	5.10	12.0	05.09.68	Schiedam		Wageningen								
				£80,000	21.02.91	Port Vale	53+8	4	1	1	9	1		
Ray Walker	5.10	12.0	28.09.63	North Shields	26.09.81	Aston Villa (A)	15+8	2+1	2					
E:Y6,FAYC'80				Loan	07.09.84	Port Vale	15				1			
				£12,000	05.08.86	Port Vale	238+3	14	16	16	23	1	3	2
FORWARDS														
Nicky Cross	5.9	11.2	07.02.61	Birmingham	12.02.79	West Brom A. (A)	68+37	6+2	5	0+1	15	2	1	
				£48,000	15.08.85	Walsall	107+2	10	12+1	6+1	45	2	3	1
				£65,000	22.01.88	Leicester City	54+4	3+2	1	1	10	1		
				£125,000	28.06.89	Port Vale	58+11	2+3	3	3	15		1	1
Martin Foyle	5.10	11.2	02.05.63	Salisbury	13.08.80	Southampton (A)	6+6	0+2			1	2		
				£10,000	03.08.84	Aldershot	98	10	8	6	35	5	5	
				£140,000	26.03.87	Oxford Utd	120+6	16	5	3+1	36	4	3	1
				£375,000	25.06.91	Port Vale	43	4	1	2	11	4		1
Keith Houchen	6.2	11.4	25.07.60	Middlesbrough		Chesterfield								
FAC'87				Free	09.02.78	Hartlepool Utd	160+10	8	4+1		65	1		
				£25,000	26.03.82	Leyton Orient	74+2	3	3	0+1	20	1		
				£151,000	22.03.84	York City	56+11	6	9+2	4	19	3	3	2
				£40,000	28.03.86	Scunthorpe Utd	9				2			
				£60,000	03.07.86	Coventry City	43+11	2+1	5+1	2+1	7		5	
				£100,000		Hibernian	51+6	5	6	4	11	1	4	1
				£100,000	09.08.91	Port Vale	18+3	2	1		4	1		
Kevin Kent	5.8	11.0	19.03.65	Stoke	31.12.82	West Brom A. (A)	1+1							
FRT'87					09.07.84	Newport Co	23+10	2	0+1	3+1	1			1
					15.08.85	Mansfield Town	223+6	10	13	21+2	35	2	4	4
				£80,000	22.03.91	Port Vale	24+10	2		1				
Brian Mills	5.9	10.10	26.12.71	Swynnerton	03.04.90	Port Vale (T)	14+9	0+3	0+1	1+1	4	1		
Paul Kerr	5.8	11.11	09.06.64	Portsmouth	18.05.82	Aston Villa	16+8	5+1	2	0+2	3	2	1	
				£50,000	17.01.86	Middlesbrough	114+11	10	9+2	13+3	13	1	3	1
				£100,000	28.03.91	Millwall	42+2	2	2	3	12		1	
				£200,000	10.07.92	Port Vale								
Bradley Sandeman	5.10	10.8	24.02.70	Northampton	14.07.88	Northampton T.	28+30	2+3	2	6+1	3			
				£10,000	22.02.91	Maidstone	55	2	1	4	7			
				Free	13.07.92	Port Vale								
ADDITIONAL CONTRACT PLAYERS														
Ian Baints					08.07.91	Port Vale								
Richard Clark						Cheltenham Town								
				Nominal Fee	14.07.92	Port Vale								
(F) Michael Harrison	6.1		19.01.73	Cannock	31.07.91	Port Vale								
Paul W. Miller						Port Vale								
				Loan	11.10.90	Hereford Utd	5				2			
Ian K Taylor						Moor Green								
				£15,000	13.07.92	Port Vale								

LEADING LEAGUE GOALSCORERS SEASONS 1985-86 – 1991-92

1985-86	**ROBBIE EARLE**	15		1986-87	**ANDY JONES**	31
1987-88	**DARREN BECKFORD**	9		1988-89	**DARREN BECKFORD**	20
1989-90	**DARREN BECKFORD**	17		1990-91	**DARREN BECKFORD**	21
	1991-92	**MARTIN FOYLE**	**11**			

VALE PARK Burslem, Stoke-on-Trent ST6 1AW

Capacity: 21,792   **Covered Standing:**   **Seating:** 12,442

Tel: Ground: 0782 814134   **Ticket Sales:** As ground number   **Clubcall:** 0898 12 16 36

All premium rate calls (0898/0891) cost 36p per minute cheap rate and 48p per minute at all other times. Call costings correct at time of going to press.

ATTENDANCES
Highest: 50,000 v Aston Villa, FA Cup Round 5, 20.2.1960
Lowest: 994 v Hereford United, Freight Rover Trophy, 22.12.1986

RECORD RECEIPTS:
£126,434 v Liverpool, Lge Cup 3 Rnd Replay, 20.11.91
£121,299 v Man. City, FA Cup 4th Rnd, 26.1.1990

VALE PARK
First game: v Newport Co., Div 3S, 24.8.1950
First floodlit game: v West Brom (Friendly), 24.9.1958

Season Tickets:
Stands: from £130 to £180
Ground: £120

Vice-Presidents: (new members) £425

Cost of Stand Tickets: Railway Stand (blocks A&B): £9 adult £6 juv/OAP; Railway Paddock: £7 adult £5.50 juv/OAP; Family Stand: £6, £4 juv/OAP; Bycars Stand: £6.50, £5.50 juv/OAP
Terraces: £6, £4 juv/OAP (home section only); Family Terrace: £5, £3.50 juv/OAP

Match and Ticket Information: Personal or postal applications to the ticket office 21 days prior to respective fixture

Car Parking: Parking (ample) behind the Railway Stand, on Hamil Road car park and street parking

Nearest Railway Station: Longport, Stoke-on-Trent (0782 411411)

How to get to the ground

From North: Use Motorway M6 until Junction 16 then join A500 S.P. Stoke. In 5.9m branch left and at roundabout take 1st exit A527. In 0.4m turn right B5051 into Newcastle Street and at end over crossroads into Moorland Road. Shortly turn left into Hamil Road for Port Vale FC
From East: Use A50 or A52 into Stoke-on-Trent then follow signs Burslem A50 into Waterloo Road. At Burslem crossroads turn right into Moorland Road. Shortly turn left into Hamil Road for Port Vale FC
From South and West: Use Motorway M6 until Junction 15 then A5006 and A500. In 6.3m branch left and at roundabout take 3rd exit A527. In 0.4m turn right B5051 into Newcastle Street and at end over crossroads into Moorland Road. Shortly turn left into Hamil Road for Port Vale FC

Value Rating: ★ ★ ★

Programme Editor: The secretary

Price of 1992-93 Programme: £1
Number of Pages: 32
Subscriptions: (Home only) £28.50, (Home and away) £53 inc postage

Local Newspapers: Staffordshire Evening Sentinel, North Staffordshire Advertiser

Local Radio Stations: Radio Stoke, Signal Radio

PRESTON NORTH END Division 2

Formed: 1881   **Turned Professional:** 1885   **Ltd Co:** 1893

SPONSORED BY: Ribble Valley Shelving Systems   **NICKNAME:** The Lillywhites

President
Tom Finney, OBE, CBE, JP

Vice-President
T C Nicholson, JP, FCIOB

Chairman
Keith W Leeming

Vice-Chairman
M J Woodhouse

Directors
E Griffith BVSc,MRCVS(Company Sec)
J E Starkie LL.B (Lond)
J T Garratt   D Shaw
M J Woodhouse (Jnr)

Life Member
A R W Jones JP,FRICS

Secretary
Derek J Allan (0772 795919)

Team Manager
Les Chapman

Youth Devolopment Officer/Coach
Sam Allardyce

Chief Executive
Paul Agnew (0772 795465,795156)

Assistant Manager
Walter Joyce

Community Development Officer
Ian Johnstone

Hon.Medical Officer
Dr.N S McCraith MB,Ch B

Physiotherapist
Mark Leather

Club Statistician for the Directory
Lawrence Bland

ANOTHER disappointing season, the third in a row struggling to avoid relegation to Division Four. The same final position as last season, and we were still in danger of the drop until the final game, as in 1989-90.

"Be patient' said the Chairman, but the fans were becoming impatient with the lack of spending and success. Perhaps we are envious of the money being spent at Blackburn, a fraction of it would do wonders at Deepdale.

North End reached the final of the pre-season Manx Lancashire Cup, but lost again, this time 1-4 at Wigan. In the Rumbelows Cup, we were leading 5-2 at one stage of the 1st leg in Round One, but lost at Scarborough after extra-time in the 2nd leg. The F.A. Cup was better, a 1-0 win at Mansfield at the second attempt, a flattering 5-1 win over Conference side Witton Albion, before outplaying Sheffield Wednesday, but losing 0-2. A poor home defeat by Hull City in Round One of the Autoglass ended our cup aspirations.

With the club losing money, prospects weren't good for the season. Pre-season transfers were Ian Bogie to Millwall and Nathan Peel to Sheffield United. Signings were few, George Berry (ex-Peterborough), but he soon moved to Aldershot (later Stafford Rangers) and Gareth Ainsworth (ex-Blackburn). After the club's slide from ninth on November 9th to 22nd on March 14th, with the fans demonstrating for some action, money was found to sign Colin Greenall from Bury. This saw a revival with only two defeats in the last ten games. The usual crop of injuries disrupted the side, and a record five players came on loan – Tim Allpress (Luton), Paul Cross (Barnsley), Julian James (Luton), Lennie Johnrose (Blackburn) and Neil Whitworth (Manchester United). Tony Hancock had his contract bought out, John Thomas was released and he eventually joined Hartlepools and Roy Tunks was sacked as coach.

The Youth Policy, now five years old, began to show some results, with Lee Ashcroft and Lee Cartwright joining Martin James as regular first teamers. Lee Cartwight was a surprise choice for the 'Player of the Season', and Lee Ashcroft came on as substitute for England under-21s in Hungary on May 12th 1992. Two more juniors – David Christie and Stephen Finney made their league debuts. The youth team again reached the final of the Lancashire Youth Cup, but another defeat, this time 0-4 at home to Manchester City.

At the end of the season, the club began a major cost-cutting and re-building programme, with captain Warren Joyce being transferred to Plymouth Argyle. The club released Gareth Ainsworth, David Burrows, Nigel Greenwood, Adrian Hughes, Matthew Lambert, Steve Senior, Adam Siddall, Gary Swann, Dave Thompson, Neil Williams, Jeff Wrightson and YTS players Kerry O'Connor, Jamie Close, Chris Williams and Chris Schofield.   **Lawrence Bland**

Back row L-R: Sam Allardyce (Youth team coach), Gary McCullough, Adam Critchley, David Flitcroft, Colin Greenall, David Christie, Ronnie Jepson (now Exeter), Mike Flynn, Ryan Kidd, Stephen Finney, David Eaves, Simon Burton, Craig Moylon, Walter Joyce (Asst. Manager). **Front row:** Martin James, Jason Kerfott, Lee Cartwright, Lee Ashcroft, John Bagnall, Les Chapman (manager), Simon Farnworth, John Tinkler, Lee Fowler, Graham Shaw (now Stoke City), Jonathan Davidson.

PRESTON NORTH END

DIVISION THREE: 17th   **FA CUP:** 3rd RND   **RUMBELOWS CUP:** 1st RND   **AUTOGLASS:** Prelim.

M	DATE		COMP.	VEN	OPPONENTS	RESULT	H/T	LGE POS	GOALSCORERS/GOAL TIMES	ATTEN-DANCE
1	A	17	BL	A	Peterborough Utd	L	0-1	0-0			(6,036)
2		20	RC 1/1	H	Scarborough	W	5-4	2-2		Wrightson 3, Swann 30, 71, Shaw 47, Joyce (pen) 61	2,683
3		24	BL	H	Torquay United	W	3-0	1-0	7	Shaw 25, Ashcroft 62, Greenwood 86	3,654
4		28	RC 1/2	A	Scarborough	L	†1-3	1-0		Joyce 18	(2,035)
5		30	BL	A	Stockport County	L	0-2	0-2	9		(5,405)
6	S	3	BL	H	Bournemouth	D	2-2	0-1		James M 76, Greenwood 83	3,170
7		7	BL	H	Bradford City	D	1-1	0-0	18	Joyce (pen) 89	4,160
8		14	BL	A	Swansea City	D	2-2	1-1	18	Shaw 35, 88	(3,170)
9		17	BL	A	Leyton Orient	D	0-0	0-0	18		(3,296)
10		21	BL	H	Stoke City	D	2-2	1-2	19	Jepson 7, Swann 60	6,345
11		28	BL	A	Birmingham City	L	1-3	1-1	20	Shaw 44	(8,760)
12	O	1	BL	H	West Bromwich A.	W	2-0	0-0	15	Swann 46, Senior 69	5,293
13		12	BL	A	Bury	W	3-2	1-2	15	Ashcroft 43, Greenwood 71, Shaw 75	(4,265)
14		19	BL	H	Huddersfield Town	W	1-0	0-0	11	James M 82	6,866
15		22	AGT Pre	A	Rochdale	D	1-1	0-0		Joyce 62	(1,255)
16		26	BL	A	Fulham	L	0-1	0-1	13		(4,022)
17	N	2	BL	A	Chester City	L	2-3	0-1	15	Shaw 47, Swann 80	(1,219)
18		5	BL	H	Wigan Athletic	W	3-0	2-0	13	Swann 6, Joyce 36, 61 (pen)	3,657
19		9	BL	H	Darlington	W	2-1	0-0	9	Thomas 76, Shaw 82	4,643
20		19	AGT Pre	H	Bolton Wanderers	W	2-1	1-0		Thomas 32, Joyce 63	2,709
21		23	BL	A	Bolton Wanderers	L	0-1	0-0	11		(7,033)
22		27	FAC 1	A	Mansfield Town	W	1-0	0-0		Thomas 90	(7,509)
23		30	BL	A	Hull City	D	2-2	0-1	11	Thomas 51, Shaw 57	(4,280)
24	D	7	FAC 2	H	Witton Albion	W	5-1	3-0		Shaw 29, Swann 31, Senior 32, Flynn 59, Greenwood 88	6,736
25		14	BL	H	Hartlepool United	L	1-4	0-2	14	Ashcroft 62	5,032
26		20	BL	A	Torquay United	L	0-1	0-1	15		(2,183)
27		26	BL	H	Stockport County	W	3-2	2-1	13	Swann 11, Shaw (pen) 26, James M 62	6,782
28		28	BL	H	Peterborough Utd	D	1-1	0-1	13	Cartwright 48	5,200
29	J	1	BL	A	Bournemouth	L	0-1	0-1	16		(5,508)
30		4	FAC 3	H	Sheffield Wed.	L	0-2	0-0			14,337
31		11	BL	A	Shrewsbury Town	L	0-2	0-0	16		(3,154)
32		14	AGT Pre	H	Hull City	L	†2-3	1-1		Thomas 35, Ainsworth 88	2,152
33		18	BL	H	Exeter City	L	1-3	0-2	18	Lambert 83	3,585
34		25	BL	A	Brentford	L	0-1	0-1	19		(7,559)
35	F	1	BL	A	Huddersfield Town	W	2-1	0-0	17	Shaw 73, Cartwright 81	(6,700)
36		8	BL	H	Fulham	L	1-2	0-2	19	Johnrose 60	3,878
37		11	BL	H	Hull City	W	3-1	1-1	17	Williams 20, Jepson 55, 59	2,932
38		15	BL	A	Hartlepool United	L	0-2	0-0	18		(2,140)
39		22	BL	H	Shrewsbury Town	D	2-2	0-0	18	James M 66, Wrightson 81	3,342
40		29	BL	A	Reading	D	2-2	0-2	18	Lambert 49, Shaw 70	(3,390)
41	M	3	BL	A	Exeter City	L	1-4	1-2	19	Ashcroft 33	(2,214)
42		7	BL	H	Brentford	W	3-2	2-2	17	Shaw 14, Thompson 39, Ashcroft 82	3,548
43		10	BL	A	Wigan Athletic	L	0-3	0-1	20		(3,364)
44		14	BL	H	Chester City	L	0-3	0-2	22		3,909
45		21	BL	A	Darlington	W	2-0	0-0	19	Jepson 46, 87	(2,270)
46		28	BL	H	Bolton Wanderers	W	2-1	1-0	20	Joyce (pen) 36, Flynn 65	7,327
47		31	BL	H	Swansea City	D	1-1	1-0	20	Greenall 34	3,637
48	A	4	BL	A	Bradford City	D	1-1	0-1	19	Shaw 58	(6,044)
49		11	BL	H	Leyton Orient	W	2-1	0-0	18	Flynn 51, Howard (og) 80	3,926
50		14	BL	H	Reading	D	1-1	1-0	18	Cartwright 24	3,203
51		18	BL	A	Stoke City	L	1-2	1-1	18	Thompson 20	(16,151)
52		21	BL	H	Birmingham City	W	3-2	2-0	17	Joyce 2, Flynn 33, Shaw 55	7,738
53		25	BL	A	West Bromwich A.	L	0-3	0-1	17		(11,318)
54	M	2	BL	H	Bury	W	2-0	1-0	17	Joyce 29, Finney 75	6,932

Best Home League Attendance: 7,738 v Birmingham City   **Smallest:** 2,932 v Hull City   **Av Home Att:** 4,729

Goal Scorers: **Compared with 90-91: -513**

League (61): Shaw 14 (1 pen), Joyce 6 (3 pens), Ashcroft 5, Jepson 5, Swann 5, James M 4, Cartwright 3, Flynn 3, Greenwood 3, Lambert 2, Thomas 2, Thompson 2, Williams, Opponents, Greenall, Senior, Finney, Wrightson, Johnrose

R/lows C (6): Swann 2, Joyce 2 (1 pen), Wrightson, Shaw

FA Cup (6): Greenwood, Shaw, Thomas, Senior, Flynn, Swann

Autoglass (5): Joyce 2, Thomas 2, Ainsworth   † = After extra-time

1991-92

Farnworth S.	Senior S.	Swann G.	Wrightson J.	Flynn M.	Berry G.	Thompson D.	Joyce W.	Jepson R.	Shaw G.	James M.	Williams N.	Lambert M.	Ashcroft L.	Greenwood N.	Kelly A.	James J. (L)	Cartwright L.	Cross P. (L)	Thomas J.	Allpress T. (L)	Hughes A.	Ainsworth G.	Whitworth N. (L)	Johnrose L. (L)	Greenall C.	Referee	
1	2	3	4	5	6	7	8	9	10	11	S	S														J Key	1
1†	2	3	4	5	6	7	8	9	10	11				S	S											**M Reed**	2
1	2		4	6	5			8	9*	10	3	7	S	11	12											J Lloyd	3
1	2*	4	6	5		14	12	8	9	10	3		7*	11												**A Wilkie**	4
1	2	8•	6	5	7			9	10	3	14	4*	12	11												R Nixon	5
	2	8	6	5	3	7*	4	9	10	11	S			12	1											K Redfern	6
	2	4	3	5	6*		8	9	10	11			12	7	1											A Dawson	7
	2	4	3	5			12	9	10	11			7		1	6	8*									K Cooper	8
	2	11	6	5			12	8		10•	3		7*		1	4	14									I Borrett	9
	2	4	3	5		12	8	9	10	11			7*		1	6	S									I Cruikshanks	10
	2	4	7	5				8	10	11					1	6	S	3	12							B Coddington	11
	2	4	7	5				8	10	11			9		1	6	S	3	S							R Poulain	12
	2•	4	7	5			12	8	10		14		11	9	1	6	3									K Breen	13
	2	4	6	5			12	8	10	11	S		7	9*	1		3									P Danson	14
	2	4	6	5			12	8	10	11*	S		7		1				3	9						**G Singh**	15
	2	4	6	5			12	8	10				7		1		11	3	9*							G Willard	16
	2*	4	3	5			9	8	10	11•	12			7	1		14			6						D Phillips	17
		4	3	5			9	8	10	11	2		7		1		S	S	6							A Smith	18
	2	4*	3	5			9•	8	10	11	14		7		1		12		6							V Callow	19
	2	4	3	5				8	10	11	S		7		1		S			9	6					**P Harrison**	20
	2	4	3*	5			8•		10	11	12		7	14	1					9	6					D Allison	21
	2	4	3	5					10	11	S		7	S	1		8			9	6					**J Key**	22
	2	4	3	5					10	11			7	12	1		8			9*	6	S				S Lodge	23
	2	4	3	5					10	11*	S		7	12	1		8			9	6					**A Smith**	24
	2	4	3	5					10		12		7	11•	1		8			9	6*	14				J Lloyd	25
	2		3	5					10		6*		7	11	1		8			9	12	4				C Wilkes	26
	2	4	3	5					10	11			7	9*	1		8			12	S	6				T West	27
	2	4	3	5					10	11			7	9*	1		8			12	S	6				P Vanes	28
	2	4	3	5			12		10•				7		1		8			9	11*	6				A Gunn	29
1	2	4	3	5			11*		10		S		7				8			9	6					**R Shepherd**	30
1	2	4	3	5					10*		S		7				8			9	6	11				P Wright	31
1	2	4	3	5•					10			12	7				8			9	6*	11				**J Rushton**	32
1	2	4	3•						10			14	7				8		9†		6	11	5			M Brandwood	33
1	2	4	S						12	11	3		7	10			8				6		5	9*		D Gallagher	34
1	2*	4	3						10•	11	12		7	9			8				6	14	5			G Singh	35
1	2	11	3	5					10	14			7•	9			8			4*	6	12				A Dawson	36
1	2	4	5				9*		10	11	3		7				8				S	6	12			G Ashby	37
1	2	S	4	5					10	11	3		7	9			8				S	6				A Flood	38
	2	S	4	5			9†		10	3	11	S	7		1		8				6					K Lupton	39
	2†	12	4	5			9		10	3	11	7•		3	14		8				6*					M Pierce	40
	2	8	6	5			12	9*	10	11	14	3•	7		1		4									R Groves	41
1	2	S	3	5			9*	8	10	11	12		7				4				6					R Hart	42
1	2		3	5			9	8	10	11	12		7				4*				6	S				G Courtney	43
1	S		3	5			9	8	12	10	11	2*	7				4				6					D Shadwell	44
1	S	6		5			11	8	9	10	3	2	7				4				S					S Bell	45
1				5			11	8	9	10	3	2		7			4				S				6	J Lloyd	46
1	S			5			11	8	9	10*	3	2	7				4						12		6	A Bennett	47
1	7*	S		5			11	8	9	10	3	2					4						12		6	T Holbrook	48
1				5			11	8	9	10	3	2	7*				4								6	W Burns	49
1		5					11	8	9	10	3	2	7				4				S				6	A Wilkie	50
1	S			5			11	8	9*	10	3	2	7				4								6	B Hill	51
1	S			5			11	8	9	10	3	2	7				4								6	K Redfern	52
1		12		5			11*	8	9•	10	3	2	7				4								6	P Durkin	53
1	S			5			11	8	9*	10	3	2	7				4								6	L Dilkes	54
23	35	28	36	43	4	18	28	23	45	36	17	7	35	16	23	6	31	5	8	7	14	2	6	1	9	**League Appearances**	
	1					7	1	1		1	9	4	3	4			2		3	2	1	3			2	**Substitute Appearances**	
2	2	2	2	2	1+1	1+1	2	2	2	2	1		1		1											**R/lows Appearances**	
1	3	3	3	3			1		3	2			3		0+1	2	3		3	2	1					**FA Cup Appearances**	
1	3	3	3	3		2		3	2		2		0+1	3		2	1	1	3	1	1	1	1			**Autoglass Appearances**	

Also Played: Posn.(Game): Kerfoot S(7,8)14(29,53)12(30,31), Christie 12(49,51)S(52), Eaves S(26,49,50), Finney 14(32)12(33,54).
Players on Loan: James J (Luton Town), Cross (Barnsley), Allpress (Luton Town), Whitworth (Man. Utd), Johnrose (Blackburn Rov.)

PRESTON NORTH END

Club Colours: White shirts, black shorts, black stockings with white & yellow trim
Change Colours: All yellow
Reserves League: Central League Div 2   **Youth Team:** Lancashire League Div 2

Previous Managers: 1919 V Hayes   1924 T Lawrence   1925 F Richards   1927 A Gibson   1931-32 L Hyde   1932-36 No Manager   1936-37 T Muirhead   1937-49 No Manager   1949-53 W Scott   1953-54 Scot Symon   1954-56 F Hill   1956-61 C Britton   1961-68 J Milne   1968-70 R Seith   1970-73 A Ball (Snr)   1973 F Lord (Caretaker)   1973-75 R Charlton   1975-77 H Catterick   1977-81 N Stiles   1981 T Docherty   1981-83 G Lee   1983-85 A Kelly   1985 T Booth   1986 B Kidd   1986 J Clark (Caretaker)   J McGrath 1986-90
Honours: Champions Div 1 *1888-89 (first winners), 1889-90   Champions Div 2, 1903-04, 1912-13, 1950-51   Champions Div 3 1970-71   FA Cup Winners *1889, 1938
*League and FA Cup Double
League Career: Original Members of Football League 1888   Relegated to Div 2 1900-01   Promoted to Div 1 1903-04
Relegated to Div 2 1911-12   Promoted to Div 1 1912-13   Relegated to Div 2 1913-14   Promoted to Div 1 1914-15
Relegated to Div 2 1924-25   Promoted to Div 1 1933-34   Relegated to Div 2 1948-49   Promoted to Div 1 1950-51
Relegated to Div 2 1960-61   Relegated to Div 3 1969-70   Promoted to Div 2 1970-71   Relegated to Div 3 1973-74
Promoted to Div 2 1977-78   Relegated to Div 3 1980-81   Relegated to Div 4 1984-85   Promoted to Div 3 1986-87

CLUB RECORDS

Most Appearances for Club: Alan Kelly (1961-75): League 447 + Cup games 65 **Total 512**
Most Capped Player: Tom Finney, 76 England
Record Goalscorer in a Match: Jimmy Ross, 8 v Hyde (h), 26-0, 1st Round FA Cup, 15.10.1887
Record League Goalscorer in a Season: Ted Harper 37, Div 2, 1932-33   **In All Competitions:** Ted Harper 37 (League 37) 1932-33
Record League Goalscorer in a Career: Tom Finney 187   **In All Competitions:** Tom Finney 210 (League 187 + FA Cup 23) 1946-60
Record Transfer Fee Received: £765,000 Manchester City for Michael Robinson, June 1979
Record Transfer Fee Paid: £250,000 to Stoke City for Tony Ellis, August 1992
Best Performances: League: Champions Div 1 (2)   **FA Cup:** Winners (2)   **League Cup:** 4th Round 1963, 1966, 1972, 1981
Most League Points: (2pts for win) 61, Div 4, 1970-71   (3pts for win) 90 1986-87
Most League Goals: 100 Div 2, 1927-28   100 Div 1, 1957-58
Record League Victory: 10-0 v Stoke City (h), Div 1, 14.9.1889
Most Goals Scored in a Cup Tie: 26-0 v Hyde, FA Cup 1st Round, 15.10.1887
Record League Defeat: 0-7 v Blackpool (h), Div 1, 1.5.1948   0-7 v Nottingham Forest (a), Div 2, 9.4.1927
Record Cup Defeat: 0-6 v Charlton Athletic, FA Cup Round 5, 1945-46
Oldest Player in a League Match: Bob Kelly 40 years 50 days, 5.1.1935 v Everton (h)
Youngest Player in a League Match: Steve Doyle, 16 years 166 days, 15.11.1974 v Tranmere Rovers (a)

LONGEST LEAGUE RUNS	
of undefeated matches: 23 (1888-89)	**of league matches without a win:** 15 (1923)
of undefeated home matches: 31 (1903-04)	**of undefeated away matches:** 11 (1888-89)
without home win: 9 (1965-66)	**without an away win:** 33 (1897-99)
of league wins: 14 (1950-51) (Joint League record)	**of home wins:** 20 (1891-92)
of league defeats: 8 (1983, 1984)	**of away wins:** 8 (1950-51)

PRESTON NORTH END

PLAYERS NAME / Honours	Ht	Wt	Birthdate	Birthplace / Transfers	Contract Date	Clubs	League	L/Cup	FA Cup	Other	Lg	L/C	FAC	Oth
GOALKEEPERS														
John A Bagnall	6.0	12.0	23.11.73		17.07.92	Preston N.E								
Simon Farnworth	5.11	11.0	28.10.63	Chorley	05.09.81	Bolton W (A)	113	11	6	8				
E: S				Loan	11.09.86	Stockport Co	10	2						
				Loan	09.01.87	Tranmere Rovers	7							
				Free	12.03.87	Bury	105	11	3	5				
				Free	01.07.90	Preston N.E	46	4	1	5				
DEFENDERS														
Jon Davidson	5.8	11.11	01.03.70	Cheadle		Derby County	7+5	1	0+2	0+1				
				£50,000	20.07.92	Preston N.E								
Lee Fowler	5.8	11.2	26.01.70	Eastwood(Notts)	15.07.88	Stoke City	42+7	5+1	2+2	6				
				Free	10.07.92	Preston N.E								
Colin Greenall	5.11	11.10	30.12.63	Billinge	17.01.81	Blackpool	179+4	12	9	2	9	2		
				£40,000	10.09.86	Gillingham	62	3	6	9	4	1	1	2
				£235,000	15.02.88	Oxford Utd	67	4	1	2	2			
				Loan	04.01.90	Bury	3			1				
				£125,000	16.07.90	Bury	66+2	3	1	8	5			1
				£50,000	27.03.92	Preston N.E	9			1				
Ryan Kidd	5.11	10.0	06.10.71	Manchester	12.07.90	Port Vale (T)	1	0+2		0+1				
				Free	15.07.92	Preston N.E								
Craig Moylon	5.10	10.10	16.10.72	Munster (Ger.)	16.07.91	Preston N.E								
MIDFIELD														
Lee Cartwright	5.8	10.6	19.09.72	Rossendale	30.07.91	Preston N.E. (T)	44+3		3	3	4			
David Eaves	5.11	11.7	13.02.73	Blackpool	16.07.91	Preston N.E. (T)	1+2			0+1				
Michael Flynn	6.0	11.0	23.02.69	Oldham	07.02.87	Oldham Ath. (T)	37+3	1+1	1	2	1			
				£100,000	22.12.88	Norwich City								
				£125,000	04.12.89	Preston N.E	99+2	4	4+1	11	5		1	
(M) Martin James	5.10	11.7	18.05.71	Formby	19.07.89	Preston N.E. (T)	70+3	4	4	7	6			
Jason Kerfoot	5.8	10.10	17.04.73	Preston	16.07.91	Preston N.E. (T)	0+4		0+1					
John Tinkler	5.8	11.7	24.08.68	Trimdon	16.12.86	Hartlepool Utd. (A)	153+17	8+2	10+1	11	7	1	1	2
				Free	14.07.92	Preston N.E								
FORWARDS														
Lee Ashcroft	5.10		07.09.72	Preston	16.07.91	Preston N.E. (T)	41+11	1	3	4+2	6			1
David Christie	6.2	12.7	26.02.73	Salford	16.07.91	Preston N.E. (T)	0+2							
Graham Shaw	5.8	10.1	07.06.67	Newcastle (Staffs)	10.06.85	Stoke City (A)	83+16	7	2+4	3+2	18	2	1	2
				£70,000	24.07.89	Preston N.E	113+8	5	5	13	29	6	1	6
ADDITIONAL CONTRACT PLAYERS														
Simon Burton					06.07.92	Preston N.E. (T)								
Adam Critchley					06.07.92	Preston N.E. (T)								
Stephen K Finney					02.05.92	Preston N.E. (T)	0+2			0+1	1			
David Flitcroft					02.05.92	Preston N.E. (T)								
Lyndon Haworth					10.11.89	Preston N.E								

LEADING LEAGUE GOALSCORERS SEASONS 1985-86 – 1991-92

1985-86	JOHN THOMAS	17	1986-87	JOHN THOMAS	21
1987-88	GARY BRAZIL	14	1988-89	TONY ELLIS	20
1989-90	WARREN JOYCE	11	1990-91	GRAHAM SHAW	10

1991-92	**GRAHAM SHAW**	**14**

DEEPDALE Preston PR1 6RU

Capacity: 15,100   **Covered Standing:**   **Seating:** 3,000

Tel: Ground: 0772 795919   **Ticket Sales:** 0772 709170

ATTENDANCES
Highest: 42,684 v Arsenal, Div 1, 23.4.1938

Lowest: 751 v Bury, Freight Rover Trophy, 29.1.1986

Record Receipts: £54,000 v Burnley, Sherpa Van Trophy Northern Area Final 1st Leg, 19.4.1988

Season Tickets:
Stands: from £101 to £147, juv/OAP £83 to £110
Ground: £92, juv/OAP £65

Executive Box Season Tickets: None available

Cost of Stand Tickets: West Stand: £7, £5 juvs/OAP;
West Stand: £7, £5 juvs/OAP; Ground: £5, £3.50 juvs/OAP

Match and Ticket Information: Postal applications with payment and SAE 14 days before match
West Stand: Admittance to Membership Card Holders Only (except Visitors section)

Car Parking: Club park on Deepdale Road (West Stand) side of ground for 500 vehicles. Limited off-street parking Cost (Match-days): £1.00

Nearest Railway Station: Preston (0772 59439)

How to get to the ground

From North: Use Motorway M6 then M55 until junction 1, leave motorway and follow signs Preston A6. In 1.9m at crossroads turn left A5085 into Blackpool Road. In 0.8m turn right A6063 into Deepdale for Preston North End FC

From East and South: Use Motorway M6 until junction 31, leave motorway and follow signs Preston A59. In 1m at roundabout take 2nd exit into Blackpool Road. In 1.3m turn left A6063 into Deepdale for Preston North End FC

From West: Use Motorway M55 until junction 1, leave motorway and follow signs Preston A6. In 1.9m at crossroads turn left A5085 into Blackpool Road. In 0.8m turn right A6063 into Deepdale for Preston North End FC

Value Rating: ★ ★ ★

Programme Editor: Paul Agnew

Price of 1992-93 Programme: £1
Number of Pages: 56
Subscriptions: Home programmes: £28 per season; Away programmes: £29 per season; Home & Away programmes: £50 per season

Local Newspapers: Lancashire Evening Post

Local Radio Stations: Red Rose Radio, Radio Lancashire

Additional Publications on Club: A Complete Record 1881-1987, (Breedon Books)

QUEENS PARK RANGERS Premier

Formed: 1885 | **Turned Professional:** 1898 | **Ltd Co:** 1899

SPONSORED BY: Classic FM | **NICKNAME:** The Rangers, The R's

Chairman
R C Thompson

Corporate Directors
R B Copus

Club Directors
A Ellis
P D Ellis
A Ingham

Secretary
Miss S F Marson

Manager
Gerry Francis

Coaches
Frank Sibley
Roger Cross
Des Bulpin

Physiotherapist
Brian Morris

Head of Marketing
Lynne Davie (081-743 0262)

Club Statistician for the Directory
Keith Westlake

THE 1991-92 season saw a slight change for the better for Rangers as they finished 11th, one place higher than the previous season, goals scored and attendances were also slightly up.

The first half of the season however, was poor, by the end of November Rangers were 21st in the League and out of the Rumbelows and ZDS Cups. In the Rumbelows an 8-1 aggregate win over Hull in the 2nd Round brought an away tie at Manchester City. After a 0-0 draw 'The R's' went down 1-3 in the replay at Loftus Road. The ZDS produced a win against Norwich City before going down to Crystal Palace. In the FA Cup a 0-2 defeat at Southampton meant that Rangers fell at the first hurdle.

Rangers, however, never really looked relegation material and if it were not for the fact that a club record 18 league games were drawn and poor home form (only six league wins) 'The R's' could and should have been higher placed, but at the end of the day Gerry Francis must have been reasonably pleased with his first season's work back at Loftus Road.

The highlights of the season had to be the two 4-1 thrashings handed out to the two United's, Manchester beaten in front of a live TV audience on New Years Day and champions Leeds in front of the Loftus Road faithful in March. These results prove Rangers can beat the best and if they can build on last season's improvements Rangers' fans can look forward to the first season of the new Premier League with high hopes.

Keith Westlake

Back row L-R: Les Ferdinand, Stephen Gallen, Garry Thompson, Michael Meaker, Jan Stejskal, Tony Witter, Alan McDonald, Peter Caldwell, Kark Ready, Darren Peacock, Danny Maddix, Gary Penrice. **Middle:** Des Bulpin (Youth Team Manager), Ron Berry (Kit Manager), Ian Holloway, Dennis Bailey, David McEnroe, Maurice Doyle, Bradley Allen, Tony Roberts, Andy Tillson, Alan McCarthy, Dougie Freedman, Gary Waddock, Roger Cross (Reserve Team Manager), Les Boyle (Trainer), Brian Morris (Physio). **Front row:** Clive Wilson, David Bardsley, Rufus Brevett, Andy Sinton, Ray Wilkins, Frank Sibley (First Team Coach) Gerry Francis (Manager), Simon Barker, Darren Finlay, Andrew Impey, Justin Channing, Roberto Herrera.

QUEENS PARK RANGERS

DIVISION ONE: 11th   **FA CUP:** 3rd RND   **RUMBELOWS CUP:** 3rd RND   **ZDS CUP:** Sth Q-FINALS

M	DATE		COMP.	VEN	OPPONENTS	RESULT		H/T	LGE POS	GOALSCORERS/GOAL TIMES	ATTEN-DANCE
1	A	17	BL	A	Arsenal	D	1-1	1-0		Bailey 15	(30,099)
2		21	BL	H	Norwich City	L	0-2	0-1	17		10,626
3		24	BL	H	Coventry City	D	1-1	0-1	17	Wegerle 69	9,393
4		28	BL	A	Liverpool	L	0-1	0-0	17		(32,700)
5		31	BL	A	Sheffield Wed.	L	1-4	0-3	21	Bailey 73	(25,022)
6	S	4	BL	H	West Ham United	D	0-0	0-0	21		16,616
7		7	BL	H	Southampton	D	2-2	0-1	21	Barker 68, Thompson 84	9,237
8		14	BL	A	Tottenham Hotspur	L	0-2	0-0	22		(30,059)
9		17	BL	A	Luton Town	W	1-0	0-0	20	Barker 47	(9,985)
10		21	BL	H	Chelsea	D	2-2	1-0	20	Wilson 21, Peacock 57	19,579
11		24	RC 2/1	A	Hull City	W	3-0	1-0		**Barker 37, 83, Thompson 87**	(4,979)
12		28	BL	A	Crystal Palace	D	2-2	1-0	19	Barker 5, Wegerle 59	(15,372)
13	O	5	BL	H	Nottingham Forest	L	0-2	0-1	19		13,058
14		9	RC 2/2	H	Hull City	W	5-1	3-0		**Bardsley 28, Thompson 29, 31, Bailey 56, 79**	5,251
15		19	BL	A	Wimbledon	W	1-0	0-0	19	Bailey 81	(4,630)
16		23	ZDS 2	A	Norwich City	W	2-1	1-1		Sinton 11, Impey 90	(4,436)
17		26	BL	H	Everton	W	3-1	1-0	18	Bailey 8, Barker 46, 90	10,002
18		29	RC 3	A	Manchester City	D	0-0	0-0			(15,512)
19	N	2	BL	H	Aston Villa	L	0-1	0-1	19		10,642
20		16	BL	A	Leeds United	L	0-2	0-0	19		(27,087)
21		20	RC 3R	H	Manchester City	L	1-3	1-1		Penrice 6	11,003
22		23	BL	H	Oldham Athletic	L	1-3	1-1	21	Ferdinand 30	8,947
23		26	ZDS S Q	H	Crystal Palace	L	2-3	0-2		Bardsley 58, Wilkins 77	4,492
24		30	BL	A	Notts County	W	1-0	0-0	19	Ferdinand 88	(8,947)
25	D	7	BL	H	Sheffield United	W	1-0	0-0	17	Wegerle 61	10,106
26		14	BL	A	Manchester City	D	2-2	0-2	17	Wegerle 54, Bailey 89	(21,437)
27		21	BL	A	Norwich City	W	1-0	0-0	14	Bailey 90	(11,436)
28		26	BL	H	Liverpool	D	0-0	0-0	14		21,693
29		28	BL	H	Sheffield Wed.	D	1-1	1-0	14	Wilkins 7	12,990
30	J	1	BL	A	Manchester United	W	4-1	2-0	13	Sinton 4, Bailey 3 (5, 58, 85)	(38,554)
31		4	FAC 3	A	Southampton	L	0-2	0-2			(13,710)
32		11	BL	A	Coventry City	D	2-2	0-1	13	Penrice 76, 84	(11,999)
33		18	BL	H	Arsenal	D	0-0	0-0	13		20,497
34	F	1	BL	H	Wimbledon	D	1-1	1-0	13	Penrice 18	9,194
35		8	BL	A	Everton	D	0-0	0-0	13		18,212
36		15	BL	A	Oldham Athletic	L	1-2	0-1	14	Wegerle 70	(13,092)
37		22	BL	H	Notts County	D	1-1	0-0	14	Ferdinand 46	8,300
38		29	BL	A	Sheffield United	D	0-0	0-0	14		(17,958)
39	M	7	BL	H	Manchester City	W	4-0	2-0	13	Ferdinand 20, 55, Wilson (pen) 39, Barker 86	10,779
40		11	BL	H	Leeds United	W	4-1	1-1	12	Ferdinand 36, Allen 63, Sinton 64, Wilson (pen) 83	16,641
41		14	BL	A	Aston Villa	W	1-0	0-0	8	Ferdinand 75	(19,630)
42		21	BL	A	West Ham United	D	2-2	0-1	9	Allen 50, 70	(20,401)
43		28	BL	H	Manchester United	D	0-0	0-0	9		22,603
44	A	4	BL	A	Southampton	L	1-2	0-1	11	Ferdinand 62	(15,102)
45		11	BL	H	Tottenham Hotspur	L	1-2	1-0	14	Sinton 26	20,678
46		18	BL	A	Chelsea	L	1-2	0-1	16	Allen 89	(18,952)
47		20	BL	H	Luton Town	W	2-1	0-0	14	Ferdinand 80, 83	10,749
48		25	BL	A	Nottingham Forest	D	1-1	0-0	14	Allen 74	(22,228)
49	M	2	BL	H	Crystal Palace	W	1-0	1-0	11	Humphrey (og) 13	14,903

Best Home League Attendance: 22,603 v Manchester United   **Smallest: 8,300 v Notts County**   **Av Home Att: 13,678**

Goal Scorers: Compared with 90-91: +187

League (48): Ferdinand 10, Bailey 9, Barker 6, Wegerle 5, Allen 5, Wilson 3 (2 pens), Penrice 3, Sinton 3, Wilkins, Peacock, Opponents Thompson

R/lows C (9): Thompson 3, Bailey 2, Barker 2, Bardsley, Penrice

FA Cup (0):

ZDS Cup (4): Impey, Wilkins, Sinton, Bardsley

Stejskal J.	Bardsley D.	Brevett R.	Wilkins R.	Peacock D.	Maddix D.	Bailey D.	Barker S.	Ferdinand L.	Wegerle R.	Sinton A.	Holloway I.	Tillson A.	Thompson G.	Wilson C.	Allen B.	McDonald A.	Roberts A.	Iorfa D.	Walsh P.	Herrera R.	McCarthy A.	Ready K.	Impey A.	Penrice G.	Channing J.	Referee	
1	2	3	4	5	6	7	8	9	10	11	12	S														R Groves	1
1	2	3		5	6	7*	8	9	10	11	4	S	12													A James	2
1	2	12		5	6	7	8	9•	10	11	4	S	12	3*												K Morton	3
1	2	S		5	6	7	8	9•	10	11	4		14	3												S Lodge	4
1	2	S		5	6	7	8	9	10		4		14	3	11•	S										P Harrison	5
1	2	3		5	6	7	8	14	10		4•	S		9	11		S									P Don	6
1	2	3		5	6	7	8		10		4	S		9	11	12										P Foakes	7
	2*	3*			6		8		10•	11	12	4		9	7	5	1		14							G Courtney	8
1	2	3*			6	14	8			11	12	4		9	7	5			9•							P Durkin	9
1	2			3	6		8			S	11	4		9	7	5			10	S						R Hamer	10
1	2			3	6		8	12	10•	11•	4		9	7	5					14						T Lunt	11
1	2			3	6		8		10•	11	4		9	7	5					S						T Aubard	12
1	2			5*	6	12	8	9	10		7	4		3							S					J Martin	13
1	2			5	6•	10	8			11•	7	4	9	3									12	14		J Carter	14
1	2	S		5	6	10	8			11	7	4	9	3									S			J Worrall	15
1	2	S		5	6	10	8			11•	7	4	9	3									12			M Bailey	16
1	2	S		5	6	10	8			11	7	4	9	3									S			H King	17
1	2	S		5	6	10	8			11	7	4	9	3									S			G Ashby	18
1	2	S		5	6	10	8			11	7	4•	9	3										12		L Shapter	19
1	2		14	5	6					11	7	4•	9•	3										10		K Breen	20
1	2	3	4	5	6	7	8	9			S	S		11										10		D Axcell	21
1	2			4	5	6	7•	8	9		11	14			3		S							10		M Pierce	22
	2		4	5		8*	9			11	12			3		6	1						14	10	7•	R Lewis	23
1	2		4	5		8	9	S		11	S			3		6					7			10		R Milford	24
1	2		4	5		8	9	S		11	12			3		6					7			9•		R Gifford	25
1	2		4	5		14	8			10	11	12		3*		6					7•			9		K Cooper	26
1	2		4	5		9	8			10	11	7	S	3	S	6										A Smith	27
1	2		4	5		9	8			10	11	7	S	3	S	6										I Borrett	28
1	2		4	5		9*	8			10	11	7	S	12	3	6										M Bodenham	29
1	2		4	5		9	8			10	11	7	S	3		6								S		K Barratt	30
1	2		4	5		10	8			11	7	S		3		6*								12		K Burge	31
1	2		4	5		9	8			10•	11	7	S	3		6								12		D Gallagher	32
1	2		4	5		9*	8			12	11	7	S	3		6								10		A Buksh	33
1		S	4	5		9	8•			14	11	7	6	3								2		10		D Elleray	34
1	2•		4	5		9*	8			12	11	7	14	3		6								10		K Hackett	35
1	2		4	5			8*			10	11	7	S	3		6							9			A Dawson	36
1	2		4	5			9	S	11	8			S	3		6							7	10		M Reed	37
1	2		7	5			9	S	11	8	4		S	3		6							S	10		N Midgley	38
1	2		7	5		14	9		11•	8			S	3		6							4	10•		M James	39
1	2		4	5		14	9		11•	7			S	3	10	6							8			K Cooper	40
1	2		7	5		S	9		11	8			S	3	10	6							4			R Nixon	41
1	2		7	5		14	9		11	8			S	3	10•	6							4			D Allinson	42
1	2		7	5		S	9		11	8			S	3	10	6							4			J Martin	43
1	2			5		7	9		11•	8			S	3	10	6							4	14		P Durkin	44
1	2		7	5		S	9•		11	8			S	3	10	6							4	14		G Singh	45
1	2		7	5		S	9		11	8			S	3	12	6							4*	10		G Ashby	46
1	2		7	5	6	S	9		11	8			S	3	10*	6							4	12		D Axcell	47
1	2		7	5		S	9		11	8			S	3	10*								4	12		P Barrett	48
1	2		7	5	S	12	11	9*			8			S	3	10	6						4		1	R Lewis	49
41	41	6	26	39	19	19	31	21	18	38	34	9	10	40	10	27	1		2		3	1	12	13		**League Appearances**	
	1	1		5	3	2	3		6	1	5		1		5			1	1		1				6	**Substitute Appearances**	
4	4	1	1	4	4	3	4	1+1	1	3	3	2	3	4		1						0+1		0+1	0+1	1	**R/lows Appearances**	
1	1		1	1		1	1		1	1	1			1		1									0+1	**FA Cup Appearances**	
1	2		1	2		1	2	1		2	1+1	1		1	2		1	1					0+2	1	1	**ZDS Cup Appearances**	

Also Played: Posn.(Game): Meaker 12(36)

Players on Loan: Walsh (Tottenham)

QUEENS PARK RANGERS

Club Colours: Blue and white hoop shirts, white shorts, white with 3 blue hoop stockings.
Change Colours: Red and black hoop shirts, black shorts, red stockings.
Reserves League: Neville Ovenden Football Combination

COMPETITIONS				
Div. 1	Div. 2	Div. 3	Div. 3S	UEFA
68-69	48-52	58-67	20-48	76-77
73-79	67-68		52-58	84-85
83-	69-73			
	79-83			

HONOURS			
Div. 2	Div. 3	Div. 3S	League Cup
82-83	66-67	47-48	66-67

MOST GOALS IN A CAREER		
GEORGE GODDARD 186 (1926-33)		
Season	League	FA Cup
1926-27	22	
1927-28	26	
1928-29	36	1
1929-30	37	2
1930-31	24	4
1931-32	17	2
1932-33	12	3
Total	**174**	**12**
Previous holder: J Birch 62 (1920-27)		

MOST APPEARANCES: TONY INGHAM 548 (1950-63)			
Year	League	FA Cup	League Cup
1950-51	24		
1951-52	17		
1952-53	43	3	
1953-54	40	4	
1954-55	38	3	
1955-56	41	1	
1956-57	46	3	
1957-58	46	3	
1958-59	46	2	
1959-60	46	3	
1960-61	46	2	2
1961-62	40	4	2
1962-63	41	2	
	514	**30**	**4**
Previous holder: P Angell 418 (1953-66)			

MANAGERS			
Name	Seasons	Best	Worst
James Cowan	1907-13		
James Howie	1913-20		
Ned Liddell	1920-25	3(3S)	22(3S)
Bob Hewison	1925-31	3(3S)	22(3S)
John Bowman	1931		
Archie Mitchell	1931-33	13(3S)	16(3S)
Mitchell O'Brien	1933-35	4(3S)	13(3S)
Billy Birrell	1935-39	3(3S)	9(3S)
Ted Vizard	1939-44		
Dave Mangnall	1944-52	13(2)	3(3S)
Jack Taylor	1952-59	10(3)	21(3S)
Alex Stock	1959-68	2(2)	15(3)
Tommy Docherty	1968		
Les Allen	1969-71	22(1)	11(2)
Gordon Jago	1971-74	4(1)	8(2)
Dave Sexton	1974-77	2(1)	14(1)
Frank Sibley	1977-78	19(1)	19(1)
Steve Burtenshaw	1978-79	20(1)	20(1)
Tommy Docherty	1979-80	5(2)	5(2)
Terry Venables	1980-84	5(1)	8(2)
Alan Mullery	1984		
Frank Sibley	1984-85	19(1)	19(1)
Jim Smith	1985-88	5(1)	16(1)
P Shreeve (Caretaker)	1988-89		
Trevor Francis	1989-90	9(1)	9(1)
Don Howe	1990-91	12(1)	12(1)

RECORD TRANSFER FEE RECEIVED			
Amount	Club	Player	Date
£1,700,000	Manchester Utd	Paul Parker	7/91
£1,300,000	Arsenal	David Seaman	7/90
£1,250,000	Arsenal	Clive Allen	6/80
£527,000	West Ham Utd	Phil Parkes	2/79

RECORD TRANSFER FEE PAID			
Amount	Club	Player	Date
£1,000,000	Luton Town	Roy Wegerle	12/89
£800,000	Southampton	Colin Clarke	3/89
£500,000	Liverpool	Nigel Spackman	2/89
£400,000	Leeds United	Tony Currie	8/79

LONGEST LEAGUE RUNS	
of undefeated matches:	20 (19.11.1966-11.4.1967)
of undefeated home matches:	25 (18.11.1972-5.2.1974)
without home win:	10 (23.11.1968-10.4.1969)
of league wins:	8 (7.11.1931-28.12.1931)
of league defeats:	9 (15.2.1969-12.4.1969)
of league matches w/out a win:	20 (23.11.1968-12.4.1969)
of undefeated away matches:	17 (27.8.1966-11.4.1967)
without an away win:	22 (27.12.1954-26.12.1955)
	(11.5.1969-13.9.1970)
of home wins:	11 (26.12.1972-28.4.1973)
of away wins:	7 (2.4.1927-4.9.1927)

PREVIOUS NAME
St. Judes 1885-87

PREVIOUS LEAGUE
Southern League

BIGGEST VICTORIES
League: 8-0 v Merthyr, Division 3S, 9.3.1929
F.A. Cup: 8-1 v Bristol Rovers (a), Round 1, 27.11.1937
7-0 v Barry Town, Round 1, 1961-62
League Cup: 8-1 Crewe, Round 2, 3.10.1983
Europe (UEFA): 7-0 v Brann Bergen, Round 1, 29-9-1976

BIGGEST DEFEATS
League: 1-8 v Mansfield, Division 3, 15.3.1965
1-8 v Manchester United, Division 1, 19.3.1969
0-7 v Southend United, Division 3S, 7.4.1928
0-7 v Coventry City, Division 3S, 4.3.1933
0-7 v Torquay United, Division 3S, 22.4.1935
0-7 v Barnsley, Division 2, 4.11.1950
F.A. Cup: 0-5 v Huddersfield, Round 4, 23.1.1932
0-5 v Derby County, Round 6, 12.3.1948
0-5 v Huddersfield (h), Round 3, 1948-49
1-6 v Burnley, Round 3, 1961-62
1-6 v Hereford, Round 2, 1957-58
League Cup: 0-4 v Reading, Round 2, 23.9.1964
0-4 v Newcastle, Round 2, 8.10.1974
Europe (UEFA): 0-4 v Partizan Belgrade, 7.11.1984

MOST POINTS
3 points a win: 85, Division 2, 1982-83
2 points a win: 67, Division 3, 1966-67

MOST GOALS
111, Division 3, 1961-62.
Bedford 36, Evans 19, Lazarus 12, Towers 12, McClelland 11, Angell 6, Collins 6, Barber 4, Keen 2, Francis 1, og 2.

MOST GOALS IN A MATCH
5. Alan Wilks v Oxford, Round 3, League Cup, 10.10.1967.

MOST GOALS IN A SEASON
Rodney Marsh, 44 (League 30, FAC 3, League Cup 11) 1966-67.
(League Only) George Goddard, 37, Div 3S, 1929-30

MOST FIRST CLASS MATCHES IN A SEASON
59 (42 League, 2 FA Cup, 7 League Cup, 8 UEFA Cup) 1976-77

MOST LEAGUE GOALS CONCEDED
95, Division 1, 1968-69

MOST LEAGUE WINS
26, Div 3S, 1947-48; Div 3, 1966-67; Div 2, 1982-83

MOST LEAGUE DRAWS
18, Division 1, 1991-92

MOST LEAGUE DEFEATS
28, Division 1, 1968-69

OLDEST PLAYER
Jimmy Langley, 38 years 96 days.

YOUNGEST PLAYER
Frank Sibley, 15 years 274 days.

MOST CAPPED PLAYER
Alan McDonald (Northern Ireland) 31

BEST PERFORMANCES BY QUEENS PARK RANGERS

League: 1966-67: Matches played 46, Won 26, Drawn 15, Lost 5, Goals for 103, Goals against 38, Points 67. First in Division 3

Highest: 1975-76: 2nd in Division 1.

F.A. Cup: 1981-82: 3rd rnd. Middlesbrough 1-1, 3-2; 4th rnd. Blackpool 0-0, 5-1; 5th rnd. Grimsby 3-1; 6th rnd. Crystal Palace 1-0; Semi-final West Bromwich Albion 1-0; Final Tottenham 1-1, 0-1.

League Cup: 1966-67: 1st rnd. Colchester 5-0; 2nd rnd. Aldershot 1-1, 2-0; 3rd rnd. Swansea 2-1; 4th rnd. Leicester 4-2; 5th rnd. Carlisle 2-1; Semi-final Birmingham 4-1, 3-1; Final West Bromwich Albion 3-2.

UEFA Cup: 1976-77: 1st rnd. Brana Bergen 4-0, 7-0; 2nd rnd. Slovan Bratislava 3-2, 5-2; 3rd rnd FC Cologne 3-0, 1-4; 4th rnd. AEK Athens 3-0, 0-3.

DIVISIONAL RECORDS

	Played	Won	Drawn	Lost	For	Against	Points
DIVISION 1	658	218	184	256	804	879	**753**
DIVISION 2	546	233	141	172	809	671	**654**
DIVISION 3	414	188	98	128	782	601	**474**
DIVISION 3S	1158	466	276	416	1781	1692	**1208**
TOTALS	**2776**	**1105**	**699**	**972**	**4176**	**3843**	**3089**

QUEENS PARK RANGERS

PLAYERS NAME Honours	Ht	Wt	Birthdate	Birthplace Transfers	Contract Date	Clubs	League	L/Cup	FA Cup	Other	Lg	L/C	FAC	Oth
GOALKEEPERS														
Peter Caldwell			05.06.72	Dorchester	09.03.90	Q.P.R								
Anthony Roberts	6.1		04.08.69	Bangor		Holyhead J								
					24.07.87	Q.P.R	19	3		2				
Jan Stejskal	6.3		15.01.62	Brunn (Czech)		Sparta Prague								
				£600,000	19.10.90	Q.P.R	67	4	2	2				
DEFENDERS														
David Bardsley	5.10	10.0	11.09.64	Manchester	05.11.82	Blackpool (A)	45	2	2			1		
E:Y.2				£150,000	23.11.83	Watford	97+3	6	13+1	1	7	1	1	
				£300,000	18.09.87	Oxford Utd	74	12	5	3	7			
				£200,000+P	15.09.89	Q.P.R	110	8	11	3	1	1		1
Rufus Brevett	5.8		24.09.69	Derby	08.07.88	Doncaster Rovers (T)	106+13	5	4	10+1	3			
				£250,000	15.02.91	Q.P.R	16+1	1						
Justin Channing	5.10	11.3	19.11.68	Reading	27.08.86	Q.P.R. (A)	40+13	3+1	2	5	4			
E:Y2														
Roberto Herrera	5.7	10.6	12.06.70	Torquay	01.03.88	Q.P.R. (A)	4+2	1+2		1+1				
				Loan	17.03.92	Torquay Utd	11							
Brain Law	6.2	11.12	01.01.70	Merthyr Tydfil	15.08.87	Q.P.R	19+1	2+1	3	1				
Daniel Maddix	5.10	11.7	11.10.66	Ashford	25.07.85	Tottenham H. (A)								
				Loan	01.11.86	Southend Utd	2							
				Free	23.07.87	Q.P.R	113+12	14	13	2+3	6	2	1	
Alan McCarthy			11.01.72	London	08.12.89	Q.P.R. (T)	4+1		0+1	2				
Alan McDonald	6.2	12.7	12.10.63	Belfast	12.08.81	Q.P.R. (A)	242+5	28	22	5	8	2	1	
NI: 33, Y.					Loan	24.03.83	Charlton Ath	9						
Darren Peacock	6.2	12.06	03.02.68	Bristol		Newport Co	24+4	2	1	1+1				
WC'90					23.03.89	Hereford Utd	56+3	6	6	6	4		1	
				£200,000	22.12.90	Q.P.R	58	4	1	2	1			
Andrew Tillson	6.2	12.7	30.06.68	Huntingdon		Kettering Town								
				f	14.07.88	Grimsby Town	104+1	8	10	5	6			
				£500,000	21.12.90	Q.P.R	27+2	2		1	2			
MIDFIELD														
Simon Barker	5.9	11.0	04.11.64	Farnworth	06.11.82	Blackburn Rov. (A)	180+2	11	12	8	35	4		2
E:u21.4,FMC'87				£400,000	20.07.88	Q.P.R	97+15	13+2	13+1	7	11	3	2	
Maurice Doyle	5.8	10.7	17.10.69	Birkenhead	11.07.88	Crewe Alexandra	6+2				2			
				£60,000	21.04.89	Q.P.R								
				Loan	17.01.91	Crewe Alexandra	6+1		2		2			
Andrew Impey			30.09.71	Hamersmith		Yeading								
					14.06.90	Q.P.R	12	0+1		0+2				1
Michael Meaker			18.08.71	Grennford	07.02.90	Q.P.R. (T)	0+9			0+1				
				Loan	20.11.91	Plymouth A	3			1				
Andy Sinton	5.7	10.7	19.03.66	Newcastle	13.04.83	Cambridge Utd. (A)	90+3	6	3	2	13	1		1
				£25,000	13.12.85	Brentford	149	8	11	14	28	3	1	2
					23.03.89	Q.P.R	124	10	11	3	15		2	1
Gary Waddock	5.10	11.12	17.03.62	Kingsbury	26.07.79	Q.P.R. (A)	191+12	21+1	14	1	8	2		
Ei: 21,u23,1,u21,1; Div2'83				Free		Charleroi (Bel)								
				£130,000	16.08.89	Millwall	51+7	5+1	5	3	2			1
				Free	20.12.91	Q.P.R								
				Loan	19.03.92	Swindon Town	5+1							
Ray Wilkins	5.8	11.02	14.09.56	Hillingdon	01.10.73	Chelsea (A)	176+3	6+1	10+1		30	2	2	
E:84,u23.2,u21.1,FA'83,SPD'90				£750,000	01.08.79	Manchester Utd	158+2	14+1	10	9	7	1	1	1
					01.07.84	A.C. Milan (Ita)								
via Paris St. Germain (Fra.) to						Glasgow Rangers	69+1	10	8+1	7	2	1		
				Free	30.11.89	Q.P.R	87+1	5	11	2	4		2	1
Clive Wilson	5.7	9.10	13.11.61	Greenleys	08.12.79	Manchester City	107+2	10	2	5	9	2		
Div.2'89;				Loan	16.10.82	Chester City	21				2			
				£250,000	19.03.87	Chelsea	68+13	3+3	4	10+2	5			
				£450,000	04.07.90	Q.P.R	51+2	6	2	2+1	4			
FORWARDS														
Bradley Allen	5.7	10.0	13.09.71	Harold Wood	30.09.88	Q.P.R. (T)	14+8	0+1	0+1	1	7			
E:Y.3														
Dennis Bailey	5.10	11.6	13.11.65	Lambeth		Farnborough		1				1		
				£10,000	02.12.87	Crystal Palace	0+5				1			
				Loan	27.02.89	Bristol Rovers	17			1+1	9			1
				£80,000	03.08.89	Birmingham City	65+10	6	6	3+3	23	2		
				Loan	28.03.91	Bristol Rovers	6				1			
				£175,000	02.07.91	Q.P.R	19+5	3	1	1	9	2		
Les Ferdinand	5.11	13.5	18.12.66	Acton		Hayes								
				£15,000	12.03.87	Q.P.R.	43+10	3+2	0+1	1	20	2		
				Loan		Brentford	3							
				Loan		Besiktas								
Ian Holloway	5.7	9.12	12.03.63	Bristol	18.03.81	Bristol Rovers	104+7	10	8	5	14	1	2	
Div.3'90					18.07.85	Wimbledon	19	3	1		2			
					21.07.86	Brentford	27+3	2	3	0+1	2			
				Loan	30.01.87	Torquay Utd	5							
					21.08.87	Bristol Rovers	179	5	10	20	26		1	3
				£230,000	12.08.91	Q.P.R	34+6	3	1	1+1				

					APPEARANCES					GOALS			
PLAYERS NAME / Honours	Ht	Wt	Birthdate	Birthplace / Transfers	Contract Date	Clubs	League	L/Cup	FA Cup	Other	Lg	L/C	FAC	Oth
FORWARDS cont.														
Gary Penrice	5.8	11.1	23.03.64	Bristol		Mangotsfield								
					06.11.84	Bristol Rovers	186+2	11	11	13+2	54	3	7	2
				£500,000	14.11.89	Watford	41+2		4	1	17		1	1
				£1,000,000	08.03.91	Aston Villa	14+6				1			
				£625,000	29.10.91	Q.P.R	13+6	1	0+1	1	3	1		
Garry L Thompson	6.1	13.13	07.10.59	Kings Heath	29.06.77	Coventry City (A)	127+7	12+1	11		38	7	4	
E:u21.6				£225,000	17.02.83	West Brom A	91	9	5		39	5	1	
				£450,000	12.08.85	Sheffield Wed	35+1	2+1	5		6	1	1	
				£450,000	05.06.86	Aston Villa	56+4	6	4	3	17	2		
				£325,000	24.12.88	Watford	24+10	0+1	7+1		8			
				£200,000	24.03.90	Crystal Palace	17+3	0+1		0+1	3	1		
					19.08.91	Q.P.R	10+5	3		1	1	3		
ADDITIONAL CONTRACT PLAYERS														
(D) Darren J Finlay					15.05.92	Q.P.R. (T)								
(F) Douglas A Freedman					15.05.92	Q.P.R. (T)								
(D) Stephen J Gallen					08.05.92	Q.P.R. (T)								
(M) David McEnroe					16.08.90	Q.P.R. (T)								
(D) Karl Ready					13.08.90	Q.P.R	1	0+1						
(D) Tony Witter	6.1		12.08.65	London	24.10.90	Crystal Palace								
				£125,000	19.08.91	Q.P.R								
				Loan	12.11.91	Millwall								
				Loan	09.01.92	Plymouth A	3+1							

MANAGER: GERRY FRANCIS

DATE OF BIRTH: 06.12.1951 **PLACE OF BIRTH:** Chiswick

DATE OF APPOINTMENT: JUNE 1991

PREVIOUS CLUBS
as Manager: Bristol Rovers
as Player: QPR, C. Palace, QPR (2nd), Coventry City, Exeter City, Cardiff City, Swansea City, Portsmouth, Bristol Rovers

HONOURS
as Manager: (Bristol Rov): Div 3 Champions 1990, Leyland Daf Finalists 1990
as Asst. Man./Coach:
as Player: (QPR): Div 1 Runners-Up 1975-76
International: England 12 (Captain), U23

Value Rating: ★ ★ ★ ★

Programme Editor: Sheila Marson

Price of 1992-93 Programme: £1.30
Number of Pages: 40
Subscriptions: Full season £38, (Overseas, please apply to club)

Local Newspapers: Shepherds Bush Gazette, Acton Gazette.

Local Radio Stations: LBC, Capital Radio.

LEADING LEAGUE GOALSCORERS
SEASONS 1979-80 – 1991-92

1979-80	CLIVE ALLEN	28	1980-81	DEAN NEAL	8
				TOMMY LANGLEY	8
1981-82	SIMON STAINROD	17	1982-83	TONY SEALY	16
1983-84	CLIVE ALLEN	14	1984-85	GARY BANNISTER	17
1985-86	GARY BANNISTER	16	1986-87	GARY BANNISTER	14
1987-88	GARY BANNISTER	8	1988-89	MARK FALCO	12
1989-90	ANDY SINTON	6	1990-91	ROY WEGERLE	18
	COLIN CLARKE	6			

1991-92	**LES FERDINAND**	**10**

RANGERS STADIUM South Africa Road, London W12 7PA

Capacity: 22,600   **Covered Standing:** 7,900   **Seating:** 14,700

Tel: Ground: 081 743 0262   **Ticket Sales:** 081 749 7798   **Clubcall:** 0898 12 11 62

All premium rate calls (0898/0891) cost 36p per minute cheap rate and 48p per minute at all other times. Call costings correct at time of going to press.

GROUNDS
Welfords Field 1885-89; London Scottish Ground, Brondesbury Home Farm, Kensall Rise Green Gun Club, Wormwood Scrubs, Kilburn C.C. 1889-99; Kensall Rise 1899-1901; Latimer Rd, Knotting Hill 1901-04; Agriculture Soc, Park Royal 1904-07; Park Royal Ground 1907-17; Loftus Rd 1917-31; White City 1931-33; Loftus Rd 1933-62; White City 1962-63; South Africa Rd 1963-

ATTENDANCES
Highest: 35,353 v Leeds United, Div 1, 12.1.1974
Lowest: 3,245 v Coventry City, Div 3, 22.5.1963

RECORD RECEIPTS
£180,963 v Manchester Utd, 28.3.1992
£143,668 v Tottenham, Div 1, 6.10.1990

SOUTH AFRICA ROAD
First game: v West Ham United, FA Cup, 8.9.1917
First floodlit game: v Arsenal, 5.10.1953
2nd Set: v Colchester, 23.8.1966

Season Tickets:
Stands: from £196 to £324
(Juvenile rates available)

Executive Box Season Tickets: Details available from the Marketing Department

Cost of Stand Tickets: South Africa Road Stand: 'A' games £15, £25; 'B' games £12; Ellerslie Road Stand: 'A' games £14, £18; 'B' games £11, £11; Loftus Road Members Stand: Centre: adult £10, juv £5; Wing: adults £9, juv £4.50; Loftus Road Terrace: £6 adult members, £4 juv members; £7, £8 adult non-members, £5 juv non-members

Match and Ticket Information: Seats bookable one month in advance of each match

Car Parking: Limited side-street parking available

Nearest Railway Station: Shepherds Bush (Tube), White City (Central Line)

How to get to the ground

From North: Use Motorway M1 and A406 North Circular Road as for Neasden. In 0.7m turn left then join A404 S.P. Harlesden then follow signs Hammersmith and turn right into White City Road then turn left into South Africa Road for Queens Park Rangers FC

From East: Use A12, A406 then A503 then join Ring Road and follow signs Oxford to join A40(M). In 2m branch left (S.P. The West) to join M41. At roundabout take 3rd exit A40 then join A4020 S.P. Acton. In 0.3m turn right into Loftus Road for Queens Park Rangers FC

From South: Use A206, A3 to cross Putney Bridge and follow signs Hammersmith. Follow signs Oxford A219 to Shepherds Bush then join A4020 S.P. Acton. In 0.3m turn right into Loftus Road for Queens Park Rangers FC

From West: Use Motorway M4 to Chiswick then A315 and A402 to Shepherds Bush, then join A4020 S.P. Acton. In 0.3m turn right into Loftus Road for Queens Park Rangers FC

READING

Division 2

Formed: 1871   **Turned Professional:** 1895   **Ltd Co:** 1895

SPONSORED BY: Autotrader (shirts), Courage (general)   **NICKNAME:** The Royals

President
J H Brooks

Chairman
R J Madejski

Managing Director/Company Sec.
M J Lewis

Directors
G J Denton

Club Secretary
Mrs Jayne Hill

Player/Manager
Mark McGhee

Coach
Colin Lee

Youth Development Officer
Colin Clarke

Youth Team Coach
Bobby Williams

Physiotherapist/Coach
J Haselden

Groundsman
Gordon Neate

Club Statistician for the Directory
David Downs

THE season proved to be yet another one of much change and readjustment, as incoming player-manager Mark McGhee worked to build a squad capable of taking the Royals back into the new First Division.

A total of thirty-five players – a club record – were used in first class games during the campaign. Although the final league position of twelfth was in some respects disappointing, there was a marked improvement as the season went on, both in terms of results and performances, and supporters can be optimistic about the future.

Nearly all the professional staff were given the opportunity to show their paces at first-team level. There was a regular influx of trialists and loan signings, notable among them being Scottish internationals Jim Leighton and Steve Archibald, as the manager attempted to bring consistency to the undoubted ability that existed within the club. The superb youth development scheme at Elm Park continued to provide a regular supply of candidates for first-team places, and the departure of old favourites like Linden Jones and Trevor Senior was balanced by the introduction of exciting newcomers such as Lea Barkus and David Bass.

The learning curve for McGhee was steep to say the least, and he took some time to win over the fans, but by May he could look back with satisfaction on all he had achieved in twelve hectic months. The experience will be valuable as he plans for next year, though one of the hardest decisions he faces may well be how to balance his own playing and managerial duties.

Other developments which took place during 1991-92 included the move to a magnificent new training base at Whitchurch, which also hosts the club's Centre of Excellence, and the decision to withdraw the reserve team, after sixty-six years, from the Football Combination. Next season will see the club's second string competing in the more localised Capital League. There will also be a return to a blue and white hooped playing strip, which should please the traditionalists among the loyal supporters of the Royals.

The demise of near neighbours Aldershot will not have gone unnoticed by the club, and the backstage organisation was stepped up to ensure that it kept pace with progress on the field. Kevin Girdler took over as Commercial Manager, Phil Chant pulled out all the financial stops as Promotions Manager, and Richard Hill was appointed to the vital post of Community Officer.

Hopes are high for 1992-93, and if the team can add consistency at home to success on its travels, then promotion can be a realistic expectation.

David Downs

Back row L-R: Colin Lee (1st Team Coach), Tom Jones, Phil Parkinson, Jeff Hopkins, Steve Francis, Jimmy Quinn, Adrian Williams, Kevin Dillon, Scott Taylor, John Haselden (Physio). **Front row:** Michael Gilkes, Mark Holzman, Keith McPherson, Mark McGhee (Manager), Stuart Lovell, Steve Richardson, Mick Godding.

READING

DIVISION THREE: 12th   **FA CUP:** 3rd RND   **RUMBELOWS CUP:** 1st RND   **AUTOGLASS:** Prelim.

M	DATE		COMP.	VEN	OPPONENTS	RESULT		H/T	LGE POS	GOALSCORERS/GOAL TIMES	ATTEN-DANCE
1	A	17	BL	H	Hull City	L	0-1	0-0	17		4,639
2		21	RC 1/1	A	Cambridge United	L	0-1	0-0			(3,701)
3		24	BL	A	Hartlepool United	L	0-2	0-1	23		(2,858)
4		28	RC 1/2	H	Cambridge United	L	0-3	0-2			3,758
5		31	BL	H	Bury	W	3-2	1-0	16	Senior 9, McPherson 88, McGhee 90	2,886
6	S	3	BL	A	Swansea City	W	2-1	0-0	11	Byrne 74, Senior 81	(3,206)
7		7	BL	H	Birmingham City	D	1-1	1-1	12	Byrne 16	6,649
8		14	BL	A	Brentford	L	0-1	0-0	17		(5,775)
9		17	BL	A	Torquay United	W	2-1	1-0	10	Senior 15, Holzman 53	(2,591)
10		24	BL	H	Bradford City	L	1-2	1-1	15	Gooding 18	3,765
11		28	BL	A	Exeter City	L	1-2	0-0	17	Lovell 57	(3,383)
12	O	5	BL	H	Bournemouth	D	0-0	0-0	17		4,033
13		11	BL	A	Wigan Athletic	D	1-1	0-0	17	Cockram 88	(1,817)
14		19	BL	H	Peterborough Utd	D	1-1	0-1	18	Dillon (pen) 66	2,954
15		22	AGT Pre	A	Leyton Orient	L	0-1	0-1			(1,054)
16		26	BL	A	Shrewsbury Town	W	2-1	0-0	16	Dillon 56, Taylor 71	(2,398)
17	N	2	BL	A	Bolton Wanderers	D	1-1	0-0	17	Gooding 52	(3,632)
18		5	BL	H	Darlington	D	2-2	0-0	18	Maskell 47, Williams 84	2,808
19		9	BL	H	West Bromwich A.	L	1-2	0-1	18	Taylor 57	5,826
20		16	FAC 1	A	Slough Town	D	3-3	0-1		Williams 71, Gooding 81, Taylor 85	(3,990)
21		20	AGT Pre	H	Northampton Town	L	0-2	0-2			1,151
22		23	BL	A	Chester City	D	2-2	1-1	19	Maskell 18, 62	(1,124)
23		27	FAC 1R	H	Slough Town	W	2-1	2-0		Williams 6, Lovell 33	6,363
24		30	BL	H	Stockport County	D	1-1	1-1	20	Maskell 2	3,511
25	D	7	FAC 2	A	Peterborough Utd	D	0-0	0-0			(5,328)
26		17	FAC 2R	H	Peterborough Utd	W	1-0	0-0		Lovell 72	4,373
27		21	BL	H	Hartlepool United	L	0-1	0-0	18		2,535
28		26	BL	A	Bury	W	1-0	0-0	17	Maskell 73	(2,333)
29		28	BL	A	Hull City	W	1-0	1-0	15	Senior 6	(3,661)
30	J	1	BL	H	Swansea City	W	1-0	0-0	14	Senior 55	5,083
31		4	FAC 3	A	Bolton Wanderers	L	0-2	0-0			(7,301)
32		11	BL	H	Huddersfield Town	W	1-0	0-0	13	Senior 83	4,732
33		18	BL	A	Stoke City	L	0-3	0-1	14		(10,835)
34	F	1	BL	A	Peterborough Utd	L	3-5	2-2	14	Richardson 18, Lee 24, Maskell (pen) 86	(3,792)
35		8	BL	H	Shrewsbury Town	W	2-1	1-0	13	Lee 42, Senior 79	3,303
36		11	BL	A	Stockport County	L	0-1	0-0	15		(3,720)
37		15	BL	H	Fulham	L	0-2	0-0	17		4,388
38		22	BL	H	Huddersfield Town	W	2-1	1-0	17	Lee 36, Williams 58	(6,259)
39		29	BL	H	Preston North End	D	2-2	2-0	16	Lee 10, 30	3,390
40	M	4	BL	H	Stoke City	L	3-4	2-2	17	Lovell 8, Williams 36, Gooding 58	4,362
41		7	BL	A	Leyton Orient	D	1-1	1-1	16	Maskell 11	(4,436)
42		10	BL	A	Darlington	W	4-2	1-0	15	Maskell 3 (41, 86, 88), Cork (og) 57	(2,388)
43		14	BL	H	Bolton Wanderers	W	1-0	1-0	14	Brown (og) 17	3,515
44		21	BL	A	West Bromwich A.	L	0-2	0-2	15		(10,707)
45		28	BL	H	Chester City	D	0-0	0-0	15		2,813
46	A	1	BL	H	Brentford	D	0-0	0-0	15		5,660
47		4	BL	A	Birmingham City	L	0-2	0-2	17		(12,229)
48		7	BL	A	Fulham	L	0-1	0-0	17		(3,499)
49		11	BL	H	Torquay United	W	6-1	4-1	16	Dillon 18, Lovell 25, Barkus 27, McGhee 33, Maskell 56, 80	3,111
50		14	BL	A	Preston North End	D	1-1	0-1	15	Maskell 86	(3,203)
51		18	BL	A	Bradford City	L	0-1	0-0	16		(5,492)
52		20	BL	H	Exeter City	W	1-0	1-0	15	McGhee 6	3,325
53		25	BL	A	Bournemouth	L	2-3	1-1	16	Watson (og) 14, Williams 77	(6,486)
54		29	BL	H	Leyton Orient	W	3-2	1-0	14	Maskell 43, 62, McGhee 77	2,690
55	M	2	BL	H	Wigan Athletic	W	3-2	0-2	12	Maskell (pen) 61, McGhee 80, Lovell 89	2,748

Best Home League Attendance: 6,649 v Birmingham City   **Smallest: 2,535 v Hartlepool Utd**   **Av Home Att: 3,858**

Goal Scorers: **Compared with 90-91: -199**

League (59): Maskell 16 (2 pens), Senior 7, Lee 5, McGhee 5, Williams 4, Lovell 4, Opponents 3, Dillon 3 (1 pen), Gooding 3, Taylor 2, Byrne 2, Holzman, Richardson, Cockram, Barkus, McPherson

R/lows C (0):

FA Cup (6): Lovell 2, Williams 2, Taylor, Gooding

Autoglass (0):

1991-92

Francis S.	Jones L.	Richardson S.	McPherson K.	Cooper N.	Williams A.	Holzman M.	Dillon K.	McGhee M.	Leworthy D.	Gilkes M.	Gooding M.	Senior T.	Seymour C.	Byrne D.	Maskell C.	Bailey D.	Streete F.	Lovell S.	Taylor S.	Cockram A.	Morrow S.	Leighton J.	Robinson D.	Barkus L.	Bass D.	Referee	
1	2	3	4	5	6	7*	8	9•	10	11	12	14														K Burge	1
1	2	3	4	5†	6	7	8†	12	10	11*	9		S													P Taylor	2
1	2		4	5•	6	12	8		10	11*	3	9		7	14											J Kirkby	3
1	2	3	4	5	6•	8	7	9	10*	14	11	12														R Hamer	4
1		3	4	S		2	8	10		11		9	7*			5	6	12								K Morton	5
1		3	4	5		2		10	S	11*	8	9	7				6	12								R Gifford	6
1	2	3	4		5	14	10*	12	11	8	9		7•				6									R Bigger	7
1	2	3	4		5	10	8		12	11*	S	9	7				6									J Moules	8
1	2	3	4		5	12	11	10•		8*	9		7	14			6									J Martin	9
1	2	3	4			14	8	10		11•	5	9*	7		12		6									C Wilkes	10
1		3	4	14	6	2	8	10*			5	9			11•		12	7								R Wiseman	11
1		3	4	8	6	2		S			5	9			11		10	7	S							K Borrett	12
1		3*	4	8•	6	2	11	14			5	9					10	7	12							S Bell	13
1			4		6	2	8	10		3	11	12				5	9*	7	S							D Shadwell	14
1			4		6	2	8	10		11	5	9				3	12	7*	S							M James	15
1			4		6	2	8	9*		11	5	12			10	3	S	7								N Midgley	16
1	2		4		6	S	8	9		11	5	S			10	7							3			A Bennett	17
1	2•		4		6	7		9	12	11	5				10*	8		14					3			G Poll	18
1		2		4	S	6	12		9	10*	11	5				7		8					3			A Gunn	19
1		2	4	S	6	3	8	9	S		5				10	7			11							P Don	20
1		2	4			3		9	14		5		6*		10•	7	8	11	12							J Carter	21
1		2	4	7	6	3		9*		8	5				10		12	11	S							M Reed	22
	2	4		6	3*				11	5		12		10	7	9	8	S								B Hill	23
		3	4		5			9*		11	7				10	8•	6		2		14	1				P Scoble	24
		3	4		5					11	7				10	8	6	9*	2	S		1				R Wiseman	25
		3	4		5					11	7				10	8	6	12	2	S		1				R Wiseman	26
		3	4		5					11	7				10	8	6	9*	2	S		1				A Buksh	27
	2	3	4		5					11	7				10	8	6	9	S			1				J Key	28
	2	3	4		5					14	7	9			10*	8	6	12	11•			1				R Dilkes	29
	2	3	4*		5					11	7	9			10	8	6	S		12		1				M Bodenham	30
	2	3	4		5					11	7	9			10•	8*	6	12			14	1				G Singh	31
	2				5				3	11	7	9			8		6	S	4	5		1				R Groves	32
	2				5			3†		11•	7	9			8	6†	10*	4	12			1				B Coddington	33
1	2	3	4					10•				9		14	8		12	7	11	1						A Smith	34
1	2		4									9		10	8		6	7	3	11						G Pooley	35
1	2	3	4	11							7	9		10	8*		6		12	S						R Hart	36
1	2	3	4	5						11	9			10	8*	6	S	7								K Cooper	37
1	2	3	9							11	S			10	8	6	S	7								M Peck	38
1	2	3	4	9		S				11	12			10	8	6		7*								M Pierce	39
1	2	3	4	9		7	12			5				10	8	6		11*	S							D Frampton	40
1	2	3	4	9		7	12			5			8•	10		6		11*	14							D Axcell	41
1	2	3	4	9		7	12			5			8*	10		6		11•	14							K Hackett	42
1	2	3	4	9		7	12			5				10	8	6		11*	14							T Ward	43
1	2	3	4	9		7	12			5		6		10	8•			11*	14							R Lewis	44
1		3	4	9		7	12			5		14		10•		6		2*				8	11			P Don	45
1		3	4	5		7	12			2	9			10	11	6		S				8*				P Taylor	46
1	2•	3	4	9		7	8*			5				10	11	6		12					14			R Dilkes	47
1*	12	3	4	5		7	14			2				10	11	6						8•	9			R Pawley	48
1		3	4	5*			8	9		2				14		6		11	12			10	7*			A Gunn	49
1	2	3	4	5			8	9				5		S		7		6	11	12			10*			A Wilkie	50
1	2	3	4	5			8	9				14		7		6		11					10*			A Dawson	51
1		3	4	5			8	9				S		7	6			11					10	S		P Vanes	52
1	3		4	5			8	9		2				7	6•			11					10*	12	14	M Pierce	53
1	2		4	5			8	9		3				7				12	11				S	10*	6	P Durkin	54
1*	2		4	5			8	10		3	9			7				12	11				S		6	A Buksh	55
32	28	38	44	6	40	11	29	23	3	19	39	20	3	7	29	23	34	16	22	2	3	8	8	4	2	**League Appearances**	
	1		1		2			3		1	1			3		5	1		8	7	4			2	1	**Substitute Appearances**	
2	2	2	2	2	2	2	2	1+1	2	1+1	2	0+1			1		5	1								**R/lows Appearances**	
1	1	5	5		5	2	1	1		4	5	1		5	3	5	2+2	4		0+1	3					**FA Cup Appearances**	
2		1	2		1	2	1	2	0+1	1	2	1		1	1		2	1+1	2	0+1						**Other Competitions**	

Also Played: Posn.(Game): Honey 1(23), Britton 12(24,25,27)9*(26), Archibald 10(32), Gray 14(33), Lee 5(34,35,36,38,39), Fealey 6*(34), Keeley 1(35,36,37,38,39,40), Kemp S(35), Giamattei S(35)12(37,51*)   †=Sent Off

Players on Loan: Bryne (Watford), Morrow (Arsenal), Leighton (Man Utd), Britton (Celtic), Lee (Chelsea), Keeley (Oldham Ath)

READING

Club Colours: Blue & white hooped shirts, white shorts and socks
Change Colours: Blue & amber hooped shirts, blue shorts and socks
Reserves League: Capital League   **Youth League:** S E Counties, Allied Counties Youth League

Previous Managers: 1923-26 Arthur Chadwick   1926-31 Angus Wylie   1931-35 Joe Smith   1935-39 Billy Butler   1939 Johnny Cochrane   1939 Joe Edelston   1947-52 Ted Drake   1952-55 Jack Smith   1955-63 Harry Johnston   1963-69 Roy Bentley   1969-72 Jack Mansell   1972-77 Charlie Hurley   1977-84 Maurice Evans   1984-89 Ian Branfoot   1989-91 Ian Porterfield
Honours: Div 3 Champions 1985-86   Div 3S Champions 1925-26   Div 4 Champions 1978-79   Div 3S Cup Winners 1937-38   Simod Cup Winners 1987-88
League Career: Original members Div 3 1920   Transferred to Div 3S 1921   Promoted to Div 2 1925-26   Relegated to Div 3S 1930-31   Transfered to Div 3 1958   Relegated to Div 4 1970-71   Promoted to Div 3 1975-76   Relegated to Div 4 1976-77   Promoted to Div 3 1978-79   Relegated to Div 4 1982-83   Promoted to Div 3 1983-84   Promoted to Div 2 1985-86   Relegated to Div 3 1987-88

CLUB RECORDS

Most Appearances for Club: Martin Hicks (1978-91): League 499 + 1 + FA Cup 38 + League Cup 38 + Others 17 + 1 **Total 592 + 2**
Most Capped Player: Billy McConnell 8 N Ireland   **For England:** Herbert Smith 4
Record Goalscorer in a Match: Arthur Bacon 6 v Stoke City (h), 7-3, Div 2, 3.4.1931
Record League Goalscorer in a Season: Ronnie Blackman 39, Div 3S 1951-52   **In All Competitions:** Trevor Senior 41 (League 36, FA Cup 1, Milk Cup 4) 1983-84
Record League Goalscorer in a Career: Ronnie Blackman 158   **In All Competitions:** Trevor Senior 186 (League 154, FA Cup 18, Lge Cup 14) 1983-92
Record Goalscorer in a Match: Arthur Bacon 6 v Stoke City (h), 7-3, Div 2, 3.4.1931
Record Transfer Fee Received: £500,000 from Wimbledon for Keith Curle, October 1988
Record Transfer Fee Paid: £250,000 to Huddersfield Town for Craig Maskell, August 1990
Best Performances: League: 13th Div 2, 1986-87   **FA Cup:** Semi-final 1927   **League Cup:** 4th Round 1965, 1966, 1978, 1988
Most League Points: (3pts a win) 94 Div 3, 1985-86   (2pts a win) 65 Div 4, 1978-79
Most League Goals: 112 Div 3S, 1951-52
Record League Victory and Most Goals Scored in a League Match: 10-2 v Crystal Palace, Div 3S, 4.9.1946   8-0 v Southport, Div 3, 22.4.1970
Record Cup Victory and Most Goals Scored in a Cup Tie: 8-3 v Corinthians, 1st Round FA Cup, 1935   6-0 v Leyton, FA Cup Rnd 2, 1925-26
Record League Defeat: 1-8 v Burnley, Div 2, 13.9.1930   0-7 v Preston North End, Div 2, 27.8.1928
Record Cup Defeat: 0-18 v Preston North End, FA Cup Rnd 1, 27.1.1894
Oldest Player in a League Match: Beaumont Ratcliffe, 39 years 336 days v Northampton Town, 1947-48
Youngest Player in a League Match: Steve Hetzke, 16 years 184 days v Darlington, 4.12.1971

LONGEST LEAGUE RUNS

of undefeated matches: 19 (1973)
of undefeated home matches: 55 (1933-36)
without home win: 8 (1954, 1991)
of league wins: 13 (1985, record for start of a season)
of league defeats: 6 (1971)

of league matches without a win: 14 (1927)
of undefeated away matches: 11 (1985)
without an away win: 21 (1952-53)
of home wins: 19 (1931-32)
of away wins: 7 (1951-52, 1985)

READING							APPEARANCES				GOALS			
PLAYERS NAME Honours	Ht	Wt	Birthdate	Birthplace Transfers	Contract Date	Clubs	League	L/Cup	FA Cup	Other	Lg	L/C	FAC	Oth
GOALKEEPERS														
Steve Francis	5.11	11.5	29.05.64	Billericay	28.04.82	Chelsea (A)	71	6	10	1				
E:Y.2,FMC'86,SC'88				£20,000	27.02.87	Reading	182	15	11	12				
Daniel Honey					04.07.19	Reading (T)			1					
DEFENDERS														
Mark Holzman	5.7	10.7	22.02.73	Bracknell	04.07.91	Reading (T)	11+5	2	2	2	1			
Jeff Hopkins	6.0	12.11	14.04.64	Swansea	10.09.81	Fulham (A)	213+6	26	12	3	4	2		
W: 16,u21.5,Y				£240,000	17.08.88	Crystal Palace	70	7	4	12	2	1	1	
				Loan	24.10.91	Plymouth A	8			1				
				Monthly	05.03.92	Bristol Rovers	4+2							
				Free	13.07.92	Reading								
Keith McPherson	5.11	11.0	10.09.63	Greenwich	12.09.81	West Ham U. (A)	1							
FAYC'81,Div.4'87				Loan	30.09.85	Cambridge Utd	11				1			
				£15,000	23.01.86	Northampton T	182	9	12	13	8	1		
					24.08.90	Reading	90	4	6	4	3			
Steve Richardson	5.7	10.3	11.02.62	Slough	13.02.80	Southampton (A)								
Div.3'86,Sc'88				f	22.07.82	Reading	362+3	25+1	32	13	3			
Adrian Williams	6.2	12.6	16.08.71	Reading	04.03.89	Reading (T)	69+2	5	8	4	6	2		1
MIDFIELD														
Danny Bailey	5.9	12.7	21.05.64	London		Bournemouth (A)	1+1							
Div.4'90						Non-League								
				Free	01.03.84	Torquay Utd	1							
via Wealdstone				Free	01.08.89	Exeter City	63+1	8	7	4+1	2			1
				£50,000	26.12.90	Reading	49+1		3		2			
				Loan	29.07.92	Fulham								
Kevin Dillon	6.0	11.0	18.12.59	Sunderland	14.07.77	Birmingham City	181+5	14	9		15	3		
E:u21.1,Y.1				£200,000	24.03.83	Portsmouth	206+9	19+2	13	8	45	6	1	4
				Free		Newcastle Utd	62	3	6+1	3+1				
					07.08.91	Reading	29	2	1	1	3			
Mick Gooding	5.9	10.7	12.04.59	Newcastle		Bishop Auckland								
Div.3'81'89					18.07.79	Rotherham Utd	90+12	9	3		10	3		
					24.12.82	Chesterfield	12							
					09.09.83	Rotherham Utd	149+7	18	13	7	32	3	4	
				£18,000	13.08.87	Peterborough U	47	8	1	4	21	2	2	2
				£85,000	20.09.88	Wolverhampton W	43+1	4		5+1	4			1
				£65,000	26.12.89	Reading	110+1	4	8	7	13		1	1
Tom Jones	5.10	11.07	07.10.64	Aldershot		Chelsea (A)								
E.SP.1						Farnboro'			2					
via Weymouth				£30,000		Aberdeen	14+14		1+2		3			
						Swindon Town	162+6	14+4	10	11	12			
				swap	09.07.92	Reading								
Stuart Lovell	5.10	11.0	09.01.72	Sydney (Aus)	13.07.90	Reading (T)	38+16		2+2	3+2	6		2	
Mark McGhee	5.10	12.0	25.05.57	Glasgow		Bristol City (A)								
S:4, u21						Morton								
					31.12.77	Newcastle Utd	21+7				5			
					28.03.79	Aberdeen	152+12	33+1	20	30+1	60	17	6	14
via Hamburg (01.07.84)					01.07.85	Celtic	62+26	4+1	10+5	4+2	27	1	4	2
				£200,000	04.08.89	Newcastle Utd	63+4	5	6	5	24	1	6	
				N.C.	23.07.91	Reading								
Phil Parkinson	6.0	11.6	01.12.67	Chorley	07.12.85	Southampton (A)								
				£12,000	08.03.88	Bury	133+12	6+1	4	13	5		1	1
				£37,500	10.07.92	Reading								
Scott D Taylor	5.10	10.0	28.11.70	Reading	22.06.89	Reading (T)	69+24	5	5+2	3+3	5	1	1	
FORWARDS														
Michael Gilkes	5.8	10.10	20.07.65	Hackney		Leicester City								
SC'88,FL X1'88				Free	10.07.84	Reading	181+19	15+3	21+2	16+2	20	6	1	1
				Loan	28.01.92	Chelsea	0+1			0+1				
				Loan	04.03.92	Southampton	4+2							
Jimmy Quinn	6.0	11.6	18.11.59	Belfast		Oswestry								
NI: 27				£10,000	31.12.81	Swindon Town	34+15	1+1	5+3	1	10		6	2
				£32,000	15.08.84	Blackburn Rovers	58+13	6+1	4	2	17	2	3	1
				£50,000	19.12.86	Swindon Town	61+3	6	5	10+1	30	8		5
				£210,000	20.06.88	Leicester City	13+18	2+1	0+1	0+1	6			
					17.03.89	Bradford City	35	2		1	14	1		
				£320,000	08.01.90	West Ham U	34+13	3	4+2	1	19	1	2	
				£40,000	05.08.91	Bournemouth	43	4	5	2	19	2	2	1
				£55,000	27.07.92	Reading								
ADDITIONAL CONTRACT PLAYERS														
Lea Barkus			07.12.74	Reading		Reading	4+2				1			
David Bass			29.11.74	Frimley		Reading	2+1							
Adrian Chatterley					07.01.89	Reading								
Dudley Gardiner					30.07.92	Reading								
Aaron Giamattei					10.07.92	Reading	0+2							
Andrew Gray					03.07.92	Reading (T)	0+1							
Daniel Henderson					13.02.91	Reading								
Chris Lambert					03.07.92	Reading								
Daren McCance					03.07.92	Reading (T)								

LEADING LEAGUE GOALSCORERS SEASONS 1985-86 – 1991-92

1985-86	**TREVOR SENIOR**	27	1986-87	**TREVOR SENIOR**	17
1987-88	**COLIN GORDON**	8	1988-89	**TREVOR SENIOR**	15
1989-90	**TREVOR SENIOR**	14	1990-91	**TREVOR SENIOR**	15

1991-92   **CRAIG MASKELL**   **16**

ELM PARK Norfolk Road, Reading RG3 2EF

Capacity: **Covered Standing:**   **Seating:**

Tel: Ground: 0734 507878   **Ticket Sales:** As ground number   **Clubcall:** 0898 12 1000

All premium rate calls (0898/0891) cost 36p per minute cheap rate and 48p per minute at all other times. Call costings correct at time of going to press.

GROUNDS
Reading Recreation Ground 1871. Reading CC 1882. Coley Park 1882-89. Caversham CC 1889-96. Elm Park 1896-

ATTENDANCES
Highest: 33,042 v Brentford, FA Cup 19.2.1927

Lowest: 1,403 v Orient, Freight Rover Trophy, 6.3.1986

Record Receipts: (with previous records)
£70,693.79 v Arsenal, FA Cup 3rd Round, 10.1.1987
£61,589 v Coventry City, Simod Cup Semi-Final, 2.3.1988
£40,456 v Chelsea, Littlewoods Cup 2, 23.9.1987
£31,631 v Aston Villa, Div 2, 19.3.1988

Season Tickets:
Stands: from £172 to £207 (no reductions)
Ground: £138, juv/OAP £80.50

Cost of Stand Tickets: Seats: £7.50 to £9
Terraces: (home) £6, juvenile/OAP £3.50; (away) £7, juvenile/OAP £4

Match and Ticket Information: Stand tickets bookable 14 days in advance of match

Car Parking: Space for 300 in Norfolk Road and Tilehurst Road. Only available on season ticket basis

Nearest Railway Station: Reading (0734 595911) and bus or Reading West (10 minutes walk)

How to get to the ground

From North: From Oxford use A423, A4074 and A4155 and cross railway bridge into Reading, follow signs Newbury A4 into Castle Hill, turn right into Tilehurst Rd. In 0.7m turn right into Cranbury Rd, turn left, then take 2nd left into Norfolk Rd for Reading FC
From East: Use Motorway M4 until J 10, leave motorway and use A329 and A4 into Reading. Follow signs Newbury into Bath Rd. Over railway bridge then take 3rd turning on right into Liebenrood Rd. At end turn left then right into Waverley Rd, and turn right into Norfolk Rd for Reading FC
From South: Use A33 into Reading then follow signs Newbury A4 into Bath Rd. Over railway bridge then take 3rd turning on right into Liebenrood Rd. At end turn left then right into Waverley Rd, and turn right into Norfolk Rd for Reading FC
From West: Use Motorway M4 until J 12, leave motorway and follow signs Reading A4. In 3.3m turn left into Liebenrood Rd. At end turn left then right into Waverley Rd, and turn right into Norfolk Rd for Reading FC

Value Rating: ★ ★ ★

Programme Editor: Maurice O'Brien

Price of 1992-93 Programme: £1.20
Number of Pages: 32
Subscriptions: Contact supporters club

Local Newspapers: Reading Evening Post, Reading Chronicle

Local Radio Stations: Radio 210

Additional Publications on Club: Biscuits and Royals – A history of Reading Football Club 1871-1986 (David Downs, hardback, £11.95)

ROCHDALE

Division 3

Formed: 1907   **Turned Professional:** 1907   **Ltd Co:** 1910

SPONSORED BY: Smith Metals Ltd   **NICKNAME:** The Dale

President
Mrs L Stoney

Chairman
D F Kilpatrick

Directors
J Marsh
G Morris
C Dunphy
T Butterworth
L Hilton
M Mace
G R Brierley

Secretary
Keith Clegg (0706 44648)

Team Manager
Dave Sutton

Coach
Mick Docherty

Commercial Manager
Stephen Walmsley

Youth Development Officer
Jimmy Robson

Club Statistician for the Directory
Stephen Birch

ROCHDALE continued the steady improvements shown over the last four seasons. The team remained undefeated in league games until mid-October and did not suffer defeat on their travels until a 6-2 hammering at Scunthorpe on Guy Fawkes night. Indeed, until mid-February Rochdale were the envy of the rest of the league with only three league defeats. Entering the final week of March with only nine games remaining, the Dale's colours had been lowered on only five occasions and promotion appeared to be a distinct possibility. But with six more losses, five of which were suffered in the final six games, Rochdale slipped badly and missed out on both promotion and the play-offs. Although fans, players and officials were all deeply disappointed with this outcome, all deserve credit for the impressive and continuing progress of a club whose existence has been threatened on several occasions in the last fifteen years.

Manager Dave Sutton, in his first full season put together a fine mix of youth and experience, backed by directors who on more than one occasion dug deep into the coffers to strengthen the squad, including a new club record transfer fee paid for Andy Flounders. Although manager Sutton expressed his deep disappointment with the low level of fan support on several occasions, attendances rose for the fourth consecutive season and are now at the highest level for twenty years.

Limited progress was made in the two major cup competitions. In the F.A. Cup Rochdale shared the spotlight with an historic first round visit to Scotland to take on Gretna. A comfortable victory in a home replay was followed by a disappointing defeat at home to Huddersfield Town in Round Two. A first round hammering of Carlisle United in the Rumbelows Cup led to a two leg tie versus first division Coventry City which brought back happy memories of the Dale's historic F.A. Cup victory over the same team 21 years ago. Although Rochdale were able to repeat the medicine, on this occasion the narrow victory came after a 4-0 first leg defeat which no doubt explained the miserable attendance.

Record signing Flounders was the teams only ever-present as well as topping the scoring list with 17 league goals, although this might well have been more but for slump of only two goals in the final 13 games. Prospects continue to be bright for the Dale with a new grandstand about to be constructed. If the club can hold on to both manager Sutton and the impressive squad of players he has put together then the long-awaited return to a higher level might be achieved.

Stephen Birch

Back row L-R: Phil Stock (Physio), Andy Milner, Jon Bowden, Alan Reeves, Kevin Rose, Paul Butler, Tony Brown, John Ryan, Jimmy Robson (Youth Team Manager). **Middle:** Andy Thackeray, Mark Payne, Andy Flounders, Mick Docherty (Asst. Manager), Dave Sutton (Manager), Steve Whitehall, Jimmy Graham, Shaun Reid. **Front:** Jason Anders, Andy Howard, Carl Parker.

ROCHDALE

DIVISION FOUR: 8th   **FA CUP:** 2nd RND   **RUMBELOWS CUP:** 2nd RND   **AUTOGLASS:** Prelim.

M	DATE		COMP.	VEN	OPPONENTS	RESULT	H/T	LGE POS	GOALSCORERS/GOAL TIMES	ATTEN-DANCE
1	A	17	BL	H	York City	D 1-1	0-1		Tutill (og) 90	2,247
2		20	RC 1/1	H	Carlisle United	W 5-1	2-1		Milner 11, 89, Whitehall 48, 57, Ryan 27	1,650
3		27	RC 1/2	A	Carlisle United	D 1-1	0-0		Ryan 82	(1,572)
4		31	BL	H	Lincoln City	W 1-0	1-0		Flounders (pen) 16	2,086
5	S	3	BL	A	Walsall	W 3-1	2-0		Flounders 14, 53 (pen), Milner 29	(3,111)
6		7	BL	A	Cardiff City	W 2-1	1-0	7	Ryan 41, Reeves 90	(4,029)
7		14	BL	H	Northampton Town	W 1-0	0-0	4	Milner 67	2,631
8		17	BL	H	Rotherham United	D 1-1	1-0		Whitehall 40	4,043
9		21	BL	A	Burnley	W 1-0	0-0	3	Milner 70	(8,633)
10		25	RC 2/1	A	Coventry City	L 0-4	0-2			(5,982)
11		28	BL	H	Doncaster Rovers	D 1-1	1-0	4	Bowden 32	2,653
12	O	8	RC 2/2	H	Coventry City	W 1-0	0-0		Milner 88	2,288
13		12	BL	H	Mansfield Town	L 0-2	0-0	6		3,871
14		19	BL	A	Maidstone United	D 1-1	0-0	5	M Brown 50	(1,016)
15		22	AGT Pre	H	Preston North End	D 1-1	0-0		Whitehall 61	1,255
16		26	BL	H	Halifax Town	W 1-0	1-0	6	Flounders 26	2,323
17	N	2	BL	H	Chesterfield	D 3-3	2-1	6	Flounders 6, Halpin 45, Kinsey 62	1,852
18		5	BL	A	Scunthorpe United	L 2-6	0-3		Bowden 50, 79	(2,331)
19		9	BL	A	Hereford United	D 1-1	0-1	6	Judge (og) 58	(2,959)
20		16	FAC 1	A	Gretna	D 0-0	0-0			(2,000)
21		23	BL	H	Barnet	W 1-0	1-0	6	Bowden 45	3,033
22		27	FAC 1R	H	Gretna	W 3-1	3-0		Jones 15, Milner 22, Flounders 44	4,300
23		30	BL	A	Scarborough	L 2-3	0-1	8	Flounders 48, Milner 69	(1,643)
24	D	7	FAC 2	H	Huddersfield Town	L 1-2	1-0		Halpin 30	5,776
25		10	AGT Pre	A	Bolton Wanderers	L 1-4	0-0		Milner 65	(1,507)
26		14	BL	H	Blackpool	W 4-2	2-1	5	Flounders 12, Milner 20, Whitehall 80, 88	2,892
27		26	BL	A	York City	W 1-0	0-0	7	Flounders 89	(2,745)
28		28	BL	A	Lincoln City	W 3-0	3-0	7	Whitehall 26, Milner 38, Flounders 44	(2,916)
29	J	1	BL	H	Walsall	D 1-1	0-1	6	Flounders (pen) 86	3,001
30		11	BL	A	Carlisle United	D 0-0	0-0	6		(2,494)
31		18	BL	H	Crewe Alexandra	W 1-0	1-0	6	Flounders 8	2,965
32	F	8	BL	A	Halifax Town	D 1-1	0-1	8	Flounders 50	(2,213)
33		11	BL	H	Scarborough	D 2-2	0-2	8	Flounders (pen) 66, Reeves 90	2,069
34		15	BL	A	Blackpool	L 0-3	0-3	9		(4,632)
35		22	BL	H	Carlisle United	W 3-1	2-1	8	Milner 12, Bowden 44, Whitehall 54	1,691
36		29	BL	H	Wrexham	L 1-2	0-0	9	Whitehall 61	(3,458)
37	M	3	BL	A	Crewe Alexandra	D 1-1	0-0		Flounders 52	(3,870)
38		7	BL	H	Gillingham	W 2-1	0-1	9	Flounders 52, Milner 74	1,941
39		10	BL	H	Scunthorpe United	W 2-0	1-0		Milner 37, Lister (og) 60	2,036
40		14	BL	A	Chesterfield	W 1-0	1-0	6	Whitehall 14	(3,231)
41		17	BL	A	Gillingham	D 0-0	0-0			(2,300)
42		21	BL	H	Hereford United	W 3-1	1-0	6	Payne 19, Whitehall 76, Flounders 83	2,122
43		28	BL	A	Barnet	L 0-3	0-2	5		(3,099)
44		31	BL	A	Northampton Town	D 2-2	1-1		Cowdrill 45, Bowden 46	(2,010)
45	A	4	BL	H	Cardiff City	W 2-0	1-0	5	Reeves 24, Milner 84	2,650
46		7	BL	H	Maidstone United	L 1-2	1-0		Flounders 18	2,248
47		11	BL	A	Rotherham United	L 0-2	0-1	5		(5,086)
48		20	BL	A	Doncaster Rovers	L 0-2	0-1			(2,255)
49		22	BL	H	Wrexham	W 2-1	1-0		Parker 9, Leonard 76	1,945
50	M	2	BL	A	Mansfield Town	L 1-2	0-0	8	Payne 88	(5,671)
51		5	BL	H	Burnley	L 1-3	1-2	8	Ryan 13	8,175

Best Home League Attendance: 8,175 v Burnley   Smallest: 1,691 v Carlisle Utd   Av Home Att: 2,784

Goal Scorers: Compared with 90-91: +545

League (57): Flounders 17 (4 pens), Milner 10, Whitehall 8, Bowden 6, Reeves 3, Opponents 3, Payne 2, Ryan 2, Leonard, Parker, Halpin, M Brown, Kinsey, Cowdrill

R/lows C (7): Milner 3, Ryan 2, Whitehall 2
FA Cup (4): Halpin, Milner, Jones, Flounders
Autoglass (2): Whitehall, Milner

Dearden K. (L)	Whitehall S.	Ryan J.	Brown A.	Reeves A.	Jones A.	Graham J.	Doyle S.	Flounders A.	Milner A.	Halpin J.	Morgan S.	Butler P.	Gary G.	Brown M.	Payne M.	Williams D. (L)	Hilditch M.	Bowden J.	Palin L. (L)	Kinsey S.	Rose K.	Kilner A. (L)	Cowdrill B. (L)	Parker C.	Referee	
1	2•	3	4	5	6	7	8	9	10*	11	12	14													J Smith	1
	2	3	4	5	6	7	8	9	10	11	S	S	1												S Bell	2
	2	3	4	5	6	7	8	9•	12	11*	14				1	10									I Cruikshanks	3
1	2	3	4	5	6	7	8	9•	10*	11	14				12										B Coddington	4
	2	3	4	5	6	7	8	9	10*	12		S			11	1									R Wiseman	5
	2	3	4	5	6	7	8	9	12	10*		S			11	1									P Durkin	6
	2*	3	4	5	6	7		9	8	10	12	S			11	1									J Kirkby	7
	2*	3	4	5	6	7		9	8	10		S			11	1									P Wright	8
	2	3	4	5	6	7		9	8	12		S			11*	1		10							I Hendrick	9
	12	3	4	5	6	7	8	9•	10*	11		14			2	1									M Brandwood	10
	2•	3	4	5	6	7*	8	9	11						12	1		14	10						T West	11
	14	3*	4	5	6	7	8	9	10			11•	1	2	12										C Trussell	12
	11*		4	5	6•	7	8	9	12	3			1	2	10			14							M Peck	13
	10		4	5	6	3	8	9	12	11		14	1	2				7*							G Poll	14
	10		4	5	6		8	9	11*	3		S	1	2				12	7						G Singh	15
	14	3*	4	5		7	8	9		6			1	2				12	10	11•					K Cooper	16
	14	3	4	5		7	8	9•		6			1	2				12	10*	11					R Nixon	17
		3	4	5	12	7*	8	9		6			1	2				14	10	11•					J Key	18
	11	7	4	5	6	3		10	12	9*			1	2				8		S					J Rushton	19
	10*	7	4	5	6	3		9•	14	11			1	2				8		12					K Redfern	20
		4	5	6*	3	8	9	12	11				2	7				10		14	1				R Poulain	21
	14		4		5	8	9•	7	11			12	1	2	6				10		3*				K Redfern	22
	3		4		S	8	9	7	11			5		2	6				10			1			R Shepherd	23
	14	7	4		3	5*	9	8	11•			12		2	6				10			1			K Lupton	24
	S	7	4		3		9	8	11			5		2	6				10	S		1			P Danson	25
	12	7	4		3		9*	8	11•			5		2	6				10		14	1			J Watson	26
	14	7	4*		3	8	9	11	12			5•		2	6				10			1			A Dawson	27
	10	7*	4		3	5	9	8	11			12		2	6					S		1			P Taylor	28
	10	7	4		3		9	8	11*	14		5		2	6•					12	1				K Lupton	29
	12		4	S	3	7	9*	8	11			5		2	6			10			1				J Lloyd	30
	12		4	S	3	7	9	8*	11			5		2	6			10			1				S Lodge	31
		4	5	S	3	7	9	8	12			5		2	6			10*			1	11			W Flood	32
		4	14		3	7	9	8	12			5		2•	6			10			1	11*			P Danson	33
	12	14	4	2		8	9		11•			5			6			10			1	7*	3		M Brandwood	34
	11	12	4	2		8	9	7*	14			5			6*			10			1		3		W Burns	35
	11	12	4	2		8	9	7*	14			5*			6			10			1		3		K Barratt	36
		11	4	5		8	9	7	S	S		2			6			10			1		3		J Kirkby	37
	12	11	4	5		8	9•	7				14		2	6*			10			1		3		I Cruikshanks	38
	12	11	4	5		8	9•	7				14		2	6*			10			1		3		D Shadwell	39
	7*	11	4	5		8	9		6			12	2		S			10			1		3		M Reed	40
	7•	11	4	5		14	8	9		6*		12	2								1	3	10		P Foakes	41
	7		4	5		11*	8•	9				12	10	2							1	3	14		P Vanes	42
	11			5		S		9				12			2			10			1	3	4	8	A Gunn	43
		11	4	5		S		9				12	5					10			1	3		8	A Buksh	44
	14	11	4	5			9	7				2*						10			1	3		8•	A Bennett	45
	12	11	4	5		2		9	7						6			10*			1	3	S	8	S Bell	46
	12	11		5		2		9	8				4•		6			10*			1	3		7	K Breen	47
	14	7	4	5		12		9	8	11•					6			10			1	3*		2	A Wilkie	48
		7	4	5		3		9	8			14	2*		6•			12			1		11	10	D Phillips	49
		7	4	5		3		9•	8			14	2*		6			12			1		11	10	R Shepherd	50
	12	7	4	5		3		9	8					2	6*			S			1		11	10	V Callow	51
2	20	29	40	33	12	29	27	42	28	22	1	22	6	18	32	6		25	3	3	28	3	15	5 9	League Appearances	
	14	13		1	1		2		5	9		11			3			2	6		3			1	Substitute Appearances	
2+2	4	4	4	4	4	4	4	3+1	3		0+1	1+1	3		2	1+1	1								R/lows Appearances	
	1	2	3	1	2	2	2	3	2	3		0+2	2	3	2			3		1+1	1				FA Cup Appearances	
	1	1	2	1	1	1	1	2	2	2		1	1	2	1			3		0+1	2		1		Autoglass Appearances	

Also Played: Posn.(Game): Stiles 7(43*,44*)12(45)14(47), Lockett S(23)

Players on Loan: Dearden (Tottenham), Kilner (Stockport), Cowdrill (Bolton Wndrs), Stiles (Doncaster), Williams (Burnley), Palin (Hull City)

ROCHDALE

Club Colours: Royal blue shirts, royal blue shorts, royal blue stockings
Change Colours: Yellow shirts, yellow shorts, yellow stockings
Reserves League: Midland Senior League

Previous Managers: 1920-21 William Bradshaw   1921-22 No appointment made   1922-23 Thomas C Wilson   1923-30 Jack Peart   1930 Harry Martin (caretaker)   1930-31 William Smith Cameron   1931-32 Vacant   1932-34 Herbert Hopkinson   1934-35 William H Smith   1935-37 Ernest Nixon (caretaker)   1937-38 Sam Jennings   1938-52 Ted Goodier   1952 Jack Warner   1953-58 Harry Catterick   1958-60 Jack Marshall   1960-67 Tony Collins   1967-68 Bob Stokoe   1968-70 Len Richley   1970-73 Dick Connor   1973-76 Walter Joyce   1976-77 Brian Green   1977-78 Mike Ferguson   1978-79 Peter Madden (caretaker)   1979 Doug Collins   1979-83 Peter Madden   1983-84 Jimmy Greenhoff   1984-86 Vic Halom   1986-88 Eddie Gray   1988-89 Danny Bergara   1989-91 Terry Dolan
Honours: None
League Career: Elected to Div 3N 1921   Transferred to Div 3 1958   Relegated to Div 4 1958-59   Promoted to Div 3 1968-69   Relegated to Div 4 1973-74

CLUB RECORDS

Most Appearances for Club: Graham Smith (1966-74): League 316+1, FA Cup 15, League Cup 13 **Total 344+1 sub**
Most Capped Player: No Rochdale player has won an international cap
Record Goalscorer in a Match: Tommy Tippett 6 v Hartlepool (a), 8-2, Div 3N, 21.4.1930
Record League Goalscorer in a Season: Albert Whitehurst 44 (1926-27)   **In All Competitions:** Albert Whitehurst, 46 (League 44 + FA Cup 2)
Record League Goalscorer in a Career: Reg Jenkins 119   **In All Competitions:** Reg Jenkins 130 (League 119 + FA Cup 5 + League Cup 6) 1964-73
Record Transfer Fee Received: £200,000 plus 25% of any future fee from Bristol City for Keith Welch, July 1991
Record Transfer Fee Paid: £80,000 to Scunthorpe Utd for Andy Flounders, July 1991
Best Performances: League: 9th Div 3, 1969-70   **FA Cup:** 5th Round, 1989-90   **League Cup:** Runners-Up 1962 (4th Div Record)
Most League Points: (2pts a win) 62 Div 3N, 1923-24   (3pts a win) 67 Div 4, 1991-92
Most League Goals: 105, Div 3N, 1926-27
Record League Victory: 8-1 v Chesterfield, Div 3N, 18.12.1926   7-0 v Walsall, Div 3N, 24.12.1921   7-0 v York City (a), Div 3N, 14.1.1939   7-0 v Hartlepool, Div 3N, 2.11.1957
Most Goals Scored in a First Class Match: Record League Victory (above)   8-2 v Crook Town (h), 1st Round FA Cup, 26.11.1927   8-2 v Hartlepool United (a), Div 3N, 22.4.1930
Record League Defeat: 1-9 v Tranmere Rovers, Div 3N, 25.12.1931   0-8 v Wrexham (a), Div 3, 28.9.1929   0-8 v Leyton Orient (a), Div 4, 20.10.1987
Record Cup Defeat: 0-6 v Wigan Atheltic, Freight Rover Trophy, 28.1.1986
Oldest Player in a League Match: Jack Warner (player/manager) 41 years 195 days v Chesterfield, Div 3N, 4.4.1953
Youngest Player in a League Match: Zac Hughes, 16 years 105 days v Exeter City, Div 4, 19.9.1987

LONGEST LEAGUE RUNS	
of undefeated matches: 20 (1923-24)	of league matches without a win: 28 (1931-32)
of undefeated home matches: 34 (1923-25)	of undefeated away matches: 9 (1923-24)
without home win: 16 (1931-32)	without an away win: 37 (1977-78)
of league wins: 8 (1969)	of home wins: 16 (1926-27)
of league defeats: 17 (1931-32)	of away wins: 4 (1923-24, 1926, 1946, 1947, 1969)

ROCHDALE

PLAYERS NAME Honours	Ht	Wt	Birthdate	Birthplace Transfers	Contract Date	Clubs	League	L/Cup	FA Cup	Other	Lg	L/C	FAC	Oth
GOALKEEPERS														
Kevin Rose	6.1	13.6	23.11.60	Evesham		Ledbury Town								
					25.08.79	Lincoln City								
						Ledbury Town								
					16.03.83	Hereford Utd	268	16	13	19				
				£25,000	07.07.89	Bolton W	10	6						
Loan Halifax Town (01.02.90)				Loan	22.03.90	Carlisle Utd	11							
Loan Rochdale (14.02.91) 3lg				Small fee	21.11.91	Rochdale	28		1	1				
DEFENDERS														
Antony J Brown	6.2	12.7	17.09.58	Thackley		5								
				f	24.03.83	Leeds Utd	24				1			
				f	03.11.84	Doncaster Rovers	85+2	4	3	3	2			
				£10,000	27.07.87	Scunthorpe Utd	46+8	7+1	2+1	3	2			
				Free		Rochdale	107+2	7	8	5				
Paul Butler	6.3	13.0	02.11.72	Manchester	05.07.91	Rochdale (T)	22+5	1+1	0+2	1				
Vincent Chapman	5.9	11.0	05.12.67	Newcastle		Tow Law Town								
					29.01.88	Huddersfield Town	4+2							
Loan York City (23.03.89)				Free		Rochdale	23+1		1		1			
James Graham	6.0	11.8	10.02.69	Glasgow	12.09.88	Bradford City	6+1							
				Loan	03.11.89	Rochdale	11		4	3				
				£15,000	09.07.90	Rochdale	55+4	8	4	3	1			
Alan Reeves	5.11		19.11.67	Birkenhead	20.09.88	Norwich City								
				Loan	09.02.89	Gillingham	18							
				£10,000	18.08.89	Chester City	31+9	1+1	3	3	2			
				Free	02.07.91	Rochdale	33+1	4	1	1	3			
John Ryan	5.10	11.7	18.02.62	Failsworth	19.02.80	Oldham Ath. (A)	77	6	2		8			
E:u21.1					05.08.83	Newcastle Utd	28	2	1		1			
					28.09.84	Sheffield Wed	5+3	1			1			
					24.08.85	Oldham Ath	20+3	2	2					
				£25,000	02.10.87	Mansfield Town	53+9	1+1	7	5+1	1		1	
					28.06.89	Chesterfield	81+1	3	1	5	6			1
					01.07.91	Rochdale	29+3	4	2	1	2	2		
MIDFIELD														
Jon Bowden	6.0	11.7	21.01.63	Stockport	22.01.80	Oldham Ath. (A)	73+9	5	4		5	1		
					06.09.85	Port Vale	64+6	3+1	5+1	6	7			
				£12,500	06.08.87	Wrexham	137+10	10	5+1	14	20		1	3
				Free	18.09.91	Rochdale	25+6		3	2	6			
Steve Doyle	5.10	11.1	02.06.58	Neath	01.06.85	Preston N.E. (A)	178+19	16+1	15+1		8		1	
W: u21(2);Div3'88				Free	03.09.82	Huddersfield Town	158+3	15	11		6			
				£57,500	18.09.86	Sunderland	99+1	4	5	6	2			
				£75,000	14.08.89	Hull City	47	5	1	1	2			
					22.11.90	Rochdale	58	4	2	3				
Carl Parker	5.9	10.10	25.03.71	Burnley		Rosendale U								
					14.08.89	Rochdale	5+1							1
Mark Payne	5.9	11.09	03.08.60	Cheltenham		Cambuur (H								
					25.08.88	Stockport Co	77+10	6	3+1	4	16			
				Swap for P	28.06.91	Rochdale	32+2	1+1	2	1	2			
Andy Thackeray	5.9	11.0	13.02.68	Huddersfield	15.02.86	Manchester City (A)								
FAYC				Free	01.08.86	Huddersfield Town	2			0+1				
					27.03.87	Newport Co	53+1	3+1	1	2+1	4			1
				£5,000	20.07.88	Wrexham	139+13	10	6	13+2	14	1		
				£15,000	15.07.92	Rochdale								
FORWARDS														
Andrew Flounders	5.9	11.3	13.12.63	Hull	24.12.81	Hull City (A)	126+33	6+2	10+3	6+3	54	3	4	2
					05.03.87	Scunthorpe Utd	186+10	14	11+2	19	87	6	3	4
					09.08.91	Rochdale	42	4	3	2	17		1	
Andy Howard				Monthly		Blackpool								
					01.08.92	Rochdale								
Mark Leonard	5.11	11.10	27.09.62	St Helens		Witton Alb								
					24.02.82	Everton								
				Loan	24.03.83	Tranmere Rovers	6+1							
				Free	01.06.83	Crewe Alexandra	51+3	4	2	3+1	15	2		
				Free	13.02.85	Stockport Co	73	5	1	2	23	2		3
				£40,000	27.09.86	Bradford City	120+37	13+5	6+3	6+5	29	6	1	3
				Nominal	27.03.92	Rochdale	9				1			
Andrew Milner	6.0	11.12	10.02.67	Kendal		Netherfield								
					24.01.89	Manchester City								
				£20,000	18.01.90	Rochdale	72+12	6+1	4+1	4	19	5	1	2
Shaun Reid	5.8	11.10	13.10.65	Huyton	20.09.83	Rochdale (A)	126+7	10	5	12	4	2	1	
				Loan	12.12.85	Preston N.E	3							
				£32,500	23.12.88	York City	76+2	5	1	3	6			1
				Free	12.12.85	Rochdale								
Steve Whitehall	5.10	11.0	08.12.66	Birmingham		Southport								
					23.07.91	Rochdale	20+14	2+2	1	1	8	2		1

ADDITIONAL CONTRACT PLAYERS

Dave Allen, Jason Anders, Tony Colletton, Paul Hardcock.

LEADING LEAGUE GOALSCORERS SEASONS 1985-86 – 1991-92

1985-86	**STEVE TAYLOR**	25	1986-87	**LYNDON SIMMONDS**	10
1987-88	**LYNDON SIMMONDS**	12	1988-89	**DAVID FRAIN**	12
1989-90	**STEVE O'SHAUGHNESSY**	8	1990-91	**PETER COSTELLO**	10

1991-92   **ANDREW FLOUNDERS**   17

SPOTLAND   Willbutts Lane, Rochdale OL11 5DS

Capacity: 10,000   **Covered Standing:**   **Seating:** 1,852

Tel: Ground: 0706 44648   **Ticket Sales:** As ground number   **Clubcall:** 0898 12 15 03

All premium rate calls (0898/0891) cost 36p per minute cheap rate and 48p per minute at all other times. Call costings correct at time of going to press.

ATTENDANCES
Highest: 24,231 v Notts County, FA Cup Round 2, 10.12.1949

Lowest: 588 v Cambridge United, Div 3, 5.2.1974 (played on a Thursday afternoon during power cuts)

Record Receipts: v Burnley, Div 4, 5.5.1992

SPOTLAND
First game: v Oldham Ath., Friendly, 3.9.1907
First floodlit game: v St. Mirren, 16.2.1954

Season Tickets:
Stands: Not available
Ground: £90, juv/OAP £45

Executive Box Season Tickets: Apply to club for details

Cost of Tickets: Stand: Not availabe until Christmas 1992
Ground: £5 (£2.50 OAPs/Juv)

Match and Ticket Information: Seats bookable in advance

Car Parking: At the ground (£1) and in adjacent streets

Nearest Railway Station: Rochdale

How to get to the ground

From North: Use A680 S.P. Rochdale then turn right into Willbutts Lane for Rochdale FC

From East and West: Use Motorway M62 until junction 20 then follow signs Rochdale. In 1.5m at roundabout take 2nd exit into Roch Valley Way and in 1.5m turn right into Willbutts Lane for Rochdale FC

Value Rating: ★ ★ ★

Programme Editor: Stephen Walmsley

Price of 1992-93 Programme: £1
Number of Pages: 32
Subscriptions: £31 for home matches

Local Newspapers: Rochdale Observer, Manchester Evening News

Local Radio Stations: Radio Manchester, Radio Piccadilly

ROTHERHAM UNITED

Division 2

Formed: 1884   **Turned Professional:** 1905   **Ltd Co:** 1920

SPONSORED BY: Parkgate Retail World (Stadium Development) **NICKNAME:** The Merry Millers

President
Sir J Layden

Chairman
K F Booth

Vice-Chairman
R Hull

Directors
C Luckock
J A Webb

Secretary
N Darnill (0709 562434)

Team Manager
Phil Henson

Assistant Manager
John Breckin

Physiotherapist
Ian Bailey

Commercial Manager
D Nicholls (0709 562760)

Club Statistician for the Directory
Mike Smith

SWEET success after last years' disappointments – but no hint of things to come in the close-season, indeed it was not until the last minute that any signings were made.

The season started well with the defeat of a physical Burnley side, though Grimsby handed us an early exit from the Rumbelows Cup. Through September and October we maintained a top ten position while going through a very difficult period with many injuries. Into November results improved, culminating in that exciting, first-ever F.A. Cup penalty shoot-out.

The turn of the year saw us string together some good results, none better than the wins at Burnley and Crewe within the space of three days. However, after this burst, came a period when the team found scoring difficult – even missing five penalties in a row – and rock bottom was reached at Gillingham. Burnley saw us out of the Autoglass Trophy, again on penalties, but this seemed to be the turning point. From then to the end of the season there were to be only two defeats and several well-earned wins. Out of these I would select the Rochdale match as the best team performance and that against Blackpool as the most exciting, with the home fans creating an atmosphere the 'Tangerines' could not live with.

So it's congratulations to all, but especially to 'Player of the Year' and 'King of Tivoli' Nicky Law – an absolute rock in defence; also to groundsman Bill Corby for the super playing surface and to all the 'reserves' who most ably 'filled in' through the injury crisis, yet still managed to retain their Pontin's League Division One spot – just!

Here's wishing everyone well in the new season – players, officials and spectators – Up the Millers!

Mike Smith

Back row L-R: M Ridenton, T Cunningham, N Richardson, N Law, B Mercer, M Clarke, N Johnson, J Rockett, S Goater, L Curtis.
Middle row: B Russell (Youth Team Coach), D Hazel, J Howard, I Banks, J Breckin (Asst. Manager), A Pickering, S Gleeson, D Page, I Bailey (Physio). **Front row:** A Taylor, M Todd, C Hutchings, P Henson (Manger), S Goodwin, D Barrick, I Hathaway.

ROTHERHAM UNITED

DIVISION FOUR: RUNNERS-UP **FA CUP:** 2nd RND **RUMBELOWS CUP:** 1st RND **AUTOGLASS:** 2nd RND

M		DATE	COMP.	VEN	OPPONENTS	RESULT		H/T	LGE POS	GOALSCORERS/GOAL TIMES	ATTEN-DANCE
1	A	17	BL	H	Burnley	W	2-1	0-1		Johnson 73, Cunningham 79	6,042
2		20	RC 1/1	H	Grimsby Town	L	1-3	0-1		Robinson 69	3,839
3		24	BL	A	Lincoln City	W	2-0	0-0	3	Cunningham 53, Robinson 78	(4,134)
4		27	RC 1/2	A	Grimsby Town	L	0-1	0-1			(3,637)
5		31	BL	H	Crewe Alexandra	L	1-2	1-1	7	Johnson 42	4,362
6	S	3	BL	A	Carlisle United	W	3-1	1-1	5	Goodwin 42, Richardson 64, Page 89	(2,346)
7		7	BL	H	Hereford United	D	0-0	0-0	6		3,778
8		13	BL	A	Halifax Town	W	4-0	0-0	1	Cunningham 53, Goater 61, Hutchings 64, Wilson 75	(2,653)
9		17	BL	A	Rochdale	D	1-1	0-1	3	Hutchings 50	(4,033)
10		21	BL	H	Maidstone United	D	3-3	1-1	5	Hazel 13, Page 69, 82	3,870
11		28	BL	A	Blackpool	L	0-3	0-1	7		(5,356)
12	O	12	BL	A	Chesterfield	D	1-1	0-1	9	Cunningham 87	(6,133)
13		25	BL	H	York City	W	4-0	1-0	8	Page 34, Hutchings 58, Cunningham 81, 85	4,676
14	N	2	BL	H	Northampton Town	W	1-0	0-0	4	Cunningham 61	3,146
15		6	BL	A	Doncaster Rovers	D	1-1	0-0	5	Wilson 52	(3,507)
16		10	BL	A	Scunthorpe United	L	0-1	0-0	5		(4,175)
17		16	FAC 1	A	Scunthorpe United	D	1-1	1-0		Cunningham 13	(4,511)
18		22	BL	H	Walsall	W	2-1	1-0	5	Cunningham 22, Watts 72	4,192
19		20	FAC 1R	H	Scunthorpe United	W	†3-3	1-0		Page 24, 113, Goodwin 54 (Won 7-6 on pens)	4,829
20		30	BL	A	Cardiff City	L	0-1	0-1	6		(3,551)
21	D	7	FAC 2	A	Burnley	L	0-2	0-0			(9,775)
22		14	BL	H	Gillingham	D	1-1	0-1	6	Cunningham 69	3,137
23		21	BL	H	Lincoln City	D	1-1	0-1	6	Cunningham 74	3,293
24		26	BL	A	Burnley	W	2-1	0-0	6	Cunningham 46, Page 77	(13,812)
25		28	BL	A	Crewe Alexandra	W	1-0	1-0	6	Hazel 23	(4,490)
26	J	1	BL	H	Carlisle United	W	1-0	0-0	5	Page 50	4,850
27		4	BL	A	Scarborough	L	0-2	0-0	5		4,497
28		11	BL	A	Barnet	W	5-2	3-0	5	Todd 13, Page 3 (32, 38, 86), Goodwin 88	(3,552)
29		18	BL	H	Mansfield Town	D	1-1	0-1	5	Hazel 89	6,454
30		21	AGT 1	H	Chester City	W	3-0	2-0		Wilson 3, Page 42, Goater 89	2,543
31	F	8	BL	A	York City	D	1-1	1-0	5	Todd 14	(3,526)
32		11	BL	H	Cardiff City	L	1-2	0-1	6	Hazel 58	3,827
33		15	BL	A	Gillingham	L	1-5	1-4	6	Goater 7	(2,486)
34		18	AGT 2	H	Burnley	D	†1-1	0-1		Hazel 71 (Lost 4-2 on pens)	2,578
35		22	BL	H	Barnet	W	3-0	1-0	6	Hutchins 36, Page 55, Cunningham 78	3,841
36		29	BL	A	Scarborough	W	3-0	0-0	5	Richardson 57, Hazel 66, Page 70	(2,604)
37	M	3	BL	A	Mansfield Town	L	0-1	0-0	7		(5,713)
38		7	BL	H	Wrexham	W	3-0	0-0	4	Cunningham 63, 68, Howard 74	3,562
39		10	BL	H	Doncaster Rovers	W	3-1	0-0	4	Howard 54, Cunningham 77, 88	4,883
40		14	BL	A	Northampton Town	W	2-1	2-0	4	Barrick 25, Goodwin 27	(2,561)
41		21	BL	H	Scunthorpe United	W	5-0	2-0	4	Goater 3 (44, 47, 87), Goodwin 45, Howard 58	4,528
42		28	BL	A	Walsall	W	2-0	0-0	4	Hazel 68, Goater 90	(3,524)
43		31	BL	H	Halifax Town	W	1-0	0-0	4	Wilson 49	4,517
44	A	4	BL	A	Hereford United	L	0-1	0-0	4		(1,868)
45		11	BL	H	Rochdale	W	2-0	1-0	4	Goater 33, Goodwin 7	5,086
46		18	BL	A	Maidstone United	D	0-0	0-0	3		(1,744)
47		20	BL	H	Blackpool	W	2-0	1-0	2	Hazel 7, Cunningham 60	8,992
48		28	BL	A	Wrexham	W	3-0	1-0	2	Goater 45, 80, Hazel 85	(3,477)
49	M	2	BL	H	Chesterfield	D	1-1	1-0	2	Cunningham 33	8,852

Best Home League Attendance: 8,992 v Blackpool   **Smallest:** 3,137 v Gillingham   **Av Home Att:** 4,780

Goal Scorers: **Compared with 90-91: +184**

League (70):   Cunningham 18, Page 11, Goater 9, Hazel 8, Goodwin 5, Hutchings 3, Wilson 3, Howard 3, Johnson 2, Richardson 2, Todd 2, Barrick, Robinson, Hutchins, Watts

R/lows C (1):   Robinson
FA Cup (4):   Page 2, Goodwin, Cunningham
Autoglass (4):   Hazel, Wilson, Page, Goater   †=After extra-time)

1991-92

Mercer W.	Hutchings C.	Robinson R.	Richardson N.	Johnson N.	Law N.	Goodwin S.	Barrick D.	Cunningham A.	Page D.	Hazel D.	Watts J.	Goater L.	Hathaway I.	Ford S.	Taylor A.	Todd M.	Wilson R.	Pickering A.	Russell W.	Thompson S.	McKnight	Ridenton	Barlow	Snodin G.		Referee	
1	2	3*	4	5	6	7	8	9	10	11	S	S														G Poll	1
1	**2**	**3**	**4**	**5**	**6**	**7**	**8***	**9**	**10**	**11**	**S**	**12**														**T Lunt**	**2**
1	2	3	4	5	6	7	8	9	10	11	S	S														B Hill	3
1	**2**	**3**	**4**	**5**	**6**	**7**	**8**	**9**	**10***	**11**	**S**	**12**														**R Hart**	**4**
1	2	3	4	5	6	7	8	9	10	11	S	S														D Allison	5
1	2	3	4	5	6	7•	8	9	10	11*	14	12														I Hendrick	6
1	2	3	4*	5	6		8	9	10		12	11	7													N Midgley	7
	2			5	6		8	9	10	11*		12		1	3	4	7	S								P Harrison	8
	2				6		8	9	10		5	11		1	3		7	4	S	S						P Wright	9
	2				6	7*	8	9	10	11	5	12		1	3			4		S						J Lloyd	10
	2				6	7	8	9	10	11	5	S		1	3	4		S								M Peck	11
1*	3				6	7	S	9	10	11	5	12				4	8	2								P Jones	12
	3			5	6	7*	12	9	10	11		S				4	8	2			1					W Flood	13
	3			5	6	7	S	9	10	11		S				4	8	2			1					I Cruikshanks	14
	3				6	7	12		10	11	5	9				4*	8	2			1	S				A Dawson	15
1	3				6	7	8	9	10	11	5	4						2		S		S				J Moules	16
1	**3**				**6**	**7**	**8**	**9**	**10**	**11**	**5**	**4**						**2**		**S**		**S**				**W Burns**	**17**
1	3			S	6	7	8	9	10	11	5	S				4		2								M Bailey	18
1	**3**			**S**	**6**	**7**	**8**	**9**	**10**	**11***	**5**	**12**				**4**		**2**								**W Burns**	**19**
1	3			5	6	7	8	9	10*	11	S	12				4		2								R Lewis	20
1	**3**			**5**	**6**	**7**	**8***	**9**	**10**	**11**		**12**			**S**	**4**		**2**								**J Watson**	**21**
1	3			5	6	7	8*	9	10•	12		11	14			4		2								R Nixon	22
1	3			5	6	7	S	9	S	10		11	8			4		2								J Parker	23
1	3			5	6	7	8	9	10	11		S	S			4		2								J Rushton	24
1	3			5	6	7	8	9	10	11		S	S			4		2								J Smith	25
1	3			5*	6	7	8	9	10	11	12	S				4		2								T West	26
1	3			5	6	7	8	9	10*	11	S	12				4		2								M Brandwood	27
1	3			5	6	7	8	9	10	11		S				4	S	2								R Hamer	28
1	3			5	6	7	8*	9	10	11		12				4		2					S			K Lupton	29
1	**3**			**5**	**6**		**8**	**9***	**10•**	**11**		**14**				**4**	**7**	**2**					**12**			**R Dilkes**	**30**
1	3			5	6	7	8	9	10	11						4*	12	2					S			R Poulain	31
1	3			5	6	7	8*	9	10	11		S	12				4	2								J Watson	32
1	3			5	6	7*	8	9	S	11		10	12				4	2								P Alcock	33
1	**3**		**7**	**5**	**6**		**8**	**9**	**14**	**11**		**10•**	**12**				**4***	**2**								**R Nixon**	**34**
1	3		8	5	6	7		9	10	11		S	S			4		2								A Wilkie	35
1	3		8	5	6	7		9	10	11		S	S			4		2								G Courtney	36
1			8	5	6	7		9	10	11		S	S			4		2						3		D Allison	37
1	3		S	5	6	7		9	10*	11						4		2						8	12	G Singh	38
1	3		S	5	6	7		9		11		S				4		2						8	10	K Redfern	39
1	3		4	5	6	7	8	9*				11	12•				14	2							10	R Pawley	40
1	3		8	5	6	7	11					9	14			4*	12	2•							10	I Cruikshanks	41
1	3		8	5	6	7*	11			12		9			S		4		2						10	K Burge	42
1	3•		8*	5	6	7	11			12		9	14				4		2						10	K Barratt	43
1	3		8*	5	6	7	11			12		9			S		4		2						10	J Worrall	44
1	3		4	5	6	7	8	S		11		9					S		2						10	K Breen	45
1	3		4	5	6	7	8	12		11		9*					S		2						10	K Morton	46
1	3		4	5	6	7	8	12	14	11		9							2*						10•	P Danson	47
1	2		4	5	6	7	8	10	S	11		9	S		3											R Gifford	48
1	3		4	5	6	7	8	9	12	11		10*			2							S				D Gallagher	49
35	41	5	18	35	42	39	32	34	29	34	7	17	2	4	6	23	11	27	6		3			3	9	**League Appearances**	
							2	2	2	4	3	7	6				3								1	**Substitute Appearances**	
2	2	2	2	2	2	2	2	2	2	2		0+2														**R/lows Appearances**	
3	3			1	3	3	3	3	3	3	2	1				2		3								**FA Cup Appearances**	
2	2		1	2	2		2	2	1+1	2		1+1	0+1			1	2	2					0+1			**Other Competitions**	

ROTHERHAM UNITED

Club Colours: Red shirts, white collar, red sleeves, white shorts with red trim, red stockings
Change Colours: Yellow shirts with blue trim, blue shorts with yellow trim, yellow stockings
Reserves League: Pontins Central League Div 1   **Youth Team:** Northern Intermediate

Previous League: Midland League
Previous Names: Thornhill United (1884), Rotherham County (1905), amalgamated in 1925 with Rotherham Town as Rotherham United
Previous Managers: (Since 1946): Reg Freeman Andy Smailes Tom Johnston Danny Williams Jack Mansell Tommy Docherty Jimmy McAnearney Jimmy McGuigan Ian Porterfield Emlyn Hughes George Kerr Norman Hunter Dave Cusack
Honours: Div 3N Champions 1950-51 Div 3 Champions 1980-81 Div 4 Champions 1988-89
League Career: Rotherham Town: Elected to Div 2 1893 Not re-elected to Div 2 1896
Rotherham County: Elected to Div 2 1919 Relegated to Div 3N 1923 Promoted to Div 2 1951 Relegated to Div 3 1968
Relegated to Div 4 1973 Promoted to Div 3 1975 Promoted to Div 2 1981 Relegated to Div 3 1983
Relegated to Div 4 1988 Promoted to Div 3 1989 Relegated to Div 4 1991

CLUB RECORDS

Most Appearances for Club: Danny Williams (1946-60): 459
Most Capped Player: Harold Millership, 6 Wales
Record Goalscorer in a Match: No player has scored more than four goals
Record League Goalscorer in a Season: Wally Ardron, 38, Div 3N, 1946-47
Record League Goalscorer in a Career: Gladstone Guest, 130, 1946-56
Record Transfer Fee Received: £180,000 from Everton for Bobby Mimms, May 1985
Record Transfer Fee Paid: £100,000 to Cardiff City for Ronnie Moore, August 1980
Best Performances: League: 3rd Div 2, 1954-55 **FA Cup:** 5th Round 1952-53, 1967-68   **League Cup:** Finalists 1960-61
Most League Points: (2pts for win) 71, Div 3N, 1950-51   (3pts a win) 82, Div 4, 1988-89
Most League Goals: 114, Div 3N, 1946-47
Record League Victory: 8-0 v Oldham Athletic, Div 3N, 26.5.1947
Record Cup Victory and Most Goals Scored in a Cup Tie: 6-0 v Spennymoor United, FA Cup Round 2, 1977-78 6-0 v Wolverhampton Wanderers, FA Cup Round 1, 16.11.1985
Record League Defeat: 1-11 v Bradford City, Div 3N, 25.8.1928*
* First match of the season. Rotherham United won their second match – at home!
Record Cup Defeat: 0-15 v Notts County, FA Cup Round 1, 24.10.1885
Oldest Player in a League Match:
Youngest Player in a League Match: Kevin Eley, 16 years 72 days v Scunthorpe (h), 3-0, 15.5.1984

LONGEST LEAGUE RUNS	
of undefeated matches: 18 (1950-51)	of league matches without a win: 14 (1934, 1977-78)
of undefeated home matches: 27 (1939-46-47)	of undefeated away matches: 16 (1950-51)
without home win: 9 (1983)	without an away win: 33 (1894-96-1919 – Non-League club)
of league wins: 9 (1982)	of home wins: 22 (1939-46-47)
of league defeats: 8 (1956)	of away wins: 8 (1948)

BARCLAYS

LOCAL BRANCH
Rotherham Branch
PO Box No. 56
Bridgegate
Rotherham
South Yorkshire S60 1PG
Tel: 0709 373721 & 364243

BARCLAYBANK MACHINE

BARCLAYS BUSINESS CENTRE
Sheffield: Fitzalan Square
PO Box No. 43
Commercial Street
Sheffield S1 1NG
Tel: 0742 729162

BARCLAYBANK MACHINE

ROTHERHAM UNITED

PLAYERS NAME Honours	Ht	Wt	Birthdate	Birthplace Transfers	Contract Date	Clubs	League	L/Cup	FA Cup	Other	Lg	L/C	FAC	Oth
							\<APPEARANCES\>				\<GOALS\>			
GOALKEEPERS														
Billy Mercer	6.1	11.0	22.05.69	Liverpool		Liverpool								
						Rotherham Utd	50	2	6	4				
DEFENDERS														
Shaun Goodwin Div.4'89	5.7	8.0	14.06.69	Rotherham	01.07.87	Rotherham Utd. (T)	142+13	5+6	10+1	9+2	18	1	1	
Nigel Johnson Div.4'89	6.2	12.8	23.06.64	Rotherham	02.08.82	Rotherham Utd. (A)	89	11	5	3	1			
					01.07.85	Manchester City	4			3				
				£75,000	22.07.87	Rotherham Utd	141+3	11	11	10	7		1	1
				Free										
Nicholas Law	6.0	13.5	08.09.61	Greenwich	17.07.79	Arsenal (A)								
				Free	04.08.81	Barnsley	113+1	5	6		1			
				Free	28.08.85	Blackpool	64+2	2	2	3	1			
					12.03.87	Plymouth A	37+1	2	2	0+1	5			
					17.06.88	Notts County	44+3	4	1	4	4			
Loan Scarborough (10.11.89) 12lg, 1FAC					01.08.90	Rotherham Utd	72+2	4	7	4	2			
Albert Pickering	5.9	10.08	22.06.67	Manchester		Buxton								
				£18,500	02.02.90	Rotherham Utd	37+1	1	4	3				
Neil Richardson	5.10	13.05	03.03.68	Sunderland	18.08.89	Rotherham Utd	36	3	1	2	4	1		
Billy Russell S: Y; Div.4'89	5.10	11.4	14.09.59	Glasgow	14.07.77	Everton (A)								
						Celtic								
				£15,000	24.07.79	Doncaster Rovers	241+3	17	16	5	15			
				Free	17.08.85	Scunthorpe Utd	113+4	10	9+1	8	7	1	3	
					11.08.88	Rotherham Utd	97+2	8	5+1	6	2			
					22.07.91	Rotherham Utd	6							
Andy Taylor	5.9	10.7	19.01.73	Wath, Rotherhay	01.07.91	Rotherham Utd. (T)	11							
MIDFIELD														
Ian F Banks	5.9	11.13	09.01.61	Mexborough	11.01.79	Barnsley (A)	158+6	19	11		37	3	1	
				£100,000	01.06.83	Leicester City	78+15	3+1	6		14	1		
				£45,000	19.09.86	Huddersfield Town	78	4	4	1	17	1		
				£180,000	21.07.88	Bradford City	26+4	5	1	1	3	3		
				£100,000	24.03.89	West Brom A	2+2							
				£100,000	02.08.89	Barnsley	87+6	6	5+1	4+1	7			4
				Free	30.07.92	Rotherham Utd								
Dean Barrick	5.9	11.4	30.09.69	Hemsworth	07.05.88	Sheffield Wed. (T)	11				2			
				£50,000	14.02.91	Rotherham Utd	51	2	3	2	3			
Chris Hutchings	5.10	11.0	05.07.57	Winchester		Southall								
						Harrow Bor								
				£10,000	19.07.80	Chelsea	83+4	7	7		3			
				£50,000	25.11.83	Brighton & H.A	153	7	11	3+1	4	1	1	
				£25,000	04.12.87	Huddersfield Town	110	6	8	7	10			
				Free	13.08.90	Walsall	40	4	2	3		1	1	
				Free	01.08.91	Rotherham Utd	41	2	3	2	3			
Mark Todd NI:u23.1	5.7	10.2	04.12.67	Belfast	07.08.85	Manchester Utd								
					01.07.87	Sheffield Utd	62+8	5+1	10+1	5+1	5		1	
				Loan	14.03.91	Wolverhampton W	6+1							
				£35,000	15.11.91	Rotherham Utd	23		2	1	2			
FORWARDS														
Tony Cunningham	6.1	13.2	12.11.57	Jamaica		Stourbridg								
				£20,000	11.05.79	Lincoln City	111+12	13	5+1		32	8		
				£85,000	23.09.82	Barnsley	40+2	2	1		11			
					10.11.83	Sheffield Wed	26+2		4+1		5			
					30.07.84	Manchester City	16+2	2	0+1		2	3		
					07.02.85	Newcastle Utd	37+10	2	1+1		4	2		
					04.08.87	Blackpool	71	8	5	6	17	3	2	2
				£40,000	02.08.89	Bury	55+3	4	1	9	17	1		4
				£70,000	28.03.91	Bolton W	9			3	4			
				£50,000	14.08.91	Rotherham Utd	34+2	2	3	2	18		1	
Shaun Goater	5.11	11.04	25.02.70	Bermunda		Manchester Utd								
				Loan	25.10.89	Rotherham Utd								
					19.01.90	Rotherham Utd	35+23	1+3	5+1	1+4	13		2	1
Ian Hathaway	5.8	10.06	22.08.68	Worsley		Bedworth								
				£8,000	08.02.89	Mansfield Town	21+23	1+1	1	3+1	2			1
					22.03.91	Rotherham Utd	5+8			0+1	1			
Desmond Hazel Div.4'89	5.10	10.4	15.07.67	Bradford	29.07.85	Sheffield Wed. (A)	5+1	1		0+1				
				Loan	23.10.86	Grimsby Town	9				2			
				£45,000	13.07.88	Rotherham Utd	131+21	11	14	12	20	2	1	4
Jonathan Howard	5.10	11.7	07.10.71	Sheffield	10.07.90	Rotherham Utd. (T)	9+2				3			
Donald Page	5.11	11.0	18.01.64	Manchester		Altrincham		1						
						Runcorn		7					1	
					23.03.89	Wigan Ath	62+12	5	5	4+2	15	2	2	3
					16.08.91	Rotherham Utd	29+2	2	3	1+1	11		2	1
ADDITIONAL CONTRACT PLAYERS														
Matthew Clarke					28.07.92	Rotherham Utd. (T)								
Stephen Gleeson					28.07.92	Rotherham Utd. (T)								
Michael Ridenton					10.10.91	Rotherham Utd								
Jason Rockett					25.03.92	Rotherham Utd								

LEADING LEAGUE GOALSCORERS SEASONS 1985-86 – 1991-92

1985-86	**TOMMY TYNAN**	**13**	1986-87	**GARETH EVANS**	**9**
1987-88	**PAUL HAYCOCK**	**12**	1988-89	**BOBBY WILLIAMSON**	**27**
1989-90	**BOBBY WILLIAMSON**	**19**	1990-91	**CLIVE MENDONCA**	**10**

1991-92   **TONY CUNNINGHAM**   **18**

MILLMOOR GROUND   Rotherham, South Yorks YO12 4HF

Capacity: 13,037   **Covered Standing:** 8,455   **Seating:** 4,582

Tel: Ground: 0709 562434   **Ticket Sales:** As ground number   **Clubcall:** 0890 12 16 37

All premium rate calls (0898/0890) cost 36p per minute cheap rate and 48p per minute at all other times. Call costings correct at time of going to press.

ATTENDANCES
Highest: 25,000 v Sheffield United, Div 2, 13.12.1952

Lowest: 1,182 v Scarborough, Leyland Daf Cup, 27.11.1990

Record Receipts: £44,091.75 v Manchester Utd, Littlewoods Cup, 28.9.1988

MILLMOOR GROUND
First game: v Tranmere Rov, 31.8.1925
First floodlit game: v Bristol Rovers, League Cup 2nd Rnd, 23.11.1960

Season Tickets:
Stands: from £120 to £150, juv/OAP £90 to £120
Ground: £100, juv/OAP £80

Executive Box Season Tickets: None

Cost of Stand Tickets: Main Stand: adults £7.50, junior/OAP £5.50; Millmoor Lane Stand: adult £6, junior/OAP £4.50; Enclosure seats: adults £6.50, junior/OAP £5
(Ground): adult £5, junior/OAP £3.80

Match and Ticket Information: Seats can be reserved one month before match.

Car Parking: There are parks within easy distance of the ground in Kimberworth Road and Main Street

Nearest Railway Station:
Rotherham Central (Town Centre)

How to get to the ground

From North: Use Motorway M1 until junction 34, leave Motorway and follow signs Rotherham A6109. Cross railway bridge and then turn right into Millmoor Lane for Rotherham United FC

From East: Use A630 into Rotherham and then follow signs Sheffield into Masborough Street, then turn left into Millmoor Lane for Rotherham United FC

From South and West: Use Motorway M1 until junction 34, leave motorway and follow signs Rotherham A6178. At roundabout take 1st exit into Ring Road and at next roundabout 1st exit in Masborough Street A6109. Take 1st turning left into Millmoor for Rotherham United FC

Value Rating: ★ ★ ★

Programme Editor: Dave Nicholls

Price of 1992-93 Programme: £1
Number of Pages: 40
Subscriptions: £35 for full season (includes postage)

Local Newspapers: Sheffield Morning Telegraph, Sheffield Star (including Saturday Special)

Local Radio Stations: Radio Hallam (194 medium wave), Radio Sheffield (290 medium wave)

Additional Publications on Club: Millmoor Personalities 1946-1986, (David Watson), paperback £6.95, A Post-War Who's Who

SCARBOROUGH

Division 3

Formed: 1879   **Turned Professional:** 1926   **Ltd Co:** 1933

SPONSORED BY: Ronson Plc   **NICKNAME:** The Boro

President & Chief Executive
J R Birley

Chairman
G Richmond

Director
J Fawcett MIPR
M Bramham
A Jenkinson
B Connolly

Secretary
K E Sheppard, MLIA, MISM

Team Manager
Ray McHale

Youth Team Coach
Phil Chambers

Club Statistician for the Directory
Andrew Whowell

PRE-SEASON aquisitions meant that Scarborough opened up the 1991-92 season with the youngest side in Football League history, an average age of 20.

To be fair, the season wasn't one that will be remembered for years to come, but the youngsters who were pitched in at the deep end worked hard and a final position of 12th is probably an apt reward.

Much earlier in the season, Boro' looked anything but a mid-table side. They went six games, from the beginning of the season, without a league win and the defeat against Aldershot on the 14th of September, left Boro' propping up the rest of the Football League for the first time ever.

Slowly results improved. With wins over Doncaster, Burnley, Northampton and Wrexham (all at home), plus very good away results at Crewe (3-3) and Blackpool (1-1), Boro' stood in a much healthier position of 14th.

The Christmas period, once again promised to turn Boro' into probable play-off candidates. After winning their first away game of the season, at Lincoln on the 17th of December, both Mansfield and Rotherham were beaten away and the outlook was much healthier, Boro' now stood 9th.

Unfortunately, the winter took its toll and by the time Scarborough got back into league action, well after a month, they had dropped back to mid-table.

To try and recover lost ground was beyond Boro's reach, but towards the end of the season, results did improve and only one of the last 10 games was lost.

In the cups, Boro' once again lost in the First Round of the F.A. Cup, but managed to survive the qualifying round of the Autoglass Trophy, before losing to Burnley in the First Round Proper. It was in the Rumbelows Cup where Boro' found success. Coming back from 2-5, a certain defeat, against Preston at Deepdale, to only losing 4-5, provided the spur Boro' needed and they won 7-6 on aggregate. Unfortunately, they lost at Southampton in the Second Round.

Andrew Whowell

![First Team Squad photograph]

First Team Squad 1992-93 *(Caption not received at time of going to press)*

SCARBOROUGH

DIVISION FOUR: 12th   **FA CUP:** 1st RND   **RUMBELOWS CUP:** 2nd RND   **AUTOGLASS:** 1st RND

M	DATE		COMP.	VEN	OPPONENTS	RESULT	H/T	LGE POS	GOALSCORERS/GOAL TIMES	ATTEN-DANCE
1	A	17	BL	H	Mansfield Town	D 0-0	0-0	12		2,343
2		20	RC 1/1	A	Preston North End	L 4-5	2-2		Ashdjian 4, Mooney 18, Hirst 85, Foreman 89	(2,683)
3		24	BL	H	Hereford United	L 1-4	1-4	19	Lowndes 27	(2,600)
4		28	RC 1/2	H	Preston North End	W †3-1	0-1		Foreman (pen) 47, Jules 89, Mooney 119	2,035
5		31	BL	H	Walsall	L 2-3	1-2	21	Mooney 17, Ashdjian 88	2,002
6	S	3	BL	A	Scunthorpe United	D 1-1	0-1	20	Mudd 51	(3,185)
7		7	BL	A	Gillingham	L 0-2	0-0	21		(3,375)
8		18	BL	H	Doncaster Rovers	W 1-0	1-0	19	Meyer 8	1,506
9		21	BL	A	Cardiff City	L 1-2	1-1	21	Ashdjian 31	(3,227)
10		24	RC 2/1	H	Southampton	L 1-3	0-2		Mooney 2	2,302
11		28	BL	H	Burnley	W 3-1	2-1	18	Meyer 17, Mooney 21, Ashdjian 69	2,596
12	O	5	BL	A	York City	L 1-4	1-3	20	Ashdjian 4	(2,971)
13		9	RC 2/2	A	Southampton	D 2-2	0-2		Himsworth 48, Mockler (pen) 74	(4,036)
14		12	BL	H	Northampton Town	W 2-1	0-0	15	Mockler (pen) 46, Lee 88	2,023
15		19	BL	A	Crewe Alexandra	D 3-3	0-2	16	Jules 85, Meyer 89, Mooney 90	(2,696)
16		26	BL	H	Barnet	L 0-4	0-2	17		1,942
17	N	2	BL	A	Blackpool	D 1-1	1-1	17	Meyer 10	(3,057)
18		5	BL	H	Wrexham	W 4-1	0-1	14	Sertori 49, Ashdjian 65, Jules 69, 75	1,164
19		9	BL	H	Carlisle United	D 2-2	2-0	15	Fletcher 11, Mockler (pen) 14	1,501
20		16	FAC 1	H	Wigan Athletic	L 0-2	0-1			1,889
21		19	AGT Pre	A	Huddersfield Town	D 1-1	0-0		Jules 85	(1,134)
22		22	BL	A	Halifax Town	L 0-1	0-1	16		(1,395)
23		30	BL	H	Rochdale	W 3-2	1-0	15	Himsworth 9, Fletcher 52, 59	1,643
24	D	7	BL	A	Northampton Town	L 2-3	0-0	15	Foreman 71, Ashdjian 72	(1,815)
25		17	BL	A	Lincoln City	W 2-0	2-0	13	Mockler (pen) 5, Mooney 44	(1,752)
26		26	BL	H	Mansfield Town	W 2-1	0-0	13	Thompson 72, Ashdjian 89	(4,012)
27		28	BL	A	Walsall	D 0-0	0-0	13		(3,488)
28	J	1	BL	H	Scunthorpe United	W 4-1	1-1	11	Fletcher 6, Mooney 59, 73, Foreman 85	2,237
29		4	BL	A	Rotherham United	W 2-0	0-0	9	Law 75, Thompson 80	(4,497)
30		8	AGT Pre	H	Wigan Athletic	D 1-1	0-0		Meyer 62	636
31	F	4	AGT 1	A	Burnley	L 1-3	0-0		Jules 71	(2,956)
32		8	BL	A	Barnet	L 1-5	0-2	12	Jules 69	(2,851)
33		11	BL	A	Rochdale	D 2-2	2-0	13	Brown 16, Mooney 25	(2,069)
34		15	BL	H	Lincoln City	D 1-1	0-1	14	Meyer 85	1,614
35		18	BL	H	Crewe Alexandra	W 2-1	0-1	10	Mockler (pen) 57, Moore 74	1,352
36		22	BL	A	Chesterfield	L 0-1	0-0	13		(2,749)
37		29	BL	H	Rotherham United	L 0-3	0-0	14		2,604
38	M	7	BL	A	Maidstone United	L 1-2	0-0	14	Jules 46	(1,019)
39		10	BL	A	Wrexham	L 0-2	0-1	15		(2,044)
40		14	BL	H	Blackpool	L 1-2	1-2	17	Price 9	1,965
41		17	BL	H	Chesterfield	W 3-2	2-2	15	Holmes 9, Himsworth (pen) 31, Ashdjian 84	1,302
42		21	BL	A	Carlisle United	D 2-2	0-0	15	Jules 46, 55	(1,813)
43		28	BL	H	Halifax Town	W 3-0	3-0	12	Marshall 11, Mooney 38, Thompson 44	1,363
44	A	4	BL	H	Gillingham	W 2-1	0-0	11	Himsworth (pen) 57, Jules 90	1,174
45		7	BL	H	Hereford United	D 1-1	0-0	11	Hirst 80	1,008
46		11	BL	A	Doncaster Rovers	L 2-3	0-2	13	Curran 51, Fletcher 90	(1,638)
47		18	BL	H	Cardiff City	D 2-2	1-0	13	Gabbiadini 19, Curran 90	935
48		20	BL	A	Burnley	D 1-1	1-1	12	Hirst 34	(12,312)
49		25	BL	H	York City	W 1-0	0-0	12	Ashdjian 88	2,108
50		29	BL	H	Maidstone United	W 2-0	0-0	11	Lee 72, Himsworth (pen) 86	939

Best Home League Attendance: 2,604 v Rotherham United   **Smallest:** 935 v Cardiff City   **Av Home Att:** 1,682

Goal Scorers: **Compared with 90-91:** +82

League (64): Ashdjian 9, Mooney 8, Jules 8, Meyer 5, Fletcher 5, Himsworth 4 (3 pens), Mockler 4 (4 pens), Thompson 3, Curran 2, Foreman 2, Hirst 2, Lee 2, Gabbiadini, Law, Marshall, Mudd, Sertori, Holmes, Moore, Brown, Price, Lowndes

R/lows C (10): Mooney 3, Foreman 2 (1 pen), Mockler (1 pen), Himsworth, Jules, Hirst, Ashdjian

FA Cup (0):

Autoglass (3): Jules 2, Meyer   † = Sent Off

500

Priestley J.	James C.	Mudd P.	Mockler A.	Hirst L.	Mayer A.	Ashdjian J.	Lee C.	Mooney T.	Foreman D.	Himsworth G.	Moore J.	Jules M.	Carter S.	Logan D.	Ash M.	Fletcher A.	Reed J.	Hughes P.	Holmes D.	Thompson S.	Ironside I.	Curran C.	McGee O.	Gabbiadini R.	Ford S.	Referee	
1	2	3	4	5	6	7*	8	9	10*	11	12	14														R Poulain	1
1	2	3	8*	5	6	7*	4	9	10	11	12	14														M Reed	2
1	2	3	14	5•	6		4	9	10	11	8	12	7*													A Smith	3
1	2	5		6		12	4	9	10*	11	8†	14	7*		3											A Wilkie	4
1	2	5	8•	6	7		4	9	14	11*	10	12			3											T Fitzharris	5
1	12	7	5	6*	14		4	9	10•	11	8				3	2										A Dawson	6
1	5	7	S	6	S		4	9	10	11	8				3	2										M James	7
1	2	7	8	5	6	S	4	9	10	11	S				3											I Cruickshanks	8
1	2	8*		5	6	7	4	9	10	11•		14			3	12										D Gallagher	9
1	2	8		5	6	7	4	9	10*	11•		14			3	12										K Redfearn	10
1		8		5	6	10	4	9•	14	11		12			3	2†	7*									S Bell	11
1	S	8		5	6	10	4	9	12	11					3*	2	7									K Lupton	12
	2	8		5	6	10	4	9	14	12		11•			3		7*	1								K A Cooper	13
	2	8*		5	6	10	4	9	S	11		12			3		7	1								R Hart	14
	2•	8		5	6	11	4	9	10†	12					3	14	7*	1								R Hamer	15
		8		5	6	10*	4	9		11•	7				3	2	14	12	1							P Wright	16
		3	8	5	6	12	4*	9		11					2	10	7	1	S							K Barratt	17
		3	8	6	5	7	4	9*	12	14		11			2	10•		1								J Watson	18
		3	8	5	6	7•	4	9	12	11					2	10*		1	14							A Bennett	19
		3	8	5	6	7*	4	9	12	11					2	10•		1	14							D Phillips	20
	2	3	8	5	6		4	9	12	11	7*					10•		1	14							P Vanes	21
	2	3	8	5	6		4	9	14	12	11	7*				10•		1								T West	22
	2	3	8	5	6		4	9*	12	7*	11			14		10		1								R Shepherd	23
	2*	3	8	5	6	14	4	9	12	7*	11					10		1								K Burge	24
	2	3	8*	5	6	12	4	9	S	7	11					10		1								I Hendrick	25
		5			6	7	4	9*	12	8		11			3	2	10•	1	14							G Singh	26
		5			6		4	9	12	8		14			3	2	10•	1	11•							D Phillips	27
		5			6	7*	4	9	14	8		12			3	2	10•	1	11							P Don	28
		5			6	12	4	9*	14	8		7			3	2	10•	1	11							M Brandwood	29
		5	3*		6	12	4	9	10*	8		7			2		14		11							M Peck	30
		5			6	14	4	9	12	8		7			3	2	10*	1	11•							T Holbrook	31
		5			6	14	4	9	12	8		7			3	2	10•	1	11*							P Scoble	32
		5	14		6	11*	4	9•	10	8	12	7			3			1	2							P Danson	33
		5	12		6	7*	4	9	10	8	S	11			3			1	2							J Worrall	34
		5	11		6	14	4	9	10*	8*	12	7			3				2							M Bailey	35
		5			6	14	4	9	12	8	10*	7			3	2			11•							K Cooper	36
		5	14		6	12	4	9•	10	8		7			3	2*			11							G Courtney	37
		11	4	6	5*			9	10•	8	12			3	2	14	7	1								P Taylor	38
		5	8	6		12	4•		11						9*			10	7	1						E Parker	39
		6	5				4	9	11						12			10*	14	7	1					D Phillips	40
		5		6		14	4	9	11						12			10	7	1						L Dilkes	41
		6	8	5		7	4	9	10						12			2	1							J Kirkby	42
		3		5		7	4	9•		11					14			2		6	8		12			P Jones	43
		3		5			4		8	11					14	9*		7	1	6	2		12			I Hendrick	44
		3		5			4	9•	8	11					14			7		6	2		12	1		R Bigger	45
		3		5			4	9*	8	11					14			7		6	2		12	1		C Trussell	46
		3		5		14	4	9*	8	11		12						7		6	2		10•	1		J Lloyd	47
		3		5		14	4	9	8	11		12					7•			6	2		10*	1		K Breen	48
		3		5		14	4	9	8	11*		12					7			6	2		10•	1		A Dawson	49
		3		5		10*	4	9	8	11		12					7			6	2			1		R Hart	50
9	12	36	20	30	30	18	41	40	12	33	3	30	2	21	16	14	5	17	3	22	7	8	8	3	6	**League Appearances**	
1			4			14			12	3	4	11	1		3	7	1		6	1				4		**Substitute Appearances**	
3	4	2	3	3	4	3+1	4	4	3+1	3+1	1+1	1+3	1		3	0+1	1	1								**R/lows Appearances**	
	1	1	1	1	1	1	1		1			1			1	1			1	0+1						**FA Cup Appearances**	
1	3	1	2	3	3	0+2	3	1	2	3	1	2	2		2	0+1	2									**Autoglass Appearances**	

Also Played: Posn.(Game): Price 14(39)8(40,41*)S(50), Hewitt 1(30,35,36), Rocca 2(39,40•,41*), Marshall 10(43*,44•,45*,46•), Swales 3(39,40,41,42*). **Players on Loan:** Priestley (Carlisle), Reed (Sheff Utd)   †=Sent Off

SCARBOROUGH

Club Colours: All white with red trim and shorts
Change Colours: All red
Reserves League: Midland Intermediate

Previous Leagues: Northern (1898-1910)   Yorkshire Combination (1910-14)   Northern (1914-26)   Yorkshire (1926-27)   Midland (1927-40)   Scarborough & District (1945-46)   Midland (1946-60)   Northern Counties (1960-62)   North Eastern (1962-63)   Midland (1963-68)   Northern Premier (1968-79)   Alliance Premier (1979-87)   Football League (1987-)
Previous Managers: (Since the war): G Hall   H Taylor   F Taylor   A Bell   R Halton   C Robson   G Higgins   A Smailes   E Brown   A Frank   S Myers   G Shaw   C Appleton   K Houghton   C Appleton   J McAnearney   J Cottam   H Dunn   N Warnock   R McHale
Honours: FA Trophy Winners 1973, 1976, 1977 (Record) GM Vauxhall Conferenece Champions 1987   Midland League Champions 1930   Scarborough & District League Champions 1946   North Easter League Champions 1963   Vauxhall Floodlit League Winners 1973, 1975   Northern Premier League Cup Winners 1977   Bob Lord Trophy Winners 1984   North Eastern Counties League Cup Winners 1963   East Riding Cup Winners (8 times) 1888, 1889, 1891, 1892, 1893, 1897, 1901, 1902   North Riding Senior Cup Winners 1909, 1929, 1939, 1948, 1956, 1959, 1961, 1962, 1969, 1973, 1974, 1977, 1978, 1981, 1982, 1985, 1988   Festival of Football Winners 1990

CLUB RECORDS

Most Appearances for Club: Steve Richards (1987-91): (League 164 + FA Cup 5 + League Cup 15 + Others 12) **Total 196**
Most Capped Player: None (Neil Sellars 9 caps for England Semi-Professional)
Record Goalscorer in a Match: No player has scored more than two in a Football League game
Record League Goalscorer in a Season: (Football League only) Paul Dobson, 15, Div 4, 1989-90   **In All Competitions:** Gary Brook 17 (League 12, Lge Cup 1, FA Cup 1, AMC 3) 1988-89
Record League Goalscorer in a Career: (Football League only) Paul Dobson, 22, 1989-91   **In All Competitions:** Paul Dobson 23 (League 22, League Cup 1) 1989-91
Record Transfer Fee Received: £240,000 from Notts County for Chris Short, August 1990
Record Transfer Fee Paid: £100,000 to Leicester City for Martin Russell, February 1989
Best Performances: League: 5th Division 4, 1988-89   **FA Cup:** Third Round (1931, 1938, 1976, 1978)   **League Cup:** Third Round, 1989, 1990
Most League Goals: 67, Division 4, 1988-89
Most League Points: (3pts for win) 77, Division 4, 1988-89
Record League Victory & Most Goals Scored in a League Match: 4-0 v Bolton Wanderers, Division 4, 29.8.1987   4-0 v Newport County (a), Division 4, 12.4.1988   5-2 v Torquay Utd, Division 4, 29.9.1988
Most Goals Scored in a First Class Cup Tie: 6-0 v Rhyl Athletic, FA Cup Round 1, 29.11.1930
Record League Defeat: 1-5 v Barnet, Division 4, 8.2.1992
Record Cup Defeat: 0-7 v Oldham Athletic, League Cup Rnd 3, 25.10.1989
Oldest Player in a League Match: Ernie Moss, 38 years 117 days v Cambridge Utd, Div 4, 13.2.1988
Youngest Player in a League Match: David Holmes, 17 years 154 days v Peterborough, Div 4, 25.4.1990

LONGEST LEAGUE RUNS	
of undefeated matches: 9 (1988, 1990, 1990-91)	**of league matches without a win:** 6 (1989)
of undefeated home matches: 12 (1987, 1988)	**of undefeated away matches:** 5 (1989, 1991)
without home win: 4 (1987, 1990)	**without an away win:** 11 (1990)
of league wins: 3 (twice 1987-88, 1988-89, twice 1989-90)	**of home wins:** 6 (1987)
of league defeats: 6 (1989)	**of away wins:** 2 (three 1988-89, 1989-90, 1990-91, 1991-92)

SCARBOROUGH

PLAYERS NAME / Honours	Ht	Wt	Birthdate	Birthplace / Transfers	Contract Date	Clubs	League	L/Cup	FA Cup	Other	Lg	L/C	FAC	Oth
GOALKEEPERS														
Stuart Ford	5.11	11.0	20.07.71	Sheffield	01.07.89	Rotherham Utd. (T)	1							
				Free	01.08.92	Scarborough								
Anthony Outhart					28.11.88	Scarborough		0+1		1				
DEFENDERS														
Geoffrey Horsefield					26.03.92	Scarborough								
Lee Hirst	6.2	12.07	26.01.69	Sheffield	02.02.90	Scarborough	72	3	2	6	4	1		
Adrian Meyer	5.11	11.4	22.09.70	Bristol	10.06.89	Scarborough	65	6	1	3	8			1
Brendan Ormsby	5.11	11.3	01.10.60	Birmingham	01.10.78	Aston Villa (A)	115+2	11+1	3+1	7	4	2		1
E: Y.12, S				£65,000	28.02.86	Leeds Utd	46	1	4	6	5		1	1
Loan 18.01.90 Shrewsbury T. 1lg				Free	25.07.90	Doncaster Rovers	43	2	2	3	4			
				Free	01.08.92	Scarborough								
Steve Swales			26.12.73	Whitby		Scarborough (T)	4							
MIDFIELD														
Chris Lee	5.10	11.10	18.06.71	Batley	01.07.89	Bradford City (T)								
					14.06.90	Rochdale	24+2	4	2	3	2	1		
				Free	14.03.91	Scarborough	49+1	4	1	3	2			
Andrew Mockler	5.11	12.6	18.11.70	Stockton-on-Tees	19.11.88	Arsenal (T)								
				Free	01.08.90	Scarborough	52+6	3	2	3	9	1		
Paul Mudd	5.9	11.4	13.11.70	Hull	01.07.89	Hull City (T)	1							
					25.07.90	Scarborough	57+3	4	2	4	1			
Aidan Murphy	5.10	10.10	17.09.67	Manchester	19.09.84	Manchester Utd. (A)								
E:Y8,S				Loan	03.10.86	Lincoln City	2							
					01.05.87	Crewe Alexandra	93+14	7+1	10+2	9+1	12	1	3	1
				Free	01.08.92	Scarborough								
FORWARDS														
John Ashdjian						Northampton T								
				Free	24.07.91	Scarborough	18+14	3+1	1	0+2	9	1		
Stephen Carter	5.8	12.0	13.04.72	Sunderland		Manchester Utd								
					31.07.90	Scarborough	33+4	3	1	3	3			1
Christopher Curran	6.1		06.01.71	Manchester	23.09.89	Crewe Alexandra (T)	1+3	0+1						
				N.C.	01.08.92	Scarborough								
Darren Foreman	5.11	11.2	12.02.68	Southampton	03.11.86	Barnsley	33+14	2+1	2+3	1	8			
E:S				£80,000	08.03.90	Crewe Alexandra	19+4	1+2			4			
				Loan	08.03.91	Scarborough								
					10.04.91	Scarborough	26+12	3+1		1	7	2		
Gary Himsworth	5.8	10.6	19.12.69	York	27.01.88	York City (T)	74+14	5		5+2	8			
				Free	05.12.90	Scarborough	56+3	3+1		3	5	1		
Mark Jules	5.10	11.1	05.09.71	Bradford	03.07.90	Bradford City (T)		0+1						
				Free	14.08.91	Scarborough	30+12	1+3	1	3	8	1		2
Owen McGee	5.5	10.8	29.10.70	Middlesborough	05.07.88	Middlesbrough (A)	18+3	0+1	0+1	3+3	1			
				N.C.		Scarborough								
Thomas J Mooney	5.11	12.6	11.08.71	Stockton-on-Tees	23.11.89	Aston Villa (T)								
				Free	01.08.90	Scarborough	57+10	4+2	2	4	19	3		
Mark Price			15.10.73	Keighley		Scarborough (T)	3+1				1			
Simon Thompson	5.9	10.6	07.01.68	Sheffield	01.07.88	Rotherham Utd. (T)	12+16	2+2	4+2	1+3				1
					24.12.91	Scarborough	22+1			2	3			
ADDITIONAL CONTRACT PLAYERS														
(D) Matthew Jarman						Scarborough (T)								
(M) David Manderson						Scarborough (T)								
(M) Martin Gill						Hartlepool								
						Scarborough								
(M) Darran Edmonds						Ipswich								
				Free		Scarborough								

LEADING LEAGUE GOALSCORERS SEASONS 1985-86 – 1991-92

1985-86	NOT IN LEAGUE			1986-87	NOT IN LEAGUE	
1987-88	STEWART MELL	8		1988-89	GARY BROOK	12
1989-90	PAUL DOBSON	15		1990-91	GEORGE OGHANI	14

1991-92 **JOHN ASHDIJAN** 9

THE McCAIN STADIUM Seamer Road, Scarborough YO12 4HF

Capacity: 7,176   **Covered Standing:** 1,500   **Seating:** 840

Tel: Ground: 0723 375094   **Ticket Sales:** As ground number

---

ATTENDANCES
Highest: 11,162 v Luton Town, FA Cup Round 3, 1938

Lowest:

Record Receipts: £19,758 v Wolverhampton Wanderers, Division 4, 15.8.1987

Season Tickets:
Stands: £116.25, juv/OAP £85.20
Ground: £77.50, juv/OAP £46.50

Executive Box Season Tickets: None

Cost of Stand Tickets: Seats: £8.50, juniors/OAP £6
Terraces: £6, juniors/OAP £3

Match and Ticket Information: Phone club

Social Facilities: Food available

Car Parking: In streets around the ground and at ground

Nearest Railway Station: Scarborough Central (2 miles)

How to get to the ground

The Ground is situated on the main Scarborough-York Road (A64), 0.5 mile on left past Plaxton's Coach Works coming from Town

Value Rating: ✷ ✷ ✷

Programme Editor: Mark Staniforth

Price of 1992-93 Programme: £1
Number of Pages: 32
Subscriptions: £30

Local Newspapers: Scarborough Evening News, The Mercury

Local Radio Stations: Radio York, TFM Radio

SCUNTHORPE UNITED Division 3

Formed: 1904   **Turned Professional:** 1912   **Ltd Co:** 1912

SPONSORED BY: Brikenden   **NICKNAME:** The Iron

President
Sir Reginald Sheffield BT

Vice-Presidents
I T Botham   G Johnson
R Ashman   G Alston
B Heywood   A Harvey
Dr Zacharias

Chairman
T E Belton

Deputy Chairman
D M Fletton

Directors
B Borrill   R Garton
J Hayes   C Plumtree

Chief Executive/Secretary
A D Rowing (0724 848077)

Team Manager
W Green

Assistant Manager
D Moore

Physiotherapist
P McLoughlin

Groundsman
G Colby

Lottery Sales Manager
A Chapman

Football in the Community Officer
R Passmoor

Club Statistician for the Directory
Michael Norton

OKAY, we've had enough! The joke is beginning to wear a little thin. Somebody up there doesn't like us. For the fourth time in five seasons we found ourselves in the play-offs and once again could not negotiate a safe path through to promotion. This time, however, there was a bonus of appearing at Wembley, but that was a minor consolation as we lost in the dreaded penalty shoot-outs. There's no denying that it was a super occasion for the fans and the players but at the end of the day we are still in the lower division travelling the same old well-worn routes.

The season began quietly but good home form, and an early away win, put us in the top third of the table and led us in nicely for a League Cup second round tie against Leeds United. Well over 8,000 squeezed into Glanford Park for the first leg to see us hold the league champions elect to a goalless draw. In the second leg we made our opponents sweat until a late penalty turned the game their way and knocked the stuffing out of us. Between those two games we showed our inconsistency when offering little resistance in a 4-0 embarrassment at Wrexham.

One highlight of the season came on bonfire night in a cracker of a game when we trounced Rochdale 6-2. Three more thrillers followed, all against Rotherham. First was the league game at Glanford Park with a glorious individual goal from Tony Daws which won the match. Then the Millers returned a week later to force a draw in an exciting F.A. Cup tie. The replay was even more exciting and proved an historic occasion, being the first F.A. Cup tie to be decided on penalties.

Four victories in a five-match unbeaten run took us to fifth place by the turn of the year, but inconsistency showed its face again over the next three months as we dropped to ninth and lost hopes of an automatic promotion place. A victory over Chesterfield on March 31st set the ball rolling again as we finished the season with an unbeaten eight-match run. That is the kind of consistency we need to achieve over the whole season if we are to reach higher divisions. A Wembley appearance would gladly be passed up if promotion could be assured!

Michael Norton

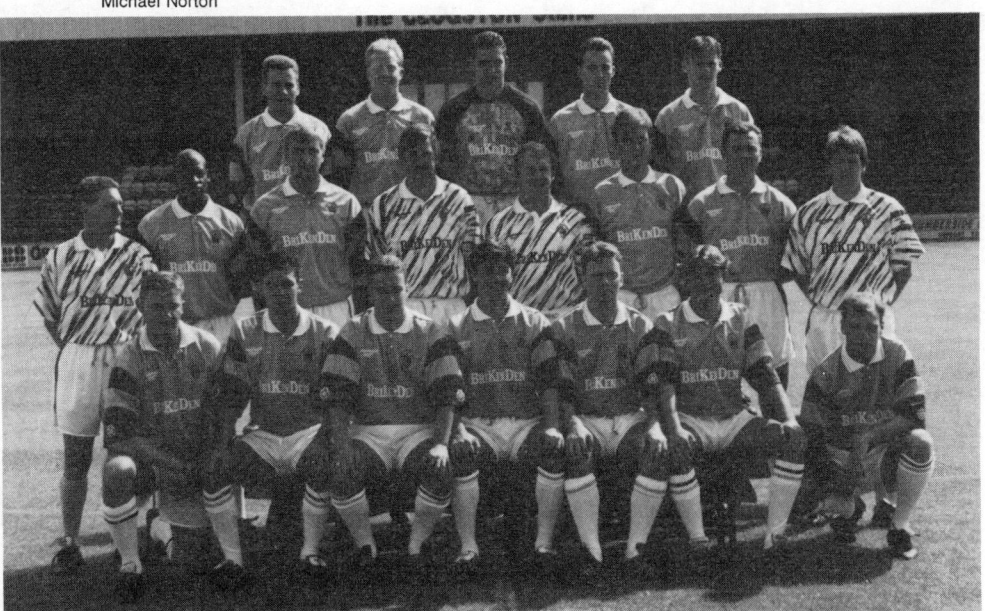

Back row L-R: Andrew Stevenson, Tony Daws, Paul Longden, Joe Joyce, John Buckley, Samuel Goodacre, Glenn Humphries. **Middle row:** Phil McLoughlin (Physio), Jason White, Matthew Elliott, Bill Green (Manager), David Moore (Asst. Manager), Ian Helliwell, Stuart Hicks, David Cowling (Youth Team Coach). **Front row:** Paul McCullagh, David Hill, Mark Samways, Dean Martin, Graham Alexander.

SCUNTHORPE UNITED

DIVISION FOUR: 5th   **FA CUP:** 1st RND   **RUMBELOWS CUP:** 2nd RND   **AUTOGLASS:** 1st RND

M	DATE		COMP.	VEN	OPPONENTS	RESULT		H/T	LGE POS	GOALSCORERS/GOAL TIMES	ATTEN-DANCE
1	A	17	BL	A	Gillingham	L	0-4	0-1			(3,480)
2		20	RC 1/1	A	Wrexham	L	0-1	0-0			(1,621)
3		24	BL	H	Doncaster Rovers	W	3-2	2-1		Helliwell 3, Alexander 17, Daws 77	3,505
4		27	RC 1/2	H	Wrexham	W	3-0	0-0		Humphries 62, Alexander 78, Helliwell 88	2,125
5		31	BL	A	Blackpool	L	1-2	1-1	19	Buckley 40	(3,273)
6	S	3	BL	H	Scarborough	D	1-1	1-0	14	Joyce 28	3,125
7		7	BL	H	Maidstone United	W	2-0	0-0	12	Hill 46, Daws 84	2,738
8		14	BL	A	Chesterfield	W	1-0	0-0	9	Humphries 62	(3,338)
9		17	BL	A	Barnet	L	2-3	1-1	10	Humphries 44, White 51	(3,094)
10		21	BL	H	Crewe Alexandra	W	1-0	1-0	8	Hamilton 33	3,021
11		24	RC 2/1	H	Leeds United	D	0-0	0-0			8,392
12		28	BL	A	Wrexham	L	0-4	0-2	9		(1,635)
13	O	5	BL	H	Hereford United	D	1-1	0-0	10	Daws (pen) 74	2,384
14		8	RC 2/2	A	Leeds United	L	0-3	0-0			(14,558)
15		12	BL	A	Carlisle United	D	0-0	0-0	11		(1,988)
16		19	BL	A	Northampton Town	W	1-0	1-0	10	Helliwell 3	(2,575)
17		22	AGT Pre	H	Bury	L	1-3	0-1		Hamilton 64	1,122
18		26	BL	H	Mansfield Town	L	1-4	0-1	11	Daws 56	3,610
19	N	2	BL	A	Cardiff City	D	2-2	0-0	11	Hill 67, Pike (og) 82	(2,356)
20		5	BL	H	Rochdale	W	6-2	3-0	9	Hamilton 4, (og) 10, Lister 42, Helliwell 59, Alexander 85, Hill 89	2,311
21		9	BL	H	Rotherham United	W	1-0	0-0	7	Daws 65	4,175
22		16	FAC 1	H	Rotherham United	D	1-1	0-1		Helliwell 85	4,511
23		23	BL	A	Lincoln City	L	2-4	1-1	9	Martin 3, Alexander 59	(3,078)
24		26	FAC 1R	A	Rotherham United	D	†3-3	0-1		Helliwell 53, Daws 78, White 109 (Lost 7-6 on pens)	(4,829)
25		30	BL	H	York City	W	1-0	0-0	9	Hamilton 57	2,887
26	D	14	BL	A	Burnley	D	1-1	0-1	9	Pender (og) 72	(8,419)
27		20	BL	A	Doncaster Rovers	W	2-1	1-1	5	Humphries 12, Alexander 59	(1,825)
28		26	BL	H	Gillingham	W	2-0	1-0	5	White 24, Martin 84	3,883
29		28	BL	H	Blackpool	W	2-1	1-1	5	White 29, 79	4,271
30	J	1	BL	A	Scarborough	L	1-4	1-1	7	White 30	(2,237)
31		7	AGT Pre	A	Halifax Town	W	2-0	0-0		White 53, Alexander 88	(646)
32		18	BL	A	Halifax Town	W	4-1	1-0	7	White 3 (39, 60, 73), Hamilton 52	(1,232)
33		21	AGT 1	A	Hartlepool United	L	1-2	1-1		Hamilton 39	(1,351)
34		25	BL	H	Walsall	D	1-1	1-0	6	White 18	3,165
35	F	8	BL	H	Mansfield Town	W	3-1	2-0	6	Alexander 11, Hamilton (pen) 18, White 72	3,469
36		11	BL	A	York City	L	0-3	0-2	7		(2,255)
37		15	BL	H	Burnley	D	2-2	2-0	8	Helliwell 31, White 37	5,303
38	M	3	BL	H	Halifax Town	W	1-0	0-0	8	Buckley 60	2,448
39		7	BL	A	Walsall	L	1-2	0-1	8	Buckley 51	(2,722)
40		10	BL	A	Rochdale	L	0-2	0-1	9		(2,036)
41		14	BL	H	Cardiff City	W	1-0	0-0	9	Buckley 80	2,766
42		21	BL	A	Rotherham United	L	0-5	0-2	9		(4,528)
43		28	BL	A	Lincoln City	L	0-2	0-1	9		3,297
44		31	BL	H	Chesterfield	W	2-0	1-0	8	Helliwell 31, Hamilton (pen) 81	2,224
45	A	4	BL	A	Maidstone United	W	1-0	0-0	7	Hamilton 76	(1,237)
46		11	BL	H	Barnet	D	1-1	0-1	8	Hamilton (pen) 69	3,361
47		14	BL	H	Northampton Town	W	3-0	2-0	7	Hill 6, Buckley 29, Daws 80	2,286
48		18	BL	A	Crewe Alexandra	D	1-1	0-0	7	Helliwell 49	(3,313)
49		20	BL	H	Wrexham	W	3-1	0-0	6	Joyce 51, Hamilton (pen) 58, Buckley 81	2,900
50		25	BL	A	Hereford United	W	2-1	1-1	5	Helliwell 22, 53	(1,587)
51	M	2	BL	H	Carlisle United	W	4-0	2-0	5	Elliott 2, Daws 43, Hill 67, Helliwell 78	3,853
52		10	PO SF1	A	Crewe Alexandra	D	2-2	2-2		Helliwell 17, 35	(6,083)
53		13	PO SF2	H	Crewe Alexandra	W	2-0	0-0		Martin 83, Hamilton 89	7,938
54		23	PO Fin	N	Blackpool	D	†1-1	0-1		Daws 52 (Lost 3-4 on pens)	(22,741)

Best Home League Attendance: 5,303 v Burnley   **Smallest:** 2,224 v Chesterfield   **Av Home Att:** 3,215

Goal Scorers:

Compared with 90-91: +101

League (64): White 11, Helliwell 9, Hamilton 9 (4 pens), Daws 7 (1 pen), Buckley 6, Hill 5, Alexander 5, Opponents 3, Humphries 3, Martin 2, Joyce 2, Elliott, Lister

R/lows C (3): Helliwell, Alexander, Humphries

FA Cup (4): Helliwell 2, Daws, White

Autoglass (4): Hamilton 2, Alexander, White

Play-Offs (9): Helliwell 2, Daws, Hamilton, Martin

† = After extra-time

506

Musselwhite P.	Joyce J.	Longden D.	Hine M.	Hicks S.	Humphries G.	Alexander G.	Hamilton I.	Daws A.	Buckley J.	Helliwell I.	Martin D.	Hyde G.	Lister S.	Stevenson A.	Hill D.	White J.	Whitehead P. (L)	Samways M. (L)	Elliott M. (L)	Batch N. (N.C.)	Goodacre S.	Evans A.	Marples C.	Referee	
	2	3	4†	5	6	7	8	9	10*	11	12		S							1				P Scoble	1
1	2	3	4	5	6	7*	8	9	10	11			12	S										K Breen	2
1	2	3	4	5	6	7	8	9	10	11			12	S										A Wilkie	3
1	2	3	4	5	6	7	8	9	10*	11			12	S										N Midgley	4
1	2	3		5	6	7*	8	9	10	11	4*	14	12											A Bennett	5
1	2	3	4	5	6	7	8	9	10	11			S	S										A Dawson	6
1	2	3	4*	5	6	7*	8	9		11		14	12		10									P Vanes	7
1	2	3	S	5*	6	7	8	9		11	4		12		10									G Poll	8
1	2	3	S		6	7	8	9		11*	4		5		10	12								J Carter	9
1	2	3	S		6	7	8	9			4	12	5		10	11*								D Phillips	10
1	2	3	S		6	7	8	9		11	4	S	5		10									I Hendrick	11
1	2	3	14		6	7*	8	9	12	11	4		5		10*									J Kirkby	12
1	2	3	8†		6*	12		9		7	11	4*		5	14	10								J Parker	13
1	2	3	14			12	8	9	7*	11	4*		5	6	10									P Danson	14
1	2	3			6	12	8	9*	7	11	4		5	S	10									B Nixon	15
1	2	3			6	S	8	9	7	11	4		S	S	10									G Willard	16
1	2	3			6*	12	8	9	7	11	4*	14	5		10									J Brandwood	17
1	2	3		5		S	8	9	7	11	4	S		6	10									S Bell	18
1	2	3		5		7	8*	9	12	11	4		6	S	10									C Wilkes	19
1	2	3		5		7	8	9	S	11	4	S	6		10									J Key	20
1	2	3			5	7	8	9	S	11	4	S	6		10									J Moules	21
1		3			5	2	8	9	7*	11	4*	12	6		10	14								W Burns	22
1		3			5	2	8	9	7	11	4	S	6		10	S								M Bullivant	23
1		3	12		5	2	8	9	7*	11	4*		6		10	14								W Burns	24
	2	3		5†		7	8	9		11	4	S	6		10	S	1							T Lunt	25
	2	3		5		7	8	9	S	11	4	6*			10	12	1							A Dawson	26
	2	3		5	6	7*	8	9*		11	4	12			10	14	1							P Harrison	27
	2	3		5	6	7*	8			4	S	S			10	11	1							W Burns	28
	2	3		5	6	7*	8	9			4	12	S		10	11	1							S Lodge	29
	2	3		5	6	7*	8	9*		12	4	14			10	11	1							P Don	30
	2	3		5		7	8	9	S		4	10	6			11	1					S		R Hart	31
	2			5	6	7	8	9	S	11	4	S			3	10	1							P Jones	32
	2		S	5	6	7	8		12	11	4	9*			3	10	1							I Hendrick	33
	2	3		5	6	7	8		S	11	4	S			10	9	1							T Ward	34
1	2	3	S		6	7	8		5	11	4				10	9						S		B Coddington	35
1	2	3	14	5		7	8	6*		11	4	12			10*	9								K Redfern	36
	2	3	14	5		7	8	12	6*	11	4				10	9*			1					J Kirkby	37
1	2	3	S	5		7	8	12	10	11	4		6			9*							1	D Gallagher	38
1	2	3		5*		7	8	12	10	11	4		6		14	9*								R Nixon	39
1	2	3	7*			S	8	9	10	11	4		6		5	12								D Shadwell	40
1	2	3	7*			14	8	9*	10	11	4		6		5	12								T Lunt	41
1	2	3			5	14	8	9*	10*	11	4		6		7	12								I Cruikshanks	42
1	2*	14			5	7*	8	9	10	11	4				3	12								K Breen	43
		2			6	7	8	S	10	11	4				3	9		1	5					D Allison	44
	2	3	S		6	7	8		10	11					4	9		1	5					I Borrett	45
	2	3			6	7*	8	12	10	11	S				4	9		1	5					T Fitzharris	46
	2	3			6	12	8	9	10	11	7*				4	S		1	5					J Watson	47
	2	3	S		6	S	8		10	11	7				4	9		1	5					R Gifford	48
	2	3	S		6	S	8		10	11	7				4	S		1	5					K Lupton	49
	2	3			6	12	8	9	10*	11	7				4	S		1	5					M Bailey	50
	2	3			6	S	8	9	10	11	7				4	S		1	5					P Danson	51
	2	3			6	12	8	9	10*	11	7				4	S		1	5					M Bodenham	52
	2	3			6	S	8	9	10	11	7				4	0+1		1	5					A Buksh	53
	2	3			6	14	8	9*	10*	11	7				4	12		1	5					K Hackett	54
League Appearances																									
24	40	40	7	21	32	30	41	32	26	38	36	1	16	1	36	15	8	8	8	1			1	League Appearances	
	1	3				6		4	2	1	1		7			1								Substitute Appearances	
4	4	4	2+1	2	3	3+1	4	4	3	4	2	0+1	2+1	1	2									R/lows Appearances	
2		2		2	2	2	2	2	2	2		2	0+2											FA Cup Appearances	
1	3	2		2	2	2+1	3	2	1+1	2	3	2	2	2										Autoglass Appearances	
	3	2		3	0+2	3	3	3	3	3		3	3											Play-Offs Appearances	

Also Played: Posn.(Game): Batch (NC) 1(1), Goodacre S(32), Evans S(36), Marples 1(38)

Players on Loan: Whitehead (Barnsley), Marples (York City), Samways (Doncaster), Elliott (Torquay)   † = Sent Off

SCUNTHORPE UNITED

Club Colours: Sky blue shirts with claret hoops on sleeves, white shorts, white socks
Change Colours: White shirts with claret design, white shorts, white socks
Reserves League: Pontins Central League Div 2   **Youth League:** Northern Intermediate

Previous League: Midland League
Previous Name: Merged with Lindsey United in 1910 to become Scunthorpe and Lindsey United. Dropped the name Lindsey in 1958
Previous Managers: Leslie Jones 1950-51   Bill Corkhill 1951-56   Ron Stuart 1956-58   Tony Macshane 1958-59   Bill Lambton (3 days) 1959   Frank Soo 1959-60   Dick Duckworth 1960-64   Freddie Goodwin 1964-67   Ron Ashman 1967-73   Ron Bradley 1973-74   Dickie Rooks 1974-76   Ron Ashman 1976-81   John Duncan 1981-83   Allan Clarke 1983-84   Frank Barlow 1984-87   Mick Buxton 1987-91   Bill Green 1991-
Honours: Div 3N Champions 1957-58
League Career: Elected to Div 3N 1950   Promoted to Div 2 1957-58   Relegated to Div 3 1963-64   Relegated to Div 4 1967-68   Promoted to Div 3 1971-72   Relegated to Div 4 1972-73   Promoted to Div 3 1982-83   Relegated to Div 4 1983-84

CLUB RECORDS

Most Appearances for Club: Jack Brownsword (1950-65): League 595 + Cup 56 **Total 651**
Most Capped Player: No Scunthorpe player has won an international cap
Record Goalscorer in a Match: Barrie Thomas 5 v Luton Town (h), 8-1, Div 3, 24.4.1965
Record League Goalscorer in a Season: Barrie Thomas 31, Div 2, 1961-62   **In All Competitions:** Barrie Thomas, 31 (all league)
Record League Goalscorer in a Career: Steve Cammack 110   **In All Competitions:** Steve Cammack 120 (League 110, FA Cup 6, League Cup 2, AMC 2) 1979-81 & 1981-86
Record Transfer Fee Received: £400,000 from Aston Villa for Neil Cox, February 1991
Record Transfer Fee Paid: £80,000 to York City for Ian Helliwell, August 1991
Best Performances: League: 4th Div 2, 1961-62   **FA Cup:** 5th Round 1957-58, 1969-70   **League Cup:** Never beyond 3rd Round
Most League Points: (3pts a win) 83, Div 4, 1982-83   (2pts a win) 66, Div 3N, 1957-58
Most League Goals: 88, Div 3N, 1957-58
Record League Victory and Most Goals Scored in a League Match: 8-1 v Luton Town, Div 3, 24.4.1965
Most Goals Scored in a Cup Tie: 9-0 v Boston United, FA Cup 1st Round, 21.11.1953
Record League Defeat: 0-8 v Carlisle United, Div 3N, 25.12.1952
Record Cup Defeat: 0-7 v Coventry City, FA Cup Round 1, 29.11.1934
Oldest Player in a League Match: Jack Brownsword, 41 years, 1965
Youngest Player in a League Match: Mike Farrell, 16 years 240 days, 8.11.1975

LONGEST LEAGUE RUNS	
of undefeated matches: 15 (1957-58, 1971-72)	**of league matches without a win:** 14 (1973-74-1974-75)
of undefeated home matches: 21 (1950-51)	**of undefeated away matches:** 9 (1981-82-1982-83)
without home win: 7 (1963-64, 1972-73)	**without an away win:** 30 (1977-78)
of league wins: 6 (1954, 1965)	**of home wins:** 7 (1984-85, 1987)
of league defeats: 7 (1972-73)	**of away wins:** 5 (1965-66)

SCUNTHORPE UNITED

PLAYERS NAME Honours	Ht	Wt	Birthdate	Birthplace Transfers	Contract Date	Clubs	League	L/Cup	FA Cup	Other	Lg	L/C	FAC	Oth
GOALKEEPERS														
Mark Samways	6.0	11.12	11.11.68	Doncaster	20.08.87	Doncaster R (A)	121	3	4	10				
				Loan	24.11.88	Leeds Utd								
				Loan	26.03.92	Scunthorpe Utd								
					19.06.92	Scunthorpe Utd	8			3				
DEFENDERS														
Graham Alexander	5.10	11.10	10.10.71	Coventry	20.03.90	Scunthorpe Utd. (T)	30+7	3+1	2	3+2	5	1		1
Matthew Elliott	6.3	13.6	01.11.68	Surrey		Epsom & Ewell								
					09.09.88	Charlton Ath		1						
				£10,000	23.03.89	Torquay Utd	123+1	9	9	16	15	2	2	1
				Loan	26.03.92	Scunthorpe Utd								
					19.06.92	Scunthorpe Utd	8			3	1			
Stuart Hicks	6.1	12.6	30.05.67	Peterborough	10.08.84	Peterborough U								
						Wisbech								
					24.03.88	Colchester Utd	57+7	2	5	5			1	
					01.10.90	Scunthorpe Utd	67	4	4	8	1		1	
Glenn Humphries E:Y6	6.0	12.0	11.08.64	Hull	19.08.82	Doncaster Rovers (A	174+6	12+1	9	7+1	8	1		
				Loan	25.03.87	Lincoln City	9							
				£20,000	23.10.87	Bristol City	81+4	3	12	9				
				£55,000	07.03.91	Scunthorpe Utd	42	3	2	5	4	1		
Joe Joyce	5.9	10.5	18.03.61	Consett	12.09.80	Barnsley	332+2	26+1	24	3	4	1	1	
				Free	20.02.91	Scunthorpe Utd	61	4		5				
Paul Longden	5.8	11.7	28.09.62	Wakefield	30.09.80	Barnsley (A)	5							
					15.08.83	Scunthorpe Utd	343+4	26+1	26	34				
Dave Moore Div3'80; FLGC'82	5.11	12.13	17.12.59	Grimsby	23.12.77	Grimsby Town (A)	136	9	7		2			
					08.08.83	Carlisle Utd	13	2			1			
				£3,500	15.12.83	Blackpool	114+1	6	5+1	4	1			
					04.12.86	Grimsby Town	3+1		1					
				m	11.08.88	Darlington	25+5	4	1	3	1	1		
				Free N.C	19.07.91	Scunthorpe Utd								
MIDFIELD														
David Cowling Div.4.80	5.9	11.0	27.11.58	Doncaster	01.11.76	Mansfield Town (A)								
					17.08.77	Huddersfield Town	331+9	26+1	25	1	43	3	2	
				Loan		Scunthorpe Utd	1							
						Reading	9+1				1			
				Free	05.11.87	Scunthorpe Utd	85+4	8	5	7	5			1
				N.C	19.07.91	Scunthorpe Utd								
David Hill	5.9	10.3	06.06.66	Nottingham	26.07.83	Scunthorpe Utd	139+1	8	9	8+2	10	2	3	
					15.02.85	Scunthorpe Utd								
				£80,000	29.07.88	Ipswich Town	54+7	6+1	1	3				
				Loan	28.03.91	Scunthorpe Utd	8+1			2	1			1
				£30,000	04.09.91	Scunthorpe Utd	36+1	2	2	5	5			
Dean Martin	5.10	10.2	09.09.67	Halifax	10.09.85	Halifax Town (A)	149+4	7	10	12	7			3
				Free	08.07.91	Scunthorpe Utd	36+1	2	2	6	2			1
Andy Stevenson	6.0	12.3	29.09.67	Scunthorpe	14.01.86	Scunthorpe Utd	53+25	7+1	4+1	12+2	1	1		1
				Loan	30.01.92	Doncaster Rovers	1							
FORWARDS														
John Buckley Div.4'89	5.9	10.7	18.05.62	East Kilbride		Read								
						Partick Thistle	42+3	1	1		5			
					19.07.84	Doncaster Rovers	79+5	3	5	3	11			
				£35,000	04.07.86	Leeds Utd	6+4		0+1	1	1			
				Loan	26.03.87	Leicester City	1+4							
				Loan	17.10.87	Doncaster Rovers	6							
					19.11.87	Rotherham Utd	85+20	8+1	5	8	13			1
				£45,000	19.10.90	Partick Thistle	26		2		5			
				£40,000	06.08.91	Scunthorpe Utd	26+2	3	2	4+1	6			
Tony Daws E:Y1	5.8	11.10	10.09.66	Sheffield	18.09.84	Notts County (A)	6+2				1			
					21.08.86	Sheffield Utd	7+4		1	0+1	3			
					02.07.87	Scunthorpe Utd	145+14	11+1	7	19+1	59	3	2	1
Samuel Goodacre E.S.F.A.u19.3	5.6	10.0	01.12.70	Sheffield	01.07.89	Sheffield Wed. (T)								
				Free	04.07.91	Scunthorpe Utd								
Ian Helliwell	6.3	13.12	07.11.62	Rotherham		Matlock Town								
				£10,000	23.10.87	York City	158+2	8	5	9+1	40	1		7
				£80,000	16.08.91	Scunthorpe Utd	38+1	4	2	5	9	1	2	2
Jason White					01.07.91	Derby County								
				Free	06.09.91	Scunthorpe Utd	15+7		0+2	2+1	11		1	1
ADDITIONAL CONTRACT PLAYERS														

LEADING LEAGUE GOALSCORERS SEASONS 1985-86 – 1991-92

1985-86	**STEVE CAMMACK**	12	1986-87	**STEVE JOHNSON**	16
1987-88	**ANDY FLOUNDERS**	24	1988-89	**TONY DAWS**	24
1989-90	**ANDY FLOUNDERS**	18	1990-91	**ANDY FLOUNDERS**	23

1991-92   **JASON WHITE**   **11**

GLANFORD PARK **Doncaster Road, Scunthorpe DN15 8TD**

Capacity: 9,200   **Covered Standing:** 2,773   **Seating:** 6,427

Tel: Ground: 0724 848077   **Ticket Sales:** As ground number   **Clubcall:** 0898 12 16 52

All premium rate calls (0898/0891) cost 36p per minute cheap rate and 48p per minute at all other times. Call costings correct at time of going to press.

ATTENDANCES
Highest: 23,935 v Portsmouth, FA Cup Round 4,
30.1.1954
(Old Showground) 8,775 v Rotherham, Div 4, 1.5.1989

Lowest: 859 v Chesterfield, Leyland Daf Cup, 18.12.1990

Record Receipts: £44,481 v Leeds Utd, Lge Cup 2nd
Rnd, 24.9.1991
£30,857 v Grimsby Town, Division 4, 26.12.1989
£28,612 v Leeds United, FA Cup Round 3 Replay, Jan
1984

GLANFORD PARK
First game: v Hereford United, League, 27.8.1988
First floodlit game: Huddersfield, League Cup, 30.8.1988

Season Tickets:
Stands: £116.25, juv/OAP £85.25
Ground: £77.50, juv/OAP £46.50

Executive Bar Season Tickets: Adult £250

Cost of Stand Tickets: Seats: £8.50, juv/OAP £6
Terraces: £6, juv/OAP £3

Match and Ticket Information: Seating tickets may be
reserved by telephone until day of match unless
otherwise notified in press

Car Parking: Club park adjacent to Ground for 800
vehicles

Nearest Railway Station: Scunthorpe

How to get to the ground

From North, South and West: Use Motorway M18 to
Junction 5, exit on to M180, at Junction 3 exit on to
M181, at roundabout take third exit. The ground can
clearly be seen on the right as you approach the
roundabout

Value Rating: ★ ★ ★

Programme Editor: M Norton

Price of 1992-93 Programme: £1
Number of Pages: 32
Subscriptions: Home & away combined £60

Local Newspapers: Scunthorpe Evening Telegraph

Local Radio Stations: Radio Humberside, Radio Viking

SHEFFIELD UNITED · Premier

Formed: 1889   **Turned Professional:** 1889   **Ltd Co:** 1889

SPONSORED BY: Arnold Laver   **NICKNAME:** The Blades

President
R Wragg M Inst BM

Chairman
P G Woolhouse

Directors
A H Laver
M A Wragg
D Dooley

Secretary
David Capper(0742 738955)

Team Manager
Dave Bassett

Coachs
Geoff Taylor
Keith Mincher

Youth Development Officer
John Dungworth

Groundsman
Glenn Nortcliffe

Physiotherapist
Derek French

Commercial Manager
Andy Daykin

Club Statistician for the Directory
Andrew Treherne

UNITED'S second season back in the top flight looked to be an action replay of the previous one. Once again the team occupied the lower reaches of the table at the start of the season with the first League win coming over Everton in the eighth match. The first Sheffield derby since 1979-80 saw United in bottom place, and having sold Tony Agana to Notts County, given little chance. However, their greater commitment and passion, especially from the two 'local boys' Carl Bradshaw and Jamie Hoyland, saw an emotional 2-0 victory gained to lift United off the bottom.

In addition to the sale of Agana, Vinnie Jones had departed to Chelsea after only four appearances. In order to strengthen the defence, Brian Gayle was signed from Ipswich Town for a club record £700,000 and he was made captain, following the departure of Jones (Chelsea) and Bob Booker to Brentford. The defeat of the old enemy in November led to further good performances and the team once again came good after Christmas. A steady climb up the table culminated in an eight match unbeaten run from mid-March, which saw the team move from seventeenth to seventh place. Also in the period was an excellent win over Liverpool which included an astonishing goal from Brian Deane following a moment of madness from Bruce Grobbelaar. Disappointing defeats by eventual champions Leeds United and Wimbledon in the final two games meant that a position of ninth was achieved.

Once again mixed fortunes were experienced in the cup competitions. A narrow victory over Wigan in Round 2 of the Rumbelows Cup was followed by a home defeat by West Ham United in Round 3. In the ZDS Cup a disastrous penalty shoot-out, with only one successful spot-kick meant another home defeat to Notts County. The one hope of glory lay in the F.A. Cup, where progress was made to Round 5 at the expense of Luton Town and Charlton Athletic. With many of the favourites falling by the wayside, an away draw at Chelsea gave the promise of glory, but the usual BBC coverage jinx led to a below par performance and a 0-1 defeat.

Injuries and loss of form meant there was never a settled side; and over the season a total of thirty-seven players appeared for the first team. A total of four goalkeepers were used, including Mervyn Day borrowed from Leeds for the last match of the season, for which special permission was required. Once again the Bassett touch was evident in the transfer market, with midfielder Paul Rogers, a £35,000 signing from non-League Sutton United, and goalkeeper Mel Rees from West Bromwich Albion proving to be astute buys. The loan market also proved successful with Bobby Davison's two goals in the 3-1 victory at Hillsborough ensuring his place in United folklore, and a derby double for the Blades.

Throughout the season United failed to be awarded a penalty. With the last spot-kick being on 2nd February 1991, that makes a total of sixty-four matches!

Andrew Treherne

Back row L-R: Matthew Cherrill, John Pemberton, Paul Rogers, Mike Lake, Jamie Hoyland, Brian Gayle (Captain), Mel Rees, Brian Deane, Dave Walton, Glynn Hodges, Paul Beesley, Alan Cork, Ian Bryson. **Middle row:** John Dungworth (Youth Development Coach), Keith Mincher (Youth Team Coach), Shane Kent, Dane Whitehouse, Carl Bradshaw, David Barnes, Simon Tracey, Nathan Peel, Alan Kelly, Charlie Hatfield, Kevin Gage, John Gannon, Ashley Fickling, Geoff Taylor (Asst. Manager), Derek French (Physio). **Front:** Brian Marwood, Tom Cowan, Andy Cale (Sports Psychologist), John Reed, Dave Bassett (Manager), Richard Lucas, John Greaves (Kit Man), Mitch Ward, Adrian Littlejohn.

SHEFFIELD UNITED

DIVISION ONE: 9th   **FA CUP:** 5th RND   **RUMBELOWS CUP:** 3rd RND   **ZDS CUP:** 2nd RND

M	DATE	COMP.	VEN	OPPONENTS	RESULT	H/T	LGE POS	GOALSCORERS/GOAL TIMES	ATTEN-DANCE
1	A 17	BL	A	Norwich City	D 2-2	1-0	9	Deane 3, Hill 75	(16,380)
2	20	BL	H	West Ham United	D 1-1	0-0	10	Beesley 49	21,463
3	24	BL	H	Southampton	L 0-2	0-1	16		18,029
4	28	BL	A	Coventry City	L 1-3	1-3	21	Bryson 14	(12,601)
5	31	BL	A	Crystal Palace	L 1-2	0-0	20	Hodges 54	(15,507)
6	S 3	BL	H	Chelsea	L 0-1	0-0	20		20,588
7	7	BL	A	Oldham Athletic	L 1-2	0-2	22	Deane 46	(15,064)
8	14	BL	A	Everton	W 2-1	0-1	20	Hoyland 64, Bryson 72	19,817
9	17	BL	H	Notts County	L 1-3	0-0	22	Agana 68	19,375
10	21	BL	A	Arsenal	L 2-5	0-4	22	Agana 55, Mendonca 89	(30,244)
11	24	RC 2/1	A	Wigan Athletic	D 2-2	1-2		Deane 11, 56	(3,647)
12	28	BL	H	Wimbledon	D 0-0	0-0	22		16,062
13	O 5	BL	A	Leeds United	L 3-4	0-3	22	Hoyland 54, Agana 76, Bradshaw 83	(28,362)
14	8	RC 2/2	H	Wigan Athletic	W 1-0	0-0		Hoyland 48	6,608
15	19	BL	H	Nottingham Forest	W 4-2	2-1	22	Whitehouse 13, Agana 27, Bryson 46, Hoyland 86	23,080
16	22	ZDS 2	H	Notts County	D †3-3	0-1		Whitehouse 54, 105, Gayle 76 (Lost 1-2 on pens)	3,291
17	26	BL	A	Manchester City	L 2-3	2-2	22	Gayle 33, 42	(25,495)
18	29	RC 3	H	West Ham United	L 0-2	0-1			11,144
19	N 2	BL	A	Manchester United	L 0-2	0-1	22		(42,942)
20	17	BL	H	Sheffield Wed.	W 2-0	1-0	21	Whitehouse 45, Deane 72	31,831
21	23	BL	A	Tottenham Hotspur	W 1-0	0-0	20	Gage 54	(28,168)
22	30	BL	H	Luton Town	D 1-1	0-0	20	Bryson 88	21,804
23	D 7	BL	A	Queens Park R.	L 0-1	0-0	21		(10,106)
24	14	BL	H	Aston Villa	W 2-0	1-0	19	Ward 40, Whitehouse 63	18,401
25	21	BL	A	West Ham United	D 1-1	0-0	19	Deane 84	(19,287)
26	26	BL	H	Coventry City	L 0-3	0-0	20		19,638
27	28	BL	H	Crystal Palace	D 1-1	1-0	19	Hoyland 14	17,969
28	J 1	BL	A	Liverpool	L 1-2	1-0	20	Deane 32	(35,993)
29	4	FAC 3	H	Luton Town	W 4-0	1-0		Hodges 44, Deane 74, Lake 85, Whitehouse 89	12,201
30	11	BL	A	Southampton	W 4-2	1-1	19	Ward 12, Lake 58, 83, Marwood 68	(13,485)
31	18	BL	H	Norwich City	W 1-0	0-0	19	Bryson 74	17,549
32	26	FAC 4	A	Charlton Athletic	D 0-0	0-0			(11,982)
33	F 1	BL	A	Nottingham Forest	W 5-2	3-1	17	Lake 11, Gannon 21, Bryson 24, Bradshaw 60, Deane 88	(22,412)
34	5	FAC 4R	H	Charlton Athletic	W 3-1	3-0		Deane 4, Gayle 9, Bradshaw 45	16,242
35	8	BL	H	Manchester City	W 4-2	3-1	15	Lake 7, Gayle 18, Deane 44, Whitehouse 81	25,839
36	15	FAC 5	A	Chelsea	L 0-1	0-1			(34,447)
37	22	BL	A	Luton Town	L 1-2	1-2	18	Bryson 11	(9,003)
38	29	BL	H	Queens Park R.	D 0-0	0-0	18		17,958
39	M 11	BL	A	Sheffield Wed.	W 3-1	2-0	15	Whitehouse 4, Davison 28, 67	(40,327)
40	14	BL	H	Manchester United	L 1-2	1-0	17	Deane 22	30,183
41	21	BL	A	Chelsea	W 2-1	1-0	17	Whitehouse 28, 61	(11,247)
42	28	BL	H	Liverpool	W 2-0	1-0	15	Deane 43, 69	26,943
43	31	BL	A	Aston Villa	D 1-1	0-0	13	Gage 79	(15,745)
44	A 4	BL	H	Oldham Athletic	W 2-0	1-0	12	Whitehouse 21, Bryson 81	19,843
45	11	BL	A	Everton	W 2-0	1-0	10	Bryson 29, Cork 66	(18,285)
46	14	BL	H	Tottenham Hotspur	W 2-0	2-0	8	Deane 30, 43	21,526
47	18	BL	A	Arsenal	D 1-1	1-0	7	Davison 25	25,034
48	20	BL	A	Notts County	W 3-1	1-1	7	Beesley 44, Hodges 55, Davison 65	(12,605)
49	26	BL	H	Leeds United	L 2-3	1-1	8	Cork 27, Chapman (og) 67	31,082
50	M 2	BL	A	Wimbledon	L 0-3	0-3	9		(8,768)

Best Home League Attendance: 31,831 v Sheffield Wed.   **Smallest: 16,062 v Wimbledon**   **Av Home Att: 22,096**

Goal Scorers: **Compared with 90-91: +645**

League (65):   Deane 12, Bryson 9, Whitehouse 8, Lake 4, Agana 4, Davison 4, Hoyland 4, Gayle 3, Ward 2, Beesley 2, Cork 2, Hodges 2, Bradshaw 2, Gage 2, Hill, Mendonca, Gannon, Opponents, Marwood

R/lows C (3):   Deane 2, Hoyland

FA Cup (7):   Deane 2, Hodges, Whitehouse, Gayle, Bradshaw, Lake

ZDS Cup (3):   Whitehouse 2, Gayle   †=After extra-time

1991-92

Tracey S.	Pemberton J.	Cowan T.	Beesley P.	Hill C.	Hoyland J.	Whitehouse D.	Agana P.	Deane B.	Bryson J.	Booker R.	Mendonca C.	Hodges G.	Hartfield C.	Barnes D.	Lake M.	Gayle B.	Kite P.	Gannon J.	Bradshaw C.	Ward M.	Gage K.	Rogers P.	Davison R.	Cork A.	Rees M.	Referee	
1	2	3	5	6	7	8*	9	10	11	12	S															P Don	1
1	2	3	5	6	7	14	9	10*	12	8		11•														I Hendrick	2
1		3	5	6	14	11*	9•		7	10																P Wright	3
1	2	3*	5	6	7	14	9		11	10	12															R Groves	4
1	2	3	12	6	5			7	4	9	10	8*														L Shapter	5
1	2	3	14	6	5			7	4	9*	10	11														W Burns	6
1	2		6†		5	8*	9	10•	7	4		11	3†													T Holbrook	7
1		5	6	8		9		7	12	14	11	4	3*	10•												A Dawson	8
1		10•	6		8		9		7	4*	14	11	3	12	5											D Allison	9
1	6•			8	3	9	10*	7	14	12	11		4	5												J Worrall	10
			6	12	11	9	10•	7*			14		3		8	5	1	4								**G Singh**	11
	2	3		6	8•		9		7	12	10*	11		14	5	1	4									K Breen	12
		3	6		8	12	9		7	10			2*	11•	5	1	4	14								K Barratt	13
		3	6		8	11•	9		7*					14	5	1	4	10	12							**P Jones**	14
	2	3	6		8	11	9•		7*		12			14	5	1	4	10								A Ward	15
	2	3	6•		8	11		7*		12				14	5	1	4	10								**T Fitzharris**	16
	2	3	6		8	11•	9		7			14			12	5	1	4	10*							R Lewis	17
	2	3	6		8	11	9		7•			14			12	5	1	4	10*							**G Courtney**	18
1	2	3	6	S	8	11	9		7						12	5		4	10*							C Trussell	19
1	2	3	6		8	11		10	9							5		4	7	S						S Lodge	20
1	2*		6	12	8	11		10	9•							5		4	7	3						J Rushton	21
1	2*		6	14	8	11		10	9						12	5		4•	7*	3						M Reed	22
1	2*		6	14	8*	11		10			9				12	5		4	7	3						R Gifford	23
1	S		6		8	11		10		S					5			4		7	2					R Milford	24
1		3	6		8	11		10	7*			12			5†			4		S	2					M Pierce	25
1		3	6		8	11		10				7			12	5		4*			2					T Fitzharris	26
1		3	6		8	11*		10	9			7•			14	5		4			2					W Flood	27
1		3	6	14	8	12		10	7			11*				5		4			2					P Wright	28
1		3	6	5	8*	11		10	14			9		2				4	7•	12						**K Barratt**	29
1	3*	6	5			11		10	9				14	8				4	7•	2						P Foakes	30
1		6	3			11•		10	9			14		8	5			4	7*	2						R Hamer	31
1		6	2			11*		10	9			7•	3	8	5			4		14						**J Worrall**	32
1		6	S			11		10	9*			12	3	8	5			4	7	2						J Martin	33
1		6•	14			12		10	9			11	3	8	5			4	7*	2						**R Gifford**	34
1		6	S			11		10	9			7*	3	8	5			4		2						A Buksh	35
		6	14			11		10	9*			12	3	8•	5	1	4	7		2					**K Burge**	36
1		6•	14	12		10		9*				7	3		5		4	11		2	8					T Holbrook	37
1		6	S			10		11	9			8*	3		5		4	7	12	2						N Midgley	38
1		6		11*		10		12	9				3		5		4	7	2	8	9•	14				R Hart	39
1	12	6				10•			11				3		5		4	7	2*	8	14	9				M Bailey	40
1		6		12	10			11*				3			5		4	7•	2	8	14	9				I Borrett	41
		6		11				10•	12			3			5		4		14	2	8	7*	9	1		A Wilkie	42
		6		11				10				3	14	5			4		7*	2	8	12	9	1		R Lewis	43
		6		11		10	12				7		3		5		4		2*	8	14	9*	1			M Reed	44
	S	6		10	11				7			3		5		4		2	8	12	9*	1				P Vanes	45
		6		14	10	11			7•			3		5		4	12	2	8	9*	1					K Breen	46
	2	6		12	10*	11			7*			3		5		4	14	8	9	1						H King	47
	2	3	6		14	10	11*			7				5		4•			8	9	1					V Callow	48
	2	6		12	10	14			7			3		5		4*	11	8	9•	1						G Courtney	49
	2	3	6		7	10	12							5		4	11•	8	9*	1						K Redfern	50
29	19	20	38	11	23	25	13	30	29	8	4	22	6	15	8	33	4	32	15	4	22	13	6	7	8	**League Appearances**	
	1		2	4	3	9			5	4	6	4	1		10				3	2			5	1		**Substitute Appearances**	
	1	2	2	1	2+1	3	3	1	3		0+2		1		1+2	3	3	3	2	0+1						**R/lows Appearances**	
3		1	4	2+2	1		3+1		4	3+1			3+1		3	4	3	1	4	2	1		2+2			**FA Cup Appearances**	
	1	1	1		1	1			1	1			0+1		0+1	1	1	1	1							**ZDS Cup Appearances**	

Also Played: Posn.(Game): Jones 4(1,2,3,4), Wood 8(3,4•,6•)14(5), Wilder 2(3,8,9,10,11), Littlejohn 12(3,27)11(5•)9(16,24,25,26,28•), Duffield 12(6)14(7), Lucas 12(7), Fickling 2(14), Reed S(20)14(50), Peel 14(21), Marwood S(26)12(30,31,32,35,48)9(38), Day 1(50)

SHEFFIELD UNITED

Club Colours: Red/white striped shirts, black shorts, red/black stockings.
Change Colours: Yellow/red trimmed shirts, yellow shorts, yellow stockings.
Reserves League: Pontins Central League Division 1

COMPETITIONS						
Div. 1	Div. 2	Div. 3	Div. 4	Texaco	Watney	A/Scot
93-34	92-93	79-81	81-82	72-73	1970	75-76
45-49	34-39	82-84		73-74	1972	77-78
53-56	49-53	88-89		74-75		78-79
61-68	56-61					79-80
71-76	68-71					80-81
90-	76-79					
	84-88					
	89-90					

HONOURS			
Div. 1	Div. 2	Div. 4	FA Cup
97-98	52-53	81-82	1899
			1902
			1915
			1925

MOST APPEARANCES: JOE SHAW 689 (1948-66)			
Year	League	FA Cup	League Cup
1948-49	19		
1949-50	37	3	
1950-51	36		
1951-52	39	5	
1952-53	42	3	
1953-54	35	2	
1954-55	41	1	
1955-56	19		
1956-57	30	1	
1957-58	41	4	
1958-59	41	6	
1959-60	39	3	
1960-61	42	7	1
1961-62	37	5	5
1962-63	40	3	1
1963-64	41	3	
1964-65	25	3	
1965-66	27	2	
	631	51	7
Previous holder: W Gillespie 448 (1911-31)			

MOST GOALS IN A CAREER		
H JOHNSON 223 (1919-31)		
Season	League	FA Cup
1919-20	12	1
1920-21	12	
1921-22	17	
1922-23	17	1
1923-24	15	
1924-25	16	5
1925-26	23	1
1926-27	23	1
1927-28	33	9
1928-29	33	
1929-30	3	
1930-31	1	
Total	205	18
Previous holder: J Kitchen 109 (1908-21)		

MANAGERS			
Name	Seasons	Best	Worst
J Wolstinholm	1898-99	16(1)	16(1)
J Nicholson	1899-32	2(1)	20(1)
J Davison	1932-52	6(1)	11(2)
R Freeman	1952-54	13(1)	1(2)
J Mercer	1954-59	22(1)	7(2)
J Harris	1959-68	5(1)	4(2)
A Rowley	1968-69	9(2)	9(2)
J Harris	1969-73	10(1)	6(2)
K Furphy	1973-76	6(1)	13(1)
J Sirrell	1976-78	22(1)	11(2)
C Coldwell	1978	12(2)	12(2)
H Haslam	1978-81	20(2)	12(3)
M Peters	1981	21(3)	21(3)
I Porterfield	1981-86	7(2)	1(4)
B McEwan	1986-88	9(2)	9(2)
D Bassett	1988-	9(1)	2(3)

RECORD TRANSFER FEE RECEIVED			
Amount	Club	Player	Date
£750,000	Notts County	Tony Agana	11/91
£575,000	Chelsea	Vinny Jones	9/91
£400,000	Leeds Utd	Alex Sabella	7/80
£250,000	Leeds Utd	Tony Currie	6/76

RECORD TRANSFER FEE PAID			
Amount	Club	Player	Date
£700,000	Ipswich Town	Brian Gayle	9/91
£650,000	Leeds United	Vinny Jones	9/90
£375,000	Leyton Orient	Paul Beesley	7/90
£250,000	Bury	Jamie Hoyland	6/90

LONGEST LEAGUE RUNS	
of undefeated matches:	22 (2.9.1899-20.1.1900)
of undefeated home matches:	27 (31.8.1936-6.11.1937)
without home win:	10 (26.3.1949-22.10.1949)
of league wins:	8 (6.2.1893-12.4.1893)(5.9.1903-31.10.1903)(1.2.1958-5.4.1958)(14.9.1960-22.10.1960)
of league defeats:	7 (19.8.1975-23.9.1975)
of league matches without a win:	19 (27.9.1975-14.2.1976)
of undefeated away matches:	11 (3.12.1892-30.10.1893)
without an away win:	20 (14.9.1975-14.4.1976)
of home wins:	11 (30.4.1960.3.12.1960)
of away wins:	6 (10.12.1891-12.4.1892)

BIGGEST VICTORIES
League: 10-0 v Port Vale (a), Div 2, 10.12.1892 (The only time a club has scored 10 Lge goals away from home)
10-0 v Burnley, Division 1, 19.1.1929
(Most goals) 11-2 v Cardiff City, 1.1.1926
F.A. Cup: 5-0 v Corinthians, Round 1, 10.1.1925
5-0 v Newcastle, Round 1, 10.1.1914
5-0 v Barrow, Round 3, 7.1.1956
League Cup: 4-0 v Fulham, Round 1, 25.9.1961
5-1 v Grimsby, Round 2, 26.10.1982
5-1 v Rotherham United, Round 1, 3.9.1985

BIGGEST DEFEATS
League: 1-8 v Arsenal, Division 1, 12.4.1930
2-9 v Arsenal, Division 1, 24.12.1932
3-10 v Middlesbrough, Division 1, 18.11.1933
0-7 v Tottenham Hotspur, Division 2, 12.11.1949
F.A. Cup: 0-13 v Bolton Wanderers, Round 2, 1.2.1890
League Cup: 0-5 v West Ham United, Round 5, 17.11.1971

MOST POINTS
3 points a win: 96, Division 4, 1981-82
2 points a win: 60, Division 2, 1952-53

MOST GOALS IN A MATCH
5. Harry Hammond v Bootle, 8-3, Division 2, 26.11.1892
5. Harry Johnson v West Ham Utd, 6-2, Division 1, 26.12.1927

MOST GOALS
102, Division 1, 1925-26.
Johnson 23, Tunstall 20, Boyle 13, Gillespie 12, Menlove 12, Mercer 8, Partridge 6, Hoyland 3, Roxborough 1, Waugh 1, Longworth 1, Grew 1, og 1.

MOST GOALS IN A SEASON
Jimmy Dunne 46 (League 41, FAC 5) 1930-31
4 goals once = 4; 3 goals 5 times = 15; 2 goals 4 times = 8; 1 goal 19 times = 19.
Previous holder: Jimmy Dunne 36, 1928-29.

MOST FIRST CLASS MATCHES IN A SEASON
61 (46 League, 7 FA Cup, 5 League Cup, 3 Sherpa Van Trophy) 1988-89

MOST LEAGUE GOALS CONCEDED
101, Division 1, 1933-34

MOST LEAGUE WINS
27, Division 4, 1981-82

MOST LEAGUE DRAWS
18, Division 1, 1920-21

MOST LEAGUE DEFEATS
26, Division 1, 1975-76

OLDEST PLAYER
Jimmy Hagan, 39 years 236 days v Derby County, 14.9.1957

YOUNGEST PLAYER
Julian Broddle, 17 years 62 days v Halifax Town, 2.1.1982

MOST CAPPED PLAYER
Billy Gillespie (Northern Ireland) 25

BEST PERFORMANCES BY SHEFFIELD UNITED

League: 1981-82: Matches played 46, Won 27, Drawn 15, Lost 4, Goals for 94, Goals against 41, Points 96. First in Division 4.

Highest: Division 1 Champions.

F.A. Cup: 1898-99: 1st rnd. Burnley 2-2, 2-0; 2nd rnd. Preston North End 2-2, 2-1; 3rd rnd. Notts County 1-0; Semi-final Liverpool 2-2, 4-4, 1-0; Final Derby 4-1.
1901-02: 1st rnd. Northampton 2-0; 2nd rnd. Bolton Wanderers 2-1; 3rd rnd. Newcastle Utd. 1-1, 2-1; Semi-final Derby County 1-1, 1-1, 1-0; Final Southampton 1-1, 2-1.
1914-15: 3rd rnd. Blackpool 2-1; 4th rnd. Liverpool 1-0; 5th rnd. Bradford 1-0; 6th rnd. Oldham 0-0, 3-0; Semi-final Bolton Wanderers 2-1; Final Chelsea 3-0.
1924-25: 3rd rnd. Corinthians 5-0; 4th rnd. Sheffield Wednesday 3-2; 5th rnd. Everton 1-0; 6th rnd. West Bromwich Albion 2-0; Semi-final Southampton 2-0; Final Cardiff 1-0.

League Cup: 1961-62: 1st rnd. Fulham 1-1, 4-0; 2nd rnd. Newcastle 2-2, 2-0; 3rd rnd. Portsmouth 1-0; 4th rnd. Bye; 5th rnd Blackpool 0-0, 0-2.
1966-67: 1st rnd. Bye; 2nd rnd. Sunderland 1-1, 1-0; 3rd rnd. Burnley 2-0; 4th rnd. Walsall 2-1; 5th rnd. Birmingham 2-3.
1971-72: 1st rnd. Bye; 2nd rnd. Fulham 3-0; 3rd rnd. York City 3-2; 4th rnd. Arsenal 0-0, 2-0; 5th rnd. West Ham United 0-5.

DIVISIONAL RECORDS

	Played	Won	Drawn	Lost	For	Against	Points
DIVISION 1	2234	839	524	871	3403	3594	**2231**
DIVISION 2	1078	477	261	340	1814	1450	**1294**
DIVISION 3	230	100	49	81	366	300	**317**
DIVISION 4	46	27	15	4	94	41	**96**
TOTALS	**3588**	**1443**	**849**	**1296**	**5677**	**5385**	**3938**

PLAYERS NAME Honours	Ht	Wt	Birthdate	Birthplace Transfers	Contract Date	Clubs	League	L/Cup	FA Cup	Other	Lg	L/C	FAC	Oth
GOALKEEPERS														
Alan Kelly	6.2	12.5	11.08.68	Preston	25.09.85	Preston N.E	142	1	8	13				
EI:u23.1				£150,000	24.07.92	Sheffield Utd								
Philip Kite	6.1	14.7	26.10.62	Bristol	31.10.80	Bristol Rovers (A)	96	12	8	2				
E:Y.5				Loan	18.01.84	Tottenham H								
					16.08.84	Southampton	4			1				
				Loan	27.03.86	Middlesbrough	2							
				Free	07.02.87	Gillingham	70	5	4	10				
				£20,000	16.08.89	Bournemouth	7	1						
				£25,000	10.08.90	Sheffield Utd	11	5	1	1				
				Loan	21.11.91	Mansfield Town	11			1				
Mel Rees	6.3	13.5	25.01.67	Cardiff	22.09.84	Cardiff City (A)	31	3	3					
W:Y				£60,000	21.07.87	Watford	3		1	1				
				Loan	24.08.89	Crewe Alexandra	6							
				Loan	22.11.89	Southampton								
				Loan	05.01.90	Leyton Orient	9			1				
				£55,000	19.09.90	West Brom A	18		1					
				Loan	29.01.92	Norwich City								
				£25,000	26.03.92	Sheffield Utd	8							
Simon Tracey	6.0	12.0	09.12.67	Woolwich	03.02.86	Wimbledon (A)	1			1				
					19.10.88	Sheffield Utd	113	4	10	5				
DEFENDERS														
David Barnes	5.10	11.4	16.11.61	London	31.05.79	Coventry City (A)	9		4					
E:Y14;UEFA.YTH'80				Free	12.04.82	Ipswich Town	16+1							
				£35,000	03.10.84	Wolverhampton W	86+2	7	6	6	4			
					22.08.87	Aldershot	68+1	2	2+2	4	1			
				£50,000	11.07.89	Sheffield Utd	67	4	11	4	1			
Paul Beesley	6.1	11.5	21.07.65	Liverpool		Marine								
					22.09.84	Wigan Ath	153+2	13	6	11	3			
				£175,000	20.10.89	Leyton Orient	32		1	2	1			1
				£300,000	10.07.90	Sheffield Utd	75+2	6	4	3	3			1
Thomas Cowan	5.8	10.8	28.08.69	Bellshill		Clyde								
						Glasgow Rangers								
				£350,000	01.08.91	Sheffield Utd	20	2	1	1				
Ashley Fickling	5.10	11.0	15.11.72	Sheffield	26.07.91	Sheffield Utd		1						
Kevin Gage	5.9	12.8	21.04.64	Chiswick	04.01.82	Wimbledon (A)	135+33	7+2	8+3	0+1	15	1	1	
EY:5,Div4'83				£100,000	17.07.87	Aston Villa	113+2	13	9	8	8	3	1	
				£150,000	15.11.91	Sheffield Utd	22		2+2		2			
Brian Gayle	6.1	12.7	06.03.65	London	03.06.85	Wimbledon (A)	76+7	7	8	2	3	1	1	
				£325,000	06.07.88	Manchester City	55	8	2	1	3			
				£330,000	19.01.90	Ipswich Town	58	3	0+1		4			
				£700,000	17.09.91	Sheffield Utd	33	3	3	1	3	1	1	1
Colin Hill	5.11	11.11	12.11.63	Uxbridge	07.08.81	Arsenal (A)	46	4	1		1			
						Maritime (Por)								
					30.10.87	Colchester Utd	64+5	2	7	3+1			2	
				£85,000	01.08.89	Sheffield Utd	77+5	5	10	3	1			
				Loan	26.03.92	Leicester City	10			3				
John Pemberton	5.11	11.9	18.11.64	Oldham		Chadderton								
				Free	26.09.84	Rochdale	1							
				Free	03.07.85	Crewe Alexandra	116+5	7	3	7	1	1		
					24.03.88	Crystal Palace	76+2	6+1	8	12	2			
				£300,000	27.07.90	Sheffield Utd	40	3		1				
Chris Wilder	5.11	10.10	23.09.67	Wortley	26.09.85	Southampton (A)								
				f	20.08.86	Sheffield Utd	89+4	8+1	7	3	1			
				Loan	02.11.89	Walsall	4		1	2				
				Loan	12.10.90	Charlton Ath	1							
				Loan	28.11.91	Charlton Ath	2							
				Loan	27.02.92	Leyton Orient	16			1	1			
				Loan	30.07.92	Rotherham Utd								
MIDFIELD														
Ian Bryson	5.11	11.11	26.11.62	Kilmarnock		Kilmarnock	194+21	12+7	14+2		40	1	3	
				£40,000	24.08.88	Sheffield Utd	129+10	10	15+3	7	33	1	4	3
John Gannon	5.8	10.10	18.12.66	London	19.12.84	Wimbledon (A)	13+3	1+1		1	2			
FAC'88				Loan	19.12.86	Crewe Alexandra	14+1			1				
					23.02.89	Sheffield Utd	8+8				1			
				Free		Sheffield Utd	90+3	7	11	4	4			
Jamie Hoyland	6.0	12.8	23.01.66	Sheffield	12.11.83	Manchester City (A)	2	0+1						
E: Y.3					11.07.86	Bury	169+3	14+1	6	12	35	5		2
				£250,000	04.07.90	Sheffield Utd	40+7	3+1	2	2	4	1		1
Michael Lake	6.1	13.07	06.11.66	Manchester		Macclesfield								
E:S.Pro.2				£60,000	11.10.89	Sheffield Utd	13+16	3+2	5	0+1	4		1	
Adrian Littlejohn	5.9	10.5	26.09.70	Wolverhampton		West Brom A. (T)								
				Free	24.05.89	Walsall	26+18	2+1	1	4	1			
				Free	06.08.91	Sheffield Utd	5+2	1						
Paul Rogers			21.03.65			Sutton Utd								
E: S.Pro				£40,000	29.01.92	Sheffield Utd	13							
Dane Whitehouse	5.9	10.12	14.10.70	Sheffield	01.07.89	Sheffield Utd. (T)	37+18	3+1	6+3	3	9		1	2
Flg.u18.1														

SHEFFIELD UNITED CONTINUED

PLAYERS NAME Honours	Ht	Wt	Birthdate	Birthplace Transfers	Contract Date	Clubs	League	L/Cup	FA Cup	Other	Lg	L/C	FAC	Oth
FORWARDS														
Carl Bradshaw	6.0	11.0	02.10.68	Sheffield	23.08.86	Sheffield Wed. (A)	16+16	2+2	6+1	1	4		3	
E:Y4				Loan	23.08.86	Barnsley	6				1			
				P.E	30.09.88	Manchester City	1+4		0+1	0+1				
				£50,000	05.10.89	Sheffield Utd	59+16	4+1	10	4	6	1	3	
Alan Cork	6.0	12.0	04.03.59	Derby	02.07.77	Derby County								
FAC'88				Loan	14.09.77	Lincoln City	5							
				Free	09.02.78	Wimbledon	352+78	29+7	30+7	3+4	145	14	8	1
				Free	09.03.92	Sheffield Utd	7+1				2			
Brian Deane	6.3	12.7	07.02.68	Leeds	14.12.85	Doncaster Rovers	59+7	3	2+1	2+2	12		1	
				£30,000	19.07.88	Sheffield Utd	156	11	15	6	68	9	8	2
Peter Duffield	5.6	10.7	04.02.69	Middlesbough	04.11.86	Middlesbrough (A)								
					20.08.87	Sheffield Utd	35+22	3+5	6+2	3	28	2	1	3
Loan Halifax Town (07.03.88) 12lg 6gls, 1oth				Loan	07.03.91	Rotherham Utd	17				5			
				Loan	23.07.92	Blackpool								
Glyn Hodges	6.0	12.3	30.04.63	Streatham	03.02.81	Wimbledon (A)	200+32	14+2	13+2	0+1	49	3	2	
W: 13, u21.5, Y; Div4'83				£200,000	15.07.87	Newcastle Utd	7							
				£300,000	01.10.87	Watford	82+4	5	8	2+1	15	2	1	1
					16.07.90	Crystal Palace	5+2	2+2				1		
					16.04.91	Sheffield Utd	34+4		3+1		6		1	
Brian Marwood	5.7	9.13	05.02.60	Seaham Harbour	09.02.78	Hull City (A)	154+4	4+1	16	5	51		1	
E: ; Div1'89; CT'89				£115,000	09.08.84	Sheffield Wed	125+3	13	19	0+1	27	5	3	
				£600,000	25.03.88	Arsenal	52	6	2	3+1	16	1		2
				£350,000	21.09.90	Sheffield Utd	13+8	3+1	0+1		3			
				Loan	18.10.91	Middlesbrough	3	1		1				
Clive Mendonca	5.10	10.7	09.09.68	Sheffield	10.09.86	Sheffield Utd. (A)	8+5	0+1		1	4			
				Loan	26.02.88	Doncaster Rovers	2							
				£15,000	25.03.88	Rotherham Utd	71+13	5+2	4+1	4+2	27	1	2	1
				£110,000	01.08.91	Sheffield Utd	4+6	0+2		0+1	1			
				Loan	19.03.92	Grimsby Town	10				3			

ADDITIONAL CONTRACT PLAYERS

(D) Charles Hartfield, (M) Richard Lucas, (F) Nathan Peel, (M) John Reed, David Walton, (D) Mitchum Ward.

MANAGER: DAVE BASSETT

DATE OF BIRTH: 04.09.1944   **PLACE OF BIRTH:** Wembley

DATE OF APPOINTMENT: 21.01.1988

PREVIOUS CLUBS
as Manager: Wimbledon; Watford
as Asst. Manager: Wimbledon
as Player: Walton & Hersham; Wimbledon; Hendon; Chelsea; Watford

HONOURS
as Manager: Wimbledon: Promotion to Div 3 1981; Division 4 Championship 1983; Promotion to Div 2 1984; Promotion to Div 1 1986. Sheffield Utd: Promotion to Div 3 1988, Promotion to Div 2 1989, Promotion to Div 1 1990
as Asst. Man./Coach:
as Player: Amateur Cup Winners Medal 1973
International: England Amateur International (10)

Value Rating: ★ ★ ★ ★

Programme Editor: Andy Pack

Price of 1992-93 Programme: £1.20

Number of Pages: 36 to 40

Subscriptions: £25.20 + £8.40 postage (homes). Double cost for aways also

Local Newspapers: Sheffield Newspapers Ltd (The Star, Morning Telegraph).

Local Radio Stations: BBC Radio Sheffield, Radio Hallam.

Additional Publications on Club: The First 100 Years by Denis Clarebrough (£17.50, published by the club)

LEADING LEAGUE GOALSCORERS
SEASONS 1979-80 – 1991-92

1979-80	**JEFF BOURNE**	**11**	1980-81	**BOB HATTON**	**18**
1981-82	**KEITH EDWARDS**	**35**	1982-83	**COLIN MORRIS**	**14**
1983-84	**KEITH EDWARDS**	**33**	1984-85	**KEITH EDWARDS**	**13**
1985-86	**KEITH EDWARDS**	**20**	1986-87	**PETER BEAGRIE**	**9**
				STEVE FOLEY	**9**
1987-88	**TONY PHILLISKIRK**	**9**	1988-89	**TONY AGANA**	**24**
1989-90	**BRIAN DEANE**	**14**	1990-91	**BRIAN DEANE**	**13**

1991-92	**BRIAN DEANE**	**12**

BRAMALL LANE GROUND Sheffield S2 4SU

Capacity: 32,213   **Covered Standing:**   **Seating:** 23,544

Tel: Ground: 0742 343122   **Ticket Sales:** 0742 738955

GROUNDS

ATTENDANCES
Highest: 68,287 v Leeds United, FA Cup 5th Round, 15.1.1936

Lowest: £1,500 v Bootle, Division 1, 10.9.1892

RECORD RECEIPTS (with previous records):
£171,095 v Manchester Utd, FA Cup 6th Rnd, 11.3.1990
£67,806 v Newcastle United, Littlewoods Cup Second Round, 27.9.1988
£65,092 v Sheffield Wednesday, Division 3, 5.4.1980
£37,500 v Arsenal, FA Cup 3rd Round, 7.1.1978
£33,000 v Newcastle United, FA Cup 3rd Round, 8.1.1977

BRAMALL LANE
First game: Sheffield Club v Hallam (Charity Match), 0-0, 28.12.1862
First Sheffield United game: v Birmingham St Georges (friendly) 0-4, 28.9.1889
First floodlit game: v Rotherham, 16.3.1954

Season Tickets:
Stands: from £156.50 to £239, juv/OAP £101.50 to £124
Ground: £143, juv/OAP £87.50

Executive Box Season Tickets: None available

Cost of Stand Tickets: Seats: £8 to £14, juv/OAP £5 to £7
Terraces: £7 to £8.50, juv/OAP £4.50 to £5

Match and Ticket Information: Sheffield United's membership scheme, which allows entry to the two members only areas of the ground, costs £3.00. Tickets bookable 14 days prior to each match. Membership areas are Spion Kop Stand, John Street Stand and John Street Terrace

Car Parking: The ground is five minutes away from car parks in the City Centre. Side-street parking is ample

Nearest Railway Station: Sheffield Midland (0742 726411)

How to get to the ground

From North: Use Motorway M1 until junction 34. Leave motorway and follow signs, Sheffield A6109. In 3.4m turn left and shortly at roundabout take 4th exit into Sheaf Street. Then at 2nd roundabout take 5th exit into St. Mary's Road (S.P. Bakewell). In 0.5m left into Bramall Lane for Sheffield United FC
From East and South: Use A57 from Motorway M1 (junction 31 or 33) then at roundabout take 3rd exit into Sheaf Street. Then at 2nd roundabout take 5th exit in St Mary's Road and proceed as above
From West: Use A57 (S.P. Sheffield) and at rounabout take 4th exit A6134 into Upper Hanover Street. Then at 2nd roundabout take 3rd exit into Bramall Lane.

SHEFFIELD WEDNESDAY Premier

Formed: 1867 | **Turned Professional:** 1887 | **Ltd Co:** 1899

SPONSORED BY: | **NICKNAME:** The Owls

AFTER the traumatic events of the summer, with the departure of Ron Atkinson, many people were concerned how the Owls would fare back in the First Division.

The appointment of Trevor Francis, the fans choice, as player/manager has proved to be a master stroke. The board and chairman Dave Richards in particular, should take a great deal of credit in their appointment of Trevor. He straight away set about the task of continuing the good football which was characteristic of the Ron Atkinson regime.

The players responded magnificently to the manager's promptings, both on and off the pitch. Trevor certainly proved he can still play, despite not being up to a full ninety minutes.

Despite a few catastrophic results, the Owls were very consistent and thoroughly deserved their third place at the end of the season. The crowds kept pouring in to Hillsborough throughout the season and the promise of the UEFA cup next season seems certain to keep the fans as committed as ever.

Of course all the players deserve credit but notably the following: David Hirst was again lethal with his finishing, as well as exciting with his skill. Roland Nilsson was sheer class throughout and Carlton Palmer deservedly capped a fine season with an England place. Chris Woods, despite a bad time in certain games had a useful first season and justified his England number one position.

It really is all happening at Hillsborough with the South Stand roof being replaced with a new modern structure. So with the new Premier League and a UEFA Cup place, exciting times lie ahead for the Owls under the leadership of Trevor Francis and Richie Barker

Michael Renshaw

Back row L-R: Peter Shirtliff, Chris Turner, Carlton Palmer, Kevin Pressman, Lawrie Madden. **Middle:** Roger Spry (Trainer), Richie Barker (Asst. Manager), John Sheridan, Dave Bennett, Phil King, Steve McCall, Nigel Worthington, David Hirst, Alan Smith (Physio). **Front:** Roland Nilsson, Darren Wood, Paul Williams, Ron Atkinson (Manager), Nigel Pearson, Danny Wilson, Trevor Francis.

SHEFFIELD WEDNESDAY

DIVISION ONE: 3rd   **FA CUP:** 4th RND   **RUMBELOWS CUP:** 3rd RND   **ZDS CUP:** 3rd RND

M	DATE	COMP.	VEN	OPPONENTS	RESULT	H/T	LGE POS	GOALSCORERS/GOAL TIMES	ATTEN-DANCE
1	A 17	BL	H	Aston Villa	L 2-3	2-1		Hirst 3, Wilson 37	36,749
2	24	BL	A	Leeds United	D 1-1	0-0	20	Hirst 49	(30,260)
3	28	BL	H	Everton	W 2-1	0-0	15	Wilson 55, Anderson 88	28,690
4	31	BL	H	Queens Park R.	W 4-1	3-0	9	Palmer 3 (6, 42, 44), Sheridan 70	25,022
5	S 3	BL	A	Notts County	L 1-2	1-1	11	Pearson 26	(12,297)
6	7	BL	H	Nottingham Forest	W 2-1	1-0	8	Williams 19, Francis 89	31,289
7	14	BL	A	Manchester City	W 1-0	0-0	5	Williams 74	(29,453)
8	18	BL	A	Norwich City	L 0-1	0-1	7		(12,503)
9	21	BL	H	Southampton	W 2-0	1-0	4	Williams 4, Worthington 66	27,291
10	24	RC 2/1	A	Leyton Orient	D 0-0	0-0			(6,231)
11	28	BL	A	Liverpool	D 1-1	0-1	4	Harkes 69	(37,071)
12	O 2	BL	A	Wimbledon	L 1-2	0-0	5	Pearson 79	(3,121)
13	5	BL	H	Crystal Palace	W 4-1	3-1	4	Worthington 8, Hirst 39, 44, Palmer 82	26,230
14	9	RC 2/2	H	Leyton Orient	W 4-1	2-0		Anderson 11, Williams 22, Francis 74, 87	14,398
15	19	BL	A	Luton Town	D 2-2	1-1	5	Hirst 44, Sheridan 89	(9,401)
16	23	ZDS 2	H	Manchester City	W 3-2	1-1		Hirst 12, Hyde 88, Jemson 89	7,951
17	26	BL	H	Manchester United	W 3-2	1-2	5	Hirst 15, Jemson 70, 81	38,260
18	30	RC 3	H	Southampton	D 1-1	1-0		Hirst 38	17,627
19	N 2	BL	H	Tottenham Hotspur	D 0-0	0-0	4		31,573
20	17	BL	A	Sheffield United	L 0-2	0-1	7		(31,803)
21	20	RC 3R	A	Southampton	L 0-1	0-0			(10,801)
22	23	BL	H	Arsenal	D 1-1	1-0	7	Hirst 19	32,174
23	26	ZDS 3	A	Notts County	L 0-1	0-0			(4,118)
24	30	BL	A	West Ham United	W 2-1	1-0	4	Harkes 24, Jemson 85	(24,116)
25	D 7	BL	H	Chelsea	W 3-0	0-0	3	Hirst 47, 59, Williams 89	27,383
26	21	BL	H	Wimbledon	W 2-0	0-0	3	Sheridan 49, 60 (pen)	20,574
27	26	BL	A	Everton	W 1-0	0-0	3	Hirst 53	(30,788)
28	28	BL	A	Queens Park R.	D 1-1	0-1	3	Hirst 89	(12,990)
29	J 1	BL	H	Oldham Athletic	D 1-1	0-0	3	Sharp (og) 63	32,679
30	4	FAC 3	A	Preston North End	W 2-0	0-0		Sheridan 62, Bart-Williams 70	(14,337)
31	12	BL	H	Leeds United	L 1-6	1-3	5	Sheridan (pen) 39	32,228
32	18	BL	H	Aston Villa	W 1-0	0-0	5	Jemson 78	(28,036)
33	F 1	BL	A	Luton Town	W 3-2	1-2	5	Hirst 18, Williams 79, Harkes 86	22,291
34	4	FAC 4	H	Middlesbrough	L 1-2	1-1		Hirst 4	29,772
35	8	BL	A	Manchester United	D 1-1	1-1	4	Hirst 4	(47,074)
36	15	BL	A	Arsenal	L 1-7	1-1	5	Worthington 44	(26,805)
37	22	BL	H	West Ham United	W 2-1	0-1	4	Palmer 80, Anderson 88	26,150
38	29	BL	A	Chelsea	W 3-0	3-0	4	Wilson 5, Worthington 21, Williams 37	(17,538)
39	M 7	BL	H	Coventry City	D 1-1	0-0	3	Anderson 83	23,959
40	11	BL	H	Sheffield United	L 1-3	0-2		King 48	40,327
41	14	BL	A	Tottenham Hotspur	W 2-0	0-0	3	Hirst 61, Williams 69	(23,027)
42	21	BL	H	Notts County	W 1-0	0-0	3	Hirst 75	23,910
43	28	BL	A	Oldham Athletic	L 0-3	0-1	3		(15,897)
44	A 4	BL	A	Nottingham Forest	W 2-0	2-0		Williams 30, Hirst 42	(26,105)
45	8	BL	A	Coventry City	D 0-0	0-0			(13,293)
46	11	BL	H	Manchester City	W 2-0	0-0	3	Hirst 56, Worthington 86	32,148
47	18	BL	A	Southampton	W 1-0	0-0	3	Hirst 70	(17,715)
48	20	BL	H	Norwich City	W 2-0	2-0		Nilsson 10, Sheridan 44	27,362
49	25	BL	A	Crystal Palace	D 1-1	1-0	3	Williams 44	(21,573)
50	M 2	BL	H	Liverpool	D 0-0	0-0	3		34,861

Best Home League Attendance: 40,327 v Sheffield United   **Smallest:** 20,574 v Wimbledon   **Av Home Att:** 29,772

Goal Scorers: **Compared with 90-91: +2,972**

League (62): Hirst 18, Williams 9, Sheridan 6 (2 pens), Palmer 5, Worthington 5, Jemson 4, Harkes 3, Wilson 3, Anderson 3, Pearson 2, Nilsson, Francis, Opponents, King

R/lows C (5): Francis 2, Williams, Hirst, Anderson

FA Cup (3): Hirst, Bart-Williams, Sheridan

ZDS Cup (3): Hyde, Hirst, Jemson

1991-92

Woods C.	Nilsson N.	King P.	Palmer C.	Warhurst P.	Pearson N.	Wilson D.	Sheridan J.	Hirst D.	Williams P.	Worthington N.	Francis T.	Harkes J.	Anderson V.	MacKenzie S.	Watson G.	Hyde G.	Jemson N.	Wood C.	Williams M.	Bart-Williams C.	Pressman K.	Shirtliff P.	Johnson D.	Referee	
1	2	3	4	5	6	7	8•	9	10*	11	12	14												R Milford	1
1	2	3	4	5	6	7	8	9•	10*	11	14				12									C Trussell	2
1	2	3	4	5		7	8	9	10*	11	12•		6	14										K Barrett	3
1	2	3	4	5		7	8	9•	10	11*	14		6		12									P Harrison	4
1		3	4	5	6	7	8	9*	10	11•	12		2	14										H King	5
1	2	3	4	5	6	7	8		10•	11	12		14		9*									A Wilkie	6
1	2	3	4	5	6	7			10	11	12		S		9*	8								J Watson	7
1	2	3	4	5	6	7			10	11	12				9•	8*	14							T Ward	8
1	2	3	4	5	6*	7			10	11		14	8	12	9•									J Parker	9
1	2	3		5		7				11	S		8	6	10	9	4	S						P Alcock	10
1	2	3	4	5	6	7			10	11	12		8	S	9*									P Danson	11
1	2	3•	4	5	6	7			10	11	12		8	14	9*									J Borrett	12
1	2	3	4	5	6	7		9*	10	11	12		8	S										A Gunn	13
1		3	4	5	6	7		9*	10	11	12		2		8•		14							I Cruikshanks	14
1	2	3	4		6	7•	8	9	10	11*			5	14	12									D Elleray	15
1	2	3	4	12				9	10	11•	7*		5		8		14	6						P Wright	16
1	2	3	4	5		7	8	9•	10	11*	14		6		12									K Breen	17
1	2	3	4			7	8	9	10*	11			5	6	12	S								D Allison	18
1	2	3•	4	5		7*	8	9	10	11	12		6	14										M Reed	19
1	2	3	4	5		7•	8	9	10	11*	14		6		12									S Lodge	20
1	2	3	4		6	7	8	9	10	S	11*		5		12									R Milford	21
1	2*	3	4	5	6		8	9	14	7	12		10•	11										V Callow	22
1	3•	4	5	6			8*	9	11	7	2		14	10	12									K Redfern	23
1	3•	4*	5	6			8	9	S	11	2		12	10	7									C Wilkes	24
	2	3	4	6*	5		8	9	14	11	12		10•	7					1					T Holbrook	25
1	2	3	4	6	5		8	9*	12	11	S		10	7										K Barratt	26
1	2	3	4	6	5	14	8•	9	12	11			10*	7										J Lloyd	27
1	2	3	4	6	5		8	9	10•	11	14		12	7*										M Bodenham	28
1		3	4	6			8•	9*	12	11	2		14	10	7	5								B Nixon	29
1	2	3	4	12			8•	11	6*	5	9		14	10	7									R Shepherd	30
1	2	3	4	5*			8	14	11•	12	6		7	10	9									P Don	31
1	2*	3	4			7				11	12		6	S	8	10						5	9	G Courtney	32
1	2	3	4	5	6			9	10	11*	12		7	S	8									P Harrison	33
1	2	3	4	5	6			9	10•	11*	12		7	14	8									D Allison	34
1	2	3	4	5	6	7		9	12	11•	14		8	10*										R Milford	35
1	2	3	4•		6	7		9	14	11	12		5	8*	10									A Gunn	36
1	2		4			7		9	14	3	11		5	8*	12	6	10•							A Wilkie	37
1	2	3	4	14		7		9	10*	11	5		8•	6	12									D Frampton	38
1	2	3	4	14		7		9	10	11*	5		12	8•	6									B Burns	39
1	2	3	4	11•		7*		9	10	14	5		8	12	6									R Hart	40
1	2	4	3	5		7		9*	10	11	8•		12	14	6									K Redfern	41
1	2	4	3	5		7*		9	10	12	11		14	8•	6									N Midgley	42
1	2	12	4	3*	5	7		9	10	14	11		8•	6										V Callow	43
1	2	3	4	5		7	8*	9	10	11	S		12	6										K Cooper	44
1	2	3	4	5		7	8	9	10•	11	14		12	6*										A Buksh	45
1	2	3	4	6	5	7	8•	9	10*	11	12	14												D Elleray	46
1	2	3	4	6	5	7	8	9*	10	11	12		14											I Borrett	47
1	2	3	4	6	5	7	8•		10	11	12		14										9*	J Worrall	48
1	2	3	4	S	5	7	8	9*	10	11	12											6		B Hill	49
1	2	3	4	6	5	7	8•	9	10*	11	14											12		J Martin	50
41	39	38	42	31	31	35	24	33	31	34			14	15		4	9	11		12	1	12	5	League Appearances	
	1		2		1			9			20	15	7	3		4	9			3			1	Substitute Appearances	
4	3	4	3	2	2	4	2	3	3	3	0+1	3	4			1	1	1+2	1+1					R/lows Appearances	
2	2	2	2	1	1	0+1	1	1	1	2			2			1+1	1	1+1	1					FA Cup Appearances	
2	1	2	2	1	1	1+1	2	2	1	2	2		0+1	1	1+1	1	0+1							ZDS Cup Appearances	

SHEFFIELD WEDNESDAY

Club Colours: Blue and white striped shirts, black shorts, blue stockings.
Change Colours: Yellow & black striped shirts, black shorts, yellow stockings.
Reserves League: Pontins Central League Division 1

COMPETITIONS

Div. 1	Div. 2	Div. 3	EUFA
92-99	99-00	75-80	61-62
00-20	20-26		63-64
26-37	37-50		
50-51	51-52		
52-55	55-56		
56-58	58-59		
59-70	70-75		
84-90	80-84		
91-	90-91		

HONOURS

Div. 1	Div. 2	FA Cup	League Cup
02-03	99-00	1896	1991
03-04	25-26	1907	
28-29	51-52	1935	C/Shield
29-30	55-56		1935
	58-59		

MOST APPEARANCES: ANDREW WILSON 546 (1900-20)

Year	League	FA Cup
1900-01	31	1
1901-02	25	1
1902-03	34	2
1903-04	29	3
1904-05	30	3
1905-06	35	5
1906-07	35	7
1907-08	34	1
1908-09	37	4
1909-10	30	2
1910-11	38	1
1911-12	37	2
1912-13	37	4
1913-14	31	5
1914-15	38	3
1919-20	1	
	502	**44**

MOST GOALS IN A CAREER
ANDREW WILSON 216 (1900-20)

Season	League	FA Cup
1900-01	13	
1901-02	9	
1902-03	12	
1903-04	10	2
1904-05	15	2
1905-06	16	2
1906-07	17	4
1907-08	19	
1908-09	18	3
1909-10	12	
1910-11	9	1
1911-12	12	
1912-13	9	2
1913-14	15	
1914-15	13	1
Total	**199**	**17**

HIGHEST TRANSFER FEE RECEIVED

Amount	Club	Player	Date
£1,700,000	Real Sociedad	Dalian Atkinson	8/90
£800,000	G. Rangers	Mel Sterland	3/89
£600,000	Arsenal	Brian Marwood	3/88
£480,000	Stoke City	Ian Cranson	7/89

HIGHEST TRANSFER FEE PAID

Amount	Club	Player	Date
£1,200,000	G. Rangers	Chris Woods	8/91
£1,000,000	Marseille	Chris Waddle	7/92
£800,000	Nott'm Forest	Nigel Jemson	9/91
£750,000	West Brom	Carlton Palmer	3/89
£750,000	Oldham Athletic	Paul Warhurst	7/91

MANAGERS

Name	Seasons	Best	Worst
Rob Brown	1920-33	1(1)	14(2)
Bill Walker	1933-37	3(2)	22(2)
Jim McMullen	1937-42	3(2)	17(2)
Eric Taylor	1942-58	14(1)	20(2)
Harry Catterick	1958-61	2(1)	5(1)
Vic Buckingham	1961-64	6(1)	6(1)
Alan Brown	1964-67	8(1)	17(1)
Jack Marshall	1967-68	19(1)	19(1)
Tom McAnearney	1968-69	15(1)	15(1)
Danny Williams	1969-71	22(1)	15(1)
Derek Dooley	1971-74	10(2)	19(2)
Steve Burtenshaw	1974-75	22(2)	20(3)
Len Ashurst	1975-77	8(3)	14(3)
Jack Charlton	1977-83	4(2)	18(3)
Howard Wilkinson	1983-88	5(1)	2(2)
Peter Eustace	1989		
Ron Atkinson	1989-91	18(1)	3(2)
Trevor Francis	1991	3(1)	3(1)

LONGEST LEAGUE RUNS

of undefeated matches:	19 (3.12.1960-17.4.1961)
of undefeated home matches:	31 (13.12.1902-29.10.1904)
without home win:	13 (7.2.1974-6.9.1975)
of league wins:	9 (14.11.1903-16.1.1904)
of league defeats:	7 (7.1.1893-25.3.1893)
of league matches without a win:	20 (6.9.1954-17.3.1955)
	(11.1.1975-6.9.1975)
of undefeated away matches:	11 (6.11.1979-12.4.1980)
without an away win:	35 (28.12.1974-16.10.1976)
of home wins:	19 (2.9.1899-6.10.1900)
of away wins:	6 (28.4.1990-6.10.1990)

PREVIOUS NAME
The Wednesday 1867-1929

PREVIOUS LEAGUE
Football Alliance

BIGGEST VICTORIES
League: 9-1 v Birmingham, Division 1, 13.12.1930
8-0 v Sunderland, Division 1, 26.12.1911
F.A. Cup: 12-0 v Halliwell, Round 1, 17.1.1891
League Cup: 8-0 v Aldershot (a), Round 2, 3.10.1989
Europe: 4-0 v Roma, Round 2, 1961-62

BIGGEST DEFEATS
League: 0-10 v Aston Villa, Division 1, 5.10.1912
F.A. Cup: 0-5 v Wolves, Round 3, 2.3.1889
1-6 v Blackburn Rovers, Final, 29.3.1890
0-5 v Everton (h), Round 3 replay, 27.1.1988
League Cup: 2-8 v Queens Park R., Round 2, 1973-74
Europe: No more than 2 goals

MOST POINTS
3 points a win: 88, Division 2, 1983-84
2 points a win: 62, Division 2, 1958-59

MOST GOALS
106, 1958-59 (Division 2).
Shiner 28, Froggatt 26, Fantham 12, Wilkinson 12, Finney 11, Curtis 5, J McAnearney 3, Kay 3, Quixall 2, Ellis 1, T McAnearney 1, Young 1, og 1.

MOST GOALS IN A MATCH
6. Douglas Hunt v Norwich, Division 2, 19.11.1938 (7-0)

MOST GOALS IN A SEASON
Derek Dooley 47, (46 League, 1 FAC) 1951-52.
5 goals once = 5; 4 goals twice = 8; 3 goals 3 times = 9; 2 goals 9 times = 18; 1 goal 7 times = 7
Previous holder: J Trotter, 37 League (1925-26 & 1926-27).

MOST FIRST CLASS MATCHES IN A SEASON
61 (46 League, 4 FA Cup, 10 League Cup, 1 ZDS) 1990-91

MOST LEAGUE GOALS CONCEDED
100, Division 1, 1954-55

MOST LEAGUE WINS
28, Division 2, 1958-59

MOST LEAGUE DRAWS
19, Division 3, 1978-79

MOST LEAGUE DEFEATS
26, Division 1, 1919-20; Division 2, 1974-75

OLDEST PLAYER
Tom Brittleton 41 years v Oldham, 1.5.1920.

YOUNGEST PLAYER
Peter Fox 15 years 269 days, 31.3.1973

MOST CAPPED PLAYER
Nigel Worthington (N. Ireland) 35

BEST PERFORMANCES BY SHEFFIELD WEDNESDAY

League: 1958-59: Matches played 42, Won 28, Drawn 6, Lost 8, Goals for 106, Goals against 48, Points 62. 1st in Division 2

Highest: 1st in Division 1

F.A. Cup: 1895-96: 1st rnd. Southampton 3-2; 2nd rnd. Sunderland 2-1; 3rd rnd. Everton 4-0; Semi-Final Bolton 3-1; Final Wolves 2-1.

1906-07: 3rd rnd. Wolves 3-2; 4th rnd. Southampton 1-1, 3-1; 5th rnd. Sunderland 0-0, 1-0; 5th rnd. Liverpool 1-0; Semi-Final Arsenal 1-0; Final Everton 2-1.

1934-35: 3rd rnd. Oldham 3-1; 4th rnd. Wolves 2-1; 5th rnd. Norwich City 1-0; 6th rnd. Arsenal 2-1; Semi-Final Burnley 3-0; Final West Bromwich A. 4-2.

League Cup: 1990-91: 2nd rnd. Brentford 2-1, 1-2; 3rd rnd. Swindon 0-0, 1-0; 4th rnd. Derby Co. 1-1, 2-1; 5th rnd. Coventry City 1-0; Semi-Final Chelsea 2-0, 3-1; Final Manchester Utd 1-0

EUFA: 1963-64: 1st rnd. Olympique Lyonnais 2-4, 5-2; 2nd rnd. AS Roma 4-0, 0-1; Q/Final Barcelona 3-2, 0-2.

DIVISIONAL RECORDS

	Played	Won	Drawn	Lost	For	Against	Points
DIVISION 1	2266	879	523	864	3567	3567	2389
DIVISION 2	1088	460	281	347	1693	1401	1285
DIVISION 3	230	83	76	71	297	266	242
TOTALS	**3584**	**1422**	**880**	**1282**	**5557**	**5234**	**3916**

SHEFFIELD WEDNESDAY

PLAYERS NAME Honours	Ht	Wt	Birthdate	Birthplace Transfers	Contract Date	Clubs	League	L/Cup	FA Cup	Other	Lg	L/C	FAC	Oth
GOALKEEPERS														
Lance Key	6.0		13.05.68	Kettering		Histon								
					14.04.90	Sheffield Wed								
Kevin Pressman	6.1	14.2	06.11.67	Fareham	07.11.85	Sheffield Wed	59	9		3				
E:u21.1,u19.3,Y.6					10.03.92	Stoke City	4			2				
Chris Woods	6.2	13.5	14.11.59	Boston	01.12.76	Nottm. Forest (A)		2						
E: 24, u21.6; Div2'86; LC'85;				£250,000	04.07.79	Q.P.R	63	8	1					
SPD'87'89'90'91,SLC'87'89'91				£250,000	12.03.81	Norwich City	216	26	19					
				£600,000	02.07.86	Glasgow Rangers	173	21	15	21				
				£1,200,000	15.08.91	Sheffield Wed	41	4	2	2				
DEFENDERS														
Viv Anderson	6.0	11.1	29.08.56	Nottingham	01.08.74	Nottm. Forest (A)	323+5	39	23+1	33	15	5	1	
E:30,u21.1,B,SC'77,Div1'78,EC'79'80,				£200,000	03.08.84	Arsenal	120	18	12		9	3	3	
ESC'79,LC'78,CS'78				£250,000	09.07.87	Manchester Utd	50+4	6+1	7	2	2	1	1	
				Free	10.01.91	Sheffield Wed	36+8	4	4+1	2	5	1	2	
Philip King	5.8	11.9	28.12.67	Bristol	07.01.85	Exeter City (A)	24+3	1		1+2				
LC'91				£3,000	14.07.86	Torquay Utd	24	2	1	2	3			
				£155,000	13.03.87	Swindon Town	112+4	11	5	13	4			
				£400,000	30.11.89	Sheffield Wed	106+1	13	8	4	1			
Roland Nilsson	6.0	11.06	27.11.63	Helsingborg		IFK Gothenburg								
				£375,000	08.12.89	Sheffield Wed	81	5	4	2	1			
Carlton Palmer	6.2	11.10	05.12.65	Oldbury	21.12.84	West Brom A. (T)	114+7	7+1	4	6	4	1		
E:B.1,u21.4				£450,000+P	23.02.89	Sheffield Wed	134	15	8	5	8			1
Nigel Pearson	6.1	12.6	21.08.63	Nottingham		Heanor Town								
LC'91				£5,000	12.11.81	Shrewsbury Town	153	19	6	3	5			
				£250,000	16.10.87	Sheffield Wed	159	14	13	7	13	5	1	
Peter Shirtliff	6.2	12.10	06.04.61	Chapeltown	31.10.78	Sheffield Wed. (A)	188	17+1	17+1		4		1	
LC'91				06.08.86	Charlton Ath	102+1	10	5	7	7			2
				£500,000	26.07.89	Sheffield Wed	84	13	6	3	4	1	2	
Paul Warhurst	6.1	12.10	26.09.69	Stockport	01.07.88	Manchester City (T)								
				£10,000	27.10.88	Oldham Ath	60+7	8	5+4	2	2			
				£750,000	17.07.91	Sheffield Wed	31+2	2	1	1				
Nigel Worthington	5.10	12.6	04.11.61	Ballymena		Ballymena								
NI:28,Y1,NILg1,UC'81,IC'81,LC'91				£100,000	01.07.81	Notts County	67	11	4		4			
				£100,000	06.02.84	Sheffield Wed	264+3	31	20	6	10			
MIDFIELD														
Chris Bart-Williams	5.8		16.06.74	Sierra Leone	18.07.91	Leyton Orient (T)	34+2	4		2	2			
				£275,000	21.11.91	Sheffield Wed	12+3		1	0+1			1	
John Harkes				USA		USSF								
				£70,000	05.11.90	Sheffield Wed	36+16	10	5+1	3	5	1		
John Sheridan	5.9	10.8	01.10.64	Stretford	02.03.82	Leeds Utd. (A)	225+5	14	11+1	11	47	3	1	1
Ei:8,u23.1,u21.21,Y,LC'91				£650,000	03.08.89	Nottm. Forest		1						
				£500,000	03.11.89	Sheffield Wed	96+1	11	7	3	18	1	2	1
Danny Wilson	5.7	10.3	01.01.60	Wigan		Wigan Ath			1					
NI:18,ASC'81,LC'88,LC'91				Free	21.09.77	Bury	87+3	4	11		8		2	
				£100,000	22.07.80	Chesterfield	100	8	9		13	1	1	
				PEE100,000	24.01.83	Nottm. Forest	9+1			0+1	1			
Loan Scunthorpe Utd 6lg 3gls				£450,000	12.01.84	Brighton & H.A	132+3	7	10	3	33	3	1	2
				£150,000	16.07.87	Luton Town	110	20	8	4	24	3	2	
				£200,000	08.08.90	Sheffield Wed	70+2	14	2+1	2+1	9	1		
FORWARDS														
Trevor Francis	5.10	11.7	19.04.54	Plymouth	01.05.71	Birmingham City	278+2	18	19		118	3	6	
E:52,u23.5,Y,EC'79,SLgC'88,LC'91				£975,000	14.02.79	Nottm. Forest	69+1	5	8	9	28		5	4
				£1,200,000	03.09.81	Manchester City	26	1	2		12		2	
				£800,000	01.07.82	Sampdoria	68				17			
						Atlanta	21				1			
				Free	01.09.87	Glasgow Rangers	8+10	1+1	0+1	2+2				
						Q.P.R	30+2	8	1	1	12	3		
				N.C	01.02.90	Sheffield Wed	28+42	5+2	2	1	5	3	1	
David Hirst	5.11	12.5	07.12.67	Barnsley	08.11.85	Barnsley	26+2	1			9			
E:u21.7,u19.3,Y9,LC'91				£200,000	11.08.86	Sheffield Wed	168+21	17+5	8+2	7	72	7	5	4
Nigel Jemson	5.10	11.10	10.08.69	Hutton	06.07.87	Preston N.E	29+3		2	5+1	8		1	5
LC'90					24.03.88	Nottm. Forest	45+2	9	3	1	13	4	3	
				Loan	23.12.88	Bolton W	4+1							
				Loan	15.03.89	Preston N.E	6+3			2	2			1
				£800,000	17.09.91	Sheffield Wed	11+9	1+2	1	1+1	4			
David A Johnson	6.2	13.8	29.10.70	Sheffield	01.07.89	Sheffield Wed. (T)	5+1							
				Loan	31.10.91	Hartlepool Utd	7		2		2		1	
Chris Waddle	6.0	11.5	14.12.60	Gateshead		Tow Law To								
E:36,u21.1,Flg				£10,000	28.07.80	Newcastle Utd	169+1	8	12		46	2	4	
				£590,000	01.07.85	Tottenham H	137+1	21	14	4	33	4	5	
				£4,250,000	01.07.89	Marseilles (Fra)								
				£1,000,000	01.07.92	Sheffield Wed								
Paul Williams	5.7	10.3	16.08.65	West Ham		Woodford T			1					
E:u21.4,LC'91				23.02.87	Charlton Ath	74+8	6	6+1		23	3	3	
				Loan	20.10.87	Brentford	7			1	3			3
				£700,000	15.08.90	Sheffield Wed	71+15	10+3	3+2	3	24	3		

PLAYERS NAME Honours	Ht	Wt	Birthdate	Birthplace Transfers	Contract Date	Clubs	League	L/Cup	FA Cup	Other	Lg	L/C	FAC	Oth
ADDITIONAL CONTRACT PLAYERS														
(G) Marlon Beresford	6.1	12.06	02.09.69	Lincoln		Sheffield Wed								
				Loan	25.08.89	Bury	1							
				Loan	29.09.89	Ipswich Town								
				Loan	27.09.90	Northampton T	13			2				
				Loan	28.02.91	Crewe Alexandra	3							
				Loan	15.08.91	Northampton T	15							
Leroy Chambers					13.06.91	Sheffield Wed								
Graham Hyde			10.11.70	Doncaster		Sheffield Wed	9 + 4	1	1 + 1	1				1
Ryan Jones					18.06.91	Sheffield Wed								
(F) Gordon Watson	6.0	12.9	20.03.71	Sidcup	05.04.89	Charlton Ath	20 + 11	2	0 + 1	1 + 1	7	1		
				£250,000	20.02.91	Sheffield Wed	5 + 4	1	1	0 + 1				
(D) Julian Watts	6.3	12.1	17.03.71	Sheffield	10.07.90	Rotherham Utd. (T)	17 + 3	1	4	2	1			
				£80,000	13.03.92	Sheffield Wed								
Michael Williams					13.02.91	Sheffield Wed								

MANAGER: TREVOR FRANCIS

DATE OF BIRTH: 19.04.1954   **PLACE OF BIRTH:** Plymouth

DATE OF APPOINTMENT: JUNE 1991

PREVIOUS CLUBS
as Player/Manager: QPR
as Player: Birmingham City, Nott'm Forest, Manchester City, Sampdoria, Atlanta (USA), Glasgow Rangers, QPR, Sheffield Wed.

HONOURS
as Manager: None
as Asst. Man./Coach:
as Player: (Nott'm Forest): European Cup; (Glasgow) Scottish Championship 1987
international: 52 England Caps

Value Rating: ✱ ✱ ✱

Programme Editor: Roger Oldfield

Price of 1992-93 Programme: £1.20
Number of Pages:
Subscriptions: 1st class £56.78, 2nd class £46.70, surface mail £57.00

Local Newspapers: Sheffield Newspapers Ltd. (The Star)

Local Radio Stations: BBC Radio Sheffield, Radio Hallam

Additional Publications on Club: A Complete Record 1867-1987 by Keith Farnsworth, Breedon Books £14.95.

LEADING LEAGUE GOALSCORERS
SEASONS 1979-80 – 1991-92

1979-80	**TERRY CURRAN**	22	1980-81	**ANDY McCULLOCH**	18
1981-82	**GARY BANNISTER**	21	1982-83	**GARY BANNISTER**	20
1983-84	**IMRE VARADI**	17	1984-85	**IMRE VARADI**	16
				LEE CHAPMAN	16
1985-86	**BRIAN MARWOOD**	13	1986-87	**LEE CHAPMAN**	19
1987-88	**LEE CHAPMAN**	19	1988-89	**DAVID HIRST**	7
1989-90	**DAVID HIRST**	14	1990-91	**DAVID HIRST**	24

1991-92 **DAVID HIRST** **18**

HILLSBOROUGH Sheffield S6 1SW

Capacity: 41,237   **Covered Standing:** 16,367   **Seating:** 23,470

Tel: Ground: 0472 343122   **Ticket Sales:** 0742 337233   **Clubcall:** 0898 12 11 86

All premium rate calls (0898/0891) cost 36p per minute cheap rate and 48p per minute at all other times. Call costings correct at time of going to press.

GROUNDS
Highfields 1867-69; Myrtle Road 1869-77; Sheaf Close 1877-87; Olive Grove 1887-99; Owlerton (changed to Hillsborough 1912) 1899-

ATTENDANCES
Highest: 72,841 v Manchester City, FA Cup 5th Round, 17.2.1934

Lowest: 2,500 v Everton, 5.4.1902

RECORD RECEIPTS (with previous records)
£398,134 Liverpool v Nottingham Forest, FA Cup Semi-Final, 9.4.1988
£395,037 Coventry City v Leeds United, FA Cup Semi-Final, 12.4.1987
£192,162 Tottenham H. v Wolverhampton, FA Cup Semi-Final, 11.4.1981
£192,152 Liverpool v Arsenal, FA Cup Semi-Final, 12.4.1980
£144,000 Manchester v Leeds, FA Cup Semi-Final, 23.4.1977
£140,300 Derby v Manchester United, FA Cup Semi-Final, 3.4.1976
£102,881 Burnley v Newcastle United, FA Cup Semi-Final, 30.3.1974
£82,500 Arsenal v Sunderland, FA Cup Semi-Final, 7.4.1973

HILLSBOROUGH
First game: v Chesterfield, Division 2, 5-1, 2.9.1899
First floodlit game: v International XI, 9.3.1955
Internationals: England v Scotland, 1920
England v France, 1962
West Germany v Switzerland, 1966
West Germany v Uruguay, 1966
Switzerland v Spain, 1966
Argentina v Switzerland, 1966

Season Tickets:
Stands: from £218 to £258, juv/OAP £158.65 to £178.60
Ground: £158.65, juv/OAP £99.28

Cost of Stand Tickets: North/South Centre: Standard £12 Premier £14, juv/OAP £8, £10; Family Enclosure £9, juv/OAP £5
Kop: £7 £9, juv/OAP £4.50 £5.50

Match and Ticket Information: South and North Stand. Applications not more than 3 weeks in advance subject to tickets being unsold. Payment and SAE must accompany application or 24hr credit card line Visa and Access

Car Parking: Street parking is available

Nearest Railway Station: Sheffield (0742 726411)

How to get to the ground

From North: Use Motorway M1 until Junction 34, leave motorway and follow signs Sheffield A6109. In 1.5m at roundabout take 3rd exit A6102. In 3.2m turn left into Harries Road South for Sheffield Wednesday FC
From East and South: Use A57 from Motorway M1 (Junction 31 or 33) then at roundabout junction with Rign Road take 3rd exit A610 into Prince of Wales Road. In 5.8m turn left into Herries Road South for Sheffield Wednesday FC
From West: Use A57 (S.P. Sheffield) then turn left A6101. In 3.8m at T road turn left A61 into Penistone Road for Sheffield Wednesday.

SHREWSBURY TOWN
Division 3

Formed: 1886   **Turned Professional:** 1905   **Ltd Co:** 1936

SPONSORED BY: Bass   **NICKNAME:** 'The Town' or 'The Shrews'

Vice-President
Dr J Millard Bryson

Chairman
K R Woodhouse

Vice-Chairman
R Bailey

Directors
F C G Fry   M J Starkey
G W Nelson   W H Richards

Director/Secretary
M J Starkey (0743 360111)

Team Manager
John Bond

Assistant Team Manager
F Davies

Physiotherapist/Coach
M Musgrove

Chief Scout
C Walker

Youth Team Coach
Richard Pratley

Youth Development Officer
P Lewis

Commercial Manager
M Thomas (0743 56316)

Medical Officer
Dr P Bottomley

Club Statistician for the Directory
Richard & Nicola Stocken

THIS was the season when the financial effects of recent year's attempts to retain division two status and then regain it resulted instead in relegation to Division Four for the first time since 1974. The entire season saw John Bond juggling with an amalgamation of out of form regulars, youngsters, trialists, loan players and a succession of injuries, resulting in some 33 players figuring in league games. A sure recipe for disaster.

It started well enough with four wins out of six including the seasons best, 6-1 over Exeter, and a win over Brentford. An inconsistent Autumn brought a mixed bag. A 1-4 home reverse to Hartlepool was followed by a 4-1 win at Stockport, a 1-3 home reverse to Bolton by a 4-1 win at Chester. It was in fact Town's home performance which did the damage. Only seven home wins and seven draws meant opposition celebrations nine times at Gay Meadow.

Three consecutive wins in January though against Stoke, Preston and Fulham left Town in 10th spot on 18th January, but by the time they next won a league game at Swansea three months later they had slipped to 22nd, where they stayed to the end. That was a new record of 17 league games without a win. Relegation was assured after Shrewsbury failed to spoil Birmingham City's promotion party in a 0-1 reverse at St Andrews.

Equally dismal were cup performances. Defeat over two legs against Wolves saw a second round exit in the Rumbelows Cup, followed by round one exits in the F.A. Cup at Hartlepool and Autoglass at Peterborough. Altogether a season to forget but like many clubs severe financial problems had to be met head on and with few promising youngsters there was little cash to spend. Indeed finances caused the eve of season sale of midfielders Tony Kelly and Michael Brown to Bolton and then central defender Mickey Heathcote to Cambridge, though the latter position was ultimately successfully filled by goalless striker Dean Spink. By the season's end his performances swept the player of the year awards, and looks set to form the basis of the defence next season.

The Board have responded to the season positively with a new share issue, persuing a move of ground and, on the field, an extensive youth policy. All this may take time to show through in results and it may be a year or two before more stability can be restored and a return up the league contemplated.

Richard Stocken

Back row L-R: Kevin Summerfield, O'Neill Donaldson, Tommy Lynch, Neil Lynne, Jim Mulvey, Steve McKenzie, Dean Spink, Howard Clark, Mark Blake, John Brough. **Middle row:** Fred Davies (Asst. Manager), Jason Evans, John Bond (Manager), Mark S Williams, Carl Griffiths, Mark Smith, Mark Taylor, Pat O'Toole, Darren Harmon, Graeme Worsley, Mark Williams, Kevin Thelwell, Kevin Seabury, Richard Pratley (Youth Team Coach), Malcolm Musgrove (Physio). **Front row:** Jason Yates, Sam Jenkins, Steve Taylor, Ashley Davies, Ian Reed, Romilly Brown, Paul Evans, Chris Hodgin.

SHREWSBURY TOWN

DIVISION THREE: 22nd   **FA CUP:** 1st RND   **RUMBELOWS CUP:** 2nd RND   **AUTOGLASS:** 1st RND

M	DATE		COMP.	VEN	OPPONENTS	RESULT		H/T	LGE POS	GOALSCORERS/GOAL TIMES	ATTEN-DANCE
1	A	18	BL	H	Wigan Athletic	W	1-0	0-0		Carr 47	3,834
2		20	RC 1/1	H	Plymouth Argyle	D	1-1	1-0		Summerfield 7	2,152
3		24	BL	A	Bury	D	0-0	0-0	6		(2,373)
4		27	RC 1/2	A	Plymouth Argyle	D	†2-2	0-1		Summerfield 58, Carr 85	(3,580)
5		31	BL	H	Exeter City	W	6-1	3-1	3	Hopkins 10, Henry 27,39(p), Summerfield 75, Lynch 78, Lyne 83	2,912
6	S	4	BL	A	Stoke City	L	0-1	0-0	5		(10,182)
7		7	BL	H	Brentford	W	1-0	0-0	4	Lyne 50	3,193
8		14	BL	A	Torquay United	W	2-1	1-1	3	Summerfield 12, Henry (pen) 64	(2,811)
9		17	BL	A	Bournemouth	L	0-1	0-0	5		(5,500)
10		21	BL	H	Swansea City	D	0-0	0-0	6		3,427
11		24	LC 2/1	A	Wolverhampton W	L	1-6	1-4		Summerfield 22	(12,229)
12		28	BL	A	Bradford City	L	0-3	0-3	7		(5,234)
13	O	5	BL	H	Birmingham City	D	1-1	0-1	8	Henry 57	7,035
14		8	LC 2/2	H	Wolverhampton W	W	3-1	1-1		Summerfield 2, Lyne 51, 90	5,784
15		12	BL	A	West Bromwich A.	L	0-2	0-1	12		(12,457)
16		19	BL	A	Darlington	D	3-3	2-0	13	Griffiths 15, 66, Henry 38	(2,188)
17		22	AGT Pre	A	West Bromwich A.	L	0-4	0-2			(6,997)
18		26	BL	H	Reading	L	1-2	0-0	14	Griffiths 62	2,398
19	N	2	BL	A	Peterborough Utd	W	2-0	0-0	12	Griffiths 62, Cash 81	1,866
20		5	BL	A	Hull City	L	0-4	0-3	15		(5,025)
21		16	FAC 1	A	Hartlepool United	L	2-3	1-1		Lyne 3, Smith 70	(2,864)
22		19	AGT Pre	H	Lincoln City	W	1-0	0-0		Griffiths 55	615
23		23	BL	A	Hartlepool United	L	1-4	0-3	18	Donaldson 86	2,368
24		26	BL	A	Stockport County	W	4-1	2-0	15	Bennett 35, 57, Summerfield 43, Lyne 74	(3,650)
25		30	BL	H	Bolton Wanderers	L	1-3	1-1	16	Smith 30	3,937
26	D	14	BL	A	Chester City	W	4-1	1-1	13	Mackenzie 16, Lightfoot (og) 73, Griffiths 77, 89	(1,016)
27		21	BL	H	Bury	D	1-1	1-1	11	Worsley 44	2,573
28		26	BL	A	Exeter City	L	0-1	0-0	14		(3,857)
29		28	BL	A	Wigan Athletic	D	1-1	1-1	14	Summerfield 18	(2,276)
30	J	1	BL	H	Stoke City	W	1-0	1-0	11	Summerfield 8	8,557
31		11	BL	A	Preston North End	W	2-0	0-0	10	Griffiths 53, Hopkins 90	3,154
32		18	BL	A	Fulham	W	1-0	0-0	10	Lyne 70	(3,440)
33		25	BL	H	Huddersfield Town	D	1-1	1-0	8	Lyne 36	3,688
34		28	BL	A	Leyton Orient	L	0-2	0-1	9		(3,197)
35		1	BL	H	Darlington	L	0-2	0-1	11		2,675
36	F	8	BL	A	Reading	L	1-2	0-1	11	Spink 53	(3,303)
37		11	BL	A	Bolton Wanderers	L	0-1	0-1	13		(5,276)
38		15	BL	H	Chester City	D	2-2	1-2	13	Summerfield 12, Taylor 53	2,807
39		18	AGT 1	A	Peterborough Utd	L	0-1	0-0			(2,049)
40		22	BL	A	Preston North End	D	2-2	0-0	14	Harmon 80, 86	(3,342)
41		29	BL	H	Leyton Orient	L	0-1	0-1	15		2,873
42	M	3	BL	H	Fulham	D	0-0	0-0	15		2,137
43		7	BL	A	Huddersfield Town	L	1-2	1-1	15	Summerfield 4	(4,674)
44		10	BL	H	Hull City	L	2-3	0-2	17	Griffiths 79, Lyne 83	1,956
45		14	BL	A	Peterborough Utd	L	0-1	0-0	20		(7,377)
46		20	BL	H	Stockport County	L	0-1	0-1	21		3,186
47		28	BL	A	Hartlepool United	L	2-4	1-2	21	Lynch 7, Bremner 77	(2,515)
48		31	BL	H	Torquay United	D	2-2	2-0	21	McKeown 30, Lyne 42	2,172
49	A	4	BL	A	Brentford	L	0-2	0-1	22		(5,561)
50		11	BL	H	Bournemouth	L	1-2	1-0	22	Lyne 13	2,586
51		17	BL	A	Swansea City	W	2-1	0-0	22	Taylor 76, Hopkins 88	(3,429)
52		21	BL	H	Bradford City	W	3-2	2-0	22	Bremner 16, Henry 37, 51	2,707
53		25	BL	A	Birmingham City	L	0-1	0-1	22		(19,868)
54	M	2	BL	H	West Bromwich A.	L	1-3	0-3	22	Donaldson 61	7,442

Best Home League Attendance: 8,557 v Stoke City   **Smallest: 1,866 v Peterborough Utd**   **Av Home Att: 3,456**

Goal Scorers: **Compared with 90-91: +18**

League (53): Griffiths 8, Lyne 8, Summerfield 7, Henry 7 (2 pens), Hopkins 3, Bremner 2, Donaldson 2, Harmon 2, Taylor 2, Bennett 2, Lynch 2, Carr, Mackenzie, Smith, Worsley, Cash, Spink, McKeown, Opponents

R/lows C (3): Summerfield 2, Carr

FA Cup (2): Smith, Lyne

Autoglass (5): Lyne 2, Summerfield 2, Griffiths   † = After extra-time

1991-92

Hughes K.	Gorman P.	Lynch T.	Henry A.	Heathcote M.	Blake M.	Smith M.	Summerfield K.	Spink D.	Carr C.	Lyne N.	Griffiths C.	Hopkins R.	O'Toole C.	Cash S.	Taylor R.	Parkin T.	Parks S.	Worsley G.	Ryan D.	Donaldson O.	Bennett D.	Mackenzie S.	Clark H.	McKeown G.	Bremner K.	Referee	
1	2	3	4	5	6	7*	8	9	10	11	12	S														J Deakin	1
1	2	3	4	5	6	7	8	9	S	11	S	10														P Danson	2
1	2	3	4	5	6	7	8	9*	S	11	12	10														W Burns	3
1	2	3	4	5	6*	7	8	9	12	11	14	10*														D Frampton	4
1	2	3	4	5*	6	7•	8	9		11	14	10	12													E Parker	5
1	2	3	4	5	6	7	8	9*		11	S	10	12													K Breen	6
1	2	3	4	5	6	7*	8		12	11	9*	14	10													H King	7
1	2	5	4		6	7	8			11*	12	9	S	3	10											J Carter	8
1	2	14	4	5		7	8			11	9*	12	10	3	6*											R Wiseman	9
1	2	S	4	5			8	9		11	S	10		3	6	7										M Bailey	10
1	2	S	4	5		7	8	9*		11	12			3	6	10										P Harrison	11
1	2	9	4*	5		7	8			11	12		14	3*	6	10										D Shadwell	12
1	2	11	4		6	7	8	12		9	S			3*	10	5										D Gallagher	13
		5	4		6	7	8	11•		9	12			3	10	14	1	2*								T Fitzharris	14
1		11	4		6	7•	8	12		9		14		3*	10	5		2								A Ward	15
1		3	4		6	7	8	9		11	S			S	10	5		2								I Hendrick	16
14		5	4		6	12	8	9		11•		7		3*	10		1	2								C Trussell	17
S		3	4		6	7*	8	9		11		5	12		10		1	2								N Midgley	18
12		3	4		6		8	14		9	11•	5		7	10*		1	2								R Groves	19
2*		3•	4†		6		8	14		9	11	5		7			1	12	10							R Hart	20
2		5			6	7	8	12		9*	11			3	10		1	4								D Allinson	21
2		5			6	7	8	12		9	11			3	10*		1	4	S							K Cooper	22
2		5	4		6	7•	8	14		9	12			3			1			10	11					B Coddington	23
2		3	4		6	11•	8	5		9		10			1					12	7*					A Wilkie	24
2		3	4		6	7•	8	5		9*	14	11		10	1					12						R Hamer	25
		3	4		6	7*	8	5		9	11	S		1	2					12		10				K Cooper	26
		3	4		6	12	8*	5		9	11	S		1	2							10	7			G Ashby	27
		3	4		6		8	5		9*	11	7		1	S					12		10	2			P Durkin	28
		3	4		6	7*	8	5		14	12	11•		1	2					9		10				T West	29
		3*	4		6		8	5		11	9•	14		1	2					7		10	12			P Taylor	30
			4		6	12	8	5		11*	9	14		1	2					7•		10	3			P Wright	31
		S	4		6		8	5		11	9	7		1	2					S		10	3			M Reed	32
		12	4		6		8	5		11	9	7		10*	1			2		S			3			R Lewis	33
		14	4		6		8	5		11•	9	7*		10	1			2		12			3			M Pierce	34
		3	4		6		8	5		11	9*	10•			1			2		12			14			C Trussell	35
			4		6		8	5		11•	9	7	12	10	1			2		14			3			G Pooley	36
			4		6		8	5		11	9	7*	4	10	1			2	S	12			3			M Brandwood	37
		3	4*		6		8	5		11				10	1					7			2			G Poll	38
		2			6		8	5			11*	7	4	10	1				12	9			3			A Buksh	39
1		3	4		6		8	5			7*	11		10					9*	12			2			K Lupton	40
1		3	4	6*			8	5			7•	14	11					12		9*			2			T Lunt	41
1		3	4				8	5		11	12	10		6	1	7		9*					2			R Poulain	42
1		3	4				8	5		10	12	9	11*	1	7								2	6		T Fitzharris	43
1		3	4				8	5		10	9	S	11	1	7*								2	6		C Wilkes	44
1		3	4*			7•	8	5		10	9	12		11									2	6		P Scoble	45
1		3•	4			7	8*	5		10		14		11					9				2	6		R Shepherd	46
1		3	4				8			10		12			7		S·					11	2*	6	9	J Key	47
1		3	4*				8	5		11	14	12		7•	2							10		6	9	S Bell	48
1		3*		10			8	5		11		S		7	2					12				6	9	I Hemley	49
1		3		6	S		8	5		11	12	10		7	2								4*		9	R Nixon	50
1		3*			6		8	5		11	10	12		7								4	2		9	R Milford	51
1		3		8	6			5		11	10†			3	7*							4	2		9	I Hendrick	52
1		3	14		6		8	5		11	10*	12		7								4	2•		9	E Parker	53
1		3			6			5		11		8		7						9		4	2*			D Allinson	54
23	14	37	39	5	39	19	44	34	1	43	20	18	13	8	29	5	22	23	2	9	2	13	21	8	7	**League Appearances**	
	1	3	1			3		6		1	7	9	14					2		10			2			**Substitute Appearances**	
2	2	2	2	2	2	2	2	2	0+1	2	0+1	2														**R/lows Appearances**	
1	1			1	1	1	0+1	1	1			1	1	1												**FA Cup Appearances**	
1	2+1	4	3		3+1	5	3+1		4	3	2+2	2	3	5	1+1	4	3	0+1	1			1				**Other Competitions**	

Also Played: Posn.(Game): Parkin 9(38), Seabury S(39), Harmon 10(41)S(42,43,52)12(44,46)14(40,45), Evans S(21),14(24)10(54), Walsh 7(35)4*(36), Williams 5(47)4(49)S(51)14(54), Barton1(54), M S Williams 12(54)

Players on Loan: Carr, Walsh (trial), Cash (Nott'm Forest), Parkin (Port Vale), Bennett (Swindon), Mackenzie (Sheff. Wed), Paskin (Wolves), McKeown (Arsenal), Williams M (Newtown), Bremner (Dundee)

SHREWSBURY TOWN

Club Colours: Amber & blue diamond shirts, blue shorts, blue socks
Change Colours: All red with white side stripes and white trim, red stockings with white trim
Reserves League: Midland Senior League   **'A' Team:** Midland Intermediate

Previous League: Birmingham League   Midland League
Previous Managers: (Since 1950): 1950-52 Sammy Crooks   1952-54 Walter Rowley   1954-56 Harry Potts   1956-57 John Spuhler
1957-68 Arthur Rowley   1968-72 Harry Gregg   1972-74 Maurice Evans   1974-78 Alan Durban   1978 Ritchie Barker   1978-84
Graham Turner   1984-87 Chic Bates   1987 Ken Brown   1987-90 Ian McNeil   1990-91 Asa Hartford   1991- John Bond
Honours: Champions Div 3 1978-79   Welsh Cup Winners (6 times)
League Career: Elected to Div 3N 1950   Reverted to Div 3S 1951   Joined Div 4 1958
Promoted to Div 3 1958-59   Relegated to Div 4 1973-74   Promoted to Div 3 1974-75   Promoted to Div 2 1978-79
Relegated to Div 3 1988-89   Relegated to Div 4 1991-92

CLUB RECORDS

Most Appearances for Club: Colin Griffin 1975-89: League 402+4 + FA Cup 30 + League Cup 25 + Others 9 **Total 466+4 subs**
Most Capped Player: Jimmy McLoughlin 5, Northern Ireland & Bernard McNally 5, Northern Ireland   **For England:** None
Record Goalscorer in a Match: Alf Wood 5 v Blackburn Rovers (h), 7-1, Div 3, 2.10.1971
Record League Goalscorer in a Season: Arthur Rowley 38, Div 3, 1958-59   **In All Competitions:** Alf Wood 40 (League 35, FA Cup 2, League Cup 3) 1971-72
Record League Goalscorer in a Career: Arthur Rowley 152, 1958-65   **In All Competitions:** Arthur Rowley 167 (League 152, FA Cup 11, League Cup 4) 1958-65
Record Transfer Fee Received: £385,000 from West Bromwich Albion for Bernard McNally, 25.7.1989
Record Transfer Fee Paid: £100,000 to Aldershot for John Dungworth in November 1979.   £100,000 to Southampton for Mark Blake, August 1990
Best Performances: League: 8th Division 2, 1983-84, 1984-85   **FA Cup:** 6th Round 1978-79, 1981-82   **League Cup:** Semi-Final 1960-61   **Welsh Cup:** Winners 1891, 1938, 1977, 1979, 1984, 1985
Most League Goals: 101, Division 4, 1958-59
Most League Points: (3pts for win) 65, Div 2, 1984-85   (2pts for win) 62, Division 4, 1974-75
Record League Victory: 7-0 v Swindon Town, Div 3S, 6.5.1955
Most Goals Scored in a League Match: 7-2 v Luton Town (a), Div 3, 10.3.1965   7-1 v Blackburn Rovers (h), Div 3, 2.10.1971   7-4 v Doncaster Rovers, Div 4, 1.2.1975
Most Goals Scored in a Cup Tie: 7-1 v Banbury Spencer (h), FA Cup 1st Round, 4.11.1961
Record League Defeat: 1-8 v Norwich City (h), Div 3S, 13.9.1952   1-8 v Coventry City, Div 2, 22.10.1963   0-7 v Bristol Rovers, Div 3, 21.3.1964
Oldest Player in a League Match: Asa Hartford, 40 years 69 days v Brentford 1.1.1991
Youngest Player in a League Match: Gerry Nardiello, 17 years 9 days, 14.5.1983

LONGEST LEAGUE RUNS	
of undefeated matches: 12 (1960)	**of league matches without a win:** 17 (1992)
of undefeated home matches: 31 (1978-79)	**of undefeated away matches:** 13 (1974)
without home win: 9 (1992)	**without an away win:** 20 (1981-82)
of league wins: 7 (1955)	**of home wins:** 8 (1955, 1975)
of league defeats: 7 (1951-52, 1987)	**of away wins:** 3 (On 5 occasions)

BARCLAYS BUSINESS CENTRE
Shrewsbury Business Centre
44-46 Castle Street
Shrewsbury SY1 2BU
Tel: 0743 232901

BARCLAYBANK MACHINE

SHREWSBURY TOWN

PLAYERS NAME / Honours	Ht	Wt	Birthdate	Birthplace / Transfers	Contract Date	Clubs	APPEARANCES League	L/Cup	FA Cup	Other	GOALS Lg	L/C	FAC	Oth
GOALKEEPERS														
Michael Barton (G)			23.09.73	Gainsborough		Shrewsbury Town	1							
DEFENDERS														
Mark Blake	6.0	12.4	19.12.67	Portsmouth	23.12.85	Southampton (A)	18	2	3	1+2	2			
E:Y7				Loan	05.09.89	Colchester Utd	4				1			
				Loan	22.03.90	Shrewsbury Town	10							
				£100,000	10.08.90	Shrewsbury Town	85	5	7	9	2			
Howard W Clark	5.11	11.1	19.09.68	Coventry	22.09.86	Coventry City	9+11	1	0+1	0+1	1			
				Loan	19.09.91	Darlington	2							
				Free	16.12.91	Shrewsbury Town	21+2			1				
Tom Lynch	6.0	12.06	10.10.64	Limerick		Limerick								
				£20,000	11.08.88	Sunderland	4		1					
				£20,000	22.02.90	Shrewsbury Town	71+8	5	7	8	4			
Jason Rowbotham	5.9		03.01.69	Cardiff	05.07.91	Plymouth A	8+1	0+1						
Loan Yeovil Town (01.10.91)				F via Penz	26.03.92	Shrewsbury Town								
Graeme Worsley	5.11	11.02	04.01.69	Liverpool		Bootle								
					21.03.89	Shrewsbury Town	63+14	4	5	7	2			
MIDFIELD														
Asa Hartford	5.6	11.2	24.10.50	Clydebank	01.11.67	West Brom A	206+7	15	9	6	18	2	2	3
S:50;u23(5);u21(1);MC'85;LC'76				£225,000	01.08.74	Manchester City	184+1	21	12	12	22	2	1	2
				£450,000	03.07.79	Nottm. Forest	3							
				£400,000	30.08.79	Everton	81	6	11		6		1	
				£350,000	02.10.81	Manchester City	75	8	5		7	1	1	
via Fort Lauderdale				Free	11.10.84	Norwich City	28	8	4		2	2		
				Free	25.07.85	Bolton W	83	4	6	10	8	1		1
				Free	10.07.87	Stockport Co	42+3	2	4	1				
						Oldham Ath	3+4							
				Play-Coach		Shrewsbury Town	22+3	3	1	0+1				
Robert Hopkins	5.7	10.8	25.10.61	Birmingham	13.07.79	Aston Villa (A)	1+2				1			
FAYC80				f	25.03.83	Birmingham City	123	13	10		21	3	2	
				£100,000	02.09.86	Manchester City	7	2			1			
				£60,000+P	17.10.86	West Brom A	81+2	3	4	2	11			
					23.03.89	Birmingham City	43+7	4+1	1+2	1	9			
				Free	29.07.91	Shrewsbury Town	18+9	2		2+2	3			
Pat O'Toole						Shelbourne								
				£25,000	07.02.90	Leicester City								
				Loan	28.12.90	Exeter City	6		1					
					27.03.91	Shrewsbury Town	24+14		1	2				
Steve MacKenzie	5.10	11.6	23.11.61	Romford	29.07.79	Crystal Palace (A)								
E: B3, u21.3, Y.15; FAYC'78; UEFA Y'80				£250,000	30.07.79	Manchester City	56+2	10	8		8		2	
				£600,000	17.08.81	West Brom A	153+3	16+2	8	2	23	1	1	
				£300,000	30.06.87	Charlton Ath	92+8	8	6+1	1+1	7			
				£100,000	08.02.91	Sheffield Wed	5+10				2			
				Free	26.03.92	Shrewsbury Town	13				1			
Kevin Summerfield	6.0	10.7	07.01.59	Walsall	01.01.77	West Brom A	5+4	2			4			
FAYC76,EY77				Free	31.05.82	Birmingham City	2+3	1	1+1		1		1	
				Free	11.02.83	Walsall	42+12	5+2	1		17	2		
				Free	06.07.84	Cardiff City	10	2			1			
				Free	21.12.84	Plymouth A	118+21	6+1	13	4	26	3	4	1
				Loan	22.03.90	Exeter City	4							
				Free	10.10.90	Shrewsbury Town	74+2	3	6+1	7	12	2		2
FORWARDS														
Carl Griffiths	5.9	10.06	15.07.71	Welshpool	26.09.88	Shrewsbury Town (T	61+31	1+3	3	5+3	22	1		1
Neil Lyne	6.1	12.2	04.04.70	Leicester		Leicester Utd								
					16.08.89	Nottm. Forest		0+1						
				Loan	22.03.90	Walsall	6+1							
				Loan	14.03.91	Shrewsbury Town	16				6			
					11.07.91	Shrewsbury Town	43+1	2	1	4	8		1	2
Dean Spink	6.1	13.6	22.01.67	Birmingham		Halesowen Town			1					
				£30,000	01.07.89	Aston Villa								
				Loan	20.11.89	Scarborough	3		1		2			
				Loan	01.02.90	Bury	6				1			
				£75,000	15.03.90	Shrewsbury Town	77+19	5+1	6+1	6+1	12		1	1
Mark Taylor	5.8	11.8	22.02.66	Birmingham	24.07.84	Walsall	101+13	7+1	3+4	10	4			
				£50,000	22.06.89	Sheffield Wed	8+1	2						
				£70,000	13.09.91	Shrewsbury Town	48		2	5	4			
Mark A Smith	5.9	10.8	16.12.64	Glasgow		Read	71+11	1	3+1		7			
SDiv1'89						Celtic	3+3	2						
						Dunfermline	48+5	3+1	4+2		6		1	
				Loan		Hamilton Accies	5							
				Loan		Stoke City	2							
				£75,000		Nottm. Forest								
				Loan	27.12.90	Reading	3							
				Loan	21.03.91	Mansfield Town	6+1							
				£25,000	13.08.91	Shrewsbury Town	19+3	2	1	3+1	1		1	

ADDITIONAL CONTRACT PLAYERS

John Brough, O'Neill Donaldson, Jason Evans, Paul Evans, Darren Harmon, Kevin Seabury, Kevin Thelwell, Kim Wassell, Mark Williams, Mark S Williams.

LEADING LEAGUE GOALSCORERS SEASONS 1985-86 – 1991-92

1985-86	COLIN ROBINSON	10	1986-87	COLIN ROBINSON	9
1987-88	DAVID GEDDIS	5	1988-89	CARL GRIFFITHS	6
	MICKEY BROWN	5			
1989-90	JOHN McGINLAY	22	1990-91	DEAN SPINK	7
	1991-92	CARL GRIFFITHS	8		

GAY MEADOW Shrewsbury

Capacity: 7,500   **Covered Standing:** 2,000   **Seating:** 3,500

Tel: Ground: 0743 360111   **Ticket Sales:** As ground number

ATTENDANCES
Highest: 18,917 v Walsall, Division 3, 26.4.1961

Lowest: 520 v Torquay Utd, 16.1.1991

Record Receipts (with previous records):
£80,610 v Arsenal, FA Cup 5th Rnd, 27.2.1991
£36,240 v Ipswich, FA Cup 5th Round, 13.2.1982
£32,270 v Ipswich, FA Cup 4th Round, 24.1.1981
£18,755 v Wolves, FA Cup 6th Round, 13.3.1979
£8,328 v Queens Park Rangers, League Cup Round 2
replay, 9.9.1975
£4,692 v Arsenal, FA Cup 3rd Round, 27.1.1968

Season Tickets:
Stands: £100 jnr to £130 adult
Ground: None

Executive Box Season Tickets: None

Cost of Stand Tickets: Wakeman Stand (Members Only): adults £6, juv/OAP £4; Centre Stand: adults £7; **Terraces:** £5, juveniles/OAP £3

Match and Ticket Information: Apply to club

Car Parking: Park adjacent to ground and a free public car park five minutes away

Nearest Railway Station: Shrewsbury (0743 64041)

How to get to the ground

From North: Use A49 or A53 and at roundabout take 2nd exit A5112 into Telford Way. In 0.8m at roundabout take 2nd exit. Then at T road turn right into Abbey Foregate A458 for Shrewsbury Town FC

From East: Use A5 then A458 into Shrewsbury and into Abbey Foregate for Shrewsbury Town FC

From South: Use A49 and follow signs Shrewsbury town centre then at end of Coleham Head turn right into Abbey Foregate for Shrewsbury Town FC

From West: Use A458 then A5 around Shrewsbury Ring Road, Roman Road, then turn left A49 into Hereford Road, and at end of Coleman Head turn right into Abbey Foregate for Shrewsbury Town FC

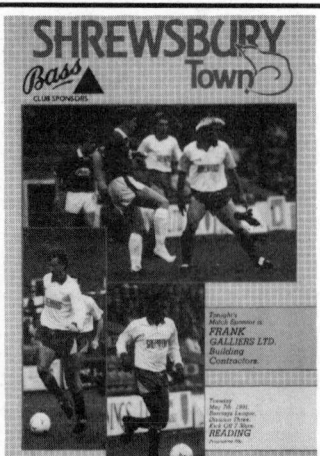

Value Rating: ★ ★ ★

Programme Editor: Pemandos A & M

Price of 1992-93 Programme: £1
Number of Pages: 32
Subscriptions: Apply to club for details

Local Newspapers: Shropshire Star, Shrewsbury Chronicle

Local Radio Stations: Radio Shropshire

SOUTHAMPTON
Premier

Formed: 1885 **Turned Professional:** 1894 **Ltd Co:** 1897

SPONSORED BY: Draper Tools Ltd **NICKNAME:** The Saints

President
John Corbett

Chairman
F G Askham FCA

Directors
F St J Wiseman (Vice-Chairman)
E T Bates
I L Gordon
B D H Hunt
M R Richards, FCA

Secretary
Brian Truscott (0703 220505)

Assistant Secretary
Barry Fox

Marketing Exective
Bob Russell

Team Manager
Ian Branfoot

Coach
Lew Chatterley

Reserve Team Coach
Ray Graydon

Physiotherapist
Don Taylor

Commercial Manager
Bob Russell

Club Statistician for the Directory
John Mason

WHEN one recalls notable seasons in the Saints history, this past campaign will not be remembered by any with a passion for the club. It will be deservedly pushed to the back of the mind like a bad dream, to be quickly forgotten.

As the season progressed, the nightmare became more vivid, until, when after three months of being entrenched at the bottom of the league, the nadir was reached at the end of February. The team had only yielded twenty-four points and produced five wins from twenty-eight starts. This ensured the spectre of relegation was shining ever brighter through the gloom at the Dell. Then as if the extra day of this leap year had some magical qualities, the Saints awoke from their torment by earning a commendable draw from the visit to Anfield on the 29th February, and then immediately went on to equal the club's record of six successive league victories. The eighteen points gained ensured a sequence of fifteen unbroken years in the top flight was maintained.

For only the third time in thirty-six years a new manager was enlisted to take charge of the team. Ian Branfoot being appointed prior to the start of the campaign. He was able to renew loyalties formed a decade past, whilst previously coaching the reserve side under Lawrie McMenemy. Out of his squad went Davis, Osman, Case, Rideout and Gotsmanov, with McLoughlin and Gittens having loans arranged, prior to permanent transfers. £1.85 million was spent to bring Lee, Dowie, Hurlock, Gray and Wood to the club. The new man also brought with him a change to a more competitive style of play throughout the team, which although stemming the flood of goals conceeded in previous years, resulted in a miserly seventeen league goals scored at the Dell.

Amongst all the trauma a visit to Wembley in the Zenith Data Cup Final was well received, especially by the younger supporters, many of whom would not have been around when the club last achieved a Wembley final in 1979, coincidently also against Nottingham Forest and also with the same scoreline. In addition under Ray Graydon, the reserve side won the Combination League and Cup double thus ensuring their place in the club's history.

The season ended with Ruddock and Horne excercising their freedom from contract and moving to Tottenham and Everton respectively and Shearer adding to his glowing reputation whilst serving England in the European Championship Finals before sadly moving to Blackburn Rovers.

The future will be for the manager to continue his rebuilding of the side and a further period of consolidation looks to the likely outcome of the new season, but hopefully a not so traumatic campaign this time. **John Mason**

Back row L-R: Jason Dodd, Jeff Kenna, Francis Benali, Neil Maddison, Tommy Widdrington, David Lee. **Middle row:** Lew Chatterley (First Team Coach), David Speedie, Richard Hall, Tim Flowers, Kerry Dixon, Ian Andrews, Iain Dowie, Matthew Le Tissier, Don Taylor (Physio). **Front row:** Stuart Gray, Micky Adams, Glenn Cockerill, Ian Branfoot (Manager), Kevin Moore, Steve Wood, Terry Hurlock.

SOUTHAMPTON

DIVISION ONE: 16th   **FA CUP:** 6th RND   **RUMBELOWS CUP:** 4th RND   **ZDS CUP:** FINALISTS

M	DATE	COMP.	VEN	OPPONENTS	RESULT	H/T	LGE POS	GOALSCORERS/GOAL TIMES	ATTEN-DANCE
1	A 17	BL	H	Tottenham Hotspur	L 2-3	1-1		Shearer 2, Hall 74	18,581
2	20	BL	A	Notts County	L 0-1	0-1			(9,613)
3	24	BL	A	Sheffield United	W 2-0	1-0	13	Shearer 45, Le Tissier 78	(18,029)
4	28	BL	H	Leeds United	L 0-4	0-1	19		15,862
5	31	BL	H	Aston Villa	D 1-1	1-1	19	Shearer 33	16,161
6	S 4	BL	A	Luton Town	L 1-2	1-2	20	Le Tissier (pen) 30	(8,055)
7	7	BL	A	Queens Park R.	D 2-2	1-0	19	Shearer 1, Dowie 81	(9,237)
8	14	BL	H	Manchester United	L 0-1	0-0	20		19,264
9	18	BL	H	Wimbledon	W 1-0	0-0	19	Cockerill 50	11,280
10	21	BL	A	Sheffield Wed.	L 0-2	0-1	19		(27,291)
11	24	RC 2/1	A	Scarborough	W 3-1	2-1		Shearer 17, 27, Cockerill 77	(2,302)
12	28	BL	H	Arsenal	L 0-4	0-1	21		18,050
13	O 5	BL	A	Oldham Athletic	D 1-1	1-0	20	Shearer 28	(13,133)
14	9	RC 2/2	H	Scarborough	D 2-2	2-0		Le Tissier 2, Cockerill 3	4,036
15	19	BL	H	Norwich City	D 0-0	0-0	20		12,516
16	22	ZDC 2	A	Bristol City	W 2-1	0-1		Shearer 69, Le Tissier 84	(5,672)
17	26	BL	A	Nottingham Forest	W 3-1	1-0	20	Le Tissier 31, 71 (pen), Shearer 72	(20,026)
18	30	RC 3	A	Sheffield Wed.	D 1-1	0-1		Shearer 81	(17,627)
19	N 2	BL	H	Manchester City	L 0-3	0-1	20		13,933
20	16	BL	A	Crystal Palace	L 0-1	0-0	20		(15,861)
21	20	RC 3R	H	Sheffield Wed.	W 1-0	0-0		Horne 69	10,801
22	23	BL	H	Chelsea	W 1-0	1-0	19	Shearer 42	14,933
23	26	ZDC 3	A	Plymouth Argyle	W 1-0	0-0		Le Tissier 70	(5,578)
24	30	BL	A	Coventry City	L 0-2	0-1	21		(8,585)
25	D 4	RC 4	A	Nottingham Forest	D 0-0	0-0			(17,939)
26	7	BL	H	Liverpool	D 1-1	0-0	20	Shearer 54	19,053
27	17	RC 4R	H	Nottingham Forest	L 0-1	0-1			10,861
28	20	BL	H	Notts County	D 1-1	1-0	21	Dowie 32	11,054
29	26	BL	A	Leeds United	D 3-3	0-2	21	Dowie 50, 85, Shearer 79	(29,053)
30	28	BL	A	Aston Villa	L 1-2	0-1	22	Shearer 73	(23,094)
31	J 1	BL	H	Everton	L 1-2	0-1	22	Adams 89	16,546
32	4	FAC 3	H	Queens Park R.	W 2-0	2-0		Wood 26, Le Tissier 39	13,710
33	7	ZDC 4	H	West Ham United	W 2-1	0-1		Shearer 67, Le Tissier (pen) 85	6,861
34	11	BL	A	Sheffield United	L 2-4	1-1	22	Le Tissier 3, Hall 59	13,689
35	18	BL	A	Tottenham Hotspur	W 2-1	1-0	21	Adams 24, Dowie 80	(23,191)
36	21	ZDC SF1	H	Chelsea	W 2-0	1-0		Shearer 15, Hurlock 79	8,726
37	27	FAC 4	H	Manchester United	D 0-0	0-0			19,506
38	29	ZDC SF2	A	Chelsea	W 3-1	2-1		Le Tissier 3 (pen 6, 20, 51)	(9,781)
39	F 1	BL	A	Norwich City	L 1-2	0-0	22	Cockerill 71	(10,660)
40	5	FAC 4R	A	Manchester United	D †2-2	2-1		Gray 8, Shearer 22 (Won 4-2 on pens)	(33,414)
41	12	BL	A	Chelsea	D 1-1	0-0	22	Horne 56	(7,148)
42	16	FAC 5	A	Bolton Wanderers	D 2-2	2-0		Hall 26, 28	(20,136)
43	22	BL	H	Coventry City	D 0-0	0-0	22		13,719
44	26	FAC 5R	H	Bolton Wanderers	W 3-2	1-1		Shearer 28, Horne 90, 108	18,009
45	29	BL	A	Liverpool	D 0-0	0-0	22		(34,449)
46	M 3	BL	H	West Ham United	W 1-0	0-0	21	Dowie 62	14,548
47	7	FAC 6	H	Norwich City	D 0-0	0-0			20,088
48	11	BL	H	Crystal Palace	W 1-0	1-0	19	Le Tissier 40	12,926
49	15	BL	A	Manchester City	W 1-0	1-0	19	Dowie 34	(24,265)
50	18	FAC 6R	A	Norwich City	L 1-2	1-0		Ruddock 44	(21,107)
51	21	BL	H	Luton Town	W 2-1	0-1	18	Shearer 68, Dowie 81	15,315
52	29	ZDC Fin	N	Nottingham Forest	L †2-3	0-2		Le Tissier 64, Moore 70	(67,688)
53	A 1	BL	A	Everton	W 1-0	1-0	19	Cockerill 24	(15,201)
54	4	BL	H	Queens Park R.	W 2-1	1-0	17	Dowie 13, Shearer (pen) 68	15,205
55	8	BL	H	Nottingham Forest	L 0-1	0-0	18		14,905
56	14	BL	A	West Ham United	W 1-0	0-0	17	Adams 88	(18,298)
57	16	BL	A	Manchester United	L 0-1	0-0	17		(43,972)
58	18	BL	H	Sheffield Wed.	L 0-1	0-0	17		17,715
59	20	BL	A	Wimbledon	W 1-0	1-0	17	Hall 24	(4,025)
60	25	BL	H	Oldham Athletic	W 1-0	0-0	13	Shearer 84	15,857
61	M 2	BL	A	Arsenal	L 1-5	0-0	16	Cockerill 63	(37,702)

Best Home League Attendance: 19,264 v Manchester Utd   **Smallest:** 11,054 v Notts County   **Av Home Att:** 15,291

Goal Scorers: **Compared with 90-91:** -1,618

League (39):   Shearer 13 (1 pen), Dowie 9, Le Tissier 6 (2 pens), Cockerill 4, Adams 3, Hall 3, Horne

R/lows C (7):   Shearer 3, Cockerill 2, Le Tissier, Horne

FA Cup (10):   Hall 2, Shearer 2, Horne 2, Le Tissier, Wood, Ruddock, Gray

ZDS Cup (12):   Le Tissier 7 (1 pen), Shearer 3, Moore, Hurlock   † = After extra-time

Flowers T.	Dodd J.	Osman R.	Horne B.	Hall R.	Ruddock N.	Le Tissier M.	Cockerill G.	Shearer A.	Rideout P.	Adams M.	Moore T.	Moody P.	McLoughlin A.	Gittens J.	Benali F.	Lee D.	Banger N.	Dowie I.	Hurlock T.	Andrews I.	Gray S.	Maddison N.	Wood S.	Kenna J.	Gilkes M.	Referee	
1	2	3	4	5	6	7	8	9	10•	11	S	14														A Gunn	1
1	2	3*	4	5	6	7	8	9	10	11				12	S											R Bigger	2
1	2	3	4	5	6	7	8	9	10	11			S			S										P Wright	3
1	2	3	4	5	6†	7*	8	9	10•	11		14				12										G Ashby	4
1	2		4	5	6	7*	8	9		3			10•	12	11	14										K Burge	5
1	2		4	5†	6	7	8	9		3			14		11•			10								A Smith	6
1	2		4	5	6	7•	8	9		3	S				11	14		10								P Foakes	7
1	2	6•	4	5		7	8	9		3			14	12				10	11•							G Pooley	8
1	2	4•	6			7*	8	9		3			5	12	11			10	14							M Bodenham	9
	2	4	12	6•		14	8	9		11			5	3•	7			10		1						E Parker	10
1	2		4	5	6	7	8	9		11					S			10			3	S				K Redfern	11
1	2		4	5	6	7	8	9		S					11	10•	12				3					P Durkin	12
1	2		4	5	6	S	8	9		11					7		S	10			3					V Callow	13
1	2		4*	5	6	7	8	9		11					S	12		10			3					K Cooper	14
1	2		S	6	11		8	9		3					7•	14		4			10			5		L Shapter	15
1	2		S	6	11		8	9		3					7		S	4			10			5		A Ward	16
1	2		S	6	11		8	9		3					7		S	4			10			5		P Don	17
1	2		12	5•	6	11	8	9		3				7		14		4	10•							D Allison	18
1	2		10		6	11	8	9		3				12	7		S	4				5*				R Gifford	19
1	2		10	6		11	8	9		3				7	12		S	4*				5				R Groves	20
1	2		10	5		7	8	9		3	11			6	S			S	4							R Milford	21
1	2		10	5		7	8	9		3				6		S		S	4				11			G Willard	22
1	2		10		5	7	8	9		3				6	S			4			S	11				J Deakin	23
1	2		10		6*	7	8	9		3				5	12			4			S	11				P Taylor	24
1	2		10	12	6	7*	8	9		3				5		14*	4		11							A Buksh	25
1	2		7		6		8	9		3*				5	12	14	10•	4				11				R Lewis	26
1	2		4		6	11	8	9		3	5*		14	7		12			10•							T Holbrook	27
1	2			6†	7*	8	9			3				S	12		10	4			11	5				P Alcock	28
1	S		7	S			8	9		3	6			5			10	4			11	2				J Watson	29
1	2		4	14			8	9		3	7•			5		12	10		11•			6				M Bailey	30
1	12		4	2			8	9		3			5•			14	10	7*	11			6				G Ashby	31
1	2		4	5		7		9		3					S	10	8		11			6	S			K Burge	32
1	2		4	5		7		9		3					12	11*	10	8				6	S			D Axcell	33
1	2		4	5		7	8*	9		3					12		10	11				6	S			P Foakes	34
1			4	5		7*	S	9		3			14		11		10	8					6	2		B Hill	35
1			4	5		7	S	9		3					11	S	10	8					6	2		R Milford	36
1			4	5	6	7	14	9		3					11		10•	8		S				2		D Elleray	37
1			4	5	6	7	S	9		3					11		10	8		S				2		V Callow	38
1			4•	5	6	7	14	9		3					11*		10	8		12				2		P Vanes	39
1			4	5	6	7	8	9		3					11		S	10•	14					2		D Elleray	40
1			4	5	6	7	8	9		3					11	S		10			S			2		P Danson	41
1			4	5	6	7	8	9		3•					11	14		S			10			2		M Peck	42
1	14		4	5	6	7								3	11•		12	8			10•			2		M Bodenham	43
1	2		4	5	6	7	8	9				14		3				11	10•					S		K Barrett	44
1	2		4		6	7	8	9		5				3			10	11			S			S		S Lodge	45
1	2		4		6	7	8	9		5				3			10	11			S			S		R Lewis	46
1	2		4		6	7	8	9		5				3			10	11			S			S		G Ashby	47
1	2		4		6	7	S	9		5				3			10	11						S	11	A Gunn	48
1	2			6		8	9		7*	5				3			10	11						S	12	R Hart	49
1	2*		4†	6	7†	8	9			5				3			10	11						12		G Ashby	50
1			4•	6		8	9			5				3			10	11			S		2	7		C Wilkes	51
1			4	6	7	8	9			5	S			3			10	11			S	2				K Hackett	52
1			12	6		8				5	S			3			10	11		4*		2	7			K Redfern	53
1			14	6		8	9			5•				3			10	11		4		2	7*			P Durkin	54
1			S	6		8*	9	4		5				3			10	11		12		2				D Elleray	55
1			4		6	7	8	9		3	5				11		10•						2	S		R Hamer	56
1			4	14	6*	7	8	9		3	5				11		12				10		2			K Cooper	57
1			5			7	8•	9		3*	6				11		10	4		14			2	12		I Borrett	58
1			4	5		7	8	9		3	6				11		14	10			S		2			J Rushton	59
1				7		9				3	5•	10*			11			4		8	6		2			M James	60
1			4	5		7	8	9		3	12				11		14	10			6*		2•			P Foakes	61

Flowers T.	Dodd J.	Osman R.	Horne B.	Hall R.	Ruddock N.	Le Tissier M.	Cockerill G.	Shearer A.	Rideout P.	Adams M.	Moore T.	Moody P.	McLoughlin A.	Gittens J.	Benali F.	Lee D.	Banger N.	Dowie I.	Hurlock T.	Andrews I.	Gray S.	Maddison N.	Wood S.	Kenna J.	Gilkes M.		
41	26	5	34	21	30	31	36	41	4	34	15	2		9	19	11		25	27	1	10	4	15	14	4	League Appearances	
	2			5		1	1				1	2	2	2	3	8	4	5	2		1	2			2	Substitute Appearances	
6	6		5+1	4+1	5	6	6	6		6	2			0+1	4			0+1	1+3	4		5				R/lows Appearances	
7	4		5	6	7	5+1	7			4	2	0+1			6	0+1	1		5		4		0+1	1	3+1	FA Cup Appearances	
6	3		5	3	4	6	3	6		5	1			1	3	1+1	1	4	6		1			4	3	ZDS Cup Appearances	

Also Played: Posn.(Game): Powell 14(51)12(54,60)7(55), Widdrington 9(53),14(56)8*(57), Bound 14(60)

Players on Loan: Gilkes (Reading)

† = Sent Off

SOUTHAMPTON

Club Colours: Red and white stripped shirts, black shorts, white stockings.
Change Colours: Blue shirts, white shorts, blue stockings.
Reserves League: Neville Ovenden Football Combination

COMPETITIONS						
Div. 1	Div. 2	Div. 3	Div. 3S	UEFA	ECWC	Texaco
66-74	22-53	20-21	21-22	69-70	76-77	74-75
78-	60-66	58-60	53-58	71-72		
	74-78			81-82		
				82-83		
				84-85		

HONOURS		
Div. 3	Div. 3S	FA Cup
59-60	21-22	75-76

MOST APPEARANCES: TERRY PAINE 805+4 (1956-74)				
Year	League	FA Cup	Lge Cup	Europe
1956-57	9			
1957-58	44	2		
1958-59	46	3		
1959-60	46	6		
1960-61	42	2	7	
1961-62	41	2	2	
1962-63	42	7	3	
1963-64	41	1	1	
1964-65	42	2	2	
1965-66	40	1	2	
1966-67	42	3	3	
1967-68	41	4	1	
1968-69	42	4	4	
1969-70	36	3	2	6
1970-71	41	4	1	
1971-72	37+3	2	2	2
1972-73	36+1	1	4	
1973-74	41	4	3	
	709+4	51	37	8
Previous holder: T Traynor 434 (1952-65)				

MOST GOALS IN A CAREER					
MIKE CHANNON 227 (1966-77 & 1979-82)					
Season	League	FAC	Lge C	Europe	Texaco
1965-66	1				
1966-67					
1967-68	7	1			
1968-69	8	1	3		
1969-70	15	2	1	3	
1970-71	18	1	1		
1971-72	14	1		1	
1972-73	16		2		
1973-74	21	1	1		
1974-75	20	1	3		5
1975-76	20	5			
1976-77	17	2	1	4	
1979-80	10	1			
1980-81	10				
1981-82	8			1	
Total	185	16	12	9	5
Previous holder: George O'Brien 154 (1956-66)					

MANAGERS			
Name	Seasons	Best	Worst
George Swift	1911-12		
James McIntyre	1919-24	5(2)	2(3S)
Arthur Chadwick	1925-31	4(2)	17(2)
G Kay	1931-36	12(2)	19(2)
George Coss	1936-37	19(2)	19(2)
T Parker	1937-War	15(2)	18(2)
W Dodgin (Snr)	War-1949	3(2)	14(2)
Sid Cann	1949-51	13(2)	21(2)
George Roughton	1952-55	3(2)	6(3)
Ted Bates	1955-73	7(1)	14(3)
Lawrie McMenemy	1973-85	2(1)	13(2)
Chris Nicholl	1985-91	7(1)	14(1)
Ian Branfoot	1991-	16(1)	16(1)

RECORD TRANSFER FEE RECEIVED			
Amount	Club	Player	Date
£3,600,000	Blackburn Rov.	Alan Shearer	7/92
£1,600,000	Leeds United	Rodney Wallace	7/91
£1,200,000	Manchester Utd	Danny Wallace	9/89
£800,000	Queens Park R	Colin Clarke	3/89

RECORD TRANSFER FEE PAID			
Amount	Club	Player	Date
£1,000,000	Swindon Town	Alan McLoughlin	12/90
£750,000	Portsmouth	Barry Horne	3/89
£600,000	Middlesbrough	David Armstrong	8/81
£400,000	Derby County	Charlie George	12/78

LONGEST LEAGUE RUNS	
of undefeated matches:	19 (5.9.1921-14.1.1922)
of undefeated home matches:	31 (22.1.1921-28.8.1922)
without home win:	10 (6.9.1969-17.1.1970)
of league wins:	6 (5.9.1964-13.10.1964) (3.3.1992-8.4.1992)
of league defeats:	5 (7.5.1927-10.9.1927)
	(12.1.1957-25.2.1957) (30.12.1967-10.2.1968)
	(31.12.1988-11.2.1989)
of league matches without a win:	20 (30.8.1969-17.1.1970)
of undefeated away matches:	9 (19.11.1977-29.3.1978)
	(17.9.1949-21.1.1950)
without an away win:	33 (22.4.1933-25.12.1934)
of home wins:	11 (10.10.1959-19.3.1960)
of away wins:	3 (On 9 different occasions)

PREVIOUS NAME
Southampton St. Mary's

PREVIOUS LEAGUE
Southern League

BIGGEST VICTORIES
League: 8-0 v Northampton, Division 3S, 24.12.1921
F.A. Cup: 7-1 v Ipswich Town, Round 3, 7.1.1961
League Cup: 5-0 v Derby County, Round 3, 8.10.1974
5-0 v Wrexham, Round 2, 28.8.1979
5-0 v Rochdale, Round 2, 25.9.1990
Europe (UEFA): 5-1 v Vittoria G, Round 2, 12.11.1969
(ECWC): 4-0 v Marseilles, Round 1, 15.9.1976

BIGGEST DEFEATS
League: 0-8 v Tottenham Hotspur, Division 2, 28.3.1936.
0-8 v Everton, Division 1, 20.11.1971.
F.A. Cup: 0-5 v Manchester City, Round 2, 5.2.1910.
League Cup: 1-7 v Watford, Round 2, 2.9.1980.
Europe: No more than 2 goal defeat.

MOST GOALS IN A MATCH
5. Charlie Wayman v Leicester, Div 2, 23.10.1948 (6-0)
5. Derek Reeves v Leeds (LC4) 5.12.1960 (5-4)

MOST POINTS
3 points a win: 77, Division 1, 1983-84.
2 points a win: 61, Division 3S, 1921-22, Division 3 1959-60.

MOST GOALS
112, 1957-58 (Division 3S).
Reeves 31, Roper 18, Hoskins 18, Raine 12, Clifton 7,
Mulgrew 8, Sydenham 4, Page 4, Walker 3, McGowan 2,
Traynor 2, McLaughlin 1, og 2.

MOST GOALS IN A SEASON
Derek Reeves 45 (League 39, FAC 6) 1959-60.
4 goals twice = 8; 3 goals twice = 6; 2 goals 3 times = 6; 1 goal
25 times = 25.
Previous holder: C Wayman 32 (1948-49).

MOST FIRST CLASS MATCHES IN A SEASON
61 (42 League, 7 FA Cup, 6 League Cup, 6 ZDS) 1991-92

MOST LEAGUE GOALS CONCEDED
92, Division 1, 1966-67

MOST LEAGUE WINS
26, Division 3, 1959-60

MOST LEAGUE DRAWS
18, Division 2, 1924-25; Division 1, 1972-73

MOST LEAGUE DEFEATS
23, Division 1, 1971-72

OLDEST PLAYER
Peter Shilton, 37 years 233 days v Coventry (Div 1) 9.5.1987.

YOUNGEST PLAYER
Danny Wallace 16 years 313 days v Manchester Utd (Div 1)
29.11.1980.

MOST CAPPED PLAYER
Peter Shilton (England) 49

BEST PERFORMANCES BY SOUTHAMPTON

League: 1921-22: Matches played 42, Won 23, Drawn 15, Lost 4, Goals for 68, Goals against 21, Points 61. 1st in Division 3S.

Highest: 1983-84: 2nd in Division 1.

F.A. Cup: 1975-76 (Div 2): 3rd rnd. Aston Villa 1-1, 2-1; 4th rnd. Blackpool 3-1; 5th rnd. West Bromwich Albion 1-1, 4-0; 6th rnd. Bradford City 1-0; Semi-final Crystal Palace 2-0; Final Manchester United 1-0.

League Cup: 1978-79 (Div 1): 2nd rnd. Birmingham City 5-2; 3rd rnd. Derby County 1-0; 4th rnd. Reading 0-0 2-0; 5th rnd. Manchester City 2-1; Semi-final Leeds United 2-2, 1-0; Final Nottingham Forest 2-3.

Europe (ECWC): 1976-77 (Div 2): 1st rnd. Marseille 4-0, 1-2; 2nd rnd Carrick R. 5-2, 4-1; 3rd rnd. Anderlecht 0-2, 2-1.

(UEFA): 1969-70: 1st rnd. Rosenburg 0-1, 2-0; 2nd rnd. Vittoria Guimariers 3-3, 5-1; 3rd rnd. Newcastle 0-0, 1-1.

DIVISIONAL RECORDS

	Played	Won	Drawn	Lost	For	Against	Points
DIVISION 1	910	314	254	342	1270	1342	**1046**
DIVISION 2	1428	559	353	516	2221	2140	**1471**
DIVISION 3	92	43	20	29	194	155	**106**
DIVISION 3S	314	150	77	87	562	368	377
TOTALS	**2744**	**1066**	**704**	**974**	**4247**	**4005**	**3000**

SOUTHAMPTON

PLAYERS NAME Honours	Ht	Wt	Birthdate	Birthplace Transfers	Contract Date	Clubs	League	L/Cup	FA Cup	Other	Lg	L/C	FAC	Oth
GOALKEEPERS														
Ian Andrews	6.2	12.02	01.12.64	Nottingham		Leicester City	126	6	7					
E:u21.1,Y.10				Loan	01.01.84	Swindon Town	1							
				£300,000	26.07.88	Celtic	5	2		1				
Loan Leeds United (15.12.88) 1lg				£200,000	15.02.90	Southampton	5			1				
Tim Flowers	6.2	14.0	03.02.67	Kenilworth	28.08.84	Wolverhampton W	63	5	2	2				
E: u21.3,Y.1				£70,000	13.06.86	Southampton	138	21	15	8				
				Loan	23.03.87	Swindon Town	7							
DEFENDERS														
Francis Benali	5.9	11.0	30.12.68	Southampton	05.01.87	Southampton (T)	54+14	7+4	11	3+1				
E: S														
Matthew Bound	6.2	12.0	09.11.72	Bradford-on-Avon	03.05.91	Southampton	0+1							
Aleksey Cherednik	5.9	11.07	12.12.60	USSR		Dneproptro								
Russia:25				£300,000	27.02.90	Southampton	19+4	3	1					
Jason Dodd	5.10	11.10	02.11.70	Bath		Bath	0+1							
				(T)	25.04.89	Southampton	63+6	14+1	10	5				
Richard Hall	6.1	12.8	14.03.72	Ipswich	20.03.90	Scunthorpe Utd. (T)	22	2	3	4	3			
				£200,000	13.02.91	Southampton	21+6	4+1	5	3	3		2	
Jeffrey Kenna	5.11	11.07	27.08.70	Dublin	25.04.89	Southampton (T)	15+1		3+1	3				
Ei:u21.4														
Steve Wood	6.1	12.7	02.02.63	Bracknell	19.02.81	Reading (A)	216+3	10	15	4	9			
Div3'86,Div2'88				£80,000	17.06.87	Millwall	108+2	1	10	3+1				
				£400,000	09.10.91	Southampton	15		1	4			1	
MIDFIELD														
Micky Adams	5.6	10.4	08.11.61	Sheffield	01.11.79	Gillingham	85+7	5	6		5			
E:Y4				£75,000	19.07.83	Coventry City	85+5	9	7	2	9	1		
				£110,000	23.01.87	Leeds Utd	72+1	4	6	6	2		1	
				£250,000	14.03.89	Southampton	86+1	12	6	6	3			
Glen Cockerill	6.0	12.4	25.08.55	Grimsby		Louth Utd								
					01.11.76	Lincoln City	65+6	2	2		10			
				£11,000	06.12.79	Swindon Town	23+3	3			1			
				£40,000	12.08.81	Lincoln City	114+1	16	7	1	25	1		
					23.03.84	Sheffield Utd	62	6	1		10	1		
				£225,000	17.10.85	Southampton	239+11	32+1	19+2	12	32	5	2	
Stuart Gray	5.10	11.10	19.04.60	Withernsea	03.12.80	Nottm. Forest	48+1	5+1	3	1	3			
				Loan		Bolton W	10							
				£40,000	03.08.83	Barnsley	117+3	7	6+1	2	23	3		1
				£150,000	25.11.87	Aston Villa	102+4	11	5+1	7+2	9	1	3	2
				£200,000	23.09.91	Southampton	10+1	5	4	1	1			
David Hughes	5.9	11.0	30.12.72	St. Albans	02.07.91	Southampton								
Terry Hurlock	5.9	13.2	22.09.58	Hackney		LOri								
E: B (3); Div2'88					28.08.80	Brentford	220	17	17	9	18	2	4	
				£90,000	20.02.86	Reading	29	3	1	2				
				£95,000	12.02.87	Millwall	103+1	9	5	5	8	2		
				£325,000	01.09.90	Glasgow Rangers								
				£400,000	09.09.91	Southampton	27+2	4	5	6				1
David Lee	5.7	10.0	05.11.67	Manchester	08.08.86	Bury (T)	203+5	15	6	19+1	35	1		4
				£350,000	27.08.91	Southampton	11+8		0+1	1+1				
Neil Maddison	5.9	11.8	02.10.69	Darlington	14.04.88	Southampton (T)	8+9	0+2	0+3	1	2			
Stephen Roast	5.6	9.10	19.09.72	London	03.05.91	Southampton								
FORWARDS														
Nicholas Banger	5.8	10.06	25.02.71	Southampton	25.04.89	Southampton (T)	0+10	1+1		1			3	
Kerry Dixon	6.0	13.10	24.07.61	Luton		Tottenham H. (A)								
E:8,u21.1; Div2'84'89; ZDC'90						Dunstable								
				£20,000	22.07.80	Reading	110+6	6+1	2+1		51			
				£175,000	04.08.83	Chelsea	331+4	40+1	18+2	25	147	24	8	12
				£575,000	19.07.92	Southampton								
Iain Dowie	6.1	12.12	09.01.65	Hatfield		Hendon			1					
NI:2,u21.1				£30,000	14.12.88	Luton Town	53+13	3+1	1+2	5	15			4
				Loan	13.09.89	Fulham	5				1			
				£480,000		West Ham U	12				4			
				£500,000	03.09.91	Southampton	25+5	1+3	4	4	9			
Matthew Le Tissier	6.0	11.10	14.10.68	Guernsey		Vale Recreation								
E: B.2,u19.2,Y.1, FLgXI.1					17.10.86	Southampton (A)	143+30	20+6	15+1	11+1	60	11	5	9
Paul Moody	6.3	12.6	13.06.67	Portsmouth		Waterlooville			1					
				£50,000	15.07.91	Southampton	2+2		0+1					
Lee Powell	5.5	8.10	02.06.73	Newport	03.05.91	Southampton	1+3	0+1						
W: u21.1														
David Speedie	5.7	10.4	20.02.60	Glenrothes	19.10.78	Barnsley	10+13							
S:5,u21.1,Div2.'84,FMC'86				Free	21.06.80	Darlington	88	4	3		21		1	
				£65,000	08.06.82	Chelsea	155+7	23+1	12	7	47	7	5	5
				£750,000	23.07.87	Coventry City	121+1	15	3+1	4	31	3		1
				£675,000	01.02.91	Liverpool	8+4		1+1		6			
				£400,000	16.08.91	Blackburn Rovers	34+2	2	2	3	23		1	2
				£400,000	24.07.92	Southampton								
ADDITIONAL CONTRACT PLAYERS														
Gary Fergusson, Callum MacDonald, Paul Tisdale, (M) Thomas Widdrington, Barry Wilson.														

SOUTHAMPTON

RECORD WIN & LOSS AGAINST EACH CLUB IN CURRENT DIVISION

(Where a score has occured on several occasions the most recent is given)

Club	Rec. Win	Season	Rec. Loss	Season
ARSENAL	3-0	1985-86	5-1	1991-92
ASTON VILLA	5-0	1986-87	4-0	1936-37
BLACKBURN ROVERS	6-1	1952-53	4-0	1937-38
CHELSEA	5-0	1968-69	4-0	1973-74
COVENTRY CITY	8-2	1983-84	5-1	1965-66
CRYSTAL PALACE	6-0	1970-71	3-0	1972-73
EVERTON	3-0	1978-79	8-0	1971-72
IPSWICH TOWN	3-0	1984-85	7-0	1973-74
LEEDS UNITED	4-0	1981-82	7-0	1971-72
LIVERPOOL	4-1	1989-90	5-0	1982-83
MANCHESTER CITY	4-1	1982-83	6-1	1927-28
MANCHESTER UNITED	4-1	1969-70 (away)	5-1	1986-87
MIDDLESBROUGH	6-0	1962-63	5-0	1960-61
NORWICH CITY	7-3	1957-58	5-0	1960-61
NOTTINGHAM FOREST	7-2	1935-36	6-0	1946-47
OLDHAM ATHLETIC	4-0	1976-77	3-1	1928-29
QUEENS PARK RANGERS	5-0	1957-58	4-0	1983-84
SHEFFIELD UNITED	4-0	1936-37	6-1	1934-35
SHEFFIELD WEDNESDAY	4-0	1969-70	4-1	1951-52 (home)
TOTTENHAM HOTSPUR	5-0	1983-84	8-0	1935-36
WIMBLEDON	1-0	1991-92	2-0	1987-88

MANAGER: IAN BRANFOOT

DATE OF BIRTH: 26.01.1947   **PLACE OF BIRTH:** Gateshead

DATE OF APPOINTMENT: 13.06.1991

PREVIOUS CLUBS
as Manager: Reading
as Asst. Man.: Crystal Palace
as Player: Sheffield Wednesday; Lincoln City; Doncaster Rovers

HONOURS
as Manager: (Reading): Promotion to 3rd Div, 3rd Div Champions, Simod Cup Winners
as Asst. Man.: (C Palace): ZDS Cup Winners, FA Cup Finalists
as Player: (Lincoln) Div 4 Champions 1975-76

Value Rating: ★ ★ ★ ★

Programme Editor: Mr J Hughes

Price of 1992-93 Programme: £1.50
Number of Pages: 48
Subscriptions: £58 for all home games

Local Newspapers: Southern Evening Echo, Portsmouth News

Local Radio Stations: Radio Solent, Ocean Sound

Additional Publications on Club: Saints! A Complete Record of Southampton Football Club 1885-1987 (Gary Chalk and Duncan Holly, hardback £15.95).
The Alphabet of the Saints. A Complete Who's Who of Southampton F.C. (Duncan Holley & Gary Chalk, hardback £17.95)

LEADING LEAGUE GOALSCORERS
SEASONS 1979-80 – 1991-92

1979-80	**PHIL BOYER**	23	1980-81	**STEVE MORAN**	18
1981-82	**KEVIN KEEGAN**	26	1982-83	**DANNY WALLACE**	12
1983-84	**STEVE MORAN**	21	1984-85	**JOE JORDAN**	12
1985-86	**DAVID ARMSTRONG**	10	1986-87	**COLIN CLARKE**	20
1987-88	**COLIN CLARKE**	16	1988-89	**ROD WALLACE**	12
1989-90	**MATTHEW LE TISSIER**	21	1990-91	**MATTHEW LE TISSIER**	19

1991-92   **ALAN SHEARER   13**

THE DELL Milton Road, Southampton SO9 4XX

Capacity: 21,909   **Covered Standing:** 3,575   **Seating:** 8,796

Tel: Ground: 0703 220505   **Ticket Sales:** 0703 337171   **Clubcall:** 0898 12 11 78

All premium rate calls (0898/0891) cost 36p per minute cheap rate and 48p per minute at all other times. Call costings correct at time of going to press.

GROUNDS
Antelope Ground 1885-1897; County Cricket Ground 1897-98; The Dell 1898-

ATTENDANCES
Highest: 31,044 v Manchester United, Division 1, 8.10.1969
30,586 v West Bromwich Albion, Division 2, 23.4.1949

Lowest: 1,875 v Port Vale, Division 2, 30.3.1936

RECORD RECEIPTS (with previous records)
£145,740 v Manchester Utd, Rumbelows Cup Q/Final, 16.1.1991
£132,585 v Tottenham H., Div 1, 26.12.1990
£128,730 v Oldham Athletic, Littlewoods Cup Quarter Final, 24.1.1990
£86,028 v Liverpool, Littlewoods Cup Semi-Final, 11.2.1987
£79,784 v Barnsley, FA Cup 5th Round, 5.3.1985
£71,202 v Sheffield Wednesday, FA Cup 6th Round, 11.3.1984
£69,690 v Liverpool, Div 1, 16.4.1983
£63,574 v Everton, FA Cup 5th Round, 14.2.1981
£43,029 v Anderlecht, ECWC, 16.3.1977

THE DELL
First game: v Brighton, (Southern League), 3.9.1898
First floodlit game: v Bournemouth, 31.10.1950

Season Tickets:
Stands: from £168 to £242 (no reductions)
Ground: from £126 (no reductions)

Executive Box Season Tickets: None

Cost of Stand Tickets: Gold Games (all ticket): Centre: £14; Wings: £12.50; Bench £10; Standing: £8, Milton/Archers Rd (juv & OAP): £2; Visitors Enc.: £8
Silver Games: Centre: £11.50; Wings: £10; Bench £8; Standing: £7; Milton/Archers Rd (juv & OAP): £2; Visitors Enc.: £7

Match and Ticket Information: Advance seat tickets 10 days before match. Terraces pay on day (unless all ticket)

Car Parking: Street parking and nearby municipal parks

Nearest Railway Station: Southampton Central (0703 229393)

How to get to the ground

From North: Use A33 S.P. Southampton via The Avenue then turn right into Northlands Road and at end turn right into Archers Road for Southampton FC

From East: Use Motorway M27 then A334 and follow signs Southampton A3024. Then follow signs The West into Commercial Road then turn right into Hill Lane and take 1st turning right into Milton Road for Southampton FC

From West: Use A35 then A3024 S.P. Southampton city centre. Forward into Fourposts Hill then turn left into Hill Lane and take 1st turning right into Milton Road for Southampton FC

SOUTHEND UNITED

Division 1

Formed: 1906   **Turned Professional:** 1906   **Ltd Co:** 1919

SPONSORED BY: ELONEX Personal Computers   **NICKNAME:** The Shrimpers

President
N J Woodcock

Chairman
V T Jobson

Vice-Chairman
J W Adams

Directors
J Bridge
J Foster
D M Markscheffel
R J Osborne (Company Secretary)

Team Manager
Colin Murphy

Coaches
Bob Houghton
Danny Greaves

Commercial Manager
J Carter

Stadium Manager
D Jobson

Club Statistician for the Directory
Dave Goody

SOUTHEND United's first ever season in the upper half of the Football League was one that promised a great deal but, due to factors out of the hands of the players themselves, ended up delivering little.

Southend's first Second Division season started with the fans and soccer pundits alike condemning them to a swift return to the League's lower echelons. But the Blues, as they had done the season before, proved everyone wrong and came very close to sealing promotion for the third consecutive season. After an emotional first game at home to Bristol City, the players travelled to Derby County for the first test of character, and how they came through with flying colours! A 2-1 victory at the Baseball Ground, with Brett Angell continuing where he left off at the end of the previous season, was thoroughly deserved and caused a few people to sit up and pay attention. A fine 3-0 victory at home to Blackburn Rovers at the start of November gave the club a top 10 position and three consecutive wins at the end of November, including one at Roker Park, where Brett Angell scored for the seventh consecutive league match, pushed the club into the top five for the first time. The final match in a seven game unbeaten sequence was at Oxford United on Boxing Day when a 90th minute goal by Brett Angell put Southend on the top of the division for the first time in their history. The occupation of the summit was, however, quite brief; about 4 hours to be precise, as Southend's match kicked off at 11.00am.

The new year saw the club go from strength to strength, with a 4-0 victory over Newcastle United followed by an unfortunate 0-1 defeat by Everton at Goodison Park in the F.A. Cup Third Round. A 1-0 victory, to complete the double over Derby County, put the Blues comfortably in 2nd place, but, just as everyone was readying themselves for the final push towards the Premier League, a large spanner was thrown into the works. The club Chairman, Vic Jobson, announced he was moving the club to Basildon as the local council had refused his planning application for a new stadium in the Southend area. The fans were outraged and demonstrations started at home matches.

After a phenomenal start, 3 wins in the last 17 league matches told the story of a club that had blown probably their best chance of ever becoming one of the Premier Clubs. The fans would have been very satisfied at the start of the season if told they were to finish in 12th position.

With Dave Webb, having served his 6 months notice, being replaced by Colin Murphy, it is hoped by all Blues fans that the new manager can persuade the players out of contract that a good future for them is still at Southend United. However, with Dean Austin already having left for Tottenham Hotspur, the next season is looking like it may be a long and hard one. **Dave Goody**

Back row L-R: Dean Austin, Ian Benjamin, Brett Angell, Andy Sussex, Spencer Prior, Pat Scully, Andy Edwards, Paul Smith. **Middle row:** David Webb (Manager), Kevin Lock (Team Coach), Steve Tilson, John Cornwell, David Martin, Paul Sansome, Tony Parks, Christian Hyslop, Steven Heffer, Danny Greaves (Youth Team Coach), Alan Raw (Physio). **Front row:** Adam Locke, Spencer Barham, Mark Hall, Andy Ansah, Jason Cook, Chris Powell, Peter Butler, Kevin O'Callaghan

SOUTHEND UNITED

DIVISION TWO: 12th   **FA CUP:** 3rd RND   **RUMBELOWS CUP:** 1st RND   **ZDS CUP:** 2nd RND

M	DATE		COMP.	VEN	OPPONENTS	RESULT		H/T	LGE POS	GOALSCORERS/GOAL TIMES	ATTEN- DANCE
1	A	17	BL	H	Bristol City	D	1-1	1-0	13	Benjamin 30	6,720
2		20	RC 1/1	A	Watford	L	0-2	0-2			(6,231)
3		24	BL	A	Derby County	W	2-1	2-0	9	Sussex 15, Angell 45	(12,284)
4		28	RC 1/2	H	Watford	D	1-1	1-1		Angell 30	3,802
5		31	BL	H	Leicester City	L	1-2	0-0	15	Martin 54	6,944
6	S	3	BL	A	Cambridge United	W	1-0	0-0		Benjamin 50	(6,413)
7		7	BL	A	Ipswich Town	L	0-1	0-0	15		(12,732)
8		14	BL	H	Bristol Rovers	W	2-0	0-0	10	Ansah 51, Angell 74	4,670
9		17	BL	H	Plymouth Argyle	W	2-1	1-0		Angell 30, Benjamin 77	4,585
10		21	BL	A	Port Vale	D	0-0	0-0	7		(5,988)
11		28	BL	H	Wolverhampton W	L	0-2	0-0	10		8,368
12	O	2	ZDS 1	A	Watford	W	1-0	1-0		**Sussex 4**	(1,700)
13		4	BL	A	Tranmere Rovers	D	1-1	1-0	12	Angell 43	(7,358)
14		12	BL	H	Millwall	L	2-3	1-2	14	Sussex 21, Tilson 54	7,266
15		19	BL	A	Watford	W	2-1	1-0	11	Sussex 3, Dublin (og) 81	(6,862)
16		22	ZDS 2	A	Crystal Palace	L	†2-4	1-0		**Jones 10, Angell 82**	(7,185)
17		26	BL	H	Charlton Athletic	D	1-1	1-0	11	Austin (pen) 34	7,320
18		30	BL	H	Oxford United	L	2-3	1-3		Angell 23, Tilson 86	4,873
19	N	2	BL	A	Middlesbrough	D	1-1	0-0	10	Angell 8	(9,664)
20		5	BL	H	Blackburn Rovers	W	3-0	1-0	10	Angell 44, 62, Benjamin 59	4,860
21		9	BL	H	Swindon Town	W	3-2	1-0	10	Angell 17, 76, Tilson 80	7,709
22		20	BL	A	Newcastle United	L	2-3	1-3	11	Angell 30, Tilson 80	(14,740)
23		23	BL	H	Barnsley	W	2-1	0-0	8	Angell 68, Tilson 73	5,060
24		30	BL	A	Sunderland	W	2-1	1-1	8	Angell 40, Scully 68	(13,575)
25	D	7	BL	H	Brighton & H A	W	2-1	1-0	5	Ansah 24, Tilson 59	6,303
26		14	BL	A	Portsmouth	D	1-1	1-1	5	Scully 17	(9,006)
27		22	BL	H	Cambridge United	D	1-1	1-1	5	Benjamin 44	9,353
28		26	BL	A	Oxford United	W	1-0	0-0	4	Angell 90	(5,601)
29		28	BL	A	Leicester City	L	0-2	0-0	5		(15,635)
30	J	1	BL	H	Newcastle United	W	4-0	2-0	3	Angell 3, 88, Jones 44, Ansah 56	9,458
31		4	FAC 3	A	Everton	L	0-1	0-1			(22,605)
32		11	BL	H	Derby County	W	1-0	1-0	2	Ansah 30	8,295
33		18	BL	A	Bristol City	D	2-2	1-0	2	Angell 4, Ansah 78	(9,883)
34	F	1	BL	H	Watford	W	1-0	0-0	2	Benjamin 69	7,581
35		8	BL	A	Charlton Athletic	L	0-2	0-0	3		(9,724)
36		15	BL	A	Barnsley	L	0-1	0-0	5		(5,328)
37		18	BL	H	Grimsby Town	L	2-3	0-1	5	Austin 48, Ansah 78	(5,337)
38		22	BL	H	Sunderland	W	2-0	2-0	3	Angell 37, Jones 39	7,473
39		29	BL	A	Brighton & H A	L	2-3	1-1	4	Benjamin 3, Angell 61	(8,271)
40	M	10	BL	A	Blackburn Rovers	D	2-2	2-1	5	Ansah 28, Angell 31	(14,404)
41		14	BL	H	Middlesbrough	L	0-1	0-0	8		7,272
42		17	BL	H	Portsmouth	L	2-3	2-2	9	Tilson 21, Jones 27	6,832
43		21	BL	A	Swindon Town	L	1-3	1-1	10	Ansah 29	(8,628)
44		28	BL	H	Grimsby Town	W	3-1	2-1	9	Angell 31, Scully 33, Ansah 57	4,591
45	A	1	BL	A	Bristol Rovers	L	1-4	1-0	9	Jones 3	(5,375)
46		4	BL	H	Ipswich Town	L	1-2	0-0	10	Prior 79	10,003
47		11	BL	A	Plymouth Argyle	W	2-0	1-0	10	Marker (og) 17, Benjamin 75	(7,060)
48		15	BL	H	Port Vale	D	0-0	0-0	1		4,462
49		20	BL	A	Wolverhampton W	L	1-3	1-1	1	Benjamin 39	(10,953)
50		25	BL	H	Tranmere Rovers	D	1-1	1-0	1	Jones 42	4,761
51	M	2	BL	A	Millwall	L	0-2	0-0	12		(7,574)

Best Home League Attendance: 10,003 v Ipswich Town   **Smallest:** 4,462 v Port Vale   **Av Home Att:** 6,729

Goal Scorers: **Compared with 90-91:** +547

League (63):   Angell 21, Benjamin 9, Ansah 9, Tilson 7, Jones 5, Sussex 3, Scully 3, Opponents 2, Austin 2 (1 pen), Martin, Prior

R/lows C (1):   Angell
FA Cup (0):
ZDS Cup (3):   Jones, Angell, Sussex   † = After extra-time

1991-92

Sansome P.	Austin D.	Powell C.	Martin D.	Edwards A.	Prior S.	Ansah A.	Sussex A.	O'Callaghan K.	Benjamin I.	Angell B.	Tilson S.	Locke A.	Cornwell J.	Scully P.	Hall M.	Cagigao	Jones K.	Hyslop C.	Butler P.	Royce S.	Referee	No.
1	2	3	4	5	6	7	8	9*	10	11	12	S									R Lewis	1
1	2	3	4	5	6	7	8	9*	10	11	12	S									I Hemley	2
1	2	3	4	5	6	7	8		10	11	9	S	S								D Frampton	3
1	2	3	4	S	6	12	8		10*	11	9	7		5							I Barrett	4
1	2	3	4	12	6	7	S		10	11	9		8	5*							A Ward	5
1	2	3	4		6	7	S		10	11	9	S	8	5							J Moules	6
1	2	3	4*		6	7	14	12	10	11	9•		8	5							A Gunn	7
1	2	3	S		6	7	4		10	11	9		8	5	S						R Wiseman	8
1	2	3	S		6	7	4		10	11	9		8	5	S						R James	9
1	2	3	S		6	7*	4		10	11	9		8	5	12						R Groves	10
1	2	3			6		4		10	11	9	12	8	5	7*	S					G Pooley	11
1	2	3			6		4	S	10		9	7	8	5	S		11				A Buksh	12
1	2	3			6		4	S	10	11	9	7	8	5	S						J Rushton	13
1	2	3			6	7	4	S	10	11	9	S	8	5							R Pawley	14
1	2	3			6	7		11*	10	12	9		8	5	S		4				M Pierce	15
1	2	3			6	7			10	11	9	S	8	5	S		4				V Callow	16
1	2	3			6	7			10	11*	9	12	8	5	S		4				K Morton	17
1	2	3	S		6	7			10	11*	9		8	5	12		4				P Danson	18
1	2	3	S		6	7			10	11	9	S	8	5			4				J Kirkby	19
1	2	3	S		6	7*			10	11	9	12	8	5			4				J Carter	20
1	2	3			6	7	S		10	11	9	S	8	5			4				A Smith	21
1	2	3			6	7	12		10*	11	9	S	8	5			4				P Harrison	22
1	2		S		6	7	S		10	11	9		8	5			4	3			R Bigger	23
1	2	3			6	7	S		10	11	9		8	5			4	S			K Hackett	24
1	2	3			6	7	S		10	11	9		8	5			4	S			P Jones	25
1	2	3			6	7	S		10	11	9		8	5			4	S			P Don	26
1	2	3			6	7			10	11	9	S	8	5			4	S			G Singh	27
1	2	3			6	7			10	11	9*	S	8	5			4	S			R Lewis	28
1	2	3			6	7			10•	11	9*	12	8	5			4	14			T Holbrook	29
1	2	3			6	7			10	11	9	S	8	5			4*	12			M James	30
1	2	3			6	7			10	11	9	S	8	5			4	S			J Key	31
1	2	3			6	7			10	11	9	S	8	5			4*	12			A Ward	32
1	2	3	S		6	7			10	11	9	S	8	5			4				I Hemley	33
1	2	3	12		6*	7*			10	11	9		8	5	14		4				R Hamer	34
1	2	3			6	7	12	14	10*		9•		8	5	11		4				K Cooper	35
1	2	3			6	7	14		10		9•	12	8	5	11*		4				T Fitzharris	36
1	2	3			6	7	11	S	10		9		8	5			4	S			D Phillips	37
1	2	3	S		6	7*			10	11	9		8	5			4	12			G Willard	38
1	2	3	S		6	7			10	11	9		8	5			4	S			M Reed	39
1	2	3	S		6	7			10	11	9		8	5			4	S			S Lodge	40
1	2	3			6	S			10	11	9	7	8	5			4	S			V Callow	41
1	2				6	S			10	11	9	7*	8	5			4	3	12		J Carter	42
1	2	3			6	7	S		10	11	9	S	8	5			4				R Pawley	43
	2	3			6	7	S	S	10	11	9		8	5			4			1	P Scoble	44
1	2	3			6	7	S	S	10	11	9		8	5			4				A Smith	45
1	2	3	S		6	7	12		10*	11	9		8	5			4				G Ashby	46
1	2	3			6	7	S		10	11	9	S	8	5			4				D Gallagher	47
1	2	3			6	7	S		10	11	9	S	8	5			4				G Poll	48
1	2	3			6	14	9		10	11•	12	7*	8	5			4				P Taylor	49
1	2	3			6	7	S	S	10	11	9		8	5			4				D Elleray	50
1		3	2		6	7		12	10	11	9*	S	8	5			4				I Borrett	51
45	45	44	5	7	42	40	12	2	45	42	44	5	43	44	1		33	2	4	1	League Appearances	
				2			3	6		1		2		5			1		5		Substitute Appearances	
2	2	2	2	1	2	1+1	2	1	2	2	1+1	1		1							R/lows Appearances	
1	1	1		1	1				1	1	1		1	1			1				FA Cup Appearances	
2	2	2			2	1	1		2	1	2	1	2	2		1	1				ZDS Cup Appearances	

SOUTHEND UNITED

Club Colours: Blue shirts with gold collar and cuff, yellow shorts, blue stockings
Change Colours: All yellow
Reserves League: (Junior Team) South Eastern Div 1

COMPETITIONS			
Div. 2	Div. 3S	Div. 3	Div. 4
91-	21-58	20-21	66-72
		58-66	76-78
		72-76	80-81
		78-80	84-87
		81-84	89-90
		87-89	
		90-91	

HONOURS
Division 4
1980-81

MOST APPEARANCES: A.W. (Sandy) ANDERSON 452 (50-63)	
Year	League
1950-51	30
1951-52	46
1952-53	23
1953-54	45
1954-55	45
1955-56	9
1956-57	27
1957-58	40
1958-59	41
1959-60	38
1960-61	43
1961-62	45
1962-63	20
	452

MOST GOALS IN A CAREER	
ROY HOLLIS 122 (1953-60)	
Season	League
1953-54	10
1954-55	27
1955-56	24
1956-57	18
1957-58	18
1958-59	18
1959-60	7
Total	122

MANAGERS			
Name	Seasons	Best	Worst
Tom Mather	1920-21	3(3S)	22(3S)
F. L. Birnie	1921-24	3(3S)	22(3S)
D. B. Jack	1924-39	10(3S)	21(3S)
Harry Warren	1946-56	3(3S)	18(3S)
Eddie Perry	1956-60	7(3S)	12(3)
Frank Broome	1960	20(3)	20(3)
Ted Fenton	1961-65	8(3)	16(2)
Alvin Williams	1965-67	21(3)	6(4)
Ernie Shepherd	1967-69	6(4)	7(4)
Geoff Hudson	1969-70	17(4)	17(4)
Arthur Rowley	1970-76	12(3)	18(4)
Dave Smith	1976-82	7(3)	10(4)
Peter Morris	1982-84	22(3)	22(3)
Bobby Moore	1984-86	9(3)	20(4)
David Webb	1986-87	7(3)	20(4)
Dick Bate	1987		
Paul Clark	1987-88	19(3)	19(3)
Dave Webb	88-	12(3)	3(4)

RECORD TRANSFER FEE RECEIVED			
Amount	Club	Player	Date
£375,000	Tottenham H	Dean Austin	7/92
£150,000	Wolves	Shane Westley	6/89
£120,000	Crystal Palace	Peter Taylor	10/73
£100,000	Chelsea	Bill Garner	9/72

RECORD TRANSFER FEE PAID			
Amount	Club	Player	Date
£175,000	Brentford	Keith Jones	10/91
£111,111	Blackpool	Derek Spence	12/79
£50,000	Tottenham H	Mike Stead	11/78
£50,000	Sheffield Wed	Dave Cusak	9/78

LONGEST LEAGUE RUNS	
of undefeated matches:	16 (20.2.1932-29.8.1932)
of undefeated home matches:	32 (16.2.1980-1.5.1981)
without home win:	8 (2.10.1948-22.1.1949)
of league wins:	7 (4.10.1924-6.11.1924)
	(24.4.1990-18.9.1990)
of league defeats:	6 (29.8.1987-19.9.1987)
of league matches without a win	17 (31.12.1983-14.4.1984)
of undefeated away matches:	9 (4.3.1972-29.4.1972)
without an away win:	27 (13.11.1920-4.2.1922)
of home wins:	18 (4.4.1980-9.1.1981)
of away wins:	5 (31.8.1931-3.10.1931) (9.4.1991-3.9.1991)

PREVIOUS LEAGUE
Southern League

BIGGEST VICTORIES
League: 9-2 v Newport Co., Div 3S, 5.9.1936
7-0 v QPR, Div 3S, 7.4.1928
8-1 v Cardiff City, Div 3S, 20.2.1937
7-0 v Workington, Div 4, 29.3.1968
F.A. Cup: 10-1 v Golders Green, Round 1, 24.11.1934
9-0 v Kings Lynn, Round 1, 16.11.1968
10-1 v Brentwood, Round 2, 7.12.1968
League Cup: 6-1 v Bournemouth, 13.8.1968

BIGGEST DEFEATS
League: 0-8 v Northampton Town, Div 3S, 22.3.1924
1-9 v Brighton, Div 3, 27.11.1965
F.A. Cup: 0-6 v Burnley, Round 2, 30.1.1915
League Cup: 0-8 v Crystal Palace, Rnd 2, 25.9.1990

MOST POINTS
3 points a win: 85, Division 3, 1990-91
2 points a win: 67, Division 4, 1980-81

MOST GOALS
92, Division 3S, 1950-51
Stubbs 19, Wakefield 15, Davies 12, Tippett 12, Grant 12, French 5, Sibley 5, Lawler 4, McAlinden 2, Anderson 1, Butler 1, Woods 1, og 3

MOST GOALS IN A MATCH
5. Jim Shankly v Merthyr Tydfil, 6-0, Div 3S, 1.3.1930
5. H. Johnson v Golders Green, 10-1, FAC Rnd 1, 24.11.1934
5. Billy Best v Brentwood, 10-1, FAC Rnd 2, 7.12.1968

MOST GOALS IN A SEASON
Jim Shankley 35 (League 34, FAC 1) 1928-29
3 goals 2 times = 6; 2 goals 6 times = 12; 1 goal 17 times = 17.
Total 35

MOST FIRST CLASS MATCHES IN A SEASON
56 (46 League, 3 FA Cup, 7 League Cup) 1979-80
56 (46 League, 5 FA Cup, 2 League Cup, 3 Football League Trophy) 1982-83
56 (46 League, 3 FA Cup, 4 League Cup, 3 Freight Rover Trophy) 1986-87
56 (46 League, 2 FA Cup, 5 League Cup, 3 Sherpa Van Trophy) 1987-88
56 (46 League, 1 FA Cup, 4 Rumbelows Cup, 5 L/Daf Cup) 1990-91

MOST LEAGUE GOALS CONCEDED
85, Division 4, 1969-70

MOST LEAGUE WINS
30, Division 4, 1980-81

MOST LEAGUE DRAWS
19, Division 4, 1976-77

MOST LEAGUE DEFEATS
26, Division 3, 1965-66

YOUNGEST PLAYER
Bobby Haddrick, 16 years 177 days, 14.10.1966

MOST CAPPED PLAYER
George McKenzie (Eire) 9

BEST PERFORMANCES BY SOUTHEND UNITED

League: 1980-81: Matches Played 46, Won 30, Drawn 7, Lost 9, Goals for 79, Goals against 31, Points 67. First in Division 4

Highest: 12th Division 2, 1991-92

F.A. Cup: 1920-21: Last sixteen

1925-26: 1st rnd. Dulwich (h) 5-1; 2nd rnd. Gillingham (h) 1-0; 3rd rnd. Southport (h) 5-2; 4th rnd. Derby County (h) 4-1; 5th rnd. Nottingham Forest (h) 0-1

1951-52: 1st rnd. Bournemouth (h) 6-1; 2nd rnd. Oldham Athletic (h) 5-0; 3rd rnd. Southampton (h) 3-0; 4th rnd. Bristol Rovers (h) 2-1; 5th rnd. Sheffield Utd (h) 1-2

1975-76: 1st rnd. Swansea City (h) 2-0; 2nd rnd. Dover (h) 4-1; 3rd rnd. Brighton (h) 2-1; 4th rnd. Cardiff City (h) 2-1; 5th rnd Derby County (a) 0-1

League Cup: Never past Round 3

DIVISIONAL RECORDS

	Played	Won	Drawn	Lost	For	Against	Points
DIVISION 2	46	17	11	18	63	63	**62**
DIVISION 3	920	319	238	363	1266	1358	**972**
DIVISION 3S	1334	503	312	519	2074	2065	**1318**
DIVISION 4	598	262	144	192	871	742	**746**
TOTALS	**2898**	**1101**	**705**	**1092**	**4274**	**4228**	**3098**

SOUTHEND UNITED

PLAYERS NAME Honours	Ht	Wt	Birthdate	Birthplace Transfers	Contract Date	Clubs	APPEARANCES				GOALS			
							League	L/Cup	FA Cup	Other	Lg	L/C	FAC	Oth
GOALKEEPERS														
Paul Sansome	6.0	13.8	06.10.61	New Addington		Crystal Palace (A)								
FLT'83				f	18.04.80	Millwall	156	12	13	9				
					24.03.88	Southend Utd	187	14	4	13				
DEFENDERS														
John Cornwell	6.4	12.2	13.10.64	Bethnal Green	15.10.82	Leyton Orient (A)	193+9	9+1	14	7	35	2	2	2
				£50,000	16.07.87	Newcastle Utd	28+5	3	1	4+1	1			
				£65,000	31.12.88	Swindon Town	7+18	2+3		0+1				
				£50,000	16.08.90	Southend Utd	56+6	4	2	3	2			
Christian Hyslop	5.10	11.13	14.06.72	Bushey	05.04.90	Southend Utd. (T)	12+1	1						
David Martin	6.1	12.2	25.04.63	East Ham	10.05.80	Millwall (A)	131+9	10+2	7	4	6	3	1	1
E: Y; FAYC'79; FLT'83				£35,000	14.09.84	Wimbledon	30+5	2	2+1		3			
				f	23.08.86	Southend Utd	186+9	23	6+1	9+1	18	4		3
Chris Powell	5.8	10.13	08.09.69	Lambeth	24.12.87	Crystal Palace	2+1	0+1		0+1				
				Loan	11.01.90	Aldershot								
				Loan	22.02.90	Aldershot	11							
					30.08.90	Southend Utd	87+2	5	2	7	1			
Spencer Prior	6.1	12.10	22.04.71	Hockley	22.05.89	Southend Utd. (T)	90	7	2	5	3			1
Patrick Scully	6.1	12.7	23.06.70	Dublin	16.09.87	Arsenal (T)								
Eire:1;B1,U23:1,U21:6				Loan	07.09.89	Preston N.E	13		1					
				Loan	23.08.90	Northampton T	15		1					
				Loan	08.01.91	Southend Utd								
				£100,000	28.03.91	Southend Utd	65	1	1	2	3			
MIDFIELD														
Peter Butler	5.9	11.1	27.08.66	Halifax		Huddersfield Town (A)	0+5							
				Loan	24.01.86	Cambridge Utd	14		1		1			
				f	08.07.86	Bury	9+2	2	1			1		
				f	10.12.86	Cambridge Utd	55	4	2	2	9			
					12.02.88	Southend Utd	135+7	12	2	11	9	1		2
				Loan	24.03.92	Huddersfield Town	7							
Andrew Edwards	6.2	12.7	17.09.71	Chigwell	14.12.89	Southend Utd. (T)	17+3	2		2	1			1
Keith Jones	5.9	10.11	14.10.65	Dulwich	16.08.83	Chelsea	43+9	9+2	1	4+1	7	3		
E:Y,2,S				£40,000	03.09.87	Brentford	167+2	15	13	16	13	1	4	1
				£175,000	21.10.91	Southend Utd	33+1		1	1	5			1
Adam Locke	5.10	12.7	20.08.70	Croydon	21.06.88	Crystal Palace								
				Free	06.08.90	Southend Utd	23+15	2	0+1	4	3			
Paul W Smith	5.11	13.7	18.09.71	London	16.03.90	Southend Utd. (T)	10+2				1			
FORWARDS														
Brett Angell	6.2	12.8	20.08.68	Malborough		Portsmouth								
						Cheltenham Town		1					1	
				£40,000	19.02.88	Derby County								
					20.10.88	Stockport Co	60+10	3	3	8	28		1	4
				£100,000	02.08.90	Southend Utd	79+6	6	2	5+1	36	3	2	8
Andrew Ansah	5.10	11.01	19.03.69	Lewisham	21.03.89	Brentford	3+5	0+1			2			
				Free	29.03.90	Southend Utd	83+4	4+2	2	4+1	19			4
Ian Benjamin	5.11	13.1	11.12.61	Nottingham	26.05.79	Sheffield Utd. (A)	4+1	1+1			3			
E: Y.3; Div4'87				£100,000	31.08.79	West Brom A	1+1							
				Free	05.02.82	Notts County								
				Free	12.08.82	Peterborough U	77+3	7+1	5		14	1		
				Free	20.08.84	Northampton T	147+3	12	9	9	59	2	3	5
				Free		Cambridge Utd	20+5		2		2		1	
				Free	28.07.88	Chester City	18+4	2	2	2	2		1	1
				Free	02.02.89	Exeter City	30+2	2	4+1	4	4	1		1
				Free	02.03.90	Southend Utd	106	6	2	7	26			4
Steven Heffer	5.9	10.12	11.01.73	Southend	04.05.91	Southend Utd								
Kevin O'Callaghan	5.8	10.9	29.10.61	London	02.11.78	Millwall (A)	15+5	2	1+2		3	2	1	
Ei:20,u21.1,Y,Xl.2;FAYC'79,Div2'88				£220,000	17.01.80	Ipswich Town	72+43	10+4	5+5	1+7	3	1		
				£90,000	01.02.85	Portsmouth	84+3	2	3	4	16	1		2
				£80,000	05.06.87	Millwall	65+11	5+1	5	2+1	14			
				Free	01.07.91	Southend Utd	2+6	1						
Andrew Sussex	6.0	11.6	23.11.64	Islington	25.11.82	Leyton Orient (A)	127+17	7+1	8	5+3	17	2	1	
				£16,000	23.06.88	Crewe Alexandra	86+16	10	7+1	5	24	6	4	2
				£100,000	04.07.91	Southend Utd	12+3	2		1	3			1
Stephen Tilson	5.11	12.6	27.07.66	Wickford		Witham Tow								
					07.02.89	Southend Utd	103+13	5+1	3	9+1	17			3
ADDITIONAL CONTRACT PLAYERS														
Scott Ashenden					01.07.92	Southend Utd. (T)								
Stephen R Brown					10.07.92	Southend Utd. (T)								
Francisco Cagigao					13.09.91	Southend Utd			1					
Melvin Capleton					01.07.92	Southend Utd. (T)								
Mark A Hall					20.08.91	Southend Utd	1+2							
Declan Perkins					15.07.92	Southend Utd								
Simon Royce						Heybridge Swifts								
				£10,000	15.10.91	Southend Utd	1							
Daniel Sains					01.07.92	Southend Utd. (T)								

SOUTHEND UNITED

RECORD WIN & LOSS AGAINST EACH CLUB IN CURRENT DIVISION
(Where a score has occured on several occasions the most recent is given)

Club	Rec. Win	Season	Rec. Loss	Season
BARNSLEY	4-1	1964-65 (home)	4-1	1959-60
BIRMINGHAM CITY	2-1	1990-91		
BRENTFORD	6-0	1983-84	6-1	1958-59
BRISTOL CITY	6-0	1934-35	6-0	1951-52
BRISTOL ROVERS	6-0	1929-30	5-1	1926-27
CAMBRIDGE UNITED	4-1	1990-91	3-2	1973-74
CHARLTON ATHLETIC	5-0	1926-27	5-0	1925-26
DERBY COUNTY	1-0	1991-92	None	
GRIMSBY TOWN	4-0	1964-65	4-1	1971-72
LEICESTER CITY	None		2-0	1991-92
LUTON TOWN	5-0	1964-65	4-0	1924-25
MILLWALL	6-0	1935-36	8-1	1925-26
NEWCASTLE UNITED	4-0	1991-92	3-2	1991-92
NOTTS COUNTY	4-0	1968-69	6-2	1987-88
OXFORD UNITED	2-0	1981-82	3-2	1965-66
PETERBOROUGH UTD	4-1	1984-85 (away)	4-0	1970-71
PORTSMOUTH	4-0	1982-83	6-0	1921-22
SUNDERLAND	2-0	1991-92	7-0	1987-88
SWINDON TOWN	8-2	1950-51	6-1	1921-22
TRANMERE ROVERS	7-1	1959-60	3-1	1990-91
WATFORD	6-1	1960-61	5-0	1935-36
WEST HAM UNITED				
WOLVERHAMPTON WNDRS	3-1	1988-89	3-0	1988-89

MANAGER: COLIN MURPHY

DATE OF BIRTH: **PLACE OF BIRTH:**

DATE OF APPOINTMENT: MAY 1992

PREVIOUS CLUBS
as Manager: Derby County; Lincoln City
as Asst.Man/Coach: Derby County; Nott'm Forest, Notts County
as Player: Cork, Hibs, Wimbledon, Hastings Utd, Crystal Palace

HONOURS
as Manager: (Lincoln) Div 4 Runners-up '81, GMVC '88
as Player:
International:

Value Rating: ★ ★ ★

Programme Editor: Kevin O'Donnell

Price of 1992-93 Programme: £1.40
Number of Pages: 36
Subscriptions:

Local Newspapers: Evening Echo, Standard Recorder, Yellow Advertiser

Local Radio Stations: Essex Radio, BBC Essex

LEADING LEAGUE GOALSCORERS
SEASONS 1979-80 – 1991-92

1979-80	**PARKER**	8	1980-81	**DEREK SPENCE**	21
1981-82	**KEITH MERCER**	13	1982-83	**STEVE PHILLIPS**	17
1983-84	**STEVE PHILLIPS**	16	1984-85	**STEVE PHILLIPS**	21
1985-86	**RICHARD CADETTE**	25	1986-87	**RICHARD CADETTE**	24
1987-88	**DAVID CROWN**	17	1988-89	**DAVID CROWN**	25
1989-90	**DAVID CROWN**	19	1990-91	**BRETT ANGELL**	15

1991-92   **BRETT ANGELL**   21

ROOTS HALL Victoria Avenue, Southend-on-Sea

Capacity: 14,428   **Covered Standing:** 2,232   **Seating:** 6,124

Tel: Ground: 0702 340707   **Ticket Sales:** 0702 435602   **Clubcall:** 0839 66 44 44

All premium rate calls (0898/0891) cost 36p per minute cheap rate and 48p per minute at all other times. Call costings correct at time of going to press.

ATTENDANCES
Highest: 31,033 v Liverpool, FA Cup Round 3, 10.1.1979

Lowest: 653 v Northampton Town, Freight Rover Trophy, 13.3.1986

Record Receipts: £36,599 v Liverpool, FA Cup Round 3, 10.1.1979

Season Tickets:
Stands: from £165 to £210 (no reductions)
Ground: not available

Executive Box Season Tickets: Vice-Presidents £500

Cost of Stand Tickets: Seats: £9-£12 (no reductions); Family Seats: £9, juv/OAP £4.50

Match and Ticket Information: Seats can be bought 14 days before match

Car Parking: Reserved car park on match days. Ample street parking is available

Nearest Railway Station: Southend Central (0702 611811) Prittlewell

How to get to the ground

From North and East: Use A127 S.P. Southend, and then at roundabout take 3rd exit into Victoria Avenue for Southend United FC

From South: Use A13 S.P. Southend and then turn left into West Road and at end turn left into Victoria Avenue for Southend United FC

STOCKPORT COUNTY

Division 2

Formed: 1883   **Turned Professional:** 1891   **Ltd Co:** 1908

SPONSORED BY: Robinson's Best Bitter   **NICKNAME:** The Hatters

Chairman
B Elwood

Vice-Chairman
J R G White

Directors
B Taylor
M Baker
M Rains
V Snell

Secretary
John Simpson, F.C.A

Assistant Secretary
Andrea Welborn

Medical Officers
Dr D Dawson
Dr P Bazley

Manager
Danny Bergara

Assistant Manager
John Sainty & David Jones

Youth Coach
David Jones

Physiotherapist
Rodger Wylde

Groundsman
Roger Edmunds

Club Statistician for the Directory
Ian Watts & Stuart Brennan

WHEN the 1991-92 season began, no Stockport County fan would have believed that their team would be going to Wembley twice within eight days in May.

But that is exactly what happened as the club had the most glorious season in its 109 year history. The only disappointment was that they lost in both Wembley appearances, to Stoke City in the Autoglass Trophy and controversially to Peterborough United in the play-off final for a place in the re-structured First Division.

Promotion would have been just reward for a team which had never been out of the top six in the division all season, despite only achieving Third Division status the season before.

The tone was set on the first day of the season as Swansea were swept aside 5-0 at Edgeley Park, and by September Stockport had hit top spot.

The traditional early exits from the League Cup, to Bradford, and the F.A. Cup, to Wigan, allowed concentration on the league, although bad results had dropped the team to sixth by Christmas.

A run of nine games without defeat boosted Stockport back into automatic promotion contention and also started them on a run in the Autoglass Trophy which was to end at Wembley.

That run interfered with the promotion bid in March and April and Stockport needed a play-off semi-final win over Stoke to stand a chance of going up. They achieved that over two-legs, but the same week lost the Autoglass final to the same team. Then eight days later they were denied victory in the play-off final by a Peterborough goal which TV replays proved did not cross the line, and by the ruling out of an 'offside' goal which the same replays proved was legitimate.

The season ended in bitterness and tears, but once the disappointment faded, fans were celebrating unexpected success.

The goals came from six feet seven inch striker Kevin Francis, who netted 26 and defender/midfielder Jim Gannon, with 21. Andy Preece, picked up for £15,000 from Wrexham reserves at Christmas, added 13 goals in 23 league games.

But this was a team effort, with young goalkeeper Neil Edwards proving a tremendous find, the defence, magnificent all season and the midfield duo of Peter Ward and David Frain proving a perfect combination.

Stockport County will approach the 1992-93 season with determination and optimism.

Stuart Brennan

Back row L-R: Bill Williams, Malcolm Brown, David Redfern, Phil Church, Paul Wheeler, Neil Matthews. **Middle row:** Dave Jones, Peter Ward, Chris Beaumont, James Gannon, Alan Finley, Andy Kilner, Tony Barras, Rodger Wydle. **Front row:** Kevin Francis, Darren Knowles, Andy Thorpe, Danny Bergara (Manager), John Sainty (Ass. Manager), David Frain, Lee Todd, Paul Williams.

STOCKPORT COUNTY

DIVISION THREE: 5th   **FA CUP:** 2nd RND   **RUMBELOWS CUP:** 1st RND   **AUTOGLASS:** FINALISTS

M	DATE	COMP.	VEN	OPPONENTS	RESULT	H/T	LGE POS	GOALSCORERS/GOAL TIMES	ATTEN-DANCE
1	A 17	BL	H	Swansea City	W 5-0	2-0	1	Kilner (pen) 16, 58 (pen), W Williams 22, Francis 52, F	4,241
2	20	RC 1/1	H	Bradford City	D 1-1	0-1		Wheeler 85	3,834
3	24	BL	A	Leyton Orient	D 3-3	2-2	5	W Williams 10, Beaumont 24, Barras 88	(3,650)
4	28	RC 1/2	A	Bradford City	L †1-3	0-1		Francis 85	(3,806)
5	30	BL	H	Preston North End	W 2-0	2-0	2	Barras 8, Gannon 41	5,405
6	S 3	BL	A	Wigan Athletic	W 3-1	0-1	2	P Williams 47, Wheeler 51, Francis 58	(3,567)
7	6	BL	H	Torquay United	W 2-1	1-0	1	Wheeler 16, Gannon 72	5,618
8	14	BL	A	West Bromwich A.	L 0-1	0-0	2		(11,845)
9	17	BL	A	Exeter City	L 1-2	1-2	4	Francis 2	(3,033)
10	21	BL	H	Bury	W 2-0	0-0	3	Francis 82, Gannon 83	5,083
11	28	BL	A	Stoke City	D 2-2	0-2	4	Lillis 55, Francis 87	(12,954)
12	O 5	BL	H	Bradford City	W 4-1	2-1	3	Paskin 13, Francis 37, Kilner 46, Mitchell (og) 59	5,825
13	12	BL	A	Birmingham City	L 0-3	0-2	5		(12,643)
14	18	BL	H	Chester City	L 0-4	0-1	6		4,820
15	25	BL	A	Huddersfield Town	W 1-0	0-0	4	Gannon 46	(9,229)
16	N 1	BL	A	Bournemouth	L 0-1	0-0	5		(4,649)
17	5	BL	H	Bolton Wanderers	D 2-2	1-2	5	Frain (pen) 17, Matthews 55	5,036
18	16	FAC 1	H	Lincoln City	W 3-1	0-0		Gannon 61, Ward (og) 68, Francis 88	3,864
19	19	AGT Pre	A	Carlisle United	L 0-4	0-3			(894)
20	23	BL	A	Fulham	W 2-1	0-0	6	Francis 49, Beaumont 68	(3,680)
21	26	BL	H	Shrewsbury Town	L 1-4	0-2	6	Lillis 82	3,650
22	30	BL	A	Reading	D 1-1	1-1	6	Wheeler 44	(3,511)
23	D 7	FAC 2	A	Wigan Athletic	L 0-2	0-1			(4,168)
24	14	BL	H	Peterborough Utd	W 3-0	1-0	6	Francis 16, Frain 47, Gannon (pen) 64	2,768
25	20	BL	H	Leyton Orient	W 1-0	0-0	6	Francis 83	2,745
26	26	BL	A	Preston North End	L 2-3	1-2	6	Flynn (og) 21, Gannon 61	(6,782)
27	28	BL	A	Swansea City	L 1-2	1-1	6	Preece 22	(4,353)
28	J 1	BL	H	Wigan Athletic	D 3-3	2-2	6	Preece 3, Francis 39, Gannon (pen) 57	4,149
29	4	BL	A	Brentford	W 2-1	0-1	6	Gannon 47, Francis 89	4,421
30	7	AGT Pre	H	York City	W 3-0	2-0		Gannon 3 (13, 32, 71 pen)	1,397
31	11	BL	A	Hull City	W 2-0	0-0	5	Preece 61, Francis 90	(3,982)
32	14	AGT 1	A	Carlisle United	W 3-1	3-0		Francis 3 (23, 32, 34)	(1,243)
33	18	BL	H	Darlington	W 2-0	0-0	4	Ward 68, Preece 88	4,186
34	F 4	AGT 2	H	Hartlepool United	W 3-0	1-0		Francis 3 (15, 50, 72)	2,255
35	7	BL	H	Huddersfield Town	D 0-0	0-0	6		7,596
36	11	BL	H	Reading	W 1-0	0-0	6	Finley 60	3,720
37	15	BL	A	Peterborough Utd	L 2-3	1-1	6	Barras (pen) 5, Preece 58	(5,301)
38	18	BL	A	Hartlepool United	W 1-0	0-0	5	Francis 75	(2,473)
39	22	BL	H	Hull City	D 1-1	0-0	4	Wheeler 78	4,490
40	29	BL	A	Brentford	L 1-2	1-2	6	Preece 6	(7,484)
41	M 3	BL	A	Darlington	W 3-1	1-1	4	Preece 3 (9, 74, 79)	(2,384)
42	6	BL	A	Hartlepool United	L 0-1	0-0	5		(7,365)
43	10	BL	A	Bolton Wanderers	D 0-0	0-0	6		(7,365)
44	13	BL	H	Bournemouth	W 5-0	3-0	4	Gannon (pen) 27, 44, Preece 29, Francis 49, Barras 60	3,576
45	17	AGT NSF	A	Crewe Alexandra	W 2-1	2-0		Ward 10, Wheeler 44	(5,594)
46	20	BL	A	Shrewsbury Town	W 1-0	1-0	2	Wheeler 38	(3,186)
47	24	BL	A	Chester City	L 2-3	0-1	3	Gannon 78, Preece 86	(3,747)
48	27	BL	H	Fulham	W 2-0	1-0	2	Gannon 12, Thomas (og) 78	4,654
49	31	BL	H	West Bromwich A.	W 3-0	1-0	2	Barras 12, Frain 63, Preece 72	6,090
50	A 4	BL	A	Torquay United	L 0-2	0-1	3		(2,693)
51	7	AGT NF1	A	Burnley	W 1-0	1-0		Francis 34	(13,259)
52	10	BL	H	Exeter City	W 4-1	1-1	3	Gannon 3 (2, 81, 86 pen), Preece 89	4,546
53	15	AGT NF2	H	Burnley	W 2-1	1-1		Francis 7, Gannon 73	8,260
54	18	BL	A	Bury	D 0-0	0-0	4		(4,546)
55	20	BL	H	Stoke City	D 0-0	0-0	4		8,129
56	25	BL	A	Bradford City	L 0-1	0-0	5		(7,099)
57	M 2	BL	A	Birmingham City	W 2-0	2-0	5	Gannon 8, Francis 12	7,840
58	10	PO SF1	H	Stoke City	W 1-0	1-0		Ward 41	7,537
59	13	PO SF2	A	Stoke City	D 1-1	1-0		Beaumont 1	(16,070)
60	16	AGT Fin	N	Stoke City	L 0-1	0-0			(48,339)
61	24	PO Fin	N	Peterborough Utd	L 1-2	0-2		Francis 87	(35,087)

Best Home League Attendance: 8,129 v Stoke City   **Smallest: 2,745 v Leyton Orient**   **Av Home Att: 4,916**

Goal Scorers: **Compared with 90-91: +1,353**

League (75):	Gannon 16 (3 pens), Francis 15, Preece 13, Barras 5 (1 pen), Wheeler 5, Frain 4 (1 pen), Opponents 3 (pen), Kilner 3 (2 pens) Lillis 2, W Williams 2, Beaumont 2, Finley, P Williams, Ward, Paskin, Matthews
R/lows C (2):	Wheeler, Francis
FA Cup (3):	Gannon, Francis, Opponents
Autoglass (14):	Francis 8, Gannon 4, Ward, Wheeler
Play-Offs (3):	Beaumont, Francis, Ward

† = After extra-time

550

Redfern D.	Thorpe A.	Williams P.	Frain D.	Williams W.	Barras A.	Gannon J.	Ward P.	Francis K.	Beaumont C.	Kilner A.	Knowles D.	Matthews N.	Wheeler P.	Todd L.	Moore C.	Paskin W.	Edwards N.	Lillis M.	Finley A.	Carstairs J.	Preece A.	Miller D.	Muir J.	Loram M.	Holmes	Referee	
1	2	3	4	5	6	7*	8	9	10	11	S	14														K Redfern	1
1	2	3	4	5	6	7*	8	9	10	11	S		14													T West	2
1	2	3	4	5	6	7	8	9•	10*		12	11	14													M Bailey	3
1	2	3	4•	5	6	7	8	9	10	S	11		14													J Lloyd	4
1	2	3	4	5	6	7	8	9	10•	11	S	14														R Nixon	5
1	6	3	4	5		7	8	9		11	2	S	10	S												C Trussell	6
1	6	3	4•	5		7	8			11	2	9	10	S	14											P Jones	7
1	6	3	4	5		7	8•	9		11*	2	14	10			12										P Taylor	8
1	8	3	4	5	6	7		9		11*	2•	14	10			12										A Smith	9
2	3	14	5	6	7	4	9			11	S		10•			8		1								K Cooper	10
4	3		5	6	7	10	9			14	2					8		1	11•	S						R Poulain	11
4	3		5	6	7	10	9			11	2					8•		1	14	S						R Hamer	12
4	3		5	6	7	10	9•	8*		11	2							1	14	12						E Parker	13
4	3*	12	5	6	7	10		11	8•			14						1	9	2						I Cruickshanks	14
4		2	5	6	7	10		8	14	11•	3							1	9	S						K Barrett	15
2	12	4	5	6	7	10		8		11	3							1	9*	S						B Hill	16
2		4	5	6	7	10		8		11	S	3•						1	9	14						M Peck	17
2	3	4	5	6	7	10	9	8	11				S					1	S							M Reed	18
2	3*	4	5	6	7	10	9	8	14				12					1	11•							T Lunt	19
2					6	7	10	9	8	S	4		S					1	11	5	3					G Poll	20
2					6	7	10	9	8	14•	4		S					1	11	5	3					A Wilkie	21
2		4	5		7	10	9	8	14	S		11•						1		6	3					P Scoble	22
S		4	5	2	7	10	9	8	14	11•		3						1		6						A Bennett	23
12		4	5*		7	8	9	10	11•		2	14						1		6	3					B Coddington	24
S		4	5		7	8	9	10	11	2			3					1		6	S					S Bell	25
S		4	5		7	8•	9	10	11	2			3					1		6	14					T West	26
		4	5	12	7	S	9	10			2		11					1		6*	3	8				J Martin	27
6•		4	5		7	8	9	10	14	2			S					1			3	11				T Holbrook	28
		4	6	5	7	8	9	10			2		3	S				1	S			11				C Wilkes	29
		4	5		7		9	10*	14	2			3	11•				1	8		12				6	J Kirkby	30
		4	5	6	7	8	9	10			2	S	3					1	S			11				J Key	31
		4	5	6	7	8	9	10		11	2		3					1	10	S	S					K Lupton	32
		4	5	6	7	8	9	10			2		3					1		S		11				T Lunt	33
		4	5	6	7	8	9	10*		11	2		3					1	12	S						V Callow	34
		4	5	6	7*	8	9	10			2		3					1	S	12		11				L Dilkes	35
S		4	5	6		8	9	10		2		S	3					1	7			11				R Hart	36
S		4	5	6		8	9	10		2		S	3					1	7			11				R Hamer	37
		4	5	6	7	8	9	10	2			S	3					1	S			11				J Rushton	38
		4	5	6	7*	8	9	10			2	14	3					1	S			11				D Allison	39
7		4	5	6		8		10		2•			9					1	S		3	11	14			J Deakin	40
2					6	7	8	9•	10	S		14						1	4	5	3	11				A Dawson	41
2					6	7	8	9•	10		12	14						1	4*	5	3	11				J Lloyd	42
2		4	5	6		7	8		10	14			9*					1	S		3	11				K Barratt	43
2		4	5			7	8	9*	10•		12	14						1		6	3	11				K Lupton	44
2		4	5			7	8	9				S	11	10				1		6	3	S				J Worrall	45
2•		4*	5			7	8	9	10		12	14						1		6	3	11				R Shepherd	46
2		4	5		12	7	8	9*	10*			14						1		6	3	11				P Wright	47
2		4	5	6	7	8		9•	10			14						1	S		3	11	9•			D Phillips	48
2		4	5	6	7	8			10•									1			3	11	S	14		K Hackett	49
2		4	5	6	7	8			10•									1		12	3	11*	9	14		C Wilkes	50
2		4	5	6	7	8	9	10		S		11	S					1			3					G Courtney	51
2		4	5	6	7	8	9•	10					S					1			3	11	14			S Bell	52
2		4	5	6	7	8	9			S		11	S					1			3					K Hackett	53
2		4	5	6	7	8	9	10					S					1			3	11	S			M Reed	54
2		4	5	6	7	8	9	10										1		3*	14	12	11•			J Watson	55
2		4	5	6	7	8		10		11*		12						1		3	14		9•			I Cruickshanks	56
		4	5	6	7	8	9	10		2•		14	3					1		S		11				G Courtney	57
S		4	5	6	7	8	9	10		2•		13	3					1				11				A Buksh	58
S		4	5	6	7	8	9	10		2		14	3					1				11•				K Hackett	59
12	14*	4	5	6	7	8	9	10		2			11•					1			3					R Hart	60
S		4	5	6	7	8•	9	10		2		14	3					1				11				M Bodenham	61
7	33	12	37	42	33	43	44	34	33	13	28	4	13	17		3		39	9	15	20	23		3	1	**League Appearances**	
1	1	2		2			1	1	5	3	5	9	2	1	2			2		3	2	3	1	3		**Substitute Appearances**	
2	2	2	2	2	2	2	2	2		1		1	0+2													**R/lows Appearances**	
1	1	2	2	2	2	2	2	2		1		1+1		1				1			2		1			**FA Cup Appearances**	
4+1	1+1	8	8	6	8	7	8	5	0+2	5	6	5+1	1	8				3+1	1	3+1					1	**Autoglass Appearances**	
		3	3	3	3	3	3	3		3			0+3	3				3				3				**Play-Offs Appearances**	

Players on Loan: J Paskin (Wolves), N Edwards (Leeds), J Carstairs (Cambridge), M Loram (Torquay)

STOCKPORT COUNTY

Club Colours: Royal blue shirts with light blue and red flecks, white shorts, white stockings
Change Colours: White shirts with thin horizontal red & blue zigzags, blue shorts, blue stockings
Reserves League: Midland Senior League   **'A' Team:** Lancashire League Division 2

Previous Name: Heaton Norris Rovers 1883-88   Heaton Norris 1988-90
Previous League: The Combination 1891-94; Lancashire League 1894-1900; Lancashire Combination 1904-05
Previous Managers: 1900-11 Fred Stewart 1911-14 Harry P Lewis 1914-19 David Ashworth 1919-24 Albert Williams 1924-26 Fred Scotchbrook 1926-31 Lincoln Hyde 1931-32 No Manager 1932-33 Andrew Wilson 1933-36 Fred Westgarth 1936-38 Bob Kelly 1938-39 No Manager 1939-49 Bob Marshall 1949-52 Andy Beattie 1952-56 Dick Duckworth 1956-60 Willie Moir 1960-63 Reg Flewin 1963-65 Trevor Porteous 1965 Bert Trautmann 1966-69 Eddie Quigley 1969 Jimmy Meadows 1969-70 Walter Galbraith 1970-71 Matt Woods 1971-72 Steve Fleet (acting) 1972-74 Brian Doyle 1974-75 Jimmy Meadows 1975-76 Roy Chapman 1976-77 Eddie Quigley 1977-78 Alan Thompson 1978-79 Mike Summerbee 1979-82 Jimmy McGuigan 1982-85 Eric Webster 1985 Colin Murphy 1985-86 Les Chapman 1986 Jimmy Melia 1986-87 Colin Murphy 1987-89 Asa Hartford 1989- Danny Bergara
Honours: Champions Div 3N 1921-22, 1936-37 Champions Div 4 1966-67 Lancashire League 1899-00 Lancashire Combination 1904-05 Divison 3N Cup Winners 1934-35 Autoglass Trophy Finalists 1992
League Career: Elected to Div 2 1900   Failed Re-election 1904   Elected to Div 2 1905
Relegated to Div 3N 1920-21 Promoted to Div 2 1921-22 Relegated to Div 3N 1925-26 Promoted to Div 2 1936-37
Relegated to Div 3N 1937-38 Transferred to Div 3 1958 Relegated to Div 4 1958-59 Promoted to Div 3 1966-67
Relegated to Div 4 1969-70 Promoted to Div 3 1990-91

CLUB RECORDS

Most Appearances for Club: Andy Thorpe 1978-86 & 1987-: Lge 484 + 5 + FAC 14 + Lge Cup 32 + 1 + Others 17 + 1. **Total 547 + 7**
Most Capped Player: Harry Hardy 1, England
Record Goalscorer in a Match: Joe Smith 5 v Southport (h), 6-3, Div 3N, 7.1.1928 Joe Smith 5 v Lincoln City (h), 7-3, Div 3N, 15.9.1928 F Newton 5 v Nelson, 6-1, Div 3N, 21.9.1929 Alf Lythgoe 5 v Southport, 6-1, Div 3N, 25.8.1934 W McNaughton 5 v Mansfield Town, 6-1, Div 3N, 14.12.1935 Jack Connor 5 v Workington (h), 6-0, Div 3N, 8.11.1952 Jack Connor 5 v Carlisle United (h), 8-1, Div 3N, 7.4.1956
Record League Goalscorer in a Season: Alf Lythgoe 46 **In All Competitions:** Alf Lythgoe 47 (League 46 + FA Cup 1) 1933-34
Record League Goalscorer in a Career: Jack Connor 132 **In All Competitions:** Jack Connor 140 (League 132 + FAC 8) 1951-56
Record Transfer Fee Received: £250,000 from West Brom for Paul A Williams, March 1991
Record Transfer Fee Paid: £70,000 to Halifax Town for Neil Matthews, June 1990   £70,000 to Sheffield Utd for Jim Gannon in instalments March 1990-Nov 1991
Best Performances: League: 10th Div 2 1905-06 **FA Cup:** 5th Round 1935, 1950 **League Cup:** 4th Round 1972-73
Most League Points: (2pts a win) 64, Div 4, 1966-67 (3pts a win) 82, Div 4, 1990-91
Most League Goals: 115, Div 3N, 1933-34
Record Victory and Most Goals Scored in a League Match: 13-0 v Halifax Town, Div 3N, 6.1.1934 (Joint League record victory)
Record First Class Cup Victory: 6-2 v West Auckland (a), FA Cup Round 1, 14.11.1959
Record League Defeat: 1-8 v Chesterfield, Div 2, 19.4.1902 0-7 v Burton Utd, Div 2, 10.10.1903 0-7 v Bristol City, Div 2, 20.1.1906 0-7 v Fulham, Div 2, 8.3.1913 0-7 v Port Vale, Div 3N, 10.4.1954 0-7 v Aldershot, Div 4, 22.2.1964 0-7 v Hull City, Div 4, 29.1.1983
Record Cup Defeat: 0-7 v Portsmouth, FA Cup Round 3, 8.1.1949 0-7 v Crystal Palace, League Cup Round 2 2nd leg, 4.9.1979 0-7 v Sheffield Wednesday, League Cup Round 2 2nd leg, 6.10.1986
Oldest Player in a League Match: Frank Worthington 39 years 150 days, 22.4.1988
Youngest Player in a League Match: David Herd 17 years 51 days, 5.5.1951

LONGEST LEAGUE RUNS

of undefeated matches: 18 (1933)	of league matches without a win: 15 (1989)
of undefeated home matches: 48 (1927-29)	of undefeated away matches: 8 (1921-22, 1929, 1929-30)
without home win: 12 (1986-87)	without an away win: 37 (1901-03)
of league wins: 8 (1927-28)	of home wins: 13 (1928-29, 1930)
of league defeats: 9 (1908-09)	of away wins: 7 (1951)

STOCKPORT COUNTY | APPEARANCES | GOALS

PLAYERS NAME / Honours	Ht	Wt	Birthdate	Birthplace / Transfers	Contract Date	Clubs	League	L/Cup	FA Cup	Other	Lg	L/C	FAC	Oth
GOALKEEPERS														
Neil Edwards	5.10	11.10	05.12.70	Aberdare	10.03.89	Leeds Utd. (T)				1				
W: Y				Loan	17.08.90	Huddersfield Town								
				Loan	03.01.91	Huddersfield Town								
				£5,000	03.09.91	Stockport Co	39		2	11				
David Redfern	6.2	13.12	08.11.62	Sheffield		Sheffield Wed. (T)								
				Loan		Doncaster Rovers								
						Rochdale	87	6	6	5				
via Gainsborough Trinity				£5,000	01.07.89	Stockport Co	42	2		2				
DEFENDERS														
Tony Barras	6.0	12.3	29.03.71	Stockton	06.07.89	Hartlepool Utd. (T)	9+3	2	1	1				
				Free	23.07.90	Stockport Co	70+5	2	2	12	5			
Jim Carstairs	6.0	12.10	29.01.71	St Andrews	23.03.89	Arsenal (T)								
				Loan	06.02.91	Brentford	8			3				
				Free	10.07.91	Cambridge Utd								
					19.02.92	Stockport Co	20			3+1				
Alan Finley	6.3	14.3	10.02.67	Liverpool		Marine								
				Free	01.07.88	Shrewsbury Town	60+3	3	2	4	2			
				Loan	24.08.90	Stockport Co	16			1	3			
				£25,000	20.09.90	Stockport Co	20+3	2	1	1	1			
James Gannon	6.2	12.6	07.09.68	London		Dundalk								
						Sheffield Utd								
				Loan	22.02.90	Halifax Town	2							
				£40,000	07.03.90	Stockport Co	91	4	3	14	23		1	5
David Miller	5.11	11.2	08.01.64	Burnley	11.01.82	Burnley (A)	27+5	2	1	2+1	3			
				Loan	18.03.83	Crewe Alexandra	3							
					16.07.85	Tranmere Rovers	25+4	1	4	2	1			1
						Colne Dynamoes								
					18.12.86	Preston N.E	50+8	6	0+1	7+2	2			
				Loan	16.02.89	Burnley	4							
				£30,000	14.09.89	Carlisle Utd	108+1	6	4	7	7			
				£25,000	31.03.92	Stockport Co	0+3							
Bill R Williams	5.10	12.7	09.10.60	Littleborough	02.09.81	Rochdale	89+6	6	4	2	2			
				Free	17.07.85	Stockport Co	104	7	5	3	1			
				£50,000	07.10.88	Manchester City	0+1							
					02.12.88	Stockport Co	124+1	7	5	16	5			
Paul R Williams	5.6	10.7	11.09.69	Leicester		Stockport Co	37+7	2	1	3+4	3			1
MIDFIELD														
David Frain	5.8	10.8	11.10.62	Sheffield	07.09.85	Sheffield Utd. (A)	35+9	3+2		2	6			
				Free	18.07.88	Rochdale	42	2	2	2	12		1	
				£50,000	21.07.89	Stockport Co	105+6	5	3+2	20	9			
Darren Knowles	5.6	10.1	08.10.70	Sheffield	01.07.89	Sheffield Utd. (T)								
				£3,000	14.09.89	Stockport Co	41+11	0+1		13+1				
FORWARDS														
Chris Beaumont	5.11	11.7	05.12.65	Denaby		Denaby Utd								
					21.07.88	Rochdale	31+3	0+1	2	2	7	1	1	
				£8,000	21.07.89	Stockport Co	97+4	3	5	15+1	22			2
Kevin Francis	6.7	15.08	06.12.67	Moseley	02.02.89	Derby County	0+10	1+2	1+2	0+1			1	
				£45,000	21.02.91	Stockport Co	45+3	2	2	11	20	1	1	9
Neil Matthews	5.11	12.0	19.09.66	Grimsby	25.09.84	Grimsby Town (A)	9+2			1				
				Loan	09.11.85	Scunthorpe Utd	1							
				Loan	10.10.86	Halifax Town	9			2				
				Loan	23.03.87	Bolton W	1							
					20.08.87	Halifax Town	99+6	4	10	9+2	29		1	5
				£70,000	03.07.90	Stockport Co	26+12	1	0+1	1	14			
				Loan	25.09.91	Halifax Town	3							
Johnny Muir	6.2		26.04.63	Sedgley		Dudley Tow								
				£5,000	19.02.90	Doncaster Rovers	64+11	3		5	18	1		1
					28.02.92	Stockport Co	3+1							
Andrew Preece	6.1		27.03.67	Evesham	31.08.88	Northampton T	0+1	0+1		0+1				
						Worcester								
					23.05.90	Wrexham	44+7	5+1	1	4	6	1	2	3
				£10,000	18.12.91	Stockport Co	23+2			3	13			
Lee Todd	5.5	10.3	07.03.72	Hartlepool		Hartlepool Utd. (T)								
				Free	23.07.90	Stockport Co	29+4	1+1	2	8+1				
Peter Ward	5.10	11.7	15.10.64	Durham		Chester le Street								
					07.01.87	Huddersfield Town	24+13	1+1	2	1	2			
				Free		Rochdale	83+1	5	7	5	10		1	
				Swap + £35	06.06.91	Stockport Co	44	2	2	10				1
Paul Wheeler	5.7	11.2	03.01.65	Caerphilly	05.01.83	Bristol Rovers (A)								
E: S.;WC'88				Free		Aberaman Ath								
				Free	29.08.85	Cardiff City	72+29	4+2	3+1	5+3	10	2	1	1
				N.C	16.10.89	Hull City	0+5							
				Free	01.02.90	Hereford Utd	34+20	0+1	0+2	5	12			
				Free	14.08.91	Stockport Co	13+9	0+2	1	6+3	5	1		1

ADDITIONAL CONTRACT PLAYERS

Jason Astley, Alan Dean, Darren Field, Carl Holmes, Neil Homer, Richard Milne, Christian Moore, Lee Nolan, Jason Robinson, Steven Salter, John Scally, (G) Wayne Shepherd, Adrian Shinn, Stephen Weir, Leigh Williams.

LEADING LEAGUE GOALSCORERS SEASONS 1985-86 – 1991-92

1985-86	MARK LEONARD	18	1986-87	VERNON ALLATT	10
1987-88	BOB COLVILLE	13	1988-89	ROGER WYLDE	12
1989-90	BRETT ANGELL	23	1990-91	CHRIS BEAUMONT	15
				PAUL A WILLIAMS	15

1991-92   **JIM GANNON   16**

EDGELEY PARK Hardcastle Road, Edgeley, Stockport, Cheshire SK3 9DD

Capacity: 8,500   **Covered Standing:**   **Seating:** 1,800

Tel: Ground: 061 480 8888   **Ticket Sales:** As ground number   **Clubcall:** 0898 12 16 38

All premium rate calls (0898/0891) cost 36p per minute cheap rate and 48p per minute at all other times. Call costings correct at time of going to press.

ATTENDANCES
Highest: 27,833 v Liverpool, FA Cup Round 5, 11.2.1950

Lowest: 1,000 v Carlisle United, Freight Rover Trophy, 8.12.1986

Record Receipts: £26,983 v Chesterfield, Div 2 Play-Off, 16.5.1990

Season Tickets:
Stands: £182 (Concessions £100)
Ground: £122.50 (Concessions £80)

Executive Box Season Tickets: £400

Cost of Stand Tickets: Main Stand: £9; juniors £5.00
Terraces: Adults £6, juveniles/OAP £4

Match and Ticket Information: Seats can be reserved in the main stand by attending the ground with remittance

Car Parking: Ample street parking around the ground

Nearest Railway Station: Edgeley (short walk to ground)

How to get to the ground

From North, South and West: Use Motorway M63 until end then join A560 S.P. Stockport. In 0.4m turn right into Edgeley Road. In 1m turn right into Caroline Street for Stockport County FC

From East: Use A6 or A560 into Stockport town centre, then turn left into Greek Street. At roundabout take 2nd exit into Castle Street then turn left into Caroline Street for Stockport County FC

Value Rating: ★ ★ ★

Programme Editor: Steve Bellis

Price of 1992-93 Programme: £1.20
Number of Pages: 52
Subscriptions: £40 inc postage

Local Newspapers: Stockport Express Advertiser, Stockport Messenger

Local Radio Stations: Radio Piccadilly, G.M.R.

STOKE CITY　　　Division 2

Formed: 1863　　　　**Turned Professional:** 1885　　　　**Ltd Co:** 1908

SPONSORED BY: Ansells　　　　**NICKNAME:** The Potters

President
Sir Stanley Matthews

Chairman
P Coates

Directors
K A Humphreys (Vice-Chairman)
R D Kenyon
P J Wright
R C Lee

Associate Director
A W Waddington

Secretary
M J Potts (0782 413511)

Team Manager
Lou Macari

Assistant Manager
Chic Bates

Reserve Team Coach
Peter Henderson

Youth Team Coach
Ashley Grimes

Commercial Manager
M Cullerton (0782 45840)

Groundsman
D Hartley

Club Statistician for the Directory
Wade Martin

A GIANT awakens.

May be this is the statement of a fan whose hopes have for so long exceeded the realities of achievement but at last the true Stokie can look back on a season of progress rather than decline.

The depths to which the club and team sank in the closing days of the 1990-91 season can only now be put in perspective and accepted because the corner has been decisively turned. That turning point was undoubtedly the directors' inspired choice of Lou Macari as manager as he vacated the manager's job at Birmingham. With an apparent dearth of players and little or no money he set about the task of achieving his initial ambitions for the club 'winning some matches'. The facts are that we maintained an automatic promotion place for a large part of the season, eventually made the play-offs and won the Autoglass Trophy at Wembley in May. Bearing in mind what had gone before the fact that, all associated with the club were deeply disappointed that promotion to the new First Division was not achieved, seems to sum up the progress made.

Macari made few of the promises of his predecessor (thankfully) but with stealth in the transfer market he added to his squad with the likes of Steve Foley (£50,000 from Swindon Town), Vince Overson (£55,000 from Birmingham City – this was close to theft!), Mark Stein (£100,000 from Oxford United – this was theft!) and Ronnie Sinclair (£25,000 from Bristol City). To these can be added players taken on loan to advantage including Jason Kearton (Everton), Kevin Russell (Leicester City), Adrian Heath (Manchester City) and Tim Steel (Wolverhampton Wanderers).

He and the rest of his excellent management and coaching team also achieved more from what they inherited with Carl Beeston playing as a powerhouse in midfield and Bertie Biggins with 28 League and Cup goals being the best haul of his career. Lee Sandford and Paul Ware also progressed over the season after slowish starts. The championship of the Second Division of the Pontins Central League was also secured as regular crowds of 2,000 saw the Reserves go on a winning and goalscoring run of the highest order.

There were numerous highlights, the two Rumbelows games with Liverpool including the draw at Anfield, the successful battles with Midlands rivals West Brom and Birmingham and of course Wembley when close on 35,000 fans cheered Stoke to the immortal strains of Deliah – it was a great day out for the Stokie family. Some how it at last sent a signal that one of the great footballing cities of the country had a team on the up and shortly to take its place with the best in the land. Thanks Lou.

Wade Martin

Back row L-R: Alex McLeish, Tony Gallimore, Carl Beeston, Vince Overson, Ian Wright, Ian Cranson, Marcus Jones, Adrian Potts, Lee Sandford, Mark Devlin. **Middle row:** Matthew Wildman, Chris Male, David Kevan, Tony Kelly, John Butler, Peter Fox, Ronnie Sinclair, Mark Reid, Gareth Jennings, Danny Martin, Tony Green, Keith Long. **Front row:** Robert Brunton, Gary Pick, Paul Ware, Paul Rennie, Mark Stein, Mike Macari, Steve Foley, Kevin Russell, Graham Harbey, Jason Percival.

STOKE CITY

DIVISION THREE: 4th **FA CUP:** 1st RND **RUMBELOWS CUP:** 2nd RND **AUTOGLASS:** WINNERS

M	DATE	COMP.	VEN	OPPONENTS	RESULT	H/T	LGE POS	GOALSCORERS/GOAL TIMES	ATTEN-DANCE
1	A 17	BL	A	Bradford City	L 0-1	0-1			(7,556)
2	21	RC 1/1	H	Chesterfield	W 1-0	1-0		Ellis 20	7,815
3	24	BL	H	Bournemouth	D 1-1	1-1	20	Biggins (pen) 17	10,011
4	27	RC 1/2	A	Chesterfield	W 2-1	1-0		Kelly 22, Beeston 66	(5,391)
5	31	BL	A	Peterborough Utd	D 1-1	1-1	20	Biggins 1	(7,174)
6	S 4	BL	H	Shrewsbury Town	W 1-0	0-0	14	Biggins 53	10,182
7	7	BL	A	Darlington	W 1-0	0-0	7	Ellis 57	(4,230)
8	14	BL	H	Fulham	D 2-2	1-0	7	Biggins 26, Cranson 53	10,567
9	17	BL	H	Hartlepool United	W 3-2	2-0	8	Biggins 37, 39, Butler 75	9,394
10	21	BL	A	Preston North End	D 2-2	1-1	8	Biggins 40, 58	(6,345)
11	25	RC 2/1	A	Liverpool	D 2-2	1-1		Cranson 28, Kelly 77	(18,389)
12	28	BL	H	Stockport County	D 2-2	2-0	8	Biggins (pen) 14, 28	12,954
13	O 5	BL	A	Chester City	D 0-0	0-0	10		(4,212)
14	9	RC 2/2	H	Liverpool	L 2-3	0-1		Biggins (pen) 77, 86	22,335
15	12	BL	H	Bolton Wanderers	W 2-0	1-0	6	Biggins 16, Scott 80	12,420
16	19	BL	A	Swansea City	L 1-2	0-2	10	Ellis 88	(3,363)
17	22	AGT Pre	A	Walsall	W 2-0	0-0		Sandford 51, 70	(3,578)
18	26	BL	H	Leyton Orient	W 2-0	1-0	6	Biggins 36, Cranson 71	9,555
19	N 2	BL	H	Huddersfield Town	L 0-2	0-2	8		10,116
20	5	BL	A	Bury	W 3-1	1-1	6	Ellis 4, 78, Overson 53	(3,245)
21	9	BL	A	Exeter City	D 0-0	0-0	5		(5,309)
22	16	FAC 1	H	Telford United	D 0-0	0-0			9,984
23	23	BL	H	Torquay United	W 3-0	2-0	5	Biggins 2, Stein 34, 59	9,124
24	26	FAC 1R	A	Telford United	L 1-2	0-1		Beeston 81	(4,032)
25	30	BL	A	West Bromwich A.	D 2-2	1-1	5	Overson 40, 52	(17,240)
26	D 14	BL	H	Wigan Athletic	W 3-0	2-0	5	Stein 18, Kelly 42, Biggins 81	8,419
27	18	AGT Pre	H	Birmingham City	W 3-1	2-1		Barnes 15, Stein (pen) 29, Ware 73	5,932
28	21	BL	A	Bournemouth	W 2-1	1-1	4	Biggins 10, Kelly 76	(5,436)
29	26	BL	H	Peterborough Utd	D 3-3	2-2	5	Kevan 7, Stein 30, Biggins 70	14,732
30	28	BL	H	Bradford City	D 0-0	0-0	5		12,208
31	J 1	BL	A	Shrewsbury Town	L 0-1	0-1	5		(8,557)
32	4	BL	H	Birmingham City	W 2-1	0-0	5	Ware 53, Biggins 77	18,914
33	11	BL	A	Brentford	L 0-2	0-1	6		(9,004)
34	14	AGT 1	H	Cardiff City	W 3-0	1-0		Biggins 31, 80 (pen), Stein 76	4,851
35	18	BL	H	Reading	W 3-0	1-0	6	Jones (og) 24, Butler 64, Stein 71	10,835
36	25	BL	A	Hull City	W 1-0	1-0	4	Russell 20	(4,996)
37	F 1	BL	A	Swansea City	W 2-1	1-0	3	Ware 41, Beeston 90	11,299
38	5	AGT 2	H	Walsall	W 3-1	3-0		Ware 18, Beeston 24, Stein 32	7,381
39	8	BL	A	Leyton Orient	W 1-0	1-0	2	Beeston 4	(7,153)
40	12	BL	H	West Bromwich A.	W 1-0	1-0	1	Stein 29	23,645
41	15	BL	A	Wigan Athletic	L 0-1	0-1	2		(5,695)
42	22	BL	H	Brentford	W 2-1	1-0	1	Butler 11, Stein 65	16,417
43	29	BL	A	Birmingham City	D 1-1	0-1	1	Barnes 89	(22,162)
44	M 4	BL	A	Reading	W 4-3	2-2	1	Stein 28, Foley 31, Ware 60, McPherson (og) 66	(4,362)
45	7	BL	H	Hull City	L 2-3	0-1	1	Barnes 53, Stein 73	13,563
46	11	BL	H	Bury	L 1-2	0-0	1	Barnes 86	12,385
47	14	BL	A	Huddersfield Town	W 2-1	2-0	1	Biggins 27, Stein 27	(10,156)
48	17	AGT SSF	A	Leyton Orient	W 1-0	1-0		Stein 24	(3,792)
49	21	BL	H	Exeter City	W 5-2	3-1	1	Biggins 16, Stein 33, Beeston 42 Grimes 61, Steele 90	13,634
50	28	BL	A	Torquay United	L 0-1	0-1	1		(3,260)
51	31	BL	A	Fulham	D 1-1	0-1	1	Stein 72	(5,779)
52	A 3	BL	H	Darlington	W 3-0	2-0	1	Biggins (pen) 10, 20, Stein 69	13,579
53	6	AGT SF1	H	Peterborough Utd	D 3-3	2-1		Biggins 3, 5, Sandford 66	14,355
54	11	BL	A	Hartlepool United	D 1-1	1-1	1	Stein 44	(4,360)
55	15	AGT SF2	A	Peterborough Utd	W 1-0	0-0		Ware 51	(12,214)
56	18	BL	H	Preston North End	W 2-1	1-1	2	Stein 44, Biggins (pen) 51	16,151
57	20	BL	A	Stockport County	D 0-0	0-0	2		(8,129)
58	25	BL	H	Chester City	L 0-1	0-0	2		18,474
59	M 2	BL	A	Bolton Wanderers	L 1-3	1-0	4	Stein 7	(9,997)
60	10	PO SF 1	A	Stockport County	L 0-1	0-1			(7,537)
61	13	PO SF 2	H	Stockport County	D 1-1	0-1		Stein 81	16,170
62	16	AGT Fin	N	Stockport County	W 1-0	0-0		Stein 65	(48,339)

Best Home League Attendance: 23,645 v West Bromwich A.   Smallest: 8,419 v Wigan Athletic   **Av Home Att: 12,982**

Goal Scorers: Compared with 90-91: +1,408

League (68): Biggins 22 (4 pens), Stein 16, Ellis 4, Ware 3, Barnes 3, Butler 3, Overson 3, Beeston 3, Cranson 2, Kelly 2, Opponents 2 Steele, Kevan, Scott, Russell, Foley

R/lows C (7): Biggins 2 (1 pen), Kelly 2, Cranson, Beeston, Ellis

FA Cup (1): Beeston

Autoglass (17): Stein 5 (1 pen), Biggins 4 (1 pen), Sandford 3, Ware 3, Barnes, Beeston

Play-Offs (1): Stein

Keaton J.	Fox P.	Butler J.	Cranson I.	Blake N.	Fowler L.	Kevan D.	Gallimore A.	Beeston C.	Kelly A.	Biggins W.	Sandford L.	Kennedy M.	Ellis A.	Scott I.	Overson V.	Barnes P.	Stein M.	Wright I.	Ware P.	Sinclair R.	Russell K.	Grimes A.	Foley S.	Steele T.	Heath A.	Referee	
1		2	3	4	5•	6	7	8	9	10	11	S	14													C Trussell	1
	1	2	3	5	11	4		8	9	10•	6	S	7			14										**H King**	2
1		2		5	11	4	14	8	9	10	6	S	7	3•												S Bell	3
	1	2	4	5	3	7		8	9•	10		6	12	11*		14										**T Fitzharris**	4
1			7	5	11	4		8	9•	10		6	14	3	2	S										J Moules	5
1			7	5	11	4		8	9•	10	S	6	14	3	2											K Breen	6
1		2	7	5	11	4		8	12•	10*	3	6	9	14												M Peck	7
1		2	7	5	11*	4		8	14	10*	3	6	9													R Shepherd	8
1		2	7	5•	14	4			10	3	6	S	11	8		9										I Hendrick	9
1		5	7	S	11	4		8		10	3	6	S	2		9										I Cruikshanks	10
	1	2	7	S	11			8	14	10	3	6	9•	4	5											**K Lupton**	11
1		2	7	S	11			8		10	3	6	S	4	5	9										R Poulain	12
1		2	7	11				8	S	10	3	6		4	5	9	S									A Dawson	13
	1	2	7*		11	14		8	9•	10	3	6		4	5	12										**A Smith**	14
1		2	7		11	4*		8		10	3	6		12	5	S	9									R Gifford	15
1		2	7	S	11•	4		8		10	3	6	9	14	5											D Frampton	16
1		2	7	S	3	11•		4		10	6		9	8	5		14									**J Key**	17
1		2	7	S	11	4		8	S	10	3	6	9	5												A Wilkie	18
1		2	7	S	11	4		8	14	10	3	6	9•	5												W Burge	19
1		2	7		11*	4		8	S	10	3	6	9	5		12										K Redfearn	20
1		2	7		11	4		8		10	3	6	S	5		9	S									M Pierce	21
	1	2*	7	S	11	4		8		10	3	6	12	5		9										**I Borrett**	22
			7		11	4		8		10•	3	6	12		14	9*		2	1							P Alcock	23
1			7	14		4		8		10	3•	6	12	11*	5	9		2								**I Borrett**	24
		3	7	S		4		8	11•	10		6		5	14	9		2	1							K Cooper	25
		3	7	S		4		8	11	10		6		5	S	9		2	1							M Reed	26
	1	3•	7	S		4		8	11			6		5	10	9		2								**K Cooper**	27
		3	7			4		8	11	10	S	6		5	S	9		2	1							G Poll	28
		3	7			4		8	11	10	12	6*		5	S	9		2	1							T Lunt	29
		3	7	S		4		8	11•	10	6			5	14	9		2	1							K Barratt	30
		3	7	S		4	6	8	11	10	S			5		9		2	1							P Taylor	31
		3	7			4*		8		10	6		S	5		9		2	1		11	S				R Milford	32
		3	7			4*		8		10	6	S	12	5		9		2	1		11					P Scoble	33
	1		7			4		8	11*	10	6	2	12	5	14	9						3•				**K Breen**	34
	3•		7			4		8		10	6			5		9			1	11	14	2				B Coddington	35
	3		7	5		4•		8			6		10			9		S	1	11	14	2				P Harrioson	36
			7	5•		4		8			6	12	10*			9		3	1	11	14	2				T Fitzharris	37
	1	3	7	14		4		8		6•			12	5	11	9		2*				10				**D Allison**	38
		3	7	S		4		8		10	6			5	14	9*		11	1		2					G Willard	39
		3	7	S		4		8		10	6			5	S	9		11	1		2					I Hendrick	40
		3	7			4		8		10	6	S		5	14	9		1			2					C Wilkes	41
		3	7			4		8		10	6			5	S	9		1	S		2	11				G Ashby	42
		3	7			4				10	6			14	9	S	5	1		2	11•					R Wiseman	43
		3	7			4				10	6			12	9*	8	5	1		S	2	11				D Frampton	44
	3*		7			4		12			6		S	5	10	9		8	1		2	11				J Worrall	45
	3	S		7		4		7			6	14		5	10	9		8			2	11•				M Peck	46
		3	7			4		6		10				5	S	9		8	1		2	11				E Parker	47
		3	7			4		8		10	6			5	S	9		11			2		S			**B Hill**	48
		3	7					8		10	6*			5	14	9		4•			12	2	11			V Callow	49
		3	7			11*				10	6			5	14	9		4			12	2				H King	50
		3	7	S		6				10				5	S	9		1			8	2	11			G Singh	51
		3	7			2		8		10	6			5*		9					12	4	11			P Don	52
		3	7			5		8		6			S	10*	9		12	1			2	4	11			**D Elleray**	53
1		3	7*	5		2		8		6				S	9		10				12	4	11			S Lodge	54
		3		12		4		8		10	6			5*	14	9		2	1		7		11•			**M Bodenham**	55
		3		5		4		8		10	6					9	7	11	1		S	2			S	B Hill	56
		3		5		4		8		10	6					9	7•	11*	1		14	2	12			J Watson	57
		3	5			4		8		10	6			S	9	S		1			11	2	7			R Pawley	58
		3	5			4*			8		10	6			9	S		1			11	2	S			K Lupton	59
		3	7	5•	8	4*				14		10	6			9			1		11	2	12			A Buksh	60
1		3	7	5*		8	4*		3				10	6			5	S	8		11	2				K Hackett	61
		3	7	5•	8	4*				14		3		7	10	6			9		S	8			3	R Hart	62
16	42	41	12	15	43	2	42	10	41	37	19	9	6	34	3	36	3	22	26	5	4	20	7	5		League Appearances	
			1	1		1	1	3		1	1	6	3	1	10		2			6				1		Substitute Appearances	
4	4	4	2	4	2+1	4	3+1	4	3	3	2+1	3	2	2+0		2	0+2		0+1							R/lows Appearances	
2	1	2	0+1	1	2		2		2	2	0+2	2	1		2		1									FA Cup Appearances	
1	5	7	8	1+1	1	8		7	3	5	8	1	1+2	1	7	2+1	7		4+1		1+2	5				Autoglass Appearances	
	2	2	2	2		1	0+1	2	2			2			2		2	1				2	1		0+1	Play-Offs Appearances	

Also Played: Posn.(Game): Rennie 14(27)11•(41), Bent 8•(50)S(51), Pressman 1(46,47,48,49,50,53)

STOKE CITY

Club Colours: Red & white striped shirts, white shorts, white stockings
Change Colours: Purple & lilac shirts with amber trim, purple shorts
Reserves League: Pontins Central League Division 1

Previous League: Southern League; Birmingham League and Football Alliance
Previous Managers: Tom Slaney 1875-82   Walter Cox 1882   Harry Lockett 1882-90   J Bradshaw 1890-92   A Reeves 1892-95   J Rowley 1895-97   A Austerberry 1897-1908   Jock Rutherford 1923   Tom Mather 1923-35   Bob McGrory 1935-52   Frank Taylor 1952-60   Tony Waddington 1960-67   George Eastham 1977-78   Alan A'Court 1978   Alan Durban 1978-81   Ritchie Barker 1981-83   Bill Asprey 1983-85   Mick Mills 1985-89   Alan Ball 1989-91   Graham Paddon 1991   Lou Macari 1991-
Honours: Champions Division 2 1932-33, 1962-63;   Champions Division 3N 1926-27;   League Cup Winners 1971-72;   Watney Cup Winners 1973;   Autoglass Trophy Winners 1991-92
League Career: Division 1 1888-90   Relegated to Div 2 1890   Promoted to Div 1 1891-92 Relegated to Div 2 1907-08   Re-elected to Div 2 1919   Promoted to Div 1 1921-22   Relegated to Div 2 1922-23 Relegated to Div 3N 1925-26   Promoted to Div 2 1926-27   Promoted to Div 1 1932-33   Relegated to Div 2 1952-53 Promoted to Div 1 1962-63   Relegated to Div 2 1976-77   Promoted to Div 1 1978-79   Relegated to Div 2 1984-85 Relegated to Div 3 1989-90

CLUB RECORDS

Most Appearances for Club: Eric Skeels (1959-76): League 495 + 12, FA Cup 42 + 2, League Cup 36 + 2, Europe 1, Texaco & Watney Cups 1 each **Total 592**
Most Capped Player: Gordon Banks, England, 36 caps
Record Goalscorer in a Match: Neville Coleman, 7 v Lincoln City 8-0 (h), Division 2, 23.2.1957
Record League Goalscorer in a Season: Freddie Steele, 33, Div 1, 1936-37   **In All Competitions:** Charles Wilson, 38 (League 32, FA Cup 6), 1927-28
Record League Goalscorer in a Career: Freddie Steele, 142, 1934-49   **In All Competitions:** John Ritchie, 171 (League 135, League Cup 18, FA Cup 15, Others 3) 1962-66 & 1969-75
Record Transfer Fee Received: £750,000 from Everton for Peter Beagrie, October 1989
Record Transfer Fee Paid: £450,000 to Sheffield Wednesday for Ian Cranson, July 1989
Best Performances: League: Fourth in Div 1, 1935-36 & 1946-47   **FA Cup:** Semi-Finals 1889-90, 1970-71, 1971-72   **League Cup:** Winners 1971-72
Most League Points: (3pts a win) 77, Div 3, 1991-92   (2pts a win) 63, Div 3N, 1926-27
Record League Victory and Most Goals Scored in a League Match: 9-0 v Plymouth Argyle, Div 2, 17.12.1960   10-3 v West Bromwich Albion, Division 1, 4.2.1937
Most Goals Scored in a First Class Cup Tie: 7-1 v Burnley, FA Cup Round 2, 20.2.1896
Record League Defeat: 0-10 v Preston North End, Div 1, 14.9.1889
European Competitions entered: UEFA Cup 1972-73, 1974-75
Oldest Player in a League Match: Sir Stanley Matthews, 50 years, 5 days v Fulham, 6.2.1965
Youngest Player in a League Match: Peter Bullock, 16 years, 163 days v Swansea Town, 19.4.1958

LONGEST LEAGUE RUNS

of undefeated matches: 18 (1962)	**of league matches without a win:** 17 (1984, 1989)
of undefeated home matches: 23 (1973-74)	**of undefeated away matches:** 11 (1978-79)
without home win: 12 (1989)	**without an away win:** 30 (1897-99)
of league wins: 9 (1895)	**of home wins:** 11 (1895)
of league defeats: 11 (1985)	**of away wins:** 5 (1922, 1947)

BARCLAYS

LOCAL BRANCH
Stoke-on-Trent
75 Church Street
Stoke-on-Trent ST4 1DG
Tel: 0782 744575

BARCLAYBANK MACHINE

BARCLAYS BUSINESS CENTRE
Hanley Business Centre
PO Box No. 202
36 Town Road
Hanley
Stoke-on-Trent ST1 2PJ
Tel: 0782 202551

BARCLAYBANK MACHINE

STOKE CITY

PLAYERS NAME Honours	Ht	Wt	Birthdate	Birthplace Transfers	Contract Date	Clubs	League	L/Cup	FA Cup	Other	Lg	L/C	FAC	Oth
APPEARANCES														
GOALS														
GOALKEEPERS														
Scott Barrett	6.0	12.11	02.04.63	Alvaston	27.09.84	Wolverhampton W	30	1	1	3				
				£10,000	24.07.87	Stoke City	51	2	3	4				
				Loan	10.01.90	Colchester Utd	13							
				Loan	22.03.90	Stockport Co	10			2				
Peter Fox	5.10	12.4	05.07.57	Scunthorpe	01.06.75	Sheffield Wed. (A)	49		3					
				Loan	22.12.77	Barnsley	1	1						
				£15,000	04.03.78	Stoke City	399	32	22	14				
Ronnie Sinclair	5.9	11.12	19.11.64	Stirling	30.10.82	Nottm. Forest (A)								
S:Y,S				Loan	01.03.84	Wrexham	11			1				
				£10,000	27.06.86	Leeds Utd	8	1						
Loan Halifax (01.03.87 4lg				Loan	23.12.88	Halifax Town	10			1				
				Free	01.09.89	Bristol City	44	3	5	3				
Loan Walsall (05.09.91) 10lg, 1oth				£25,000	09.01.92	Stoke City	26			2				
DEFENDERS														
Carl Beeston	5.9	10.3	30.06.67	Stoke	01.07.85	Stoke City (A)	154+5	10	5+1	12	9	1	1	2
E:u21.1														
John Butler	5.11	11.7	07.02.62	Liverpool		Prescot Ca								
				£100	15.01.82	Wigan Ath	238+7	17+1	20+1	18	15		2	
				£100,000	23.12.88	Stoke City	142	10	3	12	6			
Ian Cranson	5.11	12.4	02.07.64	Easington	05.07.82	Ipswich Town (A)	130+1	15	11+1	7	5			
E: u21.5				£450,000	24.03.88	Sheffield Wed	29+1	2	2	1				
				£450,000	25.07.89	Stoke City	65+2	6	5	11	4	1		
Graham Harbey	5.8	11.6	29.08.64	Chesterfield	03.08.82	Derby County (A)	35+5	5	1+2	2	1	1		
Div.2.87				£65,000	21.07.87	Ipswich Town	53+6	7+1	2	8	1	2		
				£80,000	06.12.89	West Brom A	97	5	6	5	2			
				£80,000	06.07.92	Stoke City								
Vince Overson	6.0	13.0	15.05.62	Kettering		Corby								
Div3'82, AMC'91				16.11.79	Burnley (A)	207+4	9	19	10	6	1		
				Free	11.06.86	Birmingham City	179+3	11+1	8	11	4			1
				£55,000	29.08.91	Stoke City	34+1	2	2	7	3			
Lee Sandford	6.1	12.2	22.04.68	Basingstoke	04.12.85	Portsmouth (A)	66+6	11	4	2+1	1			
E: Y.2				£140,000	22.12.89	Stoke City	92+1	6	6	12	4		1	3
MIDFIELD														
Steve Foley	5.7	10.12	04.10.62	Liverpool	02.09.80	Liverpool (A)								
				Loan	16.12.83	Fulham	2+1							
				Free	20.08.84	Grimsby Town	31	6	3		2	2	1	
				Free	17.09.85	Sheffield Utd	56+10	5	5	2+1	14	3	1	
				£40,000	24.06.87	Swindon Town	142+9	14+2	10	12+1	23	1	2	3
				£50,000	16.01.92	Stoke City	20			6	1			
David Kevan	5.8	9.10	31.08.68	Wigtown	02.09.86	Notts County (A)	82+7	4	6	9	3		1	
Loan Cardiff City (28.09.89) 6+1				£75,000	25.01.90	Stoke City	64+1	3+1	2	11+1	1			
				Loan	21.02.91	Maidstone Utd	3							
Paul Ware	5.8	11.2	07.11.70	Congleton	15.11.88	Stoke City (A)	70+16	4+1	4+1	8+1	6			3
FORWARDS														
Wayne Biggins	5.11	11.0	20.11.61	Sheffield	22.11.79	Lincoln City	8				1			
Div.2'86		via Kings Lynn & Matlock	£7,500	04.02.84	Burnley	78	6	3	7	29	1	1	5
				£40,000		Norwich City	66+13	6	4	6+2	16	2		3
				£150,000	15.07.88	Manchester City	29+3	4	2		9	1		
				£250,000	10.08.89	Stoke City	112+2	8	6	10	44	2		5
Tony Ellis	5.11	11.0	20.10.64	Salford		Horwich RMI								
via Northwich Victoria				22.08.86	Oldham Ath	5+3	1		1				
				£23,000	06.10.87	Preston N.E	80+6	3	5	11+1	26			5
				£250,000	20.12.89	Stoke City	66+11	5+1	1+4	3+2	19	1		
Tony Kelly	5.9		14.02.66	Coventry		St Albans								
				£20,000	29.01.90	Stoke City	31+20	5+2		3+1	5	3		
				Loan	30.01.92	Hull City								
Kevin Russell	5.8	10.10	06.12.66	Brighton		Brighton & H.A. (A)								
E: Y.6				Free	09.10.84	Portsmouth	3+1	0+1	0+1	1+1	1			
				£10,000	17.07.87	Wrexham	84	4	4	8	43	1		3
				£175,000	20.06.89	Leicester City	24+19	0+1	1	5	10			2
				Loan	06.09.90	Peterborough U	7				3			
				Loan	17.01.91	Cardiff City	3							
				Loan	07.11.91	Hereford Utd	3		1		1			1
				Loan	02.01.92	Stoke City								
				£95,000	16.07.92	Stoke City	5				1			
Graham Shaw	5.8	10.1	07.06.67	Newcastle (Staffs)	10.06.85	Stoke City (A)	83+16	7	2+4	3+2	18	2	1	2
				£70,000	24.07.89	Preston N.E	68+7	3	2	10	15	5		6
						Stoke City								
Mark Stein	5.6	10.0	29.01.66	S. Africa	31.01.84	Luton Town (A)	41+13	4+1	9		19		3	1
E: u19.2, Y.1, LgC'88				Loan	28.02.86	Aldershot	2				1			
				£300,000	26.08.88	Q.P.R	20+13	4	2+1	4	4	2	1	
				P.E	15.09.89	Oxford Utd	72+10	4	2+1	3	18			
				£100,000	07.11.91	Stoke City	36		2	9	16			6

ADDITIONAL CONTRACT PLAYERS

Jame Arnold, Robert Brunton, Mark Delvin, Tony Gallimore, Tony Green, Gareth Jennings, Marcus Jones, Keith Long, Michael Macari, Chris Male, Alex McLeish, James Mulligan, Jason Percival, Mark Reid, Paul Rennie, William Turley, Matt Wileman, Ian Wright.

LEADING LEAGUE GOALSCORERS SEASONS 1985-86 – 1991-92

1985-86	**KEITH BERTSCHIN**	19	1986-87	**CARL SAUNDERS**	14
1987-88	**PHIL HEATH**	8	1988-89	**PETER BEAGRIE**	8
1989-90	**WAYNE BIGGINS**	10	1990-91	**WAYNE BIGGINS**	12

1991-92   **WAYNE BIGGINS**   **22**

VICTORIA GROUND   Stoke-on-Trent, Staffs ST4 4EG

Capacity: 25,409   **Covered Standing:** 15,759   **Seating:** 9,650

Tel: Ground: 0782 413511   **Ticket Sales:** 0782 413961   **Clubcall:** 0898 888 654

All premium rate calls (0898/0891) cost 36p per minute cheap rate and 48p per minute at all other times. Call costings correct at time of going to press.

GROUNDS
Sweeting Fields 1875-78; Victoria Road 1878-

ATTENDANCES
Highest: 51,380 v Arsenal, Division 1, 29.3.1937
Lowest: 3,516 v Coventry City, Full Members Cup, 18.9.1985

RECORD RECEIPTS (with previous records)
£109,000 v Stockport Co. Play-offs, 13.5.1992
£96,000 v Liverpool, FA Cup 3rd Round, 9.1.1988
£58,000 v Manchester United, Division 1, 20.12.1981

VICTORIA ROAD
First game: Talke Rangers (Friendly), 25.3.1878
First floodlit game: v Port Vale, 10.10.1956
Internationals: England v Wales, 1889, 1893
England v Ireland, 1936

Season Tickets:
Stands: £198, juv/OAP £99
Ground: £126, juv/OAP £63

Executive Box Season Tickets: Consult Commercial Manager

Cost of Stand Tickets: Seats: £9, juv/OAP £5.50
Terraces: adults £6, juniors/OAP £4.50

Match and Ticket Information: Bookable two weeks before each match from ticket office – 0782 413961. Membership scheme – details only from club Adult/OAP £3 (for 3 seasons), Junior £1 (for 1 season)

Car Parking: Whieldon Road Car Park £1. Also street parking

Nearest Railway Station: Stoke (0782 411411)

How to get to the ground

From North, West and South: Use Motorway M6 until Junction 15, leave motorway and follow signs Stoke A5006 then join A500. In 0.8m branch left and shortly at roundabout take 2nd exit into Campbell Road for Stoke City FC

From East: Use A50 into Stoke town centre and at crossroads turn left into Lonsdale Street for Campbell Road for Stoke City FC

Value Rating: ★ ★ ★

Programme Editor: Tony Tams

Price of 1992-93 Programme: £1.20
Number of Pages: 36

Subscriptions: £36 UK, £42 Overseas

Local Newspapers: The Sentinel, North Staffordshire Advertiser

Local Radio Stations: Radio Stoke BBC, Signal Radio

SUNDERLAND

Division 1

Formed: 1879   **Turned Professional:** 1886   **Ltd Co:** 1906

SPONSORED BY: VAUX   **NICKNAME:** The Rokerites

Chairman
R S Murray FCCA

Directors
G S Wood (Vice Chairman)
J Wood
J Featherstone
G Davidson FCA

General Manager/Secretary
G Davidson FCA

Team Manager
Malcolm Crosby

Assistant Manager
Bobby Ferguson

Youth Development Officer
Jim Morrow

Reserve Team Coach
Roger Jones

Youth Team Coach
Jonathan Trigg

Commercial Manager
A King

Physiotherapist
S Smelt

Stadium Manager
A H Bailey

Club Statistician for the Directory
Eddie Brennan

SEASON 1991-92 will live long in the memories of Sunderland fans for many reasons. Nine months which saw record transfer fees shattered, a change of manager, another relegation battle and a thrilling F.A. Cup run, spearheaded by a bargain from Brighton, that swept the club to Wembley.

However, back in August, thoughts of the twin towers were a distant dream. Sunderland were strongly fancied to make a quick return to the top flight following relegation last term. No new signings were made by manager Denis Smith.

An indifferent start saw the Roker men off the pace in 15th place after seven games. A 4-1 win at Charlton lifted them to 7th, the highest achieved all season. More significantly, crowd idol Marco Gabbiadini scored a six minute hat-trick that turned out to be his last goals for the club. Six days later Crystal Palace paid £1.8m for his services.

With cash to spend, Smith signed defender Anton Rogan from Celtic and took striker Peter Beagrie on loan from Everton. Inconsistent performances abounded, none worse than the humiliating 1-6 aggregate defeat by third division Huddersfield in the Rumbelows Cup. In October, striker John Byrne arrived from Brighton but Beagrie returned to Goodison. Although Byrne proved an instant hit pressure was now mounting on Smith. He reacted by sacking his right hand man Viv Busby and promoting reserves coach Malcolm Crosby.

Defeat at Wolves in December saw Sunderland slump to 19th place despite fielding their new £900,000 record signing, striker Don Goodman from West Bromwich. He had been Smith's last throw of the dice and three weeks later the manager was sacked.

Malcolm Crosby assumed the caretaker manager's role and immediately won the divisional manager of the month award for January with four wins from four games. Suddenly the play-offs were a possibility but League form was to dip once again as an unexpected F.A. Cup run took centre stage. Port Vale, Oxford and West Ham were despatched and when Chelsea were defeated in a thrilling replay Sunderland found themselves in the semi-finals for the first time since 1973. Against Norwich at Hillsborough, John Byrne kept up his record of having scored in every round with the only goal of the game to take the club to Wembley.

Sadly there was no fairytale ending. Sunderland were beaten 2-0 by Liverpool in the final. The players received a marvellous reception the following day as half a million people lined the streets to welcome them home to Wearside. They may have lost but the fans were proud of their efforts in just getting to the final.

Malcolm Crosby was made permanent manager two weeks before Wembley when second division status was assured.   **Eddie Brennan**

Back row L-R: Anthony Smith, Ian Patterson, Richard Ord, Terry Butcher, Thomas Hauser, Gordon Armstrong, Ian Samson, Anton Rogan, Gary Owers, Don Goodman, John Byrne. **Middle:** Malcolm Crosby (Manager), Bobby Ferguson (Asst. Manager), John Colquhorn, Brian Mooney, Gareth Cronin, Anthony Robinson, Tony Norman, Tim Carter, Peter Davenport, Shaun Cunnington, John Kay, Gary Bennett, Jim Morrow (Youth Development Officer), Roger Jones (Reserve Team Coach). **Front:** Steve Smelt (Physio), Paul Williams, Craig Russell, Wayne Walls, Brian Atkinson, Keiron Brady, Kevin Ball, Michael Gray, David Rush, Steven Brodie, Warren Hawke, Martin Gray, John Trigg (Youth Team Coach).

SUNDERLAND

DIVISION TWO: 18th   **FA CUP:** FINALISTS   **RUMBELOWS CUP:** 2nd RND

M	DATE	COMP.	VEN	OPPONENTS	RESULT	H/T	LGE POS	GOALSCORERS/GOAL TIMES	ATTEN-DANCE
1	A 17	BL	H	Derby County	D 1-1	0-0		Armstrong 66	20,509
2	20	BL	A	Barnsley	W 3-0	2-0		Owers 18, Armstrong 38, Pascoe 89	(12,454)
3	24	BL	A	Millwall	L 1-4	1-3	11	Owers (pen) 30	(10,016)
4	31	BL	H	Oxford United	W 2-0	1-0	6	Gabbiadini 39, Armstrong 86	16,151
5	S 3	BL	A	Portsmouth	L 0-1	0-0	8		(9,621)
6	7	BL	H	Blackburn Rovers	D 1-1	1-1	10	Atkinson 14	17,043
7	14	BL	A	Swindon Town	L 3-5	0-3	15	Owers 52, Gabbiadini 62, Armstrong 90	(11,147)
8	17	BL	A	Charlton Athletic	W 4-1	1-1	7	Owers (pen) 12, Gabbiadini 3 (46, 50, 52)	(5,807)
9	21	BL	H	Grimsby Town	L 1-2	0-1	13	Pascoe 81	16,535
10	24	RC 2/1	H	Huddersfield Town	L 1-2	0-1		Hauser 57	8,161
11	28	BL	A	Middlesbrough	L 1-2	0-2	17	Brady 72	(19,424)
12	O 5	BL	H	Brighton & H A	W 4-2	1-2	13	Beagrie 34, Rush 48, 56, Armstrong 74	15,119
13	9	RC 2/2	A	Huddersfield Town	L 0-4	0-0			(11,177)
14	12	BL	A	Cambridge United	L 0-3	0-1	17		(7,857)
15	19	BL	A	Port Vale	D 3-3	0-1	17	Brady 58, 71, Ball 69	(7,525)
16	26	BL	H	Bristol Rovers	D 1-1	1-1	16	Bennett 34	14,746
17	N 2	BL	H	Watford	W 3-1	2-0	15	Byrne 12, 74, Armstrong 21	12,790
18	5	BL	A	Ipswich Town	W 1-0	1-0	13	Armstrong 38	(9,768)
19	9	BL	A	Bristol City	L 0-1	0-1	14		(10,570)
20	17	BL	H	Newcastle United	D 1-1	1-0	14	Davenport 21	29,224
21	23	BL	A	Plymouth Argyle	L 0-1	0-0	15		(6,007)
22	30	BL	H	Southend United	L 1-2	1-1	15	Byrne 43	13,575
23	D 7	BL	A	Wolverhampton W	L 0-1	0-0	19		(11,922)
24	14	BL	H	Leicester City	W 1-0	0-0	16	Goodman 89	15,094
25	21	BL	H	Portsmouth	W 1-0	1-0	13	Awford (og) 45	14,432
26	26	BL	A	Tranmere Rovers	L 0-1	0-1	14		(13,658)
27	28	BL	A	Oxford United	L 0-3	0-0	17		(6,140)
28	J 1	BL	H	Barnsley	W 2-0	1-0	15	Armstrong 23, Goodman 80	16,107
29	4	FAC 3	H	Port Vale	W 3-0	2-0		Atkinson 10, Davenport 44, Byrne 72	15,564
30	11	BL	H	Millwall	W 6-2	2-0	11	Hardyman 14, Byrne 55, Goodman 3 (57,59,73), Davenport 86	16,553
31	18	BL	A	Derby County	W 2-1	2-0	12	Goodman 24, Byrne 29	(15,384)
32	F 1	BL	H	Port Vale	D 1-1	1-1	12	Armstrong 39	19,488
33	5	FAC 4	A	Oxford United	W 3-2	2-0		Byrne 3, Hardyman 23, Atkinson 53	(9,968)
34	8	BL	A	Bristol Rovers	L 1-2	0-0	12	Byrne 60	(6,318)
35	11	BL	H	Tranmere Rovers	D 1-1	1-0	12	Hardyman 42	18,060
36	15	FAC 5	H	West Ham United	D 1-1	0-0		Byrne 64	25,475
37	22	BL	A	Southend United	L 0-2	0-2	12		(7,473)
38	26	FAC 5R	A	West Ham United	W 3-2	2-1		Byrne 6, 24, Rush 78	(25,830)
39	29	BL	H	Wolverhampton W	W 1-0	1-0	13	Byrne (pen) 30	20,106
40	M 9	FAC 6	A	Chelsea	D 1-1	0-1		Byrne 82	(33,948)
41	14	BL	A	Watford	L 0-1	0-1	16		(8,091)
42	18	FAC 6R	H	Chelsea	W 2-1	1-0		Davenport 20, Armstrong 88	26,039
43	21	BL	H	Bristol City	L 1-3	0-3	17	Atkinson 72	18,933
44	29	BL	A	Newcastle United	L 0-1	0-1	18		(30,306)
45	A 5	FAC SF	N	Norwich City	W 1-0	1-0		Byrne 35	(40,462)
46	8	BL	A	Leicester City	L 2-3	0-1	21	Bennett 5, Goodman 13	(16,533)
47	11	BL	H	Charlton Athletic	L 1-2	0-0	21	Bennett 56	21,326
48	14	BL	H	Ipswich Town	W 3-0	0-0	18	Goodman 53, 79, Rush 83	22,131
49	16	BL	H	Plymouth Argyle	L 0-1	0-0	18		22,813
50	18	BL	A	Grimsby Town	L 0-2	0-0	19		(8,864)
51	20	BL	H	Middlesbrough	W 1-0	1-0	18	Davenport 21	25,093
52	25	BL	A	Brighton & H A	D 2-2	2-2	18	Goodman 12, Rogan 32	(9,851)
53	27	BL	H	Swindon Town	D 0-0	0-0	18		16,716
54	29	BL	A	Blackburn Rovers	D 2-2	0-1	18	Armstrong 52, Davenport 69	(15,079)
55	M 2	BL	H	Cambridge United	D 2-2	2-1	18	Goodman 25, Rush 28	19,042
56	9	FAC Fin	N	Liverpool	L 0-2	0-0			(79,544)

Best Home League Attendance: 29,224 v Newcastle United   **Smallest:** 12,790 v Watford   **Av Home Att:** 18,330

Goal Scorers: **Compared with 90-91:** -4,204

League (61): Goodman 11, Armstrong 10, Byrne 7 (1 pen), Gabbiadini 5, Davenport 4, Owers 4 (2 pens), Rush 4, Bennett 3, Brady 3, Pascoe 2 Atkinson 2, Hardyman 2, Opponents, Beagrie, Ball, Rogan

R/lows C (1): Hauser
FA Cup (14): Byrne 7, Atkinson 2, Davenport 2, Rush, Hardyman, Armstrong
Other (0):

Norman A.	Williams P.	Hardyman P.	Bennett G.	Ord R.	Owers G.	Bracewell P.	Pascoe C.	Armstrong G.	Gabbiadini M.	Atkinson B.	Davenport P.	Sampson I.	Hauser T.	Kay J.	Ball K.	Agboola R.	Rush D.	Beagrie P.	Brady K.	Rogan A.	Cullen A.	Byrne J.	Russell C.	Goodman D.	Mooney B.	Referee	
1	2	3	4	5	6	7	8	9	10	11	S	S														D Allinson	1
1	2	3	4	5	6	7	12	9	10	8		S	11*													J Brandwood	2
1	2	3	4	5•	6	7	12	9	10	8*		14	11													J Carter	3
1		3	4		6	7	S	9	10	8	14		11•	2	5											K Been	4
1		3	4		6	7	12	9	10	8		S	11*	2	5											A Buksh	5
1			4	S	6	7	12	9	10	8*			11	2	5	3										D Phillips	6
1		3	4		6	7	11	9	10•	8*	14		12	2	5											D Elleray	7
1		3	4	S	6	7	11	9	10		8		12	2	5											T Holbrook	8
1		3	4	S	6	7	11	9	10*		8		12	2	5											J Key	9
1		3	4	14	6	7	11*	9		12	8		10•	2	5											**E Parker**	**10**
1		3	4			7		9		6*	8			2	5		10	11	12							R Hart	11
1	S				6	7		9		8	4			2	5		10	11	S	3						J Worrall	12
1	11				6	7		9		8*	4			2	5		10•		12	3	14					**T West**	**13**
1	10•				6	7		9		14	4			2	5		11		12	3	8*					R Lewis	14
1			4		6	7		9		S	10*			2	5		12	11	8	3						V Callow	15
1			4•			7	12	9		6			14	2	5		11		8*	3		10				C Trussell	16
1			4			7	11	9		12	6*			2	5			8•		3		10	14			S Bell	17
1			4			7	11	9		S	6			2	5			8	S	3		10				M Bailey	18
1			4			12	7*	11	9		6			2	5			8•		3		10	14			B Hill	19
1			4			12	7	11*	9		6*	5	14	2				8•		3		10				J Lloyd	20
1			4			12	7	11*	9		6			2	5			8		3		10•	14			K Cooper	21
1			4			11	7	12	9		6*		14	2	5					3		10	8•			K Hackett	22
1	14		4			11	7		9		6•			2	5		12			3		10	8*			K Barrett	23
1			4		6	7	14	9		11•				2	5		S			3		10	8			D Allinson	24
1	11		4		6	7		9			12			2	5		10*		S	3			8			T Lunt	25
1	9*	10•	4		6	12				11			14	2	5					3			8			M Peck	26
1	14		4		6*	7		9		12				2	5				11	3•		10	8			G Ashby	27
1	3		4		6	7		9		11	S			2	5				S			10	8			P Jones	28
1	5		4		6*	7		9		11*	8	12		2					14	3		10				**G Peck**	**29**
1	5		4			7		9		11	12	S		2						3		10	8			W Flood	30
1	5		4			7		9		11*	6*			2	12		14			3		10	8			G Pooley	31
1	5		4			7		9*		11	6*			2	12		14			3		10	8			J Kirkby	32
1	5		4	S		7	12			11	6			2	9		8			3		10*				**L Dilkes**	**33**
1	5		4	12		7•				11	14			2	9		6*			3		10	8			P Don	34
1	5		4	S			6			11	S			2	9		7			3		10	8			T Fitzharris	35
1	5		4•			7	14	9		11	6		S	2	8					3		10				**R Nixon**	**36**
12	5					7	S	9		11	6*			2	4					3		10	8			G Willard	37
1	5					7		9		11	6•	S		2	8					3		10				**R Nixon**	**38**
1	5					7		9		11	12	4		2			6*			3		10	8•			J Key	39
1	5		4*			7		9		11*	8	12		2			6			3		10				**T Holbrook**	**40**
14	5					7		9		11*	8*			2	4		6			3		10	12			R Groves	41
1	5*		12			7		9		11	8			2	4		6		S	3		10				**T Holbrook**	**42**
1		5*				7		9		11	8			2	4		6•			3		10		12	14	S Lodge	43
1		5				7		9		11	8*	S		2	4		6			3		10			14	I Hendrick	44
1		5	12			7		9		11	8			2	4*		6		S	3		10				**N Midgley**	**45**
1		5	4					9		11	8•			2			6*			3		10	7	14		T Holbrook	46
1		5	4					9		11	8•	S		2			6			3		10		7		E Parker	47
1		5	4			12		9		11	14			2			6			3		10	8*	7*		P Harrison	48
1		5*	4			12		9		11	14			2			6			3		10•	8	7		A Bennett	49
1		5	4			12	7	9		11	14			2			6•			3		10		8*		R Poulain	50
1		12	4	3		7		9•		11	8	6			14		5									G Courtney	51
1	14		4		6	7		9•		11*	12			2						3		10		8		G Poll	52
1		5	12	3		7				11	8•	6		2	4		9							10		T West	53
1		5	4				6•		10	11			2											8	7*	R Nixon	54
1			3		4	6		S		11												9		5		T Fitzharris	55
1		12	4		2	7		9•		11	8			3			6*					5		10		**P Don**	**56**
44	**4**	**29**	**38**	**5**	**24**	**39**	**12**	**40**	**9**	**29**	**25**	**7**	**5**	**41**	**31**	**1**	**20**	**5**	**4**	**33**	**1**	**27**	**1**	**20**	**6**	League Appearances	
	3	3	1	1	6		8			1	11	1	7		2		5		4			3		2	3	Substitute Appearances	
2		2	1	0+1	2	2	1	2		0+1	2	1	1	2	2		1			0+1		1		0+1		R/lows Appearances	
8		7+1	5+1	2	8	0+2	7	8		8	0+2			7	6		6			0+3	8	8				FA Cup Appearances	

Also Played: Posn.(Game): Carter 1(44,45), Martin Gray 14•(54)S(55), Hawke 10(51•,55)14(53,56)12(54), Smith 3(54)2(55)

Players on Loan: Beagrie (Everton)

SUNDERLAND

Club Colours: Red and white striped shirts, black shorts, red stockings with white band.
Change Colours: White shirts with green/blue trim, white shorts, white stockings with blue band.
Reserves League: Pontins Central League Division 1

COMPETITIONS			
Div. 1	Div. 2	Div. 3	ECWC
90-58	58-64	87-88	73-74
64-70	70-76		
76-77	77-80		
80-85	85-87		
90-91	88-90		
	91-		

HONOURS			
Div. 1	Div. 2	Div. 3	FA Cup
91-92	75-76	87-88	1937
92-93			1973
94-95			
01-02			
12-13			
35-36			

MOST APPEARANCES: JIM MONTGOMERY 611+12 (1961-77)					
Year	League	FA Cup	Lge Cup	Others	ECWC
1961-62	12		1		
1962-63	42	4	7		
1963-64	42	6	1		
1964-65	9				
1965-66	29	1	2		
1966-67	42	5	2		
1967-68	39	2	3		
1968-69	42	1	1		
1969-70	41	1	1	4	
1970-71	42	1	1		
1971-72	31	3	1	4	
1972-73	41	9	1		
1973-74	41	2	4		4
1974-75	40	1	1		
1975-76	38	5	1		
1976-77	6		4		
	537	41	33	8	4

MOST GOALS IN A CAREER		
R GURNEY 228 (1925-39)		
Season	League	FA Cup
1925-26	4	
1926-27	7	
1927-28	4	
1929-30	15	2
1930-31	31	2
1931-32	16	
1932-33	15	7
1933-34	21	1
1934-35	30	4
1935-36	31	
1936-37	20	6
1937-38	9	1
1938-39	2	
Total	205	23
League only C Buchan 209 (+15 FAC)		

HIGHEST TRANSFER FEE RECEIVED			
Amount	Club	Player	Date
£1,800,000	C. Palace	Marco Gabbiadini	9/91
£275,000	Manchester Utd.	Chris Turner	7/85
£275,000	Everton	Paul Bracewell	4/84
£275,000	Sheffield Wed.	Mark Proctor	9/87

HIGHEST TRANSFER FEE PAID			
Amount	Club	Player	Date
£900,000	West Brom	Don Goodman	12/91
£650,000	Grimsby Town	Shaun Cunnington	7/92
£350,000	Celtic	Anton Rogan	9/91
£350,000	Portsmouth	Kevin Ball	7/90

MANAGERS			
Name	Seasons	Best	Worst
Tom Watson	1890-96	1(1)	7(1)
Robert Campbell	1896-99	2(1)	15(1)
Alex Mackie	1899-05	1(1)	6(1)
Robert Kyle	1905-28	1(1)	16(1)
Johnny Cochrane	1928-39	1(1)	16(1)
William Murray	1939-57	3(1)	20(1)
Alan Brown	1957-64	21(1)	16(2)
George Hardwick	1964-65	15(1)	15(1)
Ian McColl	1965-68	15(1)	19(1)
Alan Brown	1968-72	17(1)	16(2)
Bob Stokoe	1972-76	1(2)	6(2)
Jimmy Adamson	1976-78	20(1)	6(2)
Billy Elliott	1978-79	4(2)	4(2)
Ken Knighton	1979-81	17(1)	2(2)
Alan Durban	1981-84	13(1)	19(1)
Len Ashurst	1984-85	21(1)	21(1)
Lawrie McMenemy	1985-87	18(2)	20(2)
Denis Smith	1987-91	19(1)	1(3)
Malcolm Crosby	1991-	18(2)	18(2)

LONGEST LEAGUE RUNS	
of undefeated matches:	16 (11.11.1922-24.2.1923)
of undefeated home matches:	44 (18.10.1890-6.12.1893)
without home win:	12 (5.9.1981-27.2.1982)
of league wins:	13 (14.11.1891-22.4.1892)
of league defeats:	9 (23.11.1976-15.1.1977)
of league matches without a win:	14 (16.4.1985-14.9.1985)
of undefeated away matches:	14 (25.11.1978-18.8.1979)
without an away win:	28 (15.11.1952-2.1.1954)
of home wins:	19 (10.1.1891-16.4.1892)
of away wins:	5 (1891-92, 1892, 1912-13, 1963)

BARCLAYS

PREVIOUS LEAGUE
Sunderland and District Teachers Association 1879-81

BIGGEST VICTORIES
League: 9-1 v Newcastle, Division 1, 5.12.1908
8-0 v Derby County, Division 1, 1.9.1894
F.A. Cup: 11-1 v Fairfield, Round 1, 2.2.1895
League Cup: 7-1 v Oldham Athletic, Round 2, 24.9.1962

BIGGEST DEFEATS
League: 0-8 v Sheffield Wednesday, Division 1, 26.12.1911
0-8 v West Ham Utd, Division 1, 19.10.1968
0-8 v Watford, Division 1, 25.9.1982
F.A. Cup: 2-7 v Aston Villa, Round 4, 27.1.1934
0-5 v Arsenal, Round 2, 1905-06
0-5 v Liverpool, Round 1 replay, 1921-22
0-5 v Tottenham Hotspur, Round 6 replay, 1960-61
League Cup: 0-6 v Derby County, Round 3, 31.10.1990

MOST POINTS
3 points a win: 93, Division 3, 1987-88
2 points a win: 61, Division 2, 1963-64

MOST GOALS
109, Division 1, 1935-36
Carter 31, Gurney 31, Gallagher 19, Davis 10, Conner 6,
Duns 5, Goddard 2, Hornby 2, Thompson 1, McNab 1, og 1.

MOST GOALS IN A MATCH
5. C Buchan v Liverpool, 7.12.1919 (7-0)
5. R Gurney v Bolton W., 7.12.1935 (7-2)
5. D Sharkey v Norwich, 20.2.1962 (7-1)

MOST GOALS IN A SEASON
Dave Halliday 43, 1928-29
4 goals once = 4, 3 goals twice = 6, 2 goals ten times = 20, 1
goal 13 times = 13

MOST FIRST CLASS MATCHES IN A SEASON
59 (46 League, 1 FA Cup, 8 League Cup, 1 Zenith, 3 Play-Offs) 1989-90

MOST LEAGUE GOALS CONCEDED
97, Division 1, 1957-58

MOST LEAGUE WINS
27, Division 3, 1987-88

MOST LEAGUE DRAWS
18, Division 1, 1954-55

MOST LEAGUE DEFEATS
22, Division 1, 1956-57; Division 1, 1969-70; Division 1, 1984-85

OLDEST PLAYER
Bryan 'Pop' Robson, 38 years 128 days v Leicester, 12.5.1984

YOUNGEST PLAYER
Derek Forster, 15 years 184 days v Leicester, 22.8.1964

MOST CAPPED PLAYER
Martin Harvey (Northern Ireland) 34

BEST PERFORMANCES BY SUNDERLAND

League: 1963-64: Matches played 42, Won 25, Drawn 11, Lost 6, Goals for 87, Goals against 37, Points 61. 2nd in Division 2.

Highest: First in Division 1.

F.A. Cup: 1936-37: 3rd rnd. Southampton (A) 3-2; 4th rnd. Luton Town (A) 2-2, (H) 3-1; 5th rnd. Swansea (H) 3-0; 6th rnd. Wolverhampton W. 1-1 (A), 2-2 (H), 4-0 (N); Semi-final Millwall 2-1; Final Preston North End 3-1.

1972-73: 3rd rnd. Notts County 1-1 (A), 2-0 (H); 4th rnd. Reading 1-1 (H), 3-1 (A); 5th rnd. Manchester City 2-2 (A), 3-1 (H); 6th rnd. Luton 2-0 (H); Semi-final Arsenal 2-1; Final Leeds 1-0.

League Cup: 1984-85: 2nd rnd. Crystal Palace 2-1 (H), 0-0 (A); 3rd rnd. Nottingham Forest 1-1 (A), 1-0 (H); 4th rnd. Tottenham Hotspur 0-0 (H), 2-1 (A); 5th rnd. Watford 1-0; Semi-final Chelsea 2-0 (H), 3-2 (A); Final Norwich 0-1.

Europe (ECWC): 1973-74: 1st rnd. VASAS Budapest 2-0 (A), 1-0 (H); 2nd rnd. Sporting Lisbon 2-1 (H), 0-2 (A).

DIVISIONAL RECORDS

	Played	Won	Drawn	Lost	For	Against	Points
DIVISION 1	2732	1107	621	1004	4531	4217	2889
DIVISION 2	852	355	237	260	1302	1071	1023
DIVISION 3	46	27	12	7	92	48	93
TOTALS	3630	1489	870	1271	5925	5336	4005

SUNDERLAND

PLAYERS NAME Honours	Ht	Wt	Birthdate	Birthplace Transfers	Contract Date	Clubs	League	L/Cup	FA Cup	Other	Lg	L/C	FAC	Oth
GOALKEEPERS														
Timothy Carter	6.2	13.8	05.10.67	Bristol	08.10.85	Bristol Rovers (A)	47	2	2	2				
E: Y.3				Loan	14.12.87	Newport Co	1							
					24.12.87	Sunderland	23	8	1	2				
				Loan	18.03.88	Carlisle Utd	4							
				Loan	15.09.88	Bristol City	3							
				Loan	21.11.91	Birmingham City	2	1						
Tony Norman	6.2	12.8	24.02.58	Mancot	01.08.76	Burnley								
W: 5				£30,000	14.02.80	Hull City	372	22	26	13				
				P.E.+£200K	29.12.88	Sunderland	133	5	12	6				
DEFENDERS														
Anton Rogan	5.11	12.0	25.03.66	Belfast		Celtic								
				£350,000	04.10.91	Sunderland	33	1	8		1			
Kevin Ball	5.9	11.6	12.11.68	Hastings	17.05.84	Portsmouth (A)	96+9	8+1	8	6	4			
				£350,000	16.07.90	Sunderland	64+2	5	7	2	4	1		1
Gary E Bennett	6.1	12.1	04.12.61	Manchester	08.09.79	Manchester City								
Div.3.88					16.09.81	Cardiff City	85+2	6	3		11	1		
					26.07.84	Sunderland	292+4	29	11+1	17	23	1		1
Terry Butcher	6.4	14.0	28.12.58	Singapore		Ipswich Town (A)	271	30	28	22	16	2		3
E:77, u21.7, B.1; UEFAC'81,SPD'87'89,SLC'87'89						Glasgow Rangers	127	21	11	17	10			2
				N.C	02.07.91	Coventry City	7	1						
				Monthly	15.07.92	Sunderland								
John Kay	5.10	11.6	29.01.64	Sunderland	07.08.81	Arsenal (A)	13+1							
Div.3.88				£25,000	20.07.84	Wimbledon	63	3	3	1	2			
				Loan	08.01.85	Middlesbrough	8							
				£22,500	22.07.87	Sunderland	157+3	15	10	5				
Richard Ord	6.2	12.8	03.03.70	Easington	14.07.87	Sunderland (T)	58+11	4+5	3	2+1	2		1	
				Loan	22.02.90	York City	3							
MIDFIELD														
Gordon Armstrong	6.0	11.10	15.07.67	Newcastle	10.07.85	Sunderland (A)	258+4	20+1	13	14+1	35	3	1	4
Div.3.88														
Brian Atkinson	5.10	11.6	19.01.71	Darlington	21.07.89	Sunderland	48+6	3+1	8	1+2	2			
John Colquhoun	5.7	10.0	14.07.63	Stirling		Stirling A	98+6	10+1	3+1		45	43		
						Celtic	25+6	3	1	2+1	4		1	
				£35,000		Hearts	227+4	15+1	22+1	13+1	54	2	8	1
				£400,000		Millwall	27	2	1	1	3	1		
				£220,000	09.07.92	Sunderland								
Shaun Cunnington	5.9	11.0	04.01.66	Bournemouth	11.01.84	Wrexham (A)	196+3	13	9	21	12		1	2
WC'86				£55,000	19.12.88	Grimsby Town	182	11	11	9	11		3	
				£650,000	17.07.92	Sunderland								
Warren Hawke	5.10	10.11	20.09.70	Durham	12.11.88	Sunderland (T)	7+17		1	2	1			
				Loan	26.09.91	Chesterfield								
Brian Mooney	5.11	11.2	02.07.66	Dublin		Home Farm								
Ei:B.1,u23.1,u21.3,Y					22.08.83	Liverpool		0+1						
				Loan	06.12.85	Wrexham	9		2		2			
				£40,000	09.10.87	Preston N.E	125+3	4+1	6	13+1	20			5
				Loan	31.07.90	Sheffield Wed								
				£225,000	07.02.91	Sunderland	11+4							
Gary Owers	5.11	11.10	03.10.68	Newcastle	08.10.86	Sunderland (A)	178+8	18+1	7+1	9	21			1
Div3'88														
FORWARDS														
Kieron Brady	5.9	11.13	17.09.71	Glasgow	21.07.89	Sunderland (T)	17+16	1+2	0+4		7			
Ei: Y; UEFA YC														
Stephen Brodie	5.10		14.01.73	Sunderland	01.07.91	Sunderland								
John Byrne	6.0	12.04	01.02.61	Manchester		York City (A)	167+8	10+2	10+1	1	55	5	3	
Eire: 20, Div4'84				£115,000		Q.P.R	107+16	12+1	7+2	1	30	4	2	
						Le Havre (Fra)								
				£120,000	01.09.90	Brighton & H.A	47+4	2	2	2+1	14		4	
				£225,000	23.10.91	Sunderland	27		8		7		7	
Peter Davenport	5.10	11.12	24.03.64	Birkenhead		Cammel Lai								
E: 1, B.1					05.01.82	Nottm. Forest	114+4	10	7+1	10+1	54	1	1	2
				£750,000	12.03.86	Manchester Utd	73+19	8+2	2+2		22	4		
				£750,000	03.11.88	Middlesbrough	53+6	2	4	7+1	7			1
				£350,000	19.07.90	Sunderland	52+13	5	8	13	11		2	
Don Goodman	5.10	11.7	09.05.66	Leeds	10.07.84	Bradford City	65+5	5+1	2+3	4+1	14	2	4	2
Div.3'85				£50,000	27.03.87	West Brom A	129+18	9	6	4	53			1
				£900,000	06.12.91	Sunderland	20+2				11			
Thomas Hauser	6.3	12.6	10.04.65	W. Germany		Basle O.B								
				£200,000	23.02.89	Sunderland	22+31	3+6	0+1	1+1	9	2		
Colin Pascoe	5.10	10.0	09.04.65	Aberavon	12.04.83	Swansea City (A)	167+7	11	9	7	39	3	1	1
W:10, u21.4, Y; WC'83					25.03.88	Sunderland	116+10	12	4+2	5	22	3		
David Rush	5.11	10.3	15.05.71	Sunderland	21.07.89	Sunderland (T)	28+8	1+1	7	0+1	6		1	
				Loan	15.08.91	Hartlepool Utd	8				2			

ADDITIONAL CONTRACT PLAYERS
Peter Barnes, Martin Gray, Ian Patterson, Craig Russell, Ian Sampson, Tony Smith, Wayne Walls, Paul Williams.

SUNDERLAND

RECORD WIN & LOSS AGAINST EACH CLUB IN CURRENT DIVISION

(Where a score has occured on several occasions the most recent is given)

Club	Rec. Win	Season	Rec. Loss	Season
BARNSLEY	3-0	1991-92 (away)	3-0	1988-89
BIRMINGHAM CITY	7-2	1935-36 (away)	6-1	1957-58 (home)
BRENTFORD	5-1	1935-36 (away)	4-0	1937-38
BRISTOL CITY	4-0	1909-10	4-1	1976-77
BRISTOL ROVERS	6-1	1961-62	4-0	1987-88
CAMBRIDGE UNITED	2-0	1979-80	3-0	1991-92
CHARLTON ATHLETIC	8-1	1956-57	5-0	1946-47
DERBY COUNTY	8-0	1894-95	7-2	1903-04
GRIMSBY TOWN	6-2	1962-63	6-0	1936-37
LEICESTER CITY	4-1	1931-32	5-0	1931-32
LUTON TOWN	7-1	1960-61	8-2	1955-56
MILLWALL	6-2	1991-92	4-1	1991-92
NEWCASTLE UNITED	9-1	1908-09 (away)	6-1	1955-56 (home)
NOTTS COUNTY	5-0	1911-12	6-1	1983-84
OXFORD UNITED	3-0	1971-72	5-1	1972-73
PETERBOROUGH UTD	(Never played in a League fixture)			
PORTSMOUTH	5-0	1935-36	4-0	1928-29
SOUTHEND UNITED	7-0	1987-88	2-0	1991-92
SWINDON TOWN	6-0	1963-64	4-1	1988-89
TRANMERE ROVERS	None		1-0	1991-92
WATFORD	5-0	1979-80	8-0	1982-83
WEST HAM UNITED	6-0	1976-77	8-0	1968-69
WOLVERHAMPTON WNDRS	6-0	1893-94	5-0	1957-58

MANAGER: MALCOLM CROSBY

DATE OF BIRTH: 4.7.1954   **PLACE OF BIRTH:** South Shields

DATE OF APPOINTMENT: 28.4.1992 (Caretaker from 30.12.1992)

PREVIOUS CLUBS
as Manager:
as Asst. Man./Coach: Sunderland
as Player: Aldershot, York City, Wrexham (Loan)

HONOURS
as Manager: Sunderland: FA Cup Finalists 1992
as Asst. Man./Coach:
as Player: 4th Division: Championship 1984 (York)
International:

Value Rating: ★ ★ ★ ★

Programme Editor: Stephen Rooke

Price of 1992-93 Programme: £1

Number of Pages: 32

Subscriptions: Home, 1st class £16.50; 2nd class £15.50; home and away, 1st class £24.50; overseas £27.00.

Local Newspapers: Journal/Chronicle/Sunday Sun, Sunderland Echo, Northern Echo, Sunderland and Washington Times, Shields Gazette.

Local Radio Stations: Metro Radio, Radio Tees, Radio Newcastle.

Additional Publications on Club: The History of Sunderland Football Club 1879-1986 (Bill Simmons and Bob Graham) paperback £9.95.

LEADING LEAGUE GOALSCORERS
SEASONS 1979-80 – 1991-92

1979-80	**BRYAN ROBSON**	20		1980-81	**GARY ROWELL**	10
1981-82	**GARY ROWELL**	9		1982-83	**GARY ROWELL**	16
1983-84	**COLIN WEST**	9		1984-85	**CLIVE WALKER**	10
1985-86	**ERIC GATES**	9		1986-87	**DAVID BUCHANAN**	8
					MARK PROCTOR	8
1987-88	**MARCO GABBIADINI**	21		1988-89	**MARCO GABBIADINI**	18
1989-90	**MARCO GABBIADINI**	21		1990-91	**MARCO GABBIADINI**	9

1991-92 **DON GOODMAN** 11

ROKER PARK Sunderland, Tyne & Wear SR6 9SW

Capacity: 31,222   **Covered Standing:**   **Seating:** 7,753

Tel: Ground: 091 514 0332   **Ticket Sales:** As ground number   **Clubcall:** 0898 12 11 40

All premium rate calls (0898/0891) cost 36p per minute cheap rate and 48p per minute at all other times. Call costings correct at time of going to press.

GROUNDS

ATTENDANCES
Highest: 75,118 v Derby County, FA Cup 6th Round Replay, 8.3.1933
68,004 v Newcastle United, Div 1, 4.3.1950

Lowest: 4,832 v Portsmouth, Div 1, 29.4.1935

RECORD RECEIPTS
£111,000 v Chelsea, Milk Cup Semi-Final (1st leg), 13.2.1985

GROUND NAME
First game:
First floodlit game:

Season Tickets:
Stands: £185, Family area £120
Ground: £115, juv £85, OAP £60

Executive Box Season Tickets: None available

Cost of Stand Tickets: Seats: £10 (no reductions)
Terraces: £6-£7, juv/OAP £3

Match and Ticket Information: Bookable ten days prior to a match

Car Parking: Parking for 1,500 cars 200 yards from ground

Nearest Railway Station: Seaburn

How to get to the ground

From North: Take A184 Newcastle-Sunderland road. After Boldon pass Greyhound Stadium on left. Straight on at roundabout. After 150 yards bear left (signs for Fulwell, Seaburn, and Roker). At T-junction turn left to traffic lights at Blue Bell Public House, then turn right. After about 0.5 mile ground is on the left up side street (opposite Redby School) for Sunderland FC

From South: Use A1(M) North. Take A690 to Sunderland. Head for Town Centre. Follow signs for Whitburn A183 and South Shields A1018. Pass over Wearmouth Bridge, keep in right hand lane and take signs for Roker, Seafront and Whitburn. After approximately 1 mile the ground is on the left up a side street.

From West: Take A1231 towards Sunderland (north). Follow signs for Roker, Seafront and Whitburn. After one mile ground is on left up side street

SWANSEA CITY

Division 2

Formed: 1900   **Turned Professional:** 1912   **Ltd Co:** 1912

SPONSORED BY: Action Service Stations Ltd   **NICKNAME:** The Swans

President
Ivor Pursey MBE

Chairman
D J Sharpe

Directors
M Griffiths
D G Hammond FCA MBIM (Vice-Chairman)

Chief Executive
R Sharpe

Secretary
G M Taylor (0792 474114)

Team Manager
Frank Burrows

Assistant Manager
Bobby Smith

Stadium Manager
Haydn Norman

Physiotherapist
Mike Davenport

Youth Team Coach
Jimmy Rimmer

Commercial Manager
John Gwilt

Club Statistician for the Directory
Prof. David Farmer

ONCE again Swans fans were disappointed at the outcome of a season. The club finished in 19th position in Division Three and the final home 'gate' reflected that lack of success; only 2167 bothering to come to the Vetch for the game.

Yet, Swans fans asked on the 5th November (when the club was bottom of the table) would have settled, without hesitation, for the outcome. However, results between that date and the end of February (when the Swans had risen to 12th) were such that there developed an unrealistic aspiration in the minds of supporters that the team might win its way into a play-off position. Thereafter, whilst losing only one of ten games played, only two were won. The play-off dream was exposed for what it was, whilst injuries exacerbated the problems facing manager Frank Burrows for the last games of the season.

Injuries were, indeed, at the root of the manager's difficulties throughout the season, with John Cornforth, Keith Walker, Jimmy Gilligan, Terry Connor and Russell Coughling being sidelined for long periods. Coupled with the fact that Burrows had been obliged to reduce the staff which he had inherited by half, this meant that youngsters had to be blooded earlier than they might, whilst newcomers to League football had to be given extended runs when they would have benefited by being rested.

Nevertheless, paradoxically, the season might well prove to have been an important one in the longer term in that Frank Burrows has given himself room to manoeuvre. And, if success were measured by the number of miles travelled by the likeable Scot and his number two, Bobby Smith, the new team which they will have assembled by the time this directory is published should be justifying all their hard work with some success.

As far as the 1991-92 season is concerned, there are some highlights among the general gloom. After playing their first seven away League games without a win and only winning three times in the first fifteen, the side astounded everyone by beating Bradford City 6-4 away. They also won three of the next four games to take them to sixteenth spot. After that, however, they lost to Bournemouth and drew five games in a row (to equal a club record).

John Williams's success in the search for the 'Fastest Man in Football' brought smiles to staff and supporters alike, and, on the field the lanky rookie scored eleven goals, including a hat-trick. Other hat-tricksters were Jimmy Gilligan and Steve Thornber. Reuben Agboola was capped by Nigeria, John Ford found a good level of consistency in his first season in League football; Russell Coughlin had a purple patch during which his passing was a joy to behold; John Cornforth worked hard to recover after breaking his leg and, when fit will be an excellent acquisition. Keith Walker also played outstanding football after a long lay-off, whilst Jimmy Gilligan was struck down with a back problem for the second time, just as he seemed to be running into goal-scoring form. Of the youngsters, Shaun Chappell attracted most attention, but the management believe that David Barnhouse, just 17, who was handed his debut at Hull during the final game, could prove to be a name to watch.

Prof. David Farmer

Back row L-R: Tony Cullen, Reuben Agboola, Colin Pascoe, Des Lyttle, Russell Coughlin. **Middle row:** Steven Jenkins, John Ford, Andy McFarlane, Mark Harris, Colin West, Keith Walker. **Seated:** Paul Wimbleton, Shaun Chapple, Roger Freestone, John Cornforth, James Heeps, Jason Bowen, Andrew Legg.

SWANSEA CITY

DIVISION THREE: 19th   **FA CUP:** 2nd RND   **RUMBELOWS CUP:** 2nd RND   **AUTOGLASS:** Prelim.

M	DATE		COMP.	VEN	OPPONENTS	RESULT		H/T	LGE POS	GOALSCORERS/GOAL TIMES	ATTEN-DANCE
1	A	17	BL	A	Stockport County	L	0-5	0-2			(4,241)
2		20	RC 1/1	H	Walsall	D	2-2	1-0		Thornber 10, Chalmers 87	2,029
3		24	BL	H	Bolton Wanderers	D	1-1	1-1	21	Connor 35	3,578
4		27	RC 1/2	A	Walsall	W	1-0	1-0		Thornber 6	(2,812)
5		31	BL	A	Chester City	L	0-2	0-0	23		(1,162)
6	S	3	BL	H	Reading	L	1-2	0-0	24	Williams 72	3,206
7		7	BL	A	Fulham	L	0-3	0-1	24		(3,426)
8		14	BL	H	Preston North End	D	2-2	1-1	24	Flynn (og) 20, Raynor 52	3,170
9		17	ECWC 1/	H	Monaco	L	1-2	0-2		Legg 71	6,208
10		21	BL	A	Shrewsbury Town	D	0-0	0-0	24		(3,427)
11		25	RC 2/1	H	Tottenham Hotspur	W	1-0	0-0		Gilligan 88	11,406
12		28	BL	H	Peterborough Utd	W	1-0	0-0	24	Legg 59	2,685
13	O	1	ECWC 1/	A	Monaco	L	0-8	0-5			(5,000)
14		5	BL	A	Huddersfield Town	L	0-1	0-0	24		(5,578)
15		9	RC 2/2	A	Tottenham Hotspur	L	1-5	0-1		Chapple 82	(20,198)
16		11	BL	H	Hull City	D	0-0	0-0	23		2,725
17		19	BL	H	Stoke City	W	2-1	2-0	22	Harris 9, Davies A 14	3,363
18		22	AGT Pre	A	Bournemouth	L	0-3	0-2			(1,814)
19		26	BL	A	Torquay United	L	0-1	0-0	23		(1,908)
20	N	1	BL	A	Wigan Athletic	L	0-1	0-0	23		(2,092)
21		5	BL	H	Leyton Orient	D	2-2	2-2	24	Coughlin 10, Beauchamp 39	2,081
22		8	BL	H	Bournemouth	W	3-1	1-0	23	Brazil 42, Walker 51, Williams 84	2,698
23		16	FAC 1	H	Cardiff City	W	2-1	1-1		Gilligan 29, Harris 57	9,315
24		19	AGT Pre	H	Cardiff City	D	0-0	0-0			2,955
25		23	BL	A	Bradford City	W	6-4	4-1	21	Williams 3 (17, 42, 55), Legg 38, Beauchamp 20, Gilligan 61	(5,729)
26		30	BL	A	Brentford	L	2-3	2-0	22	Williams 12, Legg 30	(6,669)
27	D	7	FAC 2	A	Exeter City	D	0-0	0-0			(4,186)
28		14	BL	H	Exeter City	W	1-0	1-0	19	Williams 7	2,848
29		18	FAC 2R	H	Exeter City	L	1-2	0-1		Walker 89	3,159
30		26	BL	A	Chester City	W	3-0	2-0	18	Gilligan 3 (12, 26, 54)	4,098
31		28	BL	H	Stockport County	W	2-1	1-1	16	Purnell 24, Gilligan 62	4,353
32	J	1	BL	A	Reading	L	0-1	0-0	18		(5,083)
33		11	BL	A	Bury	L	0-1	0-0	19		(2,161)
34		18	BL	H	Birmingham City	L	0-2	0-1	21		4,147
35		25	BL	A	West Bromwich A.	W	3-2	0-2	17	Thornber 3 (79, 81, 89)	(10,395)
36		28	BL	H	Darlington	W	4-2	3-1	15	Williams 24, 87, Legg 42, Chapple 45	2,743
37	F	1	BL	A	Stoke City	L	1-2	0-1	15	Gilligan 61	(11,299)
38		8	BL	H	Torquay United	W	1-0	1-0	14	Gilligan 22	3,418
39		12	BL	H	Brentford	D	1-1	0-1	14	Legg 51	3,582
40		15	BL	A	Exeter City	L	1-2	0-2	15	Harris 49	(2,360)
41		22	BL	H	Bury	W	2-1	0-1	15	Raynor 47, Legg 63	2,787
42		29	BL	A	Hartlepool United	W	1-0	0-0	12	Thornber 81	(2,669)
43	M	3	BL	A	Birmingham City	D	1-1	0-1	14	Williams 52	(9,475)
44		6	BL	H	West Bromwich A.	D	0-0	0-0	14		5,629
45		10	BL	A	Leyton Orient	W	2-1	1-0	11	Chalmers 38, Legg 47	(3,328)
46		14	BL	H	Wigan Athletic	W	3-0	0-0	12	Legg 54, Johnson (og) 62, Chalmers 85	3,726
47		20	BL	A	Bournemouth	L	0-3	0-2	12		(4,385)
48		28	BL	H	Bradford City	D	2-2	2-1	14	Chalmers 14, 44	3,748
49		31	BL	A	Preston North End	D	1-1	0-1	13	Chalmers 47	(3,637)
50	A	4	BL	H	Fulham	D	2-2	1-0	13	Chalmers 36, 83	3,307
51		7	BL	A	Bolton Wanderers	D	0-0	0-0	13		(3,535)
52		11	BL	A	Darlington	D	1-1	1-0	13	Williams 30	(1,507)
53		17	BL	A	Shrewsbury Town	L	1-2	1-0	14	Harris 21	3,429
54		21	BL	A	Peterborough Utd	L	1-3	0-1		Legg 70	(5,526)
55		25	BL	H	Huddersfield Town	L	0-1	0-1	16		3,964
56		28	BL	H	Hartlepool United	D	1-1	1-1	17	Chapple 4	2,167
57	M	2	BL	A	Hull City	L	0-3	0-1	19		(4,070)

Best Home League Attendance: 5,629 v West Bromwich A.   **Smallest: 2,081 v Leyton Orient**   **Av Home Att: 3,367**

Goal Scorers: **Compared with 90-91: -295**

League (55): Williams 11, Legg 9, Chalmers 7, Gilligan 7, Thornber 4, Harris 3, Opponents 2, Beauchamp 2, Chapple 2, Raynor 2, Brazil Coughlin, Purnell, Davies A, Connor, Walker

R/lows C (5): Thornber 2, Chalmers, Gilligan, Chapple
FA Cup (3): Harris, Gilligan, Walker
Autoglass (1): Legg

Bracey L.	Jenkins S.	Thornber S.	Coughlin R.	Harris M.	Hough D.	Raynor P.	Cornforth J.	Davies A.	Connor T.	Legg A.	Chalmers P.	McClean C.	Williams J.	Brazil D.	Ford J.	Freestone R.	Gilligan J.	Davey S.	Freeman C.	Chappell S.	Bowen J.	Beauchamp J.	Walker K.	Agboola R.	Purnell P.	Referee	
1	2	3	4*	5	6	7	8	9	10	11	12									S						K Redfearn	1
1	2	3	14	5	6	9*	8	7*	10	11	12	4														R Hamer	2
1	2	3		5	6	9*	8		10	11	12	4	7*		14											K Cooper	3
1	2	3		5	6	12			10	11	S	4	9		7											D Gallagher	4
1	2	3		5	6	S	8*		10	11	12	4	9		7											G Singh	5
	2	3*	8	5	6	12			10	11	S	4	9		7											R Gifford	6
	2	3	4*	5	6	14			10	11*	9•				7	8	1			12						I Borrett	7
	2	3*	4	5		9		14	10	11					7•	6	8	1		12						K Cooper	8
	2	3	4	5			8		10	11	9					7				S	S					K Nielsen	9
	2	3	4*	5		10		12		11			S	6	8	1	9	7			12					M Bailey	10
	2	3	4	5		10		S		11			7	6	8	1	9	S								L Shapter	11
	2	3	4	5		10		S		11			7*	6	8	1	9	12								M Brandwood	12
	2	3	4	5*		10		8		11						9	7*			14						A Noumentaller	13
	2	S	4	5		10		8		11			12	6	3	1	9*	7								A Wilkie	14
	2		4•	5		10		8		11			12	6	3	1	9	7*			14					G Willard	15
	2		4•	5		10		8		11				6	3	1	9	7*	12	14						P Durkin	16
	2		4	5		10		8		11				6	3	1	9	S	S	7						D Frampton	17
	2	S		5		10		8		11				6	3	1	9		7•	4	14					M Pierce	18
	2	S	4	5		10		8*		11				6	3	1	7	9	12							G Ashby	19
	2	14	4	5		12				11				6	3	1	9	7*	8•		10					W Burns	20
	2	8	4	5						11			7	6	3	1	9			S	10	S				P Danson	21
	2	8	4	5						11			7	6	3*	1	9			S	10	12				P Vanes	22
	2	8		5						11	S		7	6		1	9			S	10		3			K Cooper	23
	2	8		5						11	S		7	6		1	9			4		10	3•			A Smith	24
		4*	8	5						11	14		7*	6	2	1	9					10	12	3		K Lupton	25
		12	8*	5						11	14		7	6	2	1	9					10•	4	3		M James	26
S			8	5						11			7	2	1	9		6	10			4	3		M Bodenham	27
S		8	5							11			7	2	1	9		6			4	3	10*		G Ashby	28
12		8	5*			14				11			7	2	1	9		4	10•		6	3			M Bodenham	29
12		8	5			14				11			7•	2	1	9		6*			4	3	10		R Groves	30
S		8	5			S				11			7	2	1	9		6			4	3	10		J Martin	31
12		8*	5			14				11			7•	2	1	9		6			4	3	10		M Bodenham	32
2	14	8	5							11			7	3	1	9		6•	12		4		10*		B Coddington	33
2		8	5			12		S		11			7	3	1	9		6	10*		4				W Burge	34
2	12		5			10•	8*			11	14		7	3	1	9		6			4				A Wilkie	35
2		8	5			10	S			11	S		7	3	1	9		6			4				R Hamer	36
	12	8	5			10	S			11			7	3	1	9		6*			4	2			T Fitzharris	37
2	6	8	5			10				11			7	3	1	9		S	S		4				G Singh	38
S	6	8	5			10				11			7	3	1	9		S			4	2			P Durkin	39
14	6	8	5			10*				11			7	3	1	9		12	7		4	2•			D Frampton	40
S		8	5			10				11			7	3	1	9		6	S		4	2			D Elleray	41
7	6	8	5			10*	S			11			12	3	1	9					4	2			A Shepherd	42
6	9		5			8	10			11	12		7	3	1						4	2*			P Taylor	43
2	8		5			12	6			11	9*		7	3	1			S	10		4				K A Cooper	44
2	8	6				9				11*	10		7	3	1			5	S	12	4				R Pawley	45
2	8	6				9				11*	10		7	3	1			5	S	12	4				P Vanes	46
2*	12	6	5			9				11	10		7	3	1			8•		14	4				M Bailey	47
	14	6	5							11	10		7	3•	1			8	9*		4				K Cooper	48
	3		5			9				11*	10		12		14	1		8•			4	6			A Bennett	49
2	3	12	5			9				11	10		7		S	1		8*			4	6			J Rushton	50
2*	3		5			9				11	10		7		8	1		12	5		4	6			S Lodge	51
2	3		5			9*				11	10		7		8	1		14	12		4	6•			P Harrison	52
2	3		5			9				11	10		7		8	1		S			4	6			R Milford	53
2	3		5			9				11	10		7		8•	1		12			4	6*			D Phillips	54
	3*		5			9•				11	10		7		8	1		12	6		4	14			D Shadwell	55
	S		5			9				11	10		7		3	1		2	8		4	6			D Gallagher	56
			5			9				11	10		7		3	1		2•	8*	14	4	6			J Parker	57
3	31	26	32	44	5	18	17	6	6	46	14	4	36	12	42	42	24	3	8	17	5	5	30	20	5	**League Appearances**	
2	4	3	2+1	4	2	3+1	2	2	2	4	0+1	2	2+1	2	3	2	2	1		0+1			2	1		**Substitute Appearances**	
1+1	1	3	3				3				3	1		2	3	3			2	3			2	3		**R/lows Appearances**	
			3							3	1		2	3	3	2		1	2	3	2	1				**FA Cup Appearances**	
	3	2	4		2		3+1	1	4				1	2	1	2	3	2	1	2	0+1	1		1		**Autoglass Appearances**	

Also Played: Posn.(Game): M Coates 14(56), D Barnhouse 12(57), Trick 12(13), Kendall 1(6,9,13), Davies 6(9,13,55), Wallace 2(47,48), Hodgson 12(47,53)7(48)14(54)

Players on Loan: J Beauchamp (Oxford), P Purnell (Bristol Rov), D Brazil (Man Utd), R Wallace (Leeds)

SWANSEA CITY

Club Colours: All white
Change Colours: All yellow
Reserves League: Clifton Stockbrokers League

Previous League: Southern League
Previous Name: Swansea Town until Feb 1970
Previous Managers: 1912-14 Walter Whittaker   1914-15 William Bartlett   1919-26 Joe Bradshaw   1927-31 James Thompson 1934-39 Neil Harris   1939-47 Haydn Green   1947-55 Billy McCandless   1955-58 Ron Burgess   1958-65 Trevor Morris   1965-66 Glyn Davies   1967-69 Billy Lucas   1969-72 Roy Bentley   1972-75 Harry Gregg   1975-78 Harry Griffiths   1978-84 John Toshack 1984 Colin Appleton   1985-86 John Bond   1986-89 Terry Yorath   1989-90 Ian Evans   1990-91 Terry Yorath   1991- Frank Burrows
In addition B Watts-Jones, Joe Sykes, Walter Robins, Doug Livermore, Wyndham Evans, Les Chappel, and Tommy Hutchison all acted in a 'caretaker' capacity for short periods.
Honours: Champions Div 3S 1924-25, 1948-49   Welsh Cup Winners (10 times)
League Career: Original Members of Div 3 1920   Promoted to Div 2 1924-25   Relegated to Div 3S 1946-47   Promoted to Div 2 1948-49   Relegated to Div 3 1964-65   Relegated to Div 4 1966-67
Promoted to Div 3 1969-70   Relegated to Div 4 1972-73   Promoted to Div 3 1977-78   Promoted to Div 2 1978-79
Promoted to Div 1 1980-81   Relegated to Div 2 1982-83   Relegated to Div 3 1983-84   Relegated to Div 4 1985-86
Promoted to Div 3 1987-88

CLUB RECORDS

Most Appearances for Club: 'Wilfy' Milne (1920-37): League 585 + FA Cup 44 + Welsh Cup 28 **Total 657**
Most Capped Player: Ivor Allchurch, 42 Wales   **For England:** None
Record Goalscorer in a Match: Jack Fowler 5 v Charlton Athletic, 6-1 Div 3S, 27.9.1924
Record League Goalscorer in a Season: Cyril Pearce 35, 1931-32   **In All Competitions:** Cyril Pearce 39 (League 35 + Welsh Cup 4)
Record League Goalscorer in a Career: Ivor Allchurch 166 (1949-58 & 1965-68)   **In All Competitions:** Ivor Allchurch, 189 (League 166 + FA Cup 9 + League Cup 4 + Welsh Cup 10)
Record Transfer Fee Received: £370,000 from Leeds United for Alan Curtis, May 1979
Record Transfer Fee Paid: £340,000 to Liverpool for Colin Irwin, Aug 1981
Best Performances: League: 6th Div 1 1981-82   **FA Cup:** Semi-finals 1926, 1964   **League Cup:** 4th Round 1964-65, 1976-77
European Cup Winners Cup: 2nd round   **Welsh Cup** Winners (10)
Most League Points: (3pts a win) 70, Div 4, 1987-88   (2pts a win) 62, Div 3S, 1948-49
Most League Goals: 92, Div 4, 1976-77
Record League Victory and Most Goals Scored in a League Match: 8-0 v Hartlepool United, Div 4, 1.4.1978
Most Goals Scored in a Cup Tie: 12-0 v Sliema Wanderers (Malta), 1st rnd 1st leg, European Cup Winners Cup, 15.9.1982
Record League Defeat: 1-8 v Fulham, Div 2, 22.1.1938   1-8 v Newcastle United, Div 2, 2.9.1939   0-7 v Tottenham Hotspur, Div 2, 3.12.1932   0-7 v Bristol Rovers, Div 2, 2.10.1954   0-7 v Workington, Div 3, 4.10.1960
Record Cup Defeat: 0-8 v Liverpool, FA Cup Round 3 replay, 9.1.1990   0-8 v Monaco, ECWC 1st rnd 2nd leg, 1.10.1991
European Competitions entered: European Cup Winners Cup 1961-62, 1966-67, 1981-82, 1982-83, 1983-84, 1989-90, 1991-92
Oldest Player in a League Match: Tommy Hutchison 43 years 171 days v Southend, 12.3.91
Youngest Player in a League Match: Nigel Dalling, 15 years 10 months

---

LONGEST LEAGUE RUNS	
of undefeated matches: 19 (1970-71)	of league matches without a win: 15 (1989)
of undefeated home matches: 28 (1925-27)	of undefeated away matches: 12 (1970-71)
without home win: 9 (1938)	without an away win: 46 (1982-84)
of league wins: 8 (1961)	of home wins: 17 (1948-49)
of league defeats: 9 (1990-91)	of away wins: 4 (1955-56, 1987-88)

SWANSEA CITY

							APPEARANCES				GOALS			
PLAYERS NAME Honours	Ht	Wt	Birthdate	Birthplace Transfers	Contract Date	Clubs	League	L/Cup	FA Cup	Other	Lg	L/C	FAC	Oth
GOALKEEPERS														
Roger Freestone	6.2	14.6	19.08.68	Newport	02.04.86	Newport Co	13			1				
W: u21.1; Div2'89				£95,000	10.03.87	Chelsea	42	2	3	6				
				Loan	29.09.89	Swansea City	14			1				
				Loan	09.03.90	Hereford Utd	8							
				£50,000	05.09.91	Swansea City	42	2	3	2				
DEFENDERS														
Reuben Agboola	5.10	11.9	30.05.62	London	05.04.80	Southampton (A)	89+1	10	7	5				
Div.3.88				£150,000	10.01.85	Sunderland	129+11	12+2	6+1	9				
				Loan	30.10.86	Charlton Ath	1							
				Loan	21.11.90	Port Vale	9							
				Free	08.11.91	Swansea City	20+1		3	1				
Jonathan Ford	6.0	12.0	12.04.68	Birmingham		Cradley Town								
				£5,000	19.08.91	Swansea City	42+2	3	2	1				
Mark Harris	6.1	13.0	15.07.63	Reading		Workingham								
					18.05.88	Crystal Palace	0+2							
				Loan	07.08.89	Burnley	4	2						
				£22,500	22.09.89	Swansea City	126	6	11	11	6		3	1
MIDFIELD														
John Cornforth	6.1	12.8	07.10.67	Whitely Bay	11.10.85	Sunderland (A)	21+11	0+1		1+3	2			
				Loan	06.11.86	Doncaster Rovers	6+1			2	3			
				Loan	23.11.89	Shrewsbury Town	3			2				
				Loan	11.01.90	Lincoln City	9				1			
				£50,000	02.08.91	Swansea City	17	2						
Russell Coughlin	5.8	11.8	15.02.60	Swansea	03.03.78	Manchester City (A)								
				£40,000	26.03.79	Blackburn Rovers	22+2	1+1						
				£20,000	30.10.80	Carlisle Utd	114+16	5+1	12		13	1		
				£20,000	25.07.84	Plymouth A	128+3	8	8	5	18	2	1	1
				£75,000	11.12.87	Blackpool	100+2	9	13	10	8	1		1
				Loan	11.09.90	Shrewsbury Town	4+1	1						
					17.10.90	Swansea City	61+1	2+1	5	7	1			
David Hough	5.11	12.0	20.02.66	Crewe	27.02.84	Swansea City (A)	202+25	13+1	15+1	19	9	1	1	
W: Y; WC'89'91														
Andrew Legg	5.8	10.07	28.07.66	Neath	12.08.88	Swansea City	105+6	7+1	11	11+2	17		2	3
Keith Walker	6.0	11.09	17.04.66	Edinburgh		Falkirk	82+9	5	5		16	3	2	
						St. Mirren	41+2	3	1	3	6			
				£80,000	23.11.89	Swansea City	62+7	2	8	3	1		1	
FORWARDS														
Paul Chalmers	5.10	10.03	31.10.63	Glasgow		Celtic	0+4				1			
S: Y.; WC'91				Loan		Bradford City	2							
						St. Mirren	77+24	3	4+2	2+2	23	1	3	
				£110,000	23.11.89	Swansea City	39+19	0+1	3	2	13	1		
Jimmy Gilligan	6.2	11.2	24.01.64	Hammersmith	04.08.81	Watford (A)	18+9	2+1	5	3+1	6	2	1	2
E: Y.3; FAYC'82; WC'88				Loan	07.10.82	Lincoln City	0+3							
				£100,000	06.08.85	Grimsby Town	19+6	3	0+1	2	4	2		
					17.06.86	Swindon Town	13+4	2+1	2		5		1	
				Loan	05.02.87	Newport Co	4+1				1			
					26.03.87	Lincoln City	11				1			
				£17,500	22.07.87	Cardiff City	99	8	4	10	35	1	4	7
				£215,000	03.10.89	Portsmouth	24+8		0+1	1	5			
				£175,000	07.08.90	Swansea City	60+2	4	7	6	23	1	3	2
David Hodgson	5.10	12.12	01.11.60	Gateshead	19.08.78	Middlesbrough	116+9	6	9		16	4		
E:u21.7,Div1'83				£450,000	12.08.82	Liverpool	21+7	4+1	3	3+4	4	2	1	2
				£125,000	24.08.84	Sunderland	42+8	8+1	1	1+1	4	1		1
				Free	18.07.86	Norwich City	3+3	1	1	1	1	3		
						JCdP								
				Free	02.08.88	Sheffield Wed	6+5		1		1		1	
				Free	01.08.89	Mazda (Jap)								
				Free	26.03.92	Swansea City	1+3							
ADDITIONAL CONTRACT PLAYERS														
Jason Bowen	5.6	8.10	24.08.72		01.07.90	Swansea City (T)	6+8		3	0+1				
Shaun Chappell					15.07.91	Swansea City	17+4	0+1	2	2	2	1		
Mark Davies						Swansea City	1			2				
James Heeps			16.05.71	Luton	03.07.89	Swansea City (T)	1							
Stephens Jenkins	5.10	10.9	16.07.72	Merthyr	01.07.90	Swansea City (T)	31+4	4	1+1	4				
Lee Jones					02.08.88	Swansea City								
(M) Desmond Lyttle	5.9	12.0	24.09.71	Wolverhampton	09.01.90	Leicester City (T)								
				Free	09.07.92	Swansea City								
Christan McLean						Bath								
						Swansea City	4	2		1				
Steven McMahon						Ferguslie,								
				Free	16.08.91	Swansea City								

LEADING LEAGUE GOALSCORERS SEASONS 1985-86 – 1991-92

1985-86	ROGER GIBBINS	6	1986-87	SEAN McCARTHY	14
1987-88	COLIN PASCOE	13	1988-89	ANDY MELVILLE	10
1989-90	PAUL RAYNOR	6	1990-91	JIMMY GILLIGAN	16
	1991-92	JOHN WILLIAMS	11			

VETCH FIELD Swansea SA1 3SU

Capacity: 16,550   **Covered Standing:** 13,003   **Seating:** 3,547

Tel: Ground: 0792 474114   **Ticket Sales:** 0792 462584   **Clubcall:** 0898 12 16 39

All premium rate calls (0898/0891) cost 36p per minute cheap rate and 48p per minute at all other times. Call costings correct at time of going to press.

ATTENDANCES
Highest: 32,796 v Arsenal, FA Cup Round 4, 17.2.1968

Lowest: 1,311 v Brentford, Div 4, 26.4.1976

Record Receipts: £36,477.42 v Liverpool, Div 1, 18.9.1982

Season Tickets:
Stands: from £155 to £16, juv/OAP £100
Ground: from £90 to £95, juv/OAP £50-£55

Cost of Stand Tickets: Centre Stand: £8.50; East Stand: adult £8, 1+1 £11, 1+2 £12.50; Jewson Stand: £8, 1+1 £11, 1+2 £12.50; Wing Stand: adult £7.50, OAP £5
Terraces: East Terrace/North Bank: adult £5, OAP £3, juv £2.50

Match and Ticket Information: Tickets are on sale at the ticket office in the ground two weeks before each match

Car Parking: Car park 200 yards from ground in The Kingsway. There is also ample street parking

Nearest Railway Station: Swansea High St. (0792 46 7777)

How to get to the ground

Five minutes walk from city bus station or take South Wales Transport Co Ltd from High Street General Station to Lowere Oxford Street. Car parking near ground at Quadrant

Value Rating: ★ ★

Programme Editor: Reg Pike, I.S.M., T.D.

Price of 1992-93 Programme: £1
Number of Pages: 28
Subscriptions: Please contact club

Local Newspapers: Evening Post, Western Mail

Local Radio Stations: Swansea Sound, BBC Radio Wales

SWINDON TOWN

Division 1

SWINDON TOWN F.C.

Formed: 1881 | **Turned Professional:** 1894 | **Ltd Co:** 1894

SPONSORED BY: Burmah Petroleum Fuels Ltd | **NICKNAME:** The Robins

President
C Green

Chairman
R V Hardman

Vice-Chairman
J M Spearman

Directors
P T Archer   Sir D Seton Wills, Bt
C J Puffett
J R Hunt (Associate Director)

Chief Executive
Peter Day

Secretary
Jon Pollard (0793 430430)

Marketing Manager
Mike Sullivan

Team Manager
Glenn Hoddle

Assistant Manager
John Gorman

Reserve Team Coach
Andy Rowland

Youth Team Coach
John Trollope

Physiotherapist
Kevin Morris

Groundsman
G Warren

Club Statistician for the Directory
Tony Angell

IT will no doubt always be argued that the sale of Duncan Shearer cost Swindon any chance they may have had of winning a place in the Premier League. Certainly the loss of both recognised strikers, Steve White not playing after January due to injury, was sorely felt in the final two months when Swindon averaged less than a goal a game. Even so, only one match was lost after Shearer's departure.

Of greater significance were the 23 mid-season matches which Glenn Hoddle missed through injury and which brought only seven victories. That sequence left Swindon chasing the front runners for the remainder of the season, unable to turn a procession of away draws into victories in order to make up lost ground. The sale of Shearer removed the one man likely to score the match winning goals – but Swindon had not been winning away matches even with him in the team.

The financial situation which has forced the club to sell key players during the past two seasons is obviously no fault of the present board but inevitably supporters were becoming disillusioned and asking how many more would be sold to keep the club afloat. Fitzroy Simpson's move to Manchester City was clearly to his benefit as well as the club's but the sale of Shearer to a promotion rival was very difficult to accept. In spite of this there was much to please. The skill and influence of Hoddle was plain to see, indeed, before his injury there was even a press campaign for his recall to the England team. His pre-season signing of Shaun Taylor, together with the later return of Paul Bodin did much to strengthen the defence, Taylor forming a solid partnership with the ever reliable Calderwood. In attack Dave Mitchell, though not a prolific goalscorer, proved an able replacement for Steve White and his presence undoubtedly helped create many chances for Shearer.

In the final reckoning Swindon were probably not quite strong enough to be a genuine promotion contender especially in midfield where they won much praise for their football but lacked a ball winner.

With a little strengthening the present team is capable of mounting another challenge for promotion but the gap between top and bottom of the division is relatively narrow and Swindon's ability to survive without selling their best players will obviously be a key factor in their prospects for next season.

Tony Angell

Back row L-R: John Moncur, Darren Hall, Fraser Digby, Paul Hunt, Nicky Hammond, David Bennett, Craig Maskell, Steve White. **Middle:** John Trollope (Youth Team Manager), Ross MacLaren, Nicky Summerbee, Colin Calderwood, Shaun Taylor, Adrian Viveash, David Mitchell, Andrew Thomson, Kevin Horlock, Andy Rowland (Reserve Team Coach). **Front:** Kevin Morris (Physiotherapist), Martin Ling, David Kerslake, Wayne O'Sullivan, Glenn Hoddle (Team Manager), John Gorman (Asst. Manager), Paul Bodin, Shaun Close, Micky Hazard, Eddie Buckley (Kit Manager).

SWINDON TOWN

DIVISION TWO: 8th **FA CUP:** 5th RND **RUMBELOWS CUP:** 4th RND

M	DATE	COMP.	VEN	OPPONENTS	RESULT	H/T	LGE POS	GOALSCORERS/GOAL TIMES	ATTEN-DANCE
1	A 17	BL	H	Leicester City	D 0-0	0-0			13,238
2	20	RC 1/1	H	West Bromwich A.	W 2-0	2-0		Mitchell 5, Hazard 35	6,811
3	24	BL	A	Cambridge United	L 2-3	1-1	19	Shearer 43, Hazard (pen) 84	(6,232)
4	28	RC 1/2	A	West Bromwich A.	D 2-2	0-1		Shearer 83, 87	(7,423)
5	31	BL	H	Barnsley	W 3-1	0-1	12	White 51, Ling 69, Shearer 80	7,742
6	S 3	BL	A	Ipswich Town	W 4-1	2-1	7	White 3, Calderwood 43, Taylor 81, Hazard 88	(11,002)
7	7	BL	A	Port Vale	D 2-2	0-0	8	White 55, MacLaren 81	(7,168)
8	14	BL	H	Sunderland	W 5-3	3-0	8	White 7, Simpson 36, Hazard 38, 55 (pen), Shearer 89	11,694
9	17	BL	H	Bristol Rovers	W 1-0	1-0		Jones 40	11,162
10	21	BL	A	Wolverhampton W	L 1-2	0-1	5	White 86	(15,219)
11	25	RC 2/1	A	Millwall	D 2-2	2-0		White 3, 34	(6,048)
12	28	BL	H	Watford	W 3-1	2-0	4	Shearer 8, Simpson 44, Taylor 80	8,863
13	O 1	ZDS 1	H	Oxford United	D 3-3	2-0		White 70, 104, MacLaren 79	5,868
14	5	BL	A	Plymouth Argyle	W 4-0	2-0	3	Shearer 4 (7, 27, 61, 84)	(6,802)
15	8	RC 2/1	H	Millwall	W 3-1	0-1		Shearer 51, 76, White 54	7,137
16	12	BL	A	Derby County	L 1-2	0-1	4	Hazard (pen) 62	11,881
17	19	BL	H	Blackburn Rovers	W 2-1	0-0	4	White 64, Calderwood 90	11,008
18	23	ZDS 2	A	Chelsea	L 0-1	0-0			(5,784)
19	26	BL	A	Brighton & H A	W 2-0	1-0	4	Shearer 18, 49	(7,370)
20	29	RC 3	H	Huddersfield Town	W 4-1	2-0		Shearer 8, 76, Summerbee 15, Taylor 84	(10,088)
21	N 2	BL	H	Newcastle United	W 2-1	1-0	2	Calderwood 40, White 87	10,731
22	6	BL	A	Charlton Athletic	D 0-0	0-0	1		(5,360)
23	9	BL	A	Southend United	L 2-3	0-1	3	White 60, Shearer 81	(7,709)
24	16	BL	H	Portsmouth	L 2-3	0-0	4	White 57, 62	11,008
25	22	BL	A	Tranmere Rovers	D 0-0	0-0	4		(9,585)
26	30	BL	H	Grimsby Town	D 1-1	1-1	7	Simpson 36	8,836
27	D 7	BL	A	Middlesbrough	D 2-2	0-1	8	Simpson 60, Shearer 65	(13,300)
28	17	RC 4	H	Crystal Palace	L 0-1	0-1			10,044
29	20	BL	H	Ipswich Town	D 0-0	0-0			8,401
30	26	BL	A	Bristol City	D 1-1	1-0		Shearer 9	(14,636)
31	28	BL	A	Barnsley	D 1-1	1-0	8	Shearer 9	(8,357)
32	J 1	BL	H	Millwall	W 3-1	3-0	7	Shearer 20, 42, Ling 27	9,746
33	4	FAC 3	H	Watford	W 3-2	2-1		Shearer 3, 79, Mitchell 9	9,813
34	11	BL	H	Cambridge United	L 0-2	0-0	8		11,008
35	18	BL	A	Leicester City	L 1-3	0-1	9	Bodin 73	(14,226)
36	25	FAC 4	A	Cambridge United	W 3-0	1-0		Calderwood 45, Shearer 48, 52	(7,428)
37	28	BL	H	Oxford United	W 2-1	1-0		Kerslake 43, Shearer 61	9,707
38	F 1	BL	A	Blackburn Rovers	L 1-2	1-0	9	Mitchell 41	(14,887)
39	4	BL	A	Bristol City	W 2-0	0-0	8	Jones 51, Shearer 81	9,627
40	8	BL	A	Brighton & H A	W 2-1	0-1	4	Calderwood 70, 80	9,127
41	16	FAC 5	H	Aston Villa	L 1-2	0-1		Mitchell 80	16,402
42	22	BL	A	Grimsby Town	D 0-0	0-0	6		(6,817)
43	29	BL	H	Middlesbrough	L 0-1	0-0			10,379
44	M 7	BL	A	Oxford United	L 3-5	2-3	9	Close 1, Mitchell 41, 71	(7,995)
45	10	BL	H	Charlton Athletic	L 1-2	0-1		Shearer 25	7,196
46	14	BL	A	Newcastle United	L 1-3	0-1	10	Mitchell 60	(23,138)
47	17	BL	H	Tranmere Rovers	W 2-0	1-0	10	Shearer 20, 48	6,779
48	21	BL	H	Southend United	W 3-1	1-1	8	Shearer 13, Bodin (pen) 56, Mitchell 62	9,014
49	28	BL	A	Portsmouth	D 1-1	0-0	10	Jones 49	(16,007)
50	A 4	BL	H	Port Vale	W 1-0	1-0		Jones 5	8,567
51	8	BL	A	Millwall	D 1-1	1-1	8	Gibson 36	(6,722)
52	12	BL	A	Bristol Rovers	D 1-1	0-0	8	Taylor 75	(6,905)
53	18	BL	H	Wolverhampton W	W 1-0	1-0	8	Ling 10	10,863
54	20	BL	A	Watford	D 0-0	0-0			(9,911)
55	25	BL	H	Plymouth Argyle	W 1-0	1-0	8	Taylor 26	10,463
56	27	BL	A	Sunderland	D 0-0	0-0	8		(16,716)
57	M 2	BL	A	Derby County	L 1-2	0-1	8	Hazard 89	(22,608)

Best Home League Attendance: 13,238 v Leicester City   Smallest: 6,779 v Tranmere Rovers   Av Home Att: 9,871

Goal Scorers: Compared with 90-91: +364

League (69): Shearer 22, White 10, Hazard 6 (3 pens), Mitchell 5, Calderwood 5, Simpson 4, Taylor 4, Jones 4, Ling 3, Bodin 2 (1 pen) Gibson, MacLaren, Kerslake, Close

R/lows C (13): Shearer 6, White 3, Mitchell, Taylor, Summerbee, Hazard

FA Cup (7): Shearer 4, Mitchell 2, Calderwood

ZDS Cup (3): White 2, MacLaren

1991-92

Digby F.	Kerslake D.	Summerbee N.	Hoddle G.	Calderwood C.	Taylor S.	Hazard M.	Shearer D.	Simpson F.	MacLaren R.	Mitchell D.	Foley S.	White S.	Hammond N.	Jones T.	Viveash A.	Ling M.	Close S.	Lorenzo N.	Bodin P.	Gibson T.	Waddock G.	Moncur J.	Trollope P.	Referee	
1	2	3*	4	5	6	7	8	9	10	11•	12	14												M Pierce	1
1		3	4	5	6	7	8	9	10	11•	2*	14		12										J Moules	2
1		3	4	5	6	7	8	9	10*	11•	2			12		14								I Borrett	3
1			4	5	6	7	8	11•	10			9		2	3	S	S							A Bennett	4
1			4	5	6	7*	8	9	10			11		2	3•	12		14						M Bodenham	5
1			4	5	6	7	8	9	10			11*		2	3	12		S						P Danson	6
			4	5	6	7*	8	9	10			11	1	2	3	12		S						L Dilkes	7
	S		4	5	6	7	8	9	10			11	1	2	3	S								D Elleray	8
		3	4	5	6	7	8	9	10			11	1	2	S	S								G Singh	9
		3	4	5		7*	8	9	10			11	1	2	S		12							A Ward	10
		3†	4	5	6	7	8•	9	10			11	1	2	14		S							D Gallagher	11
	14	3	4	5		7•	8	9	10			11	1	2			S							W Burge	12
1	4	3•	14	5	6		8	9	10			11		2		7*	12							P Durkin	13
1	2	3	4*	5	6	7	8	9	10			11		14			S							K Cooper	14
1	4	3		5	6	7	8	9	10			11		2	S		S							H King	15
1	2			5	6	7	8	9•	10		14	11		4	3*	12								P Wright	16
	2	3		5	6	7	8	9	10		S	11	1	4			S							R Groves	17
	2	3		5	6	7	8	9	10		S	11	1	4			S							J Rushton	18
	2	3		5	6	7	8	9	10		S	11	1	4			S							J Carter	19
	2	3		5	6	7	8	9	10		14	11•	1	4	S									T Holbrook	20
	2	3		5	6	7	8	9	10		S	11	1	4			S							A Buksh	21
	2	3		5	6	7*	8	9	10		12	11•	1	4		14								R Pawley	22
	2	3		5	6	7	8	9	10		14	11	1	4•	S									A Smith	23
	2	3		5		7	8	9	10		S	11	1	4	6		S							A Gunn	24
	2	S		5		7	8	9	10		3	11	1	4	6		S							J Parker	25
	2	3		5		7	8	9	10		3	11	1	4•	6		S							P Don	26
	2	3		5		7	8	9	10	S	4	11	1		6		S							R Shepherd	27
	2			5	6	7	8	9	10		4•	11	1	12	3*	14								K Hackett	28
	2	14		5	6	7	8*	9	10	12	4•	11	1		3									M James	29
	2	14		5	6	7*	8	9	10	12		11*	1	3		4								R Gifford	30
	2	S		5	6	7	8	9	10	12		11*	1	3		4								P Harrison	31
	2	S		5	6	7	8	9	10	11	S		1	3		4								A Bennett	32
	2	14		5	6	7	8	9•	10	11	S		1	3		4								A Gunn	33
	2	14		5	6	7	8	9*	10	11	12		1	3		4•								R Lewis	34
1	2	14		5	6	7	8	9	10	11			S	4•					3					P Wright	35
1	2	14		5	6	7	8	9	10	11			S	4•					3					W Burns	36
1	2	S		5	6	7	8	9	10	11				12		4*			3					K Barrett	37
1	2	14		5	6	7	8*		10•	11				9		4	12		3					G Ashby	38
	2	S		5	6	7	8		10	11			1	9		4	S		3					K Burge	39
	2	S		5	6	7	8	12	10*	11			1	9		4	S		3					D Shadwell	40
	2	S		5	6	7	8	14	10	11			1	9		4•			3					R Lewis	41
	2	14		5	6	7	8	9	10•	11			1	4		S			3					R Hart	42
	2*	14		5	6	7•	8	9	10	11			1	4			12		3					P Vanes	43
	2	7*	10	5	6		8			11			1	4	S	9	12		3					D Phillips	44
	2	7	10	5	6		8						1	4*	12	9	11		3			S		B Hill	45
1	2	S		5	6	7	8			11				12		4*			3					A Flood	46
1	2	9	S	5	6	7	8			11				4		S	S		3					P Durkin	47
1	2	S	10	5	6	7	8			11				4		S			3		9			R Pawley	48
1	2	12	10*	5	6	7				11				4		S			3	8	9			D Axcell	49
1	2			5	6	7				11				4		10*	S		3	8	9	12		R Milford	50
1	2	14		5	6	7				11				4		10	S		3	8		9•		P Foakes	51
1	2	S	10	5	6	7				11				4		9	S		3	8				H King	52
1	2		10	5	6	7				11				4*		9	S		3	8	12			R Groves	53
1	2		10	5	6	7				11				4•		9	12		3	8*	S			P Jones	54
1	2		10	5	6	7				11*				4•		9	12		3	8	14			S Lodge	55
1	2	14	10	5	6	7				11				9•		12			3	8*	4			T West	56
1	2	S	10	5	6	7				11*				9		8			3	12	4			M Reed	57
21	38	16	22	46	42	44	37	29	32	24	5	21	25	37	9	17	4	2	21	8	5	1		League Appearances	
	1	11						1		3	4	2		4	1	4	8	2		1	1	2		Substitute Appearances	
3	3	4	3	6	6	6	6	6	6	1		2+1	5+1	3		4+2	2+1		0+1					R/lows Appearances	
1	3	0+2		3	3	3	3	2+1	3			2	2	3					2					FA Cup Appearances	
1	2	2	0+1	2	2	1	2	2						2	1	1*								ZDS Cup Appearances	

Players on Loan: T Gibson (Wimbledon), G Waddock (Q.P.R.)

SWINDON TOWN

Club Colours: Red shirts, white shorts, red stockings with white trim
Change Colours: Green & white shirts with navy blue & red collars, navy blue shorts, red stockings
Reserves League: Neville Ovenden Football Combination

COMPETITIONS			
Div. 2	Div. 3	Div. 3S	Div. 4
63-65	20-21	21-58	82-86
69-74	58-63		
87-	65-69		
	74-82		
	86-87		

HONOURS		
Div. 4	League Cup	Anglo/Ital
85-86	68-69	1970

MOST APPEARANCES: JOHN TROLLOPE 886+3 (60-81)				
Year	League	FA Cup	Lge Cup	Others
1960-61	44	3	3	
1961-62	46	2	3	
1962-63	46	4	2	
1963-64	42	3	4	
1964-65	42	1	1	
1965-66	46	3	1	
1966-67	46	8	5	
1967-68	46	4	2	
1968-69	19+1	1	2	
1969-70	42	4	2	7
1970-71	39	2	3	4
1971-72	42	1	1	
1972-73	34	2	1	
1973-74	36	2	3	
1974-75	46	5	1	
1975-76	46	5	4	
1976-77	35	7		
1977-78	40	4	6	
1978-79	16+2		2	
1979-80				
1980-81	14			
	767+3	61	47	11

MOST GOALS IN A CAREER		
HARRY MORRIS 230 (1926-33)		
Season	League	FA Cup
1926-27	47	1
1927-28	38	6
1928-29	27	5
1929-30	28	1
1930-31	35	
1931-32	29	
1932-33	12	1
Total	216	14

MANAGERS			
As secretary, Sam Allen took control of team matters between 1902-1948. However, a team manager was appointed in 1933.			
Name	Seasons	Best	Worst
Ted Vizzard	1933-39	8(3S)	19(3S)
Neil Harris	1939		
Lois Page	1945-53	4(3S)	18(3S)
Maurice Lindley	1953-58	4(3S)	24(3S)
Bert Head	1958-65	14(2)	16(3)
Danny Williams	1965-69	2(3)	10(3)
Fred Ford	1969-71	5(2)	12(2)
Dave Mackay	1971-72	11(2)	11(2)
Les Allen	1972-74	11(2)	22(2)
Danny Williams	1974-78	4(3)	19(3)
Bob Smith	1978-80	5(3)	10(3)
John Trollope	1980-83	17(3)	8(4)
Ken Beamish	1983-84	17(4)	17(4)
Lou Macari	1984-89	12(2)	8(4)
Osvaldo Ardiles	1989-91	4(2)	
Glenn Hoddle	1991-		

RECORD TRANSFER FEE RECEIVED			
Amount	Club	Player	Date
£1,000,000	Southampton	Alan McLoughlin	11/90
£400,000	Sheffield Wed	Phil King	11/89
£250,000	Aston Villa	Paul Rideout	5/83
£175,000	Chelsea	Alan Mayes	12/80

RECORD TRANSFER FEE PAID			
Amount	Club	Player	Date
£450,000	Bari	Nestor Lorenzo	11/90
£250,000	Huddersfield	Duncan Shearer	7/88
£150,000	Southampton	Dave Peach	3/80
£88,000	Wolverhampton	Peter Eastoe	3/74

BARCLAYS BUSINESS CENTRE
Swindon Business Centre
PO Box No. 28
28 Regent Street
Swindon SN1 1JW
Tel: 0793 512222

BARCLAYBANK MACHINE

LONGEST LEAGUE RUNS	
of undefeated matches:	22 (12.1.1986-23.8.1986)
of undefeated home matches:	26 (24.2.1968-29.3.1969)
without home win:	10 (28.2.1956-15.9.1956)
of league wins:	8 (2.1.1926-27.3.1926) (12.1.1986-15.3.1986)
of league defeats:	6 (1967) (3.5.1980-6.9.1980)
of league matches without a win:	13 (12.3.1956-8.9.1956) (1.1.1974-29.4.1974)
of undefeated away matches:	13 (18.1.1986-6.9.1986)
without an away win:	30 (25.11.1972-15.4.1974)
of home wins:	14 (26.8.1985-15.3.1986)
of away wins:	6 (18.1.1986-8.3.1986)

PREVIOUS LEAGUE
Southern League

BIGGEST VICTORIES
League: 9-1 v Luton Town, Division 3S, 28.4.1921
8-0 v Newport County, Div 3S, 26.12.1938
8-0 v Bury, Division 3, 8.12.1979
F.A. Cup: 10-1 v Farnham United Breweries FC (a), Round 1, 28.11.1925
League Cup: 4-0 v Darlington, Round 2, 1962-63
5-1 v Cardiff City, Round 2, 1977-78
4-0 v Darlington, Round 2, 9.10.1990

BIGGEST DEFEATS
League: 0-9 v Torquay United, Division 3S, 8.3.1952
F.A. Cup: 1-10 v Manchester City, Round 2, 29.1.1930
League Cup: 0-5 v Notts County, Round 3, 1962-63
0-5 v Liverpool, Round 3, 1980-81

MOST POINTS
3 points a win: 102, Division 4, 1985-86 (League record)
2 points a win: 64, Division 3, 1968-69

MOST GOALS IN A SEASON
Harry Morris 48, (47 League, 1 FA Cup) 1926-27.
5 goals once = 5; 4 goals once = 4; 3 goals 3 times = 9; 2 goals 5 times = 10; 1 goal 20 times = 20.

MOST GOALS
100, 1926-27, Division 3S.
Morris 47, Eddelston 11, Thom 8, Wall 7, Petrie 6, Denyer 5, Dickinson 3, Flood 3, Jeffries 3, Archer 1, Weston 1, Brown 1, Bailey 1, Johnson 1, Daniel 1, og 1.

MOST GOALS IN A MATCH
5. Harry Morris v Queens Park Rangers, 18.12.1927, Div 3S (6-2).
5. v Norwich City, 26.4.1930, Div 3S (5-1).
5. Keith East v Mansfield, 20.11.1965, Div 3. (6-2).

MOST FIRST CLASS MATCHES IN A SEASON
64 (46 League, 4 FA Cup, 4 League Cup, 5 Freight Rover Trophy, 5 Play-offs) 1986-87

MOST LEAGUE GOALS CONCEDED
105, Division 3S, 1932-33

MOST LEAGUE WINS
32, Division 4, 1985-86

MOST LEAGUE DRAWS
17, Division 3, 1967-68

MOST LEAGUE DEFEATS
25, Division 3S, 1956-57

OLDEST PLAYER
Alex Ferguson 43 years 103 days, v Bristol City (Div. 3S), 15.11.1947.

YOUNGEST PLAYER
Paul Rideout, 16 years 107 days v Hull (Div 3), 29.11.1980).

MOST CAPPED PLAYER
Rod Thomas (Wales) 30

BEST PERFORMANCES BY SWINDON TOWN

League: 1985-86: Matches played 46, Won 32, Drawn 6, Lost 8, Goals for 82, Goals against 43, Points 102. First in Division 4.

Highest: 1989-90: 4th Division 2.

F.A. Cup: 1910: 1st rnd. Crystal Palace 3-1; 2nd rnd. Burnley 2-0; 3rd rnd. Tottenham Hotspur 3-2; 4th rnd. Manchester City 2-0; Semi-Final Newcastle Utd. 0-2.

1912: 1st rnd. Sutton 5-0; 2nd rnd. Notts County 2-0; 3rd rnd. West Ham United 1-1, 4-0; 4th rnd. Everton 2-1; Semi-Final Barnsley 0-0, 0-1.

League Cup: 1968-69: 1st rnd. Torquay 2-1; 2nd rnd. Bradford City 1-1;4-3; 3rd rnd. Coventry City 2-2, 3-0; 4th rnd. Derby County 0-0, 1-0; Semi-Final Burnley 2-1; Final Arsenal 3-1.

DIVISIONAL RECORDS

	Played	Won	Drawn	Lost	For	Against	Points
DIVISION 2	522	178	152	192	721	727	594
DIVISION 3	828	333	220	275	1244	1067	924
DIVISION 3S	1334	491	333	510	2058	2130	1315
DIVISION 4	184	87	39	58	263	211	300
TOTALS	2868	1089	744	1035	4286	4135	3133

SWINDON TOWN

PLAYERS NAME Honours	Ht	Wt	Birthdate	Birthplace Transfers	Contract Date	Clubs	League	L/Cup	FA Cup	Other	Lg	L/C	FAC	Oth
GOALKEEPERS														
Fraser Digby	6.1	12.12	23.01.67	Sheffield	25.04.85	Manchester Utd. (A)								
E: u21.5, u19.1, Y.7				Loan	01.86	Oldham Ath								
				£32,000	23.12.86	Swindon Town	223	21	13	23				
Nicky Hammond	6.0	11.13	07.09.67	Hornchurch	12.07.85	Arsenal (A)								
				Loan	23.08.86	Bristol Rovers	3							
				Loan	01.09.86	Peterborough U								
				Loan	01.02.87	Aberdeen								
				Free	01.07.87	Swindon Town	34	6	5	4				
DEFENDERS														
Colin Calderwood	6.0	12.0	20.01.65	Stranraer	19.03.82	Mansfield Town	97+3	4	6	7	1		1	
Div.4'86				£30,000	01.07.85	Swindon Town	282+2	32	17	27	18		1	
Darren Hall	5.8		03.01.73	Grays, Essex	09.07.91	Swindon Town (T)								
Glenn Hoddle	6.0	11.6	27.10.57	Hayes		Tottenham H. (A)	370+7	44	47+1	19+4	89	10	11	1
E:53 B.2 U21.12 Y, FAC'81'82, UEFA				£800,000	01.07.87	Monaco (Fra)								
					16.08.91	Swindon Town	22	3		0+1				
Ross MacLaren	5.10	12.12	14.04.62	Edinburgh		Glasgow Rangers								
Div.2'87; WC'85				f	15.08.80	Shrewsbury Town	158+3	11	7+1		18	3	1	
				£67,000	11.07.85	Derby County	113+9	13	9	5	4	1		
				£165,000	04.08.88	Swindon Town	160	19	11	12	9	2		1
Edwin Murray	5.11		31.08.73	Wanstead	09.07.91	Swindon Town (T)	0+1							
Nicholas Summerbee	5.8	11.08	26.08.71	Altrincham	20.07.89	Swindon Town (T)	17+18	4	0+3	2		1		
Shaun Taylor	6.1	12.8	20.02.63	Bideford		Bideford								
Div.4'90					10.12.86	Exeter City	200	12	9	12	17			
				£200,000	26.07.91	Swindon Town	42	6	3	2	4	1		
MIDFIELD														
Paul Bodin	5.10	10.11	13.09.64	Cardiff	01.08.82	Cardiff City	68+7	11	4		4			
W: 1, u21.1, Y						Bath City			8				3	
				£15,000	27.01.88	Newport Co	6				1			
				£30,000	07.03.88	Swindon Town	87+6	12	6	8	9			1
				£550,000	20.03.91	Crystal Palace	8+1	1						
				Loan	05.12.91	Newcastle Utd	6							
				£225,000	10.01.92	Swindon Town	21		2		2			
Mike Hazard	5.7	10.5	05.02.60	Sunderland	02.02.78	Tottenham H. (A)	73+18	11+3	7+3	23	13	5	2	3
FAC'82,UEFA'84				£310,000	19.09.85	Chelsea	78+3	7+3	4+2	5+1	9	1	1	2
				£100,000	11.01.90	Portsmouth	8				1			
				£130,000	01.09.90	Swindon Town	75+3	7	6	2	14	1		
Paul C Hunt	5.7	10.02	08.10.71	Swindon	06.07.89	Swindon Town (T)	2+4	0+3						
David Kerslake	5.8	11.0	19.06.66	London	01.06.83	Q.P.R. (A)	38+20	6+2	2+2	2+2	6	4		
E: u21.1, u19.4, Y.27, S				£110,000	24.11.89	Swindon Town	103	9	7	9	1			
John Moncur	5.7	9.10	22.09.66	Stepney	22.08.84	Tottenham H. (T)	10+11	1+2			1			
				Loan	25.09.86	Doncaster Rovers	4							
				Loan	27.03.87	Cambridge Utd	3+1							
				Loan	22.03.89	Portsmouth	7							
				Loan	19.10.89	Brentford	5			1	1			
				Loan	24.10.91	Ipswich Town	5+1							
				Loan	18.02.92	Nottm. Forest								
				£80,000	30.03.92	Swindon Town	1+2							
Adrian Viveash	6.1	11.9	30.09.69	Swindon	14.07.88	Swindon Town (T)	32+3	5+1	0+1	1	1			
FORWARDS														
David Bennett	6.0	11.2	11.07.59	Manchester	02.08.78	Manchester City	43+9	7	5+1		9	5	1	
FAC'87				£120,000	25.09.81	Cardiff City	75+2	4	4		18	1		
				£100,000	21.07.83	Coventry City	157+15	17	12	8	25	5	3	2
				£250,000	23.03.89	Sheffield Wed	20+8	1		2				1
				£60,000	21.09.90	Swindon Town	1		1					
				Loan	21.11.91	Shrewsbury Town	2				2			
Austin Berkley	5.9		28.01.73	Dartford	13.05.91	Gillingham	0+3			0+3				
				Free	16.05.92	Swindon Town								
Shaun Close	5.8	10.1	08.09.66	Islington	22.08.86	Tottenham H. (T)	3+6	3						
				£40,000	11.03.88	Bournemouth	28+11	3	0+1	1	8			
				£70,000	08.09.89	Swindon Town	12+25	1+4			1	1		
Martin Ling	5.8	10.2	15.07.66	West Ham	13.01.84	Exeter City (A)	109+8	8	4	5	14			
				£25,000	14.07.86	Swindon Town	2	1+1						
				£15,000	16.10.86	Southend Utd	126+12	8	7	11+1	31	2	1	3
				Loan	24.01.91	Mansfield Town	3							
				Loan	28.03.91	Swindon Town	0+1							
				£15,000	15.07.91	Swindon Town	17+4		3	1	3			
Craig Maskell	5.10	11.4	10.04.68	Aldershot	15.04.86	Southampton (A)	2+4				1			
				Loan		Swindon Town								
				£20,000	31.05.88	Huddersfield Town	86+1	6	8	7	43	4	3	4
				£250,000	07.08.90	Reading	60+12	2	5+1	1	27			
				swap	09.07.92	Swindon Town								

SWINDON TOWN CONTINUED

PLAYERS NAME / Honours	Ht	Wt	Birthdate	Birthplace / Transfers	Contract Date	Clubs	APPEARANCES				GOALS			
							League	L/Cup	FA Cup	Other	Lg	L/C	FAC	Oth
David Mitchell	6.1	11.8	13.06.62	Glasgow		Cologne								
Australia: Full caps						Glasgow Rangers	18+8	6+5	2+1	2+3	6	3	1	4
						Feyenoord								
				£200,000	06.01.89	Chelsea	7			1				
				Loan		Newcastle Utd	2				1			
				£30,000	26.07.91	Swindon Town	24+3	1	3		5	1	2	
Steve White	5.10	11.4	02.01.59	Chipping Sodbury		Mangotsfield								
Div.2.82					11.07.77	Bristol Rovers	46+4	2	3		20	1	3	
				£200,000	24.12.79	Luton Town	63+9	3+1	2+1		25	1		
				£150,000	30.07.82	Charlton Ath	29	2			12			
				Loan	28.01.83	Lincoln City	2+1							
				Loan	24.03.83	Luton Town	4							
					26.08.83	Bristol Rovers	89+12	8	7+1	5+2	24	2	2	1
				Free	08.02.86	Swindon Town	178+26	19+5	8+2	21+1	76	9	2	15
ADDITIONAL CONTRACT PLAYERS														
Paul M O'Driscoll						Southampton								
				Monthly	25.07.89	Swindon Town								
Neil Pick					12.09.90	Swindon Town								
Lee Spalding					23.04.91	Swindon Town								

MANAGER: GLENN HODDLE

DATE OF BIRTH: 27.10.1957   **PLACE OF BIRTH:** Hayes

DATE OF APPOINTMENT: 04.04.1991

PREVIOUS CLUBS
  as **Manager:** None
  as **Asst. Man./Coach:** None
  as **Player:** Tottenham Hotspur, Monaco

HONOURS
  as **Manager:** None
  as **Asst. Man./Coach:** None
  as **Player:** UEFA Winners; FA Cup Winners
  International: England Youth, U21, 'B', 33 Full Caps

Value Rating: ★ ★ ★

Programme Editor: Jon Pollard

Price of 1992-93 Programme: £1.20

Number of Pages: 32

Subscriptions: £37.50

Local Newspapers: Wiltshire Newspapers (Evening Advertiser), Western Daily Press.

Local Radio Stations: GWR, BBC Wiltshire Sound.

LEADING LEAGUE GOALSCORERS
SEASONS 1979-80 – 1991-92

1979-80	ANDY ROWLAND	20		1980-81	ANDY ROWLAND	12
1981-82	PAUL RIDEOUT	14		1982-83	PAUL RIDEOUT	20
1983-84	ALAN MAYES	17		1984-85	COLIN GORDON	17
1985-86	CHARLIE HENRY	18		1986-87	STEVE WHITE	16
1987-88	JIMMY QUINN	21		1988-89	DUNCAN SHEARER	14
1989-90	DUNCAN SHEARER	20		1990-91	DUNCAN SHEARER	22

1991-92 **DUNCAN SHEARER 22**

COUNTY GROUND Swindon SN1 2ED

Capacity: 16,432   **Covered Standing:** 3,100   **Seating:** 7,200

Tel: Ground: 0793 430430   **Ticket Sales:** As ground number   **Clubcall:** 0891 12 16 40

All premium rate calls (0898/0891) cost 36p per minute cheap rate and 48p per minute at all other times. Call costings correct at time of going to press.

GROUNDS
Bradford's Field, Globe Field, The Croft (1884-1895)

ATTENDANCES
Highest: 32,000 v Arsenal, FA Cup, 15.1.1972
29,106 v Watford, Division 3, 29.3.1969

Lowest: 1,681 v Darlington, Division 4, 17.4.1984

RECORD RECEIPTS (with previous records)
£101.456 v Aston Villa, FA Cup 5th Rnd, 15.02.1992
£71,432 v Leeds United, Div 2, 04.02.1990
£56,024 v Tottenham Hotspur, FA Cup 4th Round, 28.1.1980
£24,494 v Everton, FA Cup 4th Round, 29.1.1977
£10,326 v Tottenham Hotspur, League Cup 3rd Round, 6.10.1971

COUNTY GROUND
First game: v Old St. Stephens, 13.5.1893
First floodlit game: v Bristol City, 02.04.1951

Season Tickets:
Stands: from £170 to £210, juv/OAP £100 to £120
Ground: £120, juv/OAP £80

Executive Box Season Tickets: Apply to club for details

Cost of Stand Tickets: Seats £8.50 to £10.50, juv/OAP £5 to £5.50
Terraces: £6 to £7.50

Match and Ticket Information: Available three weeks in advance. Seats only on sale to members

Car Parking: Council car park adjacent to the west end of ground off County Road

Nearest Railway Station: Swindon (0793 536804) five minutes walk

---
How to get to the ground

From all directions: Two miles towards Town Centre from M4 Junction 15

TORQUAY UNITED

Division 3

Formed: 1898   **Turned Professional:** 1921   **Ltd Co:** 1921

SPONSORED BY: Mod Dec Windows   **NICKNAME:** The Gulls

President
A J Boyce

Chairman
M Bateson

Directors
M Benney
Mrs S Bateson
W W Rogers
F M Mosley,TD
D Wilson
M Beer
I Hayman
D Turner

Company Secretary/Accountant
Clive Olney (0803 328666)

Club Secretary/General Manager
David Turner (0803 328666)

Team Manager
Paul Compton

Player/Coach
Justin Fashanu

Reserve/Youth Team Coaches
John James & Bruce Stuckey

Club Statistician for the Directory
John Lovis

AFTER nineteen long years waiting for a higher grade of football, United's fans were rewarded with just one glimpse of life in the Third.

A season of tribulation both on and off the pitch saw the Gulls with three different managers at the helm and a high profile chairman with unorthodox ideas on how to run a football club.

When they kicked off the campaign with a fine victory few would have predicted the problems to come. Seven successive league games were lost and inevitably following the usual 'chairman's backing' the popular John Impey, who had inspired promotion, was fired along with coach John Turner. Mr Bateson opted to do without a permanent manager, instead appointing inspirational defender Wes Saunders as player-coach with the experienced John Uzzell as his assistant. Results stabilised but not enough to call the experiment an unqualified success. The appointment of former Southampton defender Ivan Golac in mid-February was clearly too late to save United from the inevitable. Golac also made it clear that if the Gulls were relegated he would not be staying at the club, so after the last game of the season United were searching for their fifth boss in fourteen months.

The highs of the season were few and far between but undoubtedly the magnificent 3-0 win against Birmingham must rate as the best, followed by some impressive if narrow home victories against sides of the calibre of Stoke, West Bromwich and Stockport.

The lows were provided by the disgusting incident involving John Uzzell and Brentford's Gary Blissett which has been well documented by the national press, the terrible defensive performance at Farnborough in the F.A. Cup and United's failure to win a single away game for the first time in their history.

Justin Fashanu's arrival at the club in December certainly gave the club more attacking penetration and he along with 'Player of the Year' Paul Holmes and the rapidly improving Chris Myers did all they could to lift the depression at Plainmoor.

The new man at the helm for 1992-93 is the likeable Paul Compton who made such a courageous playing comeback last season and also did a fine job in coaching United's younger players. Compton's right-hand man will be Justin Fashanu and much will depend on how Fashanu and senior professionals like Wes Saunders and Sean Joyce inspire the promising youngsters on United's staff now that players of the calibre of Paul Holmes and Matthew Elliott have moved to pastures new.

John Lovis

Back row L-R: Arron Davis, Paul Hall, Neil Sang, Adrian Foster, Scott Colcombe, Duane Darby. **Middle row:** Bruce Stuckey (Reserve Manager), Paul Trollope, Wes Saunders, Matthew Lowe, Dave Walters, Matthew Gardiner, Darren Moore, Johm James (Chief Scout). **Front row:** Jeff Franklin, Chris Curran, Justin Fashanu (Asst. Manager), Paul Compton (Manager), Norman Medhurst (Physio), Chris Myers, Sean Joyce.

TORQUAY UNITED

DIVISION THREE: 23rd   **FA CUP:** 2nd RND   **RUMBELOWS CUP:** 2nd RND   **AUTOGLASS:** Prelim.

M	DATE		COMP.	VEN	OPPONENTS	RESULT	H/T	LGE POS	GOALSCORERS/GOAL TIMES	ATTEN-DANCE
1	A	17	BL	H	Hartlepool United	W 3-1	2-0		Elliott 4, Rowland 21, Loram (pen) 71	4,163
2		20	RC 1/1	H	Hereford United	W 2-0	1-0		Elliott 41, Loram (pen) 51	2,410
3		24	BL	A	Preston North End	L 0-3	0-1			(3,654)
4		28	RC 1/2	A	Hereford United	L 1-2	1-1		Elliott 35	(2,333)
5		31	BL	H	Fulham	L 0-1	0-0	17		3,299
6	S	4	BL	A	Exeter City	L 0-1	0-0	21		(5,772)
7		6	BL	A	Stockport County	L 1-2	0-1	21	Elliott 57	(5,618)
8		14	BL	H	Shrewsbury Town	L 1-2	1-1	23	Rowbotham 33	2,811
9		17	BL	H	Reading	L 1-2	0-1	23	Darby 84	2,591
10		21	BL	A	Hull City	L 1-4	1-2	23	Rowbotham (pen) 44	(3,093)
11		24	RC 2/1	A	Oldham Athletic	L 1-7	0-1		D Hodges 83	(7,250)
12		28	BL	H	Chester City	W 3-2	2-1	21	M Holmes 8, Darby 19, Elliott 52	2,062
13	O	5	BL	A	Bolton Wanderers	L 0-1	0-1	23		(5,092)
14		9	RC 2/2	H	Oldham Athletic	L 0-2	0-1			1,955
15		12	BL	H	Huddersfield Town	L 0-1	0-0	24		2,936
16		19	BL	A	Bradford City	L 0-2	0-0	24		(4,543)
17		23	AGT Pre	A	Exeter City	L 1-2	1-2		Edwards 14	(2,957)
18		26	BL	H	Swansea City	W 1-0	0-0	24	Elliott 50	1,908
19	N	2	BL	A	Birmingham City	L 0-3	0-1	24		(9,408)
20		6	BL	H	Bournemouth	W 1-0	0-0	23	P Holmes 85	1,884
21		9	BL	A	Leyton Orient	W 1-0	1-0	20	Whitbread (og) 24	2,388
22		16	FAC 1	H	Birmingham City	W 3-0	2-0		Loram 39, Hall 40, 55	4,123
23		19	AGT Pre	H	Hereford United	L 0-1	0-1			2,138
24		23	BL	A	Stoke City	L 0-3	0-2	23		(9,124)
25		30	BL	A	Peterborough Utd	D 1-1	0-0	24	Elliott 86	(4,007)
26	D	7	FAC 2	H	Farnborough Town	D 1-1	0-1		Loram 87	2,725
27		14	BL	H	Brentford	D 1-1	0-1	23	Rowbotham (pen) 69	2,475
28		17	FAC 2R	A	Farnborough Town	L 3-4	0-2		M Holmes 75, Rowbotham 77, Colcombe 89	(2,285)
29		20	BL	H	Preston North End	W 1-0	1-0	20	Loram (pen) 40	2,183
30		26	BL	A	Fulham	L 1-2	1-2	20	Hall 11	(4,186)
31		28	BL	A	Hartlepool United	D 1-1	1-1	21	Loram (pen) 3	(3,812)
32	J	1	BL	H	Exeter City	W 1-0	0-0		Fashanu 59	5,696
33		4	BL	H	West Bromwich A.	W 1-0	0-0	17	Fashanu 84	4,159
34		11	BL	A	Darlington	L 2-3	1-3	17	Dobbins 11, Joyce 57	(2,493)
35		18	BL	H	Bury	L 0-2	0-1	19		2,625
36	F	1	BL	H	Bradford City	D 1-1	1-0	21	Fashanu (pen) 3	2,243
37		8	BL	A	Swansea City	L 0-1	0-1	22		(3,418)
38		15	BL	A	Brentford	L 2-3	0-1		Saunders 55, Loram 64	(6,079)
39		22	BL	H	Darlington	W 3-0	2-0	21	Fashanu 13, 39, Loram 90	2,415
40		29	BL	A	West Bromwich A.	L 0-1	0-0	22		(11,669)
41	M	3	BL	A	Bury	D 0-0	0-0	23		(1,663)
42		7	BL	H	Wigan Athletic	L 0-1	0-0	23		2,198
43		10	BL	A	Bournemouth	L 1-2	0-2	23	Fashanu 76	(4,083)
44		21	BL	A	Leyton Orient	L 0-2	0-0	23		(3,636)
45		24	BL	H	Birmingham City	L 1-2	1-0	23	Myers 32	2,446
46		28	BL	H	Stoke City	W 1-0	1-0	23	Dobie 17	3,260
47		31	BL	A	Shrewsbury Town	D 2-2	0-2	23	Myers 58, Dobie 85	(2,172)
48	A	4	BL	H	Stockport County	W 2-0	1-0	23	Fashanu 23, Saunders 79	2,693
49		7	BL	A	Wigan Athletic	D 0-0	0-0	23		(1,970)
50		11	BL	A	Reading	L 1-6	1-4	23	Myers 45	(3,111)
51		14	BL	H	Hull City	W 2-1	0-1	22	Myers 58, Fashanu 81	2,339
52		20	BL	A	Chester City	L 0-2	0-1	23		(1,317)
53		25	BL	H	Bolton Wanderers	W 2-0	0-0	23	Fashanu (pen) 43, Moore 86	2,178
54		28	BL	H	Peterborough Utd	D 2-2	1-1	23	Fashanu (pen) 45, Saunders 67	1,934
55	M	2	BL	A	Huddersfield Town	L 0-4	0-2	23		(7,961)

Best Home League Attendance: 5,696 v Exeter City   **Smallest: 1,884 v Bournemouth**   **Av Home Att: 2,734**

Goal Scorers: **Compared with 90-91: -253**

League (42):   Fashanu 10 (3 pens), Loram 5 (3 pens), Elliott 5, Myers 4, Saunders 3, Rowbotham 3 (2 pens), Darby 2, Dobie 2, Moore, Rowland Dobbins, Joyce, P Holmes, Hall, Opponents, M Holmes

R/lows C (4):   Elliott 2, D Hodges, Loram (1 pen)

FA Cup (7):   Hall 2, Loram 2, Colcombe, Rowbotham, M Holmes

Autoglass (1):   Edwards

Howells G.	Myers C.	Loram M.	Whisten P.	Elliott M.	Holmes M.	Hodges D.	Colcombe S.	Rowland A.	Dobie M.	Dobbins W.	Hall P.	Joyce S.	Sang N.	Uzzell J.	Holmes P.	Rowbotham D.	Curran C.	Edwards D.	Darby D.	Compton P.	Herrera R.	Lloyd P.	Fashanu J.	Davis A.	Saunders W.	Referee	
1	2	3	4†	5	6	7	8	9	10	11			S					S								P Durkin	1
1	2	3	4	5	6	7	8	9	10	11																J Deakin	2
1	2	3	4	5	6	7	8*	9	10	11•	12	14														J Lloyd	3
1	2	3	4	5	6	7*		9	10	11	8	S	12													J Brandwood	4
1	2	3		5	6	12		9	10*	11	7	S	12	4	8											K Cooper	5
1	2	3	7	5	6		S	9	12	11*		10		4	8											P Vanes	6
1	2		3	5	6*	S		9	10	8		7	12	4	11											P Jones	7
1	2	4*		5	6			12•	10	8		9		3	11	7	14									J Carter	8
1	2	3		5	6				10			9	4*	12		11•	7		14							J Martin	9
				5	6	9	11		10	2		8*	12	3		7•			14							K Lupton	10
1		3		5	6*	10	11			7	8	S	12	4		2				9						A Wilkie	11
1	10			5	6	8*			11	12	S			7	2					9	4					M Pierce	12
1	12	10		5	6	8			11		S			7*	2					9	4					B Coddington	13
	3	7		5	6	10	11•	9*	14		8			2						12	4					C Wilkes	14
1	3	10		5	6	12			8		S			2	7					9*	4					K A Cooper	15
1	3	9		5	6	14			8		12			2	7•					10	4					J Rushton	16
1	11	3		5		S	S			8	9	6		2	7					10	4					R Gifford	17
1	11	3		5		S				8	9	6		2	7					10	S	4				G Ashby	18
1	14			5		11				8	9	6		2	7	3•				10*	12	4				T West	19
1	S	11		5	6					8	9		3	2	7					10	S	4				J Griffiths	20
1	S	11		5	6					8	9		3	2	7					10*	12	4				R Hamer	21
1	S	11		5	6					8	9		3	2	7•					10	S	4				M Bodenham	22
1	S	11		5	6					8	9		3	2	7					10	12	4				K Burge	23
1	12	11		5	6	14				8	9		3*	2	7					10		4•				P Alcock	24
1	4*	11		5	6	S		12		8	9		3	2	7					10						A Buksh	25
1	4	11		5		6	14			8	9		3	2	7•					10*	12					P Durkin	26
1		10		5	6	11		12		8	9		3*	2	7					S	4†					A Smith	27
1	S	10		5	6	11				3	8	9*		2	7					12	4					P Durkin	28
1		10		5		11	7*	8	12	6		3		2						S			4	9		C Wilkes	29
1		10		5		11		7	8	S	6	3		2*						12			4	9†		P Danson	30
1	3	10		5		11		7*	8	12	6	2		5						S			4	9		A Bennett	31
1	3	10				11		7	8	12	6*	2		5						S			4	9		J Deakin	32
1	3					11*		7	8	S	6	2		5		2							4	9	10	R Gifford	33
1	3	12		5		11		7	8	14	9•	2		6							4			10*		K Breen	34
1	4	10		5		11*		7	8	S		2		6						12			9	3		P Scoble	35
1	11			5		12		8		14		2		6•						10		4	9	3*		J Carter	36
1	11	3		5		S		8				2		6						10*		4	9		12	G Singh	37
1	2	11		5	6	10*		S	12			7	8	S						S		8	9	3	4	P Vanes	38
1	2	11		6		10			7	8	S			6						S		5	9	3	4	K Burge	39
1	2	11		5		10			7	8		6								S		3	9†	4†		E Parker	40
1	2	11		5		10			7	8		6								S		3	9		4	K Lupton	41
1	2	11		5		10			7	8	S	6		12						S		3	9		4	D Frampton	42
1	6	11		5*		10•			7	8	14		2		12		3			3		3	9		4	P Alcock	43
		10	9	5		12		14	7	8		2		6						4*	3					R Bigger	44
1	10	9				11			7	8		2								6	3			S	4	R Groves	45
1	10			12		9			7	8		2		5						6*	3•		14		4	H King	46
1	10			12		9			7*	8•	14	2		5						6			3		4	S Bell	47
1	10*					9			5	8				2						6	3	7	2•		4	C Wilkes	48
	10			12		9			5	8		S		2						6	3	7	2*		4	J Lloyd	49
	6			10		9	14	12	8*				2						5	3		7		4		A Gunn	50
	10					9	S	5	8				2							6*	3	7	12	4		J Martin	51
	10					9	12	5	8				2							3		7	S	4		C Trussell	52
	10			12		9	5*		8				2							3		7	S	4		P Durkin	53
	10					9*			5	8			2							6		12	3	7	S	4	M Pierce	54
1	10					9	7*		8				2							6		3*			12	4	T Holbrook	55
38	36	30	4	33	18	3	21	5	18	18	34	29	8	10	36	14	15	7	7	19	11	13	21	9	17	League Appearances	
	3	1			3	7	2	2	3	4	6	6					2		7					3	1	Substitute Appearances	
3	3	4	2	4	4	4	3	3	2	3+1	2	1		0+2	1	1		1		1+1	1					R/lows Appearances	
3	1		3	2	1	1+1		1	3	3				2	3	3		2		0+2	2					FA Cup Appearances	
2	1	2		2	2	1		2	2	2				2	2		2									Autoglass Appearances	

Also Played: Posn. (Game): Lange 1(10), Fillery 3(12,13)11(15,16*), Lowe 1(14,44,49to54), McNichol 8(9)4(10), Trollope 11(46,48,49,50*,51,52*,53,54,55), P Smith 14(48), K Hodges 7(36,37,38), Ginter S(41), Franklin 11(44*)14(55), Moore S(40,41)5(45,55)6(52,53,54), Bennellick S(45)12(48)

Players on Loan: T Lange (Wolves), M Fillery (Oldham), K Hodges (Plymouth), R Herrera (QPR), P Trollope (Swindon)   † = Sent Off

TORQUAY UNITED

Club Colours: Yellow & white stripes/navy & white trim shirts, navy with yellow & white trim shorts, yellow socks with navy top
Change Colours: Blue shirts with white fleck, yellow numbers and trim, white shorts
Reserves League: Great Mills League Premier Division & Neville Ovenden Football Combination Second Division

Previous League: Southern League
Previous Name: Torquay Town (1910), Amalgamated with Babbacombe in 1920
Previous Managers: (Since 1946): John Butler John McNeil Bob John Alex Massie Eric Webber Frank O'Farrell Allan Brown Jack Edwards Malcolm Musgrove Frank O'Farrell Mike Green Frank O'Farrell Bruce Rioch David Webb John Sims Stuart Morgan Cyril Knowles David Smith John Impey Ivan Golac
Honours: Sherpa Van Trophy Finalists 1989
League Career: Elected to Div 3S 1927   Original Members of Division 4 1958
Promoted to Div 3 1960   Relegated to Div 4 1962   Promoted to Div 3 1966   Relegated to Div 4 1972
Promoted to Div 3 1991   Relegated to Div 4 1992

CLUB RECORDS

Most Appearances for Club: Dennis Lewis (1947-59): League 443 + FA Cup 30 **Total 473**
Most Capped Player: None
Record Goalscorer in a Match: Robin Stubbs 5 v Newport County, 8-3, Div 4, 19.10.1963
Record League Goalscorer in a Season: Sammy Collins, 40, Div 3S, 1955-56 **In All Competitions:** Sammy Collins 42 (League 40 + FA Cup 2)
Record League Goalscorer in a Career: Sammy Collins 204, 1948-58 **In All Competitions:** 219 (League 204 + FA Cup 15)
Record Transfer Fee Received: £185,000 from Manchester United for Lee Sharpe, June 1988
Record Transfer Fee Paid: £60,000 to Dundee for Wes Saunders, July 1990
Best Performances: League: 2nd Div 3S 1956-57 **FA Cup:** 4th Round 1948-49, 1954-55, 1970-71, 1982-83, 1989-90 **League Cup:** Never past 3rd Round
Most League Points: (3pts a win) 77, Div 4, 1987-88   (2pts a win) 60, Div 4, 1959-60
Most League Goals: 89, Div 3(S), 1956-57
Record League Victory and Most Goals Scored in a League Match: 9-0 v Swindon Town, Div 3S, 8.3.1952
Record Cup Victory and Most Goals Scored in a Cup Tie: 7-1 v Northampton Town (h), FA Cup 1st Round, 14.11.1959 (all goals scored by Torquay-born players: Graham Bond (3), Ernie Pym (3), and Tommy Northcott)
6-0 v Canterbury City, FA Cup Round 1, 1964-65
Record League Defeat: 2-10 v Fulham, Div 3S, 7.9.1931   2-10 v Luton Town, Div 3S, 2.9.1933   1-9 v Millwall, Div 3S, 29.8.1927
Record Cup Defeat: 1-7 v Birmingham City (h), FA Cup Round 3, 1955-56   0-6 v Manchester City, League Cup Round 2, 25.10.1983
1-7 v Oldham Athletic, League Cup, 24.9.1991
Oldest Player in a League Match: David Webb, 38 years 8 months v Crewe Alexandra, Div 4, 5.1.1985
Youngest Player in a League Match: Lee Sharpe, 16 years 129 days v Exeter City, Div 4, 3.10.1987

LONGEST LEAGUE RUNS

of undefeated matches: 15 (1960, 1990)	**of league matches without a win:** 17 (1938)
of undefeated home matches: 31 (1956-57)	**of undefeated away matches:** 7 (1976, 1990)
without home win: 11 (1961)	**without an away win:** 26 (1991-still running)
of league wins: 6 (1953, 1990)	**of home wins:** 13 (1966-67)
of league defeats: 8 (1948, 1971)	**of away wins:** 5 (1959)

TORQUAY UNITED

PLAYERS NAME Honours	Ht	Wt	Birthdate	Birthplace Transfers	Contract Date	Clubs	APPEARANCES				GOALS			
							League	L/Cup	FA Cup	Other	Lg	L/C	FAC	Oth
GOALKEEPERS														
Matthew Lowe	6.0	11.2	25.02.74	Birmingham		Torquay Utd	7	1						
David Walter	6.3	13.3	03.09.64	Barnstaple		Bideford								
Div.4'90					02.12.88	Exeter City	44	7	2	2				
				Loan	08.03.90	Plymouth A								
				£10,000	25.07.90	Plymouth A	15	1	2	1				
				Free	01.07.92	Torquay Utd								
DEFENDERS														
Christopher Curran	5.11	11.9	17.09.71	West Midlands	13.07.90	Torquay Utd. (T)	26+5	2		3				
Arron Davis					17.08.91	Torquay Utd	9+3							
Matthew Gardiner	5.4	10.10	28.03.74			Torquay Utd								
Birmingham														
Darren M Moore						Torquay Utd	5				2			
Neil Sang	5.9	10.7	23.05.72	Liverpool	18.06.90	Everton (T)								
					21.06.91	Torquay Utd	8+6	0+2		1				
Wes Saunders	6.0	11.11	23.02.63	Sunderland	01.06.81	Newcastle Utd	79	8	6				1	
				Loan	29.03.85	Bradford City	1+3							
				Free	31.08.85	Carlisle Utd	97	7	5	7	11			1
					01.02.88	Dundee	48+2	3	4		2			
				£60,000	26.07.90	Torquay Utd	54+1	3	1	6+1	6	1		1
MIDFIELD														
Ian Bastow	5.8	9.4	12.08.71	Torquay	24.03.89	Torquay Utd. (T)	7+4		1	3				
Scott Colcombe	5.5	10.6	15.12.71	Walsall	05.07.90	West Brom A. (T)								
				Free	14.08.91	Torquay Utd	21+7	3	1+1				1	
Sean Joyce	5.8	10.5	15.02.67	Conisborough	19.09.86	Doncaster Rovers	39+2	1	2	3	2			
				Loan	28.11.86	Exeter City	1							
				Free	19.08.88	Torquay Utd	117+14	6	11	10+2	12		1	1
Chris Myers					22.08.90	Torquay Utd	60+8	4+2	2	4+3	6			
Paul J Trollope	6.0	12.2	03.06.72	Swindon	23.12.89	Swindon Town (T)								
				Loan	26.03.92	Torquay Utd	9							
				Free	17.07.92	Torquay Utd								
FORWARDS														
Duane Darby			17.10.73	West Midlands		Torquay Utd	7+7	1+1	0+2		2			
Justin Fashanu	6.1	13.01	19.02.61	Kensington		Norwich City	84+6	8	5		35	4	1	
E: Y,u21,B				£100,000		Nottingham F.	31+1	4	1		3	1		
				Loan		Southampton	9							
				£150,000		Notts County	64	3	2		20	2		
					20.11.89	West Ham U	2							
					23.10.89	Manchester City	0+2							
					20.11.89	West Ham U	2							
				m	01.03.90	Leyton Orient	3+2							
						Leatherhead								
						Southall								
				N.C	24.10.91	Newcastle Utd		0+1						
				Free	10.12.91	Torquay Utd	21				10			
Adrian Foster	5.9	11.0	19.03.71	Kidderminster	20.07.89	West Brom A. (T) ·	13+14	1+3	0+2		2			
				Free	03.07.92	Torquay Utd								
Jeffery Franklin	5.9	10.4		Darlington		Torquay Utd	1+1							
Paul Hall	5.5	9.13	03.07.72	Manchester	09.07.90	Torquay Utd. (T)	50+15	3	3+1	3+2	1		2	
ADDITIONAL CONTRACT PLAYERS														
James Bennellick						Torquay Utd	0+1							

LEADING LEAGUE GOALSCORERS SEASONS 1985-86 – 1991-92

1985-86	**STEVE PHILLIPS**	8	1986-87	**PAUL DOBSON**	16
1987-88	**PAUL DOBSON**	22	1988-89	**DEAN EDWARDS**	8
1989-90	**MARK LORAM**	12	1990-91	**DEAN EDWARDS**	15

1991-92   **JUSTIN FASHANU**   10

PLAINMOOR GROUND Torquay, Devon TQ1 3PG

Capacity: **Covered Standing:**   **Seating:**

Tel: Ground: 0792 474114   **Ticket Sales:** As ground number   **Clubcall:** 0898 12 16 39

All premium rate calls (0898/0891) cost 36p per minute cheap rate and 48p per minute at all other times. Call costings correct at time of going to press.

ATTENDANCES
Highest: 21,908 v Huddersfield, FA Cup Round 4, 29.1.1955

Lowest: 967 v Chester, Div 4, 2.5.1984
601 v Swansea, FRT, 2.12.1986

Record Receipts: £25,000 v Exeter City, Div 3, 1.1.1992

Season Tickets:
Stands: £100, juv/OAP £50
Ground: £100, juv/OAP £50

Cost of Stand Tickets: £6, £3 (OAP/child)
Terraces: £5.50 (adults), £4 (Juveniles/OAP)
Family Enclosures: £6 adults, £4 OAP/child (Stipes members £2)
Away Enclosure: £6

Match and Ticket Information: Seat bookings accepted two weeks before each match. Postal applications must include remittance and sae

Car Parking: Some street parking. Coaches park at Lymington Road Coach Station

Nearest Railway Station: Torquay (0803 295911)

How to get to the ground

From North: Use A38 then A380 to Kings Kerswell. In 1m at roundabout take 1st exit. In 1m turn left A3022 S.P. Babbacombe. In 0.8m turn left then right into Westhill Road and Warbro Road for Torquay United FC

From West: Use A380 into Torquay town centre then follow signs Teignmouth A379 into Lymington Road, then turn right into Upton Hill then keep forward into Bronshill Road. Take 2nd turning on left into Derwent Road and at end turn right then turn right again into Marnham Road for Torquay United FC

Value Rating: ★ ★ ★

Programme Editor: David Turner

Price of 1992-93 Programme: £1
Number of Pages: 32
Subscriptions: Home only £29, Away only £29, Home & away £47

Local Newspapers: Herald Express, Torbay News, Western Morning News

Local Radio Stations: BBC Radio Devon, Devon Air

TOTTENHAM HOTSPUR   Premier

Formed: 1882   **Turned Professional:** 1895   **Ltd Co:** 1898

SPONSORED BY: Holsten   **NICKNAME:** The Spurs

President
W E Nicholson

Vice-President
F P Sinclair

Chairman
Alan M Sugar

Directors
A G Berry (Vice-Chairman)
T Venables (Chief Executive)
D A Alexiou
I Yawetz

First Team Coach
Doug Livermore

Assistant First Team Coach
Ray Clemence

Secretary
Peter Barnes (081-808 6666)

Physiotherapists
John Sheridan/Dave Butler

Reserve Team Manager
Keith Waldon

Youth Team Manager
Pat Holland

Commercial Manager
Mike Rollo (081-808 0281)

P.R.O.
John Fennelly

Club Statistician for the Directory
Andy Shute

TOTTENHAM's season began promisingly with just one defeat in their opening eight games, and a top three placing by late September. Then league form began to suffer as Tottenham played fifteen games during September and October, eight of which were in cup competitions. They were mid-table by the new year and with three wins from four games during the Christmas/New Year programme optimism was high. But after Tottenham's 2-1 win at Coventry on January 1st, Spurs endured a terrible run of ten league games without a win, ending with a 4-3 home win.

As holders of the F.A. Cup Tottenham started their defence of the trophy with a difficult away tie at Aston Villa and earnt a creditable 0-0 draw but disappointingly lost the replay 0-1 at White Hart Lane. Success beckoned though in the Rumbelows Cup, beating Swansea City 5-2 on aggregate (0-1, 5-1), Grimsby Town away 3-1, Coventry City away 2-1 and Norwich City at home 2-1. In the semi-final Tottenham travelled to Nottingham Forest for the first leg and drew 1-1, but Forest gained revenge for the F.A. Cup final defeat last year, by winning 2-1 in the second leg after extra-time.

Tottenham's ventures into Europe began with a trip to Austrian side Sparkasse Stockerau in the qualifying round. Spurs won 1-0, both home and away. They then travelled back to Austria but this time to play Hadjuk Split from Yugoslavia, the tie played in Linz, Austria because of domestic unrest in Yugoslavia. Tottenham went down 0-1 in the first leg but in the second leg at home won 2-0. A home tie in the first leg of the second round against FC Porto of Portugal saw Spurs gain a 3-1 win, which remained the aggregate score after a 0-0 draw in Portugal. In the quarter-final Tottenham travelled to Dutch side Feyenoord but came away with a 0-1 defeat. In the second leg Tottenham did everything but score, drawing 0-0 and going out of the cup on aggregate.

Midway through the season Gary Lineker announced he would be leaving Tottenham in the summer to join Grampus Eight in the newly formed and ambitious Japanese league. He nevertheless finished the season with 35 goals (29 league, 7 cup). He scored four goals against Wimbledon in one game, a feat no Tottenham player has managed in the league for fourteen years.

On the transfer front, apart from Lineker to Japan and Gascoigne to Lazio, Italy, John Moncur joined Swindon (£80,000) and Peter Garland joined Newcastle (£35,000). Joining Tottenham were Andy Gray from Palace (£800,000), Jason Cundy from Chelsea (£750,000), both of whom joined in March on loan with view to permanent moves in the summer. Also signed was Gerald McMahon from Irish side Glenavon (£100,000).

During the close season manager Peter Shreeves parted company with Tottenham, leaving Terry Venables back in charge of team affairs. Darren Anderton (£1,750,000 from Portsmouth), Neil Ruddock (£750,000 from Southampton), Peter Beadle (£500,000 from Gillingham) and Dean Austin (£300,000 from Southend) all joined the club with Paul Walsh joining Portsmouth for £400,000 and Paul Stewart joining Liverpool for £2.2 million.

Andy Shute

Back row L-R: Jason Cundy, Darren Anderton, Peter Beadle, Ian Walker, David Tuttle, Erik Thorstvedt, Steve Sedgley, David Howells, Ian Hendon. **Middle:** John Sheridan (Physio), Davie Butler (Physio), Scott Houghton, Andy Gray, Gordon Durie, Nayim, Vinny Samways, Paul Moran, Keith Waldon (Reserve Coach), Roy Reyland (Kit Manager). **Front:** Doug Livermore (Coach), Justin Edinburgh, Paul Allen, Neil Ruddock, Gary Mabbutt, Dean Austin, Terry Fenwick, John Hendry, Ray Clemence (Coach).

TOTTENHAM HOTSPUR

DIVISION ONE: 15th   **FA CUP:** 3rd RND   **RUMBELOWS CUP:** SEMI-FINALISTS   **ECWC:** Q-FINALS

M	DATE		COMP.	VEN	OPPONENTS	RESULT		H/T	LGE POS	GOALSCORERS/GOAL TIMES	ATTEN-DANCE
1	A	10	C SHIEL	N	Arsenal	D	0-0	0-0			(80,000)
2		17	BL	A	Southampton	W	3-2	1-1		Lineker 40, 72, Durie 70	(18,581)
3		21	ECWC P	A	Stockerau	W	1-0	1-0		Durie 38	(15,500)
4		24	BL	H	Chelsea	L	1-3	0-2		Lineker 55	34,645
5		28	BL	A	Nottingham Forest	W	3-1	1-1	12	Lineker 37, Durie 67, Bergsson 88	(24,018)
6		31	BL	A	Norwich City	W	1-0	1-0	5	Lineker 38	(19,460)
7	S	4	ECWC P	H	Stockerau	W	1-0	1-0		Mabbutt 41	28,072
8		7	BL	A	Aston Villa	D	0-0	0-0	10		(33,096)
9		14	BL	H	Queens Park R.	W	2-0	0-0	6	Lineker 72, 75	30,059
10		17	ECWC1/1	A	Hadjuk Split	L	0-1	0-0			(7,000)
11		21	BL	A	Wimbledon	W	5-3	3-1	3	Lineker 4 (11, 32, 46, 55), Samways 39	(11,927)
12		24	RC 2/1	A	Swansea City	L	0-1	0-0			(11,416)
13		28	BL	H	Manchester United	L	1-2	1-1	7	Durie 38	35,087
14	O	2	ECWC1/2	H	Hadjuk Split	W	2-0	2-0		Tuttle 6, Durie 14	24,297
15		5	BL	A	Everton	L	1-3	1-3	12	Lineker 17	(29,505)
16		9	RC 2/2	H	Swansea City	W	5-1	1-0		Allen 15, Lineker (p) 54, Brazil (og) 60, Stewart 64, Samways 81	20,198
17		19	BL	H	Manchester City	L	0-1	0-0	13		30,102
18		23	ECWC2/1	H	F.C. Porto	W	3-1	2-0		Lineker 15, 83, Durie 31	23,621
19		26	BL	A	West Ham United	L	1-2	1-1	13	Lineker 5	(23,946)
20		29	RC 3	A	Grimsby Town	W	3-1	1-0		Howells 29, Lineker 75, Durie 84	(17,017)
21	N	2	BL	A	Sheffield Wed.	D	0-0	0-0	16		(31,573)
22		6	ECWC2/2	A	F.C. Porto	D	0-0	0-0			(55,000)
23		16	BL	H	Luton Town	W	4-1	0-1	12	Houghton 68, 75, Lineker 70, 83	27,543
24		23	BL	H	Sheffield United	L	0-1	0-0	13		28,168
25	D	1	BL	A	Arsenal	L	0-2	0-0	15		(38,892)
26		4	RC 4	H	Coventry City	W	2-1	1-0		Allen 43, Durie 83	(20,095)
27		7	BL	H	Notts County	W	2-1	1-1	13	Walsh 16, Mabbutt 90	23,364
28		14	BL	A	Leeds United	D	1-1	1-1	13	Howells 19	(31,404)
29		18	BL	H	Liverpool	L	1-2	1-1	13	Walsh 25	27,434
30		22	BL	A	Crystal Palace	W	2-1	2-0	12	Walsh 16, Lineker 35	(24,491)
31		26	BL	H	Nottingham Forest	L	1-2	0-1	12	Stewart 60	31,079
32		28	BL	H	Norwich City	W	3-0	1-0	9	Allen 32, Lineker 65, Nayim 85	27,969
33	J	1	BL	A	Coventry City	W	2-1	1-1	8	Lineker 39, Stewart 66	(19,639)
34		5	FAC 3	A	Aston Villa	D	0-0	0-0			(29,316)
35		8	RC 5	H	Norwich City	W	2-1	0-1		Walsh 78, Lineker 85	29,471
36		11	BL	A	Chelsea	L	0-2	0-1	10		(28,628)
37		14	FAC 3R	H	Aston Villa	L	0-1	0-1			25,462
38		18	BL	H	Southampton	L	1-2	0-1	12	Mabbutt 82	23,191
39		25	BL	H	Oldham Athletic	D	0-0	0-0	11		20,843
40	F	1	BL	A	Manchester City	L	0-1	0-1	11		(30,123)
41		9	RC SF 1	A	Nottingham Forest	D	1-1	1-0		Lineker (pen) 24	(21,402)
42		16	BL	H	Crystal Palace	L	0-1	0-0	12		19,834
43		22	BL	H	Arsenal	D	1-1	0-0	13	Stewart 54	33,124
44	M	1	RC SF 2	H	Nottingham Forest	L	†1-2	1-1		Lineker 15	28,216
45		4	ECWC QF	A	Feyenoord	L	0-1	0-0			(48,000)
46		7	BL	A	Leeds United	L	1-3	0-1	17	Allen 48	27,622
47		11	BL	A	Luton Town	D	0-0	0-0	17		(11,494)
48		14	BL	H	Sheffield Wed.	L	0-2	0-0	18		23,027
49		18	ECWC QF	H	Feyenoord	D	0-0	0-0			29,834
50		21	BL	A	Liverpool	L	1-2	0-0	19	Stewart 74	(36,968)
51		28	BL	H	Coventry City	W	4-3	3-1	18	Durie 3 (7, 45, 81), Lineker 32	22,744
52	A	1	BL	H	West Ham United	W	3-0	1-0	17	Lineker 3 (16, 53, 60 pen)	31,809
53		4	BL	H	Aston Villa	L	2-5	2-2	18	Lineker 6, Teale (og) 13	26,370
54		7	BL	A	Notts County	W	2-0	1-0	17	Lineker 32, 52	(9,205)
55		11	BL	A	Queens Park R.	W	2-1	0-1	13	Gray 71, Durie 79	(20,678)
56		14	BL	A	Sheffield United	L	0-2	0-2	13		(21,526)
57		18	BL	H	Wimbledon	W	3-2	2-0	12	Lineker 5, 11, Hendry 76	23,934
58		20	BL	A	Oldham Athletic	L	0-1	0-1	13		(15,443)
59		25	BL	H	Everton	D	3-3	3-0	12	Allen 18, Minton 43, Stewart 44	34,630
60	M	2	BL	A	Manchester United	L	1-3	0-1	15	Lineker 86	(44,595)

Best Home League Attendance: 35,087 v Manchester United   **Smallest: 19,834 v Crystal Palace**   Av Home Att: 27,742

Goal Scorers: Compared with 90-91: -2,888

League (58): Lineker 28, Durie 7, Stewart 5, Allen 3, Walsh 3, Mabbutt 2, Houghton 2, Nayim, Opponents, Gray, Howells, Samways, Hendry, Bergsson, Minton

R/lows C (14): Lineker 5 (2 pens), Allen 2, Durie 2, Howells, Stewart, Opponents, Walsh, Samways

FA Cup (0):

ECWC (7): Durie 3, Lineker 2, Tuttle, Mabbutt

† = After extra-time

Thorsvedt E.	Fenwick T.	Van Den Hauwe P.	Sedgley S.	Howells D.	Mabbutt G.	Stewart P.	Durie G.	Samways V.	Lineker G.	Allen P.	Naylin	Bergsson G.	Hendon I.	Hendry J.	Moran P.	Moncur J.	Houghton S.	Walsh P.	Walker I.	Edinburgh J.	Tuttle D.	Gray A.	Cundy J.	Minton J.	Dearden K.	Referee	
1	2	3	4	5	6	7		9	10	11	8	S	S					S	S	S						T Holbrook	1
1	2	3	4	5*	6	7	8	9	10	11•	12	14														A Gunn	2
1	2	3		5	6	7	8	9*	10	11	4		12													G Biguet	3
1	2•	3		5	6	7	8	9	10	11	4	14				S										P Don	4
	2	3		5	6	7	8*	9	10	11•	4	14			12				1							V Callow	5
	2	3	S	5	6	7	8	9	10		4	11			S				1							I Hemley	6
	2	3	14	5*	6	7	8	9	10•		4	11				12			1	S	S			S		M Piraux	7
	2	3	S	5	6	7	8	9	10		4	11			S				1							K Hackett	8
	2	3	14	5*	6	7	8	9*	10	12	4	11							1							G Courtney	9
	2	3	14	5•	6	7	8	9	10*	12	4	11							1							K Rothlisberger	10
	3	5	S		6	7	8	9	10	11•	4	2	12						1							P Vanes	11
	3•	5		6	7	8†	9	10	11	4		2	12	14				1								L Shapter	12
		3	12	6	7†	8	9	10	11	4•	2*						14	1		5						G Ashby	13
1		3	S	6	7	8	9	10	11•	4	2	12					S			S	5			S		E Fredriksson	14
1		3	12	6	7	8	9•	10	11	4*	2	14								5						R Milford	15
1		3	S	6	7	8	9	10	11	4	2						14			5•						G Willard	16
1	3•	7	14	6		8	9	10	11	4*	5							12		2						M Bodenham	17
1	3	4	S	6	7	8	9*	10	11		12	S						14	5•	2				S		Z Petrovic	18
1	3•	5		6	7	8	9	10	11	4*	14							12		2						D Elleray	19
1	3	4	5•	6	7	8	9	10	11*		14							12		2						K Barratt	20
1	3	4•	5	6	7	8		10*	11	9	14							12		2						M Reed	21
1	3	12	5	6	7	8*	9	10•	11		4							14		2						P Mikkelsen	22
1	3	4	5*	6			9	10	11•	12	7						14	8		2						D Frampton	23
1	3	12	5*	6		8	9	10		4•	7						14	11		2						J Rushton	24
1	2	3	S	5	6	7	8	9*		11	12	4						10								K Redfern	25
1	2	3	14	5	6	7	8	9•		11	12	4						10*								R Gifford	26
1	2	3	14	5•	6	7	8	9*		11	12	4						10								D Axcell	27
1	2	3	14	5	6	7	8•	9*		11	12	4						10								M Peck	28
1	2	3	S	5*	6	7		9	10	11	12	4						8								J Martin	29
1	2		14	5	6	7		9	10*	11	12	4						8		3•						P Foakes	30
1	2	3	14	5	6	7		9*	10	11	12	4•						8								R Bigger	31
1	2	3	4		6	7		9	10	11	5						12	8*		S						W Burge	32
1	2	3	4	5	6	7		9•	10	11							12	8*		14						J Key	33
1	2	3	4	5	6	7		9	10	11	S	S						8								I Borrett	34
1	2*	3	4		6	7	8	9•	10	11	5	12						14		8						M Bodenham	35
1	2	3	4	5•	6	7*	9		11	10	12							14		8						R Hart	36
1	2*	3	4		6	7	8•	9	10	11	14	12						5								I Borrett	37
	3*	4		6	7	8	9•	10	11		12						14	5	1	2						B Hill	38
	3	4		6	7	8		10	11	5•	S						14	9	1	2						G Willard	39
3		4	5*		7	8	9•	10	11	14	6							12	1	2						V Callow	40
1	2	3	4	5		7	8	9*	10*	11	14	6								12						D Allison	41
1	2	3	4	5•	6	7	8	9*	10	11		14								12						J Deakin	42
1	2	3	4	5	6	7	8		10	11	9*									12	S					K Barratt	43
1	2•	3	4	5	6	7	8	12	10	11	9*									14						J Worrall	44
1	2	3	4	5•	6	7	8	14	10*	11	9		S					12	S	S						P Pairetto	45
1	2	3•	4	5	6	7	8		10*	11		14						12				9				R Gifford	46
	2		4	5	6	7	8			11		12					S	10*		3		9				R Hamer	47
1	2•		4		6	7	8			11	9*	14						12	10	3		5				K Redfern	48
1		4	5•	6	7	8	S	10	11	9*	2						15	12	S	3	S					K Rothlisberger	49
1	2	10	4	5*	6	7	8			11		S						12		3		9				R Milford	50
1		2	14		6	7	8		10•	11	9							12		3	4*	5				G Courtney	51
		2•	14		6	7	8		10	11	9							12	1	3	4*	5				D Gallagher	52
		S	7		6		8*		10	11	9	2						12	1	3	4	5				R Groves	53
	2	12	9		6	7			10•	11					14			8*	1	3	4	5				I Borrett	54
	2	14	9*	6•	7	8			10	11								12	1	3	4	5				G Singh	55
14	2	6	9•		7			8*	10	11					12				1	3	4	5				K Breen	56
	2	14		6	7				10	11	9				12			8•	1	3	4*	5				T Fitzharris	57
	2*	14		6	7	8		12	10	11	9				8•				1	3	4	5				T Holbrook	58
	2	14		6	7	8			10	11								12	1	3	4*	5	9•			K Morton	59
	2	S	14	6	7	8			10	11									1	3	4	5	9•			K Hackett	60
24	22	35	21	27	40	38	31	26	35	38	22	17		1					17	18	22	2	14	10	2	League Appearances	
	1		13	4				1		1	9	11	2	4			10	12		1						Substitute Appearances	
6	4	6	6+1	4	6	7	6	6+1	6	7	4+2	3+2	1		0+1		0+1	0+2	2+1	1	1+2	1				R/lows Appearances	
2	2	2	2	1	2	2	1	2	2	2	0+1	0+1					0	2								FA Cup Appearances	
7	5	7	5+3	7	9	9	8	7	9	7+1	7	5+1	0+2		0+1			1+3	2	3	1					ECWC Appearances	

Players on Loan: A Gray (C. Palace), J Cundy (Chelsea) †= Sent Off

TOTTENHAM HOTSPUR

Club Colours: White shirts, blue shorts, white stockings.
Change Colours: All Yellow.
Reserves League: Neville Ovenden Football Combination

COMPETITIONS

Div. 1	Div. 2	Euro C	ECWC	UEFA	Texaco
09-15	08-09	61-62	62-63	71-72	70-71
20-28	15-20		63-64	72-73	
33-35	28-33		67-68	73-74	
50-77	35-50		81-82	83-84	
78-	77-78		82-83	84-85	
			91-92		

HONOURS

Div. 1	Div. 2	FAC	ECWC	UEFA	Lge C	C/S'ld
50-51	19-20	00-01	62-63	71-72	70-71	1920
60-61	49-50	20-21		83-84	72-73	1951
		60-61				1961
		61-62				1962
		66-67				1967
		80-81				1981
		81-82				1992
		90-91				shared

MOST APPEARANCES: STEVE PERRYMAN 860+4 (1969-86)

Year	League	FAC	Lge C	Europe	C/S'ld	Other
1969-70	21	4				
1970-71	42	5	6			3
1971-72	40	5	6	12		2
1972-73	41	3	10	10		
1973-74	40	1	1	12		
1974-75	42	2	1			
1975-76	40	2	6			
1976-77	42	1	2			
1977-78	42	2	2			
1978-79	42	7	2			
1979-80	40	6	2			
1980-81	42	9	6			
1981-82	42	7	8	8	1	
1982-83	32+1	3	2	2+1		
1983-84	41	4	3	9	+1	
1984-85	42	3	5	8		
1985-86	22+1	5	4			5
	653+2	69	66	61+1	1+1	10

Previous holder: Pat Jennings 472 (1964-77)

MOST GOALS IN A CAREER
JIMMY GREAVES 266 (1961-70)

Season	League	FAC	Lge C	Europe
1961-62	21	9		
1962-63	37			5
1963-64	35			1
1964-65	29	4		
1965-66	15	3		
1966-67	25	6		
1967-68	23	3		3
1968-69	27	4	5	
1969-70	8	3		
Total	**220**	**32**	**5**	**9**

RECORD TRANSFER FEE RECEIVED

Amount	Club	Player	Date
£5,500,000	Lazio	Paul Gascoigne	7/91
£4,500,000	Marseille	Chris Waddle	6/89
£1,500,000	Rangers	Richard Gough	9/87
£1,500,000	Barcelona	Steve Archibald	7/84

RECORD TRANSFER FEE PAID

Amount	Club	Player	Date
£2,200,000	Chelsea	Gordon Durie	8/91
£2,000,000	Newcastle Utd	Paul Gascoigne	7/88
£1,700,000	Manchester City	Paul Stewart	6/88
£800,000	Aberdeen	Steve Archibald	5/80

MANAGERS

Name	Seasons	Best	Worst
Frank Brettall	1895-88		
John Cameron	1898		
Fred Kirkham	1898-07		
Pete McWilliam	1907-08		
Billy Minter	1927-30	21(2)	12(2)
Percy Smith	1930-35	3(1)	8(2)
Jack Tresadern	1935-38	5(2)	10(2)
Pete McWilliam	1938-45	8(2)	8(2)
Joe Hulme	1945-49	5(2)	8(2)
Arthur Rowe	1949-55	1(1)	1(2)
Jim Anderson	1955-58	2(1)	18(1)
Bill Nicholson	1958-74	1(1)	11(1)
Terry Neill	1974-76	9(1)	19(1)
Keith Burkinshaw	1976-84	4(1)	3(2)
Peter Shreeves	1984-86	3(1)	10(1)
David Pleat	1986-87	3(1)	3(1)
Terry Venables	1987-91	3(1)	13(1)
Peter Shreeve	1991-92	15(1)	15(1)
Doug Livermore	1992-		

LONGEST LEAGUE RUNS

of undefeated matches:	22 (31.8.1949-31.12.1949)
of undefeated home matches:	33 (2.1.1932-23.9.1933)
without home win:	8 (26.1.1935-13.4.1935)
of league wins:	13 (23.4.1960-1.10.1960)
of league defeats:	5 (27.4.1912-21.9.1912)
	(1.10.1955-29.10.1955) (18.2.1975-22.3.1975)
of league matches without a win	16 (29.12.1934-13.4.1935)
of undefeated away matches:	16 (10.11.1984-21.8.1985)
without an away win:	22 (25.2.1928-16.3.1929)
of home wins:	14 (24.1.1987-3.10.1987)
of away wins:	10 (15.4.1960-29.10.1960)

PREVIOUS NAME
Hotspur F.C. 1882-84

BIGGEST VICTORIES
League: 9-0 v Bristol Rovers, Division 2, 22.10.1977
F.A. Cup: 13-2 v Crewe Alexandra, Round 4, 3.2.1960
League Cup: 5-0 v West Brom. Alb, Round 3, 28.10.1970
7-2 v Doncaster Rovers, Round 5, 3.12.1975
5-0 v Birmingham City, Round 3, 1986-87
5-0 v West Ham United, Round 5, 2.2.1987
5-0 v Hartlepool Utd, Round 1, 26.9.1990
Europe (UEFA): 9-0 v Keflavic, Round 1, 28.9.1971

BIGGEST DEFEATS
League: 0-7 v Liverpool, Division 1, 2.9.1979
F.A. Cup: 0-5 v Stoke City, Round 1, 1.2.1896
1-6 v Huddersfield, Round 6, 3.3.1928
League Cup: 0-4 v Middlesbrough (h), Round 2, 1974-75
Europe (UEFA): 1-4 v Bayern Munich, Round 2, 3.11.1982
1-4 v Manchester Utd, Cup Winners Cup Round 2, 10.12.1963

MOST POINTS
3 points a win: 77, Division 1, 1984-85
2 points a win: 70, Division 2, 1919-1920 (Div 2 record)

MOST GOALS IN A SEASON
Clive Allen 49 (League 33, League Cup 12, FAC 4) 1986-87
3 goals 3 times = 9; 2 goals 9 times = 18; 1 goal 22 times = 22
League Goals Only: Jimmy Greaves 37, Div 1, 1962-63

MOST GOALS
115, 1960-61 (Division 1)
Smith 28, Allen 22, Jones 15, White 13, Dyson 12,
Blanchflower 6, Medwin 5, Norman 4, Mackay 4, Saul 3,
Baker 1, og 2

MOST GOALS IN A MATCH
5. Ted Harper v Reading, Division 2, 30.8.1930 (7-1)
5. Alf Stokes v Birmingham, Division 1, 18.9.1957 (7-1)
5. Les Allen v Crewe Alex., FAC Round 4, 3.2.1960 (13-2)
5. Bobby Smith v Aston Villa, Division 1, 29.3.1958 (6-2)
5. V Woodwood v West Ham Utd, 1904-05
Jack Rowley netted 7 in war-time games

MOST FIRST CLASS MATCHES IN A SEASON
68 (42 League, 5 FA Cup, 7 League Cup, 12 UEFA Cup, 2 Anglos-Ital. Cup Winners Cup) 1971-72

MOST LEAGUE GOALS CONCEDED
95, Division 1958-59

MOST LEAGUE WINS
32, Division 2, 1919-20

MOST LEAGUE DRAWS
17, Division 1, 1968-69

MOST LEAGUE DEFEATS
22, Division 1, 1934-35

OLDEST PLAYER
Jimmy Cantrell, 40 years 349 days v Birmingham, 24.4.1923

YOUNGEST PLAYER
Ally Dick, 16 years 301 days v Manchester City, 20.2.1982

MOST CAPPED PLAYER
Pat Jennings (Northern Ireland) 74

BEST PERFORMANCES BY TOTTENHAM HOTSPUR

League: 1919-20: Matches played 42, Won 32, Drawn 6, Lost 4, Goals for 102, against 32, Points 70. Division 2 Champions.
Highest: 1950-51, 1960-61: Division 1 Champions.
F.A. Cup: 1900-01: 1st rnd. Preston North End 1-1, 4-2; 2nd rnd. Bury 2-1; 3rd rnd. Reading 1-1, 3-0; Semi-final West Bromwich Albion 4-0; Final Sheffield United 2-2, 3-1
1920-21: 1st rnd. Bristol Rov. 6-2; 2nd rnd. Bradford City 4-0; 3rd rnd. Southend 4-1; Semi-final Preston N E 2-1; Final Wolverhampton Wndrs 1-0
1960-61: 3rd rnd. Charlton Athletic 3-2; 4th rnd. Crewe Alexandra 5-1; 5th rnd. Aston Villa 2-0; 6th rnd. Sunderland 1-1, 5-0; Semi-final Burnley 3-0; Final Leicester 2-0
1961-62: 3rd rnd. Birmingham City 3-3, 4-2; 4th rnd. Plymouth 5-1; 5th rnd. West Brom. Alb 4-2; 6th rnd. Aston Villa 2-0; Semi-final Manchester United 3-1; Final Burnley 3-1
1966-67: 3rd rnd. Millwall 0-0, 1-0; 4th rnd. Portsmouth 3-1; 5th rnd. Bristol City 2-0; 6th rnd. Birmingham City 0-0, 6-0; Semi-final Nottingham Forest 2-1; Final Chelsea 2-1
1980-81: 3rd rnd. Queens Park Rangers 0-0, 4-1; 4th rnd. Hull City 2-0; 5th rnd. Coventry City 3-1; 6th rnd. Exeter City 2-0; Semi-final Wolverhampton W. 2-2, 3-0; Final Manchester City 1-1, 3-2
1981-82: 3rd rnd. Arsenal 1-0; 4th rnd. Leeds United 1-0; 5th rnd. Aston Villa 1-0; 6th rnd. Chelsea 3-2; Semi-final Leicester City 2-0; Final Queens Park Rangers 1-1, 1-0
1990-91: 3rd rnd. Blackpool 1-0; 4th rnd. Oxford Utd 4-2; 5th rnd. Portsmouth 2-1; 6-1 rnd. Notts County 2-1; Semi-Final Arsenal 3-1; Final Nottingham Forest 2-1
League Cup: 1970-71: 2nd rnd. Swansea City 3-0; 3rd rnd. Sheffield United 2-1; 4th rnd. West Bromwich Albion 5-0; 5th rnd. Coventry 4-1; Semi-final Bristol City 1-1, 2-0; Final Aston Villa 2-0
1972-73: 2nd rnd. Huddersfield 2-1; 3rd rnd Middlesbrough 1-1, 0-0, 2-1; 4th rnd Millwall 2-0; 5th rnd. Liverpool 1-1, 3-1; Semi-final Wolverhampton W. 2-1, 2-2; Final Norwich 1-0
ECWC: 1962-63: 2nd rnd. Rangers 3-2, 5-2; 3rd rnd Slovan Bratisl., 0-2, 6-0; Semi-final OFK Belgrade 2-1, 3-1; Final Athletico Madrid 5-1
UEFA: 1971-72: 1st rnd. Keflavic 6-1, 9-0; 2nd rnd. Nantes 0-0, 1-0; 3rd rnd. Rapid Bucharest 3-0, 2-0; 4th rnd. UT Arad 2-0, 1-1; Semi-final AC Milan 2-1, 1-1; Final Wolverhampton W. 2-1, 1-1
1983-84: 1st rnd. Drogheda 6-0, 8-0; 2nd rnd. Feyenoord 4-2, 2-0; 3rd rnd. Bayern Munich 0-1, 2-0; 4th rnd. FK Austria 2-0, 2-2; Semi-final Hadj. Split 1-2, 1-0; Final Anderlecht 1-1, 1-1, won on pens

DIVISIONAL RECORDS

	Played	Won	Drawn	Lost	For	Against	Points
DIVISION 1	2356	964	563	829	3812	3441	**2683**
DIVISION 2	668	311	172	185	1253	851	**794**
TOTALS	**3024**	**1275**	**735**	**1014**	**5065**	**4292**	**3477**

TOTTENHAM HOTSPUR

							APPEARANCES				GOALS			
PLAYERS NAME / Honours	Ht	Wt	Birthdate	Birthplace / Transfers	Contract Date	Clubs	League	L/Cup	FA Cup	Other	Lg	L/C	FAC	Oth
GOALKEEPERS														
Kevin Dearden	5.11	12.8	08.03.70	Luton	05.08.88	Tottenham H. (T)		2						
Loan Cambridge City (09.03.89) 15lg				Loan	31.08.89	Hartlepool Utd	10							
Loan Oxford United (14.12.89)				Loan	20.03.90	Swindon Town	1							
Loan Peterborough U (24.08.90) 7lg				Loan	10.01.91	Hull City	3							
Loan Rochdale (16.08.91) 2lg				Loan	19.03.92	Birmingham City	12							
Erik Thorstvedt	6.3	12.01	28.10.68	Stavanger		Viking Stavanger								
Nor:						IFK Gothenburg								
				£400,000	22.12.88	Tottenham H	113	18	8	7				
Ian Walker	6.1	11.9	31.10.71	Herts	04.12.89	Tottenham H. (T)	19	1		2				
E: Y.17, S; FAYC'90				Loan	31.08.90	Oxford Utd	2	1						
DEFENDERS														
Dean Austin	5.11	11.11	26.04.70	Hemel Hempstead		St Albans								
				£12,000	22.03.90	Southend Utd	96	4	2	7	2	1		
				£300,000	04.06.92	Tottenham H								
Jason Cundy	6.1	13.07	12.11.69	Wimbledon	01.08.88	Chelsea (T)	40+1	6	6	4	2			
				Loan	26.03.92	Tottenham H								
				£750,000	02.07.92	Tottenham H	10							
Justin Edinburgh	5.9	11.06	18.12.69	Brentwood	05.08.88	Southend Utd. (T)	36+1	2+1	2	4+1				1
				Loan	11.01.90	Tottenham H								
				£120,000	30.07.90	Tottenham H	22+3	6+2	5	3	1			
Terry Fenwick	5.10	10.11	17.11.59	Durham	01.12.76	Crystal Palace (A)	62+8	4+1	7				1	
E: 20, u21.11, Y.7; Div2 '79'83; FAYC'77'78; UEFA 0.80'82					17.12.80	Q.P.R	256	28+1	18	5	33	6	6	
				£550,000	31.12.87	Tottenham H	87+1	14	7	5	8	2		
				Loan	25.10.90	Leicester City	8		1	1	1			
Ian Hendon	6.0	12.10	05.12.71	Ilford, Essex	20.12.89	Tottenham H. (T)	0+4	1		0+2				
E: Y.10; FAYC'90				Loan	16.01.92	Portsmouth	1+3							
				Loan	26.03.92	Leyton Orient	5+1							
John Hendry	5.11		06.01.70	Glasgow		Dundee	0+2							
				£50,000	31.07.90	Tottenham H	3+6	0+1			3			
				Loan	27.02.92	Charlton Ath	1+4				1			
Gary Mabbutt	5.10	10.6	23.08.61	Bristol	09.01.79	Bristol Rovers (A)	122+9	10	5+1		10	1	1	
E: 13, B.4, u21.7, Y.11; UEFA'84; UEFA Y'80 £105,000					11.08.82	Tottenham H	326+13	49+2	28+2	29+4	25	2	3	4
Neil Ruddock	6.2	12.0	09.05.68	Battersea	03.03.86	Millwall (A)			3+1					1
E:u21.4,u19.5,Y.6				£50,000	14.04.86	Tottenham H	7+2		1+1				1	
				£300,000	29.06.88	Millwall	0+2	2		1+1	1	3		
				£250,000	13.02.89	Southampton	100+7	14+1	10	6	9		4	
				£750,000	29.07.92	Tottenham H								
Pat Van den Hauwe	5.10	10.8	16.12.60	Dundermonde	02.08.78	Birmingham City (A)	119+4	12	5		1			
W: 13, CS'85, Div1'85'87, ECWC'85				£100,000	24.09.84	Everton	134+1	20	30	14+1	2		1	
				£575,000	25.08.89	Tottenham H	97+1	14	7	7				
MIDFIELD														
Paul Allen	5.7	9.12	28.08.62	Aveley	29.08.79	West Ham U. (A)	149+3	20+4	15+3	2+1	6	2	3	
E: u21.3, Y.27, FAC'80, EUFA Y'80 £400,000					19.06.85	Tottenham H	238+15	38+2	21+1	12+1	20	4	1	
Mohamed Amar	5.8	11.04	05.11.66	Morocco		Barcelona (Spa) (A)								
Nayim				Loan	14.11.88	Tottenham H	8+3				2			
				£250,000	01.06.89	Tottenham H	72+11	9+6	3+3	7	6	3	1	
Peter Beadle	6.1	11.12	13.05.72	London	05.05.90	Gillingham (T)	42+25	2+4	1+1	1	14	2		
				£500,000	04.06.92	Tottenham H								
Gudni Bergsson	5.10	10.07	21.07.65	Iceland		Valur (Iceland)								
Ice:						Tottenham H	51+15	4+2	2+1	5+1	2			
Andy Gray	5.10	10.2	22.02.64	Brixton		Corinthian		2						
E:u21.2			Dulwich Hamlet	£2,000	08.11.84	Crystal Palace	91+7	9+1	3	0+1	27	2		
				£150,000	25.11.87	Aston Villa	34+3	3	3+1	0+2	4	1	1	
				£425,000	02.02.89	Q.P.R	11				2			
				£500,000		Crystal Palace	87+3	15	11	14	12	4	2	4
					27.02.92	Tottenham H	14				1			
Vinny Samways	5.8	9.0	27.10.68	Bethnal Green	09.11.85	Tottenham H	92+28	19+4	7+1	7	8	3		
E: u21.5, u19.3, Y.6														
Steve Sedgley	6.1	12.6	26.05.68	Enfield	02.06.86	Coventry City (A)	81+3	9	2+2	5+1	3	2		
E: u21.11				£750,000	28.07.89	Tottenham H	85+15	16+3	7+1	5+3		1		
FORWARDS														
Darren Anderton	6.0	11.7	03.03.72	Southampton	05.02.90	Portsmouth (T)	53+9	3+2	7+1	2	7	1	5	
E:Y.1				£1,750,000	03.06.92	Tottenham H								
Gordon Durie	5.10	13.0	06.12.65	Paisley		EstF	66+15	8+1	5+1		26			
S: 7, B.1, u21.4; Div2'89; ZDC'90						Hibernian	45+2	6	5		14	8		
				£381,000	25.04.86	Chelsea	115+8	11	6	12	51	7	1	3
				£2,200,000	16.08.91	Tottenham H	31	6	1	8	7	2		3
David Howells	5.11	11.1	15.12.67	Guildford	28.01.85	Tottenham H	106+28	16+2	6+2	7	14	2		
E: u19.2,Y.8														
Paul Moran	5.10	11.0	22.05.68	Enfield	15.07.85	Tottenham H	14+14	1+5	3+1	0+1	2			
Loan Portsmouth (11.01.89) 3lg				Loan	02.11.89	Leicester City	10				2			
				Loan	14.02.91	Newcastle Utd	1							
				Loan	21.03.91	Southend Utd	1							

ADDITIONAL CONTRACT PLAYERS

Nicholas Barmby, Darren Caskey, David Culverhouse, Michael Heath, Lee Hodges, Scott Houghton, Paul Mahorn, Andrew Marlowe, David MacDonald, Gerry McMahon, Jeffery Minton, Olisa Morah, Stuart nethercoft, Anthony Potts, Jeff Thompson-Minton, Andrew Turner, David Tuttle, Ian Walker, Kevin Watson, Neil Young.

TOTTENHAM HOTSPUR

RECORD WIN & LOSS AGAINST EACH CLUB IN CURRENT DIVISION
(Where a score has occured on several occasions the most recent is given)

Club	Rec. Win	Season	Rec. Loss	Season
ARSENAL	5-0	1982-83	6-0	1934-35 (home)
ASTON VILLA	6-2	1960-61	4-0	1982-83
BLACKBURN ROVERS	5-0	1924-25	7-2	1963-64
CHELSEA	5-0	1920-21	4-1	1989-90
COVENTRY CITY	5-0	1919-20 (away)	4-0	1938-39
CRYSTAL PALACE	3-0	1971-72	1-0	1990-91
EVERTON	10-4	1958-59	4-0	1976-77
IPSWICH TOWN	5-0	1962-63	4-0	1974-75
LEEDS UNITED	5-1	1956-57	4-1	1959-60
LIVERPOOL	7-2	1963-64	7-0	1978-79
MANCHESTER CITY	5-1	1957-58	5-0	1976-77
MANCHESTER UNITED	6-1	1932-33	5-0	1909-10
MIDDLESBROUGH	7-1	1952-53	4-1	1980-81
NORWICH CITY	4-0	1989-90	4-0	1979-80
NOTTINGHAM FOREST	9-2	1963-64	4-0	1979-80
OLDHAM ATHLETIC	5-1	1977-78	4-1	1914-15
QUEENS PARK RANGERS	5-0	1984-85	4-0	1983-84
SHEFFIELD UNITED	7-0	1948-50	6-1	1938-39
SHEFFIELD WEDNESDAY	7-2	1954-55	5-1	1946-47 (home)
SOUTHAMPTON	8-0	1935-36	5-0	1983-84
WIMBLEDON	4-2	1990-91	5-1	1990-91

FIRST TEAM COACH: DOUG LIVERMORE

DATE OF BIRTH: 27.12.1947   **PLACE OF BIRTH:** Liverpool

DATE OF APPOINTMENT: MARCH 1992

PREVIOUS CLUBS
  as Manager: None
  as Asst. Man./Coach: Norwich, Tottenham
  as Player: Liverpool, Norwich, Bournemouth, Cardiff, Chester City

HONOURS
  as Manager: None
  as Player: None

Value Rating: ★ ★ ★ ★ ★

Programme Editor: John Fennelly

Price of 1992-93 Programme: £1.50

Number of Pages: 48

Subscriptions: UK/BFPO £45, Overseas please contact club

Local Newspapers: Tottenham Herald, Waltham Forest Guardian, North London News.

Local Radio Stations: LBC, Radio London, Hospital Broadcasts.

Additional Publications on Club: A Complete Record 1882-1987, Breedon Books.
Glory, Glory Nights – A History of Spurs in Europe, hardback £14.95.
A Compilation of contemporary newspaper reports of all Spurs games in European competitions.

LEADING LEAGUE GOALSCORERS
SEASONS 1979-80 – 1991-92

1979-80	**GLENN HODDLE**	18		1980-81	**STEVE ARCHIBALD**	20
1981-82	**GARTH CROOKS**	13		1982-83	**STEVE ARCHIBALD**	11
1983-84	**STEVE ARCHIBALD**	21		1984-85	**MARK FALCO**	22
1985-86	**MARK FALCO**	19		1986-87	**CLIVE ALLEN**	33
1987-88	**CLIVE ALLEN**	11		1988-89	**CHRIS WADDLE**	14
1989-90	**GARY LINEKER**	24		1990-91	**GARY LINEKER**	13

1991-92   **GARY LINEKER**   **28**

WHITE HART LANE 748 High Road, Tottenham, London N17 0AP

Capacity: 32,786   **Standing:** 7,407   **Seating:** 25,379

Tel: Ground: 081 808 6666   **Ticket Sales:** 081 808 8080   **Clubcall:** 0898 100 300

All premium rate calls (0898/0891) cost 36p per minute cheap rate and 48p per minute at all other times. Call costings correct at time of going to press.

GROUNDS
Tottenham Marshes, 1882-1885. Northumberland Park
1885-1898, White Hart Lane 1898-

ATTENDANCES
Highest: 75,038 v Sunderland, FA Cup 6th Round,
5.3.1938

Lowest: 5,000 v Sunderland, Division 1, 19.12.1914

RECORD RECEIPTS (with previous records):
£336,702 v Manchester United, Div 1, 28.9.91
£245,682 v Anderlecht, UEFA, 23.5.1984
£136,407 v West Bromwich Albion, League Cup Semi-Final, 10.2.1982
£49,920 v Feyenoord, UEFA, 21.5.1974
£48,000 v Wolverhampton Wanderers, League Cup,
17.5.1972
£30,000 v Manchester United, ECWC, 2.12.1963

WHITE HART LANE
First game: v Notts County (Friendly), 4-1, 4.9.1899
Internationals: England v France 1935
England v Germany, 1935
England v Czechoslovakia, 1937
England v Italy, 1949

Season Tickets:
Stands: from £390 to £442, juv/OAP £117 to £247

Executive Box Season Tickets: Between £14,000-
£17,500 (West); £19,000-£33,000 (East)

Cost of Stand Tickets: Seats £8 to £19 (no reductions)
Terraces £6, juv/OAP £4

Match and Ticket Information: Seats for League
matches available one calendar month in advance. Seats
are available on match days at the Park Lane ticket office.
Dial a seat 081-808 3030

Car Parking: No street parking within a 0.25 mile radius
of the ground

Nearest Railway Station: White Hart Lane (from
Liverpool Street, Central London), Northumberland Park
(Liverpool St)

How to get to the ground

From North, East, South and West: Use A406 North
Circular Road to Edmonton then at traffic signals follow
signs to Edmonton then at traffic signals follow signs
Tottenham A1010 into Fore Street for Tottenham Hotspur
FC

TRANMERE ROVERS

Division 1

Formed: 1885   **Turned Professional:** 1912   **Ltd Co:** 1912

SPONSORED BY: Wirral Borough Council   **NICKNAME:** The Rovers

President
H B Thomas

Chairman
Peter Johnson

Vice-Chairman & Chief Executive
Frank Corfe

Directors
G Higham
F Williams   A J Adams
J Holsgrove   H Jones

Secretary
Norman Wilson (051-652 2578)

Team Manager
John King

Coach
Ronnie Moore

Trainer
Kenny Jones

Youth Development Officer
Warwick Rimmer

Physiotherapist
Alec McLellan

Commercial Manager
Nigel Coates (051-608 4194/0371)

Groundsman
Andy Quayle

Honorary Medical Officer
Dr. John Delaney & Dr. Mike Azurdia

Training Complex Manager
Ray Mathias

Club Statistician for the Directory
Peter Bishop

WITH Tranmere back in the Second Division for the first time in 53 years, expectation was high that they could complete their remarkable rise through the divisions, particularly after they signed world class striker John Aldridge from Real Sociedad during the summer.

But while Aldridge was an unqualified success, equalling the clubs 59 year old scoring record with 40 goals in all competitions, Rovers' overall record, which included 19 draws, meant they had to settle for mid-table security when a handful of extra victories could have pushed them into the play-off zone.

Nevertheless, there were many memorable matches for the Prenton Park faithful to savour. Newcastle, Millwall and Derby County were beaten home and away, the latter after Derby had held a 3-1 lead at one stage – Aldridge scoring a hat-trick in a 4-3 victory.

Rovers' Cup campaign also provided plenty of thrills. In the Rumbelows Cup, Halifax proved stubborn opposition only succumbing 8-6 on aggregate before first division Chelsea were vanquished 3-1 at Prenton Park after a first leg draw at Stamford Bridge. However, a third round trip to eventual champions Leeds United proved a bridge too far, though Leeds' winning margin was much closer than the 3-1 scoreline would suggest.

The Zenith Data Cup witnessed an incredible live televised 6-6 draw with Newcastle, Rovers getting the verdict on penalties to set up a home tie with Grimsby which gave Rovers their biggest victory of the season, 5-1. When Tranmere became the first side to win at Middlesbrough thanks to another Aldridge goal, hopes were high of a return to Wembley but on a foggy night at Prenton, Nottingham Forest, the ultimate winners, and Roy Keane conspired to deny them.

In the F.A. Cup, Tranmere were forced to start at the first round, along with Grimsby, and overcame Runcorn and York (at the second attempt) before crashing out 1-3 at Oxford United in the third round.

While there were plenty of highlights to enjoy, the depths were plumbed at Oxford and Portsmouth, the latter result prompting John King to abandon his favoured sweeper system in favour of playing with two wingers, including Pat Nevin on loan from Everton, which helped Aldridge become the Football League' top marksman for the season.

Tranmere though ended the season on a winning note with the victory in the Liverpool Senior Cup Final at Goodison Park. The reserves also won the Midland Senior League title.

Given that the younger players will have gained a years' experience in the rarified atmosphere of the second division, and that John King hopes to strengthen his squad in the close season, Tranmere fans can look forward to the new season with optimism and confidence.

    Peter Bishop

Back row L-R: Alan Morgan, Mike Foster, Dave Higgins, Ged Brannan, John McGreal, Mike Smith, Kenny Irons, John Morrissey, Tony Thomas. **Middle row:** Norman Wilson (Secretary), Kenny Jones (Trainer), Graham Branch, Steve Vickers, Chris Malkin, Eric Nixon, Danny Coyne, Shaun Garnett, Mark Hughes, Ronnie Moore (First team coach), Ray Mathias (Reserve team coach). **Front row:** Neil McNab, Steve Cooper, Ian Muir, Steve Mungall, John King (Manager), John Aldridge, Dave Martindale, Ian Nolan, Tony Draper.

TRANMERE ROVERS

DIVISION TWO: 14th   **FA CUP:** 3rd RND   **RUMBELOWS CUP:** 3rd RND   **ZDS CUP:** 4th RND

M	DATE		COMP.	VEN	OPPONENTS	RESULT	H/T	LGE POS	GOALSCORERS/GOAL TIMES	ATTEN-DANCE
1	A	17	BL	A	Brighton & H A	W 2-0	2-0		Aldridge 33, 35	(9,679)
2		20	RC 1/1	A	Halifax Town	W 4-3	2-3		Irons 18, Aldridge 3 (19, 65, 76)	(4,285)
3		23	BL	H	Bristol Rovers	D 2-2	1-1	4	Aldridge (pen) 44, Steel 79	10,150
4		27	RC 1/2	H	Halifax Town	W †4-3	1-2		Aldridge 11, 120, Steel 56, 105	4,285
5		31	BL	A	Grimsby Town	D 2-2	1-0	8	Aldridge 16, Thomas 75	(7,018)
6	S	3	BL	H	Charlton Athletic	D 2-2	1-0	9	Malkin 18, Hughes 90	7,609
7		7	BL	H	Newcastle United	W 3-2	1-2	6	Malkin 18, Thomas 60, Vickers 86	11,465
8		14	BL	A	Bristol City	D 2-2	1-2	9	Brannan 26, Irons 48	(11,235)
9		17	BL	A	Middlesbrough	L 0-1	0-0	13		(16,550)
10		21	BL	H	Barnsley	W 2-1	1-0	9	Aldridge 24, Higgins 48	8,482
11		25	RC 2/1	A	Chelsea	D 1-1	0-0		Aldridge 52	(11,311)
12		28	BL	A	Blackburn Rovers	D 0-0	0-0	8		(11,449)
13	O	1	ZDS 1	H	Newcastle United	D †6-6	2-2		McNab 7, Aldridge 3 (18, 94, 120 pen), Steel 75, Martindale 95 (Won 3-2 on pens)	4,056
14		4	BL	H	Southend United	D 1-1	0-1	8	Steel 50	7,358
15		8	RC 2/2	H	Chelsea	W †3-1	1-0		Steel 36, Aldridge (pen) 116, Malkin 120	11,165
16		12	BL	A	Oxford United	L 0-1	0-0	13		(5,760)
17		18	BL	H	Cambridge United	L 1-2	0-2	16	Aldridge 85	7,625
18		22	ZDS 2	H	Grimsby Town	W 5-1	2-1		Aldridge 3 (6, 22, 90), Martindale 60, Steel 81	4,053
19		26	BL	A	Wolverhampton W	D 1-1	0-1	15	Steel 75	(12,266)
20		29	RC 3	A	Leeds United	L 1-3	0-0		Aldridge 85	(18,266)
21	N	2	BL	A	Derby County	W 1-0	1-0	14	Aldridge 38	(11,501)
22		5	BL	H	Millwall	W 2-1	1-0	12	Irons 45, Aldridge (pen) 55	6,108
23		8	BL	H	Plymouth Argyle	W 1-0	0-0	12	Aldridge (pen) 72	7,490
24		16	FAC 1	A	Runcorn	W 3-0	1-0		Irons 2, Aldridge 46, 66	(6,563)
25		22	BL	H	Swindon Town	D 0-0	0-0	12		9,585
26		26	ZDS 3	A	Middlesbrough	W 1-0	0-0		Aldridge 75	(6,952)
27		30	BL	A	Ipswich Town	L 0-4	0-2	14		(11,072)
28	D	7	FAC 2	A	York City	D 1-1	1-0		Morrissey 28	(4,646)
29		10	ZDS 4	H	Nottingham Forest	L 0-2	0-1			8,034
30		13	BL	A	Port Vale	D 1-1	1-1	14	Cooper 36	(6,426)
31		17	FAC 2	H	York City	W 2-1	1-0		Aldridge 45, Irons 77	5,546
32		26	BL	H	Sunderland	W 1-0	1-0	12	Irons 27	13,658
33		28	BL	H	Grimsby Town	D 1-1	1-0	13	Aldridge 27	7,900
34	J	1	BL	A	Watford	D 0-0	0-0	14		(9,892)
35		4	FAC 3	A	Oxford United	L 1-3	0-2		Malkin 71	(6,027)
36		11	BL	A	Bristol Rovers	L 0-1	0-0	16		(7,138)
37		17	BL	H	Brighton & H A	D 1-1	0-0	15	Muir 77	7,179
38		24	BL	H	Watford	D 1-1	1-0	15	Morrissey 44	6,187
39		31	BL	A	Cambridge United	D 0-0	0-0	14		(5,491)
40	F	8	BL	H	Wolverhampton W	W 4-3	2-2	14	Aldridge (pen) 3, Malkin 6, Morrissey 63, 90	11,371
41		11	BL	A	Sunderland	D 1-1	0-1	14	Aldridge 48	(18,060)
42		21	BL	H	Ipswich Town	L 0-1	0-1	15		9,161
43		29	BL	A	Portsmouth	L 0-2	0-2	16		(16,644)
44	M	6	BL	H	Port Vale	W 2-1	0-0	16	Harvey 58, Aldridge 67	8,477
45		11	BL	A	Millwall	W 3-0	2-0	13	Morrissey 24, Aldridge 31, 79	(6,456)
46		14	BL	H	Derby County	W 4-3	1-1	12	Aldridge 3 (16, 64 pen, 68), Irons 61	10,386
47		17	BL	A	Swindon Town	L 0-2	0-1	12		(6,780)
48		21	BL	A	Plymouth Argyle	L 0-1	0-0	13		(7,447)
49		27	BL	H	Leicester City	L 1-2	1-0	15	Muir 9	9,061
50		31	BL	H	Bristol City	D 2-2	0-0	16	Nolan 52, Steel 70	5,797
51	A	4	BL	A	Newcastle United	W 3-2	2-1	15	Aldridge 33, 38, Morrissey 73	(21,215)
52		7	BL	H	Portsmouth	W 2-0	1-0	15	Irons 44, Thomas 84	6,692
53		10	BL	H	Middlesbrough	L 1-2	0-1	13	Muir 84	8,842
54		15	BL	A	Leicester City	L 0-1	0-0	13		(18,555)
55		18	BL	A	Barnsley	D 1-1	1-1	14	Muir 12	(5,811)
56		20	BL	H	Blackburn Rovers	D 2-2	1-1	14	Muir 34, Irons 61	13,705
57		25	BL	A	Southend United	D 1-1	0-1	15	Irons 56	(4,761)
58		28	BL	A	Charlton Athletic	W 1-0	1-0	13	Aldridge 34	(7,645)
59	M	2	BL	H	Oxford United	L 1-2	0-0	14	Aldridge 60	9,173

Best Home League Attendance: 13,705 v Blackburn Rovers   **Smallest: 5,797 v Bristol City**   **Av Home Att: 8,846**

Goal Scorers: **Compared with 90-91: +2,107**

League (56):   Aldridge 22 (4 pens), Irons 7, Muir 5, Morrissey 5, Steel 4, Thomas 3, Malkin 3, Nolan, Brannan, Harvey, Hughes, Cooper, Vickers, Higgins

R/lows C (13):   Aldridge 8 (1 pen), Steel 3, Irons, Malkin
FA Cup (7):   Aldridge 3, Irons 2, Morrissey, Malkin
ZDS Cup (12):   Aldridge 7, Steel 2, Martindale 2, McNab

                                                                                                          † = After extra-time

598

Nixon E.	Higgins D.	Brannan G.	Irons K.	Hughes M.	Garnett S.	Morrissey	Aldridge J.	Steel W.	Martindale D.	Thomas T.	Malkin C.	McNab N.	Mungall S.	Vickers S.	Harvey J.	Nolan I.	Cooper S.	Muir I.	Branch G.	Nevin P. (L)	Collings	McGreal J.	Referee	
1	2	3●	4	5	6	7*	8	9	10	11	12	14											A Buksh	1
1	2	3	4	5	6	7	8	9*	10	11	12	S											A Flood	2
1	2	3	4	5	6	7	8	9	10	11	S	S											N Midgley	3
1	2	3	4	5†	6*	7	8	9	10	11	S	12											G Singh	4
1	2	3	4*	5	6	7	8		10	11	9	12					S						G Courtney	5
1	2	3	4	5		7*	8		10●	11	9	14				6	12						M Reed	6
1	2	3	4*	5		7*	8		10	11	9	12				6		14					I Hendrick	7
1	2	3	4			7*	8		10	11	9	14	5	6			12●						P Vanes	8
1	2	3	4*	5●		7	8		10	11	9	12				6			14				S Bell	9
1	2	3	4	5		7	8	12	10	11	9*	S				6							B Hill	10
1	2	3	4	5		7	8	9	10	11	S	S				6							G Pooley	11
1	2	3	4*	5		7●	8	9	10	11	14	12				6							K Redfearn	12
1	2	3*	4	5			8	9	10		7	11	12	6●					14				J Key	13
1	2	3*	4	5			8	9	10†		7	12	11	6			S						J Rushton	14
1	2	3	4*	5		7	8	9	10*		14	12	11	6									P Harrison	15
1	2†	3	4*	5		7*	8	9			14	12	11	6*									P Alcock	16
1		3	4	5	2	7	8	9			12	10	11	6*	S								J Brandwood	17
1	2	3	4	5			8	9	10		S		11*	6	12								T Holbrook	18
1		3	4	5		7	8	9	10		12		11*	6	S		2						J Deakin	19
1		3	4●	5		7	8	2*	10		9		11	6	12		14						V Callow	20
1		3	4*	5		7	8	2	10		9		11	6	S	2	12						A Ward	21
1	2	3*	4	5		7	8		10		9			6	S	11	12						D Allison	22
1	2	3	4	5		7	8		10		9*			6	S	11	12						D Phillips	23
1	2	3	4	5*		7	8		10		9●			6	12	11	14						S Bell	24
1	2		4	5		7	8	14	10		9●		3*	6	12	11							J Parker	25
1	2	3	4	5		7	8	9	10		S			6	12	11*							T Fitzharris	26
1	2	3	4	5*		7	8	9	10●		12			6	14	11							I Hemley	27
1	2	3	4	5		7	8				S	9		6	S	11	10						P Harrison	28
1	2	3	4	5*		7	8	S				9		6	12	11	10						K Barratt	29
1	2	3*	4	5		7	8	S				9		6	12	11	10						D Gallagher	30
	2		4	5*		7	8	14	12				3	6	9	11	10●				1		P Harrison	31
1	2		4	5		7	8				S	S	3	6	9	11	10						M Peck	32
1	2		4	5*		7	8*				12	S	3	6	9	11	10						B Coddington	33
1	2		4	5		7	8				12	S	3	6	9	11	10*						V Callow	34
1	2†		4	5		7	8				12	14	3*	6	9	11	10●						P Jones	35
1	2		4	5*		7		9			10	3		6	8	11		12					A Gunn	36
1	2		4	5*		7		9			10	S	3	6	8	11		12					J Kirkby	37
1			4	5	2	7		9	8	11			S	6	S	3	10						J Key	38
1			4	5	2	7	8		10	11	9		S	6		3		S					M Pierce	39
1				5	2*	7	8		10	11	9		3	6	4	3		12					R Shepherd	40
1	2			5		7*	8		10	11	9		3	6	S	4		12					T Fitzharris	41
1	2		4	5*		7	8		9●	11	12			6	14	3	10						I Cruikshanks	42
1	2		4	5●			8			11	9*		7	6	10	3		12	14				R Groves	43
1	2		4			7	8	9		11			S	6	5	3		12		10*			J Watson	44
1	2		4			7	8			11			S	6	5	3	S	10		9			A Smith	45
1	2		4			7	8	S		11			S	6	5	3	10			9			N Midgley	46
1	2					7	8	12	4●	11			14	6	5	3	10*			9			P Durkin	47
1	2		4			7	8	S		11			S	6	5	3	10			9			K Cooper	48
1	2		4			7	8	12	S	11				6	5	3	10*			9			K Lupton	49
1	2					7*	8	9		11	12			6	5	3		10					R Dilkes	50
1	2†		4*			7	8	9		12	11	S		6	5	3		10					S Lodge	51
1	2		4			7	8	9	S	11	10			6	5	3	S			10			A Dawson	52
1	2		4	2		7	8	9*	14	11	10			6	5●	3		12					R Poulain	53
1			4	5	2*		8	12	7	11	9			6		3		10	S				T West	54
1			4	5			8	S	7*		9		2	6		3		10	12				A Flood	55
1		4*		5		7	8	2	11	12			S	6	9	3		10					A Bennett	56
1		4	S			7*	8		9	11	12		2	6		3		10				5	D Elleray	57
1		4	S			8		9	11	7			2	6		3		10	S			5	J Carter	58
1		4	S			8		9	11	7*			2	6		3		10	12			5	A Wilkie	59
46	33	18	43	33	8	40	43	16	29	30	23	3	17	43	19	34	4	13		8		3	**League Appearances**	
								5	2		12	9	1				5		5	7	4		**Substitute Appearances**	
5	4	5	5	5	2	5	5	5		3	1+2	0+2	2		3		0+1			0+1			**R/lows Appearances**	
3	4	2	4	4		4	4		0+1	1+1		1+1	1+1	2	4	2	4	3				1	**FA Cup Appearances**	
4	4	4	4	4		3	4		3	3		1	2	1+1	4	0+3	2	1		0+1			**ZDS Cup Appearances**	

Players on Loan: Pat Nevin (Everton)

† = Sent Off

TRANMERE ROVERS

Club Colours: All white with blue trim
Change Colours: All royal blue or Yellow shirts, green shorts, yellow socks
Reserves League: Midland Senior   **Youth League:** Lancashire League

COMPETITIONS			
Div. 2	Div. 3N	Div. 3	Div. 4
38-39	21-38	58-61	61-67
91-	39-58	67-75	75-76
		76-79	79-89
		89-91	

HONOURS		
Div. 3N	Leyland Daf	Welsh Cup
1937-38	1990	1934-35

MOST APPEARANCES: RAY MATHIAS 626+10 (1967-84)				
Year	League	FA Cup	Lge Cup	Others
1967-68	13			
1968-69	26	1	5	
1969-70	20+4			
1970-71	46	3	3	
1971-72	46	7	3	
1972-73	45	2	1	
1973-74	38+1	2	3	
1974-75	40	1	3	
1975-76	46	1	2	
1976-77	46	1	3	
1977-78	46	2	2	
1978-79	45	3	2	
1979-80	38+4	3	4	
1980-81	37	3	4	
1981-82	1		1	
1982-83	16		3	1+1
1983-84	6+1	1		
1984-85	2			
	557+10	29+1	40	1+1

Harold Bell, 631, 1946-64 (incl. record 401 consecutive
League appearances)

MOST GOALS IN A CAREER					
IAN MUIR 159 (1985-92)					
Season	League	FAC	Lge C	AMC	P/Offs
1985-86	14	1			
1986-87	20	3		2	
1987-88	27	2			
1988-89	21	5	2	1	
1989-90	23		4	7	1
1990-91	13			8	
1991-92	5				
Total	123	11	6	18	1
Previous holder: Bunny Bell, 115 (1931-36)					

MANAGERS			
Name	Seasons	Best	Worst
Bert Cooke	1912-35	4(3N)	21(3N)
Jack Carr	1935-36	3(3N)	3(3N)
Jim Knowles	1936-39	22(2)	19(3N)
Bill Ridding	1939-45		
Ernie Blackburn	1946-55	4(3N)	19(3N)
Noel Kelly	1955-57	16(3N)	23(3N)
Peter Farrall	1957-60	7(3)	20(3)
Walter Galbraith	1961	21(3)	21(3)
Dave Russell	1961-69	7(3)	15(4)
Jackie Wright	1969-72	16(3)	20(3)
Ron Yeats	1972-75	10(3)	22(3)
John King	1975-80	12(3)	15(4)
Bryan Hamilton	1980-85	6(4)	21(4)
Frank Worthington	1985-87	19(4)	20(4)
Ronnie Moore	1987		
John King	1987-	14(2)	20(4)

RECORD TRANSFER FEE RECEIVED			
Amount	Club	Player	Date
£120,000	Cardiff City	Ronnie Moore	2/79
£60,000	Manchester Utd	Steve Coppell	3/75
£34,000	West Brom Alb.	Jim Cumbes	8/69
£23,000	Derby County	Roy McFarland	8/67

RECORD TRANSFER FEE PAID			
Amount	Club	Player	Date
£250,000	Real Sociedad	John Aldridge	6/91
£125,000	Manchester City	Neil McNab	1/90
£60,000	Manchester City	Eric Nixon	7/88
£50,000	Wrexham	Jim Steel	11/87

LONGEST LEAGUE RUNS	
of undefeated matches:	18 (16.3.1970-4.9.1970)
of undefeated home matches:	26 (24.10.1988-10.11.1989)
without home win:	11 (19.2.1979-9.5.1979)
of league wins:	9 (9.2.1990-19.3.1990)
of league defeats:	8 (29.10.1938-17.12.1938)
of league matches without a win:	15 (19.2.1979-18.4.1979)
of undefeated away matches:	10 (27.12.1983-21.4.1984)
without an away win:	35 (19.11.1977-14.4.1979)
of home wins:	18 (22.8.1964-28.3.1965)
of away wins:	4 (17.2.1990-17.3.1990)

PREVIOUS NAME
Belmont 1884-85

PREVIOUS LEAGUE
Central League 1919-21

BIGGEST VICTORIES
League: 11-1 v Durham City, Div 3N, 7.1.1928
13-4 v Oldham, Div 3N, 26.12.1935
F.A. Cup: 13-0 v Oswestry, 10.10.1914
League Cup: 4-0 v Crewe Alex., Rnd 1, 19.8.1970

BIGGEST DEFEATS
League: 2-9 v Q.P.R., Div 3, 3.12.1960
0-8 v Grimsby Town, Div 3N, 14.9.1925
0-8 v Bradford City, Div 3N, 6.3.1929
0-8 v Lincoln City, Div 3N, 21.4.1930
0-8 v Bury, Div 3, 10.1.1970
F.A. Cup: 1-9 v Tottenham, Rnd 3 replay, 14.1.1953
League Cup: 0-6 v Q.P.R., Rnd 3, 23.9.1969
0-6 v West Ham Utd, Rnd 2, 11.9.1974

MOST POINTS
3 points a win: 80, Division 4, 1988-89, Div 3, 1989-90
2 points a win: 60, Division 4, 1964-65

MOST GOALS
111, Division 3N, 1930-31
J Kennedy 34, Dixon 32, Watts 27, Meston 8, Urmson 7,
Barton 1, Lewis 1, og 1

MOST GOALS IN A MATCH
9. Robert 'Bunny' Bell v Oldham Athletic, 26.12.1935

MOST GOALS IN A SEASON
Robert 'Bunny' Bell 40 (League 35, FA Cup 5,) 1933-34
4 goals twice = 8; 3 goals 4 times = 12; 1 goal 12 times = 12.
Total 40
John Aldridge 40 (League 22, Lge Cup 8, FA Cup 3, AMC 7)
1991-92
3 goals 4 times = 12; 2 goals 5 times = 10, 1 goal 18
times = 18. Total 40

MOST FIRST CLASS MATCHES IN A SEASON
65 (46 League, 1 FA Cup, 7 League Cup, 8 Leyland Daf, 3
Play-Offs) 1989-90

MOST LEAGUE GOALS CONCEDED
115, Division 3, 1960-61

MOST LEAGUE WINS
27, Division 4, 1964-65

MOST LEAGUE DRAWS
22, Division 3, 1970-71

MOST LEAGUE DEFEATS
31, Division 2, 1938-39

OLDEST PLAYER
George Payne, 39 years 202 days, Div 3, 11.3.1961

YOUNGEST PLAYER
William 'Dixie' Dean, 16 years 355 days, Div 3N, 12.1.1924

MOST CAPPED PLAYER
John Aldridge (Eire) 8

BEST PERFORMANCES BY TRANMERE ROVERS

League: 1937-38: Matches Played 42, Won 23, Drawn 10, Lost 9, Goals for 81, Goals against 41, Points 56. First in Division 3N

Highest: 14th Division 2, 1991-92

F.A. Cup: 1967-68: 1st rnd. Rochdale (h) 5-1; 2nd rnd. Bradford P.A. (a) 3-2; 3rd rnd. Huddersfield (h) 2-1; 4th rnd. Coventry City 1-1, 2-0; 5th rnd. Everton (a) 0-2

League Cup: 1960-61: 1st rnd. Bye; 2nd rnd. Port Vale 2-0, 3rd rnd Crewe 2-0, 4th rnd. Everton 0-4
1981-82: 1st rnd. Burnley 4-2, 3-3, 2nd rnd. Port Vale 2-0, 2-1, 3rd rnd. Colchester 1-0, 4th rnd. Nottingham Forest 0-2
1988-89: 1st rnd. Stockport 1-0, 1-1; 2nd rnd. Middlesbrough 0-0, 1-0; 3rd rnd. Blackpool 1-0; 4th rnd. Bristol City 0-1
1989-90: 1st rnd. Preston North End (a) 4-3, (h) 3-1; 2nd rnd. Ipswich Town (a) 1-0, (h) 1-0; 3rd rnd. Millwall (h) 3-2; 4th rnd. Tottenham Hotspur (h) 2-2, (a) 0-4

DIVISIONAL RECORDS

	Played	Won	Drawn	Lost	For	Against	Points
DIVISION 2	88	20	24	44	95	155	**78**
DIVISION 3	736	242	213	281	980	1028	**743**
DIVISION 3N	1240	506	255	479	2073	1987	**1267**
DIVISION 4	780	318	185	277	1179	1057	**955**
TOTALS	**2844**	**1086**	**677**	**1081**	**4327**	**4227**	**3043**

TRANMERE ROVERS

PLAYERS NAME Honours	Ht	Wt	Birthdate	Birthplace Transfers	Contract Date	Clubs	APPEARANCES				GOALS			
							League	L/Cup	FA Cup	Other	Lg	L/C	FAC	Oth
GOALKEEPERS														
Eric Nixon	6.4	14.3	04.10.62	Manchester		Curzon Aston								
LDC'90				£1,000	10.12.83	Manchester Utd	58	8	10	8				
				Loan	29.08.86	Wolverhampton W	16							
				Loan	28.11.86	Bradford City	3							
				Loan	23.12.86	Southampton	4							
				Loan	23.01.87	Carlisle Utd	16							
				£60,000	26.07.88	Tranmere Rovers	188	20	11	29				
DEFENDERS														
Shaun Garnett	6.2	11.0	22.11.69	Wallasey	15.06.88	Tranmere Rovers (A)	28+1	3		6+2	1			
LDC'90														
Dave Higgins	6.0	11.0	19.08.61	Liverpool		Galw								
				Free	22.08.83	Tranmere Rovers	27+1		2	5				
				Free		South Liverpool			1					
						Caernarfon			5					
					20.07.87	Tranmere Rovers	185+2	17	14	23	6			
Mark Hughes	6.0	12.8	02.02.62	Port Talbot	05.02.80	Bristol Rovers (A)	73+1	1	9+1	3	3			1
W: Y. LDC'90				Loan	24.12.82	Torquay Utd	9		3		1		1	
					30.07.84	Swansea City	12							
					07.02.85	Bristol City	21+1	1		3				
				£3,000	19.09.85	Tranmere Rovers	244+3	21	10+2	34	9	1		1
Steve Mungall	5.8	11.5	22.05.58	Bellshill		Motherwell	14+6	11+2	14+1					
LDC'90					03.07.79	Tranmere Rovers	420+13	28+2	26+1	32+1	10	2		1
Michael Smith	6.0	11.09	28.10.58	Sunderland		Lincoln City	20+5	2						
				£12,500		Wimbledon	203+2	10	14		14		2	
				Loan		Aldershot	7							
						Bath City			5				1	
						Seaham Red Star								
				£5,000	06.10.89	Hartlepool Utd	53+2	2		2	6			
				Free	22.05.92	Tranmere Rovers								
Tony Thomas	5.11	12.5	12.07.71	Liverpool		South Liverpool								
LDC'90				YTS	01.02.89	Tranmere Rovers	113+1	10	1	19	10			1
Steve Vickers	6.3	12.0	13.10.67	Bishop Auckland		Spennymoor Utd								
LDC'90					11.09.85	Tranmere Rovers	257+1	18+1	16	29	11	4	2	1
MIDFIELD														
Dave Martindale	5.11	11.10	09.04.64	Liverpool		Liverpool (A)								
						Southport								
						Caernarfon			4					
				£1,500	20.07.87	Tranmere Rovers	98+29	12+3	8+1	11+3	7		1	2
Neil McNab	5.7	10.10	06.06.57	Greenock		Morton	11+3	4	1			1		
S:u21.1,S; FAYC74; LDC'90				£75,000	01.02.74	Tottenham H	63+9	5	2		3			
				£250,000	01.11.78	Bolton W	33+2	2	2		4			
				£225,000	07.02.80	Brighton & H.A	100+3	7	5		4		1	
				Loan	17.12.82	Leeds Utd	5		1					
				£30,000	21.07.83	Manchester City	216+5	20	15	10	16	2	1	
				£125,000	05.01.90	Tranmere Rovers	64+10	2+2	3+1	17	4			2
				Loan	26.01.92	Huddersfield Town	11		1					
FORWARDS														
John Aldridge	5.11	10.4	18.09.58	Liverpool		South Liverpool								
EI:47;Div1'88;Div2'85;LC'86;WC'80;CS'88				£3,500	02.05.79	Newport Co	159+11	11	12+1	4	69	5	7	2
				£78,000	21.03.84	Oxford Utd	111+3	17	5	5	72	14	2	2
				£750,000	27.01.87	Liverpool	69+14	7+1	12	1	50	3	8	2
				£1,100,000	01.09.89	Real Sociedad								
				£250,000	11.07.91	Tranmere Rovers	43	5	4	4	22	8	3	7
Graham Branch	6.2		12.02.72	Liverpool		Heswell At								
				Free	02.07.91	Tranmere Rovers	0+4			0+1				
Steve Cooper	6.1	11.10	22.06.64	Birmingham	10.11.83	Birmingham City								
				Loan	23.12.83	Halifax Town	7				1			
				Free	28.09.84	Newport Co	38		2	5	11			
				Free	09.08.85	Plymouth A	58+15	2+3	5+1	0+1	15		3	
				£100,000	28.07.88	Barnsley	62+15	5	9	1	13	1	3	
				£100,000	13.12.90	Tranmere Rovers	13+13	0+1	3	5+2	3			3
				Loan	26.03.92	Peterborough U	2+7			0+4				
Chris Malkin	6.3	12.0	04.06.67	Bebington		Stork AFC								
LDC'90					27.07.87	Tranmere Rovers	80+45	7+5	2+4	13+6	28	5	1	5
John Morrissey	5.8	11.9	08.03.65	Liverpool	10.03.83	Everton (A)	1			0+1				
E: Y.2				Free	02.08.85	Wolverhampton W	5+5	1			1			
				£8,000	02.10.85	Tranmere Rovers	239+25	21	18+1	24+3	38		3	4
Ian Muir	5.8	11.0	05.05.63	Coventry	03.09.80	Q.P.R. (A)	2				2			
E: Y.1; LDC'90				Loan	08.10.82	Burnley	1+1				1			
				Free	27.08.83	Birmingham City	1	1						
				Free	15.02.84	Brighton & H.A	3+1							
				Loan	28.01.85	Swindon Town	2			1				
				Free	26.07.85	Tranmere Rovers	254+14	21	14	25+1	123	6	11	19

PLAYERS NAME Honours	Ht	Wt	Birthdate	Birthplace Transfers	Contract Date	Clubs	APPEARANCES				GOALS			
							League	L/Cup	FA Cup	Other	Lg	L/C	FAC	Oth
Pat Nevin	5.6	11.9	06.09.63	Glasgow		Clyde	60+13	5+3	10		17		3	
S:14, B.3, u21.5, Y; SDiv2'82; Div2'84; FMC'86				£95,000	14.07.83	Chelsea	190+3	25+1	8+1	13	36	5	1	4
				£925,000	13.07.88	Everton	81+28	7+1	14+6	9+3	16	2	2	1
				Loan	04.03.92	Tranmere Rovers	8							
				£300,000	18.09.92	Tranmere Rovers								
Jim Steel	6.3	14.0	04.12.59	Dumfries		Oldham Ath. (A)	101+7	9+1	6		24	1		
LDC'90; WC'86				Loan	11.11.82	Wigan Ath	2				2			
				Loan	26.01.83	Wrexham	9				6			
				£5,000	17.03.83	Port Vale	27+1	2+1	1		6	1		
				£10,000	13.01.84	Wrexham	164	10	7	21	51	2	2	4
				£60,000	21.11.87	Tranmere Rovers	161+13	16+2	7+1	26	29	6	2	10
ADDITIONAL CONTRACT PLAYERS														
(M) Gerald Brannan	6.0	13.3	15.01.72	Liverpool	03.07.90	Tranmere Rovers (T)	32+4	5	4	11	2			1
Daniel Coyne					08.05.92	Tranmere Rovers (T)								
Anthony J Draper					08.05.92	Tranmere Rovers (T)								
Kenneth Irons	5.9	11.0	04.11.70	Liverpool	09.11.89	Tranmere Rovers	43+9	31+9	4+1	11+4	13	1	3	
(D) John McGreal	6.1	12.0	02.06.72	Liverpool	03.07.90	Tranmere Rovers (T)	3							
Alan M Morgan					08.05.92	Tranmere Rovers (T)								
Ian Nolan	6.0	11.10	09.07.70	Liverpool	31.08.88	Preston N.E								
						Northwich Victoria			2					
						Maritime (Por)								
				£10,000	02.08.91	Tranmere Rovers	34		4	2	1			
Terry Wilson					29.11.89	Tranmere Rovers								

MANAGER: JOHN KING

DATE OF BIRTH: 15.04.1938   **PLACE OF BIRTH:** London

DATE OF APPOINTMENT: 13.04.1987

PREVIOUS CLUBS
as Manager: Tranmere Rovers, Northwich Vic, Caernarvon Town
as Asst.Man/Coach:
as Player: Everton, Bournemouth, Tranmere Rov, Port Vale

HONOURS
as Manager: (Tranmere) Promotion to Div 3 1976, 1989, Leyland DAF Cup 1990, Promotion to Div 2 1991
as Player: Promotion with Tranmere 1967, Promotion with Port Vale 1970

Value Rating: ★ ★ ★ ★

Programme Editor: Peter Bishop

Price of 1992-93 Programme: £1
Number of Pages: 32
Subscriptions: Details available from Club

Local Newspapers: Liverpool Daily Post & Echo, Wirral News, Wirral Globe

Local Radio Stations: BBC Radio Merseyside, City Talk and City FM (Radio City), MFM (Marcher Sound)

Additional Publications on Club: 'The A-Z of Tranmere Rovers' (Peter Bishop) Softback, £4.95
Tranmere Rovers 1881-1921 (Gilbert Upton) published 1992, £5.95

LEADING LEAGUE GOALSCORERS
SEASONS 1979-80 – 1991-92

1979-80	KEN BEAMISH	9	1980-81	JIM LUMBY	18
1981-82	JOHN KERR	13	1982-83	OWEN BROWN	11
1983-84	JOHN ASPINALL	14	1984-85	JOHN CLAYTON	31
1985-86	FRANK WORTHINGTON	18	1986-87	IAN MUIR	20
1987-88	IAN MUIR	27	1988-89	IAN MUIR	21
1989-90	IAN MUIR	23	1990-91	IAN MUIR	13

1991-92   **JOHN ALDRIDGE**   22

PRENTON PARK   Prenton Road West, Birkenhead, Merseyside L42 9PN

Capacity: 17,393   **Covered Standing:** 7,578   **Seating:** 3,978

Tel: Ground: 051 608 3677   **Ticket Sales:** 051 609 0137   **Clubcall:** 0989 12 16 46

All premium rate calls (0898/0891) cost 36p per minute cheap rate and 48p per minute at all other times. Call costings correct at time of going to press.

ATTENDANCES
Highest: 24,424 v Stoke City, FA Cup Round 4, 5.2.1972

Lowest: 937 v Halifax, Associate Members Cup, 20.2.1984

Record Receipts
£68,000.00 v Liverpool, Friendly, 12.8.1991

PRENTON PARK
First game: v Lancaster, 8-0, 9.3.1912
First Floodlit game: v Rochdale, 2-1, 29.9.1958

Season Tickets:
Stands: £160, juv/OAP £130
Ground: £120, juv/OAP £80

Executive Box Season Tickets: Vice-Presidents
£300+VAT
Tranmere Suite £250+VAT
Dixie Dean Suite £500+VAT

Cost of Stand Tickets: Stand: adult £8.00, junior/OAP £6.50; Ground: adult £6.00, junior/OAP £5.00; Family Area: adult stand £8.00, junior stand £4.00

Match and Ticket Information: Bookable in advance.

Car Parking: No car parking available at ground on match days, except for visiting coaches.
Car park tickets cost £50 for season.

Nearest Railway Station: Hamilton Square, Rock Ferry (1 mile)
Liverpool Lime Street (Main Line)

How to get to the ground

From North: Use Mersey Tunnel and Motorway M53 until junction 3. Leave motorway and at roundabout take 1st exit A552. In 1.3m at Half-way House crossroads turn right B5151 then turn left into Prenton Road West for Tranmere Rovers FC

From South: Use Motorway M53 until junction 4, leave motorway and at roundabout take 4th exit B5151. In 2.5m turn right into Prenton Road West for Tranmere Rovers FC
*Away should use the Kop end of the ground. Entrance from main car park

WALSALL

Division 3

Formed: 1888 **Turned Professional:** 1888 **Ltd Co:** 1921

SPONSORED BY: Sign Specialists Ltd **NICKNAME:** The Saddlers

Chairman
J W Bonser

Directors
K R Whalley
M N Lloyd
C Welch

Secretary/Commercial Manager
Roy Whalley (0922 22791)

Team Manager
Kenny Hibbitt

General Manager
Paul Taylor

Physiotherapist
Tom Bradley

Youth Team Coach
Eric McManus

Chief Scout
Ken Gutteridge

Club Chaplain
Rev. M Butt

Stadium Manager
Roger Johnson

Club Statistician for the Directory
Mervyn Sargeant

THE season proved to be yet another disappointment for Walsall supporters as a club once renowned for the quality of its football in the lower divisions continued to produce a series of poor performances.

With no money available for new players Kenny Hibbitt was forced to juggle with a succession of loan players and trialists in his efforts to build a decent team. It was with two loan players in particular, Ron Sinclair and Paul McLoughlin, that Walsall made a reasonable start to the season. Sinclair brought confidence to a defence that had made a shaky start and McLoughlin fitted in well in attack, and, linking up with Rod McDonald, seemed to have solved Walsall's long standing goal scoring problems. A new chairman was appointed whilst these players were at the club and many fans hoped that money would be found to make their moves permanent. It was not be though, and with the loss of influential midfielder Kevin MacDonald through injury, Walsall soon slipped from being 5th in the table in October to the lower reaches of the division, where they remained all season. Defeat at home to Yeovil in the F.A. Cup First Round, who were themselves at the foot of the G. M. Conference at the time, seemed to confirm the level to which Walsall had fallen.

Only the Autoglass Trophy provided relative success, defeating holders Birmingham City at St Andrews before losing to eventual winners Stoke City in the Second Round.

Average attendances fell by nearly 800 on the previous season, and, more alarmingly, from January onwards gates rarely topped 3,000. Maidstone attracted a record low to Bescot of 2,045 in March, beating the previous record set the season before – for the visit of Maidstone!

An encouraging factor was the emergence of several promising young players towards the end of the season. One of them, Neil Tolson, was sold to Oldham for a reported £150,000. If the club can retain the others, or sell them to raise funds for team building, there just might be a flicker of light at the end of the tunnel.

Mervyn Sargeant

Back row: T Bradley (Physio), S Ollerenshaw, K MacDonald, C Methven, S O'Hara, M Gayle, J Norris, W Clarke, D Smith, S Ryder, C Ntamark, E McManus. **Front row:** C Marsh, M Cecere, R Brown, C Demetrios, D Edwards, K Hibbitt (Manager), R McDonald, S Winter, R Knight D Statham, W Williams.

WALSALL

DIVISION FOUR: 15th **FA CUP:** 1st RND **RUMBELOWS CUP:** 1st RND **AUTOGLASS:** 2nd RND

M	DATE	COMP.	VEN	OPPONENTS	RESULT	H/T	LGE POS	GOALSCORERS/GOAL TIMES	ATTEN-DANCE
1	A 17	BL	A	Blackpool	L 0-3	0-1	20		(4,141)
2	20	RC 1/1	A	Swansea City	D 2-2	0-1		Ntamark 57, MacDonald (pen) 70	(2,029)
3	24	BL	H	Wrexham	D 0-0	0-0	20		3,307
4	27	RC 1/2	H	Swansea City	L 0-1	0-1			2,812
5	31	BL	A	Scarborough	W 3-2	2-1	13	McDonald 21, 39, Cecere 68	(2,002)
6	S 3	BL	H	Rochdale	L 1-3	0-2	15	McDonald 62	3,111
7	7	BL	H	Halifax Town	W 3-0	1-0	11	MacDonald 12, McLoughlin 51, McDonald 87	2,981
8	14	BL	A	Maidstone United	L 1-2	1-2	13	Methven 1	(1,139)
9	17	BL	A	Chesterfield	W 1-0	0-0	9	McLoughlin 65	(2,690)
10	21	BL	H	Hereford United	W 3-0	2-0	7	Marsh 30, Anderson 40, McLoughlin 56	4,509
11	28	BL	A	Carlisle United	D 3-3	0-1	8	McDonald 61, Anderson 62, McLoughlin 80	(2,148)
12	O 5	BL	H	Barnet	W 2-0	2-0	7	Methven 26, McDonald 28	4,981
13	11	BL	A	Crewe Alexandra	W 1-0	1-0	5	McDonald 3	(4,749)
14	19	BL	A	Burnley	L 0-2	0-2	6		(7,289)
15	22	AGT Pre	H	Stoke City	L 0-2	0-0			3,578
16	N 2	BL	A	York City	L 0-2	0-0	8		(1,605)
17	5	BL	H	Lincoln City	D 0-0	0-0	6		2,555
18	16	FAC 1	A	Yeovil Town	D 1-1	0-0		Tolson 79	(4,635)
19	22	BL	A	Rotherham United	L 1-2	0-1	9	McDonald 61	(4,192)
20	27	FAC 1R	H	Yeovil Town	L 0-1	0-0			3,869
21	30	BL	A	Mansfield Town	L 1-3	0-2	12	McDonald 75	(3,398)
22	D 20	BL	A	Wrexham	L 1-2	0-1	12	Cecere 78	(2,571)
23	26	BL	H	Blackpool	W 4-2	2-0	12	McDonald 3 (23, 45, 55), MacDonald 61	4,675
24	28	BL	H	Scarborough	D 0-0	0-0	12		3,488
25	J 1	BL	A	Rochdale	D 1-1	1-0	12	McDonald 22	(3,001)
26	4	BL	H	Doncaster Rovers	L 1-3	0-2	12	O'Hara 85	3,444
27	7	AGT Pre	A	Birmingham City	W 1-0	0-0		Ntamark 73	(5,239)
28	11	BL	A	Gillingham	L 0-4	0-4	14		(2,715)
29	18	BL	H	Cardiff City	D 0-0	0-0	13		3,654
30	21	AGT 1	A	Hereford United	W †1-0	0-0		Marsh 100	(1,503)
31	25	BL	A	Scunthorpe United	D 1-1	0-1	12	Ntamark 83	(3,165)
32	28	BL	H	Northampton Town	L 1-2	1-2	13	Cecere 33	2,399
33	F 1	BL	H	Burnley	D 2-2	1-0	14	Cecere 5, O'Hara 47	5,287
34	5	AGT 2	A	Stoke City	L 1-3	0-3		Marsh 49	(7,381)
35	11	BL	H	Mansfield Town	D 3-3	0-1	14	Cecere 49, 51, Ntamark 82	2,963
36	15	BL	A	Northampton Town	W 1-0	1-0	12	McDonald 1	(2,480)
37	22	BL	H	Gillingham	L 0-1	0-1	14		2,987
38	29	BL	A	Doncaster Rovers	W 1-0	0-0	12	Cecere 67	(1,919)
39	M 3	BL	A	Cardiff City	L 1-2	0-1	13	Perry (og) 41	(7,517)
40	7	BL	H	Scunthorpe United	W 2-1	1-0	12	Edwards 8, Cecere 77	2,722
41	11	BL	A	Lincoln City	L 0-1	0-1	13		(2,021)
42	14	BL	H	York City	D 1-1	1-1	13	Tolson 32	2,541
43	28	BL	H	Rotherham United	L 0-2	0-0	17		3,524
44	31	BL	H	Maidstone United	D 1-1	1-1	17	Ntamark 25	2,045
45	A 3	BL	A	Halifax Town	L 0-1	0-1	17		(1,006)
46	11	BL	H	Chesterfield	D 2-2	1-1	17	McDonald 4, 76	2,472
47	18	BL	A	Hereford United	W 2-1	1-1	15	McDonald 34, Cecere 49	(2,291)
48	21	BL	H	Carlisle United	D 0-0	0-0			2,406
49	25	BL	A	Barnet	W 1-0	1-0		MacDonald 12	(3,207)
50	M 2	BL	H	Crewe Alexandra	L 2-3	0-3	15	McDonald 61, O'Hara 69	4,995

Best Home League Attendance: 5,287 v Burnley **Smallest: 2,045 v Maidstone United** **Av Home Att: 3,383**

Goal Scorers: **Compared with 90-91: -761**

League (48):	McDonald 18, Cecere 9, McLoughlin 4, MacDonald 3, Ntamark 3, O'Hara 3, Anderson 2, Methven 2, Tolson, Edwards, Opponents, Marsh
R/lows C (2):	Ntamark, MacDonald (1 pen)
FA Cup (1):	Tolson
Autoglass (3):	Marsh 2, Ntamark

†=After extra-time

Gayle M.	Williams W.	Statham D.	Methven C.	Musker R.	Smith D.	MacDonald K.	Ntamark C.	Jackson R.	Cecere M.	McDonald R.	Marsh C.	Lane M.	Anderson C.	Grealish A.	O'Hara S.	Sinclair R.	Hobson G.	McLoughlin P.	Walsh A.	Essers P.	McKnight A.	Tolson N.	Edwards D.	Winter S.	Brown R.	Referee	
1	2	3†	4	5	6	7	8	9•	10*	11	12	14														R Hart	1
1	2	3	4	5	6	7	8	S	10	11	12	9*														R Hamer	2
1	2	3	4	5•	6	7	8	12	10	11	14		9*													C Wilkes	3
1	2	3	4	S	6	7	8	9	10	11	12	5*														D Gallagher	4
1	2				6	7	8*	S	10	11		5	3	9	12											T Fitzharris	5
1	2	3	4	5	6	7	8	S	10	11			9		S											R Wiseman	6
	2	3	4		6	7	8	S	11	10				S		1	5	9								K Cooper	7
	2	3	4			7	8	S	11	12			10*		6	1	5	9								P Scoble	8
	2	3	4			7	8	S	11	10		12			6	1	5*	9								T West	9
	2	3	4			7†	8	S	S	10		5			6	1		9								D Frampton	10
	2	3*	4		S	7	8		12	11		10	5		6	1		9								P Wright	11
	2	3	4				8		12	11•		10	5		6	1		9*	7							I Hendrick	12
	2	3	4				8		S	11		10	5	S	6	1		9	7							I Hemley	13
	2	3*	4				8†		12	11		10	5	S	6	1		9	7							B Coddington	14
	2	3	4			11	8	12	9			10	S	5*	6	1				7						J Key	15
	2	3†	4			7		14	11†	10	12		8*		6	1		9	5•							R Pawley	16
	2	3	4			7	8		12	11		10	S		6	1		9*								A Flood	17
	2		4	14		7	8	9•		11*		10	3	5	6						1	12				J Deakin	18
	2		4			7	8	9•		11		10	3	5	12	6*					1	14				M Bailey	19
	2		4			7	8	9*	12	11		10	3	5	S	S	6				1					J Deakin	20
	2		4			7	8	9	12	11		10*	3	5	S	6					1					C Trussell	21
	2		4			7	8	9*	10	11		3	S	5	6						1		12			J Worrall	22
	2		4			7*	8	9•	10	11		3	14	5	6						1		12			J Carter	23
	2		4				8	9		3	10*	5	S	6							1	7	11	12		D Phillips	24
	2		4				8	9		11	10	3	S	5	6						1	7	S	S		K Lupton	25
	2		4				8	9*	10	11•		3	5	6							1	7	12	14		G Poll	26
	2	3*	4				8		10			5	14	6							1	9•	7	11	12	S Bell	27
	2	3*	4				8		10	11		5		6							1	14	7•	9	12	I Borrett	28
1	2		4				8		10	11	9		5		6							7*		14	3	R Poulain	29
1	2		4				8		10*	11	9		5		6							12	S	7	3	R Groves	30
1	2		4				8		10	11	9		5*		6							S	12	7	3	A Ward	31
1	2		4				8		10	11	9		5		6							S	12	7*	3	J Rushton	32
1	2		4*				8		10	11	9		5		6							14	12	7•	3	P Durkin	33
1	2						8		10	11	9	4	5•		6							14	12	7*	3	D Allison	34
1	2	3	4				8		10	11	9		5		6								S	7	3	A Buksh	35
1	2	3	4				8		10	11	9		5		6								S	7	S	P Foakes	36
1	2	3	4				8		10	11*	9		5		6							12		7	S	R Milford	37
1	2	3	4				8		10		9		5		6							11*	12	7		W Burns	38
1	2	3	4				8		10		9†	14			6							11*	5	7*		G Ashby	39
1	2	3	4				8		10	11	9	S			6							5		7*		R Nixon	40
1	2	3	4				8		10	11	9	S			6							12	5	7*		K Morton	41
1	2	3	4				8		10	11*	9	S			6							7	5	12		P Taylor	42
1	2	3	4	S			8	12	10	11					6							5	7*			K Burge	43
1	2	3	4	6*			8		10	11•	9				12							5				P Harrison	44
1	2	3	4	S			8		10*	12	9				6							5				P Wright	45
1	2	3	4	S	5*		8		10	11	9				6							12				J Lloyd	46
1	2	3	4	6	5		8		10*	11	9							7•				12				J Deakin	47
1	2	3	4	6	5		8		10*	11	9							7•				12				P Alcock	48
1	2	3	4	6	5		8		10	11	9							7					S		6	H King	49
1	2	3	4		5		8	S	10	11	9							7					S		6	R Groves	50
24	42	29	42	3	9	20	41	7	29	38	34	6	25	3	35	10	3	9	4	1	8	3	13	13	6	**League Appearances**	
								2	6	1	3	4	1	2	2							5	9	3	3	**Substitute Appearances**	
2	2	2	2	1	2	2	2	1	2	2	0+2	2														**R/lows Appearances**	
	2	2	0+1		2	2	2	1+1	2	2	2		2		2						2	0+1				**FA Cup Appearances**	
2	4	2	3		1	4	0+1	4	2	3	1	4	0+1	4	1			1			1	1+2	1+1	3	2+1	**Autoglass Appearances**	

Also Played: Posn.(Game): Robinson 12•(29), May 11(45)12(39,40)14(44)S(38), Chine 9(43)7(44,45,46)S(47)14(48), Demetrios S(49)

†=Sent Off

WALSALL

Club Colours: Red shirts with white trim, red shorts, black socks with red tops & white trim
Change Colours: Yellow shirts with black and red trim, yellow shorts, yellow socks with red trim
Reserves League: Midland Senior League   **Youth Team:** Purity Youth League

Previous Name: Walsall Swifts (1877) and Walsall Town (1879) amalgamated and played as Walsall Town Swifts until 1895
Previous Managers: 1921-26 J Burchell   1926-27 D Ashworth   1927-28 J Torrance   1928-29 J Kerr   1929-30 S Scholey   1930-32 P O'Rourke   1932-34 W Slade   1934-37 Andy Wilson   T Lowes 1937-44   1944-51 Harry Hibbs   1951-52 G McPhee   1952-53 Brough Fletcher   1953-56 Frank Buckley   1956-57 John Love   1957-64 Bill Moore   1964 Alf Wood   1964-68 Ray Shaw   1968 Dick Graham   1968-69 Ron Lewin   1969-72 Bob Moore   1972-73 John Smith   1973 Jim McEwan   1973 Ronnie Allen   1973-77 Doug Fraser   1977-78 Dave Mackay   1978 Alan Buckley   1978 Alan Ashman   1978 Frank Sibley   1978-81 Alan Buckley   1981-82 Neil Martin   1982-86 Alan Buckley   1986-88 Tommy Coackley   1988-89 Ray Train   1989-90 John Barnwell   1990 Paul Taylor   1990- Kenny Hibbitt
Honours: Champions Div 4 1959-60
League Career: Elected to Div 2 1892   Failed to gain re-election 1895   Rejoined Div 2 1896
Failed re-election 1901   Elected as original members of Div 3N 1921   Transferred to Div 3S 1927
Transferred to Div 3N 1931   Transferred to Div 3S 1936   Joined Div 4 1958   Promoted to Div 3 1959-60
Promoted to Div 2 1960-61   Relegated to Div 3 1962-63   Relegated to Div 4 1978-79   Promoted to Div 3 1979-80
Promoted to Div 2 1987-88   Relegated to Div 3 1988-89   Relegated to Div 4 1989-90

CLUB RECORDS

Most Appearances for Club: Colin Harrison (1964-82): League 452 + 15 + FA Cup 36 + League Cup 19 **Total 507 + 15 subs**
Most Capped Player: Mick Kearns 15, Eire   **For England:** None
Record Goalscorer in a Match: Johnny Devlin 5 v Torquay United (h), 7-1, Div 3S, 1.9.1949   Gilbert Alsop 5 v Carlisle Utd (a), 6-1, Div 3N, 2.2.1935   W. Evans 5 v Mansfield Town, 7-0, Div 3N, 5.10.1935
Record League Goalscorer in a Season: Gilbert Alsop 40, Div 3N, 1933-34, 1934-35   **In All Competitions:** Gilbert Alsop 44 (League 40 + FA Cup 4) 1934-35
Record League Goalscorer in a Career: Tony Richards 184, 1954-63   **In All Competitions:** Alan Buckley 204 (League 174 + Cups 30) 1973-84
Record Transfer Fee Received: £600,000 from West Ham United for David Kelly, August 1988
Record Transfer Fee Paid: £175,000 to Birmingham City for Alan Buckley, June 1979
Best Performances: League: 6th Div 2 1898-99   **FA Cup:** 5th Round 1939, 1975, 1978 and last sixteen 1889   **League Cup:** Semi-Final 1983-84
Most League Points: (3pts for win) 82, Div 3, 1987-88   (2pts for win) 65, Div 4, 1959-60
Most League Goals: 102, Division 4, 1959-60
Record League Victory and Most Goals Scored in a League Match: 10-0 v Darwen, Div 2, 4.3.1899
Most Goals Scored in a First Class Cup Tie: 6-1 v Leytonstone (a), Round 1, 30.11.1946   6-1 v Margate, Round 1, 24.11.1955
Record League Defeat: 0-12 v Small Heath, Div 2, 17.12.1892   0-12 v Darwen, Div 2, 26.12.1896
Record Cup Defeat: 0-6 v Wednesday Town, FA Cup Round 2, 1883-84   0-6 v West Bromwich Albion, FA Cup Rnd 1 replay, 1899-1900   0-6 v Aston Villa, FA Cup Round 1, 1911-12
Oldest Player in a League Match: Des Bremner 37 years 240 days v Bristol City, 5.5.1990
Youngest Player in a League Match: Geoff Morriss 16 years 218 days v Scunthorpe, 14.9.1965

LONGEST LEAGUE RUNS	
of undefeated matches: 21 (1979-80)	of league matches without a win: 18 (1988-89)
of undefeated home matches: 26 (1960-61)	of undefeated away matches: 13 (1979-80)
without home win: 10 (1988-89, 1989-90)	without an away win: 29 (1953-54)
of league wins: 7 (1933-34)	of home wins: 9 (1973)
of league defeats: 15 (1988-89)	of away wins: 5 (1979-80)

BARCLAYS

BARCLAYS BUSINESS CENTRE
Walsall: The Bridge
The Bridge
Walsall WS1 1RN
Tel: 0922 720020

BARCLAYBANK MACHINE

WALSALL

PLAYERS NAME Honours	Ht	Wt	Birthdate	Birthplace Transfers	Contract Date	Clubs	League	L/Cup	FA Cup	Other	Lg	L/C	FAC	Oth
GOALKEEPERS														
Mark Gale	6.2	12.0	21.10.69	Birmingham	01.07.88	Leicester City (T)								
				Free		Blackpool		1						
				Free		Worcester City								
				£15,000	08.05.91	Walsall	24	2		2				
DEFENDERS														
Richard C Brown					17.06.92	Walsall (T)	6+3			2+1				
Colin Methven	6.2	12.7	10.12.55	Kirkcaldy (India)		EFif	144	16	8		14			
FRT85				£30,000	02.10.79	Wigan Ath	295+1	21	23	14	21	3	4	
				£21,000	24.07.86	Blackpool	166+7	14	12+1	13	11	1	1	1
				Loan	02.09.90	Carlisle Utd	12	3						
						Walsall	74	2	4	5	1	3		
Dean Smith	6.1	12.0	19.03.71	West Bromwich	01.07.89	Walsall (T)	63+1	4	3	3				
Derek Statham	5.5	11.7	24.03.59	Wolverhampton	01.01.77	West Brom A	298+1	33	28	14	8	1	2	
E: 3, B.2, u21.6, Y; FAYC'76				£100,000	19.08.87	Southampton	64	7	4	3	2		1	
				£75,000	18.08.89	Stoke City	41	5	3		1			
				Free	15.08.91	Walsall	29	2		2				
Wayne Williams	5.9	11.10	17.11.63	Telford	20.11.81	Shrewsbury Town (A	212+9	24	8+1	3	7	4		
WC84'85				Loan	10.11.88	Northampton T	3			1	1			
				£32,000	12.01.89	Northampton T	47+5	5+1	1	5				
				Free	06.08.91	Walsall	42	2	2	4				
MIDFIELD														
David Edwards					13.01.92	Walsall (T)	13+9			1+1	1			
Kevin MacDonald	6.1	11.11	27.12.60	Inverness		Inverness Caley								
Div.1'86;FAC'86;CS'86				£40,000	09.05.80	Leicester City	133+5	10	4		8			
				£400,000	24.11.84	Liverpool	29+11	1+3	9	10+1	1	1	1	2
				Loan	23.12.87	Leicester City	3							
				Loan	25.11.88	Glasgow Rangers	2+1							
				Free	13.07.89	Coventry City	26+5	6+3	3+2	1		1		
				Loan	28.03.91	Cardiff City	8							
				Free	15.07.91	Walsall	20	2	2	1	3			
Charles Ntamark	5.10	11.3	22.07.64	Cameroon		Boreham Wood								
Cameroon Int.					22.10.90	Walsall	81+2	4	4	7	6	1		1
Stephen O'Hara	6.1	12.2	21.01.71	Bellshill	01.07.89	Walsall (T)	67+8	2	2	5				
Steven D Winter	5.7	10.6	26.10.71	Bristol	13.03.92	Walsall	13+6			3				
FORWARDS														
Michele Cecere	6.0	11.4	04.01.68	Chester	17.01.86	Oldham Ath	35+17	4+1	1+2	2+1	8		1	1
				£100,000	11.11.88	Huddersfield Town	50+4	4	7+1	5	8	1	3	1
				Loan	22.03.90	Stockport Co	0+1							
				Loan	23.08.90	Walsall								
				£25,000	21.09.90	Walsall	55+12	6	3+1	6	15			
Wayne Clarke	6.0	11.8	28.02.61	Wolverhampton	13.03.78	Wolverhampton W (A	129+19	8+2	9+2	0+1	30	2	1	
E:Y.4,S,CS'87				£80,000	24.08.84	Birmingham City	92	6	5	2	38	4		1
					06.03.87	Everton	46+11	3+3	2+8	3	18	1		3
				£500,000	27.07.89	Leicester City	10+1	1			1	1		
				£500,000	12.01.90	Manchester City	7+14		1	1	2			
				Loan	17.10.90	Shrewsbury Town	7			1	6			
				Loan	07.03.91	Stoke City	9				3			
				Loan	26.09.91	Wolverhampton W	1							
					30.07.92	Walsall								
Chris Marsh	6.0	12.10	14.01.70	Dudley		Walsall (A)	61+26	1+2	6+1	5	3			2
Rodney McDonald	5.10	12.0	20.03.67	Liverpool		Colne Dynamoes								
					24.08.90	Walsall	69+6	3	3	4	23	1	1	
ADDITIONAL CONTRACT PLAYERS														
Athumani Chine	5.8	10.05	12.03.67	Dar Es Salaam	26.03.92	Walsall	4+1							
Robert Jackson					24.04.91	Walsall	8+2	1	2	0+1	2			
(D) Richard Knight					26.03.92	Walsall (T)								
(F) Leroy May						Worcester								
					20.02.92	Walsall	1+3							

LEADING LEAGUE GOALSCORERS SEASONS 1985-86 – 1991-92

1985-86	**NICKY CROSS**	21		1986-87	**DAVID KELLY**	23
1987-88	**DAVID KELLY**	20		1988-89	**STUART RIMMER**	8
1989-90	**STUART RIMMER**	10		1990-91	**STUART RIMMER**	13
	1991-92	**ROD McDONALD**	**18**			

BESCOT STADIUM Bescot Crescent, Walsall WS1 4SA

Capacity: 10,400   **Covered Standing:**   **Seating:** 4,500

Tel: Ground: 0922 22791   **Ticket Sales:** As ground number   **Clubcall:** 0898 12 11 04

All premium rate calls (0898/0891) cost 36p per minute cheap rate and 48p per minute at all other times. Call costings correct at time of going to press.

ATTENDANCES (Fellows Park)
Highest: 25,433 v Newcastle United, Div 2, 29.8.1961
(Bescot Stadium) 10,628 England 'B' v Switzerland, 20.5.1991

Lowest: 500 v Bootle, Div 2, 24.12.1892
(Bescot Stadium) 2,045 v Maidstone United, 31.3.1992

Record Receipts: (Fellows Park) £50,926.50 v Watford, FA Cup 5th Round Second Replay, 2nd March 1987

BESCOT STADIUM
First game: v Aston Villa, Friendly, 18.8.1991
First floodlit game: v Cambridge Utd, Lge Cup, 28.8.1991

Season Tickets:
Stands: from £120 to £165, juv/OAP £60 to £110
Ground: from £110, juv/OAP £60 to £110

Swifts Executive Club: £400

Cost of Stand Tickets: Stand (Centre): £8.50; Centre Stand (seats) £7.50; Wing Stand: £7.50, jun/OAP £5, Family Seating Area: 1 adult & 1 child £7.50

Match and Ticket Information: Seats bookable at any time by postal, telephone or personal application

Car Parking: Car park for 1,200 vehicles at ground

Nearest Railway Station: Bescot Stadium Station 50 yards from Ground

---

How to get to the ground

From North: Use A461 S.P. Walsall then join A4148 Broadway North around Ring Road. Turn left at traffic lights into Bescot Crescent, ground on left

From East, South and West: Use Motorway M6 until junction 9, leave motorway and follow signs Walsall A461, then turn right A4148 into Broadway West. Turn right at first set of traffic lights into Bescot Crescent Stadium on left

Value Rating: ★ ★ ★

Programme Editor: Don Stanton

Price of 1992-93 Programme: £1
Number of Pages: 32
Subscriptions: Apply to club shop

Local Newspapers: Wolverhampton Express & Star, Birmingham Evening Mail, Birmingham Post, Mail, Walsall Observer (Wooke's)

Local Radio Stations: BBC Radio West Midlands, BRMB Radio, Beacon Radio

WATFORD

Division 1

Formed: 1891   **Turned Professional:** 1897   **Ltd Co:** 1909

SPONSORED BY: RCI Europe   **NICKNAME:** The Hornets

Chairman
Jack Petchey

Vice-Chairman
Geoff Smith

Directors
Mervyn Winwood   Stuart L Rogers
Dr Stuart R. Timperley, PhD
Elton John   Charles Lissack

Hon Vice-Presidents
Mayor of Watford
Douglas N Broad

Chief Executive/Company Secretary
Eddie Plumley, FAAI (0923 230933)

Assistan Secretary
John Alexander

Team Manager
Steve Perryman, MBE

Assistant Manager
Peter Taylor

Reserve Team Coach
Stuart Murdoch

Physiotherapist
Billy Hails

Youth Team Coach
Kenny Jackett

Commercial Manager
Alan Robson (0923 225761)

Groundsman
Les Simmons

Community Officer
John McDermott (0923 210618)

Club Statistician for the Directory
Audrey Adams

WATFORD'S official Centenary season began with defeat at the hands of League champions Arsenal on a nostalgic August evening marred by torrential rain. It ended with a glittering dinner held at the Wembley Conference Centre, attended by everyone who is anyone in English football. Somehow the two events encapsulated Watford's season, which once again swung from the damply depressing to the bright and optimistic. For the second year running, the team put their supporters through all sorts of relegation phobias during the first half of the season, only to come good at the end with a run which almost saw the club into the play-offs.

Sporting their eye-catching new Centenary strip, Watford got under way without Paul Wilkinson, leading scorer for the past three seasons, who had departed for Middlesbrough. Luther Blissett, one of the most popular players ever to appear at Vicarage Road, returned for his third spell with the club, bringing with him the same old zest and enthusiasm: by the end of the season he had overtaken Tommy Barnett as Watford's all-time leading scorer. Elton John was back too, restored to a revamped board of directors.

Despite such optimistic portents, the turn of the year found Watford down in the nether regions of division two, and already eliminated from all three cup competitions. Just when the fans were resigned to another long hard winter, and the letters page of the Watford Observer was filling up with irate and despairing correspondence, mainly directed at chairman Jack Petchey, the team suddenly embarked on an extraordinary run of 13 matches with only one defeat, including wins over Ipswich, Leicester, Middlesbrough, Blackburn and Sunderland. The reasons for this sudden surge of form were hard to fathom, though it must have helped that manager Steve Perryman was able to field a largely unchanged team over this period.

Right-back Nigel Gibbs, who seldom puts a foot wrong, gained some overdue recognition by being voted Watford's player of the season, and there were honourable mentions for ever-present Keith Dublin, the increasingly confident Jason Drysdale and the talented Darren Bazeley. David James survived a protracted and unsettling period of transfer speculation to confirm his standing as the best goalkeeper in the division, surely destined for higher things, and David Holdsworth returned to his best after nearly a year's absence with a serious knee injury. Of the new recruits, Andy Hessenthaler never stopped running and looked a snip at £65,000 from non-league Redbridge Forest, and Lee Nogan finished the season strongly after a quiet start.

Audrey Adams

CLUB SPONSOR 1992/93

Back row L-R: Ken Brooks (Kit Manager), Alex Inglethorpe, Julian Alsford, Barry Ashford, Steve Butler, Andy Kennedy, Jason Coloman, Jason Drysdale, Trevor Putney, Billy Hails (Physio). **Middle row:** Kenny Jackett (Youth Team Manager), Perry Suckling, Luther Blissett, Darren Bazeley, Richard Johnson, David Holdsworth, Paul Furlong, Joe Gallen, Gerard Lavin, Simon Sheppard, Stuart Murdoch (Reserve Team Manager). **Front row:** James Meara, Gary Porter, Daniel Nwaokolo, Lee Nogan, Nigel Gibbs, Peter Taylor (Asst. Manager), Steve Perryman (Manager), Joe McLaughlin, Keith Dublin, Andy Hessenthaler, Rod Thomas, David Byrne. (Not in picture: Keith Waugh) *Copyright: Watford Football Club.*

WATFORD

DIVISION TWO: 10th   **FA CUP:** 3rd RND   **RUMBELOWS CUP:** 2nd RND   **ZDS CUP:** 1st RND

M	DATE		COMP.	VEN	OPPONENTS	RESULT		H/T	LGE POS	GOALSCORERS/GOAL TIMES	ATTEN- DANCE
1	A	17	BL	H	Wolverhampton W	L	0-2	0-0			13,547
2		20	RC 1/1	H	Southend United	W	2-0	2-0		Blissett 29, Porter 38	6,231
3		24	BL	A	Newcastle United	D	2-2	1-1	22	Nicholas 18, Blissett 56	(22,440)
4		28	RC 1/2	A	Southend United	D	1-1	1-1		Kennedy 34	(3,802)
5		31	BL	H	Cambridge United	L	1-3	0-1	22	Blissett 82	8,902
6	S	3	BL	A	Barnsley	W	3-0	1-0	17	Bazeley 33, Blissett 63, Kennedy 86	(6,500)
7		7	BL	H	Middlesbrough	L	1-2	0-2	20	McLaughlin 86	8,715
8		14	BL	A	Brighton & H A	W	1-0	1-0	18	Butler 26	(8,741)
9		17	BL	A	Blackburn Rovers	L	0-1	0-1	19		(9,542)
10		21	BL	H	Charlton Athletic	W	2-0	2-0	17	Butler 2, Hessenthaler 35	8,459
11		24	RC 2/1	A	Everton	L	0-1	0-0			(8,284)
12		28	BL	A	Swindon Town	L	1-3	0-2	18	Porter 69	(8,863)
13	O	2	ZDC 1	H	Southend United	L	0-1	0-1			1,700
14		5	BL	H	Grimsby Town	W	2-0	2-0	16	Hessenthaler 20, Putney 38	6,930
15		8	RC 2/2	H	Everton	L	1-2	0-0		Baseley 71	11,561
16		12	BL	A	Bristol City	L	0-1	0-1	20		(7,882)
17		19	BL	H	Southend United	L	1-2	0-1	20	Porter (pen) 80	6,862
18		26	BL	A	Plymouth Argyle	W	1-0	1-0	17	Bazeley 21	(4,090)
19		29	BL	H	Millwall	L	0-2	0-0	18		7,366
20	N	2	BL	A	Sunderland	L	1-3	0-2	19	Porter 77	(12,790)
21		6	BL	H	Oxford United	W	2-0	1-0	19	Porter (pen) 17, Bazeley 82	4,785
22		9	BL	H	Leicester City	L	0-1	0-1	19		9,271
23		16	BL	A	Bristol Rovers	D	1-1	1-1	16	Blissett 8	(5,064)
24		23	BL	H	Portsmouth	W	2-1	1-0	17	Blissett 25, 46	8,135
25		30	BL	A	Port Vale	L	1-2	0-0	16	Porter 57	(5,777)
26	D	7	BL	H	Derby County	L	1-2	0-1	21	Blissett 82	8,302
27		22	BL	H	Barnsley	D	1-1	0-1	21	Nogan 58	7,522
28		26	BL	A	Millwall	W	4-0	2-0	17	Porter 31, Butler 35, 84, Drysdale 58	(9,237)
29		29	BL	A	Cambridge United	W	1-0	0-0	15	Butler 84	(8,439)
30	J	1	BL	H	Tranmere Rovers	D	0-0	0-0	16		9,892
31		4	FAC 3	A	Swindon Town	L	2-3	1-2		Blissett 45, 58	(9,817)
32		11	BL	H	Newcastle United	D	2-2	2-1	15	Holdsworth 1, Porter (pen) 4	9,811
33		18	BL	A	Wolverhampton W	L	0-3	0-0	17		(14,175)
34		24	BL	A	Tranmere Rovers	D	1-1	0-0	16	Butler 90	(6,187)
35	F	1	BL	A	Southend United	L	0-1	0-0	17		(7,581)
36		8	BL	H	Plymouth Argyle	W	1-0	0-0	16	Blissett 68	7,260
37		22	BL	H	Port Vale	D	0-0	0-0	18		6,602
38		29	BL	A	Derby County	L	1-3	0-2	18	Nogan 69	(14,052)
39	M	7	BL	H	Ipswich Town	L	0-1	0-0	18		9,199
40		11	BL	A	Oxford United	D	0-0	0-0	20		(5,808)
41		14	BL	H	Sunderland	W	1-0	1-0	19	Porter (pen) 24	8,091
42		17	BL	A	Ipswich Town	W	2-1	0-0	16	Drysdale 69, 85	(12,484)
43		21	BL	A	Leicester City	W	2-1	2-0	16	Butler 23, Nogan 25	(14,519)
44		28	BL	H	Bristol Rovers	W	1-0	0-0	13	Drysdale (pen) 72	7,496
45		31	BL	H	Brighton & H A	L	0-1	0-0	13		7,589
46	A	4	BL	A	Middlesbrough	W	2-1	1-1	12	Holdsworth 46, Butler 64	(13,669)
47		11	BL	H	Blackburn Rovers	W	2-1	1-1	12	Bazeley 42, 52	10,522
48		18	BL	A	Charlton Athletic	D	1-1	1-0	12	Nogan 11	(6,483)
49		20	BL	H	Swindon Town	D	0-0	0-0	13		9,911
50		22	BL	A	Portsmouth	D	0-0	0-0	12		(14,417)
51		25	BL	A	Grimsby Town	W	1-0	1-0	12	Nogan 24	(6,483)
52	M	2	BL	H	Bristol City	W	5-2	1-1	10	Drysdale 32, Bazeley 53, Putney 59, Blissett 88, Gibbs 89	10,582

Best Home League Attendance: 13,547 v Wolverhampton W   **Smallest:** 4,785 v Oxford United   **Av Home Att:** 8,511

Goal Scorers: **Compared with 90-91:** -932

League (51): Blissett 9, Porter 8 (4 pens), Butler 8, Bazeley 6, Nogan 5, Drysdale 5 (1 pen), Putney 2, Hessenthaler 2, Holdsworth 2, McLaughlin, Gibbs, Nicholas, Kennedy

R/lows C (4): Blissett, Porter, Kennedy, Baseley

FA Cup (2): Blissett 2

ZDS Cup (0):

612

James D.	Gibbs N.	Morrow S.	Dublin K.	McLaughlin J.	Putney T.	Thomas R.	Porter G.	Kennedy A.	Butler S.	Nicholas P.	Blissett L.	Ashby B.	Solomon J.	Bazeley D.	Hessenthaler A.	Drysdale J.	Devonshire A.	Holdsworth D.	Lavin G.	Nogan L.	Johnson R.	Waugh K.	Inglethorpe A.	Referee	
1	2	3	4	5†	6	7*	8	9*	10	11	12	14												P Foakes	1
1	2		4	5	6	12	10	8*	9	11	7	S	3											S Hemley	2
1	2	3	4	5	6	12	8		9	11	10•		14	7*										A Shepherd	3
1	2		4	5	6		10	8	9	11	7	S	3	S										I Borrett	4
1	2	3	4		6		10	8•	9	11	7	5*	12	14										P Alcock	5
1	2	3	4	5	6		10	8	12	11	7*		14	9•										T West	6
1	2	3•	4	5	6		10	8*	12	11	7		14	9										C Wilkes	7
1	2	3	4	5	6		10•	12	8	11	7*		14	9										M Bailey	8
1	2	3•	4	5	6*		10	12	9	11	7		14		8									J Watson	9
1	2		4	5			10	12	9	11	8*	14	3•	6	7									P Don	10
1	2		4	5	6		10		12	11	8*	S	3	9	7									R Hart	11
1	2		4	5	12		10		9	11	8		14	6•	7	3*								K Burge	12
1	2*	3	4	5•	6		10		9	11	12		14	8	7									A Buksh	13
1	2	S	4	5	6		10		9	11	8			S	7	3								G Ashby	14
1	2		4	5	6		10		9	11	8			12	7*	3	S							R Bigger	15
1	2		4	5	6		10		9	11	8•			12	7*	3	14							H King	16
1	2	12	4	5	6		10		9*	11	8		S		7	3								M Pierce	17
1	2†		4	5	6		10		14	11	8•		S		7	3		9						A Smith	18
1	2		4	5	6•		10		14	11	8		S		7	3		9						D Phillips	19
1	2		4	5	6		10		14	11	8		S		7	3•		9						S Bell	20
1	2		4	5	6		10		9*	11	8		S	12	7	3								J Martin	21
1			4	5*	6•		10		9	11	8		3	12	7	14		2						M Brandwood	23
1			4			12	10	8*		9	6	2	11		7	3		5	S					R Gifford	24
1			4			14	10*	12		11	9	6	2	8•	7	3		5						D Allison	25
1	2		4			14	10			11	9	6	S	8*	7	3		5						J Worrall	26
1	2		4				10	14		11•	9	6*	12	8	7	3		5						R Pawley	27
1	2		4				14	10	9	11•		6	12	7	3		5	8*						D Axcell	28
1	2		4			S	10	8		12		6	9*	7	3		5			11				K Cooper	29
1	2		4			6	10•	8	11•	9		12	7	3		5					14			V Callow	30
1	2		4			6	10	8	11*	9		S	12	7	3		5							A Gunn	31
	2		4		6		10	12	11•	9*			14	7	3		5		8	1				J Deakin	32
	2		4	6	11		10*		12	S	9			7	3		5		8	1				L Dilkes	33
	2		4*	6	11		10		12	S	9			7	3		5		8	1				K Barratt	34
1	2		4	6	11		10		12		9		14	7	3		5		8*					R Hamer	35
1	2		4	6	11		10*		12		9		S	7	3		5		8					J Moules	36
1	2		4	6	11		10		12	5•			9	14	7	3*		5		8				P Scoble	37
1	2		4	6	11*		14		10				9	12	7	3•		5		8				P Harrison	38
1	2		4		S		10		11		9	6	7	S		3		5		8				J Rushton	39
1	2		4		S		10		12	9*		6	11		7	3		5		8				G Singh	40
1	2		4				10•		12	9*		6	11		7	3		5	14	8				R Groves	41
1	2		4		S		10		9	6		11	12	7	3		5		8*					A Gunn	42
1	2		4		S		10		S	6		11	9	7	3		5		8					W Burns	43
1	2		4				14		10*		12	6	11	9	7	3		5		8				P Foakes	44
1	2		4				14		10			6*	11•	9	7	3		5		8			12	R Bigger	45
1	2		4				12		10		14	6	11	9•	7	3*		5		8				M Peck	46
1	2		4				14		10		12	6	11	9•	7	3		5		8*				M Brandwood	47
1	2		4				14		10*			6	11	9•	7	3		5		8			12	A Gunn	48
1	2		4				14		10*		12	6	11	9•	7	3		5		8				P Jones	49
1	2		4		6		12		S		10	11*	9		7	3		5		8				R Lewis	50
1	2		4		11*		12		10		14	6		9•	7	3		5		8				S Lodge	51
1	2		4		11		14		10•		12	6*		9	7	3		5		8				K Morton	52
43	43	7	46	22	26	1	34	4	28	25	34	18	19	25	35	36		33		23	1	3		League Appearances	
	1				2		4		10	3	15	8	3	10	9		1		1		1		3	Substitute Appearances	
4	4		4	4	4	0+1	4	2	3+1	4	4		3		1+1	2		1						R/lows Appearances	
1	1		1	1		1	1		1	1	1				1	1		1						FA Cup Appearances	
1	1	1	1	1		1	1		1	1			0+1	0+1	1	1								ZDS Cup Appearances	

Players on Loan: Morrow (Arsenal)

† = Sent Off

WATFORD

Club Colours: Yellow shirts – black/red trim, red shorts – yellow trim, red stockings – yellow/black tops
Change Colours: Blue/white shirts, dark blue shorts with light blue trim, dark blue stockings with light blue tops
Reserves League: Neville Ovenden Football Combination

COMPETITIONS					
Div. 1	Div. 2	Div. 3	Div. 3S	Div. 4	UEFA
82-88	69-72	20-21	21-58	58-60	83-84
	79-82	60-69		75-78	
	88-	72-75			
		78-79			

HONOURS		
Div. 3	Div. 4	Div. 3S Cup
68-69	77-78	36-37 (shared)

MOST APPEARANCES: LUTHER BLISSETT 443+52				
(1975-92 3 spells)				
Year	League	FA Cup	Lge Cup	FMC
1975-76	1+2			
1976-77	1+3			
1977-78	17+16			
1978-79	40+1	1	6+1	
1979-80	40+2	4	2	
1980-81	42	3	8	
1981-82	40	3	6	
1982-83	41	4	3	
1984-85	38+3	5	5	
1985-86	20+3		3	
1986-87	35	5	1	1
1987-88	17+8	4+2	1+2	
1988-89	3		1	
1991-92	34+8	1	4	0+1
	369+46	32+2	41+3	1+1
Previous holder: D Welbourne 449+8 (1963-74)				

MOST GOALS IN A CAREER			
LUTHER BLISSETT 180 (1975-92 3 spells)			
Season	League	FA Cup	Lge Cup
1975-76	1		
1976-77			
1977-78	6		
1978-79	21		7
1979-80	10	1	
1980-81	11		2
1981-82	19		3
1982-83	27	2	1
1984-85	21	6	1
1985-86	7		1
1986-87	11	4	
1987-88	4		1
1988-89	1		
1991-92	9	2	1
Total	148	15	17

HIGHEST TRANSFER FEE RECEIVED			
Amount	Club	Player	Date
£1,000,000	A C Milan	Luther Blissett	6/83
£1,000,000	Manchester City	Tony Coton	7/90
£1,000,000	Aston Villa	Gary Penrice	3/91
£1,000,000	Liverpool	David James	6/92

HIGHEST TRANSFER FEE PAID			
Amount	Club	Player	Date
£550,000	A C Milan	Luther Blissett	8/84
£500,000	Bristol Rovers	Gary Penrice	11/89
£300,000	Charlton Ath.	Joe McLaughlin	8/90
£250,000	Tottenham H.	Gerry Armstrong	11/80

MANAGERS			
Name	Seasons	Best	Worst
John Goodhall	1903-10		
Harry Kent	1910-26	6(3S)	20(3S)
Fred Pagnam	1926-29	8(3S)	21(3S)
Neil McBain	1929-37	4(3S)	16(3S)
Bill Findlay	1937-47		
Jack Bray	1947-48	15(3S)	15(3S)
Eddie Hapgood	1948-50	6(3S)	17(3S)
Ron Gray	1950-51	23(3S)	23(3S)
Haydn Green	1951-52	21(3S)	21(3S)
Len Goulden	1952-55	4(3S)	10(3S)
John Paton	1955-56	21(3S)	21(3S)
Len Goulden	1956		
Neil McBain	1956-59	11(3S)	15(4)
Ron Burgess	1959-63	4(3)	4(4)
Bill McGarry	1963-64	3(3)	3(3)
Ken Furphy	1964-71	18(2)	12(3)
George Kirby	1971-73	22(2)	19(3)
Mike Keen	1973-77	7(3)	8(4)
Graham Taylor	1977-87	2(1)	1(4)
Dave Bassett	1987-88		
Steve Harrison	1988-90	20(1)	4(2)
Colin Lee	1990	15(2)	15(2)
Steve Perryman	1990-	10(2)	20(2)

LONGEST LEAGUE RUNS	
of undefeated matches:	15 (27.10.1934-2.2.1935)
	(11.11.1978-10.3.1979)
of undefeated home matches:	27 (15.10.1963-19.12.1964)
without home win:	9 (14.12.1971-15.4.1872)
	(25.8.1990-1.12.1990)
of league wins:	7 (17.11.1934-29.12.1934)
	(26.12.1977-28.1.1978)
of league defeats:	9 (26.12.1972-27.2.1973)
of league matches without a win:	19 (27.11.1971-8.4.1972)
of undefeated away matches:	12 (17.3.1977-16.9.1978)
without an away win:	32 (17.4.1971-25.11.1972)
of home wins:	8 (29.8.1931-21.11.1931)
	(3.11.1934-2.2.1935) (6.9.1977-12.11.1977)
of away wins:	5 (25.4.1981-22.9.1981)

PREVIOUS NAMES
Watford Rovers until 1891 or amalgamation of West Herts & Watford St. Marys in 1898

PREVIOUS LEAGUE
Southern League

BIGGEST VICTORIES
League: 8-0 v Sunderland, Division 1, 25.9.1982
F.A. Cup: 10-1 v Lowestoft, Round 1, 27.11.1927
League Cup: 8-0 v Darlington, Round 2, 6.10.1987
Europe: 3-0 v Kaiserslauten, Round 1, 28.9.1983

BIGGEST DEFEATS
League: 1-8 v Crystal Palace, Division 4, 23.9.1959
0-8 v Aberdare, Division 3S, 2.1.1926
0-7 v Port Vale, Division 3S, 15.9.1947
F.A. Cup: 0-10 v Wolverhampton W., Round 1, 13.12.1912
League Cup: 0-5 v Coventry City, Round 1, 9.12.1980
Europe: 0-4 v Sparta Prague, UEFA 3, 1983-84

MOST POINTS
3 points a win: 80, Division 2, 1981-82
2 points a win: 71, Division 4, 1977-78

MOST GOALS
92, 1959-60 (Division 4).
Holton 42, Uphill 29, Hartle 6, Benning 5, Gregory 3, Bunce 2, Walter 2, Chung 1, og 1.

MOST GOALS IN A MATCH
5, Eddie Mummery v Newport County (8-2), Div 3(S), 1.1.1924

MOST GOALS IN A SEASON
Cliff Holton, 48 (42 League, 6 FA Cup), 1959-60

MOST FIRST CLASS MATCHES IN A SEASON
60 (46 League, 6 FA Cup, 2 League Cup, 4 Simod Cup, 2 Play-Offs) 1988-89

MOST LEAGUE GOALS CONCEDED
89, Division 3S, 1925-26

MOST LEAGUE WINS
30, Division 4, 1977-78

MOST LEAGUE DRAWS
18, Division 3S, 1921-22

MOST LEAGUE DEFEATS
28, Division 2, 1971-72

OLDEST PLAYER
Joe Calvert 42 years 25 days

YOUNGEST PLAYER
Keith Mercer 16 years 125 days.

MOST CAPPED PLAYER
John Barnes (England) 31 & Kenny Jackett (Wales) 31

BEST PERFORMANCES BY WATFORD

League: 1977-78: Matches played 46, Won 30, Drawn 11, Lost 5, Goals for 85, Goals against 38, Points 71. First in Division 4.

Highest: 1982-83: Second in Division 1.

F.A. Cup: 1983-84: 3rd rnd. Luton Town 2-2, 4-3; 4th rnd. Charlton Athletic 2-0; 5th rnd. Brighton & HA 3-1; 6th rnd. Rotherham 3-1; Semi-final Plymouth 1-0; Final Everton 0-2.

League Cup: 1978-79: 1st rnd. Brentford 4-0, 3-1; 2nd rnd. Newcastle 2-1; 3rd rnd. Manchester United 2-1; 4th rnd. Exeter City 2-0; 5th rnd. Stoke City 0-0, 3-1; Semi-Final Nottingham Forest 0-0, 1-3.

Europe (UEFA): 1983-84: 1st rnd. Kaiserslautern 1-3, 3-0; 2nd rnd. Levski Spartak 1-1, 3-1; 3rd rnd. Sparta Prague 2-3, 0-4.

DIVISIONAL RECORDS

	Played	Won	Drawn	Lost	For	Against	Points
DIVISION 1	250	93	58	99	386	372	337
DIVISION 2	436	141	123	172	499	540	494
DIVISION 3	598	241	164	193	886	766	646
DIVISION 3S	1334	488	333	513	1972	2029	1309
DIVISION 4	230	110	51	69	387	296	271
TOTALS	2848	1073	729	1046	4130	4003	3057

WATFORD							APPEARANCES				GOALS			
PLAYERS NAME Honours	Ht	Wt	Birthdate	Birthplace Transfers	Contract Date	Clubs	League	L/Cup	FA Cup	Other	Lg	L/C	FAC	Oth
GOALKEEPERS														
Perry Suckling	6.1	11.2	12.10.65	Leyton	19.10.83	Coventry City	27	2						
E: u21.10, Y.14				P.E	05.06.86	Manchester City	39	3	1	3				
				£100,000	14.01.88	Crystal Palace	59	4	1	7				
15.12.89 Loan West Ham U. 6 Lg Apps.				Loan	11.10.91	Brentford	8			1				
				Free	13.07.92	Watford								
Keith Waugh	6.1	13.0	27.10.56	Sunderland	01.07.74	Sunderland (A)								
FRT86,Div.4.82				Free	01.07.76	Peterborough U	195	22	10					
				£90,000	27.08.81	Sheffield Utd	99	12	6	1				
09.11.84 Loan Cambridge Utd. 4 Lg Apps.				Free	15.07.85	Bristol City	170	15	15	24				
18.08.92 £40,000 Coventry 1 Lg+ 1LC App				Free	07.02.91	Watford	3							
DEFENDERS														
Barry Ashby	6.2	13.2	21.11.70	Brent	01.12.88	Watford (T)	52+10	1	4	0+1	1			
FAYC'89														
Jason Drysdale	5.10	12.0	17.11.70	Bristol	08.09.88	Watford (T)	79+8	2+1	1	2	5			
E: Y. FAYC'89														
Keith Dublin	5.7	10.0	29.01.66	Brent	28.01.84	Chelsea (A)	50+1	6	5	5+1				
E: Y, u19.4					14.08.87	Brighton & H.A	132	5	7	7	5		1	
				£275,000	17.07.90	Watford	89	5	2	2				
Nigel Gibbs	5.7	11.11	20.11.65	St.Albans	23.11.83	Watford (A)	261+3	15	25+1	12+1	3	2		
E: u21.5, u19.3, Y.6; FAYC'82														
David Holdsworth	6.1	12.4	08.11.68	Walthamstow	08.11.86	Watford (A)	119+6	6	6+1	5+2	8			
E: u21.1, Y.6														
Joe McLaughlin	6.3	13.7	02.06.60	Greenock		Morton	134	19	9		3			
S: u21.10; Div2'84'89; FMC'86					01.05.83	Chelsea	220	23	9	16	5	1		1
				£600,000	17.08.89	Charlton Ath	31	3	3					
				£300,000	09.08.90	Watford	46	5	1	1	2			
Jason Soloman	6.0	11.10	06.10.70	Welwyn Gdn City	01.02.88	Watford (T)	24+13	3		1+1				
E: Y.6; FAYC'89														
MIDFIELD														
Andrew Hessenthaler	5.7	11.0	17.08.65	Gravesend		Dartford								
via Redbridge Forest to				£65,000	12.09.91	Watford	35	2	1	1	2			
Gary Porter	5.6	10.6	06.03.66	Sunderland	06.03.84	Watford (A)	219+29	15+2	19+2	9+1	34	3	2	2
E: u21.12, Y.13; FAYC'82														
Trevor Putney	5.9	11.8	11.02.61	Harold Hill		Brentwood								
					19.09.80	Ipswich Town	94+9	15	9		8	1		
					13.06.86	Norwich City	76+6	4	8	6	9		1	
				£300,000	14.08.89	Middlesbrough	45+3	5	2	5	1			
				£150,000	15.08.91	Watford	26+2	4	1	1	2			
FORWARDS														
Darren Bazeley	5.10	10.9	05.10.72	Northampton	06.05.91	Watford (T)	26+16	2+2		1+1	6	1		
Luther Blissett	5.11	12.3	01.02.58	Jamaica	01.07.75	Watford	222+24	26+1	17		95	13	3	
E:14,B1,u21.4; Div4'78				£1,000,000	01.06.83	A.C. Milan (Ita)								
				£550,000	23.08.84	Watford	113+14	11+2	14+2	1	44	3	10	
				£60,000	25.11.88	Bournemouth	121	8	10	3	56	2	2	1
				£40,000	14.08.91	Watford	34+8	4	1	0+1	9	1	2	
Steve Butler	6.2	13.0	27.01.62	Birmingham		Wokingham Town								
E:Semi.Pro.3,GMVC'89	via Windsor & Eton to					Brentford	18+3			2	3			
					28.07.89	Maidstone Utd	76	4	18	10	41	3	7	4
				£150,000	12.04.91	Watford	38+15	3+1	1	1	9			
David Byrne	5.9	10.12	05.03.61	Hammersmith		Kingstonian								
Div2'88					15.08.85	Gillingham	18+5	2	0+3	1+1	3			
				£5,000	04.08.86	Millwall	52+11	5+1	3	4	6	1		
08.09.88 Loan Cambridge Utd. 4 Lg App				Loan	23.02.89	Blackburn Rovers	4							
					16.03.89	Plymouth A	52+7	5+1	1	1	2			
01.02.90 Loan Bristol R. 0+2 Lg, 0+1 Oth App				£50,000	16.11.90	Watford	16+1			1	2			
21.08.91 Loan Reading 7 Lg App, 2 G.				Loan	15.01.92	Fulham	5							
Paul Furlong	6.0	11.8	01.10.68	Wood Green		Enfield			4				1	
E: S-P.5, F.A.T'88.				£130,000	31.07.91	Coventry City	27+10	4	1+1	1	4	1		
				£250,000	24.07.92	Watford								
Andy Kennedy	6.1	11.10	08.10.64	Stirling		Glasgow Rangers	12+3	1+1	3		3		1	
S: Y					28.03.85	Birmingham City	51+25	8	2	1	18	2		
20.03.87 Loan Sheff. Utd. 8+1 Lg App, 1G.				£50,000	02.06.88	Blackburn Rovers	49+10	4	3	4+1	23		1	3
				£60,000	01.08.90	Watford	17+8	2	0+1	1	4	1		
				Loan	24.10.91	Bolton W	1							
Lee Nogan	5.10	11.0	21.05.69	Cardiff	25.03.87	Oxford Utd. (A)	57+7	4+1	2+1	4+1	10		1	1
W: B.1,u21.1				Loan	25.03.87	Brentford	10+1				2			
				Loan	01.09.88	Southend Utd	6	2		1	1			1
				£350,000	12.12.91	Watford	23				5			
Roderick Thomas	5.6	10.6	10.10.70	Park Royal (Lon)	03.05.88	Watford (T)	62+21	3+5	0+1	3+1	9			
E: u21.1, Y.8; FAYC'89				Loan	27.03.92	Gillingham	8				1			
ADDITIONAL CONTRACT PLAYERS														
(F) Alex Inglethorpe	5.11	11.0	14.11.71	Epsom	01.07.90	Watford	1+3	1+1						
Richard M Johnson					11.05.92	Watford (T)	1+1							
Gerard Lavin					11.05.92	Watford (T)	8+6							

Julian Alsford (D), Joseph Gallen, James Meara (M), Daniel Nwaokolo, Simon Shepherd (G).

WATFORD

RECORD WIN & LOSS AGAINST EACH CLUB IN CURRENT DIVISION

(Where a score has occured on several occasions the most recent is given)

Club	Rec. Win	Season	Rec. Loss	Season
BARNSLEY	4-0	1988-89	4-0	1964-65
BIRMINGHAM CITY	3-0	1985-86	4-1	1971-72
BRENTFORD	6-1	1960-61	5-0	1929-30
BRISTOL CITY	4-0	1934-35	5-0	1926-27
BRISTOL ROVERS	5-1	1930-31 (away)	3-0	1951-52
CAMBRIDGE UNITED	3-0	1973-74	4-0	1976-77
CHARLTON ATHLETIC	4-1	1986-87	5-2	1934-35
DERBY COUNTY	6-1	1981-82	3-2	1981-82
GRIMSBY TOWN	7-1	1967-68	3-0	1921-22
LEICESTER CITY	5-1	1986-87	4-1	1983-84
LUTON TOWN	3-0	1984-85	5-0	1925-26
MILLWALL	3-0	1963-64 (away)	6-0	1962-63
NEWCASTLE UNITED	4-1	1985-86	3-0	1987-88
NOTTS COUNTY	4-0	1962-63	4-0	1948-49
OXFORD UNITED	4-0	1988-89 (away)	2-1	1970-71
PETERBOROUGH UTD	4-1	1967-68	5-1	1967-68
PORTSMOUTH	4-0	1969-70	5-0	1970-71
SOUTHEND UNITED	5-0	1935-36	6-1	1960-61
SUNDERLAND	8-0	1982-83	5-0	1979-80
SWINDON TOWN	6-1	1935-36	7-1	1951-52 (home)
TRANMERE ROVERS	4-0	1978-79	3-0	1975-76
WEST HAM UNITED	5-0	1984-85	2-0	1984-85
WOLVERHAMPTON WNDRS	5-0	1983-84 (away)	3-0	1991-92

MANAGER: STEVE PERRYMAN

DATE OF BIRTH: 21.12.1951   **PLACE OF BIRTH:** Ealing

DATE OF APPOINTMENT: 27.11.1990

PREVIOUS CLUBS
as Manager: Brentford
as Asst. Man./Coach:
as Player: Tottenham Hotspur, Oxford United, Brentford

HONOURS
as Manager:
as Asst. Man./Coach:
as Player: FA Cup 1980, 1981; Lge Cup (2); UEFA 1972
International: England 1 full cap, 17 U23, Youth

Value Rating: ★ ★ ★ ★ ★

Programme Editor: Ed Coan

Price of 1992-93 Programme: £1.50

Number of Pages: 32

Subscriptions: £39 all home games plus postage and handling charge

Local Newspapers: Watford Observer, Watford Review, Watford Herald and Post

Local Radio Stations: Chiltern Radio, BBC Radio Bedfordshire, LBC, Radio London, Capital Radio.

LEADING LEAGUE GOALSCORERS
SEASONS 1979-80 – 1991-92

1979-80	LUTHER BLISSETT	10		1980-81	MALCOLM POSKETT	13
1981-82	LUTHER BLISSETT	19		1982-83	LUTHER BLISSETT	27
1983-84	MO JOHNSTON	20		1984-85	LUTHER BLISSETT	21
1985-86	COLIN WEST	13		1986-87	MARK FALCO	14
1987-88	LUTHER BLISSETT	4		1988-89	PAUL WILKINSON	19
1989-90	PAUL WILKINSON	16		1990-91	PAUL WILKINSON	18

1991-92 **LUTHER BLISSETT** 9

VICARAGE ROAD STADIUM Watford WD1 8ER

Capacity: 24,886   **Covered Standing:** 4,705   **Seating:** 6,906

Tel: Ground: 0923 230933   **Ticket Sales:** 0923 220393   **Clubcall:** 0898 12 10 30

All premium rate calls (0898/0891) cost 36p per minute cheap rate and 48p per minute at all other times. Call costings correct at time of going to press.

GROUNDS
Cassio Road 1899-1922; Vicarage Road 1922-

ATTENDANCES
Highest: 34,099 v Manchester United, FA Cup, 3.2.1969
Lowest: 1,700 v Southend Utd, ZDS Cup, 2.10.1991

RECORD RECEIPTS (with previous records)
£104,347 v Liverpool, FA Cup 6th Round, 17.3.1986
£89,836 v West Ham Utd, Div 2, 12.1.1991
£74,505 v Brighton & H.A. FA Cup 5th Round, 18.2.1984
£61,684 v West Ham United, FA Cup 4th Round, 23.1.1982
£48,743 v Coventry City, League Cup 5th Round, 2.12.1980
£44,542 v Arsenal, FA Cup 6th Round, 8.3.1980

VICARAGE ROAD
First game: v Millwall, Div 3S, 0-0, 30.8.1922
First floodlit game: v Luton Town, Friendly, October 1953

Season Tickets:
Stands: from £192 to £240, juv/OAP £133.50 to £210
Ground: £120, juv/OAP £85

Executive Box Season Tickets: Consult Marketing Manager

Cost of Stand Tickets: Seating £10 & £8; Family Area: £8, juv £5
Terraces: Vicarage Road £6, Rookery £7; Family Area £6, juv £3

Match and Ticket Information: Seats for league matches available any time in advance

Car Parking: No public parking available at ground. There are several multi-story parks nearby and Street parking

Nearest Railway Station: Watford Junction or Watford High Street (0923 245001)

How to get to the ground

From North: Use Motorway M1 until Junction 6. Leave motorway and follow signs Watford A405/A41 and A411. Follow signs Slough A412 and in 0.7m turn left into Harwoods Road. At end of T Road turn left into Vicarage Road for Watford FC

From East and South: Use Motorway M1 until Junction 5. Leave motorway and follow signs Watford A41 and A412. Then follow signs Slough A412 and in 0.7m turn left into Harwoods Road. At end of T road turn left into Vicarage Road for Watford FC

From West: Use A412 S.P. Watford and pass Croxley Green Station then in 0.9m turn right into Harwoods Road. At end of T road turn left into Vicarage Road for Watford FC

WEST BROMWICH ALBION Division 2

Formed: 1878-79 **Turned Professional:** 1885 **Ltd Co:** 1892

SPONSORED BY: Sandwell **NICKNAME:** The Throstles, The Baggies, The Albion

President
F A Millichip

Vice-President
J S Lucas

Chairman
T J Summers

Directors
J W Brandrick   M C McGinnity
A B Hale   C M Stapleton

Secretary
Dr. John Evans
(021-525 8888)

Team Manager
Ossie Ardiles

Assistant Manager
Keith Burkinshaw

Reserve Team Coach
Dennis Mortimer

Youth Coach
Cyril Lea

Chief Scout
Norman Bodell

Physiotherapist
Danny Thomas

Football in the Community Officer
John Trewick

Youth Development Officer
Derek Mann

Club Statistician for the Directory
Tony Matthews

THE 1991-92 season was the most turbulent in the club's history and it ended in sheer frustration and total disappointment as Albion missed out on the play-offs, finishing 7th in the Third Division – their lowest position ever.

Manager Bobby Gould had attempted to win promotion with the same band of players who had been relegated from Division Two the year before.

He domineered his staff, introducing maverick ideas which worked initially, but after selling star striker Don Goodman to Sunderland for £900,000 and after topping the table in early February, following an emphatic 3-0 win at Birmingham, there followed a shattering demise with the fans calling for both the manager and the board to resign.

The team simply disintegrated under pressure. Results were disastrous and when Gould sacked his coach, Stuart Pearson, there was uproar amongst the fans. Things went from bad to worse after that and soon after the season ended, Gould and club chairman John Silk resigned their posts, to be replaced by the 1978 Argentinian World Cup star, Ossie Ardiles and local businessman Trevor Summers respectively.

The Baggies started off 1991-92 as favourites to regain their Second Division status at the first attempt – and indeed, in their opening League game they looked sharp and purposeful when whipping Exeter City 6-3 at The Hawthorns. Early exit from the Rumbelows Cup hardly mattered as the League results continued, but then came that collapse . . . which gutted the stunned fans! Yet, surprisingly the supporters stayed loyal throughout and the average home attendance was almost 13,000, up by around 1,000 on the previous season.

A staggering 34 players were used by Gould during the campaign with only one ever-present, left-back Graham Harbey. The defence at times looked solid; the midfield battled hard and long, but scoring goals (certainly after Goodman's departure) proved difficult, and one reflects that of the 46 matches played, 14 were drawn (only Bradford and Bolton drew more) and eight matches were lost by the odd goal!

The new boss will have his work cut out to restore some stability to a team which has struggled to a certain extent over the past four or five years. But as one fan said after a quite humiliating home defeat at the hands of Hartlepool United in mid-March when victory was imperative: "We have reached rock bottom now – surely things can only get better", and hopefully they will under the new partnership of Ardiles and former Tottenham manager, Keith Burkinshaw.

Even Albion's reserve side were relegated from the Pontins League Division 1 – to be replaced by arch rivals Wolves! **Tony Matthews**

Back row L-R: I Hamilton, C Heggs, R Raven, S Naylor, G Strodder, D Burgess, R Taylor. **Middle row:** D Thomas (Physio), S Hodson, R Hunter, W Fereday, D Bradley, S Lilwall, D Mortimer (Reserve Team Coach). **Front row:** B McNally, G Robson, K Ampadu, K Burkinshaw (Asst. Manager), O Ardiles (Manager), C Shakespeare, S Coldicott, G Hackett.

WEST BROMWICH ALBION

DIVISION THREE: 7th   **FA CUP:** 2nd RND   **RUMBELOWS CUP:** 1st RND   **AUTOGLASS:** 1st RND

M	DATE		COMP.	VEN	OPPONENTS	RESULT	H/T	LGE POS	GOALSCORERS/GOAL TIMES	ATTEN-DANCE
1	A	17	BL	H	Exeter City	W 6-3	2-1	2	Shakespeare (2p) 30,45, Goodman 62,64, Foster 76, Williams 77	12,892
2		20	RC 1/1	A	Swindon Town	L 0-2	0-2			(6,611)
3		24	BL	A	Darlington	W 1-0	0-0	1	Goodman 86	(5,658)
4		28	RC 1/2	H	Swindon Town	D 2-2	1-0		Goodman 20, Shakespeare (pen) 86	8,522
5		31	BL	H	Wigan Athletic	D 1-1	1-1	4	McNally 29	12,053
6	S	3	BL	A	Fulham	D 0-0	0-0	3		(4,523)
7		7	BL	A	Bolton Wanderers	L 0-3	0-1	6		(7,980)
8		14	BL	H	Stockport County	W 1-0	0-0	6	Williams 70	11,845
9		17	BL	H	Peterborough Utd	W 4-0	2-0	3	Robson 5, 68, Williams 14, Bowen 58	10,037
10		21	BL	A	Chester City	W 2-1	1-1	1	Robson 43, Burgess 86	(3,895)
11		28	BL	H	Hull City	W 1-0	0-1	1	Burgess 50	11,932
12	O	1	BL	A	Preston North End	L 0-2	0-0	1		(5,293)
13		12	BL	H	Shrewsbury Town	W 2-0	1-0	3	Goodman 30, West 85	12,437
14		19	BL	A	Brentford	W 2-1	1-0	1	Ampadu 16, Goodman 87	(8,575)
15		22	AGT Pre	H	Shrewsbury Town	W 4-0	2-0		Rogers 28, West 38, Shakespeare 56, Ampadu 87	6,997
16		26	BL	A	Birmingham City	L 0-1	0-0	3		26,168
17	N	2	BL	H	Bury	D 1-1	0-1	3	Robson 87	8,439
18		5	BL	A	Hartlepool United	D 0-0	0-0	4		(2,810)
19		9	BL	A	Reading	W 2-1	1-0	4	Robson 29, Goodman 47	(5,826)
20		16	FAC 1	H	Marlow	W 6-0	3-0		Stodder 22, Goodman 31, Shakespeare 44, 56 (pen), McNally 62, Robson 63	11,082
21		23	BL	H	Huddersfield Town	W 2-1	2-1	3	Robson 25, Harbey 41	14,029
22		30	BL	A	Stoke City	D 2-2	1-1	3	Shakespeare 17, Goodman 83	17,207
23	D	4	AGT Pre	A	Lincoln City	W 2-1	0-0		Williams 48, Robson 89	(1,861)
24		9	FAC 2	A	Leyton Orient	L 1-2	1-1		Williams 50	(6,189)
25		14	BL	A	Bradford City	D 1-1	0-1	3	Bradley 59	(7,195)
26		22	BL	H	Darlington	W 3-1	2-0	3	Strodder 31, Sinclair 59, Fereday 66	13,261
27		26	BL	A	Wigan Athletic	W 1-0	0-0	3	Shakespeare (pen) 63	(5,068)
28		28	BL	A	Exeter City	D 1-1	0-0	1	Shakespeare (pen) 73	(5,830)
29	J	1	BL	H	Fulham	L 2-3	1-2	3	Robson 5, Shakespeare (pen) 76	16,442
30		4	BL	A	Torquay United	L 0-1	0-0	4		(4,159)
31		11	BL	H	Bournemouth	W 4-0	1-0	2	Robson 17, Bannister 62, 85, Williams 89	10,932
32		14	AGT 1	H	Exeter City	L 0-1	0-1			6,034
33		18	BL	A	Leyton Orient	D 1-1	1-1	3	Bradley 35	(6,328)
34		25	BL	H	Swansea City	L 2-3	0-1	3	Roberts 18, 38 (pen)	10,395
35	F	1	BL	H	Brentford	W 2-0	2-0	2	Taylor 11, Fereday 45	15,984
36		8	BL	A	Birmingham City	W 3-0	2-0	1	Robson 26, Taylor 44, 71	(27,508)
37		12	BL	A	Stoke City	L 0-1	0-1	2		(23,645)
38		15	BL	H	Bradford City	D 1-1	1-1	3	Shakespeare 29	12,607
39		22	BL	A	Bournemouth	L 1-2	0-1	3	Taylor 88	(7,721)
40		29	BL	H	Torquay United	W 1-0	0-0	3	Hunter 82	11,669
41	M	3	BL	H	Leyton Orient	L 1-3	0-3	3	Bannister 83	11,165
42		6	BL	A	Swansea City	D 0-0	0-0	3		(5,629)
43		11	BL	H	Hartlepool United	L 1-2	0-1	3	Williams 84	10,307
44		14	BL	A	Bury	D 1-1	1-1	5	Taylor 10	(3,810)
45		21	BL	H	Reading	W 2-0	2-0	3	Strodder 29, Raven 35	10,707
46		28	BL	H	Huddersfield Town	L 0-3	0-1	5		(7,428)
47		31	BL	A	Stockport County	L 0-3	0-1	7		(6,090)
48	A	4	BL	H	Bolton Wanderers	D 2-2	1-1	8	Ampadu 16, Taylor 72	10,287
49		11	BL	A	Peterborough Utd	D 0-0	0-0	9		(9,040)
50		18	BL	H	Chester City	D 1-1	0-1	9	Rogers 86	10,137
51		20	BL	A	Hull City	L 0-1	0-1	10		(4,815)
52		25	BL	H	Preston North End	W 3-0	1-0	8	Taylor 32, Ampadu 75, West 82	11,318
53	M	2	BL	A	Shrewsbury Town	W 3-1	3-0	7	Strodder 19, Shakespeare 33, Taylor 37	(7,442)

Best Home League Attendance: 26,168 v Birmingham City   **Smallest: 8,439 v Bury**   **Av Home Att: 12,707**

Goal Scorers: **Compared with 90-91: +706**

League (64): Robson 9, Shakespeare 8 (5 pens), Taylor 8, Goodman 7, Williams 5, Bannister 3, Strodder 3, Ampadu 3, Roberts 2 (1 pen) West 2, Bradley 2, Burgess 2, Fereday 2, Hunter, Raven, Sinclair, Foster, McNally, Bowen, Rogers, Harbey

R/lows C (2): Shakespeare (1 pen), Goodman

FA Cup (7): Shakespeare 2 (1 pen), Stodder, Goodman, Robson, McNally, Williams

Autoglass (6): Robson, Shakespeare, Williams, Rogers, Ampadu, West

Bradley D.	Harbey G.	Ford T.	Strodder G.	Burgess D.	Bannister G.	Goodman D.	Foster A.	Shakespeare C.	Ampadu P.	McNally B.	Williams P.	Naylor S.	Hodson S.	Parkin S.	Bowen S.	Robson G.	Hackett G.	West C.	Rogers D.	White W.	Fereday W.	Roberts D.	Taylor R.	Dibble A.	Raven P.	Referee	
2	3	4	5	6	7	8•	9	10	11*	12	14															K Breen	1
2	3	4	5	6	7	8	9*	10	11•	12	14	1														J Moules	2
2	3	4	5	6		8		10	11	7	14		S													D Phillips	3
2	3	4	5	6*	12	8*	14	10	11	7	9	1														A Bennett	4
2	3	4	5		8		12	10	11	7	9*		6	S												S Lodge	5
2	3	4	5	6	8		11•	10	14	7*	9	1		12												M Pierce	6
	3	4	5	6	S		9	10	11	7	14	1		2												J Lloyd	7
	3	4	5	6	7*			10			12	1	2	8	11•	9										P Taylor	8
	3	4	5	6				10*		7		1	2	8	11•	9	12									P Danson	9
12	3	4	5	6				10		7		1	2*	8	11•	9										H King	10
	3	4	5	6		7		10		12		1	2	8	11•	9*										G Poll	11
S	3	4	5	6				10		8*		1	2	7	11	9										R Poulain	12
	3	4	5	6		8*		10		12		1	2	7	11•	9										A Ward	13
7	3	4	5	6*		8		10	11	12	S	1	2			9										M Bailey	14
6	3	4			8*		10*	11	7	14		1	2		12	9		5								C Trussell	15
6	3	4	5		8		10	11*	7	12		1	2			9	S									R Gifford	16
14	3	4	5	6		8		10				1	2		11•	9*	12									M Bodenham	17
7	3	4	5	6	14	8		10	11•		S	1	2			9										P Wright	18
4*	3		5	6		8		10		7		1	2			9•				12	11					A Gunn	19
4•	3	2	5	6		8		10	14	7		1				9•				12	11					I Hemley	20
4	3		5	6		8		10	14	7		1	2			9•				S	11					J Martin	21
4	3	5*		6		8		10	14	7		1	2			9				12	11•					K Cooper	22
4	3	5	6			14		10		7	8	1	2			9				S	11•					G Pooley	23
4	3	5	6			14		10		7	8	1	2			9•				S	11					K Morton	24
4	3	5	S					10	14	7	8	1	6			9					11•					K Redfearn	25
4	3	5	6	14				10	S	7	8	1				9					11•					P Scoble	26
4	3	5	6				14	10	12	7	8	1				9•				11						R Hart	27
4	3	5				9*		10	12	7	8	1							14	11•						P Alcock	28
4	3	5*						10	14	7*	8	1				9			6	11	12					P Harrison	29
4	3		9•					10	14	7	8	1		11*					6	12	5					R Gifford	30
4	3	5	6	8				10•	11*	14	1	2			9				12	7						D Elleray	31
4	3	5	6	8						14	1	2	10•		9	11*			7							R Milford	32
4	3	5	6	8				S		1	2				9	11			7	10						J Carter	33
4	3	5	6	8•				12		14	1	2			9	11			7*	10						A Wilkie	34
4	3		6					5	12	14	1	2			9•	11			7	10	8•					B Coddington	35
4	3		6					5	12	S	1	2			9	11			7*	10	8					K Barratt	36
4	3		6	14				5			1	2•			9	11	S		7	10	8					I Hendrick	37
4*	3		6				14	5			1	2			9	11•	12		7	10	8					R Groves	38
4	3		6				14	5			1	2*	11•	9			12		7	10	8					P Don	39
4†	3		6					5		14			9		11•		7		10*	8	1	2				E Parker	40
4	3•		6	8				5	11*	14						7				10	9	1	2			J Lloyd	41
4	3		6	9				5	11	S				7					2*	10	8	1	2			K Cooper	42
4	3	5	6	9				12	11•	14				7					2*	10	8	1	2			A Ward	43
	3		4	6				5	S	9									10		8	1	2			R Shepherd	44
4	3		5	6				10		14					12				7•		8	1	2			R Lewis	45
4	3		5	6				10		14				12					7		8	1	2		12	N Midgley	46
	3		5	6				10	11•	14		2*		9	7					12	8	1		1*		J Hackett	47
4	3		5	6				10	11		9		S	7					2		8	1				J Deakin	48
4	3		5	6				10	11		9†	1		14	7•				2		8					A Flood	49
4†	3		5					10	11*		9	1		6	7•	12	14		2		8					D Frampton	50
4	3		5					10	11*		9*	1		6	7	12	14		2		8					R Hill	51
4*	3		5						11•			1		10	7	9	6		2		8					P Durkin	52
	3		5				S	4	11			1		10	7		6		2		8					D Allison	53
35	46	15	37	36	11	11	4	42	15	17	16	34	25	8	8	29	13	5	4	9	19	12	19	9	6	**League Appearances**	
2					4		4	2	6	4	18				1		3	2	2	6	1	3			1	**Substitute Appearances**	
2	2	2	2	2	1+1	2	1+1	2	2	1+1	1	2				2										**R/lows Appearances**	
2	2	1	2	2		1		2		1	2	1	2	1		2				0+1	2					**FA Cup Appearances**	
3	3	1	2	2	1	1	0	2	1	2	1+2	3	3	1		2+1	1	1	1	1	2					**Autoglass Appearances**	

Also Played: Posn.(Game): Miller 1(1,3,5), Piggott 9(3•53)8•(7)14(10,52), Pritchard 14(8,11,13)12(12)7(17), Palmer 14(9), Sinclair 2(25,26,27, 28†,29,30), Cartwright 12(32)S(33)7(44)9(45*,46*), Hunter 12(40,41,45,52)S(42,44,53)4(47)2(48), Heggs 11(44,45*,46), Coldicott S(49)

Players on Loan: Miller (Arsenal), Sinclair (Chelsea), Fereday (Bournemouth), Dibble (Man. City)   † = Sent Off

WEST BROMWICH ALBION

Club Colours: Navy blue/white striped shirts, white shorts, white stockings
Change Colours: Red and yellow striped shirts, red shorts, yellow stockings
Reserves League: Pontins Central League Division 2

Previous Name: West Bromwich Strollers 1878-80
Previous Managers: (Secretary/Managers) 1885-87 Thomas Foster 1887-90 Louis Ford 1890-92 W. Pierre Dix 1892-94 Henry Jackson 1894-95 Edward Stephenson 1895 Clement Keys 1896-1902 Frank Heaven 1902-48 Fred Everiss (Managers) 1948-52 Jack Smith 1952-53 Jesse Carver 1953-59 Vic Buckingham 1959-61 Gordon Clark 1961-63 Archie Macauley 1963-67 Jimmy Hagan 1967-71 Alan Ashman 1971-75 Don Howe 1975-77 Johnny Giles 1977 Ronnie Allen 1978-81 Ron Atkinson 1981-82 Ronnie Allen 1982-83 Ron Wylie 1983-85 Johnny Giles 1985-86 Nobby Stiles 1986-87 Ron Saunders 1987-88 Ron Atkinson 1988-91 Brian Talbot 1990-92 Bobby Gould 1992- Ossie Ardiles
Honours: Champions Division 1 1919-20 Champions Division 2 1901-02, 1910-11 FA Cup Winners 1887-88, 1891-92, 1930-31, 1953-54, 1967-68 League Cup Winners 1965-66 Charity Shield 1920, 1954 (shared)
League Career: Founder Members of Football League 1888 Relegated to Div 2 1900-01 Promoted to Div 1 1901-02 Relegated to Div 2 1903-04 Promoted to Div 1 1910-11 Relegated to Div 2 1926-27 Promoted to Div 1 1930-31 Relegated to Div 2 1937-38 Promoted to Div 1 1948-49 Relegated to Div 2 1972-73 Promoted to Div 1 1975-76 Relegated to Div 2 1985-86 Relegated to Div 3 1990-91

CLUB RECORDS

Most Appearances for Club: Tony Brown (1963-80): League 561+13, FA Cup 53+1, League Cup 46+1, Europe 14+1, Charity Shield 1 **Total 675+16**
Most Capped Player: Stuart Williams (Wales) 33 **For England:** 25 Jesse Pennington
Record Goalscorer in a Match: Jimmy Cookson, 6 v Blackpool, 6-3, Div 2, 17.9.1927
Record League Goalscorer in a Season: William Richardson, 39, 1935-36 **In All Competitions:** Williams Richardson, 40 (League 39, FA Cup 1) 1935-36
Record League Goalscorer in a Career: Tony Brown, 218, 1963-80 **In All Competitions:** Tony Brown, 271 (League 218, FA Cup 27, League Cup 18, Europe 8) 1963-80
Record Transfer Fee Received: £1,500,000 from Manchester United for Bryan Robson, October 1981
Record Transfer Fee Paid: £748,000 to Manchester City for Peter Barnes, July 1979
Best Performances: League: Champions Div 1 1919-20 **FA Cup:** Winners (5) **League Cup:** Winners 1965-66
Most League Points: (3pts for win) 72, Division 2, 1988-89 (2pts for win) 60, Division 1, 1919-20
Most Goals: 105, Division 2, 1929-30
Record League Victory and Most Goals Scored in a League Match: 12-0 v Darwen, Division 1, 4.4.1892 (Joint Div 1 record)
Record Victory and Most Goals Scored in a Cup Tie: 10-1 v Chatham (a), FA Cup Round 3, 2.3.1889
Record League Defeat: 0-7 v Bolton Wndrs, Div 1, 7.12.1889 1-8 v Notts County, Div 1, 19.11.1892 1-8 v Sunderland, Div 1, 22.10.1892 1-8 v Derby County, Div 1, 25.12.1896 1-8 v Port Vale, Div 2, 9.3.1929 3-10 v Stoke City, Div 1, 4.2.1937 0-7 v Wolverhampton Wndrs, Div 1, 16.3.1963 0-7 v Manchester United, Div 1, 8.4.1970 0-7 v Ipswich Town, Div 1, 6.11.1976
Record Cup Defeat: 0-5 v Leeds Utd, FA Cup Rnd 4, 1966-67 0-5 v Tottenham Hotspur, League Cup Rnd 4, 1970-71 1-6 v Nottingham Forest, League Cup Rnd 2, 6.10.1982
European Competitions entered: Fairs Cup 1966-67 European Cup Winners Cup 1968-69 UEFA Cup 1978-79, 1979-80, 1981-82
Oldest Player in a League Match: Jesse Pennington, 38 years 256 days v Liverpool, 6.5.1922
Youngest Player in Any Match: Frank Hodgetts, 16 years 26 days v Notts County, Div 2, 26.10.1940 (war time)
Youngest Player in League Match: Charlie Wilson, 16 years 73 days v Oldham Athletic, Div 1, 1.10.1921

LONGEST LEAGUE RUNS	
of undefeated matches: 17 (1901-02)	of league matches without a win: 13 (1985)
of undefeated home matches: 19 (1901-02, 1908-09)	of undefeated away matches: 11 (1957, 1980)
without home win: 9 (1921, 1971)	without an away win: 27 (1969-71)
of league wins: 11 (1930)	of home wins: 11 (1906-07)
of league defeats: 9 (1985)	of away wins: 7 (1953)

BARCLAYS

WEST BROMWICH ALBION

PLAYERS NAME Honours	Ht	Wt	Birthdate	Birthplace Transfers	Contract Date	Clubs	League	L/Cup	FA Cup	Other	Lg	L/C	FAC	Oth
GOALKEEPERS														
Jonathon Gould					16.10.90	Halifax Town	32	2	5	5				
				Free	30.01.92	West Brom A								
Stuart Naylor	6.4	11.3	06.12.62		19.06.80	Lincoln City	48	4	2	6				
E: B.3, Y.1				Loan	23.02.83	Peterborough U	8							
				Loan	06.10.83	Crewe Alexandra	55	2	2	3				
				£100,000	18.02.86	West Brom A	234	13	6	9				
DEFENDERS														
Daryl Burgess	5.11	12.03	24.01.71	Birmingham	01.07.89	West Brom A. (T)	91+4	5+2	4	3	2			
Simeon Hodson	5.10	11.0	05.02.66	Lincoln	14.03.84	Notts County (A)	27	3						
				f	01.04.85	Charlton Ath	5							
				f	10.01.86	Lincoln City	54+2	4	1	5				
				f	10.08.87	Newport Co	34	4	1	3	1			
				£25,000	25.03.88	West Brom A	77+4	5	1	3				
Gary Strodder	6.1	11.4	01.04.65	Spenborough	08.04.83	Lincoln City	122+10	7+1	2+1	5+1	6			
				20.03.87	West Ham U	59+6	8	4+2	2	2				
				£190,000	22.08.90	West Brom A	67+4	4	3	3	4		1	
MIDFIELD														
Darren Bradley	5.7	11.10	24.11.65	Birmingham	19.12.83	Aston Villa (A)	16+4	3						
E: u19.3, Y.3				P.E	14.03.86	West Brom A	160+12	6	4	5	6	1	1	1
Neil.A Cartwright			20.02.71	Stourbridge	01.07.89	West Brom A. (T)	143+18	11	7	5+1	60	1	1	1
Wayne Fereday	5.9	11.8	16.06.63	London	03.09.80	Q.P.R. (A)	167+30	23+3	11+3	6	21	3		1
E:u21.5				£300,000	08.06.89	Newcastle Utd	27+6	3+1	1	1+2				
				P.E	30.11.90	Bournemouth	20+3	0+2	1+1				1	
				£60,000	12.12.91	West Brom A	19+3			2				
Gary Hackett	5.8	10.1	11.10.62	Stourbridge		Bromsgrove								
WC'85				£5,000	21.07.83	Shrewsbury Town	142+8	15	6	2+1	17	2	1	
				£80,000	16.07.87	Aberdeen	6+9	1+2	2	0+2				
				£110,000	11.03.88	Stoke City	64+9	3+1	3+1	3	7			
				£70,000	01.03.90	West Brom A	22+12	0+2		1	2	1		
Ian Hamilton	5.9	11.3	14.12.67	Stevenage	24.12.85	Southampton (A)								
				29.03.88	Cambridge Utd	23+1	1	2	2	1			
				23.12.88	Scunthorpe Utd	139+6	6	6+1	11+4	18			3
				19.06.92	West Brom A								
Bernard McNally	5.7	9.11	17.02.63	Shrewsbury	19.02.81	Shrewsbury Town (A	278+4	22	13	1	23	3		
NI:5,WC84				£385,000	27.07.89	West Brom A	78+9	5+1	6	4	7	1	1	
Paul Raven			28.07.70	Salisbury	06.06.88	Doncaster Rovers (A	52	2	5	2	4			
				£100,000	23.03.89	West Brom A	27+3	1		1	1			
				Loan	27.11.91	Doncaster Rovers	7		1					
Gary Robson	5.7	10.12	06.07.65	Durham	05.05.83	West Brom A. (A)	168+28	10+2	8+1	6+4	26		2	3
FLgXI.1														
Craig Shakespeare	5.10	12.5	26.10.63	Birmingham	05.11.81	Walsall (A)	276+8	31	22	18	45	6	6	2
				£300,000	19.06.89	Sheffield Wed	15+2	3		0+1	1			
				£275,000	08.02.90	West Brom A	92+6	4	4	2	10	1	2	1
Winston White	5.8	11.2	26.10.58	Leicester		Leicester City (A)	10+2			2	1			
				Free		Hereford Utd	169+6	6	10		21	1		
via Hong Kong and Chesterfield 0+1 Lg Apps to						Port Vale	0+1							
via Stockport Co.(4 Lg + 1 FAC App) to						Bury	126	6	7	6+1	11			1
via Loan Rochdale 4 Lg Apps. to						Colchester Utd	64+1	4	3	6	8	1		3
					21.10.88	Burnley	93+11	6	10	6+2	14	1	3	3
				£35,000	28.03.91	West Brom A	13+3				1			
FORWARDS														
Kwame Ampadu	5.10	10.10	20.12.70	Bradford	19.11.88	Arsenal (T)								
Ei: u21.3,u17(2),Y(1)				Loan	31.10.90	Plymouth A	6		1	1	1			
28.03.91 Loan W.B.A. 3+4 Lg App, 1 G				£50,000	24.06.91	West Brom A	18+10	2		1	4			1
Simon Garner	5.10	11.4	23.11.59	Boston		Boston Uni								
FMC'87					05.07.78	Blackburn Rovers	455+29	32+2	24+5	17+1	173	11	7	6
				£30,000		West Brom A								
Bob Taylor	5.10	11.9	03.02.67	Horden	27.03.86	Leeds Utd	33+9	5+1	1	4+1	9	3		1
				£175,000	23.03.89	Bristol City	96+10	6+1	9	3	50	2	5	1
				£300,000	31.01.92	West Brom A	19				8			
Paul Williams	5.7	10.0	11.09.69	Leicester	29.11.88	Leicester City (T)								
				08.09.90	Stockport Co	2+5			1+2					
				28.03.91	West Brom A								
Paul A Williams	6.4	14.0	08.09.63	Sheffield		Distillery								
via Leeds United to				18.12.86	Preston N.E	1+1			1+1					
				12.08.87	Newport Co	26	2		2	3			
				06.07.88	Sheffield Utd	6+2			2+1				
					Hartlepool Utd	7+1		1	1				
					Stockport Co	24	2		3	14	1		1
				£250,000		West Brom A	10							
ADDITIONAL CONTRACT PLAYERS														

Carl Heggs (F) 3 Lg App, **Roy Hunter (M)** 2+4 Lg Apps, 1 G, **Steve Lilwall (D)** £60,000 from Kidderminster Harriers, **Marc Sinfield (D)** 6 Lg Apps, 1 G, **Stacy Coldicott (M)**, **Alex Grace (M)**, **Kirk Hammond (F)**, **Matthew Nelson (D)**.

LEADING LEAGUE GOALSCORERS SEASONS 1985-86 – 1991-92

1985-86	**IMRE VARADI**	**9**		1986-87	**GARTH CROOKS**	**11**
1987-88	**ANDY GRAY**	**10**		1988-89	**DON GOODMAN**	**15**
1989-90	**DON GOODMAN**	**21**		1990-91	**GARY BANNISTER**	**13**

1991-92   **GARY ROBSON**   **9**

THE HAWTHORNS West Bromwich B71 4LF

Capacity: 33,781   **Covered Standing:** 10,970   **Seating:** 10,959

Tel: Ground: 021 525 8888   **Ticket Sales:** 021 553 5472   **Clubcall:** 0898 12 11 93

All premium rate calls (0898/0891) cost 36p per minute cheap rate and 48p per minute at all other times. Call costings correct at time of going to press.

GROUNDS
Coopers Hill 1878; Dartmouth Park 1879-81; Bunns Field 1881-82; Four Acres (Darmouth CC) 1882-85; Stoney Lane 1885-1900; The Hawthorns 1900-

ATTENDANCES
Highest: 64,815 v Arsenal, FA Cup 6th Round, 6.3.1937

Lowest: 405 v Derby County, Div 1, 29.11.1890

RECORD RECEIPTS (with Previous Records)
£161,632,50 v Aston Villa, FA Cup 5th Rnd, 17.2.1990
£131,063.95 v Everton, FA Cup, 7.1.1989
£79,494 v Tottenham, League Cup Semi-Final, 3.2.1982

THE HAWTHORNS
First game: v Derby County, 3.9.1900
First floodlit game: v Chelsea, Div 1, 18.9.1957 (1-1)
Internationals: England v N Ireland, 1922
England v Belgium, 1924
England v Wales 1945

Season Tickets:
Stands: from £155 to £175, juv/OAP £100 to £105
Ground: £125, £70 (juveniles/OAP)

Executive Box Season Tickets: £3,250 + VAT (Halfords Lane Stand)
£2,750 + VAT (Rainbow Stand)

Cost of Stand Tickets: £8.50, £7.50, (juv/OAP £4.50)
Terraces: £6, (juv/OAP £3.50)

Match and Ticket Information: Two weeks in advance by post with remittance & SAE

Car Parking: Car parks of Halfords Lane and Middlemore Road, street parking in some areas within 10 minutes walk of ground

Nearest Railway Station: Rolfe St. Smethwick (1.25 miles)

How to get to the ground

From all directions: Use Motorway M5 until Junction 1. Leave motorway and follow signs Birmingham A41 for West Bromwich Albion FC

Value Rating: ★ ★ ★ ★

Programme Editor: Alan Stevenson

Price of 1992-93 Programme: £1
Number of Pages: 36

Supscriptions: (Home only): UK £43.50, Eire & Europe £46.25, Outside Europe: Air £73.75, Surface £51.75. For home & away the cost is doubled.

Local Newspapers: Sandwell Evening Mail, Birmingham Post & Evening Mail, Express and Star Wolverhampton, Sports Argus, Sporting Pink

Local Radio Stations: BRMB Radio, Radio WM, Beacon Radio, Mercia Sound, W.A.B. Radio

Additional publications on club: A Complete Record 1879-1987 by Tony Matthews and Colin Mackenzie, Breedon Books, £15.95.
WBA Who's Who, 1879-1989 by Tony Matthews, £6.95.
Unique Record (1930-31) by Tony Matthews, £1

WEST HAM UNITED

Division 1

Formed: 1900   **Turned Professional:** 1900   **Ltd Co:** 1900

SPONSORED BY: Dagenham Motors   **NICKNAME:** The Hammers

Chairman
T W Brown

Directors
L C Cearns
W F Cearns
C J Warner M.A.
P Storrie (Managing Director)
M W Cearns (Vice-Chairman)

Secretary
Tom Finn (081-472 2740)

PRO
John Helliar

Team Manager
Billy Bonds

Chief Scout
E Baily

Commercial Manager
Brian Blower (081-472 5756)

Club Statistician for the Directory
John Northcutt

IN their most troubled season in history the Hammers were relegated after finishing bottom of the league. A season long struggle on the pitch was not helped by unprecedented scenes at the ground with supporters protesting against the Bond Scheme.

The new season started without any quality signings and on the evidence of the goalless draw with Luton on the opening day it appeared it was going to be a difficult campaign. By the end of September only two league wins had been recorded, although it was encouraging that Mike Small was hitting the target and had scored 7.

In the Rumbelows Cup Bradford City were beaten 5-1 on aggregate. During October and early November fortunes changed as successive wins over Spurs and Arsenal and a Rumbelows Cup win at Sheffield United brought the smiles back to Upton Park. Unfortunately, December saw an alarming slump with defeats at Everton, Aston Villa and Notts County. In the Rumbelows Cup a debatable penalty in the last minute gave Norwich a 2-1 victory. Some light relief, however, came in wins over Cambridge and Brighton in the Zenith Data Systems Cup.

In the new year Hammers struggled in the F.A. Cup but managed to knock out non-league Farnborough and fourth division Wrexham. League form improved with successive victories over Luton and Oldham but there was no joy in the Zenith Cup as Southampton won 2-1. A sad event occured in January when Jack Helliar, the club historian and former programme editor, died. Jack was immensely popular at Upton Park and will be missed by all who knew him.

In the fifth round of the Cup Sunderland came to Upton Park after a draw at Roker. A 3-2 win for the Wearsiders saw them on the way to Wembley. In March the league form hit a new low when West Ham went four games without a goal and slumped to the bottom of the league. The purchase of Clive Allen from Chelsea came too late to make an impact.

The last month of the season showed the inconsistency of the team. Wins were recorded over Norwich, 4-0, and Manchester United, 1-0, with a creditable draw at Leeds, whilst Southampton and Crystal Palace won at Upton Park. The final home game against Nottingham Forest gave Frank McAvennie the chance to say goodbye to the fans. He came on as substitute and responded with a unique hat-trick to the delight of the home faithful.

Congratulations to skipper Julian Dicks on being voted 'Hammer of the Year' and well done to those wonderful fans who gave remarkable support considering the poor team displays.   **John Northcutt**

Back row L–R: Tony Gale, Colin Foster, Trevor Morley, Ludek Miklosko, Alvin Martin, Matthew Rush, Martin Allen. **Middle row:** Michael Small, Tim Breacker, George Parris, Frank McAvennie, Leroy Rosenior, Simon Livett. **Front row:** Kevin Keen, Chris Hughton, Julian Dicks, Ian Bishop, Mitchell Thomas, Steve Potts, Stuart Slater.
Copyright photograph – Steve Bacon – 081-552 8229

WEST HAM UNITED

DIVISION ONE: 22nd   **FA CUP:** 5th RND   **RUMBELOWS CUP:** 4th RND   **ZDS CUP:** Sth S-FINAL

M	DATE		COMP.	VEN	OPPONENTS	RESULT		H/T	LGE POS	GOALSCORERS/GOAL TIMES	ATTEN-DANCE
1	A	17	BL	H	Luton Town	D	0-0	0-0			25,079
2		21	BL	A	Sheffield United	D	1-1	0-0		Small 47	(21,463)
3		24	BL	A	Wimbledon	L	0-2	0-1			(10,081)
4		28	BL	H	Aston Villa	W	3-1	2-0		Small 66, Rosenior 68, Brown 87	23,644
5		31	BL	H	Notts County	L	0-2	0-0	16		20,093
6	S	4	BL	A	Queens Park R.	D	0-0	0-0	13		(16,616)
7		7	BL	H	Chelsea	D	1-1	0-0	17	Small 48	18,875
8		14	BL	A	Norwich City	L	1-2	1-2	18	Small 15	(15,348)
9		17	BL	A	Crystal Palace	W	3-2	0-1	16	Thomas 52, Morley 56, Small 75	(21,363)
10		21	BL	H	Manchester City	L	1-2	0-0	18	Brown 83	25,558
11		24	RC 2/1	A	**Bradford City**	D	1-1	1-1		**Small 12**	(7,034)
12		28	BL	A	Nottingham Forest	D	2-2	2-1	18	Small 16, 43	(25,613)
13	O	5	BL	H	Coventry City	L	0-1	0-0	18		21,817
14		9	RC 2/2	H	**Bradford City**	W	4-0	2-0		**Keen 9, Morley 36, Parris 56, Small 73**	17,232
15		19	BL	A	Oldham Athletic	D	2-2	1-2	18	Small 35, McAvennie 82	(14,365)
16		22	ZDS 2	H	**Cambridge United**	W	2-1	1-0		**Parris 31, McAvennie 60**	7,812
17		26	BL	H	Tottenham Hotspur	W	2-1	2-1	17	Small 12, Thomas 28	23,946
18		29	RC 3	A	**Sheffield United**	W	2-0	1-0		**McAvennie 44, Small 54**	(11,144)
19	N	2	BL	A	Arsenal	W	1-0	0-0	14	Small 76	(33,539)
20		17	BL	H	Liverpool	D	0-0	0-0	15		23,569
21		23	BL	A	Manchester United	L	1-2	0-2	16	McAvennie 76	(47,185)
22		26	ZDS 3	H	**Brighton & H A**	W	2-0	2-0		**McAvennie 9, 24**	8,146
23		30	BL	H	Sheffield Wed.	L	1-2	0-1	17	Breacker 84	24,116
24	D	4	RC 4	A	**Norwich City**	L	1-2	0-0		**Small 73**	(16,325)
25		7	BL	A	Everton	L	0-4	0-3	18		(21,563)
26		21	BL	H	Sheffield United	D	1-1	0-0	18	Dicks 87	19,287
27		26	BL	A	Aston Villa	L	1-3	0-2	19	McAvennie 64	(31,959)
28		28	BL	A	Notts County	L	0-3	0-0	21		(11,163)
29	J	1	BL	H	Leeds United	L	1-3	1-2	21	Dicks 24	21,766
30		4	FAC 3	A	**Farnborough Town**	D	1-1	0-0		**Dicks 66**	(23,449)
31		7	ZDS SSF	A	**Southampton**	L	1-2	1-0		**Bishop 35**	(6,861)
32		11	BL	H	Wimbledon	D	1-1	0-0	21	Morley 89	18,485
33		14	FAC 3R	H	**Farnborough Town**	W	1-0	0-0		**Morley 88**	23,869
34		18	BL	A	Luton Town	W	1-0	0-0	20	Small 69	(11,088)
35		25	FAC 4	H	**Wrexham**	D	2-2	1-0		**Dicks 27, Morley 74**	24,712
36	F	1	BL	H	Oldham Athletic	W	1-0	1-0	20	Thomas 33	19,012
37		4	FAC 4R	A	**Wrexham**	W	1-0	1-0		**Foster 27**	(17,995)
38		15	FAC 5	A	**Sunderland**	D	1-1	0-0		**Small 48**	(25,475)
39		22	BL	A	Sheffield Wed.	L	1-2	1-0	21	Small 14	(26,150)
40		26	FAC 5R	H	**Sunderland**	L	2-3	1-2		**Allen 38, 56**	25,830
41		29	BL	H	Everton	L	0-2	0-1	21		20,976
42	M	3	BL	A	Southampton	L	0-1	0-0	22		(14,548)
43		11	BL	A	Liverpool	L	0-1	0-1	22		(30,821)
44		14	BL	H	Arsenal	L	0-2	0-1	22		22,640
45		21	BL	H	Queens Park R.	D	2-2	1-0	22	Small 28, Breacker 75	20,401
46		28	BL	A	Leeds United	D	0-0	0-0	22		(31,101)
47	A	1	BL	A	Tottenham Hotspur	L	0-3	0-1	22		(31,809)
48		4	BL	A	Chelsea	L	1-2	1-1	22	Allen C 27	(20,684)
49		11	BL	H	Norwich City	W	4-0	2-0	22	Rush 14, 36, Dicks 71, Bishop 79	16,896
50		14	BL	H	Southampton	L	0-1	0-0	22		18,298
51		18	BL	A	Manchester City	L	0-2	0-1	22		(25,601)
52		20	BL	H	Crystal Palace	L	0-2	0-1	22		17,710
53		22	BL	H	Manchester United	W	1-0	0-0	22	Brown 66	24,197
54		25	BL	A	Coventry City	L	0-1	0-0	22		(15,398)
55	M	2	BL	H	Nottingham Forest	W	3-0	0-0	22	McAvennie 3 (60, 81, 85)	20,629

Best Home League Attendance: 25,558 v Manchester City   **Smallest:** 16,896 v Norwich City   **Av Home Att:** 21,285

Goal Scorers: **Compared with 90-91:** -1,280

League (37):   Small 13, McAvennie 6, Thomas 3, Brown 3, Dicks 3, Rush 2, Breacker 2, Morley 2, Allen C, Rosenior, Bishop

R/lows C (8):   Small 4, Parris, McAvennie, Keen, Morley

FA Cup (8):   Dicks 2, Morley 2, Allen 2, Small, Foster

ZDS Cup (5):   McAvennie 3, Bishop, Parris

Miklosko L.	Brown K.	Thomas M.	Breacker T.	Foster C.	Parris G.	Bishop I.	Slater S.	Small M.	Rosenior L.	Allen M.	Morley T.	Keen K.	Rush M.	Parks A.	Hughton C.	Potts S.	Gale A.	Dicks J.	McAvennie F.	Atteveld R.	Allen C.	Martin A.	Martin D.	Clarke S.	Livett S.	Referee	
1	2	3	4	5	6	7*	8	9	10	11	S	14														M Bodenham	1
1	2	3	4	5	6	7	8	9	10*	11*	12	14														I Hendrick	2
1	2	3	4	5	6	7	8*	9	10	11*	12		14													I Wiseman	3
1	2	3	4	5	6	7	8	9	10	11*	S		14													A Gunn	4
	2	3	4	5	6	7	8	9	10*		12	11*	1	14		10										J Deakin	5
	2	3	4	5	6	7	8	9*	14		11*	12	1			10										P Don	6
1	2	3	4	5	6	7	8	9	S	11		S				10										J Carter	7
1	2	3	4	5	6*	7	8	9	14	11*		12				10										T West	8
1	2	4	6	5	3	7	8	9	S	11		S				10										R Milford	9
1	2	3	4	5†	6	7	8	9	14	11*		S				10										K Barratt	10
1	2	4	6	5	3	7	8	9	S	11*						10	12									**R Nixon**	11
1	S	3	2	5	6	7	8	9*	14	11						10	4									J Watson	12
1	5	3*	2		6	7	8	9		12	11*	14				10	4									P Foakes	13
1		3	2	5	6	7	8	9*	S	11	10						4		14							**M James**	14
1		3	2		6	7	8*	9		12	11*	10				5	4		14							P Vanes	15
1			2		6	7		9		11	S	10	S		3	5	4		8							I Hemley	16
1		3	2		6	7	11	9		12	S	10*				5	4		8							D Elleray	17
1		3	2		6	7	11	9		12	S	10				5	4*		8							**G Courtney**	18
1	S	3	2		6	7	11	9		S		10				5	4		8							J Martin	19
1		3	2		6	7	11	9		S	S	10				5	4		8							G Ashby	20
1	S	3	2		6	7	11	9		12		10*				5	4		8							M Peck	21
1		3	2		6	7	11	9		S		10	S			5	4		8							**P Danson**	22
1		3	2		6	7	11	9		12	S	10*				5	4		8							C Wilkes	23
1	S	3	2		6	7	11	9		10		S				5	4		8							**K Morton**	24
1	S	3	2†		6*	7	11	9		10		12				5	4		8							A Wilkie	25
1	2			6	S	7	11	9*		10		14				5	4	3	8							M Pierce	26
1	S		2		6	7	11	9			12	10				5	4	3	8							L Dilkes	27
1	S		2	6		7	11	9		S		10				5	4	3	8							J Worrall	28
1	S	3	2		6	7	11	9*			12	10				5	4	3	8							R Groves	29
1		6	2			7	11	9			12	10				5*	4	3	8		S					**R Groves**	30
1	9	6	2	5		7	11	S			14	10*					4	3	8							**D Axcell**	31
1	9	6*	2	5		7	11	14			12	10*					4	3	8							R Gifford	32
1	9	6	2	5		7	11	S			10	S					4	3	8							**R Groves**	33
1	9	6	2	5		7	11*	14			10	12					4	3	8*							R Bigger	34
1	9	6	2	5			11	14			10	7	S				4	3	8*							**C Trussell**	35
	9	6	2	5			11	14			10*	7	S	1			4	3	8							K Cooper	36
	9	6	2	5			11	10*			12	7		1			4	3	8*			14				**C Trussell**	37
1	8		2	5		S	11	9		10	S	7		1		4	3			6						**R Nixon**	38
14			2	5		7	11	9		10	S	8*		1		4	3			6						T Fitzharris	39
1	S		2	5		7	11	9		10	12	8		1		4	3			6*						**R Nixon**	40
1	8	6	2*	5		7	11*	9		10	12		14	1		4	3									A Smith	41
1	8	6*		5		7	11	9		10	12		14	1		2	4*	3								R Lewis	42
1	2	6*			7	11	9		10	S	8	14			5	4	3									J Rushton	43
1	2			5	14	7	11	9		10*	12	6				4	3	8*								B Hill	44
1	2	12	14	5		7*	11	9		10		6*				4	3	8								D Allison	45
1	2	8	4	5		7	11*	9		10*						6	14	3	12							K Barratt	46
1	2*	8	6*	4		7	11	9				14				10	4	3	12							D Gallagher	47
1	2	9		5		7					12	11*				6	4	3	8			10	S			P Jones	48
1	S	6	2			7	11	9*				14	8			4		3				10	5			P Foakes	49
1	S		2			7	11	9		6	14	8*				4		3				10	5			R Hamer	50
1	S		2			7	11	9*		10	6					4	8	3					5		14	M Peck	51
1	14	6	2*			7	11			9	8					4	S	3					5		S	A Buksh	52
1	10	6				7	11	9		S	8					2	4	3					5		S	J Deakin	53
1	10*	6				7*	11	9		12	8					2	4	3					5	14		P Wright	54
1	S	6*				7	11	9		8						2	4	3	12				5	10		N Midgley	55
36	25	34	33	24	20	41	41	37	5	14	13	20	3	6		34	24	23	16	1	4	7	1			League Appearances	
	2	1	1		1			3	4	5	11	9	7		1		1		4			1	1			Substitute Appearances	
4	1	4	4	2	4	4	4	4	1+1	2	2					3	3+1		2+1					0+1		R/lows Appearances	
3	4	4	6	5		3	6	4+1		2	2+3	5		3		5	2	6	4	2				0+1		FA Cup Appearances	
3	1	2	3	1	2	3	2	2		1	0+1	3			1	2	3	1	3							ZDS Cup Appearances	

WEST HAM UNITED

Club Colours: Claret shirts with sky blue side panels and trim, white shorts and stockings with blue trim.
Change Colours: White shirts, shorts and stockings with claret and blue piping.
Reserves League: Neville Ovenden Football Combination

COMPETITIONS					
Div. 1	Div. 2	ECWC	Watney	Texaco	A/Ital
23-32	19-23	64-65	1973	74-75	1975
58-78	32-58	65-66			
81-89	78-81	75-76			
91-92	89-91	80-81			
	92-				

HONOURS			
Div. 2	FA Cup	Char. Shield	ECWC
57-58	63-64	1964	64-65
80-81	74-75		
	79-80		

MOST APPEARANCES: BILLY BONDS 781+12 (1967-88)				
Year	League	FA Cup	Lge Cup	ECWC
1967-68	37	3	2	
1968-69	42	3	2	
1969-70	42	1	2	
1970-71	37	1	2	
1971-72	42	4	10	
1972-73	39	2	2	
1973-74	40	2	1	
1974-75	31	8	3	
1975-76	17+1		5	9
1976-77	41	2	3	
1977-78	29	3		
1978-79	39	1	1	
1979-80	34	5	9	
1980-81	41	3	8	6
1981-82	29	2	4	
1982-83	34	1	4	
1983-84	27	0+1	2	
1984-85	19+3		4	
1985-86				
1986-87	13+4	3+1	1+2	
1987-88	22	2		
	655+8	46+2	65+2	15
Previous holder: R Moore 643 (1958-74)				

MOST GOALS IN A CAREER		
VIC WATSON 326 (1920-35)		
Season	League	FA Cup
1920-21	2	
1921-22	12	1
1922-23	22	5
1923-24	3	
1924-25	22	1
1925-26	20	
1926-27	34	3
1927-28	16	
1928-29	29	1
1929-30	42	8
1930-31	14	
1931-32	23	2
1932-33	23	4
1933-34	26	3
1934-35	10	
Total	298	28
Previous holder: Sid Puddefoot 72 (1919-33)		

HIGHEST TRANSFER FEE RECEIVED			
Amount	Club	Player	Date
£2,000,000	Everton	Tony Cottee	7/88
£850,000	Celtic	Frank McAvennie	10/87
£400,000	Newcastle Utd	Paul Goddard	10/86
£400,000	Tottenham H.	Paul Allen	6/85

MANAGERS			
Name	Seasons	Best	Worst
Syd King	1902-32	7(1)	7(2)
Charlie Paynter	1932-50	4(2)	20(2)
Ted Fenton	1950-61	6(1)	16(1)
Ron Greenwood	1961-77	6(1)	20(1)
John Lyall	1977-89	3(1)	7(2)
Lou Macari	1989-90		
Billy Bonds	1990-	22(1)	7(2)

HIGHEST TRANSFER FEE PAID			
Amount	Club	Player	Date
£1,250,000	Celtic	Frank McAvennie	3/89
£800,000	Queens Park R.	Paul Goddard	8/79
£600,000	Luton Town	Tim Breacker	10/90
£527,000	Queens Park R.	Phil Parkes	2/79

BARCLAYS BUSINESS CENTRE
Plaistow Business Centre
737 Barking Road
London E13 9PL
Tel: 081-410 9560

BARCLAYBANK MACHINE

LONGEST LEAGUE RUNS	
of undefeated matches:	27 (27.12.1980-10.10.1981)
of undefeated home matches:	27 (30.8.1980-21.11.1981)
without home win:	13 (29.10.1988-15.4.1989)
of league wins:	9 (19.10.1985-14.12.1985)
of league defeats:	9 (28.3.1932-29.8.1932)
of league matches without a win:	17 (31.1.1976-21.8.1976)
of undefeated away matches:	13 (10.1.1981-3.10.1981)
without an away win:	31 (12.12.1931-14.3.1933)
of home wins:	16 (30.8.1980-7.3.1981)
of away wins:	5 (16.12.1922-15.2.1923)
	(26.12.1935-15.3.1936) (5.10.1985-7.12.1985)

PREVIOUS NAME
Thames Ironworks 1895-1900

PREVIOUS LEAGUE
Southern League

BIGGEST VICTORIES
League: 8-0 v Rotherham United, Division 2, 8.3.1958
8-0 v Sunderland, Division 1, 19.10.1968
F.A. Cup: 6-0 v Bury, Round 2, 1919-20
6-0 v Arsenal, Round 3, 1945-46
League Cup: 10-0 v Bury, Round 2, 25.10.1984
Europe: No more than 4 goals

BIGGEST DEFEATS
League: 0-7 v Sheffield Wednesday, Division 1, 28.11.1959
0-7 v Everton, Division 1, 22.10.1927
0-7 v Barnsley, Division 2, 1.9.1919
F.A. Cup: 0-5 v Aston Villa, Round 2, 1912-13
0-5 v Tottenham Hotspur, Round 3, 1925-26
1-6 v Queens Park Rangers, Round 4 replay, 28.1.1978
League Cup: 0-6 v Oldham Athletic, Semi-Final, 14.2.1990
Europe (ECWC): No more than 3 goals

MOST POINTS
3 points a win: 87, Division 2, 1990-91
2 points a win: 66, Division 2, 1980-81

MOST GOALS
101, 1957-58, Division 2.
Dick 21, Keeble 19, Dare 14, Smith 11, Musgrove 9, Bond 8,
Cantwell 4, Malcolm 3, Lewis 3, Newman 2, Grice 2,
Landsowne 2, Allison 2, og 2.

MOST GOALS IN A MATCH
6. Geoff Hurst v Sunderland, 8-0, Division 1, 19.10.1968
6. Vic Watson v Leeds United, 8-2, Division 1, 9.2.1929

MOST GOALS IN A SEASON
Vic Watson 50 (League 42, FAC 8) 1929-30.
4 goals once = 4; 3 goals 3 times = 9; 2 goals 8 times = 16; 1
goal 21 times = 21.
Previous holder: Vic Watson 34, 1926-27

MOST FIRST CLASS MATCHES IN A SEASON
62 (42 League, 4 FA Cup, 10 League Cup, 6 European Cup
Winners Cup) 1965-66

MOST LEAGUE GOALS CONCEDED
107 Division 1, 1931-32

MOST LEAGUE WINS
28, Division 2, 1980-81

MOST LEAGUE DRAWS
18, Division 1, 1968-69

MOST LEAGUE DEFEATS
23, Division 1, 1931-32

OLDEST PLAYER
Billy Bonds 41 years 225 days v Southampton (Div 1),
30.4.1988

YOUNGEST PLAYER
Paul Allen, 17 years 32 days v Burnley, Div. 2, 29.9.1979

MOST CAPPED PLAYER
Bobby Moore (England) 108

BEST PERFORMANCES BY WEST HAM UNITED

League: 1980-81: Matches played 42, Won 28, Drawn 10, Lost 4, Goals for 79. Goals against 29, Points 66. First in Division 2.

Highest: 1985-86: Third in Division 1.

F.A. Cup: 1963-64: 3rd rnd. Charlton Athletic 3-0; 4th rnd. Orient 1-1, 3-0; 5th rnd. Swindon Town 3-1; 6th rnd. Burnley 3-2;
Semi-final Manchester United 3-1; Final Preston North End 3-2.

1974-75: 3rd rnd. Southampton 2-1; 4th rnd. Swindon Town 1-1, 2-1; 5th rnd. Queens Park Rangers 2-1; 6th rnd. Arsenal 2-0;
Semi-final Ipswich Town 0-0, 2-1; Final Fulham 2-0.

1979-80: 3rd rnd. West Bromwich Albion 1-1, 2-1; 4th rnd. Orient 3-2; 5th rnd. Swansea City 2-0; 6th rnd. Aston Villa 1-0; Semi-
final Everton 1-1, 2-1; Final Arsenal 1-0.

League Cup: 1965-66: 2nd rnd. Bristol Rovers 3-3, 3-2; 3rd rnd. Mansfield Town 4-0; 4th rnd. Rotherham United 2-1; 5th rnd.
Grimsby Town 2-2, 1-0; Semi-final Cardiff City 5-2, 5-1; Final West Bromwich Albion 2-1, 1-4.

Europe (ECWC): 1964-65: 1st rnd. La Gantoise 1-0, 1-1; 2nd rnd. Sparta Prague 2-0, 1-2; 3rd rnd. Lausanne 2-1, 4-3; Semi-
final Real Zaragoza 2-1, 1-1; Final Munich 1860 2-0.

DIVISIONAL RECORDS

	Played	Won	Drawn	Lost	For	Against	Points
DIVISION 1	1590	549	388	653	2427	2614	**1618**
DIVISION 2	1184	511	290	383	1877	1581	**1356**
TOTALS	**2774**	**1060**	**678**	**1036**	**4304**	**4195**	**2974**

WEST HAM UNITED

PLAYERS NAME Honours	Ht	Wt	Birthdate	Birthplace Transfers	Contract Date	Clubs	League	L/Cup	FA Cup	Other	Lg	L/C	FAC	Oth
GOALKEEPERS														
Ludek Miklosko						Banik Ostrava								
Czechoslovakia				£300,000	19.02.90	West Ham U	100	8	10	3				
DEFENDERS														
Tim Breaker	6.0	12.6	02.07.65	Bicester	15.05.83	Luton Town (A)	204+6	22+2	21	7	3			
LC'88				£600,000	12.10.90	West Ham U	56+4	4	12	3	3			
Kenny Brown	5.8	11.6	11.07.67	Barking	10.07.85	Norwich City (A)	24+1			3				
				Free	10.08.88	Plymouth A	126	9	6	3	4			
				£175,000	02.08.91	West Ham U	25+2	1	4	1	3			
Julian Dicks	5.7	11.7	08.08.68	Bristol	12.04.86	Birmingham City (A)	83+6	5+1	5	2	1			
E:u21.4					25.03.88	West Ham U	118	18	13	5	18	5		1
Colin Foster	6.4	13.10	16.07.64	Chislehurst	04.02.82	Leyton Orient (A)	173+1	12	19	5	10		5	1
					04.03.87	Nottm. Forest	68+4	8	5	2	5	1		
				£750,000	22.09.89	West Ham U	80+2	5	8	2+1	4		1	
Tony Gale	6.1	12.4	19.11.59	London	05.08.77	Fulham (A)	277	22	16		19	2		
E: u21.1, Y.7				£200,000	01.08.84	West Ham U	241+4	26+2	28	8	4	1	1	
Paul Hilton	6.1	11.6	08.10.59	Oldham	07.07.78	Bury	136+12	8+1	19+1	1	39		5	
				£75,000	02.02.84	West Ham U	47+13	6+1	3+2	2+1	7		1	
George Parris	5.9	12.7	11.09.64	Ilford	09.09.82	West Ham U. (A)	201+22	27+3	21	5+1	11	1	4	1
E: S														
Steve Potts	5.8	10.5	07.05.67	Hartford (USA)	11.05.84	West Ham U. (A)	139+10	18+1	21	8+1	1			
E: Y.11														
Mitchell Thomas	6.0	12.0	02.10.64	Luton	27.08.82	Luton Town	106+1	5	18		1			
E: B.1, u21.3, Y.3				£233,000	07.07.86	Tottenham H	136+21	28+1	12		6	1	1	
				£525,000	07.08.91	West Ham U	34+1	4	4	2	3			
MIDFIELD														
Martin Allen	5.10	11.0	18.08.65	Reading	01.06.83	Q.P.R. (A)	128+8	15+3	9	2	16	1	1	1
E: u21.2, u19, Y				£675,000	24.08.89	West Ham U	81+17	10+1	5	4	12	4	2	
Ian Bishop	5.9	10.12	29.05.65	Liverpool	01.06.83	Everton (A)	0+1							
				Loan	22.03.84	Crewe Alexandra	4							
				£15,000	11.10.84	Carlisle Utd	131+1	8	5	4	14	1		
				£35,000	14.07.88	Bournemouth	44	4	5	1	2			
				£465,000	02.08.89	Manchester City	18+1	4		1	2	1		
				P.E	28.12.89	West Ham U	94+4	7	9+1	3	7		2	1
Chris Harwood	5.11	12.0	19.04.70	Hendon	29.06.88	West Ham U								
Kevin Keen	5.6	10.3	25.03.67	Amersham	08.03.84	West Ham U. (A)	141+32	19+1	13+7	9+1	14	5	1	3
E: Y.10														
Matthew Rush					24.03.90	West Ham U. (T)	5+10	1			2			
FORWARDS														
Clive Allen	5.10	12.3	20.05.61	Stepney	20.09.78	Q.P.R. (A)	43+6	5	1		32	2		
E: 4,u21(3),Y.13,S,F.Lg;Div2'83				£1,250,000	13.06.80	Arsenal								
				£1,250,000	14.08.80	Crystal Palace	25	4			9	2		
				£425,000 +	15.05.81	Q.P.R	83+4	7	8		40	2	7	
				£750,000	16.08.84	Tottenham H	97+8	13+1	12+1	9	60	13	9	3
				£1,000,000	10.05.88	Bordeaux (Fra)								
				£1,100,000	18.08.89	Manchester City	31+22	5+2	4+2	2	16	4	1	
				£250,000	06.12.91	Chelsea	15+1		4+1	3	7		2	
				£275,000	27.03.92	West Ham U	4				2			
Trevor Morley	5.11	12.1	20.03.62	Nottingham		Derby County								
E: SP.6; Sthrn Lge'82; Div.4'87						Corby Town								
				£10,000		Nuneaton Borough			3					
				£20,000	21.06.85	Northampton T	107	10	6	7	39	4	2	
				£175,000	22.01.88	Manchester City	69+3	7	1	2	18	3		
				P.E	28.12.89	West Ham U	69+12	5	9+3	1+1	24	2	6	
Stuart Slater	5.7	10.5	27.03.69	Sudbury	02.04.87	West Ham U. (T)	134+7	16+1	16	5	11	2	3	2
Mike Small						Luton Town	0+4							
E:Y.5						Go Ahead Eagles								
						Poak Salonika								
				£50,000	24.08.90	Brighton & H.A	39	2	3	6	15	1	2	3
				£400,000	16.08.91	West Ham U	37+3	4	4	2	13	4	1	
ADDITIONAL CONTRACT PLAYERS														
(G) Steven Banks					24.03.90	West Ham U. (T)								
(F) Simon Clarke					24.03.90	West Ham U. (T)	0+2							
(D) Kevin Horlock					01.07.91	West Ham U								
(D) Paul Marquis					01.07.91	West Ham U								
(F) Dean Martin	5.8	11.0	31.08.72	London		Fisher Athletic								
				£25,000	03.06.91	West Ham U	1+1							
(D) John D Purdie					31.12.91	West Ham U. (T)								

WEST HAM UNITED

RECORD WIN & LOSS AGAINST EACH CLUB IN CURRENT DIVISION
(Where a score has occured on several occasions the most recent is given)

Club	Rec. Win	Season	Rec. Loss	Season
BARNSLEY	4-0	1955-56	7-0	1919-20
BIRMINGHAM CITY	5-0	1982-83	4-0	1961-62
BRENTFORD	4-1	1952-53 (away)	4-1	1934-35
BRISTOL CITY	5-0	1980-81	3-1	1955-56
BRISTOL ROVERS	6-1	1957-58	3-2	1954-55 (home)
CAMBRIDGE UNITED	5-0	1975-79	2-0	1979-80
CHARLTON ATHLETIC	7-3	1932-33	3-0	1987-88
DERBY COUNTY	3-0	1977-78	6-0	1928-29
GRIMSBY TOWN	5-1	1980-81 (away)	4-0	1930-31
LEICESTER CITY	6-0	1922-23 (away)	5-0	1928-29
LUTON TOWN	4-1	1978-79 (away)	6-1	1951-52
MILLWALL	3-0	1988-89	2-1	1978-79
NEWCASTLE UNITED	8-1	1985-86	4-0	1986-87
NOTTS COUNTY	6-1	1955-56	5-1	1954-55
OXFORD UNITED	3-1	1985-86	2-1	1990-91
PETERBOROUGH UTD				
PORTSMOUTH	6-0	1958-59	3-0	1931-32
SOUTHEND UNITED				
SUNDERLAND	8-0	1968-69	6-0	1976-77
SWINDON TOWN	2-0	1990-91	1-1	1989-90
TRANMERE ROVERS	6-1	1938-39	2-2	1938-39
WATFORD	2-0	1984-85	5-0	1984-85
WOLVERHAMPTON WNDRS	5-0	1964-65	5-0	1959-60

MANAGER: BILLY BONDS

DATE OF BIRTH: 17.09.46   **PLACE OF BIRTH:** Woolwich

DATE OF APPOINTMENT: 23.02.1990

PREVIOUS CLUBS
as Manager:
as Player: Charlton Athletic; West Ham United

HONOURS
as Manager: Second Div Runners-Up 1990-91, Barclays Manager of the Month 3 times
as Player: ECWC Runners-up 1976; FA Cup Winner 1975 & 1980; League Cup Runner-up 1981; Second Div Champions 1981.
International: E: U23 2

Value Rating: ✱ ✱ ✱

Programme Editor: Tony McDonald

Price of 1992-93 Programme: £1.50
Number of Pages: 40
Subscriptions: £63.50 for all 1st team home matches

Local Newspapers: Stratford Express, Ilford Recorder

Local Radio Stations: Essex Radio, LBC

Additional Publications on Club: Who's Who of West Ham 1900-1966. Tony Hogg and Jack Helliar. Paperback £6.50.
West Ham United. An Administrative History. Charles Korr. Paperback £7.95
West Ham: A Complete Record 1900-1987. John Northcutt. Hardback £14.95.

LEADING LEAGUE GOALSCORERS
SEASONS 1979-80 – 1991-92

1979-80	DAVID CROSS	13		1980-81	DAVID CROSS	22
1981-82	DAVID CROSS	16		1982-83	PAUL GODDARD	10
1983-84	TONY COTTEE	15		1984-85	TONY COTTEE	17
1985-86	FRANK McAVENNIE	26		1986-87	TONY COTTEE	24
1987-88	TONY COTTEE	13		1988-89	LEROY ROSENIOR	7
1989-90	JIMMY QUINN	13		1990-91	TREVOR MORLEY	12

1991-92   **MIKE SMALL**   **13**

UPTON PARK Green Street, London E13 9AZ

Capacity: 29,282   **Covered Standing:** 17,886   **Seating:** 11,396

Tel: Ground: 081 472 2740   **Ticket Sales:** 081 472 3322   **Clubcall:** 0898 12 11 65

All premium rate calls (0898/0891) cost 36p per minute cheap rate and 48p per minute at all other times. Call costings correct at time of going to press.

GROUNDS
Memorial Recreation Ground, Canning Town 1900-04;
Upton Park 1904-

ATTENDANCES
Highest: 42,322 v Tottenham Hotspur, Division 1,
17.10.1970
41,546 v Manchester United, Division 1, 29.3.1969

Lowest: 4,500 v Doncaster, Division 2, 24.2.1955

RECORD RECEIPTS (with previous records)
£112,268 v Manchester United, FA Cup 5th Round,
5.3.1986
£98,663 v Crystal Palace, FA Cup 4th Round, 31.1.1984
£71,455 v Aston Villa, FA Cup 5th Round, 8.3.1980
£45,397 v Watford, FA Cup 3rd Round, 7.1.1978
£33,000 v Ararat Erevan, ECWC, 5.11.1975

UPTON PARK
First game: v Millwall, Southern League, 1.9.1904
First floodlit game: v Tottenham Hotspur, 16.4.1953

Season Tickets:
Stands: (Bond holders) £220-£260, juv/OAP £150-£190;
(Standard) £300-£360, juv/OAP £225- £260
Terraces: (Bond holders) £140-£155, juv/OAP £70-£110;
(Standard) £190-£210, juv/OAP £105- £165

Executive Box Season Tickets: Apply to club for details

Cost of Stand Tickets: West Stand (Upper Tier): £18
(category 1); £16 (category 2); £14 (category 3); West
Stand (Lower Tier): £18 (category 1); £16 (category 2);

£12 (category 3); East Stand (Upper Tier): £18, juv/OAP
£12 (category 1); £12, juv/OAP £8 (category 3); Family
Seating Area: £12, juv/OAP £6
Terraces: North and South Banks: adults £8, juv/OAP £5

Match and Ticket Information: Advance bookings
personally by telephone or by post are accepted one
month before each League match

Car Parking: Ample side-street parking available

Nearest Railway Station: Upton Park (District Line Tube)

How to get to the ground

From North and West: Take North Circular (A406) to
A124 (East Ham), then on Barking Road for approx 1.5m
until you approach traffic lights on crossroads. Turn right
into Green Street, ground is on right hand side

From East: Use A13 (S.P. London) then at crossroads
turn right A117. In 0.9m at crossroads turn left A124. In
0.6m turn right into Green Street for West Ham United FC

From South: Use Blackwall Tunnel and A13 to Canning
Town, then follow signs East Ham A124. In 1.7m turn left
into Green Street for West Ham United FC

WIGAN ATHLETIC

Division 2

Formed: 1932   **Turned Professional:** 1932   **Ltd Co:** 1932

SPONSORED BY: Heinz   **NICKNAME:** The Latics

Life Vice-President
J H Farrimond

Chairman
W Kenyon

President
T Hitchen

Directors
J A Bennett   B Jeffrey
J D Fillingham   S Jackson
P Spencer   W Pearce

Chief Executive/Manager
Bryan Hamilton

Secretary
W Kenyon (0942 44433)

Assistant Secretary
Mrs Carol Banks

First Team Coach
David Philpotts

Coaches
David Crompton

Physiotherapist
Alex Cribley

Club Accountant
Mrs Brenda Spencer

Commercial Manager
Bernard Eccles

Groundsman
Dave Pinch

Club Statistician for the Directory
Geoffrey Lea

A League position of fifteenth was the final position in what was a rather difficult and disappointing season for the club.

A now seemingly customary bad start, resulted in only one league victory in thirteen matches. The club were not helped by long term injuries to close season signing Paul Gray and influential midfield skipper Neil Rimmer whose seasons' were finished by the end of September.

During November, a backroom shuffle promoted Dave Philpotts to new team manager and first team coach, with Bryan Hamilton staying on as chief executive in overall charge of the club.

Results at Springfield Park did start to improve, but it was on their travels that the club continued to struggle with heavy defeats at Brentford, Stoke and Bournemouth. The first league away win was finally achieved at the end of January with a 1-0 win at Exeter.

However the club were still in the bottom four, and further away defeats at Leyton Orient and Chester made relegation seem inevitable.

The month of March was the turning point of the season with five victories out of six and Dave Philpotts being rewarded with the manager of the month award. Only two defeats in the final month enabled the club to start the next season in the new Division Two.

The cup competitions brought disappointment as well with immediate exits from the Autoglass Trophy and defeats by first division sides Sheffield United and Notts County in both the Rumbelows Cup and F.A. Cup.

On the playing front, Peter Atherton left to join Coventry City for a club record fee of £350,000, with the only signings for the club being non-contract players and a full quota of loan transfers. Phil Daley was named 'Player of the Year' and 'Players Player of the Year' which was a just reward for his fourteen goals and dogged hard work up front. Phil Jones was named 'Young Player of the Year'.

The close season saw the sale of defender Darren Patterson to Crystal Palace for a fee of £200,000. Hopefully monies from the sale will be used to buy new players, because if the team is not strengthened then they will surely struggle again.

Geoffrey Lea

Back row L-R: John Robertson, Joe Parkinson, Alan Johnson, Tony Pennock, Nigel Adkins, John Doolan, Steve Appleton, Phil Daley. **Middle row:** Dave Crompton, Neil Rimmer, Allen Tankard, Andy Pilling, Gary Powell, Gary Worthington, Phil Jones, Paul Gray, Alex Cribley. **Front row:** Bryan Griffiths, Steve Nugent, Dave Philpotts, Kevin Langley, Brian Hamilton, Chris Sharratt, Andy Roberts.

WIGAN ATHLETIC

DIVISION THREE: 15th   **FA CUP:** 3rd RND   **RUMBELOWS CUP:** 2nd RND   **AUTOGLASS:** Prelim.

M	DATE		COMP.	VEN	OPPONENTS	RESULT	H/T	LGE POS	GOALSCORERS/GOAL TIMES	ATTEN-DANCE
1	A	18	BL	A	Shrewsbury Town	L 0-1	0-0	20		(3,834)
2		20	RC 1/1	H	Burnley	W 3-1	1-1		Patterson 4, Griffiths (pen) 53, Worthington 78	2,826
3		23	BL	H	Chester City	W 2-1	0-1	13	Worthington 65, 88	2,637
4		27	RC 1/2	A	Burnley	W 3-2	0-0		Patterson 46, Rimmer 64, Jones 86	(3,876)
5		31	BL	A	West Bromwich A.	D 1-1	1-1	11	Worthington 14	(12,053)
6	S	3	BL	H	Stockport County	L 1-3	1-0	17	Powell 6	3,567
7		7	BL	A	Peterborough Utd	D 0-0	0-0	20		(4,488)
8		14	BL	H	Hull City	L 0-1	0-1	21		2,445
9		17	BL	H	Huddersfield Town	L 1-3	1-2	22	Powell 40	3,531
10		21	BL	A	Bolton Wanderers	D 1-1	1-0	22	Kelly (og) 11	(6,923)
11		24	RC 2/1	H	Sheffield United	D 2-2	2-1		Worthington 3, Patterson 44	3,647
12		28	BL	H	Darlington	L 1-2	0-1	22	Powell 89	2,034
13	O	5	BL	A	Hartlepool United	L 3-4	1-3	22	Powell 25, Daley 49, 69	(3,047)
14		8	RC 2/2	A	Sheffield United	L 0-1	0-0			(6,608)
15		11	BL	H	Reading	D 1-1	0-0	22	Griffiths 52	1,817
16		19	BL	A	Birmingham City	D 3-3	2-1	23	Jones 5, Daley 40, 63	(9,662)
17		22	AGT Pre	H	Huddersfield Town	L 0-1	0-1			1,214
18		26	BL	H	Exeter City	W 4-1	1-1	21	Johnson 31, Powell 57, Connelly 73, Daley 80	1,761
19	N	1	BL	H	Swansea City	W 1-0	0-0	20	Johnson 63	2,092
20		5	BL	A	Preston North End	L 0-3	0-2	22		(3,657)
21		9	BL	A	Brentford	L 0-4	0-1	23		(6,675)
22		16	FAC 1	A	Scarborough	W 2-0	1-0		Pilling 40, Worthington 84	(1,889)
23		22	BL	H	Bury	W 2-0	1-0	19	Worthington 26, Griffiths 87	2,268
24		30	BL	H	Leyton Orient	D 1-1	1-0	19	Powell 2	2,066
25	D	7	FAC 2	H	Stockport County	W 2-0	1-0		Griffiths 18, Powell 47	4,168
26		14	BL	A	Stoke City	L 0-3	0-2	20		(8,419)
27		26	BL	A	West Bromwich A.	L 0-1	0-0	23		5,068
28		28	BL	H	Shrewsbury Town	D 1-1	1-1	23	Daley 34	2,276
29	J	1	BL	A	Stockport County	D 3-3	2-2	22	Connelly 40, Daley 42, 81	(4,149)
30		5	FAC 3	A	Notts County	L 0-2	0-0			(5,913)
31		8	AGT Pre	H	Scarborough	D 1-1	0-0		Sharrett 74	(636)
32		11	BL	H	Bradford City	W 2-1	2-1	23	Langley 7, Daley 38	2,548
33		18	BL	A	Bournemouth	L 0-3	0-0	23		(4,338)
34		28	BL	A	Fulham	D 1-1	1-0	23	Taylor 18	(2,456)
35	F	8	BL	H	Exeter City	W 1-0	0-0	23	Griffiths 89	(3,036)
36		11	BL	A	Leyton Orient	L 1-3	1-0	23	Taylor 38	(3,142)
37		15	BL	H	Stoke City	W 1-0	1-0	20	Griffiths (pen) 10	5,695
38		18	BL	A	Chester City	L 0-1	0-0	20		(1,065)
39		22	BL	H	Bradford City	D 1-1	0-0	20	Worthington 64	(5,621)
40		28	BL	H	Fulham	L 0-2	0-1	23		2,202
41	M	3	BL	H	Bournemouth	W 2-0	1-0	22	Johnson 6, Worthington (pen) 72	1,790
42		7	BL	A	Torquay United	W 1-0	0-0	20	Daley 79	(2,198)
43		10	BL	H	Preston North End	W 3-0	1-0	18	Worthington 28, 63, Daley 87	3,364
44		14	BL	A	Swansea City	L 0-3	0-0	22		(3,726)
45		20	BL	H	Brentford	W 2-1	1-0	17	Pilling 17, Parkinson 60	2,371
46		28	BL	A	Bury	W 4-1	1-0	18	Worthington (pen) 20, Parkinson 72, Daley 82, Powell 89	(2,618)
47		31	BL	A	Hull City	D 1-1	1-0	18	Worthington 26	(3,385)
48	A	3	BL	H	Peterborough Utd	W 3-0	1-0	15	Johnson 11, Langley 58, Worthington 69	2,485
49		7	BL	H	Torquay United	D 0-0	0-0	16		1,970
50		11	BL	A	Huddersfield Town	L 1-3	0-2	16	Daley 82	(7,058)
51		18	BL	H	Bolton Wanderers	D 1-1	1-0	17	Worthington 17	3,557
52		20	BL	A	Darlington	W 1-0	1-0	16	Worthington 24	(1,223)
53		24	BL	H	Hartlepool United	D 1-1	0-0	14	Daley 77	2,002
54		28	BL	H	Birmingham City	W 3-0	2-0	12	Worthington 22, 73, Pilling 39	5,950
55	M	2	BL	A	Reading	L 2-3	0-2	15	Patterson 9, Parkinson 13	(2,748)

Best Home League Attendance: 5,950 v Birmingham City   **Smallest:** 1,761 v Exeter City   **Av Home Att:** 2,848

Goal Scorers: Compared with 90-91: -35

League (58): Worthington 15 (2 pens), Daley 14, Powell 7, Johnson 4, Griffiths 4 (1 pen), Parkinson 3, Pilling 2, Connelly 2, Langley 2, Taylor 2, Jones, Opponents, Patterson

R/lows C (8): Patterson 3, Worthington 2, Jones, Griffiths (1 pen), Rimmer
FA Cup (4): Pilling, Worthington, Powell, Griffiths
Autoglass (1): Sharrett

Player appearance grid — season 1991-92

Adkins N.	Appleton S.	Parkinson J.	Atherton P.	Patterson D.	Langley K.	Powell G.	Rimmer N.	Daley P.	Worthington G.	Griffiths B.	Jones P.	Gray R.	Johnson A.	Tankard A.	Pilling A.	Carberry J.	Smith J.	Widdrington L. (L)	Smyth J. (N.C.)	Connelly D. (L)	Willimas W. (L)	Sharrat C.	Skipper P. (N.C.)	Collins D. (L)	Taylor C. (L)	Referee	
1	2*	3	4	5	6	7	8	9	10	11*	12	14														J Deacon	1
1	S	2	4	5	6	7	8	9	10*	11	3	12														E Parker	2
1	12	2		5	6*	7	8	9	10	11*	3	14	4													T West	3
1	12*	2		5	6		8	9*	10	11	7	14	4	3												P Harrison	4
1	S			5	6	9	8		10	11*	2		4	3	7		12									S Lodge	5
1	S			5	6	9	8		10	11*	2		4	3	7		12									C Trussell	6
1				5	6*	9	8		10	11*	2	14	4	3	7		12									D Gallagher	7
1				5	6	9	8		10	11*	2	7*	4	3	12			14	2							N Flood	8
1				5		7	8		10		6		4	3	12	11*	14	2								B Nixon	9
1				9	6	7	8		10	11*	2		4	3	S	12	5									J Rushton	10
1				9	6	7	8		10	11	2*		4	3	12	S	5									G Singh	11
1			2		6	7	8*	9	10*	11		4	3	12		5	14									B Hamer	12
1	2			5	6	7		9		11		10*	4	3			12	8	S							J Key	13
1	2			5*	6	7		9		11		10*	4	3			12	8	14							P Jones	14
1	S				6	7		9		11			4	3			12	5	2	8						S Bell	15
1	12				6	7		9		11*	10		4	3			2	8	5*							G Courtney	16
1	5*				6	7		9		11	10		4	3		12	14	2	8*							A Dawson	17
1		2			6	7		9		11	10		4	3	S		12	8	5*							I Cruikshanks	18
1		2			6	7		9	12	11*	10		4	3			14	8	5							B Burns	19
1		2		5	6	7*		9	11*		10		4	3		12	14	8								A Smith	20
1		2			10	6	7		9	12	11*		4	3			14	8*	5							L Shapter	21
1		2		5	6	7		9*		10	11		4	3	12*		14	8								D Phillips	22
1		2		5	6	7			10	11	4		3	9*			12	8	S							I Hendrick	23
1		2		5	6	7			10	11	4	12	3	9*			S	8								J Kirby	24
1		2		5	6	7	12	10*	11	4			14	3	9			8*								A Bennett	25
1		2		5	6	7*	12	10*	11	4			14	3	9			8								M Reed	26
1		2		5	6	12		9	10*	11*	4		14	3	7			8								R Hary	27
1		2		5	6	12*		9	10	11	7		4	3				8				14				T West	28
1		2		5	6	S		9	10	11	7		4	3	S			8								T Holbrook	29
1		2		5	6	12		9*	10	11	7		4	3	S			8								R Pawley	30
1		2		5	6			9	10*	11	7		4	3	S			8				12				M Peck	31
1		2		5	6	10*		9		11	7*		4	3	12							14	8			G Ashby	32
1		2		5	6	10*		9	14	11*	7		4	3	12								8			D Axcell	33
1	12	2		5	6			9	14	11	7		4	3									8*		10*	P Durkin	34
1		2		5	6			9	12	11	7		4	3							S		8		10*	J Rushton	35
1		2		5	6			9	12	11	7		4	3							S		8		10*	A Gunn	36
1		2		5*	6			9	14	11*	7		4	3							12		8		10	C Wilkes	37
1	S	2			6			9	11		7		4	3	12						5		8*		10	R Poulain	38
1	S	2			6			9	11		7		4	3							5	S	8		10	R Bigger	39
1		2			14	6		9	11*		7		4	3							5	12	8		10*	S Bell	40
1		2		11	6*	12		9	10		7		4	3	8*						5	14				K Redfearn	41
1		2		11	6	12		9	10*		7		4	3	8						5	S				D Frampton	42
1		2		11	6	12		9	10		7		4	3	8*						5	S				G Courtney	43
1		2		11	6	12		9	10*		7		4	3	8	14					5*					P Vanes	44
1	5	2		11	6	12		9	10		7		4	3	8*						5					J Key	45
1	5*	2		11	6*	14		9	10		7		4	3	8						12					S Lodge	46
1	14	2		11	6	12		9	10		7*		4	3	8*						5					I Cruikshanks	47
1	14	2		11	6			9	10	12	7		4	3	8*						5					B Coddington	48
1	S	2		11	6			9	10	S	7		4	3	8						5					J Lloyd	49
1		2		11	6	12		9	10*		7		4	3	8						5					P Jones	50
1		2		11	6	12		9	10*	S	7		4	3	8						5					K Barratt	51
1		2		11	6			9	10		7		4	3	8						5					B Burns	52
1		2		11	6	8*		9	10	14	7*		4	3	12						5					K Cooper	53
1		2		11	6	S		9	10	S			4	3	8						5					K Hackett	54
1		2		11	6	14		9	10		5		4	3	8*						12					A Buksh	55
46	4	36	1	39	45	22	9	37	34	26	40	2	41	44	21	1		5	2	12	4	15		9	7	**League Appearances**	
	5			1			7			1	7	2	1	3	3			6	4	6	1	6		3	4	**Substitute Appearances**	
4	1+1	2	1	4	4	3	3	3	3	4	3	1+2	3	3	0+1		0+1	2		0+1						**R/lows Appearances**	
3		3		3	3	2+1		2+1	3	3	2		2+1	3	1			3								**FA Cup Appearances**	
2	1	1		2	1		2	1		2	2		0+1	1			2			0+1		1				**Autoglass Appearances**	

Also Played: Posn.(Game): Nugent 9*(9)10*(15), Edwardson 14(16), Doolan S(54,55*), Robertson S(50)

Players on Loan: T Widdrington (Southampton), D Connelly (Barnsley), J Williams (Bournemouth), D Collins (Liverpool), C Taylor (Wolves)

WIGAN ATHLETIC

Club Colours: All royal blue with white and red trim
Change Colours: All red with white and blue trim
Reserves League: Pontins Central League Div 2

Previous League: Northern Premier
Previous Managers: Charlie Spencer 1932-37 Jimmy Milne 1946-47 Bob Pryde 1949-52 Ted Goodier 1952-54 Walter Crook 1954-55 Ron Suart 1955-56 Billy Cooke 1956 Sam Barkas 1957 Trevor Hitchen 1957-58 Malcom Barrass 1958-59 Jimmy Shirley 1959 Pat Murphy 1959-60 Allenby Chilton 1960 Johnny Ball 1961-63 Allan Brown 1963-66 Alf Craig 1966-67 Harry Leyland 1967-68 Alan Saunders 1968 Ian McNeill 1968-70 Gordon Milne 1970-72 Les Rigby 1972-74 Brian Tiler 1974-76 Ian McNeill 1976-81 Larry Lloyd 1981-83 Harry McNally 1983-85 Bryan Hamilton 1985-86 Ray Mathias 1986-89 Bryan Hamilton 1989-91
Honours: Freight Rover Trophy 1985
League Career: Elected to Div 4 1978   Promoted to Div 3 1982

CLUB RECORDS

Most Appearances for Club: Colin Methven (1979-86): League 295 + 1 + FA Cup 23 + League Cup 21 + Other Competitions 14 **Total 353 + 1 sub**
Most Capped Player: None
Record Goalscorer in a Match: Paul Jewell 4 v Aldershot, Div 3, 1.3.1988
Record League Goalscorer in a Season: Warren Aspinal 21, Div 3, 1985-86   **In All Competitions:** Warren Aspinal 27 (League 21 + Cup Competitions 6)
Record League Goalscorer in a Career: Peter Houghton 62, 1978-83   **In All Competitions:** Peter Houghton 68 (League 62 + FA Cup 3 + League Cup 3)
Record Transfer Fee Received: £350,000 from Coventry City for Peter Atherton, August 1991
Record Transfer Fee Paid: £65,000 to Everton for Eamonn O'Keefe, January 1982
Best Performances: League: 4th Div 3 1985-86 & 1986-87   **FA Cup:** 6th Round 1986-87   **League Cup:** 4th Round 1981-82
Most League Points: (3pts a win) 91, Div 4, 1981-82   (2pts a win) 55, Div 4, 1978-79, 1979-80
Most League Goals: 83, Div 3, 1985-86
Record League Victory and Most Goals Scored in a League Match: 7-2 v Scunthorpe Utd, (a), Div 4, 12.3.1982 5-0 v Peterborough Utd, (h), Div 4, 19.1.1982 5-0 v Swansea City, (h), Div 3, 18.1.1986 6-1 v Swansea City (a),Div 3, 6.4.1991
Most Goals Scored in a Cup Tie: 6-0 v Rochdale, Freight Rover Trophy (Northern Section), 28.1.1986
Record League Defeat: 0-5 v Bristol Rovers, Div 3, 26.2.1983 1-6 v Bristol Rovers, Div 3, 3.3.1990
Record Cup Defeat: 0-5 v Chelsea (h), FA Cup Round 3 replay, 26.1.1985
Oldest Player in a League Match: Roy Tunks, 36 years 276 days v Blackpool, Div 3, 24.10.1987
Youngest Player in a League Match: Steve Nugent, 16 years 132 days v Leyton Orient, Division 3, 16.9.1989

LONGEST LEAGUE RUNS

of undefeated matches: 21 (1981-82)	**of league matches without a win:** 14 (1989)
of undefeated home matches: 25 (1985-86)	**of undefeated away matches:** 11 (1986)
without home win: 6 (1988, 1989)	**without an away win:** 15 (1988)
of league wins: 6 (1986)	**of home wins:** 8 (1978-79)
of league defeats: 5 (1982, 1983, 1988)	**of away wins:** 4 (1987, 1988)

WIGAN ATHLETIC

PLAYERS NAME Honours	Ht	Wt	Birthdate	Birthplace Transfers	Contract Date	Clubs	League	L/Cup	FA Cup	Other	Lg	L/C	FAC	Oth
GOALKEEPERS														
Nigel Adkins	5.11	12.7	11.03.65	Birkenhead	10.03.83	Tranmere Rovers (A)	86	4	2	6				
				£3,000	01.08.86	Wigan Ath	117	11	7	9				
Anthony Pennock	5.11	10.9	10.04.71	Swansea	31.12.90	Stockport Co								
				Loan	28.12.90	Wigan Ath	2		2					
					05.06.91	Wigan Ath								
DEFENDERS														
Stephen Appleton					20.09.90	Wigan Ath	7+12	2+1		1				
Alan Johnson	6.0		19.02.71	Ince	01.04.89	Wigan Ath. (T)	111+14	3+2	7+2	6+3	11		1	2
Allen Tankard	5.10	11.7	21.05.69	Fleet	27.05.87	Southampton (A)	5			2				
				Free	04.07.88	Wigan Ath	166+2	11	10	13	3			
MIDFIELD														
Paul Crompton	5.9	10.7		Wigan		Wigan Ath. (A)	1	0+1		1				
Phillip Jones	5.8	10.9	01.12.69	Liverpool	10.06.88	Everton	0+1			1				
				Loan	22.03.90	Blackpool	6							
				Loan	31.01.91	Wigan Ath								
				Free	06.03.91	Wigan Ath	59+2	3	2	3	2	1		
Kevin Langley	6.1	11.0	24.05.64	St Helens	25.05.82	Wigan Ath	156+4	11	14	13	6	1	1	
AMC'85,FRT,CS'86,Div1'87				£100,000	11.07.86	Everton	16	4		2+1	2	1		
				£150,000	30.06.87	Manchester City	9							
				Loan	28.01.88	Chester City	9							
				£100,000	25.03.88	Birmingham City	74+2	4	5	3	2			
				£32,500	26.09.90	Wigan Ath	83+1	4	7	7	4			1
Joseph Parkinson	5.8		11.06.71	Eccles	01.04.89	Wigan Ath. (T)	102+4	7	9	8	6	1		
Andy Pilling	5.10	11.4	30.06.69	Wigan	25.07.85	Preston N.E	1							
				Free	27.07.87	Wigan Ath	104+21	3+2	5+1	9+3	16		1	
Neil Rimmer	5.6	10.3	13.11.67	Liverpool	14.04.84	Everton (A)	0+1							
E: Y.1					13.08.85	Ipswich Town	19+3	3		1+1	3			
					04.07.88	Wigan Ath	105+1	11	7	9	6	1	2	1
FORWARDS														
Phillip Daley					12.10.89	Wigan Ath	110+2	5	6+1	10	30			3
Robert P Gray	5.8	12.3	28.01.70	Portsmouth	01.07.88	Luton Town (A)	2+5			0+2	1			1
				Free	27.06.91	Wigan Ath	2+3	1+2	8+3					
Bryan Griffiths	5.5		26.01.65	Prescot		St Helens								
					02.11.88	Wigan Ath	133+12	8+2	8+2	13+1	31	2	4	4
Gary Worthington	5.10	10.5	10.11.66	Cleethorpes	21.11.84	Manchester Utd. (A)								
E:Y.1					30.07.86	Huddersfield Town								
				Free	04.08.87	Darlington	31+9	0+1	1+1	3+2	15			
				£12,000	20.06.89	Wrexham	68+4	6	2	6	18	2		2
				P.E.	22.03.91	Wigan Ath	44+9	3	3	1	20	2	1	
ADDITIONAL CONTRACT PLAYERS														
(M) John Doolan	5.9	10.10	10.11.68	Liverpool	26.04.91	Wigan Ath								
Paul Kirwan					23.07.92	Wigan Ath. (T)								
(F) Stephen Nugent	5.9	11.10	07.05.73	Orrell	14.09.91	Wigan Ath. (T)	2+2	0+1						
(M) Andrew T Roberts					20.07.92	Wigan Ath. (T)								
John N Robertson					06.07.92	Wigan Ath. (T)								
(F) Chris M Sharratt					18.12.91	Wigan Ath	0+4			0+1				1
John Whitney					13.09.89	Wigan Ath								

LEADING LEAGUE GOALSCORERS SEASONS 1985-86 – 1991-92

1985-86	WARREN ASPINALL	21	1986-87	DAVID LOWE	16
				BOBBY CAMPBELL	16
1987-88	PAUL JEWELL	12	1988-89	BRYAN GRIFFITHS	8
1989-90	BRYAN GRIFFITHS	7	1990-91	BRYAN GRIFFITHS	12
1991-92	GARY WORTHINGTON	15			

SPRINGFIELD PARK Wigan

Capacity: 9,578　　　**Covered Standing:** 3,000　　　**Seating:** 1,000

Tel: Ground: 0942 44433　　　**Ticket Sales:** As ground number　　　**Soccerline:** 0839 00 77 11

All premium rate calls (0898/0891) cost 36p per minute cheap rate and 48p per minute at all other times. Call costings correct at time of going to press.

ATTENDANCES
Highest: 27,500 v Hereford United, 2.12.1953

Lowest: 1,200 v Rochdale, Leyland Daf Cup, 22.1.1991

Record Receipts: £45,770 v Leeds United, FA Cup Round 6, 15.3.1987

Season Tickets:
Stands: £138, juv/OAP £85, under 12 £30
Ground: £115, juv/OAP £66

Executive Box Season Tickets: Five boxes accommodating 8 persons in each

Cost of Stand Tickets: Stand Members: £7, juv/OAP £5, under 12s £150
Terraces: £5.50, juv/OAP £3

Match and Ticket Information: Stand tickets bookable 14 days in advance.

Car Parking: On ground and nearby

Nearest Railway Station: Wigan Wallgate or Wigan (0942 42231)

How to get to the ground

From North: Use Motorway M6 until junction 27. Leave motorway and follow signs Wigan A5029. In 0.3m turn right B5206. In 1.1m turn left B5375. In 4.6m turn left into Springfield Road for Wigan Athletic FC

From East: Use A557 S.P. Wigan into town centre then turn left into Market Street and at end turn left into Parsons Walk B5375. In 0.7m turn right into Springfield Road for Wigan Athletic FC

From South: Use Motorway M6 until junction 25. Leave motorway and follow signs into Wigan A49. Turn left into Market Street and at end turn left into Parsons Walk B5375. In 0.7m turn right in Springfield Road for Wigan Athletic FC

Value Rating: ★ ★ ★

Programme Editor: B Eccles/S McIlwham

Price of 1992-93 Programme: £1
Number of Pages: 32
Subscriptions: £27 inc. P&P

Local Newspapers: Wigan Observer, Wigan Evening Post

Local Radio Stations: Radio Piccadilly, Radio Manchester, Red Rose Radio

WIMBLEDON

Premier

Formed: 1889 **Turned Professional:** 1964 **Ltd Co:** 1964

SPONSORED BY: **NICKNAME:** The Dons

Chairman
S G Reed

Deputy Chairman
J H Lelliott

Directors
P E Cork
PR Lloyd Cooper
S G N Hammam (Managing Director)
N Hammam

Chief Executive
David Barnard

Secretary
Steve Rooke (081-771 2233)

Team Manager
Joe Kinnear

Youth Team Manager
Terry Burton

Physiotherapist
Steve Allen

Commercial Manager
Reg Davis

Club Statistician for the Directory
Simon Case

THE season started in a reasonable way results wise for Wimbledon. Three wins in their opening six matches got the 'Dons' off to a good start. Captain John Fashanu and new signing Robbie Earle getting seven goals between them, including three a piece in the first three games. The season though not starting so well from a disciplinary angle with Phelan, Ryan and Fashanu all receiving their marching orders in games early on in the campaign. New manager, Peter Withe, brought in to replace Blackburn bound Ray Harford, tried to inject a new style in the 'Dons' play, but a slump in form, morale and once again early exits in all three cups, including a 1-0 replay loss in the F.A. Cup at home to Bristol City, saw Withe dismissed by January.

Joe Kinnear a long serving Wimbledon stalwart was given the managers role on caretaker terms. He reinstated the old Wimbledon traditional style and crazy gang spirit, sadly lacking during Withes reign, with great effect. Kinnear, with the help of consistent form from the likes of Segers, Scales, Earle and Fashanu was able to keep the 'Dons' unbeaten in seven matches, until a 5-1 crushing by Leeds, their heaviest defeat of the season, stopped their run. This form however lifted the 'Dons' into a comfortable high mid-table position, securing their Premier League status for next season.

One of the highlights, results wise, was a 3-2 away win at Liverpool, a controversial John Fashanu penalty gave Wimbledon the points. An average run of results until the season's end saw Wimbledon finish comfortably in 13th place.

On performances throughout the season, Robbie Earle had an excellent first season in the top flight scoring 15 goals in all competitions and earning an England-squad call-up. John Fashanu once again had a productive season with 19 goals (inc 17 in the league), while Terry Phelan and young defender Scott Fitzgerald (who was a regular in the side) won places in the Eire senior and 'B' team respectively and were consistent performances throughout the year. On down points Alan Cork was eventually allowed to leave the club on a free to Sheffield United after a transfer wrangle with Joe Kinnear which left a bitter taste in the mouth. Also the ground sharing with Crystal Palace didn't work out, with Wimbledon once again managing to attract crowds of only around 4,000. Players set to leave the club in the summer look to include the unsettled Terry Gibson and Detzi Kruszynski along with Northern Ireland international Lawrie Sanchez. **Simon Case**

Back row L-R: Joe Dillon (Kit Man), Neal Ardley, Steve Cotterill, Scott Fitzgerald, Paul Miller, Chris Perry, Neil Sullivan, Stewart Castledine, Dean Blackwell, Aidan Newhouse, Brian McAllister, Warren Barton, Ron Suart (Chief Scout). **Middle row:** Syd Neal (Kit Manager), Roger Joseph, John Scales, Robbie Earle, Lawrie Sanchez, Steve Athrobus, Hans Segers, John Fashanu, Alan Cork, Carlton Fairweather, Jamie McCarthy, Terry Phelan, Steve Allen (Physio). **Front row:** Don Howe (Coach), Andy Clarke, Gerald Dobbs, Paul McGee, Terry Gibson, Ray Harford (Manager), Gary Elkins, Vaughan Ryan, Justin Skinner, Mickey Bennett, Joe Kinnear (Res. Team Manager)

WIMBLEDON

DIVISION ONE: 13th   **FA CUP:** 3rd RND   **RUMBELOWS CUP:** 2nd RND   **ZDS CUP:** 2nd RND

M	DATE		COMP.	VEN	OPPONENTS	RESULT		H/T	LGE POS	GOALSCORERS/GOAL TIMES	ATTEN-DANCE
1	A	17	BL	A	Chelsea	D	2-2	1-1		Fashanu 23, Earle 56	(22,574)
2		24	BL	H	West Ham United	W	2-0	1-0		Earle 31, Fashanu 70	10,081
3		27	BL	A	Crystal Palace	L	2-3	1-2		Fashanu 10, Earle 87	(16,340)
4		31	BL	A	Coventry City	W	1-0	1-0		Cork 31	(9,469)
5	S	3	BL	H	Manchester United	L	1-2	0-2		Fashanu 82	13,824
6		7	BL	H	Luton Town	W	3-0	1-0	7	Clarke 25, Ryan 62, 75	3,231
7		14	BL	A	Nottingham Forest	L	2-4	1-2		McGee 2, Fashanu (pen) 75	(19,707)
8		18	BL	A	Southampton	L	0-1	0-0			(11,280)
9		21	BL	H	Tottenham Hotspur	L	3-5	1-3	16	Fashanu 5, Cork 60, Bennett 77	11,999
10		24	RC 2/1	H	Peterborough Utd	L	1-2	1-2		McGee 24	2,081
11		28	BL	A	Sheffield United	D	0-0	0-0			(16,062)
12	O	2	BL	H	Sheffield Wed.	W	2-1	0-0		Blackwell 50, Newhouse 70	3,121
13		5	BL	H	Norwich City	W	3-1	1-0	7	Fitzgerald 3, Fashanu 73, Clarke 75	3,531
14		8	RC 2/2	A	Peterborough Utd	D	2-2	0-1		Clarke 57, Fashanu (pen) 71	(5,939)
15		19	BL	H	Queens Park R.	L	0-1	0-0	11		4,630
16		23	ZDS 2	A	Brighton & H A	L	2-3	1-2		Scales 26, Earle 35	(2,796)
17		26	BL	A	Aston Villa	L	1-2	0-2	12	Fashanu 78	(16,928)
18	N	2	BL	H	Leeds United	D	0-0	0-0	13		7,025
19		16	BL	A	Everton	L	0-2	0-1	15		(18,762)
20		23	BL	H	Liverpool	D	0-0	0-0			13,373
21		30	BL	A	Manchester City	D	0-0	0-0			(22,429)
22	D	7	BL	H	Oldham Athletic	W	2-1	1-0	14	Earle 43, 60	4,011
23		21	BL	A	Sheffield Wed.	L	0-2	0-0			(20,574)
24		26	BL	H	Crystal Palace	D	1-1	0-0		Barton 67	15,009
25		28	BL	H	Coventry City	D	1-1	0-1	17	Earle 50	3,270
26	J	1	BL	A	Arsenal	D	1-1	1-0	17	Miller 19	(26,839)
27		4	FAC 3	A	Bristol City	D	1-1	1-0		Fashanu 38	(12,679)
28		11	BL	A	West Ham United	D	1-1	0-0	17	Sanchez 52	(18,485)
29		14	FAC 3R	H	Bristol City	L	0-1	0-1			3,747
30		18	BL	H	Chelsea	L	1-2	0-1	17	Earle 76	8,467
31	F	1	BL	A	Queens Park R.	D	1-1	0-1	18	Fashanu (pen) 48	(9,149)
32		8	BL	H	Aston Villa	W	2-0	1-0	17	Fashanu 24, Phelan 87	5,534
33		22	BL	H	Manchester City	W	2-1	2-0	16	Fashanu 2, Earle 41	5,802
34		25	BL	A	Notts County	D	1-1	1-0		Fashanu (pen) 74	(6,198)
35		29	BL	A	Oldham Athletic	W	1-0	1-0	12	McGee 35	(12,166)
36	M	7	BL	H	Notts County	W	2-0	1-0	11	Fashanu 40, Earle 80	4,196
37		10	BL	H	Everton	D	0-0	0-0			3,569
38		14	BL	A	Leeds United	L	1-5	0-3	12	Miller 51	(26,760)
39		21	BL	A	Manchester United	D	0-0	0-0			(45,428)
40		28	BL	H	Arsenal	L	1-3	0-2	16	Earle 60	11,299
41	A	2	BL	H	Nottingham Forest	W	3-0	2-0		Earle 30, Fashanu 35, 71	3,542
42		4	BL	A	Luton Town	L	1-2	1-1		Fashanu 6	(7,754)
43		8	BL	A	Liverpool	W	3-2	1-2	11	Sanchez 35, Clarke 65, Fashanu (pen) 72	(26,134)
44		18	BL	A	Tottenham Hotspur	L	2-3	1-2	14	Sanchez 1, Earle 83	(23,934)
45		20	BL	H	Southampton	L	0-1	0-1	17		4,025
46		24	BL	A	Norwich City	D	1-1	1-0	17	Elkins 52	(11,061)
47	M	2	BL	H	Sheffield United	W	3-0	3-0	13	Clarke 18, Earle 21, 36	8,768

Best Home League Attendance: 15,009 v Crystal Palace   **Smallest:** 3,121 v Sheffield Wednesday   **Av Home Att:** 7,062

Goal Scorers: **Compared with 90-91:** -368

League (53): Fashanu 17 (4 pens), Earle 14, Clarke 4, Sanchez 3, Cork 2, McGee 2, Miller 2, Ryan 2, Barton, Blackwell, Fitzgerald Phelan, Elkins, Bennett, Newhouse

R/lows C (3): Fashanu (1 pen), Clarke, McGee

FA Cup (1): Fashanu

ZDS Cup (2): Scales, Earle

1991-92

Segers N.	Joseph R.	Phelan T.	Barton W.	Scales J.	Fitzgerald S.	Clarke A.	Earle R.	Fashanu J.	Ryan V.	Fairweather C.	Cork A.	Elkins G.	Newhouse A.	Ardley N.	McGee P.	Gibson T.	Kruszynski Z.	Bennet M.	Blackwell D.	Anthrobus S.	Dobbs G.	Miller P.	Sanchez L.	McAllister B.	Hayes M.	Referee	No.
1	2	3	4	5	6*	7	8	9	10	11	12	S														T Ward	1
1	2	3	4	5	6	7*	8	9†	10	11*	12	14														R Wiseman	2
1	2	3†	4	5	6•	12	8	9*	10†	11	7	14														D Elleray	3
1	2	3	4*	5	6	12	8	9•	10	11	7		14													R Dilkes	4
1	2	3	4	5	6•	12		9	10	11	8*	7	14													M James	5
1	2	3	4	5	6	7			10	11*	9•	8	14		12											A Bennett	6
1	2		4	5	6	14	8	9			12	3			11	7*	10•									T Lunt	7
1	2		4	5	6	7	8	9	10		12	3	14		11•											M Bodenham	8
1	2	3	4	5	6*	14	8	9	10		12				11			7•								P Vanes	9
1	2	3	4	5	6*	14	8	9	10		12				11•			7								P Foakes	10
1	2	3	4•	5	6	12	8	9	10	11								7*	14							K Breen	11
1	2	3	4	5	6	12	8		10•	11			9					7*	14							I Borrett	12
1	2	3	4	5	6	12	8	9		11			10•					7*	14							R Groves	13
1	2	3	4•	5	6	11	8	9			14	7*						12	10							K Morton	14
1	2*	3	4	10	6	11	8	9			12	S						7	5							J Worrall	15
1		3	4	10	6		8	9	2		12	5			11•	7*		14								J Moules	16
1		3	4	10			8	9	6		12	5		2	11	7*	S									R Nixon	17
1		3	4	5	6	S	8	9			S	2		7	10					11•						A Gunn	18
1	14	3	4	5	6	12	8	9				2		7•	10					11*						R Shepherd	19
1	2	3	4	5	6	12	8				9*	S		7	10					11						R Pawley	20
1	2	3	4	5	6	S	8	9				14		7•	10					11						K Lupton	21
1	2	3	4	5	6		8	9			S		7		10		S			11						G Ashby	22
1	2	3	4	5	6		8	9			S		7	14						11•		10				K Barratt	23
1	2	3	4	5	6		8	9			S		7	14						11			10•			P Don	24
1	2	3	4	5	6		8	9			S		7	14						11			10•			B Hill	25
1	2*	3	4	5	6	14	8	9			12		7•							11			10			D Axcell	26
1		3	4	5	6	S	8	9			7	2								11			10	S		K Cooper	27
1		3	4	5	6	12	8	9			S	7*		2						11			10			R Gifford	28
1		3	4	5	6	12	8	9			S	7		2						11*			10			K Cooper	29
1			4	5	6	11	8	9	2		S	S										7*	10	3		C Wilkes	30
1		3	4	5	S	12	8	9	6			2										7*	10	11		D Elleray	31
1		3	4	5		14	8	9	12			2			11•							7	10*			R Bigger	32
1		3	4	5	6	12	8	9	10			2			11							7		6		G Courtney	33
1	2*	3	4	5	6	14	8	9	S						10					11		7		6*		S Lodge	34
1		3	4	5	6	14	8	9•	12		2				11*							7	10			J Lloyd	35
1		3	4	5	6	14	8	9	S		2•				11							7	10		14	M Bodenham	36
1		3	4	5	6	2	8	9	S						11•							7	10		2	D Gallagher	37
1		3	4*	5	6	12	8	9•				14			11							7	10			K Norton	38
1		3	4	5	6	12	8	9			S				11							7	10			M Peck	39
1		3	4	5	6	11	8	9	12		9*			2*								7	10		S	R Lewis	40
1	3•		4	5	6	12	8	9	2						11*							7	10	14		M Bailey	41
1		3	4	5	6	12	8	9	2						11							7	10*	S		B Hill	42
1		3	4	5	12	2	8	9	S						11							7	10	6*		J Key	43
1		3	4	5	12	2*	8	9							11•					14		7	10			T Fitzharris	44
1	11	3	4	5		2	8	9				14								S	7*		10	6		J Rushton	45
1	2		4	5•	10	11	8	9			3										7	S	6			I Hemley	46
1	2		4		5	11*	8	9			3										12	7	10•	6		K Redfearn	47
41	24	37	42	41	34	13	40	38	16	6	12	15	5	7	15	7	1	5	1	10	2	22	16	9	1	League Appearances	
	1				2	21		5			7	3	7	1	1					3		2		1	1	Substitute Appearances	
2	2	2	2	2	2	1+1	2	1			0+2	1			1					1+1	1					R/lows Appearances	
	2	2	2	2	2		2	2							2			2				2				FA Cup Appearances	
1	1	1	1	1	1	1	1			0+1	1				1		1									ZDS Cup Appearances	

Also Played: Posn.(Game): Sullivan 1(45), Castledine 14(46,47)

Players on Loan: M Hayes (Celtic)

† = Sent Off

WIMBLEDON

Club Colours: Royal blue with yellow trim
Change Colours: White with Royal blue trim
Reserves League:

COMPETITIONS			
Div. 1	Div. 2	Div. 3	Div. 4
86-	84-86	79-80 81-82 83-84	77-79 80-81 82-83

HONOURS	
Division 4	FA Cup
1982-83	1988

MOST APPEARANCES: ALAN CORK 414+96 (1977-92)				
Year	League	FA Cup	Lge Cup	Others
1977-78	17			
1978-79	45	5	3	
1979-80	41+1	5	5	
1980-81	41	5	4	
1981-82	6		2	
1982-83	7			
1983-84	41+1	2	5	1
1984-85	26+2	5	1	
1985-86	36+2	1	3	
1986-87	22+8	0+3	1	
1987-88	28+6	5+1	2+1	0+1
1988-89	9+16	1+1	2+2	0+1
1989-90	12+19	0+1	0+1	1+1
1990-91	9+16	1+1	1+1	1+0
1991-92	12+7		0+2	0+1
	352+78	30+7	29+7	3+4
Previous holder: Ian Cooke, 750 as a non-league club				

MOST GOALS IN A CAREER			
ALAN CORK 167 (1977-92)			
Season	League	FA Cup	League Cup
1977-78	4		
1978-79	22	2	1
1979-80	12		1
1980-81	23	2	1
1981-82			1
1982-83	5		
1983-84	29	2	2
1984-85	11		
1985-86	11		4
1986-87	5		2
1987-88	9	1	2
1988-89	2		
1989-90	5		
1990-91	5	1	
1991-92	2		
Total	145	8	14
Previous holder: Ian Cooke, 360 as a non-league club			

RECORD TRANSFER FEE RECEIVED			
Amount	Club	Player	Date
£2,500,000	Manchester City	Keith Curle	8/91
£1,600,000	Chelsea	Dennis Wise	7/90
£900,000	Newcastle Utd	Andy Thorn	7/88
£800,000	Newcastle Utd	Dave Beasant	6/88

MANAGERS			
Name	Seasons	Best	Worst
Allen Batsford	1977-78	13(4)	13(3)
Dario Gradi	1978-81	22(3)	4(4)
Dave Bassett	1981-87	6(1)	1(4)
Bobby Gould	1987-90	7(1)	12(1)
Ray Harford	1990-91	7(1)	7(1)
Peter Withe	1991-92		
Joe Kinnear	1992-	13(1)	13(1)

HIGHEST TRANSFER FEE PAID			
Amount	Club	Player	Date
£775,000	Port Vale	Robbie Earle	7/91
*£720,000	Brentford	Dean Holdsworth	7/92
£500,000	Reading	Keith Curle	10/88
£200,000	Manchester Utd	Terry Gibson	8/87
* = + Kruszynski & Bennett in exchange			

LOCAL BRANCH
Wimbledon: Park Branch
132-134 Arthur Road
Wimbledon Park
London SW19 8AA

Tel: 081-946 5062

BARCLAYS BUSINESS CENTRE
Wimbledon Business Centre
19-20 Morden Road
London SW19 3BN
Tel: 081-946 3091

BARCLAYBANK MACHINE

LONGEST LEAGUE RUNS	
of undefeated matches:	22 (15.1.1983-14.5.1983)
of undefeated home matches:	21 (22.1.1983-3.12.1983)
without home win:	7 (26.2.1980-15.4.1980)
	(4.4.1988-24.9.1988)
of league wins:	7 (9.4.1983-7.5.1983)
of league defeats:	4 (3.4.1982-14.4.1982)
of league matches without a win:	14 (23.2.1980-15.4.1980)
of undefeated away matches:	12 (22.1.1983-27.8.1983)
without an away win:	11 (5.4.1989-30.9.1989)
	(14.9.1991-25.2.1992)
of home wins:	8 (9.4.1983-17.9.1983)(8.4.1978-14.10.1978)
of away wins:	3 (23.12.1978-28.2.1979)
	(31.3.1984-14.4.1984) (10.4.1991-20.4.1991)

PREVIOUS NAMES
Wimbledon Old Centrals 1887-1905

PREVIOUS LEAGUES
Isthmian League, Southern League

BIGGEST VICTORIES
League: 6-0 v Newport County, Division 3, 3.9.1983
F.A. Cup: 7-2 v Windsor & Eton, Rnd 1, 22.11.1980
League Cup: 5-0 v Blackburn, Round 1, 24.9.1985

BIGGEST DEFEATS
League: 1-6 v Carlisle Utd., Division 2, 23.3.1985
1-6 v Gillingham, Division 2, 13.2.1982
F.A. Cup: 0-6 v Fulham, Rnd 1 replay, 1930-31
League Cup: 0-8 v Everton, Round 2, 29.8.1978

MOST POINTS
3 points a win: 98, Division 4, 1982-83.
2 points a win: 61, Division 4, 1978-79.

MOST GOALS IN A MATCH
4. Alan Cork v Torquay United, Division 4, 28.2.1979 (4-1).

MOST GOALS
97, 1983-84, Division 3
Cork 28, Hodges 16, Evans 12, Fishender 8, Ketteridge 7,
Downes 4, Park 4, Morris 3, Peters 3, Smith 3, Thomas 3,
Hatter 2, Galliers 1, Winterburn 1, og 2.

MOST GOALS IN A SEASON
Alan Cork 33, (League 29, FAC 2, Lge C 2) 1983-84
3 goals once = 3; 2 goals 6 times = 12; 1 goal 17 times = 17

MOST FIRST CLASS MATCHES IN A SEASON
56 (46 League, 2 FA Cup, 2 League Cup, 6 Football League
Group Cup) 1981-82

MOST LEAGUE GOALS CONCEDED
81, Division 3, 1979-80

MOST LEAGUE WINS
29, Division 4, 1982-83

MOST LEAGUE DRAWS
16, Division 1, 1977-78, 1989-90

MOST LEAGUE DEFEATS
22, Division 3, 1979-80

OLDEST PLAYER
Dave Donaldson, 37 years 4 months. v Hartlepool (Div 4)
9.2.1979.

YOUNGEST PLAYER
Kevin Gage 17 years 15 days v Bury (Div 4), 2.5.1981.

MOST CAPPED PLAYER
Terry Phelan (Eire) 6

BEST PERFORMANCES BY WIMBLEDON

League: 1982-83: Matches played 46, Won 29, Drawn 11, Lost 6, Goals for 95, Goals against 45, Points 98. First in Division 4.

Highest: 1986-87: 6th in Division 1.

F.A. Cup: 1987-88: 3rd rnd. West Bromwich Albion 4-1 (h); 4th rnd. Mansfield Town 2-1 (a); 5th rnd. Newcastle United 3-1 (a);
6th rnd. Watford 2-1 (a); Semi-final Luton Town 2-1; Final Liverpool 1-0.

League Cup: 1979-80: 1st rnd. Aldershot 4-1 (h), 2-1 (a); 2nd rnd. Orient 2-2 (a), 2-2 (h) won on pens; 3rd rnd. Plymouth
Argyle 0-0 (a), 1-0 (h); 4th rnd. Swindon Town 1-2 (a).
1983-84: 1st rnd. Southend 0-1 (a), 6-4 (h); 2nd rnd. Nott'm Forest 2-0 (h), 1-1 (a); 3rd rnd. Oldham Athletic 3-1 (h); 4th rnd.
Rotherham 0-1 (a)
1989-90: 2nd rnd. 2-1 (a), 3-0 (h); 3rd rnd. Middlesbrough 1-1 (a), 1-0 (h); 4th rnd. West Ham Utd 0-1 (a).

DIVISIONAL RECORDS

	Played	Won	Drawn	Lost	For	Against	Points
DIVISION 1	238	87	77	74	318	282	**338**
DIVISION 2	84	37	23	24	129	113	**134**
DIVISION 3	138	50	34	54	210	232	**174**
DIVISION 4	184	91	47	46	304	204	**258**
TOTALS	**644**	**265**	**181**	**198**	**961**	**831**	**904**

WIMBLEDON

PLAYERS NAME / Honours	Ht	Wt	Birthdate	Birthplace / Transfers	Contract Date	Clubs	League	L/Cup	FA Cup	Other	Lg	L/C	FAC	Oth
GOALKEEPERS														
Hans Segers	5.11	12.7	30.10.61	Eindhoven, Holland		PSV Eindhoven								
				£50,000	26.07.85	Nottm. Forest	58	4	5					
13.02.87 Loan Stoke City 1 Lg App.				Loan	01.07.87	Sheffield Utd	10			1				
01.03.88 Loan Dunfermline 4 Lg App				£125,000	28.09.88	Wimbledon	149	13	10	7				
Neil Sullivan	6.0	12101	24.02.70	London	26.07.88	Wimbledon (T)	2							
				Loan	01.05.92	Crystal Palace	1							
DEFENDERS														
Warren Barton	6.0	11.0	19.03.69	London		Leytonstone & Ilford								
					28.07.89	Maidstone Utd	41+1	0+2	3	7			1	
				£300,000	07.06.90	Wimbledon	79	4	5	2	4			
Dean Blackwell	6.1	12.10	05.12.69	London	07.07.88	Wimbledon (T)	32+10	2	3	1	1			
				Loan	15.03.90	Plymouth A	5+2							
Gary Elkins	5.9	11.03	04.05.66	Wallingford	03.12.83	Fulham (A)	100+4	6	2+2	7+1	2			
E: Y.11				Loan	23.12.89	Exeter City	5							
				£20,000	20.08.90	Wimbledon	10		0+1		1			
Scott Fitzgerald	6.0	12.02	13.08.69	London	13.07.89	Wimbledon	34+3	2	2	1	1			
Roger Joseph	5.11	11.10	24.02.65	Paddington		Southall								
				Free	04.10.84	Brentford	103+1	7	1	8	2			
				£150,000	25.08.88	Wimbledon	107+6	12	5+1	6				
Brian McAllister	5.11	12.5	30.11.70	Glasgow	01.03.89	Wimbledon	10+3			1				
				Loan	05.12.90	Plymouth A	7+1							
Terry Phelan	5.8	9.6	16.03.67	Manchester	30.03.82	Leeds Utd. (A)	12+2	3		2				
Ei: u23.1, u21.1, Y; FAC'88					30.07.86	Swansea City	45	4	5	3				
* NOW MAN. CITY £2.5m *				£100,000	29.07.87	Wimbledon	155+4	13+2	16	8	1		2	
John Scales	6.2	12.7	04.07.66	Harrogate	03.08.84	Leeds Utd								
FAC'88				Free	05.11.85	Bristol Rovers	68+4	3	6	3+1	2			
				£70,000	16.07.87	Wimbledon	163+5	11+1	12+1	7+1	10			4
MIDFIELD														
Michael R Bennett	5.11	11.3	27.07.69	London	27.04.87	Charlton Ath. (A)	24+11	4	1	6+1	2			
E: u19.2				£250,000	09.01.90	Wimbledon	12+6	1+1	0+1	1	2			
				Loan	14.07.92	Brentford								
Robbie Earle	5.9	10.10	27.01.65	Newcastle-U-Lyme	05.07.82	Port Vale	284+10	21+2	20+1	18+1	77	4	4	5
				£775,000	19.07.91	Wimbledon	40	2	2	1	14			1
Zbigniew Kruszynski	6.0	12.12	14.10.61	Diuschav		08 Homburg								
				£100,000	02.12.88	Wimbledon	65+6	4+1	6	3+2	4			
25.03.92 Loan Brentford 8 Lg Apps.				Loan	14.07.92	Brentford								
Vaughan Ryan	5.8	10.12	02.09.68	London	22.08.86	Wimbledon (A)	67+15	7	1	7+1	3			
				Loan	11.01.89	Sheffield Utd	2+1			1				
Lawrie Sanchez	5.11	12.0	22.10.59	Lambeth		Thatcham T								
NI: 3; Div4'79; FAC'88				Free	22.09.78	Reading	249+13	20+1	14	1	28		1	
				£29,000	10.12.84	Wimbledon	216+12	17	23+1	7	27		2	
FORWARDS														
Steve Anthrobus	6.2	12.13	10.11.68	Lewisham	01.10.86	Millwall (A)	19+2	3		1	4			
				£150,000	16.02.90	Wimbledon	23		2					
Andrew Clarke			22.07.67	London		Barnet			5+1				1	
E:S-P.2; APL(GMVC)'91				£150,000	21.02.91	Wimbledon	20+26	1+1			7	1		
Stephen Cotterill	6.1	12.5	20.07.64	Cheltenham		Burton Albion								
				£30,000*	27.02.89	Wimbledon	6+4	2		1+1	3			
Carlton Fairweather	5.11	11.0	22.09.61	London		Tooting & Mitcham								
				£13,000	19.12.84	Wimbledon	118+20	15+1	9+1	7+1	26	1	1	
John Fashanu	6.1	11.2	18.09.62	Kensington		Cambridge Utd								
E: 2; FAC'88				23.10.79	Norwich City	6+1				1				
via, 23.8.83, Crystal Pal. 1 Lg, 1 LC Apps to				23.09.83	Lincoln City	31+5	2	2+1	1	11			
				30.11.84	Millwall	50	4	9	2	12	2	4	1
				£125,000	27.03.86	Wimbledon	209+2	13+1	19	5	90	8	9	2
Terry Gibson	5.5	10.0	23.12.62	Walthamstow	30.01.80	Tottenham H. (A)	16+2	1	5	0+2	4	1	1	1
E: Y.10, S; UEFA Y'80; FAC'88				24.04.83	Coventry City	97+1	7	6	2	43	3	5	1
				31.01.86	Manchester Utd	14+9	0+2	1+1		1			
				£200,000	27.08.87	Wimbledon	74+4	10	10	8	20	6	2	1
				Loan	26.03.92	Swindon Town	8+1				1			
Dean Holdsworth	5.11	11.13	08.11.68	London	12.11.86	Watford (A)	2+14			0+4	3			
Div.3'92				Loan	11.02.88	Carlisle Utd	4				1			
18.03.88 Loan Port Vale 6 Lg App, 2 G.				Loan	25.08.88	Swansea City	4+1				1			
13.10.88 Loan Brentford 2+5 Lg App, 1 G.				£125,000	29.09.89	Brentford	106+4	7+1	6	12+1	53	6	7	9
				£750,000	20.07.92	Wimbledon								
Paul McGee	5.5	9.10	17.05.68	Dublin		Bohemians								
Ei: u21.4					10.02.89	Colchester Utd	3			1				
				£125,000	03.03.89	Wimbledon	53+4	3+1	5	2	9	2	1	
Paul Miller	6.0	11.0	31.01.68	Bisley	23.09.87	Wimbledon (A)	54+7	2+2	2	1	9			
via Loans at Wealdstone & Yeovil Town to				Loan	20.10.87	Newport Co	6				2			
				Loan	11.01.90	Bristol City	0+3			2				
Aidan Newhouse	6.1	13.05	23.05.72	Wallasey	01.07.88	Chester City (T)	29+15	5+1	0+2	2+3	6			1
E: Y.13				£250,000	22.02.90	Wimbledon	7+15	0+1	2	0+1	2			
ADDITIONAL CONTRACT PLAYERS														

Neal Ardley (F) 8+1 Lg Apps., **Stewart Castledine (M)** 0+2 Lg Apps., **Gerald Dobbs (F)** 2+2 Lg Apps., **Jamie McCarthy, Chris Perry, Justin Skinner, Steve Talboys (F)** £10,000 from Gloucester City.

WIMBLEDON

RECORD WIN & LOSS AGAINST EACH CLUB IN CURRENT DIVISION
(Where a score has occured on several occasions the most recent is given)

Club	Rec. Win	Season	Rec. Loss	Season
ARSENAL	3-1	1987-88	5-1	1988-89 (home)
ASTON VILLA	3-0	1990-91 (away)	2-0	1990-91 (home)
BLACKBURN ROVERS	1-0	1979-80	3-0	1979-80
CHELSEA	4-0	1986-87 (away)	2-1	1991-92
COVENTRY CITY	2-1	1986-87	2-1	1987-88
CRYSTAL PALACE	5-0	1984-85 (away)	3-0	1990-91 (home)
EVERTON	3-1	1989-90	3-0	1986-87
IPSWICH TOWN	Never played in League fixture			
LEEDS UNITED	0-0	1985-85	5-1	1991-92
LIVERPOOL	3-2	1991-92 (away)	3-1	1986-87 (home)
MANCHESTER CITY	2-1	1991-92	3-0	1984-85
MANCHESTER UNITED	2-1	1986-87	3-1	1990-91 (home)
MIDDLESBROUGH	3-0	1985-86	1-0	1988-89
NORWICH CITY	4-0	1990-91 (away)	2-0	1988-89 (home)
NOTTINGHAM FOREST	4-1	1988-89	4-2	1991-92
OLDHAM ATHLETIC	2-1	1991-92	2-1	1985-86
QUEENS PARK RANGERS	3-0	1990-91	4-3	1988-89
SHEFFIELD UNITED	5-0	1985-86	4-0	1985-86
SHEFFIELD WEDNESDAY	3-0	1986-87	3-1	1979-80
SOUTHAMPTON	2-0	1987-88	1-0	1991-92
TOTTENHAM HOTSPUR	5-1	1990-91	5-3	1991-92 (home)

MANAGER: JOE KINNEAR

DATE OF BIRTH: 27.12.1946   **PLACE OF BIRTH:** Dublin

DATE OF APPOINTMENT: JANUARY 1991

PREVIOUS CLUBS
  as Manager: None
  as Reserve team manager: Wimbledon
  as Player: Tottenham, Brighton & Hove Albion

HONOURS
  as Manager:
  as Asst. Man./Coach:
  as Player:
  International: Eire: 26 caps

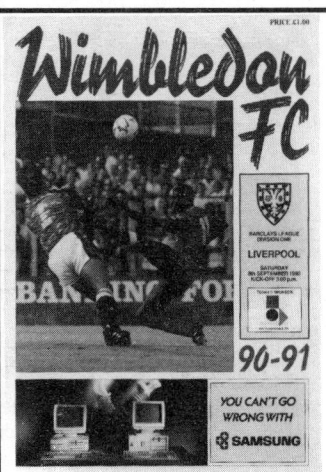

Value Rating: ★ ★ ★

Programme Editor: Reg Davies

Price of 1992-93 Programme: £1

Number of Pages: 32

Subscriptions: Home matches weekly per season £22 (postage included). Home and away matches weekly per season £33 (postage included).

Local Newspapers: Wimbledon Guardian, Surrey Comet, Wimbledon News, South London Press.

Local Radio Stations: Capital Radio, LBC.

Additional Publications on Club: Mission Impossible (Wimbledon Football Club Rise to the First Division). (Leigh Edwards & Andy Watson); Paperback £2.95.

LEADING LEAGUE GOALSCORERS
SEASONS 1979-80 – 1991-92

1979-80	**ALAN CORK**	12	1980-81	**ALAN CORK**	23
1981-82	**FRANCIS JOSEPH**	13	1982-83	**JOHN LESLIE**	23
1983-84	**ALAN CORK**	28	1984-85	**STEWART EVANS**	14
1985-86	**ALAN CORK**	11	1986-87	**JOHN FASHANU**	11
1987-88	**JOHN FASHANU**	13	1988-89	**JOHN FASHANU**	12
1989-90	**JOHN FASHANU**	20	1990-91	**JOHN FASHANU**	11

1991-92   **JOHN FASHANU**   17

SELHURST PARK London SE25 6PU

Capacity: 29,949   **Covered Standing:**   **Seating:** 15,135

Tel: Ground: 081 771 2233   **Ticket Sales:** 081 771 8841   **Clubcall:** 0898 12 11 75

All premium rate calls (0898/0891) cost 36p per minute cheap rate and 48p per minute at all other times. Call costings correct at time of going to press.

ATTENDANCES
Highest: 18,000 v H.M.S. Victory, FA Amateur Cup, Round 3, 1934-35

Lowest: Not known

RECORD RECEIPTS (with previous records):
£80,679 v Chelsea, Div 1, 1989-90
£75,244 v Arsenal, Div 1, 1988-89
£72,352 v Tottenham, FA Cup Round 6, 1986-87

PLOUGH LANE
First game: v Tooting, FA Cup, 2-0, 14.9.1912
First floodlit game: v Ilford, 25.10.1960

Season Tickets:
Stands: from £225 to £280, juv/OAP £113 to £140
Ground: £125, juv/OAP £75

Executive Box Season Tickets: None

Cost of Stand Tickets: Stand: from £15 to £20, juv/OAP £8 to £10
Terraces: £7 or £8, juv/OAP £4 or £5

Match and Ticket Information: Available 21 days prior to matches

Car Parking: In side streets and greyhound stadium quarter mile from ground

Nearest Railway Station: Haydons Road (Southern Region), Wimbledon Park (District)

How to get to the ground

From North: From Motorway M1 or A1, use A406 North Circular Road to Chiswick. Follow signs South Circular Road A205 to Wandsworth. Then use A3 to A214 and follow signs to Streatham. Join A23. In 1m turn left B273. At end turn left into High Street then forward into Whitehorse Lane for Wimbledon FC

From East: Use A232 (S.P. Croydon) to Shirley then join A215 (S.P. Norwood). In 2.2m turn left B266 into Whitehorse Lane.

From South: Use A23 (S.P. London) then follow signs Crystal Palace B266 via Thornton Heath into Whitehorse Lane.

From West: Use Motorway M4 to Chiswick then route from North or A232 (S.P. Croydon) to Beddington, then follow signs London A23. After, follow signs Crystal Palace B266 via Thornton Heath into Whitehorse Lane

WOLVERHAMPTON WDRS Division 1

Formed: 1877   **Turned Professional:** 1888   **Ltd Co:** 1892

SPONSORED BY: Goodyear   **NICKNAME:** The Wolves

President
Sir Jack Hayward

Chairman
Jonathan Hayward

Directors
Jack Harris
John Harris
Billy Wright CBE
Nic Stones
Keith Pearson, ACIS

Secretary/Accountant
Keith Pearson ACIS (0902 712181)

Assistant Secretary
Dot Wooldridge

Commercial Manager
Gary Leaver

Manager
Garham Turner

Coach
Gary Pendrey & Chris Evans

Cheif Scout/Youth Development
Ron Jukes

Physiotherapist
Paul Darby

Director of Marketing/Public Affairs
David Clayton

Groundsman
Bill Pilbeam

Club Statistician for the Directory
Les Smith

ANOTHER season ended with Wolves failing to live up to the expectations of their supporters, club directors and the media, but unlike the previous term, this time there could be no excuse of long term injuries. It was simply down to inconsistencies.

The season started well enough and at the end of September Wolves were in fifth position in Division Two. However, defeat in a poor game at Grimsby in the ZDS Cup started a run of twelve matches with two draws and ten defeats. With the club now in the relegation zone and many people feeling this was a continuation of the slump in the second part of the previous season, manager Graham Turner's job was on the line. Club owner, Sir Jack Hayward, returned from his Barbados home and stood on the terraces to ascertain the fans' mood during the league match at home to Grimsby. Wolves' victory possibly saved Turner's job as at the emergency board meeting the next day he received a vote of confidence. Subsequent results improved and a run of five consecutive league wins, with an unlucky F.A. Cup defeat at Nottingham Forest in the middle, raised hopes of a play-off place. However, another defeat at Tranmere from 3-2 up with a few minutes to go halted the run and inconsistency followed to the end of the season.

Good news off the pitch came when the club regained ownership of the ground in September and later replaced the old North Bank with a new all-seater stand named after Stan Cullis. The Billy Wright stand will follow shortly.

Steve Bull beat John Richards' all time record for goals in a career when he scored at Derby in March, and he finished the season on a total of 198 goals. He is now only six behind Billy Hartill's league goals record.

Bull also made the club's only representative appearance of the season when he played for F.L. Division Two against Italian Serie B in March. Lawrie Madden, signed at the start of the season as a stop-gap centre-half, played in all but three matches and the other new signings Derek Mountfield and Mark Ranking both impressed. Mike Stowell and Mark Venus played in every match and Paul Birch missed only one.

The reserves had an excellent season and gained promotion back to Division One of the Central League.

At the end of the season Wolves hit the headlines in the national news, but it was for a sad and worrying reason, when fires were started by arsonists and live cartridges were buried in the pitch on the eve of the last home match against Middlesbrough.

Hopefully next season these problems and the inconsistencies will be behind the club and they will make a genuine bid for promotion to the new Premier League. Otherwise the growing feeling that at least some of the players are not as good on the pitch as they are on paper will be justified.

Les Smith

Back Row L-R: Paul Cook, Mark Venus, Darren Roberts, Mike Stowell, Shane Wesley, Paul Jones, Derek Mountfield, Darren Simpkin, Laurie Madden. **Middle:** Steve Bull, Andy Mutch, Roddy Dennison, Mark Burke, Tim Steel, Mark Rankine, Tom Bennett, James Kelly. **Front:** Andy Thompson, Keith Downing, Gary Pendrie (Coach), Graham Turner (Manager), Paul Darby (Physio), Paul Birch, Kevin Ashley.

WOLVERHAMPTON WNDRS

DIVISION TWO: 11th   **FA CUP:** 3rd RND   **RUMBELOWS CUP:** 3rd RND   **ZDS CUP:** 1st RND

M	DATE		COMP.	VEN	OPPONENTS	RESULT		H/T	LGE POS	GOALSCORERS/GOAL TIMES	ATTEN DANCE
1	A	17	BL	A	Watford	W	2-0	0-0		Mutch 61, Bull 71	(13,547
2		24	BL	H	Charlton Athletic	D	1-1	1-1	5	Bull 32	16,309
3		31	BL	A	Brighton & H A	D	3-3	2-2	8	Mutch 24, 74, Bull 33	(10,621
4	S	3	BL	H	Port Vale	L	0-2	0-0	15		16,115
5		7	BL	H	Oxford United	W	3-1	3-0	9	Dennison 3, Bull 8, Steele 43	12,549
6		14	BL	A	Newcastle United	W	2-0	0-0	8	Scott (og) 39, Bull 73	(20,195
7		17	BL	A	Cambridge United	L	1-2	0-2	8	Bull 78	(6,552)
8		21	BL	H	Swindon Town	W	2-1	1-0	6	Steele 8, Bull 78	15,219
9		24	RC 2/1	H	**Shrewsbury Town**	W	6-1	4-1		**Birch 12, 35, Burke 32, Bull 44, 48, Steele 66**	**12,229**
10		28	BL	A	Southend United	W	2-0	0-0	5	Birch 61, Ashley 89	(8,368)
11	O	1	ZDS 1	A	**Grimsby Town**	L	0-1	0-1			(1,593)
12		5	BL	H	Barnsley	L	1-2	1-0	6	Cook 30	14,082
13		8	RC 2/2	A	**Shrewsbury Town**	L	1-3	1-1		**Steele 7**	**(5,784**
14		12	BL	A	Middlesbrough	D	0-0	0-0	7		(15,523
15		19	BL	A	Leicester City	L	0-3	0-2	10		(14,428)
16		26	BL	H	Tranmere Rovers	D	1-1	1-0	10	Birch 44	12,266
17		30	RC 3	A	**Everton**	L	1-4	1-2		**Bull 22**	**(19,065)**
18	N	2	BL	A	Plymouth Argyle	L	0-1	0-1	16		(4,200)
19		5	BL	A	Bristol Rovers	L	2-3	1-1		Bull 41, 78	8,536
20		9	BL	H	Derby County	L	2-3	1-1	18	Coleman (og) 22, Cook (pen) 69	15,672
21		16	BL	A	Millwall	L	1-2	1-2	20	Cook (pen) 42	(9,469)
22		23	BL	H	Ipswich Town	L	1-2	1-0	21	Birch 7	11,915
23		26	BL	H	Grimsby Town	W	2-1	1-0	18	Madden 25, Birch 82	9,378
24		30	BL	A	Portsmouth	L	0-1	0-1	20		(11,101)
25	D	7	BL	H	Sunderland	W	1-0	0-0	15	Cook 83	11,922
26		21	BL	A	Port Vale	D	1-1	1-0	17	Bull 13	(8,480)
27		26	BL	H	Blackburn Rovers	D	0-0	0-0	17		18,277
28		28	BL	H	Brighton & H A	W	2-0	2-0	15	Burke 2, Mutch 26	13,606
29	J	1	BL	A	Grimsby Town	W	2-0	1-0	11	Birch 16, Cook 81	(9,158)
30		4	FAC 3	A	**Nottingham Forest**	L	0-1	0-0			(27,068)
31		15	BL	A	Charlton Athletic	W	2-0	1-0	11	Bull 43, Bennett 84	(5,703)
32		18	BL	H	Watford	W	3-0	0-0	10	Cook 62, Bull 75, Holdsworth (og) 80	14,175
33	F	1	BL	H	Leicester City	W	1-0	1-0	10	Bull 36	18,574
34		8	BL	A	Tranmere Rovers	L	3-4	2-2	10	Cook 8, Bull 12, Burke 55	(11,371)
35		22	BL	H	Portsmouth	D	0-0	0-0	11		15,770
36		29	BL	A	Sunderland	L	0-1	0-1	12		(20,106)
37	M	7	BL	H	Bristol City	D	1-1	1-1	12	Bull 45	12,542
38		11	BL	A	Bristol Rovers	D	1-1	0-0	11	Bull 78	(6,968)
39		14	BL	H	Plymouth Argyle	W	1-0	0-0	11	Venus 70	11,556
40		17	BL	A	Bristol City	L	0-2	0-0	11		(11,623)
41		21	BL	A	Derby County	W	2-1	0-1	11	Birch (pen) 73, Bull 74	(21,024)
42		28	BL	H	Millwall	D	0-0	0-0	11		11,880
43		31	BL	H	Newcastle United	W	6-2	3-1	11	Mutch 3 (5, 10, 84), Bennett 25, Cook 48, Bull 87	14,480
44	A	4	BL	A	Oxford United	L	0-1	0-0	11		(7,165)
45		7	BL	A	Ipswich Town	L	1-2	0-0	11	Mutch 85	(17,379)
46		11	BL	H	Cambridge United	W	2-1	0-0	11	Rankine 73, Mutch 82	11,188
47		14	BL	A	Blackburn Rovers	W	2-1	0-1	10	Bull 55, Birch 90	(14,114)
48		18	BL	A	Swindon Town	L	0-1	0-1	10		(10,863)
49		20	BL	H	Southend United	W	3-1	1-1	10	Bull 37, Mountfield 52, Birch 60	10,953
50		25	BL	A	Barnsley	L	0-2	0-1	10		(7,244)
51	M	2	BL	H	Middlesbrough	L	1-2	0-0	11	Mutch 66	19,123

Best Home League Attendance: 19,123 v Middlesbrough   **Smallest:** 8,536 v Bristol Rovers   **Av Home Att:** 13,743

Goal Scorers: **Compared with 90-91: -2,099**

League (61):   Bull 20, Mutch 10, Birch 8 (1 pen), Cook 8 (2 pens), Opponents 3, Steele 2, Bennett 2, Burke 2, Madden, Rankine
Ashley, Mountfield, Dennison, Venus

R/lows C (8):   Bull 3, Steele 2, Birch 2, Burke
FA Cup (0):
ZDS Cup (0):

1991-92

Stowell M.	Ashley K.	Venus M.	Bennett T.	Madden L.	Downing K.	Birch P.	Cook P.	Bull S.	Mutch A.	Dennison R.	Steele T.	Bellamy G.	Burke M.	Clarke W.	Bradbury S.	Thompson A.	Paskin J.	Taylor C.	McLoughlin P.	Mountfield D.	Clarke N.	Rankine M.	Kelly J.	Simpkin	Howard	Referee	#
1	2	3	4	5	6	7	8	9	10	11	S					S										P Foakes	1
1	2	3	4	5	6	7•	8	9	10	11	14					S										J McGrath	2
1	2	3	4	5	6	7	8	9	10	11	S					S										R Milford	3
1	2	3	4	5	6	7	8	9	10	11•	14	S														R Lewis	4
1	2*	3	4	5	6		8	9	10	11	7	12					S									D Axcell	5
1	2	3	4	5	6•	14	8	9	10	11	7	S														W Burns	6
1	2	3	4	5	6	14	8	9	10	11•	7															P Jones	7
1	2	3	4	5	6	11	8	9		S	7*	12	10													T Ward	8
1	2	3	4	5	6	11	8	9		S	7	S	10													P Harrison	9
1	2	3	4	5	6	7	8	9		14			11			S			10•							G Pooley	10
1	2	3	4	5	6	7	8	9•		10			11	14		S										G Hill	11
1	2	3	4	5	6•	7	8	9		14	10			5		11										T Lunt	12
1	2	3	4	5		7	8			S	10	6		9		11										T Fitzharris	13
1	2	3	4	5		7	8•	9		14	6	S				11	10									D Allison	14
1	2*	3	4	5	6	7		9	10*	12	8					11		14								R Dilkes	15
1	2	3	4	5	6	7		9	10*	11	8					S		14								J Deakin	16
1	2	3	4	5	6	7		9	10	11	8	S				S										J Watson	17
1	2	3	4	5	6	7	8			11•	10	S				14		9								M Pierce	18
1	2*	3	4	5	6	7		9		11•	14	12	8						10							K Breen	19
1	2	3	4	5	6	7	11	9	10	S									10	8						D Elleray	20
1	2	3	4	5	6*	7	11	9	10	12						S				8						J Martin	21
1	2	3	4*		6	7	11	9	10	12						S				8		5				R Groves	22
1	2	3	4	5	6	7	8	9	10	S						S						11				J Moules	23
1	2	3	4•	5		7	8		10	6	14		12					9		11*						R Wiseman	24
1	2	3	4	5		7	8	9	10	11*			12					9	14	6•						K Barrett	25
1	2	3	4	5		7	8	9	10	S			11			S				6						T West	26
1	2	3	4*	5		7	8	9	10	12			11			S				6						C Wilkes	27
1	2	3		5		7	8	9	10	S			4			11				6						A Ward	28
1	2	3	12	5		7•	8	9	10	14			4*			11				6						S Bell	29
1	2	3	6	5		7	8	9	10	12	S		4*			11										G Ashby	30
1	2	3	4	5		7	8	9	10	S	S					11				6						M Bodenham	31
1	2	3	4	5		7	8	9	10*	S			12			11				6						R Dilkes	32
1	2	3	4	5		7	8*	9		S	10					11				6			12			I Cruikshanks	33
1	2	3	4	5		7	8•	9		14	10					11				6						R Shepherd	34
1	2•	3	4			7	8	9	12	14	10*					11			5	6						G Poll	35
1		3	4	6	2*	7	8	9	10	14			11•							5		12				J Kay	36
1	2	3	4		6•	7	8	9	10	11*			14							5			12			A Gunn	37
1	2	3	4	6	11	7	8	9	10*											5		10	S			P Jones	38
1	2	3	4	6	S	7	8	9	S							11				5		10				R Poulain	39
1	2	3	4	6	S	7	8	9	14							11•				5		10				P Scoble	40
1	2•	3	4	6	14	7	8	9	10							11				5					S	M James	41
1		3	4	5	12	7	8	9	10	14						11•				2		6*				M Bailey	42
1	2*	3	4	5	11	7	8	9	10	S										6			12			R Gifford	43
1	2	3	4*	5	11	7	8	9•	10											6		14	12			H King	44
1	2	3		5	11	7	8	9	10	S										6	4		S			D Axcell	45
1	2	3		5	11	7	8	9	10	S										6	4		S			D Allison	46
1	2	3		5	11	7	8	9	10	S										6	4		S			A Flood	47
1	2*	3		5	11	7	8	9	10	12										6	4				S	R Groves	48
1	2	3		5	11	7	8	9	10	S			4			S				6						P Taylor	49
1	2	3		5	11	7•	8	9	10	12			4*							6		14				P Harrison	50
1	2	3		5	11•	7	8	9	10	14			4							6			S			P Don	51
46	44	46	37	43	30	43	43	43	35	12	10	1	13	1		15	1	1	3	28	1		10			**League Appearances**	
			1			2	2			2	10	7	3	5		2	1	2				5	3			**Substitute Appearances**	
3	3	3	3	3	2	3	2	2	1	1	3	1	1			1				1						**R/lows Appearances**	
1	1	1	1	1	1		1	1	1	1			0+1			1				1						**FA Cup Appearances**	
1	1	1	1	1	1	1	1	1	1	1			0+1			1				1						**ZDS Cup Appearances**	

Also Played: Posn.(Game): D Smith S(13), Robertson S(34)

WOLVERHAMPTON WANDERERS

Club Colours: Gold Shirts, black shorts, gold stockings.
Change Colours: All white.
Reserves League: Pontins Central League Division 2

COMPETITIONS						
Div. 1	Div. 2	Div. 3N	Euro C	Texaco	Watney	C/Sld
88-06	06-23	23-24	58-59	70-71	72-73	49-50
32-65	24-32		59-60	72-73		54-55
67-76	65-67	**Div. 3**	ECWC		**F/SVT**	58-59
77-82	76-77	85-86	60-61	**A/Ital**	85-86	59-60
83-84	82-83	88-89	UEFA	69-70	86-87	60-61
	84-85		71-72		87-88	
	89-	**Div. 4**	73-74		88-89	
		86-88	74-75			
			80-81			

HONOURS						
Div. 1	Div. 2	Div. 3	Div 4	FAC	Lge C	C/Sld
53-54	31-32	23-24	87-88	92-93	73-74	49-50*
57-58	76-77	88-89		07-08	79-80	54-55*
58-59				48-49		59-60
				59-60		60-61*

*= Shared
Also won Texaco C 1970-71 & SVT 1987-88

MOST APPEARANCES: DEREK PARKIN 607+2 (1967-82)				
Year	League	FA Cup	League C	Europe
1967-68	15			
1968-69	42	2	3	
1969-70	42	1	3	
1970-71	39	2	1	
1971-72	32	2	1	7
1972-73	18	3		
1973-74	39	3	6	4
1974-75	41	1	1	2
1975-76	30	6	3	
1976-77	42	5	1	
1977-78	38	3	1	
1978-79	42	7	1	
1979-80	40	3	11	
1980-81	19+1	6+1	1	2
1981-82	21	1	2	
	500+1	**45+1**	**35**	**15**
also 7 Texaco C 70-71, 4 A/Ital 69-70, 1 Watney C 72-73				

MOST GOALS IN A CAREER						
STEVE BULL 198 (1986-92)						
Year	League	FAC	Lge C	P/Offs	FRT	ZDS
1986-87	15			1	3	
1987-88	34	3	3		13	
1988-89	37		2		11	
1989-90	24	1	2			
1990-91	26					1
1991-92	20		3			
Total	**156**	**4**	**10**	**1**	**26**	**1**
Previous holder: John Richards 194 (1969-82)						

MANAGERS			
Name	Seasons	Best	Worst
Jack Addenbrooke	1885-1922	3(1)	19(2)
George Jobey	1922-24	22(2)	1(3)
Albert Hoskins	1924-26	4(2)	6(2)
Fred Scotchbrook	1926-27	15(2)	15(2)
Major Frank Buckley	1927-44	2(1)	17(2)
Ted Vizard	1944-48	3(1)	5(1)
Stan Cullis	1948-64	1(1)	18(1)
Andy Beattie	1964-65	21(1)	21(1)
Ronnie Allen	1965-68	17(1)	6(2)
Bill McGarry	1968-76	4(1)	20(1)
Sammy Chung	1976-78	15(1)	1(2)
John Barnwell	1978-81	6(1)	18(1)
Ian Greaves	1982		
Graham Hawkins	1982-84	22(1)	2(2)
Tommy Docherty	1984-85	22(2)	22(2)
Sammy Chapman	1985		
Bill McGarry	1985		
Sammy Chapman	1985-1986	23(3)	23(3)
Brian Little	1986		
Graham Turner	1986-	10(2)	4(4)

RECORD TRANSFER FEE RECEIVED			
Amount	Club	Player	Date
£1,000,000	Manchester City	Steve Daley	9/79
£240,000	Arsenal	Alan Sunderland	11/77
£100,000	Liverpool	Alun Evans	6/68

RECORD TRANSFER FEE PAID			
Amount	Club	Player	Date
£1,175,000	Aston Villa	Andy Gray	9/80
£150,000	Hull City	Peter Daniel	3/78
£100,000	Burnley	Steve Kindon	8/72

LONGEST LEAGUE RUNS
of undefeated matches: 20 (24.11.1923-5.4.1924)
of undefeated home matches: 27 (24.3.1923-6.9.1924)
without home win: 13 (17.11.1984-27.4.1985)
of league wins:8 (13.3.1915-17.4.1915) (4.2.1967-28.3.1967)
(14.3.1987-20.4.1987) (15.10.1988-26.11.1988)
of league defeats: 8 (5.12.1981-13.2.1982)
of league matches without a win: 19 (1.12.1984-6.4.1985)
of undefeated away matches: 11 (5.9.1953-2.1.1954)
without an away win: 32 (4.3.1922-6.10.1923)
of home wins: 14 (7.3.1953-28.11.1953)
of away wins: 5 (1.1.1938-26.2.1938)
(20.8.1962-22.9.1962) (9.2.1980-7.4.1980)

BIGGEST VICTORIES
League: 10-1 v Leicester City, Division 1, 15.4.1938
9-0 v Fulham, Division 1, 16.9.1959
F.A. Cup: 14-0 v Crosswells Brewery, Rnd 2, 13.11.1886
League Cup: 6-1 v Shrewsbury, Rnd 2, 24.9.1991
Europe: 5-0 v F K Austria, 30.11.1960

BIGGEST DEFEATS
League: 1-10 v Newton Heath, Division 1, 15.10.1892
0-9 v Derby County, Division 1, 10.1.1891
F.A. Cup: 0-6 v Rotherham Utd, Rnd 1, 16.11.1985
League Cup: 0-5 v Fulham, Rnd 3, 5.10.1966
0-5 v Sunderland, Rnd 2 replay, 27.10.1982
Europe: 0-4 v Barcelona, European Cup Q-Final, 2.10.1960

MOST POINTS
3 points a win: 92, Division 3, 1988-89
2 points a win: 64, Division 1, 1957-58

MOST GOALS
115, Division 2, 1931-32.
Hartill 30, Bottrill 21, Phillips 18, Deacon 13, Lowton 9, Baraclough 7, Buttery 6, Hollingworth 4, Crook 2, Martin 1, Redfern 1, Richards 1, Smalley 1, og 1.

MOST GOALS IN A MATCH
5. J Brodie v Stoke City, 8-0, FA Cup 3, 22.2.1890
5. J Butcher v Accrington Stanley, 5-3, Div 1, 19.11.1892
5. T Phillipson v Bradford City, 7-2, Div 2, 25.12.1926
5. W Hartill v Notts County, 5-1, Div 2, 12.10.1929
5. W Hartill v Aston Villa, 5-2, Div 1, 3.9.1934

MOST GOALS IN A SEASON
Steve Bull, 52, 1987-88.
League 34, FA Cup 3, League Cup 3, SVT 12.
League only: D Westcott 38, 1946-47

MOST FIRST CLASS MATCHES IN A SEASON
61 (46 League, 3 FA Cup, 4 League Cup, 8 Sherpa Van Trophy) 1987-88

MOST LEAGUE GOALS CONCEDED
99, Division 1, 1905-06

MOST LEAGUE WINS
28, Division 1, 1957-58; Division 1, 1958-59

MOST LEAGUE DRAWS
19, Division 2, 1990-91

MOST LEAGUE DEFEATS
25, Division 1, 1964-65; Division 1, 1983-84; Division 2, 1984-85; Division 3, 1985-86

OLDEST PLAYER
Derek Dougan, 37 yrs 96 days v Manchester City, 26.4.1975

YOUNGEST PLAYER
Jimmy Mullen, 16 years 43 days v Leeds United, 18.2.1939
Wartime: Cameron Buchanan, 14 yrs 57 days v W.B.A., 26.9.1942

MOST CAPPED PLAYER
Billy Wright, 105 for England

BEST PERFORMANCES BY WOLVERHAMPTON WANDERERS

Wolverhampton are the only League Club to have been Champions of all Four Divisions: Div 1, 1954, 1958, 1959; Div 2, 1932, 1977; Div 3N 1924; Div 3, 1989; Div 4, 1988

League: 1957-58: Played 42, Won 28, Drawn 8, Lost, Goals For 103, Goals Against 47, Points 64. First in Division One
Highest: Division One Champions 3 times

F.A. Cup: 1892-93: 1st rnd. Bolton Wanderers 1-1, 1-2; 2nd rnd. Middlesbrough 2-1; 3rd rnd. Darwen 5-0; Semi-Final Blackburn Rovers 2-1; Final Everton 1-0
1907-08: 1st rnd. Bradford City 1-1, 1-0; 2nd rnd. Bury 2-0; 3rd rnd. Swindon Town 2-0; 4th rnd. Stoke City 1-0; Semi-Final Southampton 2-0; Final Newcastle United 3-1
1948-49: 3rd rnd. Chesterfield 6-0, 4th rnd. Sheffield Utd 3-0; Liverpool 3-1; 6th rnd. West Bromwich Albion 1-0; Semi-Final Manchester United 1-1, 1-0; Final Leicester City 3-1
1959-60: 3rd rnd. Newcastle United 2-2, 4-2; 4th rnd Charlton Athletic 2-1; 5th Luton Town 4-1; 6th rnd. Leicester City 2-1; Semi-Final Aston Villa 1-0; Final Blackburn Rovers 3-0

League Cup: 1973-74: 2nd rnd. Halifax Town 3-0; 3rd rnd. Tranmere Rovers 1-1, 2-1; 4th rnd. Exeter City 5-1; 5th rnd. Liverpool 1-0; Semi-Final Norwich City 1-1, 1-0; Final Manchester City 2-1
1979-80: 2nd rnd. Burnley 1-1, 2-0; 3rd rnd. Crystal Palace 2-1; 4th rnd. Queens Park Rangers 1-1, 1-0; 5th rnd. Grimsby Town 0-0, 1-1, 2-0; Semi-Final Swindon Town 1-2, 3-1; Final Nottingham Forest 1-0

UEFA Cup: 1971-72: 1st rnd. Academica 3-0, 4-1; 2nd rnd. Den Haag 3-1, 4-0; 3rd rnd. Carl Zeiss 1-0, 3-0; Quarter-Final Juventus 1-1, 2-1; Semi-Final Ferencvaros 2-2, 2-1; Final Tottenham Hotspur 1-2, 1-1

DIVISIONAL RECORDS

	Played	Won	Drawn	Lost	For	Against	Points
DIVISION 1	2270	911	506	853	3874	3671	**2344**
DIVISION 2	1194	481	263	450	1901	1731	**1302**
DIVISION 3	92	37	24	31	153	147	**135**
DIVISION 3N	42	24	15	3	76	27	**63**
DIVISION 4	92	51	16	25	151	93	**169**
TOTALS	**3690**	**1504**	**824**	**1362**	**6155**	**5669**	**3713**

WOLVERHAMPTON WANDERERS

PLAYERS NAME / Honours	Ht	Wt	Birthdate	Birthplace / Transfers	Contract Date	Clubs	League	L/Cup	FA Cup	Other	Lg	L/C	FAC	Oth
GOALKEEPERS														
Paul S Jones			18.04.67	Chirk		Shrewsbury Town								
						Bridgnorth								
						Kiddermins								
				£40,000	23.07.91	Wolverhampton W								
Michael Stowell	6.2	11.10	19.04.65	Preston		Leyland Motors								
				NC	14.02.85	Preston N.E								
					12.12.85	Everton			1					
				Loan	03.09.87	Chester City	14		2					
24.12.87 Loan York City 6 Lg Apps.				Loan		Port Vale	7		1					
17.03.89 Wolverhampton W. 7 Lg Apps.				Loan	08.02.90	Preston N.E	2							
				£250,000	28.06.90	Wolverhampton W	85	5	2	3				
DEFENDERS														
Kevin Ashley	5.7	10.4	31.12.68	Birmingham		Birmingham C.	56+1	5	3	1+1	1			
				£500,000	13.09.90	Wolverhampton W	59+1	3	1+1	1	1			
Gary Bellamy	6.2	11.5	04.07.62	Worksop	25.06.80	Chesterfield	181+3	12	7	4	7		1	1
Div.4'85'88; Div3'89; SVT'88				£17,000	21.07.87	Wolverhampton W	133	9	3	16	9			
				Loan	18.03.92	Cardiff City	9							
Thomas Bennett	5.11	11.08	12.12.69	Falkirk		Aston Villa								
					05.07.88	Wolverhampton W	91+5	7	3+1	2+1	2			
Keith Downing	5.8	11.0	23.07.65	Oldbury		Mile Oak Rovers								
Div.4'88; Div.3'89; SVT'88					16.05.84	Notts County	23				1			
				Free	06.08.87	Wolverhampton W	139+21	7+3	5	13+3	6		1	1
Rob Hindmarch	6.1	13.4	27.04.61	Stannington	05.05.78	Sunderland (A)	114+1	6+2	5		2	1		
E: Y.5; Div2'87				Loan	07.12.83	Portsmouth	2							
				Free	12.07.84	Derby County	164	13	13	6	9		1	
				£325,000	21.06.90	Wolverhampton W	40	2	1	0+1	2			
Lawrie Madden	5.11	13.1	28.09.55	London		Arsenal								
LC'91				NC	01.03.75	Mansfield Town	9+1	2	2					
					04.03.78	Charlton Ath	109+4	4+2	8		7			
via Boston United to				£10,000	25.03.82	Millwall	44+3	2	1		2			
				Free	24.08.83	Sheffield Wed	200+12	26+2	20+1	5	2	3		
				Loan	17.01.91	Leicester City	3							
				Free	15.08.91	Wolverhampton W	43	3	1	1	1			
Derek Mountfield	6.0	13.6	02.11.62	Liverpool	04.11.80	Tranmere Rovers (A)	26	2	1		1			
EB:1,u21.1,Div1'85'87,UEFA u21'84,FAC'84, CS'84'85,ECWC'85				£30,000	02.06.82	Everton	100+6	16	17	14+1	19	3	2	1
				£450,000	06.06.88	Aston Villa	88+2	13	6	11	9	2	1	5
				£150,000	07.11.91	Wolverhampton W	28				1			
Mark Venus	6.0	11.8	06.04.67	Hartlepool	22.03.85	Hartlepool Utd	4			0+1				
Div.3'89				Free	05.10.85	Leicester City	58+3	3	2	2+1	1			
					23.03.88	Wolverhampton W	131+4	4+1	2	8	3			
Shane Westley	6.2	12.10	16.06.65	Canterbury	08.06.83	Charlton Ath. (A)	8		1					
					01.03.85	Southend Utd	142+2	10+1	5	7	10	1		1
				£150,000	19.06.89	Wolverhampton W	42+1	5		1	1	1		
MIDFIELD														
Paul Birch	5.6	10.9	20.11.62	West Bromwich	15.07.80	Aston Villa (A)	153+20	21+4	9+5	5+2	16	5	3	1
ESC'82 FAYC'80				£400,000	01.02.91	Wolverhampton W	63+2	3	1	1	10	2		
Paul Cook	5.11	10.10	22.02.67	Liverpool		Marine								
					20.07.84	Wigan Ath	77+6	4	6+1	5+1	14			1
				£73,000	23.06.88	Norwich City	3+3			1+1				
				£250,000	01.11.89	Wolverhampton W	113	4	2	4	16			1
Jim Kelly	5.10		14.02.73	Liverpool	05.07.91	Wrexham (T)	11+10		2	2+2				
				Swap	21.02.92	Wolverhampton W	0+3							
Tim Steele	5.9	11.0	01.02.67	Coventry		Shrewsbury Town (A)	41+20	3+1		1+1	5	1		
				£80,000		Wolverhampton W	52+19	5	1	4	6	3		
				Loan	20.02.92	Stoke City	7				1			
Andy Thompson	5.4	10.6	09.11.67	Cannock	16.11.85	West Brom A. (A)	18+6	0+1	2	1+1	1			
Div.4'88; Div.3'89; SVT'88				£35,000	21.11.86	Wolverhampton W	204+7	11	6	24	23			1
FORWARDS														
Steve Bull	5.11	11.4	28.03.65	Tipton	24.08.85	West Brom A. (A)	2+2	2		1+2	2	1		
E: 11, B.4, u21.5; Div.4'88; Div3'89; SVT'88				£35,000	21.11.86	Wolverhampton W	247	12	6	25	155	10	4	29
Mark Burke	5.10	11.8	12.02.69	Solihull	16.02.87	Aston Villa (T)	5+2			0+1				
E:Y3				£50,000	23.12.87	Middlesbrough	32+25	3	2+1	2+1	6			
				Loan	03.10.90	Darlington	5				1			
				£15,000	14.03.91	Wolverhampton W	16+8	1	1	0+1	2	1		
Robert Dennison	5.7	11.0	30.04.63	Banbridge		Glenavon								
Div.4'88; Div3'89; SVT'88					13.09.85	West Brom A	9+7	1	2	1	1			
				£20,000	13.03.87	Wolverhampton W	193+13	12+1	6+1	21	28	3	1	4
Andy Mutch	5.10	11.3	28.12.63	Liverpool		Southport								
E: n.3, u21.1; Div.4'88; Div3'89; SVT'88					25.02.86	Wolverhampton W	243+7	12	9+1	23	88	4		4
Mark Rankine	5.10	11.08	30.09.69	Doncaster	04.07.88	Doncaster Rovers (T)	160+4	8+1	8	14	20	1	2	2
				£70,000	31.01.92	Wolverhampton W	10+5				1			
Colin Taylor	6.0	12.7	25.12.71	Liverpool	16.03.90	Wolverhampton W (T)	7+11	0+2		2				
E: u18.2				Loan	22.01.92	Wigan Ath	7				2			
ADDITIONAL CONTRACT PLAYERS														
Shaun Bradbury						Wolverhampton W		1						

Daniel Collier, Andrew de Bont, Jonathon Howard, Darren Roberts (F), Darren Simkin (D), Mark Turner (M) from Paget Rangers.

WOLVERHAMPTON WANDERERS

RECORD WIN & LOSS AGAINST EACH CLUB IN CURRENT DIVISION
(Where a score has occured on several occasions the most recent is given)

Club	Rec. Win	Season	Rec. Loss	Season
BARNSLEY	9-1	1926-27	7-1	1909-10
BIRMINGHAM CITY	7-2	1895-96	4-1	1913-14
BRENTFORD	4-0	1936-37	5-0	1935-36
BRISTOL CITY	4-0	1990-91	4-1	1927-28
BRISTOL ROVERS	5-1	1976-77 (away)	4-3	1985-86 (home)
CAMBRIDGE UNITED	3-0	1987-88	2-1	1991-92
CHARLTON ATHLETIC	6-1	1936-37	5-1	1948-49
DERBY COUNTY	7-0	1905-06	9-0	1890-91
GRIMSBY TOWN	8-1	1947-48	6-0	1926-27
LEICESTER CITY	10-1	1937-38	7-0	1922-23
LUTON TOWN	5-0	1958-59	4-0	1983-84
MILLWALL	5-0	1928-29 (away)	4-0	1929-30
NEWCASTLE UNITED	5-0	1975-76	8-0	1905-06
NOTTS COUNTY	6-1	1905-06	4-0	1985-86
OXFORD UNITED	3-1	1991-92	3-1	1984-85
PETERBOROUGH UTD	1-0	1986-87 (away)	3-0	1986-87 (home)
PORTSMOUTH	7-0	1958-59	5-0	1948-49 (home)
SOUTHEND UNITED	3-0	1988-89	3-1	1988-89
SUNDERLAND	5-0	1957-58	6-0	1893-94
SWINDON TOWN	2-1	1991-92	3-1	1989-90
TRANMERE ROVERS	3-0	1987-88	3-0	1987-88
WATFORD	3-0	1991-92	5-0	1983-84
WEST HAM UNITED	5-0	1959-60	5-0	1964-65

MANAGER: GRAHAM TURNER

DATE OF BIRTH: 05.10.1947   **PLACE OF BIRTH:** Ellesmere Port

DATE OF APPOINTMENT: OCTOBER 1986

PREVIOUS CLUBS
as Manager: Shrewsbury Town (Player/Man.); Aston Villa
as Asst. Man./Coach:
as Player: Wrexham; Chester City; Shrewsbury Town

HONOURS
as Manager: Shrewsbury Town: Division 3 Championship 1979; Wolves: Div 4 Championship 1987-88, Sherpa Van Trophy Winners 1987-88, Div 3 Championship 1988-89
International: England: Youth International Cap.

Value Rating: ★ ★ ★ ★

Programme Editor: Paper Plane Publishing

Price of 1992-93 Programme: £1.20
Number of Pages: 36
Subscriptions: Please contact Club

Local Newspapers: Express & Star, Sports Argus

Local Radio Stations: Beacon Radio, BRMB

LEADING LEAGUE GOALSCORERS
SEASONS 1979-80 – 1991-92

1979-80	JOHN RICHARDS	13		1980-81	JOHN RICHARDS	13
1981-82	MEL EVES	7		1982-83	MEL EVES	18
1983-84	WAYNE CLARKE	6		1984-85	TONY EVANS	5
					MARK BUCKLAND	5
					ALAN AINSCOW	5
1985-86	DEAN EDWARDS	14		1986-87	STEVE BULL	15
1987-88	STEVE BULL	34		1988-89	STEVE BULL	37
1989-90	STEVE BULL	26		1990-91	STEVE BULL	24
			1991-92	STEVE BULL	20	

MOLINEUX GROUND Waterloo Road, Wolverhampton WV1 4QR

Capacity: 19,500   **Covered Standing:** 5,000   **Seating:** 14,500

Tel: Ground: 0902 712181   **Ticket Sales:** 0902 25899   **Clubcall:** 0898 12 11 03

All premium rate calls (0898/0891) cost 36p per minute cheap rate and 48p per minute at all other times. Call costings correct at time of going to press.

ATTENDANCES
Highest: 61,315 v Liverpool, FA Cup Round 5, 11.2.1939

Lowest: 900 v Notts County, Division 1, 17.10.1891

RECORD RECEIPTS: (with Previous Record)
£109,655 v Aston Villa, Littlewoods Cup Rnd 2 2nd leg, 4.10.1989
£91,137 v Torquay United, Sherpa Van Trophy Area Final, 18.4.1989

MOLINEUX
First game: v Aston Villa, 2.9.1889
First floodlit game: v South Africa XI, 30.9.1953

Season Tickets:
Stands: from £110 to £145, juv/OAP £95 to £115
Ground: £110, juv/OAP £75

Executive Box Season Tickets: Apply to club for details

Cost of Stand Tickets: £8, £6, juv/OAP £8, £5
Terraces: £6, juvs/OAP £4

Match and Ticket Information: Seats available by post with payment & SAE one month before each match

Car Parking: Available around 'The West Park', in side streets and at the rear of the North Bank

Nearest Railway Station: Wolverhampton (0902 595451)

How to get to the ground

From North: Use Motorway M6 until Junction 12, leave motorway and follow signs Wolverhampton A5 then A449 and at roundabout take 2nd exit into Waterloo Road then turn left in Molineux Street for Wolverhampton Wanderers FC

From East: Use Motorway M6 until Junction 10, leave Motorway and follow signs Wolverhampton A454. Then at crossroads turn right into Stratford Street. In 0.2m turn left into Ring Road. Then at next crossroads turn right into Waterloo Road and shortly turn right into Molineux Street for Wolverhampton Wanderers FC

From South: Use Motorway M5 until junction 2, leave motorway and follow signs Wolverhampton A4123, turn right then shortly turn left into Ring Road. In 1m turn left into Waterloo Road and shortly turn right into Molineux Street for Wolverhampton Wanderers FC

From West: Use A454 S.P. Wolverhampton and at roundabout turn left into Ring Road, then turn left into Molineux Street for Wolverhampton FC

WREXHAM

Division 3

Formed: 1873   **Turned Professional:** 1912   **Ltd Co:** 1912

SPONSORED BY: Wrexham Lager   **NICKNAME:** The Robins

President
G Mytton

Chairman
W P Griffiths

Vice-Chairman
B Williams

Directors
C Griffths
S F Mackreth
D Rhodes
C G Paletta

Secretary
D Rhodes (0978 262129)

Assistant Secretary
Miss M Pike

Team Manager
Brian Flynn

Assistant Manager
Kevin Reeves

Player Coach
Joey Jones

Youth Team Coach
Cliff Sear

Physiotherapist
Steve Wade

Commercial Manager
P Stokes (0978 352536)

Club Statistician for the Directory
Gareth Davies

JANUARY 4th 1992 will remain forever in the memory of all Wrexham supporters (and a few others!) Not only, perhaps, for the never to be forgotten F.A. Cup defeat of Arsenal alone. But more significantly for the fact that the spirit within the Racecourse club seems to have been reborn.

However the season on the whole has not seen the club gain much ground, although the rise to 14th place from the previous seasons basement position must count towards progress.

The F.A. Cup success story though has at last produced some much needed cash which allows manager Brian Flynn to bring in some new blood to the Racecourse to augment the talented youngsters at the club.

Unfortunately young Lee Jones has now departed to Anfield but no one can blame the Robins for taking the financial carrot which was dangled in front of them – such is the fact of life in the lower divisions.

The fact that no less than thirty-five players were used during the course of the season embraces the problems Flynn has in producing a settled side capable of challenging for a promotion place.

The season saw the lowest ever crowd for a competitive match at the Racecourse and also the highest ever receipts, which seems to epitomise the inconsistency of Wrexham's season.

The jewel within the football club is the youth policy (which is the envy of many in the football world) and is continuing to produce promising youngsters under the guidance of Cliff Sear, B Prandle, M Buxton I Pryce and of course Joey Jones.

They are following in the footsteps of Gareth Owen, Karl Connolly, Phil Hardy, Wayne Phillips and Steve Watkin who have already broken through to become first team regulars.

The attendances at the Racecourse have improved since the cup success, having not fallen once below the 2,000 mark which was once the norm, and, in itself shows there are grounds for optimism at the Racecourse.

This, however, must be maintained in the coming season with a concerted push for promotion. The fans have been patient enough. If the club's results are not consistent, the lads who produce the official programme certainly are, with the Fourth Division best programme award going yet again to Wrexham F.C.

March 4th 1992 saw the retirement from first team football of Joey Jones, the Wrexham and Wales seventy-two times capped international, on his 37th birthday, due to persistent injury. It has often been remarked there are not enough characters in soccer these days. He is certainly one of them, and an example to all youngsters who wish to take up the game – both on and off the field. Thanks a million Joey.

Gareth M Davies

Back row L-R: Jonathan Cross, Kevin Jones, Craig Knight, Barry Jones, Tony Humes, John Paskin, Mark Sertori, Karl Connolly, Gary Bennett, Mickey Thomas. **Middle:** Mike Rigg (Community Scheme Organiser), Cliff Sear (Youth Development Officer), Stephen Pugh, Richard Laughton, Steve Watkin, Ken Hughes, Mark Morris, Scott Williams, Simon Betts, David Brammer, Joey Jones (Coach), Steve Wade (Physio). **Front:** Kieron Durkan, Phil Myddleton, Wayne Phillips, Richard McNeil, Brian Flynn (Manager), Kevin Reeves (Asst. Manager), Phil Hardy, Mel Pejic, Gareth Owen, Dave Esdaille.

WREXHAM

DIVISION FOUR: 14th **FA CUP:** 4th RND **RUMBELOWS CUP:** 1st RND **AUTOGLASS:** Sth S/FINALS

M	DATE		COMP.	VEN	OPPONENTS	RESULT	H/T	LGE POS	GOALSCORERS/GOAL TIMES	ATTEN-DANCE
1	A	17	BL	H	Hereford United	L 0-1	0-1			3,225
2		20	RC 1/1	H	Scunthorpe United	W 1-0	0-0		Thackeray 50	1,621
3		24	BL	A	Walsall	D 0-0	0-0	17		(3,307)
4		27	RC 1/2	A	Scunthorpe United	L 0-3	0-0			(2,125)
5		30	BL	H	Northampton Town	D 2-2	1-1	20	Connolly 3, Bowden (pen) 61	2,196
6	S	3	BL	A	Mansfield Town	L 0-3	0-0	21		(1,965)
7		7	BL	A	Doncaster Rovers	L 1-3	0-1	22	S Phillips 63	(1,474)
8		14	BL	H	Gillingham	W 2-1	2-1	18	Bowden 3, 15 (pen)	1,642
9		21	BL	A	York City	D 2-2	2-1	19	Owen 36, Watkin 39	(1,816)
10		28	BL	H	Scunthorpe United	W 4-0	2-0	13	Humphries (og) 24, Watkin 28, 85, Davies 59	1,635
11	O	5	BL	A	Cardiff City	L 0-5	0-2	15		(3,652)
12		12	BL	H	Burnley	L 2-6	2-4	18	Davies 3, Preece 39	3,181
13		15	AGT Pre	H	Mansfield Town	W 1-0	0-0		Preece 47	627
14		19	BL	A	Carlisle United	W 3-0	1-0	13	Watkin 17, Preece 48, Thomas 84	1,266
15		22	AGT Pre	A	Peterborough Utd	L 0-2	0-0			(1,080)
16	N	2	BL	H	Barnet	W 1-0	1-0	13	Watkin 40	1,866
17		5	BL	A	Scarborough	L 1-4	1-0	14	Watkin 42	(1,164)
18		9	BL	A	Crewe Alexandra	L 1-2	0-1	14	Owen 75	(3,596)
19		16	FAC 1	H	Winsford United	W 5-2	1-1		Watkin 3 (71, 77, 85), Connolly 8, Thomas 90	2,933
20		19	BL	A	Blackpool	L 0-4	0-2	16		(2,842)
21		23	BL	H	Chesterfield	L 0-1	0-1	17		1,636
22	D	7	FAC 2	H	Telford United	W 1-0	0-0		Watkin 71	3,897
23		13	BL	A	Halifax Town	L 3-4	1-1	20	Connolly 29, 77, Davies 52	(881)
24		20	BL	H	Walsall	W 2-1	1-0	18	Connolly 15, Watkin 49	2,571
25		26	BL	A	Hereford United	L 1-3	0-1	20	Davies 47	(3,542)
26		28	BL	A	Northampton Town	D 1-1	0-1	20	Phillips 68	(3,209)
27	J	1	BL	H	Mansfield Town	W 3-2	2-1	16	Thackeray 10, Owen 44, Connolly 64	2,442
28		4	FAC 3	H	Arsenal	W 2-1	0-1		Thomas 82, Watkin 84	13,343
29		11	BL	H	Maidstone United	D 0-0	0-0	19		3,167
30		18	BL	H	Lincoln City	D 0-0	0-0	19		(2,213)
31		25	FAC 4	H	West Ham United	D 2-2	0-1		Phillips 60, L Jones 80	(24,712)
32	F	4	FAC 4R	A	West Ham United	L 0-1	0-1			17,995
33		8	BL	H	Blackpool	D 1-1	1-1	19	Phillips 36	4,053
34		15	BL	H	Halifax Town	W 2-0	0-0	17	L Jones 63, Owen 72	2,076
35		18	AGT 1	H	Bournemouth	W 2-1	0-0		L Jones 61, 89	(2,279)
36		22	BL	A	Maidstone United	W 4-2	2-1	16	L Jones 19, Pejic 21, Thackeray 73, Owen 84	(1,491)
37		25	AGT 2	A	Fulham	W 2-0	0-0		Paskin 70, Phillips 87	(2,236)
38		29	BL	A	Rochdale	W 2-1	0-0	16	L Jones 59, Thackeray 84	3,458
39	M	3	BL	A	Lincoln City	D 1-1	0-0	16	L Jones 56	2,716
40		7	BL	H	Rotherham United	L 0-3	0-0	17		(3,562)
41		10	BL	A	Scarborough	W 2-0	1-0	14	Paskin 10, Carey 46	2,044
42		14	BL	H	Barnet	L 0-2	0-0	16		(2,917)
43		17	AGT SSF	F	Peterborough Utd	L 1-3	0-2		Connolly 51	(3,929)
44		21	BL	A	Crewe Alexandra	W 1-0	0-0	16	Owen 64	3,899
45		24	BL	H	Carlisle United	W 1-0	0-0	12	Gallimore (og) 51	(1,826)
46		28	BL	H	Chesterfield	D 1-1	1-0	13	Phillips 23	(2,961)
47		31	BL	H	Gillingham	L 1-2	0-2	13	Connolly 55	(3,078)
48	A	3	BL	A	Doncaster Rovers	L 1-2	1-2	14	Connolly 20	2,769
49		18	BL	A	York City	W 2-1	0-0	14	Connolly 75, Paskin 84	2,261
50		20	BL	A	Scunthorpe United	L 1-3	0-0	15	Longden (og) 78	(2,900)
51		22	BL	H	Rochdale	L 1-2	0-1	15	Watkin 55	(1,945)
52		25	BL	A	Cardiff City	L 0-3	0-2	15		4,002
53		28	BL	A	Rotherham United	L 0-3	0-1	15		3,477
54	M	2	BL	H	Burnley	W 2-1	0-1	14	Paskin 61, Owen 77	(21,216)

Best Home League Attendance: 4,053 v Blackpool   **Smallest:** 1,266 v Carlisle United   **Av Home Att:** 2,647

Goal Scorers: Compared with 90-91: +759

League (52): Connolly 8, Watkin 8, Owen 7, L Jones 4, Davies 4, Opponents 3, Paskin 3, Phillips 3, Thackeray 3, Bowden 3 (2 pens), Preece 2, Thomas, Pejic, Carey, S Phillips

R/lows C (1): Thackeray
FA Cup (10): Watkin 5, Thomas 2, Phillips, L Jones, Connolly
Autoglass (6): L Jones 2, Phillips, Connolly, Preece, Paskin

1991-92

O'Keefe V.	Thackeray A.	Hardy P.	Sertori M.	Beaumont N.	Jones J.	Phillips W.	Kelly J.	Owen G.	Thomas M.	Jones L.	Watkin S.	Connoly K.	Davies G.	Bowden J.	Preece A.	Lewis D.	Flynn B.	Paskin J.	Marshall C. (L)	Ireland S. (L)	Carey B. (L)	Taylor M.	Pejic M.	Humes T.	Referee	
1	2	3	4	S	6	5*			12	8	11		9	10	7										B Coddington	1
1	2	3	4		6	S		S	5	10			9	8	7	11									K Breen	2
1	2	3	4		6	S		12	5	10			9	8	7	11*									C Wilkes	3
1	2	3	4		6*	S		8	5	10			9	11	7	12									N Midgley	4
1	2	3	4		6	S			5	10			9	8	7	11									R Poulain	5
1	2	3	4			11			5*	10•			9	8	7										I Hemley	6
1	2	3	4*	12				8	5				14	10	7										T Fitzharris	7
1	2	3	6	4		S			5				9	8	7	S									R Gifford	8
1	2	3	4		6			10	8	5	14	9*	7•			12									W Burns	9
1	2	3	4		6	S		8	5		S	10	9		7	11									J Kirby	10
1	2	3	S	4	6			8	5	12		10	9		7*	11									M James	11
1	2	3		4	6	S		8	5	12		10	9		7*	11									P Vanes	12
	2	3	4	6	7	9	8	5		S	10				11							S			S Lodge	13
	2	3	S	4	6	7	9	8	5		S	10			11										D Phillips	14
	2	3	12	4	6	7*	9	8		10		14			11			5•							G Ashby	15
	2	3	6	4		9	S	8	5			10			7	11									P Harrison	16
	2	3	6	4		9	S	8	5	12		10			7	11*									J Watson	17
	2	3	5	4	6		9	8		12	10	14			7*						11•				J Parker	18
	2	3	7	4	6	11	8	5		S	10	9			S										A Bennett	19
2*	3	7	4	6		11•	8	5		12	10	9			14										S Bell	20
	2	3	8	4	6•		9		5*	14	10	12	7		11										D Shadwell	21
1	2	3	6	4		11	8	5		9	10			7	S								S		K Hackett	22
1	2	3	6	4		S	11	8	5		9*	10		7								12			C Trussell	23
1	2	3	6	4		11	8	5		10	9			7	S										J Worrall	24
1	2	3	6			12	11•	8*	5	14	10	9	7									4			R Hamer	25
1	2	3	6			S	11	8	5		10	9*	7									4			D Gallagher	26
1	2	3	6			11	S	8	5		10	9	7									4			T Lunt	27
1	2	3	6			S	11	S	8	5	10	9	7									4			K Breen	28
1	2	3	6			11	8*	5	14	10•	9	7										4	12		K Cooper	29
1	2	3	6			S	11	S	5		10	9	7									4	8		G Poll	30
1	2	3	6			11	S	8	5	12	10	9*	7•									4			C Trussell	31
1	2	3	6			11*	S	8	5	12	10	9	7									4			C Trussell	32
1	2	3	6			11	7*		5	12	10	9										4	8		P Vanes	33
1	2	3	6			11	14	5	12	10•	9		8•						5*			4	7		A Smith	34
1	2	3	6			11	8		10	12	9							5*				4			J Deakin	35
1	2	3	6			11	8		10	S	9							7				4	5		P Jones	36
1	2	3	6			11	8		10	S	9							7				4	5		A Gunn	37
1	2	3	6			11	8		10	S	9							7				4	5*		K Barratt	38
1	2	3	6			11	8		10	S	9							7				4	5*		P Danson	39
1	2	3	6			11	8		10	S	9							7				5	4		G Singh	40
1	2	3	6			11	8		10	S	9						5	7		12		4			J Parker	41
1	2	3	6			11	8		12	9•							5*	7	10			4			R Bigger	42
1	2	3	6			11	8		10*	9							5*	7	12			4			R Lewis	43
1	2	3	6			11	8		10	9						4	5*	7	12						K Cooper	44
1	2	3	6			11	8		10	9						4	5*	7*	14				12		S Lodge	45
1	2	3	6			11	8		10	9*						4		7*	12					5	T West	46
1	2	3	6			11	8			9						4	7*		12			10		5	J Martin	47
1	2	3	6			12	8			9						4	7	14	11•			10		5	K Cooper	48
1	2	3	6			11	8		12	9						4*	7		S			10		5	K Burge	49
1	2	3	6			11	8		14	9						4*	7		12			10•		5	K Lupton	50
1	2	3*	6			11	8		10	9						4	7					12		5	D Phillips	51
1	2	3	6			11	8		10	9						S	7					4		5	R Shepherd	52
1	2	3	6			11*	8	4	10	9						S	12				7				R Gifford	53
1	2	3	6			11*	8	4•	10	9						14	12				7		5		J Watson	54
36	42	42	36	13	11	28	9	33	26	11	24	33	21	6	9	8	6	14	3	2	3	13	6	6	**League Appearances**	
		1			2		3		10	4	3	1		1	1		3		3	3		3	1		**Substitute Appearances**	
2	2	2	2		2			2	2	2	2	2		1+1											**R/lows Appearances**	
4	5	5	5	2	1	3	2	5	1+2	5	5	3										3			**FA Cup Appearances**	
3	5	5	3+1	2	2	5	2	5	1	3	2+1	3		2	2	1					0+1	3			**Autoglass Appearances**	

Also Played: Posn.(Game): Morris 1(13,14,15,16,17,18,19,20,21,51,52), Knight 5(53), Skipper 6(6,7*), S Phillips 14(6)9(7), R Lunt 12(26)S(27), D Jones S(33,35,43,44,51,52)14(42), K Jones S(37)12(39), D Brammer S(40), J Griffiths 11(7,8,9), K Durkan S(5,36,38)12(6)7(35)S(37)

Players on Loan: B Carey (Manchester Utd); C Marshall (Barnsley), S Ireland (Huddersfield T)

WREXHAM

Club Colours: Red shirts, white shorts, red stockings
Change Colours: Yellow shirts with green trim, Green shorts with yellow stripes, yellow or green stockings
Reserves League: Midland Senior League   **Third Team:** Welsh National League (Wrexham area)

Previous League: The Combination, Birmingham League
Previous Managers: 1924-26 Charles Hewitt   1929-31 Jack Baynes   R Burkinshaw Dec 1931-Jan 1932   1932-36 Ernest Blackburn   Captain Logan 1937-38   1939-42 Tommy Morgan   1942-49 Tom W Williams   C Lloyd March-May 1949   1949-50 Leslie J McDowall   1951-54 Peter Jackson   1954-57 Clifford Lloyd   1957-59 John Love   1960-61 Billy Morris   1961-65 Ken Barnes   1965-66 Billy Morris   1966-67 Jack Rowley   1967 Cliff Lloyd   1967-8 Alvan Williams   1968-77 John Neal   1977-81 Arfon Griffiths   1981-82 Mel Sutton   1982-85 Bobby Roberts   Dixie McNeil 1985-89   Brian Flynn 1989-
Honours: Div 3 Champions 1977-78   Welsh Cup Winners (22)   Welsh Cup Runners-Up (22)
League Career: Original members of Div 3N 1921   Transferred to Div 3 1958   Relegated to Div 4 1959-60   Promoted to Div 3 1961-62   Relegated to Div 4 1963-64   Promoted to Div 3 1969-70   Promoted to Div 2 1977-78   Relegated to Div 3 1981-82   Relegated to Div 4 1982-83

CLUB RECORDS

Most Appearances for Club: Arfon Griffiths (1959-61 & 1962-79) **Total 586 + 6 subs** (not including Cup ties)
Most Capped Player: Joey Jones (Wales) 29   **For England:** None
Record Goalscorer in a Match: A Livingstone 7 v Tranmere Rovers, Wartime Football League North, 25.10.1943   T Bamford 6 v New Brighton (h), 11-1, Div 3N Cup, 1933-34   T H Lewis 5 v Crewe Alexandra (h) 7-0, Div 3N, 20.9.1930   T Bamford 5 v Carlisle United (h) 8-1, Div 3N, 17.3.1934
Record League Goalscorer in a Season: Tommy Bamford, 44, Div 3N, 1933-34
Record League Goalscorer in a Career: Tommy Bamford, 175, 1929-35
Record Transfer Fee Received: £300,000 from Manchester United for Mickey Thomas, Nov 1978   £300,000 from Manchester City for Bobby Shinton, July 1979
£300,000 + further £300,000 on completion of set amount of first team appearances from Liverpool for Lee Jones, March 1992
Record Transfer Fee Paid: £210,000 to Liverpool for Joey Jones, Oct 1978
Best Performances: League: 15th Div 2, 1978-79   **FA Cup:** 6th Round 1973-74, 1977-78   **League Cup:** 5th Round 1961, 1978
Welsh Cup: Winners (22), Runners-up (21). This is a record number of victories and appearances in the Final   **European Cup Winners Cup:** Quarter-Final 1975-76
Most League Points: (2pts for win) 61, Div 4, 1969-70, Div 3, 1977-78   (3pts for win) 71 Div 4, 1988-89
Most League Goals: 106, Div 3N, 1932-33
Record League Victory and Most Goals Scored in a League Match: 10-1 v Hartlepool, Div 4, 3.3.1962
Most Goals Scored in a Cup Tie: 11-1 v New Brighton (h), Div 3N Cup, 1933-34
Record League Defeat: 0-9 v Brentford, Div 3, 15.10.1963
Record Cup Defeat: 1-9 v Wolverhampton Wanderers, FA Cup Rnd 3, 1930-31
European Competitions entered: European Cup Winners Cup: 1972-73, 1975-76, 1978-79, 1979-80, 1984-85, 1986-87, 1990-91
Oldest Player in a League Match: W. Lot Jones 46 years, 1921-22
Youngest Player in a League Match: Ken Roberts 15 years 158 days v Bradford Park Avenue, 1.9.1951
Ken shares this record with Albert Geldard (Bradford P.A.) as the two youngest players to play in the Football League.

LONGEST LEAGUE RUNS

of undefeated matches: 16 (1966)	of league matches without a win: 14 (1923-24, 1950)
of undefeated home matches: 38 (1969-70)	of undefeated away matches: 8 (1961, 1966)
without home win: 10 (1980-81)	without an away win: 31 (1982-83)
of league wins: 7 (1961, 1978)	of home wins: 13 (1932-33)
of league defeats: 9 (1963)	of away wins: 7 (1961)

WREXHAM

PLAYERS NAME Honours	Ht	Wt	Birthdate	Birthplace Transfers	Contract Date	Clubs	League	L/Cup	FA Cup	Other	Lg	L/C	FAC	Oth
GOALKEEPERS														
Ken Hughes	6.0	11.8	09.01.66	Barmouth	13.08.85	Crystal Palace				1				
				Free	21.08.86	Shrewsbury	51		7	6				
				Free		Wrexham								
Mark Morris	5.11	12.0	01.08.68	Chester	03.09.87	Wrexham	55	1	2	8				
DEFENDERS														
Phil Hardy	5.10		09.04.73	Chester	24.11.90	Wrexham	75	3	6	9				
Tony Humes	5.11	11.0	19.03.66	Blyth	01.06.83	Ipswich Town (A)	107+13	6	4	10	10		1	1
				£40,000	27.03.92	Wrexham	8							
Melvin Pejic	5.7	10.6	27.04.59	Newcastle-U-Lyne	22.07.77	Stoke City (A)	1							
WC'90					13.06.80	Hereford Utd	404+9	23+2	20+1	26+1	14	3	3	
				£7,000	09.01.92	Wrexham	6+1				1			
MIDFIELD														
Gareth Owen	5.10		21.10.71	Chester	06.07.90	Wrexham (T)	65+11	1+1	6+1	12	9			
Mickey Thomas	5.6	10.7	02.12.60	Mochdre	01.04.76	Wrexham	217+13	17+1	20+4	10	33	2	2	
W: 51, u23.1, u21.2; WCx2; Div.3'78; Div.2'84					23.11.78	Manchester Utd	90	5	13	2	11	2	2	
					05.08.81	Everton	10	1						
					05.11.81	Brighton & H.A	18+2		3				1	
					26.08.82	Stoke City	57	7	3		14	1		
					13.01.84	Chelsea	43+1	7	3		9	2		
					26.09.85	West Brom A	20	5	2	1			1	
				Loan	01.04.86	Derby County	9							
				Witchita W	01.08.86	U.S. of A								
					19.08.88	Shrewsbury Town	40	1	1		1			
				£10,000	13.06.89	Leeds Utd	3							
				Loan	20.03.90	Stoke City	8							
					10.08.90	Stoke City	32+6	2+1	3	1	7			
				Free	15.08.91	Wrexham	26	2	5	1	1		2	
FORWARDS														
Gary Bennett	6.1	12.6	20.09.63	Liverpool	09.10.74	Wigan Ath.	10+10		1	3+1	3			1
FRT '85				Free	22.08.85	Chester City	109+17	6+4	8+1	10	36	1	5	5
					11.11.88	Southend Utd.	36+6	4	1	2+1	6	4		
				£20,000	01.03.90	Chester City	71+9	8	5	4	15	2	1	1
				Free		Wrexham								
Karl Connolly	6.1		09.02.70	Liverpool		Tranmere Rovers (A)								
					03.03.91	Wrexham	33+3	2	5	3	8		1	1
William Paskin	5.11	12.2	01.02.62	Capetown	29.09.88	West Brom A	14+11	1	0+2		5			
				£75,000	26.06.89	Wolverhampton W	21+13	2+1	2	0+1	2			
				Loan	11.09.91	Stockport Co	3+2				1			
				Loan	21.11.91	Birmingham City	8+2	0+1			3			
				Loan	13.02.92	Shrewsbury Town	5			1+1				
				Swap	21.02.92	Wrexham	14+3			2	3			1
Wayne Phillips			15.12.70	Bangor	23.08.89	Wrexham	54+9	4	4	10+1	3		1	1
Mark Sertori	6.3	13.04	01.09.67	Manchester	07.02.87	Stockport Co	3+1	1						
GMVC'88					01.07.88	Lincoln City	43+7	6	4	5	9		1	2
				£30,000	09.02.90	Wrexham	81+2	5	5	7+1	4			
P Mark Taylor	5.7	10.0	20.11.64	Hartlepool	16.08.82	Hartlepool Utd	42+5	0+1	2	2	4		1	
				Loan	23.12.85	Crewe Alexandra	3							
				Free	28.08.86	Blackpool	104+15	6+3	8	9+3	43	1	2	1
				Loan	21.12.90	Cardiff City	6				3			
				£30,000	24.03.92	Wrexham	6+3							
Stephen Watkin	5.10		16.06.71	Wrexham	20.06.91	Wrexham	33+4		5	3+1	9		5	
ADDITIONAL CONTRACT PLAYERS														
Andrew Carroll					16.08.89	Wrexham								
Kieron Durkan						Wrexham								
Alex Goss					03.06.91	Wrexham	3+3			0+1				
R J Hunt						Wrexham	1+7							
Kevin R Jones						Wrexham				0+1				
(D) Barry Jones	6.0	12.10	30.06.70	Liverpool		Prescot Town								
					30.06.70	Liverpool				0+1				
				Free	10.07.92	Wrexham								
Craig Knight					13.07.92	Wrexham								
Phillip Myddleton					16.07.92	Wrexham								
Carl Parrish					14.08.89	Wrexham								
Stephen Watkins					31.12.90	Wrexham								

LEADING LEAGUE GOALSCORERS SEASONS 1985-86 – 1991-92

1985-86	**STEVE CHARLES**	30	1986-87	**JIM STEEL**	17
1987-88	**KEVIN RUSSELL**	21	1988-89	**KEVIN RUSSELL**	22
1989-90	**GARY WORTHINGTON**	12	1990-91	**CHRIS ARMSTRONG**	10
	1991-92	**CARL CONNOLLY**	8		

RACECOURSE GROUND Mold Road, Wrexham

Capacity: 17,500   **Covered Standing:**   **Seating:** 5,026

Tel: Ground: 0978 262129   **Ticket Sales:** As ground number   **Clubcall:** 0898 12 16 42

All premium rate calls (0898/0891) cost 36p per minute cheap rate and 48p per minute at all other times. Call costings correct at time of going to press.

ATTENDANCES
Highest: 34,445 v Manchester United, FA Cup Round 4, 26.1.1957

Lowest: 736 v Wigan Athletic, Freight Rover Trophy, 29.1.1985

Record Receipts: £126,000 v West Ham Utd, FA Cup 4th Rnd Replay, 4.2.1992
£89,000 v Manchester Utd, European Cup Winners Cup Round 2, 2nd leg, 7.11.1990

Season Tickets:
Stands: £127, juv/OAP £80
Ground: £90, juv/OAP £72

Executive Box Season Tickets: £125

Cost of Stand Tickets: Seats: £7, juv/OAP £5
Terraces: £5, juv/OAP ££3.50

Match and Ticket Information: Tickets not bookable in advance

Membership Scheme: Our membership scheme applies to the Yale Paddock and the Centre and Town End sections of the Yale Stand

Car Parking: Parking ground at St Marks, Bodhyfryd Square, Eagles Meadows, Old Guild Hall, Hill Street, Holt Street and Town Hall (Hill Street)

Nearest Railway Station: Wrexham General

How to get to the ground

From North and West: Use A483 and Wrexham bypass until junction with A541 then branch left and at roundabout follow signs Wrexham into Mold Road for Wrexham FC

From East and South: Follow signs into Wrexham on A543 or A525 then follow signs A541 into Mold Road for Wrexham FC

Value Rating: ★ ★ ★ ★

Programme Editors: D Roberts, G Parry, P Jones

Price of 1992-93 Programme: £1
Number of Pages: 32
Fourth Division Programme of the Year 5th Year in succession. 12th overall in Football League
Subscriptions: £30 for all 1st team home programmes

Local Newspapers: Wrexham Evening Leader, Daily Post, Shropshire Star

Local Radio Stations: Radio City, Marcher Sound, Radio Clwyd

YORK CITY

Division 3

Formed: 1922   **Turned Professional:** 1922   **Ltd Co:** 1922

SPONSORED BY: Portakabin Ltd   **NICKNAME:** The Minster Men

Chairman
D M Craig
OBE, JP, BSc, FICE

Directors
B A Houghton
C Webb
E B Swallow
J E H Quickfall, F.C.A.

Club Secretary
Keith Usher (0904 624447)

Company Secretary
I R Fowler

Medical Officer
Dr G R Porter

Manager
John Ward

Coach
Alan Little

Youth Team Coach
Ricky Sbragia

Physiotherapist
Jeff Miller

Commercial Manager
Mrs Sheila Smith (0904 645941)

Groundsman
Bryan Foster

Honorary Orthopaedic Surgeon
P De Boer, MA FRCS

Club Statistician for the Directory
D Batters

SEASON 1991-92 was another very disappointing campaign for York City and for the second successive season they finished fourth from bottom of Division Four.

A poor start was made and with just two wins in 14 league and cup outings manager John Bird was dismissed in mid-October after exactly four years at the helm. John Ward was appointed as his successor. A former player with Lincoln City, Watford and Grimsby Town, he had been Graham Taylor's assistant manager and coach at Watford and Aston Villa. He is the current England under-21 manager.

Results initially improved and by late November the club were just below mid-table. A bad period around Christmas and the New Year, however, saw them again slip into the lower reaches and they were to struggle throughout the second half of the season.

Once again lack of scoring power was the major problem and in the league they only averaged a goal per game. No less than 16 games were drawn whilst the total of just 8 wins equalled a club record low set in 1987-88.

Leading marksman was Ian Blackstone and Jon McCarthy, who was the only ever-present, was voted 'Clubman of the Year'. Experienced defender Paul Stancliffe had the misfortune to miss a good deal of the season because of injury. Average league attendances of 2506 were almost identical to the previous season.

The highlight of the year was in the F.A. Cup when in the Second Round City gave Second Division Tranmere two hard battles before bowing out. It was, however, the sixth successive season that they had failed to reach the third round – the worst sequence in the club's history since they joined the Football League in 1929. There were early exits in the Rumbelows Cup and Autoglass Trophy. In the latter competition only 957 saw a Preliminary Round match against Carlisle United and this was the smallest ever recorded attendance to watch a home game.

Off the field it was brighter and in October the David Longhurst stand was officially opened with a visit from Leeds United. In readiness for 1992-93 a new Family Stand is being constructed within the maind stand.

The club's financial situation also improved considerably. Just prior to the start of the season Ian Helliwell was transferred to Scunthorpe United for £80,000 and in September when Marco Gabbiadini moved from Sunderland to Crystal Palace they received over £300,000. This was part of the deal set up when Gabbiadini was transferred to Roker Park in 1987.

Not since the mid-1980's have City tasted any success and after six lean seasons the Bootham Crescent faithful will be hoping that the tide will turn in 1992-93. **David Batters**

Back row L-R: Paul Atkin, Steve Tutill, Paul Stancliffe, Chris Marples, Dean Kiely, Ray Warburton, John Borthwick, Darren Tilley. **Middle row:** Alan Little (Coach), Paul Barnes, John McCarthy, Phil Crosby, Andy McMillan, Gary Swann, Glenn Naylor, Nigel Pepper, Ian Blackstone, Geoff Miller (Physio). **Front row:** Andy Smith, Wayne Hall, Tony Barratt, John Ward (Manager), Tony Canham, Steve Bushell, Craig Hall.

YORK CITY

DIVISION FOUR: 19th   **FA CUP:** 2nd RND   **RUMBELOWS CUP:** 1st RND   **AUTOGLASS:** Prelim.

M	DATE		COMP.	VEN	OPPONENTS	RESULT		H/T	LGE POS	GOALSCORERS/GOAL TIMES	ATTEN- DANCE
1	A	17	BL	A	Rochdale	D	1-1	1-0		Naylor 43	(2,247)
2		20	RC 1/1	A	Bolton Wanderers	D	2-2	0-1		McCarthy 67, Blackstone 72	(3,017)
3		24	BL	H	Gillingham	D	1-1	1-0	14	Naylor 34	2,328
4		27	RC 1/2	H	Bolton Wanderers	L	1-2	1-1		Canham 34	2,757
5		30	BL	A	Halifax Town	D	0-0	0-0	17		(2,167)
6	S	3	BL	H	Blackpool	W	1-0	0-0	9	McCarthy 58	2,686
7		7	BL	H	Chesterfield	L	0-1	0-1	13		2,382
8		17	BL	A	Hereford United	L	1-2	0-2	16	Stancliffe 47	(3,540)
9		21	BL	H	Wrexham	D	2-2	1-2	18	Naylor 21, Canham 82	1,816
10		28	BL	A	Maidstone United	L	0-1	0-1	21		(1,037)
11	O	5	BL	H	Scarborough	W	4-1	3-1	14	Canham 28, Naylor 33, Tutill 45, McCarthy 55	2,971
12		12	BL	A	Barnet	L	0-2	0-0	16		(4,476)
13		19	BL	H	Lincoln City	D	1-1	0-0	18	McCarthy 71	1,893
14		22	AGT Pre	H	Carlisle United	D	1-1	0-1		McCarthy 62	957
15		25	BL	A	Rotherham United	L	0-4	0-1	18		(4,677)
16	N	2	BL	H	Walsall	W	2-0	0-0	14	Reid 53, Hall 70	1,605
17		5	BL	A	Burnley	L	1-3	1-2	16	McCarthy 25	(7,389)
18		8	BL	A	Doncaster Rovers	W	1-0	1-0	14	Canham 34	(2,144)
19		16	FAC 1	A	Bridlington Town	W	2-1	0-0		Blackstone 47, 87	(1,700)
20		30	BL	A	Scunthorpe United	L	0-1	0-0	14		(2,887)
21	D	7	FAC 2	H	Tranmere Rovers	D	1-1	0-1		Hall 66	4,646
22		14	BL	H	Cardiff City	L	1-3	1-1	15	Canham 39	1,904
23		17	FAC 2R	A	Tranmere Rovers	L	1-2	0-1		McCarthy 74	(5,546)
24		21	BL	A	Gillingham	D	1-1	0-0	17	Barratt 84	(2,711)
25		26	BL	H	Rochdale	L	0-1	0-0	18		2,788
26		28	BL	H	Halifax Town	D	1-1	0-0	18	Hall 89	2,396
27	J	1	BL	A	Blackpool	L	1-3	0-2	20	Pepper 53	(3,534)
28		4	BL	H	Mansfield Town	L	1-2	0-2	20	McCarthy 73	2,666
29		7	AGT Pre	A	Stockport County	L	0-3	0-2			(1,397)
30		11	BL	A	Northampton Town	D	2-2	2-2	20	Pepper 5, Canham 17	(3,355)
31		18	BL	H	Carlisle United	W	2-0	0-0	16	Barratt 62, 74	1,953
32	F	8	BL	H	Rotherham United	D	1-1	0-1	17	Hall 90	3,526
33		11	BL	H	Scunthorpe United	W	3-0	2-0	16	Blackstone 31, Pepper (pen) 37, 47	2,255
34		15	BL	A	Cardiff City	L	0-3	0-0	16		(8,067)
35		22	BL	H	Northampton Town	D	0-0	0-0	17		2,065
36		25	BL	A	Crewe Alexandra	L	0-1	0-1	17		(3,327)
37		29	BL	A	Mansfield Town	L	2-5	1-3	18	McCarthy 10, Atkin 89	(3,290)
38	M	3	BL	A	Carlisle United	D	1-1	1-1	18	Blackstone 19	(1,681)
39		7	BL	H	Crewe Alexandra	D	1-1	1-1	18	McMillan 4	2,208
40		14	BL	A	Walsall	D	1-1	1-1	19	Blackstone 19	(2,541)
41		18	BL	A	Lincoln City	D	0-0	0-0	18		(1,875)
42		21	BL	H	Doncaster Rovers	D	1-1	0-0	18	Blackstone 89	2,127
43	A	4	BL	A	Chesterfield	W	3-1	2-1	19	Blackstone 1, Naylor 16, 65	(2,461)
44		11	BL	H	Hereford United	W	1-0	1-0	19	Blackstone 29	1,614
45		18	BL	A	Wrexham	L	1-2	0-0	19	Naylor 72	(2,261)
46		20	BL	H	Maidstone United	D	1-1	1-0	19	Naylor 31	1,638
47		25	BL	A	Scarborough	L	0-1	0-0	19		(2,108)
48		28	BL	H	Burnley	L	1-2	1-0	19	Blackstone 43	7,620
49	M	2	BL	H	Barnet	L	1-4	0-0	19	Blackstone 55	2,643

Best Home League Attendance: 7,620 v Burnley   **Smallest:** 1,605 v Walsall   **Av Home Att:** 2,528

Goal Scorers: **Compared with 90-91: +17**

League (42): Blackstone 8, Naylor 8, McCarthy 6, Canham 5, Pepper 4 (1 pen), Barratt 3, Hall 3, McMillan, Stancliffe, Atkin, Tutill, Reid

R/lows C (3): Canham, Blackstone, McCarthy

FA Cup (4): Blackstone 2, Hall, McCarthy

Autoglass (1): McCarthy

Kiely D.	McMillan L.	Crosby P.	Reid S.	Tutill S.	Stancliffe B.	McCarthy J.	Pepper N.	Blackstone I.	Naylor G.	Canham A.	Marples C.	Atkin P.	Hall W.	Osborne S.	Curtis A.	Barratt A.	Warburton R.	Bushell S.	Gosney A.	McLoughlin P.	Tilley D.	Shepstone P.	Referee	
1	2	3*	4	5	6	7	8	9	10	11		S	S										J Lloyd	1
	2	3	4	5	6*	8	7	9	10*	11	1	12	14										**C Wilkes**	2
	2	3	4	5	6	8	7	9	10	11	1	S	S										P Danson	3
	2	3			8	7	9		11*		1	5	6	10	12	S							**A Dawson**	4
	2	3	4	5	8	7	9			1	6	11*	10			12	S						A Wilkie	5
	2	3	4	5	8	7	S	11	1		S	9			10	6							I Cruikshanks	6
	2	3	4	5	8	7	12	11	1		S	9*			10	6							P Harrison	7
	2	3	4	5	6	8	7	11	1		S	12	9*			10							V Callow	8
	2		4	5	8	7	9	11	1		6	3	12	S	10*								W Burns	9
			4	5	8	7	10*	11	1		6	3	9	12	2	S							P Taylor	10
	2		4	5	8	7	10*	11	1		6	3	12	9	S								K Lupton	11
	2		4	5	6*	8	7	10	11	1	14	3		12	9*								D Gallagher	12
	2		4	5	8	7	14	11		6	3	9*	10*	12	1								A Bennett	13
	2		4	5	8	7	9	11		6	3	S	S	10	1								**E Parker**	14
	2		4	5	8	7	12	11		6	3	9	10*	S	1								A Flood	15
	2	3	4	5	8	7	9		6	10	S	11			1								R Pawley	16
	2	3	4	5	8	7	9*		6	10	12	S			1								J Lloyd	17
	2	3	4	5	8	7	9	11*		6	10	12			S	1							P Jones	18
	2	3	4	5	8	7	9	S		1	6	10	11		S								**R Dilkes**	19
	2	3	4	5	8	7	9	S	11	1	6	10			S								T Lunt	20
	2	3	4	5	8	7	9*	12	11	1	6	10			S								**P Harrison**	21
	2	3	4	5	8	7	9	12	11	1	6	10*			S								T Fitzharris	22
	2	3	4	5	8	7	9		11	1	6	10			S	S							**P Harrison**	23
	2	3	4	5	8	7	S		11	1	6	10			9	S							R Lewis	24
	2	3*	4		8	7	12		11	1	6	10			9	5	S						A Dawson	25
	2	3	4		8	7	12		11	1	6	10			9*	5	S						D Allison	26
	2	3	4		8	7	12		11	1	6	10			9*	5	S						P Danson	27
	2	3	4	5	8	7	9	S	11	1	S	10			6								I Hendrick	28
1	2	3	4	5		8		9*	12	11		S	10			7	6						**J Kirby**	29
1	2	3	4	5		8	7			11*			14			10	6			9*	12		G Willard	30
1	2	3	4	5		8		S		11		6	10			7		S			9		R Nixon	31
1	2	3	4*	5	14	8		12		11		6	10			7*					9		R Poulain	32
1	2	3		5	S	8	7	11				6	10			12		4			9*		K Redfearn	33
1	2	3		5	14	8	7	11				6*	10			12		4			9*		M Reed	34
1	2	3		5	6	8	7	11	12			S	10					4			9		S Lodge	35
1	2	3		5	6	8	7	11	12			S	10			9*		4					J Deakin	36
1	2	3		5	6*	8	7	11	9*	12		14	10					4					P Wright	37
1	2	3		5	6	8	7	11	S	9		S	10					4					C Trussell	38
1	2		5	6*	8	7	11	12	9	14	3					4*						10	B Coddington	39
1	2	4	5		8	7	11		9	6	3							S			12	10*	P Taylor	40
1	2	4	5		8	7	11		9	6	3					12	10*	S					J Key	41
1	2	4*	5*		8	7	11		9	6	3					12	14				10		T Lunt	42
1	2		5	6	8		11	9		7	3			S		S	4				10		A Wilkie	43
1	2		5	6	8		11	9		7	3	12	S			12	S	4			10*		K Lupton	44
1	2		5	6	8		11	9		7	3					12	S	4			10*		K Burge	45
1	2		5	6	8	12	11	9		7	3			S		4*					10		G Singh	46
1	2		5	6	8		11	9	12	7	3			S				4			10*		A Dawson	47
1	2		5	6	8	S	11	9	S	7	3							4			10		J Brandwood	48
1	2		5	6	8	14	11	9*	12	7	3							4			10*		J Kirkby	49
21	41	25	28	39	16	42	33	26	14	28	16	29	36	6	4	15	7	15	5	1	13	2	League Appearances	
						2			2	4	7	3		4	3	6	2	1			2		Substitute Appearances	
	2	2	2	1		1	2	2	2	1		2	2	1+1	1+1	1		0+1					R/lows Appearances	
	3	3	3	3		3	3	3		0+1	2	3	3			1							FA Cup Appearances	
1	2	1	2	2		2	1	1		1+1	2		1	2		2	1			1			Autoglass Appearances	

Players on Loan: Gosney (Portsmouth), McLoughlin (Wolves), Shepstone (Blackburn Rovers)

YORK CITY

Club Colours: Red shirts with white flash, navy blue shorts, red stockings
Change Colours: White shirts with red flash, navy blue shorts, navy blue stockings
Reserves League: Pontins Central League Div 2   **'A' Team:** Northern Intermediate League

Previous League: Midland League
Previous Name:
Previous Managers: 1929-30 John Collier   1930-33 G W Sherrington   1933-37 John Collier   1937-50 Tom Mitchell   1950-52 Dick Duckworth   1952-53 Charlie Spencer   1953-54 Jim McCormick   1956-60 Sam Bartram   1960-67 Tom Lockie   1967-68 Joe Shaw   1968-75 Tom Johnston   1975-77 Wilf McGuinness   1977-80 Charlie Wright   1980-81 Barry Lyons   1982-87 Denis Smith   1987-88 Bobby Saxton   1988-91 John Bird
Honours: Champions Div 4, 1983-84
League Career: Elected to Div 3N 1929   Transferred to Div 4 1958   Promoted to Div 3 1958-59   Relegated to Div 4 1959-60   Promoted to Div 3 1964-65   Relegated to Div 4 1965-66   Promoted to Div 3 1970-71   Promoted to Div 2 1973-74   Relegated to Div 3 1975-76   Relegated to Div 4 1976-77   Promoted to Div 3 1983-84   Relegated to Div 4 1987-88

CLUB RECORDS

Most Appearances for Club: Barry Jackson (1958-70): League 481 + FA Cup 35 + League Cup 22 **Total 538**
Most Capped Player: Peter Scott, 7 Northern Ireland   **For England:** None
Record Goalscorer in a Match: Alf Patrick 5 v Rotherham United, 6-1, Div 3, 20.11.1948
Record League Goalscorer in a Season: Bill Fenton, 31, Div 3N, 1951-52   Arthur Bottom 1954-55 and 1955-56, Div 3N   **In All Competitions:** Arthur Bottom, 39 (League 31, FA Cup 8) 1954-55
Record League Goalscorer in a Career: Norman Wilkinson, 127, 1954-66   **In All Competitions:** Norman Wilkinson, 143, (League 127, FA Cup 16) 1954-66
Record Transfer Fee Received: £80,000 Sept 87 + £350,000 Sept 91 from Sunderland for Marco Gabbiadini
Record Transfer Fee Paid: £50,000 to Aldershot for Dale Banton, Nov 1984   £50,000 to Stoke City for Paul Barnes, July 1992
Best Performances: League: 15th Div 2, 1974-75   **FA Cup:** Semi-final Replay, 1954-55 (as a Third Division club)   **League Cup:** 5th Round, 1961-2
Most League Points: (3pts a win) 101, Div 4, 1983-84   (2pts a win) 62, Div 4, 1964-65
Most League Goals: 96, Div 4, 1983-84
Record League Victory and Most Goals Scored in a League Match: 9-1 v Southport, Div 3N, 2.2.1957
Most Goals Scored in a Cup Tie: 7-1 v Horsforth (h), Prelim. Round FA Cup, 1924-25   7-1 v Stockton Malleable (h), FA Cup 3rd Qualifying Round, 1927-28   7-1 v Stockton (h), FA Cup 1st Qualifying Round, 1928-29   6-0 v South Shields (a), FA Cup 1st Round, 1968-69   7-1 v Hartlepool Utd (h), Leyland Daf Cup, 7.11.1989
Record League Defeat: 0-12 v Chester, Div 3N, 1.2.1936
Record Cup Defeat: 0-7 v Liverpool, FA Cup Round 5 replay, 20.2.1985
Oldest Player in a League Match: Matt Middleton, 42 years 6 months, May 1950
Youngest Player in a League Match: Reg Stockill, 15 years 6 months, Aug 1929

LONGEST RUNS

of undefeated matches: 21 (1973-74)	**of league matches without a win:** 17 (May-Oct 1987)
of undefeated home matches: 32 (1970-71)	**of undefeated away matches:** 10 (1973-74)
without home win: 12 (1981-82)	**without an away win:** 38 (Sept 1986-Mar 1988)
of league wins: 7 (1964)	**of home wins:** 14 (1964-65)
of league defeats: 8 (1966)	**of away wins:** 5 (1983, 1984)

YORK CITY

PLAYERS NAME Honours	Ht	Wt	Birthdate	Birthplace Transfers	Contract Date	Clubs	League	L/Cup	FA Cup	Other	Lg	L/C	FAC	Oth
GOALKEEPERS														
Dean Kiely E:Y4	6.1	11.08	10.10.70	Manchester		West Brom A. (T)								
					30.10.87	Coventry City								
				Loan	30.10.89	Ipswich Town								
					09.03.90	York City								
					18.05.90	York City	38			2				
Chris Marples Div.4'85	5.11	12.0	03.08.64	Chesterfield	21.03.84	Chesterfield	84		5	5				
					25.03.87	Stockport Co	57	2	4	2				
				£28,000	12.07.88	York City	136	10	8	8				
				Loan	14.02.92	Scunthorpe Utd	1							
DEFENDERS														
Paul Atkin E: Y	6.0	12.04	03.09.69	Nottingham		Notts County (T)								
					22.03.89	Bury	14+7			2+1	1			
				Free	01.07.91	York City	29+4	1+1	3	1	1			
Tony Barratt	5.7	10.3	18.10.65	Salford		Burnley (A)								
						Billingham								
					16.08.85	Grimsby Town	20+2	3	1	2				
						Billingham								
					04.12.86	Hartlepool Utd	93+5	4	8	6	4			
					23.03.89	York City	100+8	5	2+1	6	9			
Phil Crosby E: Y.4; Div.4'89; FLgC'82	5.9	10.8	09.11.62	Leeds	26.09.80	Grimsby Town (A)	34+5	3	1		1			
					04.08.83	Rotherham Utd	181+2	18	11	13	2			
				£42,500	17.08.89	Peterborough U	85+4	6	8	3+1				
					05.08.91	York City	25	2	3	1				
Wayne Hall	5.8	10.2	25.10.68	Rotherham	19.12.88	Darlington								
				Free	01.03.89	Hatfield								
					01.07.89	York City	104+8	4+1	6+1	6	7		1	
Andy McMillan	5.10	10.13	22.06.68	Blumfentien(S.A)	17.10.87	York City	121+8	5	7	7	2			
Paul Stancliffe Div.3'81	6.2	12.13	05.05.58	Sheffield	01.03.76	Rotherham Utd. (A)	285	10	22		8		2	
				P.E.	16.08.83	Sheffield Utd	278	21	25	13	12	4	3	
				Free	17.12.90	Wolverhampton W	17		1	2				
						Rotherham Utd	5	1						
				Free	15.07.91	York City	16+2	1			1			
Steve Tutill	5.11	11.0	01.10.69	York	27.01.88	York City	164+2	9	12	10+2	2			1
Ray Warburton	6.0	11.5	09.10.67	Rotherham	05.10.85	Rotherham Utd. (A)	3+1		2	2				
				Free		York City	72+2	6	4	5	6	1	1	
MIDFIELD														
Stephen Bushell	5.7	10.5	28.12.72	Manchester	25.02.91	York City (T)	25+6							
Tony Canham	5.9	11.8	08.06.60	Leed		Harrogate Rlwy								
					16.01.85	York City	227+20	13	15	16+2	48	2	4	3
John McCarthy	5.9	11.5	18.08.70	Middlesbrough	18.08.88	Hartlepool Utd	0+1							
				Free	22.11.90	York City	68+1	2	6	3	8	1	1	2
Nigel Pepper	5.10	10.3	25.04.68	Rotherham	26.04.86	Rotherham Utd. (A)	35+10	1	1+1	3+3	1	1		
				Free	18.07.90	York City	71+3	2+1	6	3	7		1	
Gary Swann	5.9	11.2	11.04.62	York	17.05.80	Hull City (A)	176+10	9+1	11	10	9		1	
				£10,000	27.11.86	Preston N.E	174+5	11+1	12	27	37	4	1	5
				Free	12.06.92	York City								
FORWARDS														
Paul Barnes	5.10	10.6	16.11.67	Leicester	16.11.85	Notts County (A)	36+17		0+1	4+6	14			5
				£30,000	23.03.90	Stoke City	10+14	0+2		3+1	3			2
				Loan	08.11.90	Chesterfield	1		1				1	
				£50,000	15.07.92	York City								
Ian Blackstone	6.0	13.2	07.08.64	Harrogate		Harr								
					09.09.90	York City	46+12	2	3	3+1	14	1	2	2
John Borthwick GMVC'90,Div4'91	6.0	10.12	24.03.64	Hartlepool	10.12.82	Hartlepool Utd. (A)	96+21	3	6	7+3	15		1	1
				£8,000	01.08.89	Darlington	57+18	6	6+1	4	15	1	1	2
				Free	01.07.92	York City								
Glenn Naylor	5.10	11.10	11.08.72	York	05.03.90	York City (T)	31+11	1	1+1	1+2	13			
Darren Tilley						Yate Town								
				£5,000	09.01.92	York City	13+2							
ADDITIONAL CONTRACT PLAYERS														
(M) Craig Hall					01.07.92	York City (T)								
(D) Andrew Smith					01.07.92	York City (T)								

LEADING LEAGUE GOALSCORERS SEASONS 1985-86 – 1991-92

1985-86	**KEITH WALWYN**	**22**		1986-87	**KEITH WALWYN**	**19**
1987-88	**DALE BANTON**	**16**		1988-89	**IAN HELLIWELL**	**11**
1989-90	**IAN HELLIWELL**	**14**		1990-91	**IAN HELLIWELL**	**7**

1991-92	**IAN BLACKSTONE**	**8**

BOOTHAM CRESCENT York YO3 7AQ

Capacity: 12,760   **Covered Standing:**   **Seating:** 3,059

Tel: Ground: 0904 624447   **Ticket Sales:** As ground number   **Clubcall:** 0898 12 16 43

All premium rate calls (0898/0891) cost 36p per minute cheap rate and 48p per minute at all other times. Call costings correct at time of going to press.

ATTENDANCES
Highest: 28,123 v Huddersfield Town, FA Cup Round 6, 5.3.1938

Lowest: 957 v Carlisle Utd, Autoglass Trophy Prelim. Rnd., 22.10.1991

Record Receipts: £33,000 v Burnley, Division 4, 28.4.1992

BOOTHAM CRESCENT
First game: v Stockport County, 1932
First floodlit game: v Q.P.R., Sept 1959

Season Tickets:
Stands: from £103 to £145, juv/OAP £62 to £84
Ground: £92

Hospitality Box Season Tickets: Negotiable

Cost of Stand Tickets: Main £8 (£5.00 juniors/OAP); Popular £6 (£4 juniors/OAP); Enclosure £5.50 (£3.50 juniors/OAP); Ground £5 (£3.00 juniors/OAP)

Match and Ticket Information: On sale 14 days before each match (Main stand reduction for OAPs)

Car Parking: Ample parking in side streets

Nearest Railway Station: York (0904 642155)

How to get to the ground

From North: Use A1 then A59 S.P. York. Cross railway bridge and in 1.9m turn left into Water End. At end turn right A19 (S.P. City Centre). In 0.4m turn left into Bootham Crescent for York City FC
From East: Use A1079 into York city centre and follow signs for Thirsk A19 into Bootham. Cross railway bridge and then take 2nd turning on right into Bootham Crescent for York City FC
From South: Use A64. Turn left onto by-pass and follow signs for Thirsk A19. Then turn left signposted York and then take turning on left into Bootham Crescent for York City FC
From West: Use B1224 S.P. York into city centre and follow signs Thirsk A19 into Bootham. Cross railway bridge and then take 2nd turning on right into Bootham Crescent for York City FC

Value Rating: ★ ★ ★

Programme Editor: Sheila Smith

Price of 1992-93 Programme: £1
Number of Pages: 32
Subscriptions: Apply to club

Local Newspapers: Yorkshire Evening Press

Local Radio Stations: BBC Radio York

Additional Publications on Club: 'York City – A Complete Record 1922-1990', Dave Batters, £16.95

IT'S NO GOOD SHOUTING AT THE REF!

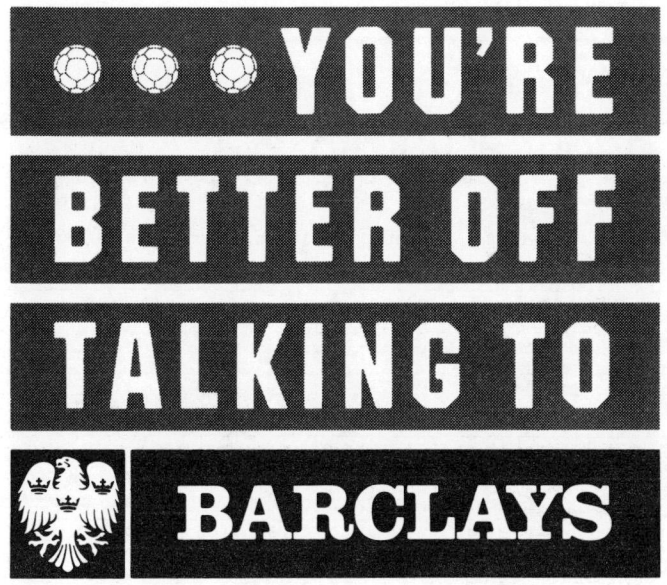

LIVERPOOL

DIVISION ONE: 6th   **FA CUP:** WINNERS   **RUMBELOWS CUP:** 4th RND   **UEFA CUP:** Q/FINALS

M	DATE	COMP.	VEN	OPPONENTS	RESULT	H/T	LGE POS	GOALSCORERS/GOAL TIMES	ATTEN-DANCE
1	S 18	UEFA 1/	H	Kuusysi Lahti	W 6-1	2-1		Saunders 4 (11, 78, 85, 87), Houghton 33, 90	17,131
2	25	RC 2/1	A	Stoke City	D 2-2	1-1		Rush 17, 71	18,839
3	O 2	UEFA 1/	A	Kuusysi Lahti	L 0-1	0-0			(8,800)
4	9	RC 2/2	A	Stoke City	W 3-2	1-0		McManaman 9, Saunders 56, Walters 84	(22,335)
5	23	UEFA 2/	H	Auxerre	L 0-2	0-1			(16,500)
6	29	RC 3	H	Port Vale	D 2-2	1-1		McManaman 8, Rush 66	21,553
7	N 6	UEFA 2/	H	Auxerre	W 3-0	2-0		Molby (pen) 4, Marsh 30, Walters 83	23,094
8	20	RC 3R	A	Port Vale	W 4-1	3-1		McManaman 21, Walters 29, Houghton 43, Saunders 62	(18,725)
9	27	UEFA 3/	A	Swarovski Tirol	W 2-0	0-0		Saunders 57, 78	(12,500)
10	D 3	RC 4	A	Peterborough Utd	L 0-1	0-1			(14,114)
11	11	UEFA 3/	H	Swarovski Tirol	W 4-0	1-0		Saunders 3 (39, 57, 68), Venison 84	16,007
12	J 6	FAC 3	A	Crewe Alexandra	W 4-0	3-0		McManaman 9, Barnes 3 (26, 28, pen 89)	(7,400)
13	F 5	FAC 4	A	Bristol Rovers	D 1-1	1-0		Saunders 38	(9,464)
14	11	FAC 4R	H	Bristol Rovers	W 2-1	0-1		McManaman 50, Saunders 77	30,142
15	16	FAC 5	H	Ipswich Town	D 0-0	0-0			(28,000)
16	26	FAC 5R	A	Ipswich Town	W †3-2	1-0		Houghton 45, Molby 98, McManaman 100	27,355
17	M 4	UEFA QF	A	Genoa	L 0-2	0-1			(40,000)
18	8	FAC 6	H	Aston Villa	W 1-0	0-0		Thomas 67	29,109
19	18	UEFA QF	H	Genoa	L 1-2	0-1		Rush 49	38,840
20	A 5	FAC SF	N	Portsmouth	D †1-1	0-0		Whelan 117	(41,869)
21	13	FAC SF	N	Portsmouth	W †0-0	0-0		(Won 3-1 on pens)	(40,097)
22	M 9	FAC Fin	N	Sunderland	W 2-0	0-0		Thomas 47, Rush 67	(79,544)

Goal Scorers:

R/lows C (11): McManaman 3, Rush 3, Saunders 2, Walters 2, Houghton

FA Cup (14): McManaman 3, Barnes 3, Saunders 2, Thomas 2, Whelan, Molby, Houghton, Rush

UEFA (16): Saunders 9, Houghton 2, Walters, Molby (1 pen), Venison, Rush, Marsh   † = After extra-time

---

PETERBOROUGH UNITED

DIVISION THREE: 6th   **FA CUP:** 2nd RND   **RUMBELOWS CUP:** 5th RND   **AUTOGLASS:** Sth FINALISTS

M	DATE	COMP.	VEN	OPPONENTS	RESULT	H/T	LGE POS	GOALSCORERS/GOAL TIMES	ATTEN-DANCE
1	A 20	RC 1/1	H	Aldershot	W 3-1	1-0		Gavin 3 (30, 68, 81)	2,731
2	27	RC 1/2	A	Aldershot	W 2-1	1-0		Gavin 15, Halsall 76	(1,601)
3	S 24	RC 2/1	A	Wimbledon	W 2-1	2-1		Charlery 28, Sterling 32	(2,081)
4	O 8	RC 2/2	H	Wimbledon	D 2-2	1-0		Kimble 35, Riley 46	5,939
5	22	AGT Pre	H	Wrexham	W 2-0	0-0		Charlery 49, Howarth 57	1,085
6	29	RC 3	H	Newcastle United	W 1-0	0-0		Charlery 85	10,382
7	N 16	FAC 1	H	Harlow	W 7-0	6-0		G Cooper 6, 18 (pen), Riley 19, Sterling 23, Halsall 27 Charlery 39, Culpin 87	4,341
8	D 3	RC 4	H	Liverpool	W 1-0	1-0		Kimble 19	14,114
9	7	FAC 2	H	Reading	D 0-0	0-0			5,328
10	17	FAC 2R	A	Reading	L 0-1	0-0			(4,373)
11	J 8	RC 5	H	Middlesbrough	D 0-0	0-0			15,302
12	F 4	AGT 1	A	Mansfield Town	W 3-0	2-0		Foster (og) 8, Gavin 16, Sterling 67	(2,578)
13	12	RC 5R	A	Middlesbrough	L 0-1	0-0			(21,073)
14	18	AGT 2	H	Shrewsbury Town	W 1-0	0-0		Costello 47	2,049
15	25	AGT SQF	H	Exeter City	W 1-0	0-0		Charlery 63	2,321
16	M 17	AGT SSF	H	Wrexham	W 3-1	2-0		Riley 7, Charlery 29, Costello 80	3,929
17	A 6	AGT SF1	A	Stoke City	D 3-3	1-2		Halsall 24, Charlery 51, Overton (og) 61	(14,355)
18	15	AGT SF2	H	Stoke City	L 0-1	0-0			12,214

Goal Scorers:

R/lows C (11): Gavin 4, Kimble 2, Charlery 2, Riley, Halsall, Sterling

FA Cup (7): G Cooper 2 (1 pen), Riley, Charlery, Halsall, Culpin, Sterling

Autoglass (13): Charlery 4, Opponents 2, Costello 2, Gavin, Howarth, Sterling, Riley, Halsall

1991-92

Grobbelaar B.	Ablett G.	Burrows D.	Nicol S.	Whelan R.	Wright M.	Saunders D.	Houghton R.	McManaman S.	Barnes J.	McMahon S.	Walters M.	Marsh M.	Tanner N.	Rosenthal R.	Harkness S.	Rush I.	Hooper M.	Jones R.	Redknapp J.	Hysen G.	Molby J.	Venison B.	Thomas M.	Kozma I.	Hutchison D.	Referee	
	2	3	4			7	8	10		11	12	5*	6		S	9	1		S						S	M Schlup	1
1	2	3	4			7*	8			11	10	5	6	12	S	9										K Lupton	2
1	2	3•	4				8			11	10	5		7*	6	9										K Hycl	3
		3	4			7	8	5		11	10	5	6		S	2	9	1								A Smith	4
1	2	3	4*				8	5		11	10	14	6	12		9			7•							J Damgaard	5
1		3				7	8*			11	10	14	6	12	2	9					4	5•				A Ward	6
1	2	3					8	7		11	10	4	6		S	9			S			5				C Valente	7
1	14	3				7	8*	9		11	10*	4	6	12					2			5				L Shapter	8
1		3	4		5	7		9		8			6						2			10				E Frederiksson	9
1	2*	3	4		5	7	8	9		11			6	12					S			10				R Bigger	10
1	8	3	4		5	7		9		11•			6	2*					12			10	14			L Spassov	11
1			4		5	7	8*	9	10		12		6		S				2	S		3	11			T Holbrook	12
1		3			5	7	8		11	9		4	6		S				2	S		10				B Hill	13
1		3			5	7	8		11				6	9*	S	12			2			10	12			B Hill	14
1		3	4		5	7	8		11	S			6			9			2			10*	12			A Buksh	15
1			4		5	7	8		11		9*		6	14	3*				2			10	12			A Buksh	16
		3	4		5	7	8		11				6	9*			1		2			10	12			H Forstinger	17
1			4	5	6	7	8		11•		10		14						2		12	3	9*			P Don	18
		3	4		6•	7			11	10		8	14			9	1		2*			5	12			F Van den Wijngaer	19
1		3*	4	5	6		8•	7	10			14				9			2			12	11			M Bodenham	20
1		3	4	5•	6	7			10		12					9			2*		8	14	11			M Bodenham	21
1		3	4		6	7	8		10	S	S					9			2			5	11			P Don	22
4	2+1	5	3		1	5	3	5		4	4	3+1	5	0+3	2+1	3	1		2			3				R/lows Appearances	
9		6	8		3	9	8	8		2+1	4+2	2	1+2	1	4+1	1	9		2		5+1	1+2	5		0+2	FA Cup Appearances	
5	6	7	7		4	5	4	8		1	5	5	7	5+1	1	3	5	3	2		1+1		5	0+3		UEFA Cup Appearances	

Also Played: Posn.(Game): Carter S(1)12(3), Jones B 14(3)S(7), Holcroft S(7)

1991-92

Barber F.	White C.	Butterworth G.	Halsall M.	Robinson D.	Welsh S.	Sterling W.	Ebdon M.	Gavin P.	Riley D.	Kimble G.	Luke N.	McInerney I.	Cooper G.	Charlery K.	Costello P.	Culpin P.	Johnson P.	Howarth L.	Robinson R.	Adcock A.	Barnes D.	Cooper S.	Salmon D.	Bennett I.	Edwards	Referee	
1	12	3	4	5	6		8	9	10	11	7	S	S													G Pooley	1
1	2	3	4	5	6		8	9	10*	11	7	12														G Willard	2
1		3	4	5	6	7		9	12	11	2		S	8	10*											P Foakes	3
1		3	4	5	6	7	12	14	9	11*	2			8	10*											K Morton	4
1	2	3	4		6	7	12	9*		11				8	10	S			5							G Ashby	5
1	14		4	5	6	7		9*		11	2			8	10			12		3						P Durkin	6
1	12		4	5	6	7*		9•		11	2			8	10			14		3						R Bigger	7
1	S		4	5	6	7		9		11	2			8	10			S		3						R Bigger	8
1	S		4	5	6	7		9*		11	2			8	10			12		3						R Wiseman	9
1			4	5	6	7	12	9		11•	2			8*	10			14		3						R Wiseman	10
1			4	5	6	7	S	9*		11	2			8	10			12		3						D Elleray	11
1	12		4	5	6	7		9		11*	2			8	10•			14		3						A Bennett	12
1	S		4	5	6	7		9		11*	2			8	10			12								K Hackett	13
1	12		4	5	6	7*		9		11•	2			8	10			14		3						A Buksh	14
1		3	4	5	6	7		9			2		S	8*	10	11					12					J Martin	15
1		3	4	5	6	7		9			2	S	8*	10	11		12									R Lewis	16
			4	5	6	7	12	9						8	10					3		14	2*	1	11•	D Elleray	17
			4	5	6	7		9						8	10					3		12		1	11•	M Bodenham	18
8	1+1	4+1	8		8	8	6	2+1	4+1	6+1	8		8	0+1	6	6	0+1	0+2		3						R/lows Appearances	
3			3	3	3	3		3	3	3			3	3			0+3	3								FA Cup Appearances	
5	1	2+3	7	6	7	6	1	2	4	3	5	1	7	7	2+2		1+1	5		0+2	1		2	2		Autoglass Appearances	

Also Played: Turner S(1), Curtis 3(13)

BARCLAYS LEAGUE Play-Off Finals
Wembley, May 23 – May 25, 1992

BLACKBURN ARE BARCLAYS PLAY-OFF FINAL VICTORS

Barclays Man of the Match Colin Hendry (centre) raises two arms in salute after Blackburn skipper Kevin Moran received the Barclays Second Division Play-Off Final trophy from Barclays Mike Pitcher, deputy managing director, Banking Division (immediately behind him). Taking Rovers into the coveted third spot for the F.A. Premier League

V for VICTORY

V-for-Victory: from double-scorer Ken Charlery whose twin-strike in the Third Division Play-Off Final took Peterborough into Division One of the new Barclays League. A happy hero for the Posh!

BLACKPOOL MAKE IT THIS TIME!

Blackpool made no mistakes this time: as they celebrate their Barclays Division Four Play-Off Final triumph to take them into Division Two of the new Barclays League!

FOOTBALL LEAGUE REFEREES LIST SEASON 1992-93

Name	Date Appointed	Previous League	Name	Date Appointed	Previous League
Paul ALCOCK	1988	Southern League	Peter JONES	1988	Southern League
David ALLISON	1980	Lancashire Combination	John KEY	1981	Northern Premier League
Gerald ASHBY	1985	West Midlands Regional League	Howard KING	1980	Welsh League
David AXCELL	1981	Football Combination	John KIRBY	1987	Alliance Premier League
Michael BAILEY	1986	Gola League	K. A. LEACH	1992	Birmingham County F.A.
Keren BARRATT	1981	West Midlands Regional League	Ray LEWIS #	1975	Isthmian League
Steven BELL	1989	Conference/Central League	John LLOYD *	1985	Northern Premier League
R. BIGGER	1989	Isthmian League	Stephen LODGE	1987	Central League
Martin BODENHAM	1981	Football Combination	Terence LUNT	1989	Northern Premier League
Ian BORRETT	1981	Football Combination	Kenneth LUPTON	1985	Northern League
John BRANDWOOD	1990	Conference/Central League	K. M. LYNCH	1992	Lincolnshire F.A.
Kevin BREEN	1985	Northern Premier League	John MARTIN	1977	Isthmian League
Alfred BUKSH	1983	Isthmian League	Roger MILFORD	1981	Western League
Keith BURGE *	1986	Gola League	Kelvin MORTON	1987	Football Combination
William BURNS	1988	Conference/Central League	John MOULES	1981	Football Combination
Vic CALLOW	1979	West Midlands Regional League	Robert NIXON	1981	Northern Premier League
John CARTER	1987	Southern League	Edward PARKER	1987	North West Counties
Brian CODDINGTON	1991	Panel Leagues	Roger PAWLEY	1988	Southern League
Keith COOPER	1982	Welsh League	Michael PECK	1977	Central League
Keith A COOPER	1987	Western League	David PHILLIPS	1985	Northern Premier League
George COURTNEY #	1971	Northern League	Michael PIERCE	1989	Football Combination
Ian CRUIKSHANKS	1989	Northern League	Graham POLL	1991	Panel Leagues
Paul DANSON	1987	Southern League	G. POOLEY	1988	Football Combination
Alan DAWSON	1988	Northern Premier League	Richard POULAIN	1991	Northern Premier League
Lawrence DILKES	1983	Northern Premier League	Kenneth REDFERN	1978	Northern League
Philip DON	1986	Southern League	Michael REED	1985	West Midlands Regional League
S. W. DUNN	1992	Gloucs County F.A.	Jim RUSHTON	1987	West Midlands Regional League
Paul DURKIN	1987	Western League	Paul SCOBLE	1990	Southern League
David ELLERAY	1986	Conference/Combination	David SHADWELL	1991	Panel Leagues
Tom FITZHARRIS	1981	Lancashire Combination	Raymond SHEPHERD	1990	Northern Counties East
Allan FLOOD	1986	Northern Premier League	Gurnam SINGH	1989	West Midlands Regional League
Peter FOAKES	1987	Eastern League	Arthur SMITH	1989	West Midland League
David FRAMPTON	1990	Southern League	Paul TAYLOR	1990	Conference
Dermot GALLAGHER	1990	Panel Leagues	Colin TRUSSELL	1985	Northern Premier League
Rodger GIFFORD *	1976	Welsh League	Paul VANES	1984	West Midlands Regional League
Ron GROVES	1984	Football Combination	Tony WARD	1980	Isthmian League
Allan GUNN #	1976	Football Combination	John WATSON	1986	Conference/Central League
Keith HACKETT #	1976	Northern Premier League	Trevor WEST	1987	Northern Premier League
Bob HAMER	1985	Gola League	Clive WILKES	1990	Football Combination
Paul HARRISON	1986	North West Counties League	Alan WILKIE	1988	Northern League
Robert HART	1986	Northern League	Gary WILLARD	1990	Conference
Ian HEMLEY	1985	Southern League	J. T. WINTER	1992	North Riding F.A.
Ian HENDRICK	1983	North West Counties	Roger WISEMAN	1986	Isthmian League
Brian HILL #	1975	Southern League	E. K. WOLSTENHOLME	1992	Lancashire F.A.
Terry HOLBROOK	1980	Central League	Joseph WORRALL #	1976	Cheshire League
Michael JAMES	1981	Southern League	Philip WRIGHT	1986	Northern Premier League

Those Referees with # beside their name are also on the English F.I.F.A. List of Referees.
Those Referees with * beside their name are also on the Welsh F.I.F.A. List of Referees.

BARCLAYS LEAGUE FINAL POSITIONS 1991-92

DIVISION ONE

	P	W	D	L	F	A	W	D	L	F	A	Pts
			Home						**Away**			
Leeds United	42	13	8	0	38	13	9	8	4	36	24	82
Manchester United	42	12	7	2	34	13	9	8	4	29	20	78
Sheffield Wednesday	42	13	5	3	39	24	8	7	6	23	25	75
Arsenal	42	12	7	2	51	22	7	8	6	30	24	72
Manchester City	42	13	4	4	32	14	7	6	8	29	34	70
Liverpool	42	13	5	3	34	17	3	1	7	13	23	64
Aston Villa	42	13	3	5	31	16	4	6	11	17	28	60
Nottingham Forest	42	10	7	4	36	27	6	4	11	24	31	59
Sheffield United	42	9	6	6	29	23	7	3	11	36	40	57
Crystal Palace	42	7	8	6	24	25	7	7	7	29	36	57
Queens Park Rangers	42	6	10	5	25	21	6	8	7	23	26	54
Everton	42	8	8	5	28	19	5	6	10	24	32	53
Wimbledon	42	10	5	6	32	20	3	9	9	21	33	53
Chelsea	42	7	8	6	31	30	6	6	9	19	30	53
Tottenham Hotspur	42	7	3	11	33	35	8	4	9	25	28	52
Southampton	42	7	5	9	17	28	7	5	9	22	27	52
Oldham Athletic	42	11	5	5	46	36	3	4	14	17	31	51
Norwich City	42	8	6	7	29	28	3	6	12	18	35	45
Coventry City	42	6	7	8	18	15	5	4	12	17	29	44
Luton Town	42	10	7	4	25	17	0	5	16	13	54	42
Notts County	42	7	5	9	24	29	3	5	13	16	33	40
West Ham United	42	6	6	9	22	24	3	5	13	15	35	38

DIVISION TWO

	P	W	D	L	F	A	W	D	L	F	A	Pts
			Home						**Away**			
Ipswich Town	46	16	3	4	42	22	8	9	6	28	28	84
Middlesbrough	46	15	6	2	37	13	8	5	10	21	28	80
Derby County	46	11	4	8	35	24	12	5	6	34	27	78
Leicester City	46	14	4	5	41	24	9	4	10	21	31	77
Cambridge City	46	10	9	4	34	19	9	8	6	31	28	74
Blackburn Rovers*	46	14	5	4	41	21	7	6	10	29	32	74
Charlton Athletic	46	9	7	7	25	23	11	4	8	29	25	71
Swindon Town	46	15	3	5	38	22	3	12	8	31	33	69
Portsmouth	46	15	6	2	41	12	4	6	13	24	39	69
Watford	46	9	5	9	25	23	9	6	8	26	25	65
Wolverhampton Wanderers	46	11	6	6	36	24	7	4	12	25	30	64
Southend United	46	11	5	7	37	26	6	6	11	26	37	62
Bristol Rovers	46	11	9	3	43	29	5	5	13	17	34	62
Tranmere Rovers	46	9	9	5	37	32	5	10	8	19	24	61
Millwall	46	10	4	9	32	32	7	6	10	32	39	61
Barnsley	46	11	4	8	27	25	5	7	11	19	32	59
Bristol City	46	10	8	5	30	24	3	7	13	25	47	54
Sunderland	46	10	8	5	36	23	4	3	16	25	42	53
Grimsby Town	46	7	5	11	25	28	7	6	10	22	34	53
Newcastle United	46	9	6	8	38	30	4	5	14	28	54	52
Oxford United	46	10	6	7	39	30	3	5	15	27	43	50
Plymouth Argyle	46	11	5	7	26	26	2	4	17	16	38	48
Brighton & Hove Albion	46	7	7	9	36	37	5	4	14	20	40	47
Port Vale	46	7	8	8	23	25	3	7	13	19	34	45

* Denotes club promoted via play-offs.

BARCLAYS LEAGUE FINAL POSITIONS 1991-92

DIVISION THREE

	P	W	D	L	F	A	W	D	L	F	A	Pts
			Home					Away				
Brentford	46	17	2	4	55	29	8	5	10	26	26	82
Birmingham City	46	15	6	2	42	22	8	6	9	27	30	81
Huddersfield Town	46	15	4	4	36	15	7	8	8	23	23	78
Stoke City	46	14	5	4	45	24	7	9	7	24	25	77
Stockport County	46	15	5	3	47	19	7	5	11	28	32	76
Peterborough Utd*	46	13	7	3	38	20	7	7	9	27	38	74
West Bromwich Albion	46	12	6	5	45	25	7	8	8	19	24	71
Bournemouth	46	13	4	6	33	18	7	7	9	19	30	71
Fulham	46	11	7	5	29	16	8	6	9	28	37	70
Leyton Orient	46	12	7	4	36	18	6	4	13	26	34	65
Hartlepool	46	12	5	6	30	21	6	6	11	27	36	65
Reading	46	9	8	6	33	27	7	5	11	26	35	61
Bolton Wanderers	46	10	9	4	26	19	4	8	11	31	37	59
Hull City	46	9	4	10	28	23	7	7	9	26	31	59
Wigan Athletic	46	11	6	6	33	21	4	8	11	25	43	59
Bradford City	46	8	10	5	36	30	5	9	9	26	31	58
Preston North End	46	12	7	4	42	32	3	5	15	19	40	57
Chester City	46	10	6	7	34	29	4	8	11	22	30	56
Swansea City	46	10	9	4	35	24	4	5	14	20	41	56
Exeter City	46	11	7	5	34	25	3	4	16	23	55	53
Bury	46	8	7	8	31	31	5	5	13	24	43	51
Shrewsbury Town	46	7	7	9	30	31	5	4	14	23	37	47
Torquay United	46	13	3	7	29	19	0	5	18	13	49	47
Darlington	46	5	5	13	31	39	5	2	16	25	31	37

DIVISION FOUR

	P	W	D	L	F	A	W	D	L	F	A	Pts
			Home					Away				
Burnley	42	14	4	3	42	16	11	4	6	37	27	83
Rotherham United	42	12	6	3	38	16	10	5	6	32	21	77
Mansfield Town	42	13	4	4	43	26	10	4	7	32	27	77
Blackpool *	42	17	3	1	48	13	5	7	9	23	32	76
Scunthorpe United	42	14	5	2	39	18	7	4	10	25	41	72
Crewe Alexandra	42	12	6	3	33	20	8	4	9	33	31	70
Barnet	42	16	1	4	48	23	5	5	11	33	38	69
Rochdale	42	12	6	3	34	22	6	7	8	23	31	67
Cardiff City	42	13	3	5	42	22	4	12	5	24	27	66
Lincoln City	42	9	5	7	21	24	8	6	7	29	20	62
Gillingham	42	12	5	4	41	19	3	7	11	22	34	57
Scarborough	42	12	5	4	39	28	3	7	11	25	40	57
Chesterfield	42	6	7	8	26	28	8	4	9	23	33	53
Wrexham	42	11	4	6	31	26	3	5	13	21	47	51
Walsall	42	5	10	6	28	26	7	3	11	20	32	49
Northampton Town	42	5	9	7	25	23	6	4	11	21	34	46
Hereford United	42	9	4	8	31	24	3	4	14	13	33	44
Maidstone United	42	6	9	6	24	22	2	9	10	21	34	42
York City	42	6	9	6	26	23	2	7	12	16	35	40
Halifax Town	42	7	5	9	23	35	3	3	15	11	40	38
Doncaster Rovers	42	6	2	13	21	35	3	6	12	19	30	35
Carlisle United	42	5	9	7	24	27	2	4	15	17	40	34

* Denotes club promoted via play-offs.

FOOTBALL LEAGUE MANAGERS DIVISIONS TWO & THREE.

BARNET

BARRY FRY since July 1986

PREVIOUS CLUBS
as Manager: Dunstable; Hillingdon Borough; Bedford Town; Barnet; Maidstone.
as Player/Coach: None
as Player: Manchester Utd; Bolton W.; Luton T.; Leyton O.; Several non-league.
HONOURS
as Manager: GM Vauxhall Conference championship.
as Player:

BLACKPOOL

BILLY AYRE since November 1990

PREVIOUS CLUBS
as Manager: Halifax Town
as Asst.Man/Coach: Halifax Town
as Player: Scarborough; Hartlepool Utd.; Halifax T.; Mansfield T.; Halifax T. (2nd)
HONOURS
as Manager:
as Player:

BOLTON WNDRS

BRUCE RIOCH since May 1992

PREVIOUS CLUBS
as Manager: Millwall.
as Player/Manager: Torquay Utd.; Middlesborough
as Player: Luton T.; Aston Villa; Derby Co.; Everton; Derby Co. (2nd); Torquay Utd.
HONOURS
as Manager: Middlesbrough: Promotion to Div 2 1987.
as Player: Scotland: 24 caps

BOURNEMOUTH

TONY PULIS since June 1992

PREVIOUS CLUBS
as Manager: None
as Player/Coach: Bournemouth
as Player: Bristol Rov.; Hong Kong; Bristol Rov. (2nd); Newport Co.; Bournemouth; Gillingham; Bournemouth (2nd).
HONOURS
as Manager:
as Player: Newport Co. Div 3 Championship 1987.

BRADFORD CITY

FRANK STAPLETON since December 1991

PREVIOUS CLUBS
as Manager: None
as Player/Coach: None
as Player: Arsenal; Manchester Utd.; Ajax; Derby Co.; Le Havre; Blackburn Rov.
HONOURS
as Manager:
as Player: Eire: 71 caps; FAC 1979, '83, '85.

BRIGHTON & H.A.

BARRY LLOYD since January 1987

PREVIOUS CLUBS
as Manager: Yeovil Town; Worthing.
as Player/Coach: Brighton & Hove Albion
as Player: Chelsea; Fulham; Hereford; Brentford; Houston Hurricane.
HONOURS
as Manager:
as Player: England: Youth; Promotion to Div 2 1970-71 & FA Cup Final sub 1975 with Fulham.

BURNLEY

JIMMY MULLEN since April 1981

PREVIOUS CLUBS
as Manager: Newport Co.; Cardiff (Joint caretaker); Blackpool.
as Asst. Manager Blackpool; Aberdeen.
as Player: Sheffield Wed.; Rotherham; Preston N. E. (loan); Cardiff City.
HONOURS
as Manager:
as Player:

BURY

MIKE WALSH since November 1990

PREVIOUS CLUBS
as Manager: None
as Player/Coach: Blackpool; Bury.
as Player: Bolton W.; Everton; Norwich (loan); Burnley (loan); Fort Lauderdale; Manchester City; Blackpool; Bury.
HONOURS
as Manager: 3rd Division play offs 1990/91
as Player: Eire: 4 caps; 2nd Division championship (Bolton) 1979/80; Promotion to Div 3 (Blackpool) 1984/85.

FOOTBALL LEAGUE MANAGERS DIVISIONS TWO & THREE.

CARDIFF CITY | **EDDIE MAY** | since July 1991

PREVIOUS CLUBS
as Manager: Al-Nahda (Saudi Arabia); Newport Co.; IFK Ravdeberg (Norway).
as Player/Coach: Leicester City; Charlton Ath.
as Player: Southend Utd.; Wrexham; Swansea City.
HONOURS
as Manager: League runners-up IFK Ravdeberg 1990
as Player: Wrexham: 4th Div. runners-up 1969-70, Welsh Cup Winners 1972, '73,'74; Swansea City: 4th Div. runners-up.

CARLISLE UTD. | **AIDAN McCAFFERY** | since April 1991

PREVIOUS CLUBS
as Manager: None
as Player/Coach: Carlisle Utd.
as Player: Newcastle Utd.; Derby Co.; Bristol Rov.; Bristol City; Exeter City; Hartlepool; Carlisle Utd.

HONOURS
as Manager:
as Player: England: Youth; Newcastle: Texaco Cup 1974, '75.

CHESTER CITY | **HARRY McNALLY** | since June 1985

PREVIOUS CLUBS
as Manager: Altrincham; Southport; Wigan Athletic.
as Asst.Man/Coach: Skelmersdale Utd; Wigan Athletic.
as Player: Skelmersdale Utd.
HONOURS
as Manager: Promotion to Div 3 85-86 (Chester City)
as Player:

CHESTERFIELD | **CHRIS McMENEMY** | since April 1991

PREVIOUS CLUBS
as Manager: None
as Player/Coach: Chesterfield; Sunderland
as Player: Southampton
HONOURS
as Manager: Manager of the Month (Division 4 - March 1991)
as Player:

COLCHESTER UTD. | **ROY McDONOUGH** | since July 1991

PREVIOUS CLUBS
as Manager: None
as Player/Coach: Colchester United
as Player: Birmingahm C.; Walsall; Chelsea; Colchester U.; Southend U.; Exeter City; Cambridge U.; Southend U. (2nd); Colchester U. (2nd).

HONOURS
as Player/Manager: GM Vauxhall Conference championship 1991/92; FA Trophy 1992.
as Player:

CREWE ALEXANDRA | **DARIO GRADI** | since May 1983

PREVIOUS CLUBS
as Manager: Wimbledon; Crystal Palace.
as Asst.Man/Coach: Chelsea; Derby County; Wimbledon; Orient (Youth Team)
as Player: Sutton United
HONOURS
as Manager: Promotion to Div 3 78-79 (Wimbledon), 1989-90 (Crewe A.)
as Player: England: Amateur.

DARLINGTON | **BILLY McEWAN** | since May 1992

PREVIOUS CLUBS
as Manager: Sheffield United; Rotherham United
as Asst.Man/Coach: Sheffield United; Rotherham United.
as Player: Hibernian, Blackpool, Brighton & H.A., Chesterfield, Mansfield Town Peterborough Utd, Rotherham Utd.

HONOURS
as Manager:
as Player: S: u23, Y; Scottish Cup with Hibernian.

DONCASTER ROV. | **STEVE BEAGLEHOLE** | since November 1991

PREVIOUS CLUBS
as Manager: None
as Asst. Manager: Doncaster Rovers.
as Player:
HONOURS
as Manager:
as Player:

FOOTBALL LEAGUE MANAGERS DIVISIONS TWO & THREE.

EXETER CITY

ALAN BALL
since August 199

PREVIOUS CLUBS
as Manager: Blackpool; Vancouver Whitecaps (as Player/Manager); Portsmouth; Stoke City.
as Asst.Man/Coach: Bristol Rovers, Portsmouth; Colchester United.
as Player: Blackpoool, Everton, Arsenal, Southampton (2 spells), Bristol Rovers
HONOURS
as Manager: Promotion to Division 1 (with Portsmouth) 1987
as Player: League Champions Medal 1970 (Everton); World Cup Winners Meda 1966, FA Cup Runners-Up 1968 (Everton), FA Cup Runners-Up 197: (Arsenal), League Cup Runners-Up 1979 (Southampton)

FULHAM

DON MACKAY
since December 199

PREVIOUS CLUBS
as Manager: Dundee; Norlesundby (Denmark); Coventry City; Blackburn Rovers
as Coach: Southend Utd.; Bristol City; Rangers (Youth & Reserves).
as Player: Forfar; Dundee Utd.; Southend Utd.
HONOURS
as Manager: Dundee: Runners-up Bells League Cup & promotion to Premier Div. Norlesundby: Promotion to Div 3.; Blackburn: Full Members Cup 1987
as Player:

GILLINGHAM

DAMIEN RICHARDSON
since May 198

PREVIOUS CLUBS
as Manager: None
as Player/Coach: None
as Player: Shamrock Rovers; Gillingham; Gravesend & other non-league.
HONOURS
as Manager:
as Player:

HALIFAX

JOHN McGRATH
since October 199

PREVIOUS CLUBS
as Manager: Port Vale; Chester City; Preston North End.
as Asst.Man/Coach: Southampton (youth Team)
as Player: Bury; Newcastle Utd.; Southampton; Brighton & H.A. (loan).
HONOURS
as Manager: Promotion to Div. 3 - Port Vale 82-83, P.N.E. 86-87.
as Player: England: u23 (1), F. Lg.(1); Div2'65 with Newcastle; Div3'61 with Bury

HARTLEPOOL

ALAN MURRAY
since March 199

PREVIOUS CLUBS
as Manager: None
as Player/Coach: None
as Player: Middlesbrough; Brentford; Wolverhampton W.; Doncaster Rov.
HONOURS
as Manager:
as Player:

HEREFORD

GREG DOWNS
since May 199

PREVIOUS CLUBS
as Manager: None
as Player/Coach: Hereford United.
as Player: Norwich City; Torquay Utd.; Coventry City; Birmingham City; Herefor Utd.
HONOURS
as Manager:
as Player: FA Cup Winner 1987 with Coventry.

HUDDERSFIELD

IAN ROSS
since March 1991

PREVIOUS CLUBS
as Manager: None
as Asst. Manager: Huddersfield Town
as Player/Coach: Hereford Utd.
as Player: Liverpool; Aston Villa; Notts Co.; Northampton T.; Peterborough U. Wolverhampton W..
HONOURS
as Manager:
as Player:

HULL CITY

TERRY DOLAN
since April 198

PREVIOUS CLUBS
as Manager: Bradford City; Rochdale.
as Asst.Man/Coach: Bradford City
as Player: Bradford P.A., Huddersfield Town, Bradford City, Rochdale
HONOURS
as Manager: Promotion to Div 2 via play-offs 1988
as Player:

FOOTBALL LEAGUE MANAGERS DIVISIONS TWO & THREE.

LEYTON ORIENT — PETER EUSTACE
since July 1991

PREVIOUS CLUBS
as Manager: Sheffield Wednesday
as Player/Coach: Sunderland; Sheffield Wednesday
as Player: Sheffield Wed.; West Ham; Sheffield Wed. (2nd); Peterborough Utd.
HONOURS
as Manager: Promotion to Div. 1 (Sunderland).
as Player: FA Cup 1966 runners-up.

LINCOLN CITY — STEVE THOMPSON
since November 1990

PREVIOUS CLUBS
as Manager: None
as Player/Coach: None
as Player: Boston Utd.; Lincoln City; Charlton Ath.; Leicester City; Sheffield Utd.
HONOURS
as Manager:
as Player: England: Semi-Professional cap.

MANSFIELD TOWN — GEORGE FOSTER
since February 1989

PREVIOUS CLUBS
as Manager: None
as Asst.Man/Coach: None
as Player: Plymouth Argyle, Torquay(L), Exeter(L), Derby County, Mansfield Town
HONOURS
as Manager:
as Player: FRT '87 (with Mansfield)

NORTHAMPTON TOWN — PHIL CHARD
since May 1992

PREVIOUS CLUBS
as Manager: None
as Player/Coach: None
as Player: Corby Town; Nottingham Forest; Peterborough Utd.; Northampton Town; Wolverhampton W.; Northampton Town (2nd).

HONOURS
as Manager:
as Player: Div 4 Championship 1987 (Northampton); Div 3 Championship 1989 (Wolverhampton W.)

PLYMOUTH ARGYLE — PETER SHILTON
since March 1992

PREVIOUS CLUBS
as Manager: None
as Player/Coach: None
as Player: Leicester City; Stoke City; Nottingham Forest; Southampton; Derby County.

HONOURS
as Manager:
as Player: England: 125, u23-3, Y, S; Nottm. Forest: Div 1 '78, Euro. Cup '79 & '80, E.S.Cup '79; Leicester: Div 2 '71.

PORT VALE — JOHN RUDGE
since December 1983

PREVIOUS CLUBS
as Manager: None
as Asst.Man/Coach: Torquay Utd.
as Player: Huddersfield T.; Carlisle Utd.; Torquay Utd.; Bristol Rov.; Bournemouth.

HONOURS
as Manager: Port Vale: Promotion to Div 3 1986; Promotion to Div 2 1989.
as Player: Bristol Rovers: Promotion to Div 2 1974.

PRESTON NORTH END — LES CHAPMAN
since April 1990

PREVIOUS CLUBS
as Manager: None
as Player/Coach: Stockport County.
as Player: Oldham Athletic; Huddersfield Town; Oldham Ath. (2nd); Stockport Co.; Bradford City; Rochdale, Stockport Co. (2nd); Preston N.E.

HONOURS
as Manager:
as Player: Div 2 Championship 69-70 (Huddersfield); Promotion to Div 3 81-82 (Bradford); Promotion to Div 3 86-87 (P.N.E.)

READING — MARK McGHEE
since May 1991

PREVIOUS CLUBS
as Manager: None
as Player/Coach: None
as Player: Bristol City; Morton; Aberdeen; SV Hamburg; Celtic; Newcastle Utd.
HONOURS
as Manager:
as Player: Scotland: u21.4.

FOOTBALL LEAGUE MANAGERS DIVISIONS TWO & THREE.

ROCHDALE

DAVID SUTTON
since February 1991

PREVIOUS CLUBS
as Manager: None
as Player/Coach: None
as Player: Plymouth Argyle; Reading; Huddersfield T.; Bolton W.; Rochdale.
HONOURS
as Manager:
as Player: Promotion to 2nd Div. and Promotion to 3rd Div.

ROTHERHAM UNITED

PHIL HENSON
since January 1991

PREVIOUS CLUBS
as Manager: None
as Asst.Man/Coach: Rotherham United
as Player: Manchester City; Sheffield Wednesday; Swansea City (loan); Sparta Rotterdam; Stockport County; Rotherham Utd.
HONOURS
as Asst. Manager: Rotherham - Div 4 Championship
as Player: Rotherham - Div. 3 Championship 1980-81

SCARBOROUGH

RAY McHALE
since November 1990

PREVIOUS CLUBS
as Manager: None
as Player/Coach: None
as Player: Chesterfield; Halifax Town; Swindon Town; Brighton & H.A.; Barnsley Sheffield Utd; Bury.

HONOURS
as Manager:
as Player:

SCUNTHORPE

BILL GREEN
since February 1991

PREVIOUS CLUBS
as Manager: None
as Asst.Man/Coach: Scunthorpe United
as Player: Hartlepool Utd.; Carlisle Utd.; West Ham Utd.; Peterborough Utd.; Chesterfield; Doncaster Rov.

HONOURS
as Manager:
as Player: Chesterfield: Anglo Scottish Cup winners; Carlisle: Promotion to Div. 1 Doncaster R.: Promotion to Div. 3.

SHREWSBURY TOWN

JOHN BOND
since January 1991

PREVIOUS CLUBS
as Manager: AFC Bournemouth; Norwich City; Manchester City; Burnley; Swansea City; Birmingham City.
as Asst.Man/Coach: None
as Player: West Ham Utd.; Torquay Utd.
HONOURS
as Manager: Norwich: Promotion to Div.1, League Cup runners-up; Man. City: FA Cup runners-up; AFC Bournemouth: Promotion to Div. 3.
as Player: England Xi v Irish League/South Africa tour; England B, FA Cup 1964.

STOCKPORT COUNTY

DANNY BERGARA
since May 1989

PREVIOUS CLUBS
as Manager: Brunei F.A.; Rochdale.
as Asst.Man/Coach: Luton Town (C); Sheffield Utd. (A.M.); Middlesbrough (C); Sheffield Utd. (C).
as Player: Racing Club Montevideo; Real Mallorca; F.C. Sevilla; F.C. Tenerife.
HONOURS
as manager: Stockport Co.: Div. 3 runners-up 1990-91.
as Player: Uruguay: Youth; Spanish Div. 2 '65 (with Mallorca), '69 (with Sevilla).

STOKE CITY

LOU MACARI
since June 1991

PREVIOUS CLUBS
as Manager: Swindon Town; West Ham Utd.; Birmingham City.
as Player/Coach: None
as Player: Celtic; Manchester United.
HONOURS
as Manager: Promotion with Swindon Town (twice); Leyland Daf Cup Winners with Birmingham City.
as Player: Scotland: 24 caps; Scottish League 3 times; Scottish Cup twice.

SWANSEA CITY

FRANK BURROWS
since March 1991

PREVIOUS CLUBS
as Manager: Portsmouth; Cardiff City.
as Asst.Man/Coach: Portsmouth; Swindon Town; Sunderland.
as Player: Raith Rovers; Scunthorpe Utd.; Swindon Town; Mansfield Town (loan).
HONOURS
as Manager:
as Player: Swindon Town: League Cup Winner 1969.

TORQUAY UTD.	**PAUL COMPTON**	since May 1992

PREVIOUS CLUBS
as Manager: None
as Coach: Torquay Utd. - Youth Dev. Officer.
as Player: Bournemouth; Aldershot; Torquay Utd.; Newport County.
HONOURS
as Manager:
as Player:

WALSALL	**KENNY HIBBITT**	since May 1990

PREVIOUS CLUBS
as Manager: None.
as Asst.Man/Coach: Bristol Rovers.
as Player: Bradford P.A.; Wolverhampton W.; Seattle Sounders; Coventry City; Bristol Rovers.

HONOURS
as Manager:
as Player: England: u23.1; League Cup 1974, 1980, Div.2 Champions 1977, UEFA Cup runners-up (Wolverhampton W.)

WEST BROMWICH A.	**OSSIE ARDILES**	since May 1992

PREVIOUS CLUBS
as Manager: Swindon Town; Newcastle United.
as Player/Coach: None
as Player: Huracan (Argentina); Tottenham Hotspur; Paris St. Germain (France); Blackburn Rovers; Q.P.R.

HONOURS
as Manager: Swindon: won Div. 2 Play-off final 1990.
as Player: Argentina : World Cup Winners 1978; Tottenham: FA Cup Winner 1981, UEFA Cup Winner 1984.

WIGAN ATHLETIC	**DAVE PHILPOTTS**	since November 1991

PREVIOUS CLUBS
as Manager: None
as Player/Coach: Wigan Athletic.
as Player: Coventry City; Southport; Tranmere Rovers; Carolina L. (USA); Tranmere Rov. (2nd).

HONOURS
as Manager:
as Player:

WREXHAM	**BRIAN FLYNN**	since November 1989

PREVIOUS CLUBS
as Manager: None.
as Player/Coach: None
as Player: Burnley; Ledds Utd.; Cardiff City; Doncaster Rov.; Bury; Limerick; Doncaster Rov. (2nd).

HONOURS
as Manager:
as Player: Wales: 66 caps, u23. 2 Schools.

YORK CITY	**JOHN WARD**	since November 1991

PREVIOUS CLUBS
as Manager: None
as Asst.Man/Coach: Watford; Aston Villa.
as Player: Lincoln City; Workington; Watford; Grimsby Town; Lincoln City.
HONOURS
as Manager:
as Player:

BARCLAYS

Your Personal Match Records

DATE	Competition	Venue	COMPETING TEAMS	Score H.T.	Score F.T.	SCORERS (with times)		Referee
			HOME:				Home	
			AWAY:				Away	
			HOME:				Home	
			AWAY:				Away	
			HOME:				Home	
			AWAY:				Away	
			HOME:				Home	
			AWAY:				Away	
			HOME:				Home	
			AWAY:				Away	
			HOME:				Home	
			AWAY:				Away	
			HOME:				Home	
			AWAY:				Away	
			HOME:				Home	
			AWAY:				Away	
			HOME:				Home	
			AWAY:				Away	
			HOME:				Home	
			AWAY:				Away	
			HOME:				Home	
			AWAY:				Away	
			HOME:				Home	
			AWAY:				Away	
			HOME:				Home	
			AWAY:				Away	
			HOME:				Home	
			AWAY:				Away	
			HOME:				Home	
			AWAY:				Away	
			HOME:				Home	
			AWAY:				Away	
			HOME:				Home	
			AWAY:				Away	
			HOME:				Home	
			AWAY:				Away	

for Season 1992-93

	1	2	3	4	5	6	7	8	9	10	11	12	14	
						PLAYERS NAMES								
H														H
A														A
H														H
A														A
H														H
A														A
H														H
A														A
H														H
A														A
H														H
A														A
H														H
A														A
H														H
A														A
H														H
A														A
H														H
A														A
H														H
A														A
H														H
A														A
H														H
A														A
H														H
A														A
H														H
A														A
H														H
A														A
H														H
A														A

Your Personal Match Records

DATE	Competition	Venue	COMPETING TEAMS	Score H.T.	Score F.T.	SCORERS (with times)		Referee
			HOME:				Home	
			AWAY:				Away	
			HOME:				Home	
			AWAY:				Away	
			HOME:				Home	
			AWAY:				Away	
			HOME:				Home	
			AWAY:				Away	
			HOME:				Home	
			AWAY:				Away	
			HOME:				Home	
			AWAY:				Away	
			HOME:				Home	
			AWAY:				Away	
			HOME:				Home	
			AWAY:				Away	
			HOME:				Home	
			AWAY:				Away	
			HOME:				Home	
			AWAY:				Away	
			HOME:				Home	
			AWAY:				Away	
			HOME:				Home	
			AWAY:				Away	
			HOME:				Home	
			AWAY:				Away	
			HOME:				Home	
			AWAY:				Away	
			HOME:				Home	
			AWAY:				Away	
			HOME:				Home	
			AWAY:				Away	
			HOME:				Home	
			AWAY:				Away	
			HOME:				Home	
			AWAY:				Away	

for Season 1992-93

		PLAYERS NAMES												
	1	2	3	4	5	6	7	8	9	10	11	12	14	
H														H
A														A
H														H
A														A
H														H
A														A
H														H
A														A
H														H
A														A
H														H
A														A
H														H
A														A
H														H
A														A
H														H
A														A
H														H
A														A
H														H
A														A
H														H
A														A
H														H
A														A
H														H
A														A
H														H
A														A
H														H
A														A

Your Personal Match Records

DATE	Competition	Venue	COMPETING TEAMS	Score H.T.	Score F.T.	SCORERS (with times)	Referee
			HOME:			Home	
			AWAY:			Away	
			HOME:			Home	
			AWAY:			Away	
			HOME:			Home	
			AWAY:			Away	
			HOME:			Home	
			AWAY:			Away	
			HOME:			Home	
			AWAY:			Away	
			HOME:			Home	
			AWAY:			Away	
			HOME:			Home	
			AWAY:			Away	
			HOME:			Home	
			AWAY:			Away	
			HOME:			Home	
			AWAY:			Away	
			HOME:			Home	
			AWAY:			Away	
			HOME:			Home	
			AWAY:			Away	
			HOME:			Home	
			AWAY:			Away	
			HOME:			Home	
			AWAY:			Away	
			HOME:			Home	
			AWAY:			Away	
			HOME:			Home	
			AWAY:			Away	
			HOME:			Home	
			AWAY:			Away	
			HOME:			Home	
			AWAY:			Away	
			HOME:			Home	
			AWAY:			Away	

for Season 1992-93

	PLAYERS NAMES													
	1	2	3	4	5	6	7	8	9	10	11	12	14	
H														H
A														A
H														H
A														A
H														H
A														A
H														H
A														A
H														H
A														A
H														H
A														A
H														H
A														A
H														H
A														A
H														H
A														A
H														H
A														A
H														H
A														A
H														H
A														A
H														H
A														A
H														H
A														A
H														H
A														A
H														H
A														A
H														H
A														A
H														H
A														A

Your Personal Match Records

DATE	Competition	Venue	COMPETING TEAMS	Score H.T.	F.T.	SCORERS (with times)		Referee
			HOME:				Home	
			AWAY:				Away	
			HOME:				Home	
			AWAY:				Away	
			HOME:				Home	
			AWAY:				Away	
			HOME:				Home	
			AWAY:				Away	
			HOME:				Home	
			AWAY:				Away	
			HOME:				Home	
			AWAY:				Away	
			HOME:				Home	
			AWAY:				Away	
			HOME:				Home	
			AWAY:				Away	
			HOME:				Home	
			AWAY:				Away	
			HOME:				Home	
			AWAY:				Away	
			HOME:				Home	
			AWAY:				Away	
			HOME:				Home	
			AWAY:				Away	
			HOME:				Home	
			AWAY:				Away	
			HOME:				Home	
			AWAY:				Away	
			HOME:				Home	
			AWAY:				Away	
			HOME:				Home	
			AWAY:				Away	
			HOME:				Home	
			AWAY:				Away	
			HOME:				Home	
			AWAY:				Away	

for Season 1992-93

	PLAYERS NAMES													
	1	2	3	4	5	6	7	8	9	10	11	12	14	
H														H
A														A
H														H
A														A
H														H
A														A
H														H
A														A
H														H
A														A
H														H
A														A
H														H
A														A
H														H
A														A
H														H
A														A
H														H
A														A
H														H
A														A
H														H
A														A
H														H
A														A
H														H
A														A
H														H
A														A
H														H
A														A

FAROE ISLES 1, AUSTRIA 0.

EUROPEAN CHAMPIONSHIPS 1990

USA 1, ENGLAND 0.

WORLD CUP FINALS 1950

WEST GERMANY 1 ALGERIA 2

WORLD CUP FINALS 1982

Arbroath 36, Bon Accord 0.

SCOTTISH CUP 1885

ARGENTINA...0 CAMEROON...1

WORLD CUP FINALS 1990

BANGOR 2 – NAPOLI 0

EUROPEAN CUP WINNERS CUP 1963

FOR MORE PREDICTABLE RESULTS SAVE WITH BARCLAYS.

Shock upsets might be interesting in football, but when it comes to your hard earned cash you want a dead cert.

For a real result from your savings why not talk to Barclays?

We have a wide range of savings schemes, to suit your individual needs, no matter how large or small the amount you have to save. From youngsters with £1, to premium rate saving accounts like Capital Advantage, when you have £10,000 or more to invest.

Just ask at your local branch for details or phone our information line – free of charge – on 0800 400 100.

You can't go wrong with Barclays behind you.

★★★ YOU'RE BETTER OFF TALKING TO BARCLAYS

MEMBER OF IMRO

Registered in London, England. Reg. Number: 1026167: Reg. Office: 54 Lombard Street, London EC3P 3AH.